HANDBOOK OF
ORGANIZATIONAL CREATIVITY

HANDBOOK OF ORGANIZATIONAL CREATIVITY

Edited by

MICHAEL D. MUMFORD
University of Oklahoma, Norman, OK

AMSTERDAM • BOSTON • HEIDELBERG • LONDON
NEW YORK • OXFORD • PARIS • SAN DIEGO
SAN FRANCISCO • SINGAPORE • SYDNEY • TOKYO
Academic Press is an imprint of Elsevier

Academic Press is an imprint of Elsevier
32 Jamestown Road, London, NW1 7BY, UK
225 Wyman Street, Waltham, MA 02451, USA
525 B Street, Suite 1800, San Diego, CA 92101-4495, USA

First edition 2012

Copyright © 2012 Elsevier Inc. All rights reserved

Notice
No responsibility is assumed by the publisher for any injury and/or damage to persons
or property as a matter of products liability, negligence or otherwise, or from any use or
operation of any methods, products, instructions or ideas contained in the material herein.
Because of rapid advances in the medical sciences, in particular, independent verification
of diagnoses and drug dosages should be made

British Library Cataloguing-in-Publication Data
A catalogue record for this book is available from the British Library

Library of Congress Cataloging-in-Publication Data
A catalog record for this book is available from the Library of Congress

ISBN : 978-0-12-374714-3

For information on all Academic Press publications
visit our website at www.elsevierdirect.com

Typeset by MPS Limited, a Macmillan Company, Chennai, India
www.macmillansolutions.com

Printed and bound in United States of America

Transferred to Digital Printing, 2012

Contents

About the Authors

EDITOR BIOSKETCH

Dr. Michael D. Mumford is the George Lynn Cross Distinguished Research Professor of Psychology at the University of Oklahoma, where he directs the Center for Applied Social Research. He received his doctoral degree from the University of Georgia in 1983 in the fields of organizational psychology and psychometrics. Dr. Mumford is a fellow of the American Psychological Association (divisions 3, 5, 10, 14), the Society for Industrial and Organizational Psychology, and the American Psychological Society. He has written more than 270 articles on creativity, leadership, planning, and ethics. He has served as senior editor of *The Leadership Quarterly*, and is on the editorial boards of the *Creativity Research Journal*, the *Journal of Creative Behavior*, *IEEE Transactions on Engineering Management*, *The International Journal of Creativity and Problem Solving*, and *Ethics and Behavior*. Dr. Mumford has served as principal investigator on grants totaling more than $30 million from the National Science Foundation, the National Institutes of Health, the Department of Defense, the Department of State, and the Department of Labor. He is a recipient of the Society for Organizational Psychology's M. Scott Myer award for applied research in the workplace.

CONTRIBUTOR BIOSKETCHES

Selcuk Acar is currently a doctoral student at the University of Georgia, studying the measurement of creativity and divergent thinking. In the past two years he has contributed several chapters to the revised edition of the Encyclopedia of Creativity (Academic Press), as well as research articles on testing of divergent thinking and quantitative studies of creativity.

Mark D. Agars, Ph.D. is a Professor of Psychology at the California State University at San Bernardino. His primary research and writing interests are in social-cognitive and contextual approaches to workplace gender issues, diversity management, and organizational creativity. Mark earned his Ph.D. in Industrial and Organizational Psychology from Penn State University in 1999.

Eunice Soriano de Alencar, Ph.D., is Professor of Psychology and Education at the Catholic University of Brasília, Brazil. Over the last 30 years, she has carried out research projects and published several books and numerous articles, especially on giftedness and creativity. Among her books are: *Psychology and Education of the Gifted, Psychology of Creativity, How to Develop the Creative Potential, Managing Creativity, The Child in the Family and in Society, Creativity and the Education of the Gifted, Creativity. Multiple Perspectives,* and *The Process of Creativity. Idea Production and Creative Techniques.* She is on the editorial board of several journals in Brazil and internationally, and is an honorary member of the Brazilian Council for Giftedness.

Deepa Aravind is Assistant Professor of Management at the Department of Business, City University of New York—College of Staten Island. She received her Ph.D. from Rutgers University. Her current research interests are in the areas of adoption and implementation of management practices/innovations in firms and corporate social responsibility initiatives.

Matthijs Baas is Assistant Professor of Work and Organizational Psychology at the University of Amsterdam. His research covers the role of mood and motivation in creativity and decision making. His work appeared in *European Review of Social Psychology*, *Journal of Personality and Social Psychology*, *Psychological Bulletin*, and *Science*.

Markus Baer is an Assistant Professor of Organizational Behavior at the Olin Business School, Washington University in St. Louis. He received his Ph.D. from the University of Illinois at Urbana-Champaign. His current research examines the determinants of the various activities (e.g., problem formulation, idea generation, solution implementation) underlying creativity and innovation in organizations.

Dr. Min Basadur began developing his insights about creative thinking and problem solving at Procter & Gamble. He received three US patents and created a corporate-wide internal consulting practice. Following his award-winning doctoral research at the University of Cincinnati, he became a Professor of Management in the Michael G. DeGroote School of Business at McMaster University. His most recent book, *The Power of Innovation,* became an instant CEO need-to-read.

Min founded Basadur Applied Creativity (formerly the Center for Research in Applied Creativity) in 1981. This now worldwide network of consulting and research associates uses his trademarked Simplex™ system to consult internationally with major organizations, including: Microsoft, Frito-Lay, PepsiCo, Goodrich Corp., Pfizer, Clemson University, Stelco, USA Today, Nav Canada, Procter & Gamble, Cancer Care Ontario, Atomic Energy of Canada, USAF Aeronautical Labs, Kimball International, Woodstream, Nabisco, Royal Bank of Canada, Tricon Global, Aera Energy, Bristol & West, Canon, and Ford.

Tim Basadur is a doctoral student in Managerial Studies at the University of Illinois at Chicago (UIC). His research interests include topics that can be said to fall under managerial cognition including individual and organizational creativity, regulatory mode orientation, and social network analysis. Prior to enrolling at UIC, Tim worked as a creativity and innovation consultant for more than 10 years, developing trainers and process leaders, and leading strategic planning, facility design and team initiatives in a variety of organizations.

George Benson is an Associate Professor of Management at the University of Texas, Arlington. He received his doctorate from the Marshall School of Business at the University of Southern California. His research interests focus on multiple aspects of leveraging human capital in organizations, including expatriates, boards, and HR practices.

Meagan Brock is an Assistant Professor of Management at West Texas A&M University. She earned her Ph.D. in Industrial/Organizational Psychology at The University of Oklahoma. Her current research is in the area of counter-productivity and time waste in the work place, with a particular focus on organizational support, incentives and culture as a catalyst for employee productivity and engagement. Her past research endeavors have been in the areas of human resources systems development, research ethics, and information systems misuse.

M. Ronald Buckley holds the JC Penney Company Chair of Business Leadership and is a Professor of Management and a Professor of Psychology in the Michael F. Price College of Business at the University of Oklahoma. He earned his Ph.D. in Industrial/Organizational Psychology from Auburn University. His research interests include, among others, work motivation, racial and gender issues in performance evaluation, business ethics, interview issues, and organizational socialization. His work has been published in journals such as the *Academy of Management Review, Personnel Psychology, Journal of Applied Psychology, Organizational Behavior and Human Decision Processes*, and the *Journal of Management*.

John F. Cabra, Ph.D. is an Assistant Professor at the International Center for Studies in Creativity. He was a former operations manager for American Airlines in Buffalo, New York. He has also held internal consulting positions for American Airlines in the fields of training and development, employee relations, and organizational development for its Miami, Caribbean, and Latin America division. Before joining American Airlines, John was a bilingual training and organizational development specialist for Fisher-Price Toys. As an external consultant, John designed and presented programs on leadership and creativity for organizations such as IBM, Cadbury Schweppes, Kraft Foods, United Airlines, ConAgra Foods, The Consortium of College and University Media Centers, Chilean Travel and Tourism Association, Boehringer Maanheim, Quaker Oats, University of Rochester, Hyatt Aruba, Transitions Optical, and El Dorado Bogotá International Airport Authority. John has presented his work in 22 countries. His research interests are organizational creativity, perceptions of creativity across cultures and the efficacy of 3D virtual platforms in the classroom. He has published articles in US and Latin American business journals. He serves as an editorial board member of Creatividad y Sociedad, a creativity journal published at the University of Barcelona, Spain. John holds a Ph.D. in Organizational Psychology from the University of Manchester, England, and a M.S. in Creativity and Change Leadership from the State University of New York, Buffalo State College.

Ingegerd M. Carlsson, is a Certified Psychologist, and got her Ph.D. in 1992 in Psychology with the thesis *The Creative Personality: Hemispheric Variation and Sex Differences in Defence Mechanisms Related to Creativity.* Since 2005, she has held the chair as Professor in Personality and Social Psychology at Lund University, Sweden. Ingegerd Carlsson is an active teacher, supervisor and researcher. She has studied creativity in the domains of personality, neuropsychology, developmental, as well as work and organizational psychology. Currently she leads a project on the importance of the dream sleep (REM) stage for creativity.

Scott Cassidy is a Ph.D. candidate in the Industrial and Organizational Psychology program at the Pennsylvania State University. His research interests include creativity and innovation management, as well as leadership and personnel selection. Within these, and other areas, he has published several journal articles and book chapters in outlets such the *Journal of Personality and Social Psychology.*

Fariborz Damanpour received his Ph.D. from the University of Pennsylvania. He is a Professor at the Department of Management and Global Business, Rutgers University, where he served as the chairperson from 1996 to 2002. His primary area of research is management of innovation and change in organizations. His recent papers have been published in the *Journal of Management Studies* (2009), *Business & Society* (2009), *Journal of Public Administration Research and Theory* (2009), *Journal of Operations Management* (2010), and *British Journal of Management* (2010).

Amanda Deane, M.S. is a Consultant with SWA Consulting in Raleigh, NC. Amanda earned her M.S. in Industrial and Organizational Psychology from California State University at San Bernardino in 2010. Her thesis research examined a model of the relationship between core self-evaluations and job satisfaction.

Triparna de Vreede is a Ph.D. student at the Department of Psychology at the University of Nebraska at Omaha. She is a research associate at the Center for Collaboration Science. She is a trained facilitator of thinkLets-based Group Support Systems workshops. Her research focuses on the psychological foundations of thinkLets-based collaboration process, cognitive processes of creativity, and creativity in groups.

Deborah Dougherty is a Professor of Management in the Management and Global Business Department, Rutgers Business School, Rutgers University, The State University of New Jersey. She earned her Ph.D. in Management from the Sloan School of Management, M.I.T. Her current research focuses on complex innovation challenges, science-based innovation, and organizing for innovation.

Carsten K.W. De Dreu is Professor of Psychology at the University of Amsterdam, fellow of the Society of Industrial and Organizational Psychology, and President of the European Association for Social Psychology. His research covers social conflict, group decision making, and the psychology of creativity. He has published over 150 research articles and scholarly book chapters, in such outlets as *Journal of Applied Psychology, Journal of Personality and Social Psychology, Psychological Bulletin*, and *Science*.

Robert Drazin is a Professor of Organization and Management at the Goizueta Business School. Professor Drazin received his Ph.D. from the Wharton School of the University of Pennsylvania in 1982. He then taught at the Graduate School of Business, Columbia University. He joined the Goizueta Business School of Emory University in 1988. His research interests include organization design, organization theory, and the management of innovation and growth in large corporations. He has

published in *Administrative Science Quarterly, Management Science, Strategic Management Journal, Academy of Management Review, Academy of Management Journal, Organization Science,* and *Organization Studies*.

Damon Drown is a Ph.D. candidate in Industrial/Organizational Psychology at Portland State University. His areas of interest include creativity in the workplace, and influences on work-team effectiveness.

Danielle D. Dunne is an Assistant Professor of Strategy in the School of Management at Binghamton University, State University of New York. She earned her Ph.D. in Management from Rutgers University, The State University of New Jersey. Her current research focuses on innovation and learning in organizations and in alliance relationships.

Mary Dzindolet is Chair and Full Professor in the Department of Psychology at Cameron University in Lawton, Oklahoma. She earned a Masters of Applied Statistics from Louisiana State University in Baton Rouge, Louisiana in 1987 and a Ph.D. in Experimental Psychology from the University of Texas at Arlington in 1992. As a graduate student she conducted research on group creativity in the laboratory of Dr. Paul B. Paulus. Since then she has published over forty articles which explore group creativity or automation reliance.

Aliyah Edwards works in human resources at SAP America. Prior to joining SAP, she earned her M.S. in Human Resource Development at Villanova University. She has also held a position at Coca Cola in Atlanta.

K. Anders Ericsson, Ph.D., is presently Conradi Eminent Scholar and Professor of Psychology at Florida State University. After completing his Ph.D. in Sweden, he collaborated with the Nobel Prize winner in Economics, Herbert A. Simon on verbal reports of thinking leading to their classic book *Protocol Analysis: Verbal Reports as Data* (1984). Currently he studies the measurement of expert performance in domains such as music, chess, nursing, law enforcement, and sports, and studies how expert performers attain their superior performance by acquiring complex cognitive mechanisms and physiological adaptations through extended deliberate practice. He has edited several books on expertise, including the influential *Cambridge Handbook of Expertise and Expert Performance* and the recent *Development of Professional Expertise*, which appeared in 2010. He has published articles in prestigious journals, such as *Science, Psychological Review, and Trends of Cognitive Science*. He is a Fellow of the Center for Advanced Study in the Behavioral Sciences, of the American Psychological Association and the Association for Psychological Science and a member of the Royal Swedish Academy of Engineering Sciences. His ideas have been recently featured in Gladwell's book *Outliers*, Colwin's *Talent is Overrated*, Coyle's *The Talent Code*, Syed's *Bounce* and Levitt & Dubner's *Superfreakonomics: The Super-illustrated Version*.

Katrina A. Graham is a doctoral student at Drexel University in the Department of Management and Organizational Behavior. Prior to beginning her doctoral work, she earned her M.S. in Human Resource Development at Villanova University, and she also worked as a Personnel Officer in the United States Air Force.

Jonathon R. B. Halbesleben is the HealthSouth Chair of Health Care Management in the Culverhouse College of Commerce and Business Administration at the University of Alabama. He received his Ph.D. in Industrial/Organizational Psychology from the University of Oklahoma. His research focuses on employee safety and well-being, performance, and health care management. His work has been published in the *Journal of Applied Psychology, Journal of Management,*

Academy of Management Learning and Education, and *Leadership Quarterly*.

Kimberly S. Hester is a doctoral student in the industrial and organizational psychology program at the University of Oklahoma. Her research interests include creativity, innovation, and leadership.

Eva V. Hoff, is a trained senior high school teacher, and got her Ph.D. at Lund University, Sweden in psychology in 2003 with the thesis: *The Creative World of Middle Childhood: Creativity, Imagination, and Self-Image from Qualitative and Quantitative Perspectives*. Since 2008, she has been the head of a European Creativity Research Group with an educational focus. Eva Hoff is an active teacher, supervisor and researcher. She has studied creativity in relation to self-esteem and imagination. She has developed creativity measurements and has studied creativity in different educational contexts, such as in higher education and in elementary school.

Sam Hunter is an Assistant Professor of Psychology at the Pennsylvania State University and received his Ph.D. in Industrial and Organizational Psychology from the University of Oklahoma in 2007. His primary research interests include leadership and innovation management. Dr. Hunter has published in outlets such as the *Journal of Applied Psychology*, the *Leadership Quarterly* and *Human Resource Management Review*. He currently serves on the editorial board of the *Leadership Quarterly*.

Keith James received a Ph.D. in Social Psychology and Organizational Behavior from the University of Arizona. He is currently a Professor of Industrial/Organizational Psychology at Portland State University and does work on: creativity and innovation in the workplace; organizational sustainability; organizations and disaster; occupational health psychology; and social–cultural influences on work outcomes. This chapter was completed while he was serving, with funding from the National Science Foundation (NSF), as a Grant Program Officer with the NSF's Education and Human Resource Development Division of NSF's Education and Human Resources Directorate.

Kimberly S. Jaussi is an Associate Professor of Organizational Behavior and Leadership in the School of Management at Binghamton University and a Fellow of the Center for Leadership Studies. She received her doctorate from the Marshall School of Business at the University of Southern California. Her research interests include creativity and leadership, strategic leadership, organizational commitment, and identity issues in diverse groups.

Anthony C. Klotz is a doctoral student in organizational behavior in the Price College of Business at the University of Oklahoma. He holds a Master of Business Administration degree from Creighton University. His past work experience includes significant management experience at a Fortune 500 firm and ownership of an entrepreneurial venture. His research interests include impression management, team conflict, counterproductive work behavior, and citizenship behavior, in organizations.

Nicholas W. Kohn is a Senior Scientist with General Dynamics in San Antonio, Texas. He is engaged in cognitive psychology research for the Department of Defense. Additionally, he is a lecturer at the University of Texas at San Antonio. He received his Ph.D. from Texas A&M University before spending time at the University of Texas at Arlington as a postdoctural research associate. His research interests include the cognitive and social mechanisms of creativity.

James C. Kaufman, Ph.D. is an Associate Professor of Psychology at the California State University at San Bernardino. He is the author/editor of 20 books and more than 175 papers. He received the 2003 Daniel E. Berlyne Award from APA's Division 10, NAGC's 2008 E. Paul Torrance Award, and the WPA's 2009 Early Career Research Award.

Robert Kazanjian is a Professor of Organization and Management at the Goizueta Business School, Emory University. Previously, he was a faculty member at the Ross School of Business, University of Michigan and a Visiting Professor at the Tuck School of Business at Dartmouth College. He received his Ph.D. in Organization and Strategy from the Wharton School of the University of Pennsylvania. His research interests center on the management of innovation and growth in both small, young firms and large, diversified firms. His particular interests relate to issues of capability creation, attaining synergies, innovation processes, and broad-scale organization design and change. He has published in *Academy of Management Journal, Academy of Management Review, Management Science, Strategic Management Journal,* and *Organization Studies*.

Gordana Licina holds an Honours Bachelor of Commerce Degree from the DeGroote School of Business at McMaster University. She is engaged in academic research focusing on the dynamics of innovation and creative problem solving within organizations. Gordana has a business background in the areas of B2B marketing, transportation logistics, and e-commerce.

Ginamarie S. Ligon is an Assistant Professor at Villanova University in the Department of Psychology and Graduate Programs in Human Resource Development. Her primary research areas are the identification and development of high level talent. She has published in *Leadership Quarterly, Journal of Creative Behavior,* and *Creativity Research Journal*. Prior to joining Villanova

University, she worked as Director of Performance Consulting at Psychological Associates in St. Louis.

Russ Marion (Clemson University) is author of the books, *The Edge of Organization* (1999) and *Leadership in Education* (2001); co-editor of the book, *Complexity Leadership*; editor of a special issue of *The Leadership Quarterly* on leadership and complexity; and author of numerous articles on leadership, including one that was honored in 2001 as best paper of the year by *The Leadership Quarterly* and the Center for Creative Leadership. Marion has provided research/consultation services on innovation for Lockheed Aeronautics, Bank of America, and Stryker Research. He co-organized workshops on complexity leadership at the Center for Creative Leadership and at George Washington University. He has presented on complexity leadership at the India Institute of Technology, the Institute for Management Development in Switzerland, in workshops on destructing complex movements at the US Department of Defense, and in a number of conference venues.

Jerad Moxley is currently a doctoral student at Florida State University. His research examines the use of long-term working memory during skilled performance, what practice activities can be considered deliberate practice, and how age affects the acquisition, maintenance, and application of skill.

Bernard A. Nijstad is Professor of Decision Making and Organizational Behavior at the University of Groningen. His research interests include (group) decision making and decision avoidance, creativity and innovation, and group dynamics and performance. His work appeared among others in *Personality and Social Psychology Review*, *Journal of Experimental Social Psychology*, *Journal of Personality and Social Psychology*, and *Organizational Behavior and Human Decision Processes*.

Greg R. Oldham is the J.F., Jr. and Jesse Lee Seinsheimer Chair in Business at the A.B. Freeman School of Business at Tulane University. He received his Ph.D. from Yale University. His research focuses on the personal and contextual conditions that prompt the creativity of individuals and teams in organizations.

Holly Osburn is an Assistant Professor of Management at the University of Central Oklahoma in Edmond, Oklahoma. Her research areas involve organizational planning, work life balance, and innovation management. She earned her Ph.D. in Industrial and Organizational Psychology from the University of Oklahoma.

Susannah Paletz has been a postdoctoral research associate at the University of Pittsburgh's Learning Research and Development Center since September 2008. From March 2004 to August 2008, she was a Research Psychologist at NASA Ames Research Center in the Human Systems Integration division, where she worked in the Distributed Team Decision Making Laboratory and the Human–Computer Interaction Laboratory. Dr. Paletz received her Ph.D. in social/personality psychology from the University of California, Berkeley in December 2003. Her research interests involve teamwork, creativity, and culture, and she has examined these topics in science, engineering, and aerospace domains.

Paul B. Paulus is Distinguished University Professor of Psychology in the Department of Psychology at the University of Texas at Arlington and director of the industrial/organizational program. He was formerly chair of that department and Dean of the College of Science. He has been a visiting scholar at the National Institute of Justice, the Uniformed Services University of the Health Sciences, University of Sidney, Carnegie Mellon University, the University of Pittsburgh and Bar Ilan University. He has conducted research on group creativity for 20 years, and on group and environmental processes for over 40 years. He has published eight books and over 100 papers and chapters on these and other topics. His most recent book is *Group Creativity: Innovation Through Collaboration* (Oxford University Press) with Bernard Nijstad. His main focus recently has been on understanding the group creative process from both social and cognitive perspectives and collaborating with cognitive scientists and computer scientists to develop a detailed neural–cognitive perspective of the group creative process.

Gerard J. Puccio, Ph.D. is Department Chair and Professor at the International Center for Studies in Creativity, Buffalo State; a unique academic department that offers the world's only master of science degree in creativity. Dr. Puccio has written more than 40 articles, chapters and books. His most recent book, co-authored with his colleagues Marie Mance and Mary Murdock, is titled *Creative Leadership: Skills that Drive Change* (2nd Edition published by Sage). In recognition of his outstanding work as a scholar, Dr. Puccio received the State University of New York Chancellor's Recognition Award for Research Excellence and the President's Medal for Scholarship and Creativity. He is also a recipient of the first ever Professor Tudor Rickards best paper award for an article published in the 2006 European journal *Creativity and Innovation Management*. As an accomplished speaker Dr. Puccio has delivered speeches and training programs to organizations around the world. Dr. Puccio holds a Ph.D. in organizational psychology from the University of Manchester, England.

Roni Reiter-Palmon, Ph.D., is the Issacson Distinguished Professor and Director of the Industrial/Organizational Psychology graduate program at the University of Nebraska at Omaha. She is also the Director of Research for the Center of Collaboration Science, a cross-disciplinary unit at the University of Nebraska at Omaha. She received her Ph.D. from George Mason University in Industrial/Organizational Psychology. Dr. Reiter-Palmon has published and has applied experiences in the areas of individual creativity and innovation, teamwork and collaboration, leadership, personality in the workplace, and job analysis. She is an Associate Editor of *Journal of Creative Behavior* and serves on the editorial board of *Journal of Organizational Behavior, The Psychology of Aesthetics, Creativity and the Arts, International Journal of Creativity and Problem Solving, Journal of Leadership and Organizational Science*, and *The Leadership Quarterly*.

David R. Peterson is a doctoral student in the industrial and organizational psychology program at the University of Oklahoma. His research interests include creativity, innovation, and leadership.

Issac C. Robledo is a doctoral student in the industrial and organizational psychology program at the University of Oklahoma. His research interests include creativity, innovation, and leadership.

Mark A. Runco is the Torrance Professor of Creativity Studies at the University of Georgia, Athens. He was Director of the Torrance Center at UGA from 2008–2010. He continues to act as Editor of the *Creativity Research Journal* and co-editor of the *Encyclopedia of Creativity*. He is Past President of the APA's Division 10 and recipient of the Lifetime Achievement Award from the National Association for Gifted Children. His textbook, *Creativity: Theories, Themes, and Implications*, is being revised by Academic Press for release in 2011.

Claudia Sacramento is a lecturer in Organizational Behavior at the Department for Work and Organizational Psychology, Aston Business School, Birmingham, England. Her current research interests are in the areas of organizational creativity and team effectiveness.

Dean Keith Simonton received his Ph.D. in social psychology from Harvard University and is currently Distinguished Professor of Psychology at the University of California, Davis. Among his approximately four hundred publications are 12 books, including *Genius, Creativity, and Leadership* (Harvard 1984), *Why Presidents Succeed* (Yale University Press, 1987), *Scientific Genius* (Cambridge University Press, 1988), *Psychology, Science, and History* (Yale University Press, 1990), *Greatness* (Guilford Press, 1994), *Origins of Genius* (Oxford University Press, 1999), *Great Psychologists and Their Times* (APA Books, 2002), *Creativity in Science* (Cambridge University Press, 2004), *Genius 101* (Springer Publications, 2009), and *Great Flicks* (Oxford University Press, 2011). Simonton's honors include the William James Book Award, the Sir Francis Galton Award for Outstanding Contributions to the Study of Creativity, the Rudolf Arnheim Award for Outstanding Contributions to Psychology and the Arts, the George A. Miller Outstanding Article Award, the Theoretical Innovation Prize in Personality and Social Psychology, the President's Award from the National Association for Gifted Children, two Mensa Awards for Excellence in Research, and the Robert S. Daniel Award for Four-Year College/University Teaching. A Fellow of nearly a dozen scientific societies, including the American Association for the Advancement of Science, he has also been elected to the presidency of three scientific organizations, namely, the Society for General Psychology (Division 1, American Psychological Association), the International Association of Empirical Aesthetics, and the Society for the Psychology of Aesthetics, Creativity and the Arts (Division 10, American Psychological Association). His research program concentrates on the cognitive, personality, developmental, and sociocultural factors behind exceptional creativity, leadership, genius, and talent.

Blackely Smith is a current graduate student in the M.S. Industrial and Organizational Psychology Program at California State University at San Bernardino. The focus of her research is cognitive control explanations of the feedback–performance relationship.

Gudmund J. W. Smith In 1949, he got his Ph.D. in Psychology with the thesis *Psychological Studies in Twin Differences. With Reference to Afterimage and Eidetic Phenomena as well as more General Personality Characteristics.* Gudmund Smith was appointed Professor in Psychology at Lund University in 1960. He has developed the Percept-genetic Theory, which claims that vital aspects of a person's perception of the world originate from and are anchored in the personality. Together with his co-workers, Gudmund Smith has developed and validated several methods to measure adaptation within this theoretical frame. Among these methods are two semi-projective tests, one of perceptual defence and anxiety, and one of creative flexibility and fluency. A recent book is: *The Process Approach to Personality: Perceptgeneses and Kindred Approaches in Focus* (Smith, 2001).

Thomas B. Ward is Professor of Psychology at the University of Alabama. His research focuses on the nature of concepts, including how they are acquired, structured, combined, and used in creative and non-creative endeavors. Dr. Ward has studied the ways in which people apply existing knowledge to new situations, including tasks as diverse as imagining life on other planets and designing practical products. His most recent line of research examines creativity and problem solving in virtual environments. He also serves as Editor of the *Journal of Creative Behavior*.

Professor Michael West is Dean at Aston Business School. He graduated from the University of Wales in 1973 and received his

Ph.D. (*The Psychology of Meditation*) in 1977. He has authored, edited or co-edited 16 books including *The Essentials of Teamworking: International Perspectives* (John Wiley & Sons Ltd, 2005), *Teamwork, Teamdiagnose, Teamentwicklung [Team work, team diagnosis, team building]* (Hogrefe, 2005), *Effective Teamwork* (Blackwell, 2004) the first edition of which has been translated into 12 languages, *Building Team-Based Working: A Practical Guide to Organizational Transformation* (Blackwell, 2004), *The Secrets of Successful Team Management* (Duncan Baird, 2004), *Developing Team Based Organisations* (Blackwell, 2004), *The International Handbook of Organizational Teamwork and Cooperative Working* (Wiley, 2003), *Effective Top Management Teams* (Blackhall, 2001), *Developing Creativity in Organizations* (BPS, 1997) and the *Handbook of Workgroup Psychology* (Wiley, 1996). He has also published over 150 articles for scientific and practitioner publications, as well as chapters in scholarly books. He is a Fellow of the British Psychological Society, the American Psychological Association (APA), the APA Society for Industrial/ Organizational Psychology, the Higher Education Academy, the International Association of Applied Psychologists and a Chartered Fellow of the Chartered Institute of Personnel and Development. He is a member of the Board of the European Foundation for Management Development and an Academician of the Academy of Social Sciences.

His areas of research interest are team and organizational innovation and effectiveness, particularly in relation to the organization of health services. He lectures widely, both nationally and internationally, about the results of his research and his ideas for developing effective and innovative healthcare organizations.

Anthony R. Wheeler is an Associate Professor of Human Resources Management in the Schmidt Labor Research Center and the College of Business Administration at the University of Rhode Island. He completed his undergraduate degree at the University of Maryland, College Park and earned both his masters and doctoral degrees at the University of Oklahoma. His research interests include the influence of HRM practices on person–environment fit and include examining issues related to alternative staffing strategies. This research has lead to the publication of several scholarly articles in outlets such as *Journal of Management Education, Work & Stress, Leadership Quarterly, Journal of Occupational and Health Psychology, Issues in Multilevel Research, Research in Personnel and Human Resources Management, International Journal of Selection and Assessment, Journal of Business Ethics, Journal of Managerial Issues.*

Ben Wigert is a graduate student and research assistant at the University of Nebraska at Omaha. He is pursuing a Ph.D. in Industrial/Organizational Psychology, and an MBA. Ben's primary research interests include creative problem solving, teamwork, and leadership.

INTRODUCTION

1

Creativity in Organizations: Importance and Approaches

Michael D. Mumford, Kimberly S. Hester, and Issac C. Robledo

The University of Oklahoma, Norman, OK

To introduce the topic of creativity and innovation in organizations it is, perhaps, appropriate to begin with the traditional view. This traditional conception of creativity and innovation in organizations is aptly summarized in a quotation from John D. Rockefeller—the founder of Standard Oil and multiple modern organizations such as Exxon:

> "I have never felt the need for scientific knowledge, have never felt it. A young man who wants to succeed in business does not require chemistry or physics. He can always hire scientists." *(Chernow, 1997, p. 182).*

Implicit in this comment is a view, a traditional view, that creativity and innovation are simply of little importance to the success of organizations. It is a stereotype that remains with us today.

However, even a cursory reading of the history of organizations points to a rather different appraisal of creativity and innovation in understanding the causes of organizational growth and performance. DuPont's growth and success as an organization was ultimately based on fundamental discoveries with regard to polymer chemistry (Morgan, 1992). Our modern electrical industry grew as a result of creative work by Edison, Tesla, Westinghouse, and Ingersoll (Hughes, 1989). Indeed, the growth of modern organizations as a social phenomenon may be traced to the work, the creative work, of Fredrick Taylor in developing the basic ideas of scientific management (Kanigel, 1997). The effects of creativity and innovation are not limited to the world of business. Creativity and innovation were also evident in the development of the modern civil service system (Morris, 1979), an innovation critical to government, and the development of non-profit organizations such as hospitals (Mumford, 2002).

Although multiple other examples might be cited, the references seem sufficient to make our basic point; creativity and innovation are critical to the growth and performance of

Handbook of Organizational Creativity.
DOI: 10.1016/B978-0-12-374714-3.00001-X

organizations—business, government, and non-profit organizations. This handbook is an examination of the variables influencing creativity and innovation in organizations. It will examine both the context in which creativity and innovation occur and the variables operating at the individual, group, and organizational levels that influence creativity and innovation. We hope it will not only provide the background needed for further research in each of these areas, but will also provide managers with some practical ideas about how to encourage creativity and innovation in their own organizations. Before turning to the topics to be covered here, however, it might useful to begin by considering exactly what we mean by the terms creativity and innovation.

CREATIVITY AND INNOVATION

Definitions

If it is granted that creativity and innovation are critical to the growth and performance of organizations, then a new question comes to the fore: What, exactly, do we mean by the terms creativity and innovation? Our intuitive conception of creativity holds that it involves the production of new ideas (Guilford, 1950). Creativity, however, is not simply a matter of idea production—although this may be an important influence on creativity. Rather, creativity is defined as the production of high quality, original, and elegant solutions to problems (Besemer & O'Quin, 1999; Christaans, 2002; Ghiselin, 1963; Mumford & Gustafson, 1988).

This rather straightforward definition of creativity has five noteworthy implications. First, creativity is a form of performance—something the individual or group does. Thus creativity should not be confused with the many variables, for example personality, motivation, and expertise that influence the production of original, high quality, and elegant problem solutions. Second, creative work, as an outcome of problem-solving is, ultimately, a product of human cognition (Finke, Ward, & Smith, 1992; Marcy & Mumford, 2007). Thus in studies of creativity we are examining a cognitive production activity—albeit an activity that may be influenced by other variables. Third, creative problem-solving is typically viewed as a form of "high-level" cognition. This, in contrast to simpler, automatic, cognitive activities such as recognition and recall, is commonly considered to be demanding (Brophy, 1998). Fourth, as a form of high-level cognition, people make a decision, a conscious decision, as to whether they are willing to invest scarce resources in generating a creative problem solution. Fifth, no reference is made in this definition with respect to the level at which problem-solving may occur—in fact, it may occur at the individual, group or organization levels.

When creativity is viewed as a form of high-level cognition resulting in the production of original, high quality, and elegant problem solutions, a new question then arises. What kind of problems call for creative thought? Mumford and Gustafson (2007) have argued that creative thought is called for by problems that are novel, complex, and ill-defined, in the sense that they can be construed and solved in multiple ways. These problems, however, come in a variety of forms. Thus insight problems call for problem structuring, whereas divergent thinking problems call for the generation of multiple original responses. The particular types of problems calling for creative thought also vary as a function of domain (Baer, 2003). Thus the problems that call for creative thought in physics are in no way identical to those that call for creative thought in the arts. Finally, novelty, complexity, and ill-definition depend on the person working on the problem. Thus the problems that call for creative thought among physics professors are not identical to those that call for creative thought among physics students.

The solutions proposed to novel, complex, ill-defined problems among those who have substantial expertise in a domain of work are, at least potentially, of great value (Ericsson & Charness, 1994). The crafting, often reworking, of creative problem solutions into new products, processes, or services is the process we refer to as innovation (Jelinek & Schoonhoven, 1990; Nyström, 1979). Thus a research design may be viewed as creative, but the production of the research to implement this design and produce a journal article is a process of innovation. Similarly, creativity may be involved in aircraft design but the production of the new aircraft depends on innovation. These observations are noteworthy because they underscore a key point with regard to discussions of creativity and innovation. Ultimately, innovation, the production of a new product, service, or process, is possible only if a creative problem solution has already been generated. Thus creativity represents a necessary but not sufficient condition for innovation.

What should be recognized here, however, is that the production of new products, services, or processes based on creative problem solutions is by no means a simple venture. In fact, most new products fail in the market place (Sharma, 1999). Thus innovation is a high risk venture. Moreover, any innovative effort will typically involve multiple parties in the organization and all these parties must understand, act on, and contribute to translating the creative problem solution into a viable product, service, or process (Cohen & Levinthal, 1990; Dougherty & Hardy, 1996). Hence innovation is an organizational social phenomenon involving exchanges among multiple parties in turning problem solutions and ideas, into viable products, services, and processes. The term "viable" is of some importance because viable products, services, or processes in organizations are inherently ambiguous. An organization may learn from an innovative effort even if the product fails in the market (Senge, 1990). By the same token organizations must invest scarce resources wisely in the development of creative ideas (Nohria & Gulati, 1996). Thus innovative efforts in organizations are subject to a host of conflicting pressures (Mumford, Bedell-Avers, & Hunter, 2008).

In discussions of organizational innovation, it is common to distinguish among innovative efforts with respect to two key variables:

1. radical versus incremental, and
2. product versus process (Chandy & Tellis, 2000; Damanpour, 1991).

Incremental innovations represent improvements in existing products, processes, and services (e.g. the iPhone) while radical innovations represent transformative products, processes, and services (e.g. the transistor). Product innovations represent new things to be sold (e.g. a new drug) while process innovation represents new ways of developing and managing the business (e.g. product evaluation procedures). Of course, radical versus incremental and product versus process, while important distinctions among various kinds of innovations, are not the only variables that might be considered in describing innovations. For example, innovations may be distinguished as exploratory versus exploitable, fundamental versus peripheral, short term versus long-term development, disruptive versus nondisruptive, and low cost versus high cost. These various forms of innovation, moreover, are of interest because they have different implications for how innovation occurs and the consequences of the innovative efforts for people and organizations (Chandy & Tellis, 2000).

Impacts

Given the definitions of creativity and innovation we have provided, it should be clear that creativity and innovation are closely linked phenomena. These definitions of creativity and innovation, however, broach a broader question. Is there value to creativity and innovation in organizations? Given the topic of this volume, and people's stereotypic reactions to the terms of creativity and innovation, the intuitive answer to this question is; "of course, creativity and innovation have value". However, from the perspectives of an organization, this intuitive answer is often incorrect.

A number of attributes of organizational operations conspire to limit the value of creativity and innovation. To begin with, not all organizations are pursuing a strategy where innovation is likely to prove of value in enhancing organizational performances (Miles & Snow, 1978). Although creativity and innovation may be valued in organizations that succeed through production of innovative products, it may not prove of much value in those where success is based on cost control (Hitt, Hoskisson, Johnson, & Moesel, 1996). Along related lines, many, although not all, organizations must make significant capital investments, which often drive the work it does. Creative ideas or innovative products that disrupt the use of this capital are unlikely to prove of much value to the organization (Dean & Sharfman, 1996). To complicate matters further, creative ideas and innovative products can often be imitated. Because the economic gains of creative and innovative efforts often go to second or third order movers (ultimately imitators, rather than the original generator of the idea or product), the difficulty of protecting creative work may limit its value to an organization (Sharma, 1999). Thus three external variables; strategy, capital intensity, and imitatability, may limit the value of creativity and innovation to organizations.

However, it is not only external variables that may limit the value of creativity and innovation. Certain internal characteristics of organizations may also act in the same way. Organizations are structured as interactive systems, where system members acquire certain roles and certain forms of expertise (Katz & Khan, 1978). Creative and innovative efforts, however, may disrupt this internal structure, and cause a loss of focus that acts to inhibit organizational performance. In fact, recognition of this point led Cohen and Levinthal (1990) to argue that organizations respond effectively to creative and innovative efforts when absorptive capacity is high. The importance of absorptive capacity is evident in an obvious attribute of organizations—certain organizations work on certain kinds of innovations. Thus Boeing focuses on innovation in aircraft and IBM on innovation in software systems. The nature of internal organizational structures, however, points to another variable that limits organizations' investment in creative ideas and innovative efforts. Creativity and innovation are expensive in both direct terms, since the people doing the creative work must be paid and equipped (Nohria & Gulati, 1996), and in indirect terms, as other investments are limited, extant organizational processes are disrupted, and current markets may be lost (Chandy & Tellis, 2000). These direct and indirect costs of creative work may simply make creativity and innovation too costly for an organization to pursue.

The many varied forces in organizations that act to inhibit creativity and innovation led Sternberg (2005) to ask a question—a fundamental question: Do we really want them in organizations? Broadly speaking, four key variables exist that appear to encourage creativity and innovation:

1. turbulence,
2. pull forces,
3. exploitation potential, and
4. competitive pressure.

The term turbulence refers to instability, or change, in the environment in which the organization operates and it is a powerful stimulus to creativity and innovation. Thus, Dean and Sharfman (1996) in a study of the development of innovative new products by 140 manufacturing firms found that environmental change was positively related ($r = 0.32$) to innovation. In a study of innovation in the broadcasting industry, Greve and Taylor (2000) found that competitor innovations, and the turbulence it induces, could in turn serve to stimulate innovative efforts among firms. Similarly, Ettlie (1983) found in a study of the food processing industry that turbulence contributed to firm innovation. However, his findings, like those of Debruyne, Moenaert, Griffin, Hart, Hultink, and Robben (2002) indicate that the effect of turbulence on innovation in a firm may be moderated by the strategy it adopts to deal with a turbulent environment.

Along with turbulence, another variable that seems to shape the willingness of organizations to innovate is the pull of market forces. In a qualitative study of urban living innovations (e.g. energy conservation, recycling), Pelz (1983) found that market forces were a stronger influence on innovation than simple technological capability. Similarly, Buzzacchi, Colombo, and Mariotti (1995) found, in a study of innovation in the finance industry, that market demands were a powerful force shaping innovation by firms.

Of course, consumers may want something, but an organization may not be capable of providing the desired product or service due to technological capabilities. These are not developed in a progressive, linear fashion, but rather, as Wise (1992) points out, technology is developed slowly over time eventually reaching the point where exploitation is possible. It is at this point that innovation becomes widespread. The impact of technological capability was illustrated by Wise (1992) in a historical analysis of the rate of innovation in the electrical industry.

Thus three key variables—technological capability, market demand, and environmental turbulence—appear to stimulate creativity and innovation on the part of organizations. What should be recognized here is that rapid technological development, the opening of new global markets and substantial environmental turbulence are the hallmarks of the conditions under which 21st century organizations operate, and it is these conditions which have given rise to the new concern over creativity and innovation in organizations (Mumford, Scott, Gaddis, & Strange, 2002).

In fact, under these conditions creativity and innovation appear critical to the economic success of organizations. For example, Eisenhardt and Tabrizi (1995) have provided evidence indicating that the rate at which new products flow to market is a critical influence on the financial performance of high technology firms. Geroski, Machin, and Van Reenen (1993), in a study of 721 firms operating in the United Kingdom, found that the firm's rate of innovation was strongly related to its profitability. Not only are real, tangible economic outcomes of innovation observed under these conditions at the organization level, but, under these conditions, they appear to be associated with economic growth. Thus Mumford, Olsen, and James (1989) examined patent awards over the last half century—an index of creativity and innovation. They found that the number of patent awards, with a lagged effect of five to seven years, was a strong positive influence on economic growth beyond the expectations established by population size, capital, and prior economic growth.

Not only do creativity and innovation have tangible outcomes for organizations under the conditions in which they operate in the 21st century, they also appear to enhance a number of other aspects of organizational functioning. Tushman and O'Reilly (1996), for example, have provided evidence which indicates that an organization's ability to respond to crisis is in part attributable to its support of creativity and innovation. Mumford et al. (2008) have argued that not only is planning critical to creativity and innovation in organizations but that organizational planning processes may improve as a result of the concern with creativity and innovation. Other work by Amabile, Schatzel, Moneta, and Kramer (2004) indicates that opportunities for creative work may lead to a more satisfied and intrinsically oriented work force. Similarly, there is reason to suspect that the need for creativity and innovation contributes to teamwork, collaboration, and organizational citizenship behavior (Ayers, Dahlstrom, & Skinner, 1997; McGourty, Tarshis, & Dominick, 1996).

When one considers the financial and organizational outcomes associated with creativity and innovation, it seems clear that they have real value in organizations. This value broaches another question: How can we go about encouraging and managing creativity and innovation in organizations? It is to this question that the present handbook is addressed. However, for reasons to be considered at some depth in this volume, we do not believe that there are simple, straightforward answers.

CONTENT

Creativity and Innovation at Work

The problem confronting organizations seeking to manage creativity and innovation arises from three sources. One source is the known complexity of most aspects of the phenomena we refer to as creativity and innovation (Sternberg, 1999). The second source is attributable to the fact that creativity and innovation are multi-level phenomena (Mumford & Hunter, 2005), influenced by variables operating at the individual, group, organizational, and environmental levels. The third source of complexity arises from the fact that these variables are not well aligned. Hence, variables that influence creativity at the individual level often conflict with those at the group and organizational levels.

Perhaps the best example of the complexity of creativity and innovation may be found in what we know about creative thought. Mumford, Mobley, Uhlman, Reiter-Palmon, and Doares (1991) identified eight core processing activities involved in the production of creative problem-solving:

1. problem definition,
2. information gathering,

3. concept selection,
4. conceptual combination,
5. idea generation,
6. idea evaluation,
7. implementation planning, and
8. monitoring.

Not only are multiple processing operations involved in creative thought, effective execution of each process involves multiple different strategies for process execution with different strategies being called for depending on the knowledge the person is working with and the nature of the idea at this stage of its development (Lonergan, Scott, & Mumford, 2004; Scott, Lonergan, & Mumford, 2005).

The complex nature of the phenomena underlying creativity and innovation is not simply a matter of individual level phenomena. For example, Mumford et al. (2008) examined the role of the organizational planning in promoting creativity and innovation. They identified thirteen organizational level variables, including scanning, exploration of themes, identification of fundamentals to be pursued, and mission definition. What is of note here is that each of these organizational operations represents a complex activity in its own right. For example, consider what must be taken into account in scanning—customer needs, gaps in current products or services, technologies currently under development, feasibility of developing these technologies, critical issues that must be addressed in technology development, competitor actions with regard to this potentially, and likely countering of responses by competitors. Clearly, planning for creativity and innovation is as complex, if not more so, than generating creative problem solutions.

The complex nature of the phenomena involved in creativity and innovation is accentuated by another aspect of the phenomena. Variables operating at different levels of analysis influence creativity and innovation in organizational settings. At the individual level, creativity and innovation are influenced not only by creative thought but also expertise (Weisberg, 2006), abilities (Plucker & Renzulli, 1999), and motivation (Jaussi, Randel, & Dionne, 2007). At the group level, creativity and innovation are influenced by phenomena such as group process (Reiter-Palmon, Herman, Yammarino, 2008), climate perceptions (Hunter, Bedell-Avers, & Mumford, 2007), and leadership (Mumford et al., 2002). At the organizational level, they are influenced by phenomena such as organizational structuring (Damanpour, 1991), organizational learning (Drazin, Glynn, & Kazanjain, 1999), and strategy (Taggar, Sulsky, & MacDonald, 2008). These many and varied influences broach a critical question for those interested in enhancing creativity and innovation in organizations: At what level and with respect to what set of variables should interventions be made in attempts to enhance creativity and innovation?

The difficulty in selecting the level at which interventions are to be made, however, is complicated by yet another observed phenomenon. Influences on creativity and innovation operating at one level are not always consistent with those operating at other levels. Of course, in some cases, these influences are internally consistent. For example, work climate variables, such as mission definition and support for creativity, are found at a group level to influence creativity and innovation (Hunter et al., 2007). Also, at an individual level, Oldham and Cummings (1996) found that creative people are especially sensitive to climate influences. Unfortunately, in many cases this kind of consistency is not observed (Mumford & Hunter, 2005); for example, at an organizational level, control and direction are positive influences on creativity and innovation (Cardinal, 2001), but at an individual level creative people seek autonomy (Feist, 1999). Similarly, collaboration and cohesion are commonly found to be positive influences on creativity in group level studies (Kessler & Chakrabarti, 1996), but at the individual level, autonomous exploration appears critical (Mumford, 2000). These at least apparently contradictory cross-level effects make the development of effective interactions to enhance creativity and innovation an uncertain undertaking—one with little assurance of success it if is not aided by the best research available.

The Present Volume

The intent of the present volume is to bring together the best research and theory which has a bearing on creativity and innovation in organizations. Our goals in this effort were twofold: first, to identify critical issues to be addressed in future research, and second, to provide organizations with guidelines for the development of interventions intended to enhance creativity and innovation. As one might suspect, based on our foregoing observations, the content of this volume follows a multi-level framework. Thus chapters are devoted to critical influences on creativity and innovation operating at the individual, group, and organizational levels of analysis. Prior to examining the influences operating at these levels, the basic phenomena of creativity and innovation in organizations are examined—who does creative work? How is research on creativity and innovation conducted? The final section of the volume considers some of the interventions that have been used in attempts to enhance creativity and innovation in organizations.

Introduction

The first section of this volume examines background considerations that must be taken into account as one considers the available research. We begin with a chapter by James and Drown (this volume) that examines trends in organizational creativity research across the last 15 years, by conducting a content analysis of publications in major organizational journals. This chapter is noteworthy in that it has aided in identifying areas which call for more investigation—such as team-level, and national culture studies. In the next chapter, Mumford, Hester, and Robledo (this volume) examine the methods used in studies of creativity and innovation. It is noted that such studies are based on four key measures of creativity and innovation: 1) product, 2) performance attributes, 3) behavior, and 4) outcomes. The major methods, qualitative, historiometric, survey, psychometric, and experimental, are then described in this chapter.

The next two introductory chapters consider two key issues that provide a context in which studies of creativity and innovation are conducted in organizations. Simonton (this volume), in his chapter, examines the fields and domains in which creative work occurs, by taking a systems perspective. One illustration he provides notes that domains can be organized hierarchically by how exact and paradigmatic they are. Alencar (this volume) examines the facilitators and inhibitors for creativity and innovation that one commonly encounters in organizational settings.

Individual Level

Traditionally, studies of creativity and innovation have focused on the individual's production of multiple new ideas or divergent thinking (Guilford, 1950). Acar and Runco (this volume) examine the basic cognitive abilities underlying creative thought. Their chapter is noteworthy in that it reminds us that creativity is not solely a matter of divergent thinking but that it also requires convergent thinking abilities such as evaluation skills. A similar point is made by Ericsson and Moxley (this volume). Their chapter contains a compelling argument for the influence of expertise on creative problem-solving. Ward (this volume) in his chapter, however, reminds us that expertise is not a fully sufficient basis for creative thought. In this chapter the various cognitive processing operations and the strategies contributing to effective process execution are examined. In one way or another, all these chapters underscore the need for both divergent and convergent thinking. Puccio and Cabra (this volume) examine an ongoing stream of research examining how divergent and convergent thinking work together in the production of new ideas and creative problem solutions, pointing out the complex interactions that exist between these two modes of thought.

Creative thought is a complex form of high-level cognition (Finke et al., 1992). As a result, people decide when and how to be creative. This rather straightforward observation implies that affect and motivation will be important influences that shape creativity at the individual level. De Dreu and Baas (this volume) consider the available research which shows how affect and motivation influence creativity. Notably, this chapter points to the complex nature of these influences with regard to timing, intensity, and direction. Of course, given the impact of these factors, one would also expect that personality would also influence creativity. Hoff, Carlsson, and Smith (this volume) examine the influence of personality variables, such as openness. The influence of affect, motivation, and personality on creativity also suggests that creativity and innovation, as individual level phenomena, will be influenced by the context confronting the individual. Agars, Kaufman, and Smith (this volume) examine how the context in which the individual is working influences creativity at the individual level.

Group Level

Of course, a critical contextual influence shaping creativity and innovation is the social context in which the creative effort occurs. Thus Reiter-Palmon, Wigert, and de Vreede (this volume) examine how group composition, cognition, and social processes influence creativity and innovation, while Paulus, Dzindlot, and Kohn (this volume) examine the influence of the nature of teams and their structure and characteristic pattern of interactions. Both these chapters are noteworthy because they remind us that creative and innovative work is typically not accomplished by an individual working alone, but rather by a group or team, and characteristics of these interactions may either facilitate or inhibit creativity and innovation.

In organizations a number of group level variables influence creativity and innovation, such as the climate and context in which work is being conducted (Hunter et al., 2007). In their chapters, West and Sacramento (this volume) and Oldham and Baer (this volume) examine the influence of climate perceptions and work context. Of course, these factors are strongly influenced by what the team is working on and how the team is lead. Paletz (this volume) in her chapter considers how project teams should be structured and managed to promote creativity and innovation, while Marion (this volume) considers the influence of the actions taken by team leaders.

Organizational Level

Our foregoing observations with regard to the influence of a leader point to the importance of organizational level influences on creativity and innovation. One critical influence in this regard is whether the organization is willing to provide a structure for engaging in creative and innovative work. Thus Damanpour and Aravind (this volume) examine aspects of organizational structure that influence creativity and innovation. They also examine historic explanations of organizational structure (e.g., mechanistic and organic) and more modern explanations of organizational structure (e.g, ambidextrous), and weigh the value of such explanations.

In organizations, effective strategic investments in creativity and innovation require marshalling knowledge, people, and resources to produce something. This observation has an important, albeit often overlooked implication; that organizational planning is likely to be a powerful influence on creativity and innovation. Hunter, Cassidy, and Ligon (this volume) examine how planning should occur to promote creativity and innovation in organizational settings. This chapter, while pointing to the importance of planning, also indicates that it is a complex, dynamic, activity. One of its critical aspects is that it provides a basis for organizational learning and acquisition of the capacity to absorb innovations. Thus, Kazanjian and Drazin (this volume) examine how organizational learning and knowledge both shape and are influenced by creativity and innovation. Organizational learning, however, also implies that a change event has occurred. In fact, change has been considered a hallmark of creativity and innovation, and there is reason to suspect that change and change management is critical to creativity and innovation at an organizational level. Dunne and Dougherty (this volume), provide a compelling argument for the impact of change management on the success of creative and innovative efforts.

Interventions

Dunne and Dougherty's (this volume) work reminds us that there are many actions that organizations can take to encourage creativity and innovation. In the final section of this volume we examine some of the interventions that organizations might take in an attempt to encourage creativity and innovation. One such intervention involves the selection of creative people and the definition of career paths creative people might follow in an organization. Jaussi and Benson (this volume) examine issues bearing on selection and career paths. Another intervention involves rewarding creative work. Although rewards for creative work are controversial (Eisenberger & Rhoades, 2001), Klotz, Wheeler, Halbesleben, Brock, and Buckley (this volume) provide a potentially viable approach for rewarding people for creative and innovative efforts. Another common intervention used to encourage creativity and innovation is training (Scott, Leritz, & Mumford, 2004). Ligon, Graham, Edwards, Osburn, and Hunter (this volume) examine the approaches that have proven most effective in creativity training, and how these approaches should be implemented in organizations. Of course, all these interventions represent aspects of broader organizational development interventions. Basadur, Basadur, and Licina (this volume) examine how systematic organizational development interventions contribute to creativity and innovation. Finally

Robledo, Hester, Peterson, and Mumford (this volume) review the critical implications of all these chapters for enhancing creativity and innovation in organizational settings.

CONCLUSIONS

Any effort, including an effort of this scope, has its limitations. Clearly, we are not attempting in this volume to describe every phenomenon that has been shown to influence creativity and innovation. For example, biology (Lumsden, 1999) and brain functioning (Cartwright, Clark-Carter, Ellis, & Matthews, 2004) have been linked to individual level creativity. Similarly, the functioning of society as a whole has been shown to influence creativity and innovation (Simonton, 1999). Although we believe these and other topics are important to understanding creativity and innovation, in the present effort we have taken a more narrow approach, focusing on creativity and innovation as they occur in the context of organizations.

This narrow focus is a potentially noteworthy limitation on the contribution of the present effort. By the same token, creativity and innovation occur in the context of organizations (Pierce & Delbecq, 1977), and are critical to their success and long-term growth (Tushman & O'Reilly, 1996). It is therefore necessary to understand the forces that shape creativity and innovation in organizations both to understand how they occur in real-world settings, and to allow organizations to capitalize on the creative and innovative capacities that exist within all organizations.

To capitalize on creativity and innovation, however, organizations must bear in mind three key considerations. First, creativity and innovation are highly complex phenomena at any given level of analysis. Second, multiple phenomena exist at the individual, group, and organizational levels. Third, the phenomena that operate at one level are not necessarily well integrated, or consistent with, those operating at other levels. Complexity, multiple levels, and inconsistencies in effects across levels present all organizations with a challenge in their attempts to encourage creativity and innovation. We hope that the present volume will provide some guidelines as to the phenomena that should be considered in attempts to understand organizational creativity and innovation and the kind of actions that should be taken to encourage them in organizations.

References

Amabile, T. M., Schatzel, E. A., Moneta, G. B., & Kramer, S. J. (2004). Leader behaviors and work environment for creativity: Perceived leader support. *Leadership Quarterly, 15,* 5–32.

Ayers, D., Dahlstrom, R., & Skinner, S. J. (1997). An exploratory investigation of organizational antecedents to new product success. *Journal of Marketing Research, 34,* 107–116.

Baer, J. (2003). Evaluative thinking, creativity, and task specificity: Separating wheat from chaff is not the same as finding needle in haystacks. In M. A. Runco (Ed.), *Critical creative processes* (pp. 129–152). Cresskill, NJ: Hampton.

Besemer, S. P., & O'Quin, K. (1999). Confirming the three-factor creative product analysis matrix model in an American sample. *Creativity Research Journal, 12,* 287–296.

Brophy, D. R. (1998). Understanding, measuring, and enhancing individual creative problem-solving efforts. *Creativity Research Journal, 11,* 123–150.

Buzzacchi, L., Colombo, M. G., & Mariotti, S. (1995). Technological regimes and innovation in services: The case of the Italian banking industry. *Research Policy, 24,* 151–168.

Cardinal, L. B. (2001). Technological innovation in the pharmaceutical industry: The use of organizational control on managing research and development. *Organizational Science, 12,* 19–37.

Cartwright, M., Clark-Carter, D., Ellis, S. J., & Matthews, C. (2004). Temporal lobe epilepsy and creativity: A model of association. *Creativity Research Journal, 16,* 27–34.

Chandy, R. K., & Tellis, G. J. (2000). The incumbent's curse? Incumbency, size and radical innovation. *Journal of Marketing, 64,* 1–17.

Chernow, R. (1997). *Titan: The life of John D. Rockefeller, Sr.* New York, NY: Vintage.

Christiaans, H. H. C. M. (2002). Creativity as a design criterion. *Creativity Research Journal, 14,* 41–54.

Cohen, W. M., & Levinthal, D. A. (1990). Absorptive capacity: A new perspective on learning and innovation. *Administrative Science Quarterly, 35,* 128–152.

Damanpour, F. (1991). Organizational innovation: A meta-analysis of effects of determinants and moderators. *Academy of Management Journal, 34,* 555–590.

Dean, J. W., Jr., & Sharfman, M. P. (1996). Does decision process matter? A study of strategic decision-making effectiveness. *Academy of Management Journal, 39,* 368–396.

Debruyne, M., Moenaert, R., Griffin, A., Hart, S., Hultink, E. J., & Robben, H. (2002). The impact of new product launch strategies on competitive reaction to industrial markets. *Journal of Product Innovation Management, 19,* 159–170.

Dougherty, D., & Hardy, B. F. (1996). Sustained innovation production in large mature organizations: Overcoming organization problems. *Academy of Management Journal, 39,* 826–851.

Drazin, R., Glynn, M. A., & Kazanjain, R. K. (1999). Multi-level theorizing about creativity in organizations: A sensemaking perspective. *Academy of Management Review, 24,* 286–329.

Eisenberger, R., & Rhoades, L. (2001). Incremental effects of reward on creativity. *Journal of Personality and Social Psychology, 81,* 728–741.

Eisenhardt, K. M., & Tabrizi, B. N. (1995). Accelerating adaptive processes: Product innovation in the global computer industry. *Administrative Science Quarterly, 40,* 84–110.

Ericsson, K. A., & Charness, W. (1994). Expert performance: Its structure and acquisition. *American Psychologist, 49,* 725–747.

Ettlie, J. E. (1983). Organizational policy and innovation among suppliers to the food-processing sector. *Academy of Management Journal, 26,* 27–44.

Feist, G. J. (1999). The influence of personality on artistic and scientific creativity. In R. J. Sternberg (Ed.), *Handbook of creativity* (pp. 273–296). Cambridge, UK: Cambridge University Press.

Finke, R. A., Ward, T. B., & Smith, S. M. (1992). *Creative cognition: Theory, research, and applications.* Cambridge, MA: The MIT Press.

Geroski, P., Machin, S., & Van Reenen, J. (1993). The profitability of innovating firms. *RAND Journal of Economics, 24,* 198–212.

Ghiselin, B. (1963). Ultimate criteria for two levels of creativity. In C. W. Taylor & F. Barron (Eds.), *Scientific creativity: Its recognition and development* (pp. 30–43). New York, NY: Wiley.

Greve, H. R., & Taylor, A. (2000). Innovations as catalysts for organizational change: Shifts in organizational cognition and search. *Administrative Science Quarterly, 45,* 54–80.

Guilford, J. P. (1950). Creativity. *American Psychologist, 5,* 444–454.

Hitt, M. A., Hoskisson, R. E., Johnson, R. A., & Moesel, D. D. (1996). The market for corporate control and firm innovation. *Academy of Management Journal, 39,* 1084–1196.

Hughes, T. P. (1989). *American genesis: A history of the American genius for invention.* New York, NY: Penguin.

Hunter, S. T., Bedell-Avers, K. E., & Mumford, M. D. (2007). Climate for creativity: A quantitative review. *Creativity Research Journal, 19,* 69–90.

Jaussi, K., Randel, A., & Dionne, S. (2007). I am, I think I can, and I do: The role of personal identity, self-efficacy, and cross-application of experiences in creativity at work. *Creativity Research Journal, 19,* 247–258.

Jelinek, M., & Schoonhoven, C. B. (1990). *Innovation marathon: Lessons from high technology firms.* Oxford, UK: Blackwell.

Kanigel, R. (1997). *The one best way: Frederick Winslow Taylor and the enigma of efficiency.* New York, NY: Penguin.

Katz, R. J., & Khan, R. (1978). *The social psychology of organizations.* New York, NY: Wiley.

Kessler, E., & Chakrabarti, A. K. (1996). Innovation speed: A conceptual model of context, antecedents, and outcomes. *Academy of Management Review, 21,* 1143–1191.

A. INTRODUCTION

Lonergan, D., Scott, G. M., & Mumford, M. D. (2004). Evaluative aspects of creative thought: Effects of appraisal and revision standards. *Creativity Research Journal, 16,* 231–246.

Lumsden, C. J. (1999). Evolving creative minds: Stories and mechanisms. In R. J. Sternberg (Ed.), *Handbook of creativity.* Cambridge, UK: Cambridge University Press.

Marcy, R. T., & Mumford, M. D. (2007). Social innovation: Enhancing creative performance through causal analysis. *Creativity Research Journal, 19,* 123–140.

McGourty, J., Tarshis, L. A., & Dominick, P. (1996). Managing innovation: Lessons from world class organizations. *International Journal of Technology Management, 11,* 354–368.

Miles, R. E., & Snow, C. C. (1978). *Organizational strategy, structure and process.* New York, NY: McGraw-Hill.

Morgan, P. W. (1992). Discovery and invention in polymer chemistry. In R. J. Weber & D. N. Perkins (Eds.), *Inventive minds: Creativity in technology* (pp. 178–193). New York, NY: Oxford University Press.

Mumford, M. D. (2000). Managing creative people: Strategies and tactics for innovation. *Human Resource Management Review, 10,* 313–351.

Mumford, M. D. (2002). Social innovation: Ten cases from Benjamin Franklin. *Creativity Research Journal, 14,* 253–266.

Mumford, M. D., Bedell-Avers, K. E., & Hunter, S. T. (2008). Planning for innovation: A multi-level perspective. In M. D. Mumford, S. T. Hunter & K. E. Bedell (Eds.), *Innovation in organizations: A multi-level perspective* (pp. 107–154). Oxford, UK: Elsevier.

Mumford, M. D., & Gustafson, S. B. (1988). Creativity syndrome: Integration, application, and innovation. *Psychological Bulletin, 103,* 27–43.

Mumford, M. D., & Gustafson, S. B. (2007). Creative thought: Cognition and problem solving in a dynamic system. In M. A. Runco (Ed.), *Creativity research handbook: Volume II* (pp. 33–77). Cresskill, NJ: Hampton.

Mumford, M. D., & Hunter, S. T. (2005). Innovation in organizations: A multi-level perspective on creativity. In F. Dansereau & F. J. Yammarino (Vol. Eds.), *Research in multi-level issues: Vol. 4. Multi-level issues in strategy and methods* (pp. 317–376). Bingley, UK: Emerald Group Publishing Limited.

Mumford, M. D., Mobley, M. I., Uhlman, C. E., Reiter-Palmon, R., & Doares, L. (1991). Process analytic models of creative capacities. *Creativity Research Journal, 4,* 91–122.

Mumford, M. D., Olsen, M. A., & James, L. R. (1989). Age-related changes in the likelihood of major contributions. *International Journal of Aging and Human Development, 29,* 9–32.

Mumford, M. D., Scott, G. M., Gaddis, B. H., & Strange, J. M. (2002). Leading creative people: Orchestrating expertise and relationships. *The Leadership Quarterly, 13,* 705–750.

Nohria, K., & Gulati, S. (1996). Is slack good or bad for innovation? *Academy of Management Journal, 39,* 799–825.

Nyström, H. (1979). *Creativity and innovation.* New York, NY: Wiley.

Oldham, G. R., & Cummings, A. (1996). Employee creativity: Personal and contextual factors at work. *Academy of Management Journal, 39,* 607–634.

Pelz, D. C. (1983). Quantitative case histories of urban innovation: Are there innovating stages? *IEEE Transactions on Engineering Management, 30,* 60–67.

Pierce, J., & Delbecq, L. A. (1977). Organizational structure, individual attitudes, and innovation. *Academy of Management Review, 2,* 27–37.

Plucker, J. A., & Renzulli, J. S. (1999). Psychometric approaches to the study of human creativity. In R. J Sternberg (Ed.), *Handbook of creativity* (pp. 35–61). New York, NY: Cambridge University Press.

Reiter-Palmon, R., Herman, A. E., & Yammarino, F. J. (2008). Creativity and cognitive processes: Multi-level linkages between individual and team cognition. In F. Dansereau & F. J. Yammarino (Series Eds.) & M. D. Mumford, S. T. Hunter, & K. E. Bedell-Avers (Vol. Eds.), *Research in multi-level issues: Vol. 7. Multi-level issues in creativity and innovation* (pp. 203–267). Bingley, UK: Emerald Group Publishing Limited.

Scott, G. M., Leritz, L. E., & Mumford, M. D. (2004). The effectiveness of creativity training: A meta-analysis. *Creativity Research Journal, 16,* 361–388.

Scott, G. M., Lonergan, D., & Mumford, M. (2005). Conceptual combination: Alternative knowledge structures, alternative heuristics. *Creativity Research Journal, 17,* 79–98.

Senge, P. M. (1990). *The fifth discipline.* London, UK: Century Business.

Sharma, A. (1999). Central dilemmas of managing innovation in large firms. *California Management Review, 41,* 65–85.

Simonton, D. K. (1999). Creativity as blind variation and selective retention: Is the creative process Darwinian? *Psychological Inquiry, 10,* 309–328.

A. INTRODUCTION

Sternberg, R. J. (1999). *Handbook of creativity*. Cambridge, UK: Cambridge University Press.

Sternberg, R. J. (2005). Creativity or creativities? *International Journal of Human-Computer Studies*, *63*, 370–382.

Taggar, S., Sulsky, L., & MacDonald, H. (2008). Subsystem configuration: A model of strategy, context, and human resources management alignment. In F. Dansereau & F. J. Yammarino (Series Eds.) & M. D. Mumford, S. T. Hunter, & K. E. Bedell-Avers (Vol. Eds.), *Research in multi-level issues: Vol. 7. Multi-level issues in creativity and innovation* (pp. 317–376). Bingley, UK: Emerald Group Publishing Limited.

Tushman, M. L., & O'Reilly, C. A. (1996). Ambidextrous organizations: Managing evolutionary and revolutionary change. *Management Review*, *38*, 8–30.

Weisberg, R. W. (2006). Expertise and reason in creative thinking: Evidence from case studies and the laboratory. In J. C. Kaufman & J. Baer (Eds.), *Creativity and reason in cognitive development* (pp. 7–42). New York, NY: Cambridge University Press.

Wise, G. (1992). Inventions and corporations in the maturing electrical industry. In R. J. Weber & D. N. Perkins (Eds.), *Inventive minds: Creativity in technology* (pp. 291–310). New York, NY: Oxford University Press.

A. INTRODUCTION

2

Organizations and Creativity: Trends in Research, Status of Education and Practice, Agenda for the Future

Keith James[1] and Damon Drown[2]
[1]Portland State University and the National Science Foundation;
[2]Portland State University, Portland, OR

"If you are out to describe the truth, leave elegance to the tailor." (*Albert Einstein*).

The pace of flux in most organizations' environments has increased substantially in recent years because of factors such as globalization, changes in technology, and increased competition. Organizations must develop the capacity to initiate or quickly adopt innovations, we hear in both the research literature and popular media, since those that do not keep up with the pace of external change will lose their ability to survive (e.g., Csikszentmihályi, 1999; Grossman, 2006; Janszen, 2000). Salient cases such as General Motors' decline—over the course of about 30 years, from better than 50% world-wide market share and vast profits to bankruptcy—certainly seem to indicate that organizations must tap employee creativity, and channel it towards innovation and change, or risk dying. In a related vein, researchers and practitioners (with Florida—see, e.g., Florida, 2002, 2004—perhaps the best example) have popularized the view that much of the value generated by businesses and for societies comes from the work of highly-creative people (individuals, groups, and "class[es]"). The consequence is that stoking creativity and managing innovation have become central topics of conversation, at least, among organizational scholars, leaders of businesses, and economic policy experts. As organizational scientists, of course, we believe that "stoking...and managing" creativity and innovation require that they be scientifically studied, and that the knowledge derived from the science of creativity and

Handbook of Organizational Creativity.
DOI: 10.1016/B978-0-12-374714-3.00002-1

innovation be used as the basis of educating for creativity, and for intervening in organizations to promote creativity and innovation in practice.

How much, however, has the contemporary popular and conceptual colloquy on creativity actually been reflected in the research, teaching, and practice of organizational science? That is, what is the state of workplace creativity as an area of scientific expertise? Further, to what extent does the scientific study of creativity actually correspond to the education of organizational scholars, practitioners, and leaders about it, and how well does it guide applied creativity and innovation in the workplace? Those topics are the first focus of the current chapter: a review of trends in the science of organizational creativity and their relationship to the teaching and practice of creativity and innovation in the workplace. The second focus of the chapter is to use the results of that review, along with some new theorizing, to generate recommendations for the future of the organizational science of creativity, and its application to practice and education.

WHERE WE HAVE BEEN AND WHERE TO FROM HERE: A SUMMARY AND THEORY OF THE SCIENCE OF CREATIVITY

What, we ask first, *is* creativity? A scientific definition of creativity that is elegant is: generation of *something* that is both *novel* and *useful* toward accomplishing *desired goals* (Amabile, 1996; Weisberg, 1993). Harking back to the Einstein quote that leads off this chapter, though, we need to complicate things a bit further. The definition just given seems a good one (but see Driver, 2008, for a contrary view), but each major part of it is meant broadly, and applying it to the real world always necessitates a certain amount of subjective judgment. *Something* does not necessary mean *an observable, concrete entity*; it can be an idea, a formula for solving a problem, or a novel approach to persuading people to try something new. Also even tangible "products" come in a wide range—for example, from a new piece of computer software, to an art or craft object, to a new type of hardware. Moreover, *novel* does not necessarily mean *completely new*; novelty is not an either–or characteristic. Instead, creative ideas and creative things can range from having a bit that is new, to being moderately new, to being massively, radically new. Creativity can potentially include anything in that range as long as *some* discernable level of novelty characterizes the "something" created. It can be a modification of something known to give it a new use, or the combining of two "old" things to produce something different than either. *Goals* are human decisions, and different individuals and different groups of people hew to different ones. Such variations mean that the *usefulness* of creative products will necessarily depend on which beholders are eyeing them (c.f., Driver, 2008; and James & Taylor, 2010). Out of those complications to the seemingly simple definition of creativity initially presented comes the possibility of some disagreement over what deserves the label "creative". There is sometimes general consensus that certain individuals or products are creative, but there is also substantial disagreement about the creativity of other individuals and products.

As in the preceding expansion of an initially simple definition of creativity, the subsequent chapters in this book explore the complexities of the influences on, generation of, and results from, creativity; and the complexities of researching creativity. In those chapters, creativity is dealt with as both an individual or social *process*, and as a distinctive type of *outcome*. Creative *processes* are the skills, and mechanisms used to translate goals and raw materials (including knowledge and abilities) into creative ideas or products. Creative *outcomes* are *products* or results that are substantially novel, useful, and goal-oriented.

Creativity as Multi-Level Phenomena

Figure 2.1 contains a model of multi-level creativity that summarizes both the conceptual and empirical contents of the current chapter. We describe below how the major constructs in the model emerged from our content analyses of organizational creativity publications. The reader will also note that the model incorporates the multiple levels (individual, group/team, organizational) that form the basis of the three sections (B, C & D) of organizational creativity sub-area chapters in this Handbook.

Note that the figure also includes *Extra-Organizational Culture and Systems* as a major component, as well as feedback among components. Creativity does not develop in a vacuum. It is always rooted in the patterns, priorities, materials, trends, and techniques of traditions and collectives even though, paradoxically, it must somehow also deviate to some extent from the collective and traditional to be truly creative. Large-scale collectives, such as societal or organizational cultures both constrain creativity by channeling it in certain directions, and provide individuals with raw materials (including knowledge, skills, and strategies) that provide starting points for creative production (James, 2005; Mar'i, 1976; Osche, 1990; Simonton, 1999).

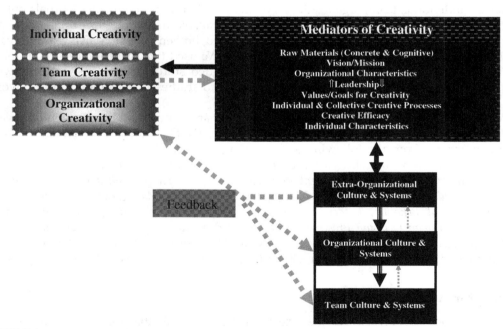

FIGURE 2.1 A model of multi-level organizational creativity.

Traditions and collectives are, themselves however, multi-level phenomena. Societal-level collectives and traditions influence organizational-level traditions and collectives; but different organizations within societies develop somewhat distinctive cultures and systems. Work groups (teams) operate creatively within an organizational context, but every team that exists for any period of time will begin to develop its own distinctive assumptions, approaches, and processes (i.e., team culture). In addition, in today's workplace (especially given modern technology-mediated communication and technology-generated complexity) many individuals do their creative work in collaboration with more than one group-level collective. Thus, the Culture and Systems label in Figure 2.1 reflects topics such as National (and Cross-National) culture, technologies, and creative norms; but also *organizational*, *team* and *inter-organizational* and *inter-group* norms, values, technologies, and procedures that inform efforts at collaborative creativity. Inter-organizational and inter-group collaborative creativity are topics of growing interest, both scientifically and in practice.

CATEGORIES OF ORGANIZATIONAL CREATIVITY SCIENCE

What follows will make it clear that the scientific study of creativity is growing and (we hope) interesting, but also still developing. The following table summarizing the last 15 years (1995–2009) of organizational creativity scholarship in leading journals. In this case, "leading journal" reflects both those organizational science journals with the highest impact rating, and those with a particular mission (or mission component) of publishing organizational creativity papers. We also tried to sample journals likely to publish studies of creativity focused on different levels (individual, team, organizational) of analysis. Certainly some other journals publish articles on organizational creativity. Limitations to available time and effort inputs required, however, that we limit the number of journals examined, broken down into five year intervals.

Description of literature search and content analysis. We used two inclusion criteria in selecting studies for this content analysis. First, we included studies that focused on the work context. Second, we restricted the content analysis to studies that included the keywords "creativity" or "innovation".

We searched for published papers in the creativity and innovation literature in two ways. First, we conducted a computerized search using *PsycINFO* (January 1995–December 2009) to obtain articles from the following journals that included the key words "creativity," or "innovation": *Academy of Management Journal, Academy of Management Review, Administrative Science Quarterly, Group and Organization Management, Journal of Applied Psychology, Journal of Business and Psychology, Journal of Management, Journal of Managerial Psychology, Journal of Organizational Behavior, Leadership Quarterly, Organizational Science,* and *Organizational Behavior and Human Decision Processes.* Next, we did a direct, article-by-article examination of all papers published in *Creativity and Innovation Management* and *Creativity Research Journal* between January 1995 and December 2009. Altogether, those searches yielded 452 papers.

Coding for Article Content

We then content-analyzed every article from those journals that focused on creativity or innovation in the workplace. Content categories were chosen based on a priori use of the major topics for leading academic organizations in Industrial/Organizational Psychology Organizational Behavior, and Human Resource Management. In particular, categories were identified from the major areas of the model curriculum identified by the Society for Industrial and Organizational Psychology (SIOP www.siop.org); the major topics identified in the Domain statement of the Organizational Behavior Division of the Academy of Management (see http://www.aomonline.org/PeopleAndCommunities/DivisionsAndInterestGroups/Domains.asp?other_code = OB#ob); and the major topics identified in the Domain statement of the Human Resources Division of the Academy of Management (see http://www.aomonline.org/PeopleAndCommunities/DivisionsAndInterestGroups/Domains.asp?other_code = HR#hr). Two Industrial/Organizational Psychology graduate students then went through the creativity articles and looked for topics that were missing from the a priori list. Topics that they agreed were missing were added; topics that they disagreed on were discussed until they either agreed that the topic was already covered by another label, or agreed to add it. From the combination of those two processes, a content coding scheme for the creativity articles was created.

Two trained undergraduate or graduate student coders then content-analyzed each study. Discrepancies were recoded by a third research assistant. When both (or 2 of the 3, where relevant) coders categorized the study the same way, the results were included in the study. The final outcome of the content analysis is shown in Table 2.1.

We see in Table 2.1 that the overall volume of publications on workplace creativity increased during the 2000–2004 time period relative to the 1995–1999 time period; and increased significantly again during the 2005–2009 time period relative to the 2000–2004 time period. The number of publications during the 2005–2009 time period was significantly higher than those in either of the other time periods. This provides quantitative support for the oft-expressed subjective view that the topic of workplace creativity has been drawing increased interest in recent years.

It is also clear from the results in Table 2.1 that there was some variation in increases across the three time frames across major subtypes of creativity publication, though. For instance, a chi-square comparison of the numbers of quantitative studies crossed with (three) time periods was significant, $\chi^2 = 24.7$, p $<$ .05. The chi-square comparison of the numbers of qualitative studies crossed with (the three) time period was non-significant, $\chi^2 = 1.76$, p $>$ .05, however. A comparison of the *total* number of quantitative versus qualitative studies was significant, $\chi^2 = 49.3$, p $<$ .05. Similarly, a time-1 versus time-3 comparison of the two types of studies yielded a marginally significant chi-square, $\chi^2 = 2.71$, p $<$ .10. Thus, there was quantitative support for the trend of increasing numbers of quantitative studies contrasted with the plateauing of qualitative studies that the raw numbers in Table 2.1 exhibit. An additional qualification of that result can be seen in the figures in Table 2.2, where studies that appeared in *Creativity and Innovation Management* (CIM) journal are contrasted with those from the other journals. The information in Table 2.2 is discussed further in a later section.

The total number of *empirical* papers on organizational creativity increased from 71 (1995–1999) to 97 (2000–2004) to 131 (2005–2009). The change was significant, $\chi^2 = 17.62$, p $<$ .05. The total number of *conceptual* papers held roughly steady between the 1995–1999 (35 conceptual papers) and 2000–2004 (33) time periods; but increased significantly to 57 in 2005–2009, $\chi^2 = 8.16$, p $<$ .05. The total growth in empirical papers was significantly greater than that in conceptual papers. That is probably to the good—if we accept that

TABLE 2.1   Organizational Creativity Content Analysis Across Five-Year Intervals.

Construct	Overall	1995–1999	2000–2004	2005–2009	Sign. Diff.
Quantitative	210	39	74	97	Yes
Qualitative	87	24	28	35	No
Conceptual	125	35	33	57	Yes
Empirical	299	71	97	131	Yes
Individual	155	39	52	64	p = .06
Team	94	26	30	38	No
Organizational	180	43	59	78	Yes
Demographics	41	11	15	15	No
Personality	45	7	20	18	Yes
Mood–Feelings–Emotions	30	5	12	13	No
Motivation	48	13	17	18	No
Creative Self Efficacy	23	8	12	3	Yes
Values	21	6	7	8	No
Cognitive Style	37	10	13	14	No
Intelligence-KSA	48	15	15	18	No
Leadership[a]	95	20	33	42	Yes
Evaluation/Feedback	35	8	20	7	Yes
Team Composition[b]	40	5	15	20	No
Team Process	66	12	26	28	No
Relationship	26	2	15	9	Yes
Job Characteristics	64	14	20	30	p = .06
Culture/Climate	85	21	37	27	Yes
Organizational Characteristics	148	36	45	67	Yes
Organizational Context	67	13	21	33	Yes
National Culture	27	6	17	4	Yes
Creative Thinking[c]	109	29	45	35	Yes

(*Continued*)

TABLE 2.1 Organizational Creativity Content Analysis Across Five-Year Intervals. (Continued)

Construct	Overall	1995–1999	2000–2004	2005–2009	Sign. Diff.
Type of Innovation	36	16	11	9	Yes
Role Model	5	2	3	0	No
Communication	44	8	22	14	Yes
PE-Fit	12	4	5	3	No
Organizational Justice	11	4	4	3	No
Organizational Support	48	10	21	17	No
Stress	21	11	5	5	Yes
Organizational Commitment	14	4	8	2	Yes
Conflict	15	3	6	6	No
Knowledge-Transfer-Exchange	59	12	28	19	Yes
Training	21	5	5	11	No
Total Papers	**452**	**121**	**134**	**197**	**Yes**

Note: N's summed across specific construct categories sometimes exceed the total N of papers because many individual papers included multiple constructs. Only full theory-development and research-based papers, not journal Editors' Editorials, were included in the construct coding. Sign. Diff. utilizes chi-square to test for a significant difference across the five year blocks. Yes indicates p<.05. No indicates p>.05.
[a]Leadership and creativity studies, as the fact that they can be partitioned into the individual, team, and organizational levels, included creative project (team) management. Some specific aspects of the latter also fell under Organizational Context (e.g., resource availability) or team process (e.g., participative versus directive decision making).
[b]Team composition includes members' organizational units, job types, and professional expertise; those overlap but even though they are sometimes treated as interchangeable, they are not necessarily always so.
[c]The generation of creative ideas, solutions, or products. For this construct, individual, organizational, and multi-level (including those that included both the team-level and some other level of analysis) idea generation are included, but intra-team-only creative thinking was placed in the Team Process construct category.

organizational creativity was relatively (compared to its scientific and practical importance) under studied in the early 90s and that it is a complex phenomenon, we needed empirical examinations of it to aid development of theories. While reviewing the *quality* of theory is beyond the scope of the current chapter, it also seems logical that the relatively rapid growth in empirical works observed in the data in Table 2.1 indicates that additional integrative theory is now needed.

Examination of the more specific categories in Table 2.1 shows many interesting and encouraging trends to the science of organizational creativity, along with a few areas of concern. It is interesting to note that raw publications numbers increased somewhat across our three coding time frames for all three major levels of analysis—individual-level, team-level, and organizational-level, but only the trend for the first and the last of those levels was statistically significant. In the sections that follow next, we consider the specific constructs falling within each level of analysis and make recommendations for the future.

Individual-Level Creativity

The individual-level analysis across the three time periods yielded a marginally significant chi-square, $\chi^2 = 5.59$, p $= .06$. Contrary to the conclusion of Kahl, Hermes da Fonseca and Witte (2009), we found that organizational scientists (c.f. Kahl, et al.'s "Business and Economics" and other categories of research) increased somewhat over time their production of works on individual-level and organizational-level creative phenomenon.

We counted Job Characteristics as an individual-level variable since it generally involves looking at how the nature of different jobs influences the creativity of the (individual) job incumbents. Studies of Job Characteristics showed a marginally significant increase across the three time periods, $\chi^2 = 5.75$, p $= .06$. Similarly, a comparison of the Personality, Affect, Motivation, Efficacy and Values constructs together between times 1 and 3 yielded a marginally significant difference of $\chi^2 = 7.65$, p $= .10$. Thus, there is some indication that the specific individual-level constructs being studied have shifted somewhat over time such that studies of Job Characteristics, personality, affect and motivation have increased somewhat; the study of value influences on creativity has held somewhat steady; and the study of creative efficacy has decreased. The latter two trends seem contrary to increased focus on values and efficacy in other areas of organizational studies. More research seems to be called for on the influence of individual values and efficacy on creativity—especially on values and efficacy as they operate within a multi-level framework.

While the general volume of studies of individual-level creativity increased over the years (see Table 2.1, row five), the study of several specific individual-level constructs of potential relevance to workplace creativity exhibits either minimal or no growth. Example constructs in that respect include cognitive-style, intelligence, role-models, and affect. Some of this may reflect the fact that the study of creativity has grown more among business and management faculty members than among Industrial/Organizational psychologists, or others who traditionally have taken more of an individual-level perspective (c.f. Kahl, et al., 2009; and the discussion of workplace creativity in education, below). In any case, the trend of limited scholarly attention to certain individual-level constructs would seem to require redress for scientific and applied advance. The same is true for the general limited growth in studies of team-creativity.

Team Creativity

Studies of team-level creativity showed, in raw numbers, a small trend of increase, but that increase was not statistically significant, $\chi^2 = 2.06$, p $> .05$. Over the fifteen-year period we examined in the content analysis, only 94 studies focused on Teams, while the individual level of analysis had 155 studies, and the organizational 180. Several organizational scientists have noted in the past that the study of team-level creativity is an under-researched area (e.g., Kurtzberg & Amabile, 2001; West, 2002). The raw numbers and non-significant chi-squares for overall team-level publications and for discrete team-level constructs that we document in

Table 2.1, immediately above and just below, support that conclusion. These findings clearly point to an increased need to focus on teams in the creativity and innovation literature.

By examining the specific team constructs present in our content analysis of the last fifteen years of creativity research, we can begin to better understand which specific constructs need further attention. Team studies examined constructs such as: group composition, group processes, communication, and conflict. In comparing these constructs we found that there were 66 studies that focused on group process, 44 on communication, 40 on group composition, and 15 on conflict. In addition, the construct of team-level collective efficacy that has become prominent in studies of non-creative team performance (see Gully, Incalcaterra, Joshi, & Beaubien's 2002 meta-analysis) and that has been argued to be—in the specific form *of team-efficacy for creativity*—relevant to creative performance by teams (see, e.g., Whyte, 1998) was essentially absent from the papers we coded. Our content analysis also showed that organizational science is paying minimal attention to constructs such as team-building and team-training (for creative effectiveness), and that our examination of applied organizational creativity (discussed further below) found it to be somewhat prominent among practitioners. These findings suggest that, despite calls for increased focus on teams doing creative work, in general, and for work on specific constructs such as conflict in teams and team-level efficacy for creativity, in particular (e.g. Kurtzberg & Amabile, 2001), little increase in such work has occurred over the last fifteen years. The discrepancies between the science of team creativity and the nature of organizational creativity interventions also need to be attended to in future works.

The dominant theoretical paradigm used to understand ineffective and effective work groups is based on an open systems theory called the input-process-output (IPO) model (Kozlowski & Illgen, 2006; Martins, Gilson, & Maynard, 2004; McGrath, 1964). In such models, inputs typically consist of the starting conditions of the group, such as the skills and personalities of individuals who make up the group. Processes are the dynamic interactions among group members that result in the translation of the team inputs into desired organizational outcomes. Therefore, this model posits that processes moderate outcomes (Kozlowski & Illgen, 2006). Outcomes are the resulting consequences of group interaction that results from interactions of inputs and processes (Martins et. al., 2004). For example, Tett and Burnett's (2003) theory of trait activation suggests that the impact of personality traits depends in large part to the person–situation interaction.

Similar to the theoretical framework shown in Figure 2.1, in recent years the IPO framework has been modified into a dynamic multi-level approach to studying work teams (Kozlowski & Illgen, 2006; Ilgen, Hollenbeck, Johnson, & Jundt, 2005), including those performing creative work (Hülsheger, Anderson & Salgado, 2009). For example, a recent study by Hirst, van Knippenberg, and Zhou (2009) utilized a cross-level perspective to examine how team learning influences the creative expression of individual goal orientation. Their findings suggest that team learning activates individual learning orientation, stimulating increased employee creativity. By utilizing a cross-level framework, as in the study by Hirst, van Knippenberg, & Zhou (2009), researchers can take a broader, more representative view of what occurs in the workplace. This type of examination might help future researchers make their research more applicable to the workplace, and provide practitioners with more points of leverage to manage creativity. The large-scale acceptance of the tenets of this theory and similar ones have led to more multi-level studies of teams that may

A. INTRODUCTION

be reflected in the growth of multi-level examinations of creativity involving teams that we outline below.

Organizational Level Creativity

The organizational level of analysis yielded the highest overall number of papers. Reflecting the general increased attention to organizational creativity, the number of organization-level papers grew most rapidly and the increase was significant, $\chi^2 = 10.23$, p $< .05$. We also see in Table 2.1 that several specific organization-level constructs (influences-on-creativity) such as organizational leadership, organizational culture/climate, and organizational characteristics also show growth as the three coded time periods progress toward the present, even though few of those trends were statistically significant when the construct was considered by itself.

Counting leadership, organizational characteristics (e.g., size; reward system), organizational climate/culture, organizational context, organizational justice, and organizational support as the organizational-level variables, we see in Table 2.1 that leadership and organizational characteristics studies increased in frequency significantly across the three time frames, organizational climate/culture studies had a curvilinear pattern that varied significantly across the three time frames, and the other organizational variables did not, when examined individually, change significantly across the three time frames. Leadership studies are discussed further, below, in the multi-level section, since leadership often implicates a crossing of levels (between, e.g., organizational mission and individual creativity).

Studies of organizational *characteristics* also increased across the three time periods we examined, $\chi^2 = 9.56$, p $< .05$. That is certainly good in that, if organizations are our target focus, it is clearly important to examine the influence of organization-level variables on creativity. Overall, organizational-creativity scholars have been, our data indicates, paying increasing attention over time to organizational-level characteristics as influences on organizational creativity. Organizational-characteristics as we employed it in our coding are, however, a portmanteau category. A separate count of the many different, specific variables used to characterize organizations was beyond the scope of what we could attempt here. Certainly attention to distinctions among organizational characteristics relative to creativity is important for the future, however. Perhaps, in fact, we need an effort to produce the equivalent of the "Big-5" personality factors to cluster aspects of the "personalities" of organizations into coherent groups.

It is perhaps somewhat disquieting that studies of organizational justice and of organizational support impacts on creativity did not increase significantly over time. Both are theoretically relevant to creativity (see, e.g., Eisenberger, Fasolo & Davis-LaMastro, 1990; and Clark & James, 1999), and both are constructs that have been more widely examined relative to non-creative outcomes. The extremely low numbers of studies of justice and creativity reflected in Table 2.1 seem especially needful to be changed, especially since organizational justice has become one of the dominant theoretical and research approaches in organizational science (Lind & Van den Bos, 2002).

Another construct that our time-coding of the organizational science literature showed to have plateaued at a relatively low level was the type or *domain* of creativity. This occurred despite that fact that Amabile's (1996) influential three-factor (motivation, domain skills, creativity skills) model of creativity clearly implies the importance of domains in whether and how creativity plays out. Feist's (1998) meta-analysis of personality relationships to creativity supports such a role for domain, by showing that specific personality factors show differential relationships to creativity across domains of creativity types. Neither Amabile's model nor Feist's meta-analysis really extends consideration of domains of creativity to creativity as a multi-level phenomenon, however, which limits their potential relevance to understanding organizational creativity. Damanpour (1988; 1991) has also presented evidence of the importance of considering domains of creativity when considering organizational-level outcomes (see also our discussion of feedback of creativity across levels, below). Studies are needed of the interactions all of the constructs in Figure 2.1 and Table 2.1 (and, possibly, constructs shown in neither) with domains of creativity.

Multi-Level Creativity

One dearth in the literature that we noted, which is not immediately obvious in Table 2.1 was the limited numbers of studies that examined multiple-levels of creativity and their cross-level influences. Coding the studies for which included multiple levels of analysis yielded the following results:

Individual/Team = 22;
Individual/Organizational = 19;
Team/Organizational = 15;
Individual/Team/Organizational = 6;
Total multi-level studies = 52.

A chi-square test of differences of level of analysis (individual-only vs. team-only versus organizational-only vs. multi-level) was significant, $\chi^2 = 83.54$, $p < .05$. A comparison of the specific types of multi-level studies (Individual/Team vs. Individual/Organizational vs. Team/Organizational vs. Individual/Team/Organizational) was also significant $\chi^2 = 9.32$, $p < .05$. If we can agree that all levels of analysis, including multi-level analysis, are equally important (which, it is granted, some people may not) for advancing the organizational science of creativity, then the numbers in Table 2.1 along with the chi-square results just presented indicate that both team-focused and multi-level studies of creativity have been relatively neglected by organizational scientists.

As an example, the relatively minimal attention to person–environment fit reflected in Table 2.1 contradicts the broad consensus that organizational context factors generally impact both individual and organizational-level outcomes differentially depending on the characteristics of the persons who experience a given context. That perspective certainly also matches the multi-level model shown in our Figure 2.1, and has implications for both the science and practice of workplace creativity. For an example of P–E fit congruent research, see George and Zhou (2001); for a multi-level P–E fit model that also includes discussion of creativity, see Tett and Burnett (2003).

On the other hand, studies of Job Characteristics, Communication and Creativity, and of knowledge-transfer increased significantly from the first coded time period, even if those two did also have something of a curvilinear trend. These studies frequently involved exchanges across levels (e.g., organizational job design as an influence on individual-level creativity; communication between organizational leadership and individual workers; knowledge sharing among individuals or teams across organizational boundaries).

As Figure 2.1 shows, it seems theoretically sound to expect the boundaries between individual, team, and organizational creativity to be permeable. Put another way, authors spanning the full range of time from James (W., 1890) to James (K., in press—see also Csikszentmihályi, 1999; Florida, 2004; Glynn, 1996; and McGrath, 1986, among others) have argued that creative people make for creative organizations, and vice-versa. It seems from our analysis of publications on creativity in organizational studies that we need more scientific attention to the how, when, and way of multi-level creativity, however.

An aspect of multi-level creativity that we found to have been virtually ignored in the literature is the feedback mechanisms shown in our Figure 2.1. The feedback elements in the figure add the theoretical notion that creativity at each level influences creativity at each other level, both *directly* (e.g., the creative ideas of individuals become the stuff from which the team that they compose spins its creativity) and *indirectly* (i.e., creativity at one level feeding back to influence creativity at other levels). The indirect effect is through the use of creativity to do things that help determine creativity at a different level, such as to attain raw materials (concrete and cognitive), change missions or goals, or affect creative efficacy or creative processes. Google, for example, makes gobs of money; that allows that company to release to employees some of their work time (resource) to pursue knowledge acquisitions and development of novel concepts; individual employees should be more creative, on average, than they would be in a company either less adept at creating wealth for itself or (partly a source of wealth and partly as a result of it), less focused on novelty.

Top–down feedback is perhaps the only type of creative feedback that is really receiving much attention (see, e.g., Damanpour's, 1991 meta-analysis of organizational innovation). The effect of leadership on innovation is an example. Figure 2.1 also positions Leadership as a mediator among mediators (see the arrows linking leadership to both creative inputs and creative processes in the mediation box). In Table 2.1 we see that attention to the role of leadership in creativity has more than quadrupled over the span of our three coding time periods. Many of the papers that deal with leadership do focus on its role in promoting other factors (such as team efficacy) and some also take a multi-level approach (see Gully, et al., 2002 for an example that addresses leadership and efficacy from a multi-level perspective). Those trends show promising progress in the organizational science of creativity.

Our review of the literature made it clear, however, that there remains much to be done relative to leadership, and to most other individual's constructs shown in Figure 2.1, as well as in advancing construct integration and multi-level understanding. For instance, studies of transformational leadership and organizational creativity/innovation have increased, which is to the good. One key mechanism through which transformational leadership is supposed to impact on creativity/innovation, however, is by way of modeling effects by leaders. The dearth of studies of role-modeling and organizational creativity shown in Table 2.1 and mentioned above indicates, however, that that particular posited mechanism of transformational leadership effects is not being directly assessed in creativity/innovation studies. Something along the lines of the gigantic GLOBE study (House, Hanges, Javidan, Dorfman & Gupta, Eds, 2004), but focused on creativity would allow for testing all of the constructs in Figure 2.1 (or some other theoretical model) together (an intermediate step would be introduction of more creativity-specific constructs *into* the GLOBE, or similar, ongoing study).

Studies of *bottom–up* multi-level effects of creativity are very few. Conceptually and practically, however, individual and team creativity often do seem to be directed toward attempting to influence organizational missions, climates, resource allocations, and other system aspects, which are then important influences on future individual and team creativity. We need to study such bottom–up feedback of creativity, both to fully understand organizational creativity, and to effectively tie creativity to other major areas of organizational science such as organizational justice (e.g., creative efforts to modify justice climates or procedures), and individual health (e.g., creative efforts to influence organizational health-related policies or organizational/leader support as influences on health). Bottom–up creativity feedback effects are also likely to differ by domain of creativity. For instance, organizational leaders may be amenable to product (service) innovation but not prepared to accept the implications of the organizational-process (administrative) innovation that can result from promoting creativity among members of the organization and that may, in fact, be necessary if product innovation is to succeed (c.f., Damanpour, 1988).

Relevant to the focus of the GLOBE study, National Culture influences on creativity was among the minority of constructs that we found to have declined in the 2004–2009 coding period, relative to preceding two categories of time (though, as can be seen in Table 2.1, studies invoking national culture and creativity did go up between the first and second time periods). This seems unfortunate, especially in the context of the globalization of businesses and the economy. See James (2005) and the *International Handbook of Creativity* (Kaufman & Sternberg, Eds, 2006) for reviews/theories of national culture and creativity.

COMPARISON OF EUROPEAN AND US APPROACHES TO ORGANIZATIONAL CREATIVITY

Reference to cultures and nations brings up another question: Do researchers from different areas of the world take different approaches to the study of creativity? Table 2.2, below, may shed some light on that question. It compares creativity paper constructs as they appeared in journals published in the United States versus those in *Creativity and Innovation Management* (*CIM*) journal, which is out of Europe. While there is some cross-publication—by some Europeans in US journals and by a few US creativity experts in *CIM*—the two regional groups of scholars are more likely to publish in the journal(s) of their own region. The 2009 Volume 18, number 1 issue of *CIM*, for instance, included *only* papers from authors at European universities. Volume 18, number 4 of *CIM*, on the other hand, had two articles by US academics, one by a Taiwanese faculty member, five by European academics, and one by European consulting/design firm members.

We see in Table 2.2, first of all, that the total number of publications (shown at the bottom of the table) is greater for *CIM* than is the number from all of the other journals combined, despite the fact that it only began publishing in 2000. That is due to the fact that *CIM* focuses exclusively on organizational creativity such that *every* article it publishes fit the criteria for this chapter whereas the majority of those from the US journals did not. *Creativity Research Journal*, while it publishes only papers that address creativity in some way, focuses

TABLE 2.2   Comparison of *Creativity and Innovation Management* (European Based) with Creativity Papers from the Selected American Journals.

Construct	Overall	CIM	Other Journals	Sign. Diff.
Quantitative	210	67	143	Yes
Qualitative	87	69	18	Yes
Conceptual	125	78	47	Yes
Empirical	299	140	159	Yes
Individual	155	65	90	Yes
Team	94	48	46	No
Organizational	180	108	72	Yes
Demographics	41	8	31	Yes
Personality	45	10	35	Yes
Mood–Feelings–Emotions	30	10	20	Yes
Motivation	48	25	23	No
Creative Self Efficacy	23	11	12	No
Values	21	12	9	No
Cognitive Style	37	18	19	No
Intelligence-KSA	48	23	25	No
Leadership	95	49	46	No
Evaluation/Feedback	35	24	11	No
Team Composition	40	20	20	No
Team Process	66	34	32	No
Relationship	26	6	20	Yes
Job Characteristics	64	28	36	No
Culture/Climate	85	44	41	No
Organizational Characteristics	148	75	73	No
External Context	67	33	34	No
National Culture	27	14	13	No
Creative Process	109	82	27	Yes
Type of Innovation	36	21	15	No
Role Model	5	0	5	Yes
Communication	44	27	17	No

(Continued)

A. INTRODUCTION

TABLE 2.2 Comparison of *Creativity and Innovation Management* (European Based) with Creativity Papers from the Selected American Journals (Continued).

Construct	Overall	CIM	Other Journals	Sign. Diff.
PE-Fit	12	5	7	No
Organizational Justice	11	2	9	Yes
Organizational Support	48	19	29	Yes
Stress	21	5	16	Yes
Organizational Commitment	14	5	9	No
Conflict	15	5	10	No
Knowledge-Transfer-Exchange	59	47	12	Yes
Training[a]	21	3	18	Yes
Total	**431**	**229**	**202**	

Note: Sign. Diff. utilizes chi-square to compare if there is a significant difference between the two categories of journals. Yes indicates $p < .05$. No indicates $p > .05$.

[a] A PsychInfo crossing of searches of "Creativity and Innovation Management Journal" and "creativity training" yielded 0 articles, but direct examination of articles published in CIM yielded 3 papers that included training for some aspect of creativity as a major construct.

on creativity in all settings, such that papers that specifically address organizational creativity are a minority among those it publishes. Readers will want to consider the imbalance toward papers from *CIM* in evaluating even the results presented in Table 2.1 and discussed above. We also see in Table 2.2 that European scholars (i.e., *CIM* as a journal) published more creativity *theory* papers than did the American journals.

We also see in Table 2.2 that papers in *CIM* (and, therefore most likely written by European academics or consultants) were significantly more likely to employ a qualitative research approach, and significantly less likely to employ a quantitative approach. This seems to reflect the general biases within organizational sciences in North America and in Europe; each approach has its potential strengths and addressing constructs with both methods should provide complimentary information that will advance understanding of workplace creativity. As we note below, however, an examination of comparisons of the frequency of use of specific constructs in *CIM* versus the other journals also yielded some significant differences. That indicates that, if the potential complimentarity of methods is to be achieved, both the European and US journals should consider encouraging more submission of research of the other type, qualitative or quantitative, to the one that they generally favor. Creativity researchers from all locales should also employ multiple (qualitative *and* quantitative) methods together in their studies where feasible. Finally, *CIM* and the US journals, along with researchers from every nation, should consider how to redress the imbalances in constructs between the two categories of journals that Table 2.2 illustrates and

A. INTRODUCTION

that we outline below. That would also help ensure the benefits of convergence of multiple methods of study of creativity.

Papers in *CIM* were significantly more likely to have an *organization-level* focus than those in the US journals we examined; while the papers in the US journals were more likely to take an *individual-level* focus. This is congruent with the differences between the "Anglo-Cluster" (which includes the US) and the other various (non-British) European clusters of cultures described by House, et al. (2004) in the Globe studies, as well as other examinations of cultural differences between the US and Europe. The US tends to be higher on individualism as a value; Europe higher on collectivism as a value, and that value difference seems to be reflected in the nature of the creativity papers appearing in *CIM* versus the US organizational science journals. We can see this reflected in certain specific constructs in Table 2.2, such as the observation that articles in the US journals were significantly more likely to focus on the individual-level variables of demographics, personality, affect, and stress. Even with the Relationship and Role-Modeling constructs significant differences seem to fit with the idea of cultural value differences between regional groups of scholars, in that both deal with one individual's relationship with another individual. European creativity scholars (*CIM* as an outlet), on the other hand, were significantly more likely to study creative *processes* (which, as we have already noted, frequently touched on organizational or multi-level processes), as well as Knowledge-Transfer. The latter, which typically reflects an *inter-organizational* level of analysis, seems to fit the way in which many organizations must operate in the modern, globalized economy and, as such, very much does need increased research attention from US scholars of organizational creativity.

Here are the explicit comparative numbers of multi-level studies between the two (*CIM*/European versus US) types of journals we examined: European publications included 10 that used an Individual/Team multi-level approach; 13 that used an Individual/Organizational approach; and 13 that had a Team/Organizational multi-level focus. US papers included 12 that were Individual/Team multi-level; 5 that were Individual/Organizational; and 2 that were Team/Organizational. The frequencies across the three subtypes of multi-level studies were marginally-significantly different between the European and US papers, $\chi^2 = 4.43$, p = .10. While we made the case above for possible cultural/value influences on such trends, it is also true that they may, at least partially, result from methodological differences. European papers (*CIM*) were more likely to use qualitative methods. Those methods, being more free form, may be more amenable to addressing questions at multiple levels of analysis. Both European and US scholars, though, need to do more to understand the interactions, as influences on creativity, especially of the individual and organizational, and the team and organizational, levels of analysis.

Our previous discussion and the model in Figure 2.1 attempt to illuminate some of the types of studies of multi-level interactions on organizational creativity that are needed. We need work, for instance, on how and when leaders apply their creativity to material, problem or task ends; versus applying it to interpersonal ends such as developing and executing creative approaches to motivating subordinates (to be creative) or developing subordinates (creative) skills; versus applying their creativity to team or organizational-level characteristics and processes (for some discussion of leadership and domains of creativity, see Ochse, 1990).

Relative to creativity as a multi-level phenomenon, as we have already noted, attention to team-level creativity has increased. This is to the good given the increased use of work teams across organizations. The constructs examined in such studies include group process, group communication, and team conflict. Even more work is clearly needed, however, that is focused on the team level of analysis and its multi-level interactions and implications.

APPLIED ORGANIZATIONAL CREATIVITY

As a method of examining how well organizational creativity practice tracks to the organizational science of creativity, we examined the first 30 links (included paid links) that appeared from a google.com search of the term "organizational creativity consulting" (we ignored websites that compiled lists of multiple creativity consulting companies and examined the first 30 that were from an individual consulting firm). This is decidedly not the only approach to this that might be taken but it seems to us to be a good starting place. The (unpaid) results of a Google search reflect (albeit from a somewhat complicated algorithm) the popularity of relevant websites, and the combination of top paid and unpaid links appearing are what other users doing the same search would find. Thus, our method should reflect, in a broad way, what approaches are actually being taken to organizational creativity interventions. From the consulting websites that resulted from our search, we coded three categories of levels of approaches (organizational, team, and individual), as well the major constructs that fell under each (the N of total constructs listed below sums to more than 30 because several consulting firms described addressing multiple constructs).

We found organizational and the individual-level approaches to creativity interventions to be somewhat better represented than were team-level approaches. We also added an inter-organizational level because it did appear multiple times in consulting descriptions. Under the organizational level, the main constructs/approaches represented were: Strategy (4 mentions), systems (4 mentions), culture/climate (4 mentions), technology (4 mentions), and finance (2 mentions). Under the individual-level, the main constructs/approaches represented were: Idea generation/implementation (6 mentions), coaching (4 mentions), goals (1 mention), and training (2 mentions). Under the team-level, the main constructs/ approaches represented were: Team building (3 mentions), and team-creative performance management/promotion (2 mentions). At the inter-organizational creativity-level, the main constructs/approaches represented were: Knowledge-sharing/knowledge-development (4 mentions), and new business development (1 mention).

We see reflected here largely constructs that also appear in the Table 2.1 data on the organizational science of creativity, though many specific constructs that are in Table 2.1 did not appear in our quick look at consulting as a representation of practice; and the consulting sites touched on a couple of constructs (finance, new-businesses) not appearing in Table 2.1. The latter is largely because our literature review focused on journals that publish mainly industrial-organizational (I/O) psychology, management, and human resource management articles. Finance and entrepreneurship tend to be different disciplines in academia and the journals in those areas certainly do include papers that address organizational creativity.

Largely absent at the individual level were direct discussions of interventions targeted to constructs such as demographics, personality, mood/feeling, general intelligence influences on creativity, and motivation/goals for creativity. Also the coaching intervention that is apparently popular in consulting was not found at all in the research studies of creativity that we examined. This certainly seems to reflect some disjunctions between the scientific and the applied areas of organizational creativity and, potentially, some opportunities for both I/O and management consultants to make use of scientific knowledge, and for I/O and management researchers to investigate topics of interest to organizations and consultants.

At the team-level, team-building interventions were present in creativity practice, but absent from the organizational science literature. Perhaps this represents an ill-informed practice of organizational creativity or, perhaps it reflects a gap in what organizational scientists are studying (or managing to get published in the leading journals). Certainly many of the constructs employed in the Hülsheger, Anderson and Salgado (2009) meta-analysis of team innovation effectiveness were not reflected in the look at consulting practices. For instance, team composition and the job-skill diversity of members had statistically significant effects on team innovation in Hülsheger, et al.'s 2009 meta-analysis, but we saw little on the consulting firms' websites that indicated direct interventions to promote effective job-skill diversity in creative teams. Effective communications among team members was stressed by consulting firms, on the other hand, and, while intra-team communications was not absent in the Hülsheger, et al. (2009) meta-analysis, its effects were relatively weak. On the other hand, the interventions that we coded as *strategy* frequently incorporated the concept of an innovation *vision*, and vision came through as a relatively powerful influence on innovation in the Hülsheger, et al. meta-analysis.

At the organizational-level, the discussion of strategy/vision and other topics, such as knowledge management or climate, typically implicated leadership. Organizational culture/climate and organizational knowledge management also appeared in both our examination of organizational creativity science, and our examination of creativity practice. Communications, which actually crossed over between the organizational and the team levels in the science literature, also appeared on the consulting websites mixed with discussions of things such as idea generation, organizational systems, and knowledge management. External environments of organizations were discussed by the consulting firms in some of the descriptions of idea development, knowledge management, and new business creation. Evaluation was covered under organizational systems (as was, to some extent, organizational support for creativity), idea development/implementation, and knowledge management. Essentially missing from the organizational-level consulting site presentations were national cultures, job characteristics/design, and organizational fairness.

Overall, we were pleasantly surprised to see a number of consulting firms citing organizational creativity science work as a foundation for their practice. Interestingly, too, the consulting sites seemed relatively more likely to take a multi-level approach to organizational creativity than did the works of organizational scientists that we examined. An example of the latter is this quote:

> "A 'thinking business' is a business with a creative culture in which creative people use a creative process to develop creative ideas" (*ThinkingBusiness, 2009*).

There were clearly still important gaps in applied multi-level approaches to organizational creativity. A specific example of a gap in the creativity literature that was also seen in descriptions from the consulting firms is the potential role of *placement* for creativity. The limited attention to person–environment fit mentioned previously partially reflects limited attention to creative tasks and skills in research among industrial (personnel) psychologists and human resource management business facilities. Placing individuals who fit the knowledge, skill, ability and motivational profiles into jobs of different sorts is clearly an important practical issue for organizations, but it was also missing from the creativity consulting websites. This is a topic about which we know a great deal about relative to many jobs (and tasks) that are relatively heavily weighted to non-creative performance. We need to begin to pay equal attention to placement and its precursors (e.g., creativity thinking skills) relative to jobs (and tasks) that are relatively heavily weighted toward *creative* performance requirements. It seems clear, then, that there are opportunities to be had relative to placement in both the organizational science of creativity, and the organizational practice of creativity.

CREATIVITY AND EDUCATION

Calls for increased efforts to promote creativity and innovation have become the norm. For example, in the economic downturn of 2007–2009, economic and social commentators repeatedly called for creative solutions to the recent problems. Moreover, with all of the technological advancements and other changes that are taking place today, it can be argued that we do not know with certainty what the world will be like in five years or what *domain* knowledge, skills, and abilities will be needed; but that we do know that adaptability—and creativity as a foundation of it—are likely to be highly necessary.

If creativity is to be the solution to organizational, economic, and social woes, is it not the case that the principles of the science and practice of creativity should be taught? Is education in organizational science reflecting that and providing students with the knowledge and skills that will help them to become scholars and practitioners expert in organizational creativity? As a first step toward answering those questions, we examined the curriculum of some leading management and industrial/organizational psychology graduate programs in North America, given that such programs purport to be training the next generation of organizational scholars to meet the current and future needs of organizations. If creativity and innovation knowledge and skills are generally important and generally needed by organizations, then such educational programs should explicitly include training in them. Moreover, one of the several goals that the full *Handbook of Organizational Creativity* is intended to achieve is to provide a resource for educating students (undergraduate and graduate) on any and all of the full range of theories, findings, and issues relevant to creativity in the workplace.

As a preliminary approach to examining the current status of formal higher education offerings on organizational creativity, we did a comparison of course catalogs of the top twenty Industrial and Organizational Psychology Ph.D. programs with the course catalogs of the top twenty graduate Management (Business School) programs. The 2010 *US News and World Report* program rankings were used to identify ten of the I/O Psychology programs, along with all 20 Management degree programs. Because the US News rankings for I/O Psychology cover only the top ten programs, however, ten other leading I/O Ph.D. programs were identified from the Oliver, Blair, Gorman and Woehr's (2007) rankings of the

I/O programs. The total research productivity index from Oliver, et al. (2007) was used to select 10 non-redundant—i.e., distinct from the 10 programs listed by *US News & World Reports*) additional I/O Psychology Ph.D. programs. US News and World Reports ranks only the top masters, not Ph.D., Management programs. All of the top twenty management graduate programs in their list are, however, in business schools that also have Ph.D. programs. Thus, we used their rankings to identify the institutions to compare to the I/O Ph.D. programs.

The presence or absence of creativity courses at each of those 40 (20 I/O psychology, 20 management) graduate programs was determined by examining the programs' course offerings as listed on their graduate degree websites. Our goal was to compare how many programs of the two different types offer explicit, formal training in creativity or innovation. While a simple examination of course offerings does not allow us to say anything about the *quality* of such training, it at least allows for an initial look at whether creativity training is being formally attempted at all.

We found that three of the top twenty I/O psychology graduate programs offered a course in creativity or innovation, all as special-topic seminars; while seven of the top twenty management programs offered such a course. Four other management programs had product development or related marketing courses listed among their electives; and one other offered a regular 1-day (2 hour 50 minute) creativity seminar for graduate students. Because of the small samples and small frequencies of creativity course offerings, a bootstrapping approach was used to estimate the difference in frequency of full-semester creativity course offerings, based on using the observed data to generate 200 Monte Carlo samples (the analysis excluded the marketing and 1-day courses offered by the management departments). The result was a significant difference for creativity course offerings by the two types of programs (I/O psychology versus management), $\chi^2 = 21.07$, $p < .05$.

The limited number of creativity/innovation courses offered by the I/O psychology doctoral programs suggests a need to re-examine the educational priorities in such programs and bring them in line with the growth in organizational creativity scholarship and practice. If creativity and innovation is truly essential to organizations, but I/O programs do not focus on developing knowledge and skills about organizational creativity among their students, they risk ineffectiveness and, at the extreme, irrelevance. Creativity is something that can be taught, that organizational conditions can help foster, and that appropriate people can be selected for. Without knowledge in this area, I/O psychologists in training will neither attain the aptitude needed to conduct sound scientific work on organizational creativity, nor the skills needed for science-based applied interventions on that topic.

CONCLUSIONS

The science of organizational creativity is growing such that our knowledge of it is increasing significantly. There are still specific areas were the science of organizational creativity is lagging, however, and organizational scholars should attempt to address those gaps. US and European scholars seem to be emphasizing somewhat different conceptual and methodological approaches to the study of organizational creativity. Greater dialogue between those two categories of organizational creativity scholars, and greater integration of their approaches seems called for.

The gulf between the *science* and the *practice* of creativity and innovation seems to have closed in some important ways, but to continue in others. Surprisingly (to the current authors, at least) practitioners' approaches to organizational creativity (or, at least, practitioners' descriptions of their approaches) appear to better reflect the scientific literature than the scientific literature reflects applied interests and applications. Moreover, the practice of organizational creativity (at least in consulting) may also be somewhat more multi-level than is the organizational science of creativity. The manifestly increasing attention being paid to creativity by organizational scientists indicates, though, that practical interest in work creativity is influencing science.

Management graduate programs are doing a better job than are I/O psychology programs of educating future scholars and practitioners in organizational creativity. If constructs in the science of organizational creativity that are currently understudied are to be better addressed in the future, and if I/O psychologists are to be able to play their role in the science and practice of organizational creativity scholarship, graduate programs in that field need to explicitly incorporate education on organizational creativity.

A better, more systematic, science of creativity will eventually, we hope, profoundly inform the education of organizational scientists, as well as the practice of creativity in the workplace. In line with the feedback components of the model in our Figure 2.1, we also urge scholars of organizational creativity to consider the implications—and potential contributions—of applied organizational creativity and creativity education to the science of organizational creativity. Our creativity and innovation need to be reflexively applied to our own discipline.

References

Amabile, T. M. (1996). *Creativity in context*. Boulder, CO: Westview Press.

Clark, K., & James, K. (1999). Justice and positive and negative creativity. *Creativity Research Journal, 12*, 311–320.

Csikszentmihályi, M. (1999). Implications of a systems perspective for the study of creativity. In R. J. Sternberg (Ed.), *The handbook of creativity* (pp. 313–335). New York, NY: Cambridge University Press.

Damanpour, F. (1988). Innovation type, radicalness, and the adoption process. *Communication Research, 15*, 545.

Damanpour, F. (1991). Organizational innovation: A meta-analysis of effects of determinants and moderators. *Academy of Management Journal, 34*, 555–590.

Driver, M. (2008). New and useless: A Psychoanalytic perspective on organizational creativity. *Journal of Management Inquiry, 17*, 187–197.

Eisenberger, R., Fasolo, P., & Davis-LaMastro, V. (1990). Perceived organizational support and employee diligence, commitment and innovation. *Journal of Applied Psychology, 75*, 51–59.

Feist, G. J. (1998). A meta-analysis of personality in scientific and artistic creativity. *Personality & Social Psychology Review, 2*, 290–309.

Florida, R. (2002). *The rise of the creative class and how it's transforming work, leisure and everyday life*. New York, NY: Basic Books.

Florida, R. (2004). America's looming creativity crisis. *Harvard Business Review, 82*, 122–136.

George, J. M., & Zhou, J. (2001). When openness to experience and conscientiousness are related to creative behavior: An interactional approach. *Journal of Applied Psychology, 86*, 513–524.

Glynn, M. A. (1996). Innovation genius: A framework for relating individual and organizational intelligence to innovation. *Academy of Management Review, 21*, 1081–1111.

Grossman, L. (2006). The next big thing is us. *Time Magazine, 167*, 64–65.

A. INTRODUCTION

Gully, S. M., Incalcaterra, K. A., Joshi, A., & Beaubien, J. M. (2002). A meta-analysis of team efficacy, potency, and performance: Interdependence and level of analysis as moderators of observed relationships. *Journal of Applied Psychology, 87*, 819–832.

Hirst, G., van Knippenberg, D., & Zhou, J. (2009). A cross-level perspective on employee creativity: Goal orientation, team learning behavior, and individual creativity. *Academy of Management Journal, 52*, 280–293.

House, R. J., Hanges, P. J., Javidan, M., Dorfman, P. W., & Gupta, V. (Eds.), (2004). *Culture, leadership and organizations: The GLOBE study of 62 societies*. Thousand Oaks, CA: Sage Publications.

Hülsheger, U. R., Anderson, N., & Salgado, J. F. (2009). Team-level predictors of innovation at work: A comprehensive meta-analysis spanning three decades of research. *Journal of Applied Psychology, 94*, 1128–1145.

Ilgen, D. R., Hollenbeck, J. R., Johnson, M., & Jundt, D. (2005). Teams in organizations: From input-process-output models to IMOI models. *Annual Review of Psychology, 56*, 517–543.

James, K. (2005). Culture and individual and group creativity in organizations. *Korean Journal of Thinking and Problem Solving, 15*, 77–95.

James, K. (in press). *Creativity and innovation: Fundamentals and applications for the workplace and beyond*. Thousand Oaks, CA: Sage Publications.

James, K., & Taylor, A. (2010). Managing the dark-side of creativity: Leadership for positive ad negative creativity. In J. Kaufman, D. Cropley, M. Runco & A. Cropley (Eds.), *The dark side of creativity* (pp. 33–56). New York, NY: Academic Press.

James, W. (1890). *The principles of psychology*. Boston, MA: Henry Holt.

Janszen, F. (2000). *In the age of innovation: Making business creativity a competence, not a coincidence*. New York, NY: Prentice Hall.

Kahl, C. H., Hermes da Fonseca, L., & Witte, E. H. (2009). Revisiting creativity research: An investigation of contemporary approaches. *Creativity Research Journal, 21*, 1–5.

Kaufman, J. C., & Sternberg, R. J. (2006). *The international handbook of creativity*. New York, NY: Cambridge University Press.

Kozlowski, S. W. J., & Ilgen, D. R. (2006). Enhancing the effectiveness of work groups and teams. *Psychological Science in the Public Interest, 7*, 77–124.

Kurtzberg, T. R., & Amabile, T. M. (2001). From Guilford to creative synergy. Opening the black box of team level creativity. *Creativity Research Journal, 13*, 285–294.

Lind, E. A., & Van den Bos, K. (2002). When fairness works: Toward a general theory of uncertainty management. In B. M. Staw & R. M. Kramer (Eds.), *Research in Organizational Behavior* (Vol. 24, pp. 181–223). Boston, MA: Elsevier.

McGrath, J. E. (1964). *Social psychology: A brief introduction*. New York, NY: Holt, Rinehart, & Winston.

McGrath, J. E. (1984). *Group: Interaction and performance*. Englewood Cliffs, NJ: Prentice Hall.

Mar'i, S. K. (1976). Toward a cross-cultural theory of creativity. *Journal of Creative Behavior, 10*, 108–116.

Martins, L. L., Gilson, L. L., & Maynard, M. T. (2004). Virtual teams: What do we know and where do we go from here? *Journal of Management, 30*, 805–835.

Ochse, R. (1990). *Before the gates of excellence: The determinants of creative genius*. New York, NY: Cambridge University Press.

Oliver, J., Blair, C. A., Gorman, C. A., & Woehr, D. J. (2007). Research productivity of I-O psychology doctoral programs in North America. *The Industrial-Organizational Psychologist, 43*. <http://www.siop.org/tip/backissues/July05/07oliver.aspx/>

Simonton, D. K. (1999). *Origins of genius*. New York, NY: Oxford University Press.

Tett, R. P., & Burnett, D. D. (2003). A personality trait-based interactionist model of job performance. *Journal of Applied Psychology, 88*, 500–517.

Thinking Business. (2009). Quoted December 21, 2009 from <http://www.thethinkingbusiness.co.uk/consulting.html/>.

Weisberg, R. W. (1993). *Creativity: Beyond the myth of genius*. New York, NY: Freeman.

West, M. A. (2002). Sparkling fountains or stagnant ponds: An integrative model of creativity and innovation implementation in work groups. *Applied Psychology: An International Review, 51*, 355–387.

Whyte, G. (1998). Recasting Janis's groupthink model: The key role of collective efficacy in decision fiascoes. *Organizational Behavior & Human Decision Processes, 73*, 185–209.

A. INTRODUCTION

3

Methods in Creativity Research: Multiple Approaches, Multiple Levels

Michael D. Mumford, Kimberly Hester, and Issac Robledo

The University of Oklahoma, Norman, OK

To study a phenomenon, any phenomenon, one must be able to say what the phenomenon of interest is (Cooke & Campbell, 1979). This issue, ultimately a definitional issue, is one that has long plagued studies of creativity and innovation or the production of new products based on creative work (Mumford & Gustafson, 1988). Some scholars take the position that intuition may be used to define creativity—I know it when I see it (e.g., Hughes, 1989). Others have argued that creativity is not a matter of intuition but rather attributions arising from a social appraisal process (e.g., Kasof, 1995). Still others have argued that creativity is reflected in the social consequences of an effort—often defining creativity in terms of its economic outcomes (e.g., Hitt, Hoskisson, Johnson, & Moesel, 1996).

In the present chapter, covering the methods employed in studies of creativity and innovation, we will base our arguments on a different conception of the creative act. More specifically, we will argue that creativity is a product of work on a particular type of problem (Mumford & Gustafson, 2007). Creative products, in our view, represent the production of viable, original, solutions to problems that call for, or permit, creativity (Ghiselin, 1963). When creativity is viewed as a product, albeit an intellectual one, arising in response to certain types of problems, the key methodological concern in studies of creativity becomes apparent. What is the criterion, or dependent variable under consideration?

It is to this issue, the criterion or dependent variables used to appraise creative performance that we will address the present chapter. We will begin by considering the types of problems that call for creative thought in solution generation. Subsequently, we will examine the key attributes of creative solutions to these problems. Having provided this context

Handbook of Organizational Creativity.
DOI: 10.1016/B978-0-12-374714-3.00003-3

we will then go on to examine how these principles are applied in each of the five major methods that have been employed in studies of creativity and innovation:

1. qualitative,
2. historiometric,
3. survey,
4. psychometric, and
5. experimental.

In the course of this discussion we will consider how each of these methods is applied at different levels of analysis.

CREATIVE WORK

Creative Problems

Above we noted that creativity is an outcome of work on certain types of problems. What should be recognized here, however, is that many problems exist in our world—and, not all of these problems call for creative thought. For example, I must plan my route to work in the morning; a problem. However, it is not a problem that calls for creative thought. The kind of problems that call for creative thought display five key characteristics, they are:

1. ill-defined,
2. novel,
3. demanding,
4. complex, and
5. exploitable.

Of these characteristics of creative problems, the concept of ill-definition (Mumford & Gustafson, 2007) has, perhaps, received the most attention. For ill-defined problems no one solution will suffice. Rather multiple different, albeit potentially viable, solutions may be generated. In fact, recognition of this point led to Guildford's (1950) development of divergent thinking tests. Ill-definition, however, is not simply a matter of multiple potential, equally viable, solutions being possible. Ill-defined problems allow the problem to be construed, or understood, in different ways. Thus an organizational purchase problem may be understood in terms of enhancing financial viability, increasing absorptive capacity, or amortizing risks. These alternative ways of framing, or approaching, the problem allow for the generation of multiple potential responses. By the same token, exactly what constitutes a viable solution may not be apparent.

Not only are creative problems ill-defined, they must also be novel (Mumford & Gustafson, 2007). The term novel as it is employed here does not imply that the individual has no familiarity with the problem or its context. Rather novel problems evidence *new* structural features or attributes (Holyoak & Thagard, 1997). These new attributes, or features, are novel from the perspective of the person working on the problem—they need not be novel in an absolute sense. The novelty of the problem from the perspective of the individual working on it implies that memory per se will not provide a sufficient basis for solution generation. Rather these new attributes or features must be understood and manipulated to arrive at a viable solution (Baughman & Mumford, 1995).These novel attributes of a problem, in turn, allow, but do not necessarily require, people to generate original solutions.

The available evidence indicates that when people are presented with new attributes, or features, in a problem, the cognitive demands made by the problem increase (Reeves & Weisberg, 1994). As the number of these new attributes or features of a problem increase, the level of demand made on the person working in this problem also increases. Thus most creative problems can be viewed as demanding. In fact, creative problem-solving, as a result of these demands, is commonly held to depend on motivation (Hennessey & Amabile, 1999). The demands made by creative problems, however, imply that new attributes of the problem, or its solution, will arise as the individual works through the problem—a phenomenon implying that in creative problem-solving, people must both generate ideas and explore the implications of these ideas (Finke, Ward, & Smith, 1992).

Because creative problems involve novel attributes, often multiple novel attributes, they also tend to be complex (Uhl-Bien & Marion, 2008). This complexity increases when it is recognized that multiple new attributes of a problem must be integrated in a way that permits both understanding of the problem and action based on this understanding (Marcy & Mumford, 2007). The resulting actions, moreover, must be used as feedback to guide and restructure the problem-solving effort in real-time where feedback cues are inherently ambiguous (Blumberg, 1994). Thus creative problem-solving is often experiential in nature, by virtue of its complexity, involving exchange with real-world feedback and constraints— which may be either internally generated or externally imposed.

Finally, creative problems are exploitable. By this we refer to the problem as a set of conditions that allow multiple solutions, which may apply in different contexts, to emerge from the problem-solving effort. Thus Finke (1990) found that creative problem-solving is enhanced when people are asked to think about the applications of new ideas. What should be recognized here, however, is that exploitability may emerge over time and involve multiple applications of an idea or imposition of an idea in different contexts. This concept of exploitability is, of course, evident in both the development of the World Wide Web, as well as the development of electrical systems (Hughes, 1989).

As stated above, creative problems evidence five key characteristics—they are:

1. ill-defined,
2. novel,
3. demanding,
4. complex, and
5. exploitable.

In this regard, however, two points should be borne in mind. First, at least conceptually, these attributes of creative problems are independent. Thus insight problems tend to be high on ill-definition but low on novelty, demand, and complexity. Divergent thinking test problems tend to be high on novelty but low on ill-definition. It can be seen that multiple, distinct types of creative problems exist. Second, when creative problems evidence all of the above attributes to a reasonable degree, creativity will become a more important determinant of performance.

A. INTRODUCTION

Our foregoing observation is noteworthy because it implies that not all jobs, or all forms of work, will necessarily call for creativity, due to the nature of the tasks presented and the characteristics of the problems posed by the tasks. For example, a train engineer is not commonly presented with problems that are ill-defined, novel, demanding, complex, or exploitable. On the other hand, a micro-biologist is commonly presented with problems evidencing novelty, demand, complexity, and exploitability. The implication of this observation is that in studies of creativity in organizations, the requirement for creativity in task execution and the nature of the creative problems presented must be taken into account.

This point is underscored in a recent study by Atwater and Carmeli (2009). In this study the effects of energy levels on creative production were examined across a wide array of jobs. It was found that energy was related to creative production in general, but was a far stronger determinant of creativity in jobs where creativity was <u>not</u> a critical aspect of the problems posed by job tasks. Thus, in drawing inferences about creativity the nature of the problems posed by job tasks must be borne in mind.

Along related lines, it should be recognized that these attributes of creative problems are not absolutes but instead are referenced against the perspective of those working on the problem. This entity-relevant framing of attributes is noteworthy for two reasons. First, a problem that is ill-defined, novel, demanding, complex, and exploitable at one point in time may not evidence these attributes at a later point in time. In fact, recognition of this point led Wise (1992) to argue that innovation and creativity comes in waves within fields. Second, the extent to which these attributes are present in a problem depends on the nature of the person responding to the problem. Thus, for a high school student, planetary motion problems may call for creative thought, but creativity is not required for an expert physicist to solve such problems (Ericsson & Charness, 1994). This point is of some importance, because it implies that studies of creativity must provide evidence that the problems presented do in fact call for creativity at this point in time within a particular population working on a particular job.

Creative Problem Solutions

Although studies of creativity and innovation are concerned with performance on a certain class of problems, another key consideration underlies the methods applied in such studies. More specifically, viable measures of performance in solving these problems must be obtained. Broadly speaking, four key types of outcome measure are employed:

1. product,
2. performance,
3. behavior, and
4. outcome measures.

Products

Product measures base the evaluation of creativity and innovation on the specific solution provided to a problem calling for creative thought. Redmond, Mumford, and Teach (1993), in a study of leader influences on creativity, asked participants to develop plans for advertising a new product, the 3-D holographic television, and these plans provided the basis for appraisals of creativity. Similarly, Scott, Lonergan, and Mumford (2005), in a study of conceptual combination, asked participants to formulate plans for running an experimental school. In another study along these lines, examining the development of artistic creativity, Rostan (1997, 2006), appraised the drawings produced by visual artists. Product-based studies of creativity and innovation are attractive because actual products are being appraised (Welling, 2007). In these studies, however, two key issues must be addressed: 1) the attributes used to appraise creativity and 2) who appraises these attributes.

To identify the attributes to be used in appraising creative products, Besemer (1998) and Besemer and O'Quin (1999) obtained chair designs from undergraduates with the resulting design being appraised on a variety of potential attributes of creative products (e.g., original, surprising, useful, understandable, well crafted). Subsequent factorings led to the identification of three key factors:

1. originality (e.g., original, surprising),
2. quality (e.g., logical, useful), and
3. elegance (e.g., organic, well crafted).

Other work by Christiaans (2002) that examined the creativity of industrial design products has provided support for this factor structure. Accordingly, most assessments of product creativity examine the quality, originality, and elegance of solutions. However, other attributes may be assessed in a given domain when these attributes are established characteristics of creative work in this arena—for example, aesthetic properties (e.g., expressiveness, reflectiveness) in the arts (Goodman, 1976).

Although it seems clear that quality, originality, and elegance, along with domain-specific attributes (when appropriate), provide a basis for evaluating creative products, the question remains as to who and how many judges should appraise these attributes. Baer, Kaufman, and Gentile (2004) examined inter-judge agreement in assessments of the writing products (e.g., stories poems, personal narratives) produced by 8th grades students. The judges were 13 experts (e.g., creative writers). The resulting appraisals produced high (low 0.90s) levels of inter-judge agreement of product creativity (Kaufman, Baer, Cole, & Sexton, 2008). Other work by Dollinger and Shafran (2005) indicates, however, that expert judges may not always be critical to obtaining reliable evaluations—with non-experts producing good convergence with expert judges. However, use of non-expert judges typically proves most effective when multiple judges, 5 to 7, are provided with extensive training in appraising products on these dimensions (Scott et al., 2005). Trained judges typically produce product appraisals evidencing adequate reliability ($r_{xx} \geq 0.70$) and validity.

Performance Attributes

Studies of creativity using a performance attribute approach do not seek to evaluate a complete creative product. Instead, in performance attribute studies some aspect of performance on a set of tasks held to be markers of creativity, or creative potential, are assessed. Thus on divergent thinking tests, people are asked to generate multiple responses to a novel, ill-defined problem—for example what would be the consequence if gravity was cut in half. Attributes of people's responses to these problems, for example the number of consequences generated (Merrifield, Guildford, Christensen, & Frick, 1962), provide the basis for appraisals of creativity.

Traditionally, in studies of creativity, divergent thinking tests, in which people are asked to generate multiple responses to novel, ill-defined problems have been scored in terms of three attributes (e.g., Kim, 2006; Madjar, Oldham, & Pratt, 2002; Sosik, Kahai, & Avolio, 1999). These are:

1. fluency or the number of responses produced,
2. flexibility or shifts in categories among responses, and
3. originality or the production of novel responses.

The available evidence indicates that these three attribute scores evidence adequate reliability ($r_{xx} \geq 0.70$) given an adequate (5 or more) number of problems, and, in the case of flexibility and originality appraisals, an adequate (3 or more) number of judges. More centrally, measures of fluency, flexibility, and originality have been shown to evidence adequate construct and predictive validity (e.g., Abedi, 2002; Runco, Dow, & Smith, 2006; Sak & Maker, 2006; Wechsler, 2006), thus justifying use of these attributes in studies of creativity.

What should be recognized in this regard, however, is that fluency, flexibility, and originality are not the only attributes of problem-solving performance that might be examined in studies of creative problem-solving. For example, Mednick and Mednick (1967) have argued that the uniqueness of solutions may be used as a marker of creativity. Stokes and Balsam (2003) have argued that indices of sustained variability may be used as attribute measures of creativity. Estes and Ward (2002) have suggested that the production of features, or principles, in solutions may represent still another attribute that can be examined in studies of creativity. All of these attributes have value. However, as Plucker, Runco, and Lim's (2006) study of time on idea generation tasks reminds us, not all attributes that are proposed will evidence adequate validity as measures of creativity—a finding pointing to the importance of systematic validation of attributes being used as a basis for appraising creativity.

Bearing in mind the point that multiple attributes of creative problem solutions exist that might be examined as markers of creativity, two key methodological questions arise concerning applications of this approach. First, attribute-based studies typically generate a pool of attributes vis-à-vis responses to a problem (Runco & Mraz, 1992). This pool of attributes must be taken into account when formulating attribute scores. Thus in appraising originality does one calculate scores based on the two or three best responses with respect to a particular attribute, or does one consider the total pool of responses? Similarly, the question arises as to whether attributes should be scored as manifest in the sample or with respect to the absolute standard.

The second question bears on the nature of the problems presented as a basis for obtaining these attribute scores (Runco et al., 2006). These problems might be presented as a general stimulus (e.g., what would happen if gravity was cut in half?) or as a domain-specific stimulus (e.g., for leaders, what would happen if your support budget was cut in half?). The merit of using domain-specific versus domain-general problems in generating attribute scores has been subject to debate (Baer, 1998; Plucker, 1998). However, the available evidence does suggest that when working with populations where a substantial domain expertise can be assumed, use of problems that are domain based, or alternatively assessment of attributes of particular importance to creative thinking in this domain, may be advantageous. Thus Mumford, Marks, Connelly, Zaccaro, and Johnson (1998) and Vincent, Decker, and Mumford (2002) found that when standard divergent thinking problems were scored for attributes of creative thought of particular importance for leaders (e.g., time frame, positive consequences, negative consequences, complexity) far stronger relationships were observed between scores on these attributes and indices of leader performance ($r \approx 0.40$) than would typically be expected.

Behavior

Behavioral measures of creativity and innovation do not attempt to appraise product or performance attributes involved in product production. Instead the acts evidenced by people in producing creative products are assessed. The frequency or intensity with which people display these behaviors across a range of problems that might call for creative thought provide the basis for assessment. Thus questions might ask, "How frequently are you a good source of creative ideas?" or "Do you suggest new ways of performing tasks?" (George & Zhou, 2001; Tierney, Farmer, & Graen, 1999).

Behaviorally based approaches for measuring creativity follow three general approaches. In the first approach, behavioral measures are developed to assess expression of creative behaviors within a particular context of interest—work, school, social relationships. An illustration of this approach may be found in Jaussi, Randel, and Dionne (2007). In this study, the interest was in whether creative self-efficacy and creative identity influenced creativity at work using the type of behavioral questions illustrated above. In the second approach behavioral measures are not referenced against performance in a specific domain. Instead, they are developed to measure known aspects of creative thought. Thus, Runco, Plucker, and Lim (2001) developed behavioral measures to assess different aspects of ideation. In the third approach, no domain referents are applied in developing the behaviors to be used in measuring creativity. Rather, creativity is treated as an aspect of personality or general behavioral tendencies (McCrae, 1987). An example of application of this approach may be found in Prabhu, Sutton, and Sauser (2008) where creativity, as measured through the general dispositional approach, was used to assess the effects of intrinsic and extrinsic motivation on creativity.

Typically, behaviorally based measures of creativity, regardless of the approach applied in measurement of development, evidence adequate reliability ($r_{xx} \geq 0.70$). Moreover, these measures often evidence some construct validity (e.g., Jaussi et al., 2007; Prabhu et al., 2008; Runco et al., 2001). With that said, four critical issues arise when behavioral measures are applied in studies of creativity.

First, behavioral measures may be completed by an individual observing their own behavior or external judges observing the behavior of others. What is critical is that the behavior to be appraised must be observable—ideally, in the case of external judges, evidencing adequate inter-judge agreement (James, James, & Ashe, 1990). Second, creativity, as a concept, involves stereotypical assumptions (Hyman, 1961). As a result, the question arises as to the extent to which these preconceptions influence behavioral evaluations. Third, in studies based on behavioral measures, all measures administered often reflect behavioral self-reports. Accordingly, in behaviorally-based studies it becomes critical to address the potential problems associated with source/method bias, so requisite methods to control such bias should be applied (Podsakoff, Mackenzie, Lee, & Podsakoff, 2003). Fourth, and finally, in behavioral studies neither creative products, nor attributes of performance in creative problem-solving, are examined. As a result, the question arises as to the efficacy of behavioral markers in reflecting behaviors actually tied to creative problem-solving activities.

Outcomes

Creativity differs from many other phenomena of interest in that creative efforts result in products that are recorded in documentary sources (Simonton, 1991). Moreover, these products are evaluated by members of the field in which the work was done, or broader socio-cultural institutions, for other manifest creativity (Csikszentmihályi, 1999). As a result, these outcome measures are often employed as a basis for appraising creativity.

In one study along these lines, Root-Bernstein, Berstein, and Garnier (1995) identified creative scientists based on whether they had been awarded the Nobel Prize—a work outcome commonly held to require creativity. Similarly, Nemeth and Goncalo (2005), in a study examining the benefits of collaboration in the production of creative products, used citation of a publication by others as a measure of its creativity. Ramey and Weisberg (2004), in a study of affective disorders on creativity, used the number of Emily Dickenson's poems included in anthologies as a measure of creativity. Simonton (2004), in a study of creativity in the film industry, used Oscar Awards as a measure of product creativity. Along somewhat different lines, Mumford, Olsen, and James (1989), in a study examining the influence of creativity on economic growth, used patent awards as a measure of creativity.

Clearly, a variety of outcome measures are available for assessing creativity. However, as implied by our foregoing observations, it should be recognized that outcome measures are necessarily field specific measures of creativity. It is not likely many scientists have won an Oscar. More centrally, it should be recognized that not all products produced, even in fields where creativity is called for, necessarily evidence creativity. These rather straightforward observations point to an important implication for outcome-based studies of creativity: Evidence must be found that the outcome measure being employed is a valid reflection of the creativity of the product and that this measure evidences adequate reliability and validity (Simonton, 1991).

Perhaps a more important consideration arises from the fact that outcome-based measures of creativity represent "hard" production measures (Muchinsky, 1993). In other words, outcome measures are analogous to criteria such as sales volume. The latter, of course, reflects not only the performance of a sales representative but also other considerations such as product quality, competitor strength, and marketing investment. In studies where sales volume is employed as a criterion, these other influences must be controlled. Accordingly, in studies of creativity based on outcome measures, inferences depend on the adequacy of the controls applied in obtaining outcome assessments (Mumford, 2006). What should be recognized here, however, is that the controls applied in outcome studies depend on both the nature of the outcome under consideration and the nature of the field from which this outcome emerges (Csikszentmihályi, 1999).

Of course, the issue of control points to the need for evidence that pertains to the reliability and validity of the outcome measure being applied. In studies based on outcome measures, however, another consideration must be taken into account. Typically outcome measures are not normally distributed (Huber, 1998). Instead, creative outcomes tend to be rare, or infrequent, events. Thus, in outcome studies the variability and distribution of scores on the outcome measure often must be established, and, moreover, comparison groups must be carefully specified (Simonton, 1990).

METHODS

Qualitative Studies

Qualitative studies focus on in-depth observation of a particular creative product, or set of products, as product production activities are observed in real-world settings. Thus qualitative studies begin with an appraisal of product creativity. As a result, demonstrating that a creative product, or products, has been produced is critical to the inferences drawn in qualitative studies. Extensive observations of the activities contributing to product production (Eckert & Stacey, 2003) or the conditions under which this occurs (Amabile, Schatzel, Moneta, & Kramer, 2004) are used to draw inferences about creativity and innovation.

Because creative and innovative products can be identified at different levels of analysis, qualitative studies have been conducted at a number of different levels of analysis. For example, in an organizational level study, Drazin, Glynn, and Kazanjian (1999) conducted observations of an organization developing a new product—in this case, an airplane. Analysis of the crisis events occurring during development of this product led to the conclusions that crises were common in the development of innovative products and that the sense-making activities engaged in by project leaders are critical to the success of these efforts. An illustrative qualitative study conducted at the group level may be found in Nemiro (2002). In this study, members of 9 virtual teams working in various organizational consulting firms were studied. A semi-structured interview was used to examine the communication strategies occurring at different phases of the product generation process. It was found that creative teams evidenced four distinct stages in their work: idea generation, development, finalization, and evaluation, with team members employing different communication strategies in each of these stages. In an individual level study, Henderson (2004) conducted interviews with inventors of new products. A combination of interviews and focus group meetings were used to draw inferences about the motivation for creative work, with findings indicating that affective pleasure in the technical aspects of creative work (e.g., problem-solving, technical perspective taking) was critical to motivating creators of new products.

Clearly, qualitative studies can be useful in enhancing our understanding of creative work at many levels. What should be recognized here, however, is that the value of such studies is to a large extent dependent on the creativity of the particular set of products being studied. Thus Mumford and his colleagues (Mumford, 2002; Mumford & Moertl, 2003) in their studies of social innovation identified clear cases where new processes and institutions provided the basis for successful innovative efforts. Similarly, Dunbar (1995) in his study of creative thinking among scientists focused expressly on the production of new research in micro-biological laboratories. Not only is clarity with regard to the particular domain of creative products being examined of critical concern in qualitative studies, but the number of cases of creative work examined within these domains is also of concern as a constraint on the generality of the conclusions flowing from these studies. Thus, in both the Dunbar (1995) and Mumford (2002) studies, 8 to 12 different cases provided the basis for subsequent analysis.

Creative work, particularly in real-world settings, which is the focus of most qualitative studies, is an inherently complex, multi-faceted, phenomenon. Accordingly, a critical question arising in qualitative studies concerns the observational methods employed. One aspect of this methods question pertains to the aspects of creativity which were observed. Thus Sawyer (1992), in his study of creativity among jazz musicians, describes in detail the interview protocol used to elicit the observational data. Similarly, McIntyre (2008) in his study of songwriting describes not only interview procedures applied but also cultural practices and participant observation techniques applied. Typically, use of multiple observational sources focused on the particular phenomenon of interest is considered desirable in qualitative studies (Hsia, 1988). The other aspect of observational method pertains to the nature of the people making the observations. In this regard, observer training, observer awareness of hypotheses, and observer influences on the observations are all issues of concern (Mace & Ward, 2002). However, the importance of these issues varies as a function of the particular observational method being applied.

Qualitative studies by virtue of their use of open-ended observations, or responses to interview questions, however, broach another concern. Specifically, exactly how are observations coded or evaluated? Some cases, for example Clydesdale's (2006) analysis of work team and competitive influences, are primarily based on a priori theoretical considerations. In other cases, for example Glück, Ernst, and Unger's (2002) study of images of creativity, theory, or expert judges are used to define thematic coding categories to be applied in appraising qualitative data. In still other cases, for example Eckert and Stacey's (2003) analysis of the representational modes used by creative knitwear designers through think aloud protocols, expert appraisal of the products produced, without direct reference to extant theory, may provide the basis for development of the themes or categories to be used in analysis.

Although qualitative studies have proven useful in studies of creativity and innovation, certain critical limitations on the utility of this method should be noted. Perhaps the first, and most obvious of these concerns is the generality of the resulting conclusions. In part, concerns with regard to generality pertain to the limited number of cases being observed in most qualitative studies (McIntyre, 2008). Generality, however, is also limited by the focus on creative performance within a particular domain and with respect to a particular product. The second limitation, however, is more subtle albeit equally important. Qualitative studies typically depend on either self observations (e.g., responses to interview questions) or the observations of external judges with regard to behaviors of interest. What should be recognized here is that not all aspects of creativity are necessarily directly observable (Eckert & Stacey, 2003). Thus qualitative procedures may not provide a viable mechanism for understanding all aspects of creativity and innovation—a case in point may be found in problem definition processes (Mumford, Reiter-Palmon, & Redmond, 1994). Third, qualitative studies often suffer because explicit comparison groups are not identified (Eckert & Stacey, 2003). Lack of appropriate comparison groups, in turn, makes it difficult to determine whether the behaviors being observed, in fact, exert unique effects on creativity and innovation.

Historiometric Studies

Historiometric studies represent an attempt to explain the sources of eminent achievement (Albert, 1996; Simonton, 1991). The term achievement is of some importance with regard to these studies since measures of the outcomes of creative work are treated as the dependent variables of interest. Thus, historiometric studies of creativity in the sciences often focus on publications and patent awards (Mumford, Connelly, Scott, Espejo, Sohl, Hunter, & Bedell, 2005). Alternatively, in studies of innovation in organizational settings technical quality, time to development, and market share attained may serve as the outcomes of interest (Keller, 2001). Although "objective" outcomes are often employed in historiometric studies, outcome measures reflecting creative achievement may also be obtained from expert judges. Thus, MacKinnon (1962) used peer nominations to identify creative professionals while Gassman and Van Zedwitz (2003) used managerial appraisals to identify creative, innovative, products.

Of course, outcomes reflecting creative achievement exist at multiple levels. As a result, historiometric studies examining influences on creative achievement have been conducted at multiple levels of analysis. In an individual level study, Root-Bernstein and Root-Bernstein (2006) defined eminence in terms of a MacArthur Foundation Fellowship Award—a genius grant. MacArthur Fellows were compared to undergraduates with respect to retrospective reports of childhood wordplay—finding that wordplay was more common among MacArthur Fellows than undergraduates in general. In a group-level study, Nemeth and Goncalo (2005) treated citation counts as a measure of eminent achievement among social scientists. They found that as the number of authors increased and the number of authors working in independent locations increased, citation rates also increased. In an organizational-level study, Chandy and Tellis (2000) identified radical 20th century innovations (e.g., the transistor). They found that these radical innovations were more likely to emerge from large rather than small firms. In another organizational-level study, Graves and Lanowitz (1993) treated new product introductions by pharmaceutical firms as the outcome of interest. They found that research and development investment contributed to new product introductions only up to a point.

These examples, at least implicitly, serve to illustrate a number of key attributes of historiometric studies. To begin with, the outcome criteria that are employed are often level specific; new product introductions are an organizational level outcome, while MacArthur Foundation Awards are an individual level outcome. Although it is possible to aggregate lower level measures (e.g., citation counts) to higher levels (e.g., organizational intellectual productivity), it is important to establish the appropriateness of these aggregations through an analysis of within-and-between effects (Mumford, Dansereau, & Yammarino, 2000). Nonetheless, due to their level dependence, historiometric studies tend to be tied to creativity as it is manifest at a particular level.

The value of historiometric studies, of course, depends on the validity of the outcome measure being applied as a measure of creative achievement. Although an outcome such as publications or new product introductions may be accepted as a measure of creative achievement based on face, or content, validity, given the foundation outcome measures provide for historiometric studies, evidence for the validity of the measure as a reflection of creative achievement is desirable. Thus Simonton (2004) in an historiometric study of creativity in the film industry, provided evidence for the validity of Academy Awards and Academy Award nominations by showing that they converged with other evaluative sources (e.g., New York Film Critics, Screen Actors Guild). Moreover, Academy Awards, and award nominations, were shown to predict movie guide ratings giving reason to suspect that they provide a valid measure of creative achievement in the film industry.

A. INTRODUCTION

Although it is desirable to validate the outcome measures employed in historiometric studies as measures of creativity, it should be recognized that not every measure employed in these studies need necessarily reflect creativity. In organizational level studies, measures such as time to product development, cost of product development, and market share gains as a result of the product are also commonly employed (Ford & Gioia, 2000; Hauschildt & Kirchmann, 2001; Keller, 2001; Lovelace, Shapiro, & Weingart, 2001). The intent of examining these outcomes, as well as the production of innovative products, is to examine the effects of predictors on derivative outcomes of creative work of interest in organizational settings. However, these derivative outcomes are not exclusively the property of organizations—although they are often examined in organizational-level studies. For example, in an individual level study one might examine costs to personal life or alternatively acceptance of non-traditional approaches by others.

What should be recognized is that the outcomes under consideration in historiometric studies, regardless of the outcome measures being employed, are typically "hard" measures. As noted earlier, "hard" measures are subject to a number of extraneous influences. As a result, controls must be given attention in historiometric studies to permit valid inferences to be made. For example Mumford et al. (2005) were interested in the factors (e.g., creative research strategy, laboratory intellectual engagement, research support) influencing the creative productivity of scientists. Potential measures of these variables were derived from the obituaries of scientists—which were used as source information because they provide a valid, comprehensive, description of the events occurring in a scientist's career. Although viable measures of these predictions were formulated, it must be borne in mind that scientists live lives of varying length, they work in different fields, follow different career paths within these fields, and have different relationships with the author of the obituary. Accordingly, measures of all these extraneous variables were formulated and inferences drawn only after taking into account the relevance of these controls. Thus in well conducted historiometric studies substantial attention is given to relevant controls.

The Mumford et al. (2005) study is also of interest because it reminds us of certain key characteristics evidenced by viable historiometric studies. First, although a variety of sources may be used in these studies to appraise creativity and/or potential predictors of creativity, viable historic studies attend to the accuracy of these sources. Second, the sample of people, products, or events used as a basis for conducting such studies is typically specially constructed with respect to the inferences to be drawn from the study (Simonton, 1991). Third, comparison groups must be defined bearing in mind the critical outcomes of concern and the nature of predictions. Thus, in the Mumford et al. (2005) study median splits were conducted within field using the creativity measure where splits were made within field, not the overall sample, due to known cross field differences in productivity.

The predictors employed in historiometric studies are typically defined with respect to theory and the nature of the outcomes of interest. For example, Feist (1997) in a study of scientific eminence, as measured by peer ratings, professional visibility, and highest honor received, was to be accounted for based on publication practices where quantity, quality, and impact of publications were used as predictors. His findings indicated that prolific scientists (high impact, high quality) but not necessarily perfectionist scientists (low quantity, high impact) tended to achieve positions of eminence. This domain specificity of predictors is also illustrated in a recent study by Simonton (2007). Here preparatory sketches of one

Picasso painting, served as the historic material, with these sketches being appraised by judges for similarity to the final picture. Structured and unstructured theories of creative product production served as predictors. The findings obtained argued for unstructured production, although there is some debate surrounding this interpretation (Mumford & Antes, 2007; Weisberg & Hass, 2007).

The specificity of outcomes and predictors evident in the Fiest (1997) and Simonton (2007) studies is noteworthy, because it points to a limitation often evident in historiometric studies. More specifically, these studies often do not allow easy generation of conclusions across outcome measures, fields, and predictors. Although principles emerging from historiometric studies have often evidenced some generality, generalization has often depended on systematic, ongoing research where theory informs both the selection of outcome measures and predictors (Simonton, 1999). Along related lines, problems arise in historiometric studies because people place faith, perhaps too much faith, in the outcome measures that provide the basis for these investigations. By the same token, however, the direct relevance of historiometric studies to real-world outcomes of creativity often recommends such studies when applied considerations are dominant concerns.

Survey Studies

The term survey, as it is used here, refers to people's reports of their own, or others', behavior. Unlike qualitative and historiometric studies, which focus on the production of creative products or the outcomes of creative work, survey studies are not tied to a particular type of criterion measure. It is true that in some studies, survey measures are used to measure both predictors and criteria (e.g., George & Zhou, 2001; Jaussi et al., 2007), but in others, surveys are used only to account for criterion measures obtained using other methods. Thus Jung (2001) measured transformational leadership through a survey measure. He found that transformational leadership influenced the number and originality of the ideas produced on a group brainstorming task—a performance attribute measure of creativity. Similarly, Engle, Mah, and Sadri (1997) administered Kirton's (1976) measure of adaptive and innovative work styles, a survey measure, and used scores on this survey to distinguish between entrepreneurs and employees—an outcome measure.

The attraction of surveys is that they provide available measures, which are often reliable and valid, of relevant constructs—either predictor or criterion constructs. The availability of these measures, their ease of administration, and the objectivity of scoring procedures, has led to the widespread use of surveys in studies of creativity—studies conducted at multiple levels. In a recent study conducted at the individual level, Muñoz-Doyague, González-Álvarez, and Nieto (2008) administered a behavioral survey measure of creativity to employees of an auto manufacturing company. Additionally survey measures examining instrinsic motivation, expertise, and cognitive style were administered. They found that intrinsic motivation and an innovative work style were effective predictors of creativity. Tierney et al. (1999), in a group-level study, administered a survey examining positive interpersonal exchange relationships between a leader and followers to a sample of chemists. They found that positive leader–follower exchange was not only related to creativity as assessed through a survey, but also formed an outcome measure of invention disclosures. In an organizational-level study, Orpen (1990) administered a climate survey, examining perceived attributes of the environment contributing to creativity, such as ownership and diversity, to employees of an innovative and a non-innovative company (outcome criteria). It was found that members of the innovative company obtained higher scores on these attributes of climate for creative work.

The first question typically raised with regard to survey studies, regardless of the level at which they are conducted, pertains to the reliability and validity of the measures being applied (Mathisen & Einarsen, 2004). In fact, most survey measures employed, due to extensive prior development, evidence adequate reliability. Validity issues, however, are typically of greater concern. One issue pertaining to validity concerns the relevance of the construct being measured to creativity at the level of analysis of concern. Thus in individual level studies, measures of leadership attributes may not be of great concern. However, in group level studies leader behavior becomes a more relevant variable for explaining creative performance (Mumford, Scott, Gaddis, & Strange, 2002). Assuming constructs have been specified at the appropriate level, the next question that comes to fore concerns the validity of the measure. Thus Hunter, Bedell, and Mumford (2007) conducted a meta-analysis examining the predictive validity of creative climate surveys. The findings obtained in this study provided evidence for the validity of these measures by showing climate appraisals were related to multiple indices of creativity obtained through various different measures (e.g., product, outcome).

As Messick (1998) has pointed out, however, validation is not simply a matter of prediction but also the justification for observed relationships. Smith (2008) makes a similar point in his analysis of the use of personality surveys in creativity research. Broadly speaking, two systems have been used to justify the application of measurement by survey in studies of creativity. The first system is essentially a construct-specific approach where the variable being measured in the survey, for example locus of control, is used to justify the relevance of this construct to creative performance. An example of this approach may be found in Pannells and Claxton's (2008) study of the influence of locus of control and happiness on a survey measure of creativity. The second system formulates justification for the variables being assessed in surveys based on the underlying process mechanisms giving rise to creative performance within the particular domain under consideration. An example of this approach may be found in the Jaussi et al. (2007) study of motivational influences on creativity. Here a compelling argument was provided for the influence of creative self-efficacy and creative identity as influences on motivation for creative work with the obtained findings indicating that creative identity added to creative self-efficacy in accounting for creative performance. Generally, substantive justifications focused on creative performance provide a stronger basis for drawing inferences with regard to creativity in survey studies.

The development of substantive systems based on the demands of creative performance at a particular level not only is of interest with regard to validation, this approach has also given rise to the development of new survey measures. Thus Proctor and Burnett (2004) developed a survey measure, based on a checklist approach, to measure constructs relevant to creative performance such as elaboration, flexibility, and risk taking. They found that these variables were related to engagement in and enjoyment of creative tasks.

In addition to substantive justification for the constructs being measured in survey studies, another concern pertains to the nature of the measure of creativity being employed. As noted earlier due to method/source bias issues, when survey measures are used as both

A. INTRODUCTION

criteria and predictors, the obtained relationships may be suspect. Thus survey studies typically yield stronger conclusions when performance, performance attributes, or outcome measures are used as the dependent variables. Thus Dollinger, Burke, and Gump (2007) and Kasof, Chen, Himsel, and Greenberger (2007) provided strong evidence of the relevance of two values, stimulation and self-determination, measured through self-report surveys, by showing that scores for these values were related to creative problem-solving performance, where the problems being examined were drawn from multiple different domains.

Along related lines, it should also be recognized that surveys, as behavioral observation measures, can be completed by different observers. Frequently, we assume that self-reports can and should be used in survey measures. However, if the behaviors of interest can be observed by others, for example, supervisors, peers, or teachers, then these sources may also be used in survey studies with the use of alternative sources limiting concerns with regard to method/source bias (Lim & Smith, 2008). Thus Madjar et al. (2002), in a study of the influence of mood states on creativity, asked external judges, judges who displayed adequate agreement, to evaluate product creativity. Similarly, Burningham and West (1995) in validation of a climate measure asked expert, external judges, to appraise the creativity of group products. Use of these external sources clearly strengthens the conclusions that may be drawn from survey studies, especially when different informants are used in collecting predictor and criterion information.

In contrast to qualitative and historiometric studies, survey studies do not typically evidence problems with regard to drawing general conclusions about influences on creativity and innovation. The ability of survey studies to produce generalizable conclusions is an outcome of the construct, or variable, oriented approach that is used in developing surveys. The key limitation applying to survey measures, however, arises from the fundamental nature of the technique. Surveys require the possibility of the self, or others, to observe behavior. Thus surveys, while useful in appraising observable aspects of creativity, are less useful in assessing unobservable attributes of creative performance and the variables shaping creative performance.

Psychometric Studies

In contrast to qualitative, historiometric, and survey studies, psychometric studies focus only on individual-level phenomena. Psychometric studies, as implied by the label, are based on tests intended to assess performance attributes linked to creative thinking (Albert & Runco, 1999). These tests are based on Guilford's (Guildford, 1950; Merrifield, Guilford, Christensen, & Frick, 1962) concept of divergent thinking. On divergent thinking tests people are presented with an ill-defined, open-ended problem—for example, think of alternative uses for a brick, or think of the consequences if gravity was cut in half. The number, number of categories, or originality of responses to these questions provide the basis for measuring creative thinking abilities.

Over the years, a number of tests intended to measure divergent thinking have been developed (Kaufman & Baer, 2006; Mumford, 2001) with many of these tests being based on the work of Guildford (e.g., Merrifield et al., 1962) and Torrance (e.g., Torrance, 1974). Accordingly, many psychometric studies have focused on the factor analysis of divergent thinking tests in the hope of identifying the abilities which underlie creative thought. For example, Michael and Bachelor (1990) factored Guilford's (Guilford, Merrifield, & Cox, 1961) divergent thinking tests, 29 tests such as alternative uses, planning elaboration, and possible jobs, using a higher order confirmatory analysis. They identified three factors that appeared to account for performance on these tests:

1. semantic,
2. symbolic, and
3. figural.

However, evidence was also obtained for the operation of a general divergent thinking factor. In another study, Abedi (2002) factored the Torrance divergent thinking measures using a different confirmatory model. He found that four factors emerged, reflecting fluency, flexibility, originality, and elaboration. Again, however, the correlations observed among these factors suggested that test performance might be accounted for by a general divergent thinking factor.

Of course, the existence, or potential existence, of a general divergent thinking factor broaches a new question—does divergent thinking predict other aspects of creative performance? The available evidence does, in fact, suggest that divergent thinking test scores are capable of predicting creative performance. For example, Plucker (1999) has shown that the Torrance creative thinking tests are an effective predictor of real-world creative achievement—producing stronger positive relationships with measures of creative achievement than measures of intelligence. Similarly, Wechsler (2006), again using measures of creative outcomes (e.g., distinctions, prizes), found that divergent thinking tests produced positive correlations, in the mid-30s, with measures of creative achievement. Other work by Vincent et al. (2002) has shown that scores on divergent thinking tests predicted creative problem-solving in a sample of army officers. Creative problem-solving, in turn, accounted for officer career achievement (e.g., medals won, critical incident performance). These effects held, moreover, even when intelligence and expertise were taken into account. Thus divergent thinking does appear to make a unique contribution to creative problem-solving and the outcome of creative work. Other studies, for example Davidovitz and Milgram (2006), have also provided evidence for the validity of divergent thinking tests in predictions of a variety of real-world performances, such as negotiation, where creativity is held to be one variable contributing to performance.

If it is granted that divergent thinking tests do in fact predict creative performance, a number of new questions come to the fore concerning the optimal procedures for applying them. The first is whether divergent thinking test content should be tailored to the performance domain at hand (Baer, 2003). Thus, in developing a divergent thinking measure for use in appraising scientists, one might present a study summary and key findings, and ask scientists to generate multiple alternative hypotheses that might account for these findings (Sak & Maker, 2006). A related issue concerns the procedures used in scoring these tests—either domain specific or domain general. Should response options be scored for general attributes (fluency, flexibility, originality, and elaboration) or key attributes of creative performance operating in this domain? Although the findings obtained by Mumford et al. (1998) suggests that the use of domain-specific scoring attributes results in stronger predictive validity coefficients than general scoring, it should be recognized that application of such procedures requires a well developed, substantive, understanding of the unique aspects of creative performance within this domain.

A related question that has been asked with regard to the use of divergent thinking tests concerns the attributes in people's performance to be scored on general, cross-domain, tests. For example, one might score divergent thinking tests for the most original response produced, the most unusual response produced, or variability in responses (e.g., Silvia, Winterstein, Willse, Barona, Cram, Hess, Martinez, & Richard, 2008; Stokes & Balsam, 2003). Although some alternative frameworks for scoring divergent thinking tests have shown some validity, other alternatives have not. For example, scoring unusual responses has proven of limited value (Plucker & Renzulli, 1999). Thus ongoing validation seems required when new attributes are proposed for scoring divergent thinking tests with such studies proving particularly valuable if evidence is provided for incremental validity on these scores above and beyond evaluations of fluency, flexibility, originality, and elaboration.

Perhaps a more fundamental question, however, lies in the variables giving rise to divergent thinking. In a recent study, Silvia et al. (2008) administered divergent thinking tests to a sample of undergraduates. A general divergent thinking factor was identified. Personality tests were also administered with two factors emerging—plasticity and stability. They found that plasticity was strongly positively related ($\beta = 0.64$) to divergent thinking while stability ($\beta = -0.32$) was negatively related. Although the findings obtained in this study are subject to some debate (Mumford, Vessey, & Barrett, 2008; Runco, 2008), they do point to the importance of studies intended to account for the origins of divergent thinking.

Although divergent thinking tests have value, two questions have been raised with regard to the value of basing studies of creativity on these measures. The first arises from the nature of all psychometric procedures that focus on variability among individuals. Because these measures focus on individual variability, sources of variation not attributable to the individual cannot be identified. Thus limitations are set on the kind of questions that can be answered through psychometric tests. Second, these tests focus on one aspect of creative production—divergent production. As Basadur, Runco, and Vega (2000) and Cropley (2006) have pointed out, however, aspects of convergent thinking may prove as, if not more, important than divergent thinking in real-world incidents of creative problem-solving and innovation. Within these limitations, however, it should also be recognized that psychometric studies often evidence some generality while producing a set of tools that not only have served to advance creativity research but also have real value for the assessment of creative potential.

Experimental Studies

Experiments, in contrast to psychometric studies which appraise individual-level variability, seek to induce variation in creativity and innovation by creating changes in the conditions under which creative performance occurs. These manipulations, of course, are time limited. Thus the measures of creativity commonly examined in these studies focus on short-term indices of creativity—creative problem-solving (e.g., Redmond et al., 1993), attributes of creative performance (e.g., Yuan & Zhou, 2008), and behaviors involved in creativity (Jausovec, 1997). Although time limited with respect to the types of creative performance measures examined, the strength of experimental studies is that they can provide a relatively unambiguous demonstration of the operation of causes through systematic manipulations of the conditions of performance. By the same token, opportunities to make manipulations are limited by the nature of the phenomena under investigation. Typically, organizations will not allow themselves to be manipulated. As a result, most experimental studies focus on individual-level (e.g., Baughman & Mumford, 1995) or group-level (e.g., Kurtzberg, 2005) phenomena.

Bearing this limitation in mind, experimental studies have been used to investigate a wide array of phenomena contributing to creativity and innovation. Experimental studies have been used:

1. to establish the role of knowledge in creative thought (Hunter, Bedell-Avers, Ligon, Hunsicker, & Mumford, 2008; Weisberg, 2006),
2. to identify the cognitive processes underlying creative thought (Estes & Ward, 2002; Finke et al., 1992) and the strategies contributing to effective execution of these processes (Lonergan, Scott, & Mumford, 2004; Scott et al., 2005),
3. to identify the kinds of errors people make in creative thought (Licuanan, Dailey, & Mumford, 2007),
4. to identify the effects of instructional set on creativity (O'Hara & Sternberg, 2001),
5. to identify the effects of motivation and mood on creativity (Kaufmann & Vosberg, 2002),
6. to identify the leadership styles contributing to creativity (Jung, 2001), and
7. to identify the effects of instructional interventions on enhancing creative thought (Scott, Leritz, & Mumford, 2004).

These examples serve to make a basic point. Experimental studies have been used to study a wide variety of phenomena relevant to understanding creativity.

As noted earlier, creativity and innovation are complex phenomena. This complexity has an important implication for experimental studies of creativity. It is simply impossible to design experimental manipulations that would influence creativity and innovation as a general phenomenon. As a result, experimental studies typically focus on a certain aspect of creativity where it is possible to formulate viable manipulations. Thus Mobley, Doares, and Mumford (1992) focused on conceptual combination and designed an experimental task where people were asked to combine categories (birds—owl, robin, sparrow and sporting equipment—bats, balls, gloves) to create a new category. Thus this study focused solely on one process, conceptual combination, held to be involved in creative thought. Similarly, in their study of the effects of mood on creativity, Kaufmann and Vosberg (2002) presented excerpts of movies intended to induce mood states before asking people to work on creative problem-solving tasks. What is noteworthy here is that movies influence only certain aspects of mood.

The need for experimental studies to formulate manipulations with respect to a specific aspect of creative thought, however, broaches another issue. More specifically, how realistic, or generalizable, is the particular aspect of creativity being examined in an experimental study? Welling (2007), in a review of experimental methods in studies of creativity, suggests that the tradeoff between isolation of manipulations and generality of the conclusions flowing from the study can be addressed through the use of low-fidelity simulations involving the production of creative products. An illustration of this approach may be found in Mumford, Baughman, Supinski, and Maher (1996). Here a series of different information cards were presented on-line where the content of the information was varied and time spent looking at each card was recorded. It was found that time spent on key facts and anomalies were related to subsequent creative problem-solving. Although not all experimental studies require a low-fidelity simulation approach (e.g., Estes & Ward, 2002), when this approach is applied it is important to bear in mind the ability of participants to think creatively within the simulation being presented. Thus the tasks used must be appropriate for the population at hand.

The strength of the findings emerging from experimental studies is often limited by need for isolation as well as necessary limitations on the length and intensity of manipulations. This point is of some importance because it suggests that while it may be useful to present effect sizes in experimental studies, effect sizes per se will rarely provide a fully adequate basis for drawing conclusions. Although educational studies might represent a noteworthy exception to this rule of thumb, the approach more commonly applied in experimental studies is to use multiple manipulations, where validation of the expected interactions among these manipulations can be used to assess the meaningfulness of the observed effects. An example of this approach may be found in a study by Marcy and Mumford (2007) examining the effects of training causal analysis skills (e.g., identification of causes that can be manipulated, identification of causes having change effects) on the production of creative solutions to social innovation problems. It was found that this training intervention induced effects on the originality of problem solutions only when people were reasonably involved in relatively familiar problems. Similarly, Lonergan et al. (2004), in a study of idea evaluation processes, found that the most creative solutions arose when people evaluated original ideas for quality and when people evaluated non-original ideas for originality. Thus idea evaluation appears to be promoted by use of a compensatory strategy.

In both the Lonergan et al. (2004) and the Marcy and Mumford (2007) studies, the emergence of these interactions strengthened the conclusions that could be drawn from the study. Thus in experimental studies of creativity the explicit specification and testing of theoretically based interactions is of some importance. What should be recognized here, however, is that not all interactions can be examined in any given study. More centrally, however, the specific interactions being examined must be those where relevant manipulations can be effectively, realistically, and appropriately embedded in the experimental task or low-fidelity simulations under consideration. Thus viable experimental studies are typically characterized by a meaningful flow of manipulations from the perspective of study participants.

In addition to interactive effects, the strength of the conclusions that may be drawn from experimental studies increases when multiple dependent variables are examined. Thus in simulation studies, it is common practice to obtain creative problem solutions and evaluate them for quality, originality, and elegance (Eubanks, Murphy, & Mumford, 2010). Similarly, Friedman, Förster, and Denzler (2007) in a study of positive, neutral, and negative moods, induced through recall of prior positive or negative life events, asked participants to list as many similarities and differences between selected television shows as they could "think of". Notably, responses were evaluated not only for the creativity and fluency but also a post-experimental survey examining motivation and liking. When the effects of mood were appraised with respect to a manipulation in task framing (e.g., the task is fun or serious), it was found that fluency, creativity, motivation, and liking were high when negative moods were induced in a serious task and when positive moods were induced in a fun task.

A. INTRODUCTION

Of course, it has traditionally been held that one key advantage of experimental studies is control. More specifically, by constructing tasks and performance conditions systematically, other extraneous influences on the performance of interest can be ruled out. Although maintenance of control in procedures is important in all experimental studies, including studies of creativity, two additional control issues are commonly addressed. First, manipulations, especially social manipulations, such as feelings of self-efficacy, may not work. As a result, manipulation checks should be conducted in many experimental studies, (Dailey & Mumford, 2006). Second, experimental studies rely on external manipulations imposed on the conditions of task performance. As a result, it is often necessary to control for individual differences variables shaping creative performance such as divergent thinking, intelligence, and expertise (e.g., Scott et al., 2005).

Our foregoing observations with regard to control of individual differences variables point to one important limitation of experimental studies of creativity. These studies, by virtue of the assumptions underlying manipulations, often have little to say about certain individual differences which are relevant to understanding creativity. Moreover, the nature of experimental studies is such that typically only two to four variables can be manipulated in any given study. Thus, a single experimental study cannot provide a complete description of all relevant variables that might shape the performance of interest. Moreover, the induction of manipulations through isolated tasks, even low-fidelity simulation tasks, brings to question the generality of the conclusions flowing from these studies. By the same token, however, the ability of experimental studies to provide relatively unambiguous conclusions about the operation of causes shaping creative performance is of great value.

CONCLUSIONS

Before turning to the broader conclusions following from the present effort certain limitations should be noted. To begin it should be clear that we have not examined every method that has been applied in studies of creativity and innovation. For example little has been said about biological methods (e.g., Cartwright, Clark-Carter, Ellis, & Mathews, 2004). Similarly, little has been said about the application of clinical research methods (e.g., Abraham & Windmann, 2008) or the potential value of longitudinal studies (e.g., Plucker, 1999). Rather, in the present effort we have focused on the methods applied in creativity research that are most directly relevant to understanding creativity and innovation in organizations—specifically, qualitative, historiometric, survey, psychometric, and experimental studies.

Along related lines, in the present effort we have focused on the methods used to conduct these studies. As a result, little has been said about the particular procedures that might, or should, be applied in analyzing the data gathered using these methods. Although, we should note that the nature of "best practice" methods often dictates the use of multivariate methods (Simonton, 1990).

It should also be recognized that we have treated both method and measures of creativity as unique aspects of study design. What should also be recognized here, however, is that often studies of creativity and innovation employ multiple criteria and multiple methods. For example, Vincent et al. (2002) in measuring creative performance considered both creative problem solutions and outcome measures. Jung (2001) used both survey methods in appraising independent variables and performance attribute measures in appraising creativity. These mixed method, mixed measure, studies are, of course, highly valuable. However, execution of these studies also requires an understanding of each method and measures being applied.

Even bearing these limitations in mind, we believe that the present effort does lead to some clear-cut conclusions about the methods applied in studies of creativity and innovation. Perhaps the most clear-cut conclusion bears on what, exactly, is being studied in this type of research. Creativity and innovation, ultimately, represent a form of performance (Ghiselin, 1963)—one of special interest due to the impact of creativity and innovation on people, groups, organizations, and society. Because studies of creativity focus on a particular form of performance, the criterion or dependent variables used to measure creativity and innovation are of particular concern.

In the present effort we have examined the four types of performance commonly used to measure creativity and innovation. More specifically, we have argued that creativity is assessed through:

1. creative problem-solving,
2. attributes of performance in producing these solutions,
3. behaviors that occur during creative work, and
4. the outcomes of creative work.

What should be recognized here is that each of these measures has its unique set of strengths and weaknesses. Thus behavioral measures can be applied across a range of contexts at low cost but are subject to biases (e.g., source/method and stereotyping). Creative problem solutions, although not subject to these problems, are subject to issues of generality depending on the nature of the problems used to assess creativity and innovation. This observation is important because it requires investigators to appraise both the appropriateness, and limitations, of the particular measure of creativity and innovation being applied in a study.

In the present effort, we have also examined the five major methods used to assess the influence of various variables on creativity and innovation as they are assessed through these criterion measures. More specifically, we have examined five key methods applied in studies of creativity and innovation:

1. qualitative,
2. historiometric,
3. survey,
4. psychometric, and
5. experimental.

What should be recognized here first, and foremost, is that each of these methods has its own unique set of strengths and weaknesses. For example, experimental studies require isolation and examine variables subject to experimental control. Psychometric studies focus only on individual variation. Qualitative studies typically require a known creative problem-solving performance but their conclusions are often limited to this particular performance. The implication of these observations is perhaps obvious but nonetheless important.

A. INTRODUCTION

No one method can provide a complete description of creative performance. Rather, in studies of creativity and innovation a multi-method, multi-measure, approach is required.

What should also be recognized is that the methods applied in studies of creativity and innovation are often bound by level. Thus psychometric studies focus on the individual level while qualitative studies cross the individual, group, and organizational levels. Moreover, the measures of creative performance applied are often level specific. Because creativity and innovation are inherently multi-level phenomena (Mumford & Hunter, 2005), this level specificity results in ambiguities in interpretation. One approach to this problem is to conduct more multi-level studies. In fact, use of multi-level approaches such as that applied by Hunter, Bedell, and Mumford (2005) have resulted in some important conclusions. For example, they found that a creative climate exerts its largest effects on performance under organizational conditions (e.g., turbulence, resource scarcity) where it is most difficult to maintain a creative climate.

Although multi-level studies have unique value in studies of creativity and innovation, the complexity of the problems applied, the level specificity methods, and the complexity of conducting multi-level studies suggests that this type of study will never be the norm. Rather, cross-level, cross-method, cross-measure integration of the findings emerging from these studies will often be based on theory—which will be examined in the remaining chapters of this book. Hopefully, this text will serve to help the reader understand the importance and significance of these substantive chapters.

References

Abedi, J. (2002). A latent-variable modeling approach to assessing reliability and validity of a creativity instrument. *Creativity Research Journal, 14*, 267–276.

Abraham, A., & Windmann, S. (2008). Selective information processing advantages in creative cognition as a function of schizotypy. *Creativity Research Journal, 20*, 1–6.

Albert, R. S. (1996). Some reasons why childhood creativity often fails to make it past puberty into the real world. In M. A. Runco (Ed.), *New directions for child and adolescent development* (pp. 43–56). San Francisco, CA: Jossey-Bass.

Albert, R. S., & Runco, M. A. (1999). A history of research on creativity. In R. J. Sternberg (Ed.), *Handbook of creativity* (pp. 16–34). Cambridge, UK: Cambridge University Press.

Amabile, T. M., Schatzel, E. A., Moneta, G. B., & Kramer, S. J. (2004). Leader behaviors and the work environment for creativity: Perceived leader support. *Leadership Quarterly, 15*, 5–32.

Atwater, L., & Carmeli, A. (2009). Leader–member exchange, feelings of energy and involvement in creative work. *The Leadership Quarterly, 20*, 264–275.

Baer, J. (1998). The case for domain specificity of creativity. *Creativity Research Journal, 11*, 173–177.

Baer, J. (2003). Evaluative thinking, creativity, and task specificity: Separating wheat from chaff is not the same as finding needle in haystacks. In M. A. Runco (Ed.), *Critical creative processes* (pp. 129–152). Cresskill, NJ: Hampton.

Baer, J., Kaufman, J. C., & Gentile, C. A. (2004). Extension of the consensual assessment technique to nonparallel creative products. *Creativity Research Journal, 16*, 113–117.

Basadur, M., Runco, M. A., & Vega, L. A. (2000). Understanding how creative thinking skills, attitudes, and behaviors work together: A causal process model. *Journal of Creative Behavior, 34*, 77–100.

Baughman, W. A., & Mumford, M. D. (1995). Process analytic models of creative capacities: Operations involved in the combination and reorganization process. *Creativity Research Journal, 8*, 37–62.

Besemer, S. P. (1998). Creative product analysis matrix: Testing the model structure and a comparison among products—Three novel chairs. *Creativity Research Journal, 11*, 333–346.

Besemer, S. P., & O'Quin, K. (1999). Confirming the three-factor creative product analysis matrix model in an American sample. *Creativity Research Journal, 12*, 287–296.

Blumberg, B. S. (1994). Scientific process and the hepatitis B virus. *Creativity Research Journal, 7*, 315–325.

Burningham, C., & West, M. A. (1995). Individual, climate, and group interaction processes as predictors of work team innovation. *Small Group Research, 26*, 106–117.

Cartwright, M., Clark-Carter, D., Ellis, S. J., & Matthews, C. (2004). Temporal lobe epilepsy and creativity: A model of association. *Creativity Research Journal, 16*, 27–34.

Chandy, R. K., & Tellis, G. J. (2000). The incumbent's curse? Incumbency, size and radical innovation. *Journal of Marketing, 64*, 1–17.

Christiaans, H. H. C. M. (2002). Creativity as a design criterion. *Creativity Research Journal, 14*, 41–54.

Clydesdale, G. (2006). Creativity and competition: The Beatles. *Creativity Research Journal, 18*, 129–139.

Cooke, T. D., & Campbell, D. T. (1979). *Quasi-experimentation: Design and analysis issues for field testing*. Chicago, IL: Rand-McNally College Publishing Company.

Cropley, A. J. (2006). In praise of convergent thinking. *Creativity Research Journal, 18*, 391–404.

Csikszentmihályi, M. (1999). Implications of a systems perspective for the study of creativity. In R. J. Sternberg (Ed.), *Handbook of creativity* (pp. 313–338). Cambridge, UK: Cambridge University Press.

Dailey, L., & Mumford, M. D. (2006). Evaluative aspects of creative thought: Errors in appraising the implications of new ideas. *Creativity Research Journal, 18*, 367–384.

Davidovitch, N., & Milgram, R. M. (2006). Creative thinking as a predictor of teacher effectiveness in higher education. *Creativity Research Journal, 18*, 385–390.

Dollinger, S. J., Burke, P. A., & Gump, N. W. (2007). Creativity and values. *Creativity Research Journal, 19*, 91–103.

Dollinger, S., & Shafran, M. (2005). Note on consensual assessment technique in creativity research. *Perceptual and motor skills, 100*, 592–598.

Drazin, R., Glynn, M. A., & Kazanjian, R. K. (1999). Multi-level theorizing about creativity in organizations: A sense-making perspective. *Academy of Management Review, 24*, 286–307.

Dunbar, K. (1995). How scientists really reason: Scientific reasoning in real-world laboratories. In R. J. Sternberg & J. E. Davidson (Eds.), *The nature of insight* (pp. 365–395). Cambridge, MA: MIT Press.

Eckert, C. M., & Stacey, M. K. (2003). Adaptation of sources of inspiration in knitwear design. *Creativity Research Journal, 15*, 355–384.

Engle, D. E., Mah, J. J., & Sadri, G. (1997). An empirical comparison of entrepreneurs and employees: Implications for innovation. *Creativity Research Journal, 10*, 45–49.

Ericsson, K. A., & Charness, W. (1994). Expert performance: Its structure and acquisition. *American Psychologist, 49*, 725–747.

Estes, Z. C., & Ward, T. B. (2002). The emergence of novel attributes in concept modification. *Creativity Research Journal, 14*, 149–156.

Eubanks, D. L., Murphy, S. T., & Mumford, M. D. (2010). Intuition as an influence on creative problem solving: The effects of intuition, positive affect, and training. *Creativity Research Journal, 22*, 170–184.

Feist, G. J. (1997). Quantity, impact, and depth of research as influences on scientific eminence: Is quantity most important? *Creativity Research Journal, 10*, 325–335.

Finke, R. A. (1990). *Creative imagery: Discoveries and inventions in visualization*. Hillsdale, NJ: Erlbaum.

Finke, R. A., Ward, T. B., & Smith, S. M. (1992). *Creative cognition: Theory, research, and applications*. Cambridge, MA: MIT Press.

Ford, C. M., & Gioia, D. A. (2000). Factors influencing creativity in the domain on managerial decision making. *Journal of Management, 26*, 705–732.

Friedman, R., Förster, J., & Denzler, M. (2007). Interactive effects of mood and task framing on creative generation. *Creativity Research Journal, 19*, 141–162.

Gassman, O., & van Zedwitz, M. (2003). Trends and determinants of managing virtual R&D teams. *R&D Management, 33*, 243–263.

George, J. M., & Zhou, J. (2001). When openness to experience and conscientiousness are related to creative behavior: An interactional approach. *Journal of Applied Psychology, 86*, 513–524.

Ghiselin, B. (1963). Ultimate criteria for two levels of creativity. In C. W. Taylor & F. Barron (Eds.), *Scientific creativity: Its recognition and development* (pp. 30–43). New York, NY: Wiley.

Glück, J., Ernst, R., & Unger, F. (2002). How creatives define creativity: Definitions reflect different types of creativity. *Creativity Research Journal, 14*, 55–67.

Goodman, N. (1976). *Languages of art*. Indianapolis, IN: Hackett.

Graves, S. B., & Lanowitz, N. S. (1993). Innovative productivity and returns to scale in the pharmaceutical industry. *Strategic Management Journal, 14*, 593–606.

A. INTRODUCTION

Guilford, J. P. (1950). Creativity. *American Psychologist, 5,* 444–454.

Guilford, J. P., Merrifield, P. R., & Cox, A. B. (1961). *Creative thinking in children at the junior high school levels.* Report of Psychological Laboratory, University of Southern California.

Hauschildt, J., & Kirchmann, E. (2001). Teamwork for innovation: The troika of promoters. *R&D Management, 31,* 41–49.

Henderson, S. T. (2004). Product inventors and creativity: The fine dimensions of enjoyment. *Creativity Research Journal, 16,* 293–312.

Hennessey, B. A., & Amabile, T. M. (1999). Consensual assessment. In M. Runco & S. Pritzker (Eds.), *Encyclopedia of creativity* (pp. 347–359). New York, NY: Academic Press.

Hitt, M. A., Hoskisson, R. E., Johnson, R. A., & Moesel, D. D. (1996). The market for corporate control and firm innovation. *Academy of Management Journal, 39,* 1084–1196.

Holyoak, K. J., & Thagard, P. (1997). The analogical mind. *American Psychologist, 52,* 35–44.

Hsia, H. (1988). *Mass communications research methods: A step by step approach.* Mahwah, NJ: Lawrence Erlbaum Associates, Inc..

Huber, J. (1998). Invention and inventivity is a random, poisson process: A potential guide to analysis of general creativity. *Creativity Research Journal, 11,* 231–241.

Hughes, T. P. (1989). *American genesis: A history of the American genius for invention.* New York, NY: Penguin.

Hunter, S. T., Bedell, K. E., & Mumford, M. D. (2005). Dimensions of creative climate: A general taxonomy. *Korean Journal of Thinking and Problem Solving, 15,* 97–116.

Hunter, S. T., Bedell, K. E., & Mumford, M. D. (2007). Climate for creativity: A quantitative review. *Creativity Research Journal, 19,* 69–90.

Hunter, S. T., Bedell-Avers, K. E., Ligon, G. S., Hunsicker, C. M., & Mumford, M. D. (2008). Applying multiple knowledge structures in creative thought: Effects on idea generation and problem-solving. *Creativity Research Journal, 20,* 137–154.

Hyman, R. (1961). On prior information and creativity. *Psychological Reports, 9,* 151–161.

James, L. R., James., L. A., & Ashe, D. K. (1990). The meaning of organizations: The role of cognition and values. In B. Schneider (Ed.), *Organizational climate and culture* (pp. 40–84). San Francisco, CA: Josey-Bass.

Jausovec, N. (1997). Differences in EEG activity during the solution of closed and open problems. *Creativity Research Journal, 10,* 317–324.

Jaussi, K., Randel, A., & Dionne, S. (2007). I am, I think I can, and I do: The role of personal identity, self-efficacy, and cross-application of experiences in creativity at work. *Creativity Research Journal, 19,* 247–258.

Jung, D. I. (2001). Transformational and transactional leadership and their effects on creativity in groups. *Creativity Research Journal, 13,* 185–195.

Kasof, J. (1995). Explaining creativity: The attribution perspective. *Creativity Research Journal, 8,* 311–366.

Kasof, J., Chen, C., Himsel, A., & Greenberger, E. (2007). Values and creativity. *Creativity Research Journal, 19,* 105–122.

Kaufman, J. C., & Baer, J. (2006). Intelligent testing with Torrance. *Creativity Research Journal, 18,* 99–102.

Kaufman, J. C., Baer, J., Cole, J. C., & Sexton, J. D. (2008). A comparison of expert and nonexpert raters using the consensual assessment technique. *Creativity Research Journal, 20,* 171–178.

Kaufmann, G., & Vosburg, S. K. (2002). The effects of mood on early and late idea production. *Creativity Research Journal, 14,* 317–330.

Keller, R. T. (2001). Cross-functional project groups in research and new product development: Diversity, communications, job stress, and outcomes. *Academy of Management Journal, 44,* 547–559.

Kim, K. H. (2006). Can we trust creativity tests: A review of the Torrance tests of creative thinking. *Creativity Research Journal, 18,* 3–14.

Kirton, M. (1976). Adaptors and innovators: A description and measure. *Journal of Applied Psychology, 61,* 622–629.

Kurtzberg, T. R. (2005). Feeling creative, being creative: An empirical study of diversity and creativity in teams. *Creativity Research Journal, 17,* 51–65.

Licuanan, B. F., Dailey, L. R., Mumford, M., & McCrae, D. (2007). Idea evaluation: Error in evaluating highly original ideas. *The Journal of Creative Behavior, 41,* 1–27.

Lim, S., & Smith, J. (2008). The structural relationships of parenting style, creative personality, and loneliness. *Creativity Research Journal, 20,* 412–419.

Lonergan, D. C., Scott, G. M., & Mumford, M. D. (2004). Evaluative aspects of creative thought: Effects of appraisal and revision standards. *Creativity Research Journal, 16,* 231–246.

A. INTRODUCTION

Lovelace, K., Shapiro, D. L, & Weingart, L. R. (2001). Maximizing cross-functional new product teams' innovativeness and constraint adherence: A conflict communications perspective. *Academy of Management Journal, 44*, 779–793.

Mace, M. A., & Ward, T. (2002). Modeling the creative process: A grounded theory analysis of creativity in the domain of art making. *Creativity Research Journal, 14*, 179–192.

MacKinnon, D. W. (1962). The nature and nurture of creative talent. *American Psychology, 17*, 484–495.

Madjar, N., Oldham, G. R., & Pratt, M. G. (2002). There's no place like home? The contributions of work and nonwork creativity support to employees' creative performance. *Academy of Management Journal, 45*, 757–787.

Marcy, R. T., & Mumford, M. D. (2007). Social innovation: Enhancing creative performance through causal analysis. *Creativity Research Journal, 19*, 123–140.

Mathisen, G. E., & Einarsen, S. (2004). A review of instruments assessing creative and innovative environments within organizations. *Creativity Research Journal, 16*, 119–140.

McCrae, R. R. (1987). Creativity, divergent thinking, and openness to experience. *Journal of Personality and Social Psychology, 52*, 1258–1265.

McIntyre, P. (2008). Creativity and cultural production: A study of contemporary western popular music songwriting. *Creativity Research Journal, 20*, 40–52.

Mednick, S. A., & Mednick, M. T. (1967). A theory and test of creative thought. In G. Neilson (Ed.), *Proceedings of the XIV international congress of applied psychology: Vol. V. Industrial and business psychology* (pp. 40–47). Oxford, UK: Munksgaard.

Merrifield, P. R., Guilford, J. P., Christensen, P. R., & Frick, J. W. (1962). The role of intellectual factors in problem solving. *Psychological Monographs, 76*, 1–21.

Messick, S. (1998). Alternative modes of assessment, uniform standards of validity. In M. D. Hakel (Ed.), *Beyond multiple choice: Evaluating alternatives to traditional testing for selection* (pp. 59–74). Mahwah, NJ: Lawrence Erlbaum.

Michael, W. B., & Bachelor, P. (1990). Higher-order structure-of-intellect creativity factors in divergent production tests: A reanalysis of a Guilford data base. *Creativity Research Journal, 3*, 58–74.

Mobley, M. I., Doares, L., & Mumford, M. D. (1992). Process analytic models of creative capacities: Evidence for the combination and reorganization process. *Creativity Research Journal, 5*, 125–156.

Muchinsky, P. (1993). Validation of personality constructs for the selection of insurance industry employees. *Journal of Business and Psychology, 7*, 475–482.

Mumford, M. D. (2001). Something old, something new: Revisiting Guilford's conception of creative problem solving. *Creativity Research Journal, 13*, 267–276.

Mumford, M. D. (2002). Social innovation: Ten cases from Benjamin Franklin. *Creativity Research Journal, 14*, 253–266.

Mumford, M. D. (2006). Pathways to outstanding leadership: A comparative analysis of charismatic: *Ideological, and pragmatic leadership*. Mahwah, NJ: Erlbaum.

Mumford, M. D., & Antes, A. L. (2007). Debates about the "general" picture: Cognition and creative achievement. *Creativity Research Journal, 19*, 367–374.

Mumford, M. D., Baughman, W. A., Supinski, E. P., & Maher, M. A. (1996). Process-based measures of creative problem-solving skills: II. Information encoding. *Creativitiy Research Journal, 9*, 77–88.

Mumford, M. D., Connelly, M. S., Scott, G. M., Espejo, J., Sohl, L., & Hunter, S. T., et al. (2005). Career experiences and scientific performance: A study of social, physical, life, and health sciences. *Creativity Research Journal, 17*, 105–129.

Mumford, M. D., Dansereau, F., & Yammarino, F. J. (2000). Motivation and followership: The case of individualized leadership. *Leadership Quarterly, 11*, 313–340.

Mumford, M. D., & Gustafson, S. B. (1988). Creativity syndrome: Integration, application, and innovation. *Psychological Bulletin, 103*, 27–43.

Mumford, M. D., & Gustafson, S. B. (2007). Creative thought: Cognition and problem solving in a dynamic system. In M. A. Runco (Ed.), *Creativity research handbook: Vol. II.* (pp. 33–77). Cresskill, NJ: Hampton.

Mumford, M. D., & Hunter, S. T. (2005). Innovation in Organizations: A multi-level perspective on creativity. In F. Dansereau & F. J. Yammarino (Eds.), *Research in multi-level issues: Vol. IV* (pp. 11–74). Oxford, UK: Elsevier.

Mumford, M. D., Marks, M. A., Connelly, M. S., Zaccaro, S. J., & Johnson, J. F. (1998). Domain-based scoring of divergent-thinking tests: Validation evidence in an occupational sample. *Creativity Research Journal, 11*, 151–163.

Mumford, M. I., Mobley, M. I., Uhlman, C. E., Reiter-Palmon, R., & Doares, L. M. (1991). Process analytic models of creative capacities. *Creativity Research Journal, 4*, 91–122.

A. INTRODUCTION

Mumford, M. D., & Moertl, P. (2003). Cases of social innovation: Lessons from two innovations in the 20th century. *Creativity Research Journal, 15*, 261–266.

Mumford, M. D., Olsen, K. A., & James, L. R. (1989). Age-related changes in the likelihood of major contributions. *International Journal of Aging and Human Development, 29*, 9–32.

Mumford, M. D., Reiter-Palmon, R., & Redmond, M. R. (1994). Problem construction and cognition: Applying problem representations in ill-defined domains. In M. A. Runco (Ed.), *Problem finding, problem solving, and creativity* (pp. 3–39). Westport, CT: Ablex.

Mumford, M. D., Scott, G. M., Gaddis, B. H., & Strange, J. M. (2002). Leading creative people: Orchestrating expertise and relationships. *Leadership Quarterly, 13*, 705–750.

Mumford, M. D., Vessey, W. B., & Barrett, J. D. (2008). Measuring divergent thinking: Is there really one solution to the problem? *Psychology of Aesthetics, Creativity, and The Arts, 2*, 86–88.

Muñoz-Doyague, M. F., González-Álvarez, N., & Nieto, M. (2008). An examination of individual factors and employees creativity: The case of Spain. *Creativity Research Journal, 20*, 21–33.

Nemeth, C. J., & Goncalo, J. A. (2005). Creative collaborations from afar: The benefits of independent authors. *Creativity Research Journal, 17*, 1–8.

Nemiro, J. E. (2002). The creative process in virtual teams. *Creativity Research Journal, 14*, 69–83.

O'Hara, L. A., & Sternberg, R. J. (2001). It doesn't hurt to ask: Effects of instructions to be creative, practical, or analytical on essay-writing performance and their interaction with students' thinking styles. *Creativity Research Journal, 13*, 197–210.

Orpen, C. (1990). Measuring support for organizational innovation: A validity study. *Psychological Report, 67*, 417–418.

Pannells, T. C., & Claxton, A. F. (2008). Happiness, creative ideation, and locus of control. *Creativity Research Journal, 20*, 67–71.

Plucker, J. A. (1998). Beware of simple conclusions: The case for the content generality of creativity. *Creativity Research Journal, 11*, 179–182.

Plucker, J. (1999). Is the proof in the pudding? Reanalyses of Torrance's (1958–present) longitudinal study data. *Creativity Research Journal, 12*, 103–114.

Plucker, J. A., & Renzulli, J. S. (1999). Psychometric approaches to the study of human creativity. In R. J. Sternberg (Ed.), *Handbook of creativity* (pp. 35–66). Cambridge, UK: Cambridge University Press.

Plucker, J. A., Runco, M. A., & Lim, W. (2006). Predicting ideational behavior from divergent thinking and discretionary time on task. *Creativity Research Journal, 15*, 55–63.

Podsakoff, P. M., MacKenzie, S. B., Lee, J., & Podsakoff, N. P. (2003). Common method biases in behavioral research: A critical review of the literature and recommended remedies. *Journal of Applied Psychology, 88*, 879–903.

Prabhu, V., Sutton, C., & Sauser, W. (2008). Creativity and certain personality traits: Understanding the mediating effect of intrinsic motivation. *Creativity Research Journal, 20*, 53–66.

Proctor, R. M. J., & Burnett, P. C. (2004). Measuring cognitive and dispositional characteristics of creativity in elementary students. *Creativity Research Journal, 16*, 421–429.

Ramey, C. H., & Weisberg, R. W. (2004). The "poetical activity" of Emily Dickinson: A further test of the hypothesis that affective disorders foster creativity. *Creativity Research Journal, 16*, 173–185.

Redmond, M. R., Mumford, M. D., & Teach, R. J. (1993). Putting creativity to work: Leader influences on subordinate creativity. *Organizational Behavior and Human Decision Processes, 55*, 120–151.

Reeves, L. M., & Weisberg, R. W. (1994). The role of content and abstract information in analogical transfer. *Psychological Bulletin, 115*, 381–400.

Root-Bernstein, R. S., Bernstein, M., & Garnier, H. (1995). Correlations between avocations, scientific style, work habits, and professional impact of scientists. *Creativity Research Journal, 8*, 115–137.

Root-Bernstein, M., & Root-Bernstein, R. (2006). Imaginary world play in childhood and maturity and its impact on adult creativity. *Creativity Research Journal, 18*, 405–425.

Rostan, S. M. (1997). A study of young artists: The development of artistic talent and creativity. *Creativity Research Journal, 10*, 175–192.

Rostan, S. M. (2006). A young artist's story: Advancing knowledge and the development of artistic talent and creativity in children. In J. C. Kaufman & J. Baer (Eds.), *Creativity and reason in cognitive development* (pp. 244–268). New York, NY: Cambridge University Press.

Runco, M. A. (2008). Divergent thinking is not synonymous with creativity. *Psychology of Aesthetics, Creativity, and the Arts, 2*, 93–96.

A. INTRODUCTION

Runco, M. A., Dow, G., & Smith, W. R. (2006). Information, experience, and divergent thinking: An empirical test. *Creativity Research Journal, 18*, 269–277.

Runco, M. A., & Mraz, W. (1992). Scoring divergent thinking tests using total ideational output and a creativity index. *Educational and Psychological Measurement, 52*, 213–221.

Runco, M. A., Plucker, J. A., & Lim, W. (2001). Development and psychometric integrity of a measure of ideational behavior. *Creativity Research Journal, 13*, 393–400.

Sak, U., & Maker, C. J. (2006). Developmental variation in children's creative mathematical thinking as a function of schooling, age, and knowledge. *Creativity Research Journal, 18*, 279–291.

Sawyer, R. K. (1992). Improvisational creativity: An analysis of jazz performance. *Creativity Research Journal, 5*, 253–263.

Scott, G. M., Leritz, L. E., & Mumford, M. D. (2004). The effectiveness of creativity training: A meta-analysis. *Creativity Research Journal, 16*, 361–388.

Scott, G. M., Lonergan, D. C., & Mumford, M. D. (2005). Conceptual combination: Alternative knowledge structures, alternative heuristics. *Creativity Research Journal, 17*, 79–98.

Silvia, P., Winterstein, B. P., Willse, J. T., Barona, C. M., Cram, J. T., & Hess, K. I., et al. (2008). Assessing creativity with divergent thinking tasks: Exploring the reliability and validity of new subjective scoring methods. *Psychology of Aesthetics, Creativity, and the Arts, 2*, 68–85.

Simonton, D. K. (1990). *Psychology, science, and history: An introduction to historiometry.* New Haven, CT: Yale University Press.

Simonton, D. K. (1991). Personality correlates of exceptional personal influence: A note on Thorndike's (1950) creators and leaders. *Creativity Research Journal, 4*, 67–78.

Simonton, D. K. (1999). Creativity from a historiometric perspective. In R. J. Sternberg (Ed.), *Handbook of creativity* (pp. 116–133). Cambridge, UK: Cambridge University Press.

Simonton, D. K. (2004). Film awards as indicators of cinematic creativity and achievement: A quantitative comparison of the Oscars and six alternatives. *Creativity Research Journal, 16*, 163–172.

Simonton, D. K. (2007). The creative process in Picasso's Guernica sketches: Monotonic improvements versus nonmonotonic variants. *Creativity Research Journal, 19*, 329–344.

Smith, S. M. (2008). Invisible assumptions and the unintentional use of knowledge and experiences in creative cognition. *Lewis & Clark Law Review, 12*, 509–525.

Sosik, J. J., Kahai, S. S., & Avolio, B. J. (1999). Leadership style, anonymity, and creativity in group decision support systems: The mediating role of optimal flow. *Journal of Creative Behavior, 33*, 227–256.

Stokes, P. D., & Balsam, P. D. (2003). Effects of early strategic hints on sustained variability levels. *Creativity Research Journal, 15*, 331–341.

Tierney, P., Farmer, S. M., & Graen, G. B. (1999). An examination of leadership and employee creativity: The relevance of traits and relationships. *Personnel Psychology, 52*, 591–620.

Torrance, E. P. (1974). *The torrance tests of creative thinking: Technical-norms manual.* Bensenville, IL: Scholastic Testing Services.

Uhl-Bien, M., & Marion, R. (2008). *Complexity leadership.* Charlotte, NC: Information Age.

Vincent, P. H., Decker, B. P., & Mumford, M. D. (2002). Divergent thinking, intelligence, and expertise: A test of alternative models. *Creativity Research Journal, 14*, 163–178.

Wechsler, S. (2006). Validity of the Torrance tests of creative thinking to the Brazilian culture. *Creativity Research Journal, 18*, 15–25.

Weisberg, R. W. (2006). *Creativity: Understanding innovation, problem solving, science, invention, and the arts.* Hoboken, NJ: Wiley & Sons.

Weisberg, R. W., & Hass, R. (2007). We are all partly right: Comment on Simonton. *Creativity Research Journal, 19*, 345–360.

Welling, H. (2007). Four mental operations in creative cognition: The importance of abstraction. *Creativity Research Journal, 19*, 163–177.

Wise, G. (1992). Inventions and corporations in the maturing electrical industry. In R. J. Weber & D. N. Perkins (Eds.), *Inventive minds: Creativity in technology* (pp. 291–310). New York, NY: Oxford University Press.

Yuan, F., & Zhou, J. (2008). Differential effects of expected external evaluation on different parts of the creative idea production process and on final product creativity. *Creativity Research Journal, 20*, 391–403.

A. INTRODUCTION

Fields, Domains, and Individuals

Dean Keith Simonton
University of California, Davis, CA

According to the poet William Wordsworth, the physicist and mathematician Isaac Newton was:

> "A mind forever / Voyaging through strange seas of thought, alone" *(quoted in Jeans, 1942, p. 711).*

Newton's supposed solitary genius allowed him to make discoveries that amazed the world. As Alexander Pope put it:

> "Nature and Nature's laws lay hid in night: / God said, *Let Newton be!* and all was light" *(quoted in Cohen & Cohen, 1960, p. 285).*

Now, no doubt Newton was very much a loner. Indeed, he may have had a disposition that might be diagnosed as Asperger's today (Fitzgerald, 2002). He never formed a truly intimate relationship with another human being, and certainly not with a woman. Even his friendships were few and often fleeting. Nevertheless, it is not quite correct to say that he was *alone*. In the first place, he himself admitted that his work built about that of his predecessors:

> "If I have seen further, it is by standing on the shoulders of giants" *(quoted in Who Said What When, 1991, p. 129).*

Among these predecessor giants were Nicolaus Copernicus, Johannes Kepler, Galileo Galilei, and René Descartes.

But even more than this, Newton was deeply embedded in a network of contemporary mathematicians and scientists in England and on the European continent. Among the most eminent of these were Jean Bernoulli, James Bradley, Abraham DeMoive, John Flamstead, Edmund Halley, Robert Hooke, Gottfried Wilhelm Leibniz, John Locke, Colin McLauren, Ole Christensen Römer, John Wallis, and Sir Christopher Wren. These associates had more

Handbook of Organizational Creativity.
DOI: 10.1016/B978-0-12-374714-3.00004-5

than a peripheral connection with Newton's life. For example, Halley facilitated the publication of Newton's masterpiece, the *Principia Mathematica*. Newton had a bitter priority dispute with Leibniz over who first invented the calculus, a dispute that was settled in Newton's favor through the aid of his friend DeMoive.

Hence, although Newton might be taken as the prototypical example of the "lone genius," he was definitely not an isolated individual. If a loner like him cannot be considered alone, then it is hard to conceive how creators in general can be viewed as persons divorced from the social context. Although it is not natural for psychologists to focus beyond the individual, more creativity researchers have increasingly come to emphasize the importance of the larger interpersonal and sociocultural milieu (e.g., Amabile, 1996; Harrington, 1990; Sawyer, 2007). However, for the purposes of this chapter, I wish to concentrate on one particular take on this issue, namely, Csikszentmihályi's (1990, 1999) *systems* perspective. I will first provide a brief overview of this perspective and then offer two illustrations of its utility.

SYSTEMS PERSPECTIVE

Csikszentmihályi (1999) argues that creativity does not take place in a singular creative person. Instead, it emerges in a system consisting of three components: the domain, the field, and the individual. The interaction of the three systemic components decides that a given contribution is in fact creative. Because Csikszentmihályi's distinction between domain and field is more precise than the terms are often used in everyday language, we will define those first. We can then discuss how the individual interacts with those two components to yield creativity.

Domain

According to Csikszentmihályi (1990), the domain represents "the parameters of the cultural symbol system" (p. 190) within a given area of creativity. More specifically, the domain constitutes "a set of rules, a vocabulary with a grammar and a syntax" (p. 200). Of course, the particulars of this definition vary from domain to domain. In quantum mechanics, for instance, we might say that the domain is characterized by such concepts as the "adiabatic hypothesis, anharmonic oscillator, Bell's inequality, blackbody radiation, collapse of the wave function, Copenhagen interpretation, correspondence principle, eigenvalue problem, electron spin, exclusion principle, Heisenberg uncertainty principle, hidden variables, indeterminacy, Josephson effect, line spectrum, magnetic dipole moment, many-worlds interpretation, photoelectric effect, Planck's constant, Planck's radiation law, positron, quanta, quantum electrodynamics, quantum oscillation frequency, renormalization, state functions, the Stern-Gerlach experiment, tunneling, virtual oscillators, wavelength, wave equation, wave-particle duality, wave-particle hypothesis, and X-ray scattering" (Simonton, 2004a, p. 44).

Speaking more generally, we could argue that the domain for a given area of creativity would be encompassed by the entries in a comprehensive encyclopedia devoted to that subject. Examples would include encyclopedias of physics, chemistry, biology, psychology, or sociology. Admittedly, it is more realistic to fragment these inclusive disciplines into subdisciplines. Most creators are specialists rather than generalists. Thus, a creative individual might work in solid-state physics or evolutionary biology or social psychology. Whatever the details, because each domain evolves over time, the specific character of any domain represents the accumulated knowledge and technique up to a given point in time. If domains cease to change, then they are stagnant, and thus no longer provide the foundation for creativity. In the terms of Kroeber (1944), the cultural pattern becomes exhausted.

Field

In contrast to the domain, "the field is composed of individuals who know the domain's grammar of rules and are more or less loosely organized to act as gatekeepers to it" (Csikszentmihályi, 1990, p. 201). To illustrate, at various times in the history of quantum mechanics the field was defined as variable subsets of the following scientists: "John Stewart Bell, Hans Bethe, Niels Bohr, Max Born, Louis-Victor de Broglie, Paul Dirac, Paul Ehrenfest, Albert Einstein, Richard Feynman, James Franck, George Gamow, Werner Heisenberg, Pascual Jordan, Brian Josephson, Hendrik A. Kramers, Rudolf W. Ladenburg, John Von Neumann, Max Planck, Erwin Schrödinger, Julian Schwinger, Tomonaga Shin'ichiro, John C. Slater, Arnold Sommerfeld, and John H. Van Vleck" (Simonton, 2004a, p. 44). If the domain can be characterized by the entries in a domain-specific encyclopedia, the field can be characterized by the entries in a field-specific biographical dictionary or who's who, with the proviso that all deceased or inactive creators are excluded from the list. Notice, too, that these reference works should correspond. For every encyclopedia of economics, architecture, or wine, there should be a corresponding biographical dictionary of economists, architects, or winemakers.

Finally, it should be obvious that the field, like the domain, changes over time. Not only do particular creators come and go, but the role of any given creator within the field may dramatically alter. An especially notorious example is how Einstein went from being an early advocate of quantum theory (via his work on the photoelectric effect) to becoming a staunch opponent of quantum theory (via his critique of the Copenhagen interpretation). Indeed, sometimes the older members of a field, in their role as gatekeepers, exert a conservative force over more innovative developments (Diamond, 1980; Hull, Tessner, & Diamond, 1978; cf. Levin, Stephan, & Walker, 1995; Sulloway, 1996). This phenomenon has been styled Planck's principle after Planck's (1949) claim that "a new scientific truth does not triumph by convincing its opponents and making them see the light, but rather because its opponents eventually die, and a new generation grows up that is familiar with it" (pp. 33–34).

Individual

Last but certainly not least (from the psychological perspective) we have the individual creator making up the third component of this tripartite system. In combination with the domain and field, the individual enters into a special kind of creativity cycle: "The domain transmits information to the person, the person produces a variation, which may or may not be selected by the field, and the field in turn will pass the selected variation to the domain" (Csikszentmihályi, 1990, p. 200). Naturally, the newly added information then is transmitted to persons operating within the domain, and the cycle goes on.

As a case in point, consider Einstein's classic 1905 paper on the photoelectric effect. In conceiving this contribution, Einstein drew upon such domain-specific ideas as Maxwell's electromagnetic theory, Wien's black-body formula, Boltzmann's probabilistic formula for entropy, Planck's quantum theory, and Lenard's experiments on the photoelectric effect (Hoffmann, 1972). His results supported the idea that light consisted of discrete quanta that much later became known as photons. He wrote up the findings, and had the paper accepted for publication in *Annalen der Physik*, the leading journal in his field, where it appeared in 1905. Although experimental verification of Einstein theory took some time— Robert Millikan managed to do so by 1916—by 1921 the theory had sufficient support to earn him a Nobel Prize for Physics. Thus recognized by his field, and his ideas having entered his domain, Einstein's paper on the photoelectric effect then became a basis for fundamental developments in quantum theory by both himself and in the field. And so the systemic cycle continued.

I should note a complication to this picture: The actual act of creative synthesis, of putting all of the domain-specific ideas into a coherent package, does not always take place within a solitary individual. Einstein was not much of a collaborator, especially in his early years, so his photoelectric effect paper was single-authored. This systemic pattern is now much less common, particularly in the sciences (Sawyer, 2007). If anything, collaboration has become a norm. This means that two or more members of the same or affiliated fields and domains will iterate ideas back and forth before the final product is presented to the rest of the field for evaluation and possible incorporation into the domain. Even if creators do not directly collaborate with others in the field, they might engage in other interactions—such as correspondence with colleagues—that might contribute to ongoing projects. Accordingly, although the systems perspective is more sophisticated than the standard individualistic analysis of creativity, it still represents a highly simplified, even schematic treatment. Nonetheless, the perspective still proves useful, as will be seen next.

TWO ILLUSTRATIONS

Below I wish to outline two illustrations of how the domain–individual–field perspective can be applied to creativity. In the first example, the application was explicit (i.e., directly based on Csikszentmihályi, 1990, albeit with modifications). For the second example, the application was only implicit because domain and field components were not explicitly separated out in line with Csikszentmihályi's original conceptions. In any case, the first concerns combinatorial models and the second disciplinary hierarchies. These two illustrations do not exhaust the possible useful applications, but because the examples are so radically different, they suffice to indicate something of the range of applicability.

Combinatorial Models

Many creative individuals have compared creativity to a combinatorial procedure (e.g., Hadamard, 1945; Poincaré, 1921). Moreover, empirical and theoretical research suggests that creativity may, in effect, operate according to a stochastic combinatorial process (Simonton, 2003, 2010). That is, creators take a set of domain-specific ideas or "mental elements" and then subject them to something akin to chance permutations (Simonton, 1988). Once a stable "configuration" is found, it is elaborated into a completed product (Simonton, 1997a). This product then is submitted for evaluation for potential publication in the vehicles appropriate for a given domain. Once published, the ideas contained in this publication can provide input into the revised domain.

This is not to say that combinatorial processes constitute the sole basis of creativity. For example, various algorithmic and heuristic methods are involved as well (see, e.g., Klahr & Simon, 1999). Moreover, the precise mix of processes and methods may vary from discipline to discipline (see, e.g., Mumford, Antes, Caughron, Connelly, & Beeler, 2010). However, because combinatorial models make the fewest assumptions and thus lend themselves to mathematical treatment, it may be useful to model creativity as a combinatorial process to provide a "chance baseline" against which we can assess the need to introduce additional processes (Simonton, 2009b). For this reason, Simonton (2004a) translated this combinatorial process into a theoretical model of creativity in science (which was later generalized to handle creativity in the arts: see also Simonton, 2009a, 2010). Like Csikszentmihályi (1990), Simonton began the translation with the scientific domain, which was defined as the set of "phenomena, facts, concepts, variables, constants, techniques, theories, laws, questions, goals, and criteria" (p. 44). During the course of education and training, individuals develop creative potential by drawing their respective samples from this domain. At the beginning of a scientist's career, the ideas making up these personalized subsets of the domain are then subjected to the combinatorial process. Those combinations that are preserved and prepared for publication are subsequently communicated to the field—the discipline's gatekeepers— who then decide which of the new ideational combinations will become incorporated into the pool of domain ideas. This decision includes both what will get published but also what will get cited by other members of the field after publication. The result of this three-component process is depicted in Figure 4.1.

As it stands, this graphic depiction of the systemic cycle is uninteresting. It does not say much more than we already know. Fortunately, the application can undergo some modifications that render the application far more useful (Simonton, 2004a, 2010). These modifications allow us to deal with variations in (a) the size of domains, field, and individual

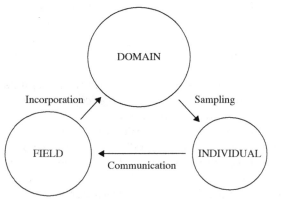

FIGURE 4.1 The creativity cycle linking domain, individual, and field. (cf. Csikszentmihályi, 1999, Figure 16.1.)

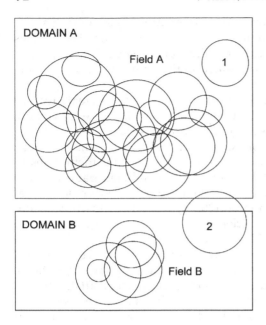

FIGURE 4.2   Domains A and B, fields A and B, and individual samples from domain-specific ideational pools. (from Simonton, 2004a.)

domain-specific samples and (b) the amount of overlap in those individual samples for those making up the same field. These complications are indicated in Figure 4.2.

Here we see two domains, A and B, demarcated by the square boundary. The two boxes contain all of the ideas that define the respective domains. Hence, domain A contains more ideas than does domain B. In comparison, the circles depict the individual samples from the domain. The larger the circle, the greater the sample for that given individual. In simple terms, some creators know more about their chosen domain than do others. The total number of circles contained totally within a domain defines the field of that domain. Thus, in the figure, field A is larger than field B, probably a representative situation if we can assume that the size of the field tends to be roughly proportional to the size of the domain. In any event, the overlap between the circles for a given field indicates the extent that the individuals share domain-specific samples (i.e., the degree that they had the same curriculum, read the same textbooks, studied under the same teachers and mentors, etc.).

Although it would certainly be the norm in the sciences for these overlapping regions to maximize, for sake of completeness Figure 4.2 shows two provocative exceptions. First, in domain A is found individual 1, a scientist who managed to obtain a sample of domain-specific ideas that do not overlap with any of the ideational samples of his or her colleagues in the same field. This person might be called the "lone wolf" in the field. Second, in domain B can be found individual 2, a scientist who has attained a sample of ideas from domain A even though most of his or her ideas come from domain B. This scientist may be considered an interdisciplinary or even multidisciplinary interloper—someone who may be able to synthesize the ideas of two previously unrelated disciplines to create a new discipline.

I realize that this conceptual scheme may seem quite abstract, but it turns out that it produces a large number of unique predictions that have undergone tests in empirical research (Simonton, 2004a, 2010). Some of these concern just the individual. For instance, the larger the domain-specific sample acquired by a particular scientist, the larger the number of potential ideational combinations that can be generated. Furthermore, the number of combinations increases as a roughly exponential function of the number of sampled ideas. That means that if the size of the domain samples is normally distributed, then the distribution of combinations will be described approximately by a highly skewed log-normal distribution. In more concrete terms, the distribution will exhibit a long upper tail so that most of the contributions will be made by a very small percentage of the individuals working in the field (Simonton, 2004a). There is abundant evidence that this distribution is actually characteristic of individual differences for creative individuals contributing to the same domain (Simonton, 1997a).

Yet from the standpoint of the current chapter, a more interesting implication concerns the consequences that operate at the level of the field (Simonton, 2004a, 2010). Clearly, fields may vary greatly in the extent to which their individual members share the same domain-specific ideas. On the one hand, in those fields where the overlap is extremely high, individuals will be subjecting the same ideas to the same stochastic combinatorial process. As a result, the probability is increased that two or more individuals will come up with the same viable combination. On the other hand, those fields in which the individual samples exhibit little overlap are less likely to see two or more individuals duplicate their efforts in this fashion.

The occasion I am describing is known as multiple discovery (Merton, 1961). Memorable instances include the calculus (Newton 1671, Leibniz 1676), the prediction of the new planet Neptune (J. C. Adams 1845, Leverrier 1846), the law of conservation of energy (J. R. von Mayer 1843, Helmholtz 1847, Joule 1847), the periodic law of the elements (DeChancourtis, Newlands, L. Meyer, and Mendeleev), the theory of evolution by natural selection (C. Darwin 1844, Wallace 1858), the ophthalmoscope (C. Babbage 1847, Helmholtz 1851, Anagnostakis 1854), and the incandescent carbon filament (Swan 1879, Edison 1878). Such cases run into the hundreds, so this is certainly not a rare event.

The multiples phenomenon is often attributed to sociocultural determinism, that is, to the notion that particular ideas become absolutely inevitable at a given moment in the history of science (e.g., Lamb & Easton, 1984). Even so, it should be evident that these events can be explicated in terms of a stochastic combinatorial process (Simonton, 2004a, 2010). Furthermore, this probabilistic rather than deterministic explanation can handle other distinctive attributes of multiples that cannot be explained by deterministic models, such as the signature distribution of the total number of scientists in a given field who are involved in a particular multiple (Simonton, 2009a, 2010). However, discussion of these niceties will take us too far from the main purpose of this essay. The main point is that the multiples phenomenon cannot be explicated without first adopting a systems perspective. Any account must begin with a domain of ideas and a field of individuals who have obtained variably overlapping samples from that domain. By definition, multiples cannot even occur at the individual level of analysis.

A. INTRODUCTION

Disciplinary Hierarchies

In the previous application of the systems perspective, it was assumed that scientific fields could differ regarding the degree to which their individual members had similar samples of domain-specific ideas. Certainly, this specific contrast does not constitute the only criterion by which fields and domains can differ from each other. At this point, it is instructive to ponder a conjecture first introduced by the philosopher August Comte (1839–1842/1855) in the mid-19th century. Comte hypothesized that scientific disciplines could be arrayed into a hierarchy. In his case, the sequence was astronomy, physics, chemistry, biology, and sociology. Although this sequence had a basis according to criteria unique to Comte's philosophy, his arrangement closely parallels more contemporary contrasts among the sciences in which they are distinguished as exact versus non-exact, hard versus soft, paradigmatic versus pre-paradigmatic, and natural versus human (e.g., Kuhn, 1970; Smith et al., 2000).

Although these disciplinary orderings are highly speculative, they have gained some empirical endorsement in recent research (Simonton, 2004b; see also Fanelli, 2010). Using objective criteria, five major scientific disciplines could be reliably ordered as follows: physics, chemistry, biology, psychology, and sociology. This ordering is depicted in Figure 4.3. Interestingly, physics and chemistry were grouped close together at the top, with biology and psychology forming a second cluster, and with sociology more distant from psychology than biology was from chemistry. More importantly, the criteria concerned the nature of the domain or the field corresponding to each discipline. In particular, these (and additional) disciplines were assessed on the following three sets of criteria:

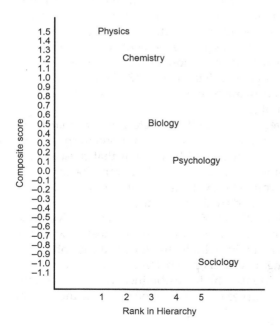

FIGURE 4.3 Hierarchy of the sciences based on objective characteristics of both field and domain. (from Simonton, D. K. (2004b.) Psychology's status as a scientific discipline: Its empirical placement within an implicit hierarchy of the sciences. *Review of General Psychology*, 8, 59–67.)

First, fields at the top of the hierarchy exhibit a tighter consensus regarding which field members are making the high-impact contributions to the domain. This consensus is revealed by:

1. the earlier impact rate for scientists under 35 (i.e., the "up and coming" are recognized sooner; Cole, 1983),
2. the lower average age at receiving the Nobel Prize for those disciplines that have the honor (Stephan & Leven, 1993; see also Manniche & Falk, 1957), and
3. the stronger agreement in peer evaluations of the relative impact of various members of the field (Cole, 1983).

Not only do the top-of-the-hierarchy fields concur on who is doing the best work, but they also can identify those contributors earlier in their careers.

Second, the foregoing consensus applies, not just to individual contributors, but also to single contributions, as indicated by the higher concentration of citations to specific research articles (Cole, 1983). Moreover, this consensus appears to delineate a well defined "research front" of "hot topics" that the field deems most important for domain advancement. This disciplinary "leading edge" is characterized by:

1. greater citation immediacy (a gauge of whether citations concentrate on the most recent publications, with rapid decay rates as a function of time; Cole, 1983),
2. faster knowledge obsolescence rates (i.e., how fast domain-specific expertise becomes out of date; McDowell, 1982), and
3. higher probabilities of research anticipation (i.e., the degree to which scientists had their research anticipated by other scientists working in the same field; Hagstrom, 1974).

Third, the field's consensus on contributors and contributions is associated with consensual understanding of the ideas that make up the discipline's domain. In disciplines lower in the hierarchy, the concepts tend to be more imprecise, ambiguous, and uncertain, with considerably more latitude for subjective interpretation. This domain-specific ideational imprecision, ambiguity, and uncertainty is reflected in:

1. higher peer consultation rates (i.e., the degree to which researchers consult with colleagues before submitting their work for publication; Suls & Fletcher, 1983),
2. higher theories-to-laws ratios, that is, greater theoretical speculation than empirically confirmed laws in the discipline's mainstream introductory textbooks (Roeckelein, 1997), and
3. higher lecture disfluency, that is, higher rates of filled pauses ("uh," "er," and "um") during classroom lectures for undergraduate courses (Schachter, Christianfeld, Ravina, & Bilous, 1991).

Incidentally, a certain conceptual concordance appears between these results and the combinatorial models discussed earlier. In disciplines with a higher magnitude of consensus, individual samples from the domain should exhibit a more conspicuous overlap. Higher sampling overlap indicates that each member of the field will be subjecting many of the same ideas to the combinatorial process. Consequently, scientists in high-consensus disciplines should have higher likelihoods of participating in multiple discoveries. There is some evidence that this is the case (Simonton, 1978, 2010). Multiples appear much more

A. INTRODUCTION

often in the physical sciences than in the biological sciences, and are rather rare in the social sciences.

Having just established the empirical existence of a Comtean hierarchy of the sciences, I would now like to use this demonstration as the basis for three consecutive extensions (cf. Simonton, 2009b, 2009c). First, I will show that the hierarchy can be interpolated within any given science as well as extrapolated beyond the sciences to encompass the arts and humanities. Second, I will indicate how this more finely differentiated and extended hierarchy correlates with the dispositional traits and developmental experiences of the creators active in a given field and domain. Third, I will examine whether the creator's magnitude of achievement within that domain depends on the degree to which his or her disposition and development match what is typical of those in the same field.

Extrapolation and Interpolation

The foregoing disciplinary hierarchy can be both extrapolated beyond the sciences to encompass the arts and humanities, and interpolated to accommodate within-discipline contrasts.

Extrapolation. Some of the criteria used to differentiate the various sciences also apply to the humanities (Simonton, 2004b, 2009c). Let me give just two examples.

1. The knowledge obsolescence rate is slower for the humanistic domains of history and English than in the scientific domains of physics, chemistry, biology, psychology, and sociology (McDowell, 1982). History and English scholars can take a break from research—such as going into administration—with much less damage to their later output than is the case for scientists, particularly a natural scientist. In fact, physics is as far above the domain average in the obsolescence rate as English is below average. In concrete terms, a high-energy physicist must work much harder to avoid falling behind his or her field than does a Chaucer scholar. In other words, the domain–individual–field creativity cycle in Figure 4.1 churns much faster in the former discipline than in the latter.

2. The lecture disfluency displayed in political science, art history, and English exceeds that exhibited in sociology and psychology (Schachter, Christenfeld, Ravina, & Bilous, 1991). Hence, the concepts that define domains in the humanities tend to be more imprecise, ambiguous, and uncertain relative to those in the social sciences. There is one fascinating exception to this generalization, however. The philosophers apparently put a premium on logical and conceptual precision because they score somewhere between psychologists and chemists on this indicator. In that limited sense, philosophy belongs in the social sciences rather than in the humanities!

Although the extrapolation is more tenuous, the disciplinary hierarchy may be extended into the arts (Bliss, 1935). The extension is more tenuous because many of the criteria would have to be defined in a broader fashion. Yet if we grant this extension, then we would expect that the psychological factors that distinguish the natural from the social sciences would also differentiate the sciences from the arts. As will be shown shortly, this turns out to be the case.

Interpolation. To be more precise, the scientific hierarchy depicted in Figure 4.3 can only be considered an approximation. The specific placement should more precisely add error bars. That is, each domain is placed according to its empirical center of gravity or central tendency, about which individual scientists will vary in significant ways. The degree of variation is even great enough to show overlap between the separate domain distributions.

Although a portion of this variation may be attributed to individual differences, a more interesting source of the variation is intra-disciplinary in nature. Again, allow me to give two illustrations.

1. *Natural-science versus human-science psychology.* According to the hierarchy presented in Figure 4.3, psychology stands somewhere between biology and sociology. Although it leans toward biology, clearly some psychologists are more favorably disposed toward the social sciences, even humanities. Empirical evidence supports this view (Coan, 1968, 1973; Simonton, 2000; see also Kimble, 1984). In particular, a study of eminent psychologists found that they formed two separable psychological orientations. On the one hand are the natural-science oriented psychologists who are objectivistic, quantitative, elementaristic, impersonal, static, and exogenist in their theory and methodology. On the other hand are the human-science oriented psychologists, who are theoretically and methodologically subjectivistic, qualitative, holistic, personal, dynamic, and endogenist. Furthermore, psychologists who represent the extremes on these dimensions tend to receive more citations than those who occupy more compromising or conciliatory positions between the extremes (Simonton, 2000). As a consequence, psychology's placement in Figure 4.3 actually represents a mean of two psychologies. It is worth pointing out the magnitude of domain consensus inspired by Skinner's radical behaviorism (as indicated by the *Journal for the Experimental Analysis of Behavior*) compares quite favorably with research published in the hard sciences (Cole, 1983).

2. *Normal versus revolutionary science.* Kuhn (1970) distinguished between sciences that were paradigmatic, such as physics and chemistry, and those that were pre- or non-paradigmatic, such as psychology and sociology. Scientists in the former domains operate with a higher level of theoretical and methodological consensus. In Kuhnian terminology, such scientists practice "normal" or "puzzle-solving" science. At the same time, Kuhn recognized that paradigmatic sciences often go through "crises" owing to the appearance of "anomalies"—findings that do not fit the accepted paradigm. During these periods, the consensus breaks down, and the science becomes, in a sense, less paradigmatic. Happily, revolutionary scientists eventually appear who introduce a new paradigm to replace the old one. The discipline then can move up to its original place in the hierarchy. Practitioners will practice normal science once again.

Note that individual practitioners of paradigmatic sciences have a strong expectation that the crisis will be temporary. Practitioners in non-paradigmatic sciences do not share that belief. Thus, natural- and human-science oriented psychologists seldom endeavor to reach some unified paradigm for the discipline.

Disposition and Development

So far, we have looked at the disciplinary hierarchy just in terms of field and domain attributes. Does the field exhibit a consensus? Does the domain consist of precise and unambiguous ideas? Yet according to the systems perspective, we have to add the individual to complete the analysis. Do the individuals who enter a given discipline display dispositional traits and developmental experiences that line up with field and domain characteristics? The relevant empirical literature appears to give an affirmative answer. To show this, I will provide a brief review of the results, starting first with disposition and then turning to development.

A. INTRODUCTION

Dispositional traits. The creative individual can be characterized by a distinctive set of motives, values, interests, and attributes (Martindale, 1989). However, these dispositional traits vary both across- and within-disciplines (Feist, 1998).

1. *Across-disciplines.* Although creativity is often associated with psychopathology, the empirical research demonstrates that the incidence and intensity of psychopathological symptoms vary according to discipline (Jamison, 1989; Ludwig, 1992, 1995; Raskin, 1936; Post, 1994; Simonton & Song, 2009). Nevertheless, Ludwig (1998) indicated a method to the madness, namely that "persons in professions that require more logical, objective, and formal forms of expression tend be more emotionally stable than those in professions that require more intuitive, subjective, and emotive forms" (p. 93). It should be immediately apparent that this distinction corresponds almost perfectly with a discipline's placement in the extended hierarchy. Ludwig went on to show that the contrasts across disciplines display the fractal pattern of "self-similarity". This pattern is found at four consecutive levels of magnification; first, scientists as a group have lower lifetime rates of mental illness than do artists as a group. Second, in the sciences, natural scientists tend to average lower rates than do social scientists, whereas in the arts, creators in the formal arts (e.g., architecture) tend to average lower rates than those in the performing arts (e.g., music and dance), who in their turn average lower rates than those in the expressive arts (e.g., literature and the visual arts). Third, within a specific expressive art such as literature, nonfiction writers are prone to display lower rates than do fiction writers, who in their turn average lower rates than poets do. Fourth and last, within any given artistic specialty (e.g., painting, sculpture, and photography), those who create in a formal style are prone to exhibit lower rates than those creating in a symbolic style, and the latter are disposed to exhibit yet lower rates than those creating in an emotive style. It must be emphasized that these interdisciplinary differences represent averages only, so that substantial individual differences exist within each discipline, a cross-sectional variation that has critical repercussions.

Individuals creating in different disciplines will tend to differ in other dispositional traits besides psychopathology. For instance, in comparison to chemists, psychologists are prone to be more introverted, unconventional, bohemian, imaginative, and creative (Chambers, 1964). Similarly, eminent social scientists tend to be less factual, more emotional, and more rebellious than do eminent physical scientists (Roe, 1953). Collating all of the findings indicates that creators in the natural sciences differ from those in the social sciences in much the same way as scientists in general differ from artistic creators (Simonton, 2009c).

2. *Within-discipline.* Returning to psychopathology, the fractal pattern observed across disciplines should also be found within disciplines, and there is evidence for this expectation within the sciences (Ko & Kim, 2008). Revolutionary scientists who overthrow the dominant paradigm tend to exhibit higher rates of mental illness than do normal scientists who conserve and extend that paradigm. Just as interesting is the evidence that psychologists who favor a natural-science orientation are prone to display a different set of personality traits relative to those who favor a human-science orientation (Johnson, Germer, Efran, & Overton, 1988). The former have a tendency to be more orderly, stable, conventional, conforming, objective, realistic, interpersonally passive, dependent, and reactive, whereas the latter are inclined to be more fluid, changing, creative, nonconforming, participative, imaginative, active, purposive, autonomous, individualistic, and environmentally integrated. Finally, another investigation has shown that eminent human-science psychologists, relative

to their natural-science colleagues, have a greater propensity for complex but integrated thinking about the discipline (Suedfeld, 1985).

Developmental experiences. I have just shown how the dispositional traits of individual creators correspond to their discipline's placement in the extended and differentiated hierarchy. The experiences that those individuals have encountered during their development exhibit a similar regularity. This again holds both across- and within-disciplines.

1. *Across-disciplines.* In terms of developmental experiences, Nobel laureates are not all cut from the same cloth (Berry, 1981). At one extreme, laureates in physics are most likely to come from highly stable, professional homes, whereas at the other extreme laureates in literature are far less so. Indeed, almost a third "lost at least one parent through death or desertion, or experienced the father's bankruptcy or impoverishment" (p. 387; see also Raskin, 1936; Simonton, 1986). Laureates in chemistry fall between these extremes, but tend to be closer to the physicists. A parallel contrast is seen the home environments of creative adolescents (Schaefer & Anastasi, 1968). Scientific talents were more likely grow up in stable homes in which their parents pursued conventional interests and hobbies, while artistic talents were more likely to come from unconventional homes that displayed conspicuous diversity with respect to geographic origins (e.g., foreign born), economic mobility, and extensive travels both in the United States and abroad. In a way, the family background of potential scientists was closer to "normal" while that of potential artists was unequivocally more deviant from the normal—more varied, unusual, and unstable.

This divergence between scientists and artists persists in educational and training experiences (Simonton, 2009c). Eminent scientists tend to have had the most formal education, eminent artists the least (Raskin, 1936; Simonton, 1986). Scientific creativity, relative to artistic creativity, appears to be associated with fewer and more homogeneous mentors and role models (Simonton, 1984, 1992b). On this score, eminent psychologists are more similar to scientists than to artists (Simonton, 1992a). Lastly, artistic creators have a higher likelihood of developing their creative potential in unstable and heterogeneous sociocultural milieus (Simonton, 1975, 1997b), whereas stable and culturally homogeneous systems are more supportive of scientific development (see also Candolle, 1873).

The foregoing concern contrasts between scientific and artistic disciplines. Still, some empirical evidence suggests that a similar pattern is found when different scientific disciplines are compared (Simonton, 2009c). For instance, relative to creative chemists, creative psychologists are disposed to have more rebellious relationships with their parents (Chambers, 1964; see also Roe, 1953). All in all, there is some reason to believe that a discipline's placement in the hierarchy corresponds to the developmental experiences of its practitioners. The higher the placement, the more stable, conventional, and homogeneous the experiences.

2. *Within-discipline.* Although very little research addresses the question of within-discipline contrasts in developmental experiences, one notable exception is Sulloway's (1996) work on the birth order of revolutionary scientists. Unlike practitioners of normal science, the scientists most favorable to revolutionary scientists tend to be laterborns. According to Sulloway's theory, firstborns tend to gravitate to conventional high-prestige and high-power professions, whereas laterborns tend to lean toward unconventional and high-risk careers. This theory falls in line with other findings regarding across-discipline birth-order effects (Simonton, 2009c). Thus, firstborns are more likely to become eminent scientists

(Eiduson, 1962; Galton, 1874; Roe, 1953; Simonton, 2008; Terry, 1989), whereas literary creators may have higher odds of being laterborns (Bliss, 1970). But composers in classical music are more prone to be firstborns (Schubert, Wagner, & Schubert, 1977). These results make sense if we assume that creators active in domains that are more logical, objective, conventional, and formal tend to be firstborns while those who create in domains that are more intuitive, subjective, individualistic, and emotional tend to be laterborns.

Sulloway (1996) maintained that birth order was by no means the only developmental factor that affects whether someone is likely to become a revolutionary scientist. Among the additional influences are some that bear a connection to placement in the disciplinary hierarchy. These include early parental loss, parent–offspring conflict, and minority status. So the fractal pattern appears applicable to developmental experiences.

Agreement and Achievement

I have just shown that an individual's dispositional traits and developmental experiences correspond with the position which his or her discipline occupies in the hierarchy. Not only may these psychological attributes distinguish the natural sciences from the social sciences, but also they differentiate the sciences from the arts and even various intra-disciplinary contrasts (e.g., natural-science versus human-science psychology). I would now like to raise an independent question: What determines the magnitude of the impact of an individual on the creator's chosen discipline? As indicated earlier when I discussed the combinatorial model, one explanation is that some individuals obtain a larger sample of domain-specific ideas. But this explanation is too simplistic. Two individuals can draw the same size samples and still differ dramatically in creative output. Where one colleague becomes a genuine creator, the other becomes a mere expert who has mastery without originality. This difference suggests that some psychological factors are involved in allowing the individual to convert his or her ideational sample into a new set of products.

Researchers have not found it difficult to identify variables that predict exceptional achievement in any given field. For instance, every high-achieving individual must boast a superlative degree of drive, motivation, determination, or persistence (Cox, 1926; Duckworth et al., 2007; Helmreich et al., 1980; Matthews et al., 1980). In this regard, a Nobel laureate in literature will be similar to a laureate in physics or chemistry. Yet a far more provocative question is whether any of the variables that influence an individual's disciplinary affiliation also affect the same person's likelihood of making high-impact contributions. To appreciate why this issue is so intriguing, consider the following three alternative possibilities (Simonton, 2009c):

1. The creators who have the highest impact on their discipline may be precisely those whose dispositional traits and developmental experiences closely approximate those that characterize most of their colleagues in the same field. The most influential psychologist, for example, would be typical of psychologists in general. By comparison, psychologists whose dispositional and developmental characteristics put them at the periphery with respect to most members of their field will be less likely to prove highly influential. Individuals in the former group may be styled *domain-typical creators*. The more the creator is like everybody else in the same field, the greater is the magnitude of that creator's production of high-impact work.

2. The creators with the highest impact on the field may be those whose disposition and development are most similar to individuals who occupy domains *higher* in the disciplinary hierarchy. Hence, high-impact psychologists may feature dispositional traits and developmental experiences that render them most similar to biologists or even chemists. As a result, natural-science orientated psychologists may actually be more influential than human-science psychologists. Such individuals may be called *domain-progressive creators*. They seemingly aspire to move their discipline up the disciplinary hierarchy. These aspirations might even adopt the form of reductionism; that is, reducing the phenomena at one level to the explanatory principles that dominate at a higher level in the hierarchy.

3. The most influential individuals just might be those whose disposition and development place them nearer to creators active in a discipline *lower* in the hierarchy. In a sense, such creators represent a regression from the objective, logical, conventional, and formal to the subjective, intuitive, individualistic, and emotional. Accordingly, we may identify these persons as *domain-regressive creators*.

The latter of the three possibilities might seem the least plausible, especially in scientific disciplines. After all, if most "soft" sciences aspire to become more "hard," and thereby move up the hierarchy, we would expect scientists to aspire to the rigor and precision of the more exact sciences. Nonetheless, a counterargument would suggest that high-impact creativity requires a relaxation of logical constraints rather than their imposition. Albert Einstein once admitted that:

> "to these elementary laws there leads no logical path, but only intuition, supported by being sympathetically in touch with experience" *(as cited in Holton, 1971–1972, p. 97).*

If so, the highest-level scientific creativity might actually have more kinship with the artistic creativity more normally exhibited at lower levels in the hierarchy. In line with this conjecture, Max Planck (1949) once observed that creative scientists:

> "must have a vivid intuitive imagination, for new ideas are not generated by deduction, but by an artistically creative imagination" *(p. 109).*

The extant research relevant to this question predominantly favors the third alternative (Simonton, 2009b, 2009c). Within any given discipline, the domain-regressive creators are the most likely to have the biggest impact on the field. This tendency is especially strong for dispositional traits. One particular manifestation of this finding concerns the artistic interests and hobbies of high-impact scientists (Root-Bernstein et al., 2008; Root-Bernstein, Bernstein, & Garnier, 1995). Not only are artistic avocations associated with scientific creativity, but the higher the level of that creativity the higher the likelihood that the scientist engages in such avocations. These interests and hobbies are also positively associated with openness to experience, a Big-Five personality factor also positively correlated with creativity (Carson, Peterson, & Higgins, 2003; Harris, 2004; McCrae, 1987).

To provide a second example, consider the relation between psychopathology and creativity. We have already seen that the incidence and intensity of mental illness relates to a discipline's placement in the extended hierarchy. Yet within a given discipline, a greater propensity toward psychopathology is positively associated with creative achievement

(Eysenck, 1995; Feist, 1998; Ludwig, 1995; Rushton, 1990). This positive relation becomes especially strong in the arts (Götz & Götz, 1979; Barron, 1963). This is not to say that madness is required for creative genius, but only that the two syndromes share some dispositional traits, such as a reduced capacity for cognitive filtering, a reduction that is also associated with higher openness to experience (Carson, Peterson, & Higgins, 2003; Peterson & Carson, 2000). Besides openness, creative individuals possess certain compensatory characteristics, such as high intelligence and ego-strength, which turn this supposed attentional deficiency into an asset (Barron, 1963; Carson, Peterson, & Higgins, 2003). Such defocused attention allows creators to "think outside the box", an ability that becomes increasingly essential toward the artistic end of the spectrum.

CONCLUSIONS

In this chapter, I have argued that we cannot fully understand individual creativity without placing the person in the context of the field and the domain—the two key aspects of the discipline to which creators make their contributions. This argument was based on Csikszentmihályi's (1990, 1999) systems perspective which situates creativity in a dynamic interaction among the domain, the field, and the individual. This perspective was then illustrated in two distinct ways, one theoretical and the other empirical.

The first illustration involved combinatorial models. In these models, the members of a particular field begin with a sample of ideas from that domain. Each individual then subjects his or her personal ideational sample to a combinatorial process. Viable combinations are then submitted to the field, which then determines which combinatorial products will enter the domain set of ideations. These models can generate a large number of verifiable predictions, but the most interesting and valuable are those entailing phenomena that cannot be explicated without adopting a systems perspective. Most notable is the multiples phenomenon where two or more scientists independently make the same contribution—a phenomenon that has no meaning at the individual level of analysis. Furthermore, certain specific attributes of both field and domain determine the odds that a creator will even participate in a multiple.

The second illustration was much less abstract and formal: disciplinary hierarchies. I began by showing how the main sciences can be ordered according to the consensus exhibited by the field and the precision of the ideas making up the domain. This ordering was then extrapolated to encompass disciplines in the humanities and interpolated to handle within-discipline contrasts. I then showed that the resulting hierarchy had a psychological basis in the dispositional traits and developmental experiences of discipline-specific practitioners. The scientists differ from artists in a manner that parallels the difference between natural scientists and social scientists. Last, but not least, I observed that individual differences in disciplinary impact were a partial consequence of the fit between individual and the discipline. The most high-impact members of a field tend to be domain-regressive in the sense that their dispositional and developmental attributes are closer to what prevails in domains lower in the hierarchy.

Taken altogether, it should be manifest that individual creators cannot be completely understood without placing their creativity in the proper disciplinary context. This context consists of two parts; the field and the domain. This two-part composition of the discipline should provide an explicit basis for the discussion of creativity beyond just the two examples given. For example, whenever collaborative research groups are established, it is critical to consider the separate domain content and methods that each member brings into the collaboration. One of the cardinal principles of collaborative creativity is that groups whose members are heterogeneous with respect to the domain-specific ideas that they bring to the table are likely to be more productive than those groups whose members are more homogeneous (Simonton, 2004a, 2010). This is not to say that a creator's source of discipline constitutes the only source of group member heterogeneity; gender, ethnicity, and age are important factors too (e.g., Andrews, 1979; Nemeth & Nemeth-Brown, 2003). Yet the crucial point remains, namely, that the individual's domain and field must be considered essential aspects of any comprehensive view of their creativity. Even the greatest creative genius does not voyage through strange seas alone.

References

Amabile, T. M. (1996). *Creativity in context: Update to the social psychology of creativity.* Boulder, CO: Westview.

Andrews, F. M. (Ed.). (1979). *Scientific productivity: The effectiveness of research groups in six countries.* Cambridge, UK: Cambridge University Press.

Barron, F. X. (1963). *Creativity and psychological health: Origins of personal vitality and creative freedom.* Princeton, NJ: Van Nostrand.

Berry, C. (1981). The Nobel scientists and the origins of scientific achievement. *British Journal of Sociology, 32,* 381–391.

Bliss, H. E. (1935). The system of the sciences and the organization of knowledge. *Philosophy of Science, 2,* 86–103.

Bliss, W. D. (1970). Birth order of creative writers. *Journal of Individual Psychology, 26,* 200–202.

Carson, S., Peterson, J. B., & Higgins, D. M. (2003). Decreased latent inhibition is associated with increased creative achievement in high-functioning individuals. *Journal of Personality and Social Psychology, 85,* 499–506.

Chambers, J. A. (1964). Relating personality and biographical factors to scientific creativity. *Psychological Monographs: General and Applied, 78*(7, Whole No. 584).

Coan, R. W. (1968). Dimensions of psychological theory. *American Psychologist, 23,* 715–722.

Coan, R. W. (1973). Toward a psychological interpretation of psychology. *Journal of the History of the Behavioral Sciences, 9,* 313–327.

Cohen, J. M., & Cohen, M. J. (Eds.). (1960). *The Penguin dictionary of quotations.* Baltimore, MD: Penguin Books.

Cole, S. (1983). The hierarchy of the sciences? *American Journal of Sociology, 89,* 111–139.

Comte, A. (1855). *The positive philosophy of Auguste Comte.* (H. Martineau, Trans.) New York, NY: Blanchard. (Original work published 1839–1842).

Cox, C. (1926). *The early mental traits of three hundred geniuses.* Stanford, CA: Stanford University Press.

Csikszentmihályi, M. (1990). The domain of creativity. In M. A. Runco & R. S. Albert (Eds.), *Theories of creativity* (pp. 190–212). Newbury Park, CA: Sage.

Csikszentmihályi, M. (1999). Implications of a systems perspective for the study of creativity. In R. J. Sternberg (Ed.), *Handbook of creativity* (pp. 313–338). Cambridge, UK: Cambridge University Press.

Diamond, A. M., Jr. (1980). Age and the acceptance of cliometrics. *Journal of Economic History, 40,* 838–841.

Duckworth, A. L., Peterson, C., Matthews, M. D., & Kelly, D. R. (2007). GRIT: Perseverence and passion for long-term goals. *Journal of Personality and Social Psychology, 92,* 1087–1101.

Eiduson, B. T. (1962). *Scientists: Their psychological world.* New York, NY: Basic Books.

Eysenck, H. J. (1995). *Genius: The natural history of creativity.* Cambridge, UK: Cambridge University Press.

Fanelli, D. (2010). "Positive" results increase down the hierarchy of the sciences. *PLoS ONE, 5*(4), e10068. doi:10.1371/journal.pone.0010068.

Feist, G. J. (1998). A meta-analysis of personality in scientific and artistic creativity. *Personality and Social Psychology Review, 2,* 290–309.

Fitzgerald, M. (2002). Asperger's disorder and mathematicians of genius. *Journal of Autism & Developmental Disorders, 32,* 59–60.

Galton, F. (1874). *English men of science: Their nature and nurture.* London, UK: Macmillan.

Götz, K. O., & Götz, K. (1979). Personality characteristics of successful artists. *Perceptual and Motor Skills, 49,* 919–924.

Hadamard, J. (1945). *The psychology of invention in the mathematical field.* Princeton, NJ: Princeton University Press.

Hagstrom, W. O. (1974). Competition in science. *American Sociological Review, 39,* 1–18.

Harrington, D. M. (1990). The ecology of human creativity: A psychological perspective. In M. A. Runco & R. S. Albert (Eds.), *Theories of creativity* (pp. 143–169). Newbury Park, CA: Sage.

Harris, J. A. (2004). Measured intelligence, achievement, openness to experience, and creativity. *Personality and Individual Differences, 36,* 913–929.

Helmreich, R. L., Spence, J. T., Beane, W. E., Lucker, G. W., & Matthews, K. A. (1980). Making it in academic psychology: Demographic and personality correlates of attainment. *Journal of Personality and Social Psychology, 39,* 896–908.

Hoffmann, B. (1972). *Albert Einstein: Creator and rebel.* New York, NY: Plume.

Holton, G. (1971–72). On trying to understand the scientific genius. *American Scholar, 41,* 95–110.

Hull, D. L., Tessner, P. D., & Diamond, A. M. (1978). Planck's principle: Do younger scientists accept new scientific ideas with greater alacrity than older scientists? *Science, 202,* 717–723.

Jamison, K. R. (1989). Mood disorders and patterns of creativity in British writers and artists. *Psychiatry, 52,* 125–134.

Jeans, J. (1942). Newton and the science of to-day. *Nature, 150,* 710–715.

Johnson, J. A., Germer, C. K., Efran, J. S., & Overton, W. F. (1988). Personality as the basis for theoretical predilections. *Journal of Personality and Social Psychology, 55,* 824–835.

Kimble, G. A. (1984). Psychology's two cultures. *American Psychologist, 39,* 833–839.

Klahr, D., & Simon, H. A. (1999). Studies of scientific creativity: Complementary approaches and convergent findings. *Psychological Bulletin, 125,* 524–543.

Kroeber, A. L. (1944). *Configurations of culture growth.* Berkeley, CA: University of California Press.

Ko, Y., & Kim, J. (2008). Scientific geniuses' psychopathology as a moderator in the relation between creative contribution types and eminence. *Creativity Research Journal, 20,* 251–261.

Kuhn, T. S. (1970). *The structure of scientific revolutions* (2nd ed.). Chicago, IL: University of Chicago Press.

Lamb, D., & Easton, S. M. (1984). *Multiple discovery.* Avebury, UK: Avebury.

Levin, S. G., Stephan, P. E., & Walker, M. B. (1995). Plancks principle revisited—A note. *Social Studies of Science, 25,* 35–55.

Ludwig, A. M. (1992). Creative achievement and psychopathology: Comparison among professions. *American Journal of Psychotherapy, 46,* 330–356.

Ludwig, A. M. (1995). *The price of greatness: Resolving the creativity and madness controversy.* New York, NY: Guilford Press.

Ludwig, A. M. (1998). Method and madness in the arts and sciences. *Creativity Research Journal, 11,* 93–101.

Manniche, E., & Falk, G. (1957). Age and the Nobel prize. *Behavioral Science, 2,* 301–307.

Martindale, C. (1989). Personality, situation, and creativity. In J. A. Glover, R. R. Ronning & C. R. Reynolds (Eds.), *Handbook of creativity* (pp. 211–232). New York, NY: Plenum Press.

Matthews, K. A., Helmreich, R. L., Beane, W. E., & Lucker, G. W. (1980). Pattern A, achievement striving, and scientific merit: Does Pattern A help or hinder? *Journal of Personality and Social Psychology, 39,* 962–967.

McCrae, R. R. (1987). Creativity, divergent thinking, and openness to experience. *Journal of Personality and Social Psychology, 52,* 1258–1265.

McDowell, J. M. (1982). Obsolescence of knowledge and career publication profiles: Some evidence of differences among fields in costs of interrupted careers. *American Economic Review, 72,* 752–768.

Merton, R. K. (1961). Singletons and multiples in scientific discovery: A chapter in the sociology of science. *Proceedings of the American Philosophical Society, 105,* 470–486.

Mumford, M. D., Antes, A. L., Caughron, J. J., Connelly, S., & Beeler, C. (2010). Cross-field differences in creative problem-solving skills: A comparison of health, biological, and social sciences. *Creativity Research Journal, 22,* 14–26.

Nemeth, C. J., & Nemeth-Brown, B. (2003). Better than individuals? The potential benefits of dissent and diversity. In P. B. Paulus & B. A. Nijstad (Eds.), *Group creativity: Innovation through collaboration* (pp. 63–84). New York, NY: Oxford University Press.

A. INTRODUCTION

Peterson, J. B., & Carson, S. (2000). Latent inhibition and openness to experience in a high-achieving student population. *Personality and Individual Differences, 28*, 323–332.

Planck, M. (1949). *Scientific autobiography and other papers* (F. Gaynor, Trans.). New York, NY: Philosophical Library.

Poincaré, H. (1921). *The foundations of science: Science and hypothesis, the value of science, science and method* (G. B. Halstead, Trans.). New York, NY: Science Press.

Post, F. (1994). Creativity and psychopathology: A study of 291 world-famous men. *British Journal of Psychiatry, 165*, 22–34.

Raskin, E. A. (1936). Comparison of scientific and literary ability: A biographical study of eminent scientists and men of letters of the nineteenth century. *Journal of Abnormal and Social Psychology, 31*, 20–35.

Roe, A. (1953). *The making of a scientist.* New York, NY: Dodd, Mead.

Roeckelein, J. E. (1997). Psychology among the sciences: Comparisons of numbers of theories and laws cited in textbooks. *Psychological Reports, 80*, 131–141.

Root-Bernstein, R., Allen, L., Beach, L., Bhadula, R., Fast, J., & Hosey, C., et al. (2008). Arts foster scientific success: Avocations of Nobel, National Academy, Royal Society, and Sigma Xi members. *Journal of the Psychology of Science and Technology, 1*, 51–63.

Root-Bernstein, R. S., Bernstein, M., & Garnier, H. (1995). Correlations between avocations, scientific style, work habits, and professional impact of scientists. *Creativity Research Journal, 8*, 115–137.

Rushton, J. P. (1990). Creativity, intelligence, and psychoticism. *Personality and Individual Differences, 11*, 1291–1298.

Sawyer, R. K. (2007). *Group genius: The creative power of collaboration.* New York, NY: Basic Books.

Schachter, S., Christenfeld, N., Ravina, B., & Bilous, R. (1991). Speech disfluency and the structure of knowledge. *Journal of Personality and Social Psychology, 60*, 362–367.

Schaefer, C. E., & Anastasi, A. (1968). A biographical inventory for identifying creativity in adolescent boys. *Journal of Applied Psychology, 58*, 42–48.

Simonton, D. K. (1975). Sociocultural context of individual creativity: A transhistorical time-series analysis. *Journal of Personality and Social Psychology, 32*, 1119–1133.

Simonton, D. K. (1978). Independent discovery in science and technology: A closer look at the Poisson distribution. *Social Studies of Science, 8*, 521–532.

Simonton, D. K. (1984). Artistic creativity and interpersonal relationships across and within generations. *Journal of Personality and Social Psychology, 46*, 1273–1286.

Simonton, D. K. (1986). Biographical typicality, eminence, and achievement style. *Journal of Creative Behavior, 20*, 14–22.

Simonton, D. K. (1988). *Scientific genius: A psychology of science.* Cambridge, UK: Cambridge University Press.

Simonton, D. K. (1992). Leaders of American psychology, 1879–1967: Career development, creative output, and professional achievement. *Journal of Personality and Social Psychology, 62*, 5–17.

Simonton, D. K. (1992). The social context of career success and course for 2,026 scientists and inventors. *Personality and Social Psychology Bulletin, 18*, 452–463.

Simonton, D. K. (1997a). Creative productivity: A predictive and explanatory model of career trajectories and landmarks. *Psychological Review, 104*, 66–89.

Simonton, D. K. (1997b). Foreign influence and national achievement: The impact of open milieus on Japanese civilization. *Journal of Personality and Social Psychology, 72*, 86–94.

Simonton, D. K. (2000). Methodological and theoretical orientation and the long-term disciplinary impact of 54 eminent psychologists. *Review of General Psychology, 4*, 13–24.

Simonton, D. K. (2003). Scientific creativity as constrained stochastic behavior: The integration of product, process, and person perspectives. *Psychological Bulletin, 129*, 475–494.

Simonton, D. K. (2004a). *Creativity in science: Chance, logic, genius, and zeitgeist.* Cambridge, UK: Cambridge University Press.

Simonton, D. K. (2004b). Psychology's status as a scientific discipline: Its empirical placement within an implicit hierarchy of the sciences. *Review of General Psychology, 8*, 59–67.

Simonton, D. K. (2008). Gender differences in birth order and family size among 186 eminent psychologists. *Journal of Psychology of Science and Technology, 1*, 15–22.

Simonton, D. K. (2009a). Scientific creativity as a combinatorial process: The chance baseline. In P. Meusburger, J. Funke & E. Wunder (Eds.), *Milieus of creativity* (pp. 39–51). Dordrecht, The Netherlands: Springer.

Simonton, D. K. (2009b). Varieties of perspectives on creativity. *Perspectives on Psychological Science, 4*, 466–467.

Simonton, D. K. (2009c). Varieties of (scientific) creativity: A hierarchical model of disposition, development, and achievement. *Perspectives on Psychological Science, 4*, 441–452.

A. INTRODUCTION

Simonton, D. K. (2010). Creativity as blind-variation and selective-retention: Constrained combinatorial models of exceptional creativity. *Physics of Life Reviews, 7*, 156–179.

Simonton, D. K., & Song, A. V. (2009). Eminence, IQ, physical and mental health, and achievement domain: Cox's 282 geniuses revisited. *Psychological Science, 20*, 429–434.

Smith, L. D., Best, L. A., Stubbs, D. A., Johnston, J., & Archibald, A. B. (2000). Scientific graphs and the hierarchy of the sciences. *Social Studies of Science, 30*, 73–94.

Stephan, P. E., & Levin, S. G. (1993). Age and the Nobel Prize revisited. *Scientometrics, 28*, 387–399.

Suedfeld, P. (1985). APA presidential addresses: The relation of integrative complexity to historical, professional, and personal factors. *Journal of Personality and Social Psychology, 47*, 848–852.

Sulloway, F. J. (1996). *Born to rebel: Birth order, family dynamics, and creative lives*. New York, NY: Pantheon.

Suls, J., & Fletcher, B. (1983). Social comparison in the social and physical sciences: An archival study. *Journal of Personality and Social Psychology, 44*, 575–580.

Terry, W. S. (1989). Birth order and prominence in the history of psychology. *Psychological Record, 39*, 333–337.

Who said what when: A chronological dictionary of quotations. (1991). New York, NY: Hippocrene Books.

A. INTRODUCTION

Creativity in Organizations: Facilitators and Inhibitors

Eunice M.L. Soriano de Alencar
Catholic University of Brasilia, Brasilia, Brazil

Creativity is a key resource for individuals, organizations and societies. It is expressed in several ways in services, work processes, products, in science, technology and cultural accomplishments. It enables the individual to take greater benefit from opportunities, to respond in a more productive way to challenges and difficulties in his/her personal and professional life, as well as to cope better with unexpected situations. This advantage was observed, for example, among US Air Force personnel who had survived extremely difficult conditions during World War II. One common trait among the successful survivors was their creative and imaginative energy for continued adaptation (Robinson & Stern, 1997). The urge to create is also a healthy part of the human being, and creative activity is usually accompanied by feelings of satisfaction and pleasure, which are fundamental elements of emotional welfare and mental health (Alencar, 2007; Csikszentmihályi, 1997; Pannells & Claxton, 2008; Runco, 2004).

At the level of the organization, creativity is an essential factor for innovation and consequent organizational success. It has been considered a critical element for the survival of many companies, in view of the challenges generated by globalization, growing competition and accelerated rhythm of change. These factors have driven organizations to remain in a continuous process of innovation, which requires better use of available resources, especially the creativity of their human resources. In this sense, Prabhu, Sutton and Sauser (2008) state that:

> "In today's competitive world, the only thing that is constant is change. A product that may be a huge success today could be extinct tomorrow. In the backdrop of such fierce competition, new ideas and new products have become a necessity, rather than a luxury. To be competitive in the global market, organizations must develop creative and high quality products and services." *(pp. 62–63)*

Regarding the concerns of the larger society, the future prosperity of countries will depend increasingly on their innovative capacity, in other words, on their ability to

Handbook of Organizational Creativity.
DOI: 10.1016/B978-0-12-374714-3.00005-7

transform ideas into new products and services, to develop new technologies and production forms, to introduce products and services in new markets and still, in a global context, to face the countless challenges of the planet in the areas of health, education and work (Smith-Bingham, 2006). It is for this reason that governments include creativity as a political priority, aware of the need to promote its fomentation in different levels of formal education, industries and in other types of organizations. It was the recognition of its importance that led the European Commission to declare 2009 as the European Year of Creativity and Innovation (Gomes & Almeida, 2009).

The main objective of this chapter is to describe different factors that help creativity to bloom in the work environment. Some of these factors refer to the employees, others to the organizations, and still others to the wider society in which individuals and organizations are embedded. Personal attributes that are associated with creativity and that may influence the individual's behavior in the workplace will be briefly outlined, as well as elements of the organizational environments that may act as incentive or obstruction to the expression of individual and work teams' creativity. In addition, some conceptual issues will also be discussed. Regarding the central topic of this chapter, it is, however, necessary to highlight that, although creativity has systematically been investigated in psychology for several decades, creativity in organizations is a relatively new area of research in the field of organizational behavior (Shalley & Zhou, 2008). It presents a lot of uncovered subjects, which require different levels of analysis for their complete understanding. Furthermore, it is extremely difficult to map out the whole constellation of elements that exert an influence on creativity in an organizational setting, due to their diversity and complexity and their multiple interactions.

CONCEPTUAL BACKGROUND

The study of creativity presents an enormous challenge, since it is a complex, dynamic, multifaceted and pluridetermined phenomenon. Thus the difficulty in reaching a precise definition, and the reason for the countless definitions already proposed for the term, which prioritize personal characteristics; or the process; or characteristics of the product or the social environment. Some of these are illustrated below:

"Creativity is the ability to produce new ideas which are novel to the idea producers themselves." *(Drabkin, 1996, p. 78)*

"Creativity is a process resulting in a product; it is the production of a novel and appropriate response, product, or solution to an open-ended task. The response must be new, but it must also be appropriate to the task to be completed or the problem to be solved. In addition, the task must be open-ended, rather than having a single, obvious solution." *(Amabile & Mueller, 2008, p. 35)*

"Creativity is a novel product that attains some level of social recognition." *(Sawyer, 2006, p. 27)*

"Creativity is not an attribute of individuals, but of social systems making judgments about individuals... The social and cultural conditions, interacting with individual potentialities, brought about the objects and behaviors we call creative." *(Csikszentmihályi, 1994, p. 144)*

The concept of creativity is closely related to the concept of innovation. These two words have been used as synonyms by scholars, such as Sawyer (2006), Simonton (2003), Smith (2003) and Shavinina and Seeratan (2003). On the other hand, other scholars, such as

Alencar (1996a), Bruno-Faria (2003), Hill and Amabile (1993), Hunter, Bedell and Mumford (2007), West and Richter (2008), and Van Gundy (1987) discuss the two constructs, making a distinction between them. Alencar emphasizes, for instance, that the term innovation has been more often used at the organizational level, whilst creativity is used to refer to an individual or team characteristic, being a fundamental factor for innovation, which interests the organization most. Creativity has been conceptualized as the component idea of innovation, an element that might be observed in different stages of the innovation process, while innovation would encompass the development, application and outcomes of new ideas. The difference between the two concepts is, however, subtle, departing more in emphasis than in substance (Mathisen & Einarsen, 2004).

Several scholars, such as Bruno-Faria (2003), analyzed how creativity in the context of organizations has been defined, signaling common aspects as, for instance, the elements of novelty and value for the organization and emphasizing creativity as originating from individuals and groups in the organization. Buno-Faria synthesized the central ideas of a great number of studies about creativity in the working environment, and proposed the following conceptualization:

> "Generation of ideas, processes, products and/or new services to an individual/group or in that context—that produce some valuable contribution for the organization and/or for the welfare of people that work in that context and that possess essential elements to their implementation." *(p.116)*

On the other hand, Alvarado (2006), in a paper that presents the conception of a creative organization as a living being, in opposition to the mechanistic conception, includes in her definition of creativity both the individual and the organization, considering it as:

> "The process and the quality that allows the human being and organizations to transform reality, and also to transform themselves through the introduction of novelty that proves to be useful, to provide responses to the needs of a changing internal and external context." *(p. 379)*

It is noticed that the initial interest of researchers devoted to the investigation of the phenomenon was centered in the personal characteristics associated with creativity, such as creative thinking abilities, together with the personality attributes of people that stand out in terms of their creative production. More recently, the environmental context has begun to receive greater attention, as fulfilling the crucial role of the individual's closest environment. In addition, another focus of interest has been the impact of political, historical and cultural features of society on the modalities of valued and exalted creative expressions, on the opportunities available for the development of creative potential, as well as on the organizational processes that facilitate or obstruct creativity and innovation (Leung, Au & Leung, 2004).

The elements that promote creativity have been addressed in several theories of creativity, such as Sternberg's (2003; Sternberg & Lubart, 1995, 1996, 1999) Investment Theory of Creativity, Amabile's (1983, 1996a; Amabile & Mueller, 2008; Amabile & Tighe, 1993) Componential Theory of Creativity and Csikszentmihályi's (1988, 1994, 1999) systems model of creativity. According to Sternberg (2003), for instance, a complete model of creativity includes the environment, and the following personal resources that may facilitate or hinder its manifestation: intellectual skills, thinking styles, personality, motivation and knowledge. Sternberg also points out that the type of environment that facilitates the expression of creativity also depends on other factors, such as personal attributes, the person's level of creative potential and the area in which creativity is expressed, highlighting that the environment that facilitates creative expression interacts with personal and situational variables in a complex way.

On the other hand, Amabile's componential theory of creativity includes three basic components within the individual and one component outside the individual. Domain-relevant skills, creativity-relevant processes and intrinsic task motivation are the individual components. The first includes several elements related to the level of expertise in a domain, such as talent, knowledge, experiences and technical abilities. The second component includes cognitive styles, the domain of strategies that favor the production of new ideas and personality characteristics that are conducive to generating new and useful ideas in any domain. The third component is task motivation, which may be primarily intrinsic or extrinsic. According to Amabile, it is the intrinsic motivation, or else, the motivation to engage in some activity primarily for its own sake, that is conducive to creativity, although informational extrinsic motivation can also be conducive, particularly if it combines with high levels of intrinsic motivation. The fourth component is the work or social environment. It comprises several factors in the environment that can block creativity or foster it (Amabile, 1983, 1996a; Amabile & Mueller, 2008; Amabile & Tighe, 1993).

Csikszentmihályi's (1994, 1999) systems approach includes, besides the individual, the field and the domain. Several characteristics of the individual, such as motivation, cognitive skills, openness to experience, persistence, curiosity, enthusiasm and other personality traits that favor breaking rules as well as the ability to convince people who belong to the field about the value of his/her own ideas, represent traits that may facilitate the occurrence of creativity. The field encompasses all the individuals that act as judges, and who decide whether an idea or product is creative. The participants in the field are those who demand, respond, judge, discourage, recognize and value the ideas and contributions of the "creator". The domain includes a group of rules and symbolic procedures of an area of knowledge, such as mathematics, physics, biology, music etc. In the case of an organization, it comprises practices accepted and implemented, production lines, market segments, among other features. Furthermore, Csikszentmihályi and Sawyer (1995) report the need to shift the focus from the creativity of the individual to its social and organizational components, bearing in mind, that creativity in organizations not only depends on internal elements, but also on other external elements, such as market characteristics and government legislation. Csikszentmihályi (1996) also notices that it is easier to develop people's creativity by changing the conditions of the environment rather than trying to make them think in a creative way, conceiving creativity both as an individual, as well as a social phenomenon.

The reciprocal influence of the person-environment has been highlighted by Sternberg (2003), Amabile (1996a; Amabile & Miller, 2008) and Csikszentmihályi (1999; Csikszentmihályi & Sawyer, 1995) and other scholars, who underscore the complex and dynamic interactions among social factors, the context and personal characteristics. This emphasizes that creativity does not occur in a vacuum, and cannot be seen as being independent of the environmental context. On the other hand, it does not exist without the individual either. Furthermore, the same environment or situation can have different impacts on different individuals, as the propeller of the creative expression for some, and a contrary effect in others.

A. INTRODUCTION

PERSONAL CHARACTERISTICS ASSOCIATED WITH CREATIVITY

Creative achievement in organizations depends not only on elements of the work environment, but also on the individual, working alone or in teams. If employees present attributes that favor the expression and development of new ideas, this may contribute to the flourishing of creativity in the workplace, particularly if creativity is valued and required in their work activities. The investigation of these attributes has gained impetus since the beginning of the second half of last century, after Guilford's (1950) presidential address to the American Psychological Association. Guilford pointed out the disregard of psychology for the study of creativity, which, by his understanding, deserved greater attention due to its social importance and crucial role for progress. Since then, research on creativity has prospered, together with greater interest in the psychological study of the personal attributes which may contribute to the expression of creativity. Since the early '80s, this interest has expanded significantly and the influence of external factors to the individual, present in his/her social environment have begun to receive greater attention, such as collaboration, social support nets, cultural background, the organization climate and cultural elements in the expression of creativity.

A vast number of studies have been carried out on the individual characteristics that facilitate creative performance. Personality attributes, cognitive abilities involved in the creative process, creative styles, motivation and expertise are among the variables that have been most examined by the literature on creativity. These will be addressed briefly below.

Personality Attributes

Individuals that present initiative, independence of judgment, flexibility, openness to new ideas, persistence, self-confidence, tolerance to ambiguity, disposition to take risks and to learn from mistakes have greater chances of taking advantage of opportunities to express and develop creative ideas. Several of these attributes were identified in biographical studies of people with outstanding contributions. They were, for instance, observed by Alencar (1998b, 2001a) in a study of a sample of Brazilian scientists recognized for their high creative production, who were interviewed about their personality traits, facilitating and inhibiting factors to their creative achievement, institutional and personal factors that promote greater creative production, as well as their aspirations for the future. To explain their high level of creative expression, these scientists signaled, among other features, their perseverance, commitment to work, initiative and independence of thinking and action. Similarly, in a study concerning the facilitating and inhibiting factors to the expression of personal creativity, conducted with a sample of engineering students and engineers (Alencar & Fleith, 2004), the participants mentioned, besides variables outside the individual, such as incentive, freedom to express ideas, opportunity and time, some personality traits, such as courage, perseverance and curiosity, considered by them as facilitating factors.

Current research has also examined, instead of the individual personality traits, the creative personality team composition, which is a measure that includes different individual creative personality variables, as well as the combination of these variables. The rationale for the advantage of its use is the recognition of the importance of team-based work systems for organizational effectiveness and creativity/innovation. This personality composition refers to a constellation of variables that might contribute to the creative achievement of the team (Baer, Oldham, Jacobsohn & Hollingshead, 2008; Mathisen, Martinsen & Einarsen, 2008).

The personality traits previously pointed out are only a sample of those that appear repeatedly in the literature on personality attributes associated with creativity (Alencar & Fleith, 2003a; Barron, 1969; Dewett, 2006; Muñoz-Doyague, González-Álvarez, & Nieto, 2008; MacKinnon, 1965, 1975; Soto, 2006; Zenasni, Besançon, & Lubart, 2008). Furthermore, it has also been stated that to be creative in one social setting does not necessarily mean that the same traits will be helpful in another setting (Talbot, 1993), that different personality traits may be needed depending on the stage of the innovation process (Mathisen, Martinsen & Einarsen, 2008), and that great differences exist among creative individuals in their personality attributes (Alencar & Fleith, 2003a; MacKinnon, 1978). Differences among people from different cultures in the extent to which they present traits associated with creativity is also a topic discussed in literature (Kim, 2007; Lubart, 1999; Leung, Au, & Leung, 2004).

Special Cognitive Abilities and Cognitive Style

The cognitive abilities most frequently reported in literature include fluency, flexibility and originality of ideas, complemented with analytical and critical reasoning, besides metaphorical and analogical thinking. It is noted that the divergent thinking abilities gained prominence with Guilford's (1967) publications on the structure of intellect theory. The assessment of these abilities has frequently been used inadequately as a general indicator of an individual's creativity (Alencar, 1996b; Alencar & Fleith, in press), in spite of Guilford's position that a constellation of multiple abilities characterizes creative thinking. According to him:

"the creative potential is very complex, and at times and in different ways involves abilities outside the divergent-production and the transformation categories, which are most important in that connection." *(Guilford, 1967, pp. 169–170)*

The role of other cognitive abilities has been increasingly recognized in creative production, as has the contribution of convergent thinking (Cropley, 2006).

In addition, Mumford, Baughman and Sager (2003) argued that creative thought also involves the identification of new and viable solutions, and considered creative thought as a form of complex problem solving, asserting that:

"the combination and reorganization of extent knowledge structures may represent the key cognitive process underlying the generation of new ideas." *(p. 24)*

These scholars have listed the following cognitive processes as appearing to play a role in creative thought: problem construction or problem definition; information encoding; category search; category selection; category combination and reorganization; idea evaluation; implementation planning; and monitoring.

The cognitive style refers to how people approach problems and their solutions, including how they generate new ideas. The perspective is on "how people are creative" or preferred ways of expressing or using one's creativity (Treffinger, 2003). The best known classification of cognitive styles was proposed by Kirton (1987), author of the theory of adaptation–innovation. It considers that any individual can be located in a continuum that varies from the ability "to do things better" to the ability "to do things in a different way". Those who present an adaptive style are characterized by precision, efficiency, discipline, attention to norms. On the other hand, the ones that present an innovative style tend to be undisciplined, rule breakers, and in face of a problem, they try to reorganize or restructure it with less predictable responses and a greater level of originality. The cognitive style that is described as innovator is the one that is linked to greater creativity levels. Other classifications of cognitive styles have been proposed by scholars, such as Sternberg (1997; Lubart & Sternberg, 1995) and Wechsler (2006).

Motivational Factors

The role of motivation for creative performance is well documented in literature. There is vast empiric evidence that calls attention to a high level of motivation, especially of intrinsic nature in creative work (Alencar, 1998b, 2001a, 2006; Amabile, 1996b; Collins & Amabile, 1999; Lewis, 1999). Alencar (1998b), for instance, in a study with scientists notable for their creative production, observed an intense enthusiasm and involvement, typical of highly motivated people. In respect to the characteristics that most contributed to their remarkable productivity, they usually reported a passion that moved them in their work, similar to that noticed by Amabile (2001) in a biographical study of John Irving, a prominent North American writer. When questioned, for example, as to the reason why he continued to work ten hours every day, even after having become a successful novelist, the response was the pleasure and love found in devoting to his writing.

However, extrinsic motivation, which characterizes the individual which gets involved in a task due to a reward or external recognition, may also have a positive effect on creative performance. In this sense, Sternberg and Lubart (1995) pointed out that both motivational types—intrinsic and extrinsic—frequently interact, mutually combining to strengthen creativity. These authors mention several empirical studies that point to the mobilizing role of both motivation types for creativity. In one of the studies, developed by Ochse (cited by Sternberg & Lubart, 1995), motivators, which were considered especially relevant for professionals that have given creative contributions in several areas, were investigated. Several factors were reported; some that reflected intrinsic motivation, and others that indicated extrinsic motivation as, for instance, the wish to obtain domain on a given problem, to be recognized by peers, to have self-esteem, to reach immortality and to discover an underlying order in things. In a similar way, Amabile (2001) proposed that certain types of extrinsic motivators, which give support to the development of competence and work involvement, complement intrinsic motivation through a process that she denominates motivational synergy.

Expertise

The term 'expert' has been used to characterize people whose performance in a domain is consistently superior to the performance of non-experts (Galvão, 1993, 2001). On the other hand, expertise can refer to the capacity, acquired through practice or deliberate individual study, to perform a specific domain task particularly well (Galvão, 2001). Several scholars (Alencar, 2009, Alencar & Galvão, 2007; Amabile, 1996a; Ericsson, 1999; Sternberg & Lubart, 1995, 1996, 1999; Weisberg, 1999) underscore the importance of expertise in a domain to the production of creative work. It has been pointed out that technical, intellectual and procedural knowledge in a specific area helps in the identification and solution of problems of real importance to the area. In relation to knowledge, Sternberg and Lubart discriminate two types: formal and informal, considering both to be important for creativity. The first would be that knowledge of a certain area or of a certain work, which is acquired through books, lectures or any other means of instruction. The informal would be the knowledge acquired when one devotes himself/herself to a certain area, and it is rarely explicitly taught. It is, most of the time, impossible even to be verbalized.

Expertise is a critical element for creative work, since new ideas are not produced in a vacuum. The greater the previous knowledge, the easier it is to acquire new knowledge and to establish links among ideas, which may result in ideas of value, appropriate to the needs of the context. However, it is also argued that experts are in danger of being entrenched in their areas of expertise, operating with the same repertoire of responses, without taking profit from external changes that might improve competencies already crystallized (Sternberg, 1996). This was evident in a study of musicians by Galvão (2000).

The role of expertise for creative production was addressed by scientists that participated in a study developed by Alencar (2001a), regarding factors that promote greater creative production. Most of them referred to the importance of the domain of the technique and knowledge, in addition to imagination, to have success in creative endeavors. Similarly, the importance of expertise was highlighted by engineering students and engineers who participated in a study, conducted by Alencar and Fleith (2004), on factors that impact creative performance.

THE WORK ENVIRONMENT FOR CREATIVITY

Organizational context variables that may affect the creativity blooming in the work place have been the target of numerous studies. The characteristics of a leader who motivates and fosters creativity, elements in groups or teams that may stimulate or inhibit creativity, the organizational climate for creativity, strategies to nurture creativity among companies that are outstanding in their innovative capacity are some topics that have been investigated and discussed (Alencar, 1996a, 1998a; Alencar & Bruno-Faria, 2007; Amabile, 1996a, 1996b, 1999; Amabile & Mueller, 2008; Bruno-Faria & Alencar, 1996; Hill & Amabile, 1993; Hitt, 1975; Locke & Kirkpatrick, 1995; Zhou & Shalley, 2008). In addition, as organizations are built-in within societies, sharing the values and suffering the influences of political, historical and cultural conditions, another focus of attention has been the influence of societal values and cultural practices on the behavior of individuals and groups in their workplace, on the management styles, and the extent to which these features enhance or inhibit creative expression. It has been underscored that national/cultural assumptions, beliefs and customs affect what happens in organizations. For this reason, it is difficult to generalize about creativity in organizations. According to Talbot (1993):

"it depends on whose creativity we mean and in what sort of organization and in which society." *(p. 187)*

This section focuses on some organizational factors that facilitate creativity and others that obstruct its expression.

A. INTRODUCTION

Facilitating Factors

The work environment conditions that have a positive impact on creativity have been discussed extensively by numerous scholars, such as Amabile (1996b, 1999; Amabile & Mueller, 2008; Amabile & Sensabaugh, 1989), Alencar (1996a), Van Gundy (1987), West and Farr (1990), Zou and Shalley (2008), among many others. They remind us that creativity, like a delicate flower, needs an ideal atmosphere to flourish (Norins, 1990). Numerous choreographies with features that characterize this atmosphere are presented in the literature, some having a few variables and others being very complex, encompassing a wide repertoire of factors that impact employees' creative performance. Although numerous variables may impact creative behavior in organizations, elements of the organizational culture and climate are among the most discussed, due to their crucial influence on creativity in the work environment. These two constructs are closely related, and both have been used to describe the organizational context that influences individuals' behavior in the workplace. They are often treated as if they were synonymous, but differences exist among them. The most critical is the greater level of abstraction at which the culture operates when compared to climate (Tesluk, Farr & Klein, 1997). Organizational culture comprises the system of beliefs, norms, feelings and values shared by its members, which are translated into actions, especially by those that hold a leadership position. Manifestations of culture might be observed in different organizational factors, such as number of hierarchies; pay levels; informal practices; values and rituals; stories, jokes and jargon; and characteristics of the physical environment (West & Richter, 2008). In discussing organizational culture, Talbot (1993) refers to the shared values (what is important), the shared beliefs (how things work), which interact with the organizational structure and control system, resulting in behavioral norms (the ways things are done in the workplace). Talbot also mentions as elements of the culture the basic assumptions on how organization problems should be solved and artifacts, which are the visible manifestations of the other cultural elements, including observable behaviors of employees, besides structures, systems, procedures, rules and characteristics of the physical environment.

On the other hand, the organizational climate refers to the shared perception of the work environment, including its policies, practices and procedures (Schneider, 1975; Tesluk, Farr & Klein, 1997). The description of the organizational climate as the "observed and recurrent patterns of behaviors, attitudes and feelings that characterize life in the organization" is offered by Isaksen, Lauer, Ekval and Britz (cited by Kwasniewska & Necka, 2004; Runco, 2007). Individuals from different organizational cultures have different experiences related to creativity. The same happens in respect to climate as perceived by employees. In addition, studies have indicated that variables such as gender, role in the organization (e.g. managers and non-managers), age and academic level influence the perception of the climate (Bruno-Faria & Alencar, 1998; Kwasniewska & Necka, 2004).

Organizational culture and the way its leaders express it were considered to be key factors for creativity in the work place by Hitt (1975) and Locke and Kirkpatrick (1995). According to these scholars, creativity needs to be explicitly valued, which requires the leader to share continually with all employees a vision that emphasizes its importance. In addition, a creative culture must be implemented according to this vision, which requires: the selection of creative people; continual training and opportunities to update knowledge and to develop creative skills; the setting of goals to reach creative products; encouragement, discussion and sharing of ideas among team members, teams, and all employees; and recognition and reward of creative ideas and products. Similar ideas are presented by Norins (1990) in describing some characteristics of an ideal environment for creativity: cultivation of a pro creativity culture; provision of incentives and recognition for creative ideas and work; provisions of the best possible tools for interchanging ideas; and the best possible training.

Numerous studies on the characteristics of organizational environments that promote creativity are available in the literature. Among the most widely known are Amabile's (1996b, 1999; Amabile & Mueller, 2008; Amabile & Sensabaugh, 1989) researches. This scholar has been recognized by a long tradition of contributions on creativity in the organizational setting. Amabile and colleagues have identified many features of organizations that promote creativity. They were initially identified through interviews with R & D scientists and were incorporated in a questionnaire—The Work Environment Inventory (Amabile & Griskiewicz, 1989). They refer to:

1. considerable freedom regarding the means available to complete the tasks necessary to reach the goals set,
2. sufficient resources, including facilities and information, as well as time to explore, mature and develop ideas,
3. challenging work, by the accomplishment of tasks that are neither too easy nor have a degree of difficulty perceived as an impediment to success in performing the task, groups/working teams characterized by diversity, with employees that have different reference structures, motivated by the tasks under their responsibility, willing to cooperate and share knowledge, prompt to recognize and incorporate contributions of the other participants,
4. supervisors' encouragement, with recognition of the employees' new ideas, efforts and successes, and
5. recognition and support by the top leaders in the organization.

Facilitating factors for creativity in the organizational environment were identified by Bruno-Faria and Alencar (1996; Alencar & Bruno-Faria, 1997), in a study of Brazilian employees from different modalities of organizations, who were interviewed about the characteristics of an organizational environment that foster creativity and those that inhibit it. Content analysis of the responses indicated the following categories as stimulants to creativity:

1. challenges—challenging tasks or missions that require creative ideas,
2. freedom and autonomy—freedom to decide how to perform tasks, with autonomy to take decisions when necessary,
3. manager's support—openness, flexibility, respect for divergent opinions, and encouragement of new ideas on the part of the manager,
4. organizational structure—limited number of hierarchies, flexible norms, power decentralization,
5. organization support—recognition and support of the creative work in the organization; availability of mechanisms to develop new ideas,

A. INTRODUCTION

6. physical environment—an environment described as agreeable, with adequate illumination, furniture, space, and ventilation,

7. salaries and benefits—adequate remuneration; a policy of benefits and reward system that encourages innovative ideas,

8. technological and material resources—availability of equipment and materials that facilitate the developmental processes of new ideas,

9. training—availability of training to all staff with the purpose of developing their creative potential and facilitating the process of innovation, and

10. work team support—dialogue and reliance among the work group; interpersonal relationships among team members that favor and stimulate new ideas.

Bruno-Faria and Alencar (1996; Alencar & Bruno-Faria, 1997) also requested that the participants should indicate, besides the characteristics of an organizational environment that promote creativity, those features in their work environment that stimulate the expression of creativity. A comparison of responses to the two questions indicated differences among them. Training, salaries and benefits, for example, were not mentioned when the participants referred to their organizations. The organization structure, freedom and autonomy and the physical environment were also much less frequently mentioned in the participants' description of their organizations, compared to their responses on the necessary stimulants for creativity in the workplace. These results suggest that the features recognized as important to creativity blooming were not always perceived to be present in the organizations where the employees actually worked. A work environment with conditions detrimental to creativity was also observed by Alencar (2001b), in a study designed to evaluate the effects of a program for fostering creativity in the workplace. The participants complained about features of their organization taken as not conducive to creativity. The practice of punishing mistakes, which prevailed in the organization, a scarcity of opportunities to express new ideas and the lack of manager's reliance on the employees inhibited creativity. Despite an awareness of the need for creativity and innovation for organizational success, deep rooted tendencies to maintain the status quo prevailed, making it difficult to introduce changes in a direction of promising conditions for creativity.

Van Gundy (1987) also described features of an organizational environment that can play a role in organizational creativity. From a review of research conducted in different work contexts, he identified several factors which facilitate creativity. Some of them converge with those previously pointed out, namely: autonomy, performance reward dependency, risk taking, tolerance of differences, personal commitment, top management support, high responsibility for initiating ideas, job security, and a moderate degree of ambiguity about the job environment.

Several instruments have been designed to assess features of the organizational climate suggested as stimulants or inhibitors to creativity. A recent description of available instruments with their psychometric characteristics is presented by Mathisen and Einarsen (2004). KEYS: Assessing the Climate for Creativity; Creative Climate Questionnaire, Team Climate Inventory, and Siegel Scale of Support for Innovation were analyzed by these scholars, who concluded that only two of them presented acceptable scientific quality and were well documented in peer-reviewed literature. One of the most cited in literature is the Work Environment Inventory, developed by Amabile and Gryskiewicz (1989), which was revised

A. INTRODUCTION

several times and is currently named KEYS. It includes the following stimulant scales: organizational encouragement; supervisory encouragement; work group support; sufficient resources; challenging work; and freedom. This instrument also includes obstacles scales which will be reported in the next section. The Creative Climate Questionnaire measures 10 climate dimensions, nine of them hypothesized as representative of a climate conducive to creativity. The promoting factors were named challenge, freedom, idea support, trust/ openness, dynamism/liveliness, playfulness/humor, debates, risk taking, and idea time. Leadership, ownership, norms for diversity, continuous development, and consistency are the dimensions measured by the Siegel Scale of Support for Innovation, while vision, participative safety, task orientation and support for innovation are the theoretical dimensions of the Team Climate Inventory. Besides describing these instruments and studies conducted with them, Mathisen and Einarsen present a critique of each questionnaire, suggesting the need for more research to reinforce their psychometric qualities, as well as more studies on the relative importance of different work environmental factors.

In Brazil, an inventory named Indicators of Climate for Creativity was developed by Bruno-Faria (in press; Bruno-Faria & Alencar, 1998). This inventory was constructed on the basis of a study of facilitating and inhibiting factors to creativity in the organizational environment (Bruno-Faria & Alencar, 1996) and a review of theory and research on creativity in the organization. The validation study, in a sample of 1,003 employees of a Brazilian state bank, resulted in eight factors with 69 items hypothesized as stimulants to creativity, and in four factors with 38 items hypothesized as obstacles to creativity in the work environment. Each item is answered on a 5-point scale, varying from totally disagree (1) to totally agree (5). The factors that represent stimulants to creativity in the work environment were labeled: adequate physical environment; favorable social climate among work colleagues; incentive to new ideas; freedom of action; challenging activities; adequate salaries and benefits; actions by managers and the organizations in support of new ideas; and availability of material resources. Cronbach's alpha varied from 0.68 to 0.88. Examples of items for each factor are: "I have enough space to keep my work material; the climate among colleagues is characterized by trust and mutual respect; my colleagues encourage me to produce new ideas; I feel at ease to act differently from my colleagues; the tasks I realize in my job require the best of myself; my salary is in agreement with the job I do; my boss encourages the employees to examine new ideas and solutions to the organization's problems. Studies conducted with this inventory indicated that the managers' and organization's actions in support of new ideas were the best predictor of teams' performance (Bruno-Faria, in press). This questionnaire is being revised to eliminate some of its weaknesses and to best adapt it to the current reality of Brazilian organizations.

An analysis of factors that promote creativity in organizations was presented by Runco (2007) based on a meta-analysis conducted by Hunter of 42 previous studies. This analysis resulted in identification of the following dimensions: positive peer-group; supervisor; resources; challenges; mission clarity; autonomy; cohesion; intellectual simulation; top management; rewards; flexibility and risk-taking; product emphasis; participation; and organizational integration. Furthermore, the most important factors indicated by the meta-analysis were those that characterize a positive interpersonal exchange, intellectual stimulants and challenges. Most of these dimensions are measured by the instruments previously pointed out, that have been designed to assess the organizational environment for creativity. Some

A. INTRODUCTION

of them overlap, for example, with the dimensions of the questionnaire labeled Indicators of Climate for Creativity (Bruno-Faria, in press; Bruno-Faria & Alencar, 1998) on elements which are promoters of creativity in the work environment, such as resources and challenges. However, flexibility and risk taking, mission clarity and organizational integration, which are some of the dimensions resulted from the meta-analysis, were not observed by Bruno-Faria and Alencar (1998).

Although the elements previously presented characterize a climate for creativity in the workplace, several variables act as moderators (Runco, 2007; Hunter, Bedell & Mumford, 2007). Runco underscores, for example, that in order to understand the influence of organizational variables on different factors, such as work satisfaction, innovation and creativity, it is essential to take into account the moderators or:

> "variables that determine how strongly a particular dimension will influence organizational and individual behavior." *(p. 165)*

As examples of individual factors that may moderate the impact of the organizational climate, Runco mentions employee job satisfaction, and even his/her mood. In addition, this scholar underscores that in team work, team factors, such as team size, cohesion and personality of its members, may moderate the impact of the organizational climate on creative achievement.

Hunter, Bedell, and Mumford (2007) conducted a meta-analysis of numerous studies, including articles, conference papers, dissertations and manuscripts, on the relationship between climate perception and creative achievement. These authors examined job, group, organization and environmental variables that may moderate the relationship between climate and creativity in organizations. Stronger relationships between climate and creative achievement were observed, for example, when employees were granted the discretion needed to do creative work in contrast to jobs with only moderate levels of discretion allowed; in groups of low and moderate cohesion compared to highly cohesive groups; in organizations with a horizontal structure in opposition to those with a vertical structure; and when the market required the development of an innovative product, in conditions of high turbulence, competitive and high production pressure as opposed to conditions of little requirement for innovative products by the market, of medium or low turbulence, and of medium or low production pressure.

Characteristics of organizations outstanding for their innovative capacity and the strategies implemented by them to nurture creativity in the workplace were described by Ferraz (2002) and Blecher (2005). Ideo, Apple, Google and Brazilian companies, for example Natura, Nutrimental, Embraco and Embraer, were some of the companies analyzed. Although differences were observed among them in relation to several characteristics previously pointed out, which promote creativity in the organizations, the following common features were reported: a culture that supports creativity; mobilization of teams from different areas to generate ideas that may generate innovations; cultivation of an atmosphere of freedom, where a feeling of safety to express and test ideas prevailed; as well as the practice of evaluating results and rewarding the team members who were responsible for successful projects. Other common features were the understanding of the market and the consumer, and the practice of "overthrowing walls", which means extending the processes for the

A. INTRODUCTION

development of new products to suppliers as well. Some differentiated practices of each of the companies analyzed were also underscored. Natura, for example, a company specializing in beauty products, maintains a net of approximately 500,000 female consultants, which generate 200,000 contacts each month. Half of these contacts feed the R & D division with suggestions that may result in product improvement or new products. On the other hand, Google's engineers have free time one day a week to develop their own products, even those which are not related to the organization's mission (Blecher, 2005).

Leadership

Among the numerous variables that impact creativity in the organizational setting, leadership has been taken as one of the most critical. This variable will be briefly discussed here. As a starting point, it might be underscored that, although leaders may be managers, supervisors or other figures with formal or informal positions in the organization, leadership and management are not always found together. Along these lines, Cyert (1988) states that it is even possible for an organization to be well managed and not well led. Leaders' influence on the characteristics of an organization, such as culture and reward systems, the leaders' impact on the behavior of their employees' creativity and motivation, the influence of leadership styles on creativity in the workplace, have all been discussed (Amabile, Schatzel, Moneta & Kramer, 2004; Cyert, 1988; Ford, 1995; Gumusluoglu & Ilsev, 2009; King, 1990; Runco, 2007; Tierney, 2008).

A more detailed analysis of leadership for creativity is offered by Tierney (2008), who pointed out this is a complex behavioral and multidimensional phenomenon. To explain the numerous ways in which a leader may contribute to foment creative action, Tierney proposed a matrix that incorporates different levels of leadership (individual, dyad, group and organization), three facets of the leader (traits, behaviors and relations) and three spheres of possible influence in those under his/her leadership (cognition, motivation and capacity).

In respect to the leader's characteristics based on an extensive literature review, Tierney (2008) points out some traits, such as emotional intelligence, intuition and sensibility regarding the diversity of cognitive and problem solving styles of subordinates; the leader's ability to apprehend the environment, to identify problems and possible consequences of different solutions proposed by subordinates; besides an innovative cognitive style and motivation to lead others towards creative performance. Regarding behaviors, the socio-emotional and instrumental support, the expression of consideration, empathy and encouragement are some leader's behaviors that relate to the employees' creative expression. With respect to relationships, it is acknowledged that leadership is a phenomenon that exists between the leader and the employees. This explains the importance of the quality of the relationship, which must be characterized by support and receptivity towards new ideas, enabling the employees to be flexible, take risks and express exploratory behaviors in their activities.

In addition, Tierney (2008) considers that leaders with certain profiles are more effective with certain types of subordinates in the process of fomenting the creative performance, adopting an interactionist perspective that calls attention to the reciprocal influence between the leader and subordinates. Furthermore, due to the presence of different leaders at several levels of the organization, the fomentation of creativity in the work environment requires that all individuals who occupy a leadership position, independent of the organization hierarchical structure level, be aligned in respect to their value and support of creativity. In support of this position, Tierney points out, for instance, that leaders in lower levels do not operate in isolation. Their capacity and motivation for fostering creativity among their subordinates are greatly determined by the higher leaders within the organization, who model and imprint elements of the cultural, structural and organizational process. However, it may also happen that, despite the creative vision of the senior management, who value and reward creativity and innovation, other people in leadership positions do not share these same values, generating a situation that is deleterious to the growth of creativity (Cyert, 1988).

Empirical evidence on the importance of perceived leader's support for employees' creativity was offered by Amabile, Schatzel, Moneta, and Kramer (2004) in a study that explored the employees' perceptual and affective reactions to the leader's behavior. These behaviors were categorized as positive (such as rewarding or giving recognition, or mentoring), negative (such as giving information in an inappropriate way), or neutral/unknown, in cases when it was not possible to determine if the leader's behaviors were positive or negative. The results obtained in this study suggested that the leader's behaviors influence the reactions of subordinates, which in turn, influence that subordinate's creative performance. Furthermore, the results also revealed that the leader's behaviors influence not only the subordinates' perceptions of the leader, but also the subordinates' perceptions of themselves, in particular their competence and the value of their work.

Moderating variables which affect the relationship between leadership and innovation have been discussed in literature. This issue was examined by Gumusluoglu and Ilsev (2009) in a study on the impact of transformational leaders, defined as those:

> "who transform followers' personal values and self-concepts, move them to higher levels of needs and aspirations and raise the performance expectations of their followers." *(p. 265)*

in terms of innovation, considered as:

> "the creation of valuable and useful new products/services within an organizational context." *(p. 266)*

The participants were employees and their leaders in micro and small-sized Turkish software development companies. A positive influence of transformational leadership on organizational innovation was observed. However, the relationship between these two variables was stronger when there were high levels of external support (technical and financial assistance). On the other hand, the moderating effect of internal support for innovation, in terms of an innovation-supporting climate and adequate resources was not significant, contrary to what was hypothesized by the researchers. These researchers went further, underscoring the importance of transformational leadership to organizational innovation. For this reason, as practical implications of their study, Gumusluoglu and Ilsev suggest that leaders should incorporate behaviors that characterize this style of leadership, such as taking into account the employees' needs, aspirations, and skills; inspiring and motivating employees towards an exciting vision; and stimulating them intellectually.

To conclude this section, it might be highlighted that much progress has been made in mapping out the wide range of features that positively impact creativity in the organizational environment. Numerous scholars have suggested ways to infuse the organizational environment with elements conducive to creativity, such as the ones previously pointed out.

A. INTRODUCTION

To have a more complete picture of the complex choreography of creativity in the organizational setting, it is also necessary to spot the potential inhibitors of creativity in this environment. This topic will be addressed below.

Inhibiting Factors to Creativity in the Organizational Setting

The numerous obstacles that may hinder the expression of the individual's creativity have been largely discussed in creativity literature. These obstacles have been classified in many ways by different authors, who have pointed out characteristics of the person, and others of the environment, which may inhibit expression of creativity. Shallcross (1981), for example, categorized the barriers to utilizing creative potential into historical, biological, physiological, social, and psychological types. Jones (1993) distinguishes strategic, values, perceptual and self-image barriers. Adams (1986) identified a list of blocks, including perceptual, emotional, cultural, environmental, intellectual, and expressive blocks. Parnes (1967) discriminated between internal and external factors that stifle creative thinking, and Alencar (2001c) identified obstacles to personal creativity, through the use of the Obstacles to Personal Creativity Inventory (Alencar, 1999). This instrument includes 66 items, which are answered on a 5-point scale, varying from totally disagree to totally agree. Examples of the items are:

I would be more creative if …

1. I were not afraid to express what I think,
2. I had more time to elaborate my ideas,
3. I had more opportunities to put my ideas into practice,
4. there was more recognition of creative work,
5. I had more opportunities to make mistakes without being criticized,
6. I had more enthusiasm, and
7. I concentrated more on the tasks I am doing.

The instrument validation study resulted in four factors that may most likely block the expression of personal creativity, named Inhibition/Shyness; Lack of Time/Opportunity; Social Repression; and Lack of Motivation. Studies conducted with this instrument in samples of Brazilian and Mexican university students and elementary, high school and higher education teachers indicated that Lack of Time/Opportunity was the most frequent cluster of obstacles among the participants of different studies (Alencar, 2001c; Alencar & Fleith, 2003b; Alencar, Fleith, & Martínez, 2003; Castro, 2007; Joly & Guerra, 2004). The items included in this factor refer to conditions external to the individual, including elements from the environment perceived as impediments for a more complete expression of the individual's creativity.

More specific to the organizational environment, the identification of potential inhibitors to creativity has been a focus of increasing attention. A description of these factors was offered by Bruno-Faria and Alencar (1996; Alencar & Bruno-Faria, 1997) from data collected from Brazilian employees from different organizations, who were interviewed on the most prevalent obstacles to creativity in any organizational environment, as well as in their own work environment. The most frequent obstacles pointed out were the organization structure, which was described as rigid, bureaucratic, with excessive hierarchies and centralized power; managers, characterized by not being receptive to the individuals' new ideas and products; organizational culture, taken as averse to risk taking, with rejection of new ideas, reinforcement of the fear of making mistakes and the fear of changes; and personal relationships in the work place characterized by lack of dialogue and group activities, lack of reliance among the staff and frequent conflicts. In describing the obstacles to creativity in the organization where these employees worked, high volume of tasks with intense time pressure, as well as frequent political changes, resulting in alterations in the norms and redirection of the organizational goals were also described. Some of these elements were similar to those reported by Brazilian engineers, who were questioned about facilitating and inhibiting factors to the expression of their creative capacity. When asked to indicate the factors that block their personal creativity, elements of the work environment, such a rigid structure, excessive pressure, bureaucracy, as well as authoritarian and centralized managers were pointed out, followed by personal characteristics, such as fear of being criticized, insecurity and lack of flexibility (Alencar & Fleith, 2004).

Other scholars who have addressed potential inhibiting factors to creativity in the organizational environment are Amabile (1999; Amabile & Mueller, 2008; Hill & Amabile, 1993), Blecher (2005), Talbot (1993) and Van Gundy (1997). Amabile has identified several factors that might inhibit creativity in the workplace, including: a conservative, low risk attitude among top management; lack of autonomy on how to do the job tasks or reach a certain goal; an inappropriate evaluation system without feedback on the tasks done and unrealistic expectations; insufficient resources, both in terms of equipment as well as people; time pressure, having too much to do in too little time; excessive emphasis on the status quo, with reluctance of managers and employees to changing the way of doing tasks and an unwillingness to take risks; competition between teams and employees, which encourages a defensive attitude; poor project management, with the presence of managers who are unable to establish clear goals; and an inadequate communication system.

Bureaucracy, risk aversion, internal disputes, lack of resources and deficient communication were the main blocks to creativity identified by Blecher (2005), who interviewed 15 innovation consultants on the enemies to creativity in organizations. On the other hand, Talbot (1993) reported that, according to engineers and scientists who participated in creativity courses conducted by him, characteristics of the boss, the colleagues and the systems were taken as creativity inhibitors in the workplace. The boss's indecision, his or her dislike for novelty, attitudes of taking credit for the ideas of employees, and playing people off against each other were some of the behaviors which were found to stifle creativity. Colleagues who do not collaborate, with no team spirit and an oppressive organizational climate, a highly centralized organizational structure and excessive formalization of rules, policies, relationships, and procedures were some other inhibitors that were pointed out.

Talbot also discussed the self as an inhibitor, identifying the course participant's own creativity-inhibiting actions in the workplace, which may stifle creativity, and that should be modified in order to help the implementation of a more promising work climate. Several of the previous inhibitors are also discussed by Van Gundy in his categorization of barriers to innovation, which included structural barriers, such as stratification, formalization and centralization; social/political barriers as, for example, norms that reinforce conformity; procedural barriers, which refer to policies, procedures, and regulations that may inhibit creativity/innovation; resource barriers, including people, time, financial supplies and

A. INTRODUCTION

information; and individual/attitudinal barriers, which refer to employees' characteristics, such as fear of risks, intolerance of uncertainty and a non cooperative attitude.

In creativity programs conducted by Alencar (1996a) in several Brazilian state companies, the inhibitors to creativity in the organizations as perceived by participants of the program was addressed as a topic. In response to the request to identify such inhibitors, the participants indicated the most frequent factors that stifle creativity to be:

1. intransigency and authoritarian attitudes, with the predominance of an unaccepting climate towards opinions different from those pre-established,
2. protectionism and paternalism, with the presence and/or people who work together to defend restrict interests, indifferent to the organization's interest as a whole,
3. lack of integration between sectors and divisions; with no common goals, excessive individualism, and lack of cooperation and team spirit,
4. lack of support to put into practice new ideas; negligence or mistrust towards new ideas, and
5. lack of encouragement of employees, who are discouraged by an oppressive climate and lack of recognition on individual efforts and production.

Inhibitors to creativity in the organizational setting may also be identified through scales included in instruments designed to measure work environment conducive to creativity. In its earlier edition, the Work Environment Inventory (Amabile & Gryskiewicz, 1989) included four scales on environment obstacles to creativity, named time pressure, evaluation, status quo and political problems. Some years later, these four scales were reduced to only two, named organizational impediments and workload pressure. The first scale comprises items on political problems, harsh criticism of new ideas, destructive internal competition, avoidance of risk, and overemphasis on the status quo. The second scale included items related to extreme time pressures, unrealistic expectations for productivity, and distractions from creative work (Amabile, Gryskiewicz, Burnside, & Koester, 1990).

Another instrument described in the literature is the Barriers for Creativity in the Workplace Questionnaire (Kwasniewska & Necka, 2004). This is a 60-item instrument, representing ten categories of work barriers. However, four factors were obtained in its validation study. Two of them reflect clearly impediments to creativity in the organizational environment, namely: bureaucratic climate, with items representing lack of encouragement, inflexibility, and negative attitude towards individual initiative; and excessive control, with items referring to a feeling of being excessively controlled by superiors, regulations, and habitual practices of the company. The two other factors were good communication and resources. They represent incentives to creativity in the organizational setting.

Indicators of Climate for Creativity Questionnaire (Bruno-Faria, in press; Bruno-Faria & Alencar, 1998) focuses on factors in the work environment that may be impediments to creativity in the work environment, besides those previously described as facilitating factors. The four impeding factors were: an excessive number of tasks and scarcity of time; blockage to new ideas; resistance to risk taking, and organizational problems. Examples of items of each of these factors are: the excessive number of tasks impedes me from having time to reflect about the best way of accomplishing them; my supervisor blocks my initiative at work; the managers do not risk new alternatives in doing the work; the approval of several hierarchical levels is necessary to implementation of a new idea.

A. INTRODUCTION

The identification of obstacles to creativity in the organizational environment, as those previously outlined, contributes to the process of fostering creativity in the workplace. The instruments described in this section may help to attain this goal. According to Cuatrecasas (1995):

> "discussions should be focused less on 'what can we do to promote creativity' and more on how we can remove those barriers that suppress the creative drive." *(p. 205),*

highlighting the importance of actions to eliminate the barriers that stifle the creative drive, which are common in many organizations. This would help in designing a promising organizational environment to creativity.

CONCLUDING REMARKS

Creativity in the organization is the result of a highly complex realm of factors. In this chapter, the central focus has been individual characteristics and organizational features, which interact amongst themselves in a dynamic and complex way in the process of promoting creativity. The report presented in this chapter does not cover all the configuration facets implied in creativity in the organizational setting. Various topics related to facilitating and inhibiting factors in the organizational environment did not receive the attention they deserve, and only a reduced number of individual and contextual variables were discussed. In addition, facilitators and inhibitors were treated as constant across domains, which is not true. The numerous components that converge for creativity to take place in a specific domain are not necessarily the same in another domain. Furthermore, several variables of outstanding importance were treated superficially.

A review of literature indicates that much progress has occurred, especially in the last two decades, in mapping out the distinct features that shape an organizational environment conducive to creativity. Personal characteristics, contextual conditions and the multiple interactions among personal and contextual features that contribute to creativity flourishing in the work environment were the focus of numerous studies. In spite of this, we are still at an early stage of understanding the extent that different variables relating to individuals, groups/teams and organizations impact creativity. Much more research is needed to fill the gaps in respect to facilitators and inhibitors to creativity in organizations. With regard to personal factors, for example, there are several other creativity-relevant characteristics not discussed in this chapter that deserve more attention in future work; mood states, self-efficacy, individuals' self-concept in relation to creative performance, abilities related with emotional intelligence are some of these. Similarly, more studies are needed with respect to the extent that organizational context variables, such as job complexity, co-workers characteristics, time deadlines, and physical work environment affect individual creative performance. The dynamic interactions among different contextual variables as well as among various personal characteristics that influence creative achievement also need more work.

A scarcity of reliable instruments to measure facilitators and inhibitors to organizational creativity is a factor that delays the development of research on this topic. Instruments of scientific quality for identifying possible barriers to creativity in organizations are still scarce, when compared to measuring facilitators. However, even in respect to creativity facilitators in organizations, there are not many reliable instruments available in the literature, as noted previously by Mathisen and Einarsen (2004). Thus, more research is needed on measurement instruments that might be used to identify facilitators and inhibitors to creativity in the workplace. The need of creativity measures is even greater in countries with a low tradition of studies on organizational creativity, as is the case for Brazil and other countries in South America. In addition, the instruments available in English or other languages need adaptation and validation before their use with employees from other countries, with varying values and cultural practices. This is a factor that needs to be taken into account by scholars in different part, of the world who are interested in identifying factors that influence organizational creativity through instruments available in the US or European literature.

The cross-cultural literature on organizational creativity is very limited. Cultural elements from different countries that promote or stifle creativity is a topic little investigated. Cross-cultural studies are necessary to reveal possible differences among different cultures in respect to creativity facilitators and inhibitors in the work setting. It is possible that a facilitator in a country may be considered as an inhibitor by employees from another country and vice-versa. But, even within a country, huge differences may be observed between the cultures prevailing in diverse regions, affecting individual characteristics and social contexts relevant to the blooming of creativity. Thus, as previously highlighted by Leung, Au and Leung (2004), it is important to evaluate the degree of generalizability of findings obtained in one society to another.

An examiantion of the literature reveals that most studies on creativity facilitators and inhibitors have adopted a quantitative approach or qualitative methods. More studies are needed that combine the two methodological approaches, getting data, for example, through inventories as well as through interview and observation. Moreover, most of the studies conducted on creativity facilitators and inhibitors have adopted a cross-sectional design. Longitudinal research design should also be adopted in future studies to identify changes or continuity of the multiples context variables that impact creativity in the organizational setting.

One issue that deserves further discussion is the optimum strategy to nurture organizational creativity: Should intentional effort to remove inhibitors occur before embracing creativity facilitating practices? Is the removal of identified barriers enough for creativity to take place in the organizational setting? Does the lack of a facilitator mean the presence of an inhibitor? Should facilitating practices be adopted in the work place without taking into account possible creativity inhibitors? It is our point of view that the identification and removal of barriers are as important as the introduction or maintenance of creativity facilitating factors. Thus, both should occur simultaneously.

It is also necessary to be aware that there are inhibitors, such as a high degree of bureaucracy and political problems, very common in public organizations from Brazil and other countries of the world, which are very difficult to remove. Much effort is required to decrease their intensity in order to prevent them impeding the flourishing of creativity in the work place. A huge challenge in many cases!

It is noteworthy that the search for individuals with characteristics associated with creativity in the job market has been a tonic in many organizations in different parts of the world. However, several authors, like Cropley (2005) and Gilson (2008), underscored the scarcity of professionals who stand out for their creativity. Cropley, for instance, presents data collected in Australia revealing that universities are not providing the necessary training for the preparation of creative professionals, characterized by the domain of efficient strategies to approach the new, to deal with the unknown, to face the everyday heterogeneous situations and to solve unexpected problems. It is reported that 75% of all newly graduated employees were pointed out by the companies that admitted them as being "deficient" in creativity, problem solving and critical and independent thinking. Also Gilson (2008) refers to an article published in one of the most well known newspapers from England—The Economist—in which it is reported that:

> "the main challenge faced by organizations nowadays is not to find or employ workers willing to earn low wages, but to hire individuals with high intellectual capacity and especially, with the ability to think creatively". *(p. 304)*

To inject creativity into organizations, however, it is not enough to ensure that professionals with the ability to think creatively are hired, as highlighted previously in this chapter. Creativity will thrive only with the intentional and determined efforts of the organizational actors in respect to receptivity, recognition and support to new ideas, besides the necessary conditions to their implementation. As it might be concluded from an analysis of the literature, the construction of a work environment that promotes creativity is an extremely complex and challenging task. However, the benefits of fostering creativity in the workplace for the individuals, organizations and society are unquestionable. It is hoped that the content presented here contributes to the discussion on how to foster creativity in the workplace. It is also hoped that it inspires those interested in investigating some of the elements of the choreography underlying the construction of a promising creativity environment.

References

Adams, J. L. (1986). *Conceptual blockbusting: A pleasurable guide to better problem solving*. New York, NY: Norton.

Alencar, E. M. L. S. (1996a). *A gerência da criatividade [Managing creativity]*. São Paulo, Brazil: Pearson/Makron Books.

Alencar, E. M. L. S. (1996b). A medida da criatividade [The measure of creativity]. In L. Pasquali (Ed.), *Teoria e método de medida em ciências do comportamento [Measurement theory and method in the behavioral sciences]* (pp. 305–316). Brasília, Brazil: INEP.

Alencar, E. M. L. S. (1998a). Promovendo um ambiente favorável à criatividade nas organizações [Promoting a favorable enviromment for creativity in organizations]. *Revista de Administração de Empresas [Journal of Organizations Administration]*, 38, 18–25.

Alencar, E. M. L. S. (1998b). Personality traits of Brazilian creative scientists. *Gifted and Talented International, 13*, 14–18.

Alencar, E. M. L. S. (2001a). Pesquisadores que se destacam por sua produção criativa: hábitos de trabalho, escolha profissional, processo de criação e aspirações [Outstanding creative researchers: Work habits, professional choice, creative process, and aspirations]. In E. M. L. S. Alencar (Ed.), *Criatividade e educação de superdotados [Creativity and gifted education]* (pp. 76–98). Petrópolis, Brazil: Vozes.

Alencar, E. M. L. S. (2001b). Fostering creativity in the work environment: a Brazilian program. In M. I. Stein (Ed.), *Creativity's global correspondents—2001* (pp. 19–28). Delfay Beach, FL: Winslow Press.

Alencar, E. M. L. S. (2001c). Obstacles to personal creativity among university students. *Gifted Education International, 15*, 133–140.

Alencar, E. M. L. S. (2006). El proceso creativo: Mecanismos subyacentes [The creative process: Underlying mechanisms]. In S. Torre & V. Violant (Eds.), *Comprender y evaluar la creatividad [Understanding and evaluating creativity]* (pp. 191–196). Málaga, Spain: Ediciones Algibe.

Alencar, E. M. L. S. (2007). O papel da escola no desenvolvimento do talento criativo [The role of school in the development of creative talent]. In D. S. Fleith & E. M. L. S. (Eds.), *Desenvolvimento de talentos e altas habilidades [Development of talent and high ability]* (pp. 151–162). Porto Alegre, Brazil: ArtMed.

Alencar, E. M. L. S. (2009). O papel da expertise na produção criativa: contribuições teóricas e empíricas [The role of expertise on the creative production: Theoretical and empirical contributions]. *Revista de Psicologia, 28,* 13–27.

Alencar, E. M. L. S., & Bruno-Faria, M. F. (1997). Characteristics of an organizational environment which stimulate and inhibit creativity. *The Journal of Creative Behavior, 31,* 271–281.

Alencar, E. M. L. S., & Bruno-Faria, M. F. (2007). Criatividade nas organizações [Creativity in organizations]. In SESI (Ed.), *Criatividade [Creativity]* (pp. 31–49). Brasília, Brazil: SESI.

Alencar, E. M. L. S., & Fleith, D. S. (2003). *Criatividade. Múltiplas perspectivas [Creativity. Multiple perspectives].* Brasília, Brazil: Editora da UnB.

Alencar, E. M. L. S., & Fleith, D. S. (2003). Barreiras à criatividade pessoal entre professores de distintos níveis de ensino [Obstacles to personal creativity among teachers from different educational levels]. *Psicologia: Reflexão e Crítica [Psychology: Reflection and Criticism], 16,* 63–69.

Alencar, E. M. L. S., & Fleith, D. S. (2004). Fatores facilitadores e inibidores à expressão da capacidade de criar segundo estudantes de engenharia e engenheiros [Facilitating and inhibiting factors to the creative capacity according to engineering students and engineers]. *Boletim da Academia Paulista de Psicologia [Paulista Academy of Psychology Bulletin], 24,* 33–41.

Alencar, E. M. L. S., & Fleith, D. S. (in press). A questão da medida em criatividade [The question of measuring creativity]. In L. Pasquali (Ed.), *Teoria e método de medida em ciências do comportamento [Measurement theory and method in the behavioral sciences]* (2nd ed.). Porto Alegre, Brazil: ArtMed.

Alencar, E. M. L. S., Fleith, D. S., & Martínez, A. M. (2003). Obstacles to creativity among Brazilian and Mexican university students: a comparative study. *The Journal of Creative Behavior, 37,* 179–192.

Alencar, E. M. L. S., & Galvão, A. (2007). Condições favoráveis à criação nas ciências e nas artes [Favorable conditions to creativity in sciences and in arts]. In A. M. R. Virgolim (Ed.), *Talento criativo. Expressão em múltiplos contextos [The creative talent. Expression in multiple contexts]* (pp. 103–120). Brasília, Brazil: Editora UnB.

Alvarado, L. D. (2006). Las organizaciones creativas como seres vivos [The creative organizations as living beings]. In S. Torre & V. Violant (Eds.), *Comprender y evaluar la creatividad [Understanding and evaluating creativity]* (pp. 375–382). Málaga, Spain: Ediciones Algibe.

Amabile, T. A. (1983). *The social psychology of creativity.* New York, NY: Springer-Verlag.

Amabile, T. A. (1996a). *Creativity in context.* Boulder, CO: Westview Press.

Amabile, T. A. (1996b). The motivation for creativity in organizations. *Harvard Business School,* January, 1–15.

Amabile, T. A. (1999). Como não matar a criatividade [How not to kill creativity]. *HSM Management, 12,* 110–116.

Amabile, T. A. (2001). Beyond talent: John Irving and the passionate craft of creativity. *American Psychologist, 56,* 333–336.

Amabile, T. A., & Gryskiewicz, N. D. (1989). The Creative Environment Scales: Work Environment Inventory. *Creativity Research Journal, 2,* 231–253.

Amabile, T. A., Gryskiewicz, N. D., Burnside, R., & Koester, N. (1990). Creative Environment Scales: Work Environment Inventory. A guide to its development and use. Center for Creative Leadership.

Amabile, T. A., & Mueller, J. S. (2008). Studying creativity, its processes, and its antecedents: An exploration of the componential theory of creativity. In J. Zhou & C. E. Shalley (Eds.), *Handbook of organizational creativity* (pp. 33–64). New York, NY: Lawrence Erlbaum.

Amabile, T. A., Schatzel, E. A., Moneta, G. B., & Kramer, S. J. (2004). Leader behaviors and the work environment for creativity: Perceived leader support. *The Leadership Quarterly, 15,* 5–32.

Amabile, T. A., & Sensabaugh, S. J. (1989). Public and private creativity. In B. G. Whiting & G. T. Salomon (Eds.), *Key issues in creativity, innovation & entrepreneurship* (pp. 101–110). Buffalo, NY: Bearly.

Amabile, T. A., & Tighe, E. (1993). Questions of creativity. In J. Brockman (Ed.), *Creativity* (pp. 7–27). New York, NY: Touchstone.

Baer, M., Oldham, G., Jacobsohn, G. C., & Hollingshead, A. B. (2008). The personality composition of teams and creativity: The moderating role of team confidence. *The Journal of Creative Behavior, 42,* 255–282.

Barron, F. (1969). *Creative person and creative process.* New York, NY: Holt, Rinehart & Winston.

Blecher, N. (2005). Idéias que viram dinheiro [Ideas that generate money]. *Exame [Exam], 39,* 22–28.

A. INTRODUCTION

Bruno-Faria, M. F. (2003). Criatividade, inovação e mudança organizacional [Creativity, innovation and organizational change]. In S. M. F. Lima (Ed.), *Mudança organizacional: Teoria e gestão [Organizational change: Theory and management]* (pp. 111–141). São Paulo, Brazil: Atlas.

Bruno-Faria, M. F. (in press). Instrumento de clima para criatividade no ambiente de trabalho [An instrument of climate for creativity in the work environment]. In E. M. L. S. Alencar, M. F. Bruno-Faria, & D. S. Fleith (Eds.), *Medidas de criatividade: Teoria e prática [Measurements of creativity: Theory and practice]*. Porto Alegre, Brazil: ArtMed.

Bruno-Faria, M. F., & Alencar, E. M. L. S. (1996). Estímulos e barreiras à criatividade no ambiente de trabalho [Stimulants and blockages to creativity in the workplace]. *Revista de Administração [Journal of Administration]*, *31*, 50–61.

Bruno-Faria, M. F., & Alencar, E. M. L. S. (1998). Indicadores de clima para a criatividade: Um instrumento de medida da percepção de estímulos e barreiras à criatividade no ambiente de trabalho [Indicators of climate for creativity: a measurement instrument of incentives and obstacles to creativity in the work environment]. *Revista de Administração [Journal of Administration]*, *33*, 86–91.

Castro, J. S. R. (2007). *Criatividade escolar: Relação entre tempo de experiência docente e tipo de escola [Creativity in schools: Relationship between teaching experience and type of school]*. Brasília, Brazil: University of Brasília. Unpublished Master Thesis.

Collins, M. A., & Amabile, T. M. (1999). Motivation and creativity. In R. J. Sternberg (Ed.), *Handbook of creativity* (pp. 297–312). New York, NY: Cambridge University Press.

Cropley, A. J. (2005). *Creativity in education and learning*. London, UK: Routledge.

Cropley, A. J. (2006). In praise of convergent thinking. *Creativity Research Journal*, *18*, 391–404.

Csikszentmihályi, M. (1988). Society, culture, and person: A systems view of creativity. In R. J. Sternberg (Ed.), *The nature of creativity* (pp. 325–329). New York, NY: Cambridge University Press.

Csikszentmihályi, M. (1994). The domain of creativity. In D. H. Feldman, M. Csikszentmihályi & H. Gardner (Eds.), *Changing the world. A framework for the study of creativity* (pp. 135–157). Westport, CT: Praeger.

Csikszentmihályi, M. (1996). *Creativity*. New York: HarperCollins.

Csikszentmihályi, M. (1997). Happiness and creativity. *Futurist*, *31*, S8–S12.

Csikszentmihályi, M. (1999). Implications of a systems view of creativity. In R. J. Sternberg (Ed.), *Handbook of creativity* (pp. 313–335). New York, NY: Cambridge University Press.

Csikszentmihályi, M., & Sawyer, K. (1995). Shifting the focus from individual to organizational creativity. In C. M. Ford & D. A. Gioia (Eds.), *Creative action in organizations. Ivory tower visions & real world voices* (pp. 167–172). Thousand Oaks, CA: Sage.

Cuatrecasas, P. (1995). Corporate America creativity held hostage. In C. M. Ford & D. A. Gioia (Eds.), *Creative actions in organizations. Ivory tower visions and real world voices* (pp. 201–205). Thousand Oaks: Sage.

Cyert, R. M. (1988). Designing a creative organization. In R. L. Kuhn (Ed.), *Handbook for creative and innovative managers* (pp. 185–195). New York, NY: McGraw-Hill.

Dewett, T. (2006). Exploring the role of risk in employee creativity. *The Journal of Creative Behavior*, *40*, 27–45.

Drabkin, S. (1996). Enhancing creativity when solving contradictory technical problems. *Journal of Professional Issues in Engineering Education and Practice*, *4*, 78–82.

Ericsson, K. A. (1999). Creative expertise as superior reproducible performance: Innovative and flexible aspects of expert performance. *Psychological Inquiry*, *10*, 329–333.

Ferraz, E. (2002). O que faz com que algumas empresas sejam brilhantes na arte de inovar [What characterizes outstanding companies in the innovation art]. *Exame [Exam]*, *36*, 47–61.

Ford, C. M. (1995). Creativity is a mystery. Clues from the investigators' notebooks. In C. M. Ford & D. A. Gioia (Eds.), *Creative actions in organizations. Ivory tower visions and real world voices* (pp. 12–49). Thousand Oaks, CA: Sage.

Galvão, A. (2000). *Practice in orchestral life: An exploratory study of string players' learning processes*. Reading, UK: Reading University. Unpublished Doctoral Dissertation.

Galvão, A. (2001). Pesquisa sobre expertise: Perspectivas e limitações [Research on expertise: Perspectives and limitations]. *Temas em Psicologia [Themes in Psychology]*, *9*, 223–238.

Gilson, L. L. (2008). Why be creative: a review of the practical outcomes associated with creativity at the individual, group, and organizational levels. In J. Zhou & C. E. Shalley (Eds.), *Handbook of organizational creativity* (pp. 303–322). New York, NY: Lawrence Erlbaum.

Gomes, J. F. S., & Almeida, R. (2009). *Os vectores da criatividade no século XXI. [The creativity vectors in XXI century]*. Lisbon, Portugal: Instituto Superior de Ciências do Trabalho e da Empresa.

A. INTRODUCTION

Guilford, J. P. (1950). Creativity. *American Psychologist*, 5, 444–454.

Guilford, J. P. (1967). *The nature of human intelligence*. New York, NY: McGraw-Hill.

Gumusluoglu, L., & Ilsev, A. (2009). Transformational leadership and organizational innovation: The roles of internal and external support for innovation. *The Journal of Product Innovation Management*, 26, 264–277.

Hill, K. G., & Amabile, T. M. (1993). A social psychology perspective in creativity: Intrinsic motivation and creativity in the classroom and workplace. In S. G. Isaksen, M. C. Murdock, R. O. Firestien & D. J. Treffinger (Eds.), *Understanding and recognizing ceativity. The emergence of a discipline* (pp. 400–432). Norwood, NJ: Ablex.

Hitt, M. A. (1975). The creative organization: Tomorrow's survivor. *The Journal of Creative Behavior*, 9, 263–290.

Hunter, S. T., Bedell, K. E., & Mumford, M. D. (2007). Climate for creativity: a quantitative review. *Creativity Research Journal*, 19, 69–90.

Joly, M. C. R., & Guerra, P. B. C. (2004). Compreensão em leitura e barreiras à criatividade: um estudo com universitários ingressantes [Reading comprehension and obstacles to creativity: a study with university students]. *Psico*, 35, 151–159.

Jones, L. (1993). Barriers to creativity and their relationship to individual, group, and organizational behavior. In S. G. Isaksen, M. C. Murdock, R. L. Firestein & D. J. Treffinger (Eds.), *Nurturing and developing creativity. The emergence of a discipline* (pp. 133–154). Norwood, NJ: Ablex.

Kim, K. H. (2007). Exploring the interactions between Asian culture (Confusionism) and creativity. *The Journal of Creative Behavior*, 41, 28–53.

King, N. (1990). Innovation at work: the research literature. In M. A. West & J. L Farr (Eds.), *Innovation ad creativity at work. Psychological and organizational strategies* (pp. 15–59). New York, NY: Wiley.

Kirton, M. J. (1987). Adaptors and innovators: Cognitive style and personality. In S. G. Isaksen (Ed.), *Frontiers of creativity research* (pp. 282–304). Buffalo, NY: Bearly.

Kwasniewska, J., & Necka, E. (2004). Perception of the climate for creativity in the workplace: the role of the level in the organization and gender. *Creativity and Innovation Management*, 13, 187–196.

Leung, K., Au, A., & Leung, B. W. C. (2004). Creativity and innovation: East–West comparison with an emphasis on Chinese societies. In S. Lau, A. N. N. Hui & G. Y. C. Ng (Eds.), *Creativity. When East meet West* (pp. 113–136). Singapore: World Scientific.

Lewis, G. (1999). Motivation for productive creativity. In A. S. Fishkin, B. Cramond & P. Olszewski-Kubilius (Eds.), *Investigating creativity in youth* (pp. 179–202). Dreskills, NJ: Hampton Press.

Locke, E. A., & Kirkpatrick, S. A. (1995). Promoting creativity in organizations. In C. M. Ford & A. Gioia (Eds.), *Creative action in organizations* (pp. 115–120). London, UK: Sage.

Lubart, T. I. (1999). Creativity across cultures. In R. J. Sternberg (Ed.), *Handbook of creativity* (pp. 339–350). New York, NY: Cambridge University Press.

Lubart, T. I., & Sternberg, R. J. (1995). An investment approach to creativity: Theory and data. In S. M. Smith, T. B. Ward & R. A. Finke (Eds.), *The creative cognitive approach* (pp. 269–302). Cambridge, MA: The MIT Press.

MacKinnon, D. W. (1965). Personality and the realization of the creative process. *American Psychologist*, 20, 273–281.

MacKinnon, D. W. (1975). IPAR's contribution to the conceptualization and study of creativity. In I. A. Taylor & J. W. Getzels (Eds.), *Perspectives in creativity* (pp. 60–89). Chicago, IL: Aldine.

MacKinnon, D. W. (1978). In *search of human effectiveness: Identifying and developing creativity*. Buffalo, NY: Bearly.

Mathisen, G. E., & Einarsen, C. A. (2004). A review of instruments assessing creative and innovative environments within organizations. *Creativity Research Journal*, 16, 119–140.

Mathisen, G. E., Martinsen, O. M., & Einarsen, S. (2008). The relationship between creative personality composition, innovative team climate, and team innovativeness: an input process–output perspective. *The Journal of Creative Behavior*, 42, 13–31.

Mumford, M. D., Baughman, W. A., & Sager, C. E. (2003). Picking the right material: Cognitive processing skills and their role in creative thought. In M. A. Runco (Ed.), *Critical creative processes* (pp. 3–18). Creskill, NJ: Hampton Press.

Muñoz-Doyague, M. F., González-Álvarez, N., & Nieto, M. (2008). An examination of individual factors and employees' creativity: the case of Spain. *Creativity Research Journal*, 20, 21–33.

Norins, H. (1990). *Traveling creative workshops*. Englewood Cliffs, NJ: Prentice Hall.

Pannells, T. C., & Claxton, A. F. (2008). Happiness, creative ideation, and locus of control. *Creativity Research Journal*, 20, 67–71.

Parnes, S. J. (1967). *Creative behavior guidebook*. New York, NY: Charles Scribners.

A. INTRODUCTION

Prabhu, V., Sutton, C., & Sauser, W. (2008). Creativity and certain personality traits: Understanding the mediating effect of intrinsic motivation. *Creativity Research Journal, 20*, 53–66.

Robinson, A. G., & Stern, S. (1997). *Corporate creativity: How innovation and improvement actually happen.* San Francisco, CA: Berrett-Koehler Publishers.

Runco, M. A. (2004). Creativity. *Annual Reviews of Psychology, 55*, 657–687.

Runco, M. A. (2007). Creativity: *Theories and themes: Research, development, and practice.* Burlington, MA: Elsevier.

Sawyer, R. K. (2006). Explaining creativity: *The science of human innovation.* New York, NY: Oxford University Press.

Schneider, B. (1975). Organizational climates: An essay. *Personnel Psychology, 28*, 447–479.

Shallcross, D. J. (1981). *Teaching creative behavior.* Englewood Cliffs, NJ: Prentice Hall.

Shalley, C. E., & Zhou, J. (2008). Organizational creativity research: a historical overview. In J. Zhou & C. E. Shalley (Eds.), *Handbook of organizational creativity* (pp. 3–32). New York, NY: Lawrence Erlbaum.

Shavinina, L. V., & Seeratan, K. L. (2003). On the nature of individual innovation. In L. V. Shavinina (Ed.), *The international handbook of innovation* (pp. 31–43). Oxford, UK: Elsevier Science.

Simonton, D. K. (2003). Exceptional creativity across life span: The emergence and manifestation of creative genius. In L. V. Shavinina (Ed.), *The international handbook of innovation* (pp. 293–308). Oxford, UK: Elsevier Science.

Smith, G. F. (2003). Toward a logic of innovation. In L. V. Shavinina (Ed.), *The international handbook of innovation* (pp. 347–365). Oxford, UK: Elsevier Science.

Smith-Bingham, R. (2006). Public policy, innovation and the need for creativity. In N Jackson, M. Oliver & J. Wisdom (Eds.), *Developing creativity in higher education. An imaginative curriculum* (pp. 10–18). London, UK: Routledge.

Soto, C. L. B. (2006). Creatividad organizacional: Elementos para la discusión [Organizational creativity: Elements for discussion]. *Recrearte, 6*, 1–14.

Sternberg, R. (1996). Costs of expertise. In K. A. Ericsson (Ed.), *The road to excellence: the acquisition of expert performance in the arts and sciences, sports and games* (pp. 347–354). NJ: LEA.

Sternberg, R. (1997). *Thinking styles.* Cambridge, UK: Cambridge University Press.

Sternberg, R. J. (2003). *Wisdom, intelligence and creativity synthesized.* Cambridge, UK: Cambridge University Press.

Sternberg, R. J., & Lubart, T. I. (1995). Defying the crowd: *Cultivating creativity in a culture of conformity.* New York, NY: The Free Press.

Sternberg, R. J., & Lubart, T. I. (1996). Investing in creativity. *American Psychologist, 51*, 677–688.

Sternberg, R. J., & Lubart, T. I. (1999). The concept of creativity: Prospects and paradigms. In R. J. Sternberg (Ed.), *Handbook of creativity* (pp. 3–15). New York, NY: Cambridge University Press.

Talbot, R. J. (1993). Creativity in the organizational context: Implications for training. In S. G. Isaksen, M. C. Murdock, R. L. Firestein & D. J. Treffinger (Eds.), *Nurturing and developing creativity. The emergence of a discipline* (pp. 177–214). Norwood, NJ: Ablex.

Tesluk, P. E., Farr, J. L., & Klein, S. R. (1997). Influences of organizational culture and climate on individual creativity. *The Journal of Creative Behavior, 31*, 27–41.

Treffinger, D. J. (2003). Assessment and measurement in creativity and creative problem solving. In J. Houtz (Ed.), *The educational psychology of creativity* (pp. 59–93). Creskill, NJ: Hampton Press.

Tierney, P. (2008). Leadership and employee creativity. In J. Zhou & C. E. Shalley (Eds.), *Handbook of organizational creativity* (pp. 95–124). New York, NY: Lawrence Erlbaum.

Van Gundy, A. (1987). Organizational creativity and innovation. In S. G. Isaksen (Ed.), *Frontiers of creativity research* (pp. 358–379). Buffalo, NY: Bearly.

Wechsler, S. M. (2006). *Estilos de pensar e criar [Thinking and creating styles].* Campinas, Brazil: LAMP/PUC.

Weisberg, R. (1999). Creativity and knowledge: a challenge to theories. In R. J. Sternberg (Ed.), *Handbook of creativity* (pp. 226–250). New York, NY: Cambridge University Press.

West, M. A., & Farr, J. L. (1990). Innovation and creativity at work: *Psychological and organizational strategies.* New York, NY: Wiley.

West, M. A., & Richter, A. W. (2008). Climates and cultures for innovation and creativity at work. In J. Zhou & C. E. Shalley (Eds.), *Handbook of organizational creativity* (pp. 211–236). New York, NY: Lawrence Erlbaum.

Zenasni, F., Besançon, M., & Lubart, T. (2008). Creativity and tolerance of ambiguity: an empirical study. *The Journal of Creative Behavior, 42*, 61–73.

Zhou, J., & Shalley, C. E. (2008). *Handbook of organizational creativity.* New York, NY: Lawrence Erlbaum.

A. INTRODUCTION

INDIVIDUAL LEVEL
INFLUENCES

6

Creative Abilities: Divergent Thinking

Selcuk Acar and Mark A. Runco
University of Georgia, Athens, GA

Organizational creativity is influenced by many things. Some are social and literally organizational. Others are brought to the organization by the individuals who comprise it. There is of course an interaction, with the social context having an impact on the performances and contributions of the individuals, as well as the organizational productivity and innovation in part being dependent on those same individuals.

One important individual factor is ability. To a certain degree, then, organizational creativity depends on the abilities of the individuals within it. *Creative ability* is a broad label and category, however, and probably for that reason most research is much more focused.[1] The focus in the present chapter is on one notable kind of creative ability, namely divergent thinking ability. The research on divergent thinking is plentiful and says a great deal about the potential for creative accomplishment, both by individuals working alone and those in organizations. Quite a bit of the research reviewed in this chapter involves divergent thinking in social settings and organizations. There is research on the divergent thinking of managers, for example, as well as entrepreneurs and individuals studying business. In order to cover all bases, we also review research outside of organizations, but of course involving divergent thinking. This will give us a full picture of divergent thinking as a potential influence on organizational creativity.

---

[1] Abilities were once a subject of much study in psychology, but seem to have fallen by the wayside in recent decades. In fact, a quick search of six major "Introduction to Psychology" collegiate textbooks revealed only one that provided a definition for the term! While research emphasis may have shifted away from discussing abilities, understanding the causes and limits of human abilities remains undoubtedly important to cognitive psychology as a whole, and it is our belief that the time is right to revisit this foundational topic.

Handbook of Organizational Creativity.
DOI: 10.1016/B978-0-12-374714-3.00006-9

EARLY THEORIES OF DIVERGENT THINKING

Although there were ambiguous references to the production of original ideas in psychological research going back at least as far as Binet, before 1900, the first detailed and empirical-based theory of divergent thinking was that of J. P. Guilford (1950, 1967). His interest was in describing the structure of the intellect (SOI), the assumption being that, just as the periodic table of elements structured the physical world, the SOI would structure the bases of cognition. Part of the SOI was *divergent production*. This allows original and varied ideas to be generated. It is in contrast to *convergent production* which leads to conventional ideas and solutions. This distinction has proven to be quite useful, for testing, as well as in organizational and educational settings. Fifty years ago there was a call for divergent thinking, the assumption being that creativity would flourish as a result. As we shall see, what is really needed for creativity is a balance of divergent and convergent thought.

Guilford's was a good theory. It was general and widely applicable, internally consistent, and testable. The last of these is critical in many ways, and not surprisingly there are a very large number of tests of divergent thinking (DT). These are used to identify individuals with creative potential and to test the impact of programs designed to enhance creative performances. All tests of DT are open-ended. They allow the individual to produce a number of ideas. Tests of convergent thinking, on the other hand, usually require one answer—and they want the conventional answer at that. Tests of DT allow originality. This can be defined in several ways, but one is highly objective. It defines original ideas as those which are produced by few people. In some circumstances originality is defined in terms of uniqueness: if an idea is produced by only one person taking the test, it is original. Other times originality is subjectively scored (Hocevar, 1981). The other common indices of DT are fluency and flexibility. The former refers to the total number of responses given by any one person. The latter represents the number of categories or themes suggested by the ideas.

One of the most important points of emphasis in this chapter can be offered at this juncture. That is that DT is useful because it involves ideas and ideation. It is not just a theory of originality, nor even just a theory of creativity. It is a theory describing the processes (e.g., associative) that lead to ideas, with data about how to direct ideation towards creativity and innovation. Tests of DT are really measures of ideation more than anything else. When they are scored for originality, they are also predictors of the potential for creative thought. That is because originality is the key ingredient in creativity. All creative things are original.

Ideational fluency, flexibility, and originality are ways of quantifying ideas and ideation. Other methods have also been proposed. Some of the subtests of the Torrance Tests of Creative Thinking (Torrance, 1995), for example, look to elaboration, or the extension of a theme. The appropriateness of ideas has also been examined (Runco & Charles, 1993), the logic being that creative things are more than just original. They are also effective, apt, fitting, or in some way "appropriate". It is also sometimes useful to take more than one index into account, to really understand an individual's potential, or when examining the impact of organizational context. Various additive, ratio, and weighted scoring methods have been tested (Runco & Acar, in press-a).

TABLE 6.1 Sample Items from Guilford's Battery (Merrifield, Guilford, Christensen & Frick, 1962).

Name of the Test	Task/Verbatim	Sample Item & Answers	Scoring	SB*
Associational fluency I	Write a number of different synonyms for each given word	*Hard:* difficult, solid.	# of acceptable similar words	.63
Brick Uses–shifts	List many uses for a common brick	*Brick:* building, pavements, drawing	# of shifts of category of use	.46
Ideational Fluency	List objects that belong to a specified class	*Name fluids that will burn:* gasoline, alcohol, hydrogen	# of acceptable responses	.77
Object Naming–shifts	List names of the objects in a given class		# of times in shifts from a subclass to another	.39
Object Synthesis III	List as many as five things that could be made by using both of two objects	*Nail–cane:* spear, hook	# of acceptable responses	.53
Similarities	Write six ways in which objects of a pair are alike	*Apple–orange:* Sweet, having seeds, growing on trees	# of acceptable similarities given	.57

DIVERGENT THINKING TESTS

This chapter draws heavily from the empirical research on divergent thinking, and for that reason it is helpful to describe how divergent thinking is measured. Early tests of intelligence actually had open ended tasks not unlike those contained in contemporary test batteries (Runco, 1999), but the popularity of DT surged after Guilford's research on the SOI (Structure of Intellect) framework (Guilford, 1967, 1988). Guilford (1967, 1971) hypothesized several abilities in the family of divergent production including creative thinking, planning, fluency, flexibility, figural–symbolic production, figural–symbolic–semantic production, transformation abilities as well as creative abilities within a particular age group. To test those abilities in different age groups, he developed many tests, and administered them to sixth, ninth grades, senior high school students as well as some others to adults (air force and naval air cadets). Our interest in this chapter is on adults, and Table 6.1 provides a sample of DT tests that have their origins in Guilford's work.

One very popular divergent thinking test that was developed by Christensen, Merrifield, and Guilford (1953) is "Consequences". Each test question asks possible outcomes of changes that could occur in the world. An example item was the question "What would happen if the world was covered in water except for a few mountaintops?" Christensen et al. reported an internal reliability of .70, and later studies (Blair & Mumford, 2007; Licuanan, Dailey, & Mumford, 2007) reported similar or higher reliabilities. The construct validity evidence was provided by Vincent, Decker, and Mumford (2002) with an adult sample. They used Consequences A test to examine the relationship of divergent thinking to creative problem solving, independently of expertise and intelligence. They asked the experts to rate the responses for quality and originality which had inter-rater reliabilities of .90, and .84, respectively. An aggregate index had an inter-rater reliability of .86. Vincent et al. found a notable relationship between creative problem solving and DT, the Consequences A test.

Guilford's battery inspired other researchers. Wallach and Kogan (1965) developed a battery with three verbal and two figural divergent thinking tests. They used two scoring indices: uniqueness and fluency (number of total responses). In a break from the preceding work by Guilford, the DT tests are administered in a game-like environment. Moreover, they are not timed. One of the verbal tests is the *Instances* test. This includes "name all the things you can think of that move on wheels as possible", "round things", "things that make noise", and "square things". The *Alternate Uses* test includes "List the different ways you could use a chair", newspaper, or shoe. This is a close approximation to the Brick Uses or Alternate Uses tests in Guilford's battery. The *Similarities* test asks respondents to find as many commonalities as possible between two verbally specified objects. This test consisted of ten questions, including "Tell me the ways in which a potato and a carrot are alike". *Pattern-meanings* test was one of the visual/figural tests. Respondents are shown cards with drawings and asked "tell me all the things you think this could be". The other figural test is the *Line Meanings* test with eight figural items. It is much like Pattern Meanings except the stimuli are more abstract and not clear cut patterns.

Reliability studies of the uniqueness and number of total responses, based on the data from 151 fifth grade students, indicated that Spearman-Brown Split-Half coefficients were above .75, with the exception of .51 for the uniqueness score from the Instances test. Item-sum correlations for the Instances test ranged between .50 to .73 for the uniqueness, and .67 to .85 for fluency. For the Alternate Uses, it ranged between .48 to 83, for the uniqueness, and .70 to .84 for the number. For Similarities test, it ranged between .42 and 77 for the uniqueness, and .70 to .85 for the number. Pattern meanings had reliability scores between .64 and 80 for the uniqueness and .69 and .85 for the number. Line meanings items had reliabilities between .59 and .68 for the uniqueness, and .68 and .84 for the number. Wallach and Kogan also reported correlations between those individual tests of divergent thinking and several tests of intelligence, including the WISC, which supported discriminant validity with only low coefficients. Only 19 out of 100 intercorrelations between the tests of divergent thinking and subtests of intelligence were significant at .05 or .01 levels, and the highest correlation was .23.

Wallach and Kogan examined the performance in children. A bit later Wallach and Wing (1969) administered those tests to college students, and found little relationship between ideation and intelligence scores (which, again served as evidence for discriminant validity). Within test correlations were above around .70 and .50 for the Uses task (fluency and uniqueness, respectively); .75 and .60 for the Pattern-Meanings task; .72 and below .52 for the Similarities task; and .70s and .53 for the Line-Meanings task. In another set of analyses, high and low intelligence groups of students were compared with respect to academic and non-academic domains. Results confirmed that intelligence did not explain their differences in leadership, arts, drama, writing, and music. However, the performance on divergent thinking tests was related to achievements in non-academic, extracurricular domains. Wallach and Kogan argued that tests that require ideational skills should be part of college admission criteria because of its importance for success in life.

The TTCT is another test of divergent thinking, and is probably the most common and popular of all the creativity tests (Hunsaker & Callahan, 1995). Even though it has some common features with the Guilford's battery, low correlations between the two batteries led to the conclusion that there is some departure. The TTCT was developed over many years, in empirical studies started when Torrance was in Minnesota. The more recent version, with figural and verbal forms, has been standardized for young children through college. (There are also adult versions of the Torrance Tests.) The figural tasks involve three activities. The first one is *Picture Construction*. It asks respondents to "think of a picture that no one else can think of". Another task was the *Picture Completion* activity with ten incomplete figures which individuals are asked to create by completing incomplete figures—and then find a title for each. The third activity was the *Lines* or *Circles* activity for the Form A and Form B, respectively. Both included many lines or circles, exactly the same, and students are encouraged to create as many figures as possible within ten minutes. The figural form had several scoring indices, including abstractness of titles and premature closure, in addition to traditionally used indices of fluency, originality, and elaboration.

The Verbal form of the TTCT has seven subtests: Asking, Guessing Causes, Guessing Consequences, Product Improvement, Unusual Uses, Unusual Questions, and Just Suppose. *Asking* requires generating as many questions as possible about a picture. *Guessing Causes* asked respondents to list possible causes about the action in the picture. *Guessing Consequences* was the same as Consequences. In *Product Improvement*, respondents were asked to improve a toy. *Unusual Uses* asked to list many different possible uses. *Unusual Questions* required asking as many possible questions as possible for a simple object, but it was dropped in later versions. *Just Suppose* asked to list possible consequences of a hypothetical and unlikely situation.

In addition to the reliability and validity evidences of the individual items in TTCT (Torrance & Safter, 1989; Torrance, Tan, & Allman, 1970), the reliability and validity of the ultimate version were around .90 for both Figural A and B. Since the TTCT requires training to score the responses, inter-rater reliability was important. Studies found a value above .95 for all five major indices of the Figural Form. The coefficient for the composite was .99 (Geoff & Torrance, 2002). TTCT was criticized for having low correlations among the subtests. Torrance defended this situation by stating the fact that creativity is multifaceted, and each subtest measures a different unit.

Longitudinal research has been reported in support of the predictive validity of the TTCT. Criteria included achievement indicators, such as the number of high school creative accomplishments, the number of post-high school creative achievements, number of "creative style of life" achievements, quality of highest creative achievements, and creativeness of future career image. In those studies, both quantity and quality indices were employed. Following the seventh (Torrance, 1969), twelfth (Torrance, 1972), and twenty-second (Torrance, 1981) years follow-up, TTCT scores still remained predictive even after forty (Cramond, Matthews-Morgan, Bandalos, & Zuo, 2005) and fifty (Runco, Millar, Acar, & Cramond, 2010) years. Those results explain the popularity of the test in the educational market.

There are newer forms of divergent thinking tests, and some have good application in adult and organizational populations. Chand and Runco (1993), for instance, developed *realistic* DT tests. The aim was to make DT tests more applied and related to the natural environment. Early versions examined college students. Here is an example: "Your friend Pat sits next to you in class. Pat really likes to talk to you and often bothers you while you are doing your work. Sometimes he distracts you and you miss an important part of the lecture, and many times you don't finish your work because he is bothering you. What should you do? How would you solve this problem? Remember to list as many ideas and solutions as you can." The scoring was no different from the Wallach and Kogan tests.

The second kind of realistic tests are *problem generation* (PG) tasks. This is an important addition, given reports in the creativity literature that problem finding is at least as important as problem solving. The first PG tasks required that students generate a number of problems about school, work, or involving friends. Okuda, Runco, and Berger (1991) found that creative performance is best predicted by problem generation scores along with standard DT test scores. An example of PG is given in the same study: "List different problems in school that are important to you. You may write down problems about the campus itself, classes, professors, policies, classmates, or whatever. Try to be specific, and take your time. Think of as many problems as you can."

It is a good idea to follow PG testing with *problem solution* (PS) tasks. Here, the respondents are redirected to the problems they themselves generated. This kind of assessment thus allows a combination of problem finding and problem solving; the examinee is involved in both. Also, PS tasks should be more engaging, and the results more meaningful, since the examinee has chosen the problem to be solved! The reliabilities of the PS tasks were about .80, with both standard and explicit instructions, for fluency, and around .46 and .62 for originality. Chand and Runco (1993) found that these tests of DT can predict creative achievement in the explicit instruction group (Rc = .70, p < .001).

Before moving on, something should be said about the Remote Associates Test (RAT) (Mednick, 1962, 1968). It requires finding associations between diverse or seemingly unrelated concepts. This same logic was used to explain how original ideas are found on DT tests. Yet unlike DT tests, the RAT has correct responses for each task, hence it also involves some convergent and evaluative skills, in contrast to the other divergent thinking tests which rely more on ideational skills. The initial form had 30 items, each having three words. The respondents are asked to find the fourth word that links all three (e.g., railroad girl class: working). Mednick summarized reliability and validity evidence that is available as he developed the RAT. It is important to note that these studies involved college students. In a study at University of California at Berkeley, creativity ratings by a faculty were strongly correlated with the performance in RAT (r = .70, p < .01). RAT scores were also found to be negatively correlated with the first two-year GPAs of the undergraduates (r = −.27, p < .05). Spearman-Brown reliability coefficient values were above .90 in different samples. Other studies indicated the differences in social attitudes and occupational interests between the high and low scorers on RAT.

Recently, Bowden and Jung-Beeman (2003) reported normative data for the 144 compound remote associates' problems. They argued that compound problems are superior to previous tasks in terms of taking shorter time (less than 1 hr), and including simpler items which controls confounding variables, having clear solutions.

Scoring DT Tests

DT tests are open-ended. This means that there can be no fixed scoring criteria. That of course fits with the definition of creativity as requiring originality, but it did mean that psychometricians needed to develop special scoring procedures for DT tests. It also means that scoring DT tests is often time-consuming. The TTCT, for example, requires training to score it. For other tests, there is no single procedure. Traditional scoring includes fluency, flexibility, and originality. Wallach and Kogan used only fluency and uniqueness. Harrington, Block and Block (1983), and Runco, Illies, and Eisenman (2005) used quality or appropriateness as another aspect of creativity. While fluency was scored by adding the total number of responses, originality was scored as the number of unique or rare responses. Rarity was mostly calculated through the percentage of the responses (those given by less than 5 or 10 percent) within a population. Cropley (1967) used a more qualitative scoring method, assigning higher scores to responses generated by statistically fewer individuals. Except for TTCT, DT tests are not normed, which make it laborious and require inter-rater reliability. For the TTCT, originality was scored based on the norms. Runco and Mraz (1994) suggested using *total ideational pools* to make scoring easier. In this method an individual's entire output of ideas is examined as a whole rather than each idea.

Mumford, Marks, Connelly, Zaccaro, and Johnson (1998) and Vincent, Decker & Mumford (2002) suggested a domain-specific scoring method for the domain of leadership. They included new indices that other DT tests have never used, such as time frame, realism, originality, complexity, use of principles, positive outcomes, and negative outcomes.

One specific problem regarding scoring is the contaminating influence of fluency (Hocevar, 1979). There tends to be a high correlation between scores for fluency, originality, and flexibility. Higher fluency scores mostly result in higher flexibility and originality scores. For this reason, flexibility was removed from the scoring grid of the TTCT. One way to minimize the influence of fluency is to use proportional scores (Hocevar and Michael, 1979; Runco et al., 1987) by dividing the original scores by the fluency scores. However, ratio scores are notoriously unreliable and a ratio does not contain exactly the same information as a raw score. A fluency score of 50 and originality score of 25, for example, gives the same ratio as a fluency score of 4 and an originality score of 2. Another method is to categorize every response as either original or popular. This removes the overlap (Milgram, Milgram, Rosenbloom, & Rabkin, 1978; Sawyers, Moran, Fu, & Milgram, 1983). Mouchiroud and Lubart (2001) used medians to suppress the influence of fluency (because they are less sensitive to means).

Runco, Okuda, and Thurstone (1987) compared four scoring systems and found that weighted fluency scores, with higher weights given to more rare ideas, were superior to the summation scores (sum of flexibility, fluency, and originality scores), common/uncommon (uncommon = generated by less than 5% of the sample), and the ratio scores (originality or flexibility divided by fluency). Limiting the number of responses (Michael and Wright, 1989; Zarnegar, Hocevar, & Michael, 1988) has also been used to diminish the influence of fluency. One thing that is often overlooked is that, if one score was to be used because of high correlations and overlap, it should be originality and not fluency. Originality is required for all creativity; fluency is not.

INFLUENCES ON IDEATION

The premise of the DT model is that ideas are good for creative thinking and innovation. Evidence suggests that ideas can be objectively measured and profiles (e.g., originality vs. fluency vs. flexibility) or ratio indicators developed. A large amount of research has also demonstrated that ideas can be manipulated. Original ideas can be encouraged, for example, and fluency—and thus the range of options and possibilities—dramatically increased. The manipulation and encouragement of ideas can occur in either of two ways. One is directed and intentional; there are strategies and programs for enhancing DT. Some of these are described towards the end of the present chapter. Before describing such strategies, it is useful to recognize how ideation is influenced by many personal and contextual variables.

There are several influences on ideation. Some of these, such as the impact of feedback, instructions, rewards, and task composition, have been tested with psychometric methods. Although that may imply that the generalization of the findings to organizations or other applied settings is questionable, psychometric research does give a clear message about the reliability and validity of the effects and the tasks and assessments themselves. Additionally, the issue of generalization is itself a topic of empirical research.

One influence on ideation is the type of problem or situation faced. This is of course suggested very generally by the distinction between DT and convergent thinking; open ended tasks allow ideation, while closed-ended tasks and situations lead to single answers and nominal options. But there is much more to it. There are, for example, differences between figural and verbal tasks (Runco & Albert, 1985; Torrance, 1995), one implication of which is that the former tend to elicit more original ideation. This may be because figural stimuli tend to be unfamiliar; it could be that familiar tasks tend to lead to rote solutions and options while unfamiliar tasks and stimuli allow original associations.

There is also a difference between tasks that allow problem definition and those that require only problem solving. The latter are sometimes called *presented problems*, the former *discovered problems* (Runco & Okuda, 1988). This is an important distinction given the role of problem finding and intrinsic motivation in creative thinking. Both of those are more likely when a task or problem is discovered, or at least defined, by the individual him- or herself.

Knowledge also has influences on DT. After all, even though DT tasks are open-ended, the individual can still draw from experience and long term memory when responding. Ideas do not come out of the blue; they are tied to knowledge. A good idea may be only loosely tied to experience, or it may be some new twist and use knowledge in a new manner, but knowledge is involved in ideation. Runco, Dow and Smith (2006) set out to determine exactly how much overlap there was between knowledge and ideation. They administered tasks that require thinking through some factual information and drawing solutions from memory, as well as traditional divergent thinking tasks. Comparisons indicated that responses in both kinds of tasks were correlated when they shared the same domain (e.g., transportation). When the domains were unrelated, there was no "experiential bias".

Later, Runco and Acar (in press-b) investigated the role of experience by administering presented problems (from the Uses DT test) and a set of highly realistic problems. One week after the research participants completed the two sets of DT tests they were given long lists of ideas, compiled from everyone involved, and they were asked to indicate which ideas they had themselves ever experienced or observed. An experiential bias was present in both kinds of tasks. In fact, even ideas that had been categorized as original tended to be tied to experience and knowledge from long term memory. That is not to say, however, that better memory leads to higher creativity. The way ideas are categorized and the text to which they are well-established can lead to only routine responses (Kilgour, 2006).

Sometimes the relevant information is suggested by the immediate environment and is not found in long term memory. Several studies have demonstrated that environmental cues can be used when faced with an open-ended task (Kilgour, 2006; Runco et al., 1991). Hence an individual may have an opportunity for DT, perhaps even be working on something at work, and may either look back and consider experience (drawing from long term memory), or look around the immediate environment for ideas, cues, possible directions. Clearly the use of the immediate environment is more useful for some kinds of tasks that others, but there are certainly implications for how the work or educational setting is designed, given that the immediate environment can have an influence on ideation (McCoy, 2000).

The topic of knowledge and experience suggests that expertise is relevant to DT. This is an important consideration because expertise has been shown to be either a contribution to creative thinking, or a hindrance. Sometimes there is a cost in expertise. This occurs when the individual is familiar with some domain or topic and thus makes assumptions about it. Those assumptions may gloss over useful details or new information.

Vincent, Decker and Mumford (2002) examined expertise by administering tests of divergent thinking, intelligence, expertise, idea generation and idea implementation to a group of organizational leaders. Vincent et al. proposed that idea implementation would be key for organizational leaders. Employees may be involved in idea generation, but the "follow through" and commitment needed to implement some idea without doubt requires good leadership. Results of this research showed that DT was strongly related to idea generation, but not to idea implementation. General intelligence and expertise were also related to idea generation. Expertise was related to idea implementation, but this was a weaker relationship than the one between expertise and idea generation. DT was related to problem solving, even after controlling general intelligence and expertise, though they too contributed to the process. All in all, DT was an important part of leadership, though as you would expect, a number of things come into play.

PERSONALITY AND ATTITUDES

Personality and attitude are also related to DT. Basadur (1994), Basadur & Finkbeiner (1985), Runco & Basadur (1993) identified four divergent thinking attitudes, and much of this research involved managers, making it directly applicable to organizations. The four attitudes were preference for ideation, tendency to avoid premature critical evaluations, valuing new ideas, and belief that creative thinking is not bizarre. Basadur subsequently developed a 24 item Preference Scale and uncovered three of the attitudes that were especially reliable and useful. These were valuing new ideas, creative individual stereotypes and too busy for new ideas (Basadur & Hausdorf, 1996). Keep in mind that each of these attitudes related to ideation.

Perhaps the best established theory of personality includes neuroticism, extraversion, openness, agreeableness, and conscientiousness (NEO-PI). McCrae (1987) administered the

NEO-PI measure and various tests of DT. The results showed that openness to experience was correlated with all divergent thinking tests except one, while none of the other traits were correlated with any of the tasks. When relationships between the six facets of openness to experience (fantasy, aesthetics, feelings, actions, ideas, and values) and divergent thinking tasks are analyzed, most of the correlations were found to be significant. The exception was the "obvious ideas" score from the Consequences task. That is not a surprising finding, at least from the perspective of creativity theory, given that obvious ideas are unrelated to remote and original ones.

Williams (2004) was also interested in openness to experience. Clearly it does relate to the potential for original ideation and DT. Openness will allow the individual to consider diverse and varied ideas. Williams examined openness, attitude toward divergent thinking (ATDT), and initiating structure in organizations. Openness to experience was related to the supervisors' and co-workers' ratings of creative performance. ATDT was related to both creativity and openness to experience, and it mediated the relationship between openness to experience and creativity. Williams also found some support for his expectation that the amount of structure initiated by supervisors influence subordinates' ATDT.

IMPROVING IDEATIONAL SKILLS

There is both theoretical and empirical support for the use of DT as an estimate of the potential for creative problem solving. Admittedly the empirical support is moderate and not astounding. Then again, most data on DT has been produced by tests of DT; and tests are never perfect—they each have some level of reliability and validity. Tests of DT probably have better than average reliability and validity (Runco, in press), compared with the full range of psychometric tests on the market. There is great variation, depending on the factors identified in this chapter (e.g., type of task). They do have clear enough reliability and validity to justify their use in research on creativity.

Not surprisingly, tests of DT are often used in research designed to test methods for enhancement. Clapham (1997), for instance, compared the effectiveness of a complete creativity training program with training much more focused on ideation. She formed three groups: creativity training, ideational skills, and control group. The TTCT was administered before and after the training. The overall training had a significant effect when a pre-training creativity index and pre-training knowledge were controlled. When two training groups are compared to the control group in terms of post-training creativity index, they significantly differed from the control group. However, the general creativity training group and the ideational skills groups were not significantly different.

Basadur, Graen, and Green (1982) assessed the effectiveness of creativity training on participants' preference for and practice of ideation, and performance in problem finding and problem solving. This research was directly tied to Basadur's own three component model (problem finding, problem solving, and solution implementation), each component involving an ideation–evaluation cycle wherein ideas are produced and then evaluated. Participants were engineers, engineering managers, and technicians of an engineering department. The post-training performances of trained, placebo, and non-placebo groups were compared, and not surprisingly the first group outperformed the other two groups.

The training was strongly effective for preference and practice for ideation in problem solving, and practice of ideation in problem finding and problem-finding performance. The training helped little for preference for ideation in problem finding and problem-solving performance.

EVALUATION OF IDEAS

The evaluative component of creativity may be particularly important when the interest is in understanding the creativity of organizations and industry. This is because only the ideas that are applicable, useful, feasible—as well as novel—are likely to lead to a concrete contribution in a market or organization. Evaluation is probably becoming even more important for organizations seeking innovation because they cannot afford to accept all new ideas. Overabundance of innovative ideas may become distracters, and evaluation can help them to identify options and solutions with noteworthy potential (Sharma, 1999).

Runco and Smith (1992) distinguished between two kinds of ideational evaluation: interpersonal and intrapersonal, both being potentially important. Intrapersonal evaluations are based on one's own subjective criteria and have been recognized in theories such as Campbell's (1960). Interpersonal evaluations take place after an idea is shared. The distinction between intra- and interpersonal evaluations is important because evaluative accuracy can vary, and research showing the direction of difference enlightens appropriate ways of judging ideas generated in organizations.

Runco and Smith compared inter- and intrapersonal evaluation and found that they are not totally distinct skills. Canonical correlations yielded significant correlations (Rc = .45). However, they found a significant relationship between intrapersonal evaluation and divergent thinking. That was not the case for interpersonal evaluation. Since an individual knows how the idea was created, appropriateness can be judged on that basis. Interpersonal evaluation was related to the preference for ideation. Others can use different information and value the idea without knowing the path which the individual has taken to generate it. The interpersonal evaluations, including those of employers, managers or supervisors, may use a rubric or guide that consists of some criteria reflecting the agreed-upon expectations. Intrapersonal evaluation was seen to be less beneficial to creativity than interpersonal evaluation (White & Owen, 1970; Poole, Williams & Lett, 1977).

The evaluative component of ideation is often viewed as a kind of convergent thinking. Whatever it is called, clearly some sort of evaluation is required for authentic creativity, otherwise there is a definite risk of *quasicreativity* or *pseudocreativity* reflecting ideas that are not adapted to reality (Cropley, 2006). It will come as no surprise, then, that theories of creativity always include some sort of evaluation or convergence, though the label varies. In fact, a number of related processes and components have been proposed. Guilford himself described four concepts that are involved "last in the cycle," after ideas have been generated (also see Mumford, 2000–2001). These were conceptual foresight, penetration, redefinition judgment, and problem sensitivity.

Conceptual foresight is a kind of prediction and uncovers future implications of an event or action (Guilford & Hoepfner, 1971). The ability to forecast the possible implications of a new idea is both generative and evaluative, because possible outcomes are projected (generative) and then standards are considered (evaluative). Mumford, Marks, Connelly, Zaccaro, and Johnson (1998) developed a specific scoring method for this process, looking specifically in the domain of leadership. One part of it concerned "time frame" and focused on decisions that bring immediate vs. long-term consequences.

Later, Mumford, Lonergan, and Scott (2002) argued that evaluation of new ideas must begin with forecasting. The possible outcomes can comply with the standards and lead to a resulting idea that can be implemented or revised based on some standards. In an organization, the first evaluative question for a new product is whether it can be sold or not, and whether it is worth it for the organization to take a risk.

Penetration is the ability of creative people to draw from their experiences and see the things under the surface level (Guilford & Hoepfner, 1971). Penetration allows us to see the implications of obscure changes in the meaning of events or information at hand (Merrifield, Guilford, Christensen, & Frick, 1962). The relationship between penetration and creativity was not clear when Guilford introduced the concept. However, recent studies have indicated that creative people, or people working in jobs requiring creativity can notice the key facts and reasons for events better, in comparison with non-creative people or those working in other regular jobs (Mumford, Peterson, & Childs, 1999; Davidson & Sternberg, 1984).

Redefinition also contributes to good idea evaluation. Redefinition concerns the reorganization of mental structures. It would, then, be involved in the oft-used measure called Uses, or Alternative Uses, that requires that the individual generate the way one uses a common object (e.g., tire, coat hanger, brick, shoe). Note that it is easy to connect this kind of thinking with innovation, especially that involving some minor change or adaptation in an existing product. Khandawalla (1993) considered reorganization a conceptual breakthrough that occurs by thinking about the meaning of the constraints. He used protocol analysis to identify several mechanisms that take place in divergent thinking and concluded that redefinition is the second most frequent (13%) thinking mechanism preceding creative solutions after "probe and example" (25%). Sensitivity to problems was defined as the awareness about the needs for change, new ways, methods or devices and deficiencies of the things that exist. A person without notable critical thinking and evaluative skills may not see the deficiencies, problems, or gaps in the currents things and finds nothing to solve. Possible ways of improving equipment has been tied to sensitivity to problems, just to name one industrial example (Merrifield et al., 1962). Titus (2000) argued that:

1. sensitivity to problems in the form of identifying unmet needs of consumers, and then
2. satisfying those needs

are the critical features of marketing. To take the advantage of this skill for marketing success, he suggested scrutinizing the environment for trends, because they provide clues for marketing opportunities.

Many other scholars also felt that an evaluational component has to be present somewhere in the creative thinking process. When creativity is defined as the production of novel and appropriate ideas and products (Amabile, 1996; Runco & Charles, 1993), for example, the appropriateness may depend on evaluation. Wallas' (1926) classic model, with preparation–incubation–illumination–verification, clearly recognizes evaluation in verification. Campbell (1960) adapted a Darwinian approach and described the creative process in terms of blind variation and selective retention (also see Simonton, 2007). Blind variation is the stage where many and various ideas, including original and unusual ones, are generated. Selective retention process filters the ideas based on their appropriateness, correctness, usefulness or value.

Recall also Basadur's (1995; see also Basadur, Graen, & Green, 1982) ideation–evaluation model of creative problem solving, mentioned above. In it, ideation is an option generation process where judgmental, rational, and convergent thoughts are deliberately delayed so that imaginative, divergent, and original thoughts can appear. In this view, evaluation may impede originality, but it is involved as some point (cf. Osborn, 1979). In the latest version of this model, ideation is tied more to the problem finding stage and evaluation to solution implementation stage. Both operate in the problem solving stage.

Lubart (1994) disagreed with the suggestion that early evaluation should be avoided. He found that students who were instructed to evaluate their work (short stories) during task production exhibited higher creativity than those who were not so instructed. This finding was not found in another task (drawing). The view that evaluation should not be postponed was also explored by Runco (1994), though his idea was that evaluation cannot be avoided. He described how evaluation is an important part of, and inherent in, all thinking and idea generation. Very recently he proposed that on the deepest level of cognition, which is likely to be preverbal and preconscious, ideas are constructed using a process that is partly evaluative. This view was used to question the idea of blind variation.

Basadur's (1995) view that the balance of ideation and evaluation is not uniform over different tasks is of great practical significance. He argued that I/E (ideation divided by evaluation) ratios can always be found but that they vary. He hypothesized that organizational members who work on basic research, training, and development will have higher I/E ratios (more ideation less evaluation) than those in marketing, advertising, and non-profit organization administration, but they will in turn have higher I/E ratios than those in secretarial/administrative support, sales, logistics, or distribution. He reported data to support this hypothesis.

Brophy (1998) looked to individual differences which argued that a majority of people have a tendency for divergent or convergent thought, and are more proficient in their preferred mode, while the majority do not alternate between divergent and convergent thinking until they attain an advanced cognitive stage. Only the minority can do both. Alternation between two the modes is mediated by one's inclination toward divergent or convergent thinking (Nyström, 2000). For Brophy the alteration is an adaptive form of metacognition. Brophy (2000–2001) compared divergent, convergent, and combination thinkers with indices of ideation versus evaluation, adaptation versus innovation, reason versus intuition, field independence versus field dependence, tolerance of ambiguity versus intolerance of ambiguity, internal control versus external control, and extraversion versus introversion. Analyses indicated that participants who had a preference for ideation had higher divergent performance than convergent performance, and those who had higher evaluation preference had higher convergent performance than divergent performance. Those who are inclined to both did not differ in their divergent and convergent performance. The same pattern was found for innovation versus adaptation, reason versus intuition, tolerance for ambiguity versus intolerance of ambiguity, extraversion versus introversion; the former relates to divergent thinking, and the latter to convergent thinking. Individuals with higher field independence had higher divergent performance than convergent performance, but

B. INDIVIDUAL LEVEL INFLUENCES

those with higher field dependence did not have higher convergent performance. Those who are inclined to both did not differ. The same pattern was found for internal versus external control. Brophy also found that divergent thinkers had more statements than combination and convergent thinkers. Additionally, they made more divergent and convergent statements than convergent thinkers.

Smilansky (1984) examined the relationship between the ability to create new problems and the ability to solve similar problems by using Raven's Standard Matrices. He found that creating problems was more difficult than solving them, and there was a low correlation between the two. Even though ideation and evaluation can lead each other (Khandwalla, 1993), those findings suggest caution when there is an assumption of distinct styles of thought.

Moneta (1993) described an optimal level balance where creativity is at the peak between the abilities for problem solving and convergent thinking, and the abilities for problem finding and divergent thinking. This is not far from Runco's (1994) description of an interactive and recursive pattern of divergent and convergent thinking that occurs throughout a creative problem solving process. Alternation from one to another at the right time would certainly be critical (Brophy, 1998). Support for this was provided by Khandwalla (1993) in his "think aloud" experiment. He asked participants to think aloud while generating solutions for a divergent thinking task. He found several subprocesses under five umbrella thinking components (problem restructuring, searching, feeling, ideating, and evaluating). He concluded that ideating is usually followed by evaluating and the recursive pattern between the two is the most frequent path in the process of creative problem solving.

Lonergan, Scott, and Mumford (2004) argued that evaluation is a special way of idea generation that allows reshaping and reforming of ideas after detecting the problematic aspects of the ideas previously generated. They argued that idea evaluation is a distinct process that involves *contextual appraisal*. An important aspect of evaluation is the criterion or criteria. They can be manipulated for different kinds of products. Runco (1991) made this point but used the labels "evaluation" for processes involved in finding what is wrong with an idea and "valuation" for processes used when finding what was creative about an idea. This makes the most sense if you remember that creative things are original, and original things are surprising and unexpected.

Lonergan, Scott, and Mumford (2004) looked to criteria and found (a) setting generative criteria associated with less original ideas and (b) implementation efficiency associated with more original ideas. Clearly, the effectiveness of the evaluation is related to the revision standards. Task complexity was also found to be involved. Evaluative accuracy was higher for highly original ideas generated for the well-structured tasks, and less original ideas for less structured and complex tasks.

Dailey and Mumford (2006) presented their research participants with three new ideas to be evaluated with respect to resource requirements, such as time and finance, and possible consequences, such as benefits or harms for the organization. The accuracy of participants' evaluations was compared with actual case events. Results showed that people tend to overestimate outcomes and underestimate resources when they are familiar with the problem, but that implementation intentions can increase accuracy of evaluations.

Idea evaluations are especially important for organizational leaders. Indeed, Mumford, Connelly, and Gaddis (2003) argued that the creative thinking of leaders differs from that of others, in that the leaders must begin an evaluation that then paves the way for new idea generation (also see Ward, Finke & Smith, 1999). Contrary to traditional modes of creative thinking, where evaluation follows ideation, evaluation is therefore the stimulus for idea generation. Strange and Mumford (2005) asked undergraduate college students to assume that they were school principals who needed to develop an implementation plan. Before the products were evaluated by judges with respect to quality and originality, half of the group received two manipulations. First, they received three models, either strong or weak, based on teachers' ratings of effectiveness. Then they were asked to write on the worksheet positive and negative experiences to allow reflection on their experiences. Quality and originality of the plans generated were higher when participants thought about the causes after reviewing strong models and reflecting on personal experiences. Reviewing weak plans followed by goal generation as well as reflecting on personal experience also yielded better plans. This study showed that evaluation, ensured by reflection on personal experiences, can contribute to the creative thinking of leaders.

A graphic depiction of evaluation working with idea generation was presented by Runco and Chand (1995) in a two-tiered model of creativity. According to this model, the first tier includes problem finding, ideation, and evaluation. A second tier consists of knowledge and motivation. Runco and Chand used the aforementioned distinction between evaluation and valuation, but included both in that third component of the primary tier. Runco and Chand went into some detail to separate evaluation from convergent and critical thinking, and thereby ensured that it is conducive to flexibility and originality. They also described how problem finding, ideation, and evaluation are all significantly influenced by knowledge and motivation. Effective evaluation will not occur, much less valuation, unless the individual sees a reason to invest the effort.

INTERPERSONAL EVALUATION

Interpersonal evaluations are quite common in the natural environment, including work in organizations. Evaluation of an idea or product by others is not easy, however. One reason is that evaluators also hold a subjective perspective, and even if they have some sort of expertise, recall here the possible biases and costs of expertise. Additionally, who is to select the judges and evaluators? That too is an evaluation (Murray, 1959)!

Evaluative accuracy varies among different divergent thinking tasks. Runco and Dow (2004) found that evaluative accuracy is the lowest in hypothetical problems and highest in Instances problems (e.g., "list as many strong things as you can"). Therefore, preparing appropriate tasks for idea evaluation is critical. Runco and Dow also found that evaluative accuracy was not related to convergent thinking, but it was related to some indices of originality. This finding provides evidence for the discriminant validity of evaluative skills and measures of them.

Lonergan, Scott, and Mumford (2004) investigated the role of standards in evaluative accuracy. They asked the participants to apply either innovative or operative standards for the evaluation of ideas with different levels of originality. They found that innovative standards that were applied to less original ideas and operative standards that were applied to highly original ideas yielded better results; in this case, plans. They also found an interaction of standards and task type. Innovative standards should probably therefore be used while revising ill-defined tasks, and operative standards used for well-defined tasks.

Evaluations can be led astray. Consider in this regard the findings from Mumford, Blair, Dailey, Leritz, and Osburn (2006). They identified various cognitive biases that led to errors in the appraisal of the ideas. In fact, they found 35 different errors! These have several sources, such as knowledge, limitations in processing capacity, patterns of information use, or strategies applied, surface evaluation, information discounting, goal fixation, overextended search, and over-optimism. Several of these errors have been tested in different empirical studies. Blair and Mumford (2007) found that people tended to like the ideas that are consistent with the social norms, complex to implement but easy to understand, and which bring desired outcomes immediately to a number of people. Rejection is likely of ideas that are original, risky, or require detailed descriptions. Time pressure and stringency were also mentioned.

Dailey and Mumford (2006) felt that the two main concerns of an organization, with respect to evaluation, are resources and consequences. With this in mind they asked participants to evaluate the ideas for the resources needed and their consequences. They found that people tend to be over-optimistic about the time and finances needed to implement new ideas. Likewise, there is a tendency to judge ideas as more complete than they really are, and to see the organization as more prepared than it really is. Judges also tend to overestimate the possible outcomes of the ideas and the extent to which the ideas will be accepted. Fortunately, asking people to list the positive as opposed to negative outcomes (implementation intention) seems to improve their evaluative accuracy.

Licuanan, Dailey, and Mumford (2007) also examined reasons for good and bad interpersonal evaluations. They asked people to evaluate the originality of the ideas generated for a marketing campaign. They found that people tended to underestimate the originality of the ideas. That is especially so in complex tasks, in unfamiliar domains, and for original ideas generated for complex problems. The good news is that the underestimation of others' ideas is probably avoidable. Licuanan et al. found that active analysis of product originality (which was done through asking participants to report the strengths and weakness of the ideas) diminished the evaluative errors.

The research of Amabile (in press), though not on DT, suggests something about interpersonal evaluations. In one study Amabile (1979) examined the influence of external evaluation by providing artists in the experimental group with instructions, but a control group had no instructions. The artists were led to expect evaluation, and their subsequent work was rated lower in creativity. Note that it was expected and therefore hypothetical evaluation rather than actual delivered evaluation.

Shalley (1995) also examined the effects of expected evaluation, goal setting, and coactions. In lack of expected evaluation situations, people performed higher when they worked alone. But the highest creativity was observed when there was a creativity goal and they worked alone under expected evaluation.

Yuan and Zhou (2008) hypothesized that expected evaluation in the variation stage, postulated by Campbell (1960) and mentioned above, would be detrimental because it inhibits the number of ideas that would be generated. Conversely they expected it to be helpful in the selective retention stage because it leads to appropriateness.

Bartis, Syzmanski, and Harkins (1988) examined the influence of evaluation expectation along with *social loafing*. Social loafing occurs when people work together, and their work is pooled, and as a result performances drop. Apparently people often assume that work will get done when they are in a group, and they do not put as much effect into the task as a result. Bartis et al. showed that evaluation expectation facilitated the performance of participants, whereas the performance of participants whose works are evaluated was lower than those whose works are pooled when they are asked to be creative.

It is, then, quite possible that interpersonal evaluations will exert a negative influence on intrinsic motivation, and thereby inhibit creative performances. Still, much of the research on evaluation and motivation has not used DT tests. Additionally, there are suggestions that interpersonal evaluations can be used to improve creative performances, and some of this work does rely on tests of DT. The research to which we are referring involves explicit instructions. These are clear and operational directions for completing a task. They have been used for years—at least since Harrington (1975)—to increase originality and flexibility on DT tests. More recent research has targeted other aspects of DT, including appropriateness evaluative accuracy.

Runco and Smith (1992) found that people are better in evaluating the popularity of ideas generated by others rather than the originality, but their accuracy in evaluating the popularity of their own ideas was the lowest. More telling is that the influence of explicit instructions can vary based on the type of tasks. Runco, Illies and Eisenmann (2005) compared four different instructions, inexplicit (or traditional), originality, appropriateness and creativity, for unrealistic and realistic tasks. They found that appropriateness scores in all four instructions were higher in realistic tasks than unrealistic tasks, while originality scores were higher in all four instructions for unrealistic tests than realistic tests. Based on those findings, Runco, Illies and Eisenmann (2005) also found that appropriateness and originality were not easy to blend. This is problematic because most definitions of creativity require both characteristics.

Runco and Charles (1993) compared participants' subjective evaluations of originality, appropriateness, and creativity with objective ratings of the same ideas. They found that originality and appropriateness were loosely connected and the lowest originality ratings were given to the most appropriate ideas. While originality seemed to be the core characteristic of creative ideas, inappropriateness did not undermine the perception of originality.

The most relevant research for designing supportive evaluations is probably that of Basadur, Runco, and Vega (2000) and Runco and Basadur (1993). Indeed, the second of these projects examined the effectiveness of training on the accuracy of the judgments given by managers. Runco and Basadur found that training improved evaluative accuracy, increasing the preference for active divergence and decreasing premature convergence. Significantly, Runco and Basadur also found moderators influencing the effectiveness of training: Creative problem solving profile ("implementor" score), ideational skills (fluency total score), and preference for active divergence post-treatment scores explained 61% of the variance in pre-and post-treatment difference. Originality was strongly correlated with correct-identification scores while the fluency score was not. It is possible that when a person has practice generating original ideas, they are also practicing the valuation of such ideas. Thus generation skill would help with evaluative accuracy.

Basadur, Wakabayashi and Graen (1990) also trained a group of people, and one of their groups was comprised of managers. They aimed to improve their skills and attitudes of divergent thinking and evaluation. They analyzed the effect with respect to profiles of the participants and found that the optimizer style of creative problem solving improves more than the other three styles (generator, conceptualizer and implementor). The training seemed to be the most helpful for managers in terms of active divergence.

In one final study with relevance to the improved evaluations of ideas, Licuanan, Dailey, and Mumford (2007) found that training that targeted creativity framing proved to be a good strategy to reduce the errors in evaluations. The active analysis of ideas, involving listing the strengths and weakness also improved evaluative accuracy (Dailey & Mumford, 2006).

ASSESSING CONVERGENT AND EVALUATIVE ABILITIES

DT is not synonymous with creative talent. It is a predictor of creative talent, or a contribution to it. Indeed, more often than not creative thinking involves at least some convergent thinking in addition to ideation. Because convergent thinking involves reasoning, logic, and evaluation, intelligence tests have been considered as a measure of convergent thinking. DeYoung and Flanders (2008), for example, used the The Wonderlic Personnel Test (WPT) which is a short test with 50 items. It had a strong correlation with WAIS-R ($r = .90$) which indicated concurrent validity (Wonderlic, 2000). Another indicator of convergent thinking is GPA. Since most of the curriculum requires students to find the best answer, and tests are often multiple choices, school works are indicative of convergent skills. Runco, Dow, and Smith (2006) for example, used GPA and reported that most of the intercorrelations between DT tasks and GPA were either non-significant or negatively corrrelated ($r = -.35$, $p < .05$), indicating discriminant validity.

Along with those measures, some specific tasks were developed to assess convergent skills. Several were part of the SOI, described earlier. Guilford (1967) developed "Correlate Completion II" to assess convergent thinking. It provides two word pairs which have a common pattern, and then the matching word for the third pair is asked. (Complete analogies where words are paired as to letter compositions: enrage-rage; correlated-late; about_____). Another test was called "Sentence Order" which asked the respondents to order three sentences to make a natural flow of events. Some of those tests or tasks have been used more recently. Brophy (2000–2001) used a Guilford (1977) task which asked respondents to use their knowledge to decide the best option for the visual figures, in the presence of goals and constraints, analyze and order the prompts, and reach a conclusion. He reported that this task had a reliability of .80 based on the KR20 formula.

Convergent thinking has been examined by two other kinds of assessment. One focuses on thinking style (rather than ability). Basadur and Finkbeiner (1985) used an eight-item Premature Critical Evaluation of Ideas scale to measure premature convergence. It included items such as "I should do some prejudgment of my ideas before telling them to others", "Quality is a lot more important than quantity in generating ideas", and "We should cut off ideas when they get ridiculous and get on with it". This factor had an internal reliability of .83. Basadur, Wakabayashi, and Graen (1990) administered this scale before and after training. They reported that Cronbach's alpha reliability of this scale ranged between .74 (before training) to .84 (after training).

The second approach is to assess evaluative ability. This is not the same as convergent thinking. Evaluative ability may be appreciative and look for what is right or original in an idea, rather than look only for it to fit with correctness or convention. As a matter of fact, Runco (1991) found a negative correlation between a measure of evaluative skills and an intelligence test. In this study, he used three lists of lexicon with both unique and non-unique responses. He created this list based on the responses of the participants in another study (Runco & Albert, 1985) where they used the tests of Instances, Uses, and Line Meanings. Each list included 25 responses, 10 of which are unique. Subjects were asked to rate the responses in terms of popularity and creativity on a 10-point scale. This test had a reliability of .77 (Cronbach alpha). The interest in the study was the inter-personal evaluative skills. Using the same method, Runco and Smith (1992) created a list for the intra-personal evaluation based on one's own responses. The Cronbach's alpha was reported as .50 for uniqueness instruction, .61 for popularity instruction.

Error management abilities were also measured by a similar procedure. Licuanan, Dailey, and Mumford (2007) used a scenario with e-mail exchanges in which ideas for advertisement campaigns are discussed. They had the participants read an e-mail conversation, and asked them to rate the originality of ideas on a five-point scale. Then they calculated the errors in this evaluation by calculating the discrepancy between the a priori originality scores and the participants' originality scores.

In another study, Dailey and Mumford (2006) used a 20-item scale of resources and outcome variables to evaluate project proposals. The items included "How difficult will it be to implement this idea?" and "How long will it take to implement this idea?" for the resources variables; and "How novel is this idea?" and "How many positive outcomes will result from this idea implementation?". Five judges rated the case descriptions by using the 20-item scale and their ratings had an inter-rate reliability of .70. For the validity, those items and the case descriptions were reviewed by a psychologist. The correlation between the objective data derived from the case materials and the evaluation of judges through the resource–outcome variables was high (r = .57). The accuracy was calculated by the difference between the participants' ratings and average ratings of the judges.

Blair and Mumford (2007) developed an instrument to measure "preference for the unoriginal". They generated a list of attributes based on the literature for the evaluation of ideas. The attributes included risky, easy to understand, original, complete description, complicated, consistent with the extant social norms, high probability of success, easy to implement, benefits a number of people, provides desired outcomes, time and effort to implement, and implementation complexity. Each idea was evaluated for those attributes on a three level scale. Experts' ratings had an average inter-rater reliability of .60. Cross-scale correlations provided the evidence for the construct validity, more specifically divergent and convergent validity, of those ratings. Ease of implementation was correlated with understandability, consistency with the extant social norms, and probability of success (r = .29, .42, and .58) while implementation difficulty was correlated with complication, risk, and perceived probability of success (r = .40, 15, and −.29). Based on the ratings of the experts for the ideas, 72 pairs of ideas were prepared, each representing a preference for an attribute.

DIVERGENT THINKING APPLIED TO ORGANIZATIONS

Divergent thinking may play several roles in organizations. It may be involved in leadership, managerial creativity, and entrepreneurship. With this in mind Sosik, Kahai, and

Avolio (1998) investigated the relationship between transformational leadership and anonymity, and divergent thinking. Four experimental groups; high versus low transformational leadership, and anonymous versus identified groups conditions, were compared with respect to fluency, flexibility, originality and elaboration. They found a main effect for transformation leadership, with the higher transformational leadership group scoring higher in originality and elaboration than the low transformational leadership group. Also, a main effect was found for anonymity. Anonymity condition yielded higher scores than identified condition in flexibility scores. They also found an interaction of transformational leadership and anonymity for flexibility. The highest flexibility was observed in the anonymous high transformational group and the lowest was identified in low transformational leadership.

Jung (2000–2001) compared transformational and transactional leadership in the conditions of real versus nominal brainstorming groups. When multivariate analyses were run by controlling for gender and group size, the significant main effects were for leadership and group conditions as well as an interaction effect of both on fluency and flexibility scores. As expected, the transformational leadership group was more flexible and fluent than the transactional group; and also nominal groups were superior to real groups in those regards.

Divergent thinking tests were also used for prediction of managerial creativity. Scratchley and Hakstian (2000–2001) used a battery of divergent thinking tests that were developed for industrial settings, including three components: the brainstorming exercise, which requires finding many solutions for a management problem; the similarities exercise, which entails finding many similarities between two different objects; and the association exercise which is about finding a word that connects three dissimilar words. They also used some other measures, including a test of intelligence and openness. The criterion involved a measure of global change and incremental criteria and a measure of general managerial creativity, both measures were domain specific. The composite of divergent thinking was correlated (both zero-order and part correlations) with the measure of global change and general managerial creativity, but not with the incremental change. They also showed that a divergent thinking test used with the openness test has validity when workplace criteria are used.

Ames and Runco (2005) tested the usefulness of SWOT (the strengths, weaknesses, opportunities and threats) analysis as an adapted version of divergent thinking tasks to predict entrepreneurship. The participants were entrepreneurs who started different numbers of businesses. The Runco Ideational Behavior Scale (RIBS) was also administered (Runco, Plucker, & Lim, 2000–2001). This is a self-report measure, assessing ideational skills in a natural environment. These analyses indicated that RIBS predicts entrepreneurship while the divergent thinking task based on SWOT analysis does not. However, scores from the SWOT are correlated with scores from the RIBS. The authors argued that skills measured by RIBS in the natural environment might come easier than a problem solving tasks. They concluded that the selection of tests is important even when they seem to measure same or similar skills.

CONCLUSIONS

The literature on DT is enormous. In this chapter we were quite selective and emphasized the research that has implications for organizational creativity and innovation. Recall here that much of the work involves entrepreneurs, managers, and organizational leaders.

Some of the research used problems—not just participant samples—that are directly relevant to organizational creativity (Basadur, 1994; Runco & Basadur, 1993; Ames & Runco, 2005).

There is an issue which may not be obvious unless we stand back from the topic. This issue reflects disagreements about the importance of ability and how it influences or determines performance. At first blush it might appear that ability is the primary determinant of performance, and therefore that individuals with more ability will perform at higher levels. This reasoning would apply to creative abilities but also more broadly to other abilities. Yet ability may not be the primary determinant of performance level. The alternative is that ability is essentially a given, at least at the individual level, and what is really important is whether or not the individual applies him- or herself. In more operational terms, this suggests that the motivation to succeed maybe more important than the ability to do so. Of course, in those terms, it is clear that performances reflect an interaction between ability and motivation. This is the only realistic view; to acknowledge the interaction. Yet motivation maybe more important in the practical sense because, if ability is a given and individuals each have a certain level of ability, then what determines whether or not they perform well is motivation. Motivation can vary, and in fact it varies quite a bit from moment to moment, or at least from one period of time to another. An individual can be interested and motivated one day, and lacking interested motivation the next. However the important point is that the motivation is what varies and is therefore of great interest and practicality. It is motivation that can be changed in a short run and manipulated through education or experimental treatments of some sort.

Still, keep in mind that quite a bit of the research reviewed in this chapter involves more than DT. That makes sense: creativity does not always depend on DT, and even when DT is involved, more than ideation is probably at work. Recall here the research pointing to motivation, knowledge, and evaluations. In fact, the research on evaluation and creativity may represent a trend in the literature. That is saying something, given that for years it was assumed that DT was good for creativity and convergent processes were bad. Fortunately we have gone beyond that simple dichotomy.

Future studies should continue to throw a broad net to take multiple factors into account. None of the abilities discussed in this chapter occurs in a vacuum; so many factors are at play, and the research on creative abilities should reflect this complexity. Chamorro-Premuzic and Reichenbacher (2008) examined the influence of personality, evaluation threat, and positive/negative affect on divergent and convergent thinking. This kind of range may be necessary for a full understanding of creative thinking. The results indicated that some of the creative abilities were strongly influenced by personality factors only under certain conditions, while other parts are not influenced by them at all. Future studies should also go beyond this, to focus on a specific ability and study their combined influence. Particularly, the facilitative and inhibitive relationship among the modes of divergent, convergent, and evaluative thinking should be part of the research agenda. The optimal combination, sequence, or interplay of those modes would be important.

Another venue is the way creative abilities are assessed. Traditional DT tests tend to assume that there is a general creative ability, namely, ideation, the general ability to produce ideas. However, as mentioned above, DT is also related to expertise, knowledge, and experience. Therefore, the domain-specific assessment of divergent thinking should allow the benefits of experience to be recognized. There is also a need for further adapted DT theory and testing in the organizational environment.

References

Amabile, T. M. (1979). Effects of external evaluation on artistic creativity. *Journal of Personality and Social Psychology, 37*, 221–233.

Amabile, T. M. (1996). *Creativity in context: Update to "The social psychology of creativity."* Boulder, CO: Westview Press.

Ames, M., & Runco, M. A. (2005). Predicting entrepreneurship from ideation and divergent thinking. *Creativity and Innovation Management, 14*, 311–315.

Bartis, S., Szymanski, K., & Harkins, S. G. (1988). Evaluation and performance: A two-edged knife. *Personality and Social Psychology Bulletin, 14*, 242–251.

Basadur, M. (1994). Managing the creative process in organizations. In M. A. Runco (Ed.), *Problem solving, problem finding, and creativity* (pp. 237–268). Norwood, NJ: Ablex Publishing Corporation.

Basadur, M. (1995). Optimal ideation–evaluation ratios. *Creativity Research Journal, 8*, 63–76.

Basadur, M., & Hausdorf, P. A. (1996). Measuring divergent thinking attitudes related to creative problem solving and innovation management. *Creativity Research Journal, 9*, 21–32.

Basadur, M., Runco, M. A., & Vega, L. (2000). Understanding how creative thinking skills, attitudes, and behaviors work together: A causal process model. *Journal of Creative Behavior, 34*, 77–100.

Basadur, M., Wakabayashi, M., & Graen, G. B. (1990). Individual problem solving styles and attitudes toward divergent thinking before and after training. *Creativity Research Journal, 3*, 22–32.

Basadur, M. S., & Finkbeiner, C. T. (1985). Measuring preference for ideation in creative problem solving training. *Journal of Applied Behavioral Science, 21*, 37–49.

Basadur, M. S., Graen, G. B., & Green, S. G. (1982). Training in creative problem solving: Effects on ideation and problem finding in an applied research organization. *Organizational Behavior and Human Performance, 30*, 41–70.

Blair, C. S., & Mumford, M. D. (2007). Errors in idea evaluation: Preference for the unoriginal? *Journal of Creative Behavior, 41*, 197–222.

Bowden, E. M., & Jung-Beeman, M. (2003). Aha! Insight experience correlates with solution activation in the right hemisphere. *Psychonomic Bulletin &.Review, 10*, 730–737.

Brophy, D. R. (1998). Understanding, measuring, and enhancing individual creative problem-solving efforts. *Creativity Research Journal, 11*, 123–150.

Brophy, D. R. (2000–2001). Comparing the attributes, activities, and performance of divergent, convergent, and combination thinkers. *Creativity Research Journal, 13*, 439–455.

Campbell, D. T. (1960). Blind variation and selective retention in creative thought as in other knowledge processes. *Psychological Review, 67*, 380–400.

Chamorro-Premuzic, T., & Reichenbacher, L. (2008). Effects of personality and threat of evaluation on divergent and convergent thinking. *Journal of Research in Personality, 42*, 1095–1101.

Chand, I., & Runco, M. A. (1993). Problem finding skills as components in the creative process. *Personality and Individual Differences, 14*, 155–162.

Christensen, P. R., Merrifield, P. R., & Guilford, J. P. (1953). *Consequences form A-1.* Beverly Hills, CA: Sheridan Supply.

Clapham, M. M. (1997). Ideational skills training: A key element in creativity training programs. *Creativity Research Journal, 10*, 33–44.

Cramond, B., Matthews-Morgan, J., Bandalos, D., & Zuo, L. (2005). A report on the 40-year follow-up of the Torrance Tests of Creative Thinking: Alive and well in the new millennium. *Gifted Child Quarterly, 49*, 283–291.

Cropley, A. J. (1967). *Creativity.* London, UK: Longmans, Green & Co. Ltd.

Cropley, A. (2006). In praise of convergent thinking. *Creativity Research Journal, 18*, 391–404.

Dailey, L. R., & Mumford, M. D. (2006). Evaluative aspects of creative thought: Errors in appraising the implications of new ideas. *Creativity Research Journal, 18*, 367–384.

Davidson, J. E., & Sternberg, R. J. (1984). The role of insight in intellectual giftedness. *Gifted Child Quarterly, 28*, 58–64.

DeYoung, C. G., Flanders, J. L., & Peterson, J. B. (2008). Cognitive abilities involved in insight problem solving: An individual differences model. *Creativity Research Journal, 20*, 278–290.

Geoff, K., & Torrance, E. P. (2002). *Abbreviated torrance test for adults.* Bensenville, IL: Scholastic Testing Service, Inc.

Guilford, J. P. (1950). Creativity. *American Psychologist, 5,* 444–454.

Guilford, J. P. (1967). *The Nature of Human Intelligence.* New York, NY: McGraw-Hill.

Guilford, J. P., & Hoepfner, R. (1971). *The analysis of intelligence.* New York, NY: McGraw–Hill.

Guilford, J. P. (1977). *Way beyond the IQ.* Buffalo, NY: Creative Education Foundation.

Guilford, J. P. (1988). Some changes in the structure-of-intellect model. *Educational and Psychological Measurement, 48,* 1–4.

Harrington, D. M., Block, J., & Block, J. H. (1983). Predicting creativity in preadolescence from divergent thinking in early childhood. *Journal of Personality and Social Psychology, 45,* 609–623.

Hocevar, D. (1979). Ideational fluency as a confounding factor in the measurement of originality. *Journal of Educational Psychology, 71,* 191–196.

Hocevar, D., & Michael, W. B. (1979). The effects of scoring formulas on the discriminant validity of tests of divergent thinking. *Educational and Psychological Measurement, 39,* 917–921.

Hocevar, D. (1981). Measurement of creativity: Review and critique. *Journal of Personality Assessment, 45,* 450–464.

Hunsaker, S. L., & Callahan, C. M. (1995). Creativity and giftedness: Published instrument uses and abuses. *Gifted Child Quarterly, 39,* 110–114.

Jung, D. I. (2000–2001). Transformational and transactional leadership and their effects on creativity in groups. *Creativity Research Journal, 13,* 185–195.

Khandwalla, P. N. (1993). An exploratory investigation of divergent thinking through protocol analysis. *Creativity Research Journal, 6,* 241–259.

Kilgour, M. (2006). Improving the creative process: Analysis of the effects of divergent thinking techniques and domain specific knowledge on creativity. *International Journal of Business and Society, 7,* 79–107.

Licuanan, B. F., Dailey, L. R., & Mumford, M. D. (2007). Idea evaluation: Error in evaluating highly original ideas. *Journal of Creative Behavior, 41,* 1–27.

Lonergan, D. C., Scott, G. M., & Mumford, M. D. (2004). Evaluative aspects of creative thought: Effects of appraisal and revision standards. *Creativity Research Journal, 16,* 231–246.

Lubart, T. I. (1994). *Product centered self-evaluation and the creative process.* Unpublished doctoral dissertation. New Haven, CT: Yale University.

McCoy, J. M. (2000). *The creative work environment: The relationship of the physical environment and creative teamwork at a state agency—A case study.* Ph.D. Dissertation. Wisconsin, University of Wisconsin-Milwaukee.

McCrae, R. R. (1987). Creativity, divergent thinking and openness to experience. *Journal of Personality and Social Psychology, 52,* 1258–1265.

Mednick, S. A. (1962). The associative basis of the creative process. *Psychology Review, 69,* 220–232.

Mednick, S. A. (1968). Remote Associates Test. *Journal of Creative Behavior, 2,* 213–214.

Merrifield, P. R., Guilford, J. P., Christensen, P. R., & Frick, J. W. (1962). The role of intellectual factors in problem solving. *Psychological Monographs, 76,* 1–21.

Michael, W. B., & Wright, C. R. (1989). Psychometric issues in the assessment of creativity. In J. A. Glover, R. R. Ronning & C. R. Reynolds (Eds.), *Handbook of creativity* (pp. 33–52). New York, NY: Plenum.

Milgram, R. M., Milgram, N. A., Rosenbloom, G., & Rabkin, L. (1978). Quantity and quality of creative thinking in children and adolescents. *Child Development, 49,* 385–388.

Moneta, G. B. (1993). A model of scientists' creative potential: The matching of cognitive structures and domain structure. *Philosophical Psychology, 6,* 23–37.

Mouchiroud, C., & Lubart, T. (2001). Children's original thinking: An empirical examination of alternative measures derived from divergent thinking tasks. *Journal of Genetic Psychology, 162,* 382–401.

Mumford, M. D. (2000–2001). Something old, something new: Revisiting Guilford's conception of creative problem solving. *Creativity Research Journal, 13,* 267–276.

Mumford, M. D., Blair, C., Dailey, L., Leritz, L. E., & Osburn, H. K. (2006). Errors in creative thought? Cognitive biases in a complex processing activity. *Journal of Creative Behavior, 40,* 75–110.

Mumford, M. D., Connelly, M. S., & Gaddis, B. (2003). How creative leaders think: Experimental findings and cases. *Leadership Quarterly, 14,* 411–432.

Mumford, M. D., Marks, M. A., Connelly, M. S., Zaccaro, S. J., & Johnson, J. F. (1998). Domain-based scoring of divergent thinking tests: Validation evidence in an occupational sample. *Creativity Research Journal, 11,* 151–163.

Mumford, M. D., Peterson, N. C., & Childs, R. A. (1999). Basic and cross-functional skills: Taxonomies, measures, and findings in assessing job skill requirements. In N. G. Peterson, M. D. Mumford, W. C. Borman, P. R.

Jeanneret & E. A. Fleishman (Eds.), *An occupational information system for the 21st century: The development of O*NET* (pp. 49–70). Washington, DC: American Psychological Association.

Mumford, M. D., Lonergan, D. C., & Scott, G. M. (2002). Evaluating creative ideas: Processes, standards, and context. *Inquiry: Critical Thinking across the Disciplines, 22,* 21–30.

Murray, H. A. (1959). Vicissitudes of creativity. In H. H. Anderson (Ed.), *Creativity and its cultivation* (pp. 203–221). New York, NY: Harper.

Nyström, H. (2000). The postmodern challenge: From economic to creative management. *Creativity and Innovation Management, 9,* 109–114.

Osborn, A. F. (1979). *Applied imagination: Principles and procedures of creative problem-solving.* New York, NY: Scribners.

Poole, M. E., Williams, A. J., & Lett, W. R. (1977). Inner-centeredness of highly creative adolescents. *Psychological Reports, 41,* 365–366.

Runco, M. A. (1991). The evaluative, valuative, and divergent thinking of children. *Journal of Creative Behavior, 25,* 311–319.

Runco, M. A. (1999). Divergent thinking. In M. A. Runco & S. Pritzker (Eds.), *Encyclopedia of creativity* (pp. 577–582). San Diego, CA: Academic Press.

Runco, M. A. (Ed.), (1994). *Problem finding, problem solving, and creativity.* Norwood, NJ: Ablex.

Runco, M. A. (Ed.), (in press). *Divergent thinking and creative potential.* Cresskill, NJ: Hampton Press.

Runco, M. A., & Acar, S. (in press-a). Divergent thinking as an indicator of creative potential. *Creativity Research Journal.*

Runco, M. A., & Acar, S. (in press-b). *Do tests of divergent thinking have an experiential bias? Psychology of Aesthetics, Creativity and the Arts.*

Runco, M. A., & Albert, R. S. (1985). The reliability and validity of ideational originality in the divergent thinking of academically gifted and non-gifted children. *Educational and Psychological Measurement, 45,* 483–501.

Runco, M. A., & Basadur, M. (1993). Assessing ideational and evaluative skills and creative styles and attitudes. *Creativity and Innovation Management, 2,* 166–173.

Runco, M. A., & Chand, I. (1995). Cognition and creativity. *Educational Psychology Review, 7,* 243–267.

Runco, M. A., & Charles, R. (1993). Judgments of originality and appropriateness as predictors of creativity. *Personality and Individual Differences, 15,* 537–546.

Runco, M. A., & Dow, G. T. (2004). Assessing the accuracy of judgment of originality on three divergent thinking tests. *Korean Journal of Thinking and Problem Solving, 14,* 5–14.

Runco, M. A., Dow, G. T., & Smith, W. R. (2006). Information, experience, and divergent thinking: An empirical test. *Creativity Research Journal, 18,* 269–277.

Runco, M. A., Millar, G., Acar, S., & Cramond, B. (2010). Torrance tests of creative thinking as predictors of personal and public achievement: A fifty-year follow-up. *Creativity Research Journal, 22,* 361–368.

Runco, M. A., & Mraz, W. (1992). Scoring divergent thinking tests using total ideational output and a creativity index. *Educational and Psychological Measurement, 52,* 213–221.

Runco, M. A., Plucker, J., & Lim, W. (2000–2001). Development and psychometric integrity of a measure of ideational behavior. *Creativity Research Journal, 13,* 393–400.

Runco, M. A., & Okuda, S. M. (1988). Problem discovery, divergent thinking, and the creative process. *Journal of Youth and Adolescence, 17,* 211–220.

Runco, M. A., & Smith, W. R. (1992). Interpersonal and intrapersonal evaluations of creative ideas. *Personality and Individual Differences, 13,* 295–302.

Runco, M. A., Illies, J. J., & Eisenman, R. (2005). Creativity, originality, and appropriateness: What do explicit instructions tell us about their relationships? *Journal of Creative Behavior, 39,* 137–148.

Runco, M. A., Okuda, S. M., & Thurston, B. J. (1987). The psychometric properties of four systems for scoring divergent thinking tests. *Journal of Psychoeducational Assessment, 5,* 149–156.

Runco, M. A., Okuda, S. M., & Thurston, B. J. (1991). Environmental cues and divergent thinking. In M. A. Runco (Ed.), *Divergent thinking* (pp. 79–85). Norwood, NJ: Ablex Publishing Corporation.

Sawyers, J. K., Moran, J. D., Fu, V. R., & Milgram, R. M. (1983). Familiar versus unfamiliar stimulus items in measurement of original thinking in young children. *Perceptual and Motor Skills, 57,* 51–55.

Scratchley, L. S., & Hakstian, A. R. (2000–2001). The measurement and prediction of managerial creativity. *Creativity Research Journal, 13,* 367–384.

Shalley, C. E. (1995). Effects of coaction, expected evaluation, and goal setting on creativity and productivity. *Academy of Management Journal, 38,* 483–503.

Sharma, R. (1999). Central dilemmas of managing innovation in large firms. *California Management Review, 41,* 146–164.

Simonton, D. K. (2007). The creative imagination in Picasso's Guernica sketches: Monotonic improvements or non-monotonic variants? *Creativity Research Journal, 19,* 329–344.

Smilansky, J. (1984). Problem solving and the quality of invention: An empirical investigation. *Journal of Educational Psychology, 76,* 377–386.

Sosik, J., Kahai, S., & Avolio, B. (1998). Transformational leadership and dimensions of creativity: Motivating idea generation in computer-mediated groups. *Creativity Research Journal, 11,* 111–121.

Strange, J. M., & Mumford, M. D. (2005). The origins of vision: Effects of reflection, models, and analysis. *The Leadership Quarterly, 16,* 121–148.

Titus, P. A. (2000). Marketing and the creative problem-solving process. *Journal of Marketing Education, 22,* 225–235.

Torrance, E. P. (1969). Prediction of adult creative achievement among high school seniors. *Gifted Child Quarterly, 13,* 223–229.

Torrance, E. P. (1972). Predictive validity of the Torrance tests of creative thinking. *Journal of Creative Behavior, 6,* 236–252.

Torrance, E. P. (1981). Predicting the creativity of elementary school children (1958–1980) and the teacher who "made a difference". *Gifted Child Quarterly, 25,* 55–62.

Torrance, E. P. (1995). *Rewarding creative behavior.* Englewood Cliff, NJ: Prentice-Hall.

Torrance, E. P., & Safter, H. T. (1989). The long range predictive validity of the Just Suppose Test. *Journal of Creative Behavior, 23,* 219–223.

Torrance, E. P., Tan, C. A., & Allman, T. (1970). Verbal originality and teacher behavior: A predictive validity study. *Journal of Teacher Education, 21,* 335–341.

Vincent, A. S., Decker, B. P., & Mumford, M. D. (2002). Divergent thinking, intelligence & expertise: A test of alternative models. *Creativity Research Journal, 14,* 163–178.

Wallach, M . A., & Kogan, N. (1965). *Modes of thinking in young children: A study of the creativity-intelligence distinction.* New York, NY: Holt, Kinnehart & Winston.

Wallach, M. A., & Wing, C. W., Jr. (1969). *The talented student: A validation of the creativity-intelligence distinction.* New York, NY: Holt, Kinehart & Winston.

Wallas, G. (1926). *The art of thought.* New York, NY: Harcourt, Brace & Co.

Ward, T. B., Smith, S. M., & Finke, R. A. (1999). Creative Cognition. In R. J. Sternberg Sternberg (Eds.), *Handbook of creativity* (pp. 189–212). Cambridge, UK: Cambridge University Press.

White, L., & Owen, D. (1970). Locus of evaluation for classroom work and the development of creative potential. *Psychology in the Schools, 7,* 292–295.

Williams, S. D. (2004). Personality, attitude, and leader influences on divergent thinking and creativity in organizations. *European Journal of Innovation Management, 7,* 187–204.

Wonderlic & Associates (2000). *Wonderlic personnel test and scholastic level exam: User's manual.* Libertyville, IL: Wonderlic Inc.

Yuan, F., & Zhou, J. (2008). Differential effects of expected external evaluation on different parts of the creative idea production process and on final product creativity. *Creativity Research Journal, 20,* 391–403.

Zarnegar, Z., Hocevar, D., & Michael, W. B. (1988). Components of original thinking in gifted children. *Educational and Psychological Measurement, 48,* 5–16.

The Expert Performance Approach and Deliberate Practice: Some Potential Implications for Studying Creative Performance in Organizations

K. Anders Ericsson and Jerad H. Moxley

Florida State University, Tallahassee, FL

The expert-performance approach (Ericsson, 2006a, 2006b; Ericsson & Smith, 1991; Ericsson & Ward, 2007) offers a unique framework for studying skill and expert performance. Whereas studies of expertise have traditionally identified highly educated and experienced individuals as experts and compared their performance to less experienced individuals, the expert-performance approach is committed to the objective study of superior performance, which captures the underlying skill in that domain and then designs controlled tasks that reproduce the relevant performance in standardized laboratory settings. Once stable individual differences in performance can be reproduced, efforts can be made to identify the mechanisms that mediate the superior performance and then to determine how the key mechanisms are either acquired by some type of practice and/or emerge during development based on innate endowment.

Recently the study of expertise and expert performance reached a point of maturity, in that a handbook was published with over 1,000 pages and over forty chapters (Ericsson, Charness, Feltovich, & Hoffman, 2006). This handbook contained chapters on the acquisition and structure of expertise in diverse domains such as medicine, transportation, software design, writing expertise, music, acting, sports, chess, memory, and mathematics. In virtually all of these domains the results have consistently supported the pivotal role that effortful training activities which are specifically designed to improve performance, or *deliberate practice*, play in the development of expert performance, as opposed to the mere accumulation of experience in the domain of expertise. More recently another edited book reviewed research studying the acquisition of objectively superior performance associated with the development of professional expertise (Ericsson, 2009a).

The expert-performance approach proposes that the most important creative innovations in a domain are typically completed during the last stage in the careers of experts, when a small number of them generate innovations to training, methods, performance or produce innovative types of products (see Ericsson, 1999, for a general discussion). In professional contexts one can track the development of individual experts where there are many contributing team members, in areas such as surgery (Ericsson, 2011), interpreting (Ericsson, 2000), music (Chaffin & Imreh, 2002; Ericsson, 2002), nursing (Whyte, Pickett-Hauber, Cormier, Grubbs, & Ward, 2010) and other domains (Ericsson, 2009b; Ericsson et al., 2006). Most of the research studies have examined the long period of acquisition of expert levels of performance rather than the apex of experts' careers, when a small number of them make major creative innovations to their domain of expertise.

OUTLINE OF CHAPTER

In their influential paper "Toward a theory of organizational creativity", Woodman, Sawyer, and Griffin (1993, p. 294) proposed that "creativity is the complex product of a person's behavior in a given situation" and proposed how creative performance in organizations might be influenced by different factors at the level of the individual, groups, and organizations. They showed that limited research on organizational creativity had been conducted in the field, but they were also pessimistic that further relevant field research would be conducted. Furthermore, they cautioned that laboratory research cannot be a valid substitute. They concluded that:

> "research on organizational creativity faces level-of-analysis problems and severe measurement and construct validity problems with operational creativity" *(p. 315).*

In their recent review of the history of organizational creativity research, Shalley and Zhou (2008) described how most research has been guided by theoretical frameworks. Given the rare occurrence of creative actions in organizations, researchers focused on reducing the amount of habitual actions (Ford, 1996). Other researchers turned the focus away from the generation of creative products to prerequisite processes, such as the attempts of individuals to engage in creative activities (Drazin, Glynn, & Kazanjian, 1999). Similarly, Mumford (2000) proposed how organizations might enhance creativity by providing organizational support and incentives for creativity. Other researchers focused on the social context and how networks might facilitate creativity (Perry-Smith & Shalley, 2003; Sawyer, 2008). Shalley and Zhou (2008) review field studies of organizational creativity, where employee's perceptions of their work context are related to their supervisors' creativity ratings. They point out, however, that only a small number of studies have used:

> "objective measures of creativity, such as number of patents, patent disclosures, technical reports and research papers, and ideas submitted to organizational suggestion systems" *(p. 19).*

Even most of these cited studies using objective measures have weaknesses—as we will show later in this chapter.

Our chapter is an attempt to address the central question of the expert-performance approach for creative performance—namely how can we identify and examine reproducibly superior performance? The successful research on expert performance has focused on a single individual's performance, such as the surgeon, the soloist or the nurse in charge of post-operational care. We recognize that one cannot repeatedly generate the same innovative idea or produce the same new type of product as a means to exhibit consistent creative performance. We will argue that the consistent creation of new (different) innovative ideas constitutes creative performance, and this can be understood in terms of the same *type* of processes as those that mediate related skilled responses to new and challenging tasks and demands (Ericsson, 1999). Consequently, we believe that repeated production of creative products should be measured as objectively as possible. Only when a superior performance has been identified in a real-world setting would it make sense to study this type of performance by capturing the phenomenon with representative tasks in the laboratory, so one can study the mediating mechanisms.

The expert-performance approach is strongly committed to objective measures of performance and actively avoids judgments and ratings by supervisors or teachers, unless they can be demonstrated to be a valid shortcut to objective measures. Our decision to impose criteria for reproducibility and quantifiably will necessarily exclude a considerable body of research on organizational creativity, and will thus limit the empirical base for our review. In the first part of our chapter we will review the traditional perspectives on professional expertise, and describe some of the empirical evidence that stimulated the development of the expert-performance approach and its commitment to objective measurement in order to avoid problems with social indicators of performance. In the subsequent sections we will attempt to apply the expert-performance approach to professional performance and its problems in varied contexts and tasks. We will discuss how we can extend the approach to the study of performance of organizations and the relation between performance of individuals and the productivity of an organization and a company. We will then review evidence about performance that is relevant to organizational creativity. In the final section of our chapter we will discuss alternative approaches to the study of creative performance and conclude with discussions about future research opportunities for those researchers interested in applying the expert-performance approach.

PROFESSIONAL EXPERTISE AND EXPERT-PERFORMANCE APPROACH

The expert-performance approach was developed as a response to traditional conceptions of expertise that were based on innate talent and/or extended experience. We will first describe the traditional approaches and how this led to the distinctions between superior and acceptable performance. After describing how the superior (expert) performance differs in its development from acceptable performance, we will focus on how deliberate practice leads to improvement over years and decades.

Traditional Perspectives on Professional Expertise: A Critical View

The traditional views of professional expertise hold that inborn abilities and capacities limit individuals' abilities to increase their performance through training and impose constraints on who can reach higher levels of success. Sir Francis Galton is often cited as this view's modern spokesperson through his book *Hereditary Genius*, (Galton, 1869/1979). According to Galton, relevant heritable capacities determine the upper range of achievement that individuals can attain through practice, and thus reflect the immutable limit that:

"Nature has rendered him capable of performing" *(p. 16)*.

Galton argued that the limiting factor for maximal performance, after all benefits of training have been gained must, by definition, reflect innate endowment. If, on the other hand, individuals are still able to improve through some new and different type of continued training, then other types of explanations for sub-maximal level of performance and arrested improvements must be considered and explored.

Galton's (1869/1979) argument for limits is compatible with the traditional model of skill acquisition proposed by Fitts and Posner (1967). Their model argues that when people initially learn a task, they first attempt to understand the task using general strategies, then they gradually learn increasingly complex habits until task performance becomes automatic. Newell and Rosenbloom (1981) identified the learning of increasingly refined chunks as the mechanism behind this type of skill acquisition, drawing on the popular chunking theory of expertise (Simon & Chase, 1973). In an important contribution, Anderson (1982) demonstrated that the phases of skill acquisition and improvements in performance could be formally described by a computer model in the form of a production system where simple rules are compiled into procedures. All of these models assume that skilled performance flows naturally from experience in the domain (Dreyfus & Dreyfus, 1986). Consequently, researchers started to study how highly experienced practitioners (experts) performed in important professional domains, such as nursing (Benner, Tanner, & Chesla, 1992).

In most professional domains of expertise, the levels of attained performance of an individual are not measured by objective methods. Consequently, levels of expertise are based on social judgments by supervisors and peers. Thus, the operational definition of who was an expert was often determined by social indicators, such as reputation and length of experience in a domain (over ten years), as well as completed education and accumulated knowledge (Chi, 2006; Chi, Glaser, & Farr, 1988).

This definition of expertise has been criticized by several reviews over the past decade (Bédard & Chi, 1992; Ericsson, 2006b; Ericsson & Lehmann, 1996; Ericsson & Smith, 1991). For instance, in many domains, decisions by two experts often disagree sharply with each other (Shanteau, 2001). Even more troubling, reviews of highly important social domains, such as clinical diagnosis, showed that statistical models nearly always outperform experts (Dawes, Faust, & Meehl, 1989). Furthermore, highly experienced computer programmers did not always outperform computer science students, and physics professors from the University of California at Berkeley were not consistently superior to students on introductory physics problems (see Ericsson and Lehmann's review, 1996, for reference to these and other studies). Recent reviews among doctors (Ericsson, 2004) and nurses (Ericsson, Whyte, & Ward, 2007) have demonstrated that, while there are some specialists who have systematically better outcomes for their patients within their specialty than non-specialists, there is little evidence of general benefits derived from extended professional experience. This effect has also been demonstrated in the military where, over a year, job performance was not found to show further increases (Wigdor & Green, 1991). A recent meta-analysis in clinical reasoning showed a similar effect—with a noticeable disadvantage for people with no experience, but little if any advantage for additional experience beyond the initial exposures (Spengler et al., 2009). In a recent review of political judgment Philip Tetlock (2005) was able to dispel the myth that professional experts' forecasts are superior to well-informed non-experts or even undergraduates.

Differences in the Acquisition of Superior and Acceptable Performance

The body of evidence outlined above demonstrates that while acceptable performance in the workplace may follow naturally from experience, exceptional performance clearly does not come automatically from extended experience in the domain. The concept of deliberate practice can account for the large individual differences between experts and novices, but also explains why experience does not equal expertise.

In a majority of tasks, most people are content with reaching a merely acceptable level of performance. Once a satisfactory level has been reached, we only need to maintain that level of performance, and often can do so with very little effort for years and even decades. As a consequence, the length of job experience is generally found to be a weak correlate of job performance beyond the first two years (McDaniel, Schmidt, & Hunter, 1988), which concept, as discussed earlier, generalizes to many professional domains (Ericsson & Lehmann, 1996; Choudhry, Fletcher, & Soumerai, 2005; Ericsson 2004; Ericsson et al., 2007).

In traditional theories of skill acquisition, expertise is fundamentally limited by basic processing capacities such as transient working memory. Therefore extended experience is hypothesized to improve performance in several ways. The first change in performance is that it becomes more fluid with faster execution times. With even more experience individuals are able to automate their performance, which reduces the processing demands of the task, saving resources to be used elsewhere (Fitts & Posner, 1967). Some individuals acquire large patterns that permit them to rapidly retrieve appropriate actions directly from memory. These acquired patterns (chunks) allow more efficient use of memory capacity (Newell & Rosenbloom, 1981) and efficient reliance of procedural knowledge (Anderson, 1982). To some extent this appears to be the case for many professional domains where experience does lead to faster, easier, but not necessarily more accurate performance (Ericsson & Lehmann, 1996).

Current theories of expertise, which focus on the reproducibly superior performance of experts, disagree with the sufficiency of the traditional Fitts-Posner model (Feltovich, Prietula, Ericsson, 2006). A wide body of research has shown that, by engaging in deliberate practice, experts continually refine their representation of their domain, building a highly organized and complex knowledge base. These representations allow experts to rapidly encode new information and integrate it with other relevant information into long-term memory. They are also able to reliably and rapidly retrieve relevant information from long-term memory for cognitive processing (Ericsson & Kintsch, 1995). This skilled use of long-term memory is called long-term working memory because it allows experts to use storage in long-term memory as rapidly and flexibly within their domain as novices use transient working memory. The acquisition of long-term working memory allow experts to meet the processing demands in their domain of expertise, and offers an explanation of how experts acquire their superior performance for representative tasks from the domain of expertise.

Most of the laboratory research related to creativity has involved undergraduates and short-term problem solving with tasks, where they lack specialized expertise. For example, Hunter, Bedell-Avers, Hunsicker, Mumford, and Ligon, (2008) demonstrated the role of organizational concepts (schemas) and associations in facilitating generated solutions to a problem of designing a hypothetical college course by undergraduates (Hunter et al., 2008). Future research will be required to tell whether these findings will generalize to experts solving problems in their domain of expertise.

Development of Elite and Expert Performers

The developmental history of international-level performers in the arts, science and sports, was shown by Bloom and his colleagues (Bloom, 1985a, 1985b) to be fundamentally different from their less accomplished peers. Based on retrospective interviews, Bloom and his colleagues found that the parents of the future elite performers helped their children from an early age to get instruction from teachers, to cover significant expenses for teachers and equipment, and to devote much of their time to transporting their child to training sessions and weekend competitions. In some cases, one of the parents or the whole family would even relocate to permit the child to study with an outstanding teacher and to have access to superior training facilities. Based on their interviews, Bloom (1985a) concluded that access to the superior training resources was necessary to give a child a reasonable chance of reaching the highest levels of competition in a given domain. However, mere access to superior teachers and training environments is not sufficient to produce the very best performers, as there are large individual differences even among children and adolescents in these favorable training environments.

If access to the best teachers and training environments is necessary, but does not sufficiently explain top performance, then we need to examine the amount and type of training activity that different students engage in on a daily basis to ascertain its correlation with individual differences in attained performance, even among the top performers.

In 1993, Ericsson et al. studied expert violinists at an internationally renowned music academy in Berlin. To gather information about their engagement in specific activities, the violin students kept a weekly diary of how much time they spent on each activity during a week. All violin students in the academy reported spending about the same amount of time (over 50 hours) per week on any type of music-related activity. However, the best violinists (the students training for a career as soloists) were found to spend more hours per week by themselves, engaged in training activities that had been specifically recommended by their teachers to improve specific aspects of their performance. Expert musicians practicing in a solitary setting in order to master specific performance goals identified by their music teachers at weekly lessons is a prime example of goal-directed efforts to reach a higher level of performance-practice activities that capture the essence of "deliberate practice" (Ericsson et al., 1993). During the weekly lessons the teachers listen to their music students' performance of particular pieces of music and then recommend that they improve some aspect of that performance, which requires the student to try to attain a level of playing that they are unable to reach at that time. A week later, and after a considerable amount of solitary practice, the musicians should have improved their performance and will be able to play at the requested level. The expert violinists were also asked to estimate how many hours of

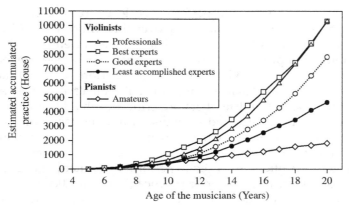

FIGURE 7.1   Estimated amount of time for solitary practice as a function of age for the middle-aged professional violinists (triangles), the best expert violinists (squares), the good expert violinists (empty circles), the least accomplished expert violinists (filled circles) and amateur pianists (diamonds). *(From "The role of deliberate practice in the acquisition of expert performance," by K. A. Ericsson, R. Th. Krampe and C. Tesch-Römer, 1993,* Psychological Review, 100(3), p. 379 and p. 384. Copyright 1993 by American Psychological Association. Adapted with permission.)

solitary (deliberate) music practice that they had engaged in per week during their musical development. The group of the most accomplished musicians (nominated by their teachers as potential international soloists) was found to have spent more time in deliberate practice during their development than the other violin soloists, as well as the group studying to become violin teachers. The accumulated hours of deliberate practice per group is shown in Figure 7.1 and, at the time of their admittance to the music academy at around age 18, the differences between groups are already significant. By the age of 20, the top violinists had spent over 10,000 hours practicing, which averages 2,500 hours more than the less accomplished group of violin soloists at the same academy (Ericsson et al., 1993). In comparison to a group of amateur pianists of the same age (Krampe & Ericsson, 1996), the top violinists from the academy had practiced 8,000 more hours.

Continued Improvement of Expert Performance with Deliberate Practice

The basic assumption of the expert performance approach (Ericsson, 1996, 2002, 2004; Ericsson et al., 1993) is that the development of increasingly superior performance can be described as a sequence of states. For example, pianists first start acquiring playing techniques with the easiest techniques that allow the student to play easy music pieces. After a few years of piano playing, teachers would begin to assign music pieces that require complex movement with non-dominant (left) hand. After 9 years of piano instruction the normal student is ready to try to master poly-rhythms, where the musicians' hands have to play with a different rhythm. For example, for every 2 beats in one hand, the other hand has to complete 3 beats and even more complex ratios of rhythms such as 4:5 and 5:6. Composers of piano music invented these complex techniques in the 18th and 19th centuries and the invented techniques keep increasing in complexity over historical time (Lehmann & Ericsson, 1998).

Similarly in individual sports, the performance levels of athletes in running, throwing, and jumping have increased dramatically over time (Ericsson, 2007). Across domains the aspiring expert performers find ways to change their currently attained maximal performance by training to improve the mediating mechanisms of performance. The key challenge to motivated performers is to identify aspects of performance that can be successfully improved by a training activity that will incrementally increase that aspect as well as the overall performance. Coaches and teachers are critical in this identification process. They can observe students' performance and recommend training tasks with known success in meeting explicit goals, based on research and their own experience with other students. For example, piano students often need to increase their speed for executing particular finger combinations and they are often instructed to perform particular finger exercises and etudes with increasing speed. Effective, deliberate practice (Ericsson, 2006b) requires that the performers try to improve achievement on tasks that are initially outside their current realm of reliable performance. Deliberate practice tasks for a given student must permit improvement on the targeted characteristic within a limited number of hours of practice or else the performer will become discouraged.

Appropriate tasks for deliberate practice for a given student will depend on the domain of expertise, the particular training goal and the individuals' pre-existing skills for monitoring and controlling their performance (Ericsson, 2006b, 2007). For example, chess players try to find the best move for presented chess positions. If they select a move different from the best move, they should analyze the position to figure out why they did not find the best move in order to avoid similar mistakes in the future. If, however, the presented position is too complex, efforts to understand the reasons for selecting the best move might fail, which in turn leads to frustration and no benefit. Being able to match the chess players with problems of appropriate difficulty is a key to deliberate practice and effective learning. Similarly, a weight-lifter attempting to increase the force of a movement might repeat the movement with too much weight and repeat it until exhaustion of the associated muscles. This defeats the purpose of gradually working up to reach attainable goals.

More generally, individuals' performances on appropriate training tasks will vary as a function of focus of their attention, their anticipation, their adopted strategy, their fatigue, and many other situational factors. If one wants to reach one's highest performance consistently or even go beyond one's initial maximal performance, one has to identify optimal circumstances to perform that task. Consequently, any type of deliberate practice depends on the performer being fresh and ready at the start of the activity. The performers should also be completely prepared for initiation of the task, be given immediate feedback on their performance and then allowed to repeat the same or similar tasks with gradual modifications. The performance of the task under these optimal conditions will be superior to the performance of the same task when it occurs spontaneously (often unexpectedly) within the natural context of performance in domain-related activities such as play and competition.

In order for deliberate practice to lead to superior performance under natural conditions, it is necessary to bridge the optimal training of performance on the task with transfer to performance under less optimal conditions. This is typically achieved by eventually embedding the trained task in its natural context, adding regular time constraints, and making its occurrence less predictable. For example, consider an amateur tennis player who misses a volley at the net during a game with a friend. The play will resume and go on until some time later a similar situation emerges unexpectedly with a similar problem for the player. Contrast this type of "on-the-job" learning with a dedicated training session with a tennis coach. The tennis coach is able to arrange situations where the player would stand at the net and be ready to execute an easy volley. Once easy volleys are mastered, the coach can increase the difficulty of the volley returns and eventually embed volley shots into extended rallies. It is easy to see that a few hours of this type of gradual training would improve a particular player's volley returns more than tens or hundreds of hours of regular tennis play against other amateurs. This process of identifying weaknesses in performance, finding solutions for those weaknesses, and then testing the solution has been compared to continuous problem solving (Ericsson, 2003). This would mean the goal is to come closer to the maximal performance for the task and the problem space that would consist of different tasks for deliberate practice and training activities that would change the structure of the individual's mental representations and skills and make them more similar to those required for maximal performance.

This continual attempt to move closer to optimal performance makes deliberate practice qualitatively different from both routine performance and playful engagement. The latter two types of activities would, if anything, merely strengthen the currently imperfect cognitive mediating mechanisms rather than modifying and refining them to allow increases in the level of performance. Within the framework of deliberate practice and expert performance, the learning involved in everyday activities such as driving a car, typing, playing golf, and many jobs is associated with a goal of reaching an acceptable level of performance. This everyday learning is consistent with traditional theories of skill acquisition (Anderson, 1982; Fitts & Posner, 1967) where learners attain an acceptable standard of performance in frequently less than 50 hours for most recreational activities. At this point of acceptable mastery, most individuals no longer make regular intentional efforts to further modify and improve their performance, which typically leads to a stable plateau of achievement that can be maintained with regular activity for months, years and decades. In direct contrast, aspiring expert performers never allow their behavior to be fully automated and continue to seek out, with the help of their teachers, new challenging training activities. In order to master these training tasks, individuals need to engage in problem solving in order to refine their cognitive representations and keep improving the mechanisms mediating performance, as illustrated by the upper arm in Figure 7.2. Some individuals will train to improve their performance for months or even years, but eventually reach a point where they stop pushing their limits and stop regular engagement in deliberate practice. For those individuals the performance level will eventually become automated and their development will be prematurely arrested at that intermediate level, as illustrated by the middle arm in Figure 7.2.

Deliberate Practice in the Workplace

Deliberate practice as we have described it can be thought of as something clearly different from most types of experience in the workplace and everyday life. This difference explains why experience in a domain of professional expertise is so weakly related to performance. When surgeons perform surgeries on patients, they need to execute the surgery in a manner that provides the best chances for recovery and health of the patient. It would be irresponsible to try out an alternative surgical method or take the time to attempt to

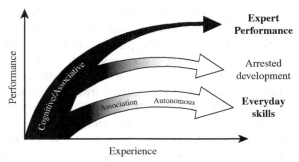

FIGURE 7.2 An illustration of the qualitative difference between the course of improvement of expert performance and of everyday activities. The goal for everyday activities is to reach as rapidly as possible a satisfactory level that is stable and "autonomous". After individuals pass through the "cognitive" and "associative" phases they can generate their performance virtually automatically with a minimal amount of effort (see the gray/white plateau at the bottom of the graph). In contrast, expert performers counteract automaticity by developing increasingly complex mental representations to attain higher levels of control of their performance and will therefore remain within the "cognitive" and "associative "phases. Some experts will at some point in their career give up their commitment to seeking excellence and thus terminate regular engagement in deliberate practice to further improve performance which results in premature automation of their performance. *(Adapted from "The scientific study of expert levels of performance: General implications for optimal learning and creativity" by K. A. Ericsson in* High Ability Studies, 9, *p. 90. Copyright 1998 by European Council for High Ability.)*

improve on some particular weakness in their surgical skills. More generally, professionals, craftsmen, and employees are expected to achieve the best possible result given their attained current level of skill during their work hours, public performances, and competitions. This does not imply that the time associated with competition or work cannot be used to improve performance. The performers can often engage in considerable preparation prior to actual performance, such as planning the surgery, preparing for playing a set of music pieces or for facing specific athletic opponents.

It is possible to re-create or simulate conditions of actual performance during practice sessions (performance practice) in anticipation of the actual (often public) performance. For instance, in surgery, recent training using simulators has provided surgical deliberate practice that has been shown to develop a different learning curve to that of merely gaining experience (Crochet et al., 2009). Recent research in the army has shown that training can rapidly plateau, but if training more like deliberate practice is undertaken, improvement either resumes or never stops. A classic example given for this is the success of the Navy's top gun program during Vietnam, when, during a break in air combat Navy pilots were trained in the air against strong pilots who would then give the pilots feedback on what they did wrong. This program led to a 10-fold improvement in combat performance for these pilots (Chatham, 2009). Additionally, training using simulators and feedback helped anti-submarine personnel to perform better after training than experienced fleet personnel, an improvement in sonar detection that would have cost billions to achieve with superior equipment (Fletcher, 2009).

More generally, skilled individuals should be able to encode significant events during the actual performance so they can recall them after the end of a performance. Alternatively it may be possible to video tape the performance and then review the tapes by themselves or with a coach or supervisor. During the review the individuals can identify problems and weaknesses that can be targeted in subsequent practice sessions. In some sports, like soccer and tennis, there may often be enough time between ball possessions or during side changes in tennis and intermissions in soccer to consider alternative tactics that will be more successful. Game film is also recorded in most major sports, allowing close inspection of performance by both the player and the coaches. At the very least, problems can be identified through performance on the field that can guide the direction of practice.

In some domains, where the focus is on increased speed and efficiency, deliberate practice will be similar to the actual work activity but the goals are different. For example, the best way to increase one's typing speed is to set aside 10–20 minutes each morning, when most individuals are most alert, to push themselves to type 10–20% faster than their normal comfortable speed of typing (Dvorak, Merrick, Dealey, & Ford, 1936). During these efforts, the typists realize which key stroke combinations are causing hesitations and thus slowing down the typing process. Once these combinations have been identified, the typists can try to overcome these problems with targeted practice. It is often helpful to type especially prepared texts, where these key stroke combinations are relatively frequent, to incorporate the improved key sequences into their integrated typing skill. Once certain combinations have been mastered then the cycle starts over with identifying new problems that are slowing the typists' elevated speed.

Summary

The expert-performance approach has been successfully applied to domains, such as sports, music and chess, where there are organized competitions that measure individual performance. The search for reproducibly superior performance has shown that peer nominations, length of professional experience and level of education are frequently not related to measurable superior performance. Given that we are not interested in studying perceptions of expertise and creativity, the expert-performance approach has made a commitment to identifying and studying objective performance rather than performance correlates of unknown validity, such as supervisor ratings.

In the next section we will explore an approach based on studying objective performance applied to professional domains. The general method will be to search for some examples of particular job performance that can be measured with objective methods. Once this type of performance is captured and repeatedly reproduced, we will proceed to study its structure and search for training activities that are related to the improvement of performance (deliberate practice). We will first discuss how the expert-performance approach can overcome challenges of studying performance in the workplace more generally. In the section that follows we will discuss how the approach can be applied to the study of the performance of groups and organizations, and then finally we will examine how this approach might be applied to study organizational creativity.

APPLYING THE EXPERT-PERFORMANCE APPROACH TO PERFORMANCE IN THE WORKPLACE

In the work environment, expert professionals encounter unique challenges under different conditions. The differences in tasks and their difficulty make it nearly impossible to compare levels of performance of different experts simply by outcomes. For example, one doctor specializing in a certain type of cancer surgery may primarily treat clients with complex and difficult conditions, whereas another doctor may treat mostly patients with relatively routine cancer conditions. How can one compare the performance of one manager assigned to resolve several serious interpersonal conflicts during the restructuring of a firm with the performance of another manager who merely has to guide an enthusiastic team? Unless professionals encounter situations with the same or comparable challenges, it will be nearly impossible to measure individual differences in performance in a meaningful manner. The first step of the expert performance approach involves searching for and identifying reproducibly superior performance and then designing representative tasks that capture the essence of expertise in the domain. Only when such superior performance has been successfully captured is it possible to study and identify the mechanisms that are responsible for the superior performance, and then examine if there are training activities that were responsible for the superior characteristics of the mechanisms and how one might be able to set up such training conditions. If we are unable to identify and capture such superior performance then there is no obvious next step. Consequently, we will start by describing how superior performance has been successfully identified and captured by standardized representative tasks, before we explore the possibility of identifying such performance in the workplace.

Capturing Reproducibly Superior Performance under Standardized Conditions

In a pioneering study, de Groot (1978) was able to examine the superior performance of experts by designing representative tasks that captured the essence of expertise in the domain of chess. Akin to the problems of finding similar tasks for experts, chess players rarely encounter the exactly same chess positions while playing games—once they have advanced the game beyond the opening. The ultimate criterion for success in chess is the ability to win games consistently at chess tournaments, where players match their chess skill in matches that last for several hours. There are statistical methods for measuring a chess player's rating on an interval scale, by an analysis of outcomes from 20–50 tournament matches with different opponents—corresponding to roughly 40–100 hours of play and over 5,000 chess moves. De Groot (1978) was able to avoid a detailed analysis of the thousands of different moves in the tournaments. He identified particular chess positions in past games between chess masters that the chess players would never have seen and where he knew (based on 100 hours of extensive analysis) the best chess move. He then presented the same set of selected positions to chess players during an individual testing session and asked them to "think aloud" while they generated the best possible next move for each of the positions. De Groot (1978) was able to confirm that world-class players reliably found the best moves for these positions, whereas skilled club players only found the best chess moves for some of them. More recent research with large groups of chess players differing widely in skill has found that the ability to select the best move for presented chess positions is highly correlated with the tournament ratings (Ericsson, Patel, & Kintsch, 2000; van der Maas & Wagenmakers, 2005). When move selections for 20–40 chess positions are aggregated, the resulting measure is highly correlated with chess ratings—thus it is possible to measure a chess player's skill after less than 15–20 minutes of testing. Of particular interest, de Groot (1978) was able to pinpoint how the thought processes of world-class players were different from highly skilled club players through an analysis of their "think aloud" protocols, that were given while they were trying to find the best move for the chess positions.

Based on a generalization of De Groot's paradigm, Ericsson and Smith (1991) proposed the *expert-performance approach*. This approach was later extended to study superior performance in many domains of expertise, such as music, sports, or medicine. It attempts to identify naturally occurring situations in a given domain of expertise that require immediate action and that capture the essence of expertise in the associated domain. For example, in the everyday life of a doctor or a nurse they will encounter emergency situations where they have to react immediately to assess the symptoms of a patient, make a diagnosis and provide the necessary treatment. Similarly, it is possible to study soccer games for situations where a given player is required to elicit an action without any delay (Ward & Williams, 2003). Once situations have been found where the correct and appropriate courses of action have been identified, it is then possible to reproduce them and present them, with an appropriate context and an immediate demand for action, under standardized conditions for all tested participants. In a controlled environment, such as a laboratory with a video screen or a simulator, it is possible to show the emergence of these representative situations to participants differing in skill. For each test, it is possible to record the participants' behavior prior to the initiation of the critical action, and then assess the correctness/appropriateness of their action. It is also possible to record process-tracing data, such as eye-fixations and concurrent or retrospective verbal reports, which allow for the determination and explication of the detailed mechanisms that account for the reproducible differences in the selection of correct actions.

The representative tasks are designed to simulate task demands and situations that a performer might encounter, and if we embed these tasks into appropriate contexts with typical demands for rapid action, it will be very likely that superior performance on the tasks will correspond to superior performance in real life situations, just like it does in chess. Figure 7.3 illustrates representative tasks in three domains, where performance on the tasks has been found to capture the essence of the associated expertise, and to correlate with everyday performance. In each case, the measured performance is closely associated with the naturally occurring performance. Chess players at different skill levels are instructed to generate the best move for identical positions, where a single superior move is available (as determined by new chess-playing programs that are superior to the best human players for tactical problems). Different typists are instructed to copy the same text and asked to type as much of the presented material as possible during a fixed time period with penalties for any errors. Musicians of different skill levels are instructed to play relatively simple pieces of music. After completing the first performance they are asked to try to play the same piece again with the same speed and interpretation. When skilled musicians perform the same piece again they are able to do so with less variation than less skilled musicians (Ericsson et al., 1993; Krampe & Ericsson, 1996).

When the empirical evidence is limited to observable superior performance, obtained under standardized controlled conditions, a couple of generalizable relations between expert performance and experience emerge across domains of expertise. First, greatly superior performance (as measured by adult standards) is only attained after extensive experience in a given domain. Second, consistent improvements in performance are only associated with engagement in some restricted types of experience, namely deliberate

B. INDIVIDUAL LEVEL INFLUENCES

Domain	Presented Information	Task
Chess		Select the best chess move for this position
Typing	OVERVIEW–NATURE AND NURTURE OF EXPERTISE The central challenge for any account of expertise is to explain how individuals attain the highest levels of achievement in a domain and why so few reach that level. However, given the continuing struggle in Psychology to explain every day (lower) levels of achievement, it may appear presumptuous to attempt to explain even more advanced levels. Consequently, the accounts of expertise have been focusing on the general characteristics of the mechanisms. In order to be able to achieve at very high (expert) levels in domains of expertise both nature and nurture are necessary. Hence, everyone agrees that experts need to have acquired the necessary domain-specific knowledge and skills (nature). Furthermore, the expert's performance often looks effortless and their most refined and insightful behavior is generated rapidly and naturally rather than the result of prolonged deliberation. It would thus appear that experts must excel in general basic characteristics, such as intelligence, memory, speed and flexibility, which have been assumed to be impossible to train and thus must be determined to a large degree by genetic factors (nature). Over the last couple of centuries, the arguments of the relative importance of nature versus nurture for expert achievement have been intricately linked to the theories of the actual processes that mediate the achievement of experts and to the conceptions of which aspects of human characteristics could be modified through development and training. Hence, this entry will briefly review the most important conceptions during the last century and then turn to a summary of our current knowledge and in conclusion the implications and connections of expert performance for creativity and genius will be outlined.	Type as much of the presented text as possible in one minute
Music		Play the same piece of music twice in same manner

FIGURE 7.3   Three examples of laboratory tasks that capture the consistently superior performance of domain experts in chess, typing and music. *(From "Expertise," by K. A. Ericsson and Andreas C. Lehmann, 1999, Encyclopedia of Creativity. Copyright by Academic Press.)*

practice. In fact, many thousands of hours of specific types of practice and training are necessary to reach the highest levels of performance.

In professional contexts, the most important outcome is the performance of the organization or group. The performance of an orchestra cannot be determined by the independent skill level of each individual member. The music produced by the orchestra will only be enjoyable for the audience when the performance of its members is integrated during prior rehearsals under the direction of a conductor. On the other hand, there is a critical role for individual skill in orchestras. Most pieces have pianists or violinists who perform solo parts, and there is need for individual skill, and for orchestra members to adapt their performance upon the direction of the conductor. Similarly, in sport competitions, national teams in soccer, basketball, or ice-hockey are virtually always made up of the top players from different club teams, who then have to integrate into their teams' performance during a few weeks prior to the competition. An expert performer is typically an individual who can rapidly adapt his/her performance to changing social contexts.

Relations of Individual Performance to Performance of Groups and Organizations

The fields of economics and human resources have looked at the issue of workplace skill, but typically they focus on outcomes and performance at the level of companies and large organizations rather than at the level of individuals. There should be close relations between individual productivity and productivity of the organization in many cases. In the first part of this review we found that individual job performance does not seem to increase beyond the first couple of years of employment (McDaniel, Schmidt, & Hunter, 1988; Wigdor & Green, 1991), and increased experience is often not associated with higher performance in professional domains (Choudhry, Fletcher, & Soumerai, 2005; Ericsson 2004; Ericsson & Lehmann, 1996; Ericsson et al., 2007). Consequently, the primary issue for managers of companies concerns if and how productivity can be increased by some interventions involving facilitating changes in the workers' activities by training. A further consideration is whether money invested in training increases productivity sufficiently to compensate for its cost, and increase the company's overall profit.

Many large scale studies have tried to assess the effects of training on worker productivity by collecting data on many companies using phone interviews and surveys. For example, in a study of 600 companies in Spain, Alba-Ramirez (1994) found that large companies trained more, but after controlling for potential confounds no significant impact of training on productivity was observed. Similarly, in a study of a large number of companies in the US, Bartel (1994) found no significant benefits of training for companies that had previously engaged in it. However, when the analysis was restricted to those companies that had not previously engaged in training, there was a significant benefit. Small but reliable increases in productivity due to training were found by Black and Lynch (1996) when the analyzed training occurred outside the working hours.

There are many differences in both the methodology of collecting data and on the variables examined that might account for the differences in the estimated benefits of training. In her meta-analysis, Bartel (2000) separated the studies into three types. The largest number of studies consisted of those which collected information about training and improvement from phone interviews and surveys. These studies tended to show variable and ambiguous results. Given that the studies rarely relied on objective data on training costs and productivity gains, the results were greatly influenced by inferences and estimates by the researchers. Furthermore, some companies appeared to start with training in response to below average productivity, raising concerns about the generalizability of training effects for average and high performing companies.

The second largest category of study consisted of econometric case studies, where the researchers had access to company records of training costs and productivity gains. Bartel (1995, 2000) found that assignment of training was related to the performance level of the worker, and that low-producing individuals received more training. A weakness of these studies is that they do not randomly determine which employees receive training or not. The third category identified by Bartel (2000) consisted of 16 case studies, where the conditions of traditional experimental studies were closely approximated by using experimental-versus-control studies, pre- and post-test studies, or time series analyses. In two of these studies, the assignment to training was randomized. For these studies Bartel (2000) estimated very large effects of training with returns on investments in the range of 100 to 200%. She acknowledges, however, that the generalization of these effects cannot be determined.

In a subsequent meta-analysis, Tharenou, Saks, and Moore (2007) discussed the fact that the results on productivity is the most valid, yet rarely used criterion for evaluating training effectiveness. Most training studies evaluate the success of training by asking participants

B. INDIVIDUAL LEVEL INFLUENCES

about their reactions to the training, and some even test knowledge and memory of training, but hardly any studies measure the effects of training on work performance (Alliger, Tannenbaum, Bennett, Traver, & Shotland, 1997). In their review Tharenou et al. (2007) found very small effects of training on the financial outcomes of the companies, but somewhat larger effects on reported attitudes and motivation. A very similar finding is reported in reviews of the effects of continuing education in medicine. Davis (2009) reviews the literature and shows that courses and lectures have no discernable effects on the doctors' clinical practice. Davis argues that continuing education should focus on activities:

"that lead to actual change in practice and improved outcomes" *(Davis & Willis, 2004, p. 142).*

Instead of describing new developments and knowledge in medicine, the doctors should get support for translating the implications of new findings into how they run their actual practice. In addition they should get training that helps them implement these changes and to learn new skills. Only in a few select medical contexts do doctors get reasonably immediate feedback on errors and problems (Ericsson, 2004). For example, in surgery a patient will often show immediate reactions to problems, such as a leaking artery, or a reaction to the surgery during the following 24 hours in the post-operational room. This is likely one important reason (Ericsson, 2011) that difficult surgeries have shown a sustained improvement for over a thousand surgeries over 7 years (McKenney et al., 2009; Vickers et al., 2008; Vickers et al., 2009).

In summary, when individuals are given training with feedback that is appropriate for improving aspects of their performance, then there is evidence of improvement of individual performance, with indirect benefits on the productivity of the organization. Unfortunately, the data on improvements reflect the sum of effects across many individuals without a detailed analysis of any of the individuals' changes in performance. To what degree the additive effects of improved performance of individuals can explain changes in the overall output of the organization will remain an interesting issue for future research. Let us now turn more specifically to the identification of individual differences in creative achievement in the work environment.

Searching for Reproducible Individual Differences in Creative Work Performance

The most common methods of assessing creativity in organizations is not to analyze and measure creative performance of individuals or groups, but rather to ask supervisors to rate the creativity of each employee (Shalley & Zhou, 2008). A smaller number of studies have attempted to measure creativity with objective measures, such as the number of patents or technical reports generated during a given time interval (Shalley & Zhou, 2008). A few of these studies have correlated objective measures, such as number of patents, with subjective supervisor ratings, generally finding reliable correlations between about 0.2 and 0.3 (Dewett, 2007; Oldham & Cummings, 1996; Tierney, Farmer, & Graen, 1999; Scott & Bruce, 1994). While these correlations are statistically significant, the subjective ratings would account for less than 10% of variance of the objective measures, and thus are too small to support a claim that objective and subjective variables are measuring the same construct. However a more fundamental concern is that objective measures of creativity, such as number of patents, follow a Poisson distribution with an extreme positive skew, which deviates markedly from a normal distribution (Huber, 1998). When Poisson-distributed variables are analyzed with traditional statistical methods, the error terms will be biased and tests of significance and associated parameters cannot be meaningfully interpreted (Gardner, Mulvey, & Shaw, 1995). If, however, the skewed variable is given a square root transformation, an approximate normally-distributed variable will result and this new variable can be analyzed with standard methods (Cohen, Cohen, West, & Aiken, 2003). Unfortunately, none of the papers cited above completed a transformation of the objective measures prior to the calculation of the correlations with the subjective ratings. Only Tierney et al. (1999) conducted the appropriate Poisson regression for the main analysis, which leaves concerns for the interpretation of the other analyses (Dewitt, 2007; Oldham & Cummings, 1996).

More generally, weak relations between subjective ratings and objective measures of performance are consistent with discrepancies between social nominations of experts and their objective performance when measured by representative tasks (Ericsson, 2006b; Ericsson et al., 2007). These findings converge to suggest that, despite their ease of collection, subjective supervisor ratings or peer nomination are not appropriate proxies for objective performance. Given our commitment to the objective measurement of performance, we will constrain our discussion to objective measures of creative performance.

In areas where we can define an individual's creative performance by the number of innovative products and discoveries, it is clear that his/her number of patents and research reports can be a biased measure of creative performance. For example, it would be possible to increase one's performance by writing many reports of low quality and publishing them in an outlet with low standards. This is less a problem for approved patents, because a successful award has to meet certain fixed criteria. Hall, Jaffe, & Trajtenberg (2005) note that current legal criteria stipulate that the patent must be new and:

> "*nonobvious* in that a skilled practitioner of the technology would not have known how to do it and it must be *useful*, meaning that it has commercial value" *(p. 18)*.

In spite of these criteria there is no assurance that all patents have a uniform commercial value. The value of the patent, even for applications that are generally recognized as valuable, will depend on many factors, such as:

> "legal strength of the rights, speed of technical advance, ease of imitation, etc." *(Hall et al., 2005, p. 18)*.

Ideally, we should be able to measure the economic value of a given patent and the scientific value of a given research report, so we can measure the productivity of each employee in terms of the generated value of their products.

There are attempts to measure the perceived value of approved patents by different indicators. For example, if the patent holder is willing to pay the fees for a renewal, if companies are willing to go to court to protect or challenge the patent, or if the patent holder is willing to seek patent rights in many different countries, then one can infer that the patent holder values the patent by their investments beyond the approval of the patent (Bessen, 2008). Another indicator is the number of times a given patent has been cited by subsequent patents. In an interesting study, Hall et al. (2005) tried to assess the value of patents indirectly by using a regression analysis to predict the market value of a company based on the amount of yearly investments in R&D, number of patents, and number of citations for their patents. They found that the number of citations of patents is related to market value of the firm. Bessen (2008) analyzed the payment of renewal fees to keep patents active, and was able to estimate the mean value of patents at over $75,000, but the median patent was only worth $7,000. The best predictor of estimated value was the degree of litigation, but number of citations also accounted for a small amount of the variance. The difficulty in measuring the values of individual patents will remain a major obstacle to efforts to identify individuals with reproducibly superior creative performance until a systematic and valid psychometric standard for scoring the difference in value of the patents is developed.

Another problem with the number of approved patents is that the distribution of the total number of patents for a given individual is extremely skewed in a positive manner. In a large database containing two million individuals with patents, Oettl (2006) identified star inventors (above two standard deviations over the mean), who had accumulated on average over 12.3 patents, whereas the remaining inventors had only generated an average of 1.7 patents. Only about a quarter of all individuals with patents had generated more than 3 patents during the recording period (Oettl, 2006). When awarded patents are such rare events for most individuals, it will be difficult to predict which of them (among those with at least one patent) will be more productive, i.e., will produce one or more patents of high value during their remaining lifetime. This raises questions about the predictability of superior creative performance that can be attributable to individual factors of skill.

While most individuals' distribution of patents is consistent with a random process (Simonton, 2003), there appears to be evidence for deviations from a random distribution for the most productive inventors. For example, Huber (1998) found that, although the rate of producing patents is generally indistinguishable from a random pattern, an analysis of only the most productive inventors showed increased deviation from a random process. Beyond this indirect evidence, there is some evidence that future patent production can be predicted from past performance. In a recent study (Audio & Goncalo, 2007) found that inventors who had been extremely productive the previous two years were 31% more likely to produce a patent during the next year compared to the inventors with the lowest productivity during the previous two years. This analysis is particularly interesting as it controlled statistically for the patenting frequency of the inventors, how frequently the inventor generated patents alone, as well as how similar the new patents were to the previously awarded patents. Nonetheless, the differences between the most productive and the least productive are small and the frequencies of successful patent application are low.

In another recent study, Oettl (2006) tried to estimate the effects of star inventors, who had produced at least two standard deviations more patents in a five-year-period compared to the effects of the average inventors. It is impossible to assess the effect of an individual inventor who keeps working in the same job environment and distinguish those effects from the environment that includes their colleagues and assistants. Oettl (2006) identified cases where the inventor had moved to a different company and monitored the performance at the new company after a star inventor or non-star inventor had arrived. Although these analyses are based on complex phenomena, and violate numerous assumptions about random assignment of star inventors to companies, it is interesting that Oettl (2006) was able to estimate relatively large effects on patent production from hiring a star inventor compared to a non-star inventor. Unfortunately, very little is known about the potential factors that mediated the influence of the star inventor. It could be the knowledge that the star inventor was able to bring to the new firm, or it could be other factors that would make the star inventor interested in moving to that firm, such as better resources, staff, and colleagues.

Marketing is another domain where creativity also should be highly important. Successful campaigns and creative marketing should be reflected in increased sales, but there are many other factors that could influence changes in sales (Britt, 2000). There are, however, impressive experiments that have been able to compare the effectiveness of different campaigns concurrently. For example, Lodish et al. (1995) were able to present different advertisements to similar audiences as well as having similar audiences not see any commercials for the products by using cable TV. These studies showed that advertising increased sales, but surprisingly the size of the budget of the campaign did not seem to matter. They did find an effect of the company altering their marketing strategy suggesting an influence of creativity (Lodish et al., 1995). Subsequent studies (El-Murad & West, 2004; Tai, 2007) have had advertisements rated for their creativity and effectiveness and have found the expected positive relationship. We caution the acceptance of these findings based on expert ratings for the same reasons that we cautioned against reliance on supervisor ratings. The findings by El-Murad and West (2004) showing a relation between creativity and effectiveness are particularly problematic, as they defined creativity as useful and appropriate and thus the two concepts are correlated by their definition. We were unable to find a large body of research on superior marketing performance; but we see a strong potential for research using controlled cable TV presentations as a means to assess the effectiveness of advertising products.

Our review was able to uncover only a few objective measures that were sufficiently reliable for meaningful findings to emerge. For example, we found that the level of attained education was related to the number of patents. At this point we do not know enough about the social structure that supports the development of patents (e.g. how much does the patent reflect a group effort or an individual effort), to permit an analysis of the causal factors mediating this relation.

The goal of the expert-performance approach is to identify the phenomenon, and then reproduce it under controlled conditions to get more detailed information about the various processes and available resources that are associated with different creative performances and generated products. Given the difficulties of identifying individual inventors or stable groups of inventors with a reproducibly superior ability to generate patents, one might want to explore another approach. In the next section we will explore the possibility of studying in retrospect the conditions that generated a particular, individual, creative product or innovation with a large commercial and societal value.

An Alternative Approach: Case Studies of the Generation of Creative Products

Although we are not aware of any detailed analyses of processes involved in inventing highly valued patents, the creative innovations by Charles Darwin, Jackson Pollack, or Pablo Picasso have been extensively analyzed and studied (Weisberg, 2006). These analyses have been conducted with respect to specific discoveries that occurred at particular historical times. For example, Faraday's discovery of the first metal colloid can be reconstructed from his detailed diaries, and reveals a process of cumulative study and learning over some years, that set the stage for the new discovery and associated reorganization of knowledge (Tweney, 2006). It is, however, difficult to fully replicate the online processes during the discovery and the diaries provide a retrospective account of the discovery after it was completed, with many sources of bias due to incomplete memory and reconstructions. It would have been desirable to study these processes by collecting concurrent thought processes such as think-aloud protocols (Klahr & Simon, 1999).

Most creative achievements and products are the culmination of many years of daily work and incremental progress. One of the most influential ideas generated in the 19th century, namely Darwin's theory of evolution, took decades to develop—as shown by Gruber's (1981) careful analysis of Darwin's note books. A more recent case-study of the extended creative process consists of the documentation of a professional musical composer who worked on a piece for over three years (Collins, 2005). This composer was thinking aloud while composing with a software system designed for music composition (akin to a text editing program). By analyzing the recorded sequence of changes to his composition, it is possible to relate his thoughts to his created piece of music. In his analysis, Collins (2005) was able to describe deep level restructuring of the musical composition, and the composer's active problem solving while trying to realize the goals for his desired music experience. This example is a superior method of conducting a case study of creativity because the behavior can be observed as it occurs without any bias from retrospective recall. However, it is very unlikely that one would be able to record a major creative innovation, given how rarely they occur. If two composers were to work on a composition, their produced music pieces would be very different. If two scientists were studying the same problem with similar background knowledge, how similar would their generated ideas and theories be? Eminent scientists are not completely unique and, in fact, there are many instances of scientists making the same discovery independently in the same time period (Merton, 1961). For example, oxygen was discovered by Carl Wilhelm Scheele, Joseph Priestly and Antoine Lavoisier in the 18th century and the theory of evolution was independently proposed by Charles Darwin and Alfred Russell Wallace, just to mention some of the best known discoveries.

If we were to apply the expert-performance approach, we would analyze the scientific or creative process to find those processing steps that seem the most difficult for others to be able to complete if a similar situation was presented as a task. Most activities of a composer and a scientist are habitual and routine. Consequently, we would thus expect most scientists or artists with the appropriate background, skill level, and training to be able to complete the easy and routine parts of the activity. We would expect that other professionals could master even moderately challenging problems. The major question concerns whether the discovering scientist would be the only one to complete the most challenging leaps or processing steps. It is possible to submit this question, at least in principle, to experimental test.

In fact, these issues have been studied with methods similar to the expert-performance approach with some success. For instance, in a study Qin and Simon (1990) provided students with information very similar to that available to the famous astronomer, Kepler, when he first discovered his third law of planetary motion. Qin and Simon (1990) found that students clearly searched a defined problem space, and used general heuristics to reduce that problem space. In their experiments, in about an hour 4 of the 14 participants were able to reproduce the formula for Kepler's law. Subsequent studies (Dunbar, 1993; Okada & Simon, 1997) provided students with opportunities to design experiments like those used in Jacob and Monod's Nobel Prize winning work. Dunbar (1993) found that if students avoided the confirmation bias and paid attention to evidence against their currently held hypothesis they could successfully recreate the targeted discovery. Okada and Simon (1997) found that when pairs of students were working together on problems they were found to be even more successful than working alone.

Additionally researchers of design have collected protocols from inventors and architects while they worked on solving a representative problem. For example, Cross (2003) collected protocols from an award winning designer while he designed a backpack carriage. He found that the expert designer used prior knowledge to limit the search space and then used basic principles to guide the development of the design that satisfied the client. Based on a series of studies with small groups, Cross (2004) found that both experts and non-experts work backwards from the constraints of product design, but experts develop hypotheses for a solution earlier and use these ideas to guide their search, which they gradually deepen and elaborate. The described search for the design is strikingly similar to the methods used by chess masters to find the best move for a chess position (de Groot, 1978).

These laboratory studies demonstrate that it is possible to reproduce some of the original innovations by reinstating the original context with all the relevant information. It is notable that unexceptional participants (college students) were able to successfully reproduce the formulas or the research designs. These studies also provide us with concurrent data on the thinking that was associated with recreating the innovations or creating new products with experts and novices. At the same time we need to acknowledge that the findings from these studies do not offer any immediate implications for how the frequency of innovation can be increased in everyday research in laboratories and industrial development centers with one possible exception. We found some parallels between search in chess and in design suggesting that similar types of practice is likely to develop the associated mental skills involved in design and other creative innovation.

CONCLUDING REMARKS

In this chapter we have explored the application of the expert-performance approach to organizational creativity. The methods of this approach differ markedly from modal research on organizational creativity, so the introduction of this chapter focused on a description of its empirical base, namely the acquisition of reproducibly superior performance in domains of expertise, such as chess, music, and sports. We emphasized the expert-performance approach's commitment to objective performance and reviewed evidence that social assessments of expertise often lacked a strong relation to objective performance.

Our chapter used Woodman et al.'s (1993) seminal paper on organizational creativity to relate individual performance to the characteristics of organizations, such as organizational creativity. We reviewed the insights from studying expert performance on what factors are related to improvement in performance and contrasted them with some of the characteristics of the acquisition of job performance. Our review examined the general lack of improved performance as a function of experience with a particular job and we attempted to demonstrate how this was compatible with both traditional skill acquisition theories (Fitts & Posner, 1967) and the theoretical framework of deliberate practice (Ericsson, 2006b; Ericsson et al., 1993). We also proposed that the most obvious hypothesis based on the expert-performance approach to increasing performance of organizations would be to examine how particular key individuals can be helped and motivated to increase their individual performance.

In the next section of the chapter we discussed how the expert-performance approach could be applied to job performance by identifying and measuring superior performance in the varied conditions of the work environment. The next issue addressed in our chapter concerned the relation between the increased performance of individuals and the resulting performance of organizations. We examined the issues related to training in organizations and how this training of individuals can be evaluated by analyzing the productivity of the organizations. After discussing some of the many methodological issues and controversies of this research we were able to identify some objective phenomena at the level of organizations and the available data did not permit an analysis at the level of performance of individuals.

Our most direct attempt to apply the expert-performance approach to organizational creativity involved an analysis of the objective performance of organizations making creative products, such as patents. Consistent with our commitment to objective performance, we found that supervisors' ratings of creativity cannot be substituted for objective creative performance measures, such as number of approved patents. Our review found that the generation of work leading to approved patents was for the most part consistent with a random process. Only for the top innovators was there evidence that some individuals were able to generate a larger number of approved patents in the future, but the superiority of their performance to lower performing colleagues was not dramatic and thus could not be easily captured with standardized tasks as recommended within the expert-performance approach. In the final section of the chapter we discussed the possibility of studying the emergence of major innovations retrospectively with the methodologies developed to reconstruct and analyze the processes mediating major scientific discoveries, such as Darwin's theory of evolution.

Our review showed that there are no low-lying fruits related to organizational creativity that can be easily harvested with the expert-performance approach when we restrict the research to help us predict the production of valuable patents. From our reading of the research on innovation we feel that the field seems to be moving towards objective measures. We were particularly impressed by Jaffe and Trajtenberg's (2002) book on the economic properties of patents that includes a dataset of over 3 million patents and 16 million citations. Our review suggested that these objective measures represent a reliable but small superiority of innovators with the highest level of productivity. To what degree these individual differences reflect primarily acquired skill is an interesting question for future research.

Based on our difficulties in applying the expert-performance approach to creativity in organizations, we would propose that it might be more promising to develop new measures of job-related flexibility and creativity that would not require a patentable outcome.

If one were to study the process of idea generation and the various stages at which a potential idea for a patent was rejected and abandoned, it should be possible to identify skills and associated performance measures that could facilitate the effectiveness of patent development. These findings should be able to reduce the work on ideas that were later rejected, or increase the probability of generating ideas that were viable. Then tests could be designed for presenting representative situations to assess whether we could identify individuals with generalizable superiority in the associated performance. At that point, we could then start a program of research that would assess the mediating mechanisms and search for any effects of relevant training activities and deliberate practice. Given the importance of continued innovation in industry and research organizations for the future competitiveness of industrialized nations this type of research should have considerable potential and value.

This type of research effort should allow us to understand the cognitive structures that lead to superior performance in organizational creativity and which will better help us understand, at a micro level, what distinguishes the innovative from the non-innovative. We predict that organizational creativity will be very similar to other skills and that the expert performance approach will allow us to understand its structure at the level of top innovators and to develop appropriate training environments that can produce the top innovators of the future.

AUTHOR NOTES

This research was supported by the FSCW/Conradi Endowment Fund of Florida State University Foundation. The authors want to thank Len Hill for the helpful comments on earlier drafts of this chapter.

References

Alba-Ramirez, A. (1994). Formal training, temporary contracts, productivity and wages in Spain. *Oxford Bulletin of Economics and Statistics, 56*, 151–170.

Alliger, G. M., Tannenbaum, S. I., Bennett, W., Traver, H., & Shotland, A. (1997). A meta-analysis of the relations among training criteria. *Personnel Psychology, 50*, 341–358.

Anderson, J. R. (1982). Acquisition of cognitive skill. *Psychological Review, 89*, 369–406.

Audio, P. G., & Goncalo, J. A. (2007). Past success and creativity over time: A study of inventors in the hard disk drive industry. *Management Science, 53*, 1–15.

Bartel, A. P. (1994). Productivity gains from the implementation of employee training programs. *Industrial Relations, 33*, 411–425.

Bartel, A. P. (1995). Training, wage growth, and job performance: Evidence from a company database. *Journal of Labor Economics, 13*, 401–425.

Bartel, A. P. (2000). Measuring the employer's return on investments in training: Evidence from the literature. *Industrial Relations, 39*, 502–524.

Bédard, J., & Chi, M. T. H. (1992). Expertise. *Current Directions in Psychological Science, 1*, 135–139.

Benner, P., Tanner, C., & Chesla, C. (1992). From beginner to expert: Gaining a differentiated clinical world in critical care nursing. *Advances in Nursing Science, 14*, 13–28.

Bessen, J. (2008). The value of US patents by owner and patent characteristics. *Research Policy, 37*, 932–945.

Black, S., & Lynch, L. (1996). Human capital investment and productivity. *American Economic Review, 86*, 263–267.

Bloom, B. S. (1985). Generalizations about talent development. In B. S. Bloom (Ed.), *Developing talent in young people* (pp. 507–549). New York, NY: Ballantine Books.

Bloom, B. S. (Ed.). (1985). *Developing talent in young people*. New York, NY: Ballantine Books.

Britt, S. H. (2000). Are so-called successful advertising campaigns really successful? *Journal of Advertising Research, 41,* 25–31.

Chaffin, R., & Imreh, G. (2002). Practicing perfection: Piano performance as expert memory. *Psychological Science, 13,* 342–349.

Chatham, R. E. (2009). The 20th-Century revolution in military training. In K. A. Ericsson (Ed.), *Development of professional expertise: Toward measurement of expert performance and design of optimal learning environments* (pp. 27–60). Cambridge, UK: Cambridge University Press.

Chi, M. T. H. (2006). Two approaches to experts' characteristics. In K. A. Ericsson, N. Charness, P. Feltovich & R. R. Hoffman (Eds.), *Cambridge handbook of expertise and expert performance* (pp. 21–38). Cambridge, UK: Cambridge University Press.

Chi, M. T. H., Glaser, R., & Farr, M. J. (Eds.), (1988). *The nature of expertise.* Hillsdale, NJ: Erlbaum.

Choudhry, N. K., Fletcher, R. H., & Soumerai, S. B. (2005). Systematic review: the relationship between clinical experience and quality of health care. *Annals of Internal Medicine, 142,* 260–273.

Cohen, J., Cohen, P., West, S. G., & Aiken, L. S. (2003). *Applied multiple regression/correlation analysis for the behavioral sciences* (3rd ed.). Mahwah, NJ: Erlbaum.

Collins, D. (2005). A synthesis process model of creative thinking in music composition. *Psychology of Music, 33,* 193–216.

Crochet, P., Aggarwal, R., Dubb, S., Ziprin, P., Rajaretnam, N., & Grantcharov, T., et al. (2009). Deliberate practice on virtual reality laparoscopic simulator improves quality of surgical skills. *Journal of the American College of Surgeons, 209,* S112.

Cross, N. (2003). The expertise of exceptional designers. In N. Cross & E. Edmonds (Eds.), *Expertise in design* (pp. 23–35). Sydney, Australia: Creativity and Cognition Press.

Cross, N. (2004). Expertise in design: An overview. *Design Studies, 25,* 427–441.

Davis, D. A. (2009). How to help professionals maintain and improve their knowledge and skills: Triangulating best practices in medicine. In K. A. Ericsson (Ed.), *The development of professional expertise: Toward measurement of expert performance and design of optimal learning environments* (pp. 180–202). New York, NY: Cambridge University Press.

Davis, D. A., & Willis, C. E. (2004). A new metric for continuing medical education credit. *Journal of Continuing Education in the Health Professions, 24,* 139–144.

Dawes, R. M., Faust, D., & Meehl, P. E. (1989). Clinical versus actuarial judgment. *Science, 243,* 1668–1674.

de Groot, A. D. (1978). Thought and choice and chess. The Hague: The Netherland Mouton. (Original work published 1946).

Dewett, T. (2007). Linking intrinsic motivation, risk taking, and employee creativity in an R&D environment. *R&D Management, 37,* 197–208.

Drazin, R., Glynn, M., & Kazanjian, R. (1999). Multi-level theorizing about creativity in organizations: A sensemaking perspective. *Academy of Management Review, 24,* 286–307.

Dreyfus, H., & Dreyfus, S. (1986). *Mind over machine: The power of human intuition and expertise in the era of the computer.* New York, NY: Free Press.

Dunbar, K. (1993). Concept discovery in a scientific domain. *Cognitive Science, 17,* 397–404.

Dvorak, A., Merrick, N. L., Dealey, W. L., & Ford, G. C. (1936). *Typewriting behavior.* New York, NY: American Book Company.

El-Murad, J., & West, D. C. (2004). The definition and measurement of creativity: What do we know? *Journal of Advertising Research, 44,* 188–201.

Ericsson, K. A. (1996). The acquisition of expert performance: An introduction to some of the issues. In K. A. Ericsson (Ed.), *The road to excellence: The acquisition of expert performance in the arts and sciences, sports, and games* (pp. 1–50). Mahwah, NJ: Erlbaum.

Ericsson, K. A. (1999). Creative expertise as superior reproducible performance: Innovative and flexible aspects of expert performance. *Psychological Inquiry, 10,* 329–333.

Ericsson, K. A. (2000). Expertise in interpreting: An expert-performance perspective. *Interpreting, 5,* 189–222.

Ericsson, K. A. (2002). Attaining excellence through deliberate practice: Insights from the study of expert performance. In M. Ferrari (Ed.), *The pursuit of excellence in education* (pp. 21–55). Hillsdale, NJ: Erlbaum.

Ericsson, K. A. (2003). The acquisition of expert performance as problem solving: Construction and modification of mediating mechanisms through deliberate practice. In J. E. Davidson & R. J. Sternberg (Eds.), *Problem solving* (pp. 31–83). New York, NY: Cambridge University Press.

Ericsson, K. A. (2004). Deliberate practice and the acquisition and maintenance of expert performance in medicine and related domains. *Academic Medicine, 10*, S1–S12.

Ericsson, K. A. (2006a). The influence of experience and deliberate practice on the development of superior expert performance. In K. A. Ericsson, N. Charness, P. Feltovich & R. R. Hoffman (Eds.), *Cambridge handbook of expertise and expert performance* (pp. 685–706). Cambridge, UK: Cambridge University Press.

Ericsson, K. A. (2006b). Protocol analysis and expert thought: Concurrent verbalizations of thinking during experts' performance on representative task. In K. A. Ericsson, N. Charness, P. Feltovich & R. R. Hoffman (Eds.), *Cambridge handbook of expertise and expert performance* (pp. 223–242). Cambridge, UK: Cambridge University Press.

Ericsson, K. A. (2007). Deliberate practice and the modifiability of body and mind: Toward a science of the structure and acquisition of expert and elite performance. *International Journal of Sport Psychology, 38*, 4–34.

Ericsson, K. A. (2009a). *Development of professional expertise: Toward measurement of expert performance and design of optimal learning environments*. New York, NY: Cambridge University Press.

Ericsson, K. A. (2009b). Enhancing the development of professional performance: Implications from the study of deliberate practice. In K. A. Ericsson (Ed.), *The development of professional expertise: Toward measurement of expert performance and design of optimal learning environments* (pp. 405–431). New York, NY: Cambridge University Press.

Ericsson, K. A. (2011). Surgical expertise: A perspective from the expert-performance approach. In H. Fry & R. Kneebone (Eds.), *Surgical education in theoretical perspective: Enhancing learning, teaching, practice and research.* Berlin, Germany: Springer, in press.

Ericsson, K. A., Charness, N., Feltovich, P., & Hoffman, R. R. (Eds.), (2006). *Cambridge handbook of expertise and expert performance*. Cambridge, UK: Cambridge University Press.

Ericsson, K. A., & Kintsch, W. (1995). Long-term working memory. *Psychology Review, 102*, 211–245.

Ericsson, K. A., Krampe, R. Th., & Tesch-Römer, C. (1993). The role of deliberate practice in the acquisition of expert performance. *Psychological Review, 100*, 363–406.

Ericsson, K. A., & Lehmann, A. C. (1996). Expert and exceptional performance: Evidence on maximal adaptations on task constraints. *Annual Review of Psychology, 47*, 273–305.

Ericsson, K. A., Patel, V. L., & Kintsch, W. (2000). How experts' adaptations to representative task demands account for the expertise effect in memory recall: Comment on Vicente and Wang (1998). *Psychological Review, 107*, 578–592.

Ericsson, K. A., & Smith, J. (1991). Prospects and limits in the empirical study of expertise: An introduction. In K. A. Ericsson & J. Smith (Eds.), *Toward a general theory of expertise: Prospects and limits* (pp. 1–38). Cambridge, UK: Cambridge University Press.

Ericsson, K. A., & Ward, P. (2007). Capturing the naturally occurring superior performance of experts in the laboratory: Toward a science of expert and exceptional performance. *Current Directions in Psychological Science, 16*, 346–350.

Ericsson, K. A., Whyte, J., & Ward, P. (2007). Expert performance in nursing: Reviewing research on expertise in nursing within the framework of the expert-performance approach. *Advances in Nursing Science, 30*, E58–E71.

Feltovich, P. J., Prietula, M. J., & Ericsson, K. A. (2006). Studies of expertise from psychological perspectives. In K. A. Ericsson, N. Charness, P. Feltovich & R. R. Hoffman (Eds.), *Cambridge handbook of expertise and expert performance* (pp. 41–67). Cambridge, UK: Cambridge University Press.

Fitts, P., & Posner, M. I. (1967). *Human performance*. Belmont, CA: Brooks/Cole.

Fletcher, J. D. (2009). The value of expertise and expert performance: A review of evidence from the military. In K. A. Ericsson (Ed.), *Development of professional expertise: Toward measurement of expert performance and design of optimal learning environments* (pp. 449–469). Cambridge, UK: Cambridge University Press.

Ford, C. M. (1996). A theory of individual creative action in multiples social domains. *Academy of Management Review, 21*, 1112–1142.

Galton, F., Sir (1869/1979). *Hereditary genius: an inquiry into its laws and consequences*. London, UK: Julian Friedman Publishers. (Originally published in 1869).

B. INDIVIDUAL LEVEL INFLUENCES

Gardner, W., Mulvey, E. P., & Shaw, E. C. (1995). Regression analyses of counts and rates: Poisson, overdispersed, and negative binomial models. *Psychological Bulletin, 118*, 392–404.

Gruber, H. E. (1981). *Darwin on man: A psychological study of scientific creativity* (2nd ed.). Chicago, IL: University of Chicago Press.

Hall, B. H., Jaffe, A., & Trajtenberg, M. (2005). Market value and patent citations. *RAND Journal of Economics, 36,* 16–38.

Huber, J. C. (1998). Invention and inventivity is a random, poisson process: A potential guide to analysis of general creativity. *Creativity Research Journal, 11*, 231–241.

Hunter, S. T., Bedell-Avers, K. E., Hunsicker, C. M., Mumford, M. D., & Ligon, G. S. (2008). Applying multiple knowledge structures in creative thought: Effects on idea generation and problem-solving. *Creativity Research Journal, 20*, 137–154.

Jaffe, A. B., & Trajtenberg, M. (2002). *Patents, citations & innovations: A window on the knowledge economy.* Cambridge, MA: The MIT Press.

Klahr, D., & Simon, H. A. (1999). Studies of scientific discovery complementary approaches and convergent findings. *Psychological Bulletin, 125,* 524–543.

Krampe, R. T., & Ericsson, K. A. (1996). Maintaining excellence: Deliberate practice and elite performance in young and older pianists. *Journal of Experimental Psychology: General, 125,* 331–359.

Lehmann, A. C., & Ericsson, K. A. (1998). The historical development of domains of expertise: Performance standards and innovations in music. In A. Steptoe (Ed.), *Genius and the mind* (pp. 67–94). Oxford, UK: Oxford University Press.

Lodish, L. M., Abraham, M., Kalmenson, S., Livelsberger, J., Lubetkin, B., & Richardson, B., et al. (1995). How TV advertising works: A meta-analysis of 389 real world split cable TV advertising experiments. *Journal of Marketing Research, 32,* 125–139.

McDaniel, M. A., Schmidt, F. L., & Hunter, J. E. (1988). Job experience correlates of job performance. *Journal of Applied Psychology, 73,* 327–330.

McKenney, M. G., Livingstone, A. S., Schulman, C., Stahl, K., Lineen, E., & Namias, N., et al. (2009). Trauma surgeon mortality rates correlate with surgeon time at institution. *Journal of American College of Surgeons, 208,* 750–754.

Merton, R. K. (1961). Singletons and multiples in scientific discovery: A chapter in the sociology of science. *Proceedings of the American Philosophical Society, 105,* 470–486.

Mumford, M. D. (2000). Managing creative people: Strategies and tactics for innovation. *Human Resources Management Review, 10,* 313–351.

Newell, A., & Rosenbloom, P. (1981). Mechanisms of skill acquisition and the law of practice. In J. R. Anderson (Ed.), *Cognitive skills and their acquisition* (pp. 1–55). Hillsdale, NJ: Erlbaum.

Okada, T., & Simon, H. A. (1997). Collaborative discovery in a scientific domain. *Cognitive Science, 21,* 109–146.

Oldham, G. R., & Cummings, A. (1996). Employee Creativity: Personal and contextual factors at work. *Academy of Management Journal, 39,* 607–634.

Oettl, A. (2006). Which stars should you reach for? Firm innovations and the mobility of scientific stars. (Working Paper). Canadian Economics Association. Retrieved December 1, 2009, from <http://economics.ca/2006/papers/0501.pdf/>.

Qin, Y., & Simon, H. A. (1990). Laboratory replication of scientific discovery processes. *Cognitive Science, 14,* 281–312.

Perry-Smith, J. E., & Shalley, C. E. (2003). The social side of creativity: A static and dynamic social network perspective. *Academy of Management Review, 28,* 89–106.

Sawyer, K. (2008). *Group genius: The creative power of collaboration.* New York, NY: Basic Books.

Scott, S. G., & Bruce, R. A. (1994). Determinants of innovative behavior: A path model of individual innovation in the workplace. *Academy of Management Journal, 37,* 580–607.

Shalley, C. E., & Zhou, J. (2008). Organizational creativity research: A historical overview. In J. Zhou & C. E. Shalley (Eds.), *Handbook of Organizational Creativity* (pp. 3–32). Mahwah, NJ: LEA.

Shanteau, J. (2001). What does it mean when experts disagree? In E. Salas & G. Klein (Eds.), *Linking expertise and naturalistic decision making* (pp. 229–244). Mahwah, NJ: LEA.

Simon, H. A., & Chase, W. G. (1973). Skill in chess. *American Scientist, 61,* 394–403.

Simonton, D. K. (2003). Scientific creativity as a constrained stochastic behavior: The integration of product, person, and process perspectives. *Psychological Bulletin, 129,* 475–494.

Spengler, P. M., White, M. J., Ægisdóttir, S., Maugherman, A. S., Anderson, L. A., & Cook, R. S., et al. (2009). The meta-analysis of clinical judgment project: Effects of experience on judgment accuracy. *The Counseling Psychologist, 20,* 350–399.

Tai, S. H. C. (2007). Correlates of successful brand advertising in China. *Asian Pacific Journal of Marketing and Logistics, 19,* 40–56.

Tharenou, P., Saks, A. M., & Moore, C. (2007). A review and critique of research on training and organizational level outcomes. *Human Resource Management Review, 17,* 251–273.

Tetlock, P. E. (2005). *Expert political judgment.* Princeton, NJ: Princeton University Press.

Tierney, P., Farmer, S. M., & Graen, G. M. (1999). An examination of leadership and employee creativity: The relevance of traits and relationships. *Personnel Psychology, 52,* 591–620.

Tweney, R. D. (2006). Discovering discovery: How Faraday found the first metallic colloid. *Perspectives on Science, 14,* 97–121.

van der Maas, H. L. J., & Wagenmakers, E. J. (2005). A psychometric analysis of chess expertise. *American Journal of Psychology, 118,* 29–60.

Vickers, A. J., Bianco, F. J., Gonen, M., Cronin, A. M., Eastham, J. A., & Schrag, D., et al. (2008). Effects of pathologic state on the learning curve for radical prostatectomy: Evidence that recurrence in organ-confined cancer is large related to inadequate surgical technique. *European Urology, 53,* 960–966.

Vickers, A. J., Hruza, M., Koenig, P., Martinez-Pinero, L., Janetschenk, G., & Guillonneau, B. (2009). The surgical learning curve for laparoscopic radical prostatectomy: A retrospective cohort study. *Lancet Oncology, 10,* 475–480.

Ward, P., & Williams, A. M. (2003). Perceptual and cognitive skill development in soccer: The multidimensional nature of expert performance. *Journal of Sport & Exercise Psychology, 25,* 93–111.

Weisberg, R. W. (2006). *Creativity: Understanding innovation in problem solving, science, invention, and the arts.* Hoboken, NJ: Wiley.

Whyte, J., Pickett-Hauber, R., Cormier, E., Grubbs, L., & Ward, P. (2010). A study of the relationship of nursing interventions and cognitions to the physiologic outcomes of care in a simulated task environment. *Applied Nursing Research, 23,* e1–e8.

Wigdor, A. K., & Green, B. F. (Eds.), *Performance assessment for the workplace* (Vol. 1). Washington, DC: National Academy Press.

Woodman, R. W., Sawyer, J. E., & Griffin, R. W. (1993). Toward a theory of organizational creativity. *Academy of Management Review, 18,* 293–321.

B. INDIVIDUAL LEVEL INFLUENCES

Problem Solving

Thomas B. Ward

University of Alabama, Department of Psychology, Birmingham, AL

INTRODUCTION

Creative behavior and problem solving have much in common. Put differently, a broad range of situations that call for creative behavior can be characterized as "problems", and the thought processes that lead to new and useful outcomes in those situations can be characterized "problem solving". Not all creative activities are reasonably called problem solving, nor can all problem solving be reasonably thought of as creative. Nevertheless, the evident commonalities at a descriptive level make a consideration of theory and research on problem solving directly relevant to a full understanding of creativity. The present chapter begins with a description of the core aspects of problems, and then examines the psychological literature on problem solving.

Problem solving is potentially one of the broadest topics in psychology. So much of what humans do in their work and personal lives could be characterized as problem solving that the boundaries of what is and what is not within the topic area are unclear. The same may be said for creativity. To illustrate; a child trying to find the sum of two numbers, a person who has lost his keys, a chess player determining the best next move, a firefighter attempting to extinguish a blaze, a manager needing to increase the motivation of her team, a military patrol needing to cross a body of water without appropriate equipment using only found materials, and an engineer wishing to increase the stability of some new structure are all confronting problems. What these situations have in common is that the person or group wants to achieve some goal and must take some set of mental steps to get there. Interestingly, there are two broad traditions in the study of problem solving, one having its roots in Gestalt Psychology (e.g., Duncker, 1945) and the other in Information Processing Theory (e.g., Ernst & Newell, 1969; Newell & Simon, 1972), but they agree on this basic characterization of a problem.

In Duncker's terms, a person has a problem when they have a goal they want to accomplish but do not know how to do so, a situation that requires thought. In information

Handbook of Organizational Creativity.
DOI: 10.1016/B978-0-12-374714-3.00008-2

processing terms, the definition of a problem is formalized in terms of **initial** or **start states** and **solution** or **goal states**. Using this terminology, a problem is a discrepancy between an initial state and a goal state. So, in either case, if there is a gap between where a person is now and where that person wants to be, then a problem exists. Most importantly, this way of characterizing problems leads to a particular way of conceptualizing problem solving, namely as the process whereby people eliminate the discrepancy between the start state and goal state or move from one to the other.

Defining problems as discrepancies between current situations and goals, and characterizing problem solving as eliminating discrepancies puts the emphasis squarely on the processes involved. Thus, understanding problem solving entails understanding the processes used in conceptualizing the problem and in moving from the beginning to the end, which has implications for how one studies problem solving. It is not enough to simply note whether or not a would-be solver has attained a solution. Instead, investigators must seek ways to look into the mind of the person to see how they go about representing the problem, how they generate solutions and how those factors might relate to their knowledge, to problem characteristics and to their likelihood of success. One relatively standard approach is to have people talk out loud as they attempt to solve the problem. These verbal protocols provide generally valid looks at the processes involved (e.g., Ericsson & Simon, 1993), and have been used by investigators in the Gestalt and information processing traditions alike.

Consider now the connection between the situations listed above and the phenomenon of creativity. A consensus view is that creativity has to include at the very least the attributes of novelty and appropriateness. Most often those attributes are mentioned in connection with the products or outcomes of an endeavor. That is, to be considered creative, a product has to be in some way novel and also relevant to the task at hand. Thus, answering "19" to the question of "how much is 7 plus 5?" would be novel, but likely not to be judged as creative because it is simply incorrect and thus inappropriate.

Important to the link between creativity and problem solving however, the attributes of novelty and appropriateness can also be considered in relation to the process by which a product is developed. For example, a child who has already committed the fact that 7 plus 5 equals 12 to memory and who gives 12 as the answer to "how much is 7 plus 5?" has developed a product that is not novel and has done so in a standard, non-novel way. On the other hand, a child who does not yet know that fact, and who achieves the answer by first trying to count on his hands and then suddenly realizes that he can take off his shoe to finish counting after he runs out of fingers has developed a non-novel product by a distinctly novel (to him) process. Thus, even the most mundane problems can be seen to be relevant to creativity when the underlying processes used to achieve solutions are considered.

The importance of process in the link between creativity and problem solving can also be seen in higher-level types of problems. The engineer who simply adapts well known materials and arrangements to the task of increasing stability would not be as likely to be identified as creative as one who sought information from some distant, as yet unused domain, such as the structure of insect creations. Again, it is the processes, and not so much the problem that determine the connection between creativity and problem solving.

Those in the Gestalt tradition were more concerned with the ways in which people might represent and restructure problems, whereas those in the information processing tradition were more concerned with the incremental steps to be followed after a particular problem representation was generated, but both were concerned with processes. As Novick and Bassok (2005) point out, more recent approaches have focused on an interaction between problem representation and the generation of solutions, but still the concern is with mental processes and the knowledge structures on which they operate. All of these aspects of process are considered in the sections that follow.

PROBLEM SOLVING AS SEARCH

In the Newell and Simon (1972) approach, the problem solver's internal representation of a problem is referred to as the **problem space**. This internal representation is distinguished from the problem solving task itself, as defined objectively or from the point of view of an omniscient observer, which is referred to as the **task environment**. The problem space contains states of knowledge, referred to as **problem states**, as well as the means of moving from one state to another, called **operators**. The states included in the problem space are the initial state, along with any of its givens, the goal state and any of its specific requirements, and all possible states in between. States can be thought of as nodes connected by links that represent possible moves or procedures that would transform one state to the other.

Newell and Simon (1971) acknowledged that the way people construct the problem space is an important aspect of problem solving, but they concentrated primarily on the movement through the problem space, once constructed. They and others that followed in the information processing tradition conceptualized problem solving as a search through the problem space, finding the path from the start state to the goal state (e.g., Atwood & Polson, 1976; Atwood, Masson, & Polson, 1980; Greeno, 1974; Kotovsky & Simon, 1990; Thomas, 1974). Within this framework, problem solving is shaped by certain characteristics of the human as an information processing system, such as serial processing, limited short-term memory and infinite long-term memory with relatively fast retrieval but slow storage. Those characteristics, as well as aspects of the task itself determine the ways in which people are able to move through problem spaces.

The operators for transforming one state into another generally fall into two classes, called algorithms and heuristics. Algorithms are rule-like procedures that, if followed correctly, will bring a person to the correct answer, whereas heuristics are rules of thumb that may guide a problem solver in the direction of a solution, or narrow the number of possibilities to be considered, but do not guarantee a correct solution.

The Newell and Simon approach was developed and tested on a relatively small range of problem types, including cryptarithmetic and chess. Consider the classic cryptarithmetic problem shown here.

```
  DONALD
+ GERALD
  ROBERT
```

In this problem, each letter corresponds to one and only one digit, and the task is to find the correct mapping between letters and digits so that the sum is correct. As a starting point, solvers are told that D = 5. The start state might include knowledge of the overall goal, the constraints of one-to-one mapping of letters to digits and that the sum must be correct, as well as the specific piece of information that D = 5. The goal state is the complete correct mapping between letters and digits. One conceivable means of representing and solving the problem would be to construct the set of all possible distinct mappings between the 10 letters and 10 digits and search that set until the one correct mapping is found. However, that set would be enormous, making the procedure impossible for any ordinary person or at the very least wildly impractical. The information processing characteristics of serial processing, limited short-term memory and minimum processing time preclude such an approach, combined with the empirical observation that some people are able to solve the problem in about 10 minutes, provides compelling evidence against the idea that people adopt that approach (Newell & Simon, 1971, 1972).

Considering how people actually go about solving cryptarithmetic problems helps to illustrate the distinction between algorithms and heuristics as well as the notion of **subgoals**. Rather than attempting to systematically go through all possible mappings until finding the one that satisfies the overall goal, people divide the problem into subgoals, such as finding the particular digit that must correspond to one of the letters. In doing so, they apply heuristics, such as "consider columns that are most constrained" to narrow the set of possibilities or to determine the starting point and subsequent steps. In this DONALD + GERALD problem, the known information is that D = 5, and the most constrained column is the rightmost one.

Having narrowed the possibilities to those relevant to the rightmost column, an algorithm in the form of addition can be applied. Adding 5 and 5 (D and D) and getting the sum of 10 leads to the conclusion, with certainty, that T = 0. Thus, a subgoal of determining the mapping for one of the letter-digit pairs is accomplished by applying that algorithm. In terms of knowledge states and operators, applying the addition operator transformed the starting knowledge state to a new one that includes not only D = 5, but also T = 0, as well as the fact that 1 is carried to the next column. The new knowledge in turn constrains the values for other columns, potentially affecting which are attempted next.

Chess also helps to illustrate the Newell and Simon approach. The start state includes the chess pieces on the board in their starting configuration and the goal state is to checkmate one's opponent. Knowledge of the rules of chess determines the possible next states from the current state. For example, from the initial configuration at the start of a game, possible next states based on a single move could include ones in which any one of the white pawns advanced by one or two squares, or in which one of the white knights advanced. Ones in which a white bishop has advanced, for example, are not initially possible given the rules of movement.

The information processing limits mentioned already preclude one from considering all possible moves and their ramifications for all possible responses by one's opponent. Instead, heuristics such as "control the center of the board" and "attempt moves that threaten an opponent's pieces with more than one of yours" narrow the set of moves considered. So, although advancing either the rightmost or leftmost pawn by one square would be a legal first move, the "control the center" heuristic would eliminate those moves from being considered and favor an initial move such as advancing the Queen's pawn two squares.

Although the information processing approach was developed for and on a narrow set of problems, the principles can apply broadly to other situations. As a simple example of an everyday problem that could be framed in this way, consider a person who has run out of gas on the way to an important meeting. There is a clear separation between the initial state of being unable to continue driving to the meeting and the goal state of being there. The internal representation of the start state might include the person's knowledge of the fact of being out of gas, the current location and time, the meeting location and time, and any other known factors. The goal state might include being physically at the meeting along with any needed materials. Heuristics, such as "don't overreact," "limit costs," or "honor social contracts" might eliminate from consideration such steps as calling 911, engaging a helicopter service or calling a friend who is known to be on his way to his own meeting in the opposite direction. Establishing subgoals might include determining whether or not one has a gas can to acquire and transport gas to the vehicle. The role of algorithms in this situation is less clear, but might be seen if one uses knowledge about walking speed, the distance to be traveled and simple mathematics to determine if walking to the meeting is a viable option.

Having constructed a problem representation, there are also heuristics that might guide progress through the space by selecting a promising next step or subgoal and determining the operator needed to achieve that move. One type of heuristic would be to choose moves that reduce the distance between the current state and the goal state or that resemble the goal state more than the current state does. Considering the problem, metaphorically, as a landscape and the goal as the highest point in the landscape, such a heuristic would lead the solver to always opt for a step that would move him or her higher, hence the term **hill climbing** for that heuristic. The problem with hill climbing is that is focuses strictly on local considerations rather than global ones. The landscape could potentially have multiple hills, and the solver could potentially reach the top of a lower one and then stop because next moves would all lead down rather than up. Barring the application of any other strategy, the solver would reach an impasse, and the search would fail.

An alternative to hill climbing is **means–ends-analysis** that takes into account the bigger picture. Like hill climbing, means–ends-analysis seeks states that reduce the difference between the current and goal state, and would ordinarily identify the next point that removes the most distant, and select an operator that will move the solver to that point. But, means–ends-analysis, with a focus on the global picture, allows for the construction of other subgoals that might potentially (and temporarily) increase the distance. If an operator cannot be applied to achieve the desired state, a new subgoal can be constructed to remove the impediment. To return to the out-of-gas example, after determining that he or she does not have a suitable container, a person might choose to walk to a hardware store in a direction opposite the nearest filling station to acquire one before moving in the direction of that station, because doing so satisfies a necessary subgoal. In hill climbing, by contrast, all movement would be in the direction of the meeting.

Evidence from a number of problem types shows that people do rely to some extent on a hill climbing heuristic, but the fact that they ultimately achieve solutions indicates that they must also apply other procedures (see, e.g., Novick & Bassok, 2005 and Mayer, 1991 for a review and interpretation of such findings). Consider a variant on the classic Luchins (1942) water jar problems. In these problems, the solver is given three jars that can hold specific quantities of water and must measure a quantity of water specified as the goal. Suppose then that the containers A, B and C can hold 8, 5 and 3 cups respectively, and that the goal is to end up with 4 cups in A and 4 in B. If the initial state includes A being full and B and C being empty, of the two possible first moves, pouring 5 cups into B is closer to the goal state than pouring 3 cups into C (i.e., it results in 3 in A and 5 in B, which is closer to the goal of 4 and 4 than 5 in A and 3 in C). Atwood and Polson's (1976) data from the 8, 5, 3 problem show that solvers have a clear preference for the former move over the latter. Consistent with other information-processing-based approaches of the time, they used the term means–ends process to describe people's approaches, but the evaluation function that identifies the "optimal" move is akin to hill climbing as described above and elsewhere (e.g., Mayer, 1991; Novick & Bassok, 2005). Note that the process described by Atwood and Polson also correctly predicts the difficulty people have in moving from the situation of $A = 6$, $B = 2$ and $C = 0$. The best move would be to empty B into C because that would allow movement to the goal in the fewest subsequent steps. Yet, that move would be identified as unacceptable because it leads to too great a deviation from the goal as measured by the evaluation function. Rather than choosing the move that leads to the fewest needed steps, people tend to favor pouring A into C, which is optimal according to the evaluation function, but increases the number of steps needed to reach the goal (Atwood & Polson, 1976).

Similar conclusions can be drawn from observations of the difficulties people have at certain points in the "Hobbits and Orcs problem". In that problem, people must use a boat that can hold two individuals at a time to transport three Hobbits and three Orcs from one side of a river to the other, subject to the constraint that the Hobbits can never be outnumbered on either side of the river; if they are, they will be eaten by the Orcs. Readers can work through initial steps, using moves of transporting two individuals to the goal side and having one individual bring the boat back to the start side, but at some point a stage will be reached in which there are two Hobbits and two Orcs on the goal side and one of each on the start side. At this point, there seems to be an impasse. If a Hobbit brings the boat back, the one on the goal side will be eaten. If an Orc brings it back, the Hobbit on the start side will be eaten when the Orc gets there. The impasse can be resolved with the realization that two individuals can bring the boat back to the start side instead of just one, and that one should be an Orc and one a Hobbit. That way, when the boat gets back to the start side, there are two Hobbits and two Orcs there as well as one Hobbit and one Orc on the goal side. Although necessary for achieving the overall goal, the step temporarily moves the solver farther from the goal state rather than closer, thereby violating the hill climbing heuristic. Empirical evidence shows that people make more errors and take longer in moving from that state than from other problem states (e.g., Greeno, 1974; Thomas, 1974).

PROBLEM SOLVING AS REPRESENTATION AND RESTRUCTURING

Although the contrast is not an absolute one, the Gestalt tradition was more concerned with the ways in which problems were represented in the solver's mind, rather than search processes through a particular representation once constructed. They extended notions of perceptual organization to problem solving and emphasized the need to restructure in order to solve some types of problems. This can be illustrated by considering the nine dot problem (Maier, 1930) shown in Figure 8.1. The task is to draw four straight lines that will connect all nine dots without lifting one's pencil and without retracing over any of the lines. For readers unfamiliar with this problem, the standard accepted solution is shown at the end of this chapter.

FIGURE 8.1   Nine dot problem.

One of the reasons this problem is difficult according to the Gestaltists is the perceptual configuration. The dots form a good figure, a square, with the result that people erroneously assume that they must stay within the square and confine their attempts to lines that stay within its boundaries. Without restructuring to overcome that constraint, achieving the standard solution is not possible. This interpretation has been challenged (e.g., Weisberg, & Alba, 1981) and the evidence shows that there may be multiple sources of difficulty (Kershaw & Ohlsson. 2004), but the possibility is mentioned here to illustrate the Gestalt view regarding perceptual organization as it may influence problem structuring.

Another example of a possible perceptual limitation on the way people represent problems is the matchstick problem in which the goal is to use six matchsticks to create four equilateral triangles with the side length of each triangle equal to the length of a match. The solution is described at the end of the chapter, but as a hint, and fitting with the current discussion, solution attempts that are limited to 2-dimensional representations as one might draw out on paper will not lead to success.

Problems need not be purely perceptual in nature to reveal the importance of representation. Consider the monk who begins a journey up along a mountain path at dawn. He walks at a steady pace, reaching a temple at the top of the mountain where he stops to rest and meditate. After a few days of contemplation he returns to the base of the mountain along the same path, of course walking at a faster pace down than he did on the way up. Can you prove that there is a place along the path that he occupies at exactly the same time on each of the two days? This is an extremely difficult problem when represented as a single monk walking up and down on two separate days. However, the answer becomes obvious by changing the representation to contain two monks making the journey on the same day, one starting at the bottom and one starting at the top. If they walk along the same mountain path, at some point they have to pass one another, so they are then at the same point at the same time of day.

Duncker's (1945) view of structuring and restructuring a problem can be described by reference to the tumor problem (see also Dunker & Krechevsky, 1939). The gist of the problem is that a patient's stomach tumor can be cured by directing a ray at it that is of sufficient intensity to destroy organic tissue, but the challenge is to do so in a way that will not harm the healthy tissue surrounding the tumor. The solver might move from broad characterizations such as avoiding contact between the rays and healthy tissue, desensitizing the healthy tissue in some way or reducing the intensity of the rays while passing through the healthy tissue, to particular implementations, such as using a free path to the stomach (e.g., the esophagus). Regressions to the broader level might occur if specific solutions as envisioned are found to be unsatisfactory, and fixation on general ranges of solutions or particular functional solutions can occur.

When theorists operating from the information processing perspective have considered changes in problem representation, they have used the notion of search. Rather than searching through states within a problem representation, however, a shift to a new way of viewing the problem can be seen as resulting from search for a different representation from among a set of possible representations (see e.g, Kaplan & Simon, 1990; Korf, 1980). Search for a new problem space or representation can be prompted by the failure to find any operators that yield progress within the current representation. Just as search within a problem space needs to be selective and guided by heuristics, so does search among possible problem representations for a new and workable problem space. Such searching is not random.

Kaplan and Simon (1990) provided evidence for the role of a number of external and internal factors that are important in directing search for a new representation. They used the mutilated checkerboard problem in which people are told that a standard 8×8 checkerboard can be covered completely using 32 dominoes. That is, since there are 64 squares and each domino can cover two horizontally or vertically adjacent squares, 32 dominoes will cover the board. Solvers must then consider a mutilated checkerboard from which two diagonally opposite corner squares have been removed. Their task is to show how 31 dominoes can be used to cover the remaining 62 squares or demonstrate logically that it is impossible to do so.

Although it might seem possible to cover the 62 squares with 31 dominoes, it is in fact impossible. The representation of the problem, which people tend to start with and which leads to the optimistic view of being able to cover the squares only considers the total number of squares and the total number of dominoes. The search space of arrangements of dominoes to test for possibility, however, would be huge, requiring solvers to try an enormous number of combinations. Thus, that representation of the problem is not viable. Solving the problem, and arriving at certainty about the impossibility requires a different problem space or representation, involving parity, in which the alternating colors of adjacent squares are considered. The pairing of alternately colored squares means that any given domino must cover one black and one white square. Removing diagonally opposite corner squares will remove two squares of the same color, leaving for example 32 black squares and 30 white squares. Thus, even if the solver constructed an arrangement of 30 dominoes covering 60 squares (30 black and 30 white), there would still be two black squares and only a divided domino could cover them.

Kaplan and Simon (1990) identified four possible sources of constraint on people's search for alternate representations; features of the problem itself or the salience of cues about relevant aspects of the problem, hints from the experimenter, both of which are external to the solver, and relevant domain knowledge and the heuristic of noticing invariants across problem situations, which are internal to the solver. They manipulated the salience of parity by using the labels bread and butter in the adjacent squares rather than alternating color and provided hints to the impossibility of the problem and to the idea of parity and found that both factors influenced performance. They also found that irrelevant domain-specific knowledge interfered with solutions. However, the most influential aspect was the heuristic of noticing invariants across situations, such as the fact that in attempts to cover the squares, the ones remaining uncovered were always the same type (e.g., black).

Findings such as those of Kaplan and Simon reveal the robustness of an information processing view. Just as search within a problem space is aided by heuristics, so too is the otherwise unmanageable task of switching to a helpful new representation if the initial one proves unworkable.

THE CREATIVE PROBLEM SOLVING MODEL

Whereas the notions of problem solving as search, and problem solving as restructuring emerged from different traditions within psychology, an alternative way of conceptualizing problem solving has its roots in more applied concerns. Specifically, the approach that has come to be labeled Creative Problem Solving (CPS), developed initially by Alex Osborn and Sidney Parnes, and subsequently refined by others, was born of the practical goal of facilitating problem solving in real world settings (see e.g., Osborn, 1957; Treffinger, Isaksen, & Stead-Dorval, 2006). CPS is comprised of stages of activity, during which solvers progressively refine their understanding of and approach to a problem from initial conceptualization through the implementation of a solution.

In CPS, there is an initial stage, exploring the challenge, during which people are supposed to identify, clarify and otherwise clearly define the problem to be confronted. Exploring the challenge itself has three substages. In the first of these, known as objective finding, mess finding, or constructing opportunities, people identify a broad goal. The goal could be based on a desire to accomplish something or dissatisfaction with the way things are. In the second substage, known as fact finding or exploring data, people determine what is known and what still needs to be known. They consider who and what is involved, and list out data ranging from known facts to assumptions and even gut feelings. The third substage, called problem finding or framing, is a critical stage during which people clarify or refine the way the problem is defined and specified. As noted earlier, the way in which problems are represented determines the ease with which they are solved and the types of solutions that are attempted, so the outcome of these initial stages is vital to progress.

The second main stage is called idea finding or idea generation. It is during this stage that people generate ideas for possible solutions to the problem as it has been defined or represented. In the CPS framework, judgment is to be deferred and as many possibilities as can be suggested, including wild ones, are welcome.

The final main stage, preparing for action, is comprised of two substages. During the first preparing-for-action substage, known as solution finding or developing solutions, people choose one of the possibilities produced during idea generation and refine it. At that stage, criticism and analysis to eliminate unworkable solutions and improve upon ones with potential would be appropriate. The final substage, acceptance finding or building acceptance, recognizes that solutions have a better chance of succeeding if the relevant parties are receptive to it. Hence, the stage includes finding ways to increase acceptance of the chosen solution. Thus, CPS goes beyond the other approaches covered in this chapter by concentrating not just on the processes involved in representing problems and generating solutions, but also on strategies for implementing the solutions and working toward their acceptance in real world settings.

PROBLEM TYPES

Well-Defined versus Ill-Defined

The types of problems we have considered so far are characteristic of the ones used in laboratory research on problem solving. They fall into a particular class of problems that can be labeled **well-defined**. Well-defined problems have clear start states and goals states, and, although some of them, such as the monk and checkerboard problems may require the solver to move beyond an initial representation to construct a more workable problem space, there is no ambiguity about the desired outcome. A specific answer or goal state is to be achieved. Thus, well-defined problems fit readily into the search framework described in the previous section. Problem solving is a matter of finding the right path in the problem space between the start and goal states once the appropriate representation has been generated.

In contrast to well-defined problems, ill-defined problems have open-ended, unclear start and goal states. Consider tasks such as making a difference in the world or creating a lasting work of art. It is difficult to identify the start state, other than perhaps noting that one has not yet made a difference or created such a work. Ill-defined problems may need different constructs than well-defined ones, such as finding a different way to represent the problem. Certainly, the early CPS stages just described may be relevant as are the constructs of problem finding or problem definition whereby people clarify a relatively ambiguous problem statement in such a way that ordinary problem solving methods or other techniques can be applied (see e.g., Basadur, 1994, 1997; Mumford, Mobley, Uhlman, Reiter-Palmon, & Doares, 1991; Mumford, Reiter-Palmon, & Redmond, 1994; Runco & Chand, 1994, 1995; Sternberg, 1988).

Three Part Classification of Problem Types

An alternative way of characterizing problems is to classify them into one of three types: **arrangement problems**, **inducing structure problems**, and **transformation problems** (Greeno, 1978). In arrangement problems, the solver has a set of objects or elements and must determine an arrangement for them that will satisfy some criterion. Consider anagram puzzles in which the solver is given a string of letters, typically in a random arrangement that does not form a word, and must arrange them in a way that forms a real word. For example, given the letters "grutohoh" one can arrange them to form the legitimate word "thorough".

Just as one can consider the role of algorithms and heuristics in other types of problems, one can see their potential roles in anagrams or other arrangement problems. In principle, it would be possible to create a problem space that included all possible arrangements of the given letters and search that set until a legal word is found. The exhaustive search approach would yield correct solutions to the problem relatively quickly for short strings that entail only a small number of possible arrangements. For example, given the string "dre", this algorithmic search would create and consider the alternative strings "der", "rde", "edr", "erd", and "red", presumably stopping as soon as red was encountered. However, as letter strings increase in length, the number of possible arrangements rapidly becomes unwieldy, making the purely algorithmic search nonviable. The need for heuristics to guide and narrow the search then becomes more evident. For example, one could use knowledge about typical spelling patterns or initial letter sequences to limit the set of possibilities considered (e.g., Novick & Sherman, 2008; Ronning, 1965).

It should also be noted that even algorithms and heuristics of the type described in the previous paragraph may not be enough for certain arrangement problems (see e.g., Finke, Ward, & Smith, 1992). Consider the following anagram problems, each involving arranging the letters of the strings to form one word. Given HTE, the algorithmic approach would easily yield THE. Adding in heuristics might help solve REARPOOT (e.g, not even considering strings such as AOEOPRRT). But what about the problem NEW DOOR? The solution (given at the end of the chapter) is startlingly easy, once seen, but requires a creative leap beyond ordinary heuristics for such problems (Finke et al., 1992).

Inducing structure problems require the problem solver to determine the relational structure present in a set of elements they are given. One need not alter the structure, but rather discover the relations at work in the situation. Consider the simple series extrapolation problem in which the solver is given the sequence 2, 4, 6, 8 and must predict the next element in the sequence. Readers can readily determine that the next element is 10, by noting that the relation involved is that each element is 2 greater than the preceding one.

Other examples of inducing structure problems are analogies of the form A:B::C:? As in series extrapolation, the solver must determine the relations involved to predict the element needed to correctly complete the problem. What is the relationship between A and B, and what entity would be related to C in the same way. For instance, given man:boy::cat:?, one might identify the relation "younger version" and choose kitten as the best answer.

Analogy is much richer than indicated by these types of reasoning problems, and can underlie creativity in a range of domains. Examples of analogies are present in science (e.g., Rutherford's use of a solar system as a model for how the hydrogen atom was structured), literature (e.g., Robbins, Laurents, Bernstein, and Sondheim's adaptation of Shakespeare's *Romeo and Juliet* to the context of a 1950s' New York City gang conflict in *West Side Story*), technology and invention (e.g., Edison's development of an electric light distribution system patterned after the gas distribution system of the day), and politics and social influence (e.g., the analogy between Iraq invading Kuwait in 1990 and Germany overrunning European countries in 1938 and 1939). What these situations have in common is that structured knowledge in the form of objects (e.g., planets and sun), relations (e.g., planets orbit the sun) and higher-order relations (gravitational force) are mapped from a more familiar domain to a new domain (e.g., electrons and nucleus, electrons orbiting the nucleus, and some type of causal attractive force). As with all good analogies, the structural aspects that are most important are the relations and higher order relations (see e.g., Gentner, 1983, 1989; Gentner, Holyoak, & Kokinov, 2001; Holyoak, 2005). For example, the power of the solar system atom analogy derives not from any similarity between the planets and electrons, but from the suggestion that, just as planets orbit around a more massive central body, the sun, electrons may orbit around a more massive central body, the nucleus.

Transformation problems involve executing a set of operations to transform one state or situation into another. The Hobbits and Orcs problem described earlier is a good example of such a problem. One must transform the situation of three Hobbits and three Orcs on one side of the river into all six on the other side of the river according to a set of constraints.

Another classic example of a transformation problem is the Tower of Hanoi, used by Kotovsky, Hayes, and Simon (1985), with variants on the task dating back at least as far as Ewert and Lambert (1932) and Peterson (1920). In a simple form of the task there are three pegs, a, b and c. At the start there are three disks of decreasing size on one of the pegs, say a, with the largest on the bottom and the smallest on the top. The goal is to recreate the stack of disks on one of the other pegs, say c, subject to specific constrains. Only one disk may be moved at a time and no disk can be placed on top of one that is smaller than it. As in the Hobbits and Orcs problem, the Tower of Hanoi also requires temporary movement away from the goal. After moving the smallest disk to the goal peg c, and moving the medium disk to b, one has to move the smallest to b to make room for the largest on c. Once again, a subgoal that involves movement away from the goal state is needed in order to reach it.

Insight versus Non-Insight Problems

Still another way of characterizing problems is to distinguish between **insight problems** and **non-insight** or analytic problems. Generally, insight problems are those that seem to involve a restructuring of information or a key realization to achieve their solution. Put differently, the initial representation of the problem by the solver is structured in a non-helpful way or contains erroneous assumptions that make achieving a solution difficult if not impossible. Restructuring or eliminating the inhibiting assumptions is necessary, though possibly not sufficient, to solve the problem. Consider the woman in a particular town who married 20 men from that town, without divorcing any of them or any of them dying, yet broke no laws even though bigamy is illegal in that town. How can this be? As long as one conceptualizes the information as specifying that she is **married to** 20 men, the answer seems to elude us. If one realizes, however, that she is of the clergy or a justice of the peace and that she performed the marriage ceremonies **for** the men, there is no problem with her marrying 20 or more. In this way, insight problems do require a re-representation.

Consider also the coin dealer who immediately called authorities when offered a supposedly ancient coin that appeared to be old, with an emperor's head on one side and the date 544 BC on the other. How did the dealer know it was a fake? Of course, BC would not have been used as a designation on coins or anything else at that point. Again, a realization seems to be required. Insight problems need not be merely verbal. More perceptual examples already discussed include the nine dot and six matchstick problems discussed earlier.

Because these problems seem to involve an initial incorrect structure or set of assumptions, and because solutions require a restructuring or relaxing those constraints, insight problems are seen as different from non-insight problems, such as algebra or logic problems, where steady plodding progress to a solution is required. The solutions to at least some insight problems seem to come quickly once they are restructured. One piece of evidence in favor of the distinction between insight and non-insight problems comes from studies in which people predict their likelihood of solving problems or rate their feelings of warmth, that is, how close they are to a solution while working on the problems (Metcalfe, 1986a; 1986b; Metcalfe & Wiebe, 1987). For example, Metcalfe and Wiebe (1987) contrasted predictions and warmth ratings for algebra problems and other incremental types (e.g., Tower of Hanoi) with those for supposed insight problems, such as determining how many socks one needs to take from a drawer of mixed proportions of brown and black socks to make sure one has a pair. A crucial finding was that feelings of warmth increased incrementally for non-insight problems as people neared the solution whereas they did not for the insight problems.

A strong interpretation of Metcalfe's findings is that the underlying processes for insight and non-insight problems are fundamentally different. Perhaps the solution to insight problems does not involve steady incremental progress as might be true if they were solved by a systematic search through a problem space as in the Newell and Simon view. Instead, the person attempts solutions within a non-workable representation of the problem until a realization is triggered leading to a better problem representation conducive to a quick solution, leading to an "Aha" moment. An alternative view is that people could be making incremental progress on both types of problems but not be consciously aware of it in insight problems. Weisberg (1992) has observed that the findings from Metcalfe's results do not conclusively rule out incremental progress that may happen outside the person's awareness.

A related issue concerning insight problems involves the role of erroneous assumptions as factors inhibiting their solution. Recall that the Gestaltists saw perceptual organization factors as affecting people's problem representations, potentially impeding their solutions. Consider the nine dot problem again, and the suggestion that the perceptual structure of the square encourages solutions that keep the lines within the boundaries of the square. However, it would be too simplistic to conclude that simply telling people that their lines should go outside the square will lead them to immediately realize the one correct solution. The reason is that that piece of information simply creates a new problem space, different from the person's original one. The solver still needs to search that new space for the correct set of lines and turns to complete the task of connecting all the dots. Data presented by Weisberg and Alba (1981) are consistent with this idea in showing that people who were told that they needed to go outside the boundaries of the square showed only a small boost in performance relative to those who were not given that clue.

Indeed, Kershaw and Ohlsson (2004) have shown that there are multiple sources of difficulty in such problems. These include perceptual factors, such as the white space where turns need to be made being ground rather than figure, process factors having to do with the sheer size of the search space in terms of possible combinations of lines, and knowledge, such as might come from experience with connect-a-dot puzzles where the lines always go through dots and do not change direction anywhere other than on dots. Such studies continue to refine our understanding of the complexities of insight problem solving.

Additional evidence contributing to a growing understanding of insight comes from studies comparing the effects of verbalization on performance on insight and non-insight problems. In an early study, Schooler, Ohlsson, and Brooks (1993) demonstrated a verbal overshadowing effect selectively for insight problems. That is, solution rates for insight problems were lower for participants who were instructed to think aloud during the task in comparison with silent controls, whereas solution rates for non-insight problems were unaffected by thinking aloud. This seminal study has since been criticized on a number of grounds, including the fact that the verbalizing participants were only given minimal training in verbalizing and it was only on non-insight problems (e.g., Fleck & Weisberg, 2004), and that the bulk of the insight problems were spatial rather than verbal, which could have produced a cost based on switching modes (e.g., Gilhooly, Fioratou, & Henretty, 2010).

B. INDIVIDUAL LEVEL INFLUENCES

Fleck and Weisberg (2004) had some participants think aloud and others not while attempting to solve Duncker's candle task. In that task, participants are given a box of tacks, matches and candles and must figure out how to attach the candle to a wall and light it (safely). The insightful solution requires the use of the box as a platform, tacking the box to wall, and melting wax to affix the candle to it. Achieving that representation involves overcoming the functional fixedness of seeing the only use for the box as being a container. Although the verbal protocols revealed clear evidence of restructuring, there was no verbal overshadowing effect on performance. In addition, Gilhooly et al. (2010) found verbalizing effects on spatial problems, both insight and non-insight, but found no effect that was specific to insight problems. As with the research on the factors that make insight problems difficult, the work on verbalization continues to reveal the complexities of the distinction between insight and non-insight problems.

It is important to note that there is evidence that insight problems share certain commonalities with one another and differ in consistent ways from non-insight problems. Gilhooly and Murphy (2005) for example had participants perform 24 tasks considered to be insight problems and 10 considered to be non-insight problems. The insight problems were a diverse set, including the nine dot, candle, multiple marriage, mutilated checkerboard, tumor and six match problems among others. The non-insight problems were also diverse, including the Tower of Hanoi, Hobbits and Orcs, cryptarithmetic, and anagrams. Participants were also given tests of various abilities, including measures of memory span, vocabulary, fluency and alternate uses. Cluster analysis showed that, in spite of the diversity within the sets, insight problems clustered with one another and non-insight problems also clustered with one another, providing evidence for a meaningful distinction between the problem types. In addition, performance on the insight problems was related to indicators of the capacity for flexible thought, such as performance on the alternate uses test. Thus, in spite of the mixed evidence on phenomena such as interference from verbalization, there does appear to be something fundamental that is shared across insight problems that makes them different in important ways from non-insight problems. Clearly, restructuring is a more salient feature for the insight problems, but there may be other factors at work as well that mesh nicely with creative approaches to problem solving.

KNOWLEDGE AND RECENT EXPOSURE

At the simplest level, knowledge clearly plays a role in how one achieves the solution to a problem. Consider for example, two different children, one of whom has memorized multiplication tables and one who has not. When confronted with a problem such as 5×9, the first child can solve it simply by retrieving a fact stored in long-term memory. Indeed, that one-step action is trivial enough that one might not even want to call it problem solving. The second child, of course, has to employ some type of computational procedure to reach an answer.

Considerable research has been devoted to documenting how knowledge influences the ways in which people represent and solve problems. There is evidence for the importance of long-term existing differences in knowledge as well as influences from recent exposure to task-relevant materials.

Knowledge Differences

Not surprisingly, there are differences between individuals that have more versus less experience in a domain in terms of the overall amount of knowledge they have about the domain, but there are also differences in terms of how they notice, organize, remember and apply problem-related information within the domain. In general, individuals with less experience rely more on surface level features, whereas those with more experience are oriented toward deeper structural properties and relations. In a well known study, for example, Chi, Feltovich and Glaser (1981) had undergraduates who had taken a physics course and advanced physics graduate students sort instances of physics problems into categories. The undergraduates tended to sort on the basis of more superficial properties, such as the apparatus used (e.g., pulleys, springs, inclined plane). In contrast, the graduate students tended to sort on the basis of the fundamental principles involved (e.g., conservation of energy).

There are corresponding differences between more and less experienced individuals in the way they solve physics problems, with more experienced individuals rapidly accessing their structured storehouse of patterns and schemata to interpret problems and generate solutions (see e.g., Larkin, 1985; Larkin, McDermott, Simon & Simon, 1980). For example, at least for problems that are well within their grasp, experts tend to use working-forward strategies, beginning with the information in the start state and performing needed calculations along the way to reach the goal state. In contrast, novice strategies involve working backward.

Evidence for reliance on more extensive, structured, or abstract representations by experts comes from a variety of other domains as well. For example, expertise in chess is associated with the accumulation of a vast storehouse of "chunks" or typical configurations of pieces that might occur during the context of a match, which guides the player's noticing of information, planning and memory for the placement of pieces on the board (e.g., Chase & Simon, 1973; de Groot, 1966). As with physics expertise, it is not just more knowledge, but organized knowledge, as revealed by the tendency to recall the position of pieces on a board in chunks, and the fact that the advantage more experienced players exhibit in memory for piece positions is greater when the arrangements studied come from ordinary mid-game situations than when the pieces are randomly placed on the board (e.g., Gobet & Simon, 1996).

The organization of knowledge by abstract principles is seen in a number of other domains, including engineering (see e.g., Moss, Kotovsky, & Cagan, 2006). Moss et al. used recall and description tasks to demonstrate that freshman and senior engineering students differed in their representations of mechanical devices. That is, patterns or recall for and descriptions of devices presented to the students revealed more evidence of abstract functional information for the seniors. In contrast to the freshman, they tended to notice not just that components of a device were connected but that the connection entailed a particular functional relationship between the parts.

Recent Exposure

Aside from any long standing effects of knowledge on problem solving, it is clear that knowledge can be activated by task factors in a way that can either facilitate or inhibit problem solving. A classic example comes from the Duncker candle problem described previously. When the candles, tacks and matches are presented in boxes, participants are less likely to come to the solution involving the use of a box as a platform than if the boxes are present but the other elements are not inside them (e.g., Duncker, 1945). One conclusion to be drawn from this is that the former condition activates knowledge about the boxes as containers, which makes it more difficult to see a different use for the box (i.e., as a platform).

Exposure-based knowledge can also take the form of very specific strategies. There is no question that learned strategies can facilitate problem solving, but there are interesting cases where they can inhibit solutions. A classic example of the latter is Luchins' (1942) finding from the water jar task that people can develop an overreliance on a particular solution strategy to the extent that they miss much simpler solutions. For instance, given that A can hold 21 cups of water, B can hold 127 cups and C can hold 3 cups, and the goal to measure out 100 cups of water, the solution is to fill B completely, empty 21 cups into A, and then 6 more cups using the 3 cup capacity of C twice. After getting a series of such problems, all of which can be solved with the same B-A-2C approach (e.g., A = 5, B = 20, C = 2, Goal = 11), people develop and apply that algorithm to such an extent that they do not readily see simpler solutions to subsequent problems for which the algorithm will not work (e.g., A = 28, B = 76, C = 3, Goal = 25). People given the simpler problem without exposure to the rule across the complex problems solve it readily.

Recent research by Hunter, Bedel-Avers, Hunsicker, Mumford, and Ligon (2008) also reveals some of the complexities involved in knowledge activation. Hunter et al. had people develop solutions to a social innovation problem in which they played the role of a teacher designing a course to reduce college dropout rates. Prior to performing that task, they were given a description of another problem and asked to generate associations (a list of things associated with the problem), schematic information (key principles that could be used to organize their representation of the problem), case-based information (specific past experiences like the problem), or a combination of these types of knowledge. Activating knowledge in the form of a single type of these structures resulted in more ideas and more high quality ideas. However, activation of a combination of structures resulted in better solutions to the social innovation problem.

SUMMARY

Problems and situations that call for creativity can both be characterized as discrepancies between one's current situation and what one wants to accomplish. Importantly, it is the processes by which one closes or eliminates the gap that are the main focus of theory and research in problem solving, and it is the focus on processes that makes work on problem solving relevant to an understanding of creativity. Although some types of problems may benefit more from creative approaches than others, it is much more the mode of attack on the problem than the problem itself that is central to creativity. Even a mundane math problem with a single correct answer can be seen to be relevant to creativity if the solver adopts a novel approach to solving it, rather than simply relying on a stored fact or well practiced procedure.

Research on problem solving stems from two separate traditions, one having roots in Gestalt psychology, the other in information processing theory. Both are deeply concerned with process, and both tend to rely on relatively simple tasks that can be performed within the confines of psychology laboratories. The Gestalt researchers focused more on how people represent problems and emphasized that the likelihood of achieving a solution was dependent on the way in which a problem was represented. The information processing researchers focused more on search through a representational space once a problem representation was generated. They noted limits on the search based on the characteristics of the human information processing system. Rather than a search through all possible problem states, problem solving is guided by certain types of heuristics.

Problem solving research and theory is also driven by the view that there are different problem types. One distinction is between well-defined problems with clear start and goal states and ill-defined problems in which the start or goal or both states are unclear. Sometimes an initial phase of problem finding or problem definition may help to turn an ill-defined problem into a well-defined one.

Another distinction is between arrangement, inducing structure and transformation problems, each with its own unique properties. Examining the ways people arrive at solutions to these types of problems can help to reveal movement through states of knowledge, as well as the use of algorithms (precise rules) and heuristics (rules of thumb). It can also help to reveal impediments to problem solving that inhibit creative problem solving, such as over-reliance on learned algorithms or the unnecessary adherence to interfering assumptions.

Still another distinction of problem types is between insight problems that seem to require problem restructuring and yield at least the conscious experience of sudden solutions, and non-insight problems which seem to give the solver an impression of more steady progress toward a solution. The differences between insight and non-insight problems is still under debate, but there do seem to be problems that cluster together into one or another type and that are differentially linked to aspects of creative capacity, such as divergent thinking.

It is also clear that knowledge affects not only the likelihood that people will solve problems but also the manner in which they represent them. More knowledgeable individuals use their knowledge to generate more abstract problem representations, for example. In addition to long term knowledge, information from recent experiences influences problem solving, and it can help or hinder people, depending on whether it helps people see possibilities or masks simpler applicable solutions.

Although there is an extensive literature on problem solving, more research would help to draw out the connections between creativity and problem solving. In particular, there is a complex interplay between the structure of problems as presented, people's knowledge, recent experiences, the ways in which people represent the problems, the processes they apply and the likelihood of achieving solutions that are novel and or appropriate. A detailed explication of that interplay would greatly advance our understanding of creativity.

PROBLEM SOLUTIONS

Matchstick problem solution is to use three matchsticks to form the base of a pyramid and the remaining three to define the sides of the pyramid rising from the base.

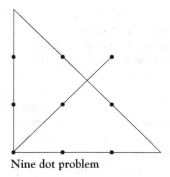

Nine dot problem

The NEW DOOR anagram solution is ONE WORD. Recall that the instructions were to unscramble the letters to make one word.

References

Atwood, M. E., & Polson, P. G. (1976). A process model for water jug problems. *Cognitive Psychology, 8*, 191–216.

Atwood, M. E., Masson, M. E., & Polson, P. G. (1980). Further explorations with a process model for water jug problems. *Memory & Cognition, 8*, 182–192.

Basadur, M. (1994). Managing the creative process in organizations. In M. A. Runco (Ed.), *Problem finding, problem solving, and creativity* (pp. 237–268). Norwood, NJ: Ablex Publishing Company.

Basadur, M. (1997). Organizational development interventions for enhancing creativity in the workplace. *Journal of Creative Behavior, 31*, 59–72.

Chase, W. G., & Simon, H. A. (1973). Perception in chess. *Cognitive Psychology, 4*, 55–81.

Chi, M. T. H., Feltovich, P. J., & Glaser, R. (1981). Categorization and representation of physics problems by experts and novices. *Cognitive Science, 5*, 121–152.

de Groot, A. D. (1966). Perception and memory versus thought. In B. Kleinmuntz (Ed.), *Problem-solving*. New York, NY: Wiley.

Duncker, K. (1945). On problem solving. *Psychological Monographs, 58*(Whole no. 270).

Duncker, K., & Krechevsky, I. (1939). On solution-achievement. *Psychological Review, 36*, 176–185.

Ericsson, K. A., & Simon, H. A. (1993). *Protocol analysis: Verbal reports as data*. Cambridge, MA: MIT Press.

Ernst, G. W., & Newell, A. (1969). *GPS: A study in generality and problem solving*. New York, NY: Academic Press.

Ewert, P. H., & Lambert, J. F. (1932). Part II: The effect of verbal instructions upon the formation of a concept. *Journal of General Psychology, 6*, 400–413.

Finke, R. A., Ward, T. B., & Smith, S. M. (1992). *Creative cognition: Theory, research and applications*. Cambridge, MA: MIT Press.

Fleck, J. I., & Weisberg, R. (2004). The use of verbal protocols as data: An analysis of insight in the candle problem. *Memory and Cognition, 32*, 990–1006.

Gentner, (1983). Structure-mapping: A theoretical framework for analogy. *Cognitive Science, 7*, 155–170.

Gentner, D., Holyoak, K., & Kokinov, B. (2001). *The analogical mind: Perspectives from cognitive science*. Cambridge, MA: MIT Press.

Gilhooly, K. J., Fioratou, E., & Henretty, N. (2010). Verbalization and problem solving: Insight and spatial factors. *British Journal of Psychology, 101*, 81–93.

Gilhooly, K. J., & Murphy, P. (2005). Differentiating insight from non-insight problems. *Thinking and Reasoning, 11*, 279–302.

Gobet, F., & Simon, H. A. (1996). Recall of rapidly presented random chess positions is a function of skill. *Psychonomic Bulleting and Review, 3*, 159–163.

Greeno, J. G. (1974). Hobbits and orcs: Acquisition of a sequential concept. *Cognitive Psychology, 6*, 270–292.

Greeno, J. G. (1978). Natures of problem solving abilities. In W. K. Estes (Ed.), *Handbook of learning and cognitive processes* (Vol. 5), pp. 239–270.

Holyoak, K. J. (2005). Analogy. In K. J. Holyoak & R. G. Morrison (Eds.), *Cambridge handbook of thinking and reasoning* (pp. 117–142). New York, NY: Cambridge University Press.

Hunter, S. T., Bedell-Avers, K. E., Hunsicker, C. M., Mumford, M. D., & Ligon, G. S. (2008). Applying multiple knowledge structures in creative thought: Effects on idea generation and problem solving. *Creativity Research Journal, 20*, 137–154.

Kaplan, C. A., & Simon, H. A. (1990). In search of insight. *Cognitive Psychology, 22*, 374–419.

Kershaw, T., & Ohlsson, S. (2004). Multiple causes of difficulty in insight: The case of the nine-dot problem. *Journal of Experimental Psychology: Learning, Memory and Cognition, 30*, 3–13.

Korf, R. E. (1980). Toward a model of representational changes. *Artificial Intelligence, 14*, 41–78.

Kotovsky, K., Hayes, J. R., & Simon, H. A. (1985). Why are some problems hard?: Evidence from Tower of Hanoi. *Cognitive Psychology, 17*, 248–294.

Kotovsky, K., & Simon, H. A. (1990). What makes some problems really hard? Explorations in the problem space of difficulty. *Cognitive Psychology, 22*, 143–183.

Larkin, J. H. (1985). Understanding problem representations and skill in physics. In S. F. Chipman, J. W. Segal & R. Glaser (Eds.), *Thinking and learning skills: Vol. 2. Research and open questions* (pp. 141–159). Hillsdale, NJ: Erlbaum.

Larkin, J., McDermott, J., Simon, D. P., & Simon, H. A. (1980). Expert and novice performance in solving physics problems. *Science, 208*, 1335–1342.

Luchins, A. S. (1942). Mechanization in problem solving. *Psychological Monographs, 54*(6) (Whole No. 248).

Mayer, R. E. (1991). *Thinking, problem solving, cognition: Second Edition.* New York, NY: W. H. Freeman.

Metcalfe, J. (1986a). Feeling of knowing in memory and problem solving. *Journal of Experimental Psychology: Learning, Memory, & Cognition, 12*, 288–294.

Metcalfe, J. (1986b). Premonitions of insight predict impending error. *Journal of Experimental Psychology: Learning, Memory, & Cognition, 12*, 623–634.

Metcalfe, J., & Wiebe, D. (1987). Intuition in insight and noninsight problem solving. *Memory & Cognition, 15*, 238–246.

Moss, J., Kotovsky, K., & Cagan, J. (2006). The role of functionality in the mental representations of engineering students: Some differences in the early stages of expertise. *Cognitive Science: A Multidisciplinary Journal, 30*, 65–93.

Mumford, M. D., Mobley, M. I., Uhlman, C. E., Reiter-Palmon, R., & Doares, L. M. (1991). Process analytic models of creative thought. *Creativity Research Journal, 4*, 91–122.

Mumford, M. D., Reiter-Palmon, R., & Redmond, M. R. (1994). Problem construction and cognition: Applying problem representations in ill-defined problems. In M. A. Runco (Ed.), *Problem finding, problem solving, and creativity* (pp. 3–39). Norwood, NJ: Ablex Publishing Company.

Newell, A., & Simon, H. A. (1972). Human problem solving: The state of the theory in 1970. *American Psychologist, 26*, 145–159.

Newell, A., & Simon, H. A. (1972). *Human problem solving.* Englewood Cliffs, NJ: Prentice-Hall.

Novick, L. R., & Bassok, M. (2005). Problem solving. In K. J. Holyoak & R. G. Morrison (Eds.), *The Cambridge handbook of thinking and reasoning* (pp. 320–350). New York, NY: Cambridge University Press.

Novick, L. R., & Sherman, S. J. (2008). The effects of superficial and structural information on online problem solving for good versus poor anagram solvers. *Quarterly Journal of Experimental Psychology, 61*, 1098–1112.

Osborn, A. F. (1957). *Applied imagination.* New York, NY: Scribner.

Peterson, J. C. (1920). The higher mental processes in learning. *Psychological Monographs, 28*(7).

Runco, M. A., & Chand, I. (1994). Conclusions concerning problem finding, problem solving, and creativity. In M. A. Runco (Ed.), *Problem finding, problem solving, and creativity* (pp. 217–290). Norwood, NJ: Ablex Publishing Company.

Schooler, J. W., Ohlsson, S., & Brooks, K. (1993). Thoughts beyond words: When language overshadows insight. *Journal of Experimental Psychology: General, 122*, 166–183.

Sternberg, R. J. (1988). A three-facet model of creativity. In R. J. Sternberg (Ed.), *The nature of creativity: Contemporary psychological perspectives* (pp. 125–147). Cambridge, UK: Cambridge University Press.

Thomas, J. C., Jr. (1974). An analysis of behavior in the hobbits–orcs problem. *Cognitive Psychology, 6*, 257–269.

Treffinger, D. J., Isaksen, S. I., & Stead–Dorval, K. B. (2006). *Creative problem solving: An introduction.* Waco, TX: Prufrock Press.

Weisberg, R. W. (1992). Metacognition and insight during problem solving: Comment on Metcalfe. *Journal of Experimental Psychology: Learning, Memory, & Cognition, 18*, 426–431.

Weisberg, R. W., & Alba, An examination of the alleged role of "fixation" in the solution of several "insight" problems. *Journal of Experimental Psychology: General, 110*, 169–192.

B. INDIVIDUAL LEVEL INFLUENCES

Idea Generation and Idea Evaluation: Cognitive Skills and Deliberate Practices

Gerard J. Puccio and John F. Cabra

State University of New York, International Center for Studies in Creativity, Buffalo State, Buffalo, NY

INTRODUCTION

How does an individual come up with a breakthrough idea? What serves as the catalyst for the production of ideas that are so original and valuable that their successful introduction results in the transformation of an organization, market or domain? In Greek mythology it was the muses, goddesses and spirits that served as intermediaries on behalf of the gods, who provided inspiration for creative acts, such as the production of literature and art. Creativity was bestowed upon humans from some external force, thus the creative process originated from outside the individual. As Dacey (1999) said of the Greeks:

> "They believed their ideas were inspired by the gods, but by gods who existed in proliferation and who cared little about the lives of humans" *(p. 312)*.

Although the Greeks may have attributed the inspiration for their creative process to an ethereal source, Dacey eloquently described the unique qualities of the Greek culture that served to support individual creativity.

Despite the fact that the origin of the word "museum" can be traced back to the Greek "mouseion", which refers to a temple to the works of the muses, few eminently creative individuals of our modern era are likely to credit their creative breakthroughs to a muse.

Handbook of Organizational Creativity.
DOI: 10.1016/B978-0-12-374714-3.00009-4

Though rare is the occasion when creative insights are attributed to a heavenly force, some contemporary great creators have persistently cited external stimuli as the source of their inspiration, but rather than ethereal creatures many of these stimuli take physical form. Mathematician Poincare (1985) credited strong coffee, while poet A. E. Housman (1985) attributed his inspiration to beer. Author Rudyard Kipling worked only with the blackest of ink. Kipling reported that even blue-black ink was an insufficient spark for his creative process (Kipling, 1985).

To be fair, not all eminently creative individuals have given such credence to external factors. Numerous anecdotal stories have been collected in which, through reflection, well-known creators have described their respective creative processes (Ghiselin, 1985). Unfortunately even the musings of contemporary creative luminaries have done little to illuminate the precise nature of the creative process, and to the contrary, often serve to reinforce its mystery. For instance, educational reformer, social activist and bestselling author, Dorothy Canfield (1985) observed:

> "I have no idea whence this tide comes, or where it goes, but when it begins to rise in my heart, I know that a story is hovering in the offing" *(p. 174)*.

Perhaps it should not be a surprise when eminently creative individuals are unable to shed clarity on the creative process; after all they are immersed in the very phenomenon they are trying to describe. The creative process has perplexed even those who are trained to study the human condition; psychologists. Carl Jung (1985), the well-known Swiss psychologist, once stated:

> "Any reaction to stimulus may be causally explained; but the creative act, which is the absolute antithesis of mere reaction, will forever elude the human understanding. It can only be described in its manifestation; it can be obscurely sensed, but never wholly grasped." *(p. 218)*.

Davis (1986), an educational psychologist who devoted much of his research and writing to the topic of creativity, suggested that although much is known about the nature of creativity, there are aspects that remain a mystery. Since these views were expressed, we believe much has been learned about the creative process. Indeed a number of models now exist through which the creative process is described and successfully taught (Basadur, 1994; Gordon, 1961; Kelley & Littman, 2001; Puccio, Mance, & Murdock, 2011; Scott, Leritz, & Mumford, 2004). The purpose of this chapter is to explore two key areas of the creative process, namely idea generation and evaluation.

In this chapter we delve into this precise aspect of the creative process, reviewing descriptions, skills and practices associated with idea generation and idea evaluation. We begin this chapter by providing a broad description of the creative process, within which we locate and define these two phases of the process. In this same section, we also describe the interplay between idea generation and idea evaluation. We then summarize the literature related to idea generation and idea evaluation, and the skills and practices that promote effective use of both. The chapter closes with recommendations for future research.

IDEA GENERATION AND IDEA EVALUATION: DEFINITIONS AND ROLES WITHIN THE CREATIVE PROCESS

Before delving headlong into a review of idea generation and idea evaluation, it is important first to define these terms, and then to locate these constructs within the network of related creativity concepts. By proceeding in this manner we hope to clearly communicate the scope of this chapter, and to position the terms "idea generation" and "idea evaluation" within the field of creativity studies. We start with the broadest terms and work our way towards definitions of idea generation and idea evaluation.

What is creativity? Though variously phrased, there has been consensus in defining creativity as the manifestation of ideas that are both novel and useful (see for example, Barron, 1988; Hennessey & Amabile, 1988; MacKinnon, 1978; Milgram, 1993; Mumford, Reiter-Palmon, & Redmond, 1994; Murray, 1959; Perkins, 1988; Puccio et al., 2011, Talbot, 1997). The misconception that creativity is mainly about original expression, being different or generating shocking ideas, appears to be on the decline, if not long dead. Rather, true creative behavior involves a balance, tension or synthesis between originality and usefulness. As Beghetto, Dow, and Plucker (2004) concluded from their exhaustive review of creativity definitions:

> "Overwhelmingly, the combination of novelty and usefulness were the most prevalent facets of both explicit and implicit definitions of creativity" (p. 91).

Puccio et al. (2011) indicated that originality without usefulness results in a fad (i.e., the idea disappears as its novelty wears off), while low originality combined with high levels of usefulness relates to an action, idea, product or service that is utilitarian (i.e., it stands the test of time as long as it remains useful). They described an action, idea, product or service that is not new and has long outlived its value, as a way of repeating past mistakes. Examples here include old policies, organizational practices, or laws that at one time served some purpose, but as situations changed are no longer relevant and may even be unnecessarily limiting.

The various combinations of originality and usefulness described above may provide insight into why creativity is rare, and so highly valued. First, by way of example, if we treat originality and usefulness as two separate and orthogonal, dichotomous dimensions each ranging from low to high, we produce a two-by-two matrix with four quadrants, of which high originality and high usefulness represents one combination. The one in four chance that outcomes will possess the qualities necessary to be considered creative seems to highlight the rarity of true creative acts. Second, even if an individual produces an idea that is both highly original and useful, he or she must possess the requisite motivation and skills to bring this idea to fruition. In particular, pursuit of a novel idea is fraught with risk. Sternberg and Lubart's (1995) investment theory of creativity underscored this challenge. As they noted, people who are attracted to novel ideas may not pursue them to fruition for fear of being ostracized; that is the perceived risks associated with buying into a rare idea may simply be too high. To quote these authors:

> "To the extent that we see less creativity than we would like, this risk aversion may be the cause" (p. 46).

Finally, the qualities of a creative idea are temporal; originality is especially fleeting and thus the value associated with a creative idea can diminish over time as its novelty wanes.

A recent study designed to test economic theory among free-ranging vervet monkeys highlights how market value is gained and lost in relationship to novelty. Fruteau, Voelkl, van Damme and Noe (2009) selected a low-status female monkey and provided this monkey with a novel, and useful, skill, i.e., the ability to open a container of food. This animal's status, as measured by the time other members of the community spent grooming her, jumped dramatically after she was taught this novel and useful behavior. However, when a second low ranking female was provided with the same skill, the first monkey's status declined. This study may serve as an analogy for why so many organizations in today's fast-changing and highly competitive global business environment see innovation as a top priority (Andrew, Sirkin, Haandes, & Michael, 2007); one way to remain competitive is to differentiate oneself in the marketplace by producing original and useful products and services. Innovation relies on the generation of creative ideas, and higher levels of innovation yield greater market share for organizations (Soo, Devinney, Midgley, & Deering, 2002).

In attempting to define creativity, many scholars have concluded that it is a multi-faceted concept (MacKinnon, 1978; Mumford & Gustafson, 1988; Rhodes, 1961; Stein, 1968). In general, these authors have identified four discrete, yet highly interrelated, facets of creativity, namely person, process, product, and environment. The view that creativity is the manifestation of novel ideas that are made useful would appear to align best with the product facet. Indeed, MacKinnon (1978) referred to the creative product as the "bedrock" to the study of creativity. He argued that creative people, processes and environments can be identified only when they lead to the creation of an original idea that is recognized as being useful. The concepts of idea generation and idea evaluation are generally thought of as aspects of the process facet of creativity. The creative process refers to the stages of thought an individual or team engages in to produce an outcome that is original and useful (Feldhusen, 1993). Thus, before individuals and teams successfully introduce a creative outcome, they generally have spent some period of time generating original ideas and then evaluating these ideas to select and develop the most promising.

Ward, Smith and Finke (1999) proposed a heuristic model of cognitive functioning associated with the creative process. Their model, called Geneplore, has two main elements: 1) Generation of Preinventive Structures; and 2) Preinventive Exploration and Interpretation. These authors indicated that creative cognition is initiated by a generative phase that involves the:

"generation of candidate ideas or solutions followed by extensive exploration of those ideas" *(p. 191)*.

This is an iterative process by which the insights gained through the exploration phase can serve to refine the initial idea or lead to new discoveries. According Ward et al., the to and fro thinking that occurs between these two phases of the creative process continues until initial insights are revised into a final creative idea or product. This model highlights the interplay between idea generation and idea evaluation, and the central role these phases of the creative process play in producing a creative outcome. Indeed, the interaction between idea generation and idea evaluation mirrors the interplay between the two fundamental elements found in the definition of creativity shared earlier. Idea generation could be thought of as a search for novelty, while its process partner, idea evaluation, might be thought of as an effort to make novel thinking practical, useful or relevant. As Cropley (2006) summarized in a recent article:

> "The idea of a two-step process is now widely accepted. In my terms, this would involve novelty generation followed by (or accompanied by) exploration of the novelty from the point of view of workability, acceptability, or similar criteria to determine if it is effective. Only then would we speak of creativity." *(p. 398)*

This balance between the generation of novelty and the exploitation of novelty, served as the cornerstone to Campbell's (1960) oft-cited theory of the creative process. Based on evolutionary biology, Campbell described the creative process as possessing two forces, blind variation followed by selective retention. Blind variation involves the introduction of a novel concept. According to Campbell, true blind variation occurs only when the outcome of an idea is unknown when first generated. Campbell suggested that if the outcome of a proposed variation is known, then the idea being introduced was not novel and, therefore, could not generate new knowledge. Selective retention involves the evaluation of blind variations to determine which concepts best fit a goal or could be adapted to reality. Those blind variations that successfully pass through the evaluation process are then selectively retained for future use. Simonton (1999) based his evolutionary theory of creative thinking, in part, on the work of Campbell. Like Campbell, he proposed a two-phase process that involved variation and selective retention; however, unlike Campbell he concluded that variation did not have to be blind or random. Simonton argued that the generation of variation could be guided by knowledge that could be combined into new variations. With respect to the evaluation phase of the creative process, Simonton indicated that selection is initially carried out in the mind of the creator, where new ideas are tested against pertinent criteria useful in determining appropriateness.

Campbell's classic description of the creative process, and Ward et al.'s Geneplore model, underscore the interplay between two fundamental phases of the creative process, one focused on the generation of novelty and the other focused on the evaluation of novel insights. Extending this line of thought, and borrowing from Puccio et al. (2011), we define idea generation as the production of "original mental images and thoughts that respond to important challenges" and idea evaluation as "assessing the reasonableness and quality of ideas in order to develop workable solutions" (p. 50). Our definitions locate idea generation and idea evaluation as conjoined phases within the confines of the creative process. We do so to avoid participating in the muddled discourse that often invokes the terms idea generation and idea evaluation as if they were synonymous with creative and critical thinking, respectively. They are not, as the latter set of terms represent much broader constructs. For example Vervalin (1971) defined creative thinking as the:

> "process of bringing a problem before one's mind clearly (as by imagining, visualizing, supposing, musing, contemplating, etc.) and then originating or inventing an idea, concept, realization, or picture along new or unconventional lines" *(p. 59),*

B. INDIVIDUAL LEVEL INFLUENCES

while O'Tuel and Bullard (1993) indicated that critical thinking:

> "is the intellectually disciplined process of actively and skillfully conceptualizing, applying, analyzing, synthesizing, or evaluating information gathered from or generated by, observation, experience, reflection, reasoning, or communication, as a guide to belief or action" *(p. 84)*.

Indeed, Cohen (1971) and Presseisen (2001) consider both creative and critical thinking to be complex thinking processes, thus subsuming other, more specific thinking skills. To further underscore this point, Marzano et al. (1988) provided a thoughtful description of the misconceptions of creative and critical thinking when they stated:

> "People tend to view critical thinking as primarily evaluative and creative as primarily generative. But the two types of thinking are not opposite; they complement each other and even share many attributes… Critical thinkers generate ways to test assertions; creative thinkers examine newly generated thoughts to assess their validity and utility." *(p. 17)*

While we position idea generation and idea evaluation within the context of the creative process, we must quickly point out that these two phases of thought do not fully embody the creative process. Rather they represent two phases of a complex cognitive process. Starting with an early description of the creative process by Wallas (1926), to more recent research into the cognitive phases of problem solving (Johnson & Jennings, 1963; Kaufmann, 1988; Simon, 1965, 1977), scholars have been able to identify discrete stages of thought related to efforts designed to generate creative solutions. For instance, Mintzberg, Duru and Theoret (1976) summarized the major phases of real-life problem solving efforts as follows: identification, which involves developing an understanding of the problem at hand; development, which focuses on creating potential solutions to the problem; and selection, which refers to making decisions among the solutions. Our own work in teaching and training creativity skills draws on a creative process model called Creative Problem Solving (CPS). This model, which has been developed and researched over a 50-year period (Isaksen & Treffinger, 2004; Osborn, 1953; Puccio, Murdock, & Mance, 2005), reflects and extends these phases of the problem solving process and includes four stages: Assessing the Situation, Clarification, Transformation, and Implementation (Puccio et al., 2011). In the CPS framework the specific steps of idea generation and idea evaluation occur within the Transformation stage. Once it is determined that the situation requires creative thinking (i.e., Assessing the Situation), and the exact nature of the challenge to be addressed has been defined (i.e., Clarification), the individual or team then begins to generate novel ideas that are then selected and refined into workable solutions. In the final stage of this process, plans are developed to ensure the successful introduction and adoption of the newly devised creative solution (i.e., Implementation). Other creative process models used in creativity training programs and applied work share similar features, in that idea generation and idea evaluation are elements of a larger set of process stages. See, for example, SIMPLEX® (Basadur, 1994), TRIZ (Altshuller, 2001), Design Thinking (Kelley & Littman, 2001), and Synectics (Gordon, 1961).

Our intent so far has been to locate idea generation and idea evaluation within a network of related creativity constructs, and, especially, highlight the interplay between these phases of thought within the context of the creative process. We now turn our attention to delineating the nature of idea generation and idea evaluation.

IDEA GENERATION SKILLS AS SEEN THROUGH THE LENS OF DIFFERENT THEORETICAL FAMILIES

Earlier we defined idea generation as the production of original mental images and thoughts that respond to important challenges (Puccio et al., 2011). The purpose of this section is to review and describe some of the skills that promote effective idea generation, beginning with those skills most often associated with idea generation, and we then use a classification of creativity theories, originally proposed by Gowan (1972), to more closely examine idea generation skills and practices as viewed from different conceptual vantage points.

The skills most often associated with idea generation can be drawn from Guilford's delineation and description of divergent thinking. The notion of divergent thinking stemmed from Guilford's research on the nature of intelligence. Through his work, Guilford set out to challenge the assumption that intelligence could be narrowly viewed, and tested, as a broad, unitary ability. To that end, Guilford (1977) devised a three dimensional model he referred to as the Structure of Intellect (SOI) theory. That is, intellectual abilities are depicted as a type of operation (e.g., divergent thinking, convergent thinking, memory, evaluation, cognition), that is triggered by a kind of content (e.g., visual, auditory, semantic, symbolic, behavioral) for the purpose of processing or organizing information into meaningful products (e.g., units, classes, relations, systems, transformations, implications). The SOI cube provides a classification system for 160 different aptitudes, which stem from combining subcategories from each of these three major dimensions. As noted above, divergent production was located within the operations dimension and was described by Guilford (1977) as a broad search that responds to the need to generate or produce an answer. According to Guilford, this broad search results in the production of alternative options that are intended to satisfy a general requirement.

Influenced by Guilford's work, Torrance (1966) designed the widely used measures of divergent thinking called the Torrance Tests of Creative Thinking (TTCT). These measures present individuals with a number of open-ended situations for which they are asked to provide either written or visual responses. The four primary cognitive skills assessed through respondents' answers are fluency (the total number of relevant responses), flexibility (the number of categories associated with the relevant responses), originality (the number of infrequent or uncommon responses), and elaboration (the enrichment or extension of responses) (Millar, 1995; Runco, 1999; Torrance, 1966). It is these four cognitive abilities that are most often associated with idea generation. As a result of longitudinal studies carried out over 20, 30 and 40-year periods (Torrance, 1972, 1980, 1999), Torrance (2000), extended the original four cognitive abilities to 14 additional indicators of creative behavior, namely: abstractedness of titles, resistance to premature closure, emotional expressiveness, story articulateness, movement, expressiveness of titles, synthesis of ideas, unusual visualization, internal visualization, extending or breaking boundaries, fantasy, humor, colorfulness of imagery, and richness of imagery.

Mumford (2000–2001) revisited Guilford's three main elements of divergent thinking, namely fluency, flexibility, and originality, and provided a refined description of each. Although Guilford maintained that speed of idea generation within a period of time would essentially create an advantage point for the idea generator, Mumford coupled speed of idea generation with speed of process execution as essential to creative thought. Just speed alone was not enough for creative output. The speed with which an individual applied a creative process was a key determinant of perceiving and comprehending ideas, reasoning and remembering. Flexibility, which initially was viewed as an approach to getting one's thinking unstuck or out of a particular pattern, was refined by highlighting empirical studies that suggest flexibility relies heavily on one's heuristics that have been crystallized through domain experience and expertise. Accordingly, domain experience proffers a wide menu of heuristics and strategies from which to choose, to solve a problem. Mumford also asserts that these types of heuristics are more central than the spontaneous trial-and-error approaches most commonly demonstrated by neophytes. Originality, a construct predominantly associated with creating a statistically infrequent response is now believed to rely on the process of combining and building upon prearranged constructs. That is to say, old ideas, previous trial and error efforts, and heuristics serve as a seedbed for creative thought.

Mumford (2000–2001) highlighted other attributes conducive to creative problem solving, which he categorized into early and late cycle capabilities. Early cycle stages relate more to idea generation, where late cycle capabilities involve the evaluation and implementation of ideas. According to Mumford, some of the additional abilities that are found in the early cycle stages of the process include analogical reasoning, category construction and identification, symbol manipulation and symbol substitution.

We wish to broaden our review of idea generation skills beyond the classic description of the skills associated with divergent thinking. To do so, we use Gowan's (1972) classification of creativity theories to examine different perspectives on idea generation. The theoretical categories to be examined are as follows:

1. Cognitive, Rational, and Semantic approaches,
2. Personality and Environmental approaches,
3. Motivational approaches,
4. Psychoanalytic or Psychodynamic approaches, and
5. Personal Exploration approaches.

We start with the Cognitive, Rational and Semantic approaches; here we share some of the additional mental operations that support idea generation. Afterwards we explore the theoretical families that move away from a strictly cognitive understanding of idea generation.

Cognitive, Rational, and Semantic Approaches

The set of theories subsumed by this approach to creativity generally take the view that creativity is a logical and understandable thought process that is primarily concerned with the use of verbal concepts and representations (Treffinger, Isaksen, & Firestien, 1983). Hunter, Bedell-Avers, Hunsicker, Mumford and Ligon (2008) described three knowledge structures conducive to the creative process. One is Schematic Knowledge, which is a principle-based knowledge that emerges from past experiences. These past experiences help form a heuristic rubric for categorizing information and can be retrieved by executing analogical mapping and search processes. This is a slow and methodical thought process, since it takes time to cluster and highlight ideas. Another knowledge structure is called Associational Knowledge, which is a relationship-based knowledge structure that emerges from a nexus made among likely events or experiences. In contrast to Schematic Knowledge, this is a faster thought process as it happens with modest conscious processing. This knowledge is typically accessed rather incidentally (Haider & Rose, 2007) and through network activation that helps produce remote or unusual associations (Hunter et al., 2008). The third knowledge structure is Case-Based, which is the formation of mental models based on past practices. This type of knowledge entails accessing contextual experiences or personal case studies that can be used as a reference for taking action when a similar context arises. This kind of knowledge can serve as a precedent or schema that enables an individual to understand a complicated situation. Below, we use these three knowledge structures to further examine skills and practices associated with idea generation.

Skills and Practices Based on Schematic Knowledge

Analogies are fed by schematic knowledge structures and accordingly can be used as design tools for generating design concepts. In particular, as suggested by Hey, Lindsey, Agogino and Wood (2008), they can be applied to keep premature judgment at bay, judgment that can get in the way of freeing the imagination. In their examination of the use of metaphor and analogy in the design process, these researchers found that in the early phases designers tended to use metaphors to frame and organize challenges, while analogies were used later to generate concepts. Designers applied metaphors to understand and explain user's reactions to a product's attributes. Analogies, on the other hand, were applied to chart attributes of a product's structure and then contrasted against a desired structure. These processes of comparison served as primers to new inferences and subsequent insightful connections (Hey et al., 2008). In a sense, the charting benefits of metaphors and analogies helped create thematic principles that were used as a starting point for concept development.

Skills and Practices Based on Associational Knowledge

Mednick's (1962) associative theory posited that a more creative person has stored information and working memories that have been crystallized from a variety of different sources. Since these sources are varied, that is to say they are dispersed broadly, Mednick suggested that a more creative person draws novel associations from a flat hierarchy of sources. A less creative person would in effect draw their associations from a peaked, more concentrated hierarchy of sources. These hierarchies are produced through diverse and rich life experiences, and thus serve as a reserve from which to build more remote interconnections. Ramachandran and Hubbard (2005) offer a fascinating explanation. In studying synesthetes, they suggested that remote interconnections are spawned at a higher rate by the cross wiring of different regions of the brain. Synesthesia is a neurological condition in which a stimulation of one cognitive sensory overlaps with a secondary one such as seeing colored letters of the alphabet, hearing sounds as motions or certain days of the week trigger certain personalities. Synesthesia permits associations among seemingly unrelated cognitive sensations. According to Ramachandran and Hubbard (2005), synesthesia is seven or eight times more common in artists, poets and novelists and explains why they are very good at generating metaphors, and at linking seemingly unrelated constructs. These authors suggested that all individuals have some degree of synesthesia and that this skill can be further developed through training in humor, art, metaphor and poetry.

Elsewhere, Gryskiewicz (1999) has suggested that organizational members should actively seek to develop the skill of receptivity, which involves, first, the absorption of information and ideas from a variety of different sources, and then the deliberate application of this exposure to identify original ways of resolving work-related challenges. Gryskiewicz, for example, suggested that people attend conferences outside their field, join professional networks external to their present field, travel to other countries, switch departments and roles, take sabbaticals, and subscribe to varied magazines. Gruszaka and Necka's (2002) study may indirectly lend support to the practices suggested by Gryskiewicz. Their study found that creative thought can be prompted from a multifaceted network of abstract facts stored as semantic memory. This network, therefore, can form and be enriched through a reception of information and ideas from a variety of different sources and experiences. Leung, Maddux, Galinsky and Chiu (2008) found that multicultural experiences correlated positively to problem solving performance, namely insight learning, remote association, and fluency in generating ideas.

Skills and Practices Based on Case-Based Knowledge

Case-Based Knowledge is derived from episodic memories, which are long-term memories of events, past performance or life experiences. They can easily be recalled through a process called amplification, in connection with an emotion or by a connection with another memory (Prater, 1995). In close examination of the amplification process, Abelson (1979) was able to show that episodic memory recall allowed an individual to break a cognitive set associated with existing beliefs, which subsequently led the individual to reconsider problems or issues from a new perspective. Rapaille (2006) has helped organizations to develop new innovative ideas by getting consumers, clients or others to express their deepest feelings about a product or service. Experience coupled with its accompanying emotion creates what Rapaille calls an imprint. The notion here is to extract the imprint from the unconscious level by evoking memories of various stages of one's life. These imprints serve as a silent system of codes, which condition thoughts and determine future actions. Some methods useful at unearthing imprints include storytelling, meaning making through collage work, and meditation. Rapaille has been credited with decoding imprints that have helped many Fortune 500 companies produce breakthrough products.

Design-Thinking Skills

To the cognitive skill areas described above, we wish to add one more area for review. Over the last decade or so a new cognitive process for guiding creative thought in teams and organizations has gained in popularity. Catapulted into the main stream primarily by work carried out at the design firm IDEO (Kelley, 2001), design thinking has been quickly adopted into numerous organizations and universities around the United States. Design thinking benefits from a user-centric approach to problem solving, in which careful observations of consumers are used to spawn idea generation and concept development through such practices as sketching, prototyping, and storytelling. Unfortunately, practice and training related to design thinking has far outpaced research efforts. Nevertheless, design research, as it is related to idea generation, has been carried out albeit at a low level. For example, Finke, Ward and Smith (1992) conducted a study of the underlying elements of design creativity. When strong constraints were applied to the experimental treatment, only those participants, who were instructed to identify a combination of shapes and figures (an analogy) that best represented the devices under observation, generated more original solutions than those participants who did not receive these instructions. Similarly, Bonnardel and Marmeche (2005) identified in their study that analogical reasoning distinguished performance of a seasoned designer from the novice. Moreover, expert designers found sources of inspiration (i.e., the re-use of aspects derived from previous sources of inspiration) more relevant and useful than did the novice designers.

Van der Lugt (2002) explored the role that sketching played in design-thinking. He suggested that sketching has a positive impact on reinterpretation, which in turn creates new knowledge. This process progresses in a cyclical manner as new knowledge spawns more reinterpretation. According to Van der Lugt, sketching is beneficial to idea generation in two specific ways. First, by engaging in a process of iterative sketching, each iteration produces insight into a new pattern or a schematic by way of metaphors and analogies. Second, sketches pinpoint possible consequences of one's thinking. Based on the summary of these studies, it is clear that analogies and experience were closely related to a designer's performance.

Personality and Environmental Approaches

The Personality and Environmental approach emphasizes affective dispositions and their effect on creative behavior (Treffinger et al., 1983). In recent years, affective constructs have received growing attention in the media under the label of emotional intelligence. A main area of concern for theories located in this category is either the facilitative or detrimental effect which attitude has on creative performance. Torrance (1979) maintained that emotions and non-rational factors are more important than solely cognitive, semantic and rational factors. In other words, "aha" moments are emotional occurrences that are then checked with thinking; that even if deliberate thought came first, it is emotion that gives power to ideas (de Bono, 1976).

Ivcevic, Brackett, and Mayer (2007) asserted that positive affect can increase flexibility and breadth of thinking. When individuals are able to maintain a positive mood they are more likely to extract more information from memory. In this manner, the information they extract is less likely to have stemmed from unsubstantiated cues in response to potential threats (Morse, 2006), what Bazerman and Chugh (2006) coined the phenomena of bounded awareness, when cognitive blinders block a person from seeing, seeking, using, and sharing key data that support idea generation.

Isen, Daubman, and Nowicki (1987) found that exposure to a comedy film or offering sweets to the research participants enhanced creative responses on the Remote Associates Test (Mednick, Mednick, & Mednick, 1964) and an insight problem (Duncker, 1945). These findings point to a cueing effect; that positive affect or induced mood serves as a memory retrieval mechanism to more information that is varied and has positive undertones, giving the individual more information to work with in generating ideas (Isen et al., 1987; Lubart, & Getz, 1997; Russ, 2000–2001; Weisberg, 2006).

B. INDIVIDUAL LEVEL INFLUENCES

The relationship between emotion and creativity is not so straightforward, however, as other studies have provided contradictory evidence. For example, Zenasni and Lubart (2009) examined relationships between emotion identification and creative performance. Using a performance-based measure, they found that as difficulty in identifying emotions arose or identified emotions varied from the emotion of others (emotional idiosyncrasy), the better the research participants performed on idea generation. Similarly, Kaufmann and Vosburg (1997) found a negative relationship between positive mood and idea generation. They found that positive affect can have a negative effect on idea generation, namely when an individual is satisfied with the first or few ideas that he or she generated. Conversely, others, who were dissatisfied with their initial responses, pushed their thinking further, thus generating more creative ideas.

Ivcevic et al. (2007) found a correlation between emotional creativity, which is the ability to express a richness of appropriate, original and authentic combinations of emotions, and openness to experience. Openness appears to prevent an individual from prematurely arriving at a conclusion (Torrance, 1979). It also puts in abeyance the cognitive blinders that prevent discovering new information of import to new thinking (Bazerman & Chugh, 2006).

Motivational Approaches

Motivational approaches involve the pursuit of personal fulfillment, personal growth and as Goble (1970) defined it, it is the desire to become everything that an individual is capable of becoming. Theories related to self-actualization have been the cornerstone to this theoretical family.

Lovelace (1986), in studying R&D managers, theorized that creativity enhancement stems from fulfilling self-actualized needs, such as growth needs (e.g., development of competence), relatedness needs (e.g., satisfactory relationship with others), and existence needs (e.g., physical well-being). Lovelace theorized that when individuals are sufficiently motivated as a result of these needs being met, they produce novel ideas, combine old ideas in a novel way, or apply knowledge from one field to another.

Another concern within the Motivational approach has been referred to as meaningfulness; the practice of asking, "Who am I?" and "Why am I here?" According to Cohen-Meitar, Carmelli, and Waldman (2009), seeking workplace meaningfulness (e.g., organizational identity, prestige, challenge, or freedom) can enhance the process variation capacity that is necessary for new and useful idea generation. Results from their study of employees working in two multinational companies highlighted the positive and significant relationship between organizational identification (i.e., meaningfulness at work and in working) and feelings of vitality, sense of positive regard, organizational and employee reciprocity, and organization-based self-esteem as factors that led to employee creativity. Employee creativity was measured using a supervisory assessment, developed by Tierney, Farmer, and Graen (1999), which focuses on the degree to which an employee demonstrates originality in his or her work (e.g., risk-taking in producing new ideas in doing a job, finding new uses for existing methods, trying out new ideas and approaches, generating novel, but operable work-related ideas, generating revolutionary ideas in their field).

Psychoanalytic or Psychodynamic Approaches

The Psychoanalytic approach to creative thought historically drew much of its inspiration from the work of Freud. The creative process is, according to Freud, a defense against neurosis (i.e., clashes between unsatisfied and unconscious biological drives and reality-based conscious processes), which in turn leads to a production of socially acceptable creations instead of socially unacceptable behavior (Treffinger et al., 1983). Unfortunately, this view of creativity conjures images of couches and, when perceived in this manner, does little to assist the field of organizational creativity to examine more closely the skills needed to foster idea generation. Overlooked are the theories offered by Freud (1925), Kris (1952), and Kubie (1958), for example, which explore how idea generation unfolds through preconscious, drive-related impulses by sanctioning daydreams, fantasy and play that subsequently enlightens the conscious (Driver, 2008).

A study conducted out of the University of British Columbia (2009) found that daydreaming permits individuals to sort through their day-to-day problems and challenges. In this study research participants underwent fMRI scanning. What scientists found is that regions of the brain mostly associated with high-level, complex problem-solving became activated while individuals were engaged in daydreaming. This finding points to an opportunity to make a space for daydreaming as a stimulus to individual idea generation and to provide resources, such as idea notebooks, to capture the output of daydreaming. In another study, Boynton (2001) was able to enhance creative flexibility (as measured by the TTCT), and well-being, by deliberately inducing hypnagogia, which is a restful state between wakefulness and sleep. Interestingly, Cai, Mednick, Harrison, Kanady, and Mednick (2009) argued that sleep states involving rapid eye movement (REM) improved creativity. In their study, they found that it was REM sleep that initiated associative networks and assimilation of unassociated information.

A number of studies have provided support for the value of an incubation break during the creative process. Kohn and Smith (2009) found that redirecting one's mind completely away from a Remote Association Test resulted in more effective responses to a problem. In a study by Smith and Blankenship (1989), they found that longer intervals of incubation provided a greater likelihood in reaching a problem resolution.

Brown (2009), in supporting the value of play in the workplace, argued that fantasy play redirects the reality of ordinary lives and in the process generates new ideas. Organizational members involved in play experience a suspension of self consciousness, open up to improvisation (which leads to new behaviors, thoughts, strategies, and movements), are anticipative or curious, and display a shift in perspective. Brown (2009) asserted that a way to screen potential hires for their creativity is to examine the extent of their playfulness when reacting or learning from mistakes, while taking risks, and or by assessing their enjoyment of novelty.

Personal Exploration Approaches

The development of cognitive, semantic and rational approaches to creative thought has been almost exclusively driven by a Western mindset (Puccio & Cabra, 2009). As globalization has pushed organizations to consider more Eastern ways of thinking and behaving, so too the approaches to facilitate creative thought must consider how to expand beyond its cognitive, rational and semantic orientation. In this section we consider the ramifications of

Personal Exploration approaches to idea generation. This approach to creativity stresses the expansion of consciousness as a way of unearthing vast and untapped resources and experiences. As Treffinger et al. (1983) explained:

> "A fundamental assumption underlying these theories is that most people seldom (or never) tap the most potent, creative dimensions of the mind; they learn from early childhood to restrict their experiences" (p. 16).

So (1995) found that practice of transcendental meditation (TM) led to significantly better scores, when compared with control group participants, on the Test for Creative Thinking-Drawing Production (TCT-DP). Orme-Johnson and Granieri (1975) studied the impact of transcendental meditation by conducting a pre- and post-test of the Torrance Test of Creative Thinking. In comparing research participants trained in TM against a control group, the TM-trained group members demonstrated significant increases in originality and fluency of visuospatial creativity, which comprises the construction of mental models for the purpose of solving problems.

EFFECTIVE IDEA EVALUATION

When engaging in idea evaluation, individuals and teams turn their attention away from the production of novel ideas, to the selection and development of a new insight into a workable solution. In keeping with the definition of creativity shared earlier, the goal at this juncture of the creative process is to ensure that the novelty of the idea is balanced against practicality. As noted by Simonton (1999), novelty is necessary for creativity to occur but it is not sufficient. Without novelty it is not possible to have a creative outcome; however, novelty alone does not guarantee the realization of a creative outcome. Thus, evaluative thinking is required to ensure that a novel idea holds some tangible or intangible value for the creator, a team, an organization or for society.

It is important to point out that idea quality is not contingent upon the novelty of the idea. As Dean, Hender, Rodgers, and Santanen (2006) pointed out, the three fundamental characteristics of high-quality ideas are:

1. the applicability of the idea to the problem at hand,
2. effectiveness as a solution to the problem, and
3. the degree to which the idea is implementable.

To be sure, in order for ideas to be effective, it is not necessary that they also be original. However, when engaged in a creative process, one that involves idea generation and idea evaluation, the expected outcome is to produce a creative solution, which by definition must be both novel and useful. Thus, novelty cuts across both idea generation and idea evaluation. Where the former is focused on the generation of novelty, the latter must focus on the exploration and eventual exploitation of novelty. Since novelty implies that the idea departs from existing paradigms and practices, evaluative thinking is crucial in determining how much promise the idea holds and then to refine the idea so this promise can be fully realized. It is through the effective application of both idea generation and idea evaluation that creative outcomes are achieved.

In a 2006 article, Cropley provided an excellent description of the interplay between idea generation and evaluation, and the consequences when one or the other of these two phases of the creative process are missing or ineffectively carried out. According to Cropley (2006) there are two potential outcomes when the generation of novelty is not partnered with the exploration of novelty. When novelty is implemented without evaluation, which Cropley described as blind insertion, the result is either "reckless variability" (if the idea is not effective) or "blindly lucky creativity" (if the idea is effective). In the latter case, although a positive end result might be achieved, there is a danger that success can lead to over confidence. True creativity occurs only when novelty is generated and then refined through a selection and evaluation process.

The mere presence of the idea generation and idea evaluation phases in the creative process does not guarantee creative outcomes; both operations must be employed effectively. Assuming the efforts to generate novelty yielded some new ideas with inherent promise, evaluation skills must then be effective at selecting and developing the alternatives that possess the greatest potential value. Returning to Cropley (2006), poor evaluation can lead to at least two detrimental outcomes. First, evaluation that leads to the rejection of a novel idea that actually has promise results in "stifled creativity" and as a consequence is a lost opportunity. Second, ineffective evaluation that leads to the acceptance of a novel idea that is actually ineffective runs the risk of producing disastrous change. We now turn our attention to the components, skills and practices associated with effective idea evaluation.

Criteria Useful for Evaluating Creative Ideas

There has been a large number of research studies that have applied evaluation criteria for the purpose of assessing creative outcomes. The focus of these studies can be divided into two broad sets. Those studies that developed or applied criteria to evaluate ideas, i.e., tentative solutions generated to resolve a proposed problem. For example, a group of university students are asked to generate solutions to a hypothetical problem, a problem for which they generally do not have ownership, and then either the students or external raters judge the quality of the ideas generated. The other category of studies has applied evaluation criteria to creative products, i.e., concepts and designs that have been embodied into a tangible form or communicated through images and other intangible forms. Here, judges are provided with criteria that are to be used to compare or evaluate the level of creativity associated with particular products. For purposes of this chapter, we will limit our review to two sets of researchers who have conducted thorough reviews of the dimensions used to evaluate either ideas or products, and who subsequently tested the efficacy of these dimensions through the use of quantitative measures.

Dean et al. (2006) carried out an exhaustive analysis of studies that employed criteria to evaluate creative ideas. These authors set out first to understand the various criteria used to evaluate ideas, then to use this analysis to identify and define a set of requirements that could be universally applied in future studies. Although their analysis of the existing literature showed some variation, the studies that evaluated the creativity of ideas focused on two broad dimensions; not surprisingly, they were novelty and usefulness. For purposes of their quantitative evaluation tool, and based on their literature review, Dean et al. further broke these evaluative constructs into more specific and measurable terms. Table 9.1 provides a summary of the four major constructs, the

TABLE 9.1   Constructs Useful in Evaluating the Creativity of Ideas.

Construct	Sub-dimensions	Anchors Used to Evaluate Ideas along Sub-dimension (arranged from low to high)
Novelty Definition: The degree to which an idea is original and modifies a paradigm.	Originality Definition: The degree to which an idea is not only rare but is also ingenious, imaginative, or surprising.	Low—Common, mundane, boring High—Not expressed before (ingenious, imaginative or surprising; may be humorous).
	Paradigm Relatedness Definition: The degree to which an idea is paradigm preserving (PP) or paradigm modifying (PM). PM ideas are sometimes radical or transformational.	PP—Elements remain same, relationship between elements remain same. PM—Elements extended, relationship between elements either redesigned or transformed.
Workability Definition: An idea is workable if it can be easily implemented and does not violate known constraints.	Acceptability Definition: The degree to which the idea is socially, legally, or politically acceptable.	Low—Radically violate law or sensibilities. High—Common strategies that violate no norms or sensibilities.
	Implementability Definition: The degree to which the idea can be easily implemented.	Low—Totally infeasible to implement or extremely financially nonviable. High—Easy to implement at low cost or non-radical changes.
Relevance Definition: The idea applies to the stated problem and will be effective at solving the problem.	Applicability Definition: The degree to which the idea clearly applies to the stated problem.	Low—Intervention is not stated or does not produce a useful outcome. High—Solves an identified problem that is directly related to the stated problem.
	Effectiveness Definition: The degree to which the idea will solve the problem.	Low—Solves an unrelated problem. High—Reasonable and will solve the stated problem without regard for workability.
Specificity Definition: An idea is specific if it is clear (worked out in detail).	Implicational Explicitness Definition: The degree to which there is a clear relationship between the recommended action and the expected outcome.	Low—Implication is not stated, even though relevant (do X without a stated Y). High—Implication is clearly stated and makes sense (do X so that Y).
	Completeness Definition: The number of independent subcomponents into which the idea can be decomposed, and the breadth of coverage with regard to who, what, where, when, why and how.	Low—Contains one or two parts from the same dimension (who, what, why, when, where, how), and usually the "what". High—Comprehensive, with three or more parts from at least two of the 5 Ws and H.
	Clarity Definition: The degree to which the idea is clearly communicated with regard to grammar and word usage.	Low—Vague or ambiguous words or use of poor language structure. High—Crisp, with standard usage, including complete sentences or well-developed phrases, and every word is commonly understood.

sub-dimensions subsumed by each construct, and the anchors used to quantitatively evaluate ideas along each sub-dimension. These authors tested the veracity of their proposed criteria by having judges apply them to two different sets of ideas generated by university students. Inter-rater reliability was analyzed using Chronbach's alpha; results showed all coefficients exceeded .60, with approximately half exceeding .70. Factor analysis of the sub-dimensions revealed that all scales loaded with their respective construct, with the exception of Clarity, which did not load with any of the constructs and was subsequently eliminated as a measure of idea quality.

The results of this study hold great promise for both research and practice in the field of creativity. With respect to research, this study demonstrated that a well-defined set of criteria could be reliably applied to evaluate the creativity, novelty and usefulness, of a set of ideas. This should be extremely beneficial for future studies that need a reliable and valid measure of ideas. With respect to creativity practitioners, the criteria for evaluating ideas could be useful in applied settings. Creativity consultants who run idea generation sessions or product concept workshops, as well as organizational teams involved in brainstorming sessions, could apply the sub-dimensions created by Dean et al. (2006), and the respective rubrics for each, to converge on the most creative solutions to a specified task.

Dean and his colleagues' (2006) exhaustive review, and subsequent development of a rating tool, was focused primarily on the evaluation of ideas. In contrast Besemer (2006) and her colleagues have developed and tested a set of criteria aimed at evaluating the creativity of products, i.e., ideas that have been embodied into some tangible form or design. According to Besemer, this evaluation metric is useful for both making final judgments about the level of creativity of products, thus allowing for proposed products to be compared against one another, as well as providing formative feedback to the creator so that modifications might be made to improve the proposed product.

The criteria used by Besemer to evaluate creative products were generated through a literature review conducted at the beginning of the 1980s (Besemer & Treffinger, 1981). The findings of this review led Besemer and Treffinger (1981) to propose the Creative Product Analysis Model, a theoretical framework that captured the three most important indicators of creativity in products. This model was put into operation later through a quantitative measure called the *Creative Product Semantic Scale* (CPSS). The CPSS is comprised of 55 adjective pairs that allow:

> "products from different locations or times (or even products from different industries) to be compared to each other" *(O'Quin & Besemer, 2006, p. 36)*

across eight criteria that are organized into three dimensions. Specifically, the CPSS assesses Novelty, which is characterized by two criteria: Originality (i.e., uniqueness); and Surprise (i.e., acceptance and appreciation). The next dimension is referred to as Resolution. This dimension is comprised of four criteria: Logical (i.e., adherence to established standards); Useful (i.e., clear and practical applications); Valuable (i.e., meets intended needs); and Understandable (i.e., ease of use). The final dimension is called Style and is measured through three criteria: Organic (i.e., elements form a complete whole); Well-Crafted (i.e., attention to detail); and Elegant (i.e., elements are refined). According to O'Quin and Besemer (2006):

B. INDIVIDUAL LEVEL INFLUENCES

"The model and the CPSS can be used with any idea or product, because they are aimed at a level of abstraction that is generally higher than that of other consumer surveys that may be used at a particular company. The purpose of the CPSS is to improve judgments made by raters or evaluators, so that they carefully consider all elements of the product (broadly defined as an idea, proposal, process, prototype or actual product)." (p. 36)

The broad applicability of the CPSS as an evaluation tool can be seen in a number of research studies that have adopted this measure or the criteria subsumed by it. Besemer (2000) found the CPSS to be useful in predicting consumers' willingness to buy. Results of this study showed that purchasing decisions were primarily driven by value and elegance, and less by novelty. Similarly, Im and Workman (2004) found that new product success was highly related to the attributes of value and resolution. Andrews and Smith (1996) found the dimensions of the CPSS to be useful in understanding the factors that predicted the effectiveness of marketing programs. Finally, Puccio, Treffinger, and Talbot (1995) used the CPSS dimensions to have employees evaluate the level of creative performance they exhibited in the workplace. Their findings showed a significant relationship between certain product qualities and the creativity styles expressed by the employees.

It should be noted that there is an approach to the evaluation of creative ideas that does not employ explicit criteria, such as those proffered by Dean et al. (2006) and Besemer (2006). Amabile put forward a method called the Consensual Assessment Technique (CAT) that is based on the assertion that domain experts are implicitly aware of the qualities that distinguish creative products from those that are less creative. As Amabile (1996) explained:

"A product or response is creative to the extent that appropriate observers independently agree it is creative. Appropriate observers are those familiar with the domain in which the product was created or the response articulated. Thus, creativity can be regarded as the quality of products or responses judged to be creative by appropriate observers, and it can also be regarded as the process by which something so judged is produced." (p. 33)

Since the introduction of CAT, Amabile has used the subjective evaluation of experts to evaluate such creative products as collages (Amabile, 1982), stories (Amabile, Hennessey, & Grossman, 1986), and poems (Amabile, 1985). CAT has been widely adopted by other researchers interested in evaluating the creative products of their research participants. Some recent studies that have used, or adapted this method, include an investigation of culinary creativity (Horng & Lin, 2009), music composition (MacDonald, Byrne, & Carlton, 2006), sentence captions (Kaufman, Joohyun, Baer, & Soonmook, 2007) and new product ideas (Piller & Walcher, 2006). Kaufman, Baer, Cole, and Sexton (2008) undertook an investigation comparing expert and non-expert judges' evaluations of poems. These researchers found that inter-rater agreement did not reach an acceptable level among non-experts, thus underscoring the value of expert judges.

Cognitive Processes Involved in Idea Evaluation

Thus far we have discussed criteria and methods that might be useful in evaluating creative ideas and products; however, we have not described the specific cognitive operations involved in the evaluation of ideas. Mumford and his colleagues have engaged in a series of research studies that have illuminated the phases and aspects of evaluative thought as they unfold within the creative process (Dailey & Mumford, 2006; Lonergan, Scott & Mumford, 2004; Mumford, 2002; Mumford, Lonergan, & Scott, 2002; Mumford & Moertl, 2003). First, Mumford has argued that idea evaluation is a distinct process, in contrast to idea generation, and as such involves uniquely identifiable mental operations. Lonergan, Scott, and Mumford distinguished idea generation from idea evaluation by noting that where the former is focused on using insight to formulate an idea, the latter is concerned primarily with the manifestation or implementation of the proposed idea. Second, as suggested earlier in this paper, although idea generation and evaluation can be isolated, there is much interplay between these two phases of the creative process. As Lonergan et al. (2004) observed:

> "Idea evaluation is typically seen as an integrative process involving potentially the testing of the idea and the generation of new ideas to handle problems encountered, or problems expected to be encountered, in idea implementation" (p. 232).

Also, Mumford's own research has demonstrated that evaluative processes do improve the quality and originality of solutions to problems that require creative responses (Mumford, Scott & Gaddis, 2003).

According to Mumford and his colleagues, there are three cognitive operations associated with the evaluation of creative ideas. Idea evaluation begins with forecasting. In this operation the individual anticipates the likely outcomes or consequences of carrying forward with a particular idea. In a sense, it is like conducting a thought experiment in which the problem solver imagines the idea being implemented in the intended context, and as such the reactions and implications associated with this proposed action (Mumford, 2000–2001). The insights gained through forecasting lead to an appraisal of the idea, the consequences and expected outcomes are weighed against the desired performance standards, and a decision is reached as to whether to go forward or not. Finally, as original ideas are often conceptual, poorly formed, and lack detail, the problem solver must revise the idea. At this juncture much creative thought may go into recasting and expanding the original concept with the overall intent of improving its effectiveness and increasing the likelihood of success. Problem sensitivity, awareness of gaps and shortcomings, would seem to support the operation of revising and recasting potential solutions.

Lonergan et al. (2004) examined the appraisal and revision processes within idea evaluation and found that different standards for revision were more or less effective given the nature of the problem. In the case of an ill-defined task, a problem scenario more open to creative solutions, more innovative revision standards produced better implementation plans. While in the case of a more well-defined task, revision standards which focused on efficiency generated better plans (see Blair & Mumford, 2007, for another study on the effects of different evaluation criteria under different conditions). These, and other findings, led the authors to conclude that standards used for appraisal and revision will vary according to the nature of the problem and the context (see also Blair & Mumford, 2007, for a description of the different effects of evaluation criteria under different conditions). Lonergan et al. (2004) also concluded that to be effective creativity enhancement programs must focus both on idea production skills and idea evaluation skills.

B. INDIVIDUAL LEVEL INFLUENCES

A number of researchers have examined the relationship between idea generation skills and idea evaluation skills. Runco (1991) conducted one of the earliest investigations of the relationship between these two phases of the creative process. He found that children who produced higher scores on indices of divergent thinking, such as fluency and originality, demonstrated higher levels of effectiveness in evaluative thinking, such as accuracy in identifying highly creative responses as well as popular responses. More recently, Grohman, Wodniecka, and Klusak (2006) examined idea generation (i.e., proposed solutions) on problems commonly faced by adolescents and two forms of evaluation, i.e., intrapersonal evaluation (judgment of one's own ideas) and interpersonal evaluation (judgment of others' ideas). In contrast to the expected relationship between idea generation and idea evaluation, statistical analysis showed that participants in the lowest quartile for originality in ideas generated were much more accurate, when compared with those in the highest quartile, at evaluating the uniqueness of ideas generated by others. Similar results were found for fluency, with highly fluent respondents being less accurate in judging the originality of their own ideas. When examining a composite score for divergent thinking against the two forms of evaluation, intrapersonal and interpersonal, the findings showed that in general participants were more accurate in evaluating the uniqueness of their own ideas versus the ideas generated by others. And those with high divergent thinking scores were particularly poor at judging the uniqueness of others' ideas. These, and other findings, led Groham et al. to conclude that the relationship between idea generation and idea evaluation is much more complex than originally conceived.

Skills and Strategies to Improve Idea Evaluation in Teams

Our discussion of idea evaluation has focused almost exclusively on the individual. Before we end this chapter we wish to briefly describe some recommendations for enhancing idea evaluation in teams. Paulus (Paulus, Nakui, & Putnam, 2006; Paulus & Yang, 2000) has carried out a program of research focused on understanding the process of idea generation in teams. He has also examined approaches which individuals and teams take when evaluating ideas (Paulus, 2008). In general, it is believed that selection of ideas in a team, due to diverse perspectives, will enhance the probability of retaining the most promising and creative solutions. Unfortunately this is not always the case, as groups can suffer from particular dysfunctions. Paulus, for example, explained that teams often suffer from a feasibility bias; that is the tendency to select the most feasible ideas over those that are more novel. This may occur because the individual team members may be biased towards ideas that fit their a priori perspectives or paradigms. Conversely, Paulus noted that on occasions teams can under-evaluate their own ideas; this is the tendency to avoid being overly critical of their own thinking, thereby falling into the potential trap Cropley (2006) described of pursuing "reckless variability", i.e., accepting ineffective novelty that leads to disastrous change.

Paulus offered a number of strategies to counter the potential pitfalls teams can experience when evaluating ideas. First, teams must approach idea evaluation in a methodical manner, one that allows for sufficient time to evaluate all alternatives that have been generated. Second, idea evaluation should occur over multiple meetings. In this manner incubation, reflection and second thoughts can be used to enhance the evaluation process. Finally, when possible, it is recommended that outside experts should be involved in the evaluation to ensure that all of the pertinent issues and criteria have been incorporated or considered into the selection and development of the most promising ideas.

Teams can also employ thinking tools,

"a structured strategy to focus, organize and guide an individual or group's thinking" (Puccio et al., 2011, p. 121–122),

to assist them in selecting and transforming ideas into effective solutions. The purpose of these tools is to help individuals and teams to move beyond intuitive decision making when converging in the creative process. In their creative process framework, called *Creative Problem Solving: The Thinking Skills* model, Puccio and his colleagues introduce and describe a set of thinking skills and commensurate thinking tools, useful in applying creative thinking to resolve complex problems (Puccio et al., 2011). The thinking skills that most closely align with the evaluation and development of ideas, as described in this chapter, are evaluative thinking (i.e., assessing the reasonableness and quality of ideas in order to develop workable solutions), contextual thinking (i.e., understanding the interrelated conditions and circumstances that will support or hinder success), and tactical thinking (i.e., devising a plan that includes specific and measurable steps for attaining a desired end and methods for monitoring its effectiveness).

Plusses, Potential, Concerns, and Overcoming Concerns (PPCO), for example, is used as an itemized evaluation tool that provides a balanced and thorough examination of the strengths, future possibilities, and shortcomings of a tentative solution. This structured strategy concludes with the identification of ideas that will address the most significant shortcomings of the proposed solution. In this manner, the PPCO provides an individual or team with a structured method to engage in the appraisal and revision processes described by Lonergan et al. (2004). Puccio et al. (2011) contend that the explicit application of such thinking tools can reduce conflict in teams, enhance the quality of decision making, and improve the probability of success. Puccio, Firestien, Coyle, and Masucci (2006) provide a thorough review of the effectiveness of Creative Problem Solving in organizations.

CONCLUSION AND FUTURE RESEARCH

The purpose of this chapter was to explore the nature of two crucial phases of the creative process; idea generation and idea evaluation. To that end, we examined various skills associated with both operations. To conclude, we wish to highlight the fact that a growing body of research has provided evidence that the skills associated with idea generation and idea evaluation can be enhanced. In describing the skills associated with his SOI model Guilford (1977) observed that:

"With so many procedures designed to help in problem solving and creative thinking...the prospects would seem to be good for improving the skills of individuals in these operations. The methods can clearly be taught, and that is being done on an increasing scale" (p. 180).

More recently, Scott, Leritz, and Mumford (2004) provided empirical evidence that supported Guilford's claim. These researchers conducted a meta-analysis of studies that evaluated creativity-training programs, and their findings demonstrated that practice in idea generation and idea evaluation contributed significantly to the success of these programs.

Creativity studies is a young field, and within this field the topic of organizational creativity is a recent area of interest. With the increased concern for innovation among corporations, it would be useful to engage in more field studies, such as Amabile's diary study (Amabile, Schatzel, Moneta, & Kramer, 2004), to better understand how organizational members' idea generation and evaluation skills directly contribute to innovative outcomes. The Boston Consulting Group's innovation survey of more than 2,000 corporate leaders pointed to a risk-averse culture as the main obstacle to innovation (Andrew, Sirkin, Haanꝺes, & Michael, 2007). Future studies might wish to more closely examine the leadership behaviors and practices that support idea generation, and then the selection and implementation of novel ideas, in such risk-averse corporate settings. Finally, within the field of creativity, idea generation in general and the usefulness of idea generation methods, has received much greater attention than idea evaluation. As noted in this chapter, both are crucial to creativity—the yin and yang of the creative process—where the former creates novelty, the latter renders it practical, useful and applicable. Idea evaluation research needs to catch up to the body of literature dedicated to idea generation; what training approaches work best, to what degree does training transfer to the workplace, what are the most effective approaches for organizations to vet and develop the most promising ideas, what idea evaluation tools are most useful to individuals and teams, and what dynamics impact successful idea evaluation in teams. These are just a few of the questions that might be useful to explore in future research.

References

Abelson, R. P. (1979). Differences between belief and knowledge systems. *Cognitive Science, 3,* 355–366.

Altshuller, G. (2001). *And suddenly the inventor appeared: TRIZ, the theory of inventive problem solving.* Worcester, MA: Technical Innovation Center. (L. Shulyak, Trans.)

Amabile, T. M. (1982). Social psychology of creativity: The consensual assessment technique. *Journal of Personality and Social Psychology, 43,* 997–1013.

Amabile, T. M. (1985). Motivation and creativity: Effects of motivational orientation on creative writers. *Journal of Personality and Social Psychology, 48,* 393–399.

Amabile, T. M. (1996). *Creativity in context.* Boulder, CO: Westview.

Amabile, T. M., Hennessey, B. A., & Grossman, B. S. (1986). Social influences on creativity: The effects of contracted-for-reward. *Journal of Personality and Social Psychology, 50,* 14–23.

Amabile, T. M., Schatzel, E. A., Moneta, G. B., & Kramer, S. J. (2004). Leader behaviors and the work environment for creativity: Perceived leader support. *Leadership Quarterly, 15,* 5–32.

Andrew, J. P., Sirkin, H. L., Haanæs, K., & Michael, D. C. (2007). *Innovation 2007: A BCG senior management survey (BCG Report).* Boston, MA: Boston Consulting Group.

Andrews, J., & Smith, D. C. (1996). In search of the marketing imagination: Factors affecting the creativity of marketing programs for mature products. *Journal of Marketing Research, 33,* 174–178.

Barron, F. (1988). Putting creativity to work. In R. J. Sternberg (Ed.), *The nature of creativity* (pp. 76–98). Cambridge, UK: Cambridge University Press.

Basadur, M. (1994). *Simplex®: A flight to creativity.* Buffalo, NY: Creative Education Foundation.

Bazerman, M. H., & Chugh, D. (2006). Decisions without blinders. *Harvard Business Review, January,* 88–97.

Beghetto, R. A., Dow, G. T., & Plucker, J. A. (2004). Why isn't creativity more important to educational psychologists? Potentials, pitfalls, and future directions in creativity research. *Educational Psychologist, 39*, 83–96.

Besemer, S. P. (2000). To buy or not to buy: Predicting the willingness to buy from creative product variables. *Korean Journal of Thinking and Problem-Solving, 10*, 5–18.

Besemer, S. P. (2006). *Creating products in the age of design: How to improve your new product ideas.* Stillwater, OK: New Forums Press.

Besemer, S. P., & Treffinger, D. J. (1981). Analysis of creative products: Review and synthesis. *The Journal of Creative Behavior, 15*, 158–178.

Blair, C. S., & Mumford, M. D. (2007). Errors in idea evaluation: Preference for the unoriginal? *The Journal of Creative Behavior, 41*, 197–222.

Bonnardel, N., & Marmèche, E. (2005). Towards supporting evocation processes in creative design: A cognitive approach. *International Journal Human-Computer Studies, 63*(45), 422–435.

Boynton, T. (2001). Applied research using alpha/theta training for enhancing creativity and well-being. *Journal of Neurotherapy, 5*, 5–18.

Brown, S. (2009). *Play: How it shapes the brain, opens the imagination, and invigorates the soul.* New York, NY: Avery.

Cai, D. J., Mednick, S. A., Harrison, E. M., Kanady, J. C., & Mednick, S. C. (2009). REM, not incubation, improves creativity by priming associative networks. *PNAS, 106*(25), 10130–10134. Retrieved January 20, 2010, from <http://www.pnas.org/content/106/25/10130.full.pdf+html/>.

Campbell, D. T. (1960). Blind variation and selective retention in creative thought as in other knowledge processes. *Psychological Review, 67*, 380–400.

Canfield, D. (1985). How flint and fire started and grew. In B. Ghiselin (Ed.), *The creative process: Reflections of invention in the art and sciences* (pp. 173–180). Berkeley, CA: University of California Press.

Cohen, J. (1971). *Thinking.* Chicago, IL: Rand McNally.

Cohen-Meitar, R., Carmeli, A., & Waldman, D. A. (2009). Linking meaningfulness in the workplace to employee creativity: The intervening role of organizational identification and positive psychological experiences. *Creativity Research Journal, 21*, 361–375.

Cropley, A. (2006). In praise of convergent thinking. *Creativity Research Journal, 18*, 391–404.

Dacey, J. (1999). Concepts of creativity: A history. In M. A. Runco & S. R. Pritzker (Eds.), *Encyclopedia of creativity* (pp. 309–322). San Diego, CA: Academic Press.

Dailey, L., & Mumford, M. D. (2006). Evaluative aspects of creative thought: Errors in appraising the implications of new ideas. *Creativity Research Journal, 18*, 385–390.

Davis, G. A. (1986). *Creativity is forever* (2nd Ed.). Dubuque, IA: Kendall/Hunt Publishing Company.

Dean, D. L., Hender, J. M., Rodgers, T. L., & Santanen, E. L. (2006). Identifying quality, novel, and creative ideas: Constructs and scales for idea evaluation. *Journal of the Association of Information Systems, 7*, 647–695.

De Bono, E. (1976). *Thinking action.* Dorset, UK: Direct Education Services.

Driver, M. (2008). New and useless: A psychoanalytic perspective on organizational creativity. *Journal of Management Inquiry, 17*(3), 187–197.

Duncker, K. (1945). On problem solving. *Psychological monographs, 58* (5, Whole No. 270).

Feldhusen, J. F. (1993). Conceptions of creative thinking and creativity training. In S. G. Isaksen, M. C. Murdock, R. L. Firestien & D. J. Treffinger (Eds.), *Nurturing and developing creativity* (pp. 31–50). Norwood, NJ: Ablex.

Finke, R., Ward, T. B., & Smith, S. M. (1992). *Creative cognition: Theory, research and applications*: Boston, MA. MIT Press.

Freud, S. (1925). *Creativity and the unconscious.* New York, NY: Harper.

Fruteau, C., Voelkl, B., van Damme, E., & Noe, R. (2009). Supply and demand determine the market value of food providers in wild vervet monkeys. *Proceedings of the National Academy of Sciences of the United States of America, 106*, 12007–12012.

Ghiselin, B. (Ed.). (1985). *The creative process: Reflections of invention in the art and sciences.* Berkeley, CA: University of California Press.

Goble, F. (1970). *The third force: The psychology of Abraham Maslow a revolutionary new view of man.* New York, NY: Pocket Books.

Gordon, W. J. J. (1961). *Synectics.* New York, NY: Harper & Row.

Gowan, J. C. (1972). *The Development of the creative individual.* San Diego, CA: Knapp.

Grohman, M., Wodniecka, Z., & Klusak, M. (2006). Divergent thinking and evaluation skills: Do they always go together. *The Journal of Creative Behavior, 40*, 125–145.

B. INDIVIDUAL LEVEL INFLUENCES

Gruszka, A., & Necka, E. (2002). Priming and acceptance of close and remote associations by creative and less creative people. *Creativity Research Journal, 14*, 174–192.

Gryskiewicz, S. S. (1999). *Positive turbulence*. San Francisco, CA: Jossey Bass.

Guilford, J. P. (1977). *Way beyond the IQ: Guide to improving intelligence*. Buffalo, NY: Creative Education Foundation.

Haider, H., & Rose, M. (2007). How to investigate insight: A proposal. *Methods, 42*, 49–57.

Hennessey, B. A., & Amabile, T. M. (1988). The conditions of creativity. In R. J. Sternberg (Ed.), *The nature of creativity* (pp. 11–38). Cambridge, UK: Cambridge University Press.

Hey, J., Linsey, J., Agogino, A. M., & Wood, K. L. (2008). Analogies and metaphors in creative design. *International Journal of Engineering Education, 24*(2), 283–294.

Horng, J. S., & Lin, L. (2009). The development of a scale to evaluating creative culinary products. *Creativity Research Journal, 21*, 54–63.

Housman, A. E. (1985). The name and nature of poetry. In B. Ghiselin (Ed.), *The creative process: Reflections of invention in the art and sciences* (pp. 85–91). Berkeley, CA: University of California Press.

Hunter, S. T., Bedell-Avers, K. E., Hunsicker, C. M., Mumford, M., & Ligon, G. S. (2008). Applying multiple knowledge structures in creative thought: Effects on idea generation and problem-solving. *Creativity Research Journal, 20*(2), 137–154.

Im, S., & Workman, J. P. (2004). Market orientation, creativity and new product performance in high-technology firms. *Journal of Marketing, 68*, 114–132.

Isaksen, S. G., & Treffinger, D. J. (2004). Celebrating 50 years of reflective practice: Versions of Creative Problem Solving. *The Journal of Creative Behavior, 38*, 75–101.

Isen, A. M., Daubman, K., & Nowicki, G. P. (1987). Positive affect facilitates creative problem solving. *Journal of Personality and Social Psychology, 52*, 1122–1131.

Ivcevic, Z., Brackett, M. A., & Mayer, J. D. (2007). Emotional intelligence and emotional creativity. *Journal of Personality, 75*, 199–235.

Johnson, D. M., & Jennings, J. W. (1963). Serial analysis of three problem solving processes. *Journal of Psychology, 56*, 43–52.

Jung, C. G. (1985). Psychology and literature. In B. Ghiselin (Ed.), *The creative process: Reflections of invention in the art and sciences* (pp. 217–232). Berkeley, CA: University of California Press.

Kaufmann, G. (1988). Problem solving and creativity. In K. Grønhaug & G. Kaufmann (Eds.), *Innovation: A cross-disciplinary perspective* (pp. 87–137). Oslo, Norway: Norwegian University Press.

Kaufman, J. C., Baer, J., Cole, J., & Sexton, J. D. (2008). A comparison of expert and nonexpert raters using the Consensual Assessment Technique. *Creativity Research Journal, 20*, 171–178.

Kaufman, J. C., Joohyun, L., Baer, J., & Soonmook, L. (2007). Captions, consistency, creativity and the Consensual Assessment Technique: New Evidence of Reliability. *Thinking Skills and Creativity, 2*, 96–106.

Kaufmann, G., & Vosburg, S. K. (1997). "Paradoxical" mood effects on creative problem-solving. *Cognition and Emotion, 11*, 151–170.

Kipling, R. (1985). Working-tools. In B. Ghiselin (Ed.), *The creative process: Reflections of invention in the art and sciences* (pp. 161–163). Berkeley, CA: University of California Press.

Kelley, T., & Littman, J. (2001). *The art of innovation: Lessons in creativity from IDEO, America's leading design firm*. New York, NY: Currency.

Kohn, N., & Smith, S. M. (2009). Partly versus completely out of your mind: Effects of incubation and distraction on resolving fixation. *The Journal of Creative Behavior, 43*, 102–118.

Kris, E. (1952). *Psychoanalytic exploration in art*. New York, NY: International University Press.

Kubie, L. S. (1958). *Neurotic distortion of the creative process*. Lawrence, KS: University of Kansas.

Leung, A. K. -Y., Maddux, W. W., Galinsky, A. D., & Chiu, C. Y. (2008). Multicultural experience enhances creativity: The when and how. *American Psychologist, 63*(3), 169–181.

Lonergan, D. C., Scott, G. M., & Mumford, M. D. (2004). Evaluative aspects of creative thought: Effects of appraisal and revision standards. *Creativity Research Journal, 16*, 231–246.

Lovelace, R. F. (1986). Stimulating creativity through managerial intervention. *R&D Management, 16*, 161–174.

Lubart, T. I., & Getz, I. (1997). Emotion, metaphor, and the creative process. *Creativity Research Journal, 10*, 285–301.

MacDonald, R., Byrne, C., & Carlton, L. (2006). Creativity and flow in musical composition: An empirical investigation. *Psychology of Music, 34*, 292–306.

MacKinnon, D. W. (1978). *In search of human effectiveness*. Buffalo, NY: Creative Education Foundation.

Marzano, R. J., Brandt, R. S., Hughes, C. S., Jones, B. F., Presseisen, B. Z., Rankin, S. C., & Suhor, C. (1988). *Dimensions of thinking: A framework for curriculum and instruction.* Alexandria, VA: Association for Supervision and Curriculum Development.

Mednick, M. T. (1962). The associative basis of the creative process. *Psychological Review, 69,* 220–232.

Mednick, M. T, Mednick, S. A., & Mednick, E. V. (1964). Incubation of creative performance and specific associative priming. *Journal of Abnormal and Social Psychology, 69,* 84–88.

Milgram, R. M. (1993). Predicting outcomes of giftedness through intrinsically motivated behavior in adolescence. In S. G. Isaksen, M. C. Murdock, R. L. Firestien & D. J. Treffinger (Eds.), *Nurturing and developing creativity* (pp. 314–330). Norwood, NJ: Ablex.

Millar, G. W. (1995). *E. Paul Torrance: The Creativity Man.* Norwood, NJ: Ablex Publishing Company.

Mintzberg, H., Duru, R., & Theoret, A. (1976). The structure of unstructured decision processes. *Administrative Science Quarterly, 21,* 246–247.

Morse, G. (2006). Decisions and desire. *Harvard Business Review, January,* 42–51.

Mumford, M. D. (2000–2001). Something old, something new: Revisiting Guilford's conception of creative problem solving. *Creativity Research Journal, 13,* 267–276.

Mumford, M. D. (2002). Social innovation: Ten cases from Benjamin Franklin. *Creativity Research Journal, 14,* 253–266.

Mumford, M. D., & Gustafson, S. B. (1988). Creativity syndrome: Integration, application, and innovation. *Psychological Bulletin, 103,* 27–43.

Mumford, M. D., Lonergan, D. C., & Scott, G. M. (2002). Evaluating creative ideas: Processes, standards, and context. *Inquiry, 22,* 21–30.

Mumford, M. D., & Moertl, P. (2003). Cases of social innovation: Lessons from two innovations in the 20th century. *Creativity Research Journal, 15,* 261–266.

Mumford, M. D., Reiter-Palmon, R., & Redmond, M. (1994). Problem construction and cognition: Applying problem representations in ill-defined domains. In M. A. Runco (Ed.), *Problem finding, problem solving, and creativity* (pp. 3–39). Norwood, NJ: Ablex.

Mumford, M. D., Scott, G. M., & Gaddis, B. (2003). Leadership in scientific organizations. In J. Hurley (Ed.), *Scientific research effectiveness: The organizational dimensions* (pp. 69–100). Dordrecht, The Netherlands: Kluwer.

Murray, H. A. (1959). Vicissitudes of creativity. In H. H. Anderson (Ed.), *Creativity and its cultivation* (pp. 96–118). New York, NY: Harper.

O'Quin, K., & Besemer, S. P. (2006). Using the Creative Product Semantic Scale as a metric for results-oriented business. *Creativity and Innovation Management, 15,* 34–44.

Orme-Johnson, D. W., & Granieri, B. (1975). The effects of the age of enlightenment governor training courses on field independence, creativity, intelligence, and behavioral flexibility. In D. Orme-Johnson & J. T. Farrow (Eds.), *Scientific research on the transcendental meditation program* (Vol. 1, pp. 713–717). New York, NY: Maharishi International University.

Osborn, A. F. (1953). *Applied imagination: Principles and procedures of creative problem-solving.* New York, NY: Scribner.

O'Tuel, F., & Bullard, R. (1993). *Developing higher-order thinking in the content areas.* Pacific Grove, CA: Critical Thinking Books and Software.

Paulus, P. B. (2008). Fostering creativity in groups and teams. In J. Zhou & C. E. Shalley (Eds.), *Handbook of organizational creativity* (pp. 165–188).

Paulus, P. B., Nakui, T., & Putman, V. L. (2006). Group brainstorming and teamwork: Some rules for the road to innovation. In L. Thompson & H. Choi (Eds.), *Creativity and innovation in organizational teams* (pp. 69–86). Mahwah, NJ: Lawrence Erlbaum Associates.

Paulus, P. B., & Yang, H. C. (2000). Idea generation in groups: A basis for creativity in organizations. *Organizational Behavior and Human Decision Processing, 82,* 76–87.

Perkins, D. N. (1988). The possibility of invention. In R. J. Sternberg (Ed.), *The nature of creativity* (pp. 362–385). Cambridge, UK: Cambridge University Press.

Piller, F. T., & Walcher, D. (2006). Toolkits for idea competitions: A novel method to integrate users in new product development. *R&D Management, 36,* 307–318.

Poincare, H. (1985). Mathematical creation. In B. Ghiselin (Ed.), *The creative process: Reflections of invention in the art and sciences* (pp. 22–31). Berkeley, CA: University of California Press.

B. INDIVIDUAL LEVEL INFLUENCES

Prater, M. (1995). *Episodic memory and creativity in drawing*. Lubbock, TX: Texas Tech University. An unpublished doctoral dissertation thesis.

Presseisen, B. Z. (2001). Thinking skills: Meanings and models revisted. In A. L. Costa (Ed.), *Developing minds: A resource book for teaching thinking* (pp. 47–57). Alexandria, VA: Association for Supervision and Curriculum Development.

Puccio, G. J., & Cabra, J. F. (2009). Creative problem solving: Past, present and future. In T. Rickards, H. A. Runco & S. Moger (Eds.), *The Routledge companion to creativity* (pp. 327–337). Oxford, UK: Routledge.

Puccio, G. J., Firestien, R. L., Coyle, C., & Masucci, C. (2006). A review of the effectiveness of Creative Problem Solving training: A focus on workplace issues. *Creativity and Innovation Management, 15*, 19–33.

Puccio, G. J., Mance, M., & Murdock, M. C. (2011). *Creative leadership: Skills that drive change (2nd Ed.)*. Thousand Oaks, CA: SAGE.

Puccio, G. J., Murdock, M. C., & Mance, M. (2005). Current developments in creative problem solving for organizations: A focus on thinking skills and styles. *The Korean Journal of Thinking & Problem Solving, 15*, 43–76.

Puccio, G. J., Treffinger, D. J., & Talbot, R. J. (1995). Exploratory examination of relationships between creativity styles and creative products. *Creativity Research Journal, 8*, 25–40.

Ramachandran, V. S., & Hubbard, E. M. (2005). The emergence of the human mind: some clues from synesthesia. In L. C. Robertson & N. Sagiv (Eds.), *Synesthesia: Perspectives from cognitive neuroscience* (pp. 147–192). New York NY: Oxford University Press.

Rapaille, C. (2006). *The culture code: An ingenious way to understand why people around the world live and buy as they do*. New York NY : Broadway Books.

Rhodes, M. (1961). An analysis of creativity. *Phi Delta Kappan, 42*, 305–310.

Runco, M. A. (1991). The evaluative, valuative, and divergent thinking of children. *The Journal of Creative Behavior, 25*, 311–319.

Runco, M. (1999). Divergent thinking. In M. A. Runco & S. Pritzker (Eds.), *Encyclopedia of creativity* (Vol. I, pp. 577–582). San Diego, CA: Academic Press.

Russ, S. W. (2000–2001). Primary-process thinking and creativity: Affect and cognition. *Creativity Research Journal, 13*, 27–36.

Scott, G. M., Leritz, L. E., & Mumford, M. D. (2004). The effectiveness of creativity training: A meta-analysis. *Creativity Research Journal, 16*, 361–388.

Simon, H. A. (1965). *The shape of automation*. New York, NY: Harper & Row.

Simon, H. A. (1977). *The new science of management decisions*. Englewood Cliffs, NJ: Prentice-Hall.

Simonton, D. K. (1999). Creativity as blind variation and selective retention: Is the creative process Darwinian? *Psychological Inquiry, 10*, 309–328.

Smith, S. M., & Blankenship, S. E. (1989). Incubation effects. *Bulletin of the Psychonomic Society, 27*, 311–314.

So, K. T. (1995). *Testing and improving intelligence and creativity in the Chinese cultures with Maharashi's vedic psychology: Toward a holistic and universal assessment*. Maharishi International University, IA. Unpublished doctoral thesis.

Soo, C., Devinney, T., Midgley, D., & Deering, A. (2002). Knowledge management: Philosophy, processes, and pitfalls. *California Management Review, 44*, 129–150.

Stein, M. I. (1968). Creativity. In E. F. Boragatta & W. W. Lambert (Eds.), *Handbook of personality theory and research* (pp. 900–942). Chicago, IL: Rand McNally.

Sternberg, R. J., & Lubart, T. I. (1995). *Defying the crowd: Cultivating creativity in a culture of conformity*. New York, NY: The Free Press.

Talbot, R. J. (1997). Taking style on board. *Creativity and Innovation Management, 6*, 177–184.

Tierney, P., Farmer, S. M., & Graen, G. B. (1999). An examination of leadership and employee creativity: The elevance of traits and relationships. *Personnel Psychology, 52*, 591–620.

Torrance, E. P. (1966). *Torrance Tests of Creative Thinking*. Bensenville, IL: Scholastic Testing.

Torrance, E. P. (1972). Predictive validity of the Torrance tests of creative thinking. *The Journal of Creative Behavior, 6*, 236–252.

Torrance, E. P. (1979). *The search for satori & creativity*. Buffalo, NY: Creative Education Foundation & Bearly Limited.

Torrance, E. P. (1980). Empirical validation of criterion-referenced indicators of creative ability through a longitudinal study. *Creative Child and Adult Quarterly, 6*, 136–140.

Torrance, E. P. (1999). Forty years of watching creative ability and creative achievement. *Newsletter of the Creative Division of the National Association for Gifted Children, 10*, 3–5.

Torrance, E. P. (2000). *Research review for the Torrance Tests of Creative Thinking: Verbal and Figural Forms A and B.* Bensenville, IL: Scholastic Testing Service.

Treffinger, D. J., Isaksen, S. G., & Firestien, R. L. (1983). Theoretical perspectives on creative learning and its facilitation. *The Journal of Creative Behavior, 17*, 9–17.

University of British Columbia, (2009, May 12). Brain's problem-solving function at work when we daydream. *ScienceDaily.* Retrieved January 19, 2010, from <http://www.sciencedaily.com/releases/2009/05/090511180702.htm/>

Van der Lugt, L. (2002). Proceedings of the 4th conference on creativity & Cognition. In E. Edmonds, L. Candy, T. Kavanagh. & T. Hewett (Eds.), *Functions of sketching in design idea generation meetings* (pp. 72–79). Loughborough, UK: ACM Press.

Vervalin, C. H. (1971). Just what is creativity? In G. A. Davis & J. A. Scott (Eds.), *Training creative thinking* (pp. 59–63). New York, NY: Holt, Rinehart, & Winston.

Wallas, G. (1926). *The art of thought.* New York, NY: Franklin Watts.

Ward, T. B., Smith, S. M., & Finke, R. A. (1999). Creative cognition. In R. J. Sternberg (Ed.), *Handbook of creativity* (pp. 189–212). Cambridge, UK: Cambridge University Press.

Weisberg, R. W. (2006). *Creativity: Understanding innovation in problem solving, science, invention, and the arts.* Hoboken, NJ: John Wiley & Sons.

Zenasni, F., & Lubart, T. (2009). Perception of emotion, emotional creativity and creative potential. *Personality and Individual Differences, 46*, 353–358.

B. INDIVIDUAL LEVEL INFLUENCES

The Emotive Roots of Creativity: Basic and Applied Issues on Affect and Motivation

Carsten K.W. De Dreu[1], Matthijs Baas[1], and Bernard A. Nijstad[2]

[1]University of Amsterdam, Amsterdam, The Netherlands; [2]University of Groningen, Groningen, The Netherlands

INTRODUCTION

Creativity helps us deal with changes in our environment, and with the opportunities and threats of everyday life (e.g., Runco, 2004). Being creative helps to sustain and promote a positive mood and sense of well-being (Hirt, Devers, & McCrea, 2008), it makes people more attractive mating partners (Griskevicius, Cialdini, & Kenrick, 2006; Miller, 2000), and it helps them to win conflicts and debates (De Dreu & Nijstad, 2008). Creativity also is core to successful entrepreneurship, and to companies establishing and expanding their market share (Baer & Frese, 2003). Creativity is intimately connected with innovation, and innovations are of great importance to organizational effectiveness and survival (e.g., Tellis, Prabhu, & Chandy, 2009). In short, both within and outside work organizations, creativity helps humans to survive, adapt, and prosper.

To achieve creativity, managers and organizational leaders collectively believe employees should feel relaxed and positive, distracted from their day-to-day hassles, and free to explore and venture out into the great wide open (e.g., Elsbach & Hargadon, 2006; Mainemelis & Ronson, 2006). The question is whether these beliefs are accurate and in line with scientific evidence. In this chapter we review this evidence, focusing on the role of moods and motives in creativity. We seek answers to questions like "do positive moods stimulate creativity more than negative moods?", "does intrinsic motivation—enjoying the task for its own sake—promote creativity to a greater extent than extrinsic motivation?", "does setting high goals and aspirations help or hinder creative performance?", "how does the motivational orientation towards gain and pleasure (approach), as contrasted to away from pain and losses (avoidance) relate to creativity?", and "how is open versus closed-mindedness related to creativity?".

Rather than providing a fact sheet listing the various research findings pertaining to the above questions, we seek to provide an overarching theoretical model of creative performance that ties these various moods and motives together, highlighting their common factors, thus arriving at a relatively succinct yet comprehensive modeling of creativity. Accordingly, we begin this chapter with the Dual Pathway to Creativity Model (Baas, De Dreu, & Nijstad, 2008; De Dreu, Baas, & Nijstad, 2008a; De Dreu, Nijstad, & Baas, 2011a; Nijstad, De Dreu, Rietzschel, & Baas, 2010 Rietzschel, De Dreu, & Nijstad, 2007a). This model provides the basis of our subsequent review of two broad classes of antecedents to creativity, namely affect, mood, and emotions on the one hand, and motivational strength and orientations on the other. In the concluding section of this chapter we highlight some avenues for new research and discuss practical implications for managers and organizational leaders seeking to enhance workplace creativity.

Before moving on, we should explicate a number of a priori choices we made when writing this chapter. First of all, we chose to focus our review on relatively recent work, published since the beginning of the 21st century, and do not cover in depth the more classic view of motivation (e.g., on achievement, power, and affiliated motives; McClelland, 1961). As such, the current review nicely builds on Ambrose and Kulik's (1999) critical essay on motivational research in the 1990s and their conclusion that the interface between motivation and creativity is among the three emerging areas (together with groups, and culture). Second, we focus our review on individual creativity and do not delve into the rich and burgeoning area of group creativity. We chose to do so because of space constraints and because the currently central Dual Pathway to Creativity Model has been related to group creativity in recent reviews published elsewhere (e.g., De Dreu, Nijstad, Bechtoldt, & Baas, 2011b; Rietzschel, De Dreu, & Nijstad, 2009; also see Gilson & Shalley, 2004; Perry-Smith & Shalley, 2003). Third, we emphasize basic research and mention only in passing more applied work relying on more qualitative case analyses. This reflects our assumption that such basic research enables more general conclusions, with broader applicability. Fourth, and finally, we deliberately focus on mood and motives rather than their possible antecedents such as climate factors (see e.g., Hunter, Bedell, & Mumford, 2007), organizational support or properties of the work environment (e.g., Oldham & Cummings, 1996; Shalley, Zhou, & Oldham, 2004) and leadership styles (e.g., Mumford, Scott, Gaddis, & Strange, 2002; Somech, 2006). These antecedents may have their effects on creativity through their effects on moods and motives, but alternative mediating pathways cannot be excluded beforehand. Nevertheless, the reader may keep in mind how the various moods and motives we discuss in the present chapter relate to specific antecedent conditions as we find them in contemporary organizations.

DUAL PATHWAY TO CREATIVITY MODEL

We define creative performance as the generation of insights, problem solutions, and ideas that are novel and potentially useful (Amabile, 1996; also Mumford & Gustafson,

1988). In social and organizational psychology, creative performance is commonly decomposed into fluency, originality, and flexibility (Guilford, 1967; Torrance, 1966). *Fluency* refers to the generated number of non-redundant ideas, insights, problem solutions, or products. *Originality* is one of the defining characteristics of creativity and refers to the uncommonness or infrequency of the ideas, insights, problem solutions, or products that are being invented (Guilford, 1967). *Flexibility* manifests itself in the use of different cognitive categories and perspectives, and the use of broad and inclusive cognitive categories (Amabile, 1996; Mednick, 1962).

Although fluency, originality, and flexibility are all considered to be dimensions of "creative performance", they are not necessarily highly correlated. Fluency and originality may be correlated (e.g., quantity breeds quality; Osborn, 1957), but they need not be. For example, fluency may manifest itself in a relatively large number of solved insight or perception problems, with the solutions themselves not being particularly new or uncommon (Förster, Friedman, & Liberman, 2004). Moreover, states or traits that influence fluency do not necessarily also influence originality, and vice versa. Taking different approaches and using more cognitive categories (i.e., high flexibility) will, all other things being equal, be associated with more ideas overall (i.e., increased fluency; Nijstad, Stroebe, & Lodewijkx, 2002, 2003) as well as with the generation of ideas in categories that are not usually thought of (i.e., originality; Murray, Sujan, Hirt, & Sujan, 1990). However, it is also possible to generate many ideas without being flexible (e.g., generating many ideas within a limited number of cognitive categories), and some of these ideas may also be original (Rietzschel, Nijstad, & Stroebe, 2007b).

These various facets of creativity are sequentially and causally ordered in the Dual Pathway to Creativity Model (DPCM; Baas et al., 2008; De Dreu et al., 2008a, 2011a, b; Nijstad et al., 2010; Rietzschel et al., 2007a, 2009). Responding to Mumford's (2003) call for integrative theory-building, the model denotes as end-states of the creative process two variables, namely the *number* (i.e., fluency) and *originality* of ideas, insights, and solutions. Figure 10.1 shows that both fluency and originality can be achieved through two distinct processes, namely (1) flexible thinking, set-breaking, and divergent processing of information, and through (2) persistent analytical probing and systematically and incrementally combining elements and possibilities. The flexibility route captures set-breaking (Smith & Blankenship, 1991), and the use of flat, associative hierarchies (Mednick, 1962). It manifests itself in the use of many different cognitive categories when generating ideas, in a high number of remote associates, in broad and inclusive cognitive categories, and in a tendency to approach problems from various angles and perspectives. The persistence route captures the notion that creative fluency and originality need hard work, perseverance, and the deliberate, persistent, and in-depth exploration of a few cognitive categories or perspectives (Boden, 1998; Schooler, Ohlsson & Brooks, 1993; Simonton, 1997). Persistence will manifest itself in the generation of many ideas within a few categories (i.e., within-category fluency; Nijstad & Stroebe, 2006), in longer time on task (De Dreu et al., 2008a), and in more bottom–up, effortful and almost analytical processing of material (Newell & Simon, 1972). Whereas DPCM combines earlier work on both divergent (flexible) and convergent (persistent) processing as key antecedents to creative performance, it does not cover aspects of the creative process such as problem finding and idea evaluation, and it remains an open issue whether flexible versus persistent processing affects problem finding and idea evaluation in similar or quite different ways. Another issue is that within DPCM the critical distinction

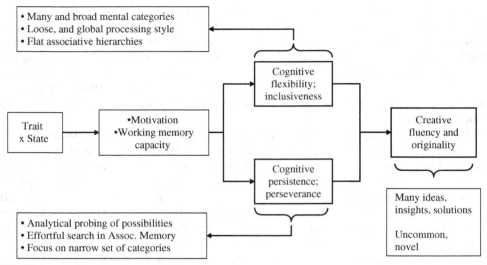

FIGURE 10.1   Dual pathway to creativity.

is in terms of the cognitive and motivational pathways that people take (or not) when performing creative tasks. As will be seen when reviewing the evidence, such different routes to creative performance operate in a variety of different tasks, including insight tasks, divergent thinking tasks, and ideation tasks. This attests to the generality of the model, yet should not be taken as if the creativity in these various tasks is identical—there are some intricate differences between insight and ideation, for example.

The distinction between these two different pathways to creativity should not be taken to mean that either one or the other pathway is engaged. In fact, creative performance often requires both pathways, either sequentially or simultaneously. Such a mixed strategy is reminiscent of what has been called "flow"—an almost automatic, effortless, yet highly focused state of consciousness (Csikszentmihályi, 1996, p. 110). Flow facilitates persistent activity and enables cognitive flexibility. In terms of DPCM, flow thus merges the cognitive flexibility and persistence pathways to creative performance. Seen this way, flow resembles the notion of engagement, a motivational state that we return to below. First, however, we examine the role of affect, mood, and emotions in driving creativity through enhanced cognitive flexibility and/or persistence.

AFFECT, MOOD, AND EMOTIONS

In many writings, the terms affect, mood, and emotions tend to be used interchangeably to reflect that an individual can feel positive or negative. In the present chapter, we adopt a more hierarchical approach, with affect denoting the most general and abstract level, essentially distinguishing between positive and negative affect. At a lower level of abstraction we have mood states that are more subject to change and due to situational pressures. Moods not only vary in valence, but also in terms of the extent to which they activate or de-activate the individual—we return to this below. Emotions, finally, are more specific than moods and include physiological reactions and action tendencies towards or away from the emotion-triggering object (Lazarus, 1991; also see Frijda, 1993; Russell & Barrett, 1999).

To understand creativity as a function of mood, research has long relied on the distinction between positive and negative affect. However, DPCM argues that, for both flexibility and cognitive persistence, the individual needs to be cognitively activated (see Figure 10.1). This is a critical deviation from the widely shared notion that creativity results from being relaxed, unfocused, and unengaged (e.g., Bransford & Stein, 1984; Martindale, 1999). Rather, and consistent with the idea that performance relates to stress in a curvilinear way (Staw, Sandelands, & Dutton, 1981), DPCM proposes that, at moderate levels of activation and arousal, both cognitive flexibility and persistence can be facilitated more than under excessively low or high activation and arousal. First, being activated leads to task engagement and motivation to consider the issue at hand (Dietrich, 2004). Second, moderately high levels of cognitive arousal are associated with the release of certain neurotransmitters, such as dopamine and noradrenalin, in the prefrontal cortex, which improves a number of cognitive functions, including working memory performance, cognitive flexibility, and sustained attention (e.g., Dreisbach & Goschke, 2004).

According to DPCM, different traits, states, and their combinations, may lead to cognitive activation. More importantly, some traits or states will be mainly of influence on creativity because they impact cognitive flexibility. Other traits or states will mainly affect creativity through their effect on cognitive persistence. One prominent case is that of the effects of mood states on creative performance (e.g., Shalley et al., 2004). In general, positive moods seem to stimulate creativity, but this positive relation has not always been obtained. Effects of negative mood states are even more inconsistent, with some studies finding negative effects, others finding no effects at all, and still others even finding positive effects on creative performance (for a review see Baas et al., 2008). To explain these different findings, De Dreu et al. (2008a) distinguish between the *activating* or *de-activating* effects of different mood states (Russell & Barrett, 1999; Watson, Clark, & Tellegen, 1988). Activating moods can be positively (e.g., feeling happy or elated) or negatively toned (e.g., anger, fear); similarly, de-activating moods can have positive (feeling relaxed or serene) or negative (sadness, feeling down) hedonic tone.

According to DPCM, both positive and negative activating moods lead to higher creative performance than de-activating moods, but *how* depends on hedonic tone. Specifically, work in both cognitive neurosciences and social cognition suggests that when feeling positive, the individual feels safe to explore the environment, is more likely to use broad and inclusive cognitive categories, and more easily engages in divergent thinking—a positive feeling engenders cognitive flexibility (e.g., Dreisbach & Goschke, 2004; George & Zhou, 2007; Hirt et al., 2008; Murray et al., 1990). These same sources also suggest that when feeling negative, the individual becomes more inward focused, more analytical, and processes information in a more bottom–up fashion—a negative feeling engenders cognitive persistence (e.g., Ambady & Gray, 2002; Derryberry & Reed, 1998; Schwarz & Clore, 2007). Put differently, whereas activating moods lead to more creativity than de-activating moods, it is because of flexibility when these activating moods are positive in tone, and because of persistence when these activating moods are negative in tone.

B. INDIVIDUAL LEVEL INFLUENCES

De Dreu et al. (2008a) tested this hypothesis in a series of studies using a variety of creativity tasks, including brainstorming and perceptual insight problems. Through self-generated imagery (i.e., writing a story about an occasion in which they experienced a particular emotion), participants were induced to experience activating or de-activating mood states that were either positive (happy, elated versus serene, relaxed) or negative (angry, anxious versus sad, depressed) in tone. Across four studies, results were consistent with the overall hypothesis that activating moods (e.g., anger, fear, happy, elated) lead to more creative fluency and originality than de-activating moods (e.g., sad, depressed, relaxed, serene); people in activating moods generated more ideas that were of greater originality, and solved more insight problems than those in de-activating moods. Furthermore, activating moods influence fluency and originality because of enhanced cognitive flexibility when the tone is positive, but because of enhanced persistence when tone is negative. For example, participants in a positive activating mood used more cognitive categories in a brainstorming task (i.e., flexibility) whereas participants in a negative activating mood explored a few cognitive categories in greater depth (i.e., persistence).

To further examine the robustness of these findings, Baas and colleagues (2008) conducted a meta-analysis of the mood–creativity literature. Consistent with DPCM, and the findings reported in De Dreu et al. (2008a), positive effects were found when studies induced activating rather than de-activating mood states. For example, happy but not relaxed mood states were associated with higher levels of creativity (see Figure 10.2). Similarly, sadness (a de-activating state) was unrelated to creativity. However, an important qualification was that this distinction applied to activating mood states associated with an approach orientation (i.e., happy) and not to activating mood states associated with an avoidance orientation (i.e., fear). Indeed in the meta-analysis, fear associated with reduced cognitive flexibility. Perhaps fear associates with more focused cognitive activity, which may promote creativity through persistence given enough time-on-task but not through flexibility (De Dreu & Nijstad, 2008). Unfortunately, not enough studies were available to assess the effects of other mood states, such as anger. Anger is an interesting case, because it is an activating mood state that associates with an approach orientation but is negative in hedonic tone. Examining the effects of anger on creative

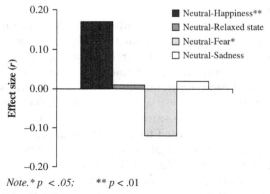

Note. * $p < .05;$ ** $p < .01$

FIGURE 10.2 Meta-analysis of the relationship of happiness, relaxed state, fear, and sadness with creative performance.

performance would therefore allow for a test of the hypothesis that activating approach-related mood states enhance creativity regardless of the mood state's hedonic tone. We return to the role of approach versus avoidance motivation in the next section.

The meta-analysis of the mood-creativity relationship also allowed for a test of the effects of important moderator variables. For example, grounded in the mood as input model (Martin & Stoner, 1996; see also Schwarz & Clore, 2007), it has been argued that if a person's mood is congruent with the task framing, more energy and time is put into the task with enhanced creative performance as a result. The problem signal elicited by negative moods motivates to solve problems and to invest more effort in order to meet performance standards. In corresponding fashion, the safety signal elicited by positive affect motivates to seek stimulation and to pursue incentives, activities that would be ill-advised under less benign circumstances (Martin & Stoner, 1996; Schwarz & Clore, 2007). By implication, whereas individuals in a negative mood benefit from a task that is framed as serious, and in which performance standards and extrinsic rewards are emphasized, those in a positive mood benefit from a task that is framed as funny and in which enjoyment and intrinsic rewards are emphasized (Hirt, Melton, McDonald, & Harackiewicz, 1996). Accordingly, in the meta-analysis, studies were coded as being serious or involving performance standards versus being silly and fun or involving enjoyment standards. It was found that when the creativity task was framed in terms of fun and enjoyment, participants in a happy mood were more creative than those in a negative mood. When the task was framed as serious or performance-related, however, participants in a negative mood tended to be more creative (although the latter effect failed to reach significance). This result supports the mood-as-input frameworks that effects of moods on creativity may substantially depend on the task context. It also supports the general idea that a fit between an internal state (mood) and external constraints (task framing) may yield high levels of creativity.

Taken together, the extant literature on mood and emotions and recent primary and meta-analytic research allow for the following conclusions: First, activating moods promote creativity more than de-activating moods, either because they facilitate cognitive flexibility (e.g., happiness, joy, elation) or because they engender effortful, persistent cognitive activity (e.g., anger, anxiety). That these influences appear stronger when mood states associate with an approach orientation is something we return to in the next section on motivation. Second, and related, the effects of mood and emotion on creative performance appear less due to purely cognitive effects such as spreading activation and "mood-as-input"—motivational influences (e.g., approach versus avoidance dimensions underlying a particular mood state) appear at least as important. Third, and finally, the literature suffers from glaring gaps—there is virtually no research on the role of anger (with the exception of the studies of De Dreu et al., 2008a), and almost all studies on the relationship between fear and creativity are correlational and focused on trait-level anxiety. Clearly, and especially when it comes to negatively toned mood states, more research is badly needed.

MOTIVATION STRENGTH AND ORIENTATION

At a very general level, motivation refers to the initiation, choice, or persistence in specific actions (Mook, 1987). Typically, researchers distinguish between motivational orientation and motivational strength. Motivational orientation refers to the tendency to approach positive outcomes, such as pleasure and gain, versus the tendency to avoid negative outcomes, such as pain and loss. Strength refers to the intensity and energy that is mobilized and thus varies from low to high. The motivation–creativity literature centers around several basic issues:

1. the role of approach versus avoidance orientation,
2. the role of intrinsic versus extrinsic motivation,
3. the role of engagement and flow,
4. the impact of goal setting and achievement motivation, and
5. the role of cognitive motivation to achieve structure and closure versus to be open-minded.

Each of these areas of inquiry will be reviewed subsequently.

Approach versus Avoidance

The term motivational orientation refers to the different outcome foci of two fundamental bio-behavioral systems: approach and avoidance (e.g., Elliot & Thrash, 2002). The motivational orientation is towards approach when the individual is moving towards, or anticipates aspired goals and positive outcomes; the motivational orientation is towards avoidance when the individual is moving away from, or anticipates aversive stimulation and negative end-states. This basic distinction between avoidance and approach orientation resonates with work on regulatory focus, showing that people operating under a prevention focus are oriented towards security, responsibilities, and avoiding aversive outcomes, while those operating under a promotion focus are oriented towards opportunities, accomplishing goals, and approaching desired outcomes (e.g., Higgins, 2000).

From DPCM it follows that both approach and avoidance oriented motivational states promote creativity to the extent that they engage and cognitively activate the individual. However, the research on approach and avoidance shows inconsistent findings. On the one hand, there is evidence that approach-related states lead to more originality and insights than avoidance-related states (Friedman & Förster, 2000, 2001). For example, Friedman and Förster (2000, 2001) manipulated motivational states by asking participants to perform approach behavior (pulling a lever towards them), or avoidance behavior (pushing a lever away), and subsequently had them perform creativity tasks. Results showed that approach behaviors indeed bolstered memory search for new responses and produced more originality and greater insight problem solving than avoidance behaviors. On the other hand, experimentally induced activating avoidance-related states (such as anxiety and the anticipation of conflict) have been found to promote creative performance (e.g., Cretenet & Dru, 2009; De Dreu et al., 2008a; De Dreu & Nijstad, 2008).

To solve this apparent conundrum, Baas, De Dreu, and Nijstad (2011) argued that the extent to which approach and avoidance oriented states engage and cognitively activate the individual depends on regulatory success—is the desired end-state achieved or not? Approach states engage the individual because the desired end-state is not attained and frustration and annoyance signal that additional effort is needed, or because the desired end-state is achieved and the concomitant joy and excitement activates in and of itself. Avoidance states engage the individual as long as the undesirable end-state is not successfully avoided; but when successfully avoided, the individual experiences relief, is deactivated and disengaged (Carver, 2004; Higgins, 2000). Accordingly, in five experiments the basic hypothesis was tested that in the case of regulatory failure, both approach and avoidance oriented individuals would show high levels of creative fluency, originality, and insight performance; in case of regulatory success, however, avoidance-oriented individuals were expected to show lower levels of creativity than those with an approach orientation.

The results confirmed this basic prediction, and showed that in the case of regulatory failure, avoidance-oriented individuals produced similar levels of creativity as approach-oriented individuals. However, in the case of regulatory success, avoidance-oriented individuals produced lower levels of creativity than approach-oriented individuals. Supporting DPCM, this effect was mediated by self-reported motivational engagement. Thus, greater originality and more creative insights emerge when the individual is activated and engaged, regardless whether the motivational orientation is towards approach or towards avoidance. After successful avoidance, however, the individual experiences relief and is deactivated and disengaged, resulting in lower levels of creativity.

A second question pertains to the way in which approach and avoidance orientations achieve their creativity-enhancing effects. It has been suggested that an approach orientation associates with a broad and global attentional focus, which facilitates conceptual access to more remote informational links. In terms of DPCM, an approach orientation may promote creativity primarily because of enhanced flexibility (Förster, Friedman, Özelsel, & Denzler, 2006). Therefore, situational factors and personality correlates that are associated with an approach orientation are expected to lead to enhanced levels of creativity through cognitive flexibility. This is indeed what the available evidence seems to suggest; states and traits that have in common that they are associated with a broad attentional focus and a willingness to explore alternative courses of action to reach some desired end-state are positively related to flexibility. Examples for which positive effects on flexibility and creativity have been found include approach motor actions (Förster et al., 2006), primes of desired outcomes (Friedman & Förster, 2001), exposure to a blue (rather than the fear-inducing red) background (Mehta & Zhu, 2009), romantic motives (Griskevicius et al., 2006), and individual differences in openness to experience (e.g., McCrae, 1987; also see below) and extraversion (e.g., Feist, 1998).

Avoidance-oriented traits and states, on the other hand, associate with the recruitment of cognitive resources and enhanced cognitive control (Koch, Holland, Hengstler & Van Knippenberg, 2009), and a narrowed scope of attention that is focused on local perceptual details (Derryberry & Reed, 1998; Förster et al., 2006). Avoidance orientation may therefore associate with creativity primarily through cognitive persistence (De Dreu & Nijstad, 2008). For example, the anticipation of conflict (Carnevale & Probst, 1998), aversive arousal (Derryberry & Reed, 1998), avoidance motor actions and prevention focus (Friedman & Förster, 2000, 2001; Förster et al., 2006), and neuroticism (Muris, De Jong, & Engelen, 2004) seem to lead to a narrow focus of attention. However, as we have argued above, also narrow and systematic processing may eventually lead to creativity. For example, De Dreu and Nijstad (2008) have recently shown that the anticipation of conflict leads to lower cognitive flexibility and creativity for tasks that are unrelated to the conflict. However, they also found that participants who anticipated a severe conflict were in fact very fluent and creative where conflict-related material was considered (e.g., in designing strategies to beat the opponent). Thus, these participants focused their attention on the upcoming conflict (and were less creative in conflict-unrelated tasks), but within the conflict domain were capable of creative thinking. Likewise, aversive arousal has been linked to greater levels of creativity through the use of many ideas within a few cognitive categories (i.e., persistence; Baas et al., 2009). Thus, under some circumstances, avoidance-related states may associate with creativity through persistent and focused processing, but future research is needed to provide more conclusive evidence.

Intrinsic versus Extrinsic Motivation and the Role of Reward

There is a rich and longstanding research tradition linking creativity to intrinsic motivation versus extrinsic motivation (Amabile, 1979; Deci & Ryan, 1985; Eisenberger & Aselage, 2009; Oldham & Cummings, 1996; Zhou, 2003). Intrinsic motivation refers to the inner-directed interest and involvement in a task (Amabile, 1979, 1996) and is associated with elevated levels of task interest, task enjoyment, and persistence on a task (Utman, 1997). Extrinsic motivation, on the other hand, refers to task engagement stemming primarily from external goals, such as rewards or the expectation of evaluation (Amabile, 1996).

The evidence for the creativity-enhancing effects of intrinsic motivation is abundant (Amabile, 1996). For example, in an interview study, creative professionals mentioned intrinsic motivation as an important determinant of creativity more frequently than any other characteristic (Amabile & Gryskiewicz, 1989). A meta-analysis of 24 studies showed positive effects of intrinsic motivation on a wide range of performance measures including creativity (Utman, 1997). Moreover, numerous field experiments have shown that creativity is stimulated by variables that are conducive to intrinsic motivation, including supporting and informative evaluations (Deci & Ryan, 1985), autonomy (e.g., Amabile, 1996; Baylin, 1985), and challenging work conditions (e.g., Amabile, Conti, Coon, Lazenby, & Herron, 1996). Intrinsic motivation leads to elevated levels of creativity, because it is associated with focused and persistent task engagement, and because intrinsically motivated individuals are more likely to take risks, to be playful with ideas and materials, and to flexibly explore new cognitive pathways (Amabile, 1996; Deci & Ryan, 1985; Oldham & Cummings, 1996; Zhou, 2003).

The relationship between extrinsic motivation and creativity is less consistent. On the one hand, research evidence suggests that external goals, such as rewards and the expectation of evaluation, have detrimental effects on creativity (Amabile, 1996; De Vet & De Dreu, 2007). For example, independent expert judges rated the poems of individuals who were primed with extrinsic reasons to write as less creative than those primed with internal reasons to write, and creativity was lowered when individuals expected evaluation of external judges and when individuals were competing for prizes (see Amabile, 1996, for an overview). These effects are commonly explained by arguing that performance evaluation and reward expectancy reduce autonomy and intrinsic motivation, which are conducive to creative thinking (Amabile et al., 1996; Deci, Koestner, & Ryan, 1999). Also, the motivation to achieve extrinsic ends is associated with greater feelings of pressure and distraction from task engagement (Deci & Ryan, 1985; Utman, 1997), which, in turn, reduce spontaneity and flexibility (Amabile, 1996).

Other findings, in contrast, suggest that expectation of performance evaluation is not necessarily bad for creativity (Shalley, 1995), and when delivered in an informative and supportive way, it can enhance it (Deci et al., 1999; Oldham & Cummings, 1996). Similarly, reward and recognition of creativity sometimes helps to stimulate it, especially if seen as a bonus or confirmation of competence (Amabile, 1996; Cummings, 1965). Moreover, a meta-analysis of the effects of reward on intrinsic motivation, measured as persistence and task enjoyment, has shown that rewards are not necessarily detrimental to intrinsic motivation (Cameron & Pierce, 1994, but see Deci et al., 1999). The meta-analytic results showed that verbal rewards actually increased persistence and task enjoyment, and the only negative effects on intrinsic motivation were found for rewards that were tangible, expected, and delivered regardless of level of performance.

Consistent with these meta-analytic results, Eisenberger and colleagues (Eisenberger & Armeli, 1997; Eisenberger & Rhoades, 2001) argued that it is crucial whether people know what is required to obtain the reward. The contingency between performance and reward informs individuals about appropriate behavior besides supplying an incentive for performing this behavior. The earlier mentioned studies that found detrimental effects of reward on creativity typically promised reward without reference to the nature of required performance. However, if instructions are more explicit; that novel performance is required to get the reward, individuals invest more effort and increase their focus on the task (Eisenberger & Armeli, 1997; Eisenberger & Rhoades, 2001). This in turn increases creativity (Czikszentmihályi, 1996; De Dreu et al., 2009; Shalley, 1995). Indeed, if individuals were instructed that novel performance is required for obtaining a reward on one task (that is, if an explicit positive association is established between rewards and novel performance), individuals increased their subsequent creative performance in an entirely different task (e.g., Eisenberger & Armeli, 1997; Eisenberger & Rhoades, 2001). Likewise, promised reward increased the creativity of stories and story titles if task instructions clarified the necessity of creative performance (Eisenberger & Rhoades, 2001). Finally, results showed that rewards for novel performance led to greater levels of creativity, because individuals display a greater intrinsic interest in the creativity task and feel more driven to carry out the task (Eisenberger & Aselage, 2009; Eisenberger & Rhoades, 2001).

In summary, intrinsic and extrinsic motivation may both lead to greater levels of creativity, because they both are associated with elevated levels of task engagement. This finding is consistent with DPCM in that it highlights that, for creativity to come about, the individual first and foremost needs to be activated and engaged in the task. The findings further suggest that intrinsic motivation produces creativity through playful combination of ideas and materials and the flexible exploration of new cognitive pathways. In other words, intrinsic motivation might primarily engage the flexibility pathway, but future work is needed to be more conclusive. Furthermore, although it has been shown that extrinsic goals sometimes lead to more creativity through increased autonomy and intrinsic task interest, this mechanism is subject to continued debate (Eisenberger & Rhoades, 2001; Eisenberger & Aselage, 2009 vs. Amabile, 1996; Deci et al., 1999). By specifically focusing on two cognitive pathways, DPCM offers an alternative approach to further our understanding of the ways extrinsic motivation could enhance creativity. Testing whether extrinsic motivation engages the flexibility and/or persistence pathway might be a fruitful avenue for future research.

Engagement and Value-from-Fit

Work on intrinsic and extrinsic motivation relates to recent studies on so-called engagement. Engagement refers to a heightened state of arousal paired to a strong sense of task commitment, sustained focus and alertness, and enjoyment. According to value-from-fit theory (Higgins, 2000, 2006) people derive value from the regulatory fit that they experience when an activity sustains their goal orientation, mood, or interests regarding that activity. For example, sad people prefer deliberate thinking, whereas happy people prefer intuitive reasoning. De Vries, Holland, and Witteman (2008) asked participants in a sad (happy) mood to make decisions after deliberate (intuitive) reasoning. They found greater satisfaction and subjective value when the thinking strategy matched rather than mismatched the mood state (i.e., sad/deliberate and happy/intuitive > sad/intuitive and happy/deliberate).

Fit-induced engagement is one of the core ingredients of "flow"—an almost automatic, effortless, yet highly focused state of consciousness (Csikszentmihályi, 1996, p. 110). Flow, in turn, has been argued to promote creative performance because it motivates persistent activity and enables cognitive flexibility. In terms of DPCM, flow merges the cognitive flexibility and persistence pathways to creative performance. And indeed, compared to non-fit, regulatory fit increases cognitive flexibility (Worthy, Maddox, & Markman, 2007) as well as cognitive persistence and fluency (Vaugh, Malik, Schwartz, Petkova, & Trudeau, 2006). Likewise, flow is related to greater perceived fit between individuals' skills and task demands, to longer time-on-task and greater fluency (Keller & Bless, 2008). Put differently, fit rather than non-fit produces positive feelings and a sense of engagement that constitutes flow. Flow, in turn, facilitates cognitive flexibility and persistence and should thereby produce more creativity than misfit.

De Dreu et al. (2011a) tested this "creative flow-from-fit" prediction in a series of experiments focusing on creativity in brainstorming, perceptual insight tasks, and conceptual problem solving. In all studies, individual differences in behavioral approach were assessed prior to the experiment. Behavioral approach is captured by such items as "I go out of my way to get things I want" and "I crave excitement and new sensations" (Carver & White, 1994). Individual differences in activation (vs. inhibition, see Carver & White, 1994) are conceptually related to approach tendencies (vs. avoidance) discussed in the previous sections. However, there is growing evidence that behavioral activation and approach orientations are weakly correlated (Robinson, Meier, Tamir, Wilkowski, & Ode, 2009), indicating that work on approach versus avoidance motivation cannot be used to predict and understand possible relationships between behavioral activation and inhibition on the one hand, and creative performance on the other.

Behavioral activation does, however, associate with extraversion and such positive emotions as hope and optimism. Both extraversion (e.g., Feist, 1998; Furnham & Bachtiar, 2008) and positive emotions (Frederickson & Branigan, 2005) associate with tendencies toward more global and abstract thinking, whereas low levels of extraversion and lack of positive emotions associate with more local, detail-oriented thinking and information processing. From this follows that people with strong behavioral activation would experience stronger fit and concomitant engagement when primed with a global thinking style (e.g., focus on the forest rather than the trees; see Förster & Higgins, 2005), whereas those with weak behavioral activation would experience stronger fit and concomitant engagement when primed with a local thinking style.

To test this value-from-fit hypothesis, De Dreu and colleagues (2011a) manipulated task requirements and thinking styles to induce in participants either a global or local processing mode, and had them subsequently perform a series of creativity tasks. For example, in one study, participants filled out the behavioral activation measure and then proceeded to generate ideas about a broadly defined problem (e.g., how to improve university education) or about a narrowly defined problem (e.g., how to improve classroom teaching). The broad topic was expected to "fit" better individuals with strong behavioral activation whereas the narrow topic was expected to "fit" better individuals with weak behavioral activation. Indeed, individuals reported stronger engagement when there was a fit rather than non-fit between the strength of their behavioral activation and the breadth of the brainstorming topic. Moreover, engagement was associated with greater creativity, as evidenced in greater fluency as well as enhanced originality. Finally, and quite consistent with DPCM, there was some evidence that engagement enacted both the persistence and flexibility pathways to creativity.

Goal Setting and Goal Orientation

One way to enhance and direct motivation in work settings is through goal setting. Specific and moderately difficult goals increase performance because they direct and sustain attention and effort toward goal-related activities (Locke & Latham, 1990). Cast within the context of DPCM, goal setting thus promotes, at the least, creativity through enhanced persistence, effort, and sustained task-focused activity. Perhaps goal setting may also enhance creativity through enhanced cognitive flexibility—we return to this at the end of this section.

Work on goal setting distinguishes between three critical components of goals—goal level and specificity, goal commitment, and goal orientation. The basic idea is that employees are productive to the extent that they are given, or self-set relatively *difficult* yet *specific* goals (i.e., generate more than 50 ideas on how to market product X) to which they are *committed* and receive *feedback* about progress (Locke & Latham, 1990). Commitment refers to the individual's determination to reach a goal (Klein, Wesson, Hollenbeck, & Alge, 1999). Each of these components may be relevant to creative performance (for a review and discussion see Litchfield, 2008). For example, individuals generated more non-redundant ideas when they were given specific, challenging goals compared to when they received no goals (Paulus & Dzindolet, 1993), or compared to non-challenging or do-your-best goals (Latham, Erez, & Locke, 1988). This resonates with the findings from a large scale study on work environment and creativity (Amabile et al., 1996), showing that challenge and supervisory encouragement were important differentiators between projects that were high and low in creativity.

Consistent with goal-setting theory, this general effect appears to be moderated by goal commitment (also referred to as *goal acceptance*). Individuals can be as committed to assigned goals as to self-set goals *if* the authority figure assigning the goals provides a reasonable explanation of the goals and makes supportive statements about the possibility of goal attainment (Latham et al., 1988). Challenging yet specific goals boost creative performance to the extent that there is high goal commitment, either because goals were self-set or because the authority figure assigning these goals used a "tell and sell" (rather than "tell") approach (Latham et al., 1988).

As predicted by goal-setting theory, there is circumstantial evidence that the relationship between challenging goals and creative performance is moderated by the presence versus absence of feedback. Fodor and Carver (2000) had students complete the Thematic Apperception Test, which was scored for achievement motivation (with higher achievement motivation corresponding to higher self-set goals and aspirations). Participants later participated in an experiment in which they first provided a solution to an engineering problem. In two conditions the experimenter gave participants preprogrammed, written feedback on how well they performed (positive or negative feedback); in a third condition there was no feedback. Participants then rendered solutions to a second engineering problem. External ratings of creativity correlated with achievement motivation in the positive- and negative-feedback conditions but not in the no-feedback condition. Work by Zhou (1998) revealed similar results. In her study, positive feedback enhanced creative performance more than negative feedback but only when it was delivered in an "informational style" and not in a "controlling" style. This effect may have emerged because positive feedback in an informational style boosts intrinsic motivation and self-efficacy.

Resonating with the work on intrinsic versus extrinsic motivation is research on different types of goals people may be assigned to, or set themselves. First, Shalley (1991) compared productivity goals (difficult, do-your-best, no goal) and creativity goals (difficult, do-your-best, no goal) on productivity and creative performance. High levels of creativity emerged when either a difficult or do-your-best creativity goal was paired to a difficult productivity goal.

Other work decomposed goal orientations into a performance goal orientation, focused on the demonstration of competence to others, and a learning goal orientation, focused on the development of competence and task mastery (e.g., Amabile, 1996; Dweck & Leggett, 1988; Elliot, 1999). Thus, resonating with our above discussion of extrinsic motivators, people may also be motivated by extrinsic factors such as competing against others, receiving rewards, acknowledgement, or avoiding criticism (VandeWalle, 1997). A learning goal orientation resonates with the concept of intrinsic motivation. It fosters an intrinsic interest in the task itself, because challenging work provides a means to develop skills and knowledge, and leads people to invest effort to complete complex tasks in the absence of extrinsic rewards (Dweck & Leggett, 1988). However, a learning orientation not only provides the intrinsic motivation to perform creatively, but also promotes skill acquisition and people's willingness to solicit and use feedback to improve their skills and creativity. Specifically, as Elliot (1999) argued, a learning orientation focuses the individual on the acquisition of new knowledge and the development of "deep-processing strategies." Further, a learning orientation associates with a preference for challenging and demanding tasks (VandeWalle, 1997). Accordingly, individuals with a stronger learning orientation may be expected to seek out creative activities that, by definition, involve uncertain and untried approaches that possess a high likelihood of error or potential failure. And indeed, a number of studies established a positive association between learning orientation on the one hand, and creativity on the other (Hirst, Van Knippenberg, & Zhou, 2009; Janssen & Van Yperen, 2004).

Several issues remain unclear when linking work on goal setting to individual creativity. First of all, it remains unclear *why* challenging goals promote creativity—is it because of enhanced cognitive flexibility, enhanced persistence, or perhaps some combination? At first blush, it seems that goal setting drives persistence and bottom–up, effortful work more than top–down, flexible processing. However, we are unaware of any research evidence and here clearly lays an important task for future research. This is all the more pressing when we realize that the link between goal setting and creative performance is evidenced when it comes to creative fluency. Little has been done to systematically examine the effects of goal setting and goal commitment on originality of thought, the undisputed hallmark of creativity (e.g., Guilford, 1967). Finally, and related, the link between goal setting and creative performance has been examined in the context of idea generation but not, as far as we know, in the adjacent domains of creative insight and problem solving (e.g., Runco, 2004). In short, there is substantial work needed to further specify the (motivating) effects of goal setting on creative performance and its mediating psychological mechanisms (also see Litchfield, 2008).

Cognitive Motivation: Closed- versus Open-Mindedness

Cognitive motivation refers to the related concepts of epistemic motivation and that of closed-versus open-mindedness. Epistemic motivation may be defined as the willingness to expend effort to reach a thorough, rich, and accurate understanding of the world, including the task at hand (De Dreu, Nijstad, & Van Knippenberg, 2008b). According to Kruglanski and Webster (1996), one important dimension underlying epistemic motivation is the need for cognitive closure: a desire for a definitive and firm answer rather than face ambiguity. A high need for cognitive closure is related to a tendency to reach quick closure on an issue ("seizing"), and a desire to maintain closure after it has been reached ("freezing"). A high need for cognitive closure (and low epistemic motivation) is associated with closed- rather than open-mindedness, in particular after initial closure has been reached.

Epistemic motivation has been argued to be both trait and state based. For example, epistemic motivation is presumably positively related to individual differences in need for cognition (Petty & Cacioppo, 1986), and the Big Five factor openness to experience (McCrae, 1987), whereas it is negatively related to individual differences in need for cognitive closure (Webster & Kruglanski, 1994). In addition, situational variables, such as importance of an issue (Mayseless & Kruglanski, 1987), or accountability (Tetlock, 1992), may raise the level of epistemic motivation, while other factors, such as fatigue, ambient noise, or time pressure, lower the level of epistemic motivation (for overviews: De Dreu et al., 2008b; Kruglanski & Webster, 1996). The question, however, is: how do epistemic motivation and open-versus closed-mindedness relate to creativity? There are two lines of research available to answer this question. The first focuses on individual differences, whereas the second focuses on situational factors. They will be discussed in turn.

Individual differences. Dispositional open- versus closed-mindedness has, in addition to the factors mentioned above, been studied in the literatures on authoritarianism, tolerance of ambiguity, uncertainty avoidance, conservatism, and dogmatism (see Kruglanski, 2004, for an overview). Most recent research, however, has been performed with the Big Five personality factor openness to experience. Openness to experience refers to a tendency towards intellectual curiosity, aesthetic sensitivity, liberal values, and emotional differentiation (McCrae, 1987). In general, this literature suggests that openness to experience is positively related to creativity. For example, McCrae (1987) has found that of the factors of the Big Five, openness to experience was most consistently positively related to scores on divergent thinking tasks (in particular fluency) and scores on Gough's (1979) creative personality scale. In a meta-analysis, Feist (1998) found that openness to experience was positively related to scientific and artistic creativity, a finding that seems to generalize to workplace creativity as well (e.g., Baer & Oldham, 2006; George & Zhou, 2001). Additionally, Butler, Scherer, and Reiter-Palmon (2003) found that Need for Cognition—a positive correlate of openness to experience—related to both cognitive flexibility and creative fluency.

Furthermore, a negative relation with creativity has been found for measures of closed-mindedness. For example, Ip, Chen, and Chiu (2006) found that need for cognitive closure is negatively related to creativity, Dollinger (2007) found that conservatism negatively relates to creative accomplishments and creativity of photo-essays and drawings, and Rubinstein (2003) observed a negative relation between authoritarianism and creativity.

The question, however, is how these results may be interpreted. One line of reasoning is that openness to experience and related personality constructs predispose people to seek out and enjoy novel situations and experiences. Firstly, having more experiences would give open people a 'richer' background to work with during a creative task. This is consistent with work showing that multicultural experiences lead to enhanced levels of creativity, but only for those people who are high in openness to experience (e.g., Leung, Maddux, Galinsky, & Chiu, 2008). Presumably, open people are motivated to adopt practices and ideas from other cultures, which predispose them to higher levels of creativity only after exposure to different cultures. Secondly, open people may enjoy creative tasks more, and experience higher levels of intrinsic motivation while working on them. Indeed, Prabhu, Sutton, and Sauser (2008) found that the relation between openness to experience and creativity was partially mediated by intrinsic motivation.

Another line of evidence suggests that the effects of openness to experience on creative performance are due to cognitive factors. Peterson, Smith, and Carson (2002) have shown that openness to experience associates with reduced levels of latent inhibition. Latent inhibition is a cognitive mechanism that allows individuals to cease responding to stimuli with no apparent motivational or emotional value. In other words, latent inhibition is a filtering mechanism that keeps irrelevant thoughts and stimuli out of awareness. Reduced levels of latent inhibition have in turn been associated with higher levels of creativity (Carson, Peterson, & Higgins, 2003). These authors argued that reduced latent inhibition implies that more stimuli are considered during task performance (i.e., they are not filtered out), including stimuli that are more original, which makes people more creative.

In terms of the DPCM, we would hypothesize that open-mindedness associates with the flexibility pathway to creativity: both intrinsic motivation to perform a task and reduced levels of latent inhibition would lead to a broad attentional focus and the consideration of remote associations during creative performance. However, given the logic of the DPCM, some facets of closed-mindedness may in fact associate with the persistence pathway: they lead to a narrow attentional focus and a systematic exploration of problem space, which, given persistence, may also result in creativity.

This possibility was explored by Rietzschel et al. (2007a), who examined the relation between creativity and a personality trait called personal need for structure (PNS). PNS refers to a chronic aversion to ill-structured situations and a longing for certainty and predictability (Thompson, Naccarato, Parker, & Moskowitz, 2001), and associates with closed- rather than open-mindedness. For example, PNS is negatively related to openness to experience (Neuberg & Newsom, 1993) and positively to authoritarianism (Thompson et al., 2001). Based on the previous, one would therefore expect PNS to be negatively related to creativity, but this is not what Rietzschel et al. (2007a) observed. Rather, they found that PNS was only negatively related to creativity for those participants who habitually worry about the correctness of their responses, as measured with Thompson et al.'s (2001) Personal Fear of Invalidity (PFI) scale. For those participants low on PFI, a *positive* relation between PNS and creativity was observed. Moreover, evidence was obtained that this was due to persistence rather than flexibility: in a brainstorming task, participants high in PNS and low in PFI did not survey more categories of ideas, but rather surveyed a few categories in greater depth. Apparently, people high in PNS engaged in a deep and systematic search within categories of ideas, which led to creativity when they were not hampered by worries over their responses.

In conclusion, the evidence indicates that open-minded people tend to be creative. We suggested that this relation might primarily be mediated by cognitive flexibility, but future studies will have to provide more conclusive evidence for this. However, we also suggested that closed-minded people may be creative, because they take a structured approach to a task which, after persistence, may also lead to creativity. However, the latter effect was only found when people did not worry about the correctness of their creative responses.

Situational factors. As argued, epistemic motivation is not only a function of personality, but also of situational factors. Of the situational factors that influence epistemic motivation, we will discuss the effect of time pressure on creativity, because this factor has been most heavily investigated. Time pressure in general will reduce epistemic motivation, and lead to a high need for cognitive closure: because extensive information processing becomes costly, people prefer to end information processing and reach a definitive conclusion (e.g., Kruglanski, 2004). The above discussion of open-mindedness and creativity may lead one to assume that the relation between time pressure and creativity is negative: as time pressure increases, people become less open-minded and therefore less creative. And indeed, authors have argued that time pressure will stifle creativity (e.g., Andrews & Smith, 1996). However, time pressure may also serve to increase one's level of arousal and cognitive activation, and according to DPCM, such activation is needed to perform creatively. However, this will mainly be true under moderate levels of arousal and time pressure, which leads to the hypothesis that time pressure relates to creativity in a curvilinear way (also Gardner, 1986).

Several studies have looked at the relation between time pressure and creativity, mostly in samples of employees. Studies examining a linear relation between time pressure and creativity have been somewhat inconsistent. For example, Andrews and Smith (1996) found a negative relation between time pressure and the creativity of marketing plans developed by product managers, Andrews and Farris (1972) found a positive relation between scientists' perceived time pressure and the innovativeness of their work, and Amabile and Gryskiewicz (1989) found a non-significant relation between time pressure and creativity in a number of different groups. More recent work, however, has obtained evidence for a curvilinear relation between time pressure and employee creativity or innovation. For example, Janssen (2001) found that the relation between job demands and supervisor-rated innovative performance of employees followed an inverted U-shape. A similar result was obtained by Ohly, Sonnentag, and Pluntke (2006) in a sample of employees of a high technology company in Germany: the relation between time pressure and both creativity and innovativeness followed an inverted U-shape.

Baer and Oldham (2006) have recently reported a study that also looked at a potential curvilinear relation between time pressure and employee creativity. They more in particular looked at experienced creative time pressure, defined as the degree to which employees experience time pressure to develop creative ideas at work. Indeed, they found evidence for a curvilinear relation between creative time pressure and employee creativity (again, following an inverted U-shape), but in addition found that this relation was moderated by openness to experience and support for creativity (from both coworkers and supervisors). More specifically, a curvilinear relation between time pressure and creativity was only obtained for employees high in openness to experience who also perceived high support for creativity. Apparently, these employees were able to convert their task engagement and arousal (resulting from intermediate levels of time pressure) into creative behaviors, while employees low in openness to experience and those not receiving support for creativity were unwilling or unable to do so.

It therefore seems that time pressure does not necessarily undermine (epistemic) motivation, but may instead lead to task engagement and optimal levels of arousal if time pressure is moderate rather than low or extremely high. Furthermore, it may be the case that especially those individuals who are willing and able to be creative benefit from moderate levels of time pressure. One hypothesis would be that moderate time pressure will only relate to creative performance if people engage in flexible thinking. Indeed, employing the persistence pathway under time pressure may be ill-advised, because this pathway by definition takes more time to arrive at creative responses.

CONCLUSIONS AND PRACTICAL IMPLICATIONS

In this chapter we reviewed classic and contemporary work on the role of mood and motivation in creativity. Our guiding principle was the Dual Pathway to Creativity Model (DPCM), and throughout we related findings to this theoretical perspective. In this concluding section we first of all summarize these insights. We then elaborate upon possible practical implications of the research findings of the emotive roots of creativity.

Theoretical Integration and Practical Implications

Research on emotive roots of creativity has been relatively disconnected, with some researchers focusing on moods and others on motives. Within mood research, most studies focused on positive versus negative moods, with explanations being cast in terms of the mood's hedonic tone. In our own work we showed that the mood's hedonic tone indeed matters for the way creative performance comes about—through flexible thinking in the case of positive tone, and persistent activity in the case of negative tone. But what matters most is whether moods activate and engage the individual, because without engagement no effects on creativity emerge whatsoever (Baas et al., 2008; De Dreu et al., 2008a). And this conclusion resonates with much of the work on motivation. That is, engagement is likely to be higher when the task is intrinsically motivating (Amabile, 1996), when specific, targeted rewards for being creative are offered (Eisenberger & Rhoades, 2001), or when challenging goals for creative performance are being set (Shalley, 1991). And all these motivating factors have indeed been related to improved creative performance, sometimes because of enhanced cognitive flexibility (e.g., under intrinsic motivation), sometimes because of enhanced persistence (e.g., under extrinsic motivation, and with challenging goals).

Whereas DPCM thus offers a parsimonious framework to both understand which moods and motives influence creativity, and why, it cannot be simply applied to understand research findings on motivational orientations—whether the individual has an approach or an avoidance orientation, a performance instead of learning goal, and so on. What matters, first of all, is whether the motivational orientation in and of itself engages and activates the individual. Thus, approach orientation engages more generally, whereas avoidance orientation engages especially when specific (threatening) goals are activated (Baas et al., 2009). Second, what seems to matter is the "fit" between the motivational orientation and some exogenous variable—when a learning orientation emerges in a environment where making errors is accepted and experimentation is welcomed, the individual may experience "fit" related engagement, which turns into elevated creative performance (De Dreu et al., 2011a).

The above reveals that DPCM offers a perspective on creativity that allows us to incorporate, integrate, and understand the effects of different moods, motivations, and motivational orientations. DPCM also allows us to see where, and why, certain creativity-enhancing interventions may be introduced. For example, as we noted at the outset, many managers and organizational leaders believe employees should feel relaxed and positive, distracted from their day-to-day hassles, and free to explore and venture out into the great wide open (e.g., Elsbach & Hargadon, 2006; Mainemelis & Ronson, 2006). Our review shows such beliefs are ill-informed and mislead organizational practice. Organizational leaders spent tremendous amounts of money to create "relaxation rooms" stuffed with cushions and fancy design, thus hoping to stimulate employee creativity. It is burnt money, as creativity does not come about when people are relaxed, and free-floating. Creativity is a function of challenging goals, which are accepted and engage the individual. It comes about when people are activated and focused on their tasks either because they feel happy and excited, or because they feel frustrated and annoyed—either way (albeit through different mechanisms) they are more creative than when they sink into deep fluffy cushions in some fancy relaxation room, where their mind wanders away only to return to reality when closing time arrives. It may feel great to disengage, and it may be good for your health, but it won't make you more creative.

The question of how to stimulate employees to be creative thus largely is a question of how to create task engagement. As argued by other organizational researchers (Woodman, Sawyer, & Griffin, 1993), creating task engagement and creativity requires taking both the organizational context and the individual into account. Some people (e.g., those high in openness to experience) may be stimulated to be creative by creating moderate amounts of time pressure (Baer & Oldham, 2006), because they are able to convert the activation and arousal associated with time pressure to higher levels of creativity. Others (e.g., those high in conscientiousness, or those high in personal need for structure) may dislike ambiguity and prefer structured tasks; these individuals may therefore be stimulated more when asked to perform highly structured tasks with minimal levels of ambiguity (cf. George & Zhou, 2001; Ohly et al., 2006). These same individuals may actually stifle when given much autonomy, while autonomy is often cited as an important contextual facilitator of creativity (e.g., Amabile & Gryskiewicz, 1989; Zhou, 1998). In short, contextual variables need to fit with the employee's personality to create task engagement, activation, and concomitant high levels of creativity.

Concluding Thoughts

We do not doubt that occasionally a flash of insight or a particularly creative idea may occur while riding a bus, sitting in the bathtub, or letting one's mind wander in a relaxation room. However, we do argue that this is more likely to happen when being activated and engaged, rather than relaxed and disengaged. Creativity may come about with a smile on one's face, through intrinsic motivation, and flexible processing, but it may also come about with a frown on one's face, to achieve external rewards and praise, and through persistent and systematic processing.

References

Amabile, T. M. (1979). Effects of external evaluation on artistic creativity. *Journal of Personality and Social Psychology, 37*, 221–233.

Amabile, T. M. (1996). *Creativity in context: update to the social psychology of creativity.* Boulder, CO: Westview.

Amabile, T. M., Conti, R., Coon, H., Lazenby, J., & Herron, M. (1996). Assessing the work environment for creativity. *Academy of Management Journal, 39*, 1154–1184.

Amabile, T. M., & Gryskiewicz, N. D. (1989). The creative environment scales: Work environment inventory. *Creativity Research Journal, 2*, 231–252.

Ambady, N., & Gray, H. M. (2002). On being sad and mistaken: Mood effects on the accuracy of thin-slice judgments. *Journal of Personality and Social Psychology, 83*, 947–961.

Ambrose, M. L., & Kulik, C. T. (1999). Old friends, new faces: Motivation research in the 1990s. *Journal of Management, 25*, 231–292.

Andrews, F., & Farris, G. F. (1972). Time pressure and performance of scientists and engineers: A five-year panel study. *Organizational Behavior and Human Performance, 8*, 185–200.

Andrews, J., & Smith, D. C. (1996). In search of the marketing imagination: Factors affecting the creativity of marketing programs for mature products. *Journal of Marketing Research, 33*, 174–187.

Baas, M., De Dreu, C. K. W., & Nijstad, B. A. (2008). A meta-analysis of 25 years of mood-creativity research: Hedonic tone, activation, or regulatory focus? *Psychological Bulletin, 134*, 779–805.

Baas, M., De Dreu, C. K. W., & Nijstad, B. A. (2011). When prevention focus promotes creativity: The role of Mood, regulatory focus, and regulatory closure. *Journal of Personality and Social Psychology, 100*, 794–809.

Baer, M., & Frese, M. (2003). Innovation is not enough: Climates for initiative and psychological safety, process innovations, and firm performance. *Journal of Organizational Behavior, 24*, 45–69.

Baer, M., & Oldham, G. R. (2006). The curvilinear relation between experienced creative time pressure and creativity: Moderating effects of openness to experience and support for creativity. *Journal of Applied Psychology, 91*, 963–970.

Bailyn, L. (1985). Autonomy in the industrial R&D laboratory. *Human Resource Management, 24*, 129–146.

Boden, M. A. (1998). Creativity and artificial intelligence. *Artificial Intelligence, 103*, 347–356.

Bransford, J. D., & Stein, B. S. (1984). *The ideal problem solver.* New York, NY: Freeman.

Butler, A. B., Scherer, L., & Reiter-Palmon, R. (2003). Effects of solution elicitation aids and need for cognition on the generation of solutions to ill-structured problems. *Creativity Research Journal, 15*, 235–244.

Cameron, J., & Pierce, W. D. (1994). Reinforcement, reward, and intrinsic motivation: A meta-analysis. *Review of Educational Research, 64*, 342–363.

Carnevale, P. J. D., & Probst, T. M. (1998). Social values and social conflict in creative problem solving and categorization. *Journal of Personality and Social Psychology, 74*, 1300–1309.

Carson, S. H., Peterson, J. B., & Higgins, D. M. (2003). Decreased latent inhibition is associated with increased creative achievement in high-functioning individuals. *Journal of Personality and Social Psychology, 85*, 499–506.

Carver, C. S. (2004). Negative affects deriving from the behavioral approach system. *Emotion, 4*, 3–22.

Carver, C. S., & White, T. L. (1994). Behavioral inhibition, behavioral activation, and affective responses to impending reward and punishment: The BIS/BAS Scales. *Journal of Personality and Social Psychology, 67*, 319–333.

Cretenet, J., & Dru, V. (2009). Influence of peripheral and motivational cues on rigid–flexible functioning: Perceptual, behavioral, and cognitive aspects. *Journal of Experimental Psychology: General, 138*, 201–217.

Cummings, L. L. (1965). Organizational climates for creativity. *Journal of the Academy of Management, 3*, 220–227.

Csikszentmihályi, M. (1996). *Creativity: Flow and the psychology of discovery and invention.* Boston, MA: Harper Collins.

De Dreu, C. K. W., Baas, M., & Nijstad, B. A. (2008). Hedonic tone and activation level in the mood–creativity link: Toward a dual pathway to creativity model. *Journal of Personality and Social Psychology, 94*, 739–756.

De Dreu, C. K. W., & Nijstad, B. A. (2008). Mental set and creative thought in social conflict: Threat rigidity versus motivated focus. *Journal of Personality and Social Psychology, 95*, 648–661.

De Dreu, C. K. W., Nijstad, B. A., & Baas, M. (2011a). Behavioral activation links to creativity because of increased cognitive flexibility. *Social Psychology and Personality Science, 2,* 72–80.

De Dreu, C. K. W., Nijstad, B. A., Bechtoldt, M. N., & Baas, M. (2011b). Group creativity and innovation: A motivated information processing perspective. *Psychology of Aesthetics, Creativity, and the Arts, 5,* 81–89.

De Dreu, C. K. W., Nijstad, B. A., & Van Knippenberg, D. (2008). Motivated information processing in group judgment and decision making. *Personality and Social Psychology Review, 12,* 22–49.

De Vet, A. J., & De Dreu, C. K. W. (2007). The influence of articulation, self-monitoring ability, and sensitivity to others on creativity. *European Journal of Social Psychology, 37,* 747–760.

De Vries, M., Holland, R. W., & Witteman, C. L. M. (2008). Fitting decisions: Mood and intuitive versus deliberative decision strategies. *Cognition and Emotion, 22,* 931–943.

Deci, E. L., Koestner, R., & Ryan, R. M. (1999). A meta-analytic review of experiments examining the effects of extrinsic rewards on intrinsic motivation. *Psychological Bulletin, 125,* 627–668.

Deci, E. L., & Ryan, R. M. (1985). *Intrinsic motivation and self-determination in human behavior.* New York, NY: Plenum.

Derryberry, D., & Reed, M. A. (1998). Anxiety and attentional focusing: Trait, state, and hemispheric influences. *Personality and Individual Differences, 25,* 745–761.

Dietrich, A. (2004). The cognitive neuroscience of creativity. *Psychonomic Bulletin & Review, 11,* 1011–1026.

Dollinger, S. J. (2007). Creativity and conservatism. *Personality and Individual Differences, 43,* 1025–1035.

Dreisbach, G., & Goschke, T. (2004). How positive affect modulates cognitive control: Reduced perseveration at the cost of increased distractibility. *Journal of Experimental Psychology: Learning, Memory, and Cognition, 30,* 343–353.

Dweck, C. S., & Leggett, E. L. (1988). A social-cognitive approach to motivation and personality. *Psychological Review, 95,* 256–273.

Eisenberger, R., & Armeli, S. (1997). Can salient reward increase creative performance without reducing intrinsic creative interest? *Journal of Personality and Social Psychology, 72,* 652–663.

Eisenberger, R., & Aselage, J. (2009). Incremental effects of reward on experienced performance pressure: Positive outcomes for intrinsic interest and creativity. *Journal of Organizational Behavior, 30,* 95–117.

Eisenberger, R., & Rhoades, L. (2001). Incremental effects of reward on creativity. *Journal of Personality and Social Psychology, 81,* 728–741.

Elliot, A. J. (1999). Approach and avoidance motivation and achievement goals. *Educational Psychologist, 34,* 169–189.

Elliot, A. J., & Thrash, T. M. (2002). Approach-avoidance motivation in personality: Approach and avoidance temperaments and goals. *Journal of Personality and Social Psychology, 82,* 804–818.

Elsbach, K. D., & Hargadon, A. B. (2006). Enhancing creativity through "mindless" work: A framework of workday design. *Organization Science, 17,* 470–483.

Feist, G. J. (1998). A meta-analysis of the impact of personality on scientific and artistic creativity. *Personality and Social Psychology Review, 2,* 290–309.

Fodor, E. M., & Carver, R. A. (2000). Achievement and power motives, performance feedback, and creativity. *Journal of Research in Personality, 34,* 380–396.

Förster, J., Friedman, R. S., & Liberman, N. (2004). Temporal construal effects on abstract and concrete thinking: Consequences for insight and creative cognition. *Journal of Personality and Social Psychology, 87,* 177–189.

Förster, J., Friedman, R. S., Özelsel, A., & Denzler, M. (2006). Enactment of approach and avoidance behavior influences the scope of perceptual and conceptual attention. *Journal of Experimental Social Psychology, 42,* 133–146.

Förster, J., & Higgins, E. T. (2005). How global vs. local processing fits regulatory focus. *Psychological Science, 16,* 631–636.

Fredrickson, B. L., & Branigan, C. (2005). Positive emotions broaden the scope of attention and thought–action repertoires. *Cognition and Emotion, 19,* 313–332.

Friedman, R. S., & Förster, J. (2000). The effects of approach and avoidance motor actions on the elements of creative insight. *Journal of Personality and Social Psychology, 79,* 477–492.

Friedman, R. S., & Förster, J. (2001). The effects of promotion and prevention cues on creativity. *Journal of Personality and Social Psychology, 81,* 1001–1013.

Frijda, N. H. (1993). Moods, emotion episodes, and emotions. In M. Lewis & J. M. Haviland (Eds.), *Handbook of emotions* (pp. 381–403). New York, NY: Guilford.

Furnham, A., & Bachtiar, V. (2008). Personality and intelligence as predictors of creativity. *Personality and Individual Differences, 45,* 613–617.

Gardner, D. G. (1986). Activation theory and task design: An empirical test of several new predictions. *Journal of Applied Psychology, 71,* 411–418.

George, J. M., & Zhou, J. (2001). When openness to experience and conscientiousness are related to creative behavior: An interactional approach. *Journal of Applied Psychology, 86*, 513–524.

George, J. M., & Zhou, J. (2007). Dual tuning in a supportive context: Joint contributions of positive mood, negative mood, and supervisory behaviors to employee creativity. *Academy of Management Journal, 50*, 605–622.

Gilson, L. L., & Shalley, C. E. (2004). A little creativity goes a long way: An examination of teams' engagement in creative processes. *Journal of Management, 30*, 453–470.

Gough, H. G. (1979). A creative personality scale for the Adjective Check List. *Journal of Personality and Social Psychology, 37*, 1398–1405.

Griskevicius, V., Cialdini, R. B., & Kenrick, D. T. (2006). Peacocks, Picasso, and parental investment: The effects of romantic motives on creativity. *Journal of Personality and Social Psychology, 91*, 52–66.

Guilford, J. P. (1967). *The nature of human intelligence*. New York, NY: McGraw-Hill.

Higgins, E. T. (2000). Making a good decision: Value from fit. *American Psychologist, 55*, 1217–1233.

Higgins, E. T. (2006). Value from hedonic experience and engagement. *Psychological Review, 113*, 439–460.

Hirst, G., van Knippenberg, D., & Zhou, J. (2009). A multi-level perspective on employee creativity: Goal orientation, team learning behavior, and individual creativity. *The Academy of Management Journal, 52*, 280–293.

Hirt, E. R., Devers, E. E., & McCrea, S. M. (2008). I want to be creative: Exploring the role of hedonic contingency theory in the positive mood-cognitive flexibility link. *Journal of Personality and Social Psychology, 94*, 214–230.

Hirt, E. R., Melton, R. J., McDonald, H. E., & Harackiewicz, J. M. (1996). Processing goals, task interest, and the mood–performance relationship: A mediational analysis. *Journal of Personality and Social Psychology, 71*, 245–261.

Hunter, S. T., Bedell, K. E., & Mumford, M. D. (2007). Climate for creativity: A quantitative review. *Creativity Research Journal, 19*, 69–90.

Ip, G. W. M., Chen, J., & Chiu, C. Y. (2006). The relationship of promotion focus, need for cognitive closure, and categorical accessibility in American and Hong Kong Chinese university students. *Journal of Creative Behavior, 40*, 201–215.

Janssen, O. (2001). Fairness perceptions as a moderator in the curvilinear relationship between job demands, and job performance and job satisfaction. *Academy of Management Journal, 44*, 1039–1050.

Janssen, O., & Van Yperen, N. W. (2004). Employees' goal orientations, the quality of leader-member exchange, and the outcomes of job performance and job satisfaction. *Academy of Management Journal, 47*, 368–384.

Keller, J., & Bless, H. (2008). Flow and regulatory compatibility: An experimental test of the flow model of intrinsic motivation. *Personality and Social Psychology Bulletin, 34*, 196–209.

Klein, H. J., Wesson, M. J., Hollenbeck, J. R., & Alge, B. J. (1999). Goal commitment and the goal setting process: Conceptual clarification and empirical synthesis. *Journal of Applied Psychology, 84*, 885–896.

Koch, S., Holland, R. W., Hengstler, M., & Van Knippenberg, A. (2009). Body locomotion as regulatory process: Stepping backward enhances cognitive control. *Psychological Science, 20*, 549–550.

Kruglanski, A. W. (2004). *The psychology of closed mindedness*. New York, NY: Psychology Press.

Kruglanski, A. W., & Webster, D. M. (1996). Motivated closing of the mind: "Seizing and "freezing". *Psychological Review, 103*, 263–283.

Latham, G. P., Erez, M., & Locke, E. A. (1988). Resolving scientific disputes by the joint design of crucial experiments by the antagonists: Application to the Erez-Latham dispute regarding participation in goal setting. *Journal of Applied Psychology, 73*, 753–772.

Lazarus, R. S. (1991). *Emotion and adaptation*. Oxford University Press.

Leung, A. K. Y., Maddux, W. W., Galinsky, A. D., & Chiu, C. Y. (2008). Multicultural experience enhances creativity: The when and how. *American Psychologist, 63*, 169–181.

Litchfield, R. C. (2008). Brainstorming reconsidered: A goal-based view. *Academy of Management Review, 33*, 649–668.

Locke, E. A., & Latham, G. P. (1990). *A theory of goal-setting and task performance*. Englewood Cliffs, NJ: Prentice-Hall.

Mainemelis, C., & Ronson, S. (2006). Ideas are born in fields of play: Towards a theory of play and creativity in organizational settings. *Research on Organizational Behavior, 27*, 81–131.

Martin, L. L., & Stoner, P. (1996). Mood as input: What we think about how we feel determines how we think. In L. L. Martin & A. Tesser (Eds.), *Striving and feeling: Interactions among goals, affect, and selfregulation* (pp. 279–301). Mahwah, NJ: Erlbaum.

Martindale, C. (1999). The biological basis of creativity. In R. J. Sternberg (Ed.), *Handbook of creativity* (pp. 137–152). Cambridge, UK: Cambridge University Press.

Mayseless, O., & Kruglanski, A. W. (1987). What makes you so sure? Effects of epistemic motivation on judgmental confidence. *Organizational Behavior and Human Decision Processes, 39*, 162–183.

McClelland, D. C. (1961). *The achieving society*. Princeton, NJ: Van Nostrand.

McCrae, R. R. (1987). Creativity, divergent thinking, and openness to experience. *Journal of Personality and Social Psychology, 52,* 1258–1265.

Mednick, S. A. (1962). The associative basis of the creative process. *Psychological Review, 69,* 220–232.

Mehta, R., & Zhu, R. J. (2009). Blue or red? Exploring the effect of color on cognitive task performances. *Science, 323,* 1226–1229.

Miller, G. F. (2000). *The mating mind: How sexual choice shaped the evolution of human nature*. New York, NY: Doubleday.

Mook, D. G. (1987). *Motivation: The organisation of action*. New York, NY: Norton.

Mumford, M. D. (2003). Where have we been, where are we going? Taking stock of creativity research. *Creativity Research Journal, 15,* 107–120.

Mumford, M. D., & Gustafson, S. B. (1988). Creativity syndrome: Integration, application, and innovation. *Psychological Bulletin, 103,* 27–43.

Mumford, M. D., Scott, G. M., Gaddis, B., & Strange, J. M. (2002). Leading creative people: Orchestrating expertise and relationships. *Leadership Quarterly, 13,* 705–750.

Muris, P., De Jong, P. J., & Engelen, S. (2004). Relationships between neuroticism, attentional control, and anxiety disorders symptoms in non-clinical children. *Personality and Individual Differences, 37,* 789–797.

Murray, N., Sujan, H., Hirt, E. R., & Sujan, M. (1990). The influence of mood on categorization: A cognitive flexibility interpretation. *Journal of Personality and Social Psychology, 59,* 411–425.

Neuberg, S. L., & Newsom, J. (1993). Personal need for structure: Individual differences in the desire for simple structure. *Journal of Personality and Social Psychology, 65,* 113–131.

Newell, A., & Simon, H. A. (1972). *Human problem solving*. Englewood Cliffs, NJ: Prentice Hall.

Nijstad, B. A., De Dreu, C. K. W., Rietzschel, E. F., & Baas, M. (2010). The Dual-Pathway to Creativity model: Creative ideation as a function of flexibility and persistence. In W. Stroebe & M. Hewstone (Eds.), *European review of social psychology*. (Vol. 21, pp 34–77). London, UK: Psychology Press.

Nijstad, B. A., & Stroebe, W. (2006). How the group affects the mind: A cognitive model of idea generation in groups. *Personality and Social Psychology Review, 10,* 186–213.

Nijstad, B. A., Stroebe, W., & Lodewijkx, H. F. M. (2002). Cognitive stimulation and interference in groups: Exposure effects in an idea generation task. *Journal of Experimental Social Psychology, 38,* 535–544.

Nijstad, B. A., Stroebe, W., & Lodewijkx, H. F. M. (2003). Production blocking and idea generation: Does blocking interfere with cognitive processes? *Journal of Experimental Social Psychology, 39,* 531–548.

Ohly, S., Sonnentag, S., & Pluntke, F. (2006). Routinization, work characteristics and their relationships with creative and proactive behaviors. *Journal of Organizational Behavior, 27,* 257–279.

Oldham, G. R., & Cummings, A. (1996). Employee creativity: Personal and contextual factors. *Academy of Management Journal, 39,* 607–634.

Osborn, A. F. (1957). *Applied imagination* (2nd ed.). New York, NY: Scribner's.

Paulus, P. B., & Dzindolet, M. T. (1993). Social influence processes in group brainstorming. *Journal of Personality and Social Psychology, 64,* 575–586.

Perry-Smith, J. E., & Shalley, C. E. (2003). The social side of creativity: A static and dynamic social network perspective. *Academy of Management Review, 28,* 89–106.

Peterson, J. B., Smith, K. W., & Carson, S. (2002). Openness and extraversion are associated with reduced latent inhibition: Replication and commentary. *Personality and Individual Differences, 33,* 1137–1147.

Petty, R. E., & Cacioppo, J. T. (1986). The elaboration likelihood model of persuasion. In L. Berkowitz (Ed.), *Advances in Experimental Social Psychology* (Vol. 19), pp. 123–205. New York, NY: Academic Press.

Prabhu, V., Sutton, C., & Sauser, W. (2008). Creativity and certain personality traits: Understanding the mediating role of intrinsic motivation. *Creativity Research Journal, 20,* 53–66.

Rietzschel, E. F., De Dreu, C. K. W., & Nijstad, B. A. (2007). Need for structure and creative performance: The moderating role of Fear of Invalidity. *Personality and Social Psychology Bulletin, 33,* 855–866.

Rietzschel, E. F., De Dreu, C. K. W., & Nijstad, B. A. (2009). What are we talking about when we talk about creativity? Group creativity as a multifaceted, multistage phenomenon. In E. A. Mannix, M. A. Neale & J. A. Goncalo (Eds.), *Creativity in groups* (pp. 1–27). Bingley, UK: Emerald.

Rietzschel, E. F., Nijstad, B. A., & Stroebe, W. (2007). The effects of knowledge activation on the quantity and quality of ideas. *Journal of Experimental Social Psychology, 43,* 933–946.

Robinson, M. D., Meier, B. P., Tamir, M., Wilkowski, B. M., & Ode, S. (2009). Behavioral facilitation: A cognitive model of individual differences in approach motivation. *Emotion, 9,* 70–82.

B. INDIVIDUAL LEVEL INFLUENCES

Rubinstein, G. (2003). Authoritarianism and its relation to creativity: A comparative study among students of design, behavioral sciences and law. *Personality and Individual Differences, 34,* 695–705.

Runco, M. A. (2004). Creativity. *Annual Review of Psychology, 55,* 657–687.

Russell, J. A., & Barrett, L. F. (1999). Core affect, prototypical emotional episodes, and other things called emotion: Dissecting the elephant. *Journal of Personality and Social Psychology, 76,* 805–819.

Schooler, J. W., Ohlsson, S., & Brooks, K. (1993). Thoughts beyond words: When language overshadows insight. *Journal of Experimental Psychology: General, 122,* 166–183.

Schwarz, N., & Clore, G. L. (2007). Feelings and phenomenal experiences. In E. T. Higgins & A. Kruglanski (Eds.), *Social psychology. A handbook of basic principles* (2nd Ed.) (pp. 385–407). New York, NY: Guilford Press.

Shalley, C. E. (1991). Effects of productivity goals, creativity goals, and personal discretion on individual creativity. *Journal of Applied Psychology, 76,* 179–185.

Shalley, C. E. (1995). Effects of coaction, expected evaluation, and goal setting on creativity and productivity. *Academy of Management Journal, 38,* 483–503.

Shalley, C., Zhou, J., & Oldham, G. (2004). The effects of personal and contextual characteristics on creativity: Where should we go from here? *Journal of Management, 30,* 933–958.

Simonton, D. K. (1997). Creative productivity: A predictive and explanatory model of career trajectories and landmarks. *Psychological Review, 104,* 66–89.

Smith, S. M., & Blankenship, S. E. (1991). Incubation and the persistence of fixation in problem solving. *The American Journal of Psychology, 104,* 61–87.

Somech, A. (2006). The effects of leadership style and team processes on performance and innovation in functionally heterogeneous teams. *Journal of Management, 32,* 132–157.

Staw, B. M., Sandelands, L. E., & Dutton, J. E. (1981). Threat-rigidity effects in organizational behavior: A multilevel analysis. *Administrative Science Quarterly, 26,* 501–524.

Tellis, G. J., Prabhu, J. C., & Chandy, R. K. (2009). Radical innovation across nations: The pre-eminence of corporate culture. *Journal of Marketing, 73,* 3–23.

Tetlock, P. E. (1992). The impact of accountability on judgment and choice: Toward a social contingency model. In L. Berkowitz (Ed.), *Advances in Experimental Social Psychology* (Vol. 25) (pp. 331–376). New York, NY: Academic Press.

Thompson, M. M., Naccarato, M. E., Parker, K. C. H., & Moskowitz, G. B. (2001). The personal need for structure and personal fear of invalidity measures: Historical perspectives, current applications, and future directions. In G. B. Moskowitz (Ed.), *Cognitive social psychology: The Princeton symposium on the legacy and future of social cognition* (pp. 19–39). Mahwah, NJ: Erlbaum.

Torrance, E. P. (1966). *Torrance tests of creativity*. Princeton, NJ: Personnel Press.

Utman, C. H. (1997). Performance effects of motivational state: A meta-analysis. *Personality and Social Psychology Review, 1,* 170–182.

Van de Walle, D. M. (1997). Development and validation of a work domain achievement goals instrument. *Educational and Psychological Measurement, 8,* 995–1015.

Watson, D., Clark, L. A., & Tellegen, A. (1988). Development and validation of brief measures of positive and negative affect: The PANAS scales. *Journal of Personality and Social Psychology, 54,* 1063–1070.

Webster, D., & Kruglanski, A. W. (1994). Individual differences in need for cognitive closure. *Journal of Personality and Social Psychology, 67,* 1049–1062.

Worthy, D. A., Maddox, W. T., & Markman, A. B. (2007). Regulatory fit effects in a choice task. *Psychonomic Bulletin & Review, 14,* 1125–1132.

Zhou, J. (1998). Feedback valence, feedback style, task autonomy, and achievement orientation: Interactive effects on creative performance. *Journal of Applied Psychology, 83,* 261–276.

Zhou, J. (2003). When the presence of creative coworkers is related to creativity: Role of supervisor close monitoring, developmental feedback, and creative personality. *Journal of Applied Psychology, 88,* 413–422.

Personality

Eva V. Hoff, Ingegerd M. Carlsson, and Gudmund J.W. Smith

Lund University, Lund, Sweden

The ultimate origin of the concept of personality was traced by Gordon Allport (1937) to *persona*, the mask whereby the actor tried to depict a role in the ancient Roman theatre. Of more immediate interest to contemporary readers are probably the applications of personality among 19th and early 20th century psychiatrists (Charcot; Janet, 1927) and psychologists (Ribot, 1885), the true pioneers in the field. When it comes to defining personality a particularly important place should be reserved for the German philosopher and psychologist William Stern (1938) and his theory of *critical personalism.* For Stern, personality should be treated as a superordinate concept, a *unitas multiplex,* not as a unit beside other equivalent units like perception or emotion.

In order to understand what personality means to most students in the field, one might again turn to Allport (1937). The basic elements in his description of what characterizes personality are *traits.* Trait psychology has remained one fundamental theory, not only for laypersons but within scientific psychology as well. There are several influential trait theorists; today the most used trait model is Paul Costa and Robert McCrae's five-factor model to be discussed in this chapter as a part of a descriptive approach.

Besides the descriptive approach, personality scholars also need to understand the processes "behind" what shows on the surface of personality. The psychoanalytic pioneers Sigmund Freud (1905/1953) and Anna Freud (1936/1961) provided a theoretic base for several questions including what motivates a person and what the drives are behind different personality types. How personality develops is another important question. The dynamic-process approach highlights these aspects of personality, and is discussed in this chapter exemplified by both the psychodynamic theory and a more recent process approach to personality called the percept-genetic model of personality.

Yet another question is to what extent nature or nurture influences personality. The trait perspective argues for a biologically predisposed personality, whereas the social approach regards environmental influences on personality as decisive. The social approach will be represented by the behaviorist and social-cognitive approaches in this chapter. Among

Handbook of Organizational Creativity.
DOI: 10.1016/B978-0-12-374714-3.00011-2

pioneer behaviorists, Burrhus Skinner (1971) and John Watson (1924) may be mentioned, and among the advocates for the Social–Cognitive Approach, Albert Bandura (1997) and Walter Mischel (Bandura & Mischel, 1965; Mischel & Shoda, 2008) are influential.

Before going into the different theories, we need to consider what should be demanded of any theory. Pervin & Cervone (2010) stated that theory should:

1. use scientific methods referring to the use of instruments that produce valid results,
2. be systematic in the sense that not only good descriptions should be obtained but also predictions and explanations, and
3. be comprehensive so that it covers all psychologically significant aspects of persons.

We will discuss to what extent these demands are met by different theories of personality.

Psychological theories may, depending on their perspective, be divided into different classes. In this chapter we have chosen the headings *Descriptive Trait Approach; Dynamic Process Approach;* and *Social-Cognitive and Learning Approach.*

THE DESCRIPTIVE TRAIT APPROACH

Trait words are the natural units in personality descriptions. They were introduced into psychology by Allport (1937) and later adopted by Cattell (1965; 1979) who was also a pioneer in the systematic measurement of traits, soon followed in Europe by Eysenck (1970). Traits capture a person's typical behavior, and thus describe what a person is generally like. As an example of a definition of traits, we take one from a personality textbook (Pervin & Cervone, 2010):

"Personality traits refer to consistent patterns in the way individuals behave, feel, and think" *(p. 228).*

In most definitions, both consistency and distinctiveness are present. Traits indicate regularity in the person's behavior, so that he or she is predisposed to act in the way described by the traits (consistency) and these features also make the person distinct compared to others (distinctiveness).

The enormous variety of traits, or trait names in use have tempted scholars of personality to construct typological schemata—sometimes termed superfactors—of which the most popular include both psychological traits and somatic attributes. These sets of traits are purported to be universal, in the sense that everyone would have them to a greater or lesser degree. Most trait theorists rely on self-report questionnaires and different kinds of multivariate statistical techniques to capture the traits. Factor analysis is the dominating statistical tool.

Cattell (1979) found 16 factors necessary for a complete description of personality. Despite Cattell's conviction that the 16-factor range was necessary, many of his followers tried to construct a simpler and more general theory, since it is difficult to track such a large number of traits. Eysenck (1990) was of the opinion that only three factors were enough; emotional stability/instability (or neuroticism), extraversion/introversion and psychoticism, the latter implying aggressiveness and antisocial behavioral tendencies. These three superfactors were discerned from secondary factor analyses and were statistically independent. However, soon Costa and McCrae (1992) appeared on the scene as champions of a five-factor model, baptized *The Big Five* by Goldberg (1990). Factor analysis now seemed to provide a firm and objective base for a five-factor model of personality. The five super-ordinate factors were named openness, conscientiousness, extraversion, agreeableness, and neuroticism (OCEAN). Different questionnaires have been developed by five-factor researchers to measure the factors: Goldberg's (1992) instrument is named the Transparent Bipolar Inventory (see Table 11.1) and Costa and McCrae's the NEO-PI-R (1992).

Descriptions of personality traits (may it be factors of traits or not) as a base for a science of personality is, however, not sufficient. Severe criticism has been directed towards the five-factor model (Block, 1995). According to Block, factor analysis is far from the reliable foundation for

TABLE 11.1   The Big-Five Factors and Examples of Underlying Traits (from Goldberg, 1992).

Main factor	Traits
Introversion versus Extroversion:	Unenergetic–energetic
	Silent–talkative
	Timid–bold
	Unassertive–assertive
	Unadventurous–adventurous
Antagonism versus Agreeableness:	Cold–warm
	Uncooperative–cooperative
	Selfish–unselfish
	Distrustful–trustful
	Stingy–generous
Lack of direction versus Conscientiousness	Disorganized–organized
	Irresponsible–responsible
	Impractical–practical
	Careless–thorough
	Lazy–hardworking
Emotional stability versus Neuroticism	Tense–relaxed
	Nervous–at ease
	Unstable–stable
	Discontented–contented
	Emotional–unemotional
Closedness versus Openness to experience	Unreflective–reflective
	Unanalytical–analytical
	Uninquisitive–curious
	Unimaginative–imaginative
	Uncreative–creative

B. INDIVIDUAL LEVEL INFLUENCES

the five-factor model that its followers purported. It could easily be manipulated, for example, by prestructuring or by clever choice of descriptive adjectives. Furthermore, other scholars have argued that the factors are not statistically independent, and that many trait items in fact load high on several of the factors (Bäckström, Larsson, & Maddux, 2009). Still, the strengths of the empirical basis of the five-factor model should not be unrecognized. Consensus is often high between raters and across various rating methods.

Block's conclusions after his critical scrutiny remained negative though:

> "After many years of research and measure development there still appears to be marked deviation empirically from the posited orthogonal five-factor structure" (p. 206).

He further stated:

> "The faith of the five factor adherents…that the field of personality psychology can confidently rely on the factor analytic paradigm as an appropriate and sufficient basis for objective deciding on the theoretical constructs to be used by personologists is in my view unwarranted, naïve, and limiting" (p.191).

McCrae and Costa (2008) have fought back vigorously. They have argued that the five-factor personality structure is a human universal. One argument they used was the fundamental lexical hypothesis, meaning that the most important individual differences in human behavior will be encoded in some of the world's languages, and the fact that the same trait dimensions appear in many different languages is a proof of the structure's universality. However, even when supported by an elaborate illustration of the theoretical substance of the five-factor model, their defense is not watertight. Researchers that did not translate the items from the English version have come to other conclusions. Di Blas and Forzi (1999; others too e.g., de Raad & Peabody, 2005) investigated whether the five-factor structure would appear when indigenous Italian concepts (not translated English items) were used, but only three of them (extraversion, agreeableness and conscientiousness) did so.

In order to make trait theory move from mere description to explanation, trait theorists have attempted to identify biological factors which underlie different traits. People with high or low assessments on a specific trait are believed to differ systematically in their neural or biochemical systems (De Fruyt, Wiele, & van Heeringen, 2000; Eysenck, 1990). Of Eysenck's three factors, extraversion/introversion is the factor for which most convincing evidence of biological differences has been found. Introverts are for instance believed to be more easily cortically aroused from outside events. Intense social interaction makes them over-aroused—a negative state they want to avoid. McCrae and Costa (2008) also treat the trait as something that truly exists. It is seen as a personality structure that everyone possesses. It is purported to be determined by genetic influences on neural structures and brain chemistry. The biological basis is considered so strong that it is more or less independent of environmental influences (McCrae et al., 2000). Little scientific evidence has been presented so far, though, for this assumption. The fact that personality changes between different decades in modern history (Bandura, 2006; Twenge, 2000, 2001) is but one argument against Costa and McCrae's position.

The major tools in this kind of research—self-report questionnaires—have obvious disadvantages. Besides the risk of all-too-positive self-reporting, there is also reason to suspect that implicit aspects of experience are out of sight of the reporter, who is usually bound by explicit aspects (Wolke, 2008). Some people do not have a sound perception of their feelings and anxiety reactions, and will therefore not be able to report them accurately. For example, when measuring stress using physiological indicators (Sonnby-Borgström, 2002; Sonnby-Borgström & Jönsson, 2004: Weinberger & Davidson, 1994; Weinberger, Schwartz & Davidson, 1979), higher anxiety levels have been found for a personality type called "repressor" when compared to what he or she reports verbally on questionnaires. Furthermore, proving a theory by use of factor analysis of measurements is risky. The measurement might not cover all aspects of personality. Some researchers have suggested that morality is a missing factor (see Pervin & Cervone, 2010) and others that openness to hypnosis and supernatural experiences (including religious beliefs and parapsychological phenomena) is an independent factor (Cardena & Terhune, 2008; Cloninger, Skravic, & Przybeck, 1993; Gillespie, Cloninger, Heath, & Martin, 2003).

A last objection is that conceptual circles can easily arise when the causes of behavior and the behavior itself derive from the same concept. The explanation is unsatisfactory that someone is behaving agreeably because she has the trait of agreeableness.

The Trait Theory in the Organizational Context.

In recent years, Big-Five theory has been applied within organizations of different kinds. Conscientiousness especially has been related to reliable performance (though often negatively related to creative performance), but also Agreeableness has been found to be connected, for instance, to success as a salesperson (as related in Kaufmann & Kaufmann, 2005).

To Sum Up

The advantages of the Descriptive Trait Approach and especially the Big Five model is that easily administered, and widely accepted tools for assessing individual differences have been developed—and are used by employers, educators and psychologists. Some evidence for the universality of some of the traits has also been found cross-culturally. However, the five-factor model still remains more a way of describing persons using trait names than a fully systematic and comprehensive theory that also explains behavior satisfactorily. It says little about how personality functions, develops (and changes) and the impact of environment on personality.

Trait or Structure

What term should be used to designate enduring personality characteristics? There is no doubt, to most of us, that trait seems to be a practical designation, and looking at the accumulated research, much is done in the field of trait and personality. However, on second thoughts, it may not be as practical as presumed by advocates of the Descriptive Trait Approach in the investigation of personality. Above all, trait does not fit naturally into the individual's historical context, as is necessary to comprehend how distinctive personality features have come about. The main reason for this is that trait is a static concept, a reified once-and-for-all designation. In the present context we suggest the concept of *structure*, once described by Rapaport (1967) as a process with a slow rate of change, or even as a "standing wave", to use a metaphor from computer terminology. This view of the enduring aspects of personality preserves the connection with process, with change and growth.

THE DYNAMIC PROCESS APPROACH

The Psychodynamic Theory

In order for a theory of personality to be satisfactory, scholars in favor of some other perspectives have argued that descriptions of traits are not enough. There is need for a central organizing principle; a *unitas multiplex* as understood by Stern (1938) as a better way of understanding personality (Smith, 2001). Most personologists with an inclination to use process-oriented or dynamic explanations would also prefer a personality theory to have a historical perspective, a vertical perspective, as well as a process perspective.

In other words, for advocates of a dynamic and process-oriented perspective it is essential to use personal history and unconscious determinants as explanatory factors for individual differences in people's behavior. The prime candidate for inclusion in this domain is of course the psychoanalytic theory. Sjöbäck (1988) maintained that psychoanalysis has always tried to understand human beings in their complex entirety. At the same time, in its isolated existence for a very long time from mainstream academic psychology, psychoanalysis has in many respects become an oddity. This oddness, for one thing, implies that psychoanalytic theory lacks a functional theory of perception, and also that it clings to a mechanistic theory of association. At the same time there are areas where psychoanalysts usually know more than other psychologists, areas that need to be included within the psychology of personality. As we name three of them—*intrapsychic conflict, drive,* and *defense*—we also move them out of the particular enclosure of psychoanalysis and reformulate this field as *psychodynamic theory.* This implies, at the same time, that psychodynamic theory is not seen as being of foremost concern for the clinical domain of psychic illness. In recent years important additions to our understanding of inner motives and wishes have been made by *attachment theory*, formulated by Ainsworth (1967) and Bowlby (1969, 1973) and by *emotion theory*, pioneered by Tomkins (1962).

Intrapsychic drive and conflict. Fundamental to this view of drive and conflict is that the dynamic importance of a mental event depends on its distance from consciousness. In psychodynamic theory, this distance is represented by the main divide in mental life between primary and secondary processes (Freud, 1911/1986). The tension between these processes, between the paralogical dreamlike thinking which characterizes primary process functioning, and the more rational thinking at the level of secondary process functioning, remains a major explanatory factor even within non-psychoanalytic personality theory. As an example, there may be a conflict between our hidden, sometimes forbidden, childish wishes (e.g. to get immediate satisfaction of a childlike wish for attention) and our conscious self-regulatory thinking in different social contexts (to refrain, or wait for the right moment to attract attention). An analogous discrepancy characterizes experiences originating from our early years or later in life. Drives as a source of human motivation have always been exploited as fundamental determinants in personality psychology. Underlying drives can be multifarious; sexuality (Freud, 1905/1953), moods (Baas, DeDreu, & Nijstad, 2008), emotions (Tomkins, 1962), curiosity (Bowlby, 1969, 1973), need for recognition (Kohut, 1971) and close attachments (Bowlby, 1969, 1973).

Defense mechanisms. The concept of defense was an early and fundamental topic in psychodynamic theory, particularly after repression had been split up into more applicable subcomponents (Freud, 1936/1961). As made evident by a recent survey of research in the field (Hentschel, Kiessling, Teubner-Berg, & Dreier et al., 2004) the psychology of defensive processes now belongs to the sphere of everyday psychology, particularly the psychology of personality. We will present some illustrations of how defense mechanisms can be revealed by means of test methods when we continue to present process approaches to personality.

The Process Approach

As a pure approach to personality, the process perspective is relatively novel. It is however based on assumptions formulated in 1920s Germany; but at that time as part of general psychology rather than as a personality concept (for a thorough description of this so-called Aktualgenese, see Draguns, 2008). This early German theory later split into two branches independent of each other, one termed *percept-genesis* and one called *microgenesis* . The latter, microgenetic theory, was formulated by the neurologist Jason Brown using neuro-terminology as his main explanatory vehicle (Brown, 2001, 2008). The former percept-genetic (PG) theory is primarily a psychology of human perception closely connected since the 1950s and 60s with the development of a large variety of experimental methods. In the case of microgenesis, reference should first of all be made to publications by Brown. In the case of percept-genetic theory and methodology we refer to the thorough account edited by Smith and Carlsson (2008).

Both theories refer to the individual's experience or action as dependent on mental, psychological, constructions (representations). These range from very rapid and unconscious (neuro-) psychic processes, to later, visual and verbal preconscious and conscious mental constructions, which are possible to reconstruct by means of special methods. These so-called percept-genetic processes are steered by the stimulus context that is actually present, and at the same time also marked by the individual's personal history. One major experimental method to make the preconscious layers of a person's percept-genesis available for observation implies that a perceptual stimulus is served piecemeal. The testing starts with exposure values well below the consciousness threshold and continues with stepwise, very slowly prolonged exposures. The person is not told that he is in fact only shown one single stimulus, and is asked to report what he/she has seen after each presentation. The individual's series of reports is assumed to mirror a part of his or her total perceptual construction process (this naturally can never be captured in its entirety). What Pachalska and McQueens (2008) have written with special reference to microgenesis might also be used for the percept-genetic model; a mental state becomes manifest as a result of a process that proceeds from depth to surface, which implies that in every mental state there are older and more primitive reactions from which the manifest percepts and behavior emerge. To exemplify this, we might envision our own reactions to certain stimuli. The smell (sight, or taste) of apple cake is connected to positive childhood memories for some and negative ones for others. This will affect our perception of apple cakes during our whole life. In the presence of this stimulus, long before we are aware of having sensed the smell, it has already evoked positive or negative processes (e.g., emotional or defensive) in us depending on our individual experiences. Personality in this process perspective is thus understood as encompassing both childlike, emotion-laden primary process cognitions and well-adapted, reality-oriented, cognitive functions.

It should be noted that even if a person's perceptual processes encompass dense reflections of his or her own personal history, they are usually, and normally, very much abbreviated upon repetition. As demonstrated by laboratory experiments this *habituation* serves our adaptive economy (Smith & Henschel, 2004).

The study of defensive properties. As Freud (1905/1953) saw it, when a forbidden impulse draws near consciousness, anxiety signals are released and defenses activated to prevent the signal from disclosure. Among the defenses, repression long remained the dominating one. Studying the major defenses associated with neuroses, Sandler and Joffe (1965) concluded that they represented general cognitive strategies but were on a functional level corresponding to forbidden impulses:

> "Defenses are part of potentially pathogenic intrapsychic conflict" *(Westerlundh, 2004, p. 91)*.
>
> "From a microgenetic point of view, the fantasy images evoked by the drive are incomplete perceptgeneses /.../ On this view, in principle all defenses that are used against the representatives of impulses can be used against psychic representations of outer stimuli" *(Westerlundh, 2004, p. 98)*.

We will only see what we are ready to see in the exterior world. This principle has been taken advantage of in percept-genetic experimentation, by using subliminal threatening and anxiety-arousing stimulation, that is presumed to activate a person's defenses. It has been found that measurements of the individual defensive structure with such process methods are important diagnostic tools not only in the clinical domain, but also very valuable for selection purposes. During several decades they have been used in the selection of applicants to pilot education in the Swedish air force. Furthermore, systematic laboratory studies with children and teenagers, clinical as well as normal, have made it possible to describe defense mechanisms in a hierarchical manner, from the immature, childlike pole to the more mature levels common in adults (Smith & Carlsson, 1990; see also Vaillant (1993) for a similar conception of the defenses).

Adaptive strategies. Personality differences in adaptive processes can furthermore be shown as individual variations in time patterns needed when the individual tries repeatedly to adapt to a conflicting situation. An example of a test situation in which conflict adaption is measured is the process application and development of the well known Stroop Color Word Test. This so called Serial Color Word Test requires the participant to name the colors of words on several sheets of words printed in incongruent hues (for instance the word red printed with blue letters). By following the process and measuring the time taken to read each successive "chunk" of 20 such color words (in all 500 words), the experimenter is able to follow the adaptive strategy of the participant. The Serial Color Word test has proved to be diagnostically very useful in the clinical field (as accounted in the manual by Smith, Nyman, Hentschel, & Rubino, 2001).

The Dynamic Process Approach in the organizational context. Psychodynamic theory has had a substantial influence in organizational contexts, as related by Kaufmann and Kaufmann (2005). In their book, Kaufmann and Kaufmann describe research done by de Vries and Miller, who discerned five different neurotic leader personalities: the paranoid, the depressive, the dramatic, the compulsive, and finally the schizoid leader. The first leader personality, the paranoid leader is often hypersensitive, on guard and prone to attack and punish.

This organization is characterized by hostility and destructive competition. The depressive leader is dominated by feelings of worthlessness and incompetence in his or her leader role, and tends not to take responsibility. In this organization avoidance and resignation prevail. The dramatic leader type loves to be at the centre of attention and is on the surface often charming and attractive. The members may idealize such a leader and may become unreflective, submissive and may follow the leader uncritically. A compulsive and perfectionistic leader needs to dominate the organization in terms of details, rules, and has no vision. The members have little power in decision making. The last, schizoid, leader type is extremely introverted, with a strong need to distance himself or herself from the organizational life. Obviously, all of these personalities are more or less unable to contribute to a creative and efficient organization. As further described by Kaufmann and Kaufmann, new research has made connections between leadership styles and differences in childhood experiences of upbringing and to attachment patterns.

To Sum Up

Models of the Dynamic Process Approach explain some of the missing links that the Descriptive Trait Approach left out: How the individual developmental history affects personality, and what dynamic and motivational processes are at work in building up the personality structure. Psychodynamic theory highlights the interaction between environment and biological prerequisites in the development of personality. However, the Dynamic Process Approach will not stand without flaws in a final evaluation of the theory. Parts of the theory are difficult to investigate scientifically (e.g. terms as primary and secondary process), and the test instruments are not as easily administered as self-rating questionnaires. The validity and reliability of some of the tests used within the psychodynamic tradition have also been called into question (Zuber & Ekehammar, 1997). There are problems with different raters' agreement on the assessment of projective tests. Most percept-genetic tests have shown to be reliable between raters, but are still not much used in applied contexts, probably due to demanding individual test procedures (Smith & Carlsson, 1990; ref to manuals).

THE SOCIAL-COGNITIVE AND LEARNING APPROACH

The third perspective to be discussed has addressed some of the issues which are major problems with the Descriptive Trait Approach, and some of the unsolved riddles of the dynamic-process theories. The trait theorists' assumption of stability of personality over situations is refuted by both behaviorists and cognitivists. Social-cognitive theorists have also found ingenious ways of testing the unconscious—or implicit as they have named it, influence on conscious behavior. Perhaps the primary process thinking that psychodynamic researchers failed to test adequately can be detected by measures of implicit cognition within the social-cognitive theoretical framework.

For social approaches, environmental factors are naturally considered to be more important than for the previous theoretical approaches, and to some extent the stability of personality has been questioned within both the Learning Approach and the Social-Cognitive Approach. Fleeson (2002) investigated individuals by using the Big Five measurement over different situations and found very little stability. The same people rated themselves from the low to the high end of a seven-point scale on extraversion, openness and conscientiousness in different situations. Thus, the social context can make people change radically. For the Social-Cognitive Approach not only environmental influences will produce change in a person's behavior, but behavior is also affected by the individual cognition (how people perceive something), as evoked by different contexts (Hennessey, 2003). There will be different behavioral outcomes depending on how we process the environmental influences. For example, if a researcher presents a drawing competition to participants in order see how that affects their creative performance, the influence will vary in different individuals. One participant might see the competition as a challenge, because she thinks she is good at drawing and wants to know how drawing experts evaluate her work. She has a high expectancy of success and will try hard to show her best performance. Another participant will be stressed due to feelings of inferiority in drawing ability and will hardly try to make something creative. Most probably the first participant will outperform the second in creativeness. The first approach to be reviewed is, however, not concerned with internal cognitive processes, but focuses merely on external influences on behavior.

The Learning Approach

Scholars from the Learning Approach (also called behaviorism) focus solely on the question of how environmental factors causally determine people's behavior. Roughly, and in the extreme, they do not believe in the free will, but that the environment shapes people's thoughts, feelings and behavior. Hence different environments will cause people to act differently. Maladaptive behavior is caused by maladaptive environments to which a person has been exposed. Therapeutic activities will be directed at changing environmental factors instead of internal processes within individuals (Skinner, 1971).

People learn behavior by different forms of association processes in which stimuli and response are linked to each other; so called conditioning. Watson (1924) and Pavlov (1927) developed the concept of classical conditioning, and Skinner (1971) developed the concept of operant conditioning. Classical conditioning is more passive and is established when automatic or emotional responses are linked to stimuli (that they were not previously associated with). In operant conditioning the person (or animal) is actively involved in the association process. The individual will get a reinforcement when the strived for behavior appears. Behavior is thus controlled by the manipulation of rewards and punishments.

To Sum Up

Personality is formed by environmental factors through positive or negative reinforcements. According to behaviorists, the contents of scientific research should only be observable variables and not invisible personality structures, which are not considered possible to study scientifically. They thus oppose personality theorists, in which all depict some form of structures in the heads of individuals that explain their consistent styles of behavior.

The Social-Cognitive Approach

Social-cognitive researchers are critical of all the other personality theories. They believe that psychodynamic scholars exaggerate the importance of the unconscious and the personal history of people. They also question the idea that personality can be understood merely in terms of people's traits, since personality also includes patterns of variability of behavior in different situations (Mischel & Shoda, 2008). Finally they also disagree with the behaviorist stand point that people are entirely controlled by environmental forces. Social-cognitivists argue that people have a capacity to influence their destinies and that their thinking capacity can be used to self-regulate and motivate actions. The construction of personal meaning and beliefs of the self is considered important for human beings (Bandura, 2006).

Mischel and Shoda (2008) have presented a set of social-cognitive personality concepts as a complex system of cognitive and affective processes which are alleged to explain human personality. Their model is named Cognitive-Affective Processing System (CAPS). The personality structures included in CAPS are competencies, expectancies, beliefs, personal goals, behavioral norms and evaluative standards. These are all interdependent. Our actions will be contingent on what beliefs and expectancies we have concerning our competencies in a certain context (e.g., to see oneself as socially competent at a party). These actions will also be influenced by what we consider to be the right thing to do in any given situation (e.g., adapting to social norms at parties) and further depends on what personal goals we have in this domain of life (e.g., to make acquaintances). Social-cognitive theory rejects context-free competencies. People will not be looked upon as more or less competent in general. Any individual's competence will vary from one situation to another and from one knowledge domain to another. Most important of all for what kind of actions we will undertake are our expectations about the future. Beliefs of self-competence are sometimes termed beliefs of self-efficacy (Bandura, 1997). Beliefs of self-efficacy will affect goals, effort and emotions. Individuals with high self-efficacy will choose more challenging goals, put more effort into a task, and approach tasks with more positive moods (less anxiety).

The Social-Cognitive Approach in the organizational context. A social-cognitive theory of motivation is Self-Determination Theory, proposed by Deci and Ryan (Ryan & Deci, 2000), which among others has often been applied to organizational research. The theory emphasizes the need for motivation for achievement, and most of all the need for intrinsic motivation. The theorists assert that understanding motivation requires taking into account three basic human needs:

1. autonomy—freedom of external constraints on behavior,
2. competence—the need to feel capable, and
3. relatedness—the need to feel involved with others.

The main idea of self-determination theory is that when individuals (such as employees in a company) feel that their basic needs are reasonably well met, they tend to perceive their actions to be intrinsically motivated or self-determined, and this will raise the quality of their performance. However, the self-determination theory emphasizes a person's perception of freedom, rather than the presence or absence of actual constraints. An individual feels free, even if he or she is also operating within certain external constraints.

To Sum Up

Social-cognitive and learning approaches have helped us gain insight into some of the unanswered questions of the other perspectives. They have focused on the environmental influences on personality and question the stability of the personality. Even if the social-cognitivists have developed scientific ways of studying unconscious processes, there is little systematic knowledge of the influence of mental conflict and the unconscious levels of cognition. This theory will not alone stand up as a systematic and comprehensive theory of personality. It lacks a unifying conceptual network which ties together elements of all different parts of this approach. There is no comprehensive test instrument that can capture the main ideas of the theory. There are also several other gaps to be filled; there is no complete developmental perspective and little attention is directed at the influence of individual history on personality functioning. Furthermore, biological influences on personality have been sparsely studied within this perspective. Considering the approaches presented here, no single theory can cover alone the whole spectrum of human personality.

TOWARDS AN ECLECTIC APPROACH?

The Descriptive Trait Approach provides us with a good description of personality through different traits, the Dynamic Process Approach suggests several processes (the influence of individual history, mental conflict and development) that affect personality, and the Social-Cognitive and Learning Approach throw light on the impact of the environment on personality. Taken together they give a fairly complete view of human personality. One assessment technique (the Time Perspective Inventory), presented by Zimbardo and Boyd (1999), might be seen as an embryo of new, more eclectic theoretical thinking within the social-cognitive tradition (and with roots in the life space model presented by Lewin, 1951 as cited in Zimbardo & Boyd). Instead of dividing people in different descriptive traits, this research group suggested that systematic individual differences can be found between people on their time orientation, or *time perspectives* as the authors termed these personality styles. There are people who are more focused on processing the past (past positive perspective or past negative perspective), others have a present orientation (present-fatalistic or present-hedonistic), and a third group is more directed towards the future. Situational factors will also influence time perspectives, so that some contexts make people orient towards future thinking and others towards past thinking. Perhaps the time perspective theory thinking can encompass:

1. a good description of personality,
2. easily manufactured tools (as the Descriptive Trait Approach sports),
3. an interest in individual history of development and interest in personality processes (as Dynamic Process Approaches has developed), without denying
4. the environmental influences of personality (as the social-cognitive and learning approach has specialized in).

Further development of the "time perspective theory", may give it the potential to address the full range of aspects of personality theory. Individual developmental history would be part of it, and the focus of present situation as well as how thinking of the future affects people. Recent studies within this theoretical field have suggested new time perspectives, one of which is called the balanced perspective, implying that focusing too much on either past or future will not be conducive in the long run (Boniwell & Zimbardo, 2004; Boniwell, Osin, Alex, & Ivanchenko, 2010). Then, within the area of psychopathology and treatment, it would be possible to see whether different people depending on their time perspective will benefit from different therapeutic approaches—psychodynamic, cognitive behavioral therapy or perhaps even medical treatment. Could for instance, the "past perspective" people best be helped by psychodynamic therapy (e.g. focusing on coming to terms with their developmental background)? Individuals with present-fatalistic perspective might be best helped by medication, as they seem to have a lack of faith in their potential to influence their own lives. Another possibility is that both past- and present-oriented people would be helped by a therapeutic effort directed at reorientating them toward a balance between past, present and future perspectives (Boniwell et al., 2010), either through dynamic or cognitive therapy. Last, future-oriented people would be those that would benefit most from cognitive behavioral therapy because they are inclined to focus on having positive images—expectancies or goals—of the future and to reformulate dysfunctional thinking. In fact, social-cognitive researchers have also asserted that self-control—conceptualized by delay of gratification, among other concepts—is an important factor for social and cognitive functioning (Bandura & Mischel, 1965; Barber, Munz, Bagsby, & Grawitch, 2009). Delay of gratification enables individuals to work for a long time to attain a goal in the future. It has been shown that those pre-schoolers who could refrain from immediately getting a reward (to not take a piece of candy on a table in front of them when left alone in a room) were found as adolescents to be more skilful, better at planning, more able to concentrate, and to express more sophisticated ideas, when compared to groups with low delay ability (Shoda, Mischel, & Peake, 1990).

THE CREATIVE PERSONALITY

The creative personality is actualized wherever artists, innovators or other forerunners have lived and worked. But they are not a uniform crowd, neither in interests nor in destinies. They do not even present a mainly sunlit picture. Pioneering achievements are mixed with unsuccessful dreams; proud expectations are stopped by lack of resources or by personal limitations. Hero tales run side by side with stories of self-delusion. These tales come from different theoretic perspectives. A large amount of research has been undertaken in many different theoretical directions.

What kind of personality traits are believed to be associated with a creative person? Before answering this question we need to discuss what a creative person is. Many researchers focus on creative geniuses (Csikszentmihályi, 1997; Gardner, 1997) and argue that creativity should be studied among the extraordinary. But creativity can be found among excellent practitioners in different scientific and artistic domains, and also among ordinary people in their everyday lives (Craft, 2000; Cropley, 1992). Creative personalities have been studied among both ordinary and extraordinary participants.

By relating personality questionnaires to individuals' creativity scores (ordinary people) or creative practitioners (recognized as extraordinary), researchers have identified creative characteristics (Barron, 1963; Barron & Harrington, 1981; Eysenck, 1995; Martindale, 1989). In this kind of study, particularly creative people are generally depicted as having a good deal of self-confidence, allowing them to trust their own ideas and to endure critical opinions (Martindale, 1989). Creative individuals are also described as being inventive, enthusiastic, hard-working, tolerant of ambiguity, risk-taking, and low on interpersonal competitiveness, but also as emotional, labile, hostile and bitter (Barron, 1963; Barron & Harrington, 1981; Feist, 1998; Mumford, Costanza, Threlfall, Baughman, & Reiter-Palmon, 1993;

Sternberg & Lubart, 1999). Eysenck (1995) pointed out that there is considerable contradiction in the descriptions given of creative persons. They are described as having social presence and poise, but are also said to be antisocial and irritable. Furthermore, they have been reported both as dominant and introverted, despite the fact that dominance is generally considered a trait of extraversion. Csikszentmihályi (1997) solved this puzzle by presenting the creative personality as one that contains opposites. Many of the 91 creative exceptional people that he interviewed demonstrated ten opposite trait-pairs: 1) They had large amounts of physical energy, as they worked hard for long periods of time in order to achieve their exceptional work. But they were also good at charging their batteries when needed. They took rests and slept a lot. They appreciated *focused activity* as much as *idleness* or reflection time. They were 2) both *smart* and *naïve*, 3) *disciplined* and *playful*, and 4) bound to both *reality* and *imagination* (for the relationship between imagination and creativity see also Hoff, 2005, and in press). Csikszentmihályi argued that these aspects were all needed in different parts of the creative process. Furthermore, the exceptional people were 5) both *extraverted* and *introverted,* 6) *humble* as well as *proud*, and 7) showed both *male* and *female* characteristics (see also Carlsson, Hoff, & Jönsson, 2004). 8) They demonstrated tendencies of both *rebellion* and independence at the same time as they were conservative and *traditional*. 9) They were passionate and *subjective* at the same time as they could manifest *objectiveness*. 10) Lastly, they were *open* to joy as well as suffering sometimes. For example, they were mocked for their intense beliefs in their new ideas and worried about that at times. However, in other situations, they *could close everything off* to concentrate on their work without consideration of what people would think.

Certain studies have investigated implicit theories of creativity by looking at notions of what constitute typical creative traits according to different participant groups (Dawson, 1997; Dawson, D'Andrea, Affinito, & Westby, 1999; Runco, Johnson, & Bear, 1993; Sternberg, 1985; Westby & Dawson, 1995). People in general consider creative individuals to be impulsive, emotional, someone who makes up the rules as he or she goes along and someone who likes to be alone when creating something new. Other groups of participants did not share this view; for example, teachers consider conforming characteristics—such as being reliable, logical, responsible and good-natured—characteristics that facilitate classroom management—to be indicative of creative pupils (Westby & Dawson, 1995).

Studies using the five-factor model have found two strong relationships. High scores on openness to experience and low scores on conscientiousness are associated with creativity (Batey, Chamorro-Premuzic, & Furnham, 2010; see also the meta-analysis of Feist, 1998). Creative people are open to new ideas, experiences and their inner feelings. They like to explore new ways of solving problems rather than following routines. Creative people show fluency and flexibility of thought. A rigidly conscientious person may set too stringent standards for evaluating their problem-solving process, making them unwilling to consider the full range of possibilities, which in its turn will screen out new and original solutions. Associations with the other factors have also been demonstrated, but not as consistently as for the above mentioned. Creative people are generally described as *low on extraversion* (Eysenck, 1995; Feist, 1998; Kemp, 1981)—having a desire to remove themselves from social interaction, *low on agreeableness* (Dudek, Bernèche, Bérubé, & Royer, 1991; Eysenck, 1995)—meaning that they commonly do not adapt to others, but go their own way, and finally *high on neuroticism* (Bakker, 1991; Eysenck, 1995)—signifying that creative people are emotionally unstable. However, to some extent there is variation between different subgroups. Feist demonstrated in his meta-study that neuroticism was higher in creative artists than in creative scientists. Kemp found musicians high on conscientiousness and Furnham and Bachtiar (2008) found extroverted creative people. Mixed results can be explained by the fact that the Big Five factors include items of different type. For instance, within Extraversion there is a confidence component and a sociability component. The confidence component includes items such as dominance, self-acceptance, ambitiousness, et cetera, and these are often related to creative individuals, whereas the sociability components seldom are (Feist, 1998).

Within the Dynamic Process Approach, scholars have also been attracted to the study of creative personalities. Creativity, as they see it, flourishes in a zone between so-called primary and secondary processes. The primary process provides the free associations that may furnish new and pioneering ideas, the secondary process provides the necessary tools of communication and reality adaptation, which might include evaluation of an idea and how it can be developed into something that will actually be of use. Kris (1952) coined the term regression in the service of the ego as an important characteristic for the creative artist dipping his/her beak in the flow of primitive ideation, but just managing not to get caught and drown. It seems to be typical of genuinely creative people that they are cognizant of their own inner world, to vague and evasive ideas, often termed intuitions, which are particularly difficult to grasp in their early phases. Dreams are also likely to attract their interest and not be easily dismissed as artifacts. However, at one stage of the creative process the subjective primary process needs to be alternated with secondary thought (reasoning, planning) to realize a creative project.

For creative people, associative connections do not yield to conventional signposts but often digress in unexpected directions, tightly interwoven with emotions and personal reminiscences.

The level of creativity shown by an individual might be classified. A recent study by Thompson, Keehn, and Gumpel (2009) illustrates one such classification (see also Kirton 1976, for another distinction between what he terms adaptors and innovators). In a sample of people working within the performing arts, they distinguished between generators and interpreters; that is between composers and opera singers, playwrights and actors, choreographers and dancers, et cetera, and found differences between these two subgroups: interpreters scored higher than generators on total dissociation, absorption/changeability and depersonalization/derealization. Unfortunately, most test instruments were of the self-descriptive variety, which are perhaps not the most valid of creativity tests.

Not only in traditional endeavors like writing, painting, composing, will creativity be found, but also in technical innovations, novel attempts at theory construction, even in the fields of politics, and in the use of well-known instruments in new ways.

THE ROLE OF MOODS AND EMOTIONS IN THE CREATIVE PERSONALITY

Some researchers have shown how affective processes (moods and emotions) are decisive in creativity. Lieberman (1977) has emphasized positive affect (enjoyment) as an important part of creativity. Russ (1993, 1999) has been interested in different affective components in play and their impact on creativity. Some of the affective processes are:

1. access to affect-laden thoughts and openness to affective states, and
2. augmented positive affect in challenges and the problem-solving activity.

Access and openness refers to a willingness to associate, and the flexibility in thought that allows people to be inspired by less controlled states of thinking—such as fantasies (affect-laden non-realistic imagination)—and the thinking termed primary process in dynamic theory.

Augmented positive affect can refer to several aspects of the creative process. Creative people like tension and challenge, and will be intrigued by being involved in something that is difficult. The challenge needs to be optimal, according to flow theory (Csikszentmihályi, 1991), which means that an individual's entire capacity in the involved area will have to be employed to meet the challenge. Creative activities can be experienced as totally absorbing and flow-like. They involve intensive emotions at least in some parts of the process.

In the social-cognitive tradition, mood induction studies have demonstrated that particularly positive affect will enhance creativity (DeDreu, Baas, & Nijstad, 2008; Isen, Daubman, & Nowicki, 1987).

Positive affect is also central to a process that pretend play and creativity have in common, namely intrinsic motivation (Amabile, 1996; Lieberman, 1977). Doing something for the fun of it is an important component of creativity—there is a mostly intrinsic value in attaining the creative solution (Lieberman, 1977). Extrinsic motivational factors (rewards, competition, and evaluation) have been shown to thwart the creative process (Amabile, 1996; Collins & Amabile, 1999), since they reduce task involvement and creative quality.

Another demonstration of the importance of the affective components of the creative process is seen in the effects of affect training. In an intervention study involving 45 preschoolers, Russ, Moore, and Pearson (as cited in Moore & Russ, 2008) used standardized instructions and props designed to elicit affects together with modeling and reinforcement of affect expression in play in the training phase of their investigation. In the test phase, higher levels of creativity were found in the Unusual Uses Test in the experimental group that had received affect training.

The effect of negative emotion is complex. Some studies that have induced very strong negative emotions have found no influence on levels of creativity (as cited in Russ, 1999). Other studies with less strong negative emotions have shown some relationship with enhanced problem-solving abilities (Russ). Also the variability of moods might affect creativity in a positive way.

Richards (1993) argues that the mood swings experienced by people with bipolar mood disorder may form a motivational force in creativity.

Anger and aggressiveness. Early investigators in the area of creativity (MacKinnon, 1962, 1965; Barron, 1968) suggested that creative people are more openly aggressive, power-seeking, or ruthless than others. This was, however, definitely not the case in a sample of Swedish idea generators in a Swedish industry (Ekvall, 1971). Similar discrepancies regarding the role of aggression in creative work continue to appear in later publications. They may depend on how aggression is understood.

Since aggression, in the eyes of most of us, represents the evil side of human nature, then its unbridled pathology and its problems may appear to belong to psychiatry rather than normal psychology. But modern semi-projective techniques to investigate aggression make possible a differentiation of adaptive and maladaptive forms. Such a differentiation could make it possible to study the association, on the one hand, between adaptive anger and creativity and, on the other, between maladaptive aggressiveness and typical examples of psychosomatic ailments and cancerous diseases. We will only consider the former kind in the present context.

In a famous paper by the psychoanalysts Hartmann, Kris, and Loewenstein (1949) the authors attempted to distinguish between an unmodified and a modified aggressive drive where only the former aims at destructiveness. Even if Klein (1975) did not see aggression as a primary drive, her statement that aggression is part of all productive human activity agrees in a general way with the concept of modified aggression.

Instead of defining aggression as violence and destruction, Markovitz (1973) viewed it as a hierarchy of behavior ranging from such adaptive forms as curiosity. At this point the present authors find it appropriate to distinguish *aggressiveness*, implying belligerence and hostility, from the more inclusive term *aggression,* which refers to self-assertion and boldness. Affect theory views anger, in its broad meaning, as a motivating force serving self-preservation. Aggressiveness is hence seen as a maladaptive development of the original affect.

In an attempt to study the relation between aggression, in its modified form, and creativity, Smith, Carlsson, and Danielsson (1986) used the CFT (a creativity measure which will be explained below) and the percept-genetic Identification Test (IT). The stimulus picture in the IT test is a drawing of two male persons facing each other. One is an "aggressor", with clenched fists and arms bent at the elbows. The other is a "victim" of aggression holding his arms stretched downwards in a gesture of dejection. Their mouths are half open as it they are talking, and that of the aggressor is twisted in a snarl. Crucial to the test is a subliminal prime, which is the word "Me" presented at the place of either the Aggressor or the Victim in two short series, each in random order after a baseline series with no subliminal prime. The experimenter is unaware of the randomized order.

The participant is instructed to report their impressions and feelings in a free verbal report after each exposure. The results were scored by two independent judges, in three categories:

1. clear anger or gradually increasing aggression reported in the aggressor primed series,
2. no anger in any series, and
3. evasive or no reports of aggression in the aggressor primed series but at least indications of anger in the victim primed series.

In an initial study of 16-year-olds, the more creative were more prone to describe anger in the picture when primed to identify with the Aggressor, whereas low creative youngsters were more likely to describe what they saw in terms of anger-related words when primed on the Victim. It may be added that the most creative subjects were characterized by the MCT as sensitive, and inclined to use imaginative interpretations of the threatening stimuli, but lacking signs of compulsion or depressive stereotypy. Approximately the same results were found in another study with 10–12-year-olds. Thus in both groups, creative individuals showed more identification with the angry person than less creative ones. This should not lead to the conclusion that these children are necessarily more boisterous, power-seeking, or ruthless. In the particular situation created by the IT, with the opposing roles of aggressor and victim, they prefer the angry person, apparently because he is more likely to be able to uphold his autonomy and exploit a freedom that the victim is less likely to enjoy. For the less creative ones such a freedom is not a natural alternative.

THE CREATIVE PERSONALITY IN A
DEVELOPMENTAL PERSPECTIVE

Are we born with different traits that make us creative? A trait theorist would assume this to be indicated by high scores on openness to new experiences and low on conscientiousness on a Big Five measurement, or are there also environmental factors that will bring about different paths of development, as is the belief of the Dynamic Process Approach and the Social-Cognitive and Learning Approach?

When can a child be really creative? Different criteria might be the starting-point for such a judgment task. According to Smith and Carlsson (1990), it takes place when the child starts to differentiate between private fantasies and outside reality. Then primary process content can be separated from secondary process material, so that the two can be combined in a fruitful way in the creative process. When do children reach enough consciousness and intentionality to realize a creative process? Some creativity scholars argue that very young children show signs of creativity (for example Amabile, 1982; Hoff, in press; Urban, 2004, measure creativity in 5-year-olds), while others place the creativity debut in the early school years (Smith & Carlsson, 1990), but others again assert that true creativity is not possible until well into adolescence, due to the fact that abstract cognitive and intentional planning abilities have to be well developed (Vygotskij, 1995/1930; Weisberg, 2006). Hoff contends that some form of executive function needs to be developed, but that might begin to develop in the late pre-school years.

According to the dynamic process perspective, some forms of dynamic change will take place in all individuals. However, there are factors that will limit the level of creativity that each individual can develop. These factors are both the genetic equipment and environmental conditions. Through processes of identification (parents' values will be taken over) and internalization (external becomes internal), what is considered important in an individual child's family will constitute a base for the personality functioning of the child. Is both primary process thinking and secondary process valued in the family? Do parents tell their dreams and reflect upon their possible meaning? Is imagination something that is encouraged as a source of life quality in the family? These factors will be influential regarding creative development.

From a social-cognitive perspective, outside influences such as social context will also be of great importance for how personality is shaped (Bandura, 1997). The social psychology of creativity has been outlined by Amabile and her collaborators (Amabile, 1982, 1996). She has shown how environmental factors are decisive for creativity. For several decades she performed studies of how extrinsic motivational factors, such as competition, rewards and evaluation can thwart creativity, whereas the creative ability of people who are intrinsically motivated—that is, are doing something for the fun of it—will be intact. However, some of Amabile's co-workers (Hennessey & Zbikowski, 1993) have demonstrated that the relationship is more complex. In the social-cognitive theory, expectations and beliefs are important determinants of behavioral outcomes. Depending on how people regard extrinsic motivational factors, they can have the opposite influence—a positive one. When people perceive a reward as an additional bonus on top of having fun with a task, it may in fact boost creativity. In line with earlier works of Deci (1971) and Lepper, Greene, and Nisbett (1973), performance is reduced when rewards are regarded as the main goal instead of the task itself. By immunizing children (through modeling) to not have their main focus on the reward, but on the thrill of exploring new things and the fun of performing the task, Hennessey and Zbikowski demonstrated an additive effect of extrinsic and intrinsic motivation. The "immunized" (intrinsic plus extrinsic) participants showed greater creativity compared to those who were in the intrinsic motivation group, and who in their turn outperformed the reward (extrinsic motivation) group.

Another view of the effects of environmental factors was put forward by Csikszentmihályi (1997). He stated that people are born with two ways of functioning—a tendency to preserve and a tendency to change. However, some people will predominantly adapt a more conservative functioning, made up of self-preservation, self-aggrandizement and energy-saving activities (e.g. sticking to habits), whereas others will to a greater extent manifest a tendency to explore and to enjoy novelty and risk. We need both these tendencies, however the first needs little encouragement, and the second—which leads to creative functioning—can easily be throttled if not cultivated (Csikszentmihályi, 1997).

Some mutual environmental factors were found among the (1997) extraordinary individuals interviewed by Csikszentmihályi (ibid.) that might be indicative of an environment beneficial to the creative personality. Most of the creative individuals grew up in fairly stable, supportive families, and a majority pointed out the importance of having had certain teachers acting as mentors to stimulate them and acknowledge their special talents. Many developmental descriptions of creativity emphasize the role of models. Apart from these special teachers, school in general was more a negative experience for most of the exceptionally creative individuals. Their parents tended to treat them more as fellow adults, taking them to the library, to museums, and to concerts. Parents were often good at "introducing the world" to the children. Few individuals were child prodigies in what would turn out to be their expert domain as adults. However, one mutual childhood trait of these exceptional people was their keen interest and curiosity about the mysteries of life.

Other environmental prerequisites have also been identified. It has been found that children need enough free time, enough psychological space and to have access to a special place in order to develop their creative imagination (Singer & Singer, 1992).

A less structured school setting is often considered better then overly structured ones (Runco, 2007). Creativity research on schools has found that self-initiated learning, student influence and encouragement of originality are important for developing children's creativity (Cremin, Burnard, & Craft, 2006; Soh, 2000; Runco, 2007; Niu & Sternberg, 2003).

Multi-cultural experiences also increase the likelihood of being creative (Leung & Chiu, 2010; Maddux & Galinsky, 2009). Evidence for this was found in studies of individuals growing up in multi-cultural families (Leung & Chiu, 2008) and in individuals having lived abroad for a period of their life (Maddux & Galinsky, 2009).

Can creativity thus be taught? Most researchers agree on the fact that creativity can be developed (Nickerson, 1999). There are environmental squelchers—often found in schools— that can stifle the development of creativity. Some examples are sticking to regulations, strict adherence to lesson plans and curriculum, asserting that there is only one way of doing things, compartmentalization of knowledge, and the discouragement of curiosity (Nickerson, 2010). However, in an encouraging environment most individuals can increase their creativity. Cropley (1992) asserts that all students, regardless of IQ, are able to think divergently, but they may have been made to think merely in convergent ways as a result of experience. Numerous specific techniques have been developed to practice creativity. Two examples might be mentioned; Osborn's (1963) *brainstorming* which develops people's capacity for association, and Debono's six thinking hats (1999), that encourage individuals to see things from many perspectives. Different creativity enhancement programs have been developed for use in schools and they have had mixed effects (See Runco, 2007; Nickerson, 1999 for overviews).

Creativity and Aging

Creativity and aging has been the subject of more speculation than empirical research. To some scholars, aging should be of no consequence for creativity, with Verdi often being cited as an example. Others, on the other hand, say that it hardly survives middle age, and genius by definition is a sign of youth. When Smith and van der Meer (1990) tested groups of elderly people in the age span of 61 to 86 years, a sizeable group of their subjects scored highly in the CFT. Among 173 adolescents, 29% got top scores, whereas only 12% in a group of 59 adults group scored similarly. The number of top-scoring in the combined group of elderly was 10%.

While the variation within the group of elderly people was still sizeable, even more noteworthy was the difference in other respects between the subgroups. Creative people treated problems of aging and declining health with more equanimity than less creative ones. They were less bored with their present situation, even found life meaningful and were more empathic with the fate of other, less successful groups of people. It was wholly in agreement with our notion of creative people as relying on reconstruction of early experiences for the generation of new ideas, that creative elderly subjects, when confronted with very rapid pictures of a face, more often than their less creative counterparts said that it depicted a youngster or even a child. It would undoubtedly be of special interest for an organization to keep their creative, elderly collaborators as long as possible.

THE CREATIVE PERSONALITY IN ORGANIZATIONS

Research has been undertaken within the organizational context to investigate what personality components are more conducive to creative team work. In general, organizations rely more and more on the use of teams for problem-solving and product development (Baer, Oldham, Costa-Jacobsohn, & Hollingshead, 2008). In the research literature, there are indications that team diversity is conducive to creativity (often diversity in competence more than in personality, e.g., described in Paulus & Nijstad, 2003), but also that more homogenous teams are superior (Baer et al., 2008; Taggar, 2001). However, regardless of the composition of the team, several studies have emphasized the importance of the beliefs of the members, group norms and the processes taking place during the creative group work, and indicated that these will affect the group's performance as much as the individuals' personalities. These studies thus combine ideas from the social-cognitive perspective and the trait approach. Adarves-Yorno, Postmes, and Haslam (2007) showed that group identity made individuals produce creative products in line with group norms, whereas those members who had a stronger personal identity went against the group norm. Another research group demonstrated that group norms can be oriented towards originality or conformity and that this fact influenced to what extent creative work was actually performed (Bechtoldt, De Dreu, Nijstad, Choi, & Nijstad, 2010).

Concerning research on what specific personalities are more likely to produce creative team work, Taggar (2001) found that the more creative group members that were included in a team, the more creative results were obtained. However, again this was only true if the processes taking place in the group were team creativity-relevant ones, such as efficient management, communication and conflict resolution. In accordance with what is said about the five-factor traits, scholars have also demonstrated that people with certain traits (high in openness, extraversion, and low in conscientiousness) contribute to group creativity to a greater extent (Baer et al., 2008; Robert & Cheung, 2010). However, Baer et al.'s study also showed that the belief concerning the effectiveness of the group was important for the increase of creativity level. When team creative confidence was high, the creativity of the group increased quadratically as the number of members characterized by high openness, high extraversion or low conscientiousness increased. There is also contradicting evidence put forward by other research groups, who assert that a combination of different personalities is conducive to creativity—in other words group diversity stimulates creativity (West, 2003).

Organizational creativity has also been studied from the perspective of the Dynamic Process Approach. In a project studying 149 teachers at a new university in Sweden (Andersson & Ryhammar, 1999; Ekvall & Ryhammar, 1999; Ryhammar & Andersson, 2001; Ryhammar & Smith, 1999), variables related to the individual (creativity, defense mechanisms, extroversion) and to the organization (for example creative climate) were investigated. Both questionnaires and percept-genetic, process instruments were used. One of the results found that individual creativity as measured by the CFT was associated with opinions of the organization as a place of openness and with experiences of diversity. Also, anxiety and defense repression correlated positively with creativity, while so-called identity defense, for example denial, was negatively correlated. In a perceptual test measuring the subjective/objective dimension, people with high creativity more often got scores on the two extreme poles in this test, that is, they were reacting either very subjectively, or with extreme objectification of their perceptual world. Another result was that the creative people regarded a high workload as stimulating to their creativity. Maybe the fact that it was a new, expanding workplace contributed to the positive experience of workload (as discussed in Smith & Carlsson, 2006).

The discussion of whether changing an environment or organizational climate will make people more creative has been dealt with in more detail in another chapter of this handbook (West & Sacramen, this volume), but here we may ask the question whether a change of creativity can be produced through interventions with the goal to change personality.

In a comparison between 70 studies of different creativity training programs, Scott, Leritz, and Mumford (2004) found that those aimed at problem-solving training and divergent thinking training were the most effective. Those creativity training efforts with the goal of changing people's personalities into more creative ones were less effective, even though all the creativity training that Scott and colleagues analyzed had some effect, meaning that the sessions indeed improved the creative capabilities of the participants. Creativity training sessions in work life were more successful than those set up in schools in this comparison. The largest effects were seen in training sessions in small groups (with a maximum of 12). In Karwowski and Soszynski's (2008) comparison between 137 different creativity development programs in Poland, the largest effect was demonstrated by those programs focusing on the development of imaginative skills and verbal skills.

TESTING CREATIVITY

There is an arsenal of tests for measuring creativity, which can be divided into personality, process, product, and place assessments. In the first category there is focus on measuring *personality traits* or behaviors with personality tests. The test methods used are often self-rating instruments and are thus predominantly scored by the participants themselves. For example, if using the Big Five measurement, NEO-PI-R (Costa & McCrae, 1992), scholars might look for the trait "openness to experience" to find creative people. On some personality questionnaires, there are more specific scales, for example on Marsh and O'Neill's (1984) Self Description Questionnaire, there is a scale called problem-solving that concerns creativity-relevant items. Examples of items are "I like to come up with new solutions to problems" and "I am an imaginative person".

The second type of test is aimed at tapping the *creative process* through some of its identified aspects, such as divergent thinking, flexible thinking, and associative ability. *Divergent thinking* is an ability that is distinguished from analytic convergent thinking (logical thinking), through its production of less expected ideas. It is most commonly measured by the Unusual Uses Test (UUT but also sometimes named alternate uses test) described by Wallach and Kogan (1965) or the more extensive battery by Torrance, Torrance Test of Creative Thinking—TTCT (1965, 1990). In the UUT, the test leader asks the participants to enumerate as many uses of an every-day object as possible, such as a newspaper, a paperclip or a milk carton. In the TTCT, other tasks (both verbal and figural) are also included, apart from the UUT, such as that the participants are requested to complete stories, pictures, ask questions about pictures, and try to develop a toy to make it interesting to play with. These tasks are evaluated on different dimensions, as described by Torrance (1990), which are fluency, flexibility, elaboration, and originality, but sometimes also usefulness. Fluency is a quantitative measure and flexibility denotes the variation of different themes of the suggested uses (for instance, a hamster house and a mouse house would go into the same theme, if they are considered as uses for a milk carton), elaboration describes the complexity and amount of detail of each use, and originality refers to how often this use has been suggested by participants—a use is scored as very original if no one else has produced that response before.

Flexibility is measured for example by Lubart, Jacquet, Pacteau, and Zenasni's (2000) morphing technique, which they assert is something different from Torrance's flexibility (1965). In this morphing test, a picture is shown on a computer screen and then gradually transformed into another picture. Those participants who recognise the new picture at an early stage are considered to have a flexible thinking style and to be creative. Another test of flexibility is the Creative Functioning Test (CFT) by Smith and Carlsson (1999, 2001) which might lean on similar assumptions as Lubart et al.'s morphing technique (Hoff & Carlsson,

2008). In the CFT, the participant is shown a series of systematically prolonged exposures of a stimulus picture (a still-life made by an artist) on a computer screen. The viewer is instructed to report his/her impressions after each exposure. When the perceptual process has advanced to the objective level, that is when the participant has reported a correct description of the stimulus picture, the testing continues uninterruptedly with a reversed exposure series; that is the time for each exposure is systematically abbreviated down to the shortest time levels. The two main scoring dimensions are *fluency* and *flexibility*, assessed respectively in the first, increasing, or, the second, reversed series. Fluency is scored as the total number of different interpretations, deviant from the correct content of the picture, given in the prolonged picture series. The inclination to again replace the correct description of the stimulus with a subjective one in the reverted series is taken as a sign of cognitive flexibility. Even if fluency and flexibility are moderately correlated, as expected, they differ in important respects.

Fluency implies that associative paths are easily accessible provided that the basic prerequisites are not violated; that is, you are free to guess as long as you do not know the correct alternative. Flexibility, on the other hand, shows how far you are willing to depart from the secure level of correctness and revert to a renewed exploitation of subjective potentialities. In the reversed series it is possible to distinguish a person's ability to shift from logical, reality-oriented thinking to more primary process oriented cognition. Comparing Smith and Carlsson's (2001) definition of flexibility with Lubart et al's (2000), the morphing technique appoints those who see the new picture early as the more flexible (and thus creative). In the CFT, those who shift from viewing the stimulus objectively, and who return to subjective interpretations, are regarded as more flexible (Hoff & Carlsson, 2008). A common denominator may be the degree of inhibition in the brain. A stimulus-bound person that is quick to form habits will be less prone to consciously perceive the small signs of an emerging new picture in Lubart et al's test. In the CFT such a person, with high inhibition, having just made a correct perception, will be more prone to inhibit the subjective and weak interpretations, even though the stimulus once more becomes ambiguous and vague during very rapid exposures.

Associative ability refers to an ability to come up with many different associations. Quantity or fluency of thought is considered more likely to also produce more quality or more original answers. Furthermore, according to Mednick (1962), individuals differ in their associative ability. Some produce steep hierarchies of association, meaning that they only have a few strong associations to each word (chair might be associated with wood, legs and table), whereas others have flat hierarchies of association, referring to them also having a large number of remote association to words (fabric, cubby hole, punishment). Mednick asserts that the most distant and the last associations often are more original, thus individuals with flat hierarchies are more likely to be creative. Associative ability can be measured by the fluency criteria in UUT, TTCT, and CFT. Mednick (1962) has also constructed a test to indicate associative ability, called the Remote Assocation Test (RAT). In this test, participants are asked to find a fourth word that is associated to three enumerated words. For example an item might contain electric, high and wheel and the sought for answer is chair.

A third category of tests measures *creative products*. Two examples of product tests are Amabile's Collage test and Urban's Test of Creative Thinking—Drawing-Production (TCT-DP, Urban, 2004). The collage test involves participants in the production of a collage out of a set of paper shapes (about 60 squares, triangles and circles) that they glue onto a cardboard paper. The collages are rated by a number of judges according to the Consensual Assessment Technique, CAT (Amabile, 1982). CAT is a rating system in which ten or more judges indicate their subjectively decided creativity level for each collage. Together, these ratings constitute a firm ground for "objective" creativity scores according to Amabile. The collage test has also a verbal sibling, the Cinquain Test; in which a poem is constructed from one supplied word (Amabile, 1982). The TCT-DP is a picture production test in which the participants get a sheet of paper with four small non-figurative fragments (a dot, half-circle, a dotted line and an angle) inside a frame and one (a square) outside the frame and are asked to complete the drawing. These pictures are judged according to a set of criteria presented by Urban (2004, 1996), such as whether the fragments are interconnected and whether they form a whole. Drawing outside the frame and/or including the box outside the frame give extra points in the assessment of creativity.

Finally, tests measuring *place* or climate will also be treated here. They concern environmental factors that are believed to affect creativity in people (Amabile, Conti, Coon, Lazenby, & Herron, 1996; Ekvall, 1996). In Ekvall's Creative Climate Questionnaire (CCQ), which is a questionnaire filled out by the employees themselves, there are ten creative environmental dimensions: challenge, freedom, idea support, trust/openness, dynamism/liveliness, playfulness/humor, debates, conflicts, risk-taking, and idea time. Nine of the dimensions are beneficial for creativity and one (conflicts) is not. In Amabile et al.'s (1996) questionnaire (KEYS), there are also dimensions measuring organizational encouragement and impediments to creativity. Among the encouragements, this research group includes: *organizational encouragement* (refers to an organization that values and encourages risk-taking, idea generation/creativity, and gives feedback and rewards for creativity and collaboration), *Supervisory encouragement* (meaning that the leader presents clear goals, encourages open dialogues between supervisor and subordinates and gives support to the team's work and ideas) and *Work group encouragement* (referring to the fruitful diversity of team members' backgrounds, openness to new ideas, and shared commitment to the work). Other creativity stimulating dimensions are freedom, enough resources, and challenge (which is a positive side of pressure, meaning that the employee has to put effort into the work). Among the impediments are: excessive workload pressure, internal conflicts, conservatism, and rigid organizational structures.

References

Adarves-Yorno, I., Postmes, T., & Haslam, S. A. (2007). Creative innovation or crazy irrelevance: The contribution of group norms and social identity to creative behavior. *Journal of Experimental Social Psychology, 43*, 410–416.

Ainsworth, M. (1967). *Infancy in Uganda: Infancy and the growth of love.* Baltimore, MD: John Hopkins University Press.

Allport, G. W. (1937). *Personality: A psychological interpretation.* New York, NY: Holt.

Amabile, T. M. (1982). Social psychology of creativity: A consensual assessment technique. *Journal of Personality and Social Psychology, 43*, 997–1013.

Amabile, T. M. (1996). *Creativity in context: Update to the social psychology of creativity.* Boulder, CO: Westview Press.

Amabile, T. M., Conti, R., Coon, H., Lazenby, J., & Herron, M. (1996). Assessing the work environment for creativity. *The Academy of Management Journal, 39*, 1154–1184.

Andersson, A. L., & Ryhammar, L. (1999). Personality of university teachers according to the defense mechanism technique modified (DMTm) as related to their assessment of their university as an organizational setting. *Social Behavior and Personality, 27*, 575–586.

Baer, M., Oldham, G. R., Jacobsohn-Costa, G., & Hollingshead, A. B. (2008). The personality composition of teams and creativity: The moderating role of team creative confidence. *Journal of Creative Behavior, 42*, 255–282.

Bakker, F. C. (1991). Development of personality in dancers: A longitudinal study. *Personality and Individual Differences, 12*, 671–681.

Bandura, A. (1997). *Self-efficacy: The exercise of control*. New York, NY: Freeman.

Bandura, A. (2006). Toward a psychology of human agency. *Perspectives on Psychological Science, 1*, 164–180.

Bandura, A., & Mischel, W. (1965). Modification of self-imposed deal of reward through exposure to live and symbolic models. *Journal of Personality and Social Psychology, 2*, 698–705.

Barber, L. K., Munz, D. C., Bagsby, P. G., & Grawitch, M. J. (2009). When does time perspective matter: Self-control as a moderator of time perspective and academic achievement. *Personality and Individual Differences, 46*, 250–253.

Barron, F. (1963). *Creativity and psychological health*. New York, NY: D. Van Nostrand.

Barron, F. (1968). *Creativity and personal freedom*. Princeton, NJ: D. Van Nostrand.

Barron, F., & Harrington, D. M. (1981). Creativity, intelligence and personality. *Annual Review of Psychology, 32*, 439–476.

Batey, M., Chamorro-Premuzic, T., & Furnham, A. (2010). Individual differences in ideational behavior: Can the big five and psychometric intelligence predict creativity scores? *Creativity Research Journal, 22*, 90–97.

Bechtoldt, M. N., De Dreu, C. K. W., Choi, H. -S., & Nijstad, B. A. (2010). Motivated information processing, social tuning, and group creativity. *Journal of Personality and Social Psychology, 99*, 622–637.

Block, J. (1995). A contrarian view to the five-factor approach to personality description. *Psychological Bulletin, 117*, 187–215.

Boniwell, I., Osin, E., Alex, L. P., & Ivanchenko, G. V. (2010). A question of balance: time perspective and well-being in British and Russian samples. *Journal of Positive Psychology, 5*, 24–40.

Boniwell, I., & Zimbardo, P. G. (2004). Balancing time perspective in pursuit of optimal functioning. In P. A. Linley & J. Stephen (Eds.), *Positive psychology in practice* (pp. 165–178). Hoboken, NJ: John Wiley & Sons Inc.

Bowlby, J. (1969). *Attachment and Loss, Vol. 1: Attachment*. New York, NY: Basic Books.

Bowlby, J. (1973). *Attachment and Loss, Vol. 2: Separation, anxiety and anger*. New York, NY: Basic Books.

Brown, J. W. (2001). Foreword. In G. J. W. Smith (Ed.), *The process approach to personality: Percept-geneses and kindred approaches in focus*. New York, NY: Kluwer Academic/Plenum Publishers.

Brown, J. W. (2008). Actualization and causality. In G. J. W. Smith & I. Carlsson (Eds.), *Process and personality: Actualization of the personal world with process-oriented methods* (pp. 263–289). Heusenstamm, Germany: Ontos Verlag.

Bäckström, M., Larsson, M. R., & Maddux, R. E. (2009). A structural validation of an inventory based on the abridged five factor circumplex model (AB5C). *Journal of Personality Assessment, 91*, 462–472.

Cardena, E., & Terhune, D. (2008). A distinct personality trait: The relationship between hypnozability, absorption, self-transcendence, and mental boundaries. *Proceedings of the 51st Annual Convention of Parapsychological Association, 61*–73.

Carlsson, I., Hoff, E. V., & Jönsson, P. (2004). The creative personality in a gender perspective. In J. W. Lee (Ed.), *Focus on gender identity* (pp. 81–96). New York, NY: Nova Science publishers.

Cattell, R. B. (1965). *The scientific analysis of Personality*. Baltimore, MD: Penguin.

Cattell, R. B. (1979). *Personality and learning theory*. New York, NY: Springer.

Cloninger, C. R., Svrakic, D. M., & Przybeck, T. R. (1993). Psychobiological model of temperament and character. *Archives of General Psychiatry, 50*, 975–990.

Collins, M. A., & Amabile, T. M. (1999). Motivation and creativity. In R. J. Steinberg (Ed.), *Handbook of creativity* (pp. 297–312). New York, NY: Cambridge University Press.

Costa, P. T., & McCrae, R. R. (1992). *NEO-PI-R: professional manual*. Odessa, FL: Psychological Assessment Resources.

Craft, A. (2000). Creativity across the primary curriculum: Framing and developing practice. London: Routledge.

Cremin, T., Burnard, P., & Craft, A. (2006). Pedagogy and possibility thinking in the early years. *Thinking Skills and Creativity, 1*, 108–119.

Cropley, A. J. (1992). *More ways than one: fostering creativity*. Norwood, NJ: Ablex.

Csikszentmihályi, M. (1991). *Flow: The psychology of optimal experience*. New York, NY: Harper Perennial.

Csikszentmihályi, M. (1997). *Creativity: Flow and the psychology of discovery and invention*. New York, NY: Harper Perennial.

Dawson, V. L. (1997). In search of the wild bohemian: Challenges in the identification of the creatively gifted. *Roeper Review, 19*(3), 148–152.

Dawson, V. L., D'Andrea, T., Affinito, R., & Westby, E. L. (1999). Predicting creative behavior: A reexamination of the divergence between traditional and teacher-defined concepts of creativity. *Creativity Research Journal, 12*, 57–66.

B. INDIVIDUAL LEVEL INFLUENCES

Debono, E. (1999). *Sex tänkande hattar* (Six thinking hats). Jönköping, Sweden: Brain books. (first published 1985).

Deci, E. L. (1971). Effects of externally mediated rewards on intrinsic motivation. *Journal of Personality and Social Psychology, 18,* 105–115.

DeDreu, C. K. W., Baas, M., & Nijstad, B. A. (2008). Hedonistic tone and activation level in the mood creativity link: Toward a dual pathway to creativity model. *Journal of Personality and Social Psychology, 94,* 739–756.

De Fruyt, F., Wiele, L. V., & Van Heeringen, C. (2000). Cloninger's psychobiological model of temperament and character and the five-factor model of personality. *Personality and Individual Differences, 29,* 441–452.

De Raad, B., & Peabody, D. (2005). Cross-culturally recurrent personality factors: Analyses of three factors. *European Journal of Personality, 19,* 451–474.

Di Blas, L., & Forzi, M. (1999). Refining a descriptive structure of personality attributes in the Italian language: The abridged big three circumplex structure. *Journal of Personality and Social Psychology, 76,* 451–481.

Draguns, J. (2008). Perceptgenesis: its origins, accomplishments and prospects. In G. J. W. Smith & I. Carlsson (Eds.), *Process and Personality: Actualization of the personal world with process-oriented methods* (pp. 23–51). Heusenstamm, Germany: Ontos Verlag.

Dudek, S. Z., Bernèche, R., Bérubé, H., & Royer, S. (1991). Personality determinants of the commitment to the profession of art. *Creativity Research Journal, 4,* 367–389.

Ekvall, G. (1971). *Creativity at the place of work. Report 62.* Stockholm, Sweden: Swedish Council for Personnel Administration.

Ekvall, G. (1996). Organizational climate for creativity and innovation. *European Journal of Work and Organizational Psychology, 5,* 105–123.

Ekvall, G., & Ryhammar, L. (1999). The creative climate: Its determinants and effects at a Swedish university. *Creativity Research Journal, 12,* 303–310.

Eysenck, H. J. (1970). *The structure of human personality* (3rd ed.). London, UK: Methuen.

Eysenck, H. J. (1990). Biological dimensions of personality. In L. A. Pervin (Ed.), *Handbook of personality. Theory and research* (pp. 244–276). New York, NY: Guilford Press.

Eysenck, H. J. (1995). Genius: The natural history of creativity. In J. Gray (Ed.), *Problems in the behavioral sciences, 12. Monograph.* Cambridge, UK: Cambridge University Press.

Feist, G. J. (1998). A meta-analysis of personality in scientific and artistic creativity. *Personality and Social Psychology Review, 2,* 290–309.

Fleeson, W. (2002). Toward a structure- and process-integrated view of personality: Traits as density distribution of states. *Journal of Personality and Social Psychology, 80,* 1011–1027.

Freud, A. (1961). *The ego and the mechanisms of defence.* New York, NY: International Universities Press. (Original work published 1936).

Freud, S. (1953). Three essays on the theory of sexuality. In *Standard Edition, Vol. 7* (pp. 123–243). New York, NY: Hogarth. (Original work published 1905).

Freud, S. (1986). Formulations regarding two principles of mental functioning. In J. Strachey (Ed. And Trans.), *The standard edition of the complete psychological works of Sigmund Freud* (Vol. 12), pp. 213–226. London, UK: Hogarth press. (Original work published 1911).

Furnham, A., & Bachtiar, V. (2008). Personality and intelligence as predictors of creativity. *Personality and Individual Differences, 45,* 613–617.

Gardner, H. (1997). *Extraordinary minds.* New York, NY: Basic Books.

Gillespie, N. A., Cloninger, C. R., Heath, A. C., & Martin, N. G. (2003). The genetic and environmental relationships between Cloninger's dimensions of temperament and character. *Personality and Individual Differences, 35,* 1931–1946.

Goldberg, L. R. (1990). An alternative "description of personality": The Big-Five factor structure. *Journal of Personality and Social Psychology, 59,* 1216–1229.

Goldberg, L. (1992). The development of markers for the Big-Five factor structure. *Psychological Assessment, 4,* 26–42.

Hartmann, H., Kris, E., & Loewenstein, R. M. (1949). Notes on the theory of aggression. *Psychoanalytic Study of the Child, 3,* 9–36.

Hennessey, B. A. (2003). The social psychology of creativity. *Scandinavian Journal of Educational Research, 47,* 253–271.

Hennessey, B. A., & Zbikowski, S. M. (1993). Immunizing children against the negative effects of reward: A further examination of intrinsic motivation training techniques. *Creativity Research Journal, 6,* 297–307.

Hentschel, U., Kiessling, M., Teubner-Berg, H., & Dreier, H. (2004). Intellectual performance and defense mechanisms in depression. In U. Hentschel, G. Smith, J. G. Draguns & W. Ehlers (Eds.), *Defense mechanism: Theoretical, research, and clinical perspectives* (pp. 431–451). Amsterdam, The Netherlands: Elsevier.

Hoff, E. V. (2005). Imaginary companions, creativity, and self-image in middle childhood. *Creativity Research Journal, 17,* 167–181.

Hoff, E. (in press). The relationship between pretend play and creativity. In M. Taylor (Ed.), *Oxford Handbook of Imagination.* New York, NY: Oxford University Press.

Hoff, E., & Carlsson, I. (2008). Vision forming and brain storming: different aspects of creativity captured by a percept-genetic measurement and other measurements of creativity. In G. J. W. Smith & I. Carlsson (Eds.), *Process and Personality: Actualization of the personal world with process-oriented methods* (pp. 221–239). Heusenstamm, Germany: Ontos Verlag.

Isen, A. M., Daubman, K. A., & Nowicki, G. P. (1987). Positive affect facilitates creative problem solving. *Journal of Personality and Social Psychology, 52,* 1122–1131.

Janet, P. (1927). *La pensée interieure et ses troubles.* Oxford, UK: Chahine.

Karwowski, M., & Soszynski, M. (2008). How to develop creative imagination? Assumptions, aims and effectiveness of Role Play Training in Creativity (RPTC). *Thinking Skills and Creativity, 3,* 163–171.

Kaufmann, G., & Kaufmann, A. (1996). *Psykologi i organization och ledning, 2nd ed. (Psychology in organization and management).* Lund, Sweden: Studentlitteratur.

Kemp, A. (1981). The personality structure of the musician: Identifying a profile of traits for the performer. *Psychology of Music, 9,* 3–4.

Kirton, M. (1976). Adaptors and innovators: A description and measure. *Journal of Applied Psychology, 61,* 622–629.

Klein, M. (1975). Love, guilt and reparation. In *The writings of Melanie Klein, vol. 1.* London, UK: The Hogarth Press. (Original work published 1937.)

Kohut, H. (1971). *The analysis of the self.* New York, NY: International Universities Press.

Kris, E. (1952). *Psychoanalytic explorations in art.* New York, NY: International universities Press.

Lepper, M., Greene, D., & Nisbett, R. (1973). Undermining children's intrinsic interest with extrinsic rewards: A test of the 'overjustification hypothesis'. *Journal of Personality and Social Psychology, 28,* 129–137.

Leung, A. K. -y., & Chiu, C-y. (2008). Interactive effects of multicultural experiences and openness to experience on creativity. *Creativity Research Journal, 20,* 376–382.

Leung, A. K. -y., & Chiu, C-y. (2010). Multicultural experience, idea receptiveness, and creativity. *Journal of Cross–Cultural Psychology, 41,* 723–741.

Lieberman, J. N. (1977). *Playfulness: Its relationship to imagination and creativity.* New York, NY: Academic Press.

Lubart, T. I., Jacquet, A. Y., Pacteau, C., & Zenasni, F. (2000). Creativity in children's drawings and links with flexible thinking. Abstracts of the XXVII International Congress of Psychology. *International Journal of Psychology, 35,* 178.

MacKinnon, D. W. (1962). The personality correlates of creativity: A study of American architects. *Proceedings of the Fourteenth Congress for Applied Psychology, 2,* 11–39.

MacKinnon, D. W. (1965). Personality and the realization of creative potentials. *American Psychologist, 20,* 273–281.

Maddux, W. W., & Galinsky, A. D. (2009). Cultural borders and mental barriers: The relationship between living abroad and creativity. *Journal of Personality and Social Psychology, 96,* 1047–1061.

Markovitz, E. (1973). Aggression in human adaptation. *Psychoanalytic Quarterly, 42,* 226–233.

Marsh, H. W., & O'Neill, R. (1984). Self-description questionnaire III: The construct validity of multidimensional self-concept ratings by late adolescents. *Journal of educational measurements, 21,* 153–174.

Martindale, C. (1989). Personality, situation and creativity. In J. A. Glover, R. R. Roning & C. R. Reynolds (Eds.), *Handbook of creativity.* New York, NY and London, UK: Plenum Press.

McCrae, R. R., & Costa, P. T., Jr. (2008). The five-factor theory of personality. In O. P. John, R. W. Robins & L. A. Pervin (Eds.), *Handbook of personality. Theory and research* (3rd Ed.) (pp. 159–181). New York, NY: Guilford.

McCrae, R. R., Costa, P. T., Jr., Ostendorf, F., Angleitner, A., Hrebickova, M., & Avia, M. D., et al. (2000). *Journal of Personality and Social Psychology, 78,* 173–186.

Mednick, S. A. (1962). The associative basis of the creative process. *Psychological Review, 69,* 220–232.

Mischel, W., & Shoda, Y. (2008). Toward a unified theory of personality: Integrating dispositions and processing dynamics within the cognitive-affective processing system. In O. P. John, R. W. Robins & L. A. Pervin (Eds.), *Handbook of personality: Theory and research* (pp. 208–241). New York, NY: Guilford.

Moore, M., & Russ, S. W. (2008). Follow-up of a pretend play intervention: Effects on play, creativity, and emotional processes in children. *Creativity Research Journal, 20,* 427–436.

B. INDIVIDUAL LEVEL INFLUENCES

Mumford, M. D., Costanza, D. P., Threlfall, K. V., Baughman, W. A., & Reiter-Palmon, R. (1993). Personality variables and problem-construction activities: An exploratory investigation. *Creativity Research Journal, 6,* 365–389.

Nickerson, R. S. (1999). Enhancing creativity. In R. J. Sternberg (Ed.), *Handbook of Creativity* (pp. 392–431). New York, NY: Cambridge University Press.

Nickerson, R. S. (2010). How to discourage creative thinking in the classroom. In R. A. Beghetto & J. C. Kaufman (Eds.), *Nurturing creativity in the classroom* (pp. 1–6). New York, NY: Cambridge University Press.

Niu, W., & Sternberg, R. J. (2003). Societal and school influences on student creativity: the case of China. *Psychology in the Schools, 40,* 103–114.

Osborn, A. (1963). *Applied imagination: Principles and procedures of creative thinking.* New York, NY: Scribner's.

Pachalska, M., & MacQueen, B. D. (2008). Process neuropsychology: Microgenetic theory and brain science. In M. Weber & W. Desmond (Eds.), *Handbook of whiteheadian process thought 1 & 2* (pp. 423–436). Frankfurt, Germany: Ontos Verlag.

Paulus, P. B., & Nijstad, B. A. (2003). *Group creativity: Innovation through collaboration.* New York, NY: Oxford University Press.

Pavlov, I. P. (1927). *Conditioned reflexes.* London, UK: Oxford Universities Press.

Pervin, L. A., & Cervone, D. (2010). *Personality: Theory and research* (11th ed.). Hoboken, NJ: John Wiley & Sons.

Rapaport, D. (1967). The theory of attention cathexis. In M. M. Gill (Ed.), *Collected papers of David Rapaport* (pp. 778–791). New York, NY: Basic Books.

Ribot, T. (1885). *Les maladies de la personnalité [The diseases of personality].* Paris, France: Alcan.

Richards, R. (1993). Everyday creativity, eminent creativity, and psychopathology. *Psychological Inquiry, 4,* 212–217.

Robert, C., & Cheung, Y. H. (2010). An examination of the relationship between conscientiousness and group performance on a creative task. *Journal of Research in Personality, 44,* 222–231.

Runco, M. (2007). *Creativity theories and themes: Research, development, and practice.* Burlington, MA: Elsevier Academic Press.

Runco, M. A., Johnson, D. J., & Bear, P. K. (1993). Parents' and teachers' implicit theories of children's creativity. *Child Study, 23,* 91–113.

Russ, S. W. (1999). Emotion/Affect. In M. Runco & S. R. Pritzker (Eds.), *Encyclopedia of creativity, Vol. 1* (pp. 659–668). San Diego, CA: Academic Press.

Ryan, R. M., & Deci, E. L. (2000). Self-determination theory and the facilitation of intrinsic motivation, social development, and well-being. *American Psychologist, 55,* 68–78.

Ryhammar, L., & Smith, G. J. W. (1999). Creative and other personality functions as defined by percept-genetic techniques and their relation to organizational conditions. *Creativity Research Journal, 12,* 277–286.

Ryhammar, L., & Andersson, A. L. (2001). Relations between university teachers' assessed degree of creativity and productivity and views regarding their organization. *The Journal of Creative Behavior, 35,* 199–204.

Sandler, J., & Joffe, W. G. (1965). Notes on obsessional manifestations in children. *The Psychoanalytic Study of the Child, 20,* 425–438.

Scott, G., Lertiz, L. E., & Mumford, M. (2004). The effectiveness of creativity training: A quantitative review. *Creativity Research Journal, 16,* 361–388.

Shoda, Y., Mischel, W., & Peake, P. K. (1990). Predicting adolescent cognitive and self-regulatory competencies from preschool delay of gratification: Identifying diagnostic conditions. *Developmental Psychology, 26,* 978–986.

Singer, D. J., & Singer, J. L. (1992). *The house of make-believe.* Cambridge, MA: Harvard University Press.

Sjöbäck, H. (1988). *The Freudian learning hypotheses: Psychoanalytic ideas about the scope and nature of early environmental influence on character development and pathogenesis.* Lund, Sweden: Lund University Press.

Skinner, B. F. (1971). *Beyond Freedom and Dignity.* New York, NY: Knopf.

Smith, G. J. W. (2001). *The process approach to personality: Percept-geneses and kindred approaches in focus.* New York, NY: Kluwer Academic/Plenum Publishers.

Smith, G. J. W., & Carlsson, I. M. (1990). *The creative process: A functional model based on empirical studies from early childhood to middle age.* Madison, CT: International Universities Press.

Smith, G., & Carlsson, I. (2001). *CFT The creative functioning test: Manual.* Lund, Sweden: Department of Psychology, Lund University.

Smith, G. J. W., & Carlsson, I. (2006). Creativity under the northern lights. Perspectives from Scandinavia. In J. C. Kaufman & R. J. Sternberg (Eds.), *The international handbook of creativity* (pp. 202–234). Cambridge, NY: Cambridge University Press.

Smith, G. J. W., & Carlsson, I. M. (2008). *Process and Personality: Actualization of the personal world with process-oriented methods*. Heusenstamm, Germany: Ontos Verlag.

Smith, G. J. W., Carlsson, I., & Danielsson, A. (1986). Creativity and aggression. *Psychoanalytic Psychology, 3*, 159–172.

Smith, G. J. W., & Hentschel, U. (2004). Percept-genetic identification of defense. In U. Hentschel, G. Smith, J. G. Druguns & W. Ehlers (Eds.), *Defense mechanism: Theoretical, research, and clinical perspectives* (pp. 129–152). Amsterdam, The Netherlands: Elsevier.

Smith, G. J. W., Nyman, E., Hentschel, U., & Rubino, I. A. (2001). *S-CWT: The serial color-word Test*. Frankfurt, Germany: Swets & Zeitlinger.

Smith, G. J. W., & van der Meer, G. (1990). Creativity in old age. *Creativity Research Journal, 3*, 249–267.

Soh, K. C. (2000). Indexing creativity fostering behavior: A preliminary validation study. *Journal of Creative Behavior, 34*, 118–134.

Sonnby-Borgström, M. (2002). *Between Ourselves. Automatic mimicry reactions as related to empathic ability and patterns of attachment*. Lund, Sweden: Department of Psychology, Lund University. Unpublished doctoral dissertation.

Sonnby-Borgström, M., & Jönsson, P. (2004). Dismissing-avoidant pattern of attachment and mimicry reactions at different levels of information processing. *Scandinavian Journal of Psychology, 45*, 103–113.

Stern, W. (1938). *General psychology from a pesonalistic standpoint*. New York, NY: Macmillan. (H.D. Soerl, Trans.)

Sternberg, R. J. (1985). Implicit theories of intelligence, creativity, and wisdom. *Journal of Personality and Social Psychology, 49*, 607–627.

Sternberg, R. J., & Lubart, T. I. (1999). The concept of creativity: Prospects and paradigms. In R. J. Sternberg (Ed.), *Handbook of Creativity* (pp. 3–15). New York, NY: Cambridge University Press.

Taggar, S. (2001). Group composition, creative synergy, and group performance. *Journal of Creative Behavior, 35*, 261–286.

Thompson, P., Keehn, E. B., & Gumpel, T. P. (2009). Generators and interpretors in a performing arts population: Dissociation, trauma, fantasy proneness, and affective states. *Creativity Research Journal, 21*, 72–92.

Tomkins, S. (1962). *Affect, imagery, consciousness* (2 vols.). New York, NY: Springer.

Torrance, E. P. (1965). *Rewarding creative behavior*. Englewood Cliffs, NJ: Prentice-Hall.

Torrance, E. P. (1990). *Torrance tests of creative thinking: Norms and technical manual*. Bensenville, IL: Scholastic Testing Service.

Twenge, J. (2000). The age of anxiety: Birth cohort change in anxiety and neuroticism, 1952–1993. *Journal of Personality and Social Psychology, 79*, 1007–1021.

Twenge, J. (2001). Birth cohort changes in extraversion: a cross-temporal meta-analysis, 1966–1993. *Personality and Individual Differences, 30*, 735–748.

Urban, K. K. (2004). Assessing creativity, the test for creative thinking-drawing production (TCT-DP): The concept, application evaluation and international studies. *Psychology Science, 46*, 387–397.

Urban, K. K., & Jellen, H. G. (1996). *Test for creative thinking—Drawing production (TCT-DP)*. Lisse, The Netherlands: Swets and Zeitlinger.

Vaillant, G. E. (1993). *The wisdom of the ego*. Cambridge, MA: Harvard University Press.

Vygotskij, L. S. (1995). *Fantasi och kreativitet i barndomen* [Fantasy and creativity in childhood] (K. Öberg, trans.). Göteborg, Sweden: Bokförlaget Daidalos. (Original work published 1930).

Wallach, M. A., & Kogan, N. (1965). *Modes of thinking in young children: a study of the creativity/intelligence distinction*. New York, NY: Holt, Rinehart and Winston.

Watson, J. (1924). *Behaviorism*. New York, NY: People's Institute Publishing.

Weinberger, D. A., & Davidson, M. N. (1994). Styles of inhibiting emotional expression: Distinguishing repressive coping from impression management. *Journal of Personality, 62*, 587–613.

Weinberger, D. A., Schwartz, G. E, & Davison, R. J. (1979). Low-anxious, high-anxious, and repressive coping styles. Psychometric patterns and behavioral and physiological responses to stress. *Journal of Abnormal Psychology, 88*, 369–380.

Weisberg, R. W. (2006). Expertise and reason in creative thinking: Evidence from case studies and the laboratory. In J. C. Kaufman & J. Baer (Eds.), *Creativity and reason in cognitive development* (pp. 7–42). Cambridge, UK: Cambridge University Press.

West, M. A. (2003). Innovation implementation in work teams. In P. B. Paulus & B. A. Nijstad (Eds.), *Group creativity: Innovation through collaboration* (pp. 245–276). New York, NY: Oxford University Press.

Westby, E. L., & Dawson, V. L. (1995). Creativity: Asset or burden in the classroom. *Creativity Research Journal, 8*, 1–10.

Westerlundh, B. (2004). Percept-genesis and the study of defensive processes. In U. Hentschel, G. Smith, J. G. Druguns & W. Ehlers (Eds.), *Defense mechanism: Theoretical, research, and clinical perspectives* (pp. 91–103). Amsterdam, The Netherlands: Elsevier.

Wolke, B. Z. (2008). A functional framework for the influence of implicit and explicit motives on autobiographical memory. *Personality and Social Psychology Review, 12,* 99–117.

Zimbardo, P. G., & Boyd, J. N. (1999). Putting time in perspective: A valid, reliable, individual-differences metric. *Journal of Personality and Social Psychology, 77,* 1271–1288.

Zuber, I., & Ekehammar, B. (1997). An empirical look at the Defence Mechanism Test (DMT): Stimulus effects. *Scandinavian Journal of Psychology, 38,* 85–94.

12

Fostering Individual Creativity Through Organizational Context: A Review of Recent Research and Recommendations for Organizational Leaders

Mark D. Agars[1], James C. Kaufman[1], Amanda Deane[2], and Blakely Smith[2]

[1]Learning Research Institute, California State University, San Bernardino, CA;
[2]California State University, San Bernardino, CA

Creativity in the workplace is increasingly recognized as a valuable organizational commodity (Amabile, 1996; Chen & Kaufmann, 2008; Ford & Gioia, 1995; Rosa, Qualls, & Fuentes, 2008; Shalley & Gilson, 2004). The value of a creative workforce will only increase as organizations face an ever-expanding global nature of business, continued and rapid changes in technology, increased competition for products and/or services, and regular changes to organizational structures, strategies, and environments (Egan, 2005). Indeed, creativity has been identified as the 21st century's most important economic resource (Florida, 2002). Though the value of creativity grows increasingly clear, the factors that contribute to a creative and innovative workforce are more elusive. Although much attention in the creativity literature has been paid to individual characteristics related to creative potential (Ivcevic, 2009), the business world necessarily requires an understanding of creativity that is both more considerate of organizational context and which focuses more directly on domain specific behavioral outcomes. The purpose of our chapter is to highlight the role of organizational context in the development of individual creativity, to discuss the impact of leader

Handbook of Organizational Creativity.
DOI: 10.1016/B978-0-12-374714-3.00012-4

and organizational-level factors, and to identify key steps in advancing our understanding of context so that organizations may benefit more directly from the research on individual creativity and context.

A big challenge to understanding contextual influences on individual creativity in organizations is the inconsistency with which creativity has been defined. In a review of over 90 different articles appearing in either the top two creativity journals, or from peer-reviewed journals in business, psychology, and education, which used the word "creativity" in the title, Plucker, Beghetto, and Dow (2004) found that 62% of the articles failed to explicitly define creativity in their work. While some have defined creativity as requiring something to be both novel and useful (Sternberg, 2006) others have argued that the "useful" aspect of a creative idea or product is a reference to innovation, and that the development or generation process (i.e., creativity) is separate (Amabile, 1996).

In an organizational context, the value of separating creativity and innovation is questionable. As we have noted elsewhere (Agars, Kaufman, & Locke, 2008) creativity and innovation should be considered as distinct constructs because of differences in how each may be predicted (Rank, Pace, & Frese, 2004; West, 2002). From a business perspective, however, creativity for its own sake has minimal value. If not for the useful implementation of a creative idea, product, or process, why would an organization value creativity? Fittingly, in the organizational world, creativity is most often defined as the production of novel and useful ideas (Hemlin, Allwood, & Martin, 2009; Mumford & Gustafson, 1988). Still, this definition is not without limitations when one is considering creativity in a business context. For example, what is considered "creative" in one organization may be problematic for another. Similarly, individual acts of creativity may not be supported (nor valued) in an organization where performance is largely team based. Plucker et al. (2004) addressed these concerns when they defined creativity as:

"...the interaction among aptitude, process, and environment by which an individual or group produces a perceptible product that is both novel and useful as defined within a social context" (p.90).

This definition is valuable both because it illustrates the complexity of causal factors underlying creativity, but also because it underscores the role of the general work domain (and the individual business domains that may exist therein). Indeed, others have argued the importance of defining creativity within a particular domain (Baer & Kaufman, 2005; Ford, 1996), and when thinking about the creativity product (i.e., instead of the creative person) the domain-specificity argument has received substantial support (Baer, 1991, 1994, 1998; Han, 2003; Runco, 1989). As one example, in a study of creative problem solving, Reiter-Palmon, Illies, Cross, Buboltz, and Nimps (2009) found that creativity was differentially influenced by problem type. Even though these problems were all broad examples of real life creativity, they represented separate domains at the micro level. Most relevant to the manager, Baer (1996, 1997, 1998) has argued that although person-factors are relevant, the smart manager should be primarily interested in domain-specific guidance.

We strongly endorse the domain-specific approach to creativity. One challenge to informing organizational leaders through a domain-specific pursuit, however, is in determining which lessons from the general creativity literature are appropriate for the domains of business. In their Four-C model of creativity, Kaufman and Beghetto (2009) take a lifespan view of creativity. Early in life, a typical creator might be beginning to play with her creativity and exploring personal insights (mini-c) as she discovers new things. Most people will first experience mini-c early in life. After repeated attempts and encouragements, the creator might then reach the realm of everyday creativity (little-c). As part of this process of enjoying creativity in everyday life, the creator may stumble upon the domain that she feels an initial pull of passion. With years of acquired expertise and advanced schooling, the creator may move onto the stage of professional creativity (Pro-c). Although she will still have mini-c insights, the creator has now achieved professional-level status and is capable of working on problems, projects, and ideas that affect the field as a whole. The creator may continue to create at the Pro-c level throughout her entire life, with specific peaks occurring at different ages based on the domain (e.g., Simonton, 1997). After many years have come and gone, the creator may achieve a lasting, legendary creativity (Big-C) contribution to a field (e.g., the Nobel Prize) or the creator may have passed away, and history will make the final judgment as to whether she has entered the pantheon of Big-C or has been long-forgotten.

Pro-c represents the developmental and effortful progression beyond little-c (but that has not yet attained Big-C status). Anyone who attains professional-level expertise in any creative area is likely to have attained Pro-c status. Not all working professionals in creative fields will necessarily reach Pro-c (a professional actor, for example, may make a good living on soap operas but may not necessarily be Pro-c level creative in his or her craft). Similarly, some people may reach Pro-c level without being able to necessarily quit day jobs; some areas of creative expression may not provide enough monetary sustenance to allow financial freedom from other responsibilities; many "amateur" artists are creative at the Pro-c level, even if it is not their primary means of support (Kaufman & Beghetto, 2009).

The challenge for organizational leaders is that most theories of creativity are aimed at either little-c or Big-C. People's creativity in their professional lives is often overlooked by other branches of psychological research. Consistent with Kaufman and Beghetto (2009), Styhre (2006) suggested that creativity and innovation need not be thought of as extraordinary events, but should be thought of as regularly occurring possibilities in organizations. How much this has occurred is debatable. In the remaining sections of this chapter, we provide a brief overview of the consideration of context in organizational creativity and innovation theory, followed by a discussion of insights gained from the research specific to work organizations, with a particular emphasis on leadership and organizational-level contexts. We conclude with a discussion of challenges and recommendations for fostering creativity in organizations.

CONTEXTUAL FACTORS AND INDIVIDUAL CREATIVITY

Early work on creativity focused largely on the importance of the individual to the creativity process and the production of creative products (Barron & Harrington, 1981; Ford & Gioia, 1995; Galton, 1869; Reuter, Panksepp, Schnabel, Kellerhoff, & Hennig, 2005). Increasingly, however, contextual factors have become integrated into theories and approaches to creativity in organizations. Amabile's Componential Theory of Creativity (1983a, 1983b) represents one of the earliest considerations of contextual factors in a theoretical sense. Her later Model of Creativity and Innovation in Organizations (Amabile 1997, 1998) specifically incorporated organizational resources, management practices, and an organization's orientation towards innovation as contextual predictors of creativity. Others have discussed the importance of social context. The Theory of Organizational Creativity

(Woodman, Sawyer, & Griffin, 1993), one of the first true multi-level models of creativity, included group norms, group cohesiveness, and social roles as key social predictors of creativity. The model also indentifies organizational-level factors such as culture, resources, rewards, strategy, structure, and technology as having both direct and indirect influences on individual creative behaviors. Today, major theories within organizational creativity field are consistent in their recognition of the importance of both person and contextual factors (Shalley, Zhou & Oldham, 2004). These include the Theory of Creative Action in Multiple Social Domains (Ford 1996), a Sensemaking Theory of Creativity in Organizations (Drazin, Glynn, & Kazanjian, 1999), a Propulsion Model of Creativity (Sternberg, 1999; Sternberg, Kaufman, & Pretz, 2002, 2003) and West's (2002) Integrative Model of Creativity and Innovation Implementation in Work Groups. An in-depth discussion of these is beyond our current scope (see Agars et al., 2008 for a more detailed review of these theories), though their existence is worth noting as it underscores the increased recognition that understanding creativity in the workplace requires a careful consideration of context. They further illustrate, as we will discuss, the complexities such context represents.

Of particular interest to the current chapter is the consideration of domains. In presenting the Theory of Creative Action in Multiple Social Domains, Ford (1996) noted that domains represent independent contexts within which unique norms for creative behavior may develop. As we noted earlier, however, much of our research on creativity is individual based or conducted in domains that may not be generalizable to the organization. As interesting as it may be to demonstrate improved creativity on Torrance tests of creativity (e.g. Torrance & Presbury, 1984; Torrance & Safter, 1989), such demonstrations are not the same as producing creative outcomes in an organizational domain (i.e. Pro-c; Kaufman & Beghetto, 2009). In the whimsically titled Amusement Park Theoretical (APT) Model of Creativity (Baer & Kaufman, 2005; Kaufman & Baer, 2004; Kaufman, Beghetto, Baer, & Ivcevic, 2010), the analogy of the amusement park, with multiple themed areas, is used to illustrate the importance of considering domains in understanding individual creativity. The APT model suggests that it is the intersection of individual characteristics with general thematic areas (which park we attend), domains (different themed areas within the park), and micro domains (individual rides within each themed area). In the organizational context, this may reflect different industries, specific organizations within an industry, and functional areas within a particular organization. For example, the general thematic area might be book publishing; domain might be this publisher, Cambridge; and the micro-domain could be the copyediting department. There are, of course, multiple examples in the world where domains are nested in this way (Agars, Baer, & Kaufman, 2005).

Reflected in these nested domains is the fact that there are both general factors (i.e., factors that relate to creativity in each micro-domain within a domain, or each domain within a thematic area) and unique or specific factors (i.e., factors that relate to creativity only within a particular domain or micro-domain) that determine what is or is not a creative outcome. Ultimately, the implication of this nested approach to creativity is that if we are to understand what will lead to creative outcomes among employees, we must identify and understand the general and specific factors that pertain to a particular context. Examining creativity at the micro-domain level, for example, can help in an organization with many different types of positions. For some micro-domains, such as a marketing department, personality factors such as agreeableness and extraversion might be important. For others, such as accounting, the conscientiousness personality factor might be the most essential.

B. INDIVIDUAL LEVEL INFLUENCES

As we noted earlier, much of what we have learned about creativity from the general creativity literature has limited and somewhat unknown application to creativity in organizations. What is clear is that the domains of interest in organizations require a more direct and precise examination of context than what has occurred outside of the organizational literature. Exacerbating this problem is that within the organizational literature, much of the research focus has been on group creativity/innovation, leaving the study of individual creativity to the creativity researchers themselves. But how much of what we know about creatively in general is applicable to our understanding of Pro-c? We are not saying there is nothing to be learned, but the question should be asked, particularly in light of the growing importance of domain specificity (Ford, 1996; Kaufman & Baer, 2002, 2005).

One of the key components of advancing from mini-c to little-c to Pro-c is the presence of a mentor. Sometimes this mentor can be found in a *formal apprenticeship*, such as a professor advising a student. An alternate path is the transitional period of tinkering—playing with one's creativity in a domain and improving through such experimentation, even without a structured mentorship. In these cases, the mentorship can be in the form of audience comments and feedback. In the organizational realm, the role of the mentor is essential, and is often found in supervisors. Good organizational leaders are good mentors, and they can enhance individual and group creativity.

Leadership and Creativity

Kaufman and Beghetto (2009) proposed the concept of Pro-c to distinguish creativity in the workplace from other types of creativity. In the following section, we will discuss leadership as a mechanism through which Pro-c can be encouraged and sustained in organizations. Mumford, Scott, Gaddis and Strange (2002) described a leader's role in fostering creativity as:

> "the exercise of influence to increase the likelihood of idea generation by followers and the subsequent development of these ideas into useful products" (p. 706).

We will discuss the characteristics and behaviors of leaders as well as the types of relationships they have with followers, which enable them to fulfill this role and thus cultivate an innovative organizational culture.

Creative expression at work involves a considerable investment of time and energy on the part of both the employee and the organization. Employees must be motivated to allocate a large amount of their temporal and cognitive resources to a creative project, and organizations must be willing to provide employees with the necessary support and freedom which enables them to invest said resources (Carmeli & Schaubroeck, 2007). To complicate the matter further, participation in the creative process often involves the need for both expertise and collaboration, which entails that an organization must support the continued attainment of expertise for those involved in creative projects (Mumford et al., 2002). The need for collaboration highlights the importance for leaders to have the interpersonal skills needed to facilitate group interactions in order to guide idea generation and evaluation effectively (Mumford et al., 2002). A recent theme in the leadership and creativity literature describes how transformational leadership may be an exceptionally successful mechanism by which to increase creativity and innovation in organizations (e.g., Elenkov & Manev, 2009; Jansen, Vera, & Crossan, 2009; Reuvers, Van Engen, Vinkenburg, & Wilson-Evered, 2008).

Transformational leadership, introduced by Burns (1978), influences both individual level creativity and organizational level innovation (Gumusluoglu & Islev, 2009). These leadership behaviors serve to motivate, inspire and support employees during times of uncertainty, such as when an organization is trying to increase participation in creative behaviors (Jung, Chow, & Wu, 2008; Reuvers et al., 2003). Transformational leadership tactics can also be used to direct culture change in an organization, such as when adopting a climate for supporting innovation. Kouzes and Pozner (1987) described the following five behaviors as characteristic of transformational leaders: modeling the way, inspiring a shared vision, challenging the process, enabling others to act and encouraging the heart. In an alternative description by Podsakoff, MacKenzie, Moorman, and Fetter (1990), the authors described six characteristics of transformational leadership: articulating a vision for the future, providing an appropriate role model, fostering the acceptance of goals, setting high performance expectations, providing individual support, and providing intellectual stimulation. Through these behaviors, leaders are able to enhance the psychological meaning that employees place on their work tasks and goals (Gumusluoglu & Islev, 2009). Transformational leadership inspires employees to put the needs of the organization (e.g., increased competitive advantage through innovation) before their personal needs (e.g., the desire not to risk failure or to experience discomfort associated with attempting a novel, time-consuming task) (Bass, 1996).

It is interesting to note that Jaussi and Dionne (2003) found that unconventional behavior on the part of the leader (e.g., standing on chairs) explained variability in employee creative behavior over and above that of transformational leadership. These findings imply that the "role model" aspect of transformational leadership might be especially important when attempting to inspire creativity in followers. Similarly, in an empirical study investigating the relationship between transformational leadership behaviors (as defined by Podsakoff et al., 1990), organizational culture and climate for innovation, only the Articulates Vision and Provides Individualized Support factors of transformational leadership were significantly related to climate for innovation (Sarros, 2008). These results imply that the most important characteristics of transformational leaders are their ability to simultaneously set inspiring group goals while guiding individuals through the actual creative process.

Elenkov and Manev (2009) found that expatriate managers' visionary transformational leadership behaviors were related to the rate of innovation adoption in their organizations. This study was unique, in that the effect of transformational leadership on creativity was being assessed in diverse, multinational organizations, and thus cultural intelligence was considered to be an important moderating characteristic of transformational leadership. In a multi-cultural context it is not possible to facilitate creative expression, and expertly evaluate creative products without being able to adapt one's behavior in order to interact effectively within a cultural context. This study concentrates on cultural intelligence. It highlights, however, the general need to understand the context of the organization in which a leader works and adapt strategies accordingly.

The influence of a transformational leader will inspire heightened commitment to group goals; however, it is the climate and culture for innovation that will help to support the individual throughout the creative process. The functionalist perspective of organizational culture (Schein, 1985, 1992; Trice & Beyer, 1993) suggests that leaders have a significant role (if not *the* most significant role) in molding an organization's culture (Sarros, 2008). An innovative climate or culture represents an environment that encourages collaboration and experimentation (Elenkov & Manev, 2008) which may mean rewarding failure. When an organization has a climate for innovation, the positive effects of transformational leadership on innovation are stronger (Jung, Chow, & Wu, 2003). This means that not only do transformational leaders empower their employees, but they are able to fashion an organizational climate which continues to foster that creativity (Damanpour & Schneider, 2006).

Although the research cited above paints an optimistic picture of the effects of transformational leadership on employee innovative behaviors, not all studies investigating this relationship are as encouraging. Some studies have found no relationship between these constructs (e.g., Jaussi & Dionne, 2003; Moss & Ritossa, 2007) while others have even found a negative effect of transformational leadership on both innovation (Basu & Green, 1997) and creativity (Kahai, Sosik, & Avolio, 2003). Addressing the apparent inconsistencies in the extant literature, Nederveen Pieterse, Van Knippenberg, Schippers, and Stam (2010) found that transformational leadership has a positive effect on employee innovation *only* when employee psychological empowerment is high.

The proposition that moderator variables are responsible for the mixed results reported in the leadership and creativity literature supports our argument that context must be considered when trying to understand and augment creativity in the work place. Leadership behaviors are but one of many contextual variables discussed in this chapter. It is important to consider other components of context, in addition to dispositional characteristics of individual employees when attempting to influence organizational innovation in both research and practice. Without concomitantly considering characteristics of the individual, environment, and the task itself, researchers and practitioners alike will lack all the necessary information to effect results.

Nederveen Pieterse et al. (2010) argued that transformational leadership may render employees *willing* to be innovative but unless they consider themselves *able* to be innovative (i.e., psychologically empowered), transformational leadership will not have an effect on their creative behaviors. This is an important distinction to consider when investigating any of the contextual factors described in this chapter; does the context increase an employee's willingness to be innovative, or their belief in their ability to be innovative? In this section, transformational leadership has been described as a characteristic of the environment which can potentially support and motivate an individual to be innovative; however there are other factors concerning both the person and the situation that will determine whether an individual feels that they are able to be innovative, regardless of how motivated they are to do so. It should also be noted that the role of a transformational leader is motivational in nature. The leader's task is not to take responsibility for the creative products of employees, but to encourage them to be willing to attempt innovation, and to provide them a context appropriate to take that risk.

It is not just transformational leadership that affects the creativity of employees. Simply having an identifiable leader has been shown to increase innovation in organizations (West, Borril, Dawson, & Brodbeck, 2003). Mumford et al. (2002) described additional characteristics of effective leadership, such as expertise, creative problem solving, social skills, and planning, which are essential when leading individuals engaged in creative processes. Expertise and creative problem solving skills are of increased importance because these characteristics are highly respected by creative individuals, and thus lead to increased social influence on the part of the leader. Furthermore, these characteristics enable leaders to provide guidance and structure in times of uncertainty because they are able to understand and relate to the creative process being undertaken by the employees. Without technical expertise, the leader would not be able to evaluate the products of creative processes. Other characteristics of effective leaders include the ability to plan and set goals broadly, thus creating structure without stifling employee autonomy (Mumford et al., 2002). Social skills (e.g., coaching, communication, persuasion, and social intelligence) are also important characteristics for leaders of creative groups—leaders must be able to communicate expectations, and interact with groups and individuals engaged in a stressful, emotionally charged task. It is easy to imagine how these skills would be helpful during a potentially heated debate over which employee's novel solution to a particular problem is most useful.

The characteristics discussed thus far describe ways in which leaders can most effectively express their expectations for creativity, and support employees in their attempts to reach these expectations. Concerning the expectations themselves, Carmeli and Schaubroeck (2007) conducted a study investigating the mediating effect of self-expectations for creativity on the relationship between referent group expectations for creativity and employee involvement in creative behavior at work. The authors found that leader expectations for creativity had the strongest effect on individual self expectations for creativity (compared to customer and family expectations). In addition to the proposed mediated effect, a direct effect between leader expectations and creative involvement of employees at work was found. Not only do leader expectations influence self-expectations, but employees are likely to comply to the expectations of leaders even if they do not internalize the expectations themselves (Carmeli & Schaubroeck, 2007). These results seem to be contrary to the suggestions of Mumford et al. (2002), which described conformity pressure as a detriment to creativity.

The authors also found that the relationship between self-expectations and creative involvement was stronger for individuals with high creative self-efficacy (Carmeli & Schaubroeck, 2007). This implies that individuals who do not believe they are capable of creative work are less likely to become involved in such work even if they have high expectations to participate. These results highlight the importance for leaders to not only communicate high expectations for creative work, but to also provide mechanisms for employees to enhance their belief that they are capable of meeting these high expectations. This may require that leaders utilize different behaviors when communicating high expectations—such as by setting challenging group goals, than when communicating confidence in employees' abilities—such as by providing individualized support (Carmeli & Schaubroeck, 2007).

Successful leadership for creative performance is a unique challenge. Hunter, Thoroughgood, Myer, and Ligon (2011) highlight four clusters of 14 paradoxes that face leaders who value innovation, following in the path of Csikszentmihályi's (1996) discussion of the paradoxes inherent in being creative. Hunter et al. focus on such conflicts as how to make employees intrinsically motivated in an environment tailored to extrinsic rewards and how to reduce costs while still supporting and nurturing creativity.

We have described the characteristics of leaders that enable them to inspire individuals to engage in creative work and effectively manage these individuals throughout the creative process. Next we will describe how the relationships that effective leaders have with their employees serve to encourage creativity. Atwater and Carmeli (2009) found that high quality relationships with leaders were related to feelings of high energy, which were subsequently related to increased creativity. However, this relationship was stronger for employees whose jobs had a traditionally low-level demand for creativity. This is important for the current discussion, because we are addressing a range of organizations (which may not be considered to have creative job tasks in the traditional sense) and are arguing that regardless of how "creative" the job is assumed to be, without innovation, that organization will not survive in the current ever-changing economic environment. Thus, leader-member exchange, as a mechanism for sustaining employee energy and thus facilitating creativity, is even more important for leaders in "low creativity" fields than for leaders in characteristically "creative" fields. Their study highlighted the complex nature of the relationship between leadership and employee creativity and distinguished employee feelings of energy as an important intervening variable.

Leadership is an imperative factor in strategic organizational change aimed to increase both the generation of new and useful ideas by employees and the application of these ideas in organizations. Through influence, relationships, and strategic behaviors, leaders with the characteristics discussed in this section can effectively inspire, support, direct, and evaluate the creativity of employees, resulting in organizations that are competitive in today's ever-changing business environment. Leaders can inspire employees to think more openly and engage more fully in their tasks, in order to produce novel solutions to projects ranging from everyday work tasks to market changing products. Leaders are also in a position to nurture, direct, and support the creativity of employees by molding an organizational climate and culture that is supportive of innovation. Such a climate gives individuals the safety, autonomy, and intellectual stimulation needed to actively attempt creativity while lessening the negative associations linked with such an uncertain and stressful endeavor.

Group and Organizational Level Factors

The substantial attention to leadership factors is appropriate, given a leader's centrality to organizational culture and direct impact on individual outcomes. The larger organizational context however, comprises a multi-level environment with a myriad of individual, group, social, and structural influences on creativite function (Agars et al., 2008; Hemlin et al., 2009). In this section we discuss several of those factors, focusing on research that has examined Pro-c outcomes in organizational domains.

Group Factors

A fair amount of research on creativity and innovation in the organizational world has focused on group-level phenomena (c.f.: Hulsheger, Anderson, & Salgado, 2009), and recent theories of organizational creativity have also underscored the importance of group influence (e.g., Ford, 1996; West, 2002). Much (not all) of the research underlying these concepts, however, has focused on group-level outcomes as well.

Though primarily interested in team-based creativity, Tagger (2002) examined the creativity of groups and individuals in a study of 94 groups of business students attending a Canadian university. His work revealed that group processes such as goal setting, preparation, idea synthesis, and group problem solving all increased individual group member creativity (a prelude to group-level creativity). Looking at coworker, supervisor, and personal support factors, Madjar, Oldham, and Pratt (2002) found that perceived support for creativity from coworkers and supervisors as well as friends and family members was positively related to creative performance (as assessed by supervisor perceptions). Interestingly, the impact of each group's influence was mediated by individual (positive) mood.

In one of the first cross-level examinations of team factors and individual characteristics, Hirst, Van Knippenberg, and Zhou (2009) explored the relationship between goal orientation (learning versus performance) and individual creativity. As Hirst et al. note, the characteristics associated with learning orientation have long been argued to be a prerequisite to individual creativity (Amabile 1983a, 1983b, 1996). They argued, however, that the relationship was in part determined by group-level factors; notably that the strength of the orientation–creative performance relationship was dependent upon team learning behaviors. In a study of 255 individuals comprising 25 research and development teams in the US, UK, and Sweden, Hirst et al. found that learning goal orientation was indeed related to individual creativity. However, consistent with expectations, when team learning behaviors were high, the relationships were strongest among individuals with an intermediate level of learning orientation. When team learning behavior was low, the relationship was strongest among individuals with high level of learning orientation. They also found that for individuals with an approach performance orientation (often expected to be negatively related to creative performance) creative performance was highest when team learning behaviors were high. In other words, when team learning behaviors were high, an approach performance orientation was positively related to creative performance. This finding is an important demonstration of the interaction between individual and (team) context in understanding creative outcomes.

In a more extensive examination of group-level influences, Hulsheger et al. (2009) conducted a meta-analysis of research looking at team-level predictors of innovation at the team- and individual-levels. Although effects were generally larger for the relationships at the team-level, several predictors of individual level innovation emerged. Taking Hackman's (1987) I-P-O approach to examining team level influences, Hulsheger et al. found that in terms of team characteristics, background diversity had a negative impact on creativity while job relevant diversity positively related to innovation. The authors appropriately note that many questions about the impact of diversity on creative performance remain, but also note that these findings, which are inconsistent with research on diversity and general performance, underscore the importance of looking at the multidimensionality of performance. The strongest team characteristic predictor of innovation was goal interdependence. In terms of team processes, strong relationships with innovation were found for team vision, internal and external communication, support for innovation, and task orientation.

Social Systems and Coworkers

Despite an increase in the consideration of organizational context, Perry-Smith (2006) notes that little research has examined the social context. This finding was echoed in a review of creativity-based dissertations published from 2005–2007 (Kahl, da Fonseca, & Witte, 2009). Building on a social-network approach to understanding creativity (Perry-Smith & Shalley, 2003), Perry-Smith (2006) examined the impact of social networks, finding that a greater number of weak ties relate to increased levels of individual creativity. The relationship was mediated by heterogeneity of direct contacts, supporting the importance of having interactions with and access to individuals with varying backgrounds and skill sets.

Madjar (2005) has also argued for the importance of expanding our consideration of social factors in creative performance, and has demonstrated the importance of both internal and external sources of social support (Madjar et al., 2002). More recently, Madjar (2008) demonstrated that the type of support may be differentially important depending on the social group source. Specifically, she found that while both information and emotional support from coworkers was related to creative performance, emotional support from social groups outside of the organization was not.

In advancing the interactionist perspective, Zhou, Shin, Brass, Choi, and Zhang (2009) conducted a study of Chinese organizations. They looked at how the role of social networks in the production of creative behaviors might be moderated by individual values, specifically the value for conformity. Similar to Perry-Smith (2006), Zhou et al. found that having an intermediate level of weak ties is related to increased creativity. Importantly, however, this relationship was present for individuals with low value for conformity. For individuals who highly valued, conformity weak ties did not predict creativity. Contrary to their expectations, strong ties were unrelated to creativity (i.e., not negative as expected).

Other aspects of the social context have proven to be important. In a set of two studies, Zhou (2003) looked at the impact of creative coworkers and the interaction of leader feedback and coworker creativity on individual creative performance. This was an integration of social cognitive theory and the intrinsic motivation arguments. In study 1, Zhou found that developmental feedback from the supervisor and the presence of creative coworkers interacted to influence individual creative behaviors. Specifically, creative behaviors were greatest in the presence of developmental feedback and creative coworkers. Interestingly, when the presence of creative coworkers was low, supervisor feedback did not meaningfully affect creative performance. In study 2, Zhou found that this effect was magnified for individuals with less creative personalities, underscoring the important role context may play in the development of creative behaviors even among employees who have individual characteristics that are less likely to produce individual creativity.

Choi, Anderson, and Veillette (2009) found that coworker creativity interacted with individual creative ability, but in a positive direction. Low creative ability individuals were more creative when surrounded by coworkers who had less creative ability. This goes counter to a means-efficacy explanation, which would suggest increased resources enhance creativity (Agars et al., 2008), but may reflect a heightened sense of self-efficacy because of positive relative comparisons, or a sense of importance because creative success is dependent upon a single individual.

Organizational Culture and Climate

The levels of organizational context, both formal and informal, present challenges for the study of creativity. Among these, culture and climate factors have received some attention, in part because of their relationship with leadership and other social factors. It is clear, however, that aspects of an organization's culture and/or climate matter for individual creative behaviors.

Rasulzada and Dackert (2009) looked at organizational factors and perceptions of creativity and innovation in high-technology industry in Sweden. Their results revealed that in organizations where employees perceived a creative innovative climate, and in organizations where resources were made available, employees perceived higher levels of creativity and innovation. Although their findings are somewhat limited by the concentration on perceptions of creativity (i.e., not creative performance itself), the relationships do support the basic relationships between climate and creativity.

Other research has examined the learning orientation of an organization. Indeed, there is a clear link between organizational learning culture and creativity at the organizational level (Kim & Wilemon, 2007). What implications does this relationship have, however, for learning culture and individual-level creativity? Part of the answer may be found in the research on feedback and creativity. Creativity research both within and outside of the organizational domain has shown that feedback interpreted as evaluation is detrimental to creative performance (Amabile, Goldfarb, & Brackfield, 1990; Shalley & Oldham, 1985). In organizations with a learning culture, however, feedback is central to employee development. Supporting the possibility of a positive impact of learning culture on individual creativity, several studies have found that developmental feedback (Zhou, 2003; Zhou & George, 2001) or feedback that is framed as potentially developmental (Shalley, 1995) improves creative performance. Training, another core component to a learning culture, has also shown to be related to an increase in creativity in an organizational domain (Scott, Leritz, & Mumford, 2004). Finally, again both within and outside of the organizational domain, the presence of developmental goals associated with creativity has also been related to increased creative behavior at the individual-level (Carson & Carson, 1993; Shalley, 1991, 1995).

The extent to which an organizational culture is viewed as threatening may also impact creative behaviors at the individual-level. In a study of post-merger creativity, Zhou, Shin, and Cannella (2008) found that individuals who evaluated the post-merger culture as an opportunity engaged in more creative behaviors than individuals who viewed the culture as threatening. As we have noted previously however, contextual factors often do not act independently. Zhou et al. also found that among individuals who viewed the culture as threatening, the presence of resources and a supportive culture for creativity made creative behaviors more likely.

In their review of 42 studies examining organizational climate and creativity, Hunter, Bedell, and Mumford (2007) identified several elements which have been linked to a climate for creativity. Some, such as challenge, and intellectual stimulation, reflect findings that are consistent with creativity research outside of the organizational domain (Kaufman, 2009). Others, such as the importance of positive exchanges with colleagues, fit well with Perry-Smith's argument for the importance of social context (Perry-Smith, 2006; Perry-Smith & Shalley, 2003), and further illustrate the interdependence of contextual dimensions. In that spirit, Hunter et al. (2007) also found that climate–creativity relationships were stronger when organizations were operating in high-pressure competitive environments. Consistent with their review, a recent meta-analysis examining individual-level innovation, also found climate linked with creativity (Hammond, Neff, Farr, Schwall, & Zhao, 2011).

Organizational Context as Inhibitory Factors

In response to the increased research which considers organizational factors that foster or facilitate creativity, Choi et al. (2009) examined potential contextual inhibitors of individual creativity. They focused on a range of contextual factors, including climate, coworker, and leader characteristics, with results revealing both direct and some more complex findings. Aversive leadership style and unsupportive climate emerged as the most powerful creativity inhibitors. Specifically, regardless of individual creative ability, the presence of aversive leaders diminished creative performance. Unsupportive climate also had a negative effect on creative performance, but was particularly detrimental for individuals with low creative ability. Conversely, task standardization was particularly negative for highly creative individuals.

In a similar vein, Elsbach and Hargadon (2006) argued conceptually that workload pressures may actually prohibit intrinsically oriented individuals from engaging in creative behaviors. They argue for the increase of "mindless work"—work that is low in cognitive demands and low on performance pressures—and that such work should alternate with cognitively challenging work to enhance creativity. Although theirs is clearly a work-design approach to enhancing creativity, the direct implication is that high-demand work contexts, which are all-too-common today, may be a primary inhibitor of creative performance in individuals.

The Complexity of Context and Domains

As evidenced in the current review, the literature on individual creativity in organizations considers issues of domain specificity rarely and then only nominally. Several key findings, however, point to the importance of considering domain characteristics more precisely. In their investigation of contextual inhibitors of creativity in several Canadian organizations, Choi et al. (2009) noted that aversive leadership (e.g., punishing, intimidating, and oppressive styles) interacted with leader monitoring behaviors in impacting creativity. Specifically, although there was a negative impact of aversive leadership on creativity when leaders did not engage in monitoring behaviors, this effect did not emerge among close monitoring aversive leaders. This surprising interaction illustrates the complexities of context. Compounding this complexity is how "monitoring" is defined. As Choi et al. note, the positive impact that monitoring displayed in their work was inconsistent with past studies of leader monitoring and creativity (George & Zhou, 2001; Zhou, 2003). They suggest the explanation may lie in how monitoring was put into operation. Specifically, their behavioral measurement of monitoring may have led to perceptions of support, information, and guidance, whereas perceptual measures used in prior works had negative connotations of over-monitoring embedded in the instrument itself.

The importance of domain precision is also evidenced in the differing effects of context on different forms of creativity. Reiter-Palmon et al. (2009) found that efficacy in a particular problem-solving domain resulted in increased creativity in terms of the *number* of solutions, but decreased creativity in terms of solution *originality*. Similarly, in a study on interpersonal group conflict and individual creativity, Troyer and Youngreen (2009) found that higher levels of conflict resulted in more creative ideas, but fewer ideas were generated overall. Yuan and Zhou (2008) also reported different effects of context (expected evaluation) on creativity as idea development or as improved idea appropriateness. Mostafa (2005) found that manager evaluations of what is and is not creative differed based on functional area in which one worked. Although these examples seem at first to be about how we define creativity, they have direct implications for context because different contexts will value forms of creativity differently. This distinction is therefore central to understanding how context facilitates individual creativity.

In summary, the complexities revealed in the aforementioned studies underscore how important a careful consideration of context is, both for researcher efforts to understand creativity in organizations, and equally for organizational leaders looking for guidance in how to identify the appropriate methods for inspiring creative work. For such guidance to emerge, greater attention must be paid to the complexity of organizational context and work domains.

DISCUSSION

Future Research Directions

Although it is clear from our review that the organizational context plays an important role in the facilitation of employee creativity, it is also clear that that there is much left to be understood. As we note in the beginning of this chapter, we argue for a domain specific approach to understanding workplace creativity; an approach that underscores the fundamental importance of the consideration of context and identifies several key directions for future research. To begin with, concerns about domain specificity lead directly to questions about defining the construct of creativity (Kaufman & Baer, 2005), and its value to organizations. Current definitions of creativity fail to capture the complexity of the construct as it relates to the context within which it occurs. Even the distinction between creativity and innovation can be ambiguous in certain organizational contexts. For example in a high-tech research and development firm, the development of a novel and useful product may not lead directly to implementation (i.e., innovation), but may serve as the springboard to the development and implementation of an even better product. From a creativity and innovation standpoint this is a desired outcome, yet it is unclear how such an outcome would be explained by current creativity theory and research.

Similarly, it is also necessary to explore how the domain of interest impacts our understanding and defining of creativity. For one, domains necessarily define the performance construct and thus determine the parameters for what is and is not creative. This is more than just differences in defining the specific performance construct, but also includes the fact that the overall value of creativity to a particular organization will impact what is or is not defined as creative. Lastly, the multidimensionality of performance, even within a particular job, implies that "creative" employees may produce certain outcomes that are positive and others that are negative, even within the same performance episode. Such differences may emerge simply as a function of the extent to which creativity is valued differently for different performance criteria. Clearly these are challenges, but if we are to advance our understanding of creativity in organizations, we must continue to explore how the construct of creativity is defined as a function of context.

Beyond fundamental issues with defining creativity and accounting for domain specificity, there are additional aspects of organizational context that provide fruitful avenues of pursuit. One such aspect is the climate for competition. Although some examples exist of organizations facilitating intergroup competition to foster creativity, few researchers have examined the impact of competition on creative outcomes (Baer, Leenders, Oldham, & Vadera, 2010). One lab-based study demonstrated that individuals operating in a competitive "proself" group produced more creative results than individuals in a non-competitive 'prosocial" group (Beersma & De Dreu, 2005). A second lab-based study (Baer et al., 2010) noted a "U-shaped" relationship between competition and creativity in open groups (i.e., groups where membership change was possible), but not in closed groups. Together, these studies reflect the growing awareness around the need for consideration of competition as a predictor of creative outcomes in an applied context, and the complexity inherent in such research.

Our review has also revealed the need for greater consideration of the relationship between individual characteristics and organizational context. In their examination of social networks, Zhou et al. (2009) noted the importance of the interaction between social context and individual values. Similarly, in an investigation of the impact of risk and creativity, Simmons and Ren (2009) confirmed that individuals performing in high-risk context exhibit more creativity than individuals performing in low-risk contexts, and that individual goal orientation impacted that relationship. Specifically, for individuals with an avoid performance goal orientation, creativity was lower in the high-risk context. Another study found that individuals who perceived their work to be meaningful were more likely to identify with their organization and were rated by their supervisors as displaying higher levels of creativity (Cohen-Meiter, Carmeli, & Waldman, 2009). That individual values and characteristics interact with organizational context in determining creative outcomes is clear, and consistent with a domain-specific approach (Kaufman & Baer, 2005). We are really only beginning, however, to understanding how such interactions may become manifest in organizations, and the range of individual characteristics and contexts to consider remains wide.

One additional need for future research is an expanded consideration of leadership factors. Initial examinations of trust, for example, have demonstrated a link with creative outcomes both for partners (Bidault & Castello, 2009) and for subordinate trust in leaders (Wang & Casimir, 2007). Others have found that leaders who engender empowerment beliefs in their employees inspire creative process engagement (Zhang & Bartol, 2010). In addition to direct consideration of leader characteristics, researchers should continue to extend beyond the consideration of leadership style and examine leaders in context. Indeed, many of the contextual factors that have been demonstrated to hinder or facilitate creativity, such as a controlling context (Amabile, 1986) or social support (Madjar, 2005, 2008), are often directly or indirectly impacted by leaders. It is also likely that the domain will impact the relationship between leadership factors and employee creativity. Rather than thinking about universal leadership factors that may impact creativity, a more direct examination of leader-in-context effects offers, great promise.

Recommendations for Leaders

Miettinen (2006) has argued that we need not search for "best practices" in terms of managing creativity, as they do not exist. Rather we should explore the problems and possibilities that emerge with domains and learn to develop new practices that support (develop) creativity. Our review of the literature suggests Miettinen may be right. Consequently, we present the following recommendations, which, though too broad to be considered traditional "best practices", provide guidance for organizational leaders looking to determine effective means to facilitate creativity in their own organizational environments. Despite the challenges presented by the complexity of contextual factors and the volume of creativity research completed in non-organizational populations, there are many lessons to heed.

Recommendation #1: Emphasize Leadership

Leaders are critical to creative behaviors in organizations, both because of the direct impact they have on individual behaviors, and through their influence on the development of organizational culture and climates. Leaders may model creative behavior (Jaussi & Dionne, 2003) or may inspire and encourage individual creativity by supporting employee attainment of expertise (Mumford et al., 2002). The development of transformational leadership (Mumford et al., 2009) is also a critical step, as recent evidence suggests transformational leadership to be linked to creativity and innovation (Elenkov & Manev, 2009; Jansen et al., 2009; Reuvers et al., 2008). Conversely, aversive leadership styles, including punishment and criticism, are clear inhibiters to creativity, and should be avoided (Choi et al., 2009).

Recommendation #2: Provide Social Support

Our review clearly illustrates the value of having a socially supportive work context for enhancing creative outcomes. Social networks seem to be particularly important as they increase access of employees to individuals with varying areas and levels of expertise. Consequently, facilitating the development of network ties, particularly weak ties (Perry-Smith, 2006) will have a positive impact on creativity. It is also clear that within the workplace, both informational and emotional support from colleagues is related to higher levels of creativity (Madjar, 2008), therefore organizations (or leaders) interested in generating creativity should afford strong collegial relationships among employees. Finally, the presence of creative colleagues may be necessary for leaders to realize the impact of their own efforts to enhance creativity. As found by Zhou (2003), individuals displayed the highest level of creativity in response to supervisor feedback when they were in the presence of creative coworkers. Clearly, fostering individual creativity requires a consideration not just of the individual, but of his or her social context.

Recommendation #3: Pay Attention to Culture and Climate within Domains

Organizations must define what creativity means within their organization and within particular micro-domains. Norms and expectations (including group-level) around the desired creative behaviors should be clearly evident and supported by leadership, and goal development should include those tied to creativity. Additionally, organizational leaders should create a climate that provides a sense of psychological safety as it pertains to creativity, rewarding idea generation rather than solely productivity. Creativity often requires an element of risk-taking and breaking social norms (Sternberg & Lubart, 1996). Obviously, organizations do not want counterproductive or antisocial behavior. However, creating a safe and nurturing environment where people feel able to take chances and suggest new ideas is essential. The idea of "psychological safety" has been proposed as a mutual feeling in a group that risk-taking is okay (Edmondson, 1999). One way that psychological safety can be increased is by a leader meeting with team members and talking honestly and openly with them (Roussin, 2008); another is to enable employees to speak up and voice dissatisfaction (Detert & Burris, 2007). Ford and Sullivan (2004) argue that experiencing psychological safety can aid both innovative contributions and personal satisfaction. In addition to safety, climates that are challenging and intellectually stimulating have been consistently associated with creativity (Hunter et al., 2007; Kaufman, 2009; Rasulzada & Dackert, 2009).

At the organizational level, developing a culture that is supportive of learning and development has clear benefits for creativity. Aspects of such a culture include developmental rather than evaluative feedback, opportunities for training on creativity or in general forms to increase expertise, and the incorporation of developmental goals tied to creativity. Finally, creating an organization-wide culture of innovation requires attention to strategic decisions ranging from long term goals to distribution of employee breaks. Innovative values and ideals must exude from what the company proclaims to be, who they hire and the reward systems they establish. When an innovative culture is instituted, these values percolate throughout all levels of the organization and the likely result is industry-changing applications of creativity.

Recommendation #4: Manage Resources

Creativity has a cost, and indeed this cost is one of the paradoxes identified by Hammond et al. (2011). To allow creativity to blossom, employees need to be given allotted time and materials (if needed) in pursuit of these new ideas. In addition, the motivation literature indicates that factors that raise extrinsic motivation (such as deadlines and feedback) may impede creativity. As a result, encouraging creativity may mean giving employees opportunities to pursue original ideas and solutions without the standard requirements for most work assignments that ensure accountability.

Often resources are at the hands of leaders, and research supports the concept that leaders who provide resources such as time, information, and expertise, enhance creativity in their employees (Mumford et al., 2002). Interestingly, it has even been suggested that time may be beneficial for creativity even if it means allotting it for "mindless work" so that greater energies are available for creative productivity (Elsbach & Hargadon, 2006). Team or group resources are also valuable. As noted above, a lack of creative expertise among team members limits the benefit of creativity-based feedback from leaders. Further, expertise in a domain or throughout the organization enhances the likelihood of creative behaviors. Finally, resources as straightforward as training and development on creativity have proven to enhance creativity in individuals (Mumford, Hunter, Eubanks, Bedell, & Murphy, 2007).

CONCLUSION

Organizational context plays a clear role in the emergence of individual creative behaviors. Leader factors, organizational characteristics, and the social fabric of the workplace each provide mechanisms for enhancing employee creativity. Attention must always be given to factors specific to the organizational domains of interest. Within those parameters, however, organization leaders are afforded a myriad of opportunities to foster employee creativity by attending to organizational context.

References

Agars, M. D., Kaufman, J. C., & Locke, T. R. (2008). Social influences and creativity in organizations: A multi-level lens for theory, research, and practice. In M. Mumford, S. Hunter & K. Bedell-Aviers (Eds.), *Multi-level Issues in Creativity and Innovation* (pp. 3–62). Amsterdam, The Netherlands: Elsevier.

Agars, M. D., Baer, J., & Kaufman, J. C. (2005). The many creativities of business and the APT Model of Creativity. *Korean Journal of Thinking & Problem Solving, 15,* 133–141.

Amabile, T. M. (1983). *The social psychology of creativity.* New York, NY: Springer-Verlag.

Amabile, T. M. (1983). Social psychology of creativity: A componential conceptualization. *Journal of Personality and Social Psychology, 45,* 357–376.

Amabile, T. M. (1996). Creativity in context. Boulder, CO: Westview.

Amabile, T. M. (1997). Entrepreneurial creativity through motivational synergy. *Journal of Creative Behavior, 31,* 18–26.

Amabile, T. M (1998). How to kill creativity. *Harvard Business Review,* 76–87.

Amabile, T. M., Goldfarb, P., & Brackfield, S. C. (1990). Social influences on creativity: Evaluation, coaction, and surveillance. *Creativity Research Journal, 3,* 6–21.

Atwater, L., & Carmeli, A. (2009). Leader–member exchange, feelings of energy, and involvement in creative work. *Leadership Quarterly, 20,* 264–275.

Baer, J. (1991). Generality of creativity across performance domains. *Creativity Research Journal, 4,* 23–39.

Baer, J. (1994). Divergent thinking is not a general trait: A multi-domain training experiment. *Creativity Research Journal, 7,* 35–46.

Baer, J. (1996). The effects of task-specific divergent-thinking training. *Journal of Creative Behavior, 30,* 183–187.

Baer, J. (1997). Gender differences in the effects of anticipated evaluation on creativity. *Creativity Research Journal, 10,* 25–31.

Baer, J. (1998). The case for domain specificity in creativity. *Creativity Research Journal, 11,* 173–177.

Baer, J., & Kaufman, J. C. (2005). Bridging generality and specificity: The Amusement Park Theoretical (APT) model of creativity. *Roeper Review, 27,* 158–163.

Baer, M., Leenders, R. T. A., Oldham, G. R., & Vadera, A. K. (2010). Win or lose the battle for creativity: The power and perils of intergroup competition. *Academy of Management Journal, 53,* 827–845.

Barron, F., & Harrington, D. M. (1981). Creativity, intelligence, and personality. *Annual Review of Psychology, 32,* 439–476.

Bass, B. M. (1996). *A New paradigm of leadership: An inquiry into transformational leadership.* Alexandria, VA: US Army Research Institute for the Behavioral & Social Sciences.

Basu, R., & Green, S. G. (1997). Leader–member exchange and transformational leadership: An empirical examination of innovative behaviors in leader–member dyads. *Journal of Applied Social Psychology, 27,* 477–499.

Beersma, B., & De Dreu, C. K. W (2005). Conflict's consequences: Effects of social motives on postnegotiation creative and convergent group functioning and performance. *Journal of Personality and Social Psychology, 89,* 358–374.

Bidault, F., & Castello, A. (2009). Trust and creativity: Understanding the role of trust in creativity-oriented joint developments. *R&D Management, 39,* 259–270.

Burns, J. M. (1978). *Leadership.* Oxford, UK: Harper & Row.

Carmeli, A., & Schaubroeck, J. (2007). The influence of leaders' and other referent's normative expectations on individual involvement in creative work. *Leadership Quarterly, 18,* 35–48.

Carson, P. P., & Carson, K. D. (1993). Managing creativity enhancement through goal setting and feedback. *Journal of Creative Behavior, 27,* 36–45.

Chen, M. H., & Kaufmann, G. (2008). Employee creativity and R&D: A critical review. *Creativity and Innovation Management, 17,* 71–76.

Choi, J. N., Anderson, T. A., & Veillette, A. (2009). Contextual inhibitors of employee creativity in organizations: The insulating role of creative ability. *Group & Organizational Management, 34,* 330–357.

Cohen-Meitar, R., Carmeli, A., & Waldman, D. A. (2009). Linking meaningfulness in the workplace to employee creativity: The intervening role of organizational identification and positive psychological experiences. *Creativity Research Journal, 21,* 361–375.

Csikszentmihályi, M. (1996). *Creativity: Flow and the psychology of discovery and invention.* New York, NY: HarperCollins.

Damanpour, F., & Schneider, M. (2006). Phases of the adoption of innovation in organizations: Effects of environment, organization and top managers. *British Journal of Management, 17,* 215–236.

Detert, J. R., & Burris, E. R. (2007). Leadership behavior and employee voice: Is the door really open? *Academy of Management Journal, 50,* 869–884.

Drazin, R., Glynn, M., & Kazanjian, R. K. (1999). Multilevel theorizing about creativity in organizations: A sense-making perspective. *Academy of Management Review, 24,* 286–307.

Edmondson, A. C. (1999). Psychological safety and learning behavior in work teams. *Administrative Science Quarterly, 44,* 350–383.

Egan, T. M. (2005). Factors influencing individual creativity in the workplace: An examination of quantitative empirical research. *Advances in Human Resources, 7*, 160–181.

Elenkov, D. S., & Manev, I. M. (2009). Senior expatriate leadership's effects on innovation and the role of cultural intelligence. *Journal of World Business, 44*, 357–369.

Elsbach, K. D., & Hargadon, A. B. (2006). Enhancing creativity through "mindless" work: A framework of workday design. *Organization Science, 17*, 470–483.

Florida, R. (2002). *The rise of the creative class*. New York, NY: Basic Books.

Ford, C. M. (1996). A theory of individual creativity in multiple social domains. *Academy of Management Review, 21*, 1112–1134.

Ford, C. M., & Gioia, D. A. (1995). *Creative action in organizations*. Thousand Oaks, CA: Sage.

Ford, C., & Sullivan, D. M. (2004). A time for everything: How timing of novel contributions influences project team outcomes. *Journal of Organizational Behavior, 21*, 163–183.

Galton, F. (1869). *Hereditary genius*. London, UK: Macmillan.

George, J. M., & Zhou, J. (2001). When openness to experience and conscientiousness are related to creative behavior: An interactional approach. *Journal of Applied Psychology, 86*, 514–524.

Gumusluoglu, L., & Ilsev, A. (2009). Transformational leadership, creativity, and organizational innovation. *Journal of Business Research, 62*, 461–473.

Hackman, J. R. (1987). The design of work teams. In J. W. Lorsch (Ed.), *Handbook of organizational behavior* (pp. 315–342). Englewood Cliffs, NJ: Prentice-Hall.

Hammond, M. M., Neff, N. L., Farr, J. L., Schwall, A. R., & Zhao, X. (2011). Predictors of individual-level innovation at work: A meta-analysis. *Psychology of Aesthetics, Creativity, and the Arts, 5*, 90–105.

Han, K. (2003). Domain-specificity of creativity in young children: How quantitative and qualitative data support it. *Journal of Creative Behavior, 37*, 117–142.

Hemlin, S., Allwood, C. M., & Martin, B. R. (2009). Creative knowledge environments. *Creativity Research Journal, 20*, 196–210.

Hirst, G., Van Knippenberg, D., & Zhou, J. (2009). A cross-level perspective on employee creativity: Goal orientation, team learning behavior, and individual creativity. *Academy of Management Journal, 52*, 280–293.

Hulsheger, U. R., Anderson, N., & Salgado, J. F. (2009). Team-level predictors of innovation at work: A comprehensive meta-analysis spanning three decades of research. *Journal of Applied Psychology, 94*, 1128–1145.

Hunter, S. T., Bedell, K. E., & Mumford, M. D. (2007). Climate for creativity: A quantitative review. *Creativity Research Journal, 19*, 69–90.

Hunter, S.T., Thouroughgood, C.N., Myer, A.T., & Ligon, G.S. (2011). Paradoxes of leading innovative endeavors: Summary, solutions, and future directions. *Psychology of Aesthetics, Creativity, and the Arts, 5*, 54–66.

Ivcevic, Z. (2009). Creativity map: Toward the next generation of theories of creativity. *Psychology of Aesthetics, Creativity, and the Arts, 3*, 17–21.

Jansen, J., Vera, D., & Crossan, M. (2009). Strategic leadership and exploitation: The moderating role of environmental dynamism. *The Leadership Quarterly, 20*, 5–18.

Jaussi, K. S., & Dionne, S. D. (2003). Leading for creativity: The role of unconventional leader behavior. *The Leadership Quarterly, 14*, 475–498.

Jung, D., Chow, C., & Wu, A. (2003). The role of transformational leadership in enhancing organizational innovation: Hypotheses and some preliminary findings. *Leadership Quarterly, 14*, 525–544.

Kahai, S. S., Sosik, J. J., & Avolio, B. J. (2003). Effects of leadership style, anonymity, and rewards on creative-relevant processes and outcomes in an electronic meeting system context. *Leadership Quarterly, 14*, 499–524.

Kahl, C. H., da Fonseca, L. H., & Witte, E. H. (2009). Revisiting creativity research: An investigation of contemporary approaches. *Creativity Research Journal, 21*, 1–5.

Kaufman, J. C., & Baer, J. (2002). Could Steven Spielberg manage the Yankees? Creative thinking in different domains. *Korean Journal of Thinking & Problem Solving, 12*, 5–15.

Kaufman, J. C., & Baer, J. (2004). The Amusement Park Theoretical (APT) Model of creativity. *Korean Journal of Thinking and Problem Solving, 14*, 15–25.

Kaufman, J. C., & Baer, J. (2005). *Creativity across domains: Faces of the muse*. Mahwah, NJ: Lawrence Erlbaum.

Kaufman, J. C., & Beghetto, R. A. (2009). Beyond big and little: The Four C Model of Creativity. *Review of General Psychology, 13*, 1–12.

Kaufman, J.C., Beghetto, R.A., Baer, J., & Ivcevic, Z. (2010). Creativity polymathy: What Benjamin Franklin can teach your kindergartener. *Learning and Individual Differences, 20*, 380–387.

B. INDIVIDUAL LEVEL INFLUENCES

Kim, J., & Wilemon, D. (2007). The learning organization as facilitator of complex NPD projects. *Creativity and Innovation Management*, *16*, Jun, 176–191.

Kouzes, J., & Pozner, B. (1987). *The Leadership challenge: How to get extraordinary things done in organizations*. San Francisco, CA: Jossey-Bass.

Madjar, N (2005). The contributions of different groups of individuals to employees' creativity. *Advances in Developing Human Resources*, *7*, 182–206.

Madjar, N. (2008). Emotional and informational support from different sources and employee creativity. *Journal of Occupational and Organizational Psychology*, *81*, 83–100.

Madjar, N., Oldham, G. R., & Pratt, M. G. (2002). There's no place like home? The contributions of work and nonwork creativity support to employees' creative performance. *Academy of Management Journal*, *45*, 757–767.

Miettinen, R. (2006). The sources of novelty: A cultural and systematic view of distributed creativity. *Creativity and Innovation Management*, *15*, 173–181.

Moss, S. A., & Ritossa, D. A. (2007). The impact of goal orientation on the association between leadership style and follower performance, creativity and work attitudes. *Leadership*, *3*, 433–456.

Mostafa, M. (2005). Factors affecting organizational creativity and innovativeness in Egyptian business organisations: An empirical investigation. *Journal of Management Development*, *24*, 7–33.

Mumford, M. D., & Gustafson, S. B. (1988). Creativity syndrome. Integration, application, and innovation. *Psychological Bulletin*, *103*, 27–43.

Mumford, M. S., Hunter, S. T., Eubanks, D. L., Bedell, K. E., & Murphy, S. T. (2007). Developing Leaders for creative efforts: A domain based approach for leadership development. *Human Resource Management Review*, *17*, 402–417.

Mumford, M. D., Scott, G. M., Gaddis, B., & Strange, J. M. (2002). Leading creative people: Orchestrating expertise and relationships. *Leadership Quarterly*, *13*, 705–750.

Nederveen Pieterse, A., Van Nippenber, D., Schippers, M., & Stam, D. (2010). Transformational and transactional leadership and innovative behavior: The moderating role of psychological empowerment. *Journal of Organizational Behavior*, *31*, 609–623.

Perry-Smith, J. (2006). Social Yet Creative: The role of social relationships in facilitating individual creativity. *Academy of Management Journal*, *49*, 85–101.

Perry-Smith, J., & Shalley, C. E. (2003). The social side of creativity: A static and dynamic network perspective. *Academy of Management Review*, *28*, 89–106.

Plucker, J. A., Beghetto, R. A., & Dow, G. (2004). Why isn't creativity more important to educational psychologists? Potential, pitfalls, and future directions in creativity research. *Educational Psychologist*, *39*, 83–96.

Podsakoff, P. M., MacKenzie, S. B., Moorman, R. H., & Fetter, R. (1990). Transformational leader behaviors and their effects on followers' trust in leader, satisfaction, and organizational citizenship behaviors. *Leadership Quarterly*, *1*, 107–142.

Rank, J., Pace, V. L., & Frese, M. (2002). Three avenues for future research on creativity, innovation, and initiative. *Applied Psychology: An International Review*, *53*, 518–528.

Rasulzada, F., & Dackert, I. (2009). Organizational creativity and innovation in relation to psychological well-being and organizational factors. *Creativity Research Journal*, *21*, 191–198.

Reiter-Palmon, R., Illies, M. Y., Cross, L. K., Buboltz, C. B., & Nimps, T. (2009). Creativity and domain specificity: The effect of task type on multiple indexes of creative problem solving. *Psychology of Aesthetics, Creativity, and the Arts*, *3*, 73–80.

Reuter, M., Panksepp, J., Schnabel, N., Kellerhoff, N., Kempel, P., & Hennig, J. (2005). Personality and biological markers of creativity. *European Journal of Personality*, *19*, 83–95.

Reuvers, M., Van Engel, M., Vinkenburg, C., & Wilson-Evered, E. (2008). Transformational leadership and innovative work behavior: Exploring the relevance of gender differences. *Creativity and Innovation Management*, *17*, 227–244.

Roussin, C. J. (2008). Increasing trust, psychological safety, and team performance through dyadic leadership discovery. *Small Group Research*, *39*, 224–248.

Rosa, J. A., Qualls, W. J., & Fuentes, C. (2008). Involving mind, body, and friends: Management that engenders creativity. *Journal of Business Research*, *61*, 631–639.

Runco, M. A. (1989). The creativity of children's art. *Child Study Journal*, *19*, 177–189.

Sarros, J. C. (2008). Building a climate for innovation through transformational leadership and organizational culture. *Journal of Organizational Studies*, *15*, 145–158.

Schien, E. H. (1985). *Organizational culture and leadership: A dynamic view*. San Francisco, CA: Jossey-Bass.

Schien, E. (1992). *Organizational culture and leadership*. San Francisco, CA: Jossey-Bass.

B. INDIVIDUAL LEVEL INFLUENCES

Scott, G., Leritz, L. E., & Mumford, M. D. (2004). The effectiveness of creativity training: A quantitative review. *Creativity Research Journal, 16*, 361–388.

Shalley, C. E. (1991). Effects of productivity goals, creativity goals, and personal discretion on individual creativity. *Journal of Applied Psychology, 76*, 179–185.

Shalley, C. E. (1995). Effects of coaction, expected evaluation, and goal setting on creativity and productivity. *Academy of Management Journal, 38*, 483–503.

Shalley, C. E., & Gilson, L. L. (2004). What leaders need to know: A review of social and contextual factors that can foster or hinder creativity. *Leadership Quarterly, 15*, 33–53.

Shalley, C. E., & Oldham, G. (1985). Effects of goal difficulty and expected external evaluation on intrinsic motivation: A laboratory study. *Academy of Management Journal, 28*, 628–640.

Shalley, C. E., Zhou, J., & Oldham, G. R. (2004). The effects of personal and contextual characteristics on creativity: Where should we go from here? *Journal of Management, 30*, 933–958.

Simmons, A. L., & Ren, R. (2009). The influence of goal orientation and risk on creativity. *Creativity Research Journal, 21*, 400–408.

Simonton, D. K. (1997). *Products, persons, and periods: Historiometric analyses of compositional creativity.* New York, NY: Oxford University Press.

Sternberg, R. J. (1999). A propulsion model of types of creative contributions. *Review of General Psychology, 3*, 83–100.

Sternberg, R. J. (2006). Creating a vision of creativity: The first 25 years. *Psychology of Aesthetics, Creativity, and the Arts, S*, 2–12.

Sternberg, R. J., Kaufman, J. C., & Pretz, J. E. (2002). *The creativity conundrum: A propulsion model of kinds of creative contributions.* New York, NY: Psychology Press.

Sternberg, R. J., Kauffman, J. C., & Pretz, J. E. (2003). A propulsion model of creative contributions. *The Leadership Quarterly, 14*, 455–473.

Sternberg, R. J., & Lubart, T. I. (1996). *Defying the crowd.* New York, NY: Free Press.

Styhre, A. (2006). Organization creativity and the empiricist image of novelty. *Creativity and Innovation Management, 15*, 143–149.

Tagger, S. (2002). Individual creativity and group ability to utilize individual creative resources: A multilevel model. *Academy of Management Journal, 45*, 315–330.

Torrance, E. P., & Presbury, J. (1984). The criteria of success used in 242 recent experimental studies of creativity. *Creative Child & Adult Quarterly, 9*, 238–243.

Torrance, E. P., & Safter, H. T. (1989). The long range predictive validity of the Just Suppose Test. *Journal of Creative Behavior, 23*, 219–223.

Trice, H. M., & Beyer, J. M. (1993). *The cultures of work organizations.* Englewood Cliffs, NJ: Prentice-Hall.

Wang, K. Y., & Casimir, G. (2007). How attitudes of leaders may enhance organizational creativity: Evidence from a Chinese study. *Creativity and Innovation Management, 16*, 229–238.

West, M. A. (2002). Sparkling fountains or stagnant ponds: An integrative model of creativity and innovation implementation in work groups. *Applied Psychology: An International Review, 51*, 355–424.

West, M. A., Borrill, C. S., Dawson, J. F., Brodbeck, F., Shapiro, D. A., & Haward, B. (2003). Leadership clarity and team innovation in health care. *The Leadership Quarterly, 14*, 393–410.

Woodman, R. W., Sawyer, J. E., & Griffin, R. W. (1993). Toward an organizational theory of creativity. *Academy of Management Review, 18*, 293–321.

Yuan, F., & Zhou, J. (2008). Differential effects of expected external evaluation on different parts of the creative idea production process and on final product creativity. *Creativity Research Journal, 20*, 391–403.

Zhang, X., & Bartol, K. (2010). Linking empowering leadership and employee creativity: The influence of psychological empowerment, intrinsic motivation, and creative process engagement. *Academy of Management Journal, 53*, 107–128.

Zhou, J. (2003). When the presence of creative coworkers is related to creativity: Role of supervisor close monitoring, developmental feedback, and creative personality. *Journal of Applied Psychology, 88*, 413–422.

Zhou, J., & George, J. M. (2001). When job dissatisfaction leads to creativity: Encouraging the expression of voice. *Academy of Management Journal, 44*, 682–696.

Zhou, J., Shin, S. J., Brass, D. J., Choi, J., & Zhang, Z. (2009). Social networks, personal values, and creativity: Evidence for curvilinear and interaction effects. *Journal of Applied Psychology, 94*, 1544–1552.

Zhou, J., Shin, S. J., & Cannella, A. A. (2008). Employee self-perceived creativity after mergers and acquisitions: Interactive effects of threat–opportunity perception, access to resources, and support for creativity. *Journal of Applied Behavioral Science, 44*, 397–421.

B. INDIVIDUAL LEVEL INFLUENCES

GROUP LEVEL
INFLUENCES

Team Creativity and Innovation: The Effect of Group Composition, Social Processes, and Cognition

Roni Reiter-Palmon[1], Ben Wigert[2], and Triparna de Vreede[2]

[1]University of Nebraska at Omaha, Department of Psychology and Center for Collaboration Science, Omaha, NE; [2]University of Nebraska at Omaha, Department of Psychology, Omaha, NE

Much of the early work on organizational creativity focused on the individual, and the role of individual differences in explaining creative production. Within this approach, teams were viewed as providing the social context that facilitates or inhibits individual creativity (Amabile, 1996; Woodman, Sawyer, & Griffin, 1993). While earlier work neglected the team as the unit of analysis, recently the direct role of teams in the development of creative products or ideas has been the focus of more research.

There are several reasons for the emergence of interest in team creativity and innovation. As a result of changes in technology, increased globalizations and competition, and a knowledge-based economy, the problems facing organizations are so complex that a single individual does not possess all the knowledge necessary to solve these problems, and teams have been viewed as the solution to this problem (Kozlowski & Bell, 2008). These same issues have also been suggested as underlying the need for creativity and innovation in organizations (Ford & Gioia, 1995; Shalley, Zhou, & Oldham, 2004; West, Hirst, Richter, & Shipton, 2004). A second reason for the emergence of the interest in teams is that they provide additional performance benefits, such as access to diverse information, diverse perspectives, and the ability to capitalize on the varied skills of the team members (Tesluk, Farr, & Klein, 1997). As a result, reliance on teams has increased steadily in organizations (Edmondson & Roloff, 2009).

Handbook of Organizational Creativity.
DOI: 10.1016/B978-0-12-374714-3.00013-6

Third, in recent years team adaptation has been viewed as being "at the heart of team effectiveness" (Burke, Stagl, Salas, Pierce, & Kendell, 2006). Burke et al. define team adaptation as:

> "a change in team performance, in response to a salient cue or cue stream, that leads to a functional outcome for the entire team. Team adaptation is manifested in the innovation of new or modification of existing structures, capacities, and/or behavioral or cognitive goal-directed actions" *(p. 1190).*

While team adaptation is conceptually different from team creativity and innovation, the two are related, as it can include creativity and innovation, although being broader and manifested in other ways.

Finally, another reason for the increased interest in team creativity beyond that of context is the development of models that suggest that some team properties can be emergent (Kozlowski & Klein, 2000). Kozlowski and Klein define emergence as a phenomenon that:

> "originates in the cognition, affect, behaviors, or other characteristics of individuals, is amplified by their interactions, and manifests as a higher-level, collective phenomenon" *(p. 55).*

This suggests that to understand the role of teams in creative production, we must not only view teams as background, or social context to the individual, but rather, through emergence, team creativity may be a very different phenomenon from that of the individual.

In this chapter we will review the research to date on team creativity and innovation. For the purpose of organizing this chapter, we will adopt the typical Input–Process–Output (I-P-O) model of team effectiveness (Kozlowski & Ilgen, 2006; Salas, Burke, & Stagl, 2004). We will focus on team composition in terms of individual characteristics of team members as input. Processes are the activities that team members engage in to solve the problem or carry out the task. Specifically, we will focus on two major classes of team processes; team social processes and team cognition. Team output is defined as team creativity and innovation. The interactive effect of these input and process variables will also be considered. Finally, we will provide directions for future research as well as practical implications of the research reviewed.

Before discussing team creativity and the factors that affect it, it is important to clarify two issues. The first is the distinction between teams and groups. Some researchers differentiate the two terms, but in many cases these are used interchangeably (Paulus, Nakui, Putnam, & Brown, 2005). In organizational psychology, preference is given to the concept of teams over groups (Kozlowski & Ilgen, 2006), which we will use here. The second distinction is between creativity and innovation. Some researchers use these terms interchangeably. Others suggest that creativity involves the generation of ideas, whereas innovation includes both idea generation and implementation (Anderson, De Dreu, & Nijstad, 2004). Finally, others suggest that creativity is viewed as the generation of ideas and solutions, whereas innovation is defined as the implementation of these ideas and solutions in the organization (West, 2002; West et al., 2004). For the purpose of this chapter, we will use this last approach, with creativity defined as the early phases of idea generation, and innovation as the later phases of implementation.

TEAM COMPOSITION

The composition of the team has been recognized as an important input variable in many models of team performance as well as in models of team creativity and innovation (Ilgen, Hollenbeck, Johnson, & Jundt, 2005; Woodman et al., 1993). Team composition covers a wide breadth of variables including demographics, job-relevant characteristics such as education or relevant knowledge, skills and abilities, and personality characteristics. Research on team composition tends to use one of two measurement approaches. The first focuses on aggregation or averaging a variable across team members (Stewart, 2006), and the second on the degree of diversity of team members with respect to the variables of interest (Hulsheger, Anderson, & Saldago, 2009; West & Anderson, 1996). Diversity has been defined in different ways (Harrison & Klein, 2007). In some cases it has been defined by the distribution of the characteristic in question (are all departments represented?), and in others by variance or range of scores. Early work in the area of team composition and creativity assumed that diversity in team composition would be beneficial, and increase the creative output of teams, as a result of the diverse knowledge and experiences of the team members (Guzzo & Dickson, 1996; McLeod, Lobel, & Cox, 1996).

Demographic Diversity

Much of the research on team diversity has found demographic diversity to be detrimental to team processes as well as team outcomes in general (Kirkman, Tesluk, & Rosen, 2004; Mathieu, Maynard, Rapp, & Gilson, 2008; Timmerman, 2000). Studies evaluating team creativity and innovation in relation to demographic diversity have found mixed results. For example, O'Reilly, Williams, and Barsade (1998) found moderate positive effects for racial diversity on creativity and innovation; however, gender and tenure diversity had no effect. On the other hand, Paletz, Peng, Erez, and Maslach (2004) reported no differences in creativity between ethnically diverse and ethnically homogenous teams, and McLeod et al. (1996) found ethnic diversity to hinder team creativity. Choi (2007) found that groups that were diverse in terms of gender were less creative, whereas groups with age diversity were more creative. Curseu (2010) found that team diversity (defined as gender, age, and national diversity combined) was moderately and positively related to the creativity of team output. Adding to the complexity, Baer, Oldham, Jacobson, and Hollingshead (2008) found that demographic diversity was negatively related to team creativity in an initial task, but not in a later task. Recently, a meta-analysis indicated nonsignificant effects for the relationship between demographic diversity and team creativity and innovation (Hulsheger et al., 2009).

The results of these studies suggest that the relationship between creativity and demographic diversity may be more complex than initially thought. It is possible that different variables (age vs. gender vs. ethnic diversity) will have different effects on creativity and innovation. The research by Baer et al. is also intriguing as it suggests that time and experience in a team may moderate the effects of diversity on creativity and innovation.

Functional Diversity

Demographic diversity is easily detected and observed, and therefore, may be more salient. However, differences based on attributes that are relevant to job performance, such as diversity in education, function in the organization, and job-relevant knowledge, skills, and abilities, while not initially salient can also influence team creativity (Milliken, Bartel, & Kutzberg, 2003). Models of team creativity indicate that it is this type of diversity—functional diversity—that facilitates creativity in teams (Woodman et al., 1993). Most research evaluating functional diversity found positive effects, suggesting that teams comprised of members from different and diverse functional backgrounds outperform homogeneous teams in terms of creativity and innovation (Fay, Borrill, Amir, Haward, & West, 2006; Keller, 2001). However, Ancona and Caldwell (1992), using 45 new product teams, found that functional background diversity was related to lower evaluations of innovation, that is, diverse teams were evaluated as less innovative. A recent meta-analysis suggested that functional diversity is positively related to team creativity and innovation (Hulsheger et al., 2009).

Taken together, these results indicate that functional diversity is positively related to creativity and innovation. However, researchers typically do not distinguish between various aspects of functional diversity such as educational background, function in the organization, and expertise. Additional research is needed to determine whether these variables have similar effects on creativity and innovation.

In addition to functional and demographic diversity, other forms of diversity have been hypothesized to influence creativity and innovation in teams. Individual difference variables that can influence individual and team cognitive processes as well as social processes have been speculated as having an influence on team creative output (Shalley, 2008). Specifically, individual differences in cognitive style, social skills, and personality variables that influence team interactions, such as extraversion and agreeableness, have been suggested as important for team functioning (Klein, DeRouin, & Salas, 2006; Stevens & Campion, 1994). However, research on the effects of team composition and diversity evaluating these variables is sparse (Kozlowski & Ilgen, 2006).

Cognitive Style and Personality

Kutzberg (2005), in two studies examining the effect of cognitive style on creative performance in teams, found that diversity in cognitive style was positively related to fluency (number of ideas generated), but negatively related to member perceptions of creative performance. Basadur and Head (2001) found that teams composed of members with heterogeneous cognitive styles outperformed homogeneous teams, indicating that diversity in cognitive style can have an important impact on team creativity and innovation. Additionally, teams that include more individuals who are creative tend to show greater creativity (Mathisen, Martinsen, & Einarsen, 2008; Taggar, 2002). Chirumboli, Mannetti, Pierro, Areni, and Kruglanski (2005) investigated average need for closure across team members and its relationship to team creativity. High need for closure groups relative to low need for closure groups generated more ideas, but the degree of elaboration and the creativity of those ideas was lower. The relationship is most likely due to need for closure restricting hypothesis generation as well as the production of conventional ideas.

Barry and Stewart (1997) evaluated the role of team composition, based on the proportion of extraverts and conscientiousness individuals in the group, on creative problem solving. They found that groups that had some extraverted members outperformed groups with no extraverted members, as well as groups in which more than 50% of the members were extraverted. However, no effect was found for conscientiousness. Robert and Cheung (2010) found that teams that were high in conscientiousness were less creative. In a follow-up study, Robert and Cheung found that team conscientiousness interacted with instructions such that low conscientiousness teams performed better when task instructions allowed for flexibility in how the task was completed and that high conscientiousness teams performed better when task instructions called for a systematic approach.

Results from a study by Baer et al. (2008) paint a more complex picture, suggesting that team personality composition interacts with creative confidence in predicting team creative performance. In this study, teams comprised of individuals that were high in extraversion, high in openness to experience, or low in conscientiousness, were more creative if members had a shared sense of creative confidence. Baer et al. suggest that creative confidence, i.e., the sense that the team is capable of generating creative ideas, allows team members to focus on collective, rather than individual, idea generation.

Results of these studies indicate that team composition in terms of cognitive style and the Big Five personality taxonomy may be important to understanding team creativity and innovation. However, only a limited number of studies are available. Future research needs to continue to examine the impact of these variables, but also to expand to include additional cognitive style and personality variables such as need for cognition, tolerance for ambiguity, and regulatory focus. In addition, it is important to evaluate the various approaches to conceptualizing team composition such as average, range, or proportion of individuals high and low in a particular characteristic in defining team diversity. The studies by Baer et al. (2008) and Robert and Cheung (2010) suggest that additional research needs to focus on the interactive effects of team composition variables with each other and with contextual variables.

Team Membership Change

Much of the research on teams tends to treat them as static entities; however, teams may gain or lose members (Levine, Choi, & Moreland, 2003). Teams may lose members due to retirement, layoffs, or the natural progression of the project. They may gain new members as a result of hiring, organizational restructuring, or the natural progression of the project. Membership change is detrimental to team performance because new members typically lack task-relevant skills, and interfere with the routine of the team because they are not aware of how it functions (Levine & Choi, 2004). However, it has been suggested that membership change, similar to diversity, may be beneficial for creativity, as new members provide access to new information, ideas, and perspectives (Levine et al., 2003).

Research on the effect of membership change on team creativity is limited. Choi and Thompson (2005) conducted two studies which evaluated the effect of membership change using student teams. Teams performed an idea generation task, and then some teams changed members before starting a second idea generation task. Choi and Thompson found no differences on the first task between teams; however, teams experiencing membership change generated more ideas and were more flexible in their thinking in the second task (after membership change) compared with teams that were stable. Hirst (2009), in a study of R&D teams, found that membership change interacted with team tenure, such that teams that had lower tenure benefited slightly from membership change, whereas membership change was detrimental to team performance for teams of longer tenure. Nemeth and Ormiston (2007), in a lab study, found that team membership change resulted in lower perceptions of team creativity by team members, however, membership change facilitated team creativity as measured objectively.

The results presented here indicate that additional research must be conducted to understand the relationship between membership change and team performance. Specifically, it is important to investigate the role of time and project phase in terms of the relationship between membership change and team creativity and innovation. The study by Hirst suggests that team tenure may be an important moderator. In addition, it is possible that membership change may influence team creativity differently depending on the phase of the project (regardless of team tenure).

Summary

Research findings regarding team composition and team diversity seem to be somewhat contradictory. There are several reasons for these contradictory results. The first issue is that only a limited number of empirical studies have looked at creativity and its relation to team diversity and team composition. A meta-analysis by Hulsheger et al. (2009) has identified a total of 15 different studies evaluating job-related diversity in any form and team creativity and innovation, with 10 of these studies evaluating team innovation specifically. Similarly, only eight studies evaluated the effect of background diversity. In addition to the limited number of studies, an even smaller number have evaluated each specific variable within a category. For example, studies evaluating the effect of background diversity sometimes focus on one variable such as gender or ethnic diversity, sometimes focus on multiple variables, and on some occasions combine these variables. As a result, a clear picture of the individual effect of each variable is even more limited. It is possible that the effects of one variable are masked by another. Therefore, additional research is still necessary for a better understanding of the effect of various aspects of diversity and team composition on creativity and innovation.

Second, the operationalization of diversity and team composition is not straightforward. As suggested by Harrison and Klein (2007), team diversity may be operationalized in different ways, such as the average of the construct across team members, score of the highest scoring member, or the range of scores. Each of these operationalizations may lead to different conclusions regarding the effect of diversity. Future research must evaluate the effect of diversity conceptualization on team creativity and innovation. It is possible that the best measure of diversity may vary depending on what constructs are being examined. For example, teams with a high number of creative individuals seem to perform better, but for cognitive style, diversity in styles was related to creativity. Research comparing different conceptualizations of team diversity (average, range, etc.) using the same construct is necessary to address this question.

Third, researchers evaluating team composition have typically evaluated one individual difference variable at a time (Barry & Stewart, 1997; Mathieu et al., 2008). However, past research at the individual level suggests interactions between various characteristics are predictive of creative performance (George & Zhou, 2001; King, McKee, & Broyles, 1996), and it is likely that similar results will be obtained at the team level. This point was made salient by Mathieu et al. (2008) who called for viewing:

"team composition as a complex combination of member attributes" *(p. 442)*.

However, only limited research to date has examined these interactive effects in the context of team creativity and innovation. Not only do we need to evaluate the interactive effects of various personality characteristics, but also those of functional and demographic diversity. For example, it is possible that if teams include members who are high on openness to experience, demographic diversity will have a positive effect on creativity, whereas when teams are composed of members low in openness to experience, demographic diversity will hinder creative performance.

A fourth explanation for the mixed findings regarding diversity and team composition on creativity and innovation is that these relationships are thought to be mediated by team processes such as social and cognitive processes (Miliken et al., 2003). Many of the studies summarized here have found that group composition and diversity were more effective when teams also exhibited social processes appropriate for creativity. For example, Taggar (2002) found that teams comprised of more creative members generated more creative solutions. This effect was particularly strong when teams also engaged in creativity-related team processes such as effective communication. Similarly, work by Pearsall, Ellis, and Evans (2008) found that gender diversity was not directly linked to group creativity. However, when gender was made salient through a task that was gender specific (designing a men's electric razor), gender diversity was linked to lower creativity. Further, salience of gender was also associated with increased team emotional conflict, which partially mediated the relationship between gender diversity and creativity. While many studies evaluating team composition diversity have also evaluated team social processes, the various studies tend to look at different variables, both for team composition and for social processes, making it more difficult to draw conclusions.

These results may also shed light on the interaction between team diversity and time on team creativity. It is likely that when teams are diverse, the development of effective team processes takes more time. Studies that have found that diverse teams perform better at a later task (Baer et al., 2008) provide initial support for this notion. The work by Hirst (2009), suggesting that membership change facilitates creativity for newly formed teams, but not for well established teams, also fits with this pattern. Newly formed teams are also forming their social processes. Membership change in well-established teams is much more disruptive to these social processes and therefore may hinder creativity. Future studies should evaluate the effect of diversity on team creativity and innovation directly, but also indirectly through the effect of diversity on social processes. In addition, time should be evaluated as an important dimension that influences the formation of social processes as well as team creativity and innovation.

From an applied perspective, it is important to note that many organizations turn to cross-functional teams as a way to facilitate team creativity and innovation. However, just putting different individuals together in teams may not yield creative teams. Demographic diversity may be an easy way for organizations to create diverse teams, as demographics are easily observed. However, research suggests that demographic diversity is the least appropriate approach to increase diversity for the purpose of creativity, resulting in negative or at best no effects. Other types of diversity, more directly related to the task at hand, seem to be more appropriate and result in enhanced creativity and innovation. Therefore, when organizations put together teams, it is best to evaluate diversity in terms of functional background, cognitive style, and personality.

A second implication is the importance of diversity coupled with effective social processes. The results of multiple studies suggest that team composition diversity interacts with various types of social processes in such a way that teams can capitalize on the benefits of diversity only if they engage in effective social processes such as open communication. It is therefore important that organizations provide teams with tools that facilitate these social processes such as effective leadership and training, so that the positive effects of team composition diversity may be realized.

SOCIAL PROCESSES

Most team effectiveness models include team social processes as a central feature (Hackman, 1987; Mathieu et al., 2008). In fact, many early versions of the I-P-O model included mainly social processes as the process variable (the "P" in the model), a notion criticized by Ilgen et al. (2005). Later, a distinction between taskwork and teamwork emerged (McIntyre & Salas, 1995). Taskwork describes the interactions with tools, tasks, and systems (Bowers, Braun, & Morgan, 1997). Teamwork, on the other hand, reflects processes associated with the social interaction of team members that ensure adaptive behavior and successful collective action to complete team taskwork (McIntyre & Salas, 1995; Salas, Sims, & Klein, 2004). However, different models and frameworks of teamwork include different variables (Mathieu et al., 2008; Rousseau, Aube, & Savoie, 2006; Salas, Sims, & Burke , 2005; Salas, Stagl, Burke, & Goodwin, 2007).

Recently, two different models have been suggested to integrate the different findings, variables, and frameworks of teamwork (Rousseau et al., 2006; Salas et al., 2005). While the models differ in the specific constructs they include, some commonalities exist. Both models emphasize the importance of coordination and collaboration, trust, psychological safety, support, communication, shared mental models, and performance and system monitoring. Together, these reviews identify some of the most central team social processes. It is important to note that some of these variables may be more appropriately discussed in the section on cognitive processes. For example, shared mental models facilitate social processes; however, are inherently a cognitive variable (Reiter-Palmon, Herman, & Yammarino, 2008). Additionally, some models include innovation as a process or teamwork variable (Rousseau et al., 2006), while in this chapter, creativity and innovation are viewed as an outcome. Finally, leadership is viewed by some as part of the social processes (Woodman et al., 1993); however, leadership will not be reviewed here as the topic is covered in another chapter (see Marion, this volume).

Team Collaboration

The terms collaboration, coordination, and cooperation are sometimes used interchangeably. Alternatively, coordination and cooperation have been viewed as necessary elements of collaboration, which is the approach taken here (de Vreede, Briggs, & Reiter-Palmon, 2010; Jassawalla & Sashittal, 1998). Team collaboration is particularly important under several circumstances such as in dynamic situations, for team adaptation, and when creativity is needed (Burke et al., 2006; Janssens & Brett, 2006). As task complexity and ambiguity increases and the nature of the work is more dynamic, the importance of collaboration increases (Burke et al., 2006). Creative tasks are complex and dynamic in nature, and require frequent adaptation and change due to the ambiguous nature of the task and outcome. When teams are working on tasks that require creativity, collaboration becomes important for effective team functioning. In addition, collaboration allows team members to overcome and integrate differences and diverse perspectives, therefore, allowing capitalization on the cognitive diversity that these diverse perspectives offer (Janssens & Brett, 2006; Edmondson & Roloff, 2009).

Studies evaluating creativity and innovation in organizational settings find that collaboration is critical for team creativity and innovation. Mitchell, Boyle, and Nicholas (2009), evaluating 98 teams from a variety of organizations, found that team goals which emphasized collaboration and cooperation were related to new idea generation. Specifically, the relationship between collaboration and idea generation was mediated by norms of open discussion, and by team behaviors that were inclusive and ensured a comprehensive decision. Mitchell et al. suggested that inclusive and comprehensive decision making allows team members to take advantage of the multiple perspectives available, further supporting the inter-relationships among the social process variables and between social processes, cognitive processes, and team diversity.

Similarly, Drach-Zehavy, and Somech (2001) found that collaboration, cooperation, and sharing information were positively related to team innovation. Pearce and Ensley (2004) found that team evaluations of collaboration correlated strongly with team evaluations of their own creative performance. However, perceptions of team collaboration did not correlate as strongly with management evaluations of creativity. Finally, in a longitudinal study of R&D teams, Hoegl, Weinkauf, and Gemueden (2004) found that team coordination, especially early in the project, was critical for team performance and project success. In addition, team coordination and collaboration was related to measures of teamwork quality (including cohesion, mutual support, and communication). This finding suggests that early on, while the project is still forming, coordination and sharing information is of particular importance for project success.

These results support the notion that collaboration facilitates open communication and interactions, which contribute to team creativity and innovation. Further, inclusive and comprehensive decision making allows team members to take advantage of the multiple perspectives from team members with varying expertise, perspectives, and experiences. Finally, there are some intriguing results suggesting the importance of time in team collaboration. It is important to note that research on collaboration often includes measures of communication and exchange of information. This confusion seems reasonable as the constructs are interwoven. It is hard to imagine collaboration without communication. Additional research is necessary to empirically separate these constructs, and determine their independent as well as direct and indirect effects on team creativity. Further, time has emerged as a possible moderator. Future studies should evaluate the role that time plays in the development of team collaboration and its effect on team creativity and innovation.

Finally, models that include team composition variables must be evaluated in conjunction with team collaboration to determine the effect (mediation, moderation) on team creativity.

Communication

Keller (2001) suggested that it is important to differentiate between internal team communication and external communication, that is, communication with organizational members outside the team and outside the organization. Ancona and Caldwell (1992) found that external communication was related to team innovation, as evaluated by top-level management. In addition, they found that the likelihood of engaging in external communication was related to team functional diversity, as more diverse teams engaged in more external communication. Similar results regarding the role of diversity for external communication were obtained by Keller (2001). Meta-analyses indicated that external communication was related to organizational innovation, and had a stronger relationship with innovation than internal communication, and was one of the strongest predictors of team creativity and innovation overall (Damanpour, 1991; Hulsheger et al., 2009).

Two main reasons have been suggested as to why external communication would be related to team creativity and innovation (Howell & Shea, 2006). The first focuses on the role of external communication in idea generation or creativity. External communication may provide the team with additional information that is not otherwise available, making the idea or solution more creative. The second focuses on the role of external communication for implementation. Here the focus is on external communication for the purpose of garnering support for the new idea, product, or solution to ensure smooth implementation.

Focusing on the role of external communication as a mechanism for information gathering, Perry-Smith and Shalley (2003) suggested that using a social network approach would be beneficial. Specifically, Perry-Smith and Shalley suggested that strength of network ties would be an important predictor of creativity and innovation, with weak network ties related to increased creativity and innovation. This is because weaker ties provide breadth of connections and access to more non-redundant information. These propositions have been tested at the individual level (Baer, 2010; Perry-Smith, 2006). However, evaluation of weak ties has not been conducted at the team level. For example, is it important that all team members have weak ties or only a few (or even one)? What happens with overlapping weak ties?

Howell and Shea (2006) evaluated external communication both as an informational source as well as a mechanism for garnering support from other organizational members. The results of their study using new product development teams indicated that external communication was related to creativity and innovation of team products, both at the original time of the data collection as well as a year later. Furthermore, both types of external communication—those associated with searching for information (scanning) and those associated with garnering support for innovation—were related to team creativity and innovation.

Research on external communication and team innovation and creativity provides support for the two roles of external communication. External communication provides access to additional information not available to the team members. However, additional research is needed to determine the role of diversity in access to external information. For example, does functional diversity influence external communication more than other types of diversity (such as personality or cognitive style)? Research should also investigate the relationship between weak ties and communication directly and their joint effects on team creativity. External communication seems to be important for innovation, or the implementation of creative ideas, as demonstrated by the role of external communication in obtaining support from the broader organization for the team and the creative idea. However, the research is limited. Further, the differentiation between the roles of external communication—for creativity (access to information) and innovation (support)—is important and needs to be evaluated further.

Internal communication has been viewed as one of the most important social processes that influences team performance (Caldwell & Everhart, 1998). Research suggests that high performing teams also communicate more effectively (Caldwell & Everhart, 1998; Marks Mathieu, & Zaccaro, 2001). With regards to innovation, meta-analyses by Damanpour (1991) and Hulsheger et al. (2009) found that internal communication was positively related to team creativity and innovation, although not as strongly as external communication. Additional support for the role of internal communication is provided by work that shows that increased participation and socialization, which are related to internal communication, are predictive of team creativity (Gilson & Shalley, 2004).

However, the relationship between internal communication and creativity is complex. For example, in investigating the effects of communication frequency, Kratzer, Leenders, and van Engelen (2004) found a negative relationship between communication frequency and creativity in teams. They speculated that frequent communication may reduce creativity and innovation as this leads to cognitive overload and production blocking. Further support was provided by Lovelace, Shapiro, and Weingart (2001), who found that the nature of the communication, whether collaborative or contentious, was critical. Collaborative communication was related to higher creativity and innovation, whereas contentious communication was related to lower creativity and innovation. Further, the effect of contentious communication was particularly detrimental when the frequency of communication was high.

The results regarding internal communication suggest that while it is important for creative performance of teams, there are conditions in which it may be detrimental. Specifically, the nature and tone of the communication is important. This further supports the notion that communication is a process that may support other social processes, such as collaboration or cohesion. Additional research is necessary to identify not only the conditions under which internal communication is effective for team creativity and innovation, but also its relationship to other important social processes.

One important aspect that has emerged in discussion of internal communication is the importance of open discussion and communication for team creativity (Lovelace et al., 2001). Psychological safety has been found to be related to the willingness of individuals to share information, and openly discuss information (Edmondson, 1999; Rank, Pace, & Frese, 2004).

Trust and Psychological Safety

Trust is based on a team member's belief that the team is competent and can accomplish its task and will not harm the individual (Ilgen et al., 2005). Psychological safety is defined as the shared belief that it is safe for individuals within the team to take interpersonal risks (Edmondson, 1999, 2004). Psychological safety has been found to encourage employees to take initiative, make suggestions, and to facilitate the implementation of innovation (Burke et al., 2006; Edmondson, 2004). In turn, these behaviors, termed voice behaviors, have been linked to employee idea generation, discussion of new ideas, and implementation of new ideas (Rank et al., 2004). Further, it was noted that when facing psychological threats and feeling psychologically unsafe, individuals are more likely to develop a defensive orientation and are less likely to display creativity and innovative behaviors at work (Nicholson & West, 1988; West & Richter, 2008). Additional support for the role of psychological safety in encouraging team creativity and innovation comes from research on the organizational climate that is conducive to creativity. Aspects related to psychological safety consistently emerge as important factors in organizational climate that facilitate creativity and innovation (Amabile & Grykiewicz, 1989; Ekvall, 1996; Hunter, Bedell, & Mumford, 2007).

Psychological safety has also been studied as a direct predictor of creativity (Carmeli & Spreitzer, 2009; Kark & Carmeli, 2009). Evidence for its importance for team creativity and innovation comes from West and his colleagues (Burningham & West, 1995; West & Anderson, 1996; West, Borrill, Dawson, Brodbeck, Shapiro, & Haward, 2003). In a series of studies across different industries and team types, psychological safety was found to be an important predictor of team innovation (Burningham & West, 1995; West & Anderson, 1996). However, a meta-analysis by Hulsheger et al. (2009) found that while psychological safety was predictive of team creativity and innovation, the relationship was weak.

Psychological safety and trust have both been linked to the willingness of team members to openly and freely discuss information (Salas et al., 2005). Trust and psychological safety have also been suggested to influence the interpretation of behavior of other team members, and therefore may be directly related to how conflict gets interpreted (Salas et al., 2005). When trust is low, disagreements and other ambiguous information are more likely to be interpreted in a negative way, resulting in negative responses from team members and backup and support behaviors may be more likely to be misinterpreted as micro-management (Salas et al., 2005). Additional research is necessary to identify team behaviors and processes that facilitate the development of trust and psychological safety. Further, the role of team composition and diversity should be evaluated as an antecedent to trust and safety, and the joint effects of trust, safety, and group diversity on team creativity and innovation should be evaluated. Additionally, other social processes, such as communication or conflict, may mediate the relationship between trust or safety and team creativity and innovation.

Backup and Support

Backup behavior is defined as one member of the team helping another member obtain the goals defined by his role and tasks, when it is clear that without this help those goals will not be attained (McIntyre & Salas, 1995). Backup behaviors require that team members be aware of what is required of other team members and how they contribute to the overall effort of the team. Backup behaviors also require team members to monitor the performance of other team members so that they can help when needed (Marks et al., 2001). While backup behavior has been investigated in the context of team effectiveness and has been suggested as important for team adaptation (Burke et al., 2006), very limited research has directly linked backup behaviors with team innovation. Pearce and Ensley (2004) looked at team altruism and its relation to performance in innovation teams. Team altruism refers to team members helping each other, a component of backup behaviors. Team altruism was strongly related to self perceptions of team performance ($r = .66$). Team altruism was also related to management perception of team performance, although not quite as strongly ($r = .30$).

Team support for innovation includes not only backup behaviors, but also the:

> "expectation, approval and practical support of attempts to introduce new and improved ways of doing things in the work environment" *(West, 1990, p. 315).*

Specifically, team support for innovation is seen through norms for innovation, tolerance for risk and failure when innovation is not successful, and openness and willingness to try new ideas (West & Anderson, 1996). Much of the work on team support for innovation focuses on team and organizational climate. Work on organizational climate and its effect on team creativity and innovation will not be reviewed here in detail, as it is covered elsewhere in this volume (see West & Sacramento). However, it is important to note that a consistent finding is that climate that is supportive of innovation is related to team creative performance (Griffin, Neal, & Parker, 2007; Mathisen et al., 2008; Scott & Bruce, 1994). A meta-analysis on climate factors related to creativity has suggested that team support and positive interpersonal relationships were related to team creativity (Hunter et al., 2007).

The role of team support for team creativity and innovation has been clearly demonstrated through research on team climate for creativity. Additionally, a meta-analysis which evaluated 39 studies found that support for innovation was a strong predictor of team creativity and innovation (Hulsheger et al., 2009). However, research on backup behavior and its relationship to team innovation and creativity is limited. Backup behavior has been found to be particularly important under conditions of uncertainty and stress (Salas et al., 2005). These are the conditions in which team creativity and innovation often flourish, suggesting that team backup behaviors are important for team creativity and innovation.

Team Conflict

Research on team conflict suggests that it can be distinguished by whether it is task (cognitive conflict related to the task) or relationship (socioemotional conflict as a result of interpersonal disagreement) based. However, the two are often related and conflict in one area can spill into another (Jehn, 1997). It has been suggested that task-related conflict can be particularly important for enhancing creativity and innovation, as different views are discussed, differences in approaches can be resolved, and multiple points of view can be incorporated (Kurtzberg & Amabile, 2001; Mannix & Neale, 2005). A meta-analysis by Hulsheger et al. (2009) found non-significant results for the relationship between task or relationship conflict and team creativity and innovation, however, the number of studies used was relatively small (6 for relationship conflict and 13 for task conflict).

Carnevale and Probst (1998) in a series of studies using Duncker's functional fixedness (candle) task and Rosch's categorization task manipulated participant expectations regarding the team. Some participants were led to believe that teams would be cooperative whereas others were informed that teams would be in conflict. Results indicated that when participants expected conflict they were less likely to develop novel solutions and developed more restricted categorizations, supporting the notion that conflict can hinder creativity. Similarly, Mortensen and Hinds (2001), using product development teams, found that both relationship and task conflict were negatively related to creative performance.

Furthermore, a study by De Dreu (2006) examining the impact of task conflict on creativity indicated that task conflict could facilitate as well as inhibit team creativity. Specifically, De Dreu found a curvilinear, inverted U relationship between task conflict and creativity in postal service teams. A moderate level of task conflict facilitated creative performance, but too much or too little task conflict stifled creativity. Such findings could also be partially explained by the work of Jehn and Mannix (2001), which indicate that task conflict breeds interpersonal conflict. In other words, high levels of task conflict may increase interpersonal conflict, which in turn, hinders creative performance.

Jehn (1995) evaluated the effect of relationship and task conflict on team performance and satisfaction. In addition, Jehn investigated whether the effect of conflict was moderated by the type of task the team performed, routine vs. non-routine tasks. The findings suggested that relationship conflict was detrimental, regardless of task. However, the findings regarding task conflict were more complex. When tasks were routine, task conflict was detrimental to group functioning. In contrast, when teams performed non-routine tasks, task conflict either had no effect or was beneficial for group functioning. Interviews conducted as part of the study revealed that when task conflicts in groups performing non-routine tasks were discussed openly, it resulted in re-evaluation of the tasks, ways to achieve team goals, and more creative ideas. Jehn also found a curvilinear relationship between task conflict and team performance for non-routine tasks. While this study focuses on performance in general, it is important for understanding the effect of conflict on team creativity and innovation as those tasks are non-routine. It is therefore possible that Jehn's (1995) finding regarding non-routine tasks will extend to teams involved in creative tasks. The inverted U relationship found may also explain the fact that the meta-analysis by Hulsheger et al. (2009) did not find a significant relationship between task conflict and team creativity, as curvilinear relationships were not evaluated.

Chen (2006) provided more direct support for the role of task type in moderating the relationship between conflict and team creativity and innovation in a study that investigated the relationship between task conflict, relationship conflict, and creativity in R&D teams. Chen evaluated whether the relationship between conflict and creativity is dependent on the type of project the team was working on (service vs. technology). For service oriented teams, task conflict had no effect on team creativity, but relationship conflict was significantly and negatively related to team creativity. On the other hand, for teams focusing on technology projects, no effects were found for relationship conflict, but task conflict was strongly associated with increased creativity.

Similarly, the effect of conflict and group polarity has been found to depend on the task and the timing in the project (Kratzer, Leenders, & van Engelen, 2006). In a study using R&D teams, Kratzer et al. found that team conflict had an overall negative relationship with team creativity. However, further investigation found that the relationship between team conflict and team creativity differed based on the phase of the project. During project conceptualization, an inverted U shaped relationship was found, suggesting that moderate levels of conflict are beneficial for creativity. However, during later phases of the team creative process, conflict had a negative effect on creativity.

Research that has focused on strategies that teams use to manage conflict found that conflict management is important and can minimize the negative effects of conflict. Song, Dyer, and Thieme (2006) found that techniques viewed as more positive and effective, such as integration or accommodation were positively related to constructive conflict and negatively related to destructive conflict. Similarly, more negative and less effective approaches, such as avoidance, were related to conflict in the reverse. Conflict management techniques were found to be directly and indirectly related to team innovation. Further support for the role of conflict management techniques was found by Lovelace et al. (2001). In a study of 43 cross functional teams, task disagreement was found to be beneficial for team innovation when team members felt free to express their concerns and openly discuss these concerns.

The results summarized here paint a complex picture regarding the relationship between conflict and creativity and innovation. Whether task and relationship conflict have different effects on creativity and innovation is still open to debate. It is possible that the relationship between task conflict and creativity is curvilinear. It seems likely that the type of task also influences the effect of conflict, with more complex and technical tasks benefiting from task conflict, whereas interpersonal tasks are hindered by interpersonal conflict. Finally, it seems that when there are positive effects for task conflict, these effects are possible because teams have mechanisms to handle these conflicts such as high cohesion, trust, and open communication (Lovelace et al., 2001; Mortensen & Hinds, 2001).

Future research should specifically evaluate the possibility of a curvilinear relationship between task conflict and team creativity and innovation. The studies reviewed here also suggest a possible moderated relationship between conflict, especially task conflict, and project phase or time, which needs to be evaluated further. Additional research needs to evaluate the direct effect of conflict and possible mediators of other social processes such as trust and communication, as ways to ameliorate the detrimental effects of conflict. Further, the relationship between task and relationship conflict as well as their relation to team creativity and innovation must be evaluated. It is possible that a high degree of task conflict can directly create or contribute to relationship conflict, resulting in negative effects of task conflict. Finally, the role of conflict may be particularly important when teams are diverse, as team diversity may lead to increased conflict (Mathieu et al., 2008). It is important to identify whether different types of diversity lead to different types of conflict or may be mitigated by different social processes.

Cohesion

Team cohesion is one of the most studied constructs in the team literature (Kozlowski & Ilgen, 2006). The most common definition suggested for team cohesion is that of team member attraction to the collective (Evans & Jarvis, 1980). Team cohesion has been found to improve team performance and effectiveness (Kozlowski & Ilgen, 2006). Further, a meta-analysis by Gully, Devine, and Whitney (1995) found that team cohesion was an important predictor of team performance, especially for tasks that require coordination and communication, characteristic of creative tasks.

Studies directly evaluating the effect of team cohesion on team creativity and innovation have generally found positive relationships, similar to those found for other team performance criteria (Craig & Kelly, 1999; Hoegl & Gemuenden, 2001; Keller, 1986). A meta-analysis (Hulsheger et al., 2009) identified a moderate and positive relationship between cohesion and team innovation. However, Sethi, Smith, and Park (2001) in a study investigating 141 product development teams, found a negative relationship between team cohesion and team creativity and innovation. Additionally, Jaussi and Dionne (2003) found that team cohesion interacted with team intrinsic motivation in predicting creativity of student teams. These latter results, combined with the work on team conflict and team cohesion, suggest that the relationship between team cohesion and creativity may not be simple. Future research should identify under what conditions cohesion contributes to team creativity and innovation. For example, it is possible that team cohesion may lead to rejection of criticism and less critical thinking about team suggestions and products in order to preserve team cohesion, resulting in lower team creativity and innovation. This suggests that team cohesion may interact with internal communication or task conflict in predicting team creativity and innovation.

Team Efficacy/Potency

Team efficacy and team potency are related but distinct constructs. Team efficacy is defined as:

> "a shared belief in a group's collective capability to organize and execute courses of action required to produce given levels of goal attainment" (*Kozlowski & Ilgen, 2006, p. 90*).

Team potency is defined as a collective belief in the ability of the team to be successful (Mathieu et al., 2008). The difference between the two is similar to the difference between self efficacy and self esteem. Team efficacy is task specific, whereas team potency is a more general belief (Mathieu et al., 2008).

Research on the relationship between team efficacy or potency and team creativity and innovation is limited. Pearce and Ensley (2004) found that team potency was one of the strongest predictors of team performance, as determined by the team's own evaluation as well as by evaluations made by managers. Shin and Zhou (2007), in a study of R&D teams, found that team efficacy was directly related to team creativity and also mediated the relationship between team diversity and transformational leadership with team creativity. Finally Baer, Baer et al. (2008), in a study of student teams, found that team creative confidence was predictive of team creative performance measured two weeks later. Specifically, team creative confidence ameliorated some of the negative effects of team composition in reaching a creative outcome. There is only limited research on the effects of team potency and team efficacy. The research cited suggests that these processes may be important for team creativity and innovation, however, more research on the direct effects of team potency and efficacy as well as possible moderators is necessary.

Summary

Overall, research suggests that social processes are important contributors to team creativity and innovation. There are several themes that have emerged from the research summarized here. First, the social processes described are interrelated and may have interactive effects on team creativity and innovation. For example, research suggests that team communication is related to team creativity and innovation, but only when communication is collaborative, open, and team members feel safe (Edmondson, 2004). Therefore, team communication interacts with the social process of collaboration and psychological safety in influencing team creativity and innovation. However, research evaluating these interactions is limited. Prior findings should be replicated, and additional variables should be investigated. Similarly, various social processes may influence one another. For example, communication may increase when team members feel safe, but psychological safety may also be a result of open communication (Edmondson, 2004). Similarly, team conflict can directly influence team cohesion, but cohesion may affect how conflict is interpreted (Salas et al., 2005).

A second theme that has emerged relates to the interaction between various social processes and time. In recent years, researchers have criticized the traditional I-P-O model as being static and suggested that it is important to understand temporal progression (Marks et al., 2001; Mohammed, Hamilton, & Lim, 2009). Longitudinal research suggests that the effect of social processes on team creativity and innovation are indeed dependent on time. Hoegl et al. (2004) found that team coordination was particularly important early in the project cycle when the project was still forming. Similarly, Kratzer et al. (2006) found that the effect of team conflict on team creativity and innovation depended on the phase of the project cycle. Early in the project, a moderate amount of conflict was beneficial, but later in the project conflict was detrimental. These results suggest that to fully understand how social processes influence team creativity and innovation, we must incorporate time into our models and research, as suggested by Marks et al. and Mohammed et al.

Finally, the research presented here suggests that the effect of team composition and team diversity may be mediated or moderated by social processes. Team diversity has been directly linked to the extent and diversity of external communication, which facilitates team creativity and innovation (Ancona & Caldwell, 1992; Keller, 2001). Team diversity has also been linked to increased conflict (Lovelace et al., 2001; Pelled, Eisenhardt, & Xin, 1999), which has been linked to decreases in team creativity and innovation. Finally, work by Baer et al. (2008) found that team efficacy mediated the relationship between team personality composition and team creativity. Additional research is necessary to identify these possible relationships.

These studies also have important implications for organizations trying to facilitate team creativity. First, open internal communication, trust, and psychological safety seem to be critical processes that influence team creativity and innovation directly, but also indirectly. Specifically, negative effects resulting from conflict or diversity may be mitigated by effective internal communication and feelings of trust. Organizations should find ways in which to facilitate these critical factors. Specifically, it has been suggested that training in effective communication techniques is particularly effective in improving team communication (Marks et al., 2001). Additionally, leadership that facilitates a positive and supportive climate can be important for improved communication, as well as for increased creativity and innovation (Hunter et al., 2007).

Finally, the work regarding conflict suggests that it must be managed carefully. Task conflict may be beneficial for team creativity and innovation, but it is important that this does not become personal. This means that organizations must ensure that teams can handle conflict in a constructive manner. Leaders have an important role in setting the tone and developing ways in which teams can handle conflict effectively.

COGNITIVE PROCESSES

Cognitive processes associated with creative problem solving have received much more attention at the individual level than at the team level (Reiter-Palmon et al., 2008). Further, compared to social processes, research on cognitive processes has been limited. For example, the meta-analysis on team variables influencing team creativity and innovation by Hulsheger et al. (2009) does not include cognitive processes, indicating that research, and possibly theory, is lacking.

One cognitive process that has been investigated extensively at the team level is that of idea generation or brainstorming (Paulus & Paulus, 1997). In most studies, creativity has been defined as the outcome of idea generation or brainstorming group meetings, therefore equating brainstorming with creativity (Reiter-Palmon et al., 2008). It is important to note that idea generation is only one cognitive process that can influence the outcome of creative problem solving and innovation. A review of cognitive models of creativity suggests that other processes, such as problem identification and construction, idea evaluation and selection, and implementation planning, also are important for a creative outcome; however, these processes have not received as much attention in the team literature (Mumford, Mobley, Uhlman, Doares, & Reiter-Palmon, 1991; Reiter-Palmon et al., 2008).

Idea Generation and Brainstorming

Much of the research on brainstorming in teams focuses on the number of ideas generated as the metric for creativity. As such, the research focuses on one possible outcome of the idea generation process (fluency) and ignores other possible outcomes such as quality or originality. Specifically, studies have used fluency as the criterion or outcome measure, equating number of ideas with creativity. Therefore, much of the research evaluated the predictors of idea generation, and did not treat idea generation as a predictor of creativity. However, research at the individual level, using divergent thinking tests and measures of fluency, suggests that fluency on these types of tasks is not always related to real-world creativity (Mouchiroud & Lubart, 2001; Runco & Mraz, 1992).

Research evaluating idea generation and brainstorming in teams suggests that nominal groups (when information from individuals working alone is combined) tend to outperform teams when the criterion is the number of ideas generated (Mullen, Johnson, & Salas, 1991). This surprising finding, dubbed productivity loss or process loss, led to a stream of research focusing on the factors that affect process loss and ways to overcome them (Diehl & Stroebe, 1987).

Both social and cognitive factors have been suggested to influence process loss. Individuals in teams may not speak up and offer ideas due to evaluation apprehension. Some of the work cited previously on team communication, safety, and cohesion suggests that these factors can minimize the role of evaluation apprehension and therefore minimize process loss (Paulus & Brown, 2003). Process loss can also be inherent in the process of communication between team members. When working face-to-face, team members cannot all speak at the same time. As a result process loss may occur as team members wait to take turns. This wait can result in less time to present ideas, as well as in idea loss. The need to wait, and the resulting process loss, increases as team size increases (de Vreede et al., 2010). One of the most common approaches to dealing with such process loss is the use of technology to facilitate idea generation, known as electronic brainstorming (Dennis & Williams, 2003; Gallupe, Dennis, Cooper, Valacich, Bastianutti, & Nunamaker, Jr., 1992). One way that this has been found to be beneficial is by allowing team members to simultaneously introduce ideas without having to wait. Electronic brainstorming has been found to be particularly effective for tasks requiring divergent thought (Kerr & Murthy, 2004), as well as for larger teams with more then eight members (DeRosa, Smith, & Hantula, 2007).

Another strategy evaluated in the context of improving the performance of brainstorming teams is that of facilitated brainstorming or providing instructions or guidelines to the team. Santanen, Briggs, and de Vreede (2004) examined the differential effects of either free or directed brainstorming strategies. Free brainstorming occurred without any facilitation, but the directed efforts had three different patterns of facilitation. Overall brainstorming efforts with directed facilitation resulted in more solutions generated with higher creativity ratings, higher average creativity ratings, and a greater concentration of creative solutions. When comparing the facilitation methods, some methods resulted in significantly more creative solutions than others.

Similarly, Coskun, Paulus, Brown, and Sherwood (2000) found that providing external primes improved the performance of brainstorming teams. Paulus and Brown (2003) found that providing additional guidelines for brainstorming increased the fluency of idea generation in teams. Finally, Paulus et al. (2006) found that teams that were provided rules for brainstorming generated more ideas than groups that were given no rules. The results of these studies suggest that rules, primes, and instructions can play an important role in team idea generation. Work by de Vreede, Kolfschoten, and Briggs (2006) suggests that predictable patterns result from the use of specific instructions and guidelines. However, different combinations of instructions may result in different outcomes. More research on the specific effects of different combinations of rules and instructions is still needed.

Creative Problem Solving Processes

As stated, idea generation, or brainstorming, has been the most studied cognitive process of creative problem solving at the team level. However, based on cognitive models of creative problem solving, other processes are also important. These models suggest that additional processes include problem identification and construction, information gathering, idea evaluation and selection, and implementation planning (Mumford et al., 1991; Reiter-Palmon et al., 2008). As research for these processes is limited, they will only be reviewed briefly in this section. When possible, these processes will be tied to other related team cognitive phenomena.

Problem identification and construction is defined as the process of identifying that a problem exists and identifying the goals and parameters of the problem solving effort (Mumford, Reiter-Palmon, & Redmond, 1994; Reiter-Palmon & Robinson, 2009). In the team literature the concept most closely aligned with problem identification and construction is that of shared mental models (SMMs). As more extensive literature on SMMs is available, this will be reviewed in a separate section.

Information gathering focuses on how individuals search both within and outside the team for information needed for the creative problem solving effort (Reiter-Palmon et al., 2008). The most closely aligned team concept related to information gathering is that of information sharing. Research on the cognitive aspect of information sharing typically uses the hidden profile paradigm, which identifies the conditions under which team members will be more likely to share information. These studies suggest that shared information, information that is available to all team members prior to team discussion, is more likely to be discussed, while information that is not available to all or most team members is less likely to be discussed (Mesmer-Magnus & DeChurch, 2009). Teams that are specifically asked to discuss information prior to reaching a decision are more likely to discuss unshared information (Stewart & Stasser, 1995). In addition, social processes that promote open discussion and cooperation allow team members to overcome the tendency to share only information that is already known to all team members (Mesmer-Magnus & DeChurch, 2009). However, research evaluating the effect of information sharing directly on team creativity is not available.

Once the team has generated multiple possible ideas, these ideas must be evaluated and a final idea, or set of ideas, must be selected for further development and implementation. This is seen as the first step in the innovation process. However, research in this area is limited and inconclusive, suggesting that in some cases groups perform no better or even worse than individuals when it comes to idea evaluation and selection while at other times teams perform better (Mumford, Feldman, Hein, & Nagao, 2001; Nijstad, Rietzschel, & Stroebe, 2006). The research by Mumford et al. highlights some conditions when teams do outperform individuals. First, teams tend to perform better at the idea evaluation and selection stage when fewer alternatives are available. Mumford et al. speculated that increased demands on coordination and time resulting from more alternatives were particularly problematic in teams. Second, teams that had the same training outperformed individuals. Mumford et al. suggested that shared mental models resulting from training assisted teams in gaining a shared understanding of the problem and the standards necessary to evaluate an effective solution. This in turn allowed teams to make more optimal choices.

Implementation planning is considered the last of the cognitive processes associated with creative problem solving. Implementation, which is viewed as part of the innovation phase, has received quite a bit of attention in recent years (West, 2002). Further, implementation includes both social and cognitive processes. Implementation requires coordination, typically across multiple teams or even organizations, increasing the time and effort required (West et al., 2004). In addition, external communication becomes particularly important as the team engages in persuasion and attempts to gain acceptance for the new idea. From a cognitive perspective, the team must develop an implementation plan which provides team members with an understanding of the implementation process and team member responsibilities (Janicik & Bartel, 2003; Mumford et al., 2001; Weingart, 1992).

Most of the research on planning has focused on planning as part of general team effectiveness, and not as part of the innovation process. Team planning research suggests that in-process planning, or adaptive planning, compared to planning prior to implementation, is more predictive of performance (Weingart, 1992). Additionally, most teams do not engage in planning on their own, however, external demands may lead to planning (Hackman, Brousseau, & Weiss, 1976; West et al., 2004). Planning seems to benefit teams that engage in more difficult and complex tasks such as creative tasks (Marta, Leritz, & Mumford, 2005; Weingart, 1992). Marta et al. also found that diverse teams responded more effectively than homogeneous teams to the need to adapt plans. Stout, Cannon-Bowers, Salas, and Milanovich (1999) found that planning is a way to develop shared mental models that facilitate team performance. In turn, these shared mental models can facilitate the effectiveness of implementation planning and particularly the modification and revision of plans.

The limited research on team creative cognitive processes indicates that much more research is necessary for an understanding of how processes occurring at the individual level are integrated into team processes. Future research should first establish ways to evaluate these cognitive processes at the team level. Future research should also evaluate the importance and relevance of each of these processes to the final outcome of team creativity and innovation. Additionally, research should evaluate the relationship between the various processes. For example, research by Mumford et al. (2001) found that the number of ideas available from the idea generation phase can influence the effectiveness of idea evaluation and choice. Other research is needed to determine the relationships between outcomes of the various cognitive processes and the processes that follow.

Cognitive process models at the individual level suggest that individuals can cycle between these processes and that the relationship is not linear (Mumford et al., 2001), however, it is not clear what the relationship is when these processes occur in a team. It is possible that one reason that we see differential effects due to time or project phase is because it is more difficult for teams to recognize the need to return to earlier processes or actually go back to a process they already engaged in, resulting in a more linear relationship between the processes. The effect of team composition and diversity on the effective application of these creative cognitive processes is also not clear. For example, it is expected that functionally diverse teams will likely have access to more diverse information, however, research evaluating information sharing in relation to team diversity and the link between those and team creativity and innovation does not exist.

Shared Mental Models

As indicated, problem construction, or the process of defining the problem and parameters used to structure an ill-defined problem and solve it, has some parallels with the concept of SMMs. Shared mental models are a representation of knowledge or beliefs that are shared by team members (Cannon-Bowers, Salas, & Converse, 1993; Klimoski & Mohammed, 1994). There are four primary content areas in which there are SMMs:

1. knowledge about equipment and tools,
2. knowledge about the team tasks, goals, and performance requirements,
3. knowledge about other team members' abilities, knowledge, and skills, and
4. knowledge about appropriate team interactions (Cannon-Bowers et al., 1993).

The second element or representation, knowledge about the task, is most closely aligned with the problem identification and construction process (Reiter-Palmon et al., 2008).

Much of the research on SMMs has focused on only one of these dimensions, or has collapsed these four types of SMMs into two dimensions of task (containing the first two) and team (containing the latter two). Previous empirical work has typically found a positive relationship between the degree of agreement, or sharedness, of the mental model and various measures of team effectiveness (Marks, Sabella, Burke, & Zacarro, 2002; Mathieu, Goodwin, Heffner, Salas, & Cannon-Bowers, 2000; Salas, Cooke, & Rosen, 2008). Burke et al. (2006) suggested that SMMs are particularly important for team adaptability, while Cannon-Bowers et al. (1993) hypothesized that SMMs play an important role in team performance when tasks are changing or are unpredictable. Shared mental models allow team members to anticipate the needs of other team members, identify performance gaps more quickly, make communication more effective, and predict the behavior of team members.

Research on the role of SMMs and creativity suggests that generally SMMs have a positive relationship with team creativity and innovation. Mumford et al. (2001) found that SMMs, developed through training, facilitated the generation and selection of more creative ideas by a team. Pearce and Ensley (2004) found that shared vision (a component of SMMs) was related to innovation in product and process development teams. Similarly, Gilson and Shalley (2004) found that team shared goals were related to increased creativity and innovation, and increased engagement in the creative process.

However, SMMs may lead to too much similarity and therefore conformity (Cannon-Bowers et al., 1993). It is possible that some degree of dissimilarity in SMMs, or less sharedness, would be beneficial especially for team creativity and innovation. Kellermanns, Floyd, Pearson, and Spencer (2008), in a study of decision making teams, found an interaction between constructive confrontation norms and SMMs. Specifically, in teams where norms supported discussion of disagreement and constructive confrontation, lower similarity in SMMs was related to higher decision quality. Similarity of SMMs contributed to decision quality only when teams could not share information openly. Kellermanns et al. hypothesized that teams can take advantage of diversity (fewer SMMs), and therefore utilize more diverse information when norms support open information exchange, participative safety, and when teams are able to manage conflict effectively. Teams in which these social processes are not effective or do not exist would benefit from the increased understanding and similarity afforded by the shared mental model.

The research on SMMs and team creativity and innovation is limited and somewhat inconclusive. More research is needed to identify whether differences between the four aspects of SMMs exist in relation to team creativity and innovation. The research by Kellermanns et al. (2008) suggests that it is possible that sharedness regarding team norms and behavior, especially if this facilitates effective social processes in the team, is more important than similarity of SMMs regarding the task. In addition, it is likely that open discussion will facilitate the formation of SMMs, allowing for the development of more inclusive mental models that contain components from mental models that initially were more divergent. Therefore, effective social processes may contribute to the development of more inclusive SMMs. Future research should address these issues. Finally, it is important to remember that SMMs are not static, but rather change over time, as team members acquire more information, discuss problems, or execute a plan (Burke et al., 2006). It is likely that the exchange of information between team members during all phases of the project or problem solving effort will facilitate the adaptation and refinement of SMMs. Further refinement of SMMs may influence various social and cognitive processes as well. Research that evaluates SMMs dynamically in relation to team creativity and innovation is necessary.

Team Reflexivity

Team reflexivity is defined as:

> "the extent to which group members overtly reflect upon the group's objectives, strategies, and processes and adapt them to current or anticipated endogenous or environmental circumstances" (West, 1996, p. 559).

Team reflexivity is viewed as a process of team reflection on all aspects of team performance including the task, processes used to reach the goal, social processes such as communication and coordination, and cognitive processes (Schippers, Den Hartog, & Koopman, 2007). Team reflexivity is particularly beneficial for teams working on complex and dynamic tasks (Tjosvold, Tang, & West, 2004). Team reflexivity has been suggested as an important antecedent of team creativity and innovation, as teams that are reflexive can change their strategies and processes and learn from past mistakes and achievements (Schippers et al., 2007; West, 1996).

Carter and West (1998) in a study of BBC-TV production teams found that team reflexivity was related to increased team performance and innovation. Tjosvold et al. (2004) in a study using teams in China found that team reflexivity was related to team innovation. In addition, Tjosvold et al. investigated factors that influence the natural occurrence of team reflexivity. They found that team reflexivity was higher when cooperative (vs. competitive) goals were present in the team. Muller, Herbig, and Petrovic (2009) manipulated team or individual reflection and compared those to a control condition with no manipulated reflection. The study utilized teams of students working on a product development task. Reflection, particularly team reflexivity, was found to be related to more creative ideas. This study suggests that team reflexivity is related to team creativity and innovation whether team reflection occurs naturally, or the team is instructed to engage in team reflection. Finally, De Dreu (2002) found that team reflexivity was related to team creativity and innovation overall, and that minority dissent contributed to the prediction of team creativity and innovation, but only for teams where reflexivity was high.

Summary

Empirical work on the effect of team cognition on team creativity and innovation is particularly sparse (Reiter-Palmon et al., 2008; Salas et al., 2008). While research on individual cognitive processes that lead to creativity and innovation is much more prevalent, interest in team cognition is more recent (Mohammed & Dumville, 2001). Several important themes emerge from the research reported here. First, much of the work on team cognitive processes is focused on social cognition. For example, SMMs include aspects of social cognition with dimensions of team member shared understanding about the team, appropriate social behavior, norms, and the like (Mohammed & Dumville, 2001). Second, the various dimensions of team cognitive processes are interrelated. For example, planning and team reflexivity seem to facilitate the development of more effective SMMs (Smith-Jentsch, Cannon-Bowers, Tannenbaum, & Salas, 2008). Similarly, SMMs influence the formation of task execution and planning (Stout et al., 1999).

Third, while no research directly assessed the role of time on these cognitive processes, time may play an important part. The cognitive processes associated with creative problem solving, such as problem construction, idea generation, and idea evaluation and selection, can be viewed as occurring in a natural progression. While the relationship between these processes is not necessarily linear, and individuals and teams may cycle within these processes (Mumford et al., 1991; Reiter-Palmon et al., 2008), it is likely that teams progress more linearly. Therefore, time may naturally align with cognitive processes such that earlier in the project teams are constructing the problem and generating ideas, whereas later in the processes teams are engaged in idea evaluation and implementation planning. For example, Hoegl et al. (2004) found that team coordination early in the project, when the team engages in idea generation, was more important than team coordination in later phases. In addition, SMMs have been shown to change over time as team members exchange information, and therefore gain a better understanding of other team members' perceptions and attitudes (Mohammed et al., 2009).

Fourth, team cognitive processes can also influence, be influenced by, and interact with team social processes. For example, the effect of team reflexivity was found to be higher when teams had cooperative norms (Tjosvold et al., 2004). In addition, social processes, such as psychological safety, influence idea generation in brainstorming teams (Paulus & Brown, 2003). Finally, team cognitive processes can mediate or moderate the relationship between team composition and team creativity and innovation. Several of the studies reviewed here suggested that diverse teams can execute cognitive processes more effectively, and take advantage of the diversity in information and knowledge if effective social processes are in place (De Dreu, 2002; Kellermanns et al., 2008). This specific point has been echoed by De Dreu, Nijstad, Bechtoldt, and Baas (in press). De Dreu et al. provide evidence that both epistemic motivation (the degree to which group members systematically process information) and pro-social motivation (the degree to which group members seek collective gain rather then individual gain) are important for team creativity and innovation. Additional research is necessary to address this issue more directly.

From an applied perspective, the latter point suggests two critical issues. First, diversity on cognitive variables (such as functional background, knowledge, or cognitive style) may be particularly important in allowing teams to capitalize on diversity. Second, the need for effective social processes is equally important. Leaders may be particularly effective in shaping the social climate in which team members feel safe, openly communicate, and trust other team members. In turn, these allow the team to share information, capitalize on diverse knowledge and experiences, and provide constructive criticism, all factors that facilitate the application of creative cognitive processes. Additionally, cognitive processes associated with creativity are time consuming. In a team, additional time and effort must be devoted to coordination and discussion of information or ideas. While technology may provide some help, leaders must take into account the increased time and effort demands required of creative teams. Leaders must balance operational demands and time urgency with the need to allow teams more time to fully realize creative ideas.

CONCLUSION

The purpose of this chapter was to review the literature pertaining to the effects of group composition, social processes, and cognitive processes on team creativity and innovation. Using the I-P-O model, group composition has been viewed as an important input variable and social and cognitive processes as critical process variables, with team creativity and innovation as the output. The dimensions of social and cognitive processes reviewed include some of the major dimensions, although the list is not exhaustive. The research reviewed here offers several insights into the relationship between group composition, social, and cognitive processes, and team creativity and innovation.

First, it is important to note that there is disagreement among researchers about how these categories of variables should be conceptualized. In the case of group composition, there is disagreement or multiple possible conceptualizations regarding the definition of diversity and composition and its measurement (Harrison & Klein, 2007; Mathieu et al., 2008). In the case of social processes, different theoretical approaches have conceptualized the important social processes in different ways, some of which overlap, but some do not (Rousseau et al., 2006; Salas et al., 2005). Finally, in the case of cognitive processes, there is still discussion as to what constitutes team cognitive processes, as well as lack of clarity on conceptualization and measurement issues (Cooke, Gorman, & Rowe, 2009; Reiter-Palmon et al., 2008).

A second important issue is that of limited research. Many of the variables discussed here have been researched in the context of team effectiveness and satisfaction. Only a handful of papers were identified that specified variables in relation to team creativity and innovation. This suggests that more research is needed to have a clear understanding of the effect of the constructs discussed. In addition, while much more research is available on idea generation, it is typically investigated as an outcome, and the role of idea generation in team creativity and innovation is not as well understood. Finally, studies investigating more complex relationships between multiple input or process variables and team innovation and creativity are even more limited.

Third, time has been recognized as an important aspect of team life, and one that can influence the various aspects of the I-P-O model (Marks et al., 2001; Mohammed et al., 2009). While only a few studies have used a longitudinal design, or have investigated time more explicitly, the results of such studies suggest that time indeed may be an important, but neglected, variable when it comes to understanding how group composition, social processes, and cognitive processes influence team creativity and innovation.

Another important issue emerging from the literature reviewed here is the nature of the relationships between the constructs identified. Much of the literature suggests complex interrelationships between the broad dimensions and the specific constructs in predicting creativity. Process variables, whether social or cognitive, are directly affected by the input variables associated with group composition (Ancona & Caldwell, 1992; De Dreu, 2002). In addition, various social process variables can influence each other; for example, more effective internal communication can reduce conflict or increase safety (Edmondson, 2004). Similarly, the cognitive process variables can influence each other (Mumford et al., 2001). Finally, social processes can influence cognitive processes and vice versa (Paulus & Brown, 2003). These interrelationships paint a complex picture and can be difficult to disentangle. Additional research is needed to evaluate the relationships between multiple variables from different categories so that these interrelationships can be better understood, and their effect on team creativity and innovation better explicated.

Adding to the complexity of the relationships is the interactive effects found between the delineated constructs. Not only do group composition variables influence the development and emergence of the social and cognitive processes, but they may also interact with these constructs such that the effect of composition variables is more or less pronounced in the presence of certain social or cognitive processes variables. Moreover, interactive effects can be found between the social and cognitive variables. Again, these findings suggest that the relationships between these sets of variables are complex, and further research is needed.

Research examining creativity and innovation in teams is still in its early stages, compared to the study of creativity and innovation at the individual level. Despite the complexities faced by team researchers, further research on group composition, social processes, and cognition is necessary to advance our understanding of what makes for an effective team in solving organizational problems creatively.

References

Amabile, T. M. (1996). *Creativity in context: Update to the social psychology of creativity*. Boulder, CO: Westview Press.

Amabile, T., & Gryskiewicz, N. (1989). The creative environment scales: Work environment inventory. *Creativity Research Journal, 2*, 231–253.

Ancona, D., & Caldwell, D. (1992). Demography and design: Predictors of new product team performance. *Organization Science, 3*, 321–341.

Anderson, N., De Dreu, C., & Nijstad, B. (2004). The routinization of innovation research: A constructively critical review of the state-of-the-science. *Journal of Organizational Behavior, 25*, 147–173.

Baer, M. (2010). The strength-of-weak-ties perspective on creativity: A comprehensive examination and extension. *Journal of Applied Psychology, 95*, 592–601.

Baer, M., Oldham, G., Jacobsohn, G., & Hollingshead, A. (2008). The personality composition of teams and creativity: The moderating role of team creative confidence. *Journal of Creative Behavior, 42*, 255–282.

Barry, B., & Stewart, G. (1997). Composition, process, and performance in self-managed groups: The role of personality. *Journal of Applied Psychology, 82*, 62–78.

Basadur, M., & Head, M. (2001). Team performance and satisfaction: A link to cognitive style within a process framework. *Journal of Creative Behavior, 35*, 227–248.

Bowers, C., Braun, C., & Morgan, B. (1997). Team workload: Its meaning and measurement. In M. T. Brannick, E. Salas & C. Prince (Eds.), *Team performance assessment and measurement: Theory, research, and applications* (pp. 85–108). Hillsdale, NJ: Lawrence Erlbaum.

Burke, C., Stagl, K., Salas, E., Pierce, L., & Kendall, D. (2006). Understanding team adaptation: A conceptual analysis and model. *Journal of Applied Psychology, 91*, 1189–1207.

Burningham, C., & West, M. (1995). Individual, climate, and group interaction processes as predictors of work team innovation. *Small Group Research, 26*, 106–117.

Caldwell, B., & Everhart, N. (1998). Information flow and development of coordination in distributed supervisory control teams. *International Journal of Human–Computer Interaction, 10*, 51–70.

Cannon-Bowers, J., Salas, E., & Converse, S. (1993). Shared mental models in expert team decision making. In N. J. Castellan (Ed.), Jr. *Individual and group decision making: Current issues* (pp. 221–246). Hillsdale, NJ: Lawrence Erlbaum Associates.

Carmeli, A., & Spreitzer, G. (2009). Trust, connectivity, and thriving: Implications for innovative behaviors at work. *Journal of Creative Behavior, 30*, 893–917.

Carnevale, P., & Probst, T. (1998). Social values and social conflict in creative problem solving and categorization. *Journal of Personality and Social Psychology, 74*, 1300–1309.

Carter, S., & West, M. (1998). Reflexivity, effectiveness, and mental health in BBC-TV production teams. *Small Group Research, 29*, 583–601.

Chen, M. (2006). Understanding the benefits and detriments of conflict on team creativity process. *Creativity and Innovation Management, 15*, 105–116.

Chirumboli, A., Mannetti, L., Pierro, A., Areni, A., & Kruglanski, A. (2005). Motivated closed-mindedness and creativity in small groups. *Small Group Research, 36*, 59–82.

Choi, J. (2007). Group composition and employee creative behaviour in a Korean electronics company: Distinct effects of relational demography and group diversity. *Journal of Occupational and Organizational Psychology, 80*, 213–234.

Choi, H., & Thompson, L. (2005). Old wine in a new bottle: Impact of membership change on group creativity. *Organizational Behavior and Human Decision Processes, 98*, 121–132.

Cooke, N., Gorman, J., & Rowe, L. (2009). An ecological perspective on team cognition. *Team effectiveness in complex organizations: Cross-disciplinary perspectives and approaches* (pp. 157–182). New York, NY: Routledge/Taylor & Francis Group.

Coskun, H., Paulus, P., Brown, V., & Sherwood, J. (2000). Cognitive stimulation and problem presentation in idea-generating groups. *Group Dynamics: Theory, Research, and Practice, 4*, 307–329. doi:10.1037/1089-2699.4.4.307.

Craig, T., & Kelly, J. (1999). Group cohesiveness and creative performance. *Group Dynamics: Theory, Research, and Practice, 3*, 243–256.

Curşeu, P. (2010). Team creativity in web site design: An empirical test of a systemic model. *Creativity Research Journal, 22*, 98–107.

Damanpour, F. (1991). Organizational innovation: A meta-analysis of effects of determinants and moderators. *Academy of Management Journal, 34*, 555–590.

De Dreu, C. (2002). Team innovation and team effectiveness: The importance of minority dissent and reflexivity. *European Journal of Work and Organizational Psychology, 11*, 285–298.

De Dreu, C. (2006). When too little or too much hurts: Evidence for a curvilinear relationship between task conflict and innovation in teams. *Journal of Management, 32*, 83–107.

De Dreu, C., Nijstad, B., Bechtoldt, M., & Baas, M. (in press). Group creativity and innovation: A motivated information processing perspective. *Psychology of Aesthetics, Creativity and the Arts.*

Dennis, A., & Williams, M. (2003). Electronic brainstorming: Theory, research, and future directions. *Group creativity: Innovation through collaboration* (pp. 160–178). New York, NY: Oxford University Press.

DeRosa, D., Smith, C., & Hantula, D. (2007). The medium matters: Mining the long-promised merit of group interaction in creative idea generation tasks in a meta-analysis of the electronic group brainstorming literature. *Computers in Human Behavior, 23*, 1549–1581.

Diehl, M., & Stroebe, W. (1987). Productivity loss in brainstorming groups: Toward the solution of a riddle. *Journal of Personality and Social Psychology, 53*, 497–509.

Drach-Zahavy, A., & Somech, A. (2001). Understanding team innovation: The role of team processes and structures. *Group Dynamics: Theory, Research, and Practice, 5*, 111–123.

Edmondson, A. (1999). Psychological safety and learning behavior in work teams. *Administrative Science Quarterly, 44*, 350–383.

Edmondson, A. (2004). Psychological safety, trust, and learning in organizations: A group-level lens. *Trust and distrust in organizations: Dilemmas and approaches* (pp. 239–272). New York, NY: Russell Sage Foundation.

Edmondson, A., & Roloff, K. (2009). Overcoming barriers to collaboration: Psychological safety and learning in diverse teams. *Team effectiveness in complex organizations: Cross-disciplinary perspectives and approaches* (pp. 183–208). New York, NY: Routledge/Taylor & Francis Group.

Ekvall, G. (1996). Organizational climate for creativity and innovation. *European Journal of Work and Organizational Psychology, 5*, 105–123.

Evans, C. R., & Jarvis, P. A. (1980). Group cohesion: A review and reevaluation. *Small Group Behavior, 11*, 359–370.

Fay, D., Borrill, C., Amir, Z., Haward, R., & West, M. (2006). Getting the most out of multidisciplinary teams: A multi-sample study of team innovation in health care. *Journal of Occupational and Organizational Psychology, 79*, 553–567.

Ford, C., & Gioia, D. (1995). *Creative action in organizations: Ivory tower visions & real world voices*. Thousand Oaks, CA: Sage Publications, Inc.

Gallupe, R., Dennis, A., Cooper, W., Valacich, J., Bastianutti, L., & Nunamaker, J., Jr. (1992). Electronic brainstorming and group size. *Academy of Management Journal, 35*, 350–369.

George, J., & Zhou, J. (2001). When openness to experience and conscientiousness are related to creative behavior: An interactional approach. *Journal of Applied Psychology, 86*, 513–524.

C. GROUP LEVEL INFLUENCES

Gilson, L., & Shalley, C. (2004). A little creativity goes a long way: An examination of teams' engagement in creative processes. *Journal of Management, 30*, 453–470.

Griffin, M., Neal, A., & Parker, S. (2007). A new model of work role performance: Positive behavior in uncertain and interdependent contexts. *Academy of Management Journal, 50*, 327–347.

Gully, S., Devine, D., & Whitney, D. (1995). A meta-analysis of cohesion and performance: Effects of levels of analysis and task interdependence. *Small Group Research, 26*, 497–520.

Guzzo, R., & Dickson, M. (1996). Teams in organizations: Recent research on performance and effectiveness. *Annual Review of Psychology, 47*, 307–338.

Hackman, J. (1987). The design of work teams. In J. W. Lorsch (Ed.), *Handbook of organizational behavior* (pp. 315–342). Englewood Cliffs, NJ: Prentice-Hall.

Hackman, J., Brousseau, K., & Weiss, J. (1976). The interaction of task design and group performance strategies in determining group effectiveness. *Organizational Behavior & Human Performance, 16*, 350–365.

Harrison, D., & Klein, K. (2007). What's the difference? Diversity constructs as separation, variety, or disparity in organizations. *Academy of Management Review, 32*, 1199–1228.

Hirst, G. (2009). Effects of membership change on open discussion and team performance: The moderating role of team tenure. *European Journal of Work and Organizational Psychology, 18*, 231–249.

Hoegl, M., & Gemuenden, H. (2001). Teamwork quality and the success of innovative projects: A theoretical concept and empirical evidence. *Organization Science, 12*, 435–449.

Hoegl, M., Weinkauf, K., & Gemuenden, H. (2004). Interteam coordination, project commitment, and teamwork in multiteam R&D projects: A longitudinal study. *Organization Science, 15*, 38–55.

Howell, J., & Shea, C. (2006). Effects of champion behavior, team potency, and external communication activities on predicting team performance. *Group & Organization Management, 31*, 180–211.

Hulsheger, U., Anderson, N., & Salgado, J. (2009). Team-level predictors of innovation at work: A comprehensive meta-analysis spanning three decades of research. *Journal of Applied Psychology, 94*, 1128–1145.

Hunter, S., Bedell, K., & Mumford, M. (2007). Climate for creativity: A quantitative review. *Creativity Research Journal, 19*, 69–90.

Ilgen, D., Hollenbeck, J., Johnson, M., & Jundt, D. (2005). Teams in organizations: From input–process–output models to IMOI models. *Annual Review of Psychology, 56*, 517–543.

Janicik, G. A., & Bartel, C. A. (2003). Talking about time: Effects of temporal planning and time awareness norms on groups coordination and performance. *Group Dynamics: Theory, Research, and Practice, 7*, 122–134.

Janssens, M., & Brett, J. (2006). Cultural intelligence in global teams: A fusion model of collaboration. *Group & Organization Management, 31*, 124–153.

Jassawalla, A. R., & Sashittal, H. C. (1998). An examination of collaboration in high-technology new product development processes. *Product Innovation Management, 15*, 237–254.

Jaussi, K., & Dionne, S. (2003). Leading for creativity: The role of unconventional leader behavior. *The Leadership Quarterly, 14*, 475–498.

Jehn, K. (1995). A multimethod examination of the benefits and detriments of intragroup conflict. *Administrative Science Quarterly, 40*, 256–282.

Jehn, K. (1997). Affective and cognitive conflict in work groups: Increasing performance through value-based intragroup conflict. *Using conflict in organizations* (pp. 87–100). Thousand Oaks, CA: Sage Publications, Inc.

Jehn, K., & Mannix, E. (2001). The dynamic nature of conflict: A longitudinal study of intragroup conflict and group performance. *Academy of Management Journal, 44*, 238–251.

Kark, R., & Carmeli, A. (2009). Alive and creating: The mediating role of vitality and aliveness in the relationship between psychological safety and creative work involvement. *Journal of Organizational Behavior, 30*, 785–804.

Keller, R. (1986). Predictors of the performance of project groups in R&D organizations. *Academy of Management Journal, 29*, 715–726.

Keller, R. (2001). Cross-functional project groups in research and new product development: Diversity, communications, job stress, and outcomes. *Academy of Management Journal, 44*, 547–559.

Kellermanns, F., Floyd, S., Pearson, A., & Spencer, B. (2008). The contingent effect of constructive confrontation on the relationship between shared mental models and decision quality. *Journal of Organizational Behavior, 29*, 119–137.

Kerr, D., & Murthy, U. (2004). Divergent and convergent idea generation in teams: A comparison of computer-mediated and face-to-face communication. *Group Decision and Negotiation, 13*, 381–399.

King, L., McKee Walker, L., & Broyles, S. (1996). Creativity and the five-factor model. *Journal of Research in Personality, 30*, 189–203.

Kirkman, B., Tesluk, P., & Rosen, B. (2004). The impact of demographic heterogeneity and team leader–team member demographic fit on team empowerment and effectiveness. *Group & Organization Management, 29*, 334–368.

Klein, C., DeRouin, R., & Salas, E. (2006). Uncovering workplace interpersonal skills: A review, framework, and research agenda. *International review of industrial and organizational psychology 2006* (pp. 79–126). Hoboken, NJ: Wiley Publishing.

Klimoski, R., & Mohammed, S. (1994). Team mental model: Construct or metaphor? *Journal of Management, 20*, 403–437.

Kozlowski, S., & Bell, B. (2008). Team learning, development, and adaptation. *Work group learning: Understanding, improving and assessing how groups learn in organizations* (pp. 15–44). New York, NY: Taylor & Francis Group/ Lawrence Erlbaum Associates.

Kozlowski, S., & Ilgen, D. (2006). Enhancing the effectiveness of work groups and teams. *Psychological Science in the Public Interest, 7*, 77–124.

Kozlowski, S., & Klein, K. (2000). A multilevel approach to theory and research in organizations: Contextual, temporal, and emergent processes. *Multilevel theory, research, and methods in organizations: Foundations, extensions, and new directions* (pp. 3–90). San Francisco, CA: Jossey-Bass.

Kratzer, J., Leenders, R., & van Engelen, J. (2004). Stimulating the potential: Creative performance and communication in innovation teams. *Creativity and Innovation Management, 13*, 63–71.

Kratzer, J., Leenders, R., & van Engelen, J. (2006). Team polarity and creative performance in innovation teams. *Creativity and Innovation Management, 15*, 96–104.

Kurtzberg, T., & Amabile, T. (2001). From Guilford to creative synergy: Opening the black box of team-level creativity. *Creativity Research Journal, 13*, 285–294.

Levine, J., & Choi, H. (2004). Impact of personnel turnover on team performance and cognition. *Team cognition: Understanding the factors that drive process and performance* (pp. 153–176). Washington, DC: American Psychological Association.

Levine, J., Choi, H., & Moreland, R. (2003). Newcomer innovation in work teams. *Group creativity: Innovation through collaboration* (pp. 202–224). New York, NY: Oxford University Press.

Lovelace, K., Shapiro, D., & Weingart, L. (2001). Maximizing cross-functional new product teams' innovativeness and constraint adherence: A conflict communications perspective. *Academy of Management Journal, 44*, 779–793.

Mannix, E., & Neale, M. (2005). What differences make a difference? The promise and reality of diverse teams in organizations. *Psychological Science in the Public Interest, 6*, 31–55.

Marks, M., Mathieu, J., & Zaccaro, S. (2001). A temporally based framework and taxonomy of team processes. *Academy of Management Review, 26*, 356–376.

Marks, M., Sabella, M., Burke, C., & Zaccaro, S. (2002). The impact of cross-training on team effectiveness. *Journal of Applied Psychology, 87*, 3–13.

Marta, S., Leritz, L., & Mumford, M. (2005). Leadership skills and the group performance: Situational demands, behavioral requirements, and planning. *The Leadership Quarterly, 16*, 97–120.

Mathieu, J. E., Goodwin, G. F., Heffner, T. S., Salas, E., & Cannon-Bowers, J. A. (2000). The influence of shared mental models on team processes and performance. *Journal of Applied Psychology, 85*, 273–283.

Mathieu, J., Maynard, M., Rapp, T., & Gilson, L. (2008). Team effectiveness 1997–2007: A review of recent advancements and a glimpse into the future. *Journal of Management, 34*, 410–476.

Mathisen, G., Martinsen, Ø., & Einarsen, S. (2008). The relationship between creative personality composition, innovative team climate, and team innovativeness: An input–process–output perspective. *Journal of Creative Behavior, 42*, 13–31.

McIntyre, R., & Salas, E. (1995). Measuring and managing for team performance: Emerging principles from complex environments. In R. A. Guzzo & E. Salas (Eds.), *Team effectiveness and decision making in organizations* (pp. 9–45). San Francisco, CA: Jossey-Bass.

McLeod, P., Lobel, S., & Cox, T. (1996). Ethnic diversity and creativity in small groups. *Small Group Research, 27*, 248–264.

Mesmer-Magnus, J., & DeChurch, L. (2009). Information sharing and team performance: A meta-analysis. *Journal of Applied Psychology, 94*, 535–546.

Milliken, F., Bartel, C., & Kurtzberg, T. (2003). Diversity and creativity in work groups: A dynamic perspective on the affective and cognitive processes that link diversity and performance. *Group creativity: Innovation through collaboration* (pp. 32–62). New York, NY: Oxford University Press.

Mitchell, R., Boyle, B., & Nicholas, S. (2009). The impact of goal structure in team knowledge creation. *Group Processes & Intergroup Relations, 12*, 639–651.

C. GROUP LEVEL INFLUENCES

Mohammed, S., & Dumville, B. (2001). Team mental models in a team knowledge framework: Expanding theory and measurement across disciplinary boundaries. *Journal of Organizational Behavior, 22*, 89–106.

Mohammed, S., Hamilton, K., & Lim, A. (2009). The incorporation of time in team research: Past, current, and future. *Team effectiveness in complex organizations: Cross-disciplinary perspectives and approaches* (pp. 321–348). New York, NY: Routledge/Taylor & Francis Group.

Mortensen, M., & Hinds, P. (2001). Conflict and shared identity in geographically distributed teams. *International Journal of Conflict Management, 12*, 212–238.

Mouchiroud, C., & Lubart, T. (2001). Children's original thinking: An empirical examination of alternative measures derived from divergent thinking tasks. *Journal of Genetic Psychology, 162*, 382–401.

Mullen, B., Johnson, C., & Salas, E. (1991). Productivity loss in brainstorming groups: A meta-analytic integration. *Basic and Applied Social Psychology, 12*, 3–23.

Muller, A., Herbig, B., & Petrovic, K. (2009). The explication of implicit team knowledge and its supporting effect on team processes and technical innovations: An action regulation perspective on team reflexivity. *Small Group Research, 40*, 28–51.

Mumford, M. D., Feldman, J. M., Hein, M. B., & Nagao, D. J. (2001). Tradeoffs between ideas and structure: Individuals versus group performance in creative problem solving. *Journal of Creative Behavior, 35*, 1–23.

Mumford, M., Mobley, M., Uhlman, C., & Reiter-Palmon, R. (1991). Process analytic models of creative capacities. *Creativity Research Journal, 4*, 91–122.

Mumford, M., Reiter-Palmon, R., & Redmond, M. (1994). Problem construction and cognition: Applying problem representations in ill-defined domains. In M. Runco (Ed.), *Problem finding, problem solving, and creativity* (pp. 3–39). Norwood, NJ: Ablex Publishing Corporation.

Nemeth, C., & Ormiston, M. (2007). Creative idea generation: Harmony versus stimulation. *European Journal of Social Psychology, 37*, 524–535.

Nicholson, N., & West, M. (1988). *Managerial job change: Men and women in transition.* New York, NY: Cambridge University Press.

Nijstad, B. A., Rietzschel, E. F., & Stroebe, W. (2006). Four principles of group creativity. In L. Thompson & H. S. Choi (Eds.), *Creativity and innovation in organizations teams* (pp. 161–179). Mahwah, NJ: Lawrence Erlbaum Associates, Inc.

O'Reilly, C., Williams, K., & Barsade, S. (1998). Group demography and innovation: Does diversity help? *Composition* (pp. 183–207). Elsevier Science/JAI Press.

Paletz, S., Peng, K., Erez, M., & Maslach, C. (2004). Ethnic composition and its differential impact on group processes in diverse teams. *Small Group Research, 35*, 128–157.

Paulus, P., & Brown, V. (2003). Enhancing ideational creativity in groups: Lessons from research on brainstorming. *Group creativity: Innovation through collaboration* (pp. 110–136). New York, NY: Oxford University Press.

Paulus, P., Nakui, T., Putman, V., & Brown, V. (2006). Effects of task instructions and brief breaks on brainstorming. *Group Dynamics: Theory, Research, and Practice, 10*, 206–219.

Paulus, P., & Paulus, L. (1997). Implications of research on group brainstorming for gifted education. *Roeper Review, 19*, 225–229.

Pearce, C., & Ensley, M. (2004). A reciprocal and longitudinal investigation of the innovation process: The central role of shared vision in product and process innovation teams (PPITs). *Journal of Organizational Behavior, 25*, 259–278.

Pearsall, M., Ellis, A. & Evans, J. (2008). Unlocking the effects of gender faultlines on team creativity: Is activation the key? *Journal of Applied Psychology, 93*, 225–234.

Pelled, L., Eisenhardt, K., & Xin, K. (1999). Exploring the black box: An analysis of work group diversity, conflict, and performance. *Administrative Science Quarterly, 44*, 1–28.

Perry-Smith, J. (2006). Social yet creative: The role of social relationships in facilitating individual creativity. *Academy of Management Journal, 49*, 85–101.

Perry-Smith, J., & Shalley, C. (2003). The social side of creativity: A static and dynamic social network perspective. *Academy of Management Review, 28*, 89–106.

Rank, J., Pace, V., & Frese, M. (2004). Three avenues for future research on creativity, innovation, and initiative. *Applied Psychology: An International Review, 53*, 518–528.

Reiter-Palmon, R., Herman, A., & Yammarino, F. (2008). Creativity and cognitive processes: Multi-level linkages between individual and team cognition. *Innovation: A multi-layer perspective.* New York, NY: Elsevier.

Reiter-Palmon, R., & Robinson, E. (2009). Problem identification and construction: What do we know, what is the future? *Psychology of Aesthetics, Creativity, and the Arts, 3,* 43–47.

Robert, C., & Cheung, Y. (2010). An examination of the relationship between conscientiousness and group performance on a creative task. *Journal of Research in Personality, 44,* 222–231.

Rousseau, V., Aubé, C., & Savoie, A. (2006). Teamwork behaviors: A review and an integration of frameworks. *Small Group Research, 37,* 540–570.

Runco, M., & Mraz, W. (1992). Scoring divergent thinking tests using total ideational output and a creativity index. *Educational and Psychological Measurement, 52,* 213–221.

Salas, E., Burke, C., & Stagl, K. (2004). Developing teams and team leaders: Strategies and principles. *Leader development for transforming organizations: Growing leaders for tomorrow* (pp. 325–355). Mahwah, NJ: Lawrence Erlbaum Associates Publishers.

Salas, E., Cooke, N., & Rosen, M. (2008). On teams, teamwork, and team performance: Discoveries and developments. *Human Factors, 50,* 540–547.

Salas, E., Sims, D., & Burke, C. (2005). Is there a 'Big Five' in teamwork? *Small Group Research, 36,* 555–599.

Salas, E., Sims, D., & Klein, C. (2004). Cooperation at work. In C. D. Speilberger (Ed.), *Encyclopedia of applied psychology* (pp. 497–505). San Diego, CA: Academic Press.

Salas, E., Stagl, K., Burke, C., & Goodwin, G. (2007). Fostering team effectiveness in organizations: Toward an integrative theoretical framework. *Modeling complex systems* (pp. 185–243). Lincoln, NE: University of Nebraska Press.

Santanen, E. L., Briggs, R. O., & DeVreede, G. J. (2004). Causal relationship in creative problem solving: Comparing facilitation interventions for ideation. *Journal of Management Information Systems, 20,* 167–197.

Schippers, M., Den Hartog, D., & Koopman, P. (2007). Reflexivity in teams: A measure and correlates. *Applied Psychology: An International Review, 56,* 189–211.

Scott, S., & Bruce, R. (1994). Determinants of innovative behavior: A path model of individual innovation in the workplace. *Academy of Management Journal, 37,* 580–607.

Sethi, R., Smith, D., & Park, C. (2001). Cross-functional product development teams, creativity, and the innovativeness of new consumer products. *Journal of Marketing Research, 38,* 73–85.

Shalley, C. E. (2008). Team cognition: The importance of team process and composition for the creative problem-solving process. In M. Mumford, S. Hunter & K. Bedell (Eds.), *Multilevel Issues in Creativity and Innovation* (pp. 289–304). Greenwich, CT: JAI Press.

Shalley, C., Zhou, J., & Oldham, G. (2004). The effects of personal and contextual characteristics on creativity: Where should we go from here? *Journal of Management, 30,* 933–958.

Shin, S., & Zhou, J. (2007). When is educational specialization heterogeneity related to creativity in research and development teams? Transformational leadership as a moderator. *Journal of Applied Psychology, 92,* 1709–1721.

Smith-Jentsch, K., Cannon-Bowers, J., Tannenbaum, S., & Salas, E. (2008). Guided team self-correction: Impacts on team mental models, processes, and effectiveness. *Small Group Research, 39,* 303–327.

Song, M., Dyer, B., & Thieme, R. (2006). Conflict management and innovation performance: An integrated contingency perspective. *Journal of the Academy of Marketing Science, 34,* 341–356.

Stevens, M., & Campion, M. (1994). The knowledge, skill, and ability requirements for teamwork: Implications for human resource management. *Journal of Management, 20,* 503–530.

Stewart, G. (2006). A meta-analytic review of relationships between team design features and team performance. *Journal of Management, 32,* 29–55.

Stewart, D., & Stasser, G. (1995). Expert role assignment and information sampling during collective recall and decision making. *Journal of Personality and Social Psychology, 69,* 619–628.

Stout, R., Cannon-Bowers, J., Salas, E., & Milanovich, D. (1999). Planning, shared mental models, and coordinated performance: An empirical link is established. *Human Factors, 41,* 61–71.

Taggar, S. (2002). Individual creativity and group ability to utilize individual creative resources: A multilevel model. *Academy of Management Journal, 45,* 315–330.

Tesluk, P., Farr, J., & Klein, S. (1997). Influences of organizational culture and climate on individual creativity. *Journal of Creative Behavior, 31,* 27–41.

Timmerman, T. (2000). Racial diversity, age diversity, interdependence, and team performance. *Small Group Research, 31,* 592–606.

Tjosvold, D., Tang, M., & West, M. (2004). Reflexivity for team innovation in China: The contribution of goal interdependence. *Group & Organization Management, 29,* 540–559.

C. GROUP LEVEL INFLUENCES

Vreede, de G. J., Briggs, R., & Reiter-Palmon, R. (2010). Exploring asynchronous brainstorming in large groups: A field comparison of serial and parallel subgroups. *Human Factors.*

Vreede, de G. J., Kolfschoten, G. L., & Briggs, R. O. (2006). ThinkLets: A collaboration engineering pattern language. *International Journal of Computer Applications in Technology, 25*, 140–154.

Weingart, L. (1992). Impact of group goals, task component complexity, effort, and planning on group performance. *Journal of Applied Psychology, 77*, 682–693.

West, M. (1990). The social psychology of innovation in groups. *Innovation and creativity at work: Psychological and organizational strategies* (pp. 309–333). Oxford, UK: John Wiley & Sons.

West, M. A. (1996). Reflexivity and work group effectiveness: A conceptual integration. In M. A. West (Ed.), *Handbook of work group psychology* (pp. 555–579). Chichester, UK: John Wiley & Sons.

West, M. (2002). Sparkling fountains or stagnant ponds: An integrative model of creativity and innovation implementation in work groups. *Applied Psychology: An International Review, 51*, 355–387.

West, M., & Anderson, N. (1996). Innovation in top management teams. *Journal of Applied Psychology, 81*, 680–693.

West, M., Borrill, C., Dawson, J., Brodbeck, F., Shapiro, D., & Haward, B. (2003). Leadership clarity and team innovation in health care. *The Leadership Quarterly, 14*, 393–410.

West, M., Hirst, G., Richter, A., & Shipton, H. (2004). Twelve steps to heaven: Successfully managing change through developing innovative teams. *European Journal of Work and Organizational Psychology, 13*, 269–299.

West, M., & Richter, A. (2008). Climates and cultures for innovation and creativity at work. In J. Zhou & C. E. Shalley (Eds.), *Handbook of organizational creativity* (pp. 211–237). New York, NY: Erlbaum.

Woodman, R., Sawyer, J., & Griffin, R. (1993). Toward a theory of organizational creativity. *Academy of Management Review, 18*, 293–321.

14

Collaborative Creativity—Group Creativity and Team Innovation

Paul B. Paulus[1], Mary Dzindolet[2], and Nicholas W. Kohn[1]

[1]University of Texas at Arlington, Arlington, TX; [2]Cameron University, Lawton, OK

GROUP CREATIVITY VERSUS TEAM INNOVATION

Today in the US and many other countries, governments, scientific agencies, university programs, and organizations are anxious to promote the development of innovation and creativity, since it is presumed that this will be an important basis for economic development and for solving environmental and social problems. Given the complexity of today's societal, scientific, and technical problems, it is presumed that teams with diverse expertise are required to solve them. Yet what is the scientific evidence related to creativity and innovation in teams? Fortunately, there has been an explosion of studies on team innovation or creativity (Hülsheger, Anderson, & Salgado, 2009) and a related set of studies on group creativity (Nijstad & Stroebe, 2006; Paulus, 2000; Paulus & Nijstad, 2003). Unfortunately, most of the research on team innovation involves self-reports, with few studies obtaining objective data on actual innovative outcomes (Antoni & Hertel, 2009; Hülsheger et al., 2009). The research on group creativity is mostly based on objective performance data, but often involves the use of college students in laboratory settings. So although there now is a wealth of data on team/group innovation and creativity, there remains much uncertainty in regard to our understanding of the actual innovative process in teams in organizations. However, there is considerable consistency in findings from these two different approaches. We feel that an integration of the research on team innovation and group creativity will greatly enhance our theoretical understanding of the collaborative creative process, and provide a

Handbook of Organizational Creativity.
DOI: 10.1016/B978-0-12-374714-3.00014-8

reasonable basis for practice in organizations (Paulus & Van der Zee, 2004). Before providing an empirical and theoretical summary of the literature in these two areas, we need to clarify some of the commonly used terminology.

WHAT ARE TEAMS, GROUPS, CREATIVITY, AND INNOVATION?

Groups are typically defined as collections of individuals focused on a specific goal or task (Forsyth, 2006). In this chapter we will be concerned only with groups that are performing a specific creative task, but there is also extensive literature on group task performance that is relevant to understanding the performance of such groups (e.g., Nijstad, 2009). Most research on group task performance and group creativity has examined small groups of three or four in controlled laboratory settings. This allows for the random assignment of participants to given experimental conditions, and careful observation and assessment of performance. In this way the investigators can be fairly confident about the causes and processes that underlie group creativity. There is always a concern about the relevance of findings from such research to real-world work environments, but there are several analyses that suggest that findings from laboratory studies in a number of domains have considerable applicability (Anderson, Lindsay, & Bushman, 1999; Mullen, Driskell, & Salas, 1998).

Teams are groups that typically have a long-term relationship, are embedded in an organization, and work together on some common project or goal. These teams can vary considerably in size, composition, or structure. Members of these teams are typically assigned to the teams by a superior, so there is no assurance that different teams will be comparable in their characteristics (as would be the case with random assignment). So it may be difficult to determine whether it is the process or it is the team composition that is responsible for differences in performance among teams. For the sake of empirical and theoretical clarity we will maintain the distinction in this chapter between groups and teams based on whether they are short-term task groups or longer term teams. However, in both cases creative groups and teams involve similar collaborative processes.

Collaborative processes are those that involve some degree of interaction and coordination with another person or other group or team members. Collaboration does not require a specific group or team, since any two people that coordinate their task activities are collaborators. There are a number of famous collaborative pairs (John-Steiner, 2000) who have achieved eminence in the creative domain. Collaboration is also popular in educational environments as students work together on various projects (Kanev, Kimura, & Orr, 2009). We will highlight the collaborative processes that are involved in both group creativity and team innovation.

Creativity is the generation or production of novel products or ideas. It is often differentiated from innovation which involves the actual implementation of an idea. Creativity is seen as an exploration process in which one considers alternatives, whereas innovation is more of an exploitation process in which one tries to effectively implement an idea. Most of the research on group creativity has focused on exploration of alternatives. Early research and treatments of innovation (West, 2002) focused on the implementation issue, but overall the research on team innovation has examined both exploration and exploitation (Hülsheger et al., 2009). Often there is not a clear differentiation between creativity and implementation, so it is not surprising that many of the factors that have been found to be important in group creativity have also been highlighted in the work on team innovation (Paulus, 2007; Paulus, Nakui, & Putman, 2006a). We will often use the term creativity to cover both creativity and innovation. This usage will simplify our treatment and is also consistent with our integrative perspective. In a later section we will discuss potential important differences between the two literatures and the research on the different phases of the creative process.

TEAMWORK

There is an extensive literature on teamwork that is relevant to the issues discussed in this chapter (Kozlowski & Ilgen, 2006; Salas, Goodwin, & Burke, 2009). However, these and other similar reviews pay little attention to the topic of innovation. We will use the general team literature as a context for our review, but we will focus primarily on literature dealing directly with team innovation. It is presumed any factor that would enhance teamwork in general would be advantageous to team innovation. So, in addition to the suggestions made in this chapter, practitioners of innovative teams should be knowledgeable about the broader team literature (e.g., Kozlowski & Ilgen, 2006). However, there are a number of factors that are relatively unique for creative teams (Pirola-Merlo & Mann, 2004; Taggar, 2001), or are especially important for these teams, such as the role of conflict and diversity. So in our review we will focus primarily on teams doing creative or innovative tasks, but will at times note the relevance of the broader team literature.

There is also an extensive literature on creativity in general that has important implications for creative teams (Mayer, 1999; Sternberg, 2006; Sternberg, Grigorenko, & Singer, 2004). Teams are made up of individuals and team creativity reflects to a large extent the creativity of the individual members (Pirola-Merlo & Mann, 2004; Taggar, 2001). Any approach, process, or characteristic that enhances individual creativity should also have positive effects on team creativity.

Models of Team and Group Effectiveness

Reviews of the team literature suggest a general model for team effectiveness (Kozlowski & Ilgen, 2006; Salas et al., 2009a). To be effective, teams need to have effective cognitive processes, be cohesive, have a sense of efficacy, coordinate their activities, have effective task structure, have goals and feedback, be trained, and have appropriate leadership (Salas, Rosen, Burke, & Goodwin, 2009; Tasa, Taggar, & Seijts, 2007). The models of teamwork have been primarily focused on understanding the input–process–output (IPO) connections (Hackman, 1987; Ilgen, Hollenbeck, Johnson, & Jundt, 2005). More recent theoretical efforts have focused more on adaptive processes in teams, which highlight the complex interrelationships among multiple factors over time and how the outcomes of these processes in turn feed back into the various input factors (Burke, Stagl, Salas, Pierce, & Kendall, 2006b; Ilgen et al., 2005). The research on team creativity will also need to move in that direction (Bledow, Frese, Anderson, Erez, & Farr, 2009). However, the bulk of the research in the teamwork and team innovation literatures fits neatly into the IPO framework (Hülsheger et al., 2009).

The model presented by Paulus and Dzindolet (2008) to integrate the group creativity literature is also representative of the major findings in the team creativity literature.

This model of collaborative creativity highlights how group member characteristics, group structure, group climate, and external demands influence the cognitive, social and motivational processes that underlie collaborative creativity (Figure 14.1). Most of the various factors listed for each of these categories have some degree of support in both the groups and teams literatures. In this chapter we will highlight the basic processes and those factors that influence these processes that have had the most extensive empirical support.

Social Processes

Team creativity is much more than the sum of the creative output of its individual group members. For one thing, group members influence their peers' potential to be creative by affecting cognitive and motivational processes. Hearing an idea shared by a peer has the potential to cognitively stimulate one to be creative; hearing a group member complain has the potential to lower one's motivation to work hard on the task. Thus, each individual group member's creativity affects and is affected by the other group members.

Once a group member has enough cognitive stimulation and motivation to generate an idea, he or she must determine whether or not to share that idea with the group. Several group, task, and situational variables will affect the likelihood that the group member will share the idea. For example, the individual's confidence in his or her creative ability and level of evaluation apprehension, the group's level of cohesiveness, psychological safety, and consequences associated with sharing an idea are likely to influence whether or not the group member chooses to share the generated idea. Both intrinsic and extrinsic motivational factors will also play a role in the decision to share the idea with the other group members.

In addition, the most recently shared ideas by other group members will not only cognitively stimulate the group member to generate ideas in the same category (Kohn & Smith, in press), but they will also socially stimulate a group member to generate more ideas to approximately match the level of performance of the other group members. This social comparison process affects and is affected by group, task, and situational variables (Paulus & Dzindolet, 2008). For example, individuals will be more likely to match to group members who they perceive to be similar to them, and the social comparison process is likely to play a larger role in smaller than larger groups. The exchange of information in groups may cognitively stimulate group members to generate more ideas, especially if varied viewpoints are discussed. However, the presentation of such different information may lead to conflict, which could hurt group performance if not managed properly.

Cognitive Processes

Much teamwork involves complex knowledge work and considerable mental coordination (Salas, et al., 2009a). It appears to be important that teams have some shared understanding or mental model of their various roles and expertise (Edwards, Day, Arthur, & Bell, 2006). This may include the degree to which a team has a strong transactive memory system (Ancona & Bresman, 2006; Lewis, 2003)—that is team members know who knows what in the group so that team members' skills can be utilized effectively.

A major component of the creative process is the exchange of information or ideas. Increasingly, teams are involved in knowledge work, and the exchange of information and

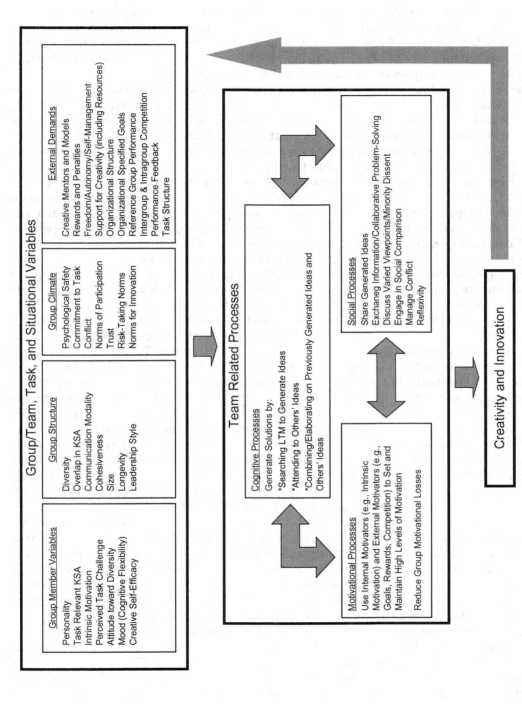

FIGURE 14.1 A model of collaborative creativity. *Reproduced with permission from Paulus and Dzindolet (2008).*

ideas is key to their innovative potential. However, little research on work team innovation has focused on these processes. Most of the relevant research and theoretical modeling has come from researchers on creativity in laboratory groups. These settings provide for the degree of control required for a careful assessment of the various mental processes related to collaborative creativity. We will briefly review this research and its relevance to team innovation.

There is an interesting contrast in focus between the laboratory research on collaborative creativity and that with work teams. The research on work teams is mostly concerned with assessing the variables that influence team creativity. It is assumed teams have much creative potential, so the focus is aimed at determining the factors that enhance it. The group literature is a bit more skeptical. Much of the group literature has highlighted the inefficiency and ineffectiveness of group performance (Kerr & Tindale, 2004; Paulus, 1989). Many of these studies use non-group comparisons to see to what extent groups can make better decisions or outperform sets of individuals. These sets of individuals are often termed nominal groups in that the performance of the interactive groups is compared to some aggregate measure of the performance of the same size group of individuals. So for creativity groups, an interactive group of four may be compared to a nominal group of four. This kind of comparison has often yielded rather negative effects, with interactive groups of brainstormers typically generating fewer good ideas and fewer total ideas than nominal groups (Diehl & Stroebe, 1987; Mullen, Johnson, & Salas, 1991). A major focus of research on group creativity has been on the basis for this production loss in groups and how to overcome it (Paulus & Brown, 2003), often using the brainstorming paradigm.

A series of studies by Stroebe and his colleagues (Diehl & Stroebe, 1991; Nijstad & Stroebe, 2006) have suggested that a critical factor is production blocking, or the inability of group members to express their ideas as they occur in their minds. That is, group members have to wait their turn to express their ideas. This limits their opportunities to contribute and interrupts their flow of ideas. Participants may forget ideas as they wait, or decide they are not longer relevant. Furthermore, there may be a tendency of group brainstormers to converge to similar topics or categories of ideas, limiting the range of ideas that are generated (Kohn & Smith, in press; Larey & Paulus, 1999; Ziegler, Diehl, & Zijlstra, 2000). Group members may also feel somewhat apprehensive in sharing their most radical or unique ideas, since others might react negatively to them. Groups that are low in social apprehension tend to be more creative (Camacho & Paulus, 1995; Diehl & Stroebe, 1987). As group size increases there may also be an increased tendency for individuals to feel less accountable for their performance and hence to loaf (Karau & Williams, 1993).

For an interactive group to demonstrate synergy, or better performance than nominal groups, it would have to overcome these negative forces (Larson, 2010). That turns out to be quite difficult for face-to-face groups because of the built-in production blocking problem. However, interactive exchanges of ideas can lead to an enhanced number of ideas relative to nominal control groups if one uses techniques which eliminate blocking (e.g., writing, computers), minimize evaluation apprehension, and have some degree of accountability (Dennis & Williams, 2003; Dugosh, Paulus, Roland, & Yang, 2000). These stimulating effects of exposure to the ideas of others may be evident even in subsequent solitary ideation sessions (Dugosh et al., 2000; Paulus & Yang, 2000) and can be enhanced if the size of the electronic brainstorming group increases (DeRosa, Smith, & Hantula, 2007).

The research demonstrating the positive effects of exchange of ideas in brainstorming supports a cognitive or semantic association perspective of the brainstorming process

(Brown & Paulus, 2002; Nijstad & Stroebe, 2006). These two models outline the nature of the process of searching one's memory for relevant ideas. This involves the search of various categories of knowledge relevant to the problem. Once one begins to tap one category, one may stay with it for a while until one feels one has exhausted its potential. At that point there will be a search for a new category to tap. The advantage of group brainstorming is that it can stimulate people to consider categories they might otherwise not have considered, and specific ideas shared can stimulate other related ideas or can be combined with one's own ideas to generate more novel or useful ideas. There have been a broad range of studies that have supported this cognitive perspective of group creativity (see Nijstad & Stroebe, 2006; Paulus & Brown, 2003 for reviews). For example, it is particularly important for brainstorming ideas to be exchanged in an efficient manner, with as little distracting material as possible (Paulus, Nakui, Putman, & Brown, 2006b; Putman & Paulus, 2009). Brainstorming rules that emphasize avoiding irrelevant discussions and staying on task lead to a much higher level of idea generation (Paulus et al., 2006b; Putman & Paulus, 2009). Presenting brainstormers with ideas while they are brainstorming individually stimulates additional ideas (Dugosh & Paulus, 2005; Dugosh et al., 2000; Nijstad, Stroebe, & Lodewijkx, 2002; Rietzschel, Nijstad, & Stroebe, 2007). Other studies have found that decomposing the task into subtasks or providing brief breaks enhances ideation. Apparently, having individuals focus on one category at a time may enhance the effectiveness of the search within specific categories (Coskun, Paulus, Brown, & Sherwood, 2000), while brief breaks may allow for rehearsal of ideas stimulated in a prior session or reduce continued focus on categories that are no longer a productive source of ideas (Paulus et al., 2006b).

Many studies on group brainstorming have attempted to find ways to enhance the synergistic effect of idea exchange. However, most of them have found that a given factor which enhances group brainstorming also enhances individual brainstorming to a similar degree. This has been the case for manipulations of goals, breaks, subtasks, additional rules, and training (Coskun et al., 2000; Paulus & Dzindolet, 1993; Paulus et al., 2006b; Putman & Paulus, 2009). This pattern of results suggests that this may be the case as well for manipulations used to enhance team creativity. Such factors as psychological safety, trust, support, and leadership are likely to have positive benefits for individual workers in an organization as well as those working in the team. Many of the studies on team innovation have only examined effects on individuals. We do not know of any study on work teams that has compared the differential effect of a key variable on individual and team creativity. Furthermore, no studies of team innovation have examined in detail the cognitive processes involved in the team creative process in comparison to individuals. So the group creativity literature provides an important theoretical and empirical reference point for understanding the collaborative creativity process (Mannix, Neale, & Goncalo, 2009; Thompson & Choi, 2006).

TEAM CHARACTERISTICS

Team Size

Teams come in many sizes and "shapes". Two dimensions are salient from both theoretical and practical points of view. Teams can vary in size and in the diversity of their group members. From a naïve perspective one might suggest that the larger and more diverse the team the better. Certainly, as one increases the size of the team, one has the benefit of more hands to do the job, and the possibility that among the team members there will be an increase in varied expertise. A review of the innovation literature suggests that large teams are related to a greater degree of innovation (Hülsheger et al., 2009). This is of course not surprising. The more members in the team, the greater is the potential for diverse perspectives on the problem (Reagans & Zuckerman, 2001). Research on electronic brainstorming in which ideas are shared using computer systems also provides support for the benefits of larger group size (DeRosa et al., 2007). Large groups generate more ideas than comparable groups of individual brainstormers. Science is increasingly being carried out in teams, and the size of the teams keeps increasing (Wuchty, Jones, & Uzzi, 2007). It has even been found that these larger science teams are more likely to be cited than smaller teams or individual scholars. This could be interpreted as support for the collaborative genius of groups (Farrell, 2001; Sawyer, 2007). However, there are some drawbacks to large teams. Individuals may tend to feel less accountable for their individual performance and therefore may be prone to social loafing (Karau & Williams, 1993). In line with this concern, Hülsheger et al.'s (2009) review found that the benefits of team size were found for team level measures but not individual ones. Large groups, in which intense interaction is required, may suffer from the competition for time to provide their individual input. This kind of competition or production blocking has been shown to be an important factor in brainstorming groups (Diehl & Stroebe, 1991; Nijstad, Stroebe, & Lodewijkx, 2003), with the larger the group size, the poorer the performance (Mullen et al., 1991) relative to similar size control groups of noninteracting individuals (nominal groups). Similarly, large teams with a high pressure to innovate experience poorer team processes (commitment to team objectives, level of participation, support for innovation, emphasis on quality) than smaller teams (Curral, Forrester, Dawson, & West, 2001).

So what are the practical implications of this mixed set of results? Obviously, for a complex task that requires multiple areas of expertise or skill, one has to involve team members with a range of skills, knowledge, and abilities (SKAs). However, it may be important to not increase the size of the group more than necessary. Moreover, interaction sessions among the team members should involve as few members as possible to allow for a more effective and complete sharing of information and ideas between specific sets of group members. The optimum size for such interactions may actually be pairs of individuals. Pairs of brainstormers exhibit little if any production deficit (Mullen et al., 1991). Analyses of collaborative creative groups suggest that much of their creative activity occurs in pairs (Farrell, 2001). Such sub-group interactions can then be integrated into the overall team project during larger meetings with other team members. Of course, team members do not spend all of their time interacting with other team members. Much of their time may be spent in solitary activities, with only periodic meetings to exchange ideas, discoveries, and information. Research on group brainstorming suggests that oscillations between such solitary and interactive sessions may be an effective procedure (Baruah & Paulus, 2008).

Diversity

One of the most straightforward ideas in regard to team innovation is that innovation is most likely in teams that are diverse in experience and expertise. One of the reasons we have people work in teams is because of the increasing complexity of many work and innovation tasks. This is particularly true in the scientific and technical fields (Wuchty et al., 2007) as well as in organizations (Salas, Goodwin, & Burke, 2009). Since many tasks can only be done by a diverse set of experts, at a practical level the benefit of team diversity is obvious. However, systematic research on the effects of diversity on team performance is rather mixed (Mannix & Neale, 2005; van Knippenberg & Schippers, 2007). Some studies find positive effects of diversity, others negative effects, and some find no effect at all. One study on creators of comic books found that individuals were better able to integrate diverse knowledge than teams, and that diversity was related to increased variance in creative performance (Taylor & Greve, 2006). Reviews have tried to determine the factors that influence these patterns of results. One reasonable suggestion is that the effects of diversity may depend on the type of diversity. Diversity that is associated with personal characteristics such as age, gender, race/ethnicity, and personality may inhibit team performance, because these may inhibit social interaction, limit communication, and reduce social cohesion (Mannix & Neale, 2005; Williams & O'Reilly, 1998). Each of these is a potentially important factor in team performance, especially on complex tasks like those involved in creativity. Furthermore, in many cases it is not clear exactly how such demographic diversity would be helpful to achieving the team goal. Those types of characteristics may not be related to differential expertise needed for a team task. Benefits of team diversity should be most likely observed when the team diversity matches the task demands. Moreover, when diversity consists primarily of differences in task-relevant expertise or experience, the social inhibitions that are often observed with demographic diversity should be minimized, since task-relevant differences should be less likely to instigate intragroup biases and feelings. However, even in that domain, there can be problematic intragroup issues among people in different fields. Of course, demographic and expertise variations may not be independent; in a group comprising nurses and engineers, it is likely that most of the nurses will be female and the engineers will be male. This situation has been termed "strong faultlines", and can be contrasted with the case in which this is not true (cross-classification) (Lau & Murnighan, 1998, 2005; Li & Hambrick, 2005). There exists evidence on the beneficial effects of cross-categorization, or weak faultlines (Lau & Murnighan, 2005; Li & Hambrick, 2005). Research suggests people anticipate that feelings will be more positive in cross-classified groups and that performance (including creativity) will be enhanced (van Oudenhoven-van der Zee, Paulus, Vos, & Parthasarathy, 2009). Pearsall, Ellis, and Evans (2008) found that activation of gender faultlines in teams reduced the number and the overall creativity of the ideas generated. Similarly, Kratzer, Leenders, and van Engelen (2004) found that subgroup formation in teams inhibited their creativity. So predicting innovation in work teams becomes a rather complex issue.

Consistent with our line of reasoning, the review by Hülsheger et al. (2009) found that background diversity was negatively related to innovation, but job-relevant diversity had a slight, positive relationship with innovation. The positive effects they obtained in contrast to the overall null effects of prior reviews may be due to the fact that their review focused only on innovation or creativity. Task diversity may be most helpful on such team tasks. However, the fact that the relationship was fairly modest suggests that the strength of this relationship may depend on a variety of factors. It appears that a positive attitude toward diversity (Bouncken, Ratzman, & Winkler, 2009; Homan, van Knippenberg, Van Kleef, &

De Dreu, 2007; Nakui, Paulus, & van der Zee, in press) and a high need for cognition (Kearney, Gebert, & Voelpel, 2009) may increase the extent to which there is careful processing or elaboration of the shared ideas or information. This may then be the basis for enhanced creativity in groups with knowledge diversity (van Knippenberg & Schippers, 2007). Furthermore, the positive effects of diversity may depend on the extent to which there is communication among the team members and with their contacts outside the team (Cummings, 2004; Cummings, Espinosa, & Pickering, 2009; Keller, 2001).

The potential benefit of diversity on innovation has been one rationale for the increased use of multidisciplinary teams in both science and industry (Fiore, 2008). Multidisciplinary teams are those in which the team members have the complementary expertise needed for the completion of a project. Such teams have an obvious benefit for the completion of various complex tasks. Although multidisciplinarity would seem to give teams an important edge, the benefits of the varied expertise may only be tapped effectively if the team has effective group processes, such as shared vision, high frequency of interaction, high levels of team reflexivity, and safety (Fay, Borrill, Amir, Haward, & West, 2006). However, the development of radically new insights or perspectives may require interdisciplinary teams in which there is integration of knowledge and expertise (Cronin & Weingart, 2007). This involves efforts by the team members to understand each others' domains, and to effectively build on this shared knowledge to develop new perspectives, approaches, or techniques. Although there are case studies of effective interdisciplinary teams (Derry, Gernsbacher, & Schunn, 2005; Dunbar, 1995), there have not been any systematic studies of the effectiveness of such teams in comparison to multidisciplinary ones. However, there has been some systematic research on the importance of "connectedness" among the team members. It appears to be important for team members to be in fairly close physical proximity to facilitate the frequent personal interactions necessary to develop enhanced shared understanding (Cummings & Kiesler, 2005). It is important for team members to communicate frequently and to develop strong interpersonal bonds (Cross & Cummings, 2004; Drach-Zahavy & Somech, 2001). However, too much communication can be associated with lower creativity, possibly because overly frequent communications may distract from the individual creative activities or indicate lack of efficacy (Kratzer et al., 2004).

One important factor in determining the effects of diversity may be the length of time over which team members have worked together. Initially, group members may be more concerned with establishing commonalities and gaining acceptance. To accomplish this they would tend to focus on ways they are similar to one another and on their shared values (van der Zee & Paulus, 2008). The common information bias found in decision-making groups in which groups focus on information they have in common rather than unique information is consistent with this point of view (Stasser & Titus, 2006). Once group members have developed some sense of social cohesion, it may be easier for them to emphasize their unique expertise and perspectives. This is supported by at least one study with business students, in which diversity was related to negative creative outcomes early in the semester but with positive outcomes later in the semester (Watson, Kumar, & Michaelsen, 1993).

One of the problems with diversity, especially background or demographic diversity, is that individuals are naturally socially inhibited in diverse settings. They may not feel free to say what comes to mind; they may feel they have to go through some diversity censoring process. People tend to have different conversations in homogenous and mixed gender settings. What may be appropriate or tolerated in one social context may receive negative reactions in other contexts. Obviously anything that inhibits the flow of thoughts or ideas may inhibit the creative process. Research on brainstorming has found that concern about performance evaluation can inhibit performance and individuals who have high levels of social interaction anxiety are particularly prone to such negative effects (Camacho & Paulus, 1995; Diehl & Stroebe, 1987). In the field of team innovation, there is similar evidence that feelings of psychological safety are important for creativity (Ancona & Bresman, 2006; Caldwell & O'Reilly, 2003; West, 1990).

FACTORS INFLUENCING TEAM CREATIVITY

Psychological or Participative Safety

Creativity implies freedom—freedom to think in new ways. But whenever someone comes up with something different, there is a chance someone else will not like it. We see this all the time as people, organizations, and governments try to gain acceptance for new ideas or initiatives. Many people are comfortable with the way things are and change may be seen as a threat. Alternatively, if the way things have been done has worked fairly well, it may seem risky to try something new no matter how promising it sounds. This type of resistance to innovations or change has been long documented in the organizational field and, of course, is at odds with the presumed interest of our society and many corporations in promoting innovation (Kilbourne & Woodman, 1999). How do we resolve this dilemma? One key factor seems to be psychological safety. That is, members of an organization or a team must feel that the organization or team is receptive to and supportive of the expression of new ideas. Unless there is this sense of psychological safety, individuals will not risk the potential ridicule or negative reactions that may accompany new ideas, especially radical ones. A number of research programs have provided strong evidence for the role of this factor in facilitating innovation (Edmonson & Roloff, 2009; West, 1990).

It is therefore important for organizational leaders to make it clear that they encourage creativity and the related risks (Kark & Carmeli, 2009). This is often highlighted as the importance of leader support for creativity (Carmeli & Schaubroeck, 2007; Hackman, 2002). A number of studies have shown that such supportive leadership is a critical factor in team innovation (Zaccaro, Heinen, & Shuffler, 2009). However, the support of one's fellow team members and that of one's family also appear to be important (Carmeli & Schaubroeck, 2007; Madjar, 2005, 2008; Madjar, Oldham, & Pratt, 2002). Although the relative importance of all these sources of support for creativity is yet to be determined, we presume that this will depend in part on the motivations of the people involved. Those whose identity is strongly related to their work should be more influenced by support derived from the work environment. Those who more strongly value family relationships may be more susceptible to family feelings about their creative activities. However, those who have a strong intrinsic motivation for a particular creative activity may not be as susceptible to these external support factors. For example, low creative individuals were more positively affected by the degree of support from home than others (Madjar et al., 2002). Madjar et al. (2002) also found that the impact of support on creativity was mediated by mood state. Thus the facilitative effects of support, psychological safety, and trust on innovation may be attributable in part to the positive mood states associated with them. Kark and Carmeli (2009) have found that the positive impact of psychological safety on innovation can be related to the increased positive feelings of vitality (positive emotions related to a high level of activation or arousal). Research indicates that positive feelings associated with high activation levels are in fact related to increased flexibility or divergent thinking (Baas, De Dreu, & Nijstad, 2008).

Further support for the importance of psychological safety comes from research on group creativity. Osborn (1963) emphasized deferment of judgment as one the important principles of group creativity and made this part of the rules of group brainstorming (don't judge or criticize ideas as they are presented). It does appear that lowering apprehension about sharing ideas can increase the generation of ideas (Diehl & Stroebe, 1987). However, research on electronic brainstorming has found little evidence that anonymity is an important factor in this process (DeRosa et al., 2007). One of the original justifications for electronic brainstorming was that it would allow participants to share ideas anonymously in the group (Nunamaker, Applegate, & Konsynski, 1987). This would eliminate the status differences that might impede a free exchange of ideas. Yet data on the effects of anonymity in electronic brainstorming are mixed. Possibly, being anonymous makes it possible for some individuals to feel less accountable for participating in the group process, and so they may be more prone to loaf (Karau & Williams, 1993). Any benefits of anonymity in increasing psychological safety may be counteracted by this social loafing effect.

This same problem may exist in organizations. Although psychological safety may reduce inhibitions for creative ideation, the feelings of safety may make one less concerned about consequences in general. That is, a highly safe and supportive environment may ironically reduce overall extrinsic motivation. This is suggested by the finding that participative safety (a combined measure of involvement in group process and a non-threatening, supportive team environment) has only a weak relationship with innovation (Hülsheger et al., 2009). Hülsheger et al. (2009) suggested that in trying to maintain a positive group atmosphere, group members may avoid conflict (and thus sharing ideas that might produce such conflict). The lethargy of many organizations has sometimes been attributed to such a tendency to maintain good relations at the expense of honest and open interactions (e.g., groupthink, Janis, 1982). So what is the solution? Certainly, it is important for organizations to encourage innovation and to make sure that team members feel free to express their ideas. However, they may also need to exert some degree of accountability or pressure on group members to be productive and come up with useful and feasible ideas in a reasonable period of time.

Leadership

Leaders are important in providing both the task and the relational context for the work environment of teams (Burke, Stagl, Klein, Goodwin, Salas, & Halpin, 2006a). On the basis of our review thus far, one would predict that the most effective leaders for creativity are those that provide a supportive environment, some degree of task structure, minimize social conflicts and effectively manage cognitive conflicts. Thus, it is important to understand how particular leadership behaviors or styles affect team creativity. Unfortunately, most studies of leader behavior have examined individual but not collaborative creativity (Ancona, Bressman, & Caldwell, 2009). Consistent with our prior suggestions, both task and person-related leadership styles appear to enhance creativity (Hülsheger et al., 2009; Hunter, Bedell-Avers, & Mumford, 2007; Zaccaro et al., 2009). Task leadership may involve initiating structure, setting clear deadlines, and close performance monitoring (Reiter-Palmon & Illies, 2004). Relational leadership may be highly participative and socially supportive. Such leaders may enhance creativity by enhancing positive moods and feelings of vitality in team members and increasing a sense of psychological safety (Atwater & Carmeli, 2009; Carmeli, Ben-Hador, Waldman, & Rupp, 2009; Kark & Carmeli, 2009), particularly if the leader is attentive. Both types of leaders may enhance the feelings of efficacy of the workers by providing encouragement and positive feedback (Carmeli & Schaubroeck, 2007) and increase their level of motivation for the task.

One type of leader that should be most encouraging for innovation is a transformational one, who inspires through a shared vision and high expectations, encourages followers to take new approaches, and provides individual consideration and support (Bass & Avolio, 1994; Shamir, House, & Arthur, 1993). Eisenbeiss, van Knippenberg, and Boerner (2008) found that this was indeed the case, but only when the organization had a strong climate for excellence. Shin and Zhou (2007) found transformational leadership was beneficial for innovation when there was diversity in the educational specialization in the research and development teams.

Since the most effective teams are self-managing (setting their own goals and even compensation, Kuipers & Stoker, 2009) and have a horizontal team structure, leadership may play different roles in such teams (Zaccaro et al., 2009). Zaccaro et al. (2009) differentiates leader-centric versus team-centric leadership. The leader-centric style involves more traditional hierarchical leadership, and the team-centric style involves more participatory or shared leadership. Presumably, most organizations that have self-managing teams have a relationally-oriented culture that emphasizes shared leadership in the team. However, Zaccaro et al. (2009) noted that in most cases, both types of leadership are needed. For example, the leader external to the team needs to set the task boundaries and may be responsible for the team composition. The focus of the team leader or the shared leadership will be the effective functioning of the team through direction setting, managing team operations, and developing leadership capacity. From this perspective a key factor differentiating the innovative success for teams should be the type of leadership within the team (Ancona et al., 2009). Moreover, since the organizational culture and support system is likely to be one consistent with the team structure (highly supportive, psychologically safe), it may be most important for the team leader or shared team leadership to have a strong task orientation. This would insure a proper balance of both a supportive environment and some degree of structure and pressure to make progress on the team goals. Moreover, there also may need to be a balance in the extent to which leadership behavior is exerted. Since creative activities involve intrinsic motivation it is important for the team members to have a degree of autonomy in their activities. Leaders should intervene only at times when task or social support is required. This may vary depending on the different phases of the exploration and exploitation process (Wageman, Fisher, & Hackman, 2009).

Conflict

If you think creative ideas may be threatening to a group or an organization, try conflict! Most people find conflict quite aversive, and therefore it is not surprising that teams in general avoid it (Tjosvold & Sun, 2002). Most of us are not well trained to handle conflict; we may be concerned about conflict escalating out of control and the related hurt feelings and anger that may ensue (De Dreu, 2008). Thus avoidance seems to be the dominant response to conflict, and much human resource training is designed to eliminate potential conflict (e.g., harassment and racism) from the workplace by emphasizing appropriate workplace protocols. Harmony in the workplace and among team members is indeed a desirable goal, and most research indicates that social conflicts in groups and teams have mostly negative consequences (De Dreu & Weingart, 2003). However, many have argued that it is important to exchange conflicting perspectives in order to stimulate innovation. Tjosvold (1991) has long championed constructive controversy as a means of stimulating innovation in organizations, and Nemeth has provided compelling evidence that exposure to conflicting perspectives can in fact increase one's creative or divergent thinking (cf., Nemeth & Nemeth-Brown, 2003). There is some evidence that a moderate degree of conflict in technological teams may be beneficial to innovation at the conceptualization stage but not at the implementation stage (Kratzer, Leenders, & Van Engelen, 2006). Chen (2006) found a positive effect of conflict on technology teams but not service teams.

Systematic reviews of informational or task conflict in co-located groups and teams (e.g., differences of opinions) have generally not found much support for the innovative impact of conflict (De Dreu & Weingart, 2003; Hülsheger et al., 2009). However, it is also clear that few significant innovations have occurred without some conflict. Most assessments of creative geniuses have found that a critical characteristic is persistence in the face of failure and negative reactions from others (Baer, 1993; Henderson, 2004; Simonton, 1999). Most of the major scientific innovations such as those by Einstein, Freud, and Darwin have been associated with many conflicts with peers during the development of their ideas (Gardner, 1993). Progress in any area requires that people get honest feedback on their ideas. So how do we balance the need for useful feedback with the potential negative reactions that may accompany such feedback? The key may be that the team must have both a strong sense of psychological safety and of social and task cohesion. That is, group members must have strong commitment to excellence in accomplishing their tasks, strong bonds of trust and respect for one another, and a culture in which openness and honesty about the group task and goals are encouraged. The exchange of honest perspectives should be done in such a way that group members see the feedback as designed to enhance the group and to build on contributions of other team members, rather than as a personal rejection or rejection of the group's goals. This kind of culture is apparently emphasized in IDEO (Sutton & Hargadon, 1996). This perspective is consistent with the finding that minority dissent in teams enhances innovation only when the teams have a high level of reflexivity or participation (De Dreu, 2002; De Dreu & West, 2001). Such groups have a high degree to which team members are open to each other's ideas and are motivated to adapt the group's goals and interaction processes to achieve a high level of functioning (see De Dreu, 2008).

Cohesion

In contrast to the conflict perspective, one of the long-held presumptions in the field is that group cohesion will enhance task performance. Cohesion is typically conceived as reflecting the extent to which group members have a strong social bond or sense of attraction (Forsyth, 2006). However, it has also been seen as a multi-dimension construct that also includes task commitment and group pride (Beal, Cohen, Burke, & McLendon, 2003; Mullen & Copper, 1994). The review of the literature by Mullen and Copper (1994) suggests that the task commitment component may be most important in predicting group task performance. Teams that have strong interpersonal bonds, a strong shared commitment to the task, and pride in their group would be expected to be more motivated than teams without such features. Given the importance of motivation in creativity, team cohesion should be a strong predictor of innovation. The review by Hülsheger et al. (2009) found that indeed this is the case. Since cohesion should take some time to develop, it is not surprising that this factor has not been found to be influential in laboratory studies of group creativity.

Even though cohesion is related to team innovation, one should not expect cohesive groups to be naturally creative. To the extent that divergent thinking processes can produce conflict, they may be avoided to maintain cohesion. Cohesion was one of the key factors in groupthink (premature consensus seeking) according to Janis (1982). However, systematic studies of groupthink have not supported this assumption (Paulus, 1998). It is likely that cohesion can have either positive or negative effects. If group cohesion involves a strong task commitment to innovation, one would expect that cohesion would be related to increased creativity. If group cohesion involves a strong commitment to maintain positive relations and feelings of superiority relative to other groups (as in the some of the classic cases of groupthink), group cohesion may be related to low innovation.

Trust

There is a significant literature on teams that has emphasized the importance of trust in innovation (Carmeli & Spreitzer, 2009). Trust is typically defined as the extent to which team members have confidence that their fellow group members will act in accordance with accepted standards of conduct and fairness. That is, team members expect their fellow group members to be honest, supportive, and to reciprocate positive exchanges and to avoid negative exchanges. Such trust inevitably takes some time to develop, so it is a meaningful construct only in longer term teams. Individuals may feel psychologically safe when there is a high level of trust, but a group can have psychological safety without a high level of trust (Carmeli & Spreitzer, 2009). Teams with a high level of trust are also likely to have a feeling of cohesion, but groups can be cohesive without having a high level of trust. So groups that have high trust should benefit from a sense of psychological safety, cohesion, as well as trust. Members of a team with these characteristics should feel highly motivated to do their fair share as a team member, be highly committed to the goals of the group, and feel free to share their ideas without fear of rejection. One would predict that such a team would have the potential to be quite innovative (Clegg, Unsworth, Epitropaki, & Parker, 2002).

Task Focus

Creativity involves performance on some type of task. Work teams typically are attempting to develop new procedures or products. Creativity requires that these products have some degree of novelty and eventually some applicability. Team creativity involves both individual and collaborative activities. Many tasks can be subdivided and individual group members may be assigned responsibility for different components of the task (disjunctive task, Steiner, 1972). Other tasks may simply involve the sum of the ideas or products of the group members, as in a brainstorming session (additive task). However, in both cases, these collaborative activities require some degree of coordination. In the case of complementary tasks, group members have to coordinate the way in which their contributions will be meshed. Not everyone may be going at the same pace, and group members may have to shift their focus from their own task to helping other group members (Hargadon & Bechky, 2006). In the case of additive tasks, coordination may be less complicated if individuals can do their tasks in isolation and then simply add the contributions at some later time (as with nominal groups). However, in many cases where group members work simultaneously together on the same task (as in a brainstorming task or completing a puzzle), individuals have to coordinate their contributions due to production blocking. They have to attend to each other's contributions and build on them when they have an opportunity. So even though the additive case is less complicated than the disjunctive or complementary case, innovative processes in any group require that the team members have a strong task focus.

What are the task skills needed in collaborative creative groups? One critical need is effective communication and information exchange (Ancona & Caldwell, 1992; Hülsheger et al., 2009). Innovation in groups and teams is related to the extent to which they effectively share ideas and information (Paulus, 2000). This requires careful attention to the shared information/ideas as well as an effective building on those ideas. Research indicates that attentional factors are in fact quite important (Paulus & Brown, 2007), but thus far little research has actively investigated the process of building on one another's ideas. To effectively coordinate with others requires some social skills, such as knowing when to contribute and when to listen. Research indicates that such social skills may be important in teamwork and innovation (Salas et al., 2009b).

Another important factor is task structure. Because collaboration is a complicated process, any procedure which simplifies the coordination and intellectual components should enhance innovation. The use of computer-mediated interactions can reduce some of the interference effects experienced in groups. Electronic brainstorming groups do not show the production losses that are found with large face-to-face groups, because the software allows individuals to contribute ideas at will and examine the shared ideas when they are interested or have run out of their own ideas (Dennis & Williams, 2003). In face-to-face groups or teams, it may be useful to structure the interaction to minimize the cognitive load. Decomposing the task so group members focus on only one subtopic or task at a time seems to enhance the number of ideas generated (Dennis, Aronson, Heninger, & Walker, 1999). Alternating between group and individual sessions may also be optimal (Baruah & Paulus, 2009). It may be useful to think through the issues before joining a group session since the group session may provide little time for private reflection. Alternatively, some period of reflection after group interaction will facilitate one's ability to build on the ideas of others as well as harvesting additional ideas stimulated by the prior interaction (Dugosh et al., 2000; Paulus & Yang, 2000).

The team literature has not focused on the details of the exchange process. It has highlighted instead the team approaches that are most helpful for innovation. West has emphasized the importance of task reflexivity, which is the extent to which the team is reflective of its goals, processes, and strategies and is able to adjust these as needed. West and others have shown that this skill is important in facilitating team innovation (Tjosvold, Tang, & West, 2004; West, 2003). A similar perspective that has been applied to teamwork in general is the adaptive perspective of Burke et al. (2006b).

The above findings imply that innovative teams need extensive training in order to perform effectively. There is a considerable literature on the benefits of team training on performance in general (Salas et al., 2008), but little if any on training for innovation. There is one laboratory study which demonstrated that training sessions with brainstorming groups can enhance the extent to which they are able to generate more creative ideas in groups (Baruah & Paulus, 2008). However, we know of no systematic study demonstrating the relative importance of different factors in the training of team innovation.

PHASES OF TEAM CREATIVITY

Although we often talk about creativity as if it were a unitary activity, the creative process in real world settings typically consists of a set of phases. The classic perspective is that creativity involves problem selection, ideation, evaluation, and implementation (Parnes, 1975). Others have emphasized the phases of exploration (idea generation) and exploitation (application of the ideas) (Bledow et al., 2009). Most laboratory studies of group creativity have focused on the ideation phase, and studies with work teams are more likely to incorporate implementation or exploitation into their measures (Anderson, De Dreu, & Nijstad, 2004). Exploration and exploitation are typically seen as distinct processes. Exploration is a divergent process that requires consideration of a wide range of perspectives and is seen as a cornerstone of the creative process. The aim of this phase is often to come up with highly novel innovations. Exploitation involves more of a convergent process of selection among alternatives, modification of alternatives, and implementing preferred ones. This phase involves more moderate novelty goals, as the main focus is on modifying or building on ideas already suggested and may involve appraisal, forecasting, and refinement (Mumford, Blair, & Marcy, 2006; Thompson, 2003). Typically these exploration and exploitation phases are seen as ones that require different orientations and possibly different people (Staw, 2009; Thompson, 2003). Some team members or teams may be good at divergent thinking (creators) while others may be better at adapting creative ideas (implementers) (Larey & Paulus, 1999). In contrast, Bledow et al. (2009) propose a dialectical perspective in which these exploration and exploitation processes do not occur in a static sequence. They support a perspective of ambidexterity (Benner & Tushman, 2003) in which these two processes can occur in any combination of ways. The Bledow et al. (2009) perspective is consistent with much of the reality in the workplace, in which there is a constant flow from one type of process to another as the situation demands. However, few research studies have examined the multiple stages of the creative process. It is not clear how long teams should stay in one phase before going to the other. Going too soon to an implementation phase may be problematic since one may not have fully tapped the idea pool. However, it may also be useful to try out ideas quickly to see if they will work and then go back to an ideation phase if needed. This approach is championed by at least one top product development company that emphasizes the need to develop rough prototypes for evaluation rather than worrying about generating highly polished ideas (Sutton & Hargadon, 1996). These prototypes can then be evaluated further and refined as needed.

Evaluation of individually generated ideas in a subsequent group discussion session was part of the Nominal Group Technique (Hegedus & Rasmussen, 1986; Van de Ven & Delbecq, 1974), but in the brainstorming literature a number of studies have examined the selection of ideas after brainstorming. These studies have found that neither individuals nor groups are particularly good at selecting the best ideas (Putman & Paulus, 2009; Rietzschel, Nijstad, & Stroebe, 2006). In comparison to the pool of available ideas, the ideas selected are not better than the average of this pool. Instead there seems to be bias to select ideas that occurred more frequently in the prior brainstorming session (Putman & Paulus, 2009). The best outcomes for selection of good ideas came from a sequence in which ideas generated as individuals were evaluated as a group, possibly in part because the nominal groups generated a bigger pool of good ideas (Putman & Paulus, 2009). Moreover, consistent with the Bledow et al. (2009) perspective, Rietzschel et al. (2006) found that it did not make a difference whether the idea generation and the selection phases were carefully separated or allowed to flow from one to another. This research suggests that team members may not be particularly good judges of the quality of the ideas generated by their own team. This may reflect a natural tendency to assess favorably ideas generated by oneself or one's group. However, Faure (2004) found that individuals were better judges of quality of their own ideas than the ideas generated by others. When groups are asked to evaluate ideas generated by others, groups can do a better job than individuals in selecting the best ideas (Larey & Paulus, 1999). The actual implementation could also be passed on to a group that specializes in that domain (possibly more technically oriented). However, those who actually came up with the ideas may better understand the nuances involved in effectively implementing them, because their collective experience as a team may allow them to tap more effectively their transactive memory or knowledge (Gino, Todorova, Miron-Spektor, & Argote, 2009; Moreland, Argote, & Krishnan, 1996).

GROUP STABILITY VERSUS TURNOVER

Since cohesiveness, psychological safety, and trust are important factors in team innovation, it might be predicted that once teams achieve these states, some degree of stability in team composition is desirable. Constant change in membership may make it hard to maintain a high level of these factors since such changes are associated with increased uncertainty, and the likelihood of conflicts in groups as they adjust to their new members (Moreland & Levine, 1989). Moreover, when group members depart they may take with them critical knowledge and skills, and the transactive memory system of the group will need to be re-developed. However, turnover in groups can also be positive, as new members can bring new perspectives and new enthusiasm to the group. The key factors in the success of group transitions are likely the pace of the transitions and the centrality of the team members being replaced. Loss of a high percentage of the group members in a short period of time is likely to be detrimental, as there is sudden loss of key expertise, a reduction in the group transactive memory, and loss of cohesion. Loss of key group leaders or those with unique expertise are also likely to negatively affect groups for a period of time until these losses can be overcome. So it would be predicted that any assessment of team stability or longevity on innovation would yield mixed results. In fact, Hülsheger et al. (2009) found no overall effect of team longevity on innovation. However, studies of laboratory brainstorming groups have found that gradual turnover in such groups over time is associated with increased creativity (Choi & Thompson, 2005; Nemeth & Ormiston, 2007). So it is predicted that gradual turnover in teams can have a positive impact on innovation, but teams may have an initial adjustment period in which their effectiveness may be reduced. Consistent with this perspective, Gilson and Shalley (2004) found that engagement in creativity was highest at moderate levels of team tenure. Future research should examine both the pace of the turnover process and obtain measures at different times after the turnover.

VIRTUAL TEAM CREATIVITY AND INNOVATION

As tasks become more and more complex, it is often necessary to choose group members with specific knowledge or skills who do not necessarily live or work near one another. Using various technologies, these individuals form a virtual team (VT). Although the use of VTs has exploded (Connaughton & Shuffler, 2007; Trzcielinski & Wypych-Zoltowska, 2008; Walvoord, Redden, Elliott, & Coovert, 2008), research focused on VT creativity is relatively scarce. However, with the increasing use of VTs, it is important to evaluate the applicability of research examining collaborative creativity to these types of teams. Like other teams, VTs are comprised of multiple individuals who have some degree of task interdependence and shared goals from an organizational setting (Horvath & Tobin, 2001). Unlike other teams, VT members are geographically dispersed and rely on technology to communicate (Gibson & Gibbs, 2006). Although most people assume that team members' geographic dispersion and electronic dependence are positively correlated, the only study that specifically measured each variable using actual teams did not find this to be the case (Gibson & Gibbs, 2006, Study 1). Some of the teams with members spread all over the globe (e.g., a team from the automotive industry) met face-to-face once a month and rarely used e-mail; some co-located teams relied extensively on e-mail.

One of the main advantages of VTs is that its members can be selected primarily on the basis of SKAs without regard to geographic location (Nemiro, 2002). Therefore, almost by definition, VTs should have members that are more likely to possess the appropriate SKAs to successfully perform creative and innovative tasks. Not only do VT members need the SKAs of their co-located counterparts, VT members must have SKA competencies regarding the use of the technology. Technical competence is likely to vary with age. For example, baby boomers may be less comfortable with some of the communication technologies frequently used in VTs than Generation Y members (Brady & Bradley, 2008; Webster & Staples, 2006). Training in the technology used for communication should alleviate this impediment (Rosen, Furst, & Blackburn, 2006). In addition, Webster and Staples (2006) found that training in "virtual teaming" skills can lead to positive effects. Several of the practitioner's guides to VTs include tips for training in certain skills and competencies to improve VT performance (e.g., Baan & Maznevski, 2008; Duarte & Snyder, 2006; Fisher & Fisher, 2001; Wesner, 2008). It also appears that VTs that are above average in creativity use different sets of media than other teams (Leenders, Kratzer, &Van Engelen, 2007; Leenders, Van Engelen, & Kratzer, 2003).

A major problem with the literature on VTs is that there is often a confound between the virtual status of the team and other characteristics (e.g., homogeneity with respect to geographic region and the culture associated with the region). In laboratory studies it is common to have face-to-face groups communicate orally and dispersed groups communicate through various technologies (Webster & Staples, 2006). Therefore, the communication medium is confounded with group type. It may be these confounds and not virtuality, per se, that are the cause of performance differences found between VT and co-located teams (c.f., Chudoba, Wynn, Lu, & Watson-Manheim, 2005). However, Nemiro (2002) concluded the processes in these VTs were similar to that of other teams. For example, the VTs tend to follow stages in the creative process: idea generation, development, finalization/closure, and evaluation. However, VTs are distinct from co-located teams in terms of archive capability and the ability to widen the creative pool of members through electronic links. In addition, Nemiro (2002) found the VTs adjusted their communication strategy with the stages of creativity. For example, nearly every VT used face-to-face communication during the idea generation stage. However, during the development stage, nearly every VT performed the work electronically. Among the VTs that included an evaluation stage, the work was often done face-to-face.

Since VTs can interact in an efficient manner like electronic brainstorming groups, they should not be as susceptible to group process losses due to production blocking. However, since they are dispersed, there may be less accountability of the extent to which team members are focusing on the key tasks unless some sort of monitoring system is in place (Aiello & Kolb, 1995). Based on the group decision support system literature, one would expect that VTs would work well for the exchange of ideas or information but not as well for more complex processes such as decision-making or negotiation (Barkhi, Jacob, & Pirkul, 1999; DeRosa, et al., 2007; Hollingshead, 1996). Consistent with this perspective, one of the common recommendations in the literature is that VTs should periodically use face-to-face meetings. The primary suggestion is that such teams should begin with face-to-face sessions and then move to virtuality, with intermittent face-to-face sessions (Duarte & Snyder, 2006; Fisher & Fisher, 2001). Presumably the initial face-to-face sessions allow for a more rapid development of group cohesion, trust, and transactive memory processes. However, one could also predict that if VTs are fine for initial information exchange, then face-to-face meetings could occur later for more complex group tasks such as decision-making. Unfortunately, no data are available to determine which is best. However, Cummings and Kiesler (2007) found that research teams that were located at the same university were more productive than those that consisted of members working at different institutions. It appears that frequent interaction and connectivity is important for the complex processes involved in scientific research projects (Cummings & Kiesler, 2005, 2008). Furthermore, much research on computer mediated groups working on decision or problem solving tasks has found that these groups tend to be less productive, slower, and less satisfied than face-to-face groups (e.g., Barkhi et al., 1999; Hollingshead, 1996; Strauss & McGrath, 1994).

One of the identifying characteristics of VTs is that they are more likely to include members who are diverse in nationality. Yet, virtuality may affect the salience of observable differences among the team members since they are not interacting face-to-face. So VTs could be associated with less negative interpersonal reactions and more effective utilization of diverse group expertise (Staples & Zhao, 2006; Webster & Staples, 2006). However, even when national diversity is not salient, it may still bring some challenges to VT performance. People of different nationalities or cultures often vary in their underlying assumptions regarding human behavior and values (Hofstede, 1997). For example, VT members from high power distance cultures may need the technology to indicate status differences within the team more than other VT members. Also people from cultures in which messages cannot be understood outside of the context (high context cultures) may require communications that provide such contextual information (Duarte & Snyder, 2006), so they may require a richer media for effective interaction and innovation.

Much of the VT literature suggests that conflict is more likely to occur in VT than co-located groups, and that this conflict will impair performance. However, only a handful of empirical studies have compared conflict and performance in VT and co-located teams. Griffith, Mannix, and Neale (2003) surveyed members of 35 teams and found that VT members had more process conflict when controlling for trust. However, they did not find VTs to have more (or less) task or relationship conflict than co-located teams. Similarly, Mortensen and Hinds (2001) found no significant differences in interpersonal or task conflict between VT and co-located teams. Hinds and Mortensen (2005) found the relationship between virtuality and conflict (both task and interpersonal) was mediated by shared identity and spontaneous communication.

In summary, members of VTs are geographically dispersed and must rely on technology to communicate. Geographic dispersion and reliance on technology affect the exchange of both task related and task unrelated information among members, and the frequency of spontaneous and planned communications. This in turn affects the role of factors such as psychological safety, conflict, cohesion, trust, and task focus in team creativity. Compared to co-located team members, VT members are more likely to possess the necessary task SKAs, have easy access to archives from prior communications, and experience less production blocking. VT members are often more nationally diverse and may experience more process conflict than co-located team members.

Due to methodological issues (e.g., confounding variables), complex results (e.g., several moderating and mediating variables), and gaps in the literature, it is difficult to provide practitioners with empirically validated suggestions to improve VT performance in a variety of organizational systems and for a variety of tasks. However, the following are likely to improve VT effectiveness:

1. select or train VT members so that they hold the task-necessary SKAs, team relevant SKAs, technology SKAs, and VT-specific SKAs,
2. select the technology (especially its media richness) based on members' computer competencies, which may vary with age, and culture,
3. consider varying face-to-face and computer-mediated phases based on the creativity phase and task requirements, and
4. guide VT task performance, providing performance feedback at key points concerning individual and team goals that foster psychological safety, cohesion, and trust.

CONCLUSIONS AND FUTURE DIRECTIONS

It is apparent that a broad range of factors can increase innovation in teams. Basically it appears that with the right people, the right supporting, motivational and task contexts, and effective social and cognitive processes, teams can be highly innovative. These results are consistent with the integrative model in Figure 14.1. This outcome is probably not surprising and to some extent states the obvious. We would expect highly creative, motivated people, who work in environments that encourage creativity, to excel. However, such excellence may not be inevitable in teams, since this configuration adds a level of complexity. Team members have to coordinate effectively, efficiently and adequately share and combine their relevant knowledge, select the best ideas, and effectively implement them. It may take considerable training and experience for teams to excel at team creativity.

Although this summary picture seems straightforward and supportive of using teams for creativity purposes, much of the evidence for this conclusion comes from studies using verbal reports of processes and outcomes. We do not know of a study that has clearly demonstrated synergy in real world work teams—that is, enhanced performance of teamwork relative to working as individuals (see also Staw, 2009). There is a need for studies that provide objective measures of processes and outcomes in real world settings with appropriate comparison groups. Laboratory studies of creativity in short-term groups suggest that groups will often underperform and will exceed non-interactive baselines only under conditions that are optimal for group idea exchange (e.g., efficient interaction patterns and mixing of group and solitary interaction). However, the fact that laboratory studies have been able to find synergy with ad-hoc groups in short-term settings suggests that teams which involve members suited for teamwork, who have worked together for some time and have the diverse perspectives needed for a problem, should also be able to achieve synergistic outcomes under the right conditions.

Another complexity for practitioners is the fact that, for practically all of the factors that have been demonstrated to influence team creativity, there are a number of limiting conditions. Moreover, in most cases there appears to be a need for some degree of balance. Teams should be cohesive but not too cohesive. Working as a VT can have benefits, but face-to-face interaction seems to be important at different times during the course of the project or task. Working as a team can have benefits, but the most effective pattern may involve a balance of teamwork, working in pairs, and working alone. Teams should be diverse, but too much diversity can be a problem. Some conflict can be stimulating if it occurs in the right context and manner, but most conflict seems to be detrimental. A supportive context in which one feels safe to try out ideas is important, but there also may need to be some external demands and goals to keep the team moving forward. Intrinsic motivation appears to be important but external incentives can also have a positive benefit. More research is needed to discover the right balance among these and the other factors we have discussed using both laboratory and field studies. However, at this point a number of practical suggestions can be made based on the literature.

PRACTICAL IMPLICATIONS

Team innovation requires a supportive context. Although team members may be capable of innovation, innovative behaviors are not likely to occur at a high level unless there is encouragement and support from the organization, leaders, and fellow team members. This includes an atmosphere of trust and psychological safety in which team members feel free to engage in some of the risky behaviors involved in creativity. Team and member characteristics are also important. Although large teams may provide a broad range of expertise, effective interaction among team members is most likely in relatively small teams, or in one-to-one exchanges. Diversity of expertise or background may facilitate creativity, but such diversity needs to be relevant to the task domain. It is important that the team members are able to understand and appreciate each other's diverse expertise and contributions. The social dynamics in the team can limit its creative potential, since there may be a tendency to conform and converge on areas of agreement. Teams need to develop a culture that encourages the exchange of diverse perspectives. Competition within teams or among teams can provide additional motivation for creative activities. However, even highly motivated teams may not be particularly successful unless they utilize effective interaction processes. Meetings should be kept as small as possible and idea exchange using writing or electronic means should be encouraged. After a period of idea exchange, there should be an allocated period for additional reflection and building on the exchanged ideas. It is also helpful if the idea generation process is structured. Decomposing the problem into subcomponents, periodic reflective breaks, and explicit instructions to combine and elaborate on the shared ideas can facilitate the generation of creative ideas. Once ideas are generated, groups or individuals need to select the best ones for implementation. There is often a bias against selecting the most innovative ideas in favor of the most useful ones. Although this may be a rational policy in the long term, procedures should be in place to maintain awareness of the most novel ideas and periodically assess their potential. For teams to achieve their creative potential, it may be important to have leaders who focus both on effective relations and appropriate task orientation. Some training on ways to work effectively as an innovative team may also be important. Although it is important for teams to develop some sense of cohesion and shared experience to work together effectively, some degree of change in membership can stimulate creative thinking in the group. Many team creative activities can be done virtually, but the process of decision making tends to be done best in face-to-face settings.

Acknowledgement

This chapter and related efforts are supported by a collaborative grant BCS 0729305 to the first author from the National Science Foundation, which includes support from the Deputy Director of National Intelligence for Analysis and a collaborative CreativeIT grant 0855825 from the National Science Foundation.

References

Aiello, J. R., & Kolb, K. J. (1995). Electronic performance monitoring and social context: Impact on productivity and stress. *Journal of Applied Psychology, 80,* 339–353.

Ancona, D., & Bresman, H. (2006). Begging, borrowing, and building on ideas from the outside to create pulsed innovation inside teams. In L. L. Thompson & H. Choi (Eds.), *Creativity and innovation in organizational teams* (pp. 87–108). Mahwah, NJ: Lawrence Erlbaum Associates.

Ancona, D., Bresman, H., & Caldwell, D. (2009). The X-factor: Six steps to leading high-performing X-teams. *Organizational Dynamics, 38*, 217–224.

Ancona, D. G., & Caldwell, D. F. (1992). Bridging the boundary: External activity and performance in organizational teams. *Administrative Science Quarterly, 37*, 634–665.

Anderson, C. A., Lindsay, J. J., & Bushman, B. J. (1999). Research in the psychological laboratory: Truth or triviality? *Current Directions in Psychological Science, 8*, 3–9.

Anderson, N., De Dreu, C. K. W., & Nijstad, B. A. (2004). The routinization of innovation research: A constructively critical review of the state-of-the-science. *Journal of Organizational Behavior, 25*, 147–173.

Antoni, C., & Hertel, G. (2009). Team processes, their antecedents and consequences: Implications for different types of teamwork. *European Journal of Work & Organizational Psychology, 18*, 253–266.

Atwater, L., & Carmeli, A. (2009). Leader–member exchange, feelings of energy, and involvement in creative work. *The Leadership Quarterly, 20*, 264–275.

Baan, A., & Maznevski, M. (2008). Training for virtual collaboration: Beyond technology competencies. In J. Nemiro, M. M. Beyerlein, L. Bradley & S. Beyerlein (Eds.), *The handbook of high-performance virtual teams: A toolkit for collaborating across boundaries* (pp. 345–365). San Francisco, CA: Jossey-Bass.

Baas, M., De Dreu, C. K. W., & Nijstad, B. A. (2008). A meta-analysis of 25 years of Mood–Creativity research: Hedonic tone, activation, or regulatory focus? *Psychological Bulletin, 134*, 779–806.

Baer, J. (1993). *Creativity and divergent thinking : A task-specific approach*. Hillsdale, N.J: L. Erlbaum Associates.

Barkhi, R., Jacob, V. S., & Pirkul, H. (1999). An experimental analysis of face to face versus computer mediated communication channels. *Group Decision and Negotiation, 8*, 325–347.

Baruah, J., & Paulus, P. B. (2008). Effects of training on idea generation in groups. *Small Group Research, 39*, 523–541.

Baruah, J., & Paulus, P. (2009). Enhancing group creativity: The search for synergy. In E. A. Mannix, M. A. Neale & J. A. Goncalo (Eds.), *Creativity in groups* (pp. 29–56). Bingley, UK: Emerald.

Bass, B. M., & Avolio, B. J. (1994). *Improving organizational effectiveness through transformational leadership*. Thousand Oaks, CA: Sage Publications.

Beal, D. J., Cohen, R. R., Burke, M. J., & McLendon, C. L. (2003). Cohesion and performance in groups: A meta-analytic clarification of construct relations. *Journal of Applied Psychology, 88*, 989–1004.

Benner, M. J., & Tushman, M. L. (2003). Exploitation, exploration, and process management: The productivity dilemma revisited. *The Academy of Management Review, 28*, 238–256.

Bledow, R., Frese, M., Anderson, N., Erez, M., & Farr, J. L. (2009). A dialectic perspective on innovation: Conflicting demands, multiple pathways, and ambidexterity. *Industrial & Organizational Psychology, 2*, 305–337.

Bouncken, R. B., Ratzman, M., & Winkler, V. A. (2009). Cross-cultural innovation teams: Effects of four types of attitudes towards diversity. *Journal of International Business Strategy, 8*, 26–36.

Brady, E., & Bradley, L. (2008). Generational differences in virtual teams. In J. Nemiro, M. M. Beyerlein, L. Bradley & S. Beyerlein (Eds.), *The handbook of high-performance virtual teams: A toolkit for collaborating across boundaries* (pp. 263–271). San Francisco, CA: Jossey-Bass.

Brown, V. R., & Paulus, P. B. (2002). Making group brainstorming more effective: Recommendations from an associative memory perspective. *Current Directions in Psychological Science, 11*, 208–212.

Burke, C. S., Stagl, K. C., Klein, C., Goodwin, G. F., Salas, E., & Halpin, S. M. (2006a). What type of leadership behaviors are functional in teams? A meta-analysis. *The Leadership Quarterly, 17*, 288–307.

Burke, C. S., Stagl, K. C., Salas, E., Pierce, L., & Kendall, D. (2006b). Understanding team adaptation: A conceptual analysis and model. *Journal of Applied Psychology, 91*, 1189–1207.

Caldwell, D. F., & O'Reilly, C. A. I. (2003). The determinants of team-based innovation in organizations. the role of social influence. *Small Group Research, 34*, 497–517.

Camacho, L. M., & Paulus, P. B. (1995). The role of social anxiousness in group brainstorming. *Journal of Personality and Social Psychology, 68*, 1071–1080.

Carmeli, A., Ben-Hador, B., Waldman, D. A., & Rupp, D. E. (2009). How leaders cultivate social capital and nurture employee vigor: Implications for job performance. *Journal of Applied Psychology, 94*, 1553–1561.

Carmeli, A., & Schaubroeck, J. (2007). The influence of leaders' and other referents' normative expectations on individual involvement in creative work. *The Leadership Quarterly, 18*, 35–48.

Carmeli, A., & Spreitzer, G. M. (2009). Trust, connectivity, and thriving: Implications for innovative behaviors at work. *Journal of Creative Behavior, 43*, 169–199.

Chen, M. (2006). Understanding the benefits and detriments of conflict on team creativity process. *Creativity and Innovation Management, 15*, 105–116.

Choi, H., & Thompson, L. (2005). Old wine in a new bottle: Impact of membership change on group creativity. *Organizational Behavior and Human Decision Processes, 98*, 121–132.

Chudoba, K. M., Wynn, E., Lu, M., & Watson-Manheim, M. B. (2005). How virtual are we? Measuring virtuality and understanding its impact in a global organization. *Information Systems Journal, 15*, 279–306.

Clegg, C., Unsworth, K., Epitropaki, O., & Parker, G. (2002). Implicating trust in the innovation process. *Journal of Occupational and Organizational Psychology, 75*, 409–422.

Connaughton, S. L., & Shuffler, M. (2007). Multinational and multicultural distributed teams. *Small Group Research, 38*, 387–412.

Coskun, H., Paulus, P. B., Brown, V., & Sherwood, J. J. (2000). Cognitive stimulation and problem presentation in idea-generating groups. *Group Dynamics: Theory, Research, and Practice, 4*, 307–329.

Cronin, M. A., & Weingart, L. R. (2007). Representational gaps, information processing, and conflict in functionally diverse teams. *Academy of Management Review, 32*, 761–773.

Cross, R., & Cummings, J. N. (2004). Tie and network correlates of individual performance in knowledge-intensive work. *Academy of Management Journal, 47*, 928–937.

Cummings, J. N. (2004). Work groups, structural diversity, and knowledge sharing in a global organization. *Management Science, 50*, 352–364.

Cummings, J. N., Espinosa, J. A., & Pickering, C. K. (2009). Crossing spatial and temporal boundaries in globally distributed projects: A relational model of coordination delay. *Information Systems Research, 20*, 420–439.

Cummings, J. N., & Kiesler, S. (2005). Collaborative research across disciplinary and organizational boundaries. *Social Studies of Science, 35*, 703–722.

Cummings, J. N., & Kiesler, S. (2007). Coordination costs and project outcomes in multi-university collaborations. *Research Policy, 36*, 1620–1634.

Cummings, J. N., & Kiesler, S. (2008). Who collaborates successfully? Prior experience reduces collaboration barriers in distributed interdisciplinary research. *Proceedings of the ACM Conference on Computer-Supported Cooperative Work*, November 10–12, San Diego, CA.

Curral, L. A., Forrester, R. H., Dawson, J. F., & West, M. A. (2001). It's what you do and the way that you do it: Team task, team size, and innovation-related group processes. *European Journal of Work & Organizational Psychology, 10*, 187–204.

De Dreu, C. K. W. (2002). Team innovation and team effectiveness: The importance of minority dissent and reflexivity. *European Journal of Work and Organizational Psychology, 11*, 285–298.

De Dreu, C. K. W. (2008). The virtue and vice of workplace conflict: Food for (pessimistic) thought. *Journal of Organizational Behavior, 29*, 5–18.

De Dreu, C. K. W., & Weingart, L. R. (2003). Task versus relationship conflict, team performance, and team member satisfaction: A meta-analysis. *Journal of Applied Psychology, 88*, 741–749.

De Dreu, C. K. W., & West, M. A. (2001). Minority dissent and team innovation: The importance of participation in decision making. *Journal of Applied Psychology, 86*, 1191–1201.

Dennis, A. R., Aronson, J. E., Heninger, W. G., & Walker, E. D. (1999). Structuring time and task in electronic brainstorming. *MIS Quarterly, 23*, 95–108.

Dennis, A. R., & Williams, M. L. (2003). Electronic brainstorming: Theory, research, and future directions. In P. B. Paulus & B. A. Nijstad (Eds.), *Group creativity* (pp. 160–178). New York, NY: Oxford University Press.

DeRosa, D. M., Smith, C. L., & Hantula, D. A. (2007). The medium matters: Mining the long-promised merit of group interaction in creative idea generation tasks in a meta-analysis of the electronic group brainstorming literature. *Computers in Human Behavior, 23*, 1549–1581.

Derry, S. J., Gernsbacher, M. A., & Schunn, C. D. (2005). *Interdisciplinary collaboration: An emerging cognitive science.* Mahwah, N.J: Lawrence Erlbaum.

Diehl, M., & Stroebe, W. (1987). Productivity loss in brainstorming groups: Toward the solution of a riddle. *Journal of Personality and Social Psychology, 53*, 497–509.

Diehl, M., & Stroebe, W. (1991). Productivity loss in idea-generating groups: Tracking down the blocking effect. *Journal of Personality and Social Psychology, 61*, 392–403.

C. GROUP LEVEL INFLUENCES

Drach-Zahavy, A., & Somech, A. (2001). Understanding team innovation: The role of team processes and structures. *Group Dynamics: Theory, Research, and Practice, 5*, 111–123.

Duarte, D. L., & Snyder, N. T. (2006). *Mastering virtual teams: Strategies, tools, and techniques that succeed* (3rd ed.). San Francisco, CA: Jossey-Bass.

Dugosh, K. L., & Paulus, P. B. (2005). Cognitive and social comparison processes in brainstorming. *Journal of Experimental Social Psychology, 41*, 313–320.

Dugosh, K. L., Paulus, P. B., Roland, E. J., & Yang, H-C. (2000). Cognitive stimulation in brainstorming. *Journal of Personality & Social Psychology, 79*, 722–735.

Dunbar, K. (1995). How scientists really reason: Scientific reasoning in real-world laboratories. In R. J. Sternberg & J. E. Davidson (Eds.), *The nature of insight* (pp. 365–395). Cambridge, MA: MIT Press.

Edmondson, A., & Roloff, K. (2009). Overcoming barriers to collaboration: Psychological safety and learning in diverse teams. In E. Salas, G. F. Goodwin & C. S. Burke (Eds.), *Team effectiveness in complex organizations: Cross-disciplinary perspectives and approaches* (pp. 183–208). Mahwah, NJ: Lawrence Erlbaum Associates. New York, NY: Routledge.

Edwards, B. D., Day, E. A., Arthur, W., & Bell, S. T. (2006). Relationships among team ability composition, team mental models, and team performance. *Journal of Applied Psychology, 91*, 727–736.

Eisenbeiss, S. A., van Knippenberg, D., & Boerner, S. (2008). Transformational leadership and team innovation: Integrating team climate principles. *Journal of Applied Psychology, 93*, 1438–1446.

Farrell, M. P. (2001). *Collaborative circles: Friendship dynamics & creative work*. Chicago, IL: University of Chicago Press.

Faure, C. (2004). Beyond brainstorming: Effects of different group procedures on selection and implementation of ideas. *Journal of Creative Behavior, 38*, 13–34.

Fay, D., Borrill, C. S., Amir, Z., Haward, R., & West, M. A. (2006). Getting the most out of multidisciplinary teams: A multi-sample study of team innovation in health care. *Journal of Occupational and Organizational Psychology, 79*, 553–567.

Fiore, S. M. (2008). Interdisciplinarity as teamwork: How the science of teams can inform team science. *Small Group Research, 39*, 251–277.

Fisher, K., & Fisher, M. D. (2001). *The distance manager: A hands-on guide to managing off-site employees and virtual teams*. New York, NY: McGraw-Hill.

Forsyth, D. R. (2006). *Group dynamics* (4th ed.). Belmont, CA: Thomson/Wadsworth.

Gardner, H. (1993). *Creating minds: An anatomy of creativity seen through the lives of Freud, Einstein, Picasso, Stravinsky, Eliot, Graham, and Gandhi*. New York, NY: Basic Books.

Gibson, C. B., & Gibbs, J. L. (2006). Unpacking the concept of virtuality: The effects of geographic dispersion, electronic dependence, dynamic structure, and national diversity on team innovation. *Administrative Science Quarterly, 51*, 451–495.

Gilson, L. L., & Shalley, C. E. (2004). A little creativity goes a long way: An examination of teams' engagement in creative processes. *Journal of Management, 30*, 453–470.

Gino, F., Todorova, G., Miron-Spektor, E., & Argote, L. (2009). When and why prior task experience fosters team creativity. In E. A. Mannix, M. A. Neale & J. A. Goncalo (Eds.), *Creativity in groups* (pp. 87–110). Bingley, UK: Emerald.

Griffith, T. L., Mannix, E. A., & Neale, M. A. (2003). Conflict and virtual teams. In C. B. Gibson & S. G. Cohen (Eds.), *Virtual teams that work: creating conditions for virtual team effectiveness* (pp. 335–352). San Francisco, CA: Jossey-Bass.

Hackman, J. R. (1987). The design of work teams. In J. W. Lorsch (Ed.), *Handbook of organizational behavior* (pp. 315–342). Englewood Cliffs, NJ: Prentice-Hall.

Hackman, J. R. (2002). *Leading teams: Setting the stage for great performances*. Boston, MA: Harvard Business School Press.

Hargadon, A. B., & Bechky, B. A. (2006). When collections of creatives become creative collectives: A field study of problem solving at work. *Organization Science, 17*, 484–500.

Hegedus, D. M., & Rasmussen, R. V. (1986). Task effectiveness and interaction process of a modified nominal group technique in solving an evaluation problem. *Journal of Management, 12*, 545.

Henderson, S. J. (2004). Inventors: The ordinary genius next door. In R. J. Sternberg, E. E. Grigorenko & J. L. Singer (Eds.), *Creativity: From potential to realization* (pp. 103–126). Washington, DC: American Psychological Association.

Hinds, P. J., & Mortensen, M. (2005). Understanding conflict in geographically distributed teams: The moderating effects of shared identity, shared context, and spontaneous communication. *Organization Science, 16*, 290–307.

Hofstede, G. (1997). *Culture's consequences, international differences in work related values.* Beverly Hills, CA: Sage.

Hollingshead, A. B. (1996). Information suppression and status persistence in group decision-making: The effects of communications media. *Human Computer Research, 23*, 193–219.

Homan, A. C., van Knippenberg, D., Van Kleef, G. A., & De Dreu, C. K. W. (2007). Bridging faultlines by valuing diversity: Diversity beliefs, information elaboration, and performance in diverse work groups. *Journal of Applied Psychology, 92*, 1189–1199.

Horvath, L., & Tobin, T. J. (2001). Twenty-first century teamwork: Defining competencies for virtual teams. In M. M. Beyerlein, D. A. Johnson & S. T. Beyerlein (Eds.), *Advances in interdisciplinary studies of work teams: Vol. 8. Virtual teams* (pp. 239–258). Oxford, UK: Elsevier Science Ltd.

Hülsheger, U. R., Anderson, N., & Salgado, J. F. (2009). Team-level predictors of innovation at work: A comprehensive meta-analysis spanning three decades of research. *Journal of Applied Psychology, 94*, 1128–1145.

Hunter, S. T., Bedell-Avers, K., & Mumford, M. D. (2007). The typical leadership study: Assumptions, implications, and potential remedies. *Leadership Quarterly, 18*, 435–446.

Ilgen, D. R., Hollenbeck, J. R., Johnson, M., & Jundt, D. (2005). Teams in organizations: From input–process–output models to IMOI models. *Annual Review of Psychology, 56*, 517–543.

Janis, I. L. (1982). *Groupthink : Psychological studies of policy decisions and fiascoes* (2nd ed.). Boston, MA: Houghton Mifflin.

John-Steiner, V. (2000). *Creative collaboration.* Oxford, UK; New York, NY: Oxford University Press.

Kanev, K., Kimura, S., & Orr, T. (2009). A framework for collaborative learning in dynamic group environments. *International Journal of Distance Education Technologies, 7*, 58–77.

Karau, S. J., & Williams, K. (1993). Social loafing: A meta-analytic review and theoretical integration. *Journal of Personality and Social Psychology, 65*, 681–706.

Kark, R., & Carmeli, A. (2009). Alive and creating: The mediating role of vitality and aliveness in the relationship between psychological safety and creative work involvement. *Journal of Organizational Behavior, 30*, 785–804.

Kearney, E., Gebert, D., & Voelpel, S. C. (2009). When and how diversity benefits teams: The importance of team members' need for cognition. *Academy of Management Journal, 52*, 581–598.

Keller, R. T. (2001). Cross-functional project groups in research and new product development: Diversity, communications, job stress, and outcomes. *Academy of Management Journal, 44*, 547–555.

Kerr, N. L., & Tindale, R. S. (2004). Group performance and decision making. *Annual Review of Psychology, 55*, 623–655.

Kilbourne, L. M., & Woodman, R. W. (1999). Barriers to organizational creativity. In R. E. Purser & A. Montuori (Eds.), *Social creativity* (pp. 125–150). Cresskill, NJ: Hampton Press.

Kohn, N. W., & Smith, S. M. (in press). Collaborative fixation: Effects of others' ideas on brainstorming. *Journal of Applied Cognitive Psychology.*

Kozlowski, S. W. J., & Ilgen, D. R. (2006). Enhancing the effectiveness of work groups and teams. *Psychological Science in the Public Interest, 7*, 77–124.

Kratzer, J., Leenders, R. T. A. J., & Van Engelen, J. M. L. (2004). Stimulating the potential: Creative performance and communication in innovation teams. *Creativity and Innovation Management, 13*, 63–70.

Kratzer, J., Leenders, R. T. A. J., & Van Engelen, J. M. L. (2006). Team polarity and creative performance in innovation teams. *Creativity and Innovation Management, 15*, 96–104.

Kuipers, B. S., & Stoker, J. I. (2009). Development and performance of self-managing work teams: A theoretical and empirical examination. *International Journal of Human Resource Management, 20*, 399–419.

Larey, T. S., & Paulus, P. B. (1999). Group preference and convergent tendencies in small groups: A content analysis of group brainstorming performance. *Creativity Research Journal, 12*, 175–184.

Larson, J. R. (2010). *In search of synergy in small group performance.* New York, NY: Psychology Press.

Lau, D. C., & Murnighan, J. K. (1998). Demographic diversity and faultlines: The compositional dynamics of organizational groups. *Academy of Management Review, 23*, 325–340.

Lau, D. C., & Murnighan, J. K. (2005). Interactions within groups and subgroups: The effects of demographic faultlines. *Academy of Management Journal, 48*, 645–659.

Leenders, R. T. A. J., Kratzer, J, & Van Engelen, J. M. L. (2007). Media ensembles and new product team creativity: A tree-based exploration. In S. P. MacGregor & T. Torress-Coronas (Eds.), *Higher creativity for virtual teams: Developing platforms for co-creation* (pp. 75–97). Harrisburg, PA: Information Science Reference.

Leenders, R. T. A. J., Van Engelen, J. M. L., & Kratzer, J. (2003). Virtuality, communication, and new product team creativity: A social network perspective. *Journal of Engineering and Technology Management, 20,* 69–92.

Lewis, K. (2003). Measuring transactive memory systems in the field: Scale development and validation. *Journal of Applied Psychology, 88,* 587–604.

Li, J., & Hambrick, D. C. (2005). Factional groups: A new vantage on demographic faultlines, conflict, and disintegration in work teams. *Academy of Management Journal, 48,* 794–813.

Madjar, N. (2005). The contributions of different groups of individuals to employees' creativity. *Advances in Developing Human Resources, 7,* 182–206.

Madjar, N. (2008). Emotional and informational support from different sources and employee creativity. *Journal of Occupational and Organizational Psychology, 81,* 83–100.

Madjar, N., Oldham, G. R., & Pratt, M. G. (2002). There's no place like home? The contributions of work and non-work creativity support to employees' creative performance. *Academy of Management Journal, 45,* 757–767.

Mannix, E. A., & Neale, M. A. (2005). What difference makes a difference: The promise and reality of diverse groups in organizations. *Psychological Science in the Public Interest, 6,* 31–55.

Mannix, E. A., Neale, M. A., & Goncalo, J. A. (2009). *Creativity in groups.* Bingley, UK: Emerald.

Mayer, R. E. (1999). Fifty years of creativity research. In R. J. Sternberg (Ed.), *Handbook of creativity* (pp. 449–458). New York, NY: Cambridge University Press.

Moreland, R. L., Argote, L., & Krishnan, R. (1996). Social shared cognition at work: Transactive memory and group performance. In J. L. Nye & A. M. Brower (Eds.), *What's social about social cognition? Research on socially shared cognition in small groups* (pp. 57–84). Thousand Oaks, CA: Sage Publications.

Moreland, R. L., & Levine, J. M. (1989). Newcomers and oldtimers in small groups. In P. B. Paulus (Ed.), *Psychology of group influence* (pp. 143–186). Hillsdale, NJ: Lawrence Erlbaum Associates.

Mortensen, M., & Hinds, P. (2001). Conflict and shared identity in geographically distributed teams. *International Journal of Conflict Management, 12,* 212–238.

Mullen, B., & Copper, C. (1994). The relation between group cohesiveness and performance: An integration. *Psychological Bulletin, 115,* 210–227.

Mullen, B., Driskell, J. E., & Salas, E. (1998). Meta-analysis and the study of group dynamics. *Group Dynamics: Theory, Research, and Practice, 2,* 213–229.

Mullen, B., Johnson, C., & Salas, E. (1991). Productivity loss in brainstorming groups: A meta-analytic integration. *Basic and Applied Social Psychology, 12,* 3–23.

Mumford, M. D., Blair, C. S., & Marcy, R. T. (2006). Alternative knowledge structures in creative thought: Schema, associations, and cases. In J. Baer (Ed.), *Creativity and reason in cognitive development* (pp. 117–136). New York, NY: Cambridge University Press.

Nakui, T., Paulus, P. B., & van der Zee, K. I. (in press). The role of attitudes in reactions to diversity in work groups. *Journal of Applied Social Psychology.*

Nemeth, C. J., & Nemeth-Brown, B. (2003). Better than individuals? The potential benefits of dissent and diversity for group creativity. In B. A. Nijstad & P. B. Paulus (Eds.), *Group creativity: Innovation through collaboration* (pp. 63–84). New York, NY: Oxford University Press.

Nemeth, C. J., & Ormiston, M. (2007). Creative idea generation: Harmony versus stimulation. *European Journal of Social Psychology, 37,* 524–535.

Nemiro, J. E. (2002). The creative process in virtual teams. *Creativity Research Journal, 14,* 69–83.

Nijstad, B. A. (2009). *Group performance.* New York, NY: Psychology Press.

Nijstad, B. A., & Stroebe, W. (2006). How the group affects the mind: A cognitive model of idea generation in groups. *Personality and Social Psychology Review, 10,* 186–213.

Nijstad, B. A., Stroebe, W., & Lodewijkx, H. F. M. (2002). Cognitive stimulation and interference in groups: Exposure effects in an idea generation task. *Journal of Experimental Social Psychology, 38,* 535–544.

Nijstad, B. A., Stroebe, W., & Lodewijkx, H. F. M. (2003). Production blocking and idea generation: Does blocking interfere with cognitive processes? *Journal of Experimental Social Psychology, 39,* 531–548.

Nunamaker, J. F., Jr., Applegate, L. M., & Konsynski, B. R. (1987). Facilitating group creativity: Experience with a group decision support system. *Journal of Management Information Systems, 3,* 5–19.

Osborn, A. F. (1963). *Applied imagination; principles and procedures of creative problem-solving* (3d rev ed.). New York, NY: Scribner.

Parnes, S. J. (1975). CPSI: A program for balanced growth. *Journal of Creative Behavior, 9*, 23–29.

Paulus, P. B. (1989). *Psychology of group influence* (2nd ed.). Hillsdale, N.J: L. Erlbaum.

Paulus, P. B. (1998). Developing consensus about groupthink after all these years. *Organizational Behavior & Human Decision Processes, 73*, 362–374.

Paulus, P. B. (2000). Groups, teams, and creativity: The creative potential of idea-generating groups. *Applied Psychology: An International Review, 49*, 237–262.

Paulus, P. B. (2007). Fostering creativity in groups and teams. In J. Zhou & C. E. Shalley (Eds.), *The Handbook of Organizational Creativity* (pp. 159–182). Boca Raton, FL: Taylor & Francis Group.

Paulus, P. B., & Brown, V. R. (2003). Enhancing ideational creativity in groups: Lessons from research on brainstorming. In P. B. Paulus & B. A. Nijstad (Eds.), *Group creativity: Innovation through collaboration* (pp. 110–136) (2nd ed.). New York, NY: Oxford University Press.

Paulus, P. B., & Brown, V. R. (2007). Toward more creative and innovative group idea generation: A cognitive-social motivational perspective of brainstorming. *Social and Personality Compass, 1*, 248–265.

Paulus, P. B., & Dzindolet, M. T. (1993). Social influence processes in group brainstorming. *Journal of Personality and Social Psychology, 64*, 575–586.

Paulus, P. B., & Dzindolet, M. T. (2008). Social influence, creativity and innovation. *Social Influence, 3*, 228–247.

Paulus, P. B., Nakui, T., & Putman, V. L. (2006a). Group brainstorming and teamwork: Some rules for the road to innovation. In L. L. Thompson & H. Choi (Eds.), *Creativity and innovation in organizational teams* (pp. 69–86). Mahwah, NJ: Lawrence Erlbaum Associates, Inc.

Paulus, P. B., Nakui, T., Putman, V. L., & Brown, V. R. (2006). Effects of task instructions and brief breaks on brainstorming. *Group Dynamics: Theory, Research, and Practice, 10*, 206–219.

Paulus, P. B., & Nijstad, B. A. (2003). *Group creativity: Innovation through collaboration.* New York, NY: Oxford University Press.

Paulus, P. B., & Van der Zee, K. I. (2004). Should there be a romance between teams and groups? *Journal of Occupational and Organizational Psychology, 77*, 475–480.

Paulus, P. B., & Yang, H. (2000). Idea generation in groups: A basis for creativity in organizations. *Organizational Behavior and Human Decision Processes, 82*, 76–87.

Pearsall, M. J., Ellis, A. P. J., & Evans, J. M. (2008). Unlocking the effects of gender faultlines on team creativity: Is activation the key? *Journal of Applied Psychology, 93*, 225–234.

Pirola-Merlo, A., & Mann, L. (2004). The relationship between individual creativity and team creativity: Aggregating across people and time. *Journal of Organizational Behavior, 25*, 235–257.

Putman, V. L., & Paulus, P. B. (2009). Brainstorming, brainstorming rules and decision making. *Journal of Creative Behavior, 43*, 23–39.

Reagans, R., & Zuckerman, E. W. (2001). Networks, diversity, and productivity: The social capital of corporate R&D teams. *Organization Science, 12*, 502–517.

Reiter-Palmon, R., & Illies, J. J. (2004). Leadership and creativity: Understanding leadership from a creative problem-solving perspective. *The Leadership Quarterly, 15*, 55–77.

Rietzschel, E. F., Nijstad, B. A., & Stroebe, W. (2006). Productivity is not enough: A comparison of interactive and nominal brainstorming groups on idea generation and selection. *Journal of Experimental Social Psychology, 42*, 244–251.

Rietzschel, E. F., Nijstad, B. A., & Stroebe, W. (2007). Relative accessibility of domain knowledge and creativity: The effects of knowledge activation on the quantity and originality of generated ideas. *Journal of Experimental Social Psychology, 43*, 933–946.

Rosen, B., Furst, S., & Blackburn, R. (2006). Training for virtual teams: An investigation of current practices and future needs. *Human Resource Management, 45*, 229–247.

Salas, E., DiazGranados, D., Klein, C., Burke, C. S., Stagl, K. C., Goodwin, G. F., & Halpin, S. M. (2008). Does team training improve team performance? A meta-analysis. *Human Factors, 50*, 903–933.

Salas, E., Goodwin, G. F., & Burke, C. S. (2009a). *Team effectiveness in complex organizations: Cross-disciplinary perspectives and approaches.* New York, NY: Routledge/Taylor & Francis Group.

Salas, E., Rosen, M. A., Burke, C. S., & Goodwin, G. F. (2009b). The wisdom of collectives in organizations: An update of the teamwork competencies. In E. Salas, G. F. Goodwin & C. S. Burke (Eds.), *Team effectiveness in complex organizations: Cross-disciplinary perspectives and approaches* (pp. 39–79). New York, NY: Routledge/Taylor & Francis Group.

Sawyer, R. K. (2007). *Group genius: The creative power of collaboration.* New York, NY: Basic Books.

Shamir, B., House, R. J., & Arthur, M. B. (1993). The motivational effects of charismatic leadership: A self-concept based theory. *Organization Science, 4,* 577–594.

Shin, S. J., & Zhou, J. (2007). When is educational specialization heterogeneity related to creativity in research and development teams? Transformational leadership as a moderator. *Journal of Applied Psychology, 92,* 1709–1721.

Simonton, D. K. (1999). *Origins of genius: Darwinian perspectives on creativity.* New York, NY: Oxford University Press.

Staples, D. S., & Zhao, L. (2006). The effects of cultural diversity in virtual teams versus face-to-face teams. *Group Decision and Negotiation, 15,* 389–406.

Stasser, G., & Titus, W. (2006). Pooling of unshared information in group decision making: Biased information sampling during discussion. In J. M. Levine & R. L. Moreland (Eds.), *Small groups: Key readings* (pp. 227–239). New York, NY: Psychology Press.

Staw, B. M. (2009). Is group creativity really an oxymoron? Some thoughts on bridging the cohesion–creativity divide. In E. A. Mannix, M. A. Neale & J. A. Goncalo (Eds.), *Creativity in groups* (pp. 311–323). Bingley, UK: Emerald.

Steiner, I. D. (1972). *Group process and productivity.* New York, NY: Academic Press.

Sternberg, R. J. (2006). Creating a vision of creativity: The first 25 years. *Psychology of Aesthetics, Creativity, and the Arts, S,* 2–12.

Sternberg, R. J., Grigorenko, E. L., & Singer, J. L. (2004). *Creativity : From potential to realization* (1st ed.). Washington, DC: American Psychological Association.

Straus, S. G., & McGrath, J. E. (1994). Does the medium matter? The interaction of task type and technology on group performance and member reactions. *Journal of Applied Psychology, 79,* 87–97.

Sutton, R. I., & Hargadon, A. B. (1996). Brainstorming groups in context: Effectiveness in a product design firm. *Administrative Science Quarterly, 41,* 685–718.

Taggar, S. (2001). Group composition, creative synergy, and group performance. *Journal of Creative Behavior, 35,* 261–286.

Tasa, K., Taggar, S., & Seijts, G. H. (2007). The development of collective efficacy in teams: A multilevel and longitudinal perspective. *Journal of Applied Psychology, 92,* 17–27.

Taylor, A., & Greve, H. R. (2006). Superman or the Fantastic Four? Knowledge combination and experience in innovative teams. *Academy of Management Journal, 49,* 723–740.

Thompson, L. (2003). Improving the creativity of organizational work groups. *Academy of Management Executive, 17,* 96–109.

Thompson, L. L., & Choi, H. (2006). *Creativity and innovation in organizational teams.* Mahwah, NJ: Lawrence Erlbaum Associates.

Tjosvold, D. (1991). *The conflict-positive organization: Stimulate diversity and create unity.* Reading, MA: Addison-Wesley.

Tjosvold, D., & Sun, H. F. (2002). Understanding conflict avoidance: Relationship, motivations, actions, and consequences. *International Journal of Conflict Management, 13,* 142–164.

Tjosvold, D., Tang, M. M. L., & West, M. A. (2004). Reflexivity for team innovation in china: The contribution of goal interdependence. *Group & Organization Management, 29,* 540–559.

Trzcieliński, S., & Wypych-Żółtowska, M. (2008). Toward the measure of virtual teams effectiveness. *Human Factors and Ergonomics in Manufacturing, 18,* 501–514.

Van de Ven, A. H., & Delbecq, A. L. (1974). The effectiveness of nominal, delphi, and interacting group decision making processes. *Academy of Management Journal, 17,* 605–621.

van der Zee, K. I., & Paulus, P. B. (2008). Social psychology and modern organizations: Balancing between innovativeness and comfort. In L. Steg, A. P. Buunk & T. Rothengatter (Eds.), *Applied social psychology: Understanding and managing social problems* (pp. 271–290). New York, NY: Cambridge University Press.

van Knippenberg, D., & Schippers, M. C. (2007). Work group diversity. *Annual Review of Psychology, 58,* 515–541.

van Oudenhoven-van der Zee, , Paulus, P. B., Vos, M., & Parthasarathy, N. (2009). The impact of group composition and attitudes towards diversity on anticipated outcomes of diversity in groups. *Group Processes & Intergroup Relations, 12,* 257–280.

Wageman, R., Fisher, C. M., & Hackman, J. R. (2009). Leading teams when the time is right: Finding the best moments to act. *Organizational Dynamics, 38*, 192–203.

Walvoord, A. A. G., Redden, E. R., Elliot, L. R., & Coovert, M. D. (2008). Empowering followers in virtual teams: Guiding principles from theory and practice. *Computers in Human Behavior, 24*, 1884–1906.

Watson, W. E., Kumar, K., & Michaelsen, L. K. (1993). Cultural diversity's impact on interaction process and performance: Comparing homogeneous and diverse task groups. *Academy of Management Journal, 36*, 590–602.

Webster, J., & Staples, D. S. (2006). Comparing virtual teams to traditional teams: An identification of new research opportunities. In J. J. Martocchio (Ed.), *Research in personnel and human resources management* (vol. 25, pp. 181–215). San Diego, CA: Elsevier Science/JAI Press.

Wesner, M. S. (2008). Assessing training needs for virtual team collaboration. In J. Nemiro, M. M. Beyerlein, L. Bradley & S. Beyerlein (Eds.), *The handbook of high-performance virtual teams: A toolkit for collaborating across boundaries* (pp. 273–294). San Francisco, CA: Jossey-Bass.

West, M. A. (1990). The social psychology of innovation in groups. Innovation and creativity at work. In M. A. West & J. L. Farr (Eds.), *Psychological and organizational strategies* (pp. 309–333). Oxford, UK: John Wiley & Sons.

West, M. A. (2002). Sparkling fountains or stagnant ponds: An integrative model of creativity and innovation implementation in work groups. *Applied Psychology: An International Review, 51*, 355–387.

West, M. A. (2003). Innovation implementation in work teams. In P. B. Paulus & B. A. Nijstad (Eds.), *Group creativity: Innovation through collaboration* (2nd ed.) (pp. 245–276). New York, NY: Oxford University Press.

Williams, K. Y., & O'Reilly, C. A. III. (1998). The complexity of diversity: A review of forty years of research. In M. Neale, E. Mannix & D. H. Gruenfeld (Eds.), *Research on managing in groups and teams* (Vol. 1). Greenwich, CT: JAI Press.

Wuchty, S., Jones, B. F., & Uzzi, B. (2007). Increasing dominance of teams in production of knowledge. *Science, 316*, 1036–1039.

Zaccaro, S. J., Heinen, B., & Shuffler, M. (2009). Team leadership and team effectiveness. In E. Salas, G. F. Goodwin & C. S. Burke (Eds.), *Team effectiveness in complex organizations: Cross-disciplinary perspectives and approaches* (pp. 83–111). New York, NY: Routledge.

Ziegler, R., Diehl, M., & Zijlstra, G. (2000). Idea production in nominal and virtual groups: Does communication improve group brainstorming. *Group Processes & Intergroup Relations, 3*, 141–158.

Creativity and Innovation: The Role of Team and Organizational Climate

Michael A. West and Claudia A. Sacramento
Aston University, Birmingham, UK

INTRODUCTION

Creativity is heralded as key for organizational survival and success. As global economic models become the norm and competitiveness assumes an international character, leaders realise that, in order to prosper in a highly challenging environment, companies must innovate. The source of organizational innovation is unquestionably the ideas generated by individuals and teams.

Perhaps driven by the organizational imperatives for creativity and innovation, scholars have in recent years made substantial progress in understanding the factors that can promote creativity in organizations (Amabile & Mueller, 2008; Shalley & Zhou, 2008), with studies demonstrating the importance of individual factors such as personality (e.g., Feist, 1998) but also of environmental variables such as leadership, team processes and organizational support (Tierney, Farmer, & Graen, 1999; West et al., 2003). Research findings consistently show that the environment plays a key influence on creativity (Oldham & Cummings, 1996; Woodman, Sawyer, & Griffin, 1993) and although a number of contextual factors have been identified (Shalley & Gilson, 2004; Shalley, Zhou, & Oldham, 2004), many scholars stress the importance of climate (Amabile, Conti, Coon, Lazenby, & Herron, 1996; Ekvall, 1996; Tesluk, Farr, & Klein, 1997; West & Anderson, 1996). So, which climate characteristics are favourable to the development of creativity? How can organizations enable people to deploy their creativity in ways that lead to progress and new understanding?

In this chapter we argue that creative, innovative organizations are places where there is a firm and shared belief among most members in an inspirational vision of what the

Handbook of Organizational Creativity.
DOI: 10.1016/B978-0-12-374714-3.00015-X

359

organization is trying to achieve. There is a high level of interaction, discussion, constructive debate, and influence among the members of the organization as they go about their work. Trust, cooperative orientations, and a sense of interpersonal safety characterize interpersonal and intergroup relationships. Members of the organization, particularly those at the upper echelons (and there are few echelons) are consistently positive and open to members' ideas for new and improved ways of working, providing both encouragement and the resources for innovation. Finally, such organizations operate in situations where the demands on them are high; they are under strong external pressure, but members see this positively as a challenge rather than an impossible burden.

In order to support these assertions, we will explore what psychological and management research suggests are the values, attitudes, and shared meanings that characterize the environment and climate of innovative organizations. We make sense of this domain of social science research by distinguishing between creativity and innovation implementation. Creativity can be seen as the development of new ideas, while innovation implementation is the application of those new ideas in practice (West, 1990, 2002). Creativity, we propose, requires individuals with creative characteristics, who feel free from threat and pressure, and work in a supportive environment. Innovation requires diversity (of knowledge particularly), integration of people's knowledge and efforts, external challenge or demand, and practical support for innovation. We also suggest that an understanding of the organizational climates that promote creativity and innovation requires a consideration of effects at the individual, team, and organizational levels.

This chapter is structured in the following way: We begin by introducing the importance of context in creativity and innovation theory. We then turn to the concept of organizational climate, and we provide a summary of different existent taxonomies of climate for creativity and innovation. After this overview, we summarize the literature looking at the impact of both team and organizational climates on individual, team, and organizational creativity and innovation. We then turn to a discussion of the role of climate in the successful implementation of top-management geared innovations. Finally we discuss some of the practical implications of creative climate research and we suggest possible avenues for future research.

THE IMPORTANCE OF CONTEXT IN CREATIVITY AND INNOVATION THEORY

Climate is a contextual feature and therefore an understanding of the role of climate in creativity theory implies an understanding of the broader role attributed to the context in general. Yet, before discussing the role of context, we should start by clarifying what we mean by creativity and innovation. Innovation can be described as:

"the intentional introduction and application within a job, work team or organization of ideas, processes, products or procedures which are new to that job, work team or organization" *(West & Farr, 1990, p. 9)*.

Innovation can be seen as encompassing two major stages, the development of ideas—creativity; followed by their implementation—the introduction of new and improved products, services, and ways of doing things at work. Although several definitions of creativity can be found in the recent organizational creativity literature, they are consensual in stressing that creativity implies novelty and usefulness (Amabile, 1988; George & Zhou, 2002; Pamela Tierney & Farmer, 2002).

In order to contextualize the importance of climate on organizational creativity and innovation it is useful to look at how this literature evolved. Organizational creativity research has its intellectual roots both in creativity research in general, which has been conducted primarily within psychology, and on macro-level approaches to the study of organizational innovation. In contrast with macro-level innovation research, which focused essentially on contextual factors but disregarded the individual (e.g., Aiken & Hage, 1971), psychology research placed less emphasis on the context and more importance on identifying the characteristics of the creative individual. For instance, the "person approach", which represented one of the dominant schools of thought in the psychological study of creativity, conceptualized creativity as the constellation of personality and intellectual traits shown by individuals who, when given sufficient autonomy, spent significant amounts of time engaged in the creative process (Findlay & Lumsden, 1988). Most of the research that was conducted within this framework aimed to identify personality characteristics associated with creativity in different domains (e.g., Barron & Harrington, 1981; James & Asmus, 2000; MacKinnon, 1962).

The development of the social psychological approach to the study of creativity was to a great extent responsible for bringing together these two research streams, integrating the importance of both individual features and contextual characteristics (Amabile, 1983). Although these efforts had already been initiated (e.g., Baldridge & Burnham, 1975), the social–psychological approach brought a new impetus to this research agenda. Next, we briefly describe two models central to this approach, with reference to the role they attribute to the context.

Amabile's Componential Model (1983) describes creativity as the product of the combination of three factors: domain relevant skills, which refer to factual knowledge and expertise in a certain domain; creativity-relevant skills, which refer to the strategies and cognitive styles that influence idea production; and intrinsic motivation, conceptualized as the individual's genuine interest in the task. Amabile attributes special relevance to intrinsic motivation because this component can make the difference between what one can do (determined by domain relevant skills and creativity-relevant skills) and what one will in fact do. In other words, intrinsic motivation determines the extent to which domain relevant skills and creativity-relevant skills will be fully and appropriately applied towards successful creative performance. Amabile gives the environment a critical role in this model. The social world is given special relevance because it has the potential to influence any of the three components that are conducive to creativity, in particular intrinsic motivation. In summary, a core contribution of Amabile's (1993) proposal is to have highlighted the role played by contextual factors such as organizational climate in influencing the individual features critical for creativity. We will refer back to this model later in this chapter when discussing organizational climate features.

The importance of context was further stressed by Woodman, Sawyer and Griffin (1993). In their multilevel, interactionist model of creativity, the authors suggest that creativity is a phenomenon that is influenced by both situational and dispositional factors. The authors propose that creativity is the product of a complex person–situation interaction influenced by events of the past as well as salient aspects of the current situation. They stress that:

C. GROUP LEVEL INFLUENCES

"individual creativity is a function of antecedent conditions (e.g., past reinforcement history, biographical variables), cognitive style and ability (e.g., divergent thinking, ideational fluency), personality factors (e.g., self-esteem, locus of control), relevant knowledge, motivation, social influences (e.g., social facilitation, social rewards), and contextual influences (e.g., physical environment, task and time constraints)" *(p. 294)*.

In addition, they argue that this interaction between person and situation is repeated at each level of analysis: group creativity is a function of individual creative inputs plus the interaction between the individuals involved in the composition of the group, group characteristics (e.g., size), group processes (e.g., conflict), and contextual influences (e.g., the larger organization, task characteristics). Finally, organizational creativity is also a function of the interaction between the creative outputs of its component groups and contextual influences (such as organizational climate and culture, reward systems, resources, or the external environment). As the componential model previously suggested, the interactionist model also stresses the role played by the context, but it further adds the notion that the effects between person and situation are not simply additive but are instead of an interactive nature. This implies that in order to fully understand creativity, one has to consider the interplay between the person and the environment. This idea is the foundation for a rich stream of research that has strongly contributed to the understanding of organizational creativity and innovation. We will return to this notion of interaction between person and situation when discussing recent developments on the effect of team climate on creativity. Note that this emphasis on the role of context in the creativity literature runs in parallel with the trend observed in the general organizational behavior literature (Johns, 2006).

Next, we turn to the concept of climate.

Organizational Climate

Central to most, if not all models of organizational behavior, are perceptions of the work environment, referred to generally as "organizational climate" (Rousseau, 1988). Organizational climate has occupied a pivotal role in the organizational sciences dating from Lewin's classic work on motivation in the 1950s (Lewin, 1951), and was formalized through the human relations movement of the 1960s (Argyris, 1958). Primarily understood as the intervening variable between the context of an organization and the responses and behavior of its members, the concept has inspired many descriptions and operationalizations. Schneider (1990) defined climate as employees':

"perceptions of the events, practices, and procedures and the kinds of behavior that are rewarded, supported, and expected in a setting" (*p. 384*).

Climate refers to the perceptions of the work environment and the term can designate descriptions and perceptions at the individual, group, or organizational level of analysis. Individual perceptions of the work environment are usually termed psychological climate, and, when shared to a level sufficient for aggregation to the group or organizational level, are labelled group or organizational climate.

Individuals can describe the organizational environment both in an overall global sense, as well as in a more specific, targeted manner. In relation to the global organizational environment, James and his colleagues (James & James, 1989) describe four dimensions of global organizational climate, which have been identified across a number of different work contexts:

1. role stress and lack of harmony (including role ambiguity, conflict and overload, subunit conflict, lack of organizational identification, and lack of management concern and awareness),
2. job challenge and autonomy (as well as job importance),
3. leadership facilitation and support (including leader trust, support, goal facilitation and interaction facilitation, and psychological and hierarchical influence), and
4. work group cooperation, friendliness, and warmth (as well as responsibility for effectiveness; James & McIntyre, 1996).

James suggests that individuals develop a global or holistic perception of their work environment (e.g., James & Jones, 1974), which could be applied to any number of contexts and industries.

More recently, researchers have departed from a general conceptualization of climate and have turned their focus to specific types or facets of climate, such as climate for safety, climate for service and climate for initiative (Baer & Frese, 2003; Schneider & Reichers, 1983; Schneider, Wheeler, & Cox, 1992). Next we briefly outline a number of climate for creativity and innovation taxonomies that, in line with this trend, have been suggested in the literature.

Climate for Creativity and Innovation: Taxonomies

Based on different theoretical frameworks, several models of climate have been developed identifying a number of dimensions that can influence creativity and innovation (cf. Hunter, Bedell, & Mumford, 2007).

West and colleagues' climate model is, in our awareness, the only model focusing on team level climate (Anderson & West, 1998; West, 1990; West & Anderson, 1996). Based on a theory of team innovation, the authors developed a four factor model including:

1. vision,
2. participative safety,
3. task orientation, and
4. support for innovation.

In contrast, Amabile and colleagues' (1996) climate model, grounded in a theory of intrinsic motivation, focuses at the broader organizational climate. Based on qualitative and quantitative work, the authors identified the following eight dimensions:

1. work group support,
2. organizational encouragement,
3. supervisory encouragement,
4. challenging work,
5. freedom,
6. resources,
7. work load pressure, and
8. organizational impediments.

Focusing on a theory of psychological processes, Ekval and colleagues (Ekvall, 1996; Ekvall & Ryhammar, 1999; Ekvall & Tangebergandersson, 1986; Isaksen, Lauer, Ekvall, & Britz, 2000) proposed a 9 dimensional model integrating:

1. challenge and involvement,
2. freedom,
3. trust and openness,
4. idea time,
5. playfulness and humor,
6. conflict,
7. idea support,
8. debate, and
9. risk-taking.

We note that other models more strongly embedded in organizational management theory have also been developed (e.g., Abbey & Dickson, 1983; Tesluk, Farr, &. Klein, 1997).

Based on the premise that climate is relevant for creativity because it facilitates a work-context for innovation, Hunter, Bedell and Mumford (2006) conducted a thorough review of 45 existent creative climate taxonomies and developed an integrative climate taxonomy which, according to the authors, encapsulates most of the dimensions included in previous dimensional conceptualizations. The 14 dimensions are:

1. positive peer group,
2. positive supervisor relations,
3. resources,
4. challenge,
5. mission clarity,
6. autonomy,
7. positive interpersonal exchange,
8. intellectual stimulation,
9. top management support,
10. reward orientation,
11. flexibility and risk taking,
12. product emphasis,
13. participation, and
14. organizational integration.

Aligned with some of the taxonomies described above, several instruments have been developed to assess a climate for creativity. To name just a few, we highlight KEYS (Amabile, et al., 1996); the Team Climate for Innovation (TCI; Anderson & West, 1998; West & Farr, 1989); the Siegal Scale of Support for Innovation (SSSI; Siegel & Kaemmerer, 1978), and the Creative Climate Questionnaire (CCQ, Ekvall, 1996). We will refer in more detail to TCI and KEYS later in this chapter (for a comprehensive review see Mathisen & Einarsen, 2004).

West's team climate model (1990) and Amabile and colleagues' work environment model (1996) are arguably the most widely validated models of climate for creativity and innovation. Moreover, they complement each other in accounting for the more proximal team climate and the more distal organizational climate influences. Thus, our following discussions on team and organizational climates will be grounded on these two frameworks. After this introductory overview, we turn to a discussion of the aspects of team and organizational climate that influence creativity and innovation.

INDIVIDUAL CREATIVITY AND INNOVATION

As discussed earlier, creativity can be seen as the development of new ideas, while innovation implementation is the application of those new ideas in practice. Creativity, we suggest, requires individuals with creative characteristics, who feel free from threat and pressure, and work in a supportive environment. Innovation requires groups and organizations with shared vision, knowledge diversity, integration of efforts and skills, external challenge or demand, and practical support for innovation.

The innovation process begins with the creativity of individuals, so the generation of a new idea is a cognitive process, located within individuals, albeit fostered by interaction processes, for example, in teams (Mumford & Gustafson, 1988). Creative cognitions occur when individuals feel "free from pressure, safe, and positive" (Claxton, 1997). Experimental manipulations of stress levels support this conclusion, since they show that high levels of stress lead to a reliance on habitual solutions. Prince (1975) considers the corollary of this and argues, on the basis of applied work in organizations focused on increasing creativity, that speculation in work settings (a critical creative process) makes us feel vulnerable because we tend to experience our workplaces as unsafe (a finding also reported by Nicholson & West, 1988, in a study of the experience of work among UK managers). Questioning the person who comes up with an idea too closely, joking about the proposal (even in a light way), or simply ignoring it can lead to the person feeling defensive, which tends to "reduce not only his speculation but that of others in the group." Prince goes on:

> "The victim of the win–lose or competitive posture is always speculation, and therefore idea production and problem solving. When one speculates he becomes vulnerable. It is easy to make him look like a loser." *(Prince, 1975).*

Moreover, psychological threats to face or identity are also associated with more rigid thinking, and time pressure increases rigidity of thinking on work-related tasks such as selection decisions.

While some theories of creativity and flow suggest that creative work is primarily sustained by intrinsic motivation (Amabile, 1997), emerging research evidence suggests that extrinsic rewards can complement intrinsic motivation. Rewards appear to be counterproductive only if they serve to displace attention from the task towards the reward. There is evidence that extrinsic rewards can encourage individual innovation implementation (Eisenberger & Cameron, 1996).

The characteristics of work roles (discernible in job descriptions and in practice) also influence both creativity and innovation implementation. Oldham and Cummings (1996) found that five job characteristics predicted levels of individual innovation at work: skill variety, task identity, task significance, autonomy, and task feedback. Skill variety refers to the degree to which a job requires different activities in order for the work to be carried out, and the degree to which the range of skills and talents of the person working within the role is used. Thus a nurse working with the elderly in their homes may need to use her professional skills of dressing wounds, listening, counselling, being empathic, and appraising the supports and dangers in the person's home. Task identity is the degree to which the job represents a whole piece of work. It is not simply adding a rubber band to the packaging of a product, but being involved in the manufacture of the product throughout the process, or at least in a meaningful part of the process. Significance of the task in terms of its impact upon other people within the organization, or in the world at large, has an influence on creativity. Monitoring the effectiveness of an organization's debt collection is less significant than addressing the well-being of elderly people in rural settings, and may therefore evoke less creativity. Autonomy refers to the freedom, independence, and discretion for the people performing tasks, in determining how to do their work and when to do it. When people receive feedback on their performance they are more likely to become aware of the "performance gaps". Consequently they are more attuned to the need to initiate new ways of working in order to fill the gaps. Of course this also implies they have clear job objectives.

Human beings minimize effort in their activities and therefore some external stimulus is necessary to prompt the extra effort required to innovate. Among individual health workers we have found, in a number of studies, that high work demands are significant predictors of individual innovation (Bunce & West, 1995, 1996; West, 1989). Indeed, studies of work role transitions show that changing role objectives, strategies, or relationships is a common response to the demands of new work environments (West, 1987). Andrews (1979) too found that moderate time pressure was generally associated with higher creativity amongst R&D scientists. Of course, excessive work demands can have detrimental effects also on stress levels, absenteeism, and turnover.

TEAM CLIMATE FOR CREATIVITY AND INNOVATION

In most organizations people work in teams, and individual creativity is often enacted in this context (Shalley, et al., 2004). Thus, team climate, as a more proximal influence than organizational climate, is likely to have a fundamental importance to the extent to which team members will engage in creative behavior, and also on the degree to which the team as a whole will be able to deliver an innovative output.

In order to understand how the climate in a team or group affects creativity and innovation, we consider first the external environment or climate of the group in relation to the level of demand or uncertainty the group faces and after we discuss the internal climate of the group.

The external context of the group's work, be it organizational climate, market environment, or environmental uncertainty, is likely to have a highly significant influence both on its creativity and innovation implementation. Borrill and colleagues (2000) explored innovation in 100 UK primary health care teams. Innovations reported by the teams were rated blind by external raters who were experts in the domain of primary health care. The external demands of the health care environment were assessed using a UK government index of health and illness for each local area (the Jarman Index). Perceived levels of participation by team members were also measured using the Team Climate Inventory (Anderson & West, 1998). Where levels of participation in the team were high, team innovation was also high, but only in environments characterized by high levels of ill health, with associated strong external demands on the health care professionals. These findings suggest that if

TABLE 15.1 Team Climate Factors for Innovation.

- Clarifying and ensuring commitment to group vision
- Participative safety and trust
- Task Orientation
- Support for innovation
- Participation in decision making
- Managing conflict and minority influence constructively
- Reflexivity

the environment of teams is demanding and uncertain, it is likely that they will innovate in order to reduce the uncertainty and level of demand. Innovation implementation involves changing the status quo, which implies resistance, conflict, and a requirement for sustained effort. A team that attempts to implement innovation is likely to encounter resistance and conflict among others in the organization, and therefore sustained effort is required to overcome these disincentives to innovate. But effort itself is aversive—like most species, we strive to achieve our goals while expending the minimum effort necessary. So the effort required to innovate has to be motivated, at least partly, by external demands.

We ground our analysis of internal team climate on West's (1990) team climate theory, which aimed to integrate extant research and to identify the critical team factors that impact team innovation. We start by focusing on the factors included in the four factor model of team climate for innovation (West & Anderson, 1998) identified earlier. While doing so, we review a number of studies that have captured team climate applying the TCI (Anderson & West, 1996, 1998). This is a four factor inventory that has been widely validated across different cultural contexts (Mathisen, Torsheim, & Einarsen, 2006; Tjosvold, Tang, & West, 2004). Then, based on West's model of team innovation (2002), we extend our discussion to include three other variables that have been shown to also affect team innovation, these are participation in decision making, conflict management and minority dissent, and team reflexivity.

Clarifying and Ensuring Commitment to Shared Vision

Ensuring clarity of and commitment to shared team objectives or vision is a sine qua non for integrating knowledge diversity to meet task requirements for teamwork. In the context of group innovation, ensuring clarity of team objectives is likely to facilitate innovation by enabling focused development of new ideas, which can be filtered with greater precision than if the team objectives are unclear. Pinto and Prescott (1987), in a study of 418 project teams, found that a clearly stated mission was the only factor which predicted success at all stages of the innovation process (conception, planning, execution, and termination). Research evidence from studies of the top management teams of hospitals (West & Anderson, 1996) and of primary health care teams (Borrill, West, Shapiro, & Rees, 2000) provides clear support for the proposition that clarity of and commitment to team goals is associated with high levels of team innovation.

Participative Safety and Trust

Intragroup safety refers to the sense of psychological or psychosocial safety which group members feel in the presence of their fellow group members, particularly during whole group interactions. It includes the related concepts of group affective tone, safety climate and conflict acceptance, which are described below. Groups that consistently develop intra-group safety, it is proposed, by encouraging positive group affect, constructive management of conflict, and creating a climate within which it is safe to learn, will be both more creative and more innovative.

George (1996) uses the term group affective tone to refer to:

> "... consistent or homogenous affective reactions within a group. If, for example, members of a group tend to be excited, energetic and enthusiastic, then the group itself can be described as being excited, energetic and enthusiastic. As another example, if members of a group tend to be distressed, mistrustful and nervous, then the group also can be described in these terms." (p. 78).

George believes that a group's affective tone will determine how innovative (and effective) the group will be. Relevant to this belief is evidence that when individuals feel positive, they tend to connect and integrate divergent stimulus materials—they are more creative (Cummings, 1998; Isen, 1984; Isen & Daubman, 1984; Isen, Daubman, & Nowicki, 1987; Isen, Johnson, Mertz, & Robinson, 1985); see inter-relatedness among diverse stimuli; and use broader, inclusive categories (Isen & Daubman, 1984; Isen, et al., 1987).

How does this affect group or team behavior? George suggests that if all or most individuals in a work group tend to feel positive at work (the group has a "high positive affective tone") then their cognitive flexibility will be amplified as a result of social influence and other group processes. As a result of these individual and group level processes, the group will develop shared (and flexible) mental models. In effect, groups with a high positive affective tone will be more creative.

Jehn (1995) found that norms reflecting the acceptance of conflict within a group, promoting an open and constructive atmosphere for group discussion, enhanced the positive effect of task based conflict on individual and team performance for 79 work groups and 75 manager groups. Members of high performing groups were not afraid to express their ideas and opinions. Such a finding further reinforces the notion that safety may be an important factor in idea generation or creativity. Indeed, Tjosvold (1998) makes a strong case, based on his considerable research, that the management of conflict in a cooperative context will lead to a greater sense of integration and safety among the parties. Safety is the consequence of the management of diversity in views rather than the cause. If we operate in situations where there is no diversity or there is no conflict, we never have the opportunity to discover safety in our psychosocial environment. In one study in the service sector (West & Wallace, 1991) cohesiveness in primary health care teams predicted levels of team innovation.

Similarly, there is evidence that teams differ in the extent to which they create a climate of safety within which it is possible to engage in group learning. Edmondson (1996) demonstrated differences between teams in a study of hospital patient care, finding significant differences across work groups in their management of medication errors. In some groups members openly acknowledged and discussed their medication errors (giving too much or too little of a drug, or administering the wrong drug) and discussed ways to avoid their occurrence. In others, members kept information about errors to themselves. Learning about the causes of these errors as a team and devising innovations to prevent future errors were only possible in groups of the former type.

Task Orientation

Task orientation can be described as a shared concern with excellence of quality of task performance in relation to shared vision or outcomes (West, 1990, p. 313). Within groups, the task orientation factor is evidenced by emphasis on individual and team accountability; control systems for evaluating and modifying performance; reacting upon work methods and team performance; intra-team advice; feedback and cooperation; mutual monitoring; appraisal of performance and ideas; clear outcome criteria; exploration of opposing opinions; constructive controversy (Tjosvold, 1982); and a concern to maximize quality of task performance. This factor hence describes a general commitment to excellence in task performance, coupled with a climate which supports the adoption of improvements to established policies, procedures, and methods. Empirical evidence supports the relevance of task orientation. In a study involving hospital top management teams, it was found that task orientation was significantly correlated with experts' ratings of radicalness of innovations. In addition, Bain, Mann, and Pirola-Merlo (2001) found that task orientation in research teams was positively correlated with a number of innovation-related outcomes, such as individual innovation and number of patents registered and also with team performance. This pattern was not so consistent for those teams involved in project development, suggesting that the relevance might be higher for teams involved in creative endeavours.

Support for Innovation

Innovation is more likely to occur in groups where there is support for innovation, and where innovative attempts are rewarded rather than punished (Amabile, 1983; Kanter, 1983). Support for innovation is the expectation, approval, and practical support for attempts to introduce new and improved ways of doing things in the work environment (West, 1990). Within groups, new ideas may be routinely rejected or ignored, or attract verbal and practical support. Such perceptions powerfully shape individual and group attitudes (for reviews see e.g., Hackman, 1992) and will encourage or discourage team members to introduce innovations. In a longitudinal study of 27 hospital top management teams, support for innovation emerged as a powerful predictor of team innovation (measured by independent evaluations of implemented innovations; West & Anderson, 1996). Further studies in TV production teams (Carter & West, 1998), primary health care teams, and community mental health teams (Borrill, et al., 2000) have also strongly supported this finding (see also Agrell & Gustafson, 1996).

In a recent study, Eisenbeiss, van Knippenberg and Boerner (2008) explored how different aspects of climate interplayed with each other to affect team innovation. In a sample including 33 research and development teams, they found that support for innovation interacted with climate for excellence, defined as shared group norms about excellence of quality of task performance, in such a way that support for innovation enhanced team innovation only when climate for excellence was high. This finding suggests that in some circumstances the positive effect of one climate dimension might only be triggered if it is in synergy with other climate dimensions. In addition, this study also explored the antecedents of team climate and found that transformational leadership was positively related with support for innovation.

Participation in Decision-Making

Participation in teams can, under appropriate conditions, lead to high levels of creativity. Group members can be motivated to perform at higher levels of creativity by social comparison processes (providing group members and teams with a comparison standard) and providing feedback on individual performance (Paulus, Dzindolet, Poletes, & Camacho, 1993; Paulus, Larey, Putman, Leggett, & Roland, 1996).

Sharing ideas with others in a team (via sustained participation) can also increase the chances of producing quite novel ideas, but this requires that group members attend to one another's ideas (Paulus, 2000). Also recent research evidence suggests that enhanced creativity can occur as a result of group participation not just during but also after group meetings (Paulus & Yang, 2000).

There are obvious reasons for supposing that participation will be linked to team innovation. To the extent that information and influence over decision-making are shared within teams, and there is a high level of interaction amongst team members, the cross fertilization of perspectives which can spawn creativity and innovation is more likely to occur (Cowan, 1986; Mumford & Gustafson, 1988; Pearce & Ravlin, 1987; Porac & Howard, 1990). More generally, high participation in decision-making means less resistance to change and therefore greater likelihood of innovations being implemented. When people participate in decision-making through having influence, interacting with those involved in the change process, and sharing information, they tend to invest in the outcomes of those decisions and to offer ideas for new and improved ways of working (Kanter, 1983; King, Anderson, & West, 1992). Studies of teams in oil companies, health care, a TV program production organization, and in top management support this proposition (Borrill, et al., 2000; Burningham & West, 1995; Carter & West, 1998; Poulton & West, 1999; West, Patterson, & Dawson, 1999).

Managing Conflict and Minority Dissent Constructively

Many scholars believe that the management of competing perspectives is fundamental to the generation of creativity and innovation (Mumford & Gustafson, 1988; Nemeth & Owens, 1996; Tjosvold, 1998). Such processes are characteristic of task-related or information conflict (as opposed to conflicts of interest, emotional or interpersonal conflict—see De Dreu & De Vries, 1997) and arise primarily from a common concern with quality of task performance in relation to shared objectives. Information conflict is evidenced by appraisal of, and constructive challenges to, the group's task processes and performance. In essence, team members are more committed to performing their work effectively and excellently than they are either to bland consensus or to personal victory in conflict with other team members over task performance strategies or decision options.

Dean Tjosvold and colleagues (Tjosvold, 1982; Tjosvold & Field, 1983; Tjosvold & Johnson, 1977; Tjosvold, Wedley, & Field, 1986) have presented cogent arguments and strong supportive evidence that such constructive (task-related) controversy in a cooperative group context improves the quality of decision-making and creativity. Constructive controversy is characterized by full exploration of opposing opinions and frank analyses of task-related issues. It occurs when decision-makers believe they are in a cooperative group context, where mutually beneficial goals are emphasized, rather than in a competitive context; where decision makers feel their personal competence is confirmed rather than questioned; and where they perceive processes of mutual influence rather than attempted dominance.

An important perspective on conflict and creativity is offered by minority influence theory. A number of researchers have shown that minority consistency of arguments over time is likely to lead to change in majority views in groups (see e.g., Maass & Clark, 1984).

The experimental evidence suggests that, while majorities bring about attitude change through public compliance prior to attitude change (i.e., the individual first publicly conforms to the majority view prior to internalizing that view), minority influence works in the opposite direction. People exposed to a confident and consistent minority change their private views prior to expressing public agreement. Minority influence researchers have labelled this process as "conversion". Research on minority influence suggests that conversion is most likely to occur where the minority is consistent and confident in the presentation of arguments. Moreover, it is a behavioral style of persistence that is most likely to lead to attitude change and innovation (Nemeth & Owens, 1996).

De Dreu and De Vries (1997) suggest that a homogenous workforce in which minority dissent is suppressed will evidence low levels of creativity, innovation, individuality, and independence (De Dreu & De Vries, 1993; Nemeth & Staw, 1989). Disagreement about ideas within a group can be beneficial, and some researchers even argue that team task or information-related conflict is valuable, whether or not it occurs in a collaborative context, since it can improve decision-making and strategic planning (Cosier & Rose, 1977; Mitroff, Barabba, & Kilmann, 1977; Schweiger, Sandberg, & Rechner, 1989). This is because task-related conflict may lead team members to re-evaluate the status quo and adapt their objectives, strategies, or processes more appropriately to their situation (Coser, 1970; Nemeth & Staw, 1989; Roloff, 1987; Thomas, 1979). From the perspective of systems theory, De Dreu (1997) invokes the concept of requisite variety to suggest that disagreement and variety are necessary for systems to adapt to their environment and perform well (Ashby, 1956).

In a study of newly formed postal work teams in the Netherlands, De Dreu and West found that minority dissent did indeed predict team innovation (as rated by the teams' supervisors), but only in teams with high levels of participation (De Dreu & West, 2001). It seems that the social processes in the team that are necessary for minority dissent to influence the innovation process are characterized by high levels of team member interaction, influence over decision-making, and information sharing. This finding has significant implications for our understanding of minority dissent in groups operating in organizational contexts.

Overall, therefore, task-related (as distinct from emotional or interpersonal) conflict within a psychosocially safe environment, and minority dissent in a participative environment will lead to innovation, by encouraging debate and consideration of alternative interpretations of information available, leading to integrated and creative solutions.

Reflexivity

Team reflexivity is:

> "the extent to which team members collectively reflect upon the team's objectives, strategies and processes as well as their wider organizations and environments, and adapt them accordingly." *(West, 1996, p. 559).*

There are three central elements to the concept of reflexivity: reflection, planning, and action or adaptation. Reflection consists of attention, awareness, monitoring, and evaluation of the object of reflection. Planning is one of the potential consequences of the indeterminacy of reflection, since during this indeterminacy, courses of action can be contemplated, intentions formed, plans developed (in more or less detail) and the potential for carrying them out is built up. High reflexivity exists when team planning is characterized by greater detail, inclusiveness of potential problems, hierarchical ordering of plans, and long as well as short range planning. The more detailed the implementation plans, the greater the likelihood that they will be manifest in innovation (Frese & Zapf, 1994; Gollwitzer, 1996). Indeed the work of Gollwitzer suggests that innovation will be implemented almost only when a team has articulated implementation intentions. This is because planning creates a conceptual readiness for and guides team members' attention towards relevant opportunities for action and means to implement the innovation. Action refers to goal-directed behaviors relevant to achieving the desired changes in team objectives, strategies, processes, organizations, or environments identified by the team. In a variety of studies, links between reflexivity and team innovation and effectiveness have been demonstrated (Borrill et al., 2000; Carter & West, 1998; Tjosvold et al., 2004).

Recent meta-analytical evidence brings additional support for the role of team climate on individual and team innovation. In a quantitative review spanning three decades of research and including 104 independent studies, Hülsheger, Anderson and Salgado (2009) found that support for innovation (.47), vision (.49), task orientation (.42), and external communication (.47) displayed the strongest relationships with an overall indicator of innovation, while team composition and structure showed weaker effect magnitudes (between .02 and .16). The effect of participative safety, although significant, was not as strong as the other group climate variables (.15). However, it should be noticed that the relationship between climate and innovation was stronger for team than individual innovation, and that these relationships were also stronger when self-ratings of innovation were employed, compared with independent ratings or objective measures of innovation. Regardless of these methodological moderators, this meta-analysis provides clear evidence for the effect of team climate on creativity and innovation. A key message for managers is that they should place greater emphasis in developing a team climate for innovation as the largest effects on innovation stem from this factor.

NEW DEVELOPMENTS IN TEAM CLIMATE RESEARCH: APPLYING PERSON–SITUATION THEORIES

In order to better understand how team climate, as a contextual feature, can influence creativity and innovation, recent work has looked at theories of person-in-situation (Hirst, van Knippenberg, Yat-Sen, & Sacramento, in press; Hirst, van Knippenberg, & Zhou, 2009). Person-in-situation theories describe how situational influences may either restrain or invite the expression of individual differences (Mischel, 1977; Tett & Burnett, 2003). Seminal work by Mischel (1977) suggests that strong contexts, of which a strong climate can be an example, limit the number of behavioral patterns that are acceptable and consequently decrease response variation between individuals. In such circumstances, individual differences in factors that promote creativity are not so relevant and the context takes a dominant role. In contrast, weak situations permit a wide range of acceptable behavior, and place little constraint on individuals. In such circumstances, individual factors that facilitate creativity are of more critical relevance. Tett and Burnett (2003) offered an alternative perspective to understand the relationship between person and situation. Their trait activation theory suggests that features of the context can promote and facilitate the expression of individual dispositions when the contextual influence is relevant to the disposition. The context can actually activate individual features that are complementary to the contextual influence, enhancing the expression of individual differences.

Based on trait-activation theory, Hirst et al. (2009) hypothesized and found support for an interaction effect between team learning behavior and individual goal orientation. Building on the premise that team context can shape the expression of individual differences, the authors argued that team learning behavior is a particularly relevant contextual factor for bringing out learning-oriented individuals' disposition to engage in learning. In line with their predictions, they found that individuals with high learning and high performance orientation responded more favourably in terms of creativity to a team climate characterized by high team learning behavior. Individuals with low learning and performance orientations were less likely to be motivated by team learning behavior, as there was no trait to be activated. In a subsequent study, Hirst et al. (in press) showed that the context may not only invite the creative expression of individual differences that can lead to creativity but also can restrain them. The authors looked at how the relationship between a team's bureaucratic climate and goal orientation affected creativity and found that learning goal orientation and performance-approach orientation were positively related to creativity primarily when two bureaucracy dimensions, centralization and formalization, were low. When centralization and formalization were high the relationships between these goal orientations and creativity were much weaker or not significant at all. These studies show that person-in-situation theories can offer a powerful framework to help in mapping the complex relationships between individual features and team climate for creativity and innovation.

In this section we have reviewed the key external and internal team climate factors that research and theory suggest will influence individual and team innovation: shared vision, participative safety, task orientation, support for innovation, participation in decision making, constructive management of conflict and dissent, and reflexivity, combined with an external environment that creates demands for innovation. However, what of organizational climate as a whole?

ORGANIZATIONAL CLIMATE FOR CREATIVITY AND INNOVATION

Several scholars have analysed how organizational climates can be conducive to innovation (Abbey & Dickson, 1983; Amabile & Gryskiewicz, 1987; Ekvall, Arvonen, & Waldenstrom-Lindblad, 1983). Amabile's componential model of creativity and innovation, introduced earlier in this chapter, (Amabile, 1988, 1997) provides a link between the work environment, individual and team creativity, and organizational innovation. Building on her seminal componential model of creativity described earlier, Amabile (1983) extended her theory to account for how individual and team creativity unfolds within a work environment (Amabile, 1988). The organizational work environment is conceptualized as having three key characteristics: organizational motivation to innovate describes an organization's basic orientation toward innovation, as well as its support for creativity and innovation; management practices include the management at all levels of the organization, but most importantly the level of individual departments and projects; supervisory encouragement and work group support are two examples of relevant managerial behavior or practices; and resources are related to everything that an organization has available to support creativity at work. Amabile proposes that the higher the concurrent levels of these three aspects of the organizational environment, the more the innovation in organizations.

The central statement of the theory is that elements of the work environment will impact individual and team creativity by influencing expertise, task motivation, and creativity skills. The influence of intrinsic task motivation on creativity is considered essential; even though the environment may have an influence on each of the three components, the impact on task motivation is thought to be the most immediate and direct. Furthermore, creativity is seen as a primary source of organizational innovation.

Amabile's (1988) componential theory of creativity and innovation offers a detailed and specific conceptual model, from which a corresponding and useful questionnaire to assess the work environment for creativity was derived. KEYS: assessing the climate for creativity provides a validated instrument to fulfill this purpose (Amabile, et al., 1996). The model and the instrument focus on individuals' perceptions of relevant organizational dimensions and their influence on creativity.

In a study examining whether and how the work environments of highly creative projects differed from the work environments of less creative projects, Amabile and colleagues found that eight sub-dimensions consistently differed between high-creativity and low-creativity projects (Amabile et al., 1996). These are encouragement of creativity, including organizational (1), supervisory (2) and work group support (3), autonomy (4), resources (5), pressures, including both the positive effect of challenge (6) and the negative effect of workload pressure (7), and organizational impediments to creativity (8). (See table 15.2 for details).

Organizational encouragement for creativity refers to several aspects within the organization. The first is encouragement of risk taking and idea generation, a valuing of innovation from the highest to the lowest levels of management. The second refers to a fair and supportive evaluation of new ideas; the authors underline this by referring to studies that showed that whereas threatening and highly critical evaluation of new ideas undermined creativity in laboratory studies, in field research supportive, informative evaluation can enhance the intrinsically motivated state that is most conducive to creativity. The third aspect of organizational encouragement focuses on reward and recognition of creativity; in a series of studies, Amabile and colleagues (1996) showed that a reward perceived as a bonus, a confirmation of one's competence, or a means of enabling one to do better, more interesting work in the future can stimulate creativity, whereas the mere engagement in an activity to obtain a reward can be detrimental. The final aspect refers to the important role of collaborative idea flow across the organization, participative management, and decision making in the stimulation of creativity. Supervisory encouragement stresses the aspects goal clarity, open supervisory interactions, and perceived supervisory support. Whereas goal clarity might have an effect on creativity by providing a clearer problem definition, Amabile et al. (1996) argue that open supervisory interactions as well as perceived supervisory support may influence creativity through preventing people from experiencing fear of negative criticism that can undermine the intrinsic motivation necessary for creativity. Work group support indicates the encouragement of activity through the particular work group. The four aspects thought to be relevant for this are team member diversity, mutual openness to

TABLE 15.2 The Conceptual Categories, KEYS-Scales, and Sample Items of the Work Environment for Creativity.

Conceptual Categories of Work Environment	Scales for Assessing Perceptions of the Work Environment (KEYS-scale)	Sample Item	
Encouragement of creativity	Organizational encouragement	People are encouraged to solve problems creatively in this organization	(+)
	Supervisory encouragement	My supervisor serves as a good working model	(+)
	Work group support	There is free and open communication within my work group	(+)
Autonomy or freedom	Freedom	I have the freedom to decide how I am going to carry out my projects	(+)
Resources	Sufficient resources	Generally, I can get the resources I need for my work	(+)
Pressures	Challenging work	I feel challenged by the work I am currently doing	(+)
	Workload pressure	I have too much work to do in too little time	(−)
Organizational impediments to creativity	Organizational impediments	There are many political problems in this organization	(−)

(Table Adapted from Amabile et al., 1996)

Note: (+) indicates stimulants to creativity; (−) indicates obstacles to creativity.

ideas, constructive challenging of ideas, and shared commitment to the project; whereas the former two may influence creativity through exposing individuals to a greater variety of unusual ideas, the latter two are thought to increase intrinsic motivation.

Freedom refers to an individual's discretion to decide upon their own work. When introducing this factor, Amabile et al. (1996) refer to previous research evidence showing that individuals produce more creative work when they perceive themselves to have choice in how to execute their tasks (Amabile & Gitomer, 1984).

Resources made available by the company are another important factor, because aside from the obvious practical limitations that lack of resources impose, individual perceptions of the adequacy of resources may also lead to beliefs about the intrinsic values of the projects undertaken, which will have obvious implications for individual commitment to the project (Amabile et al., 1996).

Challenge is regarded as a moderate degree of workload pressure that arises from the urgent, intellectually challenging problem itself (Amabile, 1988; Amabile et al., 1996). The authors carefully distinguish challenge from excessive workload pressure, which is supposed to be negatively related to creativity, and suggest that time pressure may add to the perception of challenge in the work if it is perceived as a concomitant of an important, urgent project. This challenge, in turn, may be positively related to intrinsic motivation and creativity.

In reporting the last of the eight factors, organizational impediments, Amabile et al. (1996) refer to a few studies indicating that internal strife, conservatism, and rigid, formal management structures represent obstacles to creativity. The authors suggest that, because these factors may be perceived as controlling, their likely negative influence on creativity may evolve from an increase in individual extrinsic motivation (a motivation through external factors but not the task itself) and a corresponding decrease in the intrinsic motivation necessary for creativity. However, research on impediments to creativity is still comparatively limited in comparison to research on stimulants.

In conclusion, the practical usefulness of the inventory can be seen as considerable, as was further indicated in a subsequent study during an organization's downsizing, where the KEYS-scales sensitively pictured changes in the organization's work environment relevant to creativity (Amabile & Conti, 1999).

Empirical work by Hunter, Bedell, and Mumford (2007) brings additional support to the role of organizational climate in creativity and innovation. In a meta-analytical study involving 42 independent studies, the authors examined the relationships between the 14 climate dimensions they had previously synthesized (Hunter, et al., 2006) and various indices of creative performance. They found climate dimensions to be effective predictors of creative performance across criteria, samples, and settings (overall effect size .75, with range varying between .48 and .91). The strongest predictors were positive interpersonal exchange (.91), intellectual stimulation (.88), and challenge (.85). Overall, their results suggest that creative achievement is more strongly related to individual perceptions of personally significant, local events than with general organizational influences, such as reward structures or organizational learning. This work also sheds light into the moderators of the relationship between climate and innovation. For instances, the results showed that, although climate exerted sizable effects when measures of creative achievement were obtained at the individual level, larger climate effects were obtained in studies that assessed creative achievement at the group level, mirroring the results reported by Hülsheger and colleagues (2009). In addition, these climate dimensions were especially effective predictors of creative performance in turbulent, high-pressure, and competitive environments.

IMPLEMENTING IDEAS TOP–DOWN: ORGANIZATIONAL CLIMATE FOR IMPLEMENTATION AND INNOVATION-VALUES FIT

So far we have identified a number of factors that can foster the generation and transference of ideas from lower to higher organizational units, promoting a bottom–up innovation process. There are also situations in which the innovation process is mostly characterized by a top–down approach. One example is when the top management team decides to implement a new working process, and needs to persuade employees to commit to its use. Note that these two options are not exclusive and they might very well be linked: an employee might have an idea about a new method to improve the manufacturing of a product; his or her team can further refine the initial idea, which is then communicated to the top management team. If the top management team approves it, they will then have to persuade all other teams across the organization to start using the new process. This stage can be designated as implementation of innovation (but note that implementation of innovation does not necessarily imply the involvement of the top-management team or a top–down approach).

Seeking to shed light on this side of the innovation process, Klein and Sorra (1996) developed a conceptual model describing both the determinants and consequences of implementation effectiveness, which they defined as:

" the consistency and quality of targeted organizational members' use of an innovation" *(p. 1055)*.

According to the authors, many innovations fail not because they are strategically inadequate, but because they are not effectively implemented. Implementation effectiveness is relevant because it leads to innovation effectiveness, defined as the benefits an organization receives as a result of the implementation of a given innovation, provided that the innovation adoption was strategically correct. Implementation effectiveness is influenced by two key factors.

The first factor has to do with the fit between the innovation and the employees' values. Organizational values are implicit or explicit views, shared by organizational members, about both the external adaptation of the organization and its internal integration. Innovation-values fit is the extent to which employees, who are expected to adhere to the innovation (targeted users), perceive that the use of the innovation will promote or impair the fulfilment of their values. This means that the proposed innovation needs to be aligned with the values espoused by the organizational members. Klein and Sorra (1996) provide an insightful example of a poor fit situation involving a manufacturing company's attempt to adopt a computerized inventory control system. Until then the manufacturing procedures had been very unstructured and highly flexible, allowing employees to make judgements concerning, for example, using preliminary work completed for one client to address a rushed order submitted by another client. Employees believed that customers were well served by these flexible procedures. In contrast, the new computerized system required employees to track each customer's work from start to finish, making it impossible to move work done between clients. Because this new inventory control system limited flexibility, the employees perceived a poor fit between this innovation and their values of supporting flexible production procedures, resulting in poor employee commitment to its use. The impact of a values' fit on implementation effectiveness is suggested to be mediated by employee commitment. If the innovation-values fit is low, then employees will feel less committed, and the chances of implementation effectiveness are lowered.

The second factor refers to climate for implementation, defined as the:

"targeted employees' shared summary perceptions of the extent to which their use of a specific innovation is rewarded, supported, and expected within the organization" *(Klein & Sorra, 1996, p. 1060)*.

A strong implementation climate is characterized by the existence of comprehensive and consistent implementation policies and practices that are perceived by targeted employees to encourage, cultivate, and reward their use of a given innovation. This involves three key aspects:

1. ensuring that employees have appropriate skills to use the innovation,
2. proving incentives for innovation use, and
3. removing any obstacles that might make difficult innovation use.

C. GROUP LEVEL INFLUENCES

If an organization wants to create a strong climate for implementing a particular innovation, it should engage in a number of actions beforehand: it should ensure that employees receive adequate training that empowers them to use the innovation; it should make assistance after training readily available; it also should allow for enough time for learning and transiting between systems. In addition, the company needs to make available a system to respond promptly to employees' concerns and complaints. It is also fundamental that supervisors praise and reward employees for correct adoption of the innovation. Finally, the innovation should be easily accessed. Klein and Sorra (1996) refer to a situation in which the employees reacted very positively to a new three-dimensional computer graphics program introduced by an engineering and construction company. The implementation was unsuccessful, however, because after the initial training employees had very little chance to use the new program, leading to a sharp skill decrease after training.

Implementation effectiveness is highest when there is both a strong implementation climate and good values, fit. In such circumstances, employees will be enthusiastic and there will be a committed and consistent use of the innovation. On the other hand, when implementation climate is weak and employees perceive very low values' fit, commitment to its use will be practically non-existent, resulting in very low implementation effectiveness. A situation that should be avoided is one in which employees perceive high values' fit but the implementation climate is very low. This leads to frustration and disappointment and lack of trust in any future innovations that the organization might try to implement.

Klein, Coon, and Sorra (2001) subsequently partially tested this conceptual model in a field study involving 39 manufacturing plants and 1219 employees. The authors found that financial resource availability and management support for technology implementation engendered high-quality implementation policies and practices and a strong climate for implementation, which in turn fostered implementation effectiveness. A key contribution of this research line is that it highlights the role organizations can play in developing a climate that fosters adherence to innovations geared by higher organizational echelons.

PRACTICAL IMPLICATIONS

Recent developments in the understating of how climate affects creativity and innovation have direct implications for the work of managers interested in promoting these outcomes. A key lesson is that managers can foster creativity, not only by selecting individuals with characteristics that can lead to creativity, but also by crafting environments that nurture the expression of individual differences that are conducive to creativity. Consequently, managers can have a broader scope of intervention and also a greater responsibility for their companies' creative output. While earlier research informed managers about how to select for creative potential, recent developments highlight their role in developing workplaces in which creativity is triggered.

In addition, research on creative climates has led to the development of tools that can aid managers in promoting such climates. Instruments such as KEYS or TCI enable managers to have a better understanding of the extent to which the organizational and team climates of their companies are promoting creativity or if instead they are acting against the development and implementation of new ideas. Managers can also use these instruments to plan for more specific interventions which target an aspect of climate that is particularly weak because they specify which areas are stronger and weaker at a given point in time.

These questionnaires should be applied and interpreted with great care. As with all diagnostic instruments, it is important to contextualize the results when providing feedback to managers and organizational members. This is particularly true when applying these tools in a setting different from the Western context in which they were developed. For example, although the TCI has been tested across different countries (e.g., Agrell & Gustafson, 1994; Brodbeck & Maier, 2001), more needs to be known about the validity of the instrument in different cultural backgrounds.

Another issue to take into consideration when using these instruments is the computation of the scores and their meaning. Typical applications of the TCI and KEYS aggregate the results across the different members of the unit of analysis and calculate a mean score for the team (or department/organization) for each factor. Although the factor elevation is meaningful, practitioners and managers should also pay attention to the configuration of results in each team. A team in which all six members have an average of 3 on the dimension *supervisory support* has a different climate from a team in which three members score 1 and three members score 5. Although the overall average is the same in both cases, the first example represents a team in which all members perceive supervisor support to be moderate, while the latter case suggests that half the members have a very positive perception of *supervisory support* and the other half has the opposite perception (perhaps reflecting the existence of variation in the quality of leader–member exchange across the team, Hoper & Martin, 2008). These different configurations have very different consequences for team creativity and call for different interventions in terms of improving *supervisory support*.

SUGGESTIONS FOR FUTURE RESEARCH

Although researchers have made significant progress over the last decade, many questions remain unanswered concerning climates for creativity and innovation. For instance, although cross-level research has started to analyze how team and organizational level climate constructs interplay with individual characteristics to affect creativity (e.g., Hirst et al., 2009; Hirst et al., in press), this puzzle is still far from complete. More systematic research is needed in order to understand how different climate features can enhance but also mask the effects of individual characteristics on creativity.

Furthermore, a number of terminologies identifying different climate dimensions are now available, but we know very little about the impact of these different dimensions across contexts. Although recent meta-analytical work has begun to analyze the differential strength of the different work environment dimensions (Hunter et al., 2007), further research is needed in order to understand how the impact of the different dimensions varies across contexts. For instance, it is possible that *challenge* is more relevant in routine jobs while *supervisory support* plays a greater role in jobs involving ambiguous tasks.

In addition, research evaluating the effectiveness of climate change interventions is necessary. Efforts to improve the climate for creativity and innovation have to be studied in more detail, as it is important to understand which strategies are more effective in promoting climate change. For example, should these efforts be initiated at higher, more distal, levels of the organization or should they be decentralized? Also, more research is needed to understand the antecedents of climate for creativity and innovation (Ekvall & Ryhammar, 1999). Although research has emphasised the effects of leadership (e.g., Eisenbeiss et al., 2008), other variables, such as team composition are also likely to play a role in the development of the team environment for creativity.

We also know very little about how changes in the climate for creativity occur over time. It is important to understand how climate change unfolds over time and which factors can accelerate or impede the development of a more positive climate for creativity in order to be able to intervene more effectively. Amabile and Conti (1999) found that climate for creativity significantly decreased over time during a downsizing process. It would be equally interesting to study climate changes after an intervention focusing on the development of a positive climate for creativity. Indeed, there is very little empirical evidence available concerning the lag effects of climate change interventions and more longitudinal research is needed to address this question (see also Anderson, De Dreu & Nijstad, 2004).

CONCLUSION

Findings across a range of levels and sectors make it clear that innovation only occurs where there is strong cultural support for efforts to introduce new and improved products and procedures. At the same time, opportunities to develop and implement skills in the workplace and to innovate are central to the satisfaction of people at work (Nicholson & West, 1988), while innovation is vital to the effectiveness of organizations in highly demanding and competitive environments.

This review has argued that creative, innovative organizations are those where employees perceive and share an appealing vision of what the organization is trying to achieve—one therefore that is consistent with their values. Innovative organizations have vigorous and enjoyable interactions and debates between employees at all levels about how best to achieve that vision. Conflicts are seen as opportunities to find creative solutions that meet the needs of all parties in the organizations rather than as win–lose situations. Also, people in such organizations have a high level of autonomy, responsibility, accountability, and power—they are free to make decisions about what to do, when to do it, and who to do it with. Trust, cooperativeness, warmth, and humor are likely to characterize interpersonal and intergroup interactions. There is strong practical support for people's ideas for new and improved products, ways of working or of managing the organization. Senior managers are more likely than not to encourage and resource innovative ideas, even when they are unsure of their potential value (within safe limits). Such organizations will almost certainly find themselves in uncertain, dynamic, and demanding environments, whether this is due to competition, scarcity of resources, changing markets or legislation, or to global and environmental pressures. After all, that is why innovation has always occurred—humans have adapted their organizations and ways of working to fit to the changing environments they find themselves in. That is how we have developed so astonishingly as an animal species. Continuing to encourage organizational cultures and climates that promote organizational creativity, and thereby human well being, is how we can continue this process.

References

Abbey, A., & Dickson, J. W. (1983). R&D work climate and innovation in semiconductors. *Academy of Management Journal, 26,* 362–368.

Agrell, A., & Gustafson, R. (1996). Innovation and creativity in work groups. In M. A. West (Ed.), *Handbook of work group psychology* (pp. 317–343). Chichester, UK: Wiley.

Aiken, M., & Hage, J. (1971). The organic organization and innovation. *Sociology, 5,* 63–82.

Amabile, T. M. (1983). The social-psychology of creativity: A componential conceptualization. *Journal of Personality and Social Psychology, 45,* 357–376.

Amabile, T. M. (1988). A model of creativity and innovation in organizations. In B. M. Staw & L. L. Cummings (Eds.), *Research in organizational behavior* (Vol. 10, pp. 123–167). Grenwich, CT: JAI Press.

Amabile, T. M. (1997). Motivating creativity in organizations: On doing what you love and loving what you do. *California Management Review, 40,* 39–58.

Amabile, T. M., Conti, R., Coon, H., Lazenby, J., & Herron, M. (1996). Assessing the work environment for creativity. *Academy of Management Journal, 39,* 1154–1184.

Amabile, T. M., & Gitomer, J. (1984). Childrens artistic creativity: Effects of choice in task materials. *Personality and Social Psychology Bulletin, 10,* 209–215.

Amabile, T. M., & Gryskiewicz, S. S. (1987). *Creativity in the R & D laboratory.* Greensboro, NC: Centre for Creative Leadership.

Amabile, T. M., & Mueller, J. S. (2008). Assessing creativity and its antecedents: An exploration of the componential theory of creativity. In J. Zhou & C. E. Shalley (Eds.), *Handbook of organizational creativity* (pp. 31–62). Boca Raton, FL: Taylor & Francis Group.

Anderson, N., & West, M. A. (1998). Measuring climate for work group innovation: Development and validation of the team climate inventory. *Journal of Organizational Behavior, 19,* 235–258.

Anderson, N., De Dreu, C. K. W., & Nijstad, B. A. (2004). The routinization of innovation research: A constructively critical review of the state–of–the-science. *Journal of Organizational Behavior, 25,* 147–173.

Andrews, F. M. (1979). *Scientific Productivity.* Cambridge, UK: Cambridge University Press.

Argyris, C. (1958). Some problems in conceptualizing organizational climate: A case study of a bank. *Administrative Science Quarterly, 2,* 501–520.

Ashby, W. R. (1956). *An introduction to cybernetics.* London, UK: Methuen.

Baer, M., & Frese, M. (2003). Innovation is not enough: Climates for initiative and psychological safety, process innovations, and firm performance. *Journal of Organizational Behavior, 24,* 45–68.

Bain, P. G., Mann, L., & Pirola-Merlo, A. (2001). The innovation imperative: The relationship between team climate, innovation, and performance in research and development teams. *Small Group Research, 32,* 55–73.

Baldridge, J. V., & Burnham, R. A. (1975). Organizational innovation: Individual, organizational, and environmental impacts. *Administrative Science Quarterly, 20,* 165–176.

Barron, F., & Harrington, D. M. (1981). Creativity, intelligence and personality. *Annual Review of Psychology, 32,* 439–476.

Borrill, C., West, M. A., Shapiro, D., & Rees, A. (2000). Team working and effectiveness in health care. *British Journal of Health Care, 6,* 364–371.

Borrill, C. S., Carletta, J., Carter, A. J., Dawson, J. F., Garrod, S., & Rees, A., et al. (2000). *The effectiveness of health care teams in the National Health Service.* Aston Centre for Health Service Organisational Research University of Aston, Human Communications Research Centre, Universities of Glasgow and Edinburgh, Psychological Therapies Research Centre, University of Leeds.

Brodbeck, F. C., & Maier, G. W. (2001). The Team Climate Inventory (TCI) for innovation: A psychometric test on a German sample of work groups. *Zeitschrift Fur Arbeits–Und Organisationspsychologie, 45,* 59–73.

Bunce, D., & West, M. A. (1995). Self-perceptions and perceptions of group climate as predictors of individual innovation at work. *Applied Psychology: An International Review, 44,* 199–215.

Bunce, D., & West, M. A. (1996). Stress management and innovation interventions at work. *Human Relations, 49,* 209–232.

Burningham, C., & West, M. A. (1995). Individual climate, and group-interaction processes as predictors of work team innovation. *Small Group Research, 26,* 106–117.

Carter, S. M., & West, M. A. (1998). Reflexivity, effectiveness, and mental health in BBC-TV production teams. *Small Group Research, 29,* 583–601.

Claxton, G. L. (1997). *Have brain, tortoise mind: Why intelligence increases when you think less.* London, UK: Fourth Estate.

Coser, L. A. (1970). *Continuities in the study of social conflict.* New York, NY: Free Press.

Cosier, R., & Rose, G. (1977). Cognitive conflict and goal conflict effects on task performance. *Organizational Behavior and Human Performance, 19,* 378–391.

Cowan, D. A. (1986). Developing a process model of problem recognition. *Academy of Management Review, 11,* 763–776.

Cummings, A. (1998). *Contextual characteristics and employee creativity: Affect at work.* Paper presented at the 13th Annual Conference, Society for Industrial Organizational Psychology.

De Dreu, C. K. W. (1997). Productive conflict: The importance of conflict issue and conflict management. In C. K. W. D. Dreu & E. van der Vliert (Eds.), *Using conflict in organizations* (pp. 9–22). London, UK: Sage.

De Dreu, C. K. W., & De Vries, N. K. (1997). Minority dissent in organizations. In C. K. W. De Dreu & E. van der Vliert (Eds.), *Using conflict in organizations* (pp. 72–86). London, UK: Sage.

De Dreu, C. K. W., & West, M. A. (2001). Minority dissent and team innovation: The importance of participation in decision making. *Journal of Applied Psychology, 86,* 1191–1201.

Edmondson, A. C. (1996). Learning from mistakes is easier said than done: Group and organizational influences on the detection and correction of human error. *Journal of Applied Behavioral Science, 32,* 5–28.

Eisenbeiss, S. A., van Knippenberg, D., & Boerner, S. (2008). Transformational leadership and team innovation: Integrating team climate principles. *Journal of Applied Psychology, 93,* 1438–1446.

Eisenberger, R., & Cameron, J. (1996). Detrimental effects of reward: Reality or myth? *American Psychologist, 51,* 1153–1166.

Ekvall, G. (1996). Organizational climate for creativity and innovation. *European Journal of Work and Organizational Psychology, 5,* 105–124.

Ekvall, G., Arvonen, J., & Waldenstrom-Lindblad, I. (1983). *Creative organizational climate: Construction and validation of a measuring instrument* (No. 2). Stockholm, Sweden: Swedish Council for Management and Organizational Behavior.

Ekvall, G., & Ryhammar, L. (1999). The creative climate: Its determinants and effects at a Swedish university. *Creativity Research Journal, 12,* 303–310.

Ekvall, G., & Tangebergandersson, Y. (1986). Working climate and creativity—a study of an innovative newspaper office. *Journal of Creative Behavior, 20,* 215–225.

Feist, G. J. (1998). A meta-analysis of personality in scientific and artistic creativity. *Personality and Social Psychology Review, 2,* 290–309.

Findlay, C. S., & Lumsden, C. J. (1988). The creative mind: Toward an evolutionary theory of discovery and innovation. *Journal of Biological and Social Structures, 11,* 3–55.

Frese, M., & Zapf, D. (1994). Methodological issues in the study of work stress: Objective vs subjective measurement of work stress and the question of longitudinal studies. In C. L. Cooper & R. Payne (Eds.), *Causes, coping and consequences of stress at work* (pp. 371–411). Oxford, UK: John Wiley & Sons.

George, J. M. (1996). Group affective tone. In M. A. West (Ed.), *Handbook of work group psychology* (pp. 77–94). Chichester, UK: Wiley.

George, J. M., & Zhou, J. (2002). Understanding when bad moods foster creativity and good ones don't: The role of context and clarity of feelings. *Journal of Applied Psychology, 87,* 687–697.

Gollwitzer, P. M. (1996). The volitional benefits of planning. In P. M. Gollwitzer & J. A. Bargh (Eds.), *The psychology of action: Linking cognition and motivation to behavior* (pp. 287–312). New York, NY: The Guilford Press.

Hackman, J. R. (1992). Group influences on individuals in organizations. In M. D. Dunnette & L. M. Hough (Eds.), *Handbook of industrial and organizational psychology* (Vol. 3, pp. 199–267). Palo Alto, CA: Consulting Psychology Press.

Hirst, G., van Knippenberg, D., Yat-Sen, J., & Sacramento, C. A. (in press). How does bureaucracy impact on individual creativity? A cross-level investigation of team contextual influences on goal orientation–creativity relationships. *Academy of Management Journal.*

Hirst, G., van Knippenberg, D., & Zhou, J. (2009). A cross-level perspective on employee creativity: Goal orientation, team learning behavior, and individual creativity. *Academy of Management Journal, 52,* 280–293.

Hooper, D. T., & Martin, R. (2008). Beyond personal Leader–Member Exchange (LMX) quality: The effects of perceived LMX variability on employee reactions. *The Leadership Quarterly, 19,* 20–30.

Hülsheger, U. R., Anderson, N., & Salgado, J. F. (2009). Team-level predictors of innovation at work: A comprehensive meta-analysis spanning three decades of research. *Journal of Applied Psychology, 94,* 1128–1145.

Hunter, S. T., Bedell, K. E., & Mumford, M. D. (2006). Dimension of creative climate: A general taxonomy. *Korean Journal of Thinking and Problem Solving, 15,* 97–116.

Hunter, S. T., Bedell, K. E., & Mumford, M. D. (2007). Climate for creativity: A quantitative review. *Creativity Research Journal, 19,* 69–90.

Isaksen, S. G., Lauer, K. J., Ekvall, G., & Britz, A. (2000). Perceptions of the best and worst climates for creativity: Preliminary validation evidence for the situational outlook questionnaire. *Creativity Research Journal, 13,* 171–184.

Isen, A. M. (1984). The influence of positive affect on decision-making and cognitive organization. *Advances in Consumer Research, 11,* 534–537.

Isen, A. M., & Daubman, K. A. (1984). The influence of affect on categorization. *Journal of Personality and Social Psychology, 47,* 1206–1217.

Isen, A. M., Daubman, K. A., & Nowicki, G. P. (1987). Positive affect facilitates creative problem solving. *Journal of Personality and Social Psychology, 52,* 1122–1131.

Isen, A. M., Johnson, M. M., Mertz, E., & Robinson, G. F. (1985). The influence of positive affect on the unusualness of word associations. *Journal of Personality and Social Psychology, 48,* 1413–1426.

James, K., & Asmus, C. (2000). Personality, cognitive skills, and creativity in different life domains. *Creativity Research Journal, 13,* 149–159.

James, L. A., & James, L. R. (1989). Integrating work environment perceptions: Explorations into the measurement of meaning. *Journal of Applied Psychology, 74,* 739–751.

James, L. R., & Jones, A. P. (1974). Organisational climate: A review of theory and research. *Psychological Bulletin, 81,* 1096–1112.

James, L. R., & McIntyre, M. D. (1996). Perceptions of organizational climate. In K. R. Murphy (Ed.), *Individual differences and behavior in organizations.* San Francisco, CA: Jossey-Bass.

Jehn, K. A. (1995). A multimethod examination of the benefits and detriments of intragroup conflict. *Administrative Science Quarterly, 40,* 256–282.

Kanter, R. (1983). *The change masters.* New York, NY: Simon & Schuster.

King, N., Anderson, N., & West, M. A. (1992). Organizational innovation in the UK—a case-study of perceptions and processes. *Work and Stress, 5,* 331–339.

Klein, K. J., Conn, A. B., & Sorra, J. S. (2001). Implementing computerized technology: An organizational analysis. *Journal of Applied Psychology, 86,* 811–824.

Klein, K. J., & Sorra, J. S. (1996). The challenge of innovation implementation. *Academy of Management Review, 21,* 1055–1080.

Lewin, K. (1951). *Field theory in social science.* New York, NY: Harper.

Maass, A., & Clark, R. D. (1984). Hidden impact of minorities—15 years of minority influence research. *Psychological Bulletin, 95,* 428–450.

MacKinnon, D. W. (1962). The nature and nurture of creative talent. *American Psychologist, 17,* 484–495.

Mathisen, G. E., & Einarsen, S. (2004). A review of instruments assessing creative and innovative environments within organizations. *Creativity Research Journal, 16,* 119–140.

Mathisen, G. E., Torsheim, T., & Einarsen, S. (2006). The team-level model of climate for innovation: A two-level confirmatory factor analysis. *Journal of Occupational and Organizational Psychology, 79,* 23–35.

Mischel, W. (1977). The interaction of person and situation. In D. Magnusson & N. S. Endler (Eds.), *Personality as the crossroads: Current issues in interactional psychology* (pp. 333–352). Hillsdale, NJ: Erlbaum.

Mitroff, J., Barabba, N., & Kilmann, R. (1977). The application of behaviour and philosophical technologies to strategic planning: A case study of a large federal agency. *Management Studies, 24,* 44–58.

Mumford, M. D., & Gustafson, S. B. (1988). Creativity syndrome: Integration, application, and innovation. *Psychological Bulletin, 103,* 27–43.

Nemeth, C., & Owens, P. (1996). Making work groups more effective: The value of minority dissent. In M. A. West (Ed.), *Handbook of work group psychology* (pp. 125–141). Chichester, UK: Wiley.

Nemeth, C., & Staw, B. M. (1989). The trade offs of social control and innovation within groups and organizations. In L. Berkowitz (Ed.), *Advances in experimental social psychology* (pp. 175–210). New York, NY: Academic Press.

Nicholson, N., & West, M. A. (1988). *Managerial job change: Men and women in transition.* Cambridge, UK: University Press.

Oldham, G. R., & Cummings, A. (1996). Employee creativity: Personal and contextual factors at work. *Academy of Management Journal, 39,* 607–634.

Paulus, P. (2000). Groups, teams and creativity; The creative potential for idea-generating groups. *Applied Psychology: An International Review, 49,* 237–262.

Paulus, P., Dzindolet, M. T., Poletes, G., & Camacho, L. M. (1993). Perception of performance in group brainstorming: The illusion of group productivity. *Personality and Social Psychology Bulletin, 19,* 78–89.

Paulus, P. B., Larey, T. S., Putman, V. L., Leggett, K. L., & Roland, E. J. (1996). Social influence processes in computer brainstorming. *Basic and Applied Social Psychology, 18,* 3–14.

Paulus, P. B., & Yang, H. C. (2000). Idea generation in groups: A basis for creativity in organizations. *Organizational Behavior and Human Decision Processes, 82,* 76–87.

Pearce, J. A., & Ravlin, E. C. (1987). The design and activation of self-regulating work groups. *Human Relations, 40,* 751–782.

Pinto, J. K., & Prescott, J. E. (1987). Changes in critical success factor importance over the life of a project. *Academy of Management Proceedings, New Orleans,* 328–332.

Porac, J. F., & Howard, H. (1990). Taxonomic mental models in competitor definition. *Academy of Management Review, 2,* 224–240.

Poulton, B. C., & West, M. A. (1999). The determinants of effectiveness in primary health care teams. *Journal of Interprofessional Care, 13,* 7–18.

Prince, G. (1975). Creativity, self and power. In I. A. Taylor & J. W. Getzels (Eds.), *Perspectives in creativity* (pp. 249–277). Chicago, IL: Aldine.

Roloff, M. E. (1987). Communication and conflict. In C. R. Berger & S. H. Chaffee (Eds.), *Handbook of communication science* (pp. 484–534). Newbury Park, CA: Sage.

Rousseau, D. M. (1988). The construction of climate in organizational research. In C. L. Cooper & I. T. Robinson (Eds.), *International review of industrial and organizational psychology* (Vol. 3, pp. 139–158). Chichester, UK: Wiley.

Schneider, B. (1990). The climate for service: An application of the climate construct. In B. Schneider (Ed.), *Organizational climate and culture* (pp. 383–412). San Francisco, CA: Jossey-Bass.

Schneider, B., & Reichers, A. E. (1983). On the etiology of climates. *Personnel Psychology, 36,* 19–39.

Schneider, B., Wheeler, J. K., & Cox, J. F. (1992). A passion for service—using content-analysis to explicate service climate themes. *Journal of Applied Psychology, 77,* 705–716.

Schweiger, D., Sandberg, W., & Rechner, P. (1989). Experimental effects of dialectical inquiry, devil's advocacy, and other consensus approaches to strategic decision making. *Academy of Management Journal, 32,* 745–772.

Shalley, C. E., & Gilson, L. L. (2004). What leaders need to know: A review of social and contextual factors that can foster or hinder creativity. *Leadership Quarterly, 15,* 33–53.

Shalley, C. E., & Zhou, J. (2008). Organizational creativity research: Historical overview. In C. E. Shalley & J. Zhou (Eds.), *Handbook of organizational creativity* (pp. 3–32).

Shalley, C. E., Zhou, J., & Oldham, G. R. (2004). The effects of personal and contextual characteristics on creativity: Where should we go from here? *Journal of Management, 30,* 933–958.

Siegel, S. M., & Kaemmerer, W. F. (1978). Measuring the perceived support for innovation in organizations. *Journal of Applied Psychology, 63,* 553–562.

Tesluk, P. E., Farr, J. L., & Klein, S. R. (1997). Influences of culture and climate on individual creativity. *Journal of Creative Behavior, 31,* 27–41.

Tett, R. P., & Burnett, D. D. (2003). A personality trait-based interactionist model of job performance. *Journal of Applied Psychology, 88,* 500–517.

Thomas, K. W. (1979). Organizational conflict. In S. Kerr (Ed.), *Organizational behavior* (pp. 151–184). Columbus, OH: Grid Publishing.

Tierney, P., & Farmer, S. M. (2002). Creative self-efficacy: Its potential antecedents and relationship to creative performance. *Academy of Management Journal, 45,* 1137.

Tierney, P., Farmer, S. M., & Graen, G. B. (1999). An examination of leadership and employee creativity: The relevance of traits and relationships. *Personnel Psychology, 52,* 591–620.

Tjosvold, D. (1982). Effects of approach to controversy on superiors' incorporation of subordinates' infomation on decision making. *Journal of Applied Psychology, 67,* 189–193.

Tjosvold, D. (1998). Co-operative and competitive goal approaches to conflict: Accomplishments and challenges. *Applied Psychology: An International Review, 7,* 285–342.

Tjosvold, D., & Field, R. H. G. (1983). Effects of social-context on consensus and majority vote decision-making. *Academy of Management Journal, 26,* 500–506.

Tjosvold, D., & Johnson, D. W. (1977). The effects of controversy on cognitive perspective-taking. *Journal of Education Psychology, 69,* 679–685.

Tjosvold, D., Tang, M. M. L., & West, M. (2004). Reflexivity for team innovation in China—The contribution of goal interdependence. *Group & Organization Management, 29,* 540–559.

Tjosvold, D., Wedley, W. C., & Field, R. H. G. (1986). Constructive controversy, the Vroom-Yetton Model, and managerial decision-making. *Journal of Occupational Behaviour, 7,* 125–138.

West, M. A. (1987). Role innovation in the world of work. *British Journal of Social Psychology, 26,* 305–315.

West, M. A. (1989). Innovation amongst health-care professionals. *Social Behaviour, 4,* 173–184.

West, M. A. (1990). The social psychology of innovation in groups. In M. A. West & J. L. Farr (Eds.), *Innovation and creativity at work: Psychological and organizational strategies* (pp. 309–333). Chichester, UK: Wiley.

West, M. A. (1996). Reflexivity and work group effectiveness: A conceptual integration. In M. A. West (Ed.), *Handbook of work group psychology* (pp. 555–579). Chichester, UK: Wiley.

West, M. A. (2002). Sparkling fountains or stagnant ponds: An integrative model of creativity and innovation implementation in work groups. *Applied Psychology: An International Review, 51,* 355–387.

West, M. A., & Anderson, N. R. (1996). Innovation in top management teams. *Journal of Applied Psychology, 81,* 680–693.

West, M. A., Borrill, C. S., Dawson, J., Brodbeck, F., Shapiro, D., & Haward, B. (2003). Leadership clarity and team innovation in health care. *Leadership Quarterly, 14,* 393–410.

West, M. A., & Farr, J. L. (1989). Innovation at work—psychological perspectives. *Social Behaviour, 4,* 15–30.

West, M. A., & Farr, J. L. (1990). Innovation at work. In M. A. West & J. L. Farr (Eds.), *Innovation and creativity at work: Psychological and organizational strategies* (pp. 3–14). Chichester, UK: Wiley.

West, M. A., Patterson, M. G., & Dawson, J. F. (1999). A path to profit? Teamwork at the top. *Centrepiece, 4,* 6–11.

West, M. A., & Wallace, M. (1991). Innovation in health-care teams. *European Journal of Social Psychology, 21,* 303–315.

Woodman, R. W., Sawyer, J. E., & Griffin, R. W. (1993). Toward a theory of organizational creativity. *The Academy of Management Review, 18,* 293.

Creativity and the Work Context

Greg R. Oldham[1] and Markus Baer[2]

[1]Tulane University, A. B. Freeman School of Business, New Orleans, LA;
[2]Washington University in St. Louis, Olin Business School, St. Louis, MO

Substantial evidence suggests that employee creativity contributes to an organization's growth, effectiveness, and survival (Amabile, 1996; Damanpour & Schneider, 2006; Nonaka, 1991). When employees exhibit creativity at work, they generate novel, potentially useful ideas about organizational products, practices, services, or procedures (Oldham, 2002; Shalley, Zhou, & Oldham, 2004). The production of these creative ideas increases the likelihood that the employee and his or her colleagues will informally adopt the ideas and apply them in their own jobs and that the management of the organization will formally implement the ideas and introduce them in the organization as a whole or in the marketplace. It is the use and adoption of these ideas that allows firms to adjust to shifting market conditions, respond to opportunities, and thereby, to adapt, grow, and compete (Lee, Rho, Kim, & Jun, 2007; Nonaka, 1991).

Given the potential significance of employee creativity for the growth and effectiveness of organizations, it is not surprising that a wealth of recent studies have examined the possibility that there are personal and contextual conditions that serve to enhance (or restrict) the creativity employees exhibit at work (see George, 2007; Mumford, 2000; Shalley et al., 2004). The purpose of this chapter is to summarize and integrate the literature that has addressed the effects of contextual conditions on employee creativity. Since other chapters in this handbook focus on employees' personal characteristics (e.g., abilities and personality) (see Acar & Runco, this volume; see Hoff, Carlsson, & Smith, this volume), we discuss such characteristics only to the extent that they combine or interact with contextual conditions to affect employee creativity. In addition, we discuss the effects of the context on the creativity of employees who work in both team and individual, non-team settings. We provide a synthesis of what we currently know about the effects of contextual conditions on the creativity of employees in both settings, and then suggest a number of new directions for future research.

BACKGROUND

As indicated above, most contemporary theorists define creativity as the production of ideas concerning products, practices, services, or procedures that are (a) novel or original and (b) potentially useful to the organization (see Amabile, 1996; Shalley et al., 2004). Ideas are considered *novel* if they are unique relative to other ideas currently available in the organization. Ideas are considered *useful* if they have the potential for direct or indirect value to the organization, in either the short- or long-term. Given this definition, creative ideas can range from suggestions for small, incremental refinements in procedures or processes to radical, major breakthroughs in the development of new products or policies (Mumford & Gustafson, 1988). Finally, our definition assumes that creative ideas may be generated by employees in any job and at any level of the organization (Madjar, Oldham, & Pratt, 2002).

Our review includes published studies that contain measures of either individual or team creativity. The measures of creativity used in previous studies include the number of patent disclosures or technical reports written by employees (Tierney, Farmer, & Graen, 1999), the number of ideas submitted to suggestion programs (Frese, Teng, & Wijnen, 1999; Oldham & Cummings, 1996), bonuses awarded to employees on the basis of their evaluated creativity (Liao, Liu, & Loi, 2010), ratings by external observers, supervisors, and peers of employees' overall creativity (Grant & Berry, 2011; Zhou, 1998) or of the creativity of their specific ideas (Baer, Leenders, Oldham, & Vadera, 2010; Binnewies, Ohly, & Niessen, 2008), employee self-reported creativity (Shalley, Gilson, & Blum., 2009), and employee responses to established creativity tests (e.g., Luchins' water jar problem) (Amabile, 1987). We also include studies that use measures that *combine* the creativity of ideas generated by employees and their implementation in the team, work unit, or organization (e.g., De Dreu, 2006; Zhou & George, 2001). We refer to measures that include both creativity and implementation concepts as *creativity* throughout the chapter, although these measures clearly differ from those that measure the creativity of ideas alone. We exclude studies that focus exclusively on the implementation or adoption of ideas—since those studies did not include measures of the creativity of ideas themselves. Finally, we include in our review studies that have been conducted in both laboratory and field settings, as long as those studies addressed creativity and some aspect of the context.

CONCEPTUAL FRAMEWORK

To explain the effects of the work context (i.e., the characteristics of an employee's job, the ways in which work is organized, and the patterns of social interaction) on creativity, we rely on a framework derived from previous theoretical models (Amabile, 1988, 1996; Kahn, 1990, 1992). Our framework posits that two general conditions are critical if employees are to generate creative ideas—enhanced access and exposure to new and different pockets of information (i.e., ideas, perspectives, approaches) and full engagement in the job and work role. We are not suggesting that these are the only conditions that contribute to an employee's creativity at work—research suggests that there may be several others, including an employee's domain- and creativity-relevant skills (see Amabile, 1996). However, we focus on the information and engagement components specifically as extant research and theory suggest that they contribute to creativity, and because evidence suggests that contextual conditions can have a substantial impact on them (Amabile, 1996; Atwater & Carmeli, 2009; Madjar, 2008; Perry-Smith, 2006; Shin & Zhou, 2003; Zhang & Bartol, 2010).

We propose that enhanced access and exposure to new and different pockets of information (i.e., different from each other and from the information held by the focal individual) contributes to an employee's creativity, not only by providing new ideas directly (Madjar, 2008; Perry-Smith, 2006), but also by energizing the combinatory processes that underlie the production of creative ideas (Baer, 2010; Brass, 1995; Mumford & Gustafson, 1988; Perry-Smith & Shalley, 2003). Thus, to the extent that the work context facilitates access, exposure, and the exchange of new, unique information from other sources to the focal employee, the creativity of that employee should be enhanced.

Our second condition, engagement, suggests that creativity is enhanced when individuals are fully engaged in their work. When engaged, employees should be attentive, emotionally connected, and totally focused on their full work role performance (Kahn, 1990; May, Gilson, & Harter, 2004; Rich, LePine, & Crawford, 2010). By contrast, those who are disengaged are best characterized as passive and as relatively detached from their work roles. We expect an employee's engagement at work to have substantial effects on the extent to which he or she generates ideas that are truly novel and creative. Rich et al. (2010) suggest that those who are engaged are likely to step outside the bounds of their formally defined jobs and engage in acts that might benefit the work unit or organization. Naturally, such acts might include generating ideas for improving the organization's product and service offerings. Moreover, previous research suggests that individuals who are fully engaged in their work are not only more curious but also more willing to take risks, such as engaging in exploratory behaviors and experimentation—all of which should facilitate creativity (Baer & Oldham, 2006; Zhou & Shalley, 2003). Thus, any feature of a person's work context that boosts engagement should result in elevated levels of creativity. By contrast, those contextual features that restrict or undermine engagement should contribute to lowered employee creativity.

In the pages that follow, we review those contextual characteristics that have received attention in the literature, and explain how each characteristic may affect creativity based on the perspective we have presented. If the evidence reviewed suggests that the effects of the contextual characteristics may vary as a function of personal or other contextual conditions, we also discuss these moderating variables. We conclude with a discussion of the implications of all findings for practice and future research.

CONTEXTUAL CHARACTERISTICS

Job Design

The design of jobs has long been considered an important contributor to employee creativity (Shalley et al., 2004; West & Farr, 1990). Specifically, scholars have argued that jobs that are complex and challenging in nature produce the conditions necessary for the generation of novel and creative ideas (Amabile, 1996; Oldham & Cummings, 1996). Following the conceptual framework outlined above, we propose that the structure and content of an employee's job could have an impact on employee creativity via both the information and engagement components. With regard to the former, complex, challenging jobs often offer jobholders higher levels of autonomy and personal control (Hackman & Oldham, 1980), which should provide them with the freedom and discretion necessary to seek out new sources of information that will enable them to effectively complete their own job assignments. Moreover, many complex jobs include properties that require or permit the employee to interact with others, either inside or outside the boundaries of the organization (Morgeson & Humphrey, 2006; Turner & Lawrence, 1965). This interaction, whether work-related or not, may provide new information to the jobholder and expose him or her to different ideas and perspectives (Oldham & Hackman, 2010).

We also expect the content of employees' jobs to have a substantial impact on the aforementioned engagement component. Complex, challenging jobs include such characteristics as personal control, autonomy, skill variety, task significance, and job-based feedback (Hackman & Oldham, 1980; Karasek, 1979). Previous research has shown that jobs with such characteristics are experienced by jobholders as personally rewarding and meaningful which should enhance their positive affective states and boost their involvement and engagement in the work role (Fried & Ferris, 1987; Saavedra & Kwun, 2000). As noted earlier, we expect this enhanced engagement to contribute to the development of creative ideas.

A number of early investigations provide results that are generally consistent with these arguments. For example, studies have shown positive, significant correlations between objective indicators of job complexity and challenge derived from the Dictionary of Occupational Titles (Roos & Treiman, 1980) and both supervisor-rated creativity (Tierney & Farmer, 2002, 2004) and employee self-reported creativity (Shalley et al., 2009). Other studies have obtained similar findings using either self-reports (e.g., Amabile et al., 1996; Amabile & Gryskiewicz, 1989; Coelho & Augusto, 2010; Farmer, Tierney, & Kung-McIntyre, 2003; Martin, Salanova, & Peiro, 2007) or peer ratings (Raja & Johns, 2010) of an employee's job complexity. For example, Ohly, Sonnentag, and Pluntke (2006) found positive associations between self-reported creativity and employee descriptions of their job's overall complexity and personal control. Hatcher, Ross, and Collins (1989) found a significant correlation between a measure composed of three job characteristics (autonomy, variety, and feedback) and the number of new ideas employees submitted to an organization suggestion program. Also, Zhang and Bartol (2010) found a positive relation between a supervisor rating of employee creativity and an index composed of three job characteristics: variety, identity, and significance.

Although the large majority of previous studies have demonstrated that employees exhibit high levels of creativity when they work on challenging and complex jobs, a few studies found generally weak or inconsistent relations involving job complexity and creativity. For example, Oldham and Cummings (1996) found a significant correlation between an index composed of employee descriptions of five job characteristics (autonomy, skill variety, job feedback, task identity, task significance) and a supervisory rating of employee creativity. However, this study also reported non-significant relations involving this same job index and two additional creativity measures: ideas accepted by the organization's suggestion program and number of patent disclosures written. Using the identical job complexity index, Jaskyte (2008) showed that across two samples, job complexity had non-significant relations to employee self-reports of creativity. Choi, Anderson, and Veilette (2009) showed that a job's overall routinization and standardization had a non-significant link to peer-rated creativity, not the anticipated negative relation. Finally, Grant and Berry (2011) found a positive, significant association between supervisor-rated creativity and the job characteristic of autonomy, but a non-significant association involving skill variety.

Apparently, the link between job complexity and creativity is not that straightforward and, consequently, studies have explored the potential moderating conditions shaping these effects. For example, Oldham and Cummings (1996) showed that the index of job complexity described earlier related positively to contributions to a suggestion program when employees scored high on Gough's (1979) creative personality scale (CPS) and positively to patent disclosures written when the employee's supervisor had a non-controlling, supportive leadership style. In addition, the aforementioned study by Martin et al. (2007) demonstrated that the positive link between job control and employee creativity was further enhanced when employees also experienced high job demands. A study by Binnewies et al. (2008) showed that job control in fact related negatively to creativity, but only for younger employees. The creativity of older employees, on the other hand, was largely unaffected by increasing levels of control. Finally, Choi et al. (2009) showed that decreasing task standardization had positive effects on peer-rated creativity but only when employee self-reported creative ability was high.

In summary, the studies discussed in this section suggest that complex, challenging jobs generally have positive effects on employee creativity and that these effects may in fact by amplified or strengthened if certain personal and contextual characteristics are present (e.g., creative ability, supportive supervision). However, since so few studies have examined these moderating conditions, it is not yet clear which must be in place for the creative potential of complex jobs to be unlocked. More research is needed to identify conditions that consistently moderate the effects of the work itself on creativity. Moreover, research is also needed to examine the specific job characteristics that may be responsible for increasing access to information and boosting engagement. For example, we argued that the job dimension of "required interaction" (Turner & Lawrence, 1965) may be associated with many challenging jobs and that this job feature may increase access to new perspectives, thereby enhancing creativity (Tushman, 1977). However, no previous study has directly examined this job dimension, or linked it to either a measure of new perspectives or to creativity. The same can be said for many of the other job characteristics that are associated with complex jobs. Research is now needed to address these issues.

Goal Setting

Assigning performance goals or targets to individuals is a strategy that has long been used in an effort to motivate employees to achieve higher levels of productivity (Locke & Latham, 1990). Numerous studies have established that assigning difficult, challenging performance goals yields higher levels of productivity than assigning no goals, goals that are less difficult or challenging, or general, "do your best" goals (see Locke & Latham, 1990).

A few previous studies have also focused on the possibility that goal setting may affect individuals' creativity—not only their productivity. In general, this earlier work has examined the effects on creativity of two types of goals: performance goals as described above (e.g., produce X units in 20 minutes) and creativity goals (e.g., produce novel, useful ideas in 20 minutes) (see Shalley et al., 2004). Commentators have suggested that these two goal types are likely to have different effects on creativity, with performance goals expected to limit or constrain individuals' creativity (Amabile, 1996) and creativity goals expected to boost creative idea production (Shalley et al., 2004).

These possible effects may be understood by applying our conceptual framework. When individuals are assigned challenging performance goals, they are likely to focus their attention and energy on attaining these goals and, as a consequence, have less time and energy available to seek out or attend to new ideas and perspectives. All of this should result in lowered creativity. Likewise, since those with specific, challenging performance goals are likely to focus on goal attainment, they may be less focused on appreciating the qualities of their work roles (Shalley & Oldham, 1985), resulting in lower engagement and, consequently, creativity. By contrast, those assigned creativity goals should seek out new perspectives and knowledge since this information may increase the chances that they will achieve the creativity goal that has been assigned. In addition, creativity goals are likely to cause individuals to focus their attention on the task itself, thereby enhancing engagement and creativity (Shalley et al., 2004).

Only a few previous studies have tested the arguments concerning performance goals and they provide mixed results for the expected effects (e.g., Carson & Carson, 1993; Soriano de Alencar & Bruno-Faria, 1997). For example, a laboratory study by Shalley (1991) found that the creativity of those in a no performance goal condition was slightly, albeit not significantly, higher than those assigned either a "do-your-best" or difficult performance goal. There was no difference between the latter two goal conditions. A study by Carson and Carson (1993) demonstrated that the creativity level of individuals assigned a challenging performance goal was substantially lower than those assigned a creativity goal.

Results are also mixed with regard to the effects of creativity goals. For example, Shalley (1995, Study 2) showed that those assigned "do-your-best" creativity goals produced more creative work than those assigned no creativity goals. However, Shalley (1991) obtained results that were not completely consistent with these findings—those individuals assigned either "do-your-best" or challenging creativity goals exhibited creativity levels that were not significantly higher than those not assigned creativity goals. Finally, Madjar and Shalley (2008) examined the effects of goal setting on three tasks—two that required creative solutions and a third intervening task that did not. Results showed that individuals who were assigned challenging creativity goals for the tasks requiring creative solutions exhibited higher levels of creativity across both tasks than those not assigned creativity goals.

In summary, few studies have examined the effects of performance and creativity goals on individuals' creativity and the results of these studies are mixed. Research is now needed that investigates the specific conditions that moderate the effects of both types of goals and thereby sorts out the inconsistent results presented above. One possibility is that the effects of both types of goals might vary as a function of the extent to which the individual is involved in establishing the goal itself. It may be that those who are allowed to have an impact on the goal ultimately assigned may be more committed to that goal and more likely to be engaged in achieving it (Erez & Kanfer, 1983). Another possibility is that there may be individual differences in the way individuals respond to both performance and creativity goals. For example, it may be that individuals with a "learning goal orientation" (VandeWalle, 1997; VandeWalle, Cron, & Slocum, 2001) will react more positively when given a creativity goal, since achieving the goal would involve generating new uses and learning about one's capabilities. Finally, all of the studies that have been conducted have focused on the effects of goals on individuals' creativity. Future studies are now needed that examine the effects of both performance and creativity goals on the creative work produced by teams.

Competition

Competition, which refers to mutually exclusive goal attainment where the success of one party requires the failure of another (Deutsch, 1949), has long been suggested as a condition that is likely to undermine creativity (Amabile, 1996). Given the inherent incompatibility of goals created by competition, individuals should be less motivated to share and make available relevant information or resources that may aid others in attaining their goals. Under such conditions, information is likely to be hoarded and the free exchange of ideas and perspectives is inhibited. Furthermore, even when new information is made available, individuals may be hesitant to acknowledge or accept information from competitors because doing so threatens the self and its competence and may often be perceived as being tantamount to being a "follower" and losing status relative to the competitor (Menon & Pfeffer, 2003; Menon, Thompson, & Choi, 2006). Given that creativity often emerges when new and different sets of information are reshuffled or recombined (Hargadon & Bechky, 2006), establishing conditions that foster goal conflict, such as pitting individuals against each other for a chance of obtaining scare resources (e.g., promotions, prizes), is therefore likely to stifle the production of new, useful ideas. In addition, competition is likely to limit creativity because of its inhibiting effects on engagement. Cognitive and energy resources that could be invested in the job or task are likely to be absorbed by unnecessary activities, such as monitoring the performance of a competitor or contemplating the potential negative consequences of failing to beat the competition. As a result, individuals' engagement in the task or problem at hand is likely to suffer and creativity is likely to decline.

Although we expect competition between individuals to have generally negative effects on creativity, competition between groups and teams may have more nuanced effects (Amabile, 1996). Similar to competition between individuals, we expect intergroup competition to inhibit the free exchange of information between groups and teams (Hansen, Mors, & Løvås, 2005). However, unlike competition between individuals, intergroup competition has the potential to foster creativity by providing the motivational impetus necessary for groups to compensate for some of the process losses they are likely to experience. Specifically, competition may serve to weld groups together into tight-knit social units in which members view each other as interdependent and in which the distinction between self- and group-interest becomes blurred (Bornstein & Erev, 1994; Sherif & Sherif, 1953; Staw, Sandelands, & Dutton, 1981)—all of which are likely to boost within-group collaboration and engagement in the task, thereby enhancing subsequent creativity (Baer et al., 2010).

Research on the effects of competition on individuals' creativity provides only partial support for the notion that competition has creativity-diminishing qualities. For example, Amabile (1982) found that collages made by elementary school-age girls were significantly less creative when the girls competed against each other for prizes than when there was no competition between participants. Similarly, using Lunchins' (1942) water jar problems, Amabile (1987) found that individuals were more likely to use the set breaking (i.e., creative) 2-jar solution instead of the standard 3-jar solution to solve the last of the six problems when they worked in the absence of competition than when competition was present. Providing additional support for a negative link between competition and creativity, Tjosvold, Tang, and West (2004) showed that teams in which members were competing against each other were rated lower in creativity than teams in which members were pursing the same agenda. In contrast to these findings, a laboratory study by Shalley and Oldham (1997) demonstrated that competition had generally positive effects on individuals' creativity.

Only two studies have directly investigated the effects of intergroup competition on team creativity. Discussing the factors contributing to the success of the British pop group The Beatles, Clydesdale (2006) observed that the rivalry between The Beatles and the American group the Beach Boys played in integral part in the band's success. A laboratory study by Baer et al. (2010) found that intergroup rivalry caused groups to produce ideas of greater creativity, albeit this effect was limited to low and medium levels of competition and there were no added benefits to competition becoming increasingly fierce.

In summary, only a few studies have examined the effects of competition on the creativity of individuals and teams. With respect to teams, there is some evidence to suggest that intergroup competition can boost creativity. However, since only two studies have examined the effects of intergroup competition, more research is needed before any definite conclusions can be drawn. Results of studies examining the effects of competition on individuals' creativity are somewhat inconsistent, with three studies showing negative effects and one positive. One explanation for these mixed findings involves the personal characteristics of the individuals who are competing against one another. One characteristic that may be particularly important is the competitors' gender. Specifically, it may be that women are more susceptible to the creativity-inhibiting effects of competition than men (Amabile, 1996). Examining this possibility, Conti, Collins, and Picariello (2001) asked 50 children (27 boys, 23 girls) to make collages at one of two "parties". At one party, prizes were awarded for the best collages; at the other party prizes were raffled off. Results showed that girls were less creative when competing in the prize condition, while boys were more creative in that condition—a finding that emerged only when boys and girls were segregated by gender. These results are consistent with those obtained in the Amabile (1982) study that examined the effects of competition between girls and suggest that men may thrive in competitive situations while women react negatively. More research is now needed to systematically investigate the moderating role of gender on the effects of competition on the creativity of both individuals and teams.

Evaluation

Evaluating or appraising a person's creative contributions has been suggested to have the potential to powerfully shape individual creativity (Amabile, 1996; Diehl & Stroebe, 1987). Most previous research on this topic has focused on two general types of evaluation: *judgmental* and *developmental* (Shalley et al., 2004). Judgmental evaluations involve others (e.g., a manager, subject-matter expert, or teammate) critically assessing or appraising the creativity of an individual's work and comparing it to some standard (Oldham, 2002). By contrast, developmental evaluations are non-judgmental in nature and intended to provide the focal individual with guidance or direction in developing his or her creativity-relevant skills and talents (Shalley, 1995). These latter evaluations are typically conducted by others; however, self-administered developmental evaluations are also possible and have been investigated (Zhou & Oldham, 2001).

The conceptual framework outlined earlier can be used to explain the possible effects of both types of evaluation on individuals' creativity. In terms of the first component of that framework, access and exposure to new and different sets of information, we expect that individuals who anticipate a judgmental evaluation will be relatively closed to new ideas and perspectives that might be available from the individuals conducting the evaluation. The reason is that this type of evaluation is likely to be perceived by the focal person as threatening or intimidating (Kavanagh, 1982)—causing the individual to react defensively to the evaluation itself and to dismiss any ideas that might be forthcoming. Conversely, those anticipating a developmental evaluation should be open to new perspectives and approaches from the evaluator since such information is perceived as a genuine attempt to enhance his or her creativity. A similar logic applies to the second component of our framework—engagement. Specifically, we expect those anticipating a judgmental evaluation to react defensively to it. This should cause individuals to focus their attention on managing the evaluation itself versus focusing on their work activities, resulting in lowered engagement in the work role and lowered creativity. By contrast, individuals should experience developmental evaluations as supportive and informational, which should boost their involvement in the work and enhance their creativity.

In summary, our framework posits that individuals anticipating a judgmental evaluation will be less open to new ideas and perspectives and less engaged in their work, resulting in lowered creativity. Developmental evaluation should have the opposite effect, leading to heightened creativity since individuals in such circumstances are likely to be open to new ideas and benefit from the support such an evaluation provides.

Several earlier studies provide results that are generally consistent with our argument that creativity is lower when individuals expect their work to be critically judged and evaluated (Camacho & Paulus, 1995; Cheek & Stahl, 1986; Diehl & Stroebe, 1987; Szymanski & Harkins, 1992). For example, previous research on brainstorming groups has established that the expectation of negative evaluations by others in the group leads members to self-censor their ideas and to generate fewer ideas (Diehl & Stroebe, 1987). This effect tends to be present when group members are identifiable as well as when they are anonymous. Moreover, a meta-analysis established that fewer ideas were generated in brainstorming groups when individuals felt they were being monitored by external authorities (Mullen, Johnson, & Salas, 1991). Research conducted in non-brainstorming contexts shows similar effects of anticipated judgmental evaluation. For example, Amabile (1979) showed that individuals who expected their artwork to be critically evaluated by experts produced less creative work than individuals in no-evaluation conditions. Likewise, Bartis, Szymanski, and Harkins (1988) showed that the creativity of the uses generated for a common object (a knife) was lower among individuals who expected the experimenter to evaluate their ideas than among those who expected no judgmental evaluation. Amabile, Goldfarb, and Brackfield (1990) showed that the creativity of poems and collages was significantly lower among individuals expecting a judgmental evaluation than among those expecting no critical evaluation. Finally, Yuan and Zhou (2008) demonstrated that those who expected subject-matter experts to conduct an evaluation of their work produced fewer ideas and fewer novel ideas than those not expecting a judgmental evaluation.

C. GROUP LEVEL INFLUENCES

Although the bulk of previous research suggests that expected judgmental evaluations will have adverse effects on creativity, two studies failed to provide results consistent with our arguments. Troyer and Youngreen (2009) examined individuals' creativity under three conditions: no judgmental evaluation, observing one group member negatively evaluate a second member's ideas, and observing one group member negatively evaluate the teammate who generated the idea. Consistent with previous research, those in the no evaluation condition produced *more ideas* than those in the other conditions. However, inconsistent with our arguments, the creativity of the ideas generated by individuals was higher in the idea-evaluation condition than in the no evaluation and person-evaluation conditions. Also inconsistent with our framework, Shalley (1995, Study 1) showed that individuals expecting a judgmental evaluation from experts were no less creative than those expecting no evaluation.

Only a few studies have focused directly on the effects of anticipated developmental evaluations, and these studies have provided mixed results for the expected effects of such evaluations (Shalley & Perry-Smith, 2001; Zhou & Oldham, 2001). For example, Shalley and Perry-Smith (2001) demonstrated that the creativity of individuals who anticipated a judgmental evaluation by subject-matter experts was significantly lower than those expecting a developmental evaluation provided by these experts. Zhou and Oldham (2001) contrasted the creativity of individuals expecting a self-administered developmental evaluation (i.e., they would analyze the extent to which their ideas were creative) versus those expecting either an expert developmental evaluation or no evaluation. Results showed that creativity scores in the self-administered condition were higher than those in the other two conditions. However, those anticipating an expert developmental evaluation were no more creative than those expecting no evaluation. Finally, Shalley (1995, Study 2) showed no differences in creativity among individuals expecting a developmental evaluation from experts and those expecting no evaluation.

In summary, results of earlier studies generally demonstrated that those expecting judgmental evaluations exhibited lower creativity than those expecting no evaluation. However, two studies (Shalley, 1995, Study 1; Troyer & Youngreen, 2009) failed to provide evidence that was completely supportive, suggesting that there may be specific conditions under which judgmental evaluations have negligible effects on creativity. One such condition is that identified by Troyer and Youngreen (2009)—the target of the judgmental evaluation itself. That is, it may be that when the evaluation focuses on the idea versus the person who generates it, individuals are more likely to accept the evaluation as constructive and non-threatening, and respond less negatively to it. Another possibility is that there may be individual differences in the way individuals respond to judgmental evaluations. For example, it may be that those who have a learning goal orientation (VandeWalle et al., 2001) will interpret judgmental evaluations as helpful and react positively to them. Research is now needed to test these possibilities.

Results of studies focusing on developmental evaluation were also not completely consistent with our arguments, with some studies showing positive effects of developmental evaluation on creativity (Shalley & Perry-Smith, 2001) and others showing few effects (Shalley, 1995, Study 2). Again, these mixed results suggest that moderating conditions might play a role. For example, it may be that those with a learning goal orientation (VandeWalle et al., 2001) will react most positively when offered feedback and information intended to develop their skills. It is also possible that the source of the developmental evaluation plays a role in its effectiveness. For example, individuals may react more positively when developmental feedback has been offered by a trusted colleague versus a manager. Research is now needed to examine these issues.

Financial Rewards

A good deal of attention has focused on the possible effects of monetary rewards on individuals' creativity (Amabile, 1996; Eisenberger & Aselage, 2009; Hennessey & Amabile, 2010). However, there is little agreement among scholars concerning the likely *direction* of the effects of such rewards. That is, some commentators argue that monetary rewards result in lowered creativity (Amabile, 1996); others argue that such rewards boost creativity (Eisenberger & Armeli, 1997).

Applying our framework, a case can be made for both of these expected effects. On the one hand, offering financial rewards to individuals for performing a task or assignment might result in lowered creativity if these rewards cause individuals to focus their attention and energy on the reward itself versus making an effort to access new perspectives or information that are available in the environment. Financial rewards also may reduce creativity by undermining individuals' interest and engagement in their work roles (Deci & Ryan, 2000). If monetary rewards are perceived by individuals as controlling or manipulative of their behavior, they may react by disengaging from the task and focusing their energy on the reward itself, thereby lowering their creative performance.

Alternatively, it may be that the opportunity to obtain a financial reward for producing creative work causes individuals to scan the environment for new ideas and perspectives that might facilitate the creativity of their own ideas. And these rewards might boost creativity by providing individuals with recognition that enhances their feelings of personal competence and amplifies their work role engagement (Shalley et al., 2004).

Unfortunately, early empirical research has done little to sort out which of these positions is valid. That is, some studies show positive effects of rewards on creativity (Eisenberger, Armeli, & Pretz, 1998; Eisenberger & Rhoades, 2001) and others show negative effects (Amabile, Hennessey, & Grossman, 1986; Kruglanski, Friedman, & Zeevi, 1971). Still, other studies demonstrate that extrinsic rewards have negligible effects on individuals' creativity (Hennessey, 1989; Joussemet & Koestner, 1999).

For example, among the studies showing positive effects of rewards, Eisenberger and Rhoades (2001) showed that story titles produced by students who were promised financial rewards were significantly more creative than the titles of students not promised rewards. Eisenberger and Aselage (2009, Study 3) showed that individuals who were told that they would have to return a financial reward unless they produced creative short story titles were rated by judges as producing titles that were significantly more creative than those in a control condition.

Among the studies demonstrating that financial rewards had weak effects on creativity, Eisenberger and Aselage (2009, Study 2) found that employees' performance-reward expectancies (i.e., the perception that if they perform well they will receive higher pay) had a statistically non-significant relation to supervisor-rated creativity. Similarly, Hennessey (1989) demonstrated that individuals assigned to either a reward-experimenter (the experimenter awarded a certificate for participation) or a reward-computer (they received a certificate controlled by a computer) condition produced creative work that did not differ from those in a control (no reward) condition.

Finally, among those showing negative effects of rewards, Kruglanski et al. (1971) showed that students *not* promised a reward exhibited higher creativity on two tasks than those who were promised rewards. Selart, Nordstrom, Kuvaas, and Takemura (2008) demonstrated that participants in a control group achieved higher rated creativity than participants in a performance-contingent reward group.

The mixed and inconsistent results obtained in these earlier studies suggest there is a need to understand the conditions under which expected financial rewards enhance creativity and the conditions under which they reduce creative accomplishment. One possibility is that the negative effects of financial rewards would only be observed when organizational norms are present that suggest that such rewards are inappropriate (see Staw, Calder, Hess, & Sandelands, 1980). In other circumstances, financial rewards may have positive effects on creativity. Another possibility is suggested in a study by Baer, Oldham, and Cummings (2003). These authors argued that the effects of extrinsic rewards were likely a function of individuals' cognitive styles (i.e., adaptive or innovative; Kirton, 1994) and the nature of employees' jobs. Results of their field study showed that rewards enhanced creativity only for employees with an adaptive style who worked on relatively simple, routine jobs. In contrast, those with an innovative style in complex jobs were generally unaffected by extrinsic rewards. Research is now needed that replicates these findings and that investigates the effects of other individual differences and contextual conditions on the link between extrinsic rewards and individuals' creativity.

Deadlines and Time Pressure

Early research and theory has suggested that the presence of tight deadlines for projects or work activities produced the experience of time pressure, which would undermine individuals' creativity (Amabile, Hadley, & Kramer, 2002; Andrews & Smith, 1996). Following our conceptual framework, when time is tight, individuals tend to be less likely to seek out and make use of different and potentially relevant sources of information. This may not only include exchanges with colleagues but may also apply to the extent to which individuals are likely to examine all parameters of a given problem situation in order to gain a comprehensive understanding of what it is they need to do (Andrews & Smith, 1996). As a result, ideas that emerge under tight deadlines and high time pressure should not only lack sufficient originality, as the resources required to derive unique ideas are limited, but these ideas, because they are likely to ignore key aspects of the problem situation, may prove to be of little use. In addition, severe time pressure has the potential to undermine people's engagement in the task at hand as too many fires have to be fought at the same time. Reduced task engagement, in turn, is likely to constrict people's willingness and ability to explore different combinations of existing approaches and viewpoints (Andrews & Smith, 1996; Baer & Oldham, 2006). As a consequence, individuals are likely to rely on familiar algorithms when approaching a problem situation—a tendency which is likely to produce ideas of only limited creativity.

Previous research provides mixed and inconsistent support for these arguments. Although a few studies demonstrated that time pressure had the expected negative effects on creativity (e.g., Amabile et al., 1996; Kelly & McGrath, 1985; Madjar & Oldham, 2006), others showed that it had either positive effects (Andrews & Ferris, 1972; Ohly & Fritz, 2010) or no effects (Amabile & Gryskiewicz, 1989). Among the studies showing negative effects, Andrews and Smith (1996) found that product managers who experienced high time pressure developed marketing programs that were low in creativity. Similarly, analyzing diary entries, Amabile et al. (2002) reported that on days when employees experienced very high levels of time pressure, they were 45 percent less likely to think creatively than they were on days with lower levels of experienced pressure. The studies showing positive effects of time pressure include a study of health service employees by Unsworth, Wall, and Carter (2005). These authors found that experienced time pressure produced elevated levels of creativity by creating the perception that creativity is an expected and required part of individuals' work responsibilities. Using experience sampling data, Ohly and Fritz (2010) showed that the experience of chronic time pressure (mediated by perceptions of daily levels of time pressure) produced a sense of challenge which translated into elevated levels of creativity.

The mixed results reported above have led some scholars to argue that the link between time pressure and creativity may not be linear. While too much time pressure is clearly contraindicated when it comes to the production of creative ideas, the complete lack of a sense of urgency may prove to be equally stifling. Creativity requires that people invest themselves in their work. With no pressure at all, people are unlikely to feel the level of excitement and challenge that stimulates creativity (Ohly & Fritz, 2010). If true, this line of theorizing would suggest that creativity is likely to flourish at a happy medium (Gardner & Cummings, 1988)—not too much pressure to constrict the search for new information and the reshuffling of existing approaches and viewpoints into something new, but not so little that people begin to disengage from the task at hand (Amabile et al., 2002; Baer & Oldham, 2006).

Consistent with these arguments, Baer and Oldham (2006) observed an inverted U-shaped pattern between time pressure and creativity for employees who received support for their creative endeavors and who were highly open to experience. Similarly, Ohly et al. (2006) showed a curvilinear, inverted U-shaped relation between experienced time pressure and creativity. The strongest evidence, however, that the link between time pressure and creativity follows the shape of an inverted U was provided by Byron, Khazanchi, and Nazarian (2010). Their meta-analysis of 76 experimental studies showed that stressors such as time pressure had no linear effects on creativity, but were related via an inverted U-shaped pattern—creativity was highest when stress levels were of medium intensity.

In summary, the results of early studies concerning the effects of deadlines and time pressure on creativity were generally mixed, with some showing positive and others negative effects of pressure. Recent evidence provides an explanation for these results suggesting that time pressure is only likely to enhance creativity when it is at an optimal level. At other levels, creativity is likely to suffer. More research is now needed to examine the various antecedents of pressure and the possibility that there are individual differences in the way individuals respond to different levels of pressure.

Conflict

Many commentators have suggested that conflict could have a substantial impact on both individual and team creativity (see Amabile, 1996; Jehn & Bendersky, 2003). Based on early research and theory (Amason, 1996; Jehn, 1997), we distinguish between two types of conflict—conflict in interpersonal relationships (relationship conflict) and conflict involving the task (task conflict). Relationship conflict exists when there are interpersonal incompatibilities among individuals or the members of a group; task conflict exists when there are differences in viewpoints, ideas, and opinions regarding the nature or content of the task itself. Consistent with our conceptual framework, Jehn and Bendersky (2003) and others (e.g., De Dreu & Weingart, 2003) have argued that task conflict should have positive effects on creativity, as it entails and fosters the expression and subsequent elaboration of different perspectives and viewpoints. Thus, task conflict may not only enhance the availability of new and potentially relevant information but also produce a deeper cognitive and emotional engagement in the task at hand. Relationship conflict, by contrast, is likely to undermine creativity. Not only have interpersonal problems the potential to impair individuals' cognitive functioning in processing complex information (Staw et al., 1981) but they are also likely to force individuals to disengage from the task at hand to resolve the conflict (Evan, 1965; Jehn, 1995). In addition, relationship conflict is likely to reduce individuals' willingness to accept others' ideas (Pelled, 1996). Thus, since relationship conflict is likely to limit individuals' access to new information, as well as the ability to thoroughly process this information, and forces individuals to disengage from the task at hand, creativity is likely to be undermined.

Previous research provides some support for these arguments. For example, a laboratory study by Carnevale and Probst (1998) demonstrated that individual participants in a relationship conflict condition exhibited lower creativity than those in a control condition. Similarly, a study by Van Dyne, Jehn, and Cummings (2002) showed that both work strain (subjective feelings of conflict based on tensions with coworkers and supervisors) and home strain (subjective feelings of conflict based on relationships at home) had the potential to undermine creativity, particularly when the employee–supervisor relationship was characterized by a lack of confidence and trust. In an experimental study of teams, Pearsall, Ellis, and Evans (2008) observed a negative effect of relationship conflict on the number of ideas that teams generated, although not on the overall creativity of these ideas. Chen (2006) observed a negative link between relationship conflict and creativity in service-driven teams. Also, Farh, Lee, and Farh (2010) showed that a measure of relationship conflict had a negative relation to a supervisor rating of team creativity.

However, three studies showed that relationship conflict had negligible effects on creativity. De Dreu (2006, Study 2) showed that a measure of relationship conflict had a non-significant relation to supervisor-rated creativity. Using self-reported daily measures of conflict and creativity from individuals in project teams, Kurtzberg and Mueller (2005) showed that relationship conflict had non-significant relations to individuals' reports of their own creativity on the day following the conflict and on the day the conflict occurred. Jehn, Rispens, and Thatcher (2010) reported that relationship conflict had a non-significant correlation to team member reports of the team's creativity.

Results of early studies suggest that the effects of task conflict on creativity are even less consistent than those involving relationship conflict. For example, the aforementioned study by Chen (2006) observed a positive link between task conflict and the creativity of technologically-minded project teams. And task-related minority dissent, one manifestation of task conflict in teams, has been shown to stimulate the creative thinking of the majority of members (Van Dyne & Saaverda, 1996). However, De Dreu and West (2001) and Jehn et al. (2010) demonstrated that task conflict had a non-significant relationship with team creativity. Finally, the study by Kurtzberg and Mueller (2005) showed that task conflict related positively to individuals' reports of their own creativity on the day following a task conflict but had no relation to creativity on the day the conflict occurred.

In summary, previous research provides some support for the notion that relationship conflict can depress the creativity of individuals and teams. However, the evidence concerning the expected positive effects of task conflict on creativity are somewhat less clear, with some studies showing positive effects and others negligible effects. Recent research has attempted to address these inconsistent findings and suggests that the positive effects of task conflict may be limited to situations in which conflict is of lower intensity. For example, across two studies, De Dreu (2006) showed that task conflict was positively associated with supervisor-rated team creativity but only up to a certain point, beyond which the relation became negative resulting in an inverted U-shaped pattern. In addition, this study provided evidence for the notion that task conflict is likely to exert its beneficial effects on creativity by causing individuals to exchange task-relevant information. Additional support for an inverted U-shaped relation between task conflict and creativity was provided in studies by Farh et al. (2010) and Kratzer, Leenders, and van Engelen (2006). For example, in a sample of R&D teams, Kratzer et al. (2006) showed that during the early stages (i.e., conceptualization phase) of the innovation process when creativity is especially required, team polarity—the authors' label for task conflict—resulted in elevated levels of creativity up to some optimal level beyond which the relation became negative resulting in depressed levels of creativity as task conflict increased. In addition, the authors found that task conflict generally had negative effects on creativity during the later stages of the innovation process (i.e., commercialization phase) and when the project was relatively less complex (i.e., more routine).

Overall, then, it appears that task conflict has the potential to enhance the creativity of individuals and groups, albeit only in selected circumstances. Particularly, task conflict seems to be most beneficial when at low to moderate levels of intensity and in environments that require extensive amounts of creativity, such as the early stages of the innovation process or problems characterized by sufficient complexity. Relationship conflict, by contrast, appears to have generally negative effects on creativity, both at the individual and group levels of analyses.

Social Environment

In reviewing the influence of the social environment on creativity (Amabile, 1996; Hennessey & Amabile, 2010), we broadly distinguish between the social behaviors (e.g., supportive behaviors, transformational leadership) of the individuals who constitute a focal person's social environment (i.e., supervisors, colleagues, customers and clients) and the relational (e.g., quality of leader–member exchange relationship, strength of relationship) and structural features (e.g., structural holes) of the social relationships that link the focal person to the individuals in his or her social environment.

BEHAVIORAL PARAMETERS

Previous research has examined a wide range of different social behaviors that could promote or depress creativity. Promoting behaviors range from setting expectations for creativity (Carmeli & Schaubroeck, 2007; Scott & Bruce, 1994) and subsequently delivering instrumental and socioemotional support to fulfill these expectations (Tierney & Farmer, 2004), to challenging others, inspiring them, and providing meaning to their activities (e.g., Gong, Huang, & Farh, 2009; Shin & Zhou, 2003; Zhang & Bartol, 2010). Social behaviors with a possible depressing effect on creativity range from intimidating colleagues and subordinates and dispensing punishment, to closely monitoring their activities (e.g., Choi et al., 2009; Zhou, 2003).

Consistent with our framework, we propose that a wide range of different social behaviors have the potential to satisfy the two necessary conditions for heightened creativity—full engagement in one's job and work role, and access and exposure to a wide range of different pockets of information. For example, by removing obstacles to individuals' task completion or providing resources aiding in this endeavor, employees should be more likely to fully engage in their work activities, as a result of which we expect creativity to flourish. Similarly, by inspiring others and providing meaning to their work, individuals should be more energized and willing to exert the effort needed to produce creative work (Shin & Zhou, 2003; Zhang & Bartol, 2010). In addition, directly sharing task-relevant information, or providing employees with opportunities to discuss their ideas may allow new ideas to emerge, and important feedback to be exchanged, so colleagues and supervisors extend the pool of information that is available to individuals to derive new and potentially useful ideas (Binnewies, Ohly, & Sonnentag, 2007; Madjar & Ortiz-Walters, 2008). We structure the following discussion by distinguishing between those behaviors that are generally supportive in nature (i.e., instrumental and socioemotional support) and those that have traditionally been discussed in the realms of leadership and that go beyond these purely supportive actions (e.g., empowering and transformational leadership).

Supportive Behaviors

Many earlier studies suggest that support provided by the colleagues and supervisors of an individual generally relates positively to creativity (e.g., Amabile et al., 1996; Amabile & Conti, 1999; Basu & Green, 1997; Choi, 2004; Frese et al., 1999; Janssen, 2005; Lim & Choi, 2009; Madjar et al., 2002; Oldham & Cummings, 1996; Rice, 2006; Tierney & Farmer, 2002, 2004; Unsworth et al., 2005). For example, Zhou and George (2001) observed a positive correlation between the extent to which employees received useful feedback, help, and support from their coworkers and their creativity as rated by supervisors. In addition, these authors found that support served as a powerful catalyst, channeling the dissatisfaction of committed employees into creative outcomes. Amabile, Schatzel, Moneta, and Kramer (2004) reported a positive link between support provided by supervisors and peer-rated creativity among employees working on projects in seven different companies. Similarly, in a study of employees of a large manufacturing company, Madjar (2008) found that instrumental support from the primary work unit was positively related to creativity. In addition, her results demonstrated that socioemotional support from colleagues and supervisors, located either inside or outside the focal individual's work unit, was also positively associated with creativity. Similarly, Zhou, Shin, and Cannella (2008) found that employees reported higher levels of creativity in a post-merger environment when they perceived that their organization encouraged and supported their creative efforts. In addition, these authors showed that in resource-rich environments, support compensated for the detrimental effects on creativity of perceiving the merger as a potential threat rather than as an opportunity. Finally, Wang and Cheng (2010) examined the effects on creativity of benevolent leadership, a concept akin to supportive supervision but concerned primarily with employees themselves (i.e., socioemotional support) rather than their task performance. Their study of supervisor-subordinate dyads revealed a positive link between benevolent leadership and creativity, and this relation was particularly pronounced when employees enjoyed a great deal of freedom in their jobs.

Although the majority of studies showed a positive support–creativity relationship, several investigations failed to provide evidence supporting a direct link between support and creativity (e.g., Axtell et al., 2000; George & Zhou, 2001; Jaskyte, 2008; Ohly et al., 2006; Zhou, 2003). For example, in a study of machine operators, Axtell et al. (2000) found no evidence (when controlling for implementation) for a positive correlation between support provided by management, team leaders, and team members, and the extent to which individuals had made suggestions for improvements in a number of different areas. Similarly, Ohly et al. (2006) found no relation between the extent to which supervisors encouraged employee participation, kept employees informed, and rewarded good performance and their creativity. In addition, their results revealed a negative relation between supervisor support and the number of suggestions employees had submitted to the organizational suggestion system in the three years prior to data collection. Finally, George and Zhou (2001) found a non-significant relation between employee creativity and the extent to which coworkers provided constructive help at work.

The mixed results of the studies discussed above suggest that the effects of supportive behaviors on creativity may be contingent on a number of other factors (e.g., Baer & Oldham, 2006; George & Zhou, 2007). A few earlier studies support this possibility. For example, in a sample of nurses, Binnewies et al. (2008) found no direct relationship between support and expert ratings of nurses' ideas, but a moderated relation such that a lack of support for creativity from coworkers and supervisor did damage creativity as nurses became older in age. No direct link between supervisor support and creativity was also observed in a study by Kim, Hon, and Lee (2010) who examined employee–supervisor pairs in South Korea. However, support from supervisors combined with employees' proactive personality and job creativity requirement to jointly impact creativity. Specifically, proactive employees exhibited the highest levels of creativity when their job required them to be creative and when their supervisors provided them with useful feedback and support for their creative endeavors. Finally, Zhou (2003) showed that supportive behavior on the part of supervisors had stronger, positive effects on employee creativity when coworkers were present in the work unit and they exhibited high creativity. Research is now needed to examine other personal and contextual conditions that may moderate the effects of supportive behavior on employees' creative performance at work and to sort out the specific conditions that should be in place if support is to enhance creativity.

Empowering and Transformational Leadership Behaviors

Recent research has provided evidence supporting the general notion that behaviors such as empowering and transformational leadership have the potential to enhance creativity. Empowering leadership involves highlighting the significance of the work, encouraging participation in decision-making, conveying confidence in high performance and removing bureaucratic barriers (Ahearne, Mathieu, & Rapp, 2005). Consistent with the notion that such behaviors enhance creativity to the extent that they foster engagement, Zhang and Bartol (2010) demonstrated that empowering leadership promoted creativity by deepening employees' engagement in various creativity-enhancing activities (i.e., problem identification, information searching and encoding, and idea generation) and by fostering intrinsic motivation.

Transformational leadership, which is a behavioral syndrome encompassing leader activities such as intellectual stimulation, charisma or idealized influence, inspirational motivation, and individualized consideration (Bass, 1985) also has been found to positively relate to creativity (e.g., Boerner, Eisenbeiss, & Griesser, 2007; Moss & Rotossa, 2007; Rank, Nelson, Allen, & Xu, 2009; Redmond, Mumford, & Teach, 1993, Reuvers, van Engen, Vinkenburg, & Wilson-Evered, 2008). By challenging the status quo and encouraging novel approaches to problems, energizing followers via the articulation of a compelling cause, and mentoring and developing them, transformational leaders may not only provide the informational impetus for creativity but also foster a deeper engagement in the task. Consistent with this logic, Shin and Zhou (2003) showed that transformational leadership related positively to employees' creativity and a measure of intrinsic motivation, particularly among those who were receptive to the leader's efforts, and that higher levels of intrinsic motivation translated into greater creativity. Similar findings have been observed in other studies (e.g., Gumusluoglu & Ilsev, 2009), although it appears that there may be other mediating mechanisms operative in addition to engagement. For example, Gong et al. (2009) showed that the positive relation between transformational leadership and creativity was mediated by employee creative self-efficacy. The generally positive link between transformational leadership and creativity has also been documented at the group level of analysis (Eisenbeiss, van Knippenberg, & Boerner, 2008; Jung, 2000–2001; Sosik, Kahai, & Avolio, 1998).

In contrast to these generally positive findings, Basu and Green (1997) observed a negative relation between transformational leadership and a measure of creativity. Similarly, in a laboratory study of student groups performing two decision making tasks, Kahai, Sosik, and Avolio (2003) found that transformational leadership was associated with lower solution originality than transactional leadership. Jaussi and Dionne (2003) found no empirical support for the notion that transformational leadership positively relates to creativity in a laboratory study with student subjects. And Pieterse, van Knippenberg, Schippers, and Stam (2010) showed that transformational leadership was only positively related to creativity when employees felt empowered. With the exception of these studies, however, the majority of research seems to support a positive link between transformational leadership and creativity. Research is now needed that investigates the specific circumstances under which transformational and empowering leadership behaviors have the strongest effects on employee creativity.

RELATIONAL AND STRUCTURAL PARAMETERS

An emerging stream of research has highlighted the importance, not of the characteristics and behaviors of the people who collectively constitute an individual's social environment, but rather of the nature and constellation of the *relationships* that together link the focal individual to his or her social world. Specifically, reflecting the insight that social relationships not only have the potential to foster work engagement but are the primary conduits of individuals' access and exposure to new and different pockets of information (e.g., Singh & Fleming, 2010), recent research has tried to identify (1) the types of relationships that are most likely to deliver these informational benefits and (2) the structural arrangement (i.e., the way in which a person's social network is structured) of a person's social relationships that ultimately promotes creativity.

Relational Parameters: Leader–Member Exchange

Highlighting the importance of the nature of the dyadic relationships connecting individuals to others in their social environment, research on leader–member exchange (as well as on team–member exchange) considers the quality of the exchange relationship between people as the key factor determining a variety of outcomes (Dansereau, Graen, & Haga, 1975; Graen & Scandura, 1987). For example, while some leader–subordinate relationships are characterized by interactions that are formal and impersonal in nature (i.e., low-quality leader–member exchange) other relationships, over time, develop into more mature interactions characterized by trust, mutual liking, and respect (i.e., high-quality leader–member exchange). In these high-quality exchanges, followers are not only granted greater autonomy and freedom promoting deeper engagement, but also access to more and better information, both of which should foster higher creativity (Khazanchi & Masterson, 2010; Scott & Bruce, 1994).

Consistent with this logic, in a study of leader–member dyads in a manufacturing plant, Basu and Green (1997) found that the quality of leader–member exchange relationships was not only related positively to follower autonomy, leader support of followers, and follower commitment to the organization but also to followers' creativity. Similarly, in a sample of R&D employees, Tierney et al. (1999) found that effective leader–member exchange relationships were positively associated with employee creativity, with these effects appearing to be particularly enabling for less creative individuals. Atwater and Carmeli (2009) showed that employees' perceptions of the quality of their relationships with their leaders were positively related to their subsequent feelings of energy (reflective of their task engagement), which, in turn, were positively linked to creativity. Finally, using longitudinal data from employees on 16 teams, Liao et al. (2010) found that both the quality of employees' relationships with their supervisors and with their team members had unique, indirect positive effects on employee creativity.

Relational Parameters: Strength of Ties

Rather than focusing on the overall quality of the social relationships which individuals maintain with their colleagues and supervisors, another stream of research has focused on the strength of these ties. Specifically, building on Granovetter's (1973) strength-of-weak-ties theory, researchers have suggested that "weak" ties; social relationships typified by infrequent interaction, short history, and limited (emotional) closeness, are particularly valuable to the production of creative ideas, because they allow for enhanced access and exposure to socially distant pockets of information—information that is likely to be novel and, therefore, particularly relevant to the production of new and useful ideas (Brass, 1995; Perry-Smith & Shalley, 2003). While weak ties may deliver certain informational benefits that spur creativity, the support and trust that are typically associated with "strong" ties—relationships typified by frequent interaction, long history, and high emotional closeness—may promote a deeper engagement in the task at hand that ultimately also fosters creativity.

Consistent with strength-of-weak-ties theory, Perry-Smith (2006) showed a positive link between the number of weak-tie acquaintances and the creativity of scientists—an effect that was mediated by weak ties allowing for access and exposure to a more heterogeneous set of contacts. No support was found, however, for a positive or negative relation between the number of strong ties and scientists' creativity. The relevance of weak ties was further demonstrated in a study by Cross and Cummings (2004). Their analysis of data from engineers and from consultants revealed that individuals who maintained more relationships with people outside their own department and outside the organization—ties that are likely to be weak—received higher performance ratings (e.g., capturing creativity, among other factors). Further supporting the importance of weak ties, Zhou, Shin, Brass, Choi, and Zhang (2009) showed that an increasing number of weak ties coincided with elevated levels of creativity in a sample of technology employees. However, their findings also highlighted the diminishing returns that resulted from people cultivating a growing number of weak ties eventually producing lowered levels of creativity. Thus, creativity appears to flourish when the number of weak ties is at a moderate level, and this effect was particularly pronounced when individuals were less susceptible to the forces of conformity.

Disentangling the effects of the number of ties from the strength of these relationships and the heterogeneity of contacts they provide access to, Baer (2010) showed that creativity benefited from an optimal number of weak ties but only when (1) these relationships connected people to contacts all throughout the organization and beyond its boundaries, and (2) when individuals were high on the openness to experience personality dimension, so allowing them to take advantage of the informational benefits afforded to them by their social ties. Thus, although weak ties seem to be conducive to the production of creative ideas, the full benefit of such ties is only realized when they afford people access and exposure to many different pockets of information, and when individuals are predisposed to taking advantage of these different information sets.

Structural Parameters: Structural Holes

Focusing on the structural arrangements of individuals' social relationships, Burt (1992) suggested that examining the extent to which social networks contain "structural holes"—connections between otherwise disconnected people—allows for a more accurate test of the notion that access to information that is nonredundant produces brokerage benefits that ultimately translate into higher levels of creativity. Consistent with this argument, Burt (2004) observed that managers who brokered connections across structural holes in their organization were more likely to have good ideas. Similarly, Fleming, Mingo, and Chen (2007) found that brokerage related positively to a measure of creativity—the number of previously uncombined subclasses of patents. However, a study by Tortoriello and Krackhardt (2010) revealed that ties that spanned across intra-organizational boundaries had no benefits for creativity per se, and only emerged as a significant predictor of patent generation when embedded in a dense, clique-like structure (i.e., bridging across Simmelian ties) promoting open and smooth transfer of information. Relatedly, Rodan and Galunic (2004) showed that structural holes are not necessarily correlates of greater creativity—managers who spanned structural holes were more likely to develop and implement new ideas only when their networks afforded them access and exposure to heterogeneous knowledge sets. Zhou et al. (2009) provided additional support for the notion that the mere presence of structural holes does not invariably produce higher levels of creativity. Finally, in contrast to the findings presented by Burt (2004) and Fleming et al. (2007), Obstfeld (2005) showed that the extent to which networks of automotive design employees featured structural holes correlated *negatively* with their involvement (capturing, among others, whether a person initiated a particular innovation) in a series of innovations (for a related finding at the team level of analysis, see Kratzer, Leenders, & van Engelen, 2010).

One explanation for these inconsistent findings may be found in the varying importance of structural holes for the production and implementation of creative ideas. Specifically, while brokering connections across structural holes appears to be conducive to the generation of new, useful ideas (Burt, 2004; Fleming et al., 2007), particularly when bridging ties are strong, embedded in clique-like structures, and allow for access to a great many different knowledge sets (Rodan & Galunic, 2004; Tortoriello & Krackhardt, 2010), it may be a hindrance when the primary creative activity becomes more concerned with creating and mobilizing support for the implementation of such ideas (Fleming et al., 2007; Obstfeld, 2005). Thus, to the extent that more than "just" creativity is required, the benefits of being able to connect disparate social worlds should decline. Alternatively, it is possible that brokering connections across structural holes, while enhancing access and exposure to nonredundant information, may reduce employees' engagement in their job and work roles. Indeed, it is conceivable that the time and energy needed to successfully span disparate social worlds may drain people's physical, emotional, and cognitive resources thereby undermining their full engagement in their work. Thus, while structural holes may exert a positive effect on the information component of our model, they may simultaneously negatively impact the engagement component. Future research is now needed to examine these possibilities.

Overall, it can be concluded that given certain individual qualities (i.e., low conformity or being highly open to experience), creativity should benefit from relational and structural features that promote (a) deeper task engagement, (b) access and exposure to a variety of different pockets of information, and (c) the open and smooth transfer of such information. These benefits may be achieved via different relations and structural configurations. Cultivating high quality relationships (Liao et al., 2010), developing a sustainable number of weak and diverse ties (Baer, 2010; Perry-Smith, 2006; Zhou et al., 2009), bridging structural holes (Burt, 2004; Fleming et al., 2007), and serving as a conduit for the transfer of information by occupying a central position in one's network (e.g., Cross & Cummings, 2004; Kratzer & Lettl, 2008; Perry-Smith, 2006) are all avenues that should stimulate the production of new, useful ideas.

CONCLUSIONS AND FUTURE RESEARCH DIRECTIONS

This chapter has reviewed and integrated research on the effects of characteristics of the work context on the creativity of individuals and teams in organizations. We focused our attention on a wide variety of contextual factors including job design, goal setting, competition, evaluation, financial rewards, deadlines and time pressure, conflict, and various aspects of the social environment. In addressing the potential effects of these various contextual forces, we adopted a conceptual framework that included two general components—access and exposure to new information and engagement in one's job and work role. Specifically, we posited that creativity will be fostered to the extent that the various contextual characteristics promote enhanced access and exposure to new and different pockets of information and to the extent that they produce a deeper and fuller engagement of individuals in their jobs and work roles. The contextual characteristics included in our review and their expected effects on creativity and each of the two components of the conceptual framework are presented in summary form in Table 16.1.

Overall, the results discussed in this chapter and summarized in the table suggest strongly that the work context plays a significant role in shaping the creativity of individuals and teams. That is, the creativity that individuals and teams exhibit appears to be very much a function of the contextual and environmental conditions they are exposed to at work. Therefore, continuing to examine the conditions included in this chapter and refining our understanding of their effects on creativity appears to be a fruitful avenue for future research.

Although the context clearly plays a critical role in shaping employee creativity, Table 16.1 also shows the contextual characteristics included in our review have effects on creativity that differ in direction and consistency. For example, previous studies suggest that challenging, well-designed jobs, and high quality leader–member exchange relationships have generally consistent and positive effects on employee creativity. By contrast, judgmental evaluations have been shown to have generally consistent negative effects. Finally, many of the contextual characteristics examined (e.g., financial rewards, supportive behaviors from coworkers and supervisors, developmental evaluations) have been shown to have effects on creativity that might be characterized as mixed and inconsistent, with some studies focusing on a given characteristic showing positive effects while others addressing the same characteristic showing negligible or negative effects.

There are several possible explanations for these mixed and inconsistent results. The first of these involves the two components included in our conceptual framework: engagement and exposure to new information. As shown in Table 16.1, the various contextual characteristics which we reviewed were expected to have different effects on the two components of the framework—that is, some of the characteristics were expected to restrict exposure to new pockets of information (e.g., performance goals and relationship conflict) whereas others were predicted to enhance both access to information and engagement in the work role. It may be that the different components affected by the contextual characteristics were responsible for some of the mixed and inconsistent results involving creativity. For example, it is possible that the relatively weak or inconsistent effects observed for some characteristics (e.g., performance goals and developmental evaluations) were due to the fact that only one of the two components was prompted by the contextual characteristic in question.

TABLE 16.1 Summary of Effects of Contextual Features on Framework Components and Creativity.

Contextual Feature	Expected Effects on Framework Component		Consistency of Empirical Findings
	Information	Engagement	
Job design	+	+	Consistent
Goal setting			
Performance	−	−	Inconsistent
Creativity	+	+	Inconsistent
Competition			
Between individuals	−	−	Consistent
Between teams	−	+	Consistent
Evaluation			
Judgmental	−	−	Consistent
Developmental	+	+	Inconsistent
Financial rewards	+/−	+/−	Inconsistent
Deadlines/time pressure	−	−	Inconsistent
Conflict			
Relationship	−	−	Inconsistent
Task	+	+	Inconsistent
Social environment			
Supportive behavior	+	+	Inconsistent
Empowering/transformational leadership behaviors	+	+	Consistent
LMX	+	+	Consistent
Strength of ties			
Weak	+	−	Consistent
Strong	−	+	Inconsistent
Structural holes	+	−	Inconsistent

By contrast, those characteristics shown to have strong, positive effects on creativity (e.g., job design and leader–member exchange) may have enhanced both the engagement and information components. These arguments suggest that both engagement *and* informational access and exposure may be necessary if creativity is to be enhanced. Contextual forces that foster deeper engagement but do little to enhance individuals' access to the type of information spurring the combinatory process underlying creativity may be insufficient to produce high levels of creativity and vice versa. Future research is now needed to address this possibility by directly examining the effects of the contextual conditions on each of the two components in our framework in order to determine the extent to which they are influenced by the contextual characteristics under consideration.

A second explanation for the mixed results involving the effects of the context on creativity concerns individual differences and the presence of other contextual conditions. As we noted in our discussion of several of the characteristics, it may be that a given characteristic has an effect on creativity only if the employee has certain personal qualities (e.g., high creative ability or creative personality characteristics) or if other contextual characteristics are simultaneously present (e.g., supportive supervision). If these personal or contextual conditions are not present, the contextual characteristic under consideration may have little or no effect on the employee's creative responses. This view is consistent with various interactionist perspectives that suggest that creativity only flourishes when contextual and personal characteristics are aligned (Amabile, 1996; Oldham & Cummings, 1996; Woodman, Sawyer, & Griffin, 1993). Research is now needed to examine whether there is a specific set of personal and contextual characteristics that are necessary across all contextual conditions or if these characteristics vary by the contextual variable under consideration.

In addition to the inconsistent results involving creativity and several of the contextual characteristics reviewed in this chapter, there are a number of limitations to note with regard to the conclusions we have presented. First, we treated all measures of creativity similarly, as though they all tapped the same underlying concept. Thus, in considering the effects of a contextual condition, we interpreted the effects of that characteristic on a supervisor rating of creativity as we did a self rating or an objective indicator of creativity (e.g., patent disclosure). Unfortunately, the previous studies that have examined the relationships between various creativity measures (e.g., Oldham & Cummings, 1996; Tierney et al., 1999) have demonstrated that these measures are often not highly correlated. This suggests that the effects of the characteristics on creativity may to some degree be a function of the creativity measure itself. Some evidence for this may be found in a study by Oldham and Cummings (1996). These authors showed that measures of job complexity and noncontrolling supervision were significantly related to a supervisor rating of creativity, but not to two objective indicators. Also, a study by Tierney et al. (1999) demonstrated that a measure of leader–member exchange was positively related to a supervisor rating of creativity but not to the number of research reports written. Future research is now needed to examine whether the type of the creativity measure included in the research influences the results obtained across a variety of contextual characteristics.

Second, we also treated many characteristics identically, regardless of their immediacy to the employee. For example, in concluding that transformational leadership behaviors generally have positive effects on creativity we did not take into account whether the source of transformational influence was the CEO or the employee's immediate supervisor. Also, we treated support from coworkers similarly, regardless of whether the coworkers were interacting with the employee on a day-to-day or on an occasional basis. However, it may be that an immediate contextual characteristic (e.g., a direct supervisor's empowering and transformational behavior) has a more powerful effect on an employee's creativity than the same characteristic from a less immediate source (e.g., transformational behavior on the part of a division manager or CEO). Some evidence for this is found in a study by Madjar (2008). She showed that informational support from coworkers outside the boundaries of the work unit had no impact on employee creativity, whereas informational support from coworkers inside the work unit had a significant and positive effect. More research is now needed to systematically examine whether immediacy influences the effects of a wide variety of contextual characteristics.

A final limitation concerns the duration of the contextual influence. Specifically, we assumed throughout the review that each of the contextual characteristics would affect employee creativity regardless of the length or duration of the employee's exposure to that characteristic. However, it may be that a characteristic is more likely to shape employee creativity if the employee is exposed to it over the long-term versus only the short-term. This possibility might explain the relatively weak effects observed for performance goals. The studies examining this contextual characteristic were laboratory studies and short-term goals were assigned. It may be that stronger and more substantial effects would have emerged if individuals were assigned performance goals over the long-term. Research is now needed to directly test this possibility.

Despite these limitations, results of the studies reviewed here have a number of practical implications for enhancing creativity in the workplace. For example, given the relatively strong and consistent effects observed for job design, improving the standing of an employee's job on such core job properties as autonomy, personal control, feedback, and skill variety (Hackman & Oldham, 1980) should result in enhanced engagement and exposure to new information resulting in significant improvements in the creativity an employee exhibits at work. Similarly, articulating competitive threats from external teams should result in enhanced team creativity by fostering a greater sense of engagement and by boosting team member collaboration. Interventions designed to lower relationship conflict and time pressure may also be productive and result in enhanced creativity. These are just a few examples of steps that might be taken to modify the contextual conditions described in this chapter in an effort to boost creativity in the workplace. Future studies might examine the specific strategies that are most effective in changing these contextual conditions.

A number of additional new directions for research were suggested by our review. One of these involves our conceptual framework. As mentioned earlier, we suggested that research is needed to determine if both exposure to new pockets of information and engagement in the work role are necessary to fully explain the context–creativity relation, or if only one of these components is necessary. Few studies have included direct measures of either of these components (see Atwater & Carmeli, 2009, De Dreu, 2006, and Madjar, 2008 for exceptions) and we know of no study that included measures of both. Future studies are needed to directly test the framework we presented and to contrast it with other possible frameworks. For example, a number of the reviewed studies have highlighted the importance of creative self-efficacy in explaining the link between the context and creativity (e.g., Gong et al., 2009; Tierney & Farmer, 2002). In addition, previous research has highlighted employees' intrinsic motivation (Amabile, 1996) and positive mood states (Madjar et al., 2002) as important mediating conditions that might explain the effects of the context on creativity. Research is now needed that compares and contrasts the effectiveness of these mediating mechanisms with the model presented here to determine which framework, or combination of frameworks, best explains the effects of contextual characteristics on individual and team creativity.

The fact that a number of studies have found curvilinear effects on creativity of contextual factors such as time pressure (Baer & Oldham, 2006), conflict (De Dreu, 2006), and number of weak ties (Baer, 2010; Zhou et al., 2009) also highlights the need for future work to refine the conceptual model outlined in this chapter. Specifically, while the link between engagement and creativity may well be linear, it is evident that too little pressure and conflict may seem ineffective in instilling the level of engagement required for individuals to produce creative work. In addition, there is evidence to suggest that the link between access and exposure to new and different pockets of information may not be linear as proposed in our theoretical model but curvilinear with too much information potentially producing problems of information overload (Baer, 2010; Zhou et al., 2009). Thus, we encourage future work to consider both linear and curvilinear relations between dimensions of the work context and creativity.

In addition, research is also needed that identifies other characteristics that may impact the creativity of employees at work. One that may deserve attention is the physical environment in which employees work (Dul & Ceylan, 2011). Early research established that the physical configuration of environments could influence interaction patterns among employees with open, nonpartitioned spaces encouraging more interpersonal contact and interaction than closed, partitioned spaces (Oldham, Cummings, & Zhou, 1995; Vischer, 2005). These early studies would suggest that open spaces might encourage the exchange of information among employees which, in turn, may enhance creativity. Alternatively, it may be that open spaces that encourage interactions produce more unexpected interpersonal interruptions that distract employees from their work, resulting in lowered engagement and creativity. Unfortunately, very few studies have tested the effects of the physical space on creativity and none have systematically addressed possible mediating conditions (Shalley et al., 2004). Research is now needed to investigate these issues in order to determine the physical configurations most likely to stimulate the production of creative ideas.

Most of the studies we reviewed in this chapter focused on the effects of contextual conditions inside the boundaries of the organization. But many employees in contemporary organizations may not spend the bulk of their working lives inside the physical boundaries of an organization. Instead, they may spend part or all of their time at home and telecommute to work. Or they may be independent contractors, simultaneously managing temporary or semi-permanent relationships with multiple enterprises (Oldham & Hackman, 2010). These possible changes in the nature of work suggest that it may be productive to examine the effects of environmental and social conditions outside the organization that influence employees' creative responses. To this point only a few studies have focused on contextual conditions of this type, and these studies have reported encouraging results (e.g., Baer, 2010; Madjar et al., 2002). For example, Madjar (2008) demonstrated that support and new information from family and friends had a positive relationship to employee creativity. Baer (2010) showed that contacts with customers and clients outside the organization can have a positive impact on a focal employee's creativity. More work is now needed to investigate the effects of the external organizational environment on employee creativity and the possibility that these conditions can combine with those inside the organization to affect employee creativity.

In addition to the fact that most of our reviewed studies focused on contextual conditions inside the organization's formal boundaries, most of the studies reviewed also examined the effects of the context on the creativity of employees working individually. Relatively few studies (e.g., Baer et al., 2010; Eisenbeiss et al., 2008) have examined the effects of the context on team creativity, despite the increasing prevalence of teams in contemporary organizations. Future research should address this issue and examine a variety of contextual conditions on the creativity exhibited by teams. For example, research might explore the effects on team creativity of different schemes for paying individual team members and entire teams. Also, research on the effects of team performance and creativity goals and evaluation programs could yield results that are of both theoretical and practical interest.

Throughout the chapter we have focused on the effects of the context on creativity—defined as the extent to which ideas generated by employees or teams were both novel and useful. Although this definition of creativity is consistent with that used in most contemporary research (see Amabile, 1996; Shalley et al., 2004), some research suggests that the dimensions of novelty and usefulness are not always aligned and sometimes even can be negatively related (Beersma & De Dreu, 2005; Rietzschel, Nijstad, & Stroebe, 2007). Therefore, it might be productive if future studies examined the effects of contextual conditions on the two individual elements of creativity—novelty and usefulness. It may be that certain contextual characteristics are more conducive to stimulating the novelty component whereas others contribute more to an idea's usefulness. To our knowledge, no previous studies have systematically examined this possibility.

Finally, this chapter has focused on the contextual conditions that had the potential to prompt creative ideas in the workplace. But as we noted earlier, these creative ideas are only likely to build competitive advantage if they are actually brought to fruition. Unfortunately, few studies have examined the contextual conditions that facilitate the connection between creative idea generation and idea implementation (for exceptions, see Axtell et al., 2000, Fleming et al., 2007, and Frese et al., 1999). Thus, we know little about the circumstances that must be in place if ideas are to be fully taken advantage of at work. Previous work has highlighted that the factors that contribute to the production of creative ideas may not be sufficient to guarantee the successful implementation of these ideas (Burt, 2004). Thus, future work is now needed that identifies the contextual conditions that foster the implementation of new and potentially useful ideas. Work on this topic, combined with research on contextual conditions that enhance employee creativity, might go a long way toward clarifying how organizations should be managed and structured to ensure that creative ideas are both developed and implemented.

Acknowledgement

The authors thank Michael Mumford for his helpful suggestions on an earlier draft of this chapter and Taisha Penn for her help with the literature review.

References

Ahearne, M., Mathieu, J., & Rapp, A. (2005). To empower or not to empower your sales force? An empirical examination of the influence of leadership empowerment behavior on customer satisfaction and performance. *Journal of Applied Psychology, 90*, 945–955.

Amabile, T. M. (1979). Effects of external evaluation on artistic creativity. *Journal of Personality and Social Psychology, 37*, 221–233.

Amabile, T. M. (1982). Children's artistic creativity: Detrimental effects of competition in a field setting. *Personality and Social Psychology Bulletin, 8*, 573–578.

Amabile, T. M. (1987). The motivation to be creative. In S. Isaksen (Ed.), *Frontiers of creativity research: Beyond the basics* (pp. 223–254). Buffalo, NY: Bearly Limited.

Amabile, T. M. (1988). A model of creativity and innovation in organizations. In B. Staw & L. Cummings (Eds.), *Research in organizational behavior* (Vol. 10, pp. 123–167). Greenwich, CT: JAI Press.

Amabile, T. M. (1996). *Creativity in context*. Boulder, CO: Westview Press.

Amabile, T. M., & Conti, R. (1999). Changes in the work environment for creativity during downsizing. *Academy of Management Journal, 42*, 630–640.

Amabile, T. M., & Gryskiewicz, N. D. (1989). The creative environment scales: Work environment inventory. *Creativity Research Journal, 2*, 231–252.

Amabile, T. M., Conti, R., Coon, H., Lazenby, J., & Herron, M. (1996). Assessing the work environment for creativity. *Academy of Management Journal, 39*, 1154–1184.

Amabile, T. M., Goldfarb, P., & Brackfield, S. C. (1990). Social influences on creativity: Evaluation, coaction, and surveillance. *Creativity Research Journal, 3*, 6–21.

Amabile, T. M., Hennessey, B. A., & Grossman, B. S. (1986). Social influences on creativity: The effects of contracted-for reward. *Journal of Personality and Social Psychology, 50*, 14–23.

Amabile, T. M., Schatzel, E. A., Moneta, G. B., & Kramer, S. J. (2004). Leader behaviors and the work environment: Perceived leader support. *The Leadership Quarterly, 15*, 5–32.

Amabile, T. R., Hadley, C. N., & Kramer, S. J. (2002). Creativity under the gun. *Harvard Business Review, 80*, 52–61.

Amason, A. C. (1996). Distinguishing the effects of functional and dysfunctional conflict on strategic decision making: Resolving a paradox for top management teams. *Academy of Management Journal, 39*, 123–148.

Andrews, F. M., & Farris, G. F. (1972). Time pressure and performance of scientists and engineers: A five-year panel study. *Organizational Behavior and Human Performance, 8*, 185–200.

Andrews, J., & Smith, D. C. (1996). In search of the marketing imagination: Factors affecting the creativity of marketing programs for mature products. *Journal of Marketing Research, 33*, 174–187.

Atwater, L., & Carmeli, A. (2009). Leader–member exchange, feelings of energy, and involvement in creative work. *The Leadership Quarterly, 20*, 264–275.

Axtell, C. M., Holman, D. J., Unsworth, K. L., Wall, T. D., Waterson, P. E., & Harrington, E. (2000). Shopfloor innovation: Facilitating the suggestion and implementation of ideas. *Journal of Occupational and Organizational Psychology, 73*, 265–285.

Baer, M. (2010). The strength-of-weak-ties perspective on creativity: A comprehensive examination and extension. *Journal of Applied Psychology, 95*, 592–601.

Baer, M., Leenders, R. T. A. J., Oldham, G. R., & Vadera, A. (2010). Win or lose the battle for creativity: The power and perils of intergroup competition. *Academy of Management Journal, 53*, 827–845.

Baer, M., & Oldham, G. R. (2006). The curvilinear relation between experienced creative time pressure and creativity: Moderating effects of openness to experience and support for creativity. *Journal of Applied Psychology, 91*, 963–970.

Baer, M., Oldham, G. R., & Cummings, A. (2003). Rewarding creativity: When does it really matter? *The Leadership Quarterly, 14*, 569–586.

Bartis, S., Szymanski, K., & Harkins, S. G. (1988). Evaluation and performance: A two edged knife. *Personality and Social Psychology Bulletin, 14*, 242–251.

Bass, B. M. (1985). *Leadership and performance beyond expectations*. New York, NY: Free Press.

Basu, R., & Green, S. G. (1997). Leader–member exchange and transformational leadership: An empirical examination of innovative behaviors in leader–member dyads. *Journal of Applied Social Psychology, 27*, 477–499.

Beersma, B., & De Dreu, C. K. W. (2005). Conflict's consequences: Effects of social motives on postnegotiation creative and convergent group functioning and performance. *Journal of Personality and Social Psychology, 89*, 358–374.

Binnewies, C., Ohly, S., & Niessen, C. (2008). Age and creativity at work: The interplay between job resources, age, and idea creativity. *Journal of Managerial Psychology, 23*, 438–457.

Binnewies, C., Ohly, S., & Sonentag, S. (2007). Taking personal initiative and communicating about ideas: What is important for the creative process and for idea creativity? *European Journal of Work and Organizational Psychology, 16*, 432–455.

Boerner, S., Eisenbeiss, S. A., & Griesser, D. (2007). Follower performance and organizational performance: The impact of transformational leaders. *Journal of Leadership & Organizational Studies, 13*, 15–26.

Bornstein, G., & Erev, I. (1994). The enhancing effect of intergroup competition on group performance. *International Journal of Conflict Management, 5*, 52–67.

Brass, D. J. (1995). Creativity: It's all in your social network. In C. Ford & D. Gioia (Eds.), *Creative action in organization* (pp. 94–99). Thousand Oaks, CA: Sage.

Burt, R. (2004). Structural holes and good ideas. *American Journal of Sociology, 110*, 349–399.

Burt, R. S. (1992). *Structural holes: The social structure of competition.* Cambridge, MA: Harvard University Press.

Byron, K., Khazanchi, S., & Nazarian, D. (2010). The relationship between stressors and creativity: A meta-analysis examining competing theoretical models. *Journal of Applied Psychology, 95*, 201–212.

Camacho, L. M., & Paulus, P. B. (1995). The role of social anxiousness in group brainstorming. *Journal of Personality and Social Psychology, 68*, 1071–1080.

Carmeli, A., & Schaubroeck, J. (2007). The influence of leaders' and other referents' normative expectations on individual involvement in creative work. *The Leadership Quarterly, 18*, 35–48.

Carnevale, P. J., & Probst, T. M. (1998). Social values and social conflict in creative problem solving and categorization. *Journal of Personality and Social Psychology, 74*, 1300–1309.

Carson, P. P., & Carson, K. D. (1993). Managing creativity enhancement through goal setting and feedback. *Journal of Creative Behavior, 27*, 36–45.

Cheek, J. M., & Stahl, S. S. (1986). Shyness and verbal creativity. *Journal of Research in Personality, 2*, 51–61.

Chen, M-H. (2006). Understanding the benefits and detriments of conflict on team creativity process. *Creativity and Innovation Management, 15*, 105–116.

Choi, J. N. (2004). Individual and contextual predictors of creative performance: The mediating role of psychological processes. *Creativity Research Journal, 2&3*, 187–199.

Choi, J. N., Anderson, T. A., & Veillette, A. (2009). Contextual inhibitors of employee creativity in organizations: The insulating role of creative ability. *Group & Organization Management, 34*, 330–357.

Clydesdale, G. (2006). Creativity and competition: The Beatles. *Creativity Research Journal, 18*, 129–139.

Coelho, R., & Augusto, M. (2010). Job characteristics and the creativity of frontline service employees. *Journal of Service Research, 13*, 426–438.

Conti, R., Collins, M. A., & Picariello, M. L. (2001). The impact of competition on intrinsic motivation and creativity: Considering gender, gender segregation and gender role orientation. *Personality and Individual Differences, 30*, 1273–1289.

Cross, R., & Cummings, J. N. (2004). Tie and network correlates of individual performance in knowledge intensive work. *Academy of Management Journal, 47*, 928–937.

Damanpour, F., & Schneider, M. (2006). Phases of the adoption of innovation: Effects of environment, organization and top managers. *British Journal of Management, 17*, 215–236.

Dansereau, F., Graen, G., & Haga, W. (1975). A vertical dyad linkage approach to leadership within formal organizations: A longitudinal investigation of the role-making process. *Organizational Behavior and Human Performance, 13*, 46–78.

De Dreu, C. K. W. (2006). When too little or too much hurts: Evidence for a curvilinear relationship between task conflict and innovation in teams. *Journal of Management, 32*, 83–107.

De Dreu, C. K. W., & Weingart, L. R. (2003). Task versus relationship conflict, team performance, and team member satisfaction: A meta-analysis. *Journal of Applied Psychology, 88*, 741–749.

De Dreu, C. K. W., & West, M. A. (2001). Minority dissent and team innovation: The importance of participation in decision making. *Journal of Applied Psychology, 86*, 1191–1201.

Deci, E. L., & Ryan, R. M. (2000). The "what" and "why" of goal pursuits: Human needs and the self-determination of behavior. *Psychological Inquiry, 11*, 227–268.

Deutsch, M. (1949). A theory of co-operation and competition. *Human Relations, 2*, 129–152.

Diehl, M., & Stroebe, W. (1987). Productivity loss in brainstorming groups: Toward the solution of a riddle. *Journal of Personality and Social Psychology, 53*, 497–509.

Dul, J., & Ceylan, C. (2011). Work environments for employee creativity. *Ergonomics, 54*, 12–20.

Eisenbeiss, S., van Knippenberg, D., & Boerner, S. (2008). Transformational leadership and team innovation: Integrating team climate principles. *Journal of Applied Psychology, 93*, 1438–1446.

Eisenberger, R., & Armeli, S. (1997). Can salient reward increase creative performance without reducing intrinsic creative interest? *Journal of Personality and Social Psychology, 72*, 652–663.

Eisenberger, R., Armeli, S., & Pretz, J. (1998). Can the promise of reward increase creativity? *Journal of Personality and Social Psychology, 74*, 704–714.

Eisenberger, R., & Aselage, J. (2009). Incremental effects of reward on experienced performance pressure: Positive outcomes for intrinsic interest and creativity. *Journal of Organizational Behavior, 30*, 95–117.

C. GROUP LEVEL INFLUENCES

Eisenberger, R., & Rhoades, L. (2001). Incremental effects of rewards on creativity. *Journal of Personality and Social Psychology, 81,* 728–741.

Erez, M., & Kanfer, F. H. (1983). The role of goal acceptance in goal setting and task performance. *Academy of Management Review, 8,* 454–463.

Evan, W. (1965). Conflict and performance in R&D organizations. *Industrial Management Review, 7,* 37–46.

Farh, J-L., Lee, C., & Farh, C. I. C. (2010). Task conflict and team creativity: A question of how much and when. *Journal of Applied Psychology, 95,* 1173–1180.

Farmer, S. M., Tierney, P., & Kung-McIntyre, K. (2003). Employee creativity in Taiwan: An application of role identity theory. *Academy of Management Journal, 46,* 618–630.

Fleming, L., Mingo, S., & Chen, D. (2007). Collaborative brokerage, generative creativity, and creative success. *Administrative Science Quarterly, 52,* 443–475.

Frese, M., Teng, E., & Wijnen, C. J. D. (1999). Helping to improve suggestion systems: Predictors of making suggestions in companies. *Journal of Organizational Behavior, 20,* 1139–1155.

Fried, Y., & Ferris, G. R. (1987). The validity of the job characteristics model: A review and meta-analysis. *Personnel Psychology, 40,* 287–322.

Gardner, D. G., & Cummings, L. L. (1988). Activation theory and job design: Review and reconceptualization. In B. Staw & L. Cummings (Eds.), *Research in organizational behavior* (Vol. 10, pp. 81–122). Greenwich, CT: JAI Press.

George, J. M. (2007). Creativity in organizations. *Academy of Management Annals, 1,* 439–477.

George, J. M., & Zhou, J. (2001). When openness to experience and conscientiousness are related to creative behavior: An interactional approach. *Journal of Applied Psychology, 86,* 513–524.

George, J. M., & Zhou, J. (2007). Dual tuning in a supportive context: Joint contributions of positive mood, negative mood, and supervisory behaviors to employee creativity. *Academy of Management Journal, 50,* 605–622.

Gong, Y., Huang, J.-C., & Farh, J.-L. (2009). Employee learning orientation, transformational leadership, and employee creativity: The mediating role of employee self-efficacy. *Academy of Management Journal, 52,* 765–778.

Gough, H. G. (1979). A creative personality scale for the Adjective Check List. *Journal of Personality and Social Psychology, 37,* 1398–1405.

Graen, G., & Scandura., T. (1987). Toward a psychology of dyadic organizing. In L. Cummings & B. Staw (Eds.), *Research in organizational behavior* (Vol. 9, pp. 175–208). Greenwich, CT: JAI Press.

Granovetter, M. S. (1973). The strength of weak ties. *American Journal of Sociology, 78,* 1360–1380.

Grant, A. M., & Berry, J. (2011). The necessity of others is the mother of invention: Intrinsic and prosocial motivations, perspective-taking, and creativity. *Academy of Management Journal, 54,* 73–96.

Gumusluoglu, L., & Ilsev, A. (2009). Transformational leadership, creativity, and organizational innovation. *Journal of Business Research, 62,* 461–473.

Hackman, J. R., & Oldham, G. R. (1980). *Work redesign.* Reading, MA: Addison-Wesley.

Hansen, M. T., Mors, M. L., & Løvås, B. (2005). Knowledge sharing in organizations: Multiple networks, multiple phases. *Academy of Management Journal, 48,* 776–793.

Hargadon, A. B., & Bechky, B. A. (2006). When collections of creatives become creative collectives: A field study of problem solving at work. *Organization Science, 4,* 484–500.

Hatcher, L., Ross, T. L., & Collins, D. (1989). Prosocial behavior, job complexity, and suggestion contribution under gainsharing plans. *Journal of Applied Behavioral Science, 25,* 231–248.

Hennessey, B. A. (1989). The effect of extrinsic constraints on children's creativity while using a computer. *Creativity Research Journal, 2,* 151–168.

Hennessey, B. A., & Amabile, T. M. (2010). Creativity. In S. Fiske (Ed.), *Annual Review of Psychology* (61, pp. 569–598). Palo Alto, CA: Annual Reviews.

Janssen, O. (2005). The joint impact of perceived influence and supervisor supportiveness on employee innovative behaviour. *Journal of Occupational and Organizational Psychology, 78,* 573–579.

Jaskyte, K. (2008). Employee creativity in US and Lithuanian nonprofit organizations. *Nonprofit Management & Leadership, 18,* 465–483.

Jaussi, K. S., & Dionne, S. D. (2003). Leading for creativity: The role of unconventional leader behavior. *The Leadership Quarterly, 14,* 475–498.

Jehn, K. A. (1995). A multimethod examination of the benefits and detriments of intragroup conflict. *Administrative Science Quarterly, 40,* 256–282.

Jehn, K. A. (1997). A qualitative analysis of conflict types and dimensions in organizational groups. *Administrative Science Quarterly, 42,* 530–557.

Jehn, K. A., & Bendersky, C. (2003). Intragroup conflict in organizations: A contingency perspective on the conflict-outcome relationship. In R. Kramer & B. Staw (Eds.), *Research in organizational behavior* (Vol. 25, pp. 187–242). New York, NY: Elsevier.

Jehn, K. A., Rispens, S., & Thatcher, S. M. B. (2010). The effects of conflict asymmetry on work group and individual outcomes. *Academy of Management Journal, 53*, 596–616.

Joussemet, M., & Koestner, R. (1999). Effect of expected rewards on children's creativity. *Creativity Research Journal, 12*, 231–239.

Jung, D. I. (2000–2001). Transformational and transactional leadership and their effects on creativity in groups. *Creativity Research Journal, 13*, 185–195.

Kahai, S. S., Sosik, J. J., & Avolio, B. J. (2003). Effects of leadership style, anonymity, and rewards on creativity-relevant processes and outcomes in an electronic meeting system context. *The Leadership Quarterly, 14*, 499–524.

Kahn, W. A. (1990). Psychological conditions of personal engagement and disengagement at work. *Academy of Management Journal, 33*, 692–724.

Kahn, W. A. (1992). To be fully there: Psychological presence at work. *Human Relations, 45*, 321–349.

Karasek, R. (1979). Job demands, job decision latitude and mental strain: Implications for job redesign. *Administrative Science Quarterly, 24*, 285–306.

Kavanagh, M. J. (1982). Evaluating performance. In K. Rowland & G. Ferris (Eds.), *Personnel management* (pp. 187–226). Boston, MA: Allyn & Bacon.

Kelly, J. R., & McGrath, J. E. (1985). Effects of time limits and task types on task performance and interaction in four-person groups. *Journal of Personality and Social Psychology, 49*, 395–407.

Khazanchi, S., & Masterson, S. S. (2010). Who and what is fair matters: A multi-foci social exchange model of creativity. *Journal of Organizational Behavior, 32*, 86–106.

Kim, T-Y., Hon, A. H. Y., & Lee, D-R. (2010). Proactive personality and employee creativity: The effects of job creativity requirement and supervisor support for creativity. *Creativity Research Journal, 22*, 37–45.

Kirton, M. (1994). *Adaptors and innovators: Styles of creativity and problem solving.* New York, NY: Routledge.

Kratzer, J., Leenders, R. T. A. J., & van Engleen, J. M. (2006). Team polarity and creative performance in innovation teams. *Creativity and Innovation Management, 15*, 96–104.

Kratzer, J., Leenders, R. T. A. J., & van Engleen, J. M. (2010). The social network among engineering design teams and their creativity: A case study among teams in two product development programs. *International Journal of Project Management, 28*, 428–436.

Kratzer, J., & Lettl, C. (2008). A social network perspective of lead users and creativity: An empirical study among children. *Creativity and Innovation Management, 17*, 26–36.

Kruglanski, A. W., Friedman, I., & Zeevi, G. (1971). The effects of extrinsic incentive on some qualitative aspects of task performance. *Journal of Personality, 39*, 606–617.

Kurtzberg, T. R., & Mueller, J. S. (2005). The influence of daily conflict on perceptions of creativity: A longitudinal study. *The International Journal of Conflict Management, 16*, 335–353.

Lee, K., Rho, S., Kim, S., & Jun, G. J. (2007). Creativity–innovation cycle for organizational exploration and exploitation: Lessons from Neowiz–a Korean internet company. *Long Range Planning, 40*, 505–523.

Liao, H., Liu, D., & Loi, R. (2010). Looking at both sides of the social exchange coin: A social cognitive perspective on the joint effects of relationship quality and differentiation on creativity. *Academy of Management Journal, 53*, 1090–1109.

Lim, H. S., & Choi, J. N. (2009). Testing an alternative relationship between individual and contextual predictors of creative performance. *Social Behavior and Personality, 37*, 117–136.

Locke, E. A., & Latham, G. P. (1990). *A theory of goal setting and task performance.* Englewood Cliffs, NJ: Prentice Hall.

Lunchins, A. (1942). Mechanization in problem solving: The effect of Einstellung. *Psychological Monographs, 54.* (Whole No. 248)

Madjar, N. (2008). Emotional and informational support from different sources and employee creativity. *Journal of Occupational and Organizational Psychology, 81*, 83–100.

Madjar, N., & Oldham, G. R. (2006). Task rotation and polychronicity: Effects on individuals' creativity. *Human Performance, 19*, 117–131.

Madjar, N., Oldham, G. R., & Pratt, M. G. (2002). There's no place like home? The contributions of work and non-work creativity support to employee's creative performance. *Academy of Management Journal, 45*, 757–767.

Madjar, N., & Ortiz-Walters, R. (2008). Customers as contributors and reliable evaluators of creativity in the service industry. *Journal of Organizational Behavior, 29*, 949–966.

Madjar, N., & Shalley, C. E. (2008). Multiple tasks' and multiple goals' effect on creativity: Forced incubation or just a distraction? *Journal of Management, 34,* 786–805.

Martin, P., Salanova, M., & Peiró, J. M. (2007). Job demands, job resources and individual innovation at work: Going beyond Karasek's model? *Psicothema, 19,* 621–626.

May, D. R., Gilson, R., & Harter, L. M. (2004). The psychological conditions of meaningfulness, safety and availability and the engagement of the human spirit at work. *Journal of Occupational and Organizational Psychology, 77,* 11–37.

Menon, T., & Pfeffer, J. (2003). Valuing internal vs. external knowledge: Explaining the preference for outsiders. *Management Science, 49,* 497–513.

Menon, T., Thompson, L., & Choi, H-S. (2006). Tainted knowledge vs. tempting knowledge: People avoid knowledge from internal rivals and seek knowledge from external rivals. *Management Science, 52,* 1129–1144.

Morgeson, F. P., & Humphrey, S. E. (2006). The work design questionnaire (WDQ): Developing and validating a comprehensive measure for assessing job design and the nature of work. *Journal of Applied Psychology, 90,* 399–406.

Moss, A. A., & Ritossa, D. A. (2007). The impact of goal orientation on the association between leadership style and follower performance, creativity and work attitudes. *Leadership, 3,* 433–456.

Mullen, B., Johnson, C., & Salas, E. (1991). Productivity loss in brainstorming groups: A meta-analytic integration. *Basic and Applied Psychology, 12,* 2–23.

Mumford, M. D. (2000). Managing creative people: Strategies and tactics for innovation. *Human Resources Management Review, 10,* 313–351.

Mumford, M. D., & Gustafson, S. B. (1988). Creativity syndrome: Integration, application, and innovation. *Psychological Bulletin, 103,* 27–43.

Nonaka, I. (1991). The knowledge-creating company. *Harvard Business Review, 69,* 96–104.

Obstfeld, D. (2005). Social networks, the tertius iungens orientation, and involvement in innovation. *Administrative Science Quarterly, 50,* 100–130.

Ohly, S., & Fritz, C. (2010). Work characteristics, creativity, and proactive behavior: The mediating role of challenge. *Journal of Organizational Behavior, 31,* 543–565.

Ohly, S., Sonnentag, S., & Pluntke, F. (2006). Routinization, work characteristics, and their relationships with creative and proactive behaviors. *Journal of Organizational Behavior, 27,* 257–279.

Oldham, G. R. (2002). Stimulating and supporting creativity in organizations. In S. Jackson, M. Hitt & A. DeNisi (Eds.), *Managing knowledge for sustained competitive advantage* (pp. 243–273). San Francisco, CA: Jossey-Bass.

Oldham, G. R., & Cummings, A. (1996). Employee creativity: Personal and contextual factors at work. *Academy of Management Journal, 39,* 607–634.

Oldham, G. R., Cummings, A., & Zhou, J. (1995). The spatial configuration of organizations. In G. Ferris (Ed.), *Research in personnel and human resources management* (Vol. 13, pp. 1–37). Greenwich, CT: JAI Press.

Oldham, G. R., & Hackman, J. R. (2010). Not what it was and not what it will be: The future of job design research. *Journal of Organizational Behavior, 31,* 463–479.

Pearsall, M. J., Ellis, A. P. J., & Evans, J. M. (2008). Unlocking the effects of gender faultlines on team creativity: Is activation the key. *Journal of Applied Psychology, 93,* 225–234.

Pelled, L. H. (1996). Demographic diversity, conflict, and work group outcomes: An intervening process theory. *Organization Science, 7,* 615–631.

Perry-Smith, J. E. (2006). Social yet creative: The role of social relationships in facilitating individual creativity. *Academy of Management Journal, 49,* 85–101.

Perry-Smith, J. E., & Shalley, C. E. (2003). The social side of creativity: A static and dynamic social network perspective. *Academy of Management Review, 28,* 89–106.

Pieterse, A. N., van Knippenberg, D., Schippers, M., & Stam, D. (2010). Transformational and transactional leadership and innovative behavior: The moderating role of psychological empowerment. *Journal of Organizational Behavior, 31,* 609–623.

Raja, U., & Johns, G. (2010). The joint effects of personality and job scope on in-role performance, citizenship behaviors, and creativity. *Human Relations, 63,* 981–1005.

Rank, J., Nelson, N. E., Allen, T. D., & Xu, X. (2009). Leadership predictors of innovation and task performance: Subordinates' self-esteem and self-presentation as moderators. *Journal of Occupational and Organizational Psychology, 82,* 465–489.

Redmond, M. R., Mumford, M. D., & Teach, R. (1993). Putting creativity to work: Effects of leader behavior on subordinate creativity. *Organizational Behavior and Human Decision Processes, 55,* 120–151.

Reuvers, M., van Engen, M. L., Vinkenburg, C. J., & Wilson-Evered, E. (2008). Transformational leadership and innovative work behaviour: Exploring the relevance of gender differences. *Creativity and Innovation Management, 17*, 227–244.

Rice, G. (2006). Individual values, organizational context, and self-perceptions of employee creativity. Evidence from Egyptian organizations. *Journal of Business Research, 59*, 233–241.

Rich, B. L., LePine, J., & Crawford, E. R. (2010). Job engagement: Antecedents and effects on job performance. *Academy of Management Journal, 53*, 617–635.

Rietzschel, E. F., Nijstad, B. A., & Stroebe, W. (2007). Relative accessibility of domain knowledge and creativity: The effects of knowledge activation on the quantity and originality of generated ideas. *Journal of Experimental Social Psychology, 43*, 933–946.

Rodan, S., & Galunic, C. (2004). More than network structure: How knowledge heterogeneity influences managerial performance and innovativeness. *Strategic Management Journal, 25*, 541–562.

Roos, P. A., & Treiman, D. J. (1980). Worker functions and work traits for the 1970 US census classification. In A. Miller (Ed.), *Work, jobs and occupations* (pp. 336–389). Washington, D.C: National Academy Press.

Runco, M. (in press). Abilities. In M. Mumford (Ed.), *Handbook of organizational creativity*.

Saavedra, R., & Kwun, S. K. (2000). Affective states in job characteristics theory. *Journal of Organizational Behavior, 21*, 131–146.

Scott, S. G., & Bruce, R. A. (1994). Determinants of innovative behavior: A path model of individual innovation in the workplace. *Academy of Management Journal, 37*, 580–607.

Selart, M., Nordstrom, T., Kuvaas, B., & Takemura, K. (2008). Effects of reward on self-regulation, intrinsic motivation and creativity. *Scandinavian Journal of Educational Research, 52*, 439–458.

Shalley, C. E. (1991). Effects of productivity goals, creativity goals, and personal discretion on individual creativity. *Journal of Applied Psychology, 76*, 179–185.

Shalley, C. E. (1995). Effects of coaction, expected evaluation, and goal setting on creativity and productivity. *Academy of Management Journal, 38*, 483–503.

Shalley, C. E., Gilson, L. L., & Blum, T. C. (2009). Interactive effects of growth need strength, work context, and job complexity on self-reported creative performance. *Academy of Management Journal, 52*, 489–505.

Shalley, C. E., & Oldham, G. R. (1985). Effects of goal difficulty and expected external evaluation on intrinsic motivation: A laboratory study. *Academy of Management Journal, 28*, 628–640.

Shalley, C. E., & Oldham, G. R. (1997). Competition and creative performance: Effects of competitor presence and visibility. *Creativity Research Journal, 10*, 337–345.

Shalley, C. E., & Perry-Smith, J. E. (2001). Effects of social-psychological factors on creative performance: The role of informational and controlling expected evaluation and modeling experience. *Organizational Behavior and Human Decision Processes, 84*, 1–22.

Shalley, C. E., Zhou, J., & Oldham, G. R. (2004). The effects of personal and contextual characteristics on creativity: Where should we go from here? *Journal of Management, 30*, 933–958.

Sherif, M., & Sherif, C. W. (1953). *Groups in harmony and tension: An introduction to studies in intergroup relations.* New York, NY: Harper & Brothers.

Shin, S. J., & Zhou, J. (2003). Transformational leadership, conservation, and creativity: Evidence from Korea. *Academy of Management Journal, 46*, 703–714.

Singh, J., & Fleming, L. (2010). Lone inventors as sources of breakthroughs: Myth or reality? *Management Science, 56*, 41–56.

Smith, G. J. W. (in press). Personality. In M. Mumford (Ed.), *Handbook of organizational creativity*.

Soriano de Alencar, E., & Bruno-Faria, M. (1997). Characteristics of an organizational environment which stimulate and inhibit creativity. *Journal of Creative Behavior, 3*, 271–281.

Sosik, J. J., Kahai, S. S., & Avolio, B. J. (1998). Transformational leadership and dimensions of creativity: Motivating idea generation in computer-mediated groups. *Creativity Research Journal, 11*, 111–121.

Staw, B. M., Calder, B. J., Hess, R. K., & Sandelands, L. E. (1980). Intrinsic motivation and norms about payment. *Journal of Personality, 48*, 1–14.

Staw, B. M., Sandelands, L. E., & Dutton, J. E. (1981). Threat-rigidity effects in organizational behavior: A multilevel analysis. *Administrative Science Quarterly, 26*, 501–524.

Szymanski, K., & Harkins, S. G. (1992). Self-evaluation and creativity. *Personality and Social Psychology Bulletin, 18*, 259–265.

C. GROUP LEVEL INFLUENCES

Tierney, P., & Farmer, S. M. (2002). Creative self-efficacy: Potential antecedents and relationship to creative perform-ance. *Academy of Management Journal, 45,* 1137–1148.

Tierney, P., & Farmer, S. M. (2004). The Pygmalion process and employee creativity. *Journal of Management, 30,* 413–432.

Tierney, P., Farmer, S. M., & Graen, G. B. (1999). An examination of leadership and employee creativity: The rel-evance of traits and relationships. *Personnel Psychology, 52,* 591–620.

Tjosvold, D., Tang, M. M. L., & West, M. (2004). Reflexivity for team innovation in China. *Group & Organization Management, 29,* 540–559.

Tortoriello, M., & Krackhardt, D. (2010). Activating cross-boundary knowledge: The role of Simmelian ties in the generation of innovations. *Academy of Management Journal, 53,* 167–181.

Troyer, L., & Youngreen, R. (2009). Conflict and creativity in groups. *Journal of Social Issues, 65,* 409–427.

Turner, A. N., & Lawrence, P. R. (1965). *Industrial jobs and the worker.* Boston, MA: Harvard Graduate School of Business Administration.

Tushman, M. L. (1977). Special boundary roles in the innovation process. *Administrative Science Quarterly, 22,* 587–605.

Unsworth, K. L., Wall, T. D., & Carter, A. (2005). Creative requirement: A neglected construct in the study of employee creativity? *Group & Organization Management, 30,* 541–560.

Van Dyne, L., & Saaverda, R. (1996). A naturalistic minority influence experiment: Effects on divergent thinking, conflict, and originality in work-groups. *British Journal of Social Psychology, 35,* 151–168.

Van Dyne, L., Jehn, K. A., & Cummings, A. (2002). Differential effect of strain on two forms of work performance: Individual employee sales and creativity. *Journal of Organizational Behavior, 23,* 57–74.

VandeWalle, D. (1997). Development and validation of a work domain goal orientation instrument. *Educational and Psychological Measurement, 57,* 995–1015.

VandeWalle, D., Cron, W. L., & Slocum, J. W. (2001). The role of goal orientation following performance feedback. *Journal of Applied Psychology, 86,* 629–640.

Vischer, J. C. (2005). *Space meets status: Designing workplace performance.* New York, NY: Routledge.

Wang, A-C., & Cheng, B-S. (2010). When does benevolent leadership lead to creativity? The moderating role of creative role identity and job autonomy. *Journal of Organizational Behavior, 31,* 106–121.

West, M. A., & Farr, J. L. (1990). Innovation at work. In M. West & J. Farr (Eds.), *Innovation and creativity at work: Psychological and organizational strategies* (pp. 3–13). Chichester, UK: Wiley.

Woodman, R. W., Sawyer, J. E., & Griffin, R. W. (1993). Toward a theory of organizational creativity. *Academy of Management Review, 18,* 293–321.

Yuan, R., & Zhou, J. (2008). Differential effects of expected external evaluation on different parts of the creative idea production process and on final product creativity. *Creativity Research Journal, 20,* 391–403.

Zhang, X., & Bartol, K. M. (2010). Linking empowering leadership and employee creativity: The influence of psy-chological empowerment, intrinsic motivation, and creative process engagement. *Academy of Management Journal, 53,* 107–128.

Zhou, J. (1998). Feedback valence, feedback style, task autonomy, and achievement orientation: Interactive effects on creative performance. *Journal of Applied Psychology, 83,* 261–276.

Zhou, J. (2003). When the presence of creative coworkers is related to creativity: Role of supervisor close monitor-ing, developmental feedback, and creative personality. *Journal of Applied Psychology, 88,* 413–422.

Zhou, J., & George, J. M. (2001). When job dissatisfaction leads to creativity: Encouraging the expression of voice. *Academy of Management Journal, 44,* 682–696.

Zhou, J., & Oldham, G. R. (2001). Enhancing creative performance: Effects of expected developmental assessment strategies and creative personality. *Journal of Creative Behavior, 35,* 151–167.

Zhou, J., & Shalley, C. E. (2003). Research on employee creativity: A critical review and directions for future research. In J. Martocchio (Ed.), *Research in personnel and human resource management* (pp. 165–217). Oxford, UK: Elsevier.

Zhou, J., Shin, S. J., Brass, D. J., Choi, J., & Zhang, Z-X. (2009). Social networks, personal values, and creativity: Evidence for curvilinear and interaction effects. *Journal of Applied Psychology, 94,* 1544–1552.

Zhou, J., Shin, S. J., & Cannella, A. A. (2008). Employee self-perceived creativity after mergers and acquisitions: Interactive effects of threat–opportunity perception, access to resources, and support for creativity. *Journal of Applied Behavioral Science, 44,* 397–421.

Project Management of Innovative Teams

Susannah B. F. Paletz

University of Pittsburgh, Pittsburgh, PA

In many organizations, innovation occurs in teams working within project management structures. In 2006, a design team working internally to NASA was tasked with producing software to support the reporting, tracking, and correcting problems with space flight hardware. As with most large organizations, NASA required project management principles be met. Although this software design was conducted in a fairly flexible, fast-paced, and iterative manner, clear requirements, schedules, and risks were identified and managed for the life of the project. The goal of this chapter is to outline fundamental project management concepts, and then to tie these to relevant psychological and organizational research. Not all projects lead to creative outcomes or processes but from an organizational perspective, most day-to-day creative and innovative work is project based. Because of the traditional disciplinary separation between the organizational behavior and project management communities, this area is ripe for bridging research.

This chapter examines both creativity and innovation, depending on the study reviewed. Creativity is generally defined as a person, process, product, or environment that expresses or enables both usefulness (appropriateness or correctness) and originality/novelty (e.g., Amabile, 1983, 1996; Mayer, 1999). Innovation additionally includes the elements of relative rather than absolute novelty, intentional benefit to an individual, group, organization, or to wider society, and the application or implementation of the creative idea (Anderson, De Dreu, & Nijstad, 2004; West & Farr, 1990). Occasionally, but not always, these terms will be used interchangeably.

Although there is academic research on project management (Turner, 2010), it is primarily a form of structuring work processes. Projects have real outcomes and meaningful consequences. As such, project management is simultaneously an area of research, an application, a type of practice, and a method of conducting work. Project management principles are taught in MBA programs, learned on the job, and practiced in a range of settings. Unlike much organizational psychological research, project management as a field

Handbook of Organizational Creativity.
DOI: 10.1016/B978-0-12-374714-3.00017-3

is often prescriptive, explicitly attempting to refine and advise the best work practices for conducting projects (e.g., Iyigun, 1999; Shenhar & Dvir, 2007a, 2007b). Although project management principles are more or less useful depending on the project and organization, theoretically, any task can be viewed through the lens of project management.

PROJECT MANAGEMENT CONCEPTS

This section is an overview of core project management concepts. Given the scope and goals of this chapter, this section is not intended to be an in-depth review, nor will every nuance be covered. Project management is a field in its own right, spawning many books and at least two journals. The Project Management Institute (PMI), a group that publishes and maintains project management standards, has its own journal, *Project Management Journal*, and the publisher Elsevier puts out the *International Journal of Project Management*. Over the past two decades, project management has grown to encompass more topics and has become increasingly research-focused, citing to and from a range of journals and using more rigorous methods (Turner, 2010). Interested readers are encouraged to seek out these resources. This section, instead, serves as an introduction to project management concepts for organizational creativity/innovation researchers.

In the context of project management, a *project* is a time-bounded task to create a specific outcome, be that a product or service (e.g., new software, a new medical device, a new way of getting passengers through security at airports). 'Task', as the tem is used here, is a broad set of work activities, rather than as psychologists generally use the term (e.g., McGrath, 1984). The time-bounded nature of the task means that those assembled to work on the project are dedicated to it for a limited period of time, albeit not necessarily a short or clearly defined time (Zhao & Chen, 2009). Contrast, then, project teams with typical work teams, such as a shift group at a restaurant, which generally have stable membership and may not have a specific ending to their jobs (Cohen & Bailey, 1997). Although projects may occupy only one individual, they often involve teams within and/or across organizational units. Thus, the definition of a project falls neatly into psychological research's definitions and theories of a team as a collection of interdependent individuals who are perceived by themselves and others as such (e.g., Cohen & Bailey, 1997; Guzzo & Dickson, 1996; see also McGrath, 1984). As defined by PMI, the team's outputs consist of products (e.g., infrastructure, software, physical items), and also services, business capabilities (e.g., work processes), and reports/documents. Basically, anything that can be created can be project managed. Project management, then, is the application of specific techniques and knowledge to make a project work.

Overview of Project Management Principles

In broad strokes, project management is multidimensional. On the one hand, it is a series of processes that fall under five broad categories, including tools and specific types of documentation. Along another dimension, project management emphasizes the objectives of controlling scope, cost, schedule, risk, and quality. Project management also highlights the importance of several roles, especially the project manager and the stakeholder, and pays close attention to issues of communication and human resources. PMI's (2008) standard book lists 42 project management processes under the five broad categories of "process groups" (p. 39): initiating, planning, executing, monitoring/controlling, and closing (see also Lewis, 2007). These standards are assumed to be applicable to most projects most of the time. The five categories should not be confused with the *phases* of the project. A single project may have one or more phases, each of which incorporates the five broad categories. For instance, in a typical experimental research project, the different phases might involve literature review and idea generation, experimental design, data collection, data analysis, and paper writing. The type of project determines how overlapping versus sequential these phases are. Each of these phases involves initiating, planning, executing, and so on. So, for example, literature review and data collection all require initiating, planning, etc. processes.

Managing a project also entails:

> "identifying requirements, addressing the various needs, concerns, and expectations of the stakeholders as the project is planned and carried out, [and] balancing the competing project constraints including, but not limited to: scope, quality, schedule, budget, resources, and risk" *(PMI, 2008, p. 6).*

Balancing these constraints is one of the most difficult aspects of project management. Project managers are warned that cost, time, scope, and performance are all related, such that cost is a function of the other three (Lewis, 2007). Real projects seldom have unlimited (or even extra) money, time, or people, and an increase in scope without subsequent increases in time, money, and/or personnel are doomed to lower quality. These constraints also change in different ways over the course of the project's life cycle: cost and staffing ramp up at the beginning of a project and then go down as the project is closed out, whereas stakeholder influences start off high and then decrease (PMI, 2008). Importantly, the cost of changes made to the project increase over its life. For example, after a house is mostly built, the cost of replacing inadequate supporting beams is far greater than changing the materials before they have been built or installed.

Two roles are particularly important to project management: the project manager and the stakeholder. The balancing of scope, cost, schedule, and quality is generally the job of the project manager, an individual with, ideally, both technical and managerial competence. Unlike administrative managers, who might oversee individual employees and a specific organizational unit, project managers are responsible for specific projects. Project managers tend to be middle managers, both reporting to higher-level program managers and administrative managers and leading groups of subordinate employees.

Stakeholders are those with an interest in the project, be they internal or external to the company (Lewis, 2007; PMI, 2008). Stakeholders generally include customers, clients, funders, others within the organization (e.g., program managers), and/or the public. They also include the people executing the actual work, who should be included in planning (Lewis, 2007), since they can and/or should influence the project for good or for ill. Incorrectly identifying and empowering stakeholders is sometimes a cause of a project's failure. For example, redesigning existing work processes is likely to fail if there is no buy-in by either upper management, who has the authority to make necessary changes, or the workers, who have to implement and live with such changes. Other external factors may also influence a project's success, including but not limited to industry standards, existing infrastructure and resources, economic conditions, communication channels, risk tolerance, and existing organizational structure (PMI, 2008, p. 14).

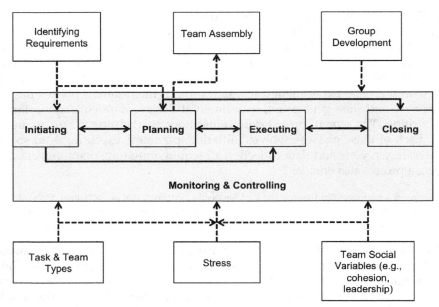

FIGURE 17.1 Applying the psychology of creativity and innovation to project management. Dotted lines are hypothesized connections between creativity constructs and project management processes; bolded lines are connections between project management processes.

The Five Project Management Process Groups

The five project management process groups are roughly sequential, although they may occur multiple times within the same project, depending on the number of phases (sub-tasks, e.g., literature review, data collection) a project has. Individual sub-processes may overlap with each other, and many processes are iterative and interactive, as feedback from one process necessitates revisiting another (Figure 17.1, grey area). During a data collection phase of an experimental research project, monitoring data collection may reveal problems that require revising the experimental design, spurring a fresh round of data collection. For simplicity, the sections written below will presume a single phased project (e.g., just data collection). Many of the processes described below also fall under the general category of project integration management, which entails a great deal of coordination, as well as decision-making about trade-offs between the different objectives (see PMI, 2008, chapter 4).

Initiating Processes

These processes entail identifying and authorizing a new project, defining the phases and high-level requirements, and identifying the relevant stakeholders. For example, NASA's Columbia Accident Investigation Board (CAIB, 2003) identified that the numerous, unconnected databases for tracking hardware problems were a distal factor in the Columbia Shuttle accident. Prior to the accident, the proliferation of unconnected databases made coherent tracking, trending, and identification of hardware problems difficult. The CAIB report motivated individuals across multiple NASA centers to obtain and fund a new, integrated software database. Projects may also be initiated due to market demand for new products, specific requests from a customer, and other ways of recognizing unmet needs. Another sub-process of initiation involves identifying stakeholders, both internal and external. As a practical matter, when one engages in a project and it is stalled due to someone's irritation and feelings of disempowerment, that incident indicates that the project planners did not adequately engage an important stakeholder. Rather than being viewed as an interloper, that stakeholder should be brought into the process in a conciliatory and productive manner.

The PMI standard (2008) also recommends that a specific project charter should formalize the project and its authorization. This charter is created on the basis of knowledge of prior resources as well as an initial statement of work. Statements of work (SOWs) are formal documents that detail work activities, deliverables (outcomes), schedule, and pricing.

Planning Processes

Most of the information necessary for the statement of work is pulled together using planning processes. These processes involve defining the *scope* of the project and determining how to go about conducting the project. There are numerous planning processes described in the PMI's standards, many of which involve gathering information that has different implications for schedule, budget, and so on. One of the most important is collecting requirements. This process entails understanding the stakeholders' needs in enough detail to know what work needs to be done. In the case of the NASA problem-reporting software, many meetings, interviews, and observations of potential users of the software went into creating a set of detailed requirements documents. These documents made explicit the needs for the new software, such as search features and flexibility with creating data entry fields.

The requirements documentation also goes into defining the scope of the project. Lack of defined scope can cause "scope creep" (also called "mission creep" and "feature creep" in the military/government and software, respectively). Scope creep is when the initial scope expands during the process of doing the work, and this can endanger the project. Imagine building an office structure; midway through building, the customer requests an extra elevator and another floor. The cost in terms of time, money, and labor in making these changes is greater than if it had been planned initially. A good statement of work helps to keep scope creep under control.

In addition to the requirements, another project management document is the work breakdown structure (WBS; Lewis, 2007; PMI, 2008; Smith, 2000). The WBS details project outcomes and work into more manageable sub-tasks. When the scope, requirements, and project objectives are defined, then the actual project activities and milestones can be formulated in detail. In the case of data collection, specific activities might include reserving a room, requesting participants from a departmental subject pool, posting times, actually running subjects, giving them subject pool credit via an online tool, and so on. Milestones might include getting institutional review board approval, getting permission to use the subject pool, collecting 50% of the desired data, etc. Working from the numerous sub-tasks, project managers can then estimate the schedules/timelines, costs/budgets, and resources. Resources here include not only physical materials and infrastructure (e.g., computers, offices), but also human resources such as number of staff, specific project roles, skills and knowledge, and personnel structure. Additional planning processes include planning for quality, such as identifying standards and metrics for assessing the project, and planning the communication and information needs for the project.

An important project management construct is the idea of *dependencies*. "Dependent" sub-tasks cannot begin until a previous sub-task has reached a certain stage of completion. In the example of the NASA software development group, code for the new software could not be written until some of the design had been created. The most obvious implication of dependencies is that if a previous sub-task is running late, it makes the entire project late. It can also increase costs and complicate logistics.

A last set of planning processes involve planning for and identifying risks, as well as conducting qualitative and/or quantitative risk analyses and planning for risk mitigations (Webb, 2000). Risk in this context is:

> "an uncertain event or condition that, if it occurs, has an effect on at least one project objective…[with objectives including] scope, schedule, cost, and quality" *(PMI, 2008, p. 275).*

Risks can have multiple causes and affect multiple objectives. Understaffing a project, a not uncommon occurrence, is a risk that can impact schedule and quality. Part of the project management process is being intensely aware of the risks for a project and planning ways to deal with them.

Executing Processes

These processes involve actually performing the work at hand. These sub-processes include doing the activities as planned, assembling and directing the project team, performing quality assurance (making sure quality standards are being met/used), communicating appropriate information, and managing stakeholder expectations. Managing stakeholder expectations is important to ensure that scope creep does not occur.

Monitoring/Controlling Processes

Many projects require (or should conduct) periodic reviewing and tracking of the project's progress, both in terms of the project's process and the project's objectives. Monitoring and controlling processes highlight areas where progress is not proceeding as planned, whether because the plan needs revisiting, the plan is deviating, or unanticipated events occur. Controlling processes entail recommending corrective or preventative actions as necessary, as well as identifying places where undesired changes from the project plan may be occurring. Monitoring and controlling processes examine each of the core project management objectives (quality, scope, cost, schedule), as well as other important intermediate processes, such as communications, performance, and risk management. NASA and other government agencies require substantial formal monitoring and controlling processes. It is common for spaceflight hardware designed by outside contractors, for example, to go through several series of reviews at different stages of design.

Closing Processes

Every project should end. Products are delivered to the customer and leave the control of their creators. These processes entail finalizing contracts and formally ending work. Some processes might include official acceptance by a customer, a final review, written documentation of lessons learned, archiving all important documents, and settling procurements.

Managing the Project

Another way to deconstruct project management is to focus on how the core objectives and other elements (e.g., risk, communication) are managed across the different process groups.

Managing Scope and Stakeholders

The scope is mainly managed via accurate requirement collection, documentation, monitoring, and verification. In fact, much 'agile' software development entails rapid prototyping, where users are introduced to new products and give feedback in very fast, iterative cycles. Human–computer interaction design principles take requirements generation to heart, using ethnographic observation, interview, and analysis techniques to generate requirements (Beyer & Holtzblatt, 1998).

Scope is directly related to managing stakeholder expectations and enabling stakeholders. If a stakeholder group is not identified early, scope may have to be expanded simply to meet what should have been part of the initial plan ('scope discovery'). In other cases, project failure may result. Imagine a children's toy that was created without identifying parents as stakeholders, such that the design was utterly unpalatable. In a dramatic example, in 2007 the British retailer Tesco sold a stripper pole, including fake money and garter, in the toy section of its stores, leading to disdain for the product and retailer (Horowitz, Jacobson, McNichol, & Thomas, 2007). This example violated the suggestion:

> "Be sure the project really satisfies the customer's needs, rather than being what the team thinks the customer needs!" *(Lewis, 2007, p. 42)*.

As stakeholders observe the development of a product, they may decide they want more features than were initially planned, leading to inappropriate scope expansion. This occasionally occurs during weddings, for example.

Managing Costs, Time, and Resources

Project management provides tools and processes to estimate, plan, monitor, and control costs, schedule, and other resources, all of which are interrelated (Lewis, 2007; PMI, 2008). Defining activities in detail is key, including anticipating dependencies. Software project management tools exist, and some companies require that their work breakdown structures or other information be presented using them (e.g., in Gantt charts, using Microsoft Project, etc.). Gantt charts involve taking the WBS and mapping sub-tasks onto a time chart including responsible individuals, anticipated schedules, and break points (Caughron & Mumford, 2008; Smith, 2000). Similarly, schedule development tools exist, such as the critical path and the critical chain method (Lewis, 2007; PMI, 2008; Smith, 2000). The latter:

> "modifies the project schedule to account for limited resources" *(PMI, 2008, p. 155)*.

Critical path analysis creates a network of related tasks in order to make dependencies more explicit (Caughron & Mumford, 2008).

Managing human resources is also benefitted by having a clear sense of the activities involved, as the first step is to determine the necessary team structure; knowledge, skills, abilities, and other characteristics; and roles and responsibilities. The next step is to assemble a project team with the necessary characteristics, often by utilizing selection techniques and team structure (e.g., team hierarchy) planning. Training and assessment are important, as are monitoring team interactions, cohesion, and environment. Performance appraisal, feedback, and conflict management are all vital aspects of managing the project team (Smith, 2000), requiring the project manager to be a leader, supervisor, and possibly a mentor as well. Some project teams are acquired rather than selected, and recruiting staff may involve negotiating with other managers and teams (PMI, 2008, p. 227).

Managing Quality

Quality is in large part a function of proper management of scope, cost, appropriate staffing and resources, schedule, and stakeholders. As with human resource management, quality assurance and management is a field unto itself. The first approach is planning for quality by identifying quality requirements and standards, and figuring out how compliance will be documented. As with other elements, various tools and methodologies exist to help project managers plan for quality, including benchmarking activities, control charts, flowcharting, and group creativity planning techniques like brainstorming. Quality control is an additional, complementary set of methods for monitoring, assessing performance, and recommending necessary changes during the implementation of the project, including validating changes and end-of-project completion checklists and lessons learned.

Managing Risk

Risk is generally a result of decisions made with regards to scope, quality, cost, staffing, and schedule, as well as factors outside of the control of the project manager. Organizations use different formal and informal mechanisms for assessing and tracking/monitoring risks, sometimes using tools stemming from safety and reliability engineering fields (e.g., probabilistic risk analysis). PMI (2008) recommends, among numerous other techniques, creating and updating a risk register that identifies the risks in the format of events that might occur, the impacts/effects, and the causes, as well as potential responses to risk events. Risks may be positive such that project objectives are impacted positively. Some of the possible responses to negative risk are to avoid the risk (e.g., pushing a deadline forward, reducing scope), transfer the risk (e.g., transferring liability for financial ruin to another group), mitigate the risk (reducing the probability or severity of the impact of the risk, e.g., including redundancy in a system), or accept the risk.

Managing Communication

Communication, be it face-to-face or written, formal or informal, is vital to managing a project, whether it is to/from project managers, stakeholders, team members, superiors, or other interested parties. Communication is the mechanism by which all of the above processes run smoothly. It is important for innovation: communication is key to sharing information that exists across different subcultures (e.g., manufacturing, planning) that may conceive of innovation in different ways (Dougherty, 1992). Social network analyses using text mining suggest that people who are more central are more involved in coordination activities (Hossain & Wu, 2009). Whether by informal or formal means, the right information must go to the relevant people at the right time and in the right way. The type of information depends on the interest/impact/concern and power/influence/authority of the parties involved. Special attention must be paid to the potential urgency of information needs. Planning communication overlaps with and at times includes planning human resources (e.g., planning work roles and staffing), infrastructure and communication technology (e.g., identifying, obtaining, and assessing the right information technology), and current work practices (e.g., virtual vs. face-to-face teams).

What about the Project Management of Creative and Innovative Teams?

Many project management principles are clearly relevant to creative and innovative teams. By their nature, many projects entail some level of creativity or innovation: The difference between creative/innovative project teams and others is more a matter of degree than type. For instance, the idea of 'dependencies', without taking into account any changes (innovations) to work process, is valid for both creative and non-creative tasks. For example, initial designs must precede prototype building, and stakeholder input is still ideal before (in addition to iteratively during) design. Managing stakeholders, scope, communication, risks, costs, schedule, and so on are concerns for creative as well as non-creative project teams. Managers still play an important role. High-level problems are similar for creative and non-creative projects, such as failing to meet performance or safety standards, violating resource constraints such as cost or schedule, unfavorable market reception, and being beaten by a similar product from a competitor (Cooper, 2003).

The Assumption of Certainty

That said, creative projects and the teams tasked with managing them may be different from less creative projects in fundamental ways that challenge the assumptions underlying project management principles. Creative projects may involve greater novelty and complexity, which may lead to higher task uncertainty (Tatikonda & Rosenthal, 2000). Technological innovation has been conceptualized as a process of uncertainty reduction, with potential sources of uncertainty including user needs, organizational resources, and technological and competitive environments (Souder & Moenaert, 1992). Psychological uncertainty is the feeling of being unsure about information that may itself be objectively indeterminate (Schunn, 2010). Uncertainty can entail inadequate understanding, incomplete information, and/or undifferentiated alternatives (Lipshitz & Strauss, 1997). Uncertainty, ambiguity, and complexity can represent risks based on inadequacy of information (Pich, Loch, & de Meyer, 2002). Managing uncertainty, novelty, and complexity is quite challenging, for example, process technological novelty (and, assumedly, task uncertainty) may lead to difficulties with keeping costs and schedule under control, even when quality is maintained (Tatikonda & Rosenthal, 2000).

It makes sense that high levels of uncertainty will lead to more dynamism in the project, as well as more risks and opportunities. Although classical project management theory points out a relationship of tradeoffs between cost, schedule, and performance, recent research suggests that already high efficiency projects experience these three as a zero sum game. Low efficiency new product development projects, on the other hand, may achieve improvements on all three constraints through restructuring and process improvements. Improvements include using an experienced project manager, explicit project goals, committed management, and overlapping (rather than strictly sequential) project activities (Swink, Talluri, & Pandejpong, 2006).

Managing Creative Projects

Managing creative projects thus should go beyond the basic project management principles to take into account high initial and ongoing uncertainty, novelty, complexity, and dynamism. These factors require changes to the as-stated processes involved with project initiation, planning, executing, monitoring/controlling, and even closing. For example, planning is difficult to achieve before a project is firmly conceptualized. Prematurely creating a plan (e.g., creating a quickly obsolete SOW) can lead to problems in executing, inaccurate monitoring, and irrelevant controlling. Imagine creating a work breakdown structure when the end product itself is still under debate: subtasks in the course of production are completely unknown. For creative, uncertain projects, one can envision project managers wincing as they attempt to describe and mitigate for risks, estimate costs, schedule, and personnel. Even worse, what would occur when a manager solicits feedback from stakeholders midway through the process, or from stakeholders who are no longer relevant? Even after closing a project, innovation can create complications: for example, drugs are often prescribed after Federal Drug Administration approval for off-label uses, potentially opening up a product to new stakeholders with different needs (e.g., teenagers, the elderly, individuals taking other drugs). Current project management principles are quiet with regards to evaluating the project's creativity or innovativeness, separate from its quality or moneymaking outcomes. Even more difficult is how to evaluate creativity as a project reaches different milestones, when creativity may occur in bursts rather than steadily.

These issues are not entirely new to the project management literature. Coming up with multiple contingent plans and targets, not punishing for failure due to uncontrollable events, planning for learning itself, evaluating and sharing learning are some of many ideas to deal with uncertainty (Pich, Loch, & de Meyer, 2002). Eisenhardt and Tabrizi (1995) suggested an experiential strategy to accelerate product development that takes uncertainty into account. This strategy in part entailed rapidly building flexible options and the intuition (expertise) to learn and adapt to dynamic situations, while on the other hand creating organizational and team structures to support motivation, pace and sensemaking. Specifically, Eisenhardt and Tabrizi (1995) recommended increasing the number of design iterations, increasing the time spent testing the product, imposing frequent milestones with less time in between them, and granting greater power to the project leader. For example, increasing the number of design iterations should encourage cognitive flexibility, enhance confidence, build understanding of the product, and offer more opportunities for success. Given the often non-linear pace of creativity, increasing milestones could decrease uncertainty as milestones motivate workers, force individuals to frequently reassess the project to internal and external standards, and provide a sense of control, accomplishment, routine, and structure.

Similarly, Tatikonda and Rosenthal (2000) suggest that to deal with uncertainty, organizations can explicitly assess novelty up front and attempt to account for it, distinguishing between product and process novelty, which is more challenging. Furthermore, organizations could lengthen planning stages in order to reduce uncertainty before project execution, and plan to acquire additional people and equipment resources from other projects as necessary during execution. All of the processes that entail multiple iterations in less creative projects require even more iterations for creative projects, be they identifying stakeholders or planning for risks. Some changes to scope and the SOW are to be expected, and planning, monitoring, etc. should adapt accordingly.

APPLYING THE PSYCHOLOGY OF CREATIVITY AND INNOVATION

For those not accustomed to formal project management methods, the processes described above can seem a combination of obvious, burdensome, and excessive. They are, however, widely used and considered in general to be best practices for most projects, much of the time (PMI, 2008). In practice, using project management principles draws needed attention to specific issues that may cause project failures. The rest of this chapter tackles some of the ways in which project management might be enhanced or informed by the research on organizational creativity. Figure 17.1 connects these issues visually to the five main project management processes, taking into account the existing interrelationships between those processes. Given the variety of factors, specific practical implications will be offered at each section.

Identifying Requirements: Project Definition and Requirements Generation

Before beginning work on a project, the project itself must be defined. Preliminary framing can influence the level of project uncertainty and complexity (Pich et al., 2002). One of the initial processes of creativity is problem finding (Getzels, 1975; Ward, Smith, & Finke, 1999). Problem finding includes four related aspects: problem identification, problem definition, problem expression, and problem construction (Runco, 1994; Runco & Nemiro, 1994). The way a problem is framed has direct implications for the creativity of its solution: artists who are good at problem finding are rated as more original (Csikszentmihályi & Getzels, 1988), and problem construction is positively associated with problem solving originality and quality (Mumford, Reiter-Palmon, & Redmond, 1994). Breaking a problem down via presenting multiple specific problem categories can enhance idea generation (Coskun, Paulus, Brown, & Sherwood, 2000). Imagine a scientist who observes a monkey eating dirt (Paletz & Peng, 2009). The scientist could wish to diagnose how the monkey is sick, or could frame the problem as an opportunity for discovering something special about the dirt or about the nutritional needs of that species of monkey. The questions that the scientist asks will necessarily focus and limit possible solutions.

Project Management Strategy: The Diamond Model

Project management is not without its own models to help in problem definition: Shenhar and Dvir (2007a, 2007b) created a model to aid project managers in strategizing before the project is started. The Diamond model ties together innovation for research and development and project management principles by assessing the product, task, and environment of the project. The model is termed thus because each project is mapped on four dimensions, radiating like a cross from a central point: technology is the top (low tech to high tech), pace is the bottom (regular development time to blitz), novelty on the right (derivative to breakthrough), and complexity on the left (assembly to array/high). The pattern of assignments on these four axes gives each project a different diamond shape. Each assignment has implications for project management. Projects using high technology require more design cycles and later design freezes; projects with faster paces require more autonomy; projects higher in complexity require more complex organizational formality; and projects higher in novelty require later market freezes and may have less market data from which to work. Creative and innovative projects can certainly learn from this contingent approach. An analysis of NASA's Mars Climate Orbiter project failure using the Diamond model revealed that, while the managers took pace somewhat into account, they did not adequately modify their processes to deal with the level of complexity, novelty, and uncertainty involved (Sauser, Reilly, & Shenhar, 2009). Although this is a post-hoc analysis benefitted by hindsight, it is suggestive of the possible utility of this and other contingency models.

In organizations, choosing which projects to fund and predicting which will be most innovative and successful is a difficult process. Ahn and colleagues (2010) modified the Diamond model to identify factors that portfolio managers can take into account when making product development decisions. In addition to the four dimensions of the Diamond model, this model highlights possible market size, market growth rates, and development costs as important factors in a possible product's profile. In a sense, this modified model maps out the socioeconomic context of potential products in order to optimize appropriateness, feasibility and novelty. Although these are high-level constructs, the Ahn et al. model reveals additional opportunities and constraints for a potentially successful product.

Overview of Requirement Generation Techniques

Identifying the specific project requirements once a general product has been defined is vital to that product's success. Usually, project ambiguity needs to be clarified, although when novelty and flexibility are project goals, ambiguity should be sustained (Brun & Saetre, 2009). PMI (2008) recommends using brainstorming, nominal group techniques, focus groups, and so on for a variety of specific planning generation tasks noted above. All of these methods have different strengths and weaknesses (Kerr, Aronoff, & Messe, 2000). Focus groups are a semistructured, moderated, interview conversation with a small group. Done correctly, they require preparation such as identifying the right population, noting which topics to cover, and scripting specific probes (Kerr et al., 20000). Brainstorming in teams has been criticized for being less effective than idea generation in nominal groups (Diehl & Stroebe, 1987; Kerr et al., 2000; Mullen, Johnson, & Salas, 1991). Nominal groups consist of the same number of individuals as an interactive group, but the individuals work independently. On the other hand, a great many of the studies examining brainstorming have not been appropriate, either because they did not use the specific prescribed brainstorming methods put forth by Osborne (e.g., to ignore evaluation, to combine ideas), did not have a properly trained facilitator, did not have the right comparison groups, and/or did not use the right tasks or adult professional samples (Isaksen, 1998; Isaksen & Gaulin, 2005). It is similarly unclear how many project management groups follow brainstorming guidelines correctly.

Recent research suggests that attending to Osborne's initial suggestions can enhance brainstorming. Using a properly trained facilitator seems to reduce process losses (e.g., Isaksen & Gaulin, 2005; Offner, Kramer, & Winter, 1996). Electronic brainstorming groups may be fulfilling the promise of brainstorming (Kerr & Tindale, 2004). Electronic brainstorming, unlike face-to-face brainstorming, minimizes production blocking by enabling several people to "talk" at the same time, as well as be anonymous, minimizing evaluation apprehension. In addition to minimizing these group process losses, larger groups can even outperform nominal groups of the same size, not because they are coming up with a greater number of wild ideas but because of the stimulating effect of being exposed to others' ideas (Kerr & Tindale, 2004).

Practical Implications for Identifying Requirements

Many requirement identification processes already exist, both in the project management (the Diamond model) and the creativity literature. This latter literature suggests that in order to optimize group brainstorming, project managers should utilize trained facilitators and electronic brainstorming media when possible. A range of other methods, such as observation and focus groups, might be useful in project definition, particularly if both the problem finding literature and advice from contingent models to understand the problem space (e.g., the Diamond model) are utilized. An important, unrelated issue is that these brainstorming teams and focus groups need to include the right stakeholders. Too many might confuse matters, but as discussed before, failing to include important groups can derail projects later. Creative project management teams may need to run additional focus groups/meetings when new stakeholders are discovered.

People as Resources: Team Assembly

Assembling the team is an important early process in project management. Although acquiring the project team is considered to be part of an executing process (PMI, 2008), thinking through who is needed should begin much earlier, during planning if not before (see Figure 17.1). More so than other teams, project teams tend to be diverse in terms of expertise and functions (Cohen & Bailey, 1997). Different individuals must also fill different roles within a project. For example, in product development, guiding a new product from beginning to end may require inventors, champions, implementers, and serial innovators (Sim, Griffin, Price, & Vojak, 2007). Successfully managing people as resources entails selection, training, feedback, and performance appraisal (PMI, 2008). As with any other task, the necessary knowledge, skills, abilities, and other characteristics both within individuals and across the team must be collected (Edwards, Scott, & Raju, 2003).

Staffing Levels

Staffing at appropriate levels is important. Although psychological research suggests that understaffed projects lead members to take on more responsibilities, work harder, and feel more involved in the group (see Cini, Moreland, & Levine, 1993; Levine & Moreland, 1994 for a review), understaffing is also a very real project management risk. Cini and colleagues (1993) studied over- and understaffing in campus student groups via interviews with group leaders. Self-reported problems with understaffing included poorer performance, fatigue and burnout, lost resources, and group homogeneity, whereas overstaffing problems included apathy and boredom, confusion, cliques, alienation, and inadequate resources (e.g., not enough music copies for everyone in a music group). Solutions for understaffing in these student groups included reorganizing the group and recruiting new members; while solutions for overstaffing included dividing the group, restricting membership, punishing deviance, and encouraging members to work hard. Many of these solutions would work in project management teams, particularly reorganization and acquiring/recruiting new members, or dividing the group, as appropriate.

Team Cognitive Composition

Team assembly is important for group functioning, innovation, and success, whether in experimental groups or long-term astronaut teams (Paletz, 2009). In addition to theory and research on the effects of cognitive and demographic diversity on team creativity (see Mannix & Neale, 2005; van Knippenberg & Schippers, 2007), some new research examines cognitive diversity in teams. Cognitive diversity between fields rather than between levels of expertise, such as multidisciplinarity, is assumed to lead to team creativity, by supplying a larger pool of information from which to make connections (Paletz & Schunn, 2010; Mannix & Neale, 2005; Williams & O'Reilly, 1998). Most projects probably entail some measure of cognitive diversity, if only because projects require multiple roles and diverse knowledge. Unfortunately, a great deal of knowledge diversity research has not lived up to its promise, revealing weak and/or inconsistent results (for reviews see Mannix & Neale, 2005; van Knippenberg, De Dreu, & Homan, 2004). As a result, some authors have suggested that new models showing moderation and/or mediation are necessary (van Knippenberg, De Dreu, & Homan, 2004; van Knippenberg & Schippers, 2007), and new models highlighting potentially important moderators have appeared (e.g., Paletz & Schunn, 2010).

One possible mitigating factor when dealing with individuals from different fields is to ensure that each person's expertise is valued (Paletz & Schunn, 2010). This can occur via instituting expertise as formal roles (Paletz & Schunn, 2010; Hart, Stasson, & Karau, 1999). Recent research examining intelligence analysis teams suggests that bringing in experts to a non-expert team is useful for team success, but only when the team has guidance about how to use member resources (Woolley, Gerbasi, Chabris, Kosslyn, & Hackman, 2008). Both collaborative planning (guidance on how to use member resources) and experts were necessary for team success, specifically through effective information integration.

A recent, fruitful area of research carefully specifies what is meant by cognitive diversity and ties it to specific roles. Woolley and colleagues (2007) composed dyads working on a maze and identification task as either homogenous or heterogeneous on object versus spatial visualization tendencies. Half the heterogeneous teams had their visualization tendency matched to their role in the task (e.g., map navigation with spatial visualization tendency), whereas the other half did not. The homogeneous groups were assigned to roles randomly. The investigators found that heterogeneous teams where individual abilities matched task roles performed better than both the homogeneous teams and heterogeneous teams where role and ability were not matched. Heterogeneous teams that had mismatched abilities and roles both collaborated more and did better when they collaborated, whereas collaboration did not make a difference for heterogeneous matched teams.

Practical Implications for Team Assembly

This research has implications for both team composition and the different needs for collaboration. Of course, in genuine project management teams, it is not always initially clear exactly what skills each team member already has and what skills are needed, suggesting a need for careful assessment and selection of team members concurrent with project planning—which is an issue for non-creative as well as creative teams. The section for staffing would suggest that while understaffing has some benefits, they might be outweighed by the risks involved. Ideally, the team would be neither over- nor understaffed, and appropriate planning would identify early on the number and types of personnel necessary. For creative groups specifically, other theory recommends that different expertise be valued within the team in order to harness cognitive diversity (Paletz & Schunn, 2010). Heterogeneous teams with mismatched abilities and roles should take advantage of each other's expertise and collaborate. Taking a recommendation from an earlier section, middle and upper management should remain flexible and be able to add extra personnel if necessary, particularly to teams tasked with innovation (Tatikonda & Rosenthal, 2000).

Group Development

An examination of the project management of creative teams must take into account that groups go through development stages over their work lives, and such development may impact any of the five project management processes (see Figure 17.1). The dominant model of group socialization involves an increase in commitment to the team over time; depending on what occurs, there is then a decrease in commitment leading to exiting the team (Levine & Moreland, 1994; Moreland & Levine, 1982). An individual joins a group, is indoctrinated into group norms (which they may then try to resist or influence), becomes a member, and then, if necessary, exits. This model focuses on voluntary, autonomous, interdependent groups (Levine & Moreland, 1994). This model of group socialization is distinct from the commonly held model of group development (Levine & Moreland, 1994; c.f. Tuckman, 1965). That model suggests that groups pass through five stages of development: forming, storming, norming, performing, and adjourning. Both Tuckman's (1965) and the Moreland and Levine (1982) models are vaguely paralleled in the PMI's (2008) model of project development, which suggests that a project starts with low levels of cost and staffing which increases over time, only to decrease as the project is closed out (p. 16).

Gersick (1988) created a specific model of group development using task-focused groups which more closely resembles what occurs in project management teams. Using grounded theory analyses of eight project teams, Gersick (1988) rejects Tuckman's (1965) idea of hierarchical stages of group development and proposes a model of punctuated equilibrium where groups very quickly (even in the first few minutes) develop norms and behavioral patterns which are then dramatically revisited during a midpoint transition. The group then settles into a second inertial phase that is followed by a completion stage, when they make an effort to satisfy external expectations.

Practical Implications of Group Development Research

Given that the second model more closely matches what occurs in project management groups, its insights should be incorporated into project management's understanding of group development. It would be a simple matter for the maintenance and monitoring processes espoused in project management to take into account a midpoint evaluation and revision. This alternate model also points out that norms solidify quite early, rather than slowly over time, suggesting that project managers should carefully prepare for the first meeting (Gersick, 1988). For creative teams, this model would suggest that norms which inspire creativity should be established for that first meeting (e.g., rewarding creativity, risk-taking, openness, goal clarity, etc., Amabile et al., 1996).

Stress in Work Groups

Stress has complex effects on performance in innovative teams—it does not just appear at the time of final delivery of a product, but is apparent throughout all five processes (Figure 17.1). One type of stress ("quantitative stress" or role overload) includes time pressure, accumulating demands, lack of resources, and workload, whereas another type ("qualitative stress" or role ambiguity) is related to task complexity and excessive performance standards (Drach-Zahavy & Freund, 2007; c.f. Caplan et al., 1975). This section focuses on the first type of stress. Factors external to the project team, such as the work context, the organization, and the environment may be a source of stress (Kanki, 1996). Stress has an impact on group and individual performance such that:

> "stress tends to increase the performance quantity with an accompanying decline in quality, to narrow attention onto more vital task features, and to prompt more simplified, heuristic information processing" (Kerr & Tindale, 2004, p. 630).

The Yerkes-Dodson Law suggests an inverted U-shaped relationship where low and high levels of stress hurt performance, but that increases in stress from low to moderate levels actually improve some types of performance (Kerr & Tindale, 2004). That said, different studies have found unambiguously negative (e.g., Drach-Zahavy & Freund, 2007) and positive (e.g., Anderson & Farris, 1972) effects of stress on team performance.

In addition to effects on task performance, related research indicates that when teams are under stress, the group's need for cognitive closure increases, resulting in group-centrism (Chirumbolo, Livi, Mannetti, Pierro, & Kruglanski, 2004; Kerr & Tindale, 2004; Kruglanski, Pierro, Mannetti, & De Grada, 2006). This group-centrism includes a desire for greater conformity to group norms and consensus, in-group favoritism, and more autocratic leadership. There is support for an Attentional Focus Model where time pressure encourages group members to filter out what they find less important or relevant in group discussions (Kelly & Loving, 2004). Given previous research on the positive effects on cognition and creativity of minority opinion influence (Martin & Hewstone, 2008; Nemeth, 1986), this finding suggests that under high levels of stress, project teams may focus on quick answers and avoid reassessments of problems to the detriment of creativity, divergent thinking, and innovation. In fact, research by Chirumbolo and colleagues (2004) found that high need for closure groups performed less creatively, and this relationship was mediated by conformity pressure. This finding is matched by a small study where undergraduates drawing imaginary space creatures under time pressure drew fewer creatures and conformed more to examples of those creatures compared to students in the self-paced conditions (Landau, Thomas, Thelen, & Chang, 2002). In getting done what is necessary and in converging around a decisive leader, last-minute opportunities and possibly necessary course corrections may be lost.

Time Pressure

In several key studies where the measures of stress were time pressure and the measures of group performance included creativity, the findings demonstrated the inverted U-shaped relationship (e.g., Karau & Kelly, 1992; Ohly, Sonnentag, Pluntke, 2006). Using self-report surveys, time pressure has been shown to have an inverted U-shaped relationship with creativity and innovation, but not with submitting suggestions, a type of organizational citizenship behavior (Ohly, Sonnentag, Pluntke, 2006).

Along with a proliferation of moderators, this U-shaped relationship may explain how the results of time pressure and innovation research are genuinely mixed. There are studies suggesting time pressure has a positive effect on creativity, where creativity was measured by self-reported idea generation at work (Noefer, Stegmaier, Molter, & Sonntag, 2009) or observer ratings of innovative performance (Anderson & Farris, 1972). On the other hand, other experimental research suggests that externally imposed deadlines hinder intrinsic motivation (Amabile, DeJong, & Lepper, 1976). Intrinsic motivation is considered key to creativity (Amabile, 1983, 1996; Amabile et al., 2002). In addition, an externally imposed deadline (time pressure) versus working at one's own pace has been negatively related to problem definition, concept selection, conceptual combination, idea generation, and idea evaluation, but not final originality (Antes & Mumford, 2009).

These studies are silent when it comes to *internally* imposed deadlines, which would assumedly also involve time pressure. Project management deadlines are often a mix of those which are imposed, accepted, and discussed by the team members. Given that autonomy is also usually associated with creativity (see below and Amabile et al., 1996; Ohly et al., 2006), it is possible the negative effects of external deadlines are being driven by the lack of autonomy rather than the deadlines themselves. In fact, when externally-imposed deadlines were co-opted, sub-deadlines were self-imposed, or more stringent deadlines were self-imposed, intrinsic motivation was not harmed as measured by free-choice time spent on tasks (Burgess, Enzle, & Schmaltz, 2004). Perceptions of partial or complete self-determination of time limits served to cancel out the negative effects of the external deadline on intrinsic motivation.

Much of the research on time pressure and team performance has involved ad hoc experimental groups and/or retrospective, single-point surveys. Single-time surveys in organizations have been criticized as possibly tapping into lay, causal theories of performance rather than genuine causal connections (Staw, 1975). Experiments are vital for testing causality, but may not represent the conditions under which project management teams actually function (e.g., people who know each other, deadlines that are both self- and externally-imposed, complex tasks). Two studies have examined time pressure and creativity over time in field data. Amabile and her colleagues (2002) set out to unpack the relationship between creativity, time pressure, and motivation in a field study. They were able to obtain a remarkable dataset of longitudinal process data, including measures of daily creativity and time pressure from 177 workers within 22 project teams working toward creative outcomes. Although the data were self-report, the methodology employed daily questionnaire items and event sampling, providing rich information about activities on the same day they occurred. Amabile and her colleagues did not find an inverted U-shape relationship; instead, using multiple measures of time pressure, they found that time pressure on a given day *negatively* predicted creative cognitive processing on the same day, the next day, and two days later. This finding was not due to the participants lacking the time to report creative activities. Intrinsic motivation did not mediate the relationship. In fact, intrinsic motivation was positively related to time pressure and unrelated to creativity.

The Amabile longitudinal study contrasts with an early study by Andrews and Farris (1972), which twice surveyed NASA scientists, their managers, and others who could evaluate them. This study found that perceived time pressure at Time One was positively correlated with innovation, usefulness, and productivity as rated by supervisors and senior colleagues at Time Two, five years later. Usefulness and productivity at Time One were not related to time pressure at Time Two, and there was a small, negative relationship between innovation at Time One and time pressure at Time Two. Interestingly, while all the performance measures and time pressure were positively related at Time One, at Time Two only usefulness was related to time pressure.

How do we make sense of the mixed literature on time pressure (Shalley, Zhou, & Oldham, 2004)? Something particular to the datasets may explain the positive relationship between time pressure and creativity. The Andrews and Farris (1972) sample were scientists in a government laboratory. Perceptions of time pressure were positively related to numbers of close colleagues and administrative duties, and negatively related to working alone, suggesting that collaboration and time pressure could be confounded. In addition, there was a negative relationship between freedom given by supervisors at Time One and experienced time pressure at Time Two, suggesting that the scientists in this sample ranged from having too little time pressure to a moderate amount. This and other studies could have been examining differences between objectively low and moderate levels of time pressure.

Similarly, the negative relationships between time pressure and creativity must also be explained. The obvious explanation, the flip side of the one above, is that the time pressure varied from moderate to high, tracing the downward relationship on the inverted U. Another possibility is that the U-shaped relationship itself is moderated, as suggested by a field study of manufacturing employees where creativity was measured by multiple supervisor ratings (Bear & Oldham, 2006). Although there was a general negative main effect for time pressure on creativity, there was a significant three-way interaction such that, for employees with strong supervisor support and high openness to experience, they experienced the inverse-U relationship between time pressure and creativity.

Findings from the time pressure literature would suggest that when coming up with schedule estimates, project managers should attempt to ensure that their team members are not overly burdened with unrealistic time constraints. They should provide a moderate amount of time pressure, especially in ways that help make their team members feel empowered to set or co-opt deadlines themselves. Too much time is rarely a problem in the working world, although undefined deadlines can make it difficult to keep on task (for a model regarding project completion in drug discovery, see Zhao & Chen, 2009; also implied by Andrews & Farris, 1972).

A second suggestion from the psychology literature comes from research on social entrainment (Kelly & Karau, 1993; Kelly & McGrath, 1985). Kelly and colleagues' (1993) study on time pressure found that if a creative task starts with a relatively longer time period, people will work more slowly but be more creative. This creativity will be maintained even if subsequent sessions of the task have subsequently shorter and shorter durations. This finding suggests that if a project team has an initial, low-time pressure time to master a creative task, subsequently increasing time pressure should not result in less creativity. A project manager could start a project slowly but thoroughly and then pick up the pace as the schedule continued.

A third suggestion comes from the literature on task switching. Task switching is widely known to hinder performance on later tasks. However, when a first task was completed, perceived time pressure on that first task led to better performance on a second task, by triggering confidence in having met the goals of the first task (Leroy, 2009). This research is in contrast to other work where the effects of time pressure are examined only on a concurrent task. Thus, a little time pressure tied to a completed task is helpful for creating a clean transition between tasks. Of course, all of these suggestions are tentative, as befits psychological research, but they provide useful directions in the absence of other guidance.

Scheduling Estimates and Temporal Perspectives

These suggestions assume that managers are making rational decisions about schedules. In fact, behavioral decision-making research suggests that there is an optimism bias for estimating task completion, such that people anticipate tasks taking less time than they do (e.g., Buehler, Messervey, & Griffin, 2005; Sanna, Parks, Chang, & Carter, 2005). Buehler and colleagues (2005) found, across three tasks, that not only does this bias exist in individuals, but it was enhanced in ad hoc groups, suggesting that bringing in others' opinions does not lessen the bias. In fact, these biased estimates were driven by groups focusing on factors that promote successful future task completion rather than by considering negative factors. Furthermore, Sanna and colleagues (2005) found that it was the *ease* of (availability) of thinking about successful task completion, not simply thinking about successful task completion per se, which caused this planning fallacy. The obvious recommendations from this line of research is for managers to consider possible threats to schedule, not just success, regardless of their cognitive availability, and to adjust their estimates to make up for what they can't anticipate. Otherwise, projects may encounter time pressure simply due to incorrectly estimated schedules.

The temporal perspective of the group is also related to time pressure. Antes and Mumford (2009) found a significant three-way interaction between time pressure, temporal perspective, and positive/negative frames, such that the generally negative effect they found for time pressure on problem definition was reversed when the temporal perspective focused on the past and the framing was negative. This finding suggested that a past orientation focused on negative events was benefitted from time pressure when defining the problem. In addition, Antes and Mumford (2009) found that information gathering was more effective when there was time pressure and a present or future orientation, whereas when a past temporal orientation was employed, no time pressure was best; idea evaluation using a future orientation did not reveal differences between time pressure and no time pressure. These findings suggest a complex pattern of orientation, framing, and time pressure that may be task-specific (Antes & Mumford, 2009). The study reminds us that time itself is socially constructed (Arrow, Henry, Poole, Wheelan, & Moreland, 2005).

Workload

Workload and time pressure are linked. Given the same number of staff, time pressure creates a heavier workload. Workload has been defined as:

"the cost incurred by a human operator to achieve a particular level of performance" *(Hart & Staveland, 1988, p. 2).*

Workload can include any combination of perceived task difficulty, time pressure, perform- ance, mental effort, physical effort, frustration, and fatigue (Hart & Staveland, 1988). Amabile and her colleagues (1996), in their model of environment/climate for creativity, proposed that workload pressure was negatively related to creativity. Workload and time pressure are also sometimes confounded. In Amabile and colleagues' (2002) longitudinal field study, workload was used as a measure of time pressure. They also found that workload pressure measured at the beginning of each half of the project negatively predicted average creative cognitive processing for the following half of the project, suggesting long-term effects.

At the level of the organization, downsizing and job insecurity can create workload pres- sure on those who remain and hurt creativity in other ways. Amabile and Conti (1999) col- lected data on their work environment scale for creativity (KEYS) at a large Fortune 500 high-technology company that was undergoing downsizing. All six environmental stimu- lants to creativity decreased (autonomy, challenge, sufficient resources, supervisory and organizational encouragement, and work group supports, see below), and obstacles to crea- tivity such as workload pressures and organizational impediments increased, although the trend started to reverse as time went on. Amabile and colleagues also observed that down- sizing decreased productivity and creativity, both subjectively and in terms of invention disclosures, and that this effect was fully mediated by the environmental stimulants and obstacles to creativity. Probst and colleagues (2007) similarly found in both an experiment and a field study that job insecurity led to lower rates of creativity measured by an insight/ functional fixedness task (experiment) and on the Remote Associates Test (field study). These findings are in line with other studies suggesting that when people are under threat, they take on a prevention rather than a promotion regulatory focus, which is relatively bad for creativity (Friedman & Forster, 2001).

Elsbach and Hargadon (2006) take intense workloads of creative professionals as a given. They recommend, given that free time is often eroded during high pressure times, that organizations redesign workdays to include legitimate, scheduled, mindless work. Mindless work involves tasks that are simple and easily mastered. They are low in both cognitive dif- ficulty and performance pressures. Tasks include routine cleaning chores or other impor- tant but simple maintenance duties. They recommend this work be conducted about half an hour every day or several days of week in order to inspire positive affect, psychological safety, and high cognitive capacity. These breaks from the normal mindful work should then encourage greater creativity.

Burnout

Chronic stress can lead to burnout, a prolonged response characterized by cynicism and detachment from a job, exhaustion, and a lack of efficacy (for a review, see Maslach, Schaufeli, & Leiter, 2001). Given that organizational creativity is positively associated with psychological well-being at work (Rasulzada & Dackert, 2009), organizational creativity researchers are right to attend to the problems of burnout. Burnout has good discriminant validity: it is distinguished from depression by being focused in one's work, specifically, afflicting people who do not normally suffer from any psychopathology (Maslach et al., 2001). Exhaustion is the most influenced by stress (Friesen & Sarros, 1989). Cynicism follows sequentially from exhaustion (Greenglass, Burke, & Fiksenbaum, 2001), but lack of efficacy develops simultaneously with the other two (Maslach et al., 2001). Burnout is associated with withdrawal from the job, but also with lower productivity and job performance, and the exhaustion dimension predicts stress-related poor health outcomes. Most of the examined predictors of burnout are situational factors, in particular experienced high workload (e.g., Greenglass et al., 2001; Kushnir & Cohen, 2006), insufficient resources, and time pressure. Role ambiguity and role conflict are also positively associated with burnout. Of course, stressful experiences occur through an individual's perception. Maslach and colleagues' (2001) review noted having low self-esteem, an avoidant coping style, poor hardiness, an external locus of control, and higher levels of neuroticism (the Big Five dimension) are all related to burnout.

Maslach and Leiter (1997) proposed six areas of mismatch between the individual and the working experience that can promote burnout; workload (including emotional workload), control (autonomy and access to resources), reward (including social rewards like appreciation), community (connection with others), fairness (e.g., transparency), and values (including conflicts between stated and normative values). There is some support for this model, suggesting that some of those factors are associated more with different dimensions of burnout (e.g., lack of recognition with lower efficacy and higher cynicism, Friesen & Sarros, 1989). Situational and organizational factors predominate in causing burnout, suggesting that focusing interventions on the individual is insufficient (Maslach et al., 2001; Maslach & Goldberg, 1998).

Practical Implications of Stress Research

All of this research suggests that high levels of stress are, in general, bad not only for performance in general, but for group creativity and motivation in particular. At the minimum, individuals under high stress will focus attention on group norms and conformity. One caveat is that at the end of a group's process, if only convergent thinking is necessary and changes are unnecessary, the focus encouraged may not be harmful, and in fact may help in task switching (Leroy, 2009). On the other hand, a little stress, be it via time pressure or a reasonable workload, may under some circumstances (e.g., with supervisor support) increase creativity, so long as the stress does not create a prevention mindset. Deadlines should be created to increase intrinsic motivation, and so be genuinely accepted and possibly initiated by the team workers themselves, rather than externally imposed. According to the literature mentioned earlier, milestones (deadlines) should occur often in order to control and mitigate for uncertainty in innovative project teams. That said, self-imposed deadlines should be created in ways that avoid common planning fallacies, such as by thoroughly considering negative factors to success. Studies on entrainment suggest that if initial, low-time pressure periods are granted to master a creative task, subsequent mild time pressure should not result in lowered creativity. Burnout should also clearly be avoided and engagement encouraged.

Task and Team Types

Projects differ a great deal in terms of the specific tasks they involve and the structures of their teams. Different projects may have different needs, interactions, and effects based on the team and task structures utilized, affecting processes at any point in the project management lifecycle and even interacting with stress (see Figure 17.1). McGrath's (1984) typology of team tasks depicts 8 types of tasks in a circumplex with four quandrants: generative tasks, which include planning and creativity; choosing tasks, which are problem-solving tasks with correct answers or decision-making tasks; negotiation tasks, which involve mixed-motive conflicts and cognitive conflicts; and executive tasks, which include competitions and relatively simpler psycho–motor tasks. Although experimental research may focus on one task type, in practice, project management teams have to perform most of these tasks at some point in their tenure.

High-Level Tasks

At a higher level of task type, projects can involve hardware or software, services or products; teams can be virtual and/or in-person, large or small, multi-functional or homogeneous, international or national. Project management strategies need to take task and team types into account and make sure that the task and team types fit the project. For example, Hertel and colleagues (2005) have a model and review of managing virtual teams. Research and development projects, which tend to be creativity-focused, often have more ambiguity and uncertainty than other projects (Iyigun, 1999), and creative projects involve more novelty, complexity, and uncertainty (Tatikonda & Rosenthal, 2000). Project management has also been criticized as being a poor fit for software development work, specifically (Yabuuchi, Kocaoglu, & Watada, 2006). That said, those issues that impact the efficiency of project management in software logically would influence project management in any domain, such as an understanding of the requirements, project scale and complexity, and the number of revisions (Yabaachi et al., 2006).

Team Structure as How the Team is Embedded in Organizations

Project management teams can vary greatly in how the teams are embedded in the organization. At one end are traditional functional organizations, which break up the project into segments to the relevant functional groups; at the other are project teams, where a project manager leads specialists from across the organization (Larson & Gobeli, 1989). These specialists may still report to their functional managers. In between are matrix organizations, where an employee may report to both a project manager and a functional manager. A functional matrix involves a project manager with a minor role, whereas a project matrix involves a project manager with authority to decide staffing and work flow. In between these is a balanced matrix. Survey research of 547 individuals suggests that, in general, the ideal project team structures are project matrix, project team, and balanced matrix, with no significant differences between them (Larson & Gobeli, 1989). These three types had the best project success in terms of controlling costs, meeting the schedule, technical performance, and overall quality. Less successful team types were traditional functional organizations and functional matrix teams. This finding suggests that project managers must be as empowered as functional managers to lead for projects to be successful.

Team structures vary in other ways as well. Gassmann and von Zedtwitz (1999) interviewed 204 Research and Development (R&D) directors and project managers about innovation and virtual (not face-to-face) teams. They found that the main determinants for organizing international R&D projects were the type of innovation (radical versus incremental), the systemic versus autonomous nature of the project, the mode of knowledge involved (tacit versus explicit), and the degree of resource bundling (complementary versus redundant). The success of virtual teams depended on considering those factors and the project scope.

Team and Individual Autonomy

Gassmann and von Zedtwitz (1999) also identified four types of virtual teams that fall along a dimension of team autonomy, from highest to lowest: decentralized self-organization, system integrator as coordinator, core team as a system architect, and a centralized venture team. If the project information is easy to share, explicit, and unambiguous, the project teams can do fairly autonomous work. Gassmann and von Zedtwitz (1999) suggest centralized projects if the knowledge is tacit, the innovation desired is radical, interdependencies between teams and components is high, and the resources needed are limited and/or restricted. Different team configurations also require different levels of involvement from the project manager. This contingent approach can also explain studies that suggest that autonomy is not associated with higher performance in project teams (for a review, see Cohen & Bailey, 1997). Those studies seem to measure autonomy at the team level, comparing self-managed versus project-managed teams, and demonstrate the need for a team leader.

This contingent approach is not entirely in conflict with Amabile and colleagues' (1996) emphasis on autonomy and freedom as important to individual creativity. Autonomy over one's own day-to-day tasks versus the level of autonomy to make team-level decisions are different constructs with different implications. Providing additional support for Amabile's (1996) model, Ohly and colleagues (2006) found that job control—having autonomy on one's tasks and influence over methods for doing a job—was positively associated with self-reported creativity and innovation on the job. Similarly, Martin and colleagues (2007) found that job resources (operationalized here as perceptions of autonomy and control and opportunities to use skills) moderated the negative effects of job demands (perceived workload and sustained effort) on self-reported work innovation. In addition to a main effect for autonomy as positively associated with innovation, high autonomy buffered against the detrimental effect of job demands on innovation. This research, among others, suggests that granting workers freedom over their day-to-day tasks is important for creativity (Amabile et al., 1996), a finding that does not conflict with the idea of having supportive, directive project management.

Routinization

Some projects involve tasks that are less complex and/or more thoroughly learned. Controlling for time pressure, job control, and a host of other background variables, routinization as measured by self-reported behavioral automaticity for commonly done tasks was positively related to self-reported creativity and innovation, suggesting that routinization on some tasks allowed employees to generate and implement new ideas (Ohly et al., 2006). This finding suggests that project managers should make sure that tasks are already well-learned. This finding is in line with other research which suggests that in order to be creative, individuals need to have a minimum level of domain expertise (Amabile, 1983).

Interactions with Stress

Task types can also interact with stress. In a model separating out role overload and role ambiguity as two very different types of stress, Drach-Zahavy and Freund (2007) suggest, and find some support for, the idea that different types of team structuring helps with these two types of stress. Mechanistic team structures (e.g., roles and tasks are clearly defined, high certainty, routinization of tasks) should help mitigate the effects of role overload whereas organic team structures (e.g., autonomy, feedback, participation) help with role ambiguity. These two types of structures were actually positively related, and an interesting pattern of interactions between structuring and stress influenced team effectiveness. When mechanistic structuring was high, team effectiveness was high regardless of level of role overload stress, whereas when mechanistic structuring was low, high role overload stress led to lower team effectiveness. When organic team structuring was low, team effectiveness was low regardless of role ambiguity, but when it was high, high levels of role ambiguity were associated with higher levels of team effectiveness. Not surprisingly, team effectiveness was highest under high levels of both types of structuring. Thus, when project managers are creating team structures, they may wish to encourage both complexity and definition of tasks. Drach-Zahavy and Freund (2007) conclude that groups with a range of modes for structuring may be able to weather different kinds of stresses.

Practical Implications of Different Task and Team Types

This section suggests that project teams may differ greatly in terms of their tasks and team structure. Not all team structures are created equal, with project matrix, project team, and balanced matrix formats displaying superior project success compared to traditional functional organizations and functional matrix teams (Larson & Gobeli, 1989). Routinized tasks can, counter-intuitively, enable creativity (Ohly et al., 2006), although this finding could be due to benefits granted by learning and/or expertise. Though individual-level autonomy is useful, particularly for creativity, teams could use strong project managers, particularly to control costs, schedule, and quality. Project teams should be structured to best match their tasks and to match the types of stress expected. For example, as noted above, when role ambiguity is high (which it may be in teams doing radical innovation), an extremely organic team structure will be associated with greater team effectiveness. The strongest advice here is that a contingent approach is necessary.

Team Social Variables: Cohesion, Morale, Leadership, Organizational Climate, and Interacting with External Groups

Several interpersonal, team social variables are important to project management success across the five different process groups, be they as correlates, causes, moderators, or outcomes. These variables are often vital buffers against or exacerbators of stress, regardless of the source (Figure 17.1). These variables include cohesion and morale, coworker support, leadership, organizational climate, and interacting with external groups.

Cohesion, Morale, and Coworker Support

Project managers are often explicitly encouraged to maintain cohesion and morale (PMI, 2008). As noted above, stress can cause a team to acquire a greater need for cognitive closure, take a group-centric stance, and be less patient with dissenters (Kruglanski et al., 2006), possibly to the detriment of creativity and elaborative thinking. Amabile and Conti's (1999) study on downsizing revealed an unsurprising relationship between anticipated downsizing and lower levels of job satisfaction and morale. Mullen and Copper's (1994) much-cited meta-analysis on performance and morale indicated, not only a positive relationship between morale and performance, but that the stronger relationship was from performance to cohesion, suggesting that teams will become more cohesive as they experience successes.

In addition to being important in their own right, one would think that morale and cohesion, if maintained in the face of downsizing and failures, might help buffer the negative effects of stress; however, this does not always seem to be the case. In a study of nurses, a significant interaction was found such that social support, including supervisor and coworker tangible and emotional support, strengthened a *positive* relationship between stressors and strains (Kaufmann & Beehr, 1986). On the other hand, emotional support from coworkers outside the primary work unit can be associated with creative performance, independent of emotional support from elsewhere (Madjar, 2008). At this time, research on coworker influences is mixed and could be further developed (see Shalley et al., 2004 for a review). Zhou and George (2001) found that when coworker help and support, useful feedback from coworkers, or perceived organizational support for creativity was high, and when continuance commitment was high, employees with high job dissatisfaction exhibited the highest creativity. Thus, coworker support may not be a useful buffer by itself, but under conditions when commitment is high, may interact with job dissatisfaction to create high creativity. Coworker support, along with cohesion and morale, should be examined for possible interactions with other characteristics.

Leadership: *Managing Down*

The project manager has an important role in guiding, encouraging, and directing project teams. Leadership of creative people can be quite complicated (see, e.g., Mumford, Scott, Gaddis, & Strange, 2002). In general, supportive, non-controlling leadership styles encourage employee creativity (see Shalley, Zhou, & Oldham, 2004 for a brief review), whereas lack of leader support can lead to burnout (Maslach et al., 2001). In a study of employees' innovative tendencies, recognition and feedback from supervisors moderated the relationship between time pressure and innovation such that when supervisor feedback was high, high time pressure lead to higher scores on self-reported idea implementation, such as securing resources (Noefer et al., 2009). Under conditions of low levels of supervisor feedback, time pressure did not have an effect on idea implementation. Bear and Oldman (2006) found a similar effect in addition to the three-way interaction effect noted above (supervisor support, employee openness to experience, and time pressure), such that when supervisor support was high, time pressure resulted in the inverse-U shaped relationship with creativity. These studies suggest the importance of leader support as a moderator as well as a direct effect.

Organizational Climate

Cultural norms are the lens through which workers interpret everything; as common knowledge, they are internalized standards for acceptable behavior, shared visions, understandings of how to implement procedures, and perceptions of social hierarchies, and are therefore important to project management (PMI, 2008). Organizational culture entails the social norms, group values, and system-level understanding of appropriate behavior within an organization, whereas organizational climate is an aggregate of the individual psychological meanings held by workers (James et al., 2008). Organizational climate and culture are both internal and external, generated by and imposed on workers. As such, they influence how projects are performed (PMI, 2008). King and colleagues (2007) surveyed over 24,000 workers from healthcare organizations across the UK to test for the effects of organizational climate for innovation on organizational performance. Climate for innovation was measured as the perception that people in the organization were searching for new ways to conduct their work. King et al. found that work demands were negatively related to performance (in line with the previous section on workload) and that a climate for innovation was positively related to organizational performance. Even more interestingly, a climate for innovation moderated the negative effect of work demands, such that a high climate for innovation combined with high work demands resulted in similar organizational performance as low work demands. However, climate for innovation and work demands were negatively related, suggesting that the configuration of high climate for innovation and high work demands, while possible, may be difficult for managers to achieve.

Amabile and colleagues (1996) created a more extensive organizational climate for creativity scale (KEYS) based on a review of the literature and critical incident interviews. They highlight organizational and supervisory encouragement, work group supports, and resources as positively related to creativity, whereas organizational impediments would be negatively related to creativity. Organizational encouragement includes encouragement to take risks, generate ideas, and value innovation at all levels of management, as well as fair, supportive assessment of new ideas, reward and appreciation of creativity, and participative decision making such that information flows across the organization. Supervisory encouragement includes goal clarity, open interactions with the supervisor, and supervisory support of the team. Work group encouragement includes team diversity and openness to ideas, as well as constructive challenging of ideas and shared commitment to the project. Adequate resources are important to projects' creativity levels, but the perception of the adequacy of resource allocation is also important (Amabile et al., 1996). Organizational impediments that require buffering against include internal organizational conflict, conservatism, and rigid management structures. Project managers thus need to shield their team from organizational strife and figure out ways to get around rigid structures that might mire down the project. On the other hand, project managers also need to seek out adequate resources and portray a climate of encouragement, the latter by rewarding and assessing creative ideas.

Managing External Groups

So far, the team variables have looked inside the team. One important social variable looks outside the team to relationships with external groups. The PMI guide (2008) warns that acquiring team members as part of planning will involve negotiating with other managers and across teams. As teams grow and require resources of time, money, information, and personnel, inter-team interactions arise, bestowing potential problems and opportunities. Some findings about how an innovative team might best interact with external groups come from Ancona and Caldwell's (1988, 1992) study. They conducted interviews with managers and team members from 38 new product teams in high technology firms to understand better the types of activities and communication that team members engage in with external others. After identifying a large number of activities (Ancona & Caldwell, 1988), they collected 409 questionnaires from product development teams not involved in the initial study and found four factors (1992). The first factor involved "ambassador" activities such as communicating frequently with those above in the hierarchy in order to lobby for resources, protect a team from outside pressure, and persuade others to support the team. The second factor was "task coordinator" activities that involved lateral communication to other groups primarily about technical or design issues. The third factor was labeled "scout activity" and represented communicating with marketing, sales, and R&D in order to scan for information about competition, the market, or technology. Finally, the fourth factor involved "guarding activities" which included internal activities to keep information from escaping the team. Among other findings, ambassadorial activities were positively related to adherence to budgets and schedules, and task-coordinator activities were positively associated with team performance, particularly innovation assessed at the end of a projects' life. Prolonged scouting activities were negatively related to adherence to budgets and schedules at project midpoints and to innovation at both times.

Practical Implications of Team Social Variables

A range of social variables has an impact on team processes and outcomes, including those of creative teams. High cohesion and morale are considered beneficial in their own right. Coworker support has had mixed effects, at times promoting creativity and at other times promoting stress, likely caused by interactions with other variables. For example, coworker support can aid in creativity when a worker is dissatisfied, if the commitment to continue at the job is high (Zhou & George, 2001). In general, supportive, non-controlling leadership styles are particularly helpful to innovation and may alleviate or moderate other factors (e.g., stress). Managers, together with project teams, can deliberately create organizational climates which are supportive of innovation via promoting organizational encouragement to take risks and generate ideas, appreciation of creativity, goal clarity, team diversity and openness to ideas, and access to adequate resources. In terms of dealing with external teams, the type and manner of external communication is also important to team performance, such as encouraging lateral communication with other groups about design issues but not excessively communicating with marketing and R&D about competitors or the market.

CONCLUSION

Project management relies on careful planning and monitoring of scope, schedules, cost, risk, and quality, with particular attention to internal and external stakeholders. The above summary of relevant psychological literature included problem finding, team cognitive composition, the effects of time pressure, workload, stress and burnout on performance, the problem of biased schedule estimates, and the importance of individual autonomy and team leadership, morale and worker support, and organizational climate. Contingency is the watchword of this area. Many factors are important as moderators, and matching the team structure and communication to the particular tasks is very important. Additional theories are important, but one of the advantages of project management as a field is that it keeps researchers solidly grounded in the realities of the working world.

Theoretical Implications

Each of the literature sections was followed by a practical implications section. This chapter—part project management principles, part review of specific creativity literature—raises theoretical implications as well, in terms of understanding both project management and creative performance in teams. From the perspective of project management, the greater uncertainty, dynamism, and novelty underlying creative projects implies that an altered approach may be necessary. A great deal simply is not known about the effectiveness of the project management approach on different kinds of creative projects. That said, the five broad process categories described above and seen in Figure 17.1 are already iterative, influencing each other. Beyond a broad contingent approach, specific methods of handling uncertainty, novelty, and complexity should be integrated into the project management principles. For example, the contingent approach to communication is apt, by and large, but what precise changes should be made to communication content and mechanisms in the face of an innovative team project? Tatikonda and Rosenthal (2000) provide various suggestions to deal with uncertainty, such as letting the project add more resources and personnel as it develops and lengthening the planning stages. Similarly, the Diamond model makes practical suggestions depending on the pattern of initial factors (e.g., Shenhar & Dvir, 2007a, 2007b). A deeper intermingling of planning, executing, and monitoring/controlling processes may be necessary, challenging some of the core assumptions about each of those phases and the specific tools used. For example, a work breakdown structure created early may be more useful as a way of identifying specific areas of uncertainty, rather than as a planning tool.

On the other side, a great deal of creativity research has ignored project management principles, either as specific or general context variables. For instance, many creativity studies examine short-term ad hoc groups rather than real project teams, with those that study group development and/or field research as important exceptions. Even beyond that criticism, project management can offer different types of framing for existing research questions. For example, practical considerations could help guide team assembly research, such as providing a focus on deep-level composition variables such as abilities and personality (Bell, 2007), particularly those that are desirable in a creative project group. The importance of stakeholders is an example of a variable rarely (if ever) examined in creativity theory and literature. Theoretically, stakeholders outside the team may be an important source of information, encouragement, and support on one hand, but also stress, resentment, and time demands on the other.

Further Gaps

Many opportunities exist for enterprising scientists. Integrating project management into creativity research could be helpful; project management concepts and principles themselves can be examined as variables. What are the effects of different kinds of planning processes on performance, cohesion, and creativity? How about on prevention versus promotion mindsets? How does a shorter time frame between initiation and planning affect creative projects, particularly those with high uncertainty? Do different tradeoffs among resources, cost, risk, and schedule impact creativity differently? How do different executing and planning processes enhance or buffer against stress? Project management can also offer possible moderators to existing frameworks. For example, are some leadership styles more useful during some processes (e.g., initiating) than others (e.g., monitoring/controlling)? Does stress have the same impact on creativity and/or innovation during one set of processes as during another? Many specific types of project management processes have not been tested for their effects on creativity, innovation, cohesion, morale, and stress.

An exception is the study by Caughron and Mumford (2008). They compared three specific types of planning techniques—Gantt charts, case-based planning, and critical path analysis—in terms of their effects on innovative solutions. Gantt charts involve laying the work breakdown structure onto a time chart and the critical path method creates a network of task dependencies, highlighting problems that might occur (Caughron & Mumford, 2008). Case-based planning involves taking a past project with similar goals and attempting to learn from its successes and failures. Caughron and Mumford (2008) experimentally tested the utility of these different planning methods with undergraduates, controlling for individual differences in creativity. The critical path method resulted in the most originality (and to a lesser degree, highest quality and elegance, as well). These results suggest that explicitly considering possible problems helps with creativity—a finding that parallels the Buehler et al. (2005) finding that focusing on the positive was related to biased schedule estimates.

In addition to more carefully examining the effects of specific project management processes on creativity, another gap is the importance of looking beyond project management to other influences on organizational creativity. For example, in addition to work support for creativity being important to creative performance, nonwork support (e.g., friends, family) has a significant and independent contribution to creative performance (Madjar, Oldham, & Pratt, 2002). Similarly, in addition to examining interactions between personal and contextual factors (and between contextual factors, e.g., Zhou, 1988), research on project management of creative teams could be benefitted by examining the effects of national culture (Shalley et al., 2004). International settings come with a host of different norms and expectations about not only teams, groups, and the self (e.g., Triandis, 1989), but nuanced similarities and differences about creativity itself (Paletz & Peng, 2008). The role of the project manager in creating, not just buffering against, organizational climate would also be a useful area of research.

Another issue that could be better studied from both a psychological and a project management perspective is the physical environment for creativity. So far, research suggests that high density, noise, and lack of physical boundaries produce more distractions and interruptions and lead to less creativity (see Shalley et al., 2004). More research could be done in this area to examine not only the effect of the environment on creativity, but also how it interacts with different project management processes and phases of work.

Although there was a great deal of literature on time pressure effects, there still needs to be more studies on the effects of time on groups (Arrow et al., 2005). In addition to empirically testing theories and models of group development, it would be useful to examine the effects of planned and unplanned change on project team outcomes (Arrow et al., 2005). Field research could also examine issues across different projects. What occurs when individuals work on a series of projects, either consecutively or in parallel, with some of the same individuals? Skilton and Dooley (2010) recently theorized that repeat collaborations between individuals within creative project teams may lead to less creativity due to (and mediated by) less creative abrasion. Creative abrasion is defined as early team processes which arise from team and task ambiguity, such as idea generation, constructive conflict, and negotiation. Repeat collaborations bring forward team mental models from previous projects, decreasing ambiguity and increasing convergence on familiar objectives and courses of action. Skilton and Dooley (2010) recommend including outsiders in new project teams in order to restructure mental models. They also warn that while process interventions like brainstorming will likely have intended effects on specific creativity, they are unlikely to change the underlying team mental models. New research could test and refine their theory, particularly in light of the problems of high project uncertainty.

Conclusion

Project management is a broad, diverse field, touching other domains such as human resources and quality assurance. The work of project management itself can seem all-encompassing. Team creativity research is similarly broad. Although a science of project management is developing, there are many areas where organizational creativity research can touch upon and enhance project management. Similarly, the structure that project management provides can raise specific questions for organizational creativity researchers. Brought together, the two areas are ripe for bridging research.

Acknowledgements

This project was supported in part by a National Science Foundation Grant #SBE-0830210 to the author through the National Science Foundation (NSF)'s Science of Science and Innovation Policy Program. The opinions expressed are those of the author and not necessarily those of NSF. The author is grateful to Justin Krill for initial assistance in finding project management articles in the IEEE database.

References

Ahn, M. J., Zwikael, O., & Bednarek, R. (2010). Technological invention to product innovation: A project management approach. *International Journal of Project Management, 28*, 559–568.

Amabile, T. M. (1983). The social psychology of creativity: A componential conceptualization. *Journal of Personality and Social Psychology, 45*, 357–376.

Amabile, T. M. (1996). *Creativity in context: Update to the social psychology of creativity.* Boulder, CO: Westview Press.

Amabile, T. M., & Conti, R. (1999). Changes in the work environment for creativity during downsizing. *Academy of Management Journal, 42*, 630–640.

Amabile, T. M., Conti, R., Coon, H., Lazenby, J., & Herron, M. (1996). Assessing the work environment for creativity. *Academy of Management Journal, 39*, 1154–1184.

Amabile, T. M., DeJong, W., & Lepper, M. R. (1976). Effects of externally imposed deadlines on subsequent intrinsic motivation. *Journal of Personality and Social Psychology, 34*, 92–98.

Amabile, T. M., Mueller, J. S., Sipson, W. B., Hadley, C. N., Kramer, S. J., & Fleming, L. (2002). *Time pressure and creativity in organizations: A longitudinal field study.* Working paper no. 02–073, Boston, MA: Harvard Business School.

Ancona, D. G., & Caldwell, D. F. (1988). Beyond task and maintenance: Defining external functions in groups. *Group & Organizational Studies, 13*, 468–494.

Ancona, D. G., & Caldwell, D. F. (1992). Bridging the boundary: External activity and performance in organizational teams. *Administrative Science Quarterly, 37*, 634–665.

Anderson, N., De Dreu, C. K. W., & Nijstad, B. A. (2004). The routinization of innovation research: A constructively critical review of the state-of-the-science. *Journal of Organizational Behavior, 25*, 147–173.

Andrews, F. M., & Farris, G. F. (1972). Time pressure and performance of scientists and engineers: A five-year panel study. *Organizational Behavior and Human Performance, 8*, 185–200.

Antes, A., & Mumford, M. D. (2009). Effects of time frame on creative thought: Process versus problem-solving effects. *Creativity Research Journal, 21*, 166–182.

Arrow, H., Henry, K. B., Poole, M. S., Wheelan, S., & Moreland, R. (2005). Traces, trajectories, and timing. In M. S. Poole & A. B. Hollingshead (Eds.), *Theories of small groups: Interdisciplinary perspectives* (pp. 313–367). Thousand Oaks, CA: Sage.

Bear, M., & Oldham, G. R. (2006). The curvilinear relation between experienced creative time pressure and creativity: Moderating effects of openness to experience and support for creativity. *Journal of Applied Psychology, 91,* 963–970.

Bell, S. T. (2007). Deep-level composition variables as predictors of team performance: A meta-analysis. *Journal of Applied Psychology, 92,* 595–615.

Beyer, H., & Holtzblatt, K. (1998). *Contextual design: Defining customer-centered systems.* San Diego, CA: Academic Press.

Brun, E., & Saetre, A. S. (2009). Managing ambiguity in new product development projects. *Creativity and Innovation Management, 18,* 24–34.

Buehler, R., Messervey, D., & Griffin, D. (2005). Collaborative planning and prediction: Does group discussion affect optimistic biases in time estimation? *Organizational Behavior and Human Decision Processes, 97,* 47–63.

Burgess, M., Enzle, M. E., & Schmaltz, R. (2004). Defeating the potentially deleterious effects of externally imposed deadlines: Practitioners' rules of thumb. *Personality and Social Psychology Bulletin, 30,* 868–877.

Caplan, R. D., & French, J. R. (1975). Relationships of cessation of smoking with job stress, personality, and social support. *Journal of Applied Psychology, 60,* 211–219.

Caughron, J. J., & Mumford, M. D. (2008). Project planning: The effects of using formal planning techniques on creative problem-solving. *Creativity and Innovation Management, 17,* 204–215.

Chirumbolo, A., Livi, S., Mannetti, L., Pierro, A., & Kruglanski, A. W. (2004). Effects of need for closure on creativity in small group interactions. *European Journal of Personality, 18,* 265–278.

Cini, M. A., Moreland, R. L., & Levine, J. M. (1993). Group staffing levels and responses to prospective and new group members. *Journal of Personality and Social Psychology, 65,* 723–734.

Cohen, S. G., & Bailey, D. E. (1997). What makes teams work: Group effectiveness research from the shop floor to the executive suite. *Journal of Management, 23,* 239–290.

Columbia Accident Investigation Board (CAIB), (2003). *Columbia accident investigation board report volume 1.* Washington, DC: National Aeronautics and Space Administration and Government Printing Office.

Cooper, L. (2003). A research agenda to reduce risk in new product development through knowledge management: A practitioner perspective. *Journal of Engineering Technology Management, 20,* 117–140.

Coskun, H., Paulus, P. B., Brown, V., & Sherwood, J. J. (2000). Cognitive stimulation and problem presentation in idea-generating groups. *Group Dynamics: Theory, Research, and Practice, 4,* 307–329.

Csikszentmihályi, M., & Getzels, J. W. (1988). Creativity and problem solving in art. In F. H. Farley & R. W. Neperud (Eds.), *The foundations of aesthetics, art, and art education* (pp. 91–116). New York, NY: Praeger.

Diehl, M., & Stroebe, W. (1987). Productivity loss in brainstorming groups: Toward the solution of a riddle. *Journal of Personality and Social Psychology, 53,* 497–509.

Dougherty, D. (1992). Interpretive barriers to successful product innovation in large firms. *Organization Science, 3,* 179–202.

Drach-Zahavy, A., & Freund, A. (2007). Team effectiveness under stress: A structural contingency approach. *Journal of Organizational Behavior, 28,* 423–450.

Edwards, J. E., Scott, J. C., & Raju, N. S. (Eds.), (2003). *The human resources program-evaluation handbook.* Thousand Oaks, CA: Sage.

Eisenhardt, K. M., & Tabrizi, B. N. (1995). Accelerating adaptive processes: Product innovation in the global computer industry. *Administrative Science Quarterly, 40,* 84–110.

Elsbach, K. D., & Hargadon, A. B. (2006). Enhancing creativity through "mindless" work: A framework of workday design. *Organization Science, 17,* 470–783.

Friedman, R. S., & Forster, J. (2001). The effects of promotion and prevention cues on creativity. *Journal of Personality and Social Psychology, 81,* 1001–1013.

Frisen, D., & Sarros, J. (1989). Sources of burnout among educators. *Journal of Organizational Behavior, 10,* 179–188.

Gassman, O., & von Zedtwitz, M. (1999). Organizing virtual R&D teams: Toward a contingency approach. *Portland International Conference on Management of Engineering and Technology, Technology and Innovation Management* (Vol. 1, pp. 198–199). Portland, OR: PICMET.

Gersick, C. J. G. (1988). Time and transition in work teams. Toward a new model of group development. *Academy of Management Journal, 31,* 9–41.

Getzels, J. W. (1975). Problem-finding and the inventiveness of solutions. *Journal of Creative Behavior, 9,* 12–18.

Greenglass, E. R., Burke, R. J., & Fiksenbaum, L. (2001). Workload and burnout in nurses. *Journal of Community and Applied Social Psychology, 11,* 211–215.

Guzzo, R. A., & Dickson, M. W. (1996). Teams in organizations: Recent research on performance and effectiveness. *Annual Review of Psychology, 47,* 307–338.

Hart, J. W., Stasson, M. F., & Karau, S. J. (1999). Effects of source expertise and physical distance on minority influence. *Group Dynamics: Theory, Research, and Practice, 3,* 81–92.

Hart, S. G., & Staveland, L. E. (1988). Development of the NASA-TLX (Task Load Index): Results of empirical and theoretical research. In P. A. Hancock & N. Meshkati (Eds.), *Human Mental Workload* (pp. 139–183). North-Holland: Elsevier Science.

Hertel, G., Geister, S., & Konradt, U. (2005). Managing virtual teams: A review of current empirical research. *Human Resource Management Review, 15,* 69–95.

Horowitz, A., Jacobson, D., McNichol, T., & Thomas, O. (2007). 101 dumbest moments in business: 99. Tesco: Kelsey's hogging the stripper pole again! *CNNMoney.com.* Retrieved from <http://money.cnn.com/galleries/2007/biz2/0701/gallery.101dumbest_2007/99.html/>.

Hossain, L., & Wu, A. (2009). Communications network centrality correlates to organisational coordination. *International Journal of Project Management, 27,* 795–811.

Isaksen, S. G. (1998). *A review of brainstorming research: Six critical issues for inquiry.* Monograph #302. Buffalo, NY: Creative Problem Solving Group.

Isaksen, S. G., & Gaulin, J. P. (2005). A reexamination of brainstorming research: Implications for research and practice. *Gifted Child Quarterly, 49,* 315–329.

Iyigun, I. (1999). Multi project management system implementation. *Portland international conference on management of engineering and technology, technology and innovation management* (Vol. 1, pp. 250–251). Portland, OR: PICMET.

James, L. R., Choi, C. C., Ko, C.-H. E., McNeil, P. K., Minton, M. K., Wright, M. A., et al. (2008). Organizational and psychological climate: A review of theory and research. *European Journal of Work and Organizational Psychology, 17,* 5–32.

Kanki, B. G. (1996). Stress and aircrew performance: A team-level perspective. In J. E. Driskell & E. Salas (Eds.), *Stress and human performance* (pp. 127–162). Hillsdale, NJ: Lawrence Erlbaum Associates.

Karau, S. J., & Kelly, J. R. (1992). The effects of time scarcity and time abundance on group performance quality and interaction process. *Journal of Experimental Social Psychology, 28,* 542–571.

Kaufmann, G. M., & Beehr, T. A. (1986). Interactions between job stressors and social support: Some counterintuitive results. *Journal of Applied Psychology, 71,* 522–526.

Kelly, J. R., & Karau, S. J. (1993). Entrainment of creativity in small groups. *Small Group Research, 24,* 179–198.

Kelly, J. R., & Loving, T. J. (2004). Time pressure and group performance: Exploring underlying processes in the Attentional Focus Model. *Journal of Experimental Social Psychology, 40,* 185–198.

Kelly, J. R., & McGrath, J. E. (1985). The effects of time limits and task types on task performance and interaction of four-person groups. *Journal of Personality and Social Psychology, 49,* 395–407.

Kerr, N. L., Aronoff, J., & Messe, L. A. (2000). Methods of small group research. In H. T. Reis & C. M. Judd (Eds.), *Handbook of research methods in social and personality psychology* (pp. 160–189). Cambridge, UK: Cambridge University Press.

Kerr, N. L., & Tindale, R. S. (2004). Group performance and decision making. *Annual Review of Psychology, 55,* 623–655.

King, E., de Chermont, K., West, M., Dawson, J. F., & Hebl, M. R. (2007). How innovation can alleviate negative consequences of demanding work contexts: The influence of climate for innovation on organizational outcomes. *Journal of Occupational and Organizational Psychology, 80,* 631–645.

Kruglanski, A. W., Pierro, A., Mannetti, L., & De Grada, E. (2006). Groups as epistemic providers: Need for closure and the unfolding of group-centrism. *Psychological Review, 13,* 84–100.

Kushnir, T., & Cohen, A. H. (2006). Job structure and burnout among primary care pediatricians. *Work, 27,* 67–74.

Landau, J. D., Thomas, D. M., Thelen, S. E., & Chang, P. K. (2002). Source monitoring in a generative task. *Memory, 10,* 187–197.

Larson, E. W., & Gobeli, D. H. (1989). Significance of project management structure on development success. *IEEE Transactions on Engineering Management, 36,* 119–125.

Leroy, S. (2009). Why is it so hard to do my work? The challenge of attention residue when switching between work tasks. *Organizational Behavior and Human Decision Processes, 109,* 168–181.

Levine, J. M., & Morland, R. L. (1994). Group socialization: Theory and research. In W. Stroebe & M. Hewstone (Eds.), *European review of social psychology* (Vol. 5, pp. 305–336). Chichester, UK: John Wiley & Sons.

Lewis, J. P. (2007). *Fundamentals of project management* (3rd ed.). New York, NY: American Management Association.

Lipshitz, R., & Strauss, O. (1997). Coping with uncertainty: A naturalistic decision-making analysis. *Organizational Behavior and Human Decision Processes, 69*, 149–163.

Madjar, N., Oldham, G. R., & Pratt, M. G. (2002). There's no place like home? The contributions of work and nonwork creativity support to employees' creative performance. *Academy of Management Journal, 45*, 757–767.

Madjar, N. (2008). Emotional and informational support from different sources and employee creativity. *Journal of Occupational and Organizational Psychology, 81*, 83–100.

Mannix, E., & Neale, M. A. (2005). What differences make a difference? The promise and reality of diverse teams in organizations. *Psychological Science in the Public Interest, 6*, 31–55.

Martin, R., & Hewstone, M. (2008). Majority versus minority influence, message processing and attitude change: The source–context–elaboration model. *Advances in Experimental Social Psychology, 40*, 237–326.

Martin, P., Salanova, M., & Peiro, J. M. (2007). Job demands, job resources and individual innovation at work: Going beyond Karasek's model? *Psicothema, 19*, 621–626.

Maslach, C., & Goldberg, J. (1998). Prevention of burnout: New perspectives. *Applied Preventative Psychology, 7*, 63–74.

Maslach, C., & Leiter, M. P. (1997). *The truth about burnout.* San Francisco, CA: Jossey-Bass.

Maslach, C., Schaufeli, W. B., & Leiter, M. P. (2001). Job burnout. *Annual Review of Psychology, 52*, 397–422.

Mayer, R. E. (1999). Fifty years of creativity research. In R. J. Sternberg (Ed.), *Handbook of creativity* (pp. 449–460). Cambridge, UK: Cambridge University Press.

McGrath, J. E. (1984). *Groups: Interaction and performance.* Englewood Cliffs, NJ: Prentice Hall.

Moreland, R. L., & Levine, J. M. (1982). Socialization in small groups: Temporal changes in individual–group relations. In L. Berkowitz (Ed.), *Advances in experimental social psychology* (Vol. 15, pp. 137–192). New York, NY: Academic Press.

Mullen, B., & Copper, C. (1994). The relation between group cohesiveness and performance: An integration. *Psychological Bulletin, 115*, 210–227.

Mullen, B., Johnson, C., & Salas, E. (1991). Productivity loss in brainstorming groups: A meta-analytic integration. *Basic and Applied Psychology, 12*, 3–23.

Mumford, M. D., Reiter-Palmon, R., & Redmond, M. R. (1994). Problem construction and cognition: Applying problem representations to ill-defined domains. In M. A. Runco (Ed.), *Problem finding, problem solving, and creativity* (pp. 3–39). Westport, CT: Ablex.

Mumford, M. D., Scott, G., Gaddis, B., & Strange, J. M. (2002). Leading creative people: Orchestrating expertise and relationships. *Leadership Quarterly, 13*, 705–750.

Nemeth, C. J. (1986). Differential contributions of majority and minority influence. *Psychological Review, 93*, 23–32.

Noefer, K., Stegmaier, R., Molter, B., & Sonntag, K. (2009). A great many things to do and not a minute to spare: Can feedback from supervisors moderate the relationship between skill variety, time pressure, and employees' innovative behavior? *Creativity Research Journal, 21*, 384–393.

Offner, A. K., Kramer, T. J., & Winter, J. P. (1996). The effects of facilitation, recording, and pauses on group brainstorming. *Small Group Research, 27*, 283–298.

Ohly, S., Sonnentag, S., & Pluntke, F. (2006). Routinization, work characteristics and their relationships with creative and proactive behaviors. *Journal of Organizational Behavior, 27*, 257–279.

Paletz, S. B. F. (2009). Individual selection and crew assembly: A gap analysis for exploration missions. In S. B. F. Paletz & M. K. Kaiser (Eds.), *Behavioral health and performance technical gap analysis white papers* (NASA Technical Memorandum NASA/TM–2009–215381, pp. 141–198). Moffett Field, CA: National Aeronautics and Space Administration Ames Research Center.

Paletz, S. B. F., & Peng, K. (2008). Implicit theories of creativity across cultures: Novelty and appropriateness in two product domains. *Journal of Cross-Cultural Psychology, 39*, 286–302.

Paletz, S. B. F., & Peng, K. (2009). Problem finding and contradiction: Examining the relationship between naïve dialectical thinking, ethnicity, and creativity. *Creativity Research Journal, 21*, 139–151.

Paletz, S. B. F., & Schunn, C. (2010). A social-cognitive framework of multidisciplinary team innovation. *Topics in Cognitive Science, 2*, 73–95.

C. GROUP LEVEL INFLUENCES

Pich, M. T., Loch, C. H., & de Meyer, A. (2002). On uncertainty, ambiguity, and complexity in project management. *Management Science, 48,* 1008–1023.

Probst, T., Stewart, S. M., Gruys, M., & Tierney, B. W. (2007). Productivity, counterproductivity and creativity: The ups and downs of job insecurity. *Journal of Occupational and Organizational Psychology, 80,* 479–497.

Project Management Institute (2008). *A guide to the project management body of knowledge (PMBOK® guide)* (4th ed.). Newtown Square, PA: PMI Publications.

Rasulzada, F., & Dackert, I. (2009). Organizational creativity and innovation in relation to psychological well-being and organizational factors. *Creativity Research Journal, 21,* 191–198.

Runco, M. A. (1994). *Problem finding, problem solving, and creativity.* Westport, CT: Ablex.

Runco, M. A., & Nemiro, J. (1994). Problem finding, creativity, and giftedness. *Roeper Review, 16,* 235–241.

Sanna, L. J., Parks, C. D., Chang, E. C., & Carter, S. E. (2005). The hourglass is half full or half empty: Temporal framing and the group planning fallacy. *Group Dynamics: Theory, Research, and Practice, 9,* 173–188.

Sauser, B. J., Reilly, R. R., & Shenhar, A. J. (2009). Why projects fail? How contingency theory can provide new insights—A comparative analysis of NASA's Mars Climate Orbiter loss. *International Journal of Project Management, 27,* 665–679.

Schunn, C. D. (2010). From uncertainty exact to certainty vague: Epistemic uncertainty and approximation in science and engineering problem solving. In B. H. Ross (Ed.), *The Psychology of Learning and Motivation* (Vol. 53, pp. 227–252). Burlington, VT: Academic Press.

Shalley, C. E., Zhou, J., & Oldham, G. R. (2004). The effects of personal and contextual characteristics on creativity: Where should we go from here? *Journal of Management, 30,* 933–958.

Shenhar, A. J., & Dvir, D. (2007). *Reinventing project management: The Diamond approach to successful growth and innovation.* Boston, MA: Harvard Business School Press.

Shenhar, A. J., & Dvir, D. (2007a). The lost link: why successful innovation needs sound project management. *Portland international conference on management of engineering and technology, technology and innovation management* (Vol. 1, pp. 597–610). Portland, OR: PICMET.

Sim, E. W., Griffin, A., Price, R. L., & Vojak, B. A. (2007). Exploring differences between inventors, champions, implementers and innovators in creating and developing new products in large, mature firms. *Creativity and Innovation Management, 16,* 422–436.

Skilton, P. F., & Dooley, K. J. (2010). The effects of repeat collaboration on creative abrasion. *Academy of Management Review, 35,* 118–134.

Smith, K. A. (2000). *Project management and teamwork.* Boston, MA: McGraw-Hill.

Souder, W. E., & Moenaert, R. K. (1992). Integrating marketing and R&D project personnel within innovation projects: An information uncertainty model. *Journal of Management Studies, 29,* 485–512.

Staw, B. M. (1975). Attribution of the "causes" of performance: A general alternative interpretation of cross-sectional research on organizations. *Organizational Behavior and Human Performance, 13,* 414–432.

Swink, M., Talluri, S., & Pandejpong, T. (2006). Faster, better, cheaper: A study of NPD project efficiency and performance tradeoffs. *Journal of Operations Management, 24,* 542–562.

Tatikonda, M. V., & Rosenthal, S. R. (2000). Technology novelty, project complexity, and product development project execution success: A deeper look at task uncertainty in product innovation. *IEEE Transactions on Engineering Management, 47,* 74–87.

Triandis, H. C. (1989). The self and social behavior in differing cultural contexts. *Psychological Review, 96,* 506–520.

Tuckman, B. W. (1965). Developmental sequence in small groups. *Psychological Bulletin, 63,* 384–399.

Turner, J. R. (2010). Editorial: Evolution of project management research as evidenced by papers published in the International Journal of Project Management. *International Journal of Project Management, 28,* 1–6.

van Knippenberg, D., De Dreu, C. K. W., & Homan, A. C. (2004). Work group diversity and group performance: An integrated model and research agenda. *Journal of Applied Psychology, 89,* 1008–1022.

van Knippenberg, D., & Schippers, M. C. (2007). Work group diversity. *Annual Review of Psychology, 58,* 515–541.

Ward, T. B., Smith, S. M., & Finke, R. A. (1999). Creative cognition. In R. J. Sternberg (Ed.), *Handbook of creativity* (pp. 189–212). Cambridge, UK: Cambridge University Press.

Webb, A. (2000). *Project management for successful product innovation.* Burlington, VT: Gower.

West, M. A., & Farr, J. L. (1990). Innovation at work. In M. A. West & J. L. Farr (Eds.), *Innovation and creativity at work: Psychological and organizational strategies* (pp. 3–13). Chichester, UK: John Wiley & Sons.

Williams, K. Y., & O'Reilly, C. A. III. (1998). Demography and diversity in organizations: A review of 40 years of research. In B. Staw & R. Sutton (Eds.), *Research in organizational behavior* (Vol. 20, pp. 77–140). Greenwich, CT: JAI Press.

Woolley, A. W., Gerbasi, M. E., Chabris, C. F., Kosslyn, S. M., & Hackman, J. R. (2008). Bringing in the experts: How team composition and collaborative planning jointly shape analytic effectiveness. *Small Group Research, 39,* 352–371.

Woolley, A. W., Hackman, J. R., Jerde, T. E., Chabris, C. F., Bennett, S. L., & Kosslyn, S. M. (2007). Using brain-based measures to compose teams: How individual capabilities and team collaboration strategies jointly shape performance. *Social Neuroscience, 2,* 96–105.

Yabuuchi, Y., Kocaoglu, D., & Watada, J. (2006). Analysis of project management in software development. In *PICMET 2006 Proceedings* (July 9–13, pp. 2809–2814). Istanbul, Turkey: PICMET.

Zhao, G., & Chen, W. (2009). Enhancing R&D in the science-based industry: An optimal stopping model for drug discovery. *International Journal of Project Management, 27,* 754–764.

Zhou, J. (1988). Feedback valence, feedback style, task autonomy, and achievement orientation: Interactive effects on creative performance. *Journal of Applied Psychology, 83,* 261–276.

Zhou, J., & George, J. M. (2001). When job dissatisfaction leads to creativity: Encouraging the expression of voice. *Academy of Management Journal, 44,* 682–696.

18

Leadership of Creativity: Entity-Based, Relational, and Complexity Perspectives

Russ Marion

Clemson University, Clemson, SC

Creativity has been extensively studied since the beginning of the 1990s and much has been learned of this critical issue for knowledge era organizations (Amabile, Schatzel, Moneta, & Kramer, 2004; Atwater & Carmeli, 2009; Basadur, 2004; Dougherty, 1996; Hirst, Van Knippenberg, & Zhou, 2009; Howell & Boies, 2004; Jaussi & Dionne, 2003; Jung, Chow, & Wu, 2003; Kahai, Sosik, & Avolio, 2005; Mumford, 2003; Mumford, Connelly, & Gaddis, 2003; Mumford, Scott, Gaddis, & Strange, 2002; Perry-Smith, 2006; Reiter-Palmon & Illies, 2004; Shalley & Gilson, 2004; Woodman, Sawyer, & Griffin, 1993; Zhou & George, 2001). This scholarship has examined where creativity comes from (Mumford et al., 2002; Rostan, 1998; Woodman, et al., 1993), the contexts that are conducive to creativity (Carmeli & Schaubroeck, 2007; George, 2007; Shalley & Gilson, 2004), how creativity occurs within teams (George, 2007; Kahai et al., 2005; Shalley & Gilson, 2004), and how to lead for creativity (Elkins & Keller, 2003; Howell & Boies, 2004; Mumford et al., 2002).

Much of this work is entity-based (Uhl-Bien, 2006), in part because creativity is a particular fascination of psychologists (George, 2007). Recently, however, some scholars have observed that little is known about team dynamics and its contribution to the emergence of creativity—what Hargadon and Bechky (2006) have called collective creativity, or instances:

> "where particular interactions yield creative insights, yet those insights cannot be attributed to particular individuals" *(p. 484).*

George (2007), summarizing this study by Hargadon and Bechky, define collective creativity as:

> "coming up with new ways to combine old or existing ideas, procedures, and processes to arrive at creative solutions to problems" *(p. 494).*

Handbook of Organizational Creativity.
DOI: 10.1016/B978-0-12-374714-3.00018-5

It is creativity that emerges from the interactions and conflicts of diverse people and ideas rather than from the mind of any given individual.

The current state of efforts in team dynamics and creativity has been largely limited to studies of group composition and conditions (George, 2007; Shalley, Zhou, & Oldham, 2004) or to categorizations of interactive behaviors (Hargadon & Bechky, 2006). Complexity theory goes beyond this, by studying just how interactive dynamics foster emergent phenomena like creativity. Complexity theory allows one to understand creativity as functions of interdependent interactions under conditions of conflicting constraints, heterogeneity, pressure, and uncertainty. Complexity describes large networks of people and ideas that are interacting and changing in a complex dance. It focuses not so much on the variables of a social system as on its processes, or social mechanisms (Hedström & Swedberg, 1998; Marion & Uhl-Bien, in press). Also, unlike traditional approaches to creativity, complexity focuses less on creativity as an individual attribute, but on the emergence, interactions, and flow of ideas themselves. Thus Hargadon and Bechky's (2006) collective creativity, from the complexity theory perspective, is not so much about a collective mind as it is about interactive, collective ideas.

This chapter describes both entity and collective (or complexity) perspectives of creativity. It begins by reviewing traditional, entity-based studies of creativity and then contrasts them with the complexity leadership approach to understanding this phenomenon. The chapter then describes studies by complexity theorists on creativity, and concludes by describing how leadership can influence creative dynamics and foster creative outcomes.

ENTITY-BASED APPROACHES TO CREATIVITY

A large body of research examines creativity as an act performed by individual persons; hence, they are called entity-based approaches. These approaches focus on the attributes of individuals acting independently or while engaged in group activities (Shalley et al., 2004; Uhl-Bien, 2006), and on the conditions that foster creativity. The conditions that foster individual creativity include contexts (such as autonomy or heterogeneity) and appropriate leadership behaviors.

Studies of Creative Individuals

One of the questions that creativity researchers are interested in is, what personal characteristics differentiate those who are creative from those who are not? Woodman et al. (1993), usefully categorized the factors that promote creativity into personality traits, cognitive factors, intrinsic motivation, and knowledge. They cite Barron and Harrington (1981) to define personality traits conducive to creativity as including:

> "high valuation of aesthetic qualities in experience, broad interests, attraction to complexity, high energy, independence of judgment, autonomy, intuition, self-confidence, ability to resolve antinomies or to accommodate apparently opposite or conflicting traits in one's self-concept, and a firm sense of self as creative" (p. 453).

Accordingly, creative people possess a high degree of achievement motivation (Mumford et al., 2002; Rostan, 1998), and they have an adaptive style of relating to problems in their environment (Baer, Oldham, & Cummings, 2003; Kirton, 1994).

Woodman et al. (1993) define the cognitive factors that underlie creative capacity as knowledge, cognitive skills, and cognitive styles/preferences. Barron and Harrington (1981) argued that the cognitive styles of creative people are characterized by associational abilities, analogical and metaphorical abilities, imagery abilities, and problem-finding abilities. Creative people have a tendency to go against the norm; that is, they tend to be divergent thinkers (Kirton, 1994).

Intrinsic motivation refers to those internal attributes that drive a person to be creative. Amabile, Conti, Coon, Lazenby, and Herron (1996) argued that creative people are motivated by the work itself and by positive engagement in their tasks. Others have identified traditional motivators that have a negative effect on creative people. Woodman, for example, observed that:

> "motivational interventions such as evaluations and reward systems may adversely affect intrinsic motivation toward a creative task because they redirect attention away from the heuristic aspects of the creative task and toward the technical or rule-bound aspects of task performance" (p. 300).

However, George (2007), along with Shalley et al. (2004) and Zhou and Shalley (2003) have observed that:

> "very few studies directly examined to what extent intrinsic motivation is an explanatory mediating process, and the few that directly tested this proposition yielded inconsistent results... Thus, research has yet to support consistently and rigorously the intuitively appealing premise that intrinsic motivation underlies creativity" (p. 444).

Finally, Woodman's knowledge category addresses what a person knows. A number of researchers have identified knowledge (in the form of expertise) as a critical factor in the creative process (Feldman, 1999; Mumford et al., 2002; Rostan, 1998; Woodman et al., 1993). As Mumford (2002) put it:

> "one of the most noteworthy characteristics of creative people is that they have a substantial investment in expertise and the ongoing development of expertise" (p. 710).

LEADERSHIP OF CREATIVE PEOPLE

The entity-based literature on leading creative people has been devoted largely to expositions on motivating, supporting, directing, and creating needed conditions for creativity.

Motivating Creativity

The literature on motivation of creativity deals with such things as leader–member exchange theory (e.g., Atwater & Carmeli, 2009) and transformational theory (Elkins & Keller, 2003; Jung et al., 2003; Jung, Wu, & Chow, 2008; Kahai et al., 2005; Murphy & Ensher, 2008; Nemanich & Keller, 2007). Atwater and Carmeli (2009) concluded that:

> "LMX was positively related to employees' feelings of energy, which in turn were related to a high level of involvement in creative work" (p. 264).

It is worth noting, as Atwater and Cameli themselves did, that the focus was on creative involvement rather than creative output.

Tierney, Farmer, and Graen (1999), however, found a strong interaction between LMX and whether a person had an innovative or creative cognitive style (Kirton, 1976; LMX was strongly related to adaptive styles but not with innovative styles); that is, innovative people seem to be creative regardless of a leader's LMX strategies (Elkins & Keller, 2003).

Creativity literature from the transformational leadership tradition is mixed. Elkins and Keller (2003) concluded from their review that the effects of transformational leadership in R&D organizations are moderated by intervening variables such as project type. Citing Keller (1992), they argued that transformational leadership had a stronger impact on research projects than on research development. They also noted the findings of Waldman and Atwater (1992), who found that the transformational leadership of higher level administrators was more effective for R&D success than it was when project managers expressed this type of leadership. This is generally consistent with the findings of Osborn and Marion (2009), who examined international innovation-seeking alliances. These researchers concluded that the transformational styles of managers in home offices that sponsored alliances were effective for producing a return to the home office, but that transformational styles were not particularly effective for the alliance itself; they further concluded that a more distributed, knowledge-based style (patterning of attention and network development) by project heads was more useful for alliance innovation.

The findings of some researchers would seem to contradict those of Osborn and Marion (2009). For example, Sosik, Kahai, and Avolio (1998) found that, for unidentified leaders, perceptions of transformational behaviors by the leaders increased the emergence of flow, which affected motivation and subsequent creativity. Mumford et al. (2002) may help explain these diverse findings. They observed that transformational leadership was not consistently related to creativity and proposed that the strong vision of a transformational leader may distract the attention of workers and limit their autonomy. This in turn could inhibit creativity. They subsequently proposed that transformational leadership *may be* (instead of is) related to creativity.

Supporting Creativity

Leaders support creativity by (among other things) championing creativity and creative ideas (Elkins & Keller, 2003; Howell & Boies, 2004), with daily interactions with employees (Amabile et al., 2004), with skill not only in managing both subordinate tasks and subordinate relationships but the ability to integrate the two simultaneously; with support for creative thinking (Nemanich & Keller, 2007); and by providing information (Reiter-Palmon & Illies, 2004).

Directing Creativity

Creative people seem to operate most effectively if some sort of frame, or structure, is constructed around their efforts (Mumford, Bedell-Avers, & Hunter, 2008). Several studies have supported this. Mumford et al. (2008) and West et al. (2003), for example, argue that leaders enhance the creative process by planning for it. Mumford et al. (2002) add that leaders of creativity envision and direct creative activities. This visioning proposal would seem to contradict the earlier referenced statement by Mumford, that a transformational leader's vision may limit the autonomy of, and distract, creative people. He agrees that vision is not consistently related to creativity, but explains that certain types of vision may create a valuable consensus among workers. He adds that a mission-oriented vision (e.g., John Kennedy's vision to land a man on the moon) may be more valuable than a less specific vision.

Creating Conditions for Creativity

Finally, leaders create conditions that are conducive to creativity by individuals. Jung et al. (2003, 2008) and Zhang and Bartol (2010), for example, argued that effective leaders of creativity create a climate of empowerment among workers. Mumford et al. (2002) proposed that creative environments thrive on a diversity of skills and outlooks, and that they require a climate of autonomy. Carmeli and Schaubroeck (2007) stated that the expectations of leaders influence creative behavior. George (2007) argued that creativity benefits from creativity prompts from leaders and from signals of safety. Byrne, Mumford, Barrett, and Vessey (2009) make the rather strong argument that leaders contribute to creative conditions by selling (or championing) creative efforts and initiatives (see also Mumford, Scott, Gaddis, & Strange, 2002). They add that organizational and technical expertise on the part of leadership is equally critical to leading creative people.

ENTITY BASED STUDIES OF GROUP CREATIVITY

Individual level analyses survey the opinions or attitudes of individuals, or they summarize such conditions as total communication, average degree of including others etc., relative to individual creativity (Hargadon & Bechky, 2006). Entity based studies of group creativity extend this basic approach, arguing that creativity comes from the individual and that the group supports those individuals. These studies do not try to capture the ways in which individuals, groups, ideas, tasks, resources, and beliefs influence one another to generate creative outcomes (Hargadon & Bechky, 2006).

The body of work on entity-based group creativity can be grouped into studies that examine creativity relative to group attributes, studies of inputs and conditions, and studies of network characteristics. Group attributes that have been examined include level of cooperation and level of participation by group members (Kahai et al., 2005). Cooperation, according to Kahai and his colleagues, is:

"defined as behaviors that help a group advance its thinking, [and] includes

a. seeking help from others by asking questions,
b. helping others by clarifying the problem or a range of solutions, and
c. assessment of peer input…

Cooperation is related to elaboration, which refers to clarification or addition of details to a problem or solution and is used to measure creativity" (p. 501).

Most entity-based studies of teams examine team inputs and conditions (Shalley et al., 2004). Scholars, for example, have found positive effects for heterogeneity conditions (in terms of skills, outlooks, etc.; Mannix & Neale, 2005), and frequency of communication (Leenders, van Engelen, & Kratzer, 2003). Taggar (2002) examined the relationships between individual dispositions to be creative, processes such as involving others, and team creativity.

Networks

Network analyses have become popular in recent years. These analyses are built from matrices of interaction (such as who socializes with whom, who does one most trust, etc.); they produce statistics about different informal leadership functions in the network (ones' centrality in the network, whether one fills a structural hole, persons through whom significant amounts of information flows) and they produce statistics about the network's capacity to learn, to function efficiently, and so forth.

Entity-based network analyses tend to correlate various network statistics with measures of system creativity. Uzzi and Spiro (2005), for example, looked at how small world networks (e.g., the six degrees of separation, like in the Kevin Bacon game) influenced creativity among Broadway artists. Small worlds are characterized by relatively short paths between network participants. They found that, up to a point, the enhanced ability to share information inherent in a small world network was conducive to creativity, but as the network grew, that advantage disappeared. Perry-Smith (2006) found that weak ties were more conducive to creativity than strong ties. She also found that persons with a high degree of centrality in the network (connected to many people with short paths through the network) benefited creatively from weak ties with external networks. Tsai (2001) found similarly that units with a high degree of centrality and that had significant absorptive capacity were more creative than units with low centrality or less significant absorptive capacity.

Mason, Jones, and Goldstone (2008) examined different network structures and their effects on problem finding, speed of solution, and problem solving. They found that people tended to converge on a single solution even when an alternative, equally valid solution was available. They also concluded that networks with spatially-based cliques tended to explore more options when a greater range of exploration was required, and that long range connections are advantageous for problems that require less exploration. Teigland, Chen, and Fey (2009), using network statistics and hierarchical linear modeling, found that people who occupy structural holes (they broker relationships between two groups) are likely to be creative.

COLLECTIVE CREATIVITY AND LEADERSHIP

In his 2007 article on creativity in organizations, George rather boldly states that creativity scholarship is working toward a perspective of *collective* creativity:

"In their review, Shalley and colleagues (2004) concluded that research has tended to focus on individual creativity, with little empirical research focused on creativity at the group or team level. This appears to continue to be true for organizational research on group creativity. While psychologists are intrigued by group creativity and are working to understand creativity as a collective phenomenon…, organizational research has been focused on the individual level of analysis…. This is somewhat paradoxical given the increasing reliance of organizations on flatter, more flexible, team-based structures…, but it is perhaps understandable given that the study of creativity in organizations is a relatively new and emerging area of research and the very real challenges of studying creativity in ongoing teams in organizations." *(p. 462)*

Hargadon and Bechky (2006) define collective creativity as:

"moments when the creative insight emerges *not* within a single individual, but rather across the interactions of multiple participants in the process" *(p. 484)*.

Several scholars have called for this type of team-based analysis. Kurtzberg and Amabile (2001) argue that:

"In all of the [current] approaches, the focus has rested squarely on the individual, highlighting individual cognitive processing, stable individual difference, and the effects of the external environment on the individual. Relatively little attention has been paid to team level creative synergy, in which ideas are generated by groups instead of being generated by one mind." *(p. 285)*

Both George (2007) and Shalley et al. (2004), in their rather extensive reviews of creativity and leadership research, argue that researchers need to learn more about team dynamics and the production of creativity (see also Boyatzis, 2006). Hargadon and Bechky (2006) ask:

"What turns collections of creative individuals into creative collectives, where particular interactions yield creative insights, yet those insights cannot be attributed to particular individuals? An answer to this question is important because the need for individual creative genius is steadily being displaced in organizations" *(p. 484)*.

These questions go beyond those asked by entity-based team level researchers. Collective creativity researchers want to know about the dynamics of interaction in networked groups, and how those dynamics foster creativity.

Complexity Theory

At present, the science of complexity is the only comprehensive theory available for systematically framing and analyzing such questions. Complexity theory analyzes the dynamics of complex interactive networks. Complexity theorists propose that when many agents (people, groups, species, etc.) interact locally, they generate a structured and patterned behavior that may be difficult to envision and impossible to predict in its long-term trajectory. Heifetz (1994) argues that one must develop the capacity to view social dynamics from the balcony (so to speak) if one is to grasp something of the dynamics that such systems engage in.

At its foundation, complexity theory is relational in nature. Uhl-Bien (2006) describes relational leadership (a particular focus within the relational perspective) as:

"a view of leadership and organization as human social constructions that emanate from the rich connections and interdependencies of organizations and their members" *(p. 484)*.

She continues:

> "In contrast to a more traditional orientation, which considers relationships from the standpoint of individuals as independent, discrete entities (i.e., individual agency) ..., a 'relational' orientation starts with processes and not persons, and views persons, leadership and other relational realities as made in processes" *(p. 484)*.

Complexity, then, is about processes more than static events, and it is about the flow of information within those processes (George, 2007; Mason et al., 2008; Saatcioglu, 2002). Complexity theorists have identified certain regularly-occurring processes that help explain the dynamics of a social system. Uhl-Bien, Marion, and McKelvey (2007), drawing from the work of Hedström and Swedberg (1998) and Davis and Marquis (2005), refer to these processes as social mechanisms. Marion and Uhl-Bien (in press) defines social mechanisms as:

> "Dynamic social processes rather than static variables (although they may include interactions among variables). The study of complexity, then, is a study of complex social mechanisms and the interactions among these mechanisms as well as their effects on system outcomes."

There are clustering mechanisms or processes that cause agents to naturally form bonds and organize into networks (Marion & Uhl-Bien, 2001). Complexity theorists study the effects of coupling strength and relationships with external networks on this clustering mechanism (Kauffman, 1993). They analyze the effects of interdependencies and conflicting constraints (Kauffman, 1995), pressure (McKelvey, 2008), simple enabling rules (Bonabeau & Meyer, 2001; Miller, 2007), and heterogeneity (Allen, 2001; George, 2007; Mary Uhl-Bien et al., 2007) on clustering.

There are catalyzing mechanisms that emerge out of the interactive, aggregating processes that enable and speed aggregation (Kauffman, 1993). Adaptive mechanisms also emerge to respond to the actions of external and internal pressures to help the system maintain fitness within its environment; as an illustration, systems self-adjust their coupling strengths to better adapt to threat (Kauffman, 1993). Enabling processes emerge, which foster conditions in which complexity can occur (Uhl-Bien et al., 2007). Learning mechanisms involve the interaction and processing of information within the system (Allen, 2001; Hannah & Lester, 2009; Tsai, 2001).

Perhaps the most important of the social mechanisms, at least for our purposes, is the change mechanism (Boyatzis, 2006). There are two different but complementary schools of thought on how this social mechanism works. One school is related to the work of biologists, who argue that complex systems are so dynamic that they function just shy of collapse; this is called "the edge of chaos" (Langston, 1986; see also Goodwin, 1994, 1997; Kauffman, 1993, 1995). Complex systems gain from this the ability to adapt, thrive, learn, and to change, and the dynamism, if properly tuned (Kauffman, 1993), is surprisingly robust and resistant to perturbation. Change occurs because of adaptive adjustments and because different dynamics occasionally step over the edge into chaos, thus forcing adjustments. Such changes occur in many different levels of intensity (and here the difference between adaptation and stepping over becomes fuzzy): most are very small, but a few are very big (as in 1989 when the USSR stepped over the edge and became a new political system). Such changes can occur with the smallest of triggers, or perturbations; that is change is non-linear, as when someone calmly says "fire", a small trigger, in a crowded room and causes massive panic.

Major changes often occur when systems are in a state of tension (McKelvey, 2008), however, and this brings us to the second perspective. This perspective of change is based on the work of physicist and Nobel Prize winner Ilya Prigogine (1997), who argued that complex systems tend to build pressures within the system, and that when the pressure reaches a level at which it can no longer be contained, change occurs to release that pressure (see also Fonseca, 2002; McKelvey, 2003). The stock market crash of 2009 can be explained in this way.

Certainly there are elements of both perspectives in the change mechanism. The perspective of biologists focuses on the nature of interaction and that of physicists focuses on the accumulation of pressure. Both are applicable to any given process, and neither perspective really excludes the other.

This non-linear change mechanism is the proximal source of creativity in the complexity dynamic. Complex change is unpredictable in form (although predictable in fact—if the right dynamics exist, it will occur). Creativity is likewise a phenomenon that cannot be predicted from prior states (Popper, 1961). Adaptability is a similar process, except here the system experiments with many different adaptive strategies until it converges on one that serves its needs.

This social change/creativity mechanism functions because the dynamically interacting, interdependent, pressured system combines, elaborates, critiques, conflicts, compares, diverges, and discards ideas (some survive the process, some don't; Goodwin, 1994; Kauffman, 1993; Marion, 1999). As people in the system engage in this dynamic, new ideas are generated that also become part of the process. Occasionally different ideas will collapse together rather dramatically and precipitously, to generate significant change/creativity events, as was the case in 1975 when ideas about microchips, processors, LEDs, print boards, transistors, and universal computing logic converged rather suddenly and the first microcomputer resulted (Anderson, 1995; Marion, 1999). That is, a complex system is an environment in which ideas interact, evolve, and new ideas emerge. Brilliant people help, but when brilliant people (or even moderately brilliant people—the advantage is in the process; Schreiber & Carley, 2006; 2008) interact over ideas, creative breakthroughs occurs. Complexity is about the interdependent interactions of ideas more than about creative individuals.

Goodwin (1997) made an interesting social/ethical observation about all of this. He observed that what complexity allows for is fulfilling creative expression:

> "[This] has intrinsic value for the members of the enterprise, as well as providing the best chance of the organizations persisting in a constantly changing corporate world. All the participants in this sector of social organization can then experience a higher quality of life, since they have greater freedom, more opportunities for creative play, and richer interactions—good for them and good for the organization." *(p. 118)*

Fletcher (2004) likewise made an interesting observation; she suggested that the feminine personality may benefit from the demands of the knowledge economy because of their greater tendency (over the masculine personality) to enable interaction and collaborative environments.

To say that creativity is entirely about the group dynamic would be incorrect, however. Complexity is about the dynamic processing of ideas, and how humans interact with that dynamic; that is, the individual mind is an important actor in the complexity process.

C. GROUP LEVEL INFLUENCES

Stacey (2001), drawing from the work of Mead (1934), argued that the mind is an independent actor but that it is shaped by interaction with the social environment, which in turn is shaped by the individual mind—a constructionist and constructivist epistemology blended. As Stacey (2001) so artfully put it:

> "All human relationships, including the communicative action of a body with itself, that is mind, and communicative action between bodies, that is the social, are interweaving storylines and propositions constructed by those relationships at the same time as those story lines and propositions constructed the relationship. They are all complex responsive processes of relating that can be thought of as the interweaving of themes, and variations on those things, that recursively form themselves." *(p. 140)*

Fonseca (2002) adds that it is this interaction between people that creates meaning, or knowledge:

> "Identity, both individual and collective, evolves and communicative interaction, learning and knowledge creation are essentially the same processes as the evolution of identity" *(p. 8)*.

Fonseca then argues that creativity is the creation of new meaning, and therefore, it evolves in the interaction of people. However, referring again to Stacy (2001), the individual mind and the collective interaction are partners in this process.

Complexity Research on Creative Collectives

Uhl-Bien et al. (2007) argue that the outcomes of complexity are creativity, adaptability, and learning. These three processual products are presented as interrelated and dependent on very similar social processes. They are all, for example, functions of interaction, interdependencies, pressure, and heterogeneity. All are variations of the change mechanism and involve non-linear processes. To wit, if you write about one, you are describing basically the same processes that drive the other two outcomes.

Research on Creativity

Complexity requires one to think and analyze relational influences rather than linear predictability. From the complexity perspective, relational influence is a foundational assumption, and people and variables are not conceptualized as independent agents (e.g., absent serial autocorrelation) as they are in typical statistical procedures. Thus statistical methodologies are only partially useful for understanding complex dynamics. Useful methodologies for analyzing relational influence include qualitative analysis and network analyses/simulations. Qualitative and network dynamic methodologies are found extensively in the research literature (e.g., Browning, Beyer, & Shetler, 1995; Carley, 1991, 1992; Carson, Tesluk, & Marrone, 2007; Graebner, 2009; Greenwood, Hinings, & Suddaby, 2002; Greenwood & Suddaby, 2006; Hollensbe, Khazanchi, & Masterson, 2008; Purdy & Gray, 2009) and describe social behaviors as relational, interactionist, and constructivist/constructionist dynamics. They offer a perspective and understanding of social dynamics that cannot be achieved through positivistic methodologies and consequently are valuable tools in our exploratory arsenal.

The body of research literature supporting the collectivist/complexity perspective is young but growing, and it is providing interesting insights into the collectivist dynamic. Much of the theoretical work in complexity leadership and creativity has focused on the role of leadership in the generation of complex dynamics (i.e., creativity, adaptability, and learning). The theory article of Uhl-Bien et al. (2007), for example, argued that a form of leadership they label "enabling leadership" fosters the conditions necessary for complexity, interactive processes and creativity to emerge. The complex interactive process that is enabled by this involves people taking initiatives to engage in interactive dynamics; this process is called adaptive leadership.

Lichtenstein and Plowman (2009), in a summary of three complexity research studies, conclude that enabling leaders:

> "Disrupt existing patterns through embracing uncertainty and creating controversy, encourage novelty by allowing experiments and supporting collective action, provide sensemaking and sensegiving through the artful use of language and symbols, and stabilize the system by integrating local constraints." (p. 617; see also Plowman, Solansky et al., 2007)

Schreiber and Carley (2008), using dynamic network analyses, show how informal leadership emerges from a dynamic interactive process. In their analysis of an army battle group, they found that a focus on informal network dynamics was more effective at fostering learning then was a culture of formal leadership. Further, they simulated the removal of selected informal leaders from the complex network and found a significant negative impact on the capacity of the group to learn, thus underscoring the importance of these functions in the effective operation of the complex network.

Schreiber, Marion, Uhl-Bien, and Carley (2006) performed a similar simulation on the effects of vision and coupling patterns on the capacity of a system to learn. The networks in the simulation were artificially constructed, so that initial conditions could be controlled. They found that moderate levels of coupling plus moderately demanding vision produced better learning then did low coupling and vision or high coupling and vision. Interestingly, they also found that as network size increased, the simulated agents began to cluster naturally into cliques, which inhibited the flow of information in the system.

On the issue of creativity itself, Koch and Leitner (2008) used a complexity dynamic to explore creativity in five Austrian semiconductor companies. They found that complex dynamics complemented top–down, managerial efforts by helping to accelerate the product development process. They also identified a bottom–up emergent dynamic in which employees, behind the backs of managers, took it upon themselves to generate and then promote their own ideas. Ethiraj and Levinthal (2004), in a somewhat similar study, examined the effects of modularity in complex tasks—breaking a task across teams—on performance.

Marion, Uhl-Bien, Arena, Sweetman, and Schreiber (2010) shed light on this bottom–up emergent process. In a grounded theory analysis of creativity in a large banking firm, they found, among other things, that creative ideas tended to emerge in small networks of interactive personnel. They also found some indication that silos—which otherwise suppress needed interactive dynamics—could actually serve to protect ideas until they were ready to present to management, thus supporting Koch and Leitner's (2008) findings above. They found, interestingly, that bureaucracy, which one would think would suppress complex dynamics and creativity, could actually serve to enhance the interactive dynamic. The logic is that, when employees are faced with bureaucratic restrictions, they may work to find ways to circumvent that restriction or re-conceptualize their efforts, thus fostering further creativity.

Hargadon and Bechky (2006), who coined the term collective creativity, advocate:

> "shifting the emphasis in research and management of creativity from identifying and managing creative individuals to understanding the social context and developing interactive approaches to creativity, and from a focus on relatively constant contextual variables to the alignment of fluctuating variables and their precipitation of momentary phenomena" (p. 484).

In their field studies of work in professional service firms, they found, as Stacey (2001) and Fonseca (2002) anticipated, that (consistent with the entity-based literature) individuals were at times responsible for creative endeavors. However, they also found evidence of a collective process. In analyzing the origins of this behavior, they found it was attributable to four types of social interaction: help seeking, help giving, reflective reframing, and reinforcing.

THE ROLE OF LEADERSHIP

We turn now to evidence in the literature on how to lead for complexity. The focus here will be on how to enable complexity and collective creativity. Uhl-Bien et al. (2007) coined the term "enabling leadership" to describe this dynamic, but others have written of leadership's role in fostering complex responses as well (Goldstein, Hazy, & Lichtenstein, 2010; Lichtenstein et al., 2007; Lichtenstein & Plowman, 2009; Marion & Uhl-Bien, 2007, in press; Osborn & Hunt, 2007; Schreiber et al., 2006; Solow, Burnetas, Piderit, & Leenawong, 2003; Surie & Hazy, 2006; Uhl-Bien & Marion, 2009; Uhl-Bien et al., 2007). Enabling leadership functions to foster conditions in which complex dynamics can emerge. Enabling leaders enable rather than control a creative future (Plowman et al., 2007). Enabling leaders can be anyone within an organization, and effective complex systems have a large web of informal enabling leaders. Formal leaders, however, are particularly well-positioned for this role because of their access to resources and authority, although one cannot assume that all positional leaders are capable of performing the enabling function.

My colleagues and I have found in our own research analyses that complexity is most dynamic and effective when everyone in the system understands and seeks to implement the principles of complex behaviors and their relationship to creativity, and when a large number of the agents (individuals or groups) in the system act as enablers who are committed to adaptive actions (e.g., Uhl-Bien et al., 2010). However, complex dynamics will evolve naturally when creative processes occur as well (Koch & Leitner, 2008).

Creativity, learning, and adaptability are emergent phenomena (Lichtenstein & Plowman, 2009). They emerge from the interaction and interdependency of ideas, tasks, information, resources, beliefs, world views, visions, and adaptive agents. Creativity is, by definition, an outcome that cannot be predicted from preceding conditions, thus it cannot be planned. It can be anticipated, not in its specific form, but in the fact that it will very likely emerge from dynamic conditions.

Many of the processes in which enabling leaders engage have also been identified by entity-based researchers (and we cite them as appropriate below), but complexity theorists focus on the role of these processes in the production of collective outcomes rather than entity outcomes. More specifically, enabling leadership enables the conditions described in this chapter under which complex dynamics thrive. Further, the model of enabling, administrative, and adaptive leadership proposed by Uhl-Bien et al. (2007) needs to be more conclusively researched, as does the issue of relationality (Bradbury & Lichtenstein, 2001), but the studies that have been conducted on complexity leadership and on complexity in general provide a foundation for projecting the functions of enabling leaders. We summarize this research relative to enabling leadership in the following, which focuses on conditions conducive to group creativity. We propose that leaders who foster collective creative processes will seek to enhance these conditions.

Enabling Interaction

Interaction is sine qua non of complexity dynamics, thus enabling leaders encourage open, formal and informal interaction among personnel, including positional administrators (Ethiraj & Levinthal, 2004; Fonseca, 2002; Koch & Leitner, 2008; Stacey, 1996). Enabling leaders pay attention to physical layout and the proximity/availability of agents with one another. Barry and Price (2004), for example, analyzed the effect of structural organization on agent connectedness and resultant creativity; they found a strong positive effect for open interactive structures on the capacity of the system to innovate. Enabling leaders provide comfortable workspaces where agents can interact (Thomke & Nimgade, 2007). Enabling leaders also foster interactions across groups—the intent here is to bridge communication channels across silos, or self-contained, largely isolated centers of behavior (Perry-Smith, 2006).

Enabling Interdependency

The network characteristic of interdependency is related to Weick's (1976) simulation research on loose and tight coupling, in that complexity theory explores the nature of coupling strength and coupling characteristics on complex dynamics (see also, Beekun & Glick, 2001; Daft, 1997; Hannah & Lester, 2009; Orton & Weick, 1990; Perry-Smith, 2006). Kauffman (1995) found, also in a series of simulations, that interdependent couplings foster tension and elaborative system changes, particularly when agents must resolve conflicting preferences that emerge from conditions in which agents depend upon one another. Perry-Smith (2006), in an analysis of relationships within university research labs, found that weaker ties are generally conducive to creativity.

Enabling leaders foster interdependent relationships in which the actions of one agent are dependent on the actions of another (Uhl-Bien et al., 2010). When the system is structured as networks of interdependent agents, a degree of complexity, or dynamism, results (Kauffman, 1995). Interdependency creates pressure on agents in a network to act. Cusumano (2001), for example, reports on a "sync and stabilize" strategy at Microsoft in which programmers are allowed to work independently or in groups for 4 days a week, but at the end of the week they must complete their code and run it against the code of other programmers. If the code does not interface other codes properly, then the programmer must work out the problem before leaving. This form of interdependency among programmers forces them to work together and to elaborate their code when inconsistencies arise.

Interdependent pressure is fostered when the successful completion of one's tasks depends upon unfulfilled actions by another person. It exists when the preference-satisfaction of one person is dependent on the patterns of behavior by one or more other persons: the success of one person's pursuit of influence may depend on others not pursuing influence; or one person's preference on how to complete a task may depend on support from another who has a vested interest in that task, or whose own task performance may be affected by how the initial person completes his or her tasks. However, excessive interdependency across a network (e.g., Weick's, 1976, tight coupling) can overwhelm it. When the patterns of interdependencies and resulting demands are so complex that none can be satisfied without disrupting the actions of numerous others, a system will tend to freeze and not take action (Kauffman, 1995).

Conflicting Constraints (Or Task-Related Conflict)

Enabling leadership fosters and supports situations in which agents differ over how tasks or preferences are to be conducted (Danneels & Sethi, 2003; Kauffman, 1995). These are called task related conflicts (Jehn, 1997), and they emerge under conditions of interdependency (Kauffman, 1995). Daneels and Sethi (2003), for example, performed a moderated regression analysis of data collected from public manufacturing firms in the US and found that constructive (i.e., task related) conflict had a positive effect on creativity in new product programs.

Task related conflicts pressure agents and networks of agents to search for adaptive solutions to differences. The ideal outcome is the _trilemma solution_: _dilemmas_ suggest a choice of mutually exclusive solutions—in a conflict between agent A or B, one wins and the other loses. In a trilemma, a third solution is suggested by the struggle between competing forces (cf. Lichtenstein et al., 2006). This third solution, while often unanticipated, elaborates the creativity, learning, and adaptability of the system beyond what was implicit in A or B's original position. A basic error of positional administrators is to step into conflicting constraints and side with one or the other of the competitors. This is the use of authority to shut down a crucial element of dynamic problem solving processes and, consequently, to curtail the adaptive capacity of networks. Administrators should inject their authority only if a task related conflict is clearly becoming personal.

Heterogeneity

Several of the studies—from both entity-based and collective-based literature—have dealt with heterogeneity (Andriani, 2001; Choi & Thompson, 2005; Levine & Choi, 2004). Allen (2001) argued what he called the fundamental importance of microdiversity in producing learning in group dynamics. George (2007) argued that diverse groups are more creative than homogeneous groups. They are able to draw on a greater diversity of knowledge and skills. Choi and Thompson (2005) performed controlled experiments in which group members were shifted among groups; they found that increased diversity increased the ability of the group to produce new ideas. Interestingly (or alarmingly), Mannix and Neale (2005) reviewed 50 years of research, and reported that differences in social or ethnic characteristics (age, race, gender) are negatively related to creativity, while underlying differences in characteristics such as skills and education positively affect creativity. Basadur (2004) proposed that:

> "teams with more heterogeneous preferences for various phases or stages of the creative process were more innovative than teams whose members were more homogeneous in preference for stages of the creative process" (p. 106).

Enabling leaders, then, embrace a diversity of skills, preferences, ethnicities, worldviews, visions and goals, knowledge, and ideas among network participants (Uhl-Bien et al., 2007). Heterogeneity feeds conflicting constraints. It injects diverse information into a system thus increasing the amount of information on which the complex network acts (as Churchill allegedly said (paraphrasing); give me two persons who think alike and I will give you one person that I don't need). Enabling leaders do not seek to have everyone on the same page; if positional, they do not inject their authority to dominate the preferences of others and they do not suppress certain agent's preferences in favor of those of others. They encourage the hiring of personnel with the goal of creating a heterogeneous workforce—not only for ethnic diversity but also for ideational diversity.

Adaptive Rules

Adaptive rules govern the actions of a system in ways that produce adaptive outcomes for the system. They are not limiting or delimiting rules as are common with bureaucracies (Hall, 1963). Cusumano's story of Microsoft's sync and stabilize strategy (above) illustrates how simple rules can foster interdependent behavior and product elaboration. Eric Bonabeau (2001) describes a simple game that illustrates this: ask a group of people to silently choose two other people in the group; when the game begins, they should move in a way that keeps the person they chose between him or her and the second choice. Then replay the game, except this time move in a way that keeps yourself between your two choices. The first will generate a tight clustering of the group and the second, a more dynamic movement with small, temporary clusters. The simple rules create two different forms of order.

Enabling leaders foster adaptive rules that enable such things as interaction, interdependency, uncertainty, and pressure (Plowman et al., 2007). Examples might include rules that evaluate collaborative initiatives more heavily than individual initiatives, or that require teams to advocate at least one creative product idea per month.

Adaptive, Creative, and/or Learning Pressure

Enabling leaders generate adaptive pressures; such pressures supplement those created by interdependency and conflicting constraints (McKelvey, 2008). Pressure can be direct or it may be enacted with adaptive rules. Excessive pressure, however, may suppress rather than enable creativity in groups (Uhl-Bien et al., 2010).

Social Dampening

Social dampening can occur when a dynamic process interacts with organizational or environmental resistors such as rules, policies, or regulations (Marion & Uhl-Bien, in press). Marion, Uhl-Bien, Arena, Sweetman, and Schreiber (2010) have found that, under such conditions, the system becomes more dynamic or complex in an effort to find work-arounds or alternative processes that skirt the resistor pressure. Inflexible or dominating pressures, however, can overcome, or suppress, social dampening (Uhl-Bien, Marion, Schreiber, Arena, & Hanson, 2010), as when regulations are particularly specific and emphatic, thus it appears there needs to be some perceived flexibility in the resistor to enable social dampening. Enabling leaders, then, perceive bureaucracy as modifiable assumptions about how business is conducted and not as non-negotiable rules.

Enabling Uncertainty

Complexity thrives on uncertainty, and enabling leaders embrace and foster that uncertainty (Andriani, 2001). Indeed, Mumford et al. (2008) observed that uncertainty characterizes creative work. Plowman et al. (2007) observed in their complexity study of a deteriorating church, that:

"The leaders did not shy away from unpredictable or unexplainable outcomes. Rather, they embraced the unknowable, and actually introduced system instability through organizational conflict, system disruptions, and open conversations about the church's uncertain future. Our study revealed that the leaders contributed to the organization's instability by disrupting existing patterns, which then made it much more likely that emergent ideas would bubble up from within the organization." (p. 349)

Enabling Information Flow and Diversity

Enabling leaders foster information flow by injecting knowledge into the interactive dynamic (George, 2007; Mason et al., 2008; Reiter-Palmon & Illies, 2004; Saatcioglu, 2002) and by providing the system with sources of diverse information. Several researchers have written on the centrality of information in complex dynamics, including Fonseca (2002), Marion et al. (2010), and Mason et al. (2008). Mumford et al. (2008), an entity researcher, likewise observed that the diversity of information imported into a firm is positively related to innovation. He cited Koberg, Uhlenbruck, and Sarason (1996), who likewise found that scanning was positively related to innovation.

Diversity of information is a more generalized expression of what happens when enabling leaders promote diversity of skills, outlooks, preferences, and educational levels. Diversity of information promotes information flow; multiple ideas to interact, combine, diverge, and elaborate within groups; and task related conflicts, all of which have been discussed as complexity-related dynamics.

Resources

Creativity is an emergent outcome that is enabled by a number of dynamic processes. When these processes "bear fruit," creativity is manifest as the unique convergence of existing ideas, resources, tasks, knowledge, and agents (among other things; Arthur, 2009). The 1975 emergence of the desktop computer is a case in point, in that it was the product of the convergence of many different technologies that were commonly available at the time. Thus emergent creativity functions best in a resource-rich environment. Enabling leaders enhance creativity by seeking to enhance the quality and scope of resources to which agents have access.

Championing

Enabling leaders champion emerging ideas, adaptive behaviors, and learning initiatives. They do this by advocating and selling the emergent dynamic, providing resources for the dynamic, helping to move it through administrative channels as appropriate, and recruiting support from others. Entity researchers have long observed this (e.g., Byrne, Mumford, Barrett, & Vessey, 2009). Howell and Boies (2004) observed in their qualitative analysis that champions promote creativity, because of their more enthusiastic support for new ideas and their ability to sell ideas to the management in a firm. Complexity researchers Marion et al. (2010) made similar observations about group dynamics in their grounded theory analysis of creativity in a banking firm.

Psychological Safety

Enabling leaders foster environments of psychological comfort, safety, trust, and risk taking (Danneels & Seth, 2003; Edmondson, 1999; Marion et al., 2010). This refers to basic interpersonal skills that have been taught in the leadership literature for much of the 20th century. We are finding in our research that the same safety that enables individual action also enables effective group dynamics (Uhl-Bien et al., 2010). That is, enabling leaders are effective at leader–member exchange, which refers not only to exchanges between positional leaders and followers, but exchanges among followers, groups, and within groups as well. Elkins and Keller (2003), for example, argued that effective leader–member exchanges are related to project success. Atwater and Carmeli (2009) found a strong relationship between LMX and involvement in creative activities.

Enabling leaders foster an atmosphere that is free from threat, abuse of power, and political favorites. A key concept is the notion of trust, referring to a climate in which one can exchange ideas freely without fear that confidences will be abused. Enabling leaders foster a climate in which individuals and groups are rewarded for initiatives rather than sanctioned for failures. In short, enablers foster psychological conditions which are conducive to the free flow of information and the conditions in which complex dynamics can operate.

SUMMARY AND DISCUSSION

Collective creativity, then, emerges from an environment in which ideas can flow and interact. Creativity is fostered by interaction, interdependency, heterogeneity, pressure, task-related conflict, and adaptive rules. It is enabled by leaders who champion creative ideas, foster sensemaking in self and others, and who provide psychologically safe environments.

Complexity dynamics allow ideas to converge and diverge; to conflict and elaborate; to spontaneously emerge when people try to reconcile differences, when they discover opportunities to merge various ideas into a uniquely different idea, or when ideas complement the usefulness of one another. Complexity isn't just a one-on-one environment, it is a networked environment in which different ideas influence and re-influence each other, in which ideas affect one another at a distance through indirect pathways of relationships, and in which higher-order ideas influence the development of lower level ideas. This is, in part, what Hargadon and Bechky (2006) meant when they defined collective creativity as a process:

> "where particular interactions yield creative insights, yet those insights cannot be attributed to particular individuals" (p. 484).

Collective creativity is a process in which individual perceptions shape collective behavior, and collective behaviors shape individual perceptions (Stacey, 2001), where meaning is created by interactions with others and with the environment, and creativity emerges from the meaning-making process.

The question is, how does leadership function in such an environment? The complexity and entity-based creativity literature agree on certain strategies: Both agree, for example, that leaders import information (Reiter-Palmon & Illies, 2004; Mason et al., 2008), foster heterogeneity (Allen, 2001; Andriani, 2001; Basadur, 2004), and champion ideas (Byrne et al., 2009; Howell & Boies, 2004). Entity-based and complexity scholars differ, however, in that the former see creativity as a variable, and the latter as a process. To the complexity theorist, the challenge of leadership is in enabling, engaging in, and managing such processes (Uhl-Bien et al., 2007). They enable by creating environments in which complexity and creativity can thrive. They engage in that every person is part of the networked process; all participants interact, conflict over ideas, engage in sensemaking, take initiatives that contribute to the creativity process, and respect the bottom–up paticipatory process. They manage by planning for creativity (Uhl-Bien et al., 2007), by fostering visions that focus the imagination and the work (Schreiber, Marion, Uhl-Bien, & Carley, 2006), and by championing to help creative ideas gain the attention of the bureaucracy.

Complexity theory is not just about ideas from one person at a time; rather it describes how ideas interact and influence one another in ways that sharpen and grow the idea. It opens new theoretical and methodological vistas for the study of creativity. It does not supplant the rich foundation of entity-based research that precedes it; rather, complexity enhances, elaborates, develops, and interacts with that research in ways that can only benefit the field.

References

Allen, P. M. (2001). A complex systems approach to learning in adaptive networks. *International Journal of Innovation Management, 5,* 149–180.

Amabile, T. M., Conti, R., Coon, H., Lazenby, J., & Herron, M. (1996). Assessing the work environment for creativity. *Academy of Management Journal, 39,* 1154–1184.

Amabile, T. M., Schatzel, E. A., Moneta, G. B., & Kramer, S. J. (2004). Leader behaviors and the work environment for creativity: Perceived leader support. *The Leadership Quarterly, 15,* 5–32.

Anderson, P. (1995). Microcomputer manufacturers. In G. R. Carroll & M. T. Hannan (Eds.), *Organizations in industry* (pp. 37–58). New York, NY: Oxford University Press.

Andriani, P. (2001). Diversity, knowledge and complexity theory: Some introductory issues. *International Journal of Innovation Management, 5*, 257.

Arthur, W. B. (2009). *The nature of technology*. New York, NY: Free Press.

Atwater, L., & Carmeli, A. (2009). Leader–member exchange, feelings of energy, and involvement in creative work. *The Leadership Quarterly, 20*, 264–275.

Baer, M., Oldham, G. R., & Cummings, A. (2003). Rewarding creativity: When does it really matter? *The Leadership Quarterly, 14*, 569–586.

Barron, F. , B., & Harrington, D. M. (1981). Creativity, intelligence, and personality. *Annual Review of Psychology, 32*, 439–476.

Barry, H., & Price, I. (2004). Quantifying the complex adaptive workplace. *Facilities, 22*, 8–18.

Basadur, M. (2004). Leading others to think innovatively together: Creative leadership. *The Leadership Quarterly, 15*, 103–121.

Beekun, R. I., & Glick, W. H. (2001). Organization structure from a loose coupling perspective: A multidimensional approach. *Decision Sciences, 32*, 227–250.

Bonabeau, E., & Meyer, C. (2001). Swarm intelligence: A whole new way to think about business. *Harvard Business Review, 79*, 107–114.

Boyatzis, R. E. (2006). An overview of intentional change from a complexity perspective. *Journal of Management Development, 25*, 607–623.

Browning, L. D., Beyer, J. M., & Shetler, J. C. (1995). Building cooperation in a competitive industry: Sematech and the semiconductor industry. *Academy of Management Journal, 38*, 113–151.

Byrne, C. L., Mumford, M. D., Barrett, J. D., & Vessey, W. B. (2009). Examining the leaders of creative efforts: What do they do, and what do they think about? *Creativity and Innovation Management, 18*, 256–268.

Carley, K. (1991). A theory of group stability. *American Sociological Review, 56*, 331–354.

Carley, K. (1992). Organizational learning and personnel turnover. *Organizational Science, 3*, 20–46.

Carmeli, A., & Schaubroeck, J. (2007). The influence of leaders' and other referents' normative expectations on individual involvement in creative work. *The Leadership Quarterly, 18*, 35–48.

Carson, J. B., Tesluk, P. E., & Marrone, J. A. (2007). Shared leadership in teams: An investigation of antecedent conditions and performance. *Academy of Management Journal, 50*, 1217–1234.

Choi, H.-S., & Thompson, L. (2005). Old wine in a new bottle: Impact of membership change on group creativity. *Organizational Behavior and Human Decision Processes, 98*, 121–132.

Cusumano, M. (2001). Focusing creativity: Microsoft's "Synch and stabilize" approach to software product development. In I. Nonaka & T. Nishiguchi (Eds.), *Knowledge emergence: Social, technical, and evolutionary dimensions of knowledge creation* (pp. 111–123). Oxford, UK: Oxford University Press.

Daft, R. L. (1997). *Organization theory and design* (2nd ed.). Cincinnatti, OH: Southwestern College Publishing.

Danneels, E., & Sethi, R. (2003). Antecedents of new product program creativity: The moderating role of environmental turbulence. [Proceeding]. A1–A6.

Davis, G. F., & Marquis, C. (2005). Prospects for organization theory in the early twenty-first century: Institutional fields and mechanisms. *Organization Science, 16*, 332–343.

Dougherty, D. (1996). Organizing for innovation. In S. R. Clegg, C. Hardy & W. Nord (Eds.), *Handbook of organization studies* (pp. 424–439). London, UK: Sage.

Edmondson, A. (1999). Psychological safety and learning behavior in work teams. *Administrative Science Quarterly, 44*, 350–383.

Elkins, T., & Keller, R. (2003). Leadership in research and development organizations: A literature review and conceptual framework. *The Leadership Quarterly, 14*, 433–487.

Ethiraj, S. K., & Levinthal, D. (2004). Modularity and innovation in complex systems. *Management Science, 50*, 159–174.

Feldman, D. H. (1999). The development of creativity. In R. J. Sternberg (Ed.), *Handbook of creativity* (pp. 169–188). Cambridge, UK: Cambridge University Press.

Fletcher, J. K. (2004). The paradox of postheroic leadership: An essay on gender, power, and transformational change. *The Leadership Quarterly, 15*, 647–661.

Fonseca, J. (2002). *Complexity and innovation in organizations*. London, UK: Routledge.

George, J. M. (2007). Creativity in organizations. *Academy of Management Annals, 1*, 439–477.

Goldstein, J., Hazy, J., & Lichtenstein, B. (2010). *Complexity and the nexus of leadership: Leveraging nonlinear science to create ecologies of innovation*. Englewood Cliffs, NJ: Palgrave Macmillan.

C. GROUP LEVEL INFLUENCES

Goodwin, B. (1994). *How the leopard changed its spots: The evolution of complexity*. New York, NY: Charles Scribner's Sons.

Goodwin, B. (1997). Complexity, creativity, and society. *Soundings, 5* (Spring) Retrieved from <amielandmelburn.org.uk/>.

Graebner, M. E. (2009). Caveat venditor: Trust asymmetries in acquisitions of entrepreneurial firms. *Academy of Management Journal, 52*, 435–472.

Greenwood, R., & Suddaby, R. (2006). Institutional entrepreneurship in mature fields: The big five accounting firms. *Academy of Management Journal, 49*, 27–48.

Greenwood, R., Hinings, C. R., & Suddaby, R. (2002). Theorizing change: The role of professional associations in the transformation of institutionalized fields. *Academy of Management Journal, 45*, 58–80.

Hall, R. H. (1963). The concept of bureaucracy: An empirical assessment. *American Journal of Sociology, 69*, 32–40.

Hannah, S. T., & Lester, P. B. (2009). A multilevel approach to building and leading learning organizations. *The Leadership Quarterly, 20*, 34–48.

Hargadon, A. B., & Bechky, B. A. (2006). When collections of creatives become creative collectives: A field study of problem solving at work. *Organization Science, 17*, 484–500.

Hedström, P., & Swedberg, R. (1998). *Social mechanisms: An analytical approach to social theory*. Cambridge, UK: Cambridge University Press.

Heifetz, R. A. (1994). *Leadership without easy answers*. Cambridge, MA: Harvard University Press.

Hirst, G., Van Knippenberg, D., & Zhou, J. (2009). A cross-level perspective on employee creativity: Goal orientation, team learning behavior, and individual creativity. *Academy of Management Journal, 52*, 280–293.

Hollensbe, E. C., Khazanchi, S., & Masterson, S. S. (2008). How do i assess if my supervisor and organization are fair? Identifying the rules underlying entity-based justice perceptions. *Academy of Management Journal, 51*, 1099–1116.

Howell, J. M., & Boies, K. (2004). Champions of technological innovation: The influence of contextual knowledge, role orientation, idea generation, and idea promotion on champion emergence. *The Leadership Quarterly, 15*, 123–143.

Jaussi, K. S., & Dionne, S. D. (2003). Leading for creativity: The role of unconventional leadership behavior. *The Leadership Quarterly, 14*, 475–498.

Jehn, K. A. (1997). A qualitative analysis of conflict types and dimensions in organizational groups. *Administrative Science Quarterly, 42*, 530–557.

Jung, D., Chow, C., & Wu, A. (2003). The role of transformational leadership in enhancing organizational innovation: Hypotheses and some preliminary findings. *The Leadership Quarterly, 12*, 525–544.

Jung, D., Wu, A., & Chow, C. (2008). Towards understanding the direct and indirect effects of CEOs' transformational leadership on firm innovation. *The Leadership Quarterly, 19*, 582–594.

Kahai, S. S., Sosik, J. J., & Avolio, B. J. (2005). Effects of leadership style, anonymity, and rewards on creativity-relevant processes and outcomes in an electronic meeting system context. *The Leadership Quarterly, 14*, 499–524.

Kauffman, S. A. (1993). *The origins of order*. New York, NY: Oxford University Press.

Kauffman, S. A. (1995). *At home in the universe: The search for the laws of self-organization and complexity*. New York, NY: Oxford University Press.

Kirton, M. J. (1976). Adaptors and innovators: A description and measure. *Journal of Applied Psychology, 61*, 622–629.

Kirton, M. J. (1994). *Adaptors and innovators: Styles of creativity and problem solving*. New York, NY: Routledge.

Koberg, C. S., Uhlenbruck, N., & Sarason, Y. (1996). Facilitators of organizational innovation: The role of life-cycle stage. *Journal of Business Venturing, 11*, 133–149.

Koch, R., & Leitner, K. (2008). The dynamics and functions of self-organization in the fuzzy front end: Empirical evidence from the Austrian semiconductor industry. *Creativity and Innovation Management, 17*, 216–226.

Kurtzberg, T. R., & Amabile, T. M. (2001). From guilford to creative synergy: Opening the black box of team level creativity. *Creativity Research Journal, 13*, 285–294.

Langston, C. G. (1986). Studying artificial life with cellular automata. *Physica, 22D*, 120–149.

Leenders, R., van Engelen, J., & Kratzer, J. (2003). Virtuality, communication, and new product team creativity: A social network perspective. *Journal of Engineering and Technology Management, 20*, 69–92.

Levine, J. M., & Choi, H.-S. (2004). Impact of personnel turnover on team performance and cognition. In E. Salas & M. S. Fiore (Eds.), *Team cognition: Process and performance at the interindividual level* (pp. 163–176). Washington, DC: American Psychological Association.

Lichtenstein, B., & Plowman, D. (2009). The leadership of emergence: A complex systems leadership theory of emergence at successive organizational levels. *The Leadership Quarterly, 20,* 617–630.

Lichtenstein, B., Uhl-Bien, M., Marion, R., Seers, A., Orton, D., & Schreiber, C. (2006). Leadership in emergent events: Exploring the interactive process of leading in complex situations. *Emergence: Complexity and Organization, 8,* 2–12.

Lichtenstein, B., Uhl-Bien, M., Marion, R., Seers, A., Orton, J. D., & Schreiber, C. (2007). Complexity leadership theory: An interactive perspective on leading in complex adaptive systems. In J. K. Hazy, J. Goldstein & B. Lichtenstein (Eds.), *Complex systems leadership theory* (pp. 129–142)

Mannix, E., & Neale, M. A. (2005). What differences make a difference: The promise and reality of diverse teams in organizations. *Psychological Science in the Public Interest, 6,* 31–55.

Marion, R. (1999). *The edge of organization: Chaos and complexity theories of formal social organizations.* Newbury Park, CA: Sage.

Marion, R., & Uhl-Bien, M. (2001). Leadership in complex organizations. *The Leadership Quarterly, 12,* 389–418.

Marion, R., & Uhl-Bien, M. (2007). Complexity and strategic leadership. In R. Hooijberg, J. Hunt, J. Antonakis, K. Boal & N. Lane (Eds.), *Being there even when you are not: Leading through structures, systems, and processes* (Vol. 4, pp. 273–287). Amsterdam, The Netherlands: Elsevier.

Marion, R., & Uhl-Bien, M. (in press). Implications of complexity science for the study of leadership. In P. Allen, S. Maquire & B. McKelvey (Eds.), *Sage handbook of complexity and management.* London, UK: Sage.

Marion, R., Uhl-Bien, M., Arena, M., Sweetman, D., & Schreiber, C. (2010). *A grounded theory of innovation in complex adaptive organizations.* Clemson University. (In process)

Mason, W. A., Jones, A., & Goldstone, R. L. (2008). Propagation of innovations in networked groups. *Journal of Experimental Psychology: General, 137,* 422–433.

McKelvey, B. (2003). Toward a 0th law of thermodynamics: Order creation complexity dynamics from physics & biology to bioeconomics. *Journal of Bioeconomics, 1,* 1–31.

McKelvey, B. (2008). Emergent strategy via complexity leadership: Using complexity science and adaptive tension to build distributed intelligence. In Uhl-Bien & R. Marion (Eds.), *Complexity leadership, part 1: Conceptual foundations* (pp. 225–268). Charlotte, NC: Information Age Publishing.

Mead, G. H. (1934). *Mind, self, and society.* Chicago, IL: University of Chicago Press.

Miller, P. (July, 2007). Swarm theory. *National Geographic, 212,* 126–147.

Mumford, M. D. (2003). Where have we been, where are we going? Taking stock in creativity research. *Creativity Research Journal, 15,* 107–120.

Mumford, M. D., Bedell-Avers, K. E., & Hunter, S. T. (2008). Planning for innovation: A multi-level perspective. In M. Mumford, S. T. Hunter & K. E. Bedell (Eds.), *Research in multi-level issues* (Vol. 7, pp. 107–154). Bingley, UK: Emerald Group Pub Ltd.

Mumford, M. D., Connelly, S., & Gaddis, B. (2003). How creative leaders think: Experimental findings and cases. *The Leadership Quarterly, 14,* 411–432.

Mumford, M. D., Scott, G. M., Gaddis, B., & Strange, J. M. (2002). Leading creative people: Orchestrating expertise and relationships. *The Leadership Quarterly, 13,* 705–750.

Murphy, S. E., & Ensher, E. A. (2008). A qualitative analysis of charismatic leadership in creative teams: The case of television directors. *The Leadership Quarterly, 19,* 335–352.

Nemanich, L. A., & Keller, R. T. (2007). Transformational leadership in an acquisition: A field study of employees. *The Leadership Quarterly, 18,* 49–68.

Osborn, R. N., & Hunt, J. G. (2007). Leadership and the choice of order: Complexity and hierarchical perspectives near the edge of chaos. *The Leadership Quarterly, 18,* 319–340.

Osborn, R., & Marion, R. (2009). Contextual leadership, transformational leadership and the performance of international innovation seeking alliances. *The Leadership Quarterly, 20,* 191–206.

Perry-Smith, J. E. (2006). Social yet creative: The role of social relationships in facilitating individual creativity. *Academy of Management Journal, 49,* 85–101.

Plowman, D. A., Solansky, S., Beck, T. E., Baker, L., Kulkarni, M., & Travis, D. V. (2007). The role of leadership in emergent, self-organization. *The Leadership Quarterly, 18,* 341–356.

Popper, K. R. (1961). *The logic of scientific discovery.* New York, NY: Basic Books.

Prigogine, I. (1997). *The end of certainty.* New York, NY: The Free Press.

Purdy, J. M., & Gray, B. (2009). Conflicting logics, mechanisms of diffusion, and multilevel dynamics in emerging institutional fields. *Academy of Management Journal, 52,* 355–380.

C. GROUP LEVEL INFLUENCES

Reiter-Palmon, R., & Illies, J. J. (2004). Leadership and creativity: Understanding leadership from the creative problem-solving perspective. *The Leadership Quarterly, 15,* 55–77.

Rostan, S. M. (1998). A study of young artists: The emergence of artistic and creative identity. *Journal of Creative Behavior, 32,* 278–301.

Saatcioglu, A. (2002). *Using grounded inquiry to explore idea management for innovativeness.* Paper presented at the Academy of Management Proceedings & Membership Directory. August.

Schreiber, C., & Carley, K. (2006). Leadership style as an enabler of organizational complex functioning. *Emergence: Complexity and Organization, 8,* 61–76.

Schreiber, C., & Carley, K. (2008). Dynamic network leadership: Leading for learning and adaptability. In Uhl-Bien & R. Marion (Eds.), *Complexity leadership, part 1: Conceptual foundations* (pp. 291–332). Charlotte, NC: Information Age Publishing.

Schreiber, C., Marion, R., Uhl-Bien, M., & Carley, K. (2006). *Multi-agent based simulation of a model of complexity leadership.* Paper presented at the International Conference on Complex Systems, Boston, MA.

Shalley, C. E., & Gilson, L. L. (2004). What leaders need to know: A review of social and contextual factors that can foster or hinder creativity. *The Leadership Quarterly, 15,* 33–53.

Shalley, C. E., Zhou, J., & Oldham, G. R. (2004). Effects of personal and contextual characteristics on creativity: Where should we go from here? *Journal of Management Development, 30,* 933–958.

Solow, D., Burnetas, A., Piderit, S., & Leenawong, C. (2003). Mathematical models for studying the value of motivational leadership in teams. *Computational & Mathematical Organization Theory, 9,* 61–81.

Sosik, J. M., Kahai, S. S., & Avolio, B. J. (1998). Transformational leadership and dimensions of creativity: Motivating idea generation in computer mediated groups. *Creativity Research Journal, 11,* 111–122.

Stacey, R. D. (1996). *Complexity and creativity in organizations.* San Francisco, CA: Berrett-Koehler Publishers.

Stacey, R. D. (2001). *Complex responsive processes in organizations: Learning and knowledge creation.* London, UK: Routledge.

Surie, G., & Hazy, J. (2006). Generative leadership: Nurturing innovation in complex systems. *Emergence: Complexity and Organization, 8,* 13–26.

Taggar, S. (2002). Individual creativity and group ability to utilize individual creative resources: A multilevel model. *Academy of Management Journal, 45,* 315–330.

Teigland, R., Chen, Y., & Fey, C. F. (2009). Contingency effects of national culture and institutions on how social networks influence creativity. *Academy of Management Proceedings,* 1–6.

Thomke, S., & Nimgade, A. (2007). *Ideo product development. Harvard business school case (9-600-143).* Boston, MA: Harvard Business School Publishing.

Tierney, P., Farmer, S. M., & Graen, G. B. (1999). An examination of leadership and employee creativity: The relevance of traits and relationships. *Personnel Psychology, 52,* 591–620.

Tsai, W. (2001). Knowledge transfer in intraorganizational networks: Effects of network position and absorptive capacity on business unit innovation and performance. *Academy of Management Journal, 44,* 996–1004.

Uhl-Bien, M. (2006). Relational leadership theory: Exploring the social processes of leadership and organizing. *The Leadership Quarterly, 17,* 654–676.

Uhl-Bien, M., & Marion, R. (2009). Complexity leadership in bureaucratic forms of organizing: A meso model. *The Leadership Quarterly, 20,* 631–650.

Uhl-Bien, M., Marion, R., & McKelvey, B. (2007). Complexity leadership theory: Shifting leadership from the industrial age to the knowledge era. *The Leadership Quarterly, 18,* 298–318.

Uhl-Bien, M., Marion, R., Schreiber, C., Arena, M., & Hanson, W. (2010). *Constraints and resistors in a creativity-oriented firm.* Lincoln, NB: University of Nebraska-Lincoln.

Uhl-Bien, M., Marion, R., Schreiber, C., Arena, M., Sweetman, D., & Olson, J. (2010). *Enabling leadership and creativity in innovative organizations: A grounded theory.* Lincoln, NB: University of Nebraska–Lincoln. (In process)

Uzzi, B., & Spiro, J. (2005). Collaboration and creativity: The small world problem. *American Journal of Sociology, 111,* 447–504.

Waldman, D., & Atwater, L. (1992). The nature of effective leadership and championing processes at different levels in a R&D hierarchy. *Journal of High Technology Management Research, 5,* 233–245.

Weick, K. E. (1976). Educational organizations as loosely coupled systems. *Administrative Science Quarterly, 21,* 1–19.

West, M. A., Borrill, C. S., Dawson, J. F., Brodbeck, F., Shapiro, D. A., & Haward, B. (2003). Leadership clarity and team innovation in health care. *The Leadership Quarterly, 14,* 393–410.

C. GROUP LEVEL INFLUENCES

Woodman, R. W., Sawyer, J. E., & Griffin, R. W. (1993). Toward a theory of organizational creativity. *Academy of Management Review, 18*, 293–321.

Zhang, X., & Bartol, K. M. (2010). Linking empowering leadership and employee creativity: The influence of psychological empowerment, intrinsic motivation, and creative process engagement. *Academy of Management Journal, 53*, 107–128.

Zhou, J., & George, J. M. (2001). When job dissatisfaction leads to creativity: Encouraging the expression of voice. *Academy of Management Journal, 44*, 682–696.

C. GROUP LEVEL INFLUENCES

ORGANIZATIONAL LEVEL INFLUENCES

Organizational Structure and Innovation Revisited: From Organic To Ambidextrous Structure

Fariborz Damanpour[1] and Deepa Aravind[2]

[1]Rutgers University, Department of Management and Global Business, NJ;
[2]City University of New York – College of Staten Island, Department of
Business, NY

Innovation is a popular area of study in a variety of fields, such as business, economics, engineering, psychology, public administration, and sociology. It is viewed as a concept central to economic growth, the creation of new industries and businesses, competitive advantage and performance of firms, and the effective management of business and public organizations (Drucker, 1985; Gopalakrishnan & Damanpour, 1997). Whereas the extraordinary breadth of innovation research has resulted in many new perspectives and theories, integrating these research results to develop compatible theories has become increasingly challenging, since researchers in each field conceptualize and operationalize innovation differently, even at a single level of analysis (e.g., the firm or organizational level). Thus, the primary goal of this chapter is to gather together the findings of empirical studies of the relationship between organizational structure and innovation, a relationship of importance to scholars for determining organizational conditions and processes conducive to innovation, and also of relevance to managers of business firms and public organizations, who design innovative organizations and manage the innovation process.

The chapter is constructed as follows. In the first section, we define innovation and distinguish it from two closely related concepts: creativity and change. In the second section, we discuss innovation as a process and distinguish between the generation and adoption processes of innovation. The section after this covers the prominent typologies of innovation and explains the differences between major innovation types. These distinctions assist

Handbook of Organizational Creativity.
DOI: 10.1016/B978-0-12-374714-3.00019-7

in a better understanding of research findings and facilitate their integration into compatible theories. In the fourth section, we review the results of the empirical studies of structure and innovation. For the studies conducted before 1990, we use the integrative findings of Damanpour's (1991) meta-analysis. We update and complement his findings with a review of the empirical studies between 1990 and 2009. In the last section we discuss the emerging trends on the design of innovative organizations since the early 1990s, and point out some of the opportunities and challenges for future research on the determinants and consequences of innovation.

CONCEPTION OF INNOVATION IN ORGANIZATIONS

Innovation in organizations is generally understood in two ways: more specifically, it is distinguished from closely-related concepts like creativity and change; more broadly, it includes all. To illustrate the diversity in the conceptualization of innovation, we summarize the definitions given for the term in twelve articles published in two concurrent special issues on innovation in management (Table 19.1). As can be seen, even in one field at one time, innovation has been used to represent a variety of concepts and phenomena, including creativity and creative problem solving (Ford, 1996), speed or extent of product introduction (Kessler & Chakrabarti, 1996), organizational change (Greenwood & Hinings, 1996), technological change (Lawless & Anderson, 1996), acquisition of new firms (Hitt, Hoskisson, Johnson, & Moesel, 1996), and so on. Hardly have any two articles from this set defined innovation similarly, yet each conceptualization overlaps with at least one other and manifests a certain view of this multidimensional, multilevel construct. Therefore, to facilitate integration of the findings of empirical studies on the structure–innovation association, we first define and distinguish three interrelated conceptions of creativity, innovation, and change that are of interest and importance for research on innovation in organizations.

Innovation

Researchers have conceived of innovations in organizations as both a discrete product and outcome, or as a process. The primary goal of the studies of innovation as an outcome is to determine the contextual, structural, and process conditions under which organizations innovate (Gopalakrishnan & Damanpour, 1994; Kimberly & Evanisko, 1981; Meyer & Goes, 1988). Innovation as outcome is intended to create a new opportunity or satisfy an existing opportunity, and thus, to contribute to the organization's effectiveness and competitiveness (Drucker, 1985). From this perspective, innovation is a means toward achieving an end, i.e., the effectiveness or competitiveness of the innovating organization. It is defined as the introduction of new products or services to the market (Dougherty & Hardy, 1996; Hitt et al., 1996) or the introduction of new policies, systems, programs, and processes in the organization (Damanpour, 1991; Klein & Sorra, 1996). Studies of innovation as a process examine how the innovation is originated, developed, implemented, and eventually terminated over time (Rogers, 1995; Van de Ven et al., 2000). Innovation process researchers treat innovation as a complex and intricate series of events involving a multitude of activities, decisions,

TABLE 19.1   Conceptions of Innovation from the Articles in Two Special Issues[a].

Study	Conception
Amabile et al. (1996)	*Creativity*: The production of novel and useful ideas in any domain.
Dougherty & Hardy (1996)	*Sustained product innovation*: The generation of multiple new products intended for customers who are unfamiliar to an organization or that require unfamiliar technologies with a reasonable rate of commercial success.
Ford (1996)	*Creative action*: A domain-specific, subjective judgment of the novelty and value of an outcome of a particular action.
Glynn (1996)	*Individual creativity*: The production of novel and useful ideas by individuals working together in an organization. *Organizational innovation*: Non-routine, significant, and discontinuous organizational change that embodies a new idea that is not consistent with the current concept of the organization's business.
Greenwood & Hinings (1996)	*Organizational change*: Occurs when an organization moves from one organizational form (e.g., democratic involvement) to another (e.g., representative democracy).
Hitt, Hoskisson, Johnson, & Moosel (1996)	*Internal innovation*: The development and introduction of new products and processes. *External innovation*: The extent of acquisition of firms that have introduced new products, developed new processes, and built new markets.
Kessler & Chakrabarti (1996)	*Innovation speed*: The time elapsed between initial development, including the conception and definition of an innovation, and ultimate commercialization, which is the introduction of a new product into the marketplace.
Klein & Sorra (1996)	*Implementation effectiveness*: The consistency and quality of targeted organizational members' use of a specific innovation. *Innovation effectiveness*: The benefits an organization receives as a result of its implementation of a specific innovation.
Lawless & Anderson (1996)	*Generational technological change*: A significant advance in technological performance within a technological regime.
Nohria & Gulati (1996)	*Innovation*: Any policy, structure, method or process, product or market opportunity that the manager of the innovative unit perceives to be new.
Pouder & John (1996)	*Innovation performance of hot spots*: Where innovation is defined as new products, services, processes, and structures that firms use to meet customer demands and compete with each other.
Wade (1996)	*Technological variation*: A phase of technological change provided by technological breakthroughs or discontinuities leading to a dominant design.

[a]*The special issues: (1) Special Research Forum on Innovation and Organizations,* Academy of Management Journal *(October 1996); and (2) Special Topic Forum on the Management of Innovation,* Academy of Management Review *(October 1996).*

individual behaviors, and social systems (Gopalakrishnan & Damanpour, 1994). Innovation is defined as encompassing multiple patterns and stages (Roberts, 1988; Rogers, 1995), but researchers do not concur on the patterns that constitute the process (Schroeder, Van de Ven, Scudder, & Polley, 2000). As will be discussed below, for parsimony we distinguish between generation and adoption processes only.

D. ORGANIZATIONAL LEVEL INFLUENCES

Creativity

Psychologists have studied the characteristics of creative persons, and the thought processes that people use to create new and novel ideas; however, most scholars who study creativity in the context of an organization depart from the traditional psychological approach and conceive of creative ideas and actions as elements of innovation (Amabile, Conti, Coon, Lazenby, & Herron, 1996; Ford, 1996). Ford (1996) defines creativity as:

"a domain-specific, subjective judgment of novelty and value of an outcome of a particular action" *(p. 1115).*

Creative ideas and acts:

"can influence processes and outcomes that affect multiple levels of analysis and can solve dilemmas that arise throughout the innovation process" *(Ford, 1996, p. 1113).*

From this perspective, creativity is different from innovation; it is an input to the innovative outcome or a part of the innovation process. Creativity requires freedom and a climate of support where individuals are unrestricted in their search for solutions (Amabile, 1988). Innovation, on the other hand, requires a more systematic (i.e., focused, purposeful, and organized) effort to succeed (Dougherty & Hardy, 1996; Drucker, 1985). As West and Richter (2008) point out, individual and team creativity feed organizational innovation.

Woodman, Sawyer, and Griffin (1993) define creativity as an outcome and distinguish between creativity at the individual and organizational levels. At the individual level, they define creativity as:

"the complex product of a person's behavior in a given situation" *(p. 294).*

At the organizational level, creativity is:

"the creation of a valuable, useful product, service, idea, procedure, or process by individuals working together in a complex social system" *(Woodman et al., 1993, p. 293).*

While these authors' definition of individual creativity is similar to definitions of creativity advanced by other scholars, their definition of organizational creativity is similar to the definition of the generation of innovation in organizations manifested in individual actions (i.e., when innovation is measured at the individual level of analysis). Amabile (1988), on the other hand, defines creativity as a process, and distinguishes it from innovation by relating creativity to the production of new ideas and innovation to their implementation. Creativity is:

"the production of novel and useful ideas by an individual or small group of individuals working together,"

while innovation is:

"the successful implementation of creative ideas within an organization" *(Amabile, 1988, p. 126).*

Creativity by individuals and teams, however, is the starting point for innovation; creativity might be necessary but is not sufficient for innovation to occur (Amabile et al., 1996).

These definitions show that, like innovation, creativity is conceived of as both outcome and process, and it is a subset or a sub-process of a broader domain of innovation (Ford, 1996). Creativity and innovation are usually applied at different levels of analysis: creativity at the individual and team levels, and innovation at the organizational unit and organizational levels. Innovation:

> "is essentially a social activity; it must involve some attempt to have an influence wider than on just the individual ..." *(King, 1990, p. 10).*

Innovation activities or outcomes are novel or new to the organization. Organizational members influence both the development and implementation of those novel acts or outcomes by their creative ideas. Thus, while creativity can influence innovation outcomes, and can help solve problems that arise throughout the innovation process, it is only one component in producing innovation outcome and a sub-process of the innovation process.

Change

While creativity is a subset or a sub-process of organizational innovation, innovation is a subset or a sub-process of organizational change. Further, while creativity can influence both the generation and adoption of innovation, as the following discussion suggests, the intersection of innovation and organizational change primarily concerns innovation adoption.

Organizational change is the introduction of behaviors that are different from those currently in use (Daft & Becker, 1978). As a process, change occurs when people or organizations evolve from old behaviors and methods of operations to new ones. It is a shift or transfer from the current state prior to change to the future state after the change (Nadler & Tushman, 1997). In this sense, change is an:

> "observation of differences in time on one or more dimensions" of an organization (Van de Ven & Rogers, 1988, pp. 638–639).

The difference between the current and future state can be the consequence of the adoption of innovation.

In distinguishing between organizational innovation and change, Daft and Becker (1978) defined innovation as adopted behaviors new to a group of organizations that share the same goals and technology, and change as behaviors which are merely new to the adopting organization. This distinction suggests that what primarily distinguishes change from innovation is "newness" to the relative unit of adoption (Slappendel, 1996). Broadly, an innovation can be perceived as being new to the individual adopter, to most people in the unit of adoption, to the organization as a whole, to most organizations in an organizational population, or to the world. The notion of newness varies in different streams of innovation research. For instance, in diffusion research, newness is typically perceived as the newness of innovation to the individual adopter (Rogers, 1995); in economics and strategic management, it is commonly the first time introduction of innovation in an industry or an organizational population (Roberts, 1988); and in organizational sociology and management, it is often newness to the adopting organization or to the organization's relevant environment (Daft & Becker, 1978; Gopalakrishnan & Damanpour, 1997). In most empirical studies, what constitutes newness has been left as an empirical question, or an issue for an executive or a

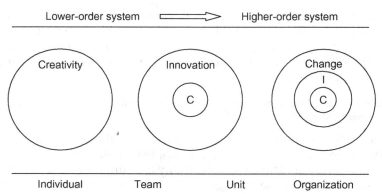

FIGURE 19.1   Locus and order of creativity, innovation, and change.

panel of experts to resolve, which, in turn, has blurred the distinction between innovation adoption and organizational change.

Based on the definition of *system* ("an assemblage or combination of parts whose relations make them interdependent" Scott, 1992; p. 77) that is used by both physical and social scientists, and Boulding's (1956) classification of systems into levels where the complexity of the system increases from the lower- to higher-order system, Figure 19.1 depicts the locus (individual, team, organization unit, organization) and order (lower to higher) of creativity, innovation, and change.

INNOVATION PROCESS

The process of innovation has been usually given a wide-scoped definition: it encompasses the entire process from the decision to begin research on a recognized or potential problem or opportunity, to its development, production, commercialization, diffusion, decision to adopt, implementation, and consequences (Rogers, 1995). This unitary perspective of the innovation process can be best applied when the level of analysis is innovation or an innovation is developed and implemented in the same organization. However, when the level of analysis is organization or multiple innovations are studied, the distinction between development process and adoption process is essential. For instance, Klein and Sorra (1996, p. 1057) distinguish between "source-based" and "user-based" process models, where in the former innovation is a new product, service, or technology that the organization produces for the market, and in the latter it is a product, service, or technology that is used for the first time by members of the organization. Similarly, we distinguish between generation (development) and adoption (use) of innovations (Tornatzky & Fleischer, 1990), on the assumption that innovations can be developed and supplied by one organization but consumed and used in another (Damanpour & Wischnevsky, 2006). In large organizations, however, the innovation-generating and innovation-adopting organizations can be two units or divisions within the same organization. In this vein, Amabile's (1988) distinction between "production" and "implementation" as two sub-processes of the innovation process associates, respectively, with innovation generation and adoption as defined here.

Generation and adoption have not been distinguished in most studies of innovation in organizations; both have usually been referred to as the innovation process. The generation

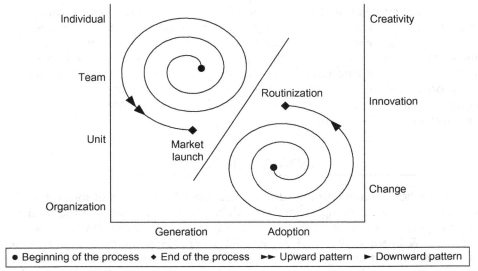

FIGURE 19.2 Locus and conceptions of innovation and patterns of the generation and adoption processes in organizations.

of innovation results in an outcome—a product, service, or technology that is at least new to an organizational population. A second organization (or unit) adopts this innovation by obtaining or acquiring it from the organization (or unit) that has produced it. As such, adoption basically means that the innovation is developed elsewhere, not in the adopting organization (Angle & Van de Ven, 2000). The adoption of innovation results in the assimilation of a product, service, or technology that is new to the adopting organization. In general, generation can be separated from adoption when the process of diffusion of the innovation among potential adopters begins (Rogers, 1995).

Generation is a creative process, in which new and existing ideas are combined in a novel way to produce an invention or a configuration that was previously unknown (Duncan, 1976). It covers all efforts and activities aimed at creating new ideas and getting them to work (Roberts, 1988). Adoption, on the other hand, is usually a problem-solving process in which an existing idea is adapted to address the recognized needs and identified problems within an organization. The generation process has been divided into several phases or stages, including recognition of opportunity, idea formulation, research, design, development, marketing, and distribution (Roberts, 1988; Tornatzky & Fleischer, 1990). The adoption process has also been divided into a variety of phases that are often grouped into three general phases of pre-adoption, adoption decision, and post-adoption, often referred to as initiation, adoption (decision), and implementation (Damanpour & Schneider, 2006; Rogers, 1995). These phases cover all activities pertaining to bringing in a new idea and adapting it to the organization and implementing it for use by organizational members or clients. Overall, the generation process is relatively disorderly and slow, and usually takes longer to complete than the adoption process (Damanpour & Wischnevsky, 2006).

Figure 19.2 shows the locus of studies of innovations in organizations in relation to the three conceptions and two processes. In innovation-generating, the pattern of innovation resembles an upward spiral (from individual to organization); in innovation–adopting, it resembles a downward spiral (from organization to individual). That is, the generation process usually begins with idea generation by individuals and small groups, and the extension and expansion of the idea across the organization until it is developed into an outcome for launch to internal or external market. The adoption process, on the other hand, usually begins by organizational leaders' awareness and decision to acquire an innovation, and adaptation and implementation of the innovation by units and members until it becomes a routine activity across the organization.

INNOVATION TYPE

Innovation scholars have introduced many conceptual typologies of innovation; however, the most widely studied typologies are the product–process typology (Abernathy & Utterback 1978; Damanpour & Aravind, 2006) and the technological–administrative typology (Daft, 1982; Kimberly & Evanisko 1981). Meeus and Edquist (2006) juxtaposed these typologies and offered a taxonomy that distinguished between two types of product innovations ("in goods" and "in services") and two types of process innovations ("technological" and "organizational"). A third widely applied typology has also been introduced, based on the dimension of innovation radicalness, which distinguishes between incremental and radical innovations (Cardinal, 2001; Germain, 1996). More recently (details below), these innovation types have been referred to as exploratory and exploitative innovations (Bierly, Damanpour, & Santoro, 2009; Jansen, Van Den Bosch, & Volberda, 2006; Smith & Tushman, 2005).

Technological Product and Process Innovations

From Meeus and Edquist's (2006) taxonomy, we define *technological innovations* as technology-based innovations that are primarily associated with firms in goods industries. Product and process innovations are technological innovations that produce changes in the organization's products and production systems, respectively. *Product innovations* have external focus, are often market driven, and their introduction results in differentiation of the organization's output for its customers or clients. *Process innovations*, on the other hand, are new elements introduced into an organization's operational systems for producing its products (Abernathy & Utterback, 1978; Damanpour & Aravind, 2006). The drivers of product innovations are customer need and demand, and a firm's aspiration to compete and grow. The drivers of process innovations are a reduction in delivery time, an increase in operational flexibility, and the lowering of production costs (Boer & During, 2001). Therefore, whereas product innovations are mainly introduced to make the firm compete more effectively in its markets, process innovations are primarily introduced to increase efficiency of its internal operations.

Service Innovations

Most studies of innovation in organizations do not distinguish between service and product innovations. Generally, services offered by organizations in the service sector are conceptualized to be similar to products introduced by organizations in the manufacturing sector (Damanpour, Walker, & Avellaneda, 2009; Miles, 2005). In this vein, like product innovations, the drivers of service innovations are clients' demand for new services and executives' desire to create new services for existing markets or to find new market niches for existing services (Miles, 2005). However, as firms in both goods and services industries offer services, we define *service innovations* as the introduction of new services to increase the effectiveness and quality of the organization's output, whether products or service, to the customers or clients.

Administrative Innovations

Administrative innovations are non-technological process innovations. They have been referred to as organizational innovations by economists (Fagerberg, 2005; Sanidas, 2005), and recently, as management innovations by management scholars (Birkinshaw, Hamel, & Mol, 2008; Vaccaro, Jansen, Van Den Bosch, & Volberda, 2010). The name notwithstanding, this innovation type is mostly compared and contrasted with technological or technical innovations. Whereas technological (process) innovations are directly related to the primary work activity of the organization and mainly produce changes in its operating systems, administrative (process) innovations are indirectly related to the organization's basic work activity and are mainly associated with its social systems (Damanpour et al., 2009; Trist & Murray 1993). These innovations pertain to changes in the organization's structure and processes, administrative systems, knowledge used in performing the work of management, and managerial skills that enable organizations to succeed by functioning efficiently and using their resources effectively. Thus, we define *administrative innovations* as new approaches and practices to motivate and reward organizational members, devise strategy and structure of tasks and units, and modify the organization's management processes and administrative systems (Birkinshaw et al., 2008; Daft, 1982; Kimberly & Evanisko, 1981). Contrary to product and service innovations that are mainly discrete, administrative innovations often permeate the entire organization and require integration across units and functions (Elenkov & Manev, 2005).

Radical and Incremental Innovations

The radicalness of an innovation is one of its important attributes, a dimension along which the radical–incremental typology is conceived. As for other innovation typologies, different perspectives govern distinguishing between these two innovation types. For example, at the industry or product class level, radical innovations can create discontinuity in the product class and can be "competence-destroying"; incremental innovations rely on existing knowledge and allow existing product or process technologies to remain competitive (Tushman & Anderson, 1986). Radical innovations disrupt an existing technological trajectory, but incremental innovations refine and improve it (Gatignon, Tushman, Smith, & Anderson, 2002). At the organizational level, radical and incremental innovations are mainly distinguished by the extent to which the innovation causes fundamental changes in the outputs or internal activities of the organization and results in a clear departure from existing activities (Cardinal, 2001; Damanpour, 1991). Overall, these distinctions suggest that *radical innovations* result in a major change whether in the technology, organization, or industry, and *incremental innovations* result in a minor change in the existing state of an entity (e.g., fine-tuning of the products or practices of a firm).

After the publication of March's (1991) seminal article on "Exploration and Exploitation in Organizational Learning", innovation scholars have used a new typology similar to the radical–incremental typology. Firms invest in creating new knowledge internally or in acquiring it from outside sources, or both. The source notwithstanding, the primary goal of learning for innovation is to gain new knowledge that is related to current areas of expertise, in order to advance the organization's existing technologies and products, or to gather new, unrelated knowledge to create untapped future opportunities (Cohen & Levinthal, 1990). These two means of learning for innovation can be related to exploration and exploitation of the knowledge, respectively. In this context, *exploration* refers to the application of learning to produce new products and technologies and *exploitation* refers to the application of learning to refine the organization's existing products and improve its processes (Bierly et al., 2009; March, 1991). The essence of exploration is experimentation with new ideas; it is associated with divergent thinking and flexibility. The essence of exploitation is the refinement of existing ideas; it is associated with convergent thinking and focus (March, 1991; Smith & Tushman, 2005). That is, the extent of departure from existing technological and administrative know-how is the primary criterion that distinguishes exploration and exploitation of knowledge for innovation. As such, *exploratory* and *exploitative innovations* can be respectively conceived as the results of exploration and exploitation for an organization's innovative outcome and processes (Bierly et al., 2009; Jansen et al., 2006; Smith & Tushman, 2005), resembling radical and incremental innovations.

EMPIRICAL STUDIES OF STRUCTURE AND INNOVATION

First Wave—Pre-1990 Studies

The empirical studies of the influence of organizational characteristics on innovation began in the 1960s and flourished in the 1970s and 1980s. Damanpour (1991) used a meta-analytical procedure and integrated the results of 23 studies published in this period, including 13 antecedents of innovation and seven moderators of the antecedent–innovation relationship. Damanpour summarized the direction of effects of each antecedent and reasons for expected effects (1991; pp558–559) and provided definitions of all variables (1991; pp588–590). His analysis resulted in:

1. positive associations between innovation and specialization, functional differentiation, professionalism, managerial attitude toward change, technical knowledge resources, administrative intensity, slack resources, and external and internal communication,
2. negative associations between innovation and centralization, and
3. non-significant associations between innovation and formalization, managerial tenure, and vertical differentiation (1991, pp. 567–569).

The moderator analyses resulted in the moderating effectiveness of "type of organization" (manufacturing vs. service, and for-profit vs. non-profit) and "scope of innovation" (studies based on a large number of innovations vs. those based on a small number of innovations), but not "type of innovation" and "stage of adoption" (Damanpour, 1991; p. 577).

Damanpour (1991) drew several conclusions from his quantitative integration of research findings. First, contrary to previous suggestions, when innovation is tightly conceptualized (e.g., at the organizational level in his study) the cumulative findings are consistent. Second, whereas innovation types (product vs. process, technical vs. administrative, radical vs. incremental) and stages of adoption (initiation vs. implementation) do not moderate the relationship between organizational factors and innovation, organizational type and scope of innovation do. Third, the results across the determinants generally provide support for the commonly held perspective, based on Burns and Staker (1961), that the characteristics associated with organic structure are more conducive to innovation than those associated with mechanistic structure.

Second Wave—Post-1990 Studies

In order to understand the additional insights of newer studies on the relations between organizational structure and innovation, we conducted a review of empirical studies published from 1990 to 2009. We followed a "systematic" procedure for selecting these studies (Tranfield, Denyer, & Smart, 2003). According to Hunter and Schmidt (1990), the efficacy of this type of procedure in extracting the information from the primary studies is between "traditional narrative" and "meta-analytical" procedures. However, while the meta-analytical procedure allows for the computation of effect size, it relies on the studies that have reported bivariate analyses. The procedure used for the second wave studies does not allow the computation of effect size; however, the results from both bivariate and multivariate analyses are included. The results from multivariate analyses help alleviate statistical bias due to the omission of explanatory variables other than the focal antecedent.

We searched electronic databases such as Business Source Complete and Academic Search Complete during the summer of 2009. We searched the title, abstract, and full text of articles published from 1990 to 2009 in these databases using keywords such as "innovation", "creativity", "organizational structure", and one or more of the 13 predictor variables from the first wave studies. We only considered peer-reviewed articles in English. We narrowed the list of articles by reading the abstract and if this was not clear, by examining the full text. We also looked at the reference list of these articles, and selected related articles. This selection process resulted in 27 articles.

Table 19.2 lists the conceptions of innovation from the second wave studies and Table 19.3 provides an overview of each of these articles. As an example of how we constructed Table 19.3, Jansen et al. (2006) examines the introduction of innovations (e.g., ATMs, Internet banking, mobile banking, p. 1665) at organizational units (e.g., bank branches) in a financial service organization. Hence we denote the conception and context as "Innovation, Service" and the innovation process as "Adoption". Also, the study examines the introduction of both exploratory and exploitative products/services and uses cross-sectional data. Thus, we

TABLE 19.2   Conceptions of Innovation from the Second Wave Studies.

Study	Conception
Burns & Wholey (1993)	*Administrative innovation*: Matrix management program, a new hybrid organizational form.
Calantone, Cavusgil, & Zhao (2002)	*Firm innovativeness:* Conceptualized from two perspectives: (1) a behavioral variable (the rate of adoption of innovations by the firm), and (2) an organization's willingness to change.
Cardinal (2001)	*Innovation outcomes:* Classified as drug enhancements or new drugs.
Damanpour & Schneider (2006)	*Innovation:* Adoption of a new product, service, process, technology, policy or structure that is new to the adopting unit.
Delaney et al. (1996)	*Innovation:* The adoption of an idea that is new to the adopting organization. The idea may involve a different approach to technology, process, product, service, administrative procedure, employees, customers or other stakeholders.
Ekvall (1996)	*Innovativeness:* Success of organizations in developing new, profitable products.
Fichman (2001)	*Innovation:* The organizational initiation, adoption and/or implementation of one or more emerging technologies.
Geiger & Makri (2006)	*Innovation process:* Can involve both exploration and exploitation. *Exploration* is experimentation with new alternatives whose returns are uncertain and distant; *exploitation* is the refinement and extension of existing competencies and technologies, exhibiting returns that are positive and proximate.
Germain (1996)	*Logistics process innovations:* Those that affect the organizational-wide flow of goods and related information encompassing physical distribution and materials management.
Goes & Park (1997)	*Service innovations:* Those that incorporate changes in the technology, design, or delivery of a particular service or bundle of services which are relatively new to the overall industry and new to the adopting firms in a particular market area.
Greve (2007)	*Exploitation innovations:* Apply known technology. *Exploration innovations:* Involve development of new technology or application of existing technology not earlier used by a firm.
Grover, Purvis, & Segars (2007)	*Radical technological innovations:* Incorporate a technology that is a clear, risky departure from existing practice. *Incremental technological innovations:* Routine enhancements to existing technology.
Hashem & Tann (2007)	*Innovation:* The adoption of an idea or behavior that is new to the adopting unit.
Herrmann & Gordillo (2001)	*Innovation:* An idea, practice, or object that has been adopted, that is, one whose actual utilization by organizational members has begun.
Jansen, Van Den Bosch, & Volberda (2006)	*Exploratory innovations:* Designed to meet the needs of emerging customers or markets; they are radical innovations that require new knowledge or depart from existing knowledge. *Exploitative innovations:* Designed to meet the needs of existing customers or markets; they are incremental innovations that build on existing knowledge and reinforce existing skills, processes, and structures.
Kivimaki et al. (2000)	*Innovation:* Creation of new strategies, new products, and new ways of manufacturing, distributing, and selling.

(Continued)

D. ORGANIZATIONAL LEVEL INFLUENCES

TABLE 19.2   Conceptions of Innovation from the Second Wave Studies (Continued).

Study	Conception
Liao (2007)	*Extent of product innovation*: Extent of innovation in terms of new products, services, and programs.
Li, Lin, & Chu (2008)	*Radical (explorative) innovations:* Designed to meet the needs of emerging customers and markets and offer new designs, create new markets, or develop new channels of distribution. *Incremental (exploitative) innovations:* Designed to meet the needs of existing customers or markets and to broaden existing knowledge and skills, improve established designs to existing products and services, and increase the efficiency of existing distribution channels.
Madjar, Oldham, & Pratt (2002)	*Employee creativity:* Production of ideas, products, or procedures at the individual level that are: (1) novel or original, and (2) potentially useful to the employing organization.
Nohria & Gulati (1996)	*Innovation:* Any policy, structure, method or process, product or market opportunity that the manager of the innovating unit perceived to be new.
Nystrom, Ramamurthy, & Wilson (2002)	*Organizational innovation:* The adoption of an idea or behavior that is new to the organization adopting it. *Innovativeness:* Determined in terms of the radicalness of innovations adopted, the extent of benefits they provide, and the number of innovations adopted over time.
Papadakis & Bourantas (1998)	*Technological innovation:* Pertains to innovation in products and services, as well as production processes and operations related to the central activities of the organization.
Pil & MacDuffie (1996)	*Adoption of high involvement work practices:* The adoption of a fundamental organizational change in the structure and organization of work that could be competence destroying.
Rego et al. (2007)	*Creativity:* The production of novel and useful ideas or solutions. It is often the starting point of innovation and a critical resource for organizational success.
Scott & Bruce (1994)	*Individual innovation:* A multi-stage process which includes: (1) problem recognition and the generation of ideas or solutions (either novel or adopted); (2) seeking sponsorship for the idea and attempting to build a coalition of supporters for it; and (3) completing the idea by producing a prototype or model of the innovation that can be diffused, mass-produced, turned to productive use, or institutionalized.
Souitaris (2001)	*Innovation:* The adoption of an internally generated or externally acquired product or manufacturing process perceived to be new by the firm.
Weigelt & Sarkar (2009)	*Innovation:* Novel devices, systems, policies, programs, processes, products, or services new to the adopting organization.

denote the innovation type as "Products/Services" and "Radical/Incremental" and the analytical method as "Cross-sectional" (see Table 19.3).

Similar to the first wave, we included organizational variables that were examined in at least two different studies in our analysis. With the exception of "administrative intensity" and "vertical differentiation", all predictor variables of the first wave were included in two or more studies of the second wave. "Functional differentiation", an indicator of structural

TABLE 19.3   Overview of the Second Wave Studies.[a]

Study	Sample Size	Conception, Context	Innovation Process	Innovation Type	Analytical Method
Burns & Wholey (1993)	1247	Innovation, Service	Adoption	Administrative	Longitudinal
Calantone et al. (2002)	187	Innovation, Mixed	Mixed (Generation, adoption)	Technological (Product, and Process)	Cross-sectional
Cardinal (2001)	57	Innovation, Manufacturing	Generation	Technological (Radical, Incremental)	Cross-sectional
Damanpour & Schneider (2006)	1276	Innovation, Service	Adoption	Administrative	Cross-sectional
Delaney et al. (1996)	45	Innovation, Service	Mixed	Mixed	Cross-sectional
Ekvall (1996)	49	Innovation, Mixed	Mixed	Mixed	Cross-sectional
Fichman (2001)	608	Innovation, Mixed	Adoption	Process	Cross-sectional
Geiger & Makri (2006)	208	Innovation, Manufacturing	Generation	Technological	Cross-sectional
Germain (1996)	183	Innovation, Manufacturing	Adoption	Technological (Process—Radical, Incremental)	Cross-sectional
Goes & Park (1997)	388	Innovation, Service	Adoption	Mixed	Longitudinal
Greve (2007)[b]	13	Innovation, Manufacturing	Generation	Technological (Product—Radical, Incremental)	Longitudinal
Grover, Purvis, & Segars (2007)	154	Innovation, Service/ Manufacturing	Adoption	Technological (Radical, Incremental)	Cross-sectional
Hashem & Tann (2007)	255	Innovation, Manufacturing	Adoption	Administrative	Cross-sectional
Herrmann & Gordillo (2001)	55	Innovation, Service	Adoption	Technological	Cross-sectional
Jansen, Van den Bosch, & Volberda (2006)	283	Innovation, Service	Adoption	Products/Services (Radical, Incremental)	Cross-sectional
Kivimaki et al. (2000)	442	Innovation, Manufacturing	Generation	Technological (Product and Process)	Cross-sectional
Liao (2007)	203	Innovation, Manufacturing	Generation	Technological, Product	Cross-sectional
Li, Lin, & Chu (2008)	227	Innovation, Manufacturing	Generation	Technological (Radical, Incremental)	Cross-sectional

(Continued)

TABLE 19.3 Overview of the Second Wave Studies[a] (Continued).

Study	Sample Size	Conception, Context	Innovation Process	Innovation Type	Analytical Method
Madjar, Oldham, & Pratt (2002)	265	Creativity (individual), Manufacturing	Generation	Mixed	Cross-sectional
Nohria & Gulati (1996)	256	Innovation, Manufacturing	Generation	Mixed	Cross-sectional
Nystrom et al. (2002)[c]	70	Innovation, Service	Adoption	Technological (Radical and Incremental mixed)	Cross-sectional
Papadakis & Bourantas (1998)	97	Innovation, Manufacturing	Generation	Technological (Process; Product—Radical, Incremental)	Cross-sectional
Pil & MacDuffie (1996)	39	Change, Manufacturing	Adoption	Administrative	Longitudinal
Rego et al. (2007)	138	Creativity (team), Mixed	Generation	Mixed	Cross-sectional
Scott & Bruce (1994)	172	Creativity (individual), R&D units	Generation	Mixed	Cross-sectional
Souitaris (2001)	105	Innovation, Manufacturing	Generation	Technological (Process; Product—Radical, Incremental)	Cross-sectional
Weigelt & Sarkar (2009)[d]	4293	Innovation, Service	Adoption	Service	Longitudinal

[a]*Conception of innovation: Creativity, innovation, change; Context: Manufacturing, service, mixed; Innovation process: Generation, adoption, mixed; Innovation types: Product, service, process, technological, administrative, radical, incremental, mixed; Analytical method: Cross-sectional, longitudinal.*

[b]*4061 observations for 273 innovations, in 13 firms.*

[c]*314 respondents in 70 hospitals.*

[d]*28,311 observations in 4293 firms.*

complexity from the first wave studies, was referred to as "complexity" in the second wave studies. Also, some studies in the second wave included antecedents that were not examined in the first wave studies. We included four that were in two or more studies: managerial attitude toward risk, managerial education, managerial age, and organizational age.

The results of the second wave studies are summarized in Table 19.4. In 85% of cases, the results reflect the direction and significance level of regression coefficients. For instance, in Cardinal (2001), regression coefficients for centralization and both radical (new drug innovations) and incremental (drug enhancements) innovations are positive and significant at the .05 level. Hence in Table 19.4, we indicate these relationships as "Radical: Positive" and "Incremental: Positive". Where the regression results were not reported in the original studies (15% of cases), we entered the direction and significance levels of the correlation coefficients.

TABLE 19.4   Accumulation of the Results from the Second Wave Studies.

Study	Results[a]
Formalization	
Cardinal (2001)	*Radical:* Positive*; *Incremental:* Negative[†]
Ekvall (1996)	Negative**
Grover, Purvis, & Segars (2007)	*Incremental:* Negative***
Hashem & Tann (2007)	Positive**
Herrmann & Gordillo (2001)	Negative*
Jansen, Van den Bosch, & Volberda (2006)	*Exploratory:* NS; *Exploitative:* Positive**
Liao (2007)	Positive*
Nohria & Gulati (1996)	NS
Souitaris (2001)	*Process:* Negative*; *Product Radical:* NS; *Product Incremental:* NS
Centralization	
Cardinal (2001)	*Radical:* Positive*; *Incremental:* Positive*
Delaney et al. (1996)	NS
Germain (1996)	*Incremental:* Negative*
Grover, Purvis, & Segars (2007)	*Incremental:* Negative***
Hashem & Tann (2007)	Positive**
Herrmann & Gordillo (2001)	NS
Jansen et al. (2006)	*Exploratory:* Negative**; *Exploitative:* NS
Liao (2007)	NS
Nohria & Gulati (1996)	NS
Professionalism	
Cardinal (2001)	*Radical:* Positive***; *Incremental:* Positive***
Ekvall (1996)	Positive**
Herrmann & Gordillo (2001)	NS
Specialization	
Cardinal (2001)	*Radical:* Positive*; *Incremental:* Positive***
Fichman (2001)[b]	*OOP Assimilation:* NS; *RDB Assimilation:* NS; *CASE Assimilation:* Positive**; *SPI Assimilation:* Positive**
Germain (1996)	*Radical:* Positive*; *Incremental:* Positive*

(Continued)

TABLE 19.4   Accumulation of the Results from the Second Wave Studies (Continued).

Study	Results[a]
Managerial attitude toward change[c]	
Damanpour & Schneider (2006)	*Initiation:* Positive*; *Adoption Decision:* NS; *Implementation:* NS
Hashem & Tann (2007)	NS
Kivimaki et al. (2000)	*Perceived Innovation Effectiveness:* Positive***; *No. of patents:* Positive*
Madjar, Oldham, & Pratt (2002)	Positive*
Scott & Bruce (1994)	Positive*
Technical Knowledge Resources	
Fichman (2001)	*OOP Assimilation:* Positive**; *RDB Assimilation:* Positive**; *CASE Assimilation:* NS; *SPI Assimilation:* Positive**
Liao (2007)	Positive**
Complexity	
Damanpour & Schneider (2006)	*Initiation:* Positive***; *Adoption Decision:* Positive***; *Implementation:* Positive**
Delaney et al. (1996)	Positive*
Grover et al. (2007)	*Incremental:* Negative*
Herrmann & Gordillo (2001)	Positive**
Jansen et al. (2006)	*Exploratory:* Positive*; *Exploitative:* NS
Kivimaki et al. (2000)	*Perceived Innovation Effectiveness:* NS; *No. of patents:* Positive*
Weigelt & Sarkar (2009)	Positive***
Slack Resources	
Burns & Wholey (1993)	*1971 or earlier:* NS; *1972–78:* NS
Delaney et al. (1996)	Positive*
Geiger & Makri (2006)	*Absorbed Slack:* Positive**; *Unabsorbed Slack:* NS
Goes & Park (1997)	*1983 or earlier:* NS; *1984–90:* Positive***
Greve (2007)	*Exploratory:* NS (absorbed slack), Positive** (unabsorbed slack); *Exploitative:* Positive[†] (absorbed slack), NS (unabsorbed slack)
Li, Lin, & Chu (2008)	*Radical:* Positive*; *Incremental:* NS
Nohria & Gulati (1996)	Positive*
Nystrom et al. (2002)	Positive[†]
Weigelt & Sarkar (2009)	NS

(Continued)

D. ORGANIZATIONAL LEVEL INFLUENCES

TABLE 19.4 Accumulation of the Results from the Second Wave Studies (Continued).

Study	Results[a]
Internal Communication	
Calantone et al. (2002)	Positive*
Germain (1996)	*Radical:* Negative[†]
Jansen et al. (2006)	*Exploratory:* Positive**; *Exploitative:* Positive**
Kivimaki et al. (2000)	*Perceived Innovation Effectiveness:* Positive*
Managerial Tenure	
Damanpour & Schneider (2006)	*Initiation:* Positive***; *Adoption Decision:* Positive***; *Implementation:* Positive**
Madjar et al. (2002)	NS
Papadakis & Bourantas (1998)	*Process:* Positive*; *New Product Introduction:* NS; *Radical Product:* NS; *Incremental Product:* NS
Pil & MacDuffie (1996)	Positive*
Rego et al. (2007)	NS
External Communication	
Damanpour & Schneider (2006)	*Initiation:* Positive***; *Adoption Decision:* Positive**; *Implementation:* Positive***
Goes & Park (1997)	*1983 or earlier:* NS; *1984–90:* Positive***
Kivimaki et al. (2000)	*No. of patents:* Positive**
Managerial Attitude Toward Risk	
Nystrom et al. (2002)	Positive**
Papadakis & Bourantas (1998)	*Process:* NS; *New Product Introduction:* NS; *Radical Product:* NS; *Incremental Product:* NS
Souitaris (2001)	*Process:* NS; *Radical Product:* NS; *Incremental Product:* Negative*
Managerial Education	
Damanpour & Schneider (2006)	*Initiation:* NS; *Adoption Decision:* NS; *Implementation:* NS
Herrmann & Gordillo (2001)	NS
Madjar et al. (2002)	NS
Scott & Bruce (1994)	NS
Papadakis & Bourantas (1998)	*Process:* NS; *New Product Introduction:* Positive*; *Radical Product:* NS; *Incremental Product:* NS
Managerial Age	
Damanpour & Schneider (2006)	*Initiation:* NS; *Adoption Decision:* NS; *Implementation:* NS
Herrmann & Gordillo (2001)	NS

(Continued)

D. ORGANIZATIONAL LEVEL INFLUENCES

TABLE 19.4   Accumulation of the Results from the Second Wave Studies (Continued)

Study	Results[a]
Madjar et al. (2002)	NS
Rego et al. (2007)	NS
Souitaris (2001)	*Process:* NS; *Radical Product:* NS; *Incremental Product:* NS
Organizational Age	
Greve (2007)	*Exploratory:* Negative*; *Exploitative:* NS
Jansen et al. (2006)	*Exploratory:* NS; *Exploitative:* NS
Nystrom et al. (2002)	NS
Weigelt & Sarkar (2009)	Negative*

[a]*The statistical significance is the significance level of regression coefficients from the original studies. If regression results were not reported the significance levels of the correlation coefficients are provided.*
[b]*OOP: Object-Oriented Programming Languages; RDB: Relational Database Management Systems; CASE: Computer-Aided Software Engineering Tools; SPI: Software Process Innovations.*
[c]*This variable has also been named management support for innovation.*
$^{\dagger}p < .10; *p < .05; **p < .01; ***p < .001.$

Comparison of the First and Second Wave Studies

Table 19.5 compares the overall findings of the first and second wave studies. To arrive at this table, we examined the directions and strengths of the relationships between each variable and innovation for each study. If two or more studies had the same findings, we reported the finding in column 3 of Table 19.5. For example, two studies (Cardinal, 2001; Ekvall, 1996) found significant, positive relationships between professionalism and innovation, and one study (Herrmann & Gordillo, 2001) found a non-significant relationship. Therefore we denoted the relationship between professionalism and innovation as positive in column 3 of Table 19.5. Furthermore, if the original studies reported both positive and negative results, we took the results that a larger number of studies had found. For instance, for the variable internal communication, the relationship with innovation was found to be positive and significant in three out of four studies, and negative in one (Germain, 1996). Hence we denoted this relationship as "Positive" in column 3 of Table 19.5.

Direct Effects

The second wave studies have used various definitions of innovation (Table 19.2); however, the majority of them have conceptualized it as innovation (23 studies) rather than creativity (3 studies) or change (1 study). As shown in Table 19.5, from 11 factors that were included in both pre- and post-1990 studies, seven showed similar effects and four (formalization, centralization, slack resources, and managerial tenure) did not. Also, with exception of organizational age, which had a negative effect on innovation in the longitudinal studies, the other three variables that were included only in the second wave studies were related to the characteristics of managers and did not significantly influence innovation (Table 19.5). In general, the cumulative results from the second wave studies support Damanpour's (1991)

TABLE 19.5   Comparison of the Results of the First Wave (Pre-1990) and Second Wave (Post-1990) Studies.

Variable	Pre-1990	Post-1990
Formalization	NS	*Technological innovation, Incremental innovation*: Negative
		Radical innovation: NS
Centralization	Negative	*Service firms, Generation of innovation, Mixed innovation type*: NS
		Incremental innovation, Adoption of innovation: Negative
Professionalism	Positive	Positive
Specialization	Positive	Positive
Technical Knowledge Resources	Positive	Positive
Complexity (Functional Differentiation)	Positive	Positive
Slack Resources	Positive	*Mixed innovation type, Cross-sectional study, Absorbed slack*: Positive (*Unabsorbed slack*: NS)
		Longitudinal study, Technological innovation: NS/Positive
Internal Communication	Positive	Positive
External Communication	Positive	Positive
Managerial Tenure	NS	*Generation of innovation, Mixed innovation type*: NS
		Administrative innovation, Adoption of innovation: Positive
Administrative Intensity	Positive	—
Vertical Differentiation	NS	—
Managerial Attitude Toward Change	Positive	Positive
Managerial Attitude Toward Risk	—	NS
Managerial Education	—	NS
Managerial Age	—	NS
Organizational Age	—	*Service firms, Incremental innovation, Adoption of innovation, Cross-sectional studies*: NS; *Longitudinal studies*: Negative

general conclusion that the findings of empirical research on the relationships between organizational factors and innovation are mainly consistent.

Some quantitative review studies report salient antecedents of a construct as determined by "effect size"—the absolute value of the corrected mean correlations in a meta-analysis (Chen, Damanpour, & O'Reilly, 2010; Henard & Szymanski, 2001). Cohen and Cohen (1983) regard 0.30 as the conventional medium effect size of a population. Accordingly, four antecedents from Damanpour's (1991) review can be considered as salient determinants of innovation: specialization ($r_c = .394$), complexity (functional differentiation) ($r_c = .337$), technical knowledge resources ($r_c = .466$), external communication ($r_c = .362$). The second wave studies supported these results (Table 19.5). In addition, three antecedents—professionalism, internal communication, and managerial attitude toward change—that had positive effects in the pre-1990 studies had also positive relationships across a majority (more than 75%) of the post-1990 studies. Hence, we also consider these variables as salient determinants of innovation.

These salient factors represent a set of structural and behavioral characteristics that have found continuous empirical support in over four decades of research. They indicate that a greater variety of expertise and knowledge base (*specialization*), as well as greater cross-functional coalition of professionals (*complexity*), increase the likelihood of cross-fertilization of ideas across organizational units leading to innovation. Moreover, greater boundary-spanning activities, a commitment to move beyond the status quo (*professionalism*) and creation of a climate conducive to dispersion of ideas across the organization (*internal communication*) all facilitate innovation. New ideas for innovation are not merely contained inside the organization; innovative organizations ought to seek, receive, and absorb information from outside. Hence, *external communication* including environmental scanning and exchange, extra-organizational professional activities, and forming cooperative alliances with other organizations are necessary. Investment in attracting technically skilled members, and training and continuously developing organizational members' knowledge resources (*technical knowledge resources*) are also among the central features of innovative firms. Finally, a favorable *attitude toward change* in managers is essential for creating a climate conducive to innovation, motivating members to engage with and stay on the usually long journey to making the innovation happen, and resolving conflicts and maintaining the balance of power to let innovation survive internal rivalries and succeed.

The inconsistent results between first and second wave studies for formalization and centralization need further explanation. Centralization is usually defined as the extent to which decisions are made by higher echelons of authority, and formalization as the extent to which formal rules and procedures are used in the organization (Zeffane, 1989). They are components of bureaucratic control, and both are expected to influence innovation negatively. Yet, the cumulative findings from the two sets of studies show a flip-flop of these variables, presumed negative effect. In the first wave studies, the influence of formalization is non-significant and that of centralization is negative (Table 19.5), we found that the effect of formalization is mostly a negative (especially for technological and incremental innovations) and that of centralization is non-significant (especially in studies of service firms, studies of generation of innovations, and those that examined a mix of technological and administrative innovations). These cumulative results suggest that, contrary to the commonly accepted views of most organizational scholars and many practitioners, bureaucracy may not necessarily inhibit innovation. Therefore, to tease out the complex relationship between bureaucratic control and innovation, researchers would need to account for various moderators and examine the aggregate effects of multiple moderators on bureaucratic control and innovation. In such an investigation based on the results of the first wave studies, Damanpour (1996) found that, for example, the organizational size positively moderates the centralization-innovation association but negatively moderates the formalization–innovation association. Similar complex analyses are needed to enable a comparison of the results of the second wave studies with those of the first wave for the relationship between these components of bureaucratic control and innovation.

Moderating Effects

Table 19.4 provides some insight into the effects of moderators on the relationships between certain determinants and innovation. Whereas our methodology does not allow a statistical retest of Damanpour's (1991) conclusion that innovation types do not moderate the relationship between organizational factors and innovation, a cursory review of the results of the second wave studies suggests that innovation type remains the most widely examined contingency factor here. Moreover, among the three typologies of innovation discussed above, innovation radicalness has received most attention in the second wave studies (Table 19.4).

To get a better sense of cumulative results on this moderator we compared the number of positive, negative, and non-significant associations between determinants with radical/exploratory and incremental/exploitative innovations. No particular pattern emerged for any of the eleven determinants where these two innovation types were distinguished. More generally, of a total of 18 associations for radical/exploratory innovations, 8 were positive, 2 were negative, and 8 were non-significant. Of the total of 22 associations for incremental/exploitative innovations, 7, 6, and 9 were positive, negative, and non-significant, respectively. From these findings we can conclude, albeit crudely, that the second wave studies support Damanpour's conclusion about the moderating role of innovation types. However, researchers' focus on innovation radicalness in the second wave studies may suggest a new trend in innovation research, which we discuss below.

DISCUSSION

Whereas empirical results from the first and second wave studies are generally similar, we observed two major trends which emerged in the post-1990 as compared to pre-1990 studies. One relates to structuring of innovative organization, and the other to consequences of innovation for organizations.

From Organic to Ambidextrous Structure

In the first wave studies, the dominant framework for distinguishing the structure of innovative from non-innovate organizations was Burns and Stalker's (1961) organic and mechanistic designs. As stated above, an overall conclusion of the integration of empirical research before 1990 was that the characteristics associated with organic structures are more conducive to innovation than those associated with mechanistic structures (Damanpour, 1991). In the second wave studies the mechanistic–organic structure has been shifted to the ambidextrous structure.

The concept of organizational ambidexterity has gained traction after March's (1991) articulation of exploration and exploitation. However, empirical research on ambidexterity is unfocused and limited, and its conceptualization, antecedents, and consequences are still evolving (Simsek, 2009). In relation to innovation, for instance, Atuahene-Gima (2005) argues that exploration and exploitation are drivers of radical and incremental innovations, respectively. He and Wong (2004) distinguish between explorative and exploitative innovation strategies and find that, whereas exploitation strategy positively affects product and process innovations, exploration strategy positively affects only product innovations. Others (Bierly et al., 2009; Jansen et al., 2006; Smith & Tushman, 2005) distinguish between exploratory and exploitative innovations, as we have in this paper, and have generally defined them synonymous to radical and incremental innovations.

The ambidextrous structure for innovation predates the surge in studies of organizational ambidexterity after March's article. For instance, innovation scholars have proposed ambidextrous structures based on the adoption process (Duncan, 1976), innovation type (Daft, 1982), and innovation radicalness (Tushman & O'Reilly, 1996). Duncan (1976) proposed an ambidextrous structure for the initiation and implementation phases of innovation adoption, arguing that initiation is facilitated by higher complexity, and lower formalization and centralization, whereas implementation is facilitated by lower complexity, and higher formalization and centralization (Duncan, 1976). Daft (1982) proposed an ambidextrous structure for technical and administrative innovations, arguing that technical innovations are enhanced by smaller size, lower bureaucratic control, and higher complexity, whereas administrative innovations are enhanced by larger size, and higher centralization and formalization. Tushman and O'Reilly (1996) proposed an ambidextrous structure for the introduction of radical and incremental innovations during the reorientation and convergence periods of organizational evolution, arguing that in innovative organizations one unit focuses on incremental innovations for short-term efficiency and another unit focuses on discontinuous innovations for long-term innovation. The former unit is more formalized, centralized, and less complex than the latter (Smith & Tushman, 2005). In the second wave studies, the ambidextrous structure proposed by Tushman and colleagues, coupled with the concept of exploration–exploitation (March, 1991), has become central in studies of the structure–innovation relationship.

The differences between the dual structures, whether based on innovation process, type, or radicalness, are analogous to the differences between the characteristics of innovative (organic) and non-innovative (mechanistic) organizations as conceived in the pre-1990 studies. For example, Tushman and Smith (2002) argue that radical innovations are associated with organizations that have experimental cultures, an entrepreneurial climate, a loose, decentralized structure, flexible work processes, heterogeneous human resource profiles, and strong technical competencies. Incremental innovations, on the other hand, are associated with organizations that have an efficiency culture, a centralized structure, engineered work processes, and formalized roles and coordinating mechanisms. Our results do not support this view of structuring organizations for radical and incremental innovations as they do not show a difference in the effects of organizational factors that promote and inhibit radical (exploratory) versus incremental (exploitative) innovations. For instance, for centralization (an inhibiting factor), we found one positive and one negative effect for radical/exploratory innovations, and one positive and two negative effects for incremental/exploitative innovations (Table 19.4). For specialization (a promoting factor), we found two positive effects for both innovation types. While these results are only suggestive, when coupled with the cumulative results of the first wave studies they indicate that the process of innovation (whether initiation and implementation, or generation and adoption) and types of innovation (whether technological and administrative, or exploratory and exploitative) are generally facilitated by the same organizational characteristics. Therefore, prevailing arguments that one phase of innovation process or one type of innovation requires more organic structure than another phase or another type would need further scrutiny. New perspectives of ambidexterity leading to new ideas for research on ambidextrous structure for innovation are called for.

A line of inquiry, for example, could be to explore ambidextrous structures that distinguish between characteristics of organizational units that "supply" or "produce" innovations and the units that "consume" or "use" those innovations (Damanpour & Wischnevsky, 2006). The supplier units can generate product and process innovations, whether radical or incremental, and the user units can assimilate and put innovations to work. The success of the ambidextrous organization requires strategic leadership and control for innovation; that is, innovation strategies and management processes that guide, coordinate, and support both suppliers and users that may have different goals, structures, and systems. The critical innovation issue for managing the ambidextrous organization is the integration of the dual structure: how the organization can take advantage of the contrasting organizational capabilities of its dual structure yet manage the connectivity between them (Benner & Tushman, 2003). Strategic and operational integrations require certain capabilities that may not exist in the supplier or user unit. These capabilities are mainly managerial, process-based and can be gained and improved by managerial innovations.

Studies of organizational ambidexterity have increased rapidly. Simsek's (2009; pp600–601) review of the definition of organizational ambidexterity lists two studies published in the 1980s, three in the 1990s, and 12 in the 2000s. However, empirical research has not sufficiently addressed the issues related to structuring and managing ambidextrous organizations, as the studies have mainly focused on the introduction of stand-alone innovations of a single type. Since innovation is an ongoing organizational process, managing the integration of the dual structures requires research into the introduction of compositions or portfolio of innovation types that facilitate strategic renewal and contribute to organizational performance over time. Therefore, an avenue for future research is to focus on the consequences, rather than only the determinants, of innovation, and to examine the characteristics of organizations that succeed in generating and/or adopting combinations of innovation types that continuously produce intended outcomes.

From Stand-Alone to Compositions of Innovations

Table 19.3 shows that most empirical studies of the structure–innovation relationship have been cross-sectional. Similarly, the studies of consequences of innovation are mainly cross-sectional, although the innovation–organizational performance relationship is path dependent and occurs over time. Roberts and Amit (2003) argued that the performance of a firm relates more to its history of innovation activity than to the introduction of certain new products or processes. Damanpour et al. (2009) also argued that, because organizations are adaptive systems and innovation is a means to facilitate adaptive changes to the external environment, the impact of innovation on performance depends on the introduction of a portfolio or composition of innovations of different types. Hence, the generation or adoption of an innovation at one point in time, or even multiple innovations of the same type over time, could not fully explain the true effect of innovation on organizational performance in the long term.

The primary goal of research on the structure–innovation association in both pre- and post-1990 studies has been to develop contingency theories to differentiate the determinants of innovation in order to address the problem of inconsistent results of characteristics of innovative organizations. With few exceptions (Damanpour et al., 2009; Roberts & Amit, 2003), innovation researchers have not examined effects of composition of different innovation types on firm performance. Roberts and Amit (2003) examined three compositions (focus, commitment, and divergence) of three innovation types (product, process, and distribution) in Australian retail banking organizations. Damanpour et al. (2009) examined compositions of three other types of innovation (service, technological, and administrative) in public service organizations in England. Whereas the types of innovation and theoretical justifications of the innovation–performance relationship in the two studies differed, both provided empirical evidence for Roberts and Amit's (2003) cogent argument that sustained organizational performance results from the firm's history of innovation activity rather than an occasional innovation success.

Whereas some scholars have considered that successful organizations introduce streams of innovations over time (e.g., Smith & Tushman, 2005), the prevailing logic in innovation research is that organizations tend to rely on knowledge in areas where they have had success. That is, prior experience with a specific type of knowledge will support further application of the same body of knowledge (Bierly et al., 2009; Cohen & Levinthal, 1990). Therefore, organizations tend to focus on excelling at a certain type of innovation (e.g., radical, product, process) because they possess knowledge in that area, and can thus more easily integrate new knowledge, and create new opportunities to gain a performance advantage from it (Roberts & Amit, 2003). The perspective of organizations as socio-technical systems (STS) challenges this logic. The STS argues that the relationship between the technical and social subsystems of an organization is not strictly a one-to-one relationship; it is a correlative relationship representing a "coupling of dissimilarities" (Trist & Murray, 1993). Any change in one subsystem sets certain constraints and requirements, and necessitates a corresponding change in the other subsystem in order to produce positive outcomes. For sustained performance, therefore, instead of innovating in one subsystem (e.g., technological process innovation in the technical system, or managerial process innovation in the social system), organizations would need to invest in introducing innovations associated with multiple systems (Damanpour et al., 2009). The STS perspective, itself based on the perspective of organizations as systems, assumes that, in addition to adaptation to the external environment, strong interdependencies among internal organizational systems are fundamental to achieving organizational effectiveness over time (Wischnevsky & Damanpour, 2006). Managing the interdependencies across a complex system requires shared culture as organizational units and members should act independently but in a unified direction within a changing and unpredictable environment.

The application of resource-based view (RBV) to innovation activity also supports the complementary role of innovation in multiple organizational subsystems. RBV emphasizes the role of internal resources and the firm's capability in integrating them for gaining distinctive competencies and sustained high performance. Organizational performance is induced by the synergistic use of the organization's internal resources (e.g., product, technological process, and administrative knowledge resources) leading to simultaneous introduction of innovations in multiple subsystems (Damanpour et al., 2009). The concepts of combinative capabilities and internal dynamic capabilities also imply that innovating across the organization would ensure that the organization renews its ability to build, reconfigure, and integrate internal and external competencies to cope with environmental change and remain effective over time (Eisenhardt & Martin, 2000; Van den Bosch, Volberda, & de Boer, 1999). Future research can build on these perspectives and contribute by empirically investigating performance consequences of innovation activity in organizations that focus on introducing innovations across subsystems and seek balance in introducing various, complementary innovation types over time.

IMPLICATIONS FOR RESEARCH AND PRACTICE

This study has considered the results of empirical research on the relationship between organizational characteristics and innovation from 1990 to 2009, and compared it with the results of a quantitative integration of similar studies from 1967 to 1988 by Damanpour (1991). We identified seven salient antecedents of innovation from the first wave and second wave studies: specialization, complexity (functional differentiation), technical knowledge resources, external communication, professionalism, internal communication, and managerial attitude toward change. Our review supported Damanpour's (1991) observation that phases of innovation process and types of innovations (including exploratory vs. exploitative innovation) do not differentiate between the structure–innovation relationships. More generally, a comparison of the findings of the two sets of studies suggest that the focus of research on structuring for innovation has shifted from Burns and Stalkers' (1961) organic–mechanistic structure to Tushman and O'Reilly's (1996) ambidextrous structure.

Coupling the findings from the pre- and post-1990 sets of studies, we recommend two lines of inquiry for future research. First, research would need to focus on the integration of the dual structures in ambidextrous organizations, because the critical innovation issue for managing an ambidextrous organization is the strategic and operational integration of units with different cultures, climate, goals, and performance management regimes. Second, in addition to examining the determinants of innovation, research should also investigate the consequences of innovation for organizational performance. In particular, we posit that since innovation is an ongoing process, its consequences cannot be truly detected unless:

1. scholars develop theoretical models explaining composite effects of innovations on performance over time, and
2. future research relies on longitudinal analytical methods to examine these conceptual models.

Our study offers several implications for organizational and team leaders who want to promote innovation and creativity in an organization, its units and project teams. First, the findings highlight the importance of both slack and technical knowledge resources. Innovation requires both financial and human-knowledge capitals and is facilitated if the resources are specifically allocated to it. For example, in allocating financial resources to units and teams, resources for knowledge acquisition and rewarding generation of novel ideas should be separated from those for operational activities. The positive effect of external communication, that is, extra-organizational professional activities of members, in both sets of studies, punctuates this point. Second, as expected, the findings highlight the importance of internal communication in fostering innovation, and the role of managers' positive attitude toward innovation. Previous research has emphasized the need for top executives' attitudinal support for innovation. We add that assignment of team and organizational leaders who are supportive of innovation and have skills to foster communication within the project teams and organizational units could be equally important. Third, the positive effect of managerial tenure in the post-1990 studies, particularly in the studies of administrative innovations and innovation adoption, coupled with the non-significant effect of managers' age, suggests that the negative effect of tenure on innovation has been overstated in the literature. If so, human resource managers can be advised not to shy away from recruiting and appointing seasoned, well-experienced managers to oversee the innovation process. This finding is also highlighted by the positive effect of professionalism on innovation. Fourth, the non-significant effects of managerial age and education suggest that demographic managerial attributes are not likely to be important predictors of innovation. Finally, contrary to the commonly accepted view, we found that the effect of bureaucratic control (formalization of procedure and centralization of decision making) on innovation is not necessarily negative. This result reminds us that innovation in organizations is an intentional, planned, and structured activity; hence, controlling the process is an important function in the management of innovation. That is, strong performance management systems, coupled with structural conditions that are supportive of innovation, will lead to successful generation and adoption of innovation in organizations.

References

Abernathy, W. J., & Utterback, J. M. (1978). Patterns of industrial innovation. *Technology Review, June/July,* 40–47.

Amabile, T. M. (1988). A model of creativity and innovation in organizations. In L. L. Cummings & B. M. Staw (Eds.), *Research in Organizational Behavior* (Vol. 10, pp. 123–167). Greenwich, CT: JAI Press.

Amabile, T. M., Conti, R., Coon, H., Lazenby, J., & Herron, M. (1996). Assessing the work environment for creativity. *Academy of Management Journal, 39,* 1154–1184.

Angle, H. L., & Van de Ven, A. H. (2000). Suggestions for managing the innovation journey. In A. H. Van de Ven, H. L. Angle & M. S. Poole (Eds.), *Research on the Management of Innovation* (pp. 663–697). Oxford, UK: Oxford University Press.

Atuahene-Gima, K. (2005). Resolving the capability–rigidity paradox in new product innovation. *Journal of Marketing, 69,* 61–83.

Benner, M. J., & Tushman, M. L. (2003). Exploitation, exploration, and process management: The productivity dilemma revisited. *Academy of Management Review, 28,* 238–256.

Bierly, P., Damanpour, F., & Santoro, M. (2009). The application of external knowledge: Organizational conditions for exploration and exploitation. *Journal of Management Studies, 46,* 481–509.

Birkinshaw, J., Hamel, G., & Mol, M. (2008). Management innovation. *Academy of Management Review, 33,* 825–845.

Boer, H., & During, W. E. (2001). Innovation, what innovation? A comparison between product, process, and organizational innovation. *International Journal of Technology Management, 22,* 83–107.

Boulding, K. (1956). *General system theory—The skeleton of science, 1,* 11–17. General systems (Yearbook of the Society for the Advancement of General Systems Theory).

Burns, T., & Stalker, G. M. (1961). *The Management of innovation.* London, UK: Tavistock Publications.

Burns, L. R., & Wholey, D. R. (1993). Adoption and abandonment of matrix management programs—Effects of organizational characteristics and interorganizational networks. *Academy of Management Journal, 36,* 106–138.

Calantone, R. J., Cavusgil, S. T., & Zhao, Y. (2002). Learning orientation, firm innovation capability, and firm performance. *Industrial Marketing Management, 31,* 515–524.

Cardinal, L. B. (2001). Technological innovation in the pharmaceutical industry: The use of organizational control in managing research and development. *Organization Science, 12,* 19–36.

Chen, J., Damanpour, F., & O'Reilly, R. R. (2010). Understanding antecedents of new product development speed: A meta-analysis. *Journal of Operations Management, 28,* 17–33.

Cohen, J., & Cohen, P. (1983). *Applied Multiple regression/correlation analysis for the behavioral sciences* (2 ed.). Hillsdale NJ: Lawrence Erlbaum Associates, Inc.

Cohen, W. M., & Levinthal, D. A. (1990). Absorptive capacity: New perspective on learning and innovation. *Administrative Science Quarterly, 35,* 128–152.

Daft, R. L., & Becker, S. W. (1978). *The innovative organization.* New York, NY: Elsevier.

Daft, R. L. (1982). Bureaucratic versus non-bureaucratic structure and the process of innovation and change. In S. B. (1982). Bacharach (Ed.), *Research in the sociology of organizations* (vol. 1, pp. 129–166). Greenwich, CT: JAI Press.

Damanpour, F. (1991). Organizational innovation: A meta-analysis of effects of determinants and moderators. *Academy of Management Journal, 34,* 555–590.

Damanpour, F. (1996). Bureaucracy and innovation revisited: Effects of contingency factors, industrial sectors, and innovation characteristics. *Journal of High Technology Innovation Management, 7,* 149–173.

Damanpour, F., & Aravind, D. (2006). Product and process innovations: A review of organizational and environmental determinants. In J. Hage & M. Meeus (Eds.), *Innovation, Science, and Institutional Change.* Oxford, UK: Oxford University Press.

Damanpour, F., & Schneider, M. (2006). Phases of the adoption of innovation in organizations: Effects of environment, organization, and top managers. *British Journal of Management, 17,* 215–236.

Damanpour, F., & Wischnevsky, J. D. (2006). Research on innovation in organizations: Distinguishing innovation-generating from innovation-adopting organizations. *Journal of Engineering and Technology Management, 23,* 269–291.

Damanpour, F., Walker, R. M., & Avellaneda, C. N. (2009). Combinative effects of innovation types on organizational performance: A longitudinal study of public services. *Journal of Management Studies, 46,* 650–675.

Delaney, J. T., Jarley, P., & Fiorito, J. (1996). Planning for change: Determinants of innovation in US national unions. *Industrial and Labor Relations Review, 49,* 597–614.

Dougherty, D., & Hardy, C. (1996). Sustained product innovation in large, mature organizations: Overcoming innovation-organization problems. *Academy of Management Journal, 39,* 1120–1153.

Drucker, P. F. (1985). The discipline of innovation. *Harvard Business Review, May–June,* 72–76.

Duncan, R. B. (1976). The ambidextrous organization: Designing dual structures for innovation. In R. H. Kilmann, L. R. Pondy & D. P. Slevin (Eds.), *The management of organizational design: Strategy implementation* (pp. 167–188). New York, NY: North-Holland.

Eisenhardt, K., & Martin, J. A. (2000). Dynamic capabilities: What are they? *Strategic management Journal, 21,* 1105–1121.

Ekvall, G. (1996). Organizational climate for creativity and innovation. *European Journal of Work and Organizational Psychology, 5,* 105–123.

Elenkov, D. S., & Manev, I. M. (2005). Senior expatriate leadership's effects on innovation and the role of cultural intelligence. *Journal of World Business, 44,* 357–369.

Fagerberg, J. (2005). Innovation: A guide to the literature. In J. Fagerberg, D. Mowery & R. Nelson (Eds.), *The Oxford handbook of innovation* (pp. 1–27). Oxford, UK: Oxford University Press.

Fichman, R. G. (2001). The role of aggregation in the measurement of IT-related organizational innovation. *MIS Quarterly, 25,* 427–455.

Ford, C. M. (1996). A theory of individual creative action in multiple social domains. *Academy of Management Review, 21,* 1112–1142.

Gatignon, H., Tushman, M. L., Smith, W., & Anderson, P. (2002). A structural approach to assessing innovation: Construct development of innovation locus, type, and characteristics. *Management Science, 48,* 1103–1122.

Geiger, S. W., & Makri, M. (2006). Exploration and exploitation innovation processes: The role of organizational slack in R&D intensive firms. *Journal of High Technology Management Research, 17,* 97–108.

Germain, R. (1996). The role of context and structure in radical and incremental logistics innovation adoption. *Journal of Business Research, 35,* 117–127.

Glynn, M. A. (1996). Innovative genius: A framework for relating individual and organizational intelligences to innovation. *Academy of Management Review, 21,* 1081–1111.

Goes, J. B., & Park, S. H. (1997). Interorganizational links and innovation: The case of hospital services. *Academy of Management Journal, 40,* 673–696.

Gopalakrishnan, S., & Damanpour, F. (1994). Patterns of generation and adoption of innovations in organizations: Contingency models of innovation attributes. *Journal of Engineering and Technology Management, 11*, 95–116.

Gopalakrishnan, S., & Damanpour, F. (1997). Innovation research in economics, sociology, and technology management. *Omega, 25*, 15–28.

Greenwood, R., & Hinings, C. R. (1996). Understanding radical organizational change: Bringing together the old and the new institutionalism. *Academy of Management Review, 21*, 1022–1054.

Greve, H. R. (2007). Exploration and exploitation in product innovation. *Industrial and Corporate Change, 16*, 945–975.

Grover, V., Purvis, R. L., & Segars, A. H. (2007). Exploring ambidextrous innovation tendencies in the adoption of telecommunications technologies. *IEEE Transactions on Engineering Management, 54*, 268–285.

Hashem, G., & Tann, J. (2007). The adoption of ISO standards within the Egyptian context: A diffusion of innovation approach. *Total Quality Management, 18*, 631–652.

He, Z., & Wong, P. (2004). Exploration vs. exploitation: An empirical test of the ambidexterity hypothesis. *Organization Science, 15*, 481–494.

Henard, D. H., & Szymanski, D. M. (2001). Why some new products are more successful than others. *Journal of Marketing Research, 38*, 362–373.

Herrmann, P., & Gordillo, M. (2001). Organizational innovation in developing countries: An empirical approach. *International Journal of Organizational Theory and Behavior, 4*, 33–55.

Hitt, M. A., Hoskisson, R. E., Johnson, R. A., & Moesel, D. D. (1996). The market for corporate control and firm innovation. *Academy of Management Journal, 39*, 1084–1119.

Hunter, J. E., & Schmidt, F. L. (1990). *Methods of meta-analysis*. Newbury Park, CA: Sage Publications.

Jansen, J. J. P., Van Den Bosch, F. A. J., & Volberda, H. W. (2006). Exploratory innovation, exploitative innovation, and performance: Effects of organizational antecedents and environmental moderators. *Management Science, 52*, 1661–1674.

Kessler, E. H., & Chakrabarti, A. K. (1996). Innovation speed: A conceptual model of context, antecedents, and outcomes. *Academy of Management Review, 21*, 1143–1191.

Kimberly, J. R., & Evanisko, M. J. (1981). Organizational innovation: The influence of individual, organizational, and contextual factors on hospital adoption of technological and administrative innovations. *Academy of Management Journal, 24*, 679–713.

King, N. (1990). Innovation at work: The research literature. In M. A. West & J. L. Farr (Eds.), *Innovation and creativity at work* (pp. 15–59). New York, NY: Wiley.

Kivimaki, M., Lansisalmi, H., Elovainio, M., Heikkila, A., Lindstrom, K., Harisalo, R. et al.,(2000). Communication as a determinant of organizational innovation. *R&D Management, 30*, 33–42.

Klein, K. J., & Sorra, J. S. (1996). The challenge of innovation implementation. *Academy of Management Journal, 21*, 1055–1080.

Lam, A. (2005). Organizational innovation. In J. Fagerberg, D. C. Mowery & R. R. Nelson (Eds.), *The Oxford handbook of innovation* (pp. 115–147). Oxford, UK: Oxford University Press.

Lawless, M. W., & Anderson, P. C. (1996). Generational technological change: Effects of innovation and local rivalry on performance. *Academy of Management Journal, 39*, 1185–1217.

Liao, Y. (2007). The effects of knowledge management strategy and organization structure on innovation. *International Journal of Management, 24*, 53–60.

Li, C., Lin, C., & Chu, C. (2008). The nature of market orientation and the ambidexterity of innovations. *Management Decision, 46*, 1002–1026.

Madjar, N., Oldham, G. R., & Pratt, M. G. (2002). There's no place like home? The contributions of work and non-work creativity support to employees' creative performance. *Academy of Management Journal, 45*, 757–767.

March, J. G. (1991). Exploration and exploitation in organizational learning. *Organization Science, 2*, 71–87.

Meeus, M. T. H., & Edquist, C. (2006). Introduction to Part I: Product and process innovation. In J. Hage & M. Meeus (Eds.), *Innovation, science, and institutional change* (pp. 23–37). Oxford, NY: Oxford University Press.

Meyer, A. D., & Goes, J. B. (1988). Organizational assimilation of innovation: A multilevel contextual analysis. *Academy of Management Journal, 31*, 897–923.

Miles, I. (2005). Innovation in services. In J. Fagerberg, D. C. Mowery & R. R. Nelson (Eds.), *The Oxford handbook of innovation* (pp. 433–458). Oxford, UK: Oxford University Press.

Nadler, D. A., & Tushman, M. L. (1997). Implementing new designs: Managing organizational change. In M. L. Tushman & P. Anderson (Eds.), *Managing strategic innovation and change* (pp. 595–606). New York, NY: Oxford University Press.

Nohria, N., & Gulati, R. (1996). Is slack good or bad for innovation? *Academy of Management Journal, 39*, 1245–1264.

Nystrom, P. C., Ramamurthy, K., & Wilson, A. L. (2002). Organizational context, climate and innovativeness: Adoption of imaging technology. *Journal of Engineering Technology Management, 19*, 221–247.

Papadakis, V., & Bourantas, D. (1998). The Chief Executive Officer as corporate champion of technological innovation: An empirical investigation. *Technology Analysis and Strategic Management, 10*, 89–109.

Pil, F. K., & MacDuffie, J. P. (1996). The adoption of high-involvement work practices. *Industrial Relations, 35*, 423–455.

Pouder, R., & John, C. H. (1996). Hot spots and blind spots: geographical clusters of firms and innovation. *Academy of Management Review, 21*, 1192–1225.

Rego, A., Sousa, F., Pina e Cunha, M., Correia, A., & Saur-Amaral, I. (2007). Leader self-reported emotional intelligence and perceived employee creativity: An exploratory study. *Creativity and Innovation Management, 16*, 250–264.

Roberts, E. B. (1988). Managing invention and innovation. *Research Management, 31*, 11–29.

Roberts, P. W., & Amit, R. (2003). The dynamics of innovative activity and competitive advantage: The case of Australian retail banking, 1981 to 1995. *Organization Science, 14*, 107–122.

Rogers, E. M. (1995). *Diffusion of innovations* (4th ed.). New York, NY: The Free Press.

Sanidas, E. (2005). *Organizational innovations and economic growth.* Cheltenham, UK: Edward Elgar.

Schroeder, R. G., Van de Ven, A. H., Scudder, G. D., & Polley, D. (2000). The development of innovation ideas. In A. H. Van de Ven, H. L. Angle & M. S. Poole (Eds.), *Research on the management of innovation: The Minnesota studies* (pp. 107–134). New York, NY: Oxford University Press.

Scott, W. R. (1992). *Organizations: Rational, natural and open systems.* Englewood Cliffs, NJ: Prentice-Hall.

Scott, S. G., & Bruce, R. A. (1994). Determinants of innovative behavior: A path model of individual innovation in the workplace. *Academy of Management Journal, 37*, 580–607.

Simsek, Z. (2009). Organizational ambidexterity: Towards a multilevel understanding. *Journal of Management Studies, 46*, 597–624.

Slappendel, C. (1996). Perspectives on innovation in organizations. *Organization Studies, 17*, 107–129.

Smith, W. K., & Tushman, M. L. (2005). Managing strategic contradictions: A top management model for managing innovation streams. *Organization Science, 16*, 522–536.

Souitaris, V. (2001). Strategic influences of technological innovations in Greece. *British Journal of Management, 12*, 131–147.

Tornatzky, L. G., & Fleischer, M. (1990). *The Processes of technological innovation.* Lexington, MA: Lexington Books.

Tranfield, D., Denyer, D., & Smart, P. (2003). Towards a methodology for developing evidence-informed management knowledge by means of systematic review. *British Journal of Management, 14*, 207–222.

Trist, E., & Murray, H. (1993). *The social engagement of social science: A Tavistock anthology* (vol. 2). Philadelphia, PA: University of Pennsylvania Press.

Tushman, M. L., & Anderson, P. (1986). Technological discontinuities and organizational environments. *Administrative Science Quarterly, 31*, 439–465.

Tushman, M. L., & O'Reilly, C. A. (1996). Ambidextrous organizations: Managing evolutionary and revolutionary change. *California Management Review, 38*, 8–30.

Tushman, M., & Smith, W. (2002). Technological change, ambidextrous organizations and organizational evolution. In J. Baum (Ed.), *The Blackwell companion to organizations* (pp. 386–414). UK: Blackwell Publishers.

Vaccaro, I. G., Jansen, J. J. P., Van Den Bosch, F. A. J., & Volberda, H. (2010). Top management team diversity and management innovation: The moderating role of social integration and environmental dynamism. Paper presented at EURAM 2010, Rome, Italy.

Van de Ven, A. H., Angle, H. L., & Poole, M. S. (2000). *Research on the management of innovation: The Minnesota studies.* New York, NY: Oxford University Press.

Van de Ven, A. H., & Rogers, E. M. (1988). Innovations and organizations. *Communication Research, 15*, 632–651.

Van den Bosch, F. A. J., Volberda, H. W., & de Boer, M. (1999). Coevolution of firm absorptive capacity and knowledge environment: Organizational forms and combinative capabilities. *Organization Science, 10*, 551–568.

Wade, J. (1996). A community-level analysis of sources and rates of technological variation in the microprocessor market. *Academy of Management Journal, 39*, 1218–1244.

Weigelt, C., & Sarkar, M. B. (2009). Learning from supply-side agents: The impact of technology solution providers' experiential diversity on client innovation adoption. *Academy of Management Journal, 52*, 37–60.

West, M. A., & Richter, A. W. (2008). Climates and cultures for innovation and creativity at work. In J. Zhou & C. E. Shalley (Eds.), *Handbook of organizational creativity*. New York, NY: Lawrence Erlbaum Associates.

Wischnevsky, J. D., & Damanpour, F. (2006). Organizational transformation and performance: An examination of three perspectives. *Journal of Managerial Issues, 18*, 104–128.

Woodman, R. W., Sawyer, J. E., & Griffin, R. W. (1993). Toward a theory of organizational creativity. *Academy of Management Review, 18*, 293–321.

Zeffane, R. M. (1989). Centralization or formalization? Indifference curve for strategies and control. *Organization Studies, 10*, 327–352.

D. ORGANIZATIONAL LEVEL INFLUENCES

Planning for Innovation: A Process Oriented Perspective

Samuel T. Hunter[1], Scott E. Cassidy[1], and Gina Scott Ligon[2]

[1]Pennsylvania State University, PA; [2]Villanova University, PA

Organizations continue to place an ever-increasing premium on innovation—the successful implementation of novel and useful ideas (Estrin, 2009; Florida, 2002; Kao, 2007). The reasons for the pursuit of innovation are seemingly quite justified. Simply put, businesses that can bring products to market before competitors stand to have a unique competitive advantage over those that lag in development (Dess & Pickens, 2000; Janssen, van de Vliert, & West, 2004; Mumford & Hunter, 2005). Moreover, organizations that continually seek new and novel ways to operate might also gain a competitive advantage over those businesses that continue to engage in outdated and inefficient practices.

Thus, for many organizations the question is not, "should we innovate?" but rather, "how do we successfully innovate?". This primary question, moreover, flows into the need to explore business practices that allow for *sustained* innovation—or continual innovation over time. Doing so clearly requires a strategic orientation toward the pursuit of new and useful ideas—a long-term commitment to innovation (Ettlie, Bridges, & O'Keefe, 1984, 2008). What remains less clear, however, is how to best roadmap or define the path to creative solutions. As such, the aim of this chapter is to consider the application of planning for innovation as part of a successful innovation strategy.

The outline of the chapter is as follows: first, given the debate around the topic of planning for innovation, we will begin with a consideration of the arguments both for and against the activity. We then turn to a careful consideration of how planning is defined, as this has notable implications for how planning is both viewed and, ultimately, conducted. We will then move to a discussion on process-oriented views of both planning and innovation activities, respectively. The two approaches are then integrated in a discussion of the sub-process plans necessary for successful innovation. Within each of the sub-plans, the key planning processes and necessary planning requirements are discussed. We round out our discussion on the keys to integrating planning activities as well as the requirements and guidelines for a broader successful plan for innovation. Finally, we conclude with a summary of the literature and discussion on avenues for future research.

THE CASE AGAINST PLANNING FOR INNOVATION: WHY IT CAN'T BE DONE

Admittedly, there is a reasonable argument against the utility of planning for innovation and, it may surprise the reader, it is not our intent to discount this argument. Many of the points made against the possibility of planning for innovation are justified and well grounded in experience and research. It must be borne in mind that successfully planning for innovation is a complex, dynamic, resource-intensive activity. Thus, unless a strong commitment is made to the endeavor, planning is likely to prove of little utility to an organization and, in fact, may actually hamper creative production.

At the heart of the case against planning is simply that innovation does not follow a prescribed path. That is, when developing something novel, new, or original, there are limited benchmarks for that process. As such, one may not be able to develop an effective plan for an unpredictable activity. This argument is made very well by Minztberg and colleagues (Minztberg & Waters, 1985; Mintzberg, Raisinghani, & Theoret, 1976) and is nicely summarized via a lively exchange between Mintzberg (1991) and Ansoff (1991).

Extending the complexity argument for planning is a second set of points against the utility of planning for creative endeavors. Illustrated by the "seed" model (Eisenhardt & Tabrizi, 1995) or the "bubble-up" argument (Miller & Osburn, 2008) the contention, broadly, is that innovation suffers if constraints are imposed. Rather, ideas and projects must be allowed to emerge in somewhat organic fashion—to "bubble up" within the organization. One of the specific mechanisms operating here is that creativity, the precursor to innovation, requires a reasonable degree of autonomy (Abbey & Dickson 1983; Hunter, Bedell-Avers, & Mumford, 2007). It may be argued that restricting the freedom to explore differing creative avenues via a specific plan of action will restrict the creativity of ideas generated. Thus a plan that is developed to solely maximize efficiency may, as a by-product, reduce innovative thinking.

Similarly, one of the fundamental components of creativity is a passion for the task—or what is typically referred to as intrinsic motivation (Collins & Amabile, 1999). A plan that is too strict may, in turn, take away from the intrinsic satisfaction of creation and discovery and will thereby limit the creativity of the ideas generated. On the whole, then, the case against planning for innovation is summarized by suggesting that innovation is too complex to plan, and that highly rigid plans can reduce essential innovation mechanisms such as freedom and intrinsic satisfaction.

We turn now to the case for why planning may be beneficial for innovation and, along the way, address many of the above concerns.

THE CASE FOR PLANNING: WHY IT MUST BE DONE

Somewhat paradoxically, the case for why planning is important for innovation—indeed as we see it, necessary—is tied directly to the case *against* planning for innovation. Consider a bit further the argument that innovation is so complex, iterative, and dynamic that it cannot be planned for. We contend that it is this complexity, inherently, that makes planning a necessary component of sustained innovation. Specifically, an initial plan—even if the initial plan is not ultimately utilized—provides movement and guidance in this deeply complex endeavor (Latham & Locke, 1991). As the leader of Nissan's innovative design group noted:

> "Since it is not possible to effect a plan without an idea, or an idea without a plan, they must be very much in sync with each other" *(Hirschberg, 1999, p. 231).*

When faced with complex and ill-defined situations, situations characterizing creative performance, many of us are resistant to change and will often choose, instead, a more familiar path (Lonergan, Scott, & Mumford, 2004; Mumford, Blair, Dailey, Leritz, & Osburn, 2006). Thus, rather than being innovative, a less risky and more predictable route is taken (Adams, Day, & Dougherty, 1998). A plan for innovation, in contrast, can provide a beacon on the horizon and facilitate movement toward a creative goal. What must be borne in mind is, that although innovation is an iterative process, it must *begin* somewhere if an end is to be achieved. Plans provide this starting point.

As alluded to earlier, perhaps the strongest case for why planning is useful for innovation begins with a reconsideration of the basic assumptions of plan development. Namely, the assumption that plans are a static set of activities—a checklist to be executed that maximizes project efficiency. As will be discussed in greater detail later in the chapter, plans need not be rigid. They can, and should in fact, be comprised of multiple contingency plans to account for emergent conditions and situations. Thus, as Mintzberg and colleagues (Mintzberg, 1990, 1991; Mintzberg & Waters, 1985) might suggest, adhering to a strict set of rules for task completion is likely to result in reduced creative performance. Instead, planning for innovation must employ the use of multiple, flexible, mid-range plans that account for a myriad of contingencies (Hayes-Roth & Hayes-Roth, 1979). What is quickly emerging from the discussion on successful planning is that this approach is resource-intensive, multifaceted and challenging. Thus, some organizations may not be willing to engage in such complex planning activities and, as a result, will not see benefits from planning.

It must also be noted that along with the somewhat disheartening realization that plans are complex and involve multiple moving components, there is the *beneficial* realization that planning actually helps *identify* these components (Berger, Guilford, & Christensen, 1957; Doerner & Schaub, 1994; Noice, 1991). Without an initial template, it is very difficult to determine what resources are required for implementing a plan. Thus, planning not only provides an initial structure and generates movement toward a challenging goal, but it can also identify what additional capabilities must be acquired for successful innovation. More specifically, a systematic approach to innovation, even one that is continually adapting, provides some guidance as to what resources are required to capitalize on ideas that do prove viable. Plans help organizations build the absorptive capacity to take advantage of opportunities that arise in the pursuit of innovation (Cohen & Levinthal, 1990).

Along similar lines, the planning process helps decision makers align efforts within a broader innovation strategy. One of the primary challenges that organizations face is how to allocate resources in such a way as to maximize profit (Estrin, 2009). Although they vary in degree of constraint, organizations all face the limitation of capital. Without some form of planning, it is possible for organizations to get stuck in a circular quagmire of development, continually draining resources in the exploration of ideas. At some point ideas must move from conception to development for profit to be realized (March, 1991). Plans allow for this movement—they provide the structure necessary for transition among the various innovation activities (Mumford, Bedell-Avers, & Hunter, 2008).

Additionally, it should be realized that because innovation is inherently a high-risk endeavor, the vast majority of ideas will simply fail. This consistent failure often represents a substantial loss to an organization's financial resources, and as such it's critical that organizations recoup some of that loss through organizational learning (Hurley & Hult, 1998). That is, product failures should not simply be discarded and the information about the failure lost in the recycling bin. It is important that the exact nature of their failure be fed back into the system—organizations must learn from failed attempts as well as successful implementations. This process, unfortunately, does not happen without sustained and purposeful effort or more directly, a plan. Moreover, learning may take the form of codification (March, 1991) where organizations impact individuals and individuals impact organizations through a dynamic "code" or through more direct influences such as face-to-face interaction (Miller, Zhao, & Calantone, 2006). Planning helps provide structure to this dynamic and multifaceted activity, allowing organizational learning in long-term innovation strategy.

One final comment on the case for why planning is beneficial in the pursuit of innovative endeavors is that guidance must not be equated with control. In a study examining leadership and its influence on subordinate performance, for example, Trevelyan (2001) gathered both qualitative and quantitative data on multiple leaders and project teams. She observed that controlling leaders were de-motivating to their subordinates, while leaders who provided guidance (i.e., involvement) facilitated motivation and satisfaction with the project. Moreover, there is evidence that moderate degrees of constraint can aid in creative thinking (Hughes, 1989; Mumford et al., 2008). Thus, on the whole it appears that organizations can provide general goals and guidance for employees without excessively restricting their paths to achieve those goals. Well-designed plans are constructed in this way and enhance, rather than inhibit, innovation.

In sum, when considering whether planning for innovation is either a help or hindrance, the answer, in complex fashion, is that it may be both. Organizations that develop rigid plans of action and stick to them despite evidence indicating they must be adjusted will see limited benefit to planning. On the other hand, organizations that choose to engage in the challenging, complex, resource-intensive act of planning and embrace the flexibility necessary for such an endeavor will likely see the substantial benefits of planning for innovation. With this in mind, we turn to defining the process of planning.

DEFINING PLANNING: A PROCESS PERSPECTIVE

Planning, as is the case with innovation, has a long and rich research history (Berger et al., 1957; Gaerling, 1996; Miller, Galanter, & Pribam, 1960). Although approaches to understanding planning certainly vary, the basic conceptualizations can be broken down into two main perspectives: 1) the structural and 2) process-oriented or generative view. The structural conceptualization of planning might best be described as generating a list of action items to engage in as a means to achieve a desired outcome or goal. The aim is to direct action and, as a result, increase efficiency (McDermott, 1978; Miller, et al., 1960). Thus, the plan is separated from the planner; tasks comprising the plan might just as readily be completed by the individual who developed the list as by the individual charged with executing the items on it. In this view of planning, the plan is a static collection of steps and tasks to be completed in general linear fashion to achieve a goal. The plan itself, then, is the product and focus of this conceptualization.

In contrast to the structural view, the process-oriented or generative view of planning emphasizes the *act* of planning (Hayes-Roth & Hayes-Roth, 1979). Thus, according to the generative view, planning involves the cognitive processes used to generate a plan of action as well as the alternative plans of action that result. Planning from this perspective is defined as:

"the active conscious construction, or mental simulation, of future action sequences, including cognitive acts, to organize effort and optimize the attainment of select goals" *(Mumford, Scott, Gaddis, & Strange, 2002, p. 5).*

This generative conceptualization has a number of implications for considering the role of planning in innovative endeavors. First, because the generative approach is process-oriented, plans are not seen as a static set of tasks to complete. Rather than being seen as the act of completing rigid action lists, planning involves the cognitive processes involved in future simulations of events (Hayes-Roth & Hayes-Roth, 1979; Keane, 1996). In this sense, planning is far more flexible and adaptive—a necessary key feature for planning creative endeavors. Second, because of the cognitive orientation in this conceptualization, knowledge and expertise play a key role in this view of planning (Berger et al., 1957; Noice, 1991). That is, whereas the structural approach emphasizes the capacity and resources necessary to execute a plan, the generative perspective relies on the experience of the planner or planning team.

As may be surmised, the generative view of planning will be used as the basis for this chapter—a choice made for several reasons. First, because creativity and innovation are, in and of themselves, processes, a process-oriented perspective would appear most appropriate for the present discussion (Baughman & Mumford, 1995). Second, a process perspective allows for a richer understanding of causality among variables and as a result, a more complete view of what is required for successful planning. Finally, the generative approach to planning does not emphasize static plans and, instead, allows for a dynamic approach to understanding the act of planning. As will be discussed later in the chapter, innovation is not a static phenomenon and, as we will argue, successfully planning for innovation will require a substantial degree of flexibility.

A PROCESS MODEL OF PLANNING

Although arguing for a process-oriented view of planning is a relatively straightforward task, describing the actual processes involved is a substantially more complex endeavor. Fortunately, there is some guidance provided by Mumford and colleagues in their discussions on planning processes (Mumford et al., 2001, 2002a). Using their framework as a foundation,

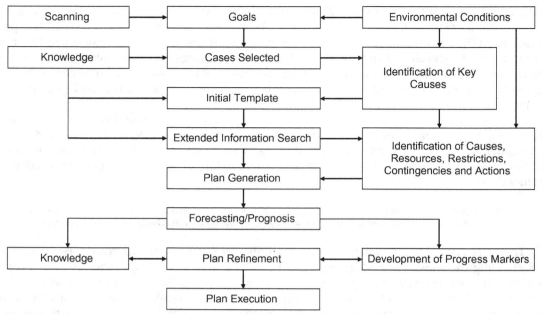

FIGURE 20.1 Planning process model. Model developed based on the works of *Mumford et al., 2001, 2002.*

planning begins with the determination of a goal or desired end-state (Earley & Perry, 1987; Gaerling, 1996). This point will be of notable importance later in the chapter when we discuss requirements for developing sub-plans required for innovation. Before we turn to this discussion, however, let us return to the model and note that once a goal is determined, a planner or planning team will select the previous experiences, or cases, to apply to understanding and developing their emerging plan. The selection of cases is driven largely by previous experience as well as basic knowledge of why such endeavors succeed or failed. With cases chosen, plans move toward an initial template or framework for the plan (Berger & DiBattista, 1992; Xiao, Milgram, & Doyle, 1997). This first framing attempt provides the basis for gathering more information and, ultimately, generating an initial plan for action.

This initial plan is critical in that it allows for consideration of what might happen should the plan be implemented in its current form. At this point in the process, a very important planning activity occurs: the development of back-up or alternative plans. By considering an initial plan along with what might influence the success of that plan, it is possible to develop secondary action plans dictating what should be done in the case of contingencies occurring (Patalano & Siefert, 1997). With respect to planning for innovation, specifically, the development of contingency plans is critical because the path to successful innovation does not follow a highly predictable route. Thus, successful planners consider multiple contingencies and have multiple back-up plans ready for implementation (Goldin & Hayes-Roth, 1980).

With back-up plans in place, the initial plan can be refined and developed further. Additionally, markers for success and progress can be developed to provide indications of whether key milestones are being met. A refined plan can then be taken to the execution stage where the plan itself is implemented. Once a plan is implemented, a careful monitoring process must also occur, in which contingency plans are put into action should they be required.

KEY INNOVATION ACTIVITIES

Before we can integrate planning and innovation, we must begin with a careful consideration of the activities characterizing innovation itself. That is, we must know what activities we are planning for as a necessary precursor to plan development. Creativity and innovation models have a long-standing history (Lubart, 2001), beginning with the work by scholars such as Dewey (1910) and largely driven by the early work of Wallas (1926). More recent models include those by Taylor, Austin and Sutton (1974), Fink, Ward and Smith (1992) and Amabile (1996). One of the most heavily researched recent approaches is the eight-stage model put forth by Mumford and colleagues (e.g., Baughman & Mumford, 1995; Mumford et al., 1991, 1996, 1997). This model emphasizes a more refined perspective on the innovation process—discussing the various sub-processes involved in innovation. Because the model offers a rather detailed perspective as well as the sizable literature base supporting the model, this eight-stage framework will serve as the basis for our discussion of innovation.

According to the eight-stage model, the primary activities involved in creativity and innovation are: opportunity identification; information gathering; concept selection; conceptual combination; idea generation; idea evaluation; implementation planning; and monitoring. It is beyond the scope of this discussion to go into detail on each of these innovation activities, yet it must be acknowledged that these activities are not suggested as being linear, rote, stages. Although there is a rough path provided, the model recognizes that each activity necessarily impacts the others. For example, in the process of evaluating a project (a later stage activity), the project team may realize the need to go back and gather further information (an earlier stage activity). Moreover, monitoring activities (a later activity) may reveal new opportunities (an early activity) for future projects. Thus, congruent with work by Fink and colleagues (1992), innovation is an iterative set of actions.

Although each of the eight stages will be discussed in our conceptualization of planning, they will be roughly categorized into four core sets of activities which will, in turn, set the stage for framing the four basic sub-plans necessary for innovation planning. These activities are:

1. identifying opportunities,
2. generating viable solutions,
3. evaluating viability of projects, and
4. successfully implementing projects.

It is important, however, to bear in mind that that these four basic activities represent a heuristic for discussion and should not be taken as being a rote plan of action for all innovative endeavors.

Project Based Activities

Although process models of creativity and innovation are useful as a starting point for understanding which activities are necessary for innovation to occur, a few additional points must be made regarding their application to understanding planning processes. First, with respect to the generation of single ideas, several activities can prove largely unpredictable and, as such, cannot be planned for with a systematic regularity. Idea generation and idea development, in particular, are notoriously challenging and unpredictable activities (Simonton, 1999). Thus, we will focus our discussion of innovation activities within a project-based framework (Mumford et al., 2008). Projects differ from simple idea generation and development in at least four key ways. First, projects involve multiple ideas revolving around a central theme or model (Mumford et al., 2008). Second, projects fit within the framework of an organization (Gruber & Wallace, 1999). Third, projects are larger in scope and, as a result, require integration among multiple parties underscoring the need for elements such as teamwork and collaboration (Abra, 1994; Dunbar, 1995). Finally, because of the complex nature of innovation, projects will prove relatively expensive and time-consuming (Nohari & Gulatti, 1996). Thus, in contrast to simple idea generation, project-based innovation activities are more suitable as a basis for a discussion on planning.

INTEGRATING PLANNING PROCESSES AND INNOVATION ACTIVITIES

Integrating planning processes and innovation activities requires careful consideration of two key points. First, each set of innovation activities have, at their core, differing—albeit inextricably related—goals. For example, early innovation activities center on finding and defining emerging opportunities (Baughman et al., 1995). Later activities, in contrast, aim to determine how to successfully implement project ideas (Mumford et al., 1991). What must also be borne in mind is that although these goals may be unique, their completion serves as key sources of input for all other innovation activities. Each of these activities, then, is inextricably bound to one another and requires input from each other for successful completion.

The second point to bear in mind is that planning begins with the identification of goals—that is, what will be planned for (Hammond, 1990; Pea, 1982; Friedman & Scholnick, 1997). As such, due to the requirements of differing goals, a single, broad innovation plan would be insufficient. Instead, to achieve each of the unique goals, multiple sub-plans are required for successful innovation—sub-plans that help to inform other on-going innovation activities. A brief view of these sub plans is presented in Table 20.1.

Before turning to a discussion of each of these sub-plans, however, it is important to address how goals are instantiated. The specific nature of goals may emerge via a number of mechanisms. Organizations might, for example, examine best practices among competitors. By examining what known innovators are doing, the exact nature of the goals necessary for beginning the planning process might emerge (Radnor & Robinson, 2000). In addition, examining the strengths and weaknesses of competitors' products and processes, new ideas may emerge as to how to innovate to gain previously-held market share. A recent example of this can be found in Target's implementation of retail groceries, a similar move made by its rival Wal-Mart over a decade before. However, Target, understanding its customer as a health-conscious and environmentally aware individual, adapted Wal-Mart's strategy to offer more organic and fresh produce—a clear innovation on what a competitor had already done. Although benchmarking may be useful for many aspects of performance, it may at times prove limited with respect to

TABLE 20.1 Sub-Plans Comprising the Broader Plan for Innovation.

Goal(s)	Sub-Plan 1	Sub-Plan 2	Sub-Plan 3	Sub-Plan 4
	Identify and define emerging opportunities	Generate viable solutions or project prototypes	Critically evaluate the viability of projects	Determine how to successfully implement projects
Foundations for goal instantiation	Fundamentals driven by broadly defined capabilities	Fundamentals emphasizing generative components	Benchmarking and fundamentals	Benchmarking and fundamentals
Innovation activities	Opportunity identification; Information gathering	Concept selection; Conceptual combination; Idea generation	Idea evaluation and refinement	Implementation planning; Monitoring
Sample of specific innovation activities	Scanning; Trend analysis; Customer feedback; Focus groups; Supplier feedback	Brainstorming sessions; Sketching; CAD model development	Focus group analysis Prototyping–testing; Sales forecasting	Market analysis; Cost determination; Supplier negotiation; Consumer follow-up
Key planning processes	Cases chosen; Identification of key causes	Back-up plan development	Identification of causes, resources, restrictions, contingencies, and actions; Forecasting/prognosis	Identification of key causes; Plan refinement
Key planning requirements	Leadership	Context and Expertise	Resources	Networks and alliances
Plan specificity	Low–Moderate	Low	Moderate	High

innovation. That is, to develop new and novel endeavors, benchmarks may simply not exist detailing how to define novel goals. Moreover, by relying only on what others are doing, an organization will inherently be bound to their competitors with little hope of radically changing the business landscape through innovation. Thus, in addition to paying attention to what competitors (and collaborators) might be doing, we also suggest that goals be determined via an explicit consideration of technical fundamentals—or problems framed very broadly and that span an organization's infrastructure (Hughes, 1989; Mumford et al., 2008). This is nicely illustrated in DuPont's success in developing synthetic fibers—a decision made after carefully considering whether it would be fruitful to pursue polymer chemistry (Smith & Hounshell, 1998). The decision was made, in part, because a pursuit of the fundamental would contribute to a number of product areas the organization had already invested in.

The use of extant technical fundamentals for the basis of developing goals (or themes) has three basic advantages. The first is that they allow organizations to ensure that successful projects can help drive success in other projects (Mumford et al., 2008). That is, because projects have a common scaffolding driven by the broadly-based fundamental, success in one area can often readily translate to other projects. Second, because fundamentals are relatively stable, they allow for a sustained and profitable approach to innovation. Along similar lines, fundamentals can be defined in emerging areas, yet their growth is typically long-term

(Simon, 1993). Finally, due to their broad nature, fundamentals help ensure congruence among products, markets, and core competences (Mumford et al., 2008). The use of fundamentals as the foundation for goal determination underscores the importance of maintaining a project portfolio—or collection of related projects (Feldman, 1999; Gruber & Wallace, 1999). Turning to our next section, we contend that the success of each of these projects, as well as the project portfolio as a whole, is driven by appropriate development of four sub-plans.

SUB-PLANS FOR INNOVATION

As may be seen in Table 20.1, the varying goals of each activity group help dictate the generation of sub-plans, labeled 1–4. The key planning processes for each sub-plan will be examined in greater detail below, but one aspect of Table 20.1 warrants immediate discussion. Namely, note that each of the sub-plans will vary with degree of specificity (Mumford et al., 2001, 2008). Generally speaking, plans developed for early innovation activities will be more loosely defined than those at later stages of development. This flexibility allows for the identification of additional opportunities and options (Berg, Strough, Calderone, Sansone, & Weir, 1998; Goldin & Hayes-Roth, 1980). In a think-aloud study on planning processes, for example, Patalano and Seifert (1997) found that participants who generated mid-range plans (i.e., less specific plans) as opposed to specific plans recognized a greater number of alternative opportunities for goal attainment. In contrast, plans for implementation can be more tightly constructed and serve to improve efficiency and maximize performance in addition to providing feedback on other ongoing planning activities.

A second point worth noting is that the development of sub-plan goals should be driven by varying emphases on fundamentals (Mumford et al., 2008). For example, determining how to identify and define emerging opportunities may be best served by focusing on fundamentals that emphasize an organization's current (and emerging) technical capabilities. In contrast, when developing the specific goals for producing unique solutions, fundamentals with a greater degree of generative potential should be used. Finally, as plans and projects move forward in the innovation process, it will be critical to focus on the use of fundamentals when developing goals and themes, but it will also serve organizations well to consider what practices other organizations are engaging in to maximize exploitative capabilities.

Turning now to the specific sub-plans required for innovation, it is important to consider that these plans should not be taken to represent the *only* set of sub-plans innovative organizations might engage in. Rather, as noted earlier, these plans represent groupings of key innovation activities that serve as heuristics for the approach organizations may take in successful implementation of an innovation strategy. In this way, they serve to guide our discussion rather than provide a prescribed set of planning tasks each organization must engage in.

Sub-Plan 1—Determining How Emerging Opportunities will be Found

Before project ideas can be generated, designers must first understand what they are developing creative solutions for (Amabile, 1996; Baughman & Mumford, 1995; Wallas, 1926). That is, creative teams must adequately understand the design problem before viable ideas come to fruition. Thus, a key innovation activity is identifying potential opportunities that require novel solutions. One means of identifying opportunities is through examination of what is happening in the broader context, a process referred to as environmental scanning. This activity is nicely illustrated by Souitaris (2001) who investigated innovation in 105 organizations, and found that environmental scanning (e.g., gathering customer and supplier feedback, monitoring competitors, analyzing market trends, and technology monitoring) was significantly related to the implementation of innovative processes.

Although gathering information and scanning for potential opportunities and threats play a key role in defining the problems to be solved, one important point should be noted: precisely how this is conducted in organizations may vary substantially. An in-depth case analysis of Nissan's design team, for example, reveals that market analysis proved of only modest utility when developing radically innovative solutions (Hirschberg, 1999). Instead, bringing customers into the design shop and discussing needs proved more useful in this particular situation. Additionally, engineers gained a great deal of insight from simply examining their own behavior as they interacted with several vehicles in the design shop. Thus, techniques, tools, and methods will vary across organizations, yet the fundamental need to view and understand innovation opportunities holds true across nearly every domain and context.

Key Planning Processes

Having established the importance of the above innovation activities, we turn now to the key planning activities that will allow for successful accomplishment of associated goals. As is the case with all four sub-plans in this chapter, each of the planning processes illustrated in Figure 20.1 will prove to be important in the achievement of specific sub-plan goals. However, two planning processes appear to be particularly important for the successful implementation of sub-plan 1. First, the nature and type of opportunities sought will be largely driven by the previous experiences, or cases, of the planners. That is, individuals tend to view the world in ways which are consistent with their previous experiences.

Consider, for example, the missed opportunity of early email by IBM's and Sears' collaborative effort, Prodigy (Christensen & Raynor, 2003). In the early 90s, Prodigy developed a digital infrastructure to enable business transaction via a network—a novel approach at the time. The organization quickly realized, however, that many of their customers were using the network to send electronic notes to one another rather than conduct business. They then made the mistake of applying their previous model of focusing on business transactions and decided to charge users who sent over 30 electronic notes per month. Not surprisingly, users were not happy with this restriction and Prodigy did not perform well as a result. In contrast, America Online (AOL) applied a more novel case to view the emerging electronic communication changes and email was, in many ways, born. This example illustrates that the cases selected for guiding the formation of this sub-plan appear to be of notable importance.

The second, particularly important planning process is the identification of key causes. Along the lines of the paragraph above, planners who are charged with identifying opportunities will make decisions as to what the key driving factors are in the opportunity. Coca-Cola's oft-cited error in decision making centering on the introduction of "New Coke" in the 1980s serves as a useful illustration (Oliver, 1986). The decision to change formulae came about, in large part, because decision makers presented focus groups blind taste tests of the original product (later branded "Coke Classic") in contrast to "New Coke", which had a notably sweeter formula. Focus groups reported an overwhelming preference for the sweeter formula. Leaders believed the driving factor (i.e., key cause) in soft-drink choice was taste and decided to change the formula based on this viewpoint. Although taste was certainly part of the consumer decision, the organization quickly realized when profits plummeted that other driving factors (e.g., brand loyalty) were non-trivial driving factors. Their error, then, rested in incorrectly determining the key driving factors in consumer choice.

In addition to decision-making, the identification of key causes has a number of implications for the type of expertise and resources obtained by the organization. That is, determining the key causes influences plan generation and, by proxy, resource allocation. These resources will play substantial roles in the capabilities of the organization in both the short and long term. The acquisition of appropriate resources—expertise in particular—is a key component of successful innovation (Ericsson & Charness, 1994; Weisberg, 1999).

Sub-Plan 2—Determining How to Generate Viable Solutions

Once opportunities are found and reasonably researched, work may begin on the generation of viable project solutions. Innovation activities pursued in this sub-plan may range from simple concept selection, choosing which ideas to focus on, to developing concrete solutions in the form of working project prototypes. The emphasis in this set of innovation activities is putting pen to paper—beginning to generate viable solutions.

Key Planning Processes

Although all planning processes will prove to be important, when determining how an organization will go about generating solutions, planners must focus on developing a host of back-up plans. It is important to keep in mind that not every idea generated by the team in the innovation stage will prove useful and as a result, planning for sessions that elicit alternative solutions or prototypes will prove critical. A few select brainstorming sessions may result in wonderfully novel solutions, for example, and other sessions may simply fall flat resulting in few workable projects. It will prove critical to try multiple means of stimulating project ideas.

As an illustration, consider a rather unique approach to facilitating idea generation employed by a number of organizations. This approach, at times referred to as a "Skunk Works", is modeled after Lockheed Martin's facility, which was utilized during WWII to develop highly innovative solutions away from potential naysayers in the larger organizational facilities. To develop a radically new mobile phone, for example, Motorola took many of its best engineers to a remote facility for approximately 12 months, resulting in a nearly revolutionary mobile phone called the "Razr" in a time period unprecedented by other phone designers (Kao, 2007). Along similar lines, Apple built a "Skunk Works" facility within the organization when designing the original iPod.

Other organizations have taken alternative approaches. Pixar, for example, works to establish a playful environment where spontaneity and collaborative idea-sharing can drive novel thinking (Catmull, 2008). Leaders at Google have set aside roughly one day a week to allow their employees to explore their own ideas. Known as the 20% rule, the results of this effort have given rise to a number of unique creative solutions at the organization (Vise & Malseed, 2007). Thus, there exists no precise template for how to generate ideas—planning for multiple approaches will be necessary as well as possessing the capacity and willingness to try several methods.

Along these lines, one particularly noteworthy point about planning for this innovation activity should be reiterated. Namely it will prove very difficult to plan exactly *how* ideas will be generated. Thus, forming a plan for this innovation activity should not place excessive weight on the specific details as to how this goal will be achieved (Hayes-Roth & Hayes-Roth, 1979; Kuipers et al., 1988). Planners must realize that some innovation activities will vary so greatly that planning for their specific occurrence will prove less than useful. In many ways, planning should emphasize the means to establish an environment where idea generation can occur and to allow emerging ideas to be captured. Again, it will be necessary for planners to develop and utilize a number of back-up plans to achieve the innovation activity goal of project idea generation. Simply put, some plans will work—others will not.

Sub-Plan 3—Determining How to Critically Evaluate the Project Viability

During the idea generation phases, several viable projects will typically be brought to the table. At this point, decision-makers must choose which ideas will receive support, and which ideas will be either discarded or shelved for future consideration. Thus, it is critical to develop a sub-plan that outlines how these evaluative decisions will be made. Failure to do so can mean an organization is continually wasting valuable resources on projects that may not prove useful. It is also important to note that these decisions are made on novel or new projects—projects that have few comparison products with which to assess value. Accordingly, the decisions made during these innovation activities may prove particularly difficult and planning, as a result, may be especially helpful (Kitchell, 1995; Licuanan, Dailey, & Mumford, 2007).

In the applied and management literatures, there has been a great deal of work put into the development and assessment of tools to help with this key innovation activity. Perhaps the most widely used is the stage gate model put forth by Cooper and colleagues (Cooper, 1994, 2000; Cooper & Kleinschmidt, 2000; Cooper, Edgett, & Kleinschmidt, 2002), although other notable tools include road-mapping (Radnor & Probert, 2004) and quality function deployment or QFD (Ettlie & Johnson, 1994). A report on the use of stage gate models suggests that nearly 70% of organizations have used some form of these tools (Griffin, 1997).

Although the approaches vary, these models may be depicted as decision-making tools that outline when, and under what conditions, ideas should be admitted to later stages of production. They are intended to guide the innovation process and limit wasted resources on projects not viewed as viable by pre-determined criteria—criteria that are often, although not exclusively, economically based.

For many organizations, models akin to the stage gate approach have proved useful in helping to determine which ideas are of value (e.g., Ettlie & Elsenbach, 2007; Ettlie & Johnson, 1994). An overemphasis on the rigid application of such models, however, is likely to hamper the generation of highly innovative or "radical" new ideas. For example, an investigation of 120 projects using the stage gate approach revealed that rigid application of evaluation criteria limited the flexibility and learning capacity of those organizations and project teams (Sethi & Iqbal, 2008). Researchers also observed that this failure to learn was found to negatively impact the market performance of new products. Thus, on the whole, evaluative tools may prove useful for those organizations that do not apply them too rigidly—a point noted by advocates of such models (e.g., Ettlie & Elsenbach, 2007).

Key Planning Processes

Two planning processes appear particularly important when determining how an organization will assess the potential value of projects and ideas. First, cases selected as starting points, typically derived from previous experience, will have a significant impact on the causes, resource restrictions, contingencies, and actions identified as critical to plan execution. For example, Hitt, Hoskisson, Johnson and Moesel (1996) found that using financial standards to appraise project ideas tended to inhibit innovative performance. However, the findings on evaluation standards are mixed. Lonergan and colleagues (2004) found that applying efficiency and quality standards to highly novel ideas lead to better results, while applying novelty and creativity standards to more rote ideas also lead to better results. It seems then, that decision makers need to be flexible in the type of standards they apply, drawing from a pool of evaluation tools to complement the idea at hand.

A second key process for the successful execution of this sub-plan is the mental simulation of how projects will "play out" in the future (i.e., forecasting/prognosis). That is, for successful evaluation of novel ideas, leaders and decision makers must be able to view new ideas with, pardon the pun, a novel perspective (Mumford et al., 2007). This point underscores the key importance of creative thinking skills in leaders (Mumford et al., 2003), nicely illustrated by O'Connor (1998) who found that the success of highly radical projects could be traced back to a leader who was able to forecast the downstream consequences of the project.

Sub-Plan 4—Determining How to Successfully Implement Projects

With a viable project chosen, planning turns to determining how these products will be manufactured, marketed, and sold. Successful planners must carefully consider, for example, which previous marketing plans functioned well and assess the current status of the business climate. Decision makers must also forecast initial sales to guide supplier relationships and manufacturing practices. Distribution activities, moreover, must be considered and price points carefully calculated. Consider, for example, the current mobile phone industry where higher end "smart phones" are typically offered at reduced rates if they are paired with a provider agreement—often up to two years (or more) in length. This contractual agreement requires a careful consideration of price point and projected sales as well as a great deal of trust, communication, and contingency planning with service providers. Clearly, implementing an innovation is not a simple matter.

Planning, moreover, does not stop when the product is sold. Once products have been distributed, organizations must carefully monitor their innovations. As an illustration, consider Nintendo's introduction of their popular gaming console, the Wii. The novel nature of the motion controls characterizing the system was new to consumers, and it was unclear how the system would, in practice, be utilized by families. Through careful monitoring, Nintendo quickly realized that some overzealous gamers were swinging the rather stout gaming controllers a bit too wildly, despite specific warnings against doing so. In response, the organization sent free rubberized safety coverings for these controllers to limit the damage to property and persons (Yam, 2007). Future releases of the consoles, moreover, included the controllers already pre-wrapped in the protective covering. Thus, successful implementation of projects does not end once the product is released—as is the case with nearly all aspects of innovation, their implementation is an ongoing, dynamic activity.

Key Planning Processes

When determining how an idea will be built, marketed, and sold at least two processes appear particularly important. First, identifying the key causes, or driving forces, to successful plan implementation are paramount. In the case of planning for project implementation, key "causes" will typically center on why the product will sell and to whom. This information, in turn, helps guide who is chosen to develop marketing plans and how the product will be sold. Take, for example, Apple's approach toward selling iPhones and Mac computers. Apple was keenly aware that, among other things, Mac, iPod, and iPhone users were a unique group who viewed themselves differently to more common PC users. Thus, given their unique identity, Apple decided to explore the idea that their customers would prefer their own stores—an approach that has proven successful (Useem, 2007). What is critical here is that Apple knew who would be buying their products, and why—they understood the key causes and developed an implementation plan around those causes.

The second key planning process is the capacity for plan refinement. Using our aforementioned examples of monitoring products after they are released, it is clear that although initial plans provide a place to begin, organizations must be prepared to make revisions to the plan (Mumford et al., 2008). In fact, in the cases of safety issues such as tire failure at Firestone, airbag malfunctions at Honda, and brake and accelerator defects at Toyota, the sooner an organization can refine their plan, the fewer lawsuits and potentially bad press may result.

INTEGRATING SUB-PLANS INTO A BROADER PLAN FOR INNOVATION

Although useful to consider each of these sub-plans independently, it is the aggregate of these efforts that comprise an organization's overall plan for innovation. More central to the present effort, however, is how these plans—and the knowledge gathered from them—inform, guide, and influence all planning processes. A core theme throughout the chapter is that planning is an on-going activity and one that requires flexibility and the capacity to adjust depending on emerging circumstances. In fact, along with several other scholars, we contend that, to sustain innovation over the long-term, organizations must be in continual states of planning and monitoring each of the sub-plans outlined earlier (Franklin & Bower, 1988; Hayes-Roth & Hayes-Roth, 1979; Patalano & Siefert, 1997). Recall that this suggestion stands in contrast to a staged or gated model where ideas move in relative lock step through the system (Cooper, 2000). Thus, we contend that successfully planning for innovation requires the purposeful and intentional integration of these ongoing activities. Unfortunately, such integration is often easier said than done.

The challenges to this integration are expressed by Hirschberg (1999) who, while leading the development of a new line of trucks at Nissan, lamented that discussing design options with sales or marketing groups was disallowed at the time. As head of design he realized that such communication was necessary and, discreetly, engaged in conversations with individuals within sales and marketing. These exchanges revealed that, although truck-owners were very knowledgeable about truck-specific capabilities (e.g., towing capacity, bed-size), most trucks were used primarily for transportation and "not as trucks" (p. 198)—owners actually used their vehicles as "trucks" only 25% of the time. This informal feedback drove the design priorities for the truck and resulted in a highly innovative, and financially successful, outcome. What must be realized here is that information from later stage planning processes, in this case marketing and sales, was critical to early and mid-stage planning processes. With this in mind, we discuss some of the key integrating activities across sub-plans.

The first key integration activity flows nicely from the above discussion, in that feedback from implementation can often serve to guide future opportunity recognition. That is, once a project has been implemented and is being monitored for success, this information can prove particularly valuable to early-stage innovation planning activities. Take another example from the Nintendo developed gaming console, the Wii, discussed earlier. Decision makers at Nintendo noticed that customers were swinging their controllers in a rather wild fashion and in the process, forgetting they were playing a game (hence the injury and property damage). This information proved useful for game developers who began to include exercise or active elements into their game designs. In fact, the exercise "games" are now a burgeoning industry (Inskeep, 2008). Thus, when planners are seeking to determine how opportunities will be found, in addition to relying on previous cases of market research and focus groups, they must also target cases emerging from late-stage monitoring activities.

The second key integration activity also centers on opportunity recognition, where planning processes can result in the identification of longer-term needs. That is, in addition to providing decision makers with input on who must be hired for designing a product or process (the next sequential stage in the innovation process), this information can cue leaders into what strategic partnerships might be required for implementing a project, or collection of projects, down the road. Planning processes involved in opportunity recognition, then, help inform both short-term and longer-term needs.

A third integration activity that will prove paramount in the planning process is the relationship between evaluation and generation (Fink et al., 1992). When projects are evaluated and decisions made as to which are worth pursuing, this feedback can have implications for revising the present project or, perhaps more critically, revising other on-going projects. An organization that designs and manufactures mobile phones, for example, may find in the testing phase that battery life negates the design of the phone. This information might help inform ways to refine that specific product, but may also have implications for other ongoing phone models or other products that employ the use of the same battery (e.g., music players, personal organizers). Thus, although ideas must be generated before they can be evaluated, highly successful projects are often brought about via feedback from the evaluation stages.

Although other integration activities are important, the above should suffice to make our basic point: neither innovation nor planning for it are linear activities (Bonissone, Dutta, & Wood, 1994; Hayes-Roth & Hayes-Roth, 1979; Patalano & Seifert, 1997). We contend that an ongoing, iterative planning approach that simultaneously engages multiple sub-plans is required for sustained innovation (Mumford et al., 2008). Specifically, two points about these sub-plans should be considered. First, early planning processes can impact longer-term processes, and not simply the next stage of the innovation activity. In this way, a staged model is limited with respect to capturing this informative feedback. Moreover, later processes help inform earlier processes and thus, feedback within the planning system is required. On the whole, in contrast to gated or stage models, we contend that planning is better characterized by Figure 20.2.

A second point partially illustrated by Figure 20.2 also warrants specific discussion. Namely, it is important to bear in mind that sustained innovation in an organization is built

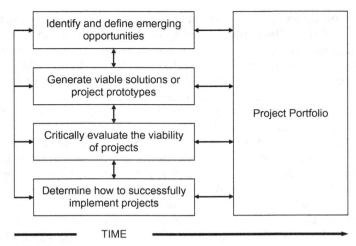

FIGURE 20.2 Simultaneous sub-plan model for innovation.

upon the development of a balanced project portfolio (Estrin, 2009). That is, organizations should have multiple projects at varying stages in the research and production pipeline (Sharma, 1999) and these projects, moreover, should be built upon some degree of common scaffolding (Topalian, 2000). By building projects around common themes and frameworks, resources can be freed for the exploration of potentially radical or disruptive (Christensen, 1997) ideas. Common scaffolding helps to allow for capital to pursue congruent ideas fully rather than many, disjointed ideas, poorly. More central to the present effort is that each of the sub-plans and their resulting information help inform not only other planning activities, but also the project portfolio itself. Moreover, the nature of the project portfolio helps to guide ongoing planning efforts (Mumford et al., 2008).

INTEGRATING PLANNING AND ONGOING ORGANIZATIONAL ACTIVITIES

Innovative endeavors do not occur in an organizational vacuum and as such it is important to bear in mind that decision makers often have pressing organizational activities to be concerned with, in addition to producing the next new and novel product. In fact, several paradox-based models of innovation suggest that its pursuit—which requires freedom, risk-permissiveness, and latitude—may run at odds with traditional organizational functions which often emphasize low cost, efficiency, and productivity (Bledow et al., 2009; Hunter, Thoroughgood, Myers, & Ligon, in press; Mumford & Hunter, 2005). For example, Hunter and colleagues (in press) reported 14 unique paradoxes that occur in the pursuit of innovation. One example is the *autonomy/control paradox* which occurs when organizations must promote autonomy in the creative process but control and efficiency in other organizational endeavors.

Perhaps the most well known paradox model of innovation and learning was put forth in the seminal work by March (1991) who used the terms exploration and exploitation to describe the, at times, opposing processes of exploring novel ideas and exploiting the ideas that have proven valuable. The exploitation/exploration model of innovation has become a foundation for understanding many of the innovation processes in organizations (Gupta, Smith, & Shalley, 2006; Jansen, Temelaar, Van den Bosch, & Valberda, 2009; Peretti & Negro, 2006; Taylor & Greve, 2006). This work underscores the importance of considering how a strategy for innovation—and planning processes more specifically—fit within a broader organizational backdrop. Not only is innovation a challenging endeavor, but its pursuit can also result in significant tension within the organization.

Not surprisingly, resolution of these tensions is a challenging affair. Fortunately, there are some noteworthy solutions emerging from academic research as well as the applied community. For example, the *autonomy/control paradox* may be resolved by permitting autonomy on some tasks but not on others. As an illustration, known innovators Google and 3M allow their employees to take approximately one day a week to work on their own ideas while working on organizational-driven ideas the remainder of their time—an approach that has proven highly valuable and profitable (Vise & Malseed, 2006). Other resolutions, such as those emerging from the exploration/exploitation paradox have been the source of fruitful academic debate. Some authors, such as Tushman and O'Reilly (1996) and Benner and Tushman (2003) have suggested that this ambidextrous balancing act be a simultaneous affair—that organizations continually explore and exploit ideas. Others have contended that the balancing act be a cyclical affair, where periods of exploration and exploitation follow one anther (Burgelman, 2002).

Other solutions to the natural tensions that can emerge when planning for innovation may be tied to an organization's business model (McGrath, 2009). Teece (2009) outlined several business models used in successful innovation that range from full production where ideas are generated and produced within the organization, to more licensing-based models, where ideas are generated and wholly sent out to be manufactured by other organizations. Nestled between these models is a hybrid approach where some combination is used. What is particularly noteworthy about the consideration of business models and innovation is that some core tensions or paradoxes may be resolved through a change in how business is conducted. If an organization is having challenges in promoting a culture that is based on efficiency, but also charged with promoting a culture that is accepting of risk and error, then it may be useful to outsource some manufacturing activities, allowing for a more natural culture and focus on creative thinking. Innovation powerhouse IDEO, for example, is able to produce highly creative thinking while not engaging in significant manufacturing activities (Kelley, 2001).

In summary, it is important to keep in mind that innovation and the process of planning for it are not isolated activities. They occur within an organization that is often made of multiple divisions with unique requirements that run counter to the needs of innovative endeavors. The development of innovation plans, then, must consider these requirements and balance the needs of all activities. This stage of the planning process may reveal that the organization is not flexible enough to pursue a strategy based around innovation, and it may simply be that innovation is not worth pursuing. This decision is a critical one and must take the broader needs of the organization into consideration when being made. Successful innovation plans, moreover, will purposefully consider broader organizational activities to identify any potential roadblocks or severe tensions that might emerge.

Although it is impossible to anticipate every problem, active engagement in problem identification can minimize the negative effects from these often opposing activities.

PLANNING REQUIREMENTS FOR ORGANIZATIONS: WHAT SUCCESSFUL PLANS NEED

Although each of the sub-plans discussed have their own unique challenges, there are some common requirements among them. Successful planning for innovation—as well as innovation itself—is contingent on at least five key organizational requirements:

1. expertise,
2. leadership,
3. context,
4. resources, and
5. networks.

We discuss each of these in greater detail below.

Expertise

At the heart of effective planning is having appropriate information to make decisions, allocate resources, and guide creative efforts. Too much information, however, can prove unwieldy. It is critical for leaders and decision makers to have information structured in such a way as to prove useful to the planning process. Experts, by having well-formed and efficient mental models, can help provide this structure and serve as essential components in plan formation. Experts are able to identify potential problems, recognize long-term needs, and know when contingency plans should be implemented. Although leaders must have a significant amount of expertise themselves (Weisberg, 1999), the complexity of innovation dictates that they cannot be experts in every area of the planning process. Thus, decision-makers must surround themselves with people who possess high levels of knowledge and expertise—and be willing to listen to them (Estrin, 2009).

Along these lines, the challenge to planners is not, generally, utilizing expertise—it is determining what type of expertise is needed, when, and then obtaining it. One of the reasons a multi-stage plan for innovation is so critical is that early processes help to identify what type of expertise will be needed down the road. Acquiring this type of talent is not a trivial endeavor, nor is it one that happens quickly. In fact, there is some indication that leaders are served well by building a cadre of expertise (Mumford et al., 2002b). This group of core experts can prove useful in the tumultuous, often unpredictable activities characterizing innovation (Root-Bernstein, Bernstein, & Garnier, 1995). Google provides an excellent example of broad expert acquisition, where a decision-maker recently met a group of voice-recognition experts outside of the company. These experts were hired by the organization without an explicit understanding of what project they would be working on. Rather, decision-makers realized that the skill set would prove useful within Google's portfolio of projects. So far, the decision has proved fruitful, leading to the development of Google's voice-driven search capacities, which are particularly popular within the burgeoning smart phone industry (Estrin, 2009).

Leadership

With respect to who is doing the planning, leaders are either the primary guiding force in the endeavor or have, at a minimum, significant input on decision making during the planning process (Farris, 1972; Tierney, Farmer, & Graen, 1999; West et al., 2003). In this regard, leaders play substantial roles in both successful planning and successful innovation. Such an observation begs the question as to which aspects of leadership are critical to the planning process.

One of primary capabilities a leader must possess in order to successfully plan for innovation is a strong set of creative thinking skills (Mumford et al., 2007; Tierney et al., 1999). These skills serve leaders well in planning for two primary reasons. First, by being able to think outside the box, to see beyond what is readily apparent, a leader can observe value in novel ideas and allocate resources to their completion. In contrast, by relying on only those cases that have worked in the past, the likelihood of radical innovation is reduced. In addition, the second way creative thinking skills help leaders is by allowing them to provide input into the design process—particularly during evaluative and revision stages.

The above paragraph flows well into the second characteristic required for leaders associated with successful planning endeavors: expertise (Barnowe, 1975; Weisberg, 1999). A leader is of little use in the generation of novel ideas if they do not fully understand the problem (or opportunity) in hand. Put another way, decision makers must possess a reasonable level of technical expertise (Mumford et al., 2007). Bill Gates and Steve Jobs, for example, were particularly adept at aiding the development process of their respective products and Microsoft and Apple in part because they possessed the requisite technical expertise to do so. Moreover, leaders cannot allocate an organization's (limited) resources with any degree of accuracy or provide guidance to idea generation efforts without requisite leadership expertise—expertise often gained from experience in making decisions in leadership roles (Andrews & Farris, 1967; Mumford et al., 2002b).

Finally, leaders must possess the social skills to work with and engage a wide array of individuals that make up the innovation system (Keller, 2001; Mumford et al., 2002b). As has been noted throughout the chapter, a host of individuals within an organization have access to the information and knowledge necessary for successful innovation—from marketing teams, to sales groups, to engineers—each of which play a key role in the planning process. Leaders must be able to connect to this wide array of personalities in order to access the knowledge required for successful plan development (Hunter et al., in press). Perhaps more importantly, leaders must also establish a climate and context that supports the exchange of ideas among such constituencies. Hence, our next requirement for innovation planning: context.

Context

Perhaps one of the most important things a leader can do in the pursuit of innovation is to establish an environment that supports creative endeavors (Anderson & West, 1998). In a recent meta-analysis of over 40 studies on creative climate, for example, Hunter et al. (2007) found an average correlation of approximately .45 between climate and creative performance. With respect to planning, specifically, a climate that supports the exchange of information across disciplines and departments is particularly critical.

Although it is clear that context matters, exactly how to establish an environment where information is shared freely and comfortably is less clear. Certainly, as was discussed above, leadership matters to innovation. In particular, role modeling can serve to establish that novel thinking is welcomed and should be shared (Jaussi & Dionne, 2003; Mouly & Sankaran, 1999). Reward systems, in addition, can help indicate the importance of sharing ideas in the planning process. Although there is some debate around the use of rewards in creativity, when used effectively they are useful tools for indicating what behavior is appropriate (Byron, Khazanchi, & Nazarian, in press). Finally, the emergence of new technology, particularly communication tools, can help bridge barriers that once existed. This area of research is still emerging, but it is clear that advances in technology have begun to impact how we share ideas (Estrin, 2009; Fairchild, Cassidy, Cushenberry, & Hunter, in press).

Resources

Innovation is a costly endeavor that entails a substantial degree of risk. The vast majority of creative projects will fail and with them, substantial capital may be lost—particularly for those ideas that have reached later stages of production. Having the funds to support these attempts, however, is only part of the planning solution. Successful planning requires access to adequate resources—the raw materials with which to craft initial and contingency plans. Certainly expertise serves as a key human resource, but other resources also play a role, including manufacturing capacity, marketing networks, and quality of the organization's retail and sales force. Planning then, will require explicit knowledge of these capabilities—leaders must be expressly aware of what is possible and not possible within the organization (Cardinal, 2001; Howell & Boies, 2004; Hunter et al., in press). This type of organizational knowledge has been shown to be related to innovation in a variety of contexts (Li & Atuahene-Gima, 2001; Mitra, 2000; Sivadas & Dwyer, 2000).

Perhaps more fundamentally, resources in an organization allow planners to obtain and gather rich sources of data (Koberg, Uhlenbruck, & Sarason, 1996). Successful planning requires that leaders must have access to issues such as market readiness, cost of project efforts, direct and indirect returns, synergies with other efforts, and strategic positioning (Mumford et al., 2007). Thus, an organization that has the resources to provide market research, trend analysis, and focus-group assessment will have, at least in part, the tools necessary for effective planning (Hirschberg, 1999).

Alliances, Networks, and Relationships

Opportunities for innovative solutions emerging, both now and in the future, will be characterized by an increasing degree of complexity. Thus, whereas previous planning efforts could remain largely within the organization, the opportunities of tomorrow will require collaborations among external agencies (Mitra, 2000). Gemunden, Heydenbreck, and Herden (1992), for example, found that alliance formation was positively related to performance in new product development efforts. Similarly, Allen and Cohen (1969) found that high performing R&D team members had a greater number of ties outside of the organization. Thus, congruent with our discussion on expertise, alliance formation or network development helps provide necessary input for planning and innovation (Adams & Day, 1998; Nellore & Balachandra, 2001).

In addition to external alliances, it is critical to have strong networks within the organization (Abra, 1994; Gassman & van Zedwitz, 2003). Recall our earlier example of Nissan's design team leader lamenting the challenges of interacting with members of other divisions within the organization (Hirschberg, 1999). By crossing organizational borders, leaders can have a much better picture of emerging opportunities and the design solutions for them.

SHIFTING REQUIREMENTS ACROSS SUB-PLANS

Although useful to discuss the requirements for successful planning as a whole, it is important to also discuss the shifts in key requirements across each of the sub-plans. As depicted in Table 20.1, although each requirement is useful for planning as a whole, they will play uniquely vital roles for each of the four sub-plans. Leadership, for example, will be particularly critical in the early phases of project development, where a vision or mission is necessary to move forward on novel projects (Mumford et al., 2003, 2007). In sub-plan two, both context and expertise will prove particularly important due to the unique nature of creativity, where the prospect of suggesting new and novel ideas can be met with some degree of apprehension. Thus, a climate that promotes psychological safety and comfort in sharing original, odd, or strange ideas is essential (Anderson & West, 1998; Hunter et al., 2007). Moreover, successful idea generation, particularly in conceptual combination activities, may also be enhanced by having reasonable diversity in expertise—teammates with unique backgrounds can help facilitate unique prototype generation (Ahuja, 2000; Taylor & Greve, 2006). Turning to sub-plan three, although resources are helpful across *all* forms of organizational functioning, they will play an even greater role in this sub-plan, where prototyping, testing, and evaluating can prove particularly costly. Additionally, resources that allow for rapid and rich evaluation can provide organizations with a significant advantage over those that might lag behind in testing and refinement (Mumford & Hunter, 2005). Finally, sub-plan four will be aided greatly by having a strong set of connections to external suppliers, customers, market analysts, and other collaborators (Adams & Day, 1998; Nellore & Balachandra, 2001) as well as effective network connections within the organization (Abra, 1994; Gassman, & van Zedwitz, 2003).

RECOMMENDATIONS FOR SUCCESSFUL PLANNING

Throughout the chapter we have outlined the key reasons why planning is important for successful innovation, presented the sub-plans necessary for an integrated innovation plan, and discussed the requirements and resources that may be useful for plan development. What has not been presented, however, is a set of guidelines for successful plan development. Although it would be useful to have an explicit list of executable tasks for innovation planning, the dynamic nature of the process precludes such concrete action items. Instead, in the following section we will outline five guidelines to aid in the planning process.

Guideline 1: Choose a Fundamental

The nature of successful innovation planning is that the plan will change as new opportunities arise, information is gathered, ideas are evaluated, and innovations are implemented. As such, pursuing—and planning for—a single idea or concept will prove less than useful for sustained innovation. Rather, innovation must be driven by something broader—a project portfolio driven by a fundamental that aligns projects and organizational strategy as well as fitting within current capabilities and organizational culture. Moreover, a fundamental (or small set of fundamentals) provides the foundation for goal instantiation which can then drive activities such as future talent and resource acquisition. Thus, leaders and decisions makers are well-served by choosing a core fundamental as a starting point for the innovation planning.

Guideline 2: Designate Leadership and Decision Making in the Planning Process

Planning requires informed decision making, typically by a single individual or relatively small leadership team. Because innovation is a process that is in a continual state of flux, information can frequently be lost in the often complex organizational system. When establishing an innovation plan, it will be critical to designate roles and responsibilities at the decision-making level with a particular emphasis on the planning process. In small organizations, the founder or CEO of the company may be the primary planning coordinator for innovation. In larger organizations, it will likely be necessary to establish heads of R&D, sales, or marketing, for example. Members of planning teams must also possess the requisite expertise described in earlier sections—technical, organizational, and leadership skills and expertise are essential for this group to succeed in identifying and developing plans for organizational innovation. What must also be kept in mind is that these decision makers must be cognizant of their roles and responsibilities in the planning process, and a direct effort must be made to enable lines of communication between these decision makers and the subordinates that work with them. It is simply too easy to become entrenched in our own activities and lose sight of the dynamic and resource intensive act of planning—it is critical to make it a priority and innovative organizations will invariably do so. Thus, formalizing roles as planning team members (through appraisal and compensation systems) should encourage members to see planning as critical components of their positions.

Guideline 3: Build Failure into the System

Although many aspects of innovation are not predictable, one thing most certainly is: successfully pursuing innovation means failing, and failing often. Bear in mind that we do not suggest that organizations actively pursue failure as an end, although this has been suggested by some. Rather, we suggest that leaders be aware that failure and innovation go hand in hand, and because of this it is critical that organizations actively manage this feature in several ways. First, organizations must learn from their mistakes—key information about a failure cannot be lost in the innovation process. Learning, however, requires that creative teams feel comfortable sharing their trials and tribulations—even those that did not turn out particularly well. It may be useful, for example, to celebrate high quality efforts that may have fallen short of commercial success—an activity engaged in by Hewlett Packard in their creative efforts (Berkun, 2007). Second, it is critical that leaders establish an environment where errors are recognized as part of the innovation process and are not to be feared. Doing so can facilitate high-risk efforts that have the potential to either pay off commercially, or feed back into the system as part of the planning process.

Guideline 4: Build Continual Evaluation into the System

As we have stressed throughout the chapter, planning is not a "set and forget" activity—it requires continual assessment about progress and resource capability. A sizable error that leaders make when planning for innovation is to spend significant time developing an initial plan and then failing to monitor progress and utilize contingency plans when it becomes necessary to do so. Successful planning, particularly with respect to innovation, requires explicit dedication to evaluation and refinement. In other words, leaders must be flexible and continually examine ways in which that flexibility is required.

Guideline 5: Build the Bottle, Don't Create the Lightning

On the surface, it may appear that planning for innovation is analogous to creating the lightning that stereotypically epitomizes creative thinking. In reality, however, a leader's job is to establish an environment where lightning *can* occur by ensuring that talented individuals are interacting with each other on a frequent basis and they have the resources around them to fully and continually pursue novel ideas. Perhaps more importantly, it is critical that leaders create an environment where, once novel ideas are generated, they can be capitalized upon. Thus, the process of innovation planning can better be thought of as building the bottle to capture the lightning. Put another way, leaders must bear in mind that they cannot set their watches to the time that lightning will strike, but can ensure that once it does, it doesn't slip away in the chaos of organizational life.

CONCLUSIONS AND FUTURE RESEARCH

Before turning to the broader conclusions of the chapter, a few key limitations must be noted. First, we have taken a cross-domain perspective in examining planning and did not address the issue of domain specificity in innovation (Baer, 2003; Csikszentmihályi, 1999). Such a discussion would have proved unwieldy and limited the practical utility of the chapter. Moreover, although certain planning processes will be more or less emphasized in varying domains, the general recommendations and observations hold consistently across markets, contexts, and organizations.

Second, we discussed four primary innovation activities and the planning requirements for their achievement. Although we used the condensed eight-stage model (Mumford et al., 1991) as our framework, other models of innovation activities may have led to varying conclusions and discussions (e.g., Amabile, 1996; Fink et al., 1992; Lubart, 2001; Taylor, Austin, & Sutton, 1974). In this way, our discussion represents one of several that may center on the topic of innovation. Even with the application of alternative models, however, the key innovation activities discussed would remain relatively consistent across conceptualizations. Thus, although labeling might change or certain tasks may be emphasized differently, the activities which are required for innovation will, broadly speaking, remain the same. Along these lines, the planning processes required for innovation are also generally congruent with varying conceptualizations of creative processes.

Third and finally, the stage gate models and related approaches to planning were discussed in a general aggregate fashion. Space did not permit examination of each approach—or their variants—in substantial detail and this terse view stands as a limitation of the chapter. With this in mind, the reader should be aware that not every stage gate, road-mapping, or quality function deployment model is equivalent. In fact, some researchers and practitioners employ the use of such models using many of the approaches discussed in this chapter. It is important, when seeking tools to aid the planning process, that each approach be viewed, and evaluated on its own merit and not dismissed based on label alone. With these limitations being noted, we turn now to the broader conclusions emerging from the present effort.

Broader Conclusions

The first and most straightforward point emerging from the present effort is that planning for innovation will lack utility for those organizations not committed to this resource-intensive activity. Planning is not a "set and forget" activity—leaders cannot develop a plan and put the innovation to function on autopilot. Planning in general requires constant monitoring. Planning for *innovation* requires even greater attention and flexibility.

For those willing to invest this time and energy, however, planning for innovation can provide leaders with a useful means to create movement toward an innovation strategy. The tendency to avoid the often risk-saturated opportunities characterizing innovation means some guidance is necessary to put organizations on a creative path. The development of innovation plans, even with their complexity and need for near constant attention, provide this "push" necessary for moving toward unknown territory.

A third broad point emerging from the present effort is that the various activities required for innovation dictate the development and execution of various sub-plans in the pursuit of an overall plan for innovation. Commitment to each of these sub-plans ensures that organizations are working toward the main activities characterizing innovation. Moreover, the point most central to this chapter is that planning processes must inform other planning activities. This exchange allows for the necessary refinement and adjustment characterizing successful planning efforts (Hayes-Roth & Hayes-Roth, 1979).

Future Research

One of the most exciting areas for future research and planning is the emergence of new technologies that may aid in the sharing of information and, in turn, facilitate novel idea exchange. The growing existence of social networking sites, instant messaging, twitter feeds, text-messaging, and even simple email means that we are nearly always in contact with potential collaborators. Moreover, in what might be seen as a revamped version of the suggestion box, emerging forms of technology allow for anonymous exchanges, limiting the potential fear of suggesting "odd", but potentially useful, ideas. Still other forms of technology are shaping the nature of the design process itself. Tools such as a concept generator (Bryant-Arnold et al., 2006) provide engineers with a database of parts, organized by characteristics chosen by the user (e.g., function, tolerance, etc.). Others, such as rapid prototyping machines, mean that organizations can move more quickly through the design process. The growing mantra of "fail faster to succeed sooner" (Kelley, 2001) means that problems can be identified more quickly and, more importantly, work can begin on solutions for them. All of the above have significant implications for future planning research and we hope efforts are made in these areas.

A second area for future research is tied to the increasingly rapid product development cycle noted above. Because products can be developed more quickly and have the potential to reach market in record time, there may be less time to evaluate the product relative to others in the portfolio. Such decisions have significant implications for current products that are in production. For example, in the early 1960s IBM made the calculated decision to pursue an operating system that had wide-ranging applicability for users. In doing so, however, they negated their entire product line (Estrin, 2009). Thus planning must consider the impact that potential projects might have on ongoing efforts. Although we recognize the importance of this issue, we know little about how planners calculate and best assess these critical decisions.

Finally, the growth of shared leadership in the leadership literature brings to the fore the emerging issue of shared planning efforts (Gronn, 2002). A recent study of 133 innovations emerging from engineering and manufacturing firms, for example, found that the quality and financial success of the innovative endeavors were stronger when multiple leaders were involved in the project (Hauschildt & Kirchmann, 2001). As organizations move toward shared leadership models, it will be important for researchers to examine the processes involved in shared decision-making and planning efforts.

In sum, although the debate surrounding the place of planning in an overall strategy for innovation is a reasonable one to have, planning represents a tool to manage the chaos that often surrounds innovation. Plans must be adaptive and flexible, and the various sub-plans must inform each other if planning is to be beneficial to organizations seeking to sustain an innovative-based competitive advantage. With a concerted and marked effort, however, we believe planning is a critical step toward an innovative end.

References

Abbey, A., & Dickson, J. (1983). R&D work climate and innovation in semiconductors. *Academy of Management Journal, 25,* 362–368.

Abra, J. (1994). Collaboration in creative work: An initiative for investigation. *Creativity Research Journal, 8,* 205–218.

Adams, J. E., & Day, G. S. (1998). Enhancing new product development performance: An organizational learning perspective. *Journal of Product Innovation Management, 15,* 403–422.

Ahuja, G. (2000). Collaboration networks, structural holes, and innovation: A longitudinal study. *Administrative Science Quarterly, 45,* 425–455.

Allen, T. J., & Cohen, S. I. (1969). Information flow in research and development laboratories. *Administrative Science Quarterly, 14,* 12–19.

Amabile, T. M. (1996). *Creativity in context: Update to "The social psychology of creativity".* Boulder, CO: Westview Press.

Anderson, N. R., & West, M. A. (1998). Measuring climate for work group innovation: Development and validation of the team climate inventory. *Journal of Organizational Behavior, 19,* 235–258.

Andrews, F. M., & Farris, G. F. (1967). Supervisory practices and innovation in scientific teams. *Personnel Psychology, 20*, 497–515.

Ansoff, H. I. (1991). Critique of Henry Mintzberg's 'the design school: Reconsidering the basic premises of strategic management'. *Strategic Management Journal, 12*, 449–461.

Baer, J. (2003). Evaluative thinking, creativity, and task specificity: Separating wheat from chaff is not the same as finding needle in haystacks. In M. A. Runco (Ed.), *Critical creative processes* (pp. 129–152). Cresskill, NJ: Hampton.

Barnowe, J. T. (1975). Leadership and performance outcomes in research organizations. *Organizational Behavior and Human Performance, 14*, 264–280.

Baughman, W. A., & Mumford, M. D. (1995). Process analytic models of creative capacities: Operations involved in the combination and reorganization process. *Creativity Research Journal, 8*, 37–62.

Benner, M., & Tushman, M. L. (2003). Exploitation, exploration and process management: The productivity dilemma revisited. *Academy of Management Review, 28*, 238–256.

Berg, C. A., Strough, J., Calderone, K. S., Sansone, C., & Weir, C. (1998). The role of problem definitions in understanding age and context effects on strategies for solving everyday problems. *Psychology and Aging, 13*, 29–44.

Berger, C. R., & Dibattista, P. (1992). Planning sources, planning difficulty, and verbal fluency. *Communication Monographs, 59*, 130–148.

Berger, R. M., Guilford, J. P., & Christensen, P. R. (1957). A factor-analytic study of planning abilities. *Psychological Monographs, 71*, 1–31.

Berkun, S. (2007). *The myths of innovation.* Sebastopol, CA: O'Reilly.

Bledow, R., Frese, M., Erez, M., Anderson, N., & Farr, J. (2009). A dialectic perspective on innovation: Conflicting demands, multiple pathways, and ambidexterity. *Industrial and Organizational Psychology: Perspectives on Science and Practice, 2*, 305–337.

Bonissone, P. P., Dutta, S., & Wood, N. C. (1994). Merging strategic and tactical planning in dynamic and uncertain environments. *Systems, Man, and Cybernetics, IEEE Transactions, 24*, 841–862.

Bryant-Arnold C.R., Pieper E., Walther B., Stone R.B., McAdams D.A., Kurtoglu T., et. al. (2006). *Software evaluation of an automated concept generator design tool.* Proceedings of the 2006 American Society for Engineering Education Annual Conference & Exhibition, Chicago, IL, Paper 2005–1758.

Burgelman, R. A. (2002). Strategy as vector and the inertia of coevolutionary lock in. *Organization Science, 2*, 239–262.

Byron, K., Khazanchi, S., & Nazarian, D. (in press). The relationship between stressors and creativity: A meta-analysis examining competing theoretical models. *Journal of Applied Psychology.*

Cardinal, L. B. (2001). Technological innovation in the pharmaceutical industry: the use of organizational control in managing research and development. *Organization Science, 12*, 19–37.

Catmull, E. (2008). How Pixar fosters creativity. *Harvard Business Review, September.*

Christensen, C. M. (1997). *The innovator's dilemma.* New York, NY: Collins.

Christensen, C., & Raynor, M. (2003). *The innovator's solution.* Boston, MA: Harvard Business School Press.

Cohen, W. M., & Levinthal, W. M. (1990). Absorptive capacity: A new perspective on learning and innovation. *Administrative Science Quarterly, 35*, 128–152.

Collins, M. A., & Amabile, T. M. (1999). Motivation and creativity. In R. J. Sternberg (Ed.), *Handbook of creativity* (pp. 297–312). New York, NY: Cambridge University Press.

Cooper, R. G. (1994). Third generation new product processes. *Journal of Product Innovation Management, 11*, 3–14.

Cooper, R. G. (2000). Product innovation and technology strategy. *Research Technology Mangament, 43*, 38–41.

Cooper, R. G., Edgett, S. J., & Kleinschmidt, E. J. (2002). Optimizing the stage-gate process: What the best practice companies do—I. *Research Technology Management, 45*, 21–28.

Cooper, R. G., & Kleinschmidt, E. J. (2000). New product performance: What distinguishes the star products. *Australian Journal of Management, 25*, 17–46.

Csikszentmihály, M. (1999). Implications of a systems perspective for the study of creativity. In R. J. Sternberg (Ed.), *Handbook of creativity* (pp. 312–338). Cambridge, UK: Cambridge University Press.

Dess, G. G., & Pickens, J. C. (2000). Changing roles: Leadership in the 21st Century. *Organizational Dynamics, 28*, 18–34.

Dewey, J. (1910). *How we think.* Lexington, MA: D.C. Heath.

Doerner, D., & Schaub, H. (1994). Errors in planning and decision-making and the nature of human information processing. *Applied Psychology: An International Review, 43*, 453.

Dunbar, K. (1995). How do scientists really reason: Scientific reasoning in real-world laboratories. In R. J. Sternberg & J. E. Davidson (Eds.), *The nature of insight* (pp. 365–396). Cambridge, MA: MIT Press.

Earley, P. C., & Perry, B. C. (1987). Work plan availability and performance: An assessment of task strategy priming on subsequent task completion. *Organizational Behavior and Human Decision Processes, 39,* 279–302.

Eisenhardt, K. M., & Tabrizi, B. N. (1995). Accelerating adaptive processes: Product innovation in the global computer industry. *Administrative Science Quarterly, 40,* 84–110.

Ericsson, K. A., & Charness, W. (1994). Expert performance: Its structure and acquisition. *American Psychologist, 49,* 725–747.

Estrin, J. (2009). *Closing the innovation gap.* New York, NY: McGraw-Hill.

Ettlie, J. E., & Elsenbach, J. M. (2007). Modified stage-gate regimes in new product development. *Journal of Production and Innovation Management, 24,* 20–33.

Ettlie, J. E., & Johnson, M. D. (1994). Product development benchmarking versus customer focus in applications of quality function deployment. *Marketing Letters, 5,* 107–116.

Ettlie, J. E., Bridges, , & O'Keefe, Organization strategy and structural differences for radical versus incremental innovation. *Management Science, 30,* 682–695.

Fairchild, J., Cassidy, S. E., Cushenbery, L., & Hunter, S. T. (in press). *Integrating technology with the creative design process.* In Mesquita, A. (Ed.), Technology for creativity and innovation: Tools, techniques and applications. Hershey, PA: IGI Publishing.

Farris, G. F. (1972). The effect of individual role on performance in innovative groups. *R&D Management, 3,* 23–28.

Finke, R. A., Ward, T. B., & Smith, S. M. (1992). *Creative cognition: Theory, research, and applications.* Cambridge, MA: MIT Press.

Feldman, D. H. (1999). The development of creativity. In R. J. Sternberg (Ed.), *Handbook of creativity* (pp. 169–188). Cambridge, UK: Cambridge University Press.

Florida, R. (2002). *The rise of the creative class.* New York, NY: Basic Books.

Franklin, N., & Bower, G. G. (1988). Retrieving actions from goal hierarchies. *Bulletin of the Psychonomic Society, 26,* 15–18.

Friedman, S. L., & Scholnick, E. K. (1997). *The developmental psychology of planning: Why, how, and when do we plan?*

Gaerling, T. (1996). Sequencing actions: An information-search of tradeoffs of priorities against spatiotemporal constraints. *Scandinavian Journal of Psychology, 37,* 282–293.

Gassman, O., & van Zedwitz, M. (2003). Trends and determinants of managing virtual R&D teams. *R&D Management, 33,* 243–263.

Gemunden, H. G., Heydebreck, P., & Herden, R. (1992). Technological interweavement: A means of achieving innovation success. *R&D Management, 22,* 359–376.

Goldin, S. E., & Hayes-Roth, B. (1980). *Individual differences in planning.* San Diego, CA: Rand.

Griffin, A. (1997). *Drivers of NPD success: The 1997 PDMA report.* Chicago, IL: Product Development Management Association.

Gronn, P. (2002). Distributed leadership as a unit of analysis. *Leadership Quarterly, 13,* 423–451.

Gruber, H. E., & Wallace, D. B. (1999). The case study method and evolving systems approach for understanding unique creative people at work. In R. J. Sternberg (Ed.), *Handbook of creativity* (pp. 93–115). Cambridge, UK: Cambridge University Press.

Gupta, A., Smith, K. G., & Shalley, C. E. (2006). The interplay between exploration and exploitation. *Academy of Management Journal, 49,* 693–706.

Hammond, K. J. (1990). Case-based planning: A framework for planning from experience. *Cognitive Science, 14,* 385–443.

Hauschildt, J., & Kirchmann, E. (2001). Teamwork for innovation—the "troika" of promotors. *R&D Management, 31,* 41–49.

Hayes-Roth, B., & Hayes-Roth, F. (1979). A cognitive model of planning. *Cognitive Science, 3,* 275–310.

Hirschberg, J. (1999). *The creative priority.* New York, NY: Harper Business.

Hitt, M. A., Hoskisson, R. E., Johnson, R. A., & Moesel, D. D. (1996). The market for corporate control and firm innovation. *Academy of Management Journal, 39,* 1084–1196.

Howell, J. M., & Boies, K. (2004). Champions of technological innovation: The influence of contextual knowledge, role orientation, idea generation, and idea promotion on champion emergence. *Leadership Quarterly, 15,* 130–149.

Hughes, T. P. (1989). *American genesis: A history of the American genius for invention.* New York, NY: Penguin.

Hunter, S. T., Bedell-Avers, K. E., & Mumford, M. D. (2007). Climate for creativity: A quantitative review. *Creativity Research Journal, 19*, 69–90.

Hunter, S. T., Thoroughgood, C., Myers, A., & Ligon, G. S. (in press). Managing the paradoxes of leading for innovation. *Psychology of Aesthetics, Creativity, and the Arts—Special issue: Innovation in Organizations.*

Hurley, R. F., & Hult, T. M. (1998). Innovation, market orientation, and organizational learning: An integration and empirical examination. *American Marketing Association, 3*, 42–54.

Inskeep, S. (Speaker) (May 18, 2008). *Nintendo's Wii fit pumps up "Active Gaming" trend.* Washington DC: National Public Radio.

Jansen, J. J. P., Tempelaar, M. P., Van den Bosch, F. A. J., & Volberda, H. W. (2009). Structural differentiation and ambidexterity: The mediating role of integration mechanisms. *Organization Science, 1287*, 1–15.

Janssen, O., van de Vliert, E., & West, M. (2004). The bright and dark sides of individual and group innovation: A special issue introduction. *Journal of Organizational Behavior, 25*, 129–146.

Jaussi, K. S., & Dionne, S. D. (2003). Leading for creativity: The role of unconventional behavior. *Leadership Quarterly, 14*, 351–368.

Kao, J. (2007). *Innovation nation: How America is losing its innovative edge, why it matters and what we can do to get it back.* New York, NY: Free Press.

Keane, M. T. (1996). On adaptation in analogy: Tests of pragmatic importance and adaptability in analogical problem solving. *Quarterly Journal of Experimental Psychology, 49*, 1062–1085.

Keller, R. T. (2001). Cross-functional project groups in research and new product development: Diversity, communications, job stress, and outcomes. *Academy of Management Journal, 44*, 547–553.

Kelley, T. (2001). The art of innovation: Lessons in creativity from IDEO: *America's leading design firm.* New York, NY: Currency/Doubleday.

Kitchell, S. (1995). Corporate culture, environmental adaptation, and innovation adoption: A qualitative/quantitative approach. *Journal of the Academy of Marketing Science, 23*, 195–205.

Koberg, C. S., Uhlenbruck, N., & Sarason, Y. (1996). Facilitators of organizational innovation: The role of life-cycle stage. *Journal of Business Venturing, 11*, 133–149.

Kuipers, B., Moskowitz, A. J., & Kassinger, J. P. (1988). Critical decision under uncertainty: Representation and structure. *Cognitive Science, 12*, 177–210.

Latham, G. P., & Locke, E. A. (1991). Self-regulation through goal-setting. *Organizational Behavior and Human Decision Processes, 50*, 212–247.

Li, H., & Atuahene-Gima, K. (2001). Product innovation strategy and the performance of technology ventures in China. *Academy of Management Journal, 44*, 1123–1134.

Licuanan, B., Dailey, L., & Mumford, M. D. (2007). Idea evaluation: Error in evaluating highly original ideas. *Journal of Creative Behavior, 41*, 1–27.

Lonergan, D. C., Scott, G. M., & Mumford, M. D. (2004). Evaluative aspects of creative thought: Effects of idea appraisal and revision standards. *Creativity Research Journal, 16*, 231–246.

Lubart, T. I. (2001). Models of the creative process: Past, present, and future. *Creativity Research Journal, 13*, 295–308.

March, J. G. (1991). Exploration and exploitation in organizational learning. *Organization Science, 2*, 71–87.

McDermott, D. (1978). Planning and acting. *Cognitive Science, 2*, 71–109.

McGrath, R. G. (2009). Business models: A discovery driven approach. *Long Range Planning, 7*, 1–15.

Miller, C., & Osburn, R. N. (2008). In M. D. Mumford, S. T. Hunter & K. E. Bedell Avers (Eds.), *Multi-level issues in creativity and innovation* (pp. 169–187). Oxford, UK: Elsevier.

Miller, G. A., Galanter, E., & Pribaum, K. H. (1960). *Plans and the structure of behavior.* New York, NY: Holt, Reinhardt & Winston.

Miller, K. D., Zhao, M., & Calantone, R. J. (2006). Adding interpersonal learning and tacit knowledge to March's exploration–exploitation model. *Academy of Management Journal, 49*, 709–722.

Mintzberg, H. (1990). The design school: Reconsidering the basic premises of strategic management. *Strategic Management Journal, 11*, 171–195.

Mintzberg, H. (1991). Learning-1, Planning-0—Reply. *Strategic Management Journal, 12*, 463–466.

Mintzberg, H., & Waters, J. (1985). Of strategies, deliberate and emergent. *Strategic Management Journal, 6*, 257–272.

Mintzberg, H., Raisinghani, D., & Theoret, A. (1976). The structure of unstructured decision processes. *Administrative Science Quarterly, 21*, 246–275.

Mitra, J. (2000). Making corrections: Innovation and collective learning in small businesses. *Education and Training*, *42*, 228–237.

Mouly, V. S., & Sankaran, J. K. (1999). The "permanent" acting leader: Insights from a dying Indian R&D organization. *The Leadership Quarterly*, *10*, 637–652.

Mumford, M. D., & Hunter, S. T. (2005). Innovation in organizations: A multi-level perspective on creativity. In F. J. Yammarino & F. Dansereau (Eds.), *Research in multi-level issues:* (Vol. IV, pp. 11–74). Oxford, UK: Elsevier.

Mumford, M. D., Baughman, W. A., Supinski, E. P., & Maher, M. A. (1996). Process-based measures of creative problem-solving skills: II. Information encoding. *Creativity Research Journal*, *9*, 77–88.

Mumford, M. D., Bedell-Avers, K. E., & Hunter, S. T. (2008). Planning for innovation: A multi-level perspective. In M. D. Mumford, S. T. Hunter & K. E. Bedell (Eds.), *Research in multi-level issues:* (Vol. VII, pp. 107–154). Oxford, UK: Elsevier.

Mumford, M. D., Blair, C., Dailey, L., Lertiz, L. E., & Osburn, H. K. (2006). Errors in creative thought? Cognitive biases in a complex processing activity. *Journal of Creative Behavior*, *40*, 75–109.

Mumford, M. D., Hunter, S. T., Eubanks, D., Bedell, K., & Murphy, S. (2007). Developing leaders for creative efforts: A domain based approach to leadership development. *Human Resource Review*, *17*, 402–417.

Mumford, M. D., Mobley, M. I., Uhlman, C. E., Reiter-Palmon, R., & Doares, L. (1991). Process analytic models of creative capacities. *Creativity Research Journal*, *4*, 91–122.

Mumford, M. D., Schultz, R. A, & Van Dorn, J. R. (2001). Performance in planning: Processes, requirements, and errors. *Review of General Psychology*, *5*, 213–240.

Mumford, M. D., Schultz, R. A., & Osburn, H. K. (2002a). Planning in organizations: Performance as a multi-level phenomenon. In F. J. Yammarino & F. Dansereau (Eds.), *Research in multi-level issues: The many faces of multi-level issues* (Vol. 1, pp. 3–36). Oxford, UK: Elsevier.

Mumford, M. D., Scott, G. M., Gaddis, B., & Strange, J. M. (2002b). Leading creative people: Orchestrating expertise and relationships. *Leadership Quarterly*, *13*, 705–750.

Mumford, M. D., Supinski, E. P., Baughman, W. A., Costanza, D. P., & Threlfall, K. V. (1997). Process-based measures of creative problem-solving skills: I. Overall prediction. *Creativity Research Journal*, *10*, 77–85.

Nellore, R., & Balachandra, R. (2001). Factors influencing success in integrated product development (IPD) projects. *IEEE Transactions on Engineering Management*, *48*, 164–173.

Noice, H. (1991). The role of explanations and plan recognition in the learning of theatrical scripts. *Cognitive Science*, *15*, 425–460.

Nohari, K., & Gulatti, S. (1996). Is slack good or bad for innovation? *Academy of Management Journal*, *39*, 799–825.

O'Connor, G. C. (1998). Market learning and radical innovation: A cross case comparison of eight radical innovation projects. *Journal of Product Innovation Management*, *15*, 131–151.

Oliver, T. (1986). *The real coke, the real story*. New York, NY: Penguin.

Patalano, A. L., & Seifert, C. M. (1997). Opportunistic planning: Being reminded of pending goals. *Cognitive Psychology*, *34*, 1–36.

Pea, R. D. (1982). What is planning development the development of? *New Directions for Child Development*, *18*, 5–27.

Peretti, F., & Negro, G. (2006). Filling empty seats: How status and organizational hierarchies affect exploration versus exploitation in team design. *Academy of Management Journal*, *49*, 759–777.

Radnor, M., & Probert, D. R. (2004). Viewing the future. *Research Technology Management*, *47*, 25–27.

Radnor, Z., & Robinson, J. (2000). Benchmarking innovation: A short report. *Creativity and Innovation Management*, *9*, 3–13.

Root-Bernstein, R. S., Bernstein, M., & Garnier, H. (1995). Correlations between avocations, scientific style, work habits, and professional impact of scientists. *Creativity Research Journal*, *8*, 115–137.

Sethi, R., & Iqbal, Z. (2008). Stage-gate controls, learning failure, and adverse effect on novel new products. *Journal of Marketing*, *72*, 118–134.

Sharma, A. (1999). Central dilemmas of managing innovation in large firms. *California Management Review*, *41*, 65–85.

Simon, H. (1993). Strategy and organizational evolution. *Strategic Management Journal*, *14*, 131–142.

Simonton, D. K. (1999). Talent and its development: An emergenic and epigenetic model. *Psychological Review*, *106*, 435–457.

Sivadas, E., & Dwyer, F. R. (2000). An examination of organizational factors influencing new product success in internal and alliance–based processes. *Journal of Marketing*, *64*, 31–49.

Smith, J. K., & Hounshell, D. A. (1998). Wallace H. Carothers and fundamental research at Du Pont. *Science, 229*, 436–442.

Souitaris, V. (2001). External communication determinants of innovation in the context of a newly industrialized country: A comparison of objective and perceptual results from Greece. *Technovation, 21*, 25–34.

Taylor, A., & Greve, H. (2006). Superman or the Fantastic Four? Knowledge combination and experience in innovative teams. *Academy of Management Journal, 49*, 723–740.

Taylor, I. A., Austin, G. A., & Sutton, D. F (1974). A note on "instant creativity" at CPSI. *Journal of Creative Behavior, 8*, 208–210.

Teece, D. J. (2009). Business models, business strategy and innovation. *Long Range Planning, 1016*, 1–23.

Tierney, P., Farmer, S. M., & Graen, G. B. (1999). An examination of leadership and employee creativity: The relevance of traits and relationships. *Personnel Psychology, 52*, 591–620.

Topalian, A. (2000). The role of innovation leaders in developing long-term products. *International Journal of Innovation Management, 4*, 149–171.

Trevelyan, R. (2001). The paradox of autonomy: The case of academic research scientists. *Human Relations, 54*, 495–525.

Tushman, M. L., & O'Reilly, C. A. (1996). Ambidextrous organizations: Managing evolutionary and revolutionary change. *California Management Review, 38*, 8–30.

Useem, J. (March 19, 2007). Apple: America's best retailer. *Fortune Magazine, 155*, 37–45.

Vise, D. A., & Malseed, M. (2006). *The Google story– Inside the hottest business, media and technology success of our time.* UK: Pan MacMillan Books.

Wallas, G. (1926). *The art of thought.* New York, NY: Harcourt Brace.

Weisberg, R. W. (1999). Creativity and knowledge: A challenge to theories. In R. J. Sternberg (Ed.), *Handbook of creativity* (pp. 226–259). Cambridge, UK: Cambridge University Press.

West, M. A., Borill, C. S., Dawson, J. F., Brodbeck, F., Shapiro, D. A., & Haward, B. (2003). Leadership clarity and team innovation. *Leadership Quarterly, 14*, 246–278.

Xiao, Y., Milgram, P., & Doyle, D. J. (1997). Capturing and modeling planning expertise in anesthesiology. Results of a field study. In C. Zsambok & G. Klein (Eds.), *Naturalistic decision making* (pp. 197–205). Hillsdale, NJ: LEA.

Yam, M. (October 2, 2007). Nintendo offers free Wii remote jackets to all Wii owners. Daily Tech. Retrieved from. <www.dailytech.com/Nintendo+Offers+Free+Wii+Remote+Jackets+to+All+Wii+Owners/article9126.htm/>

D. ORGANIZATIONAL LEVEL INFLUENCES

Organizational Learning, Knowledge Management and Creativity

Robert K. Kazanjian, and Robert Drazin

Goizueta Business School, Emory University, Atlanta, GA

INTRODUCTION

The individual level of analysis has been the focus of most theories of creativity, with much of the effort directed at describing the nature of creative people (Barron, 1955; Bennis & Biederman, 1997; Glynn, 1996; MacKinnon, 1965). Individual characteristics such as personality (Barron & Harrington, 1981; Singh, 1986), cognitive abilities (Basadur, Graen, & Green, 1982), and intelligence (Gardner, 1993; Glynn, 1996) have all been linked to creativity. Within the existing literature, creativity at the individual level has been related to constructs as varied as: team cohesiveness, diversity, tenure and degree of cooperation among group members (Andrews, 1979; King & Anderson, 1990; Payne, 1990), job design (Amabile, 1988; Kanter, 1988), supervisory style (Stahl & Koser, 1978; West, 1989), and the provision of performance feedback (Carson & Carson, 1993). Some additional research has enlarged this scope, by arguing that creative behavior results from a complex interaction between the characteristics of the individual and those of the environment (Amabile, 1983, 1996; George & Zhou, 2007; Mumford & Gustafson, 1988; Redmond, Mumford, & Teach, 1993; Woodman et al., 1993).

Correspondingly then, theories of creativity typically emphasize the role of individuals or small groups, with little or no recognition that creative tasks might well be embedded in larger organizational efforts entailing task interdependencies between units or across complex organizational systems. The bulk of research has focused primarily on examining creativity at more micro-levels of analysis (i.e., for individuals, work units, or small project teams), by modeling creativity as a discrete task largely isolated from broader organizational and operational pressures. Such studies investigate creativity in situations where an

Handbook of Organizational Creativity.
DOI: 10.1016/B978-0-12-374714-3.00021-5

individual or small team is assigned a narrow, bounded design task or problem and seem most relevant to small, team-based, new product development (Dumaine, 1993).

While recognizing the contribution of such research, we argue that these models tend to be less applicable to more recently established contexts for creativity. Increasingly, organizations pursue creativity in large settings, employing hundreds or even thousands of individuals where the activities may span many months or even years. Further, the nature of the creative task is such that any one individual or group may be highly interdependent with the creative work of others (DeMaio, Verganti, & Corso, 1994; Drazin, Glynn, & Kazanjian, 2004; Kazanjian, Drazin, & Glynn, 2000). Examples include development of a new aircraft (Horwitch, 1982; Sabbagh, 1996), new automobiles (Clark & Fujimoto, 1991; Quinn & Pacquette, 1988), space projects at NASA (Hoffman, 1997; Sayles & Chandler, 1971) and defense contracting (Scudder et al., 1989). We raise these examples to indicate that the context for creativity in many settings is heavily influenced by organizational and strategic factors that typically have not been included in existing research on creativity (Drazin, Kazanjian, & Blyler, 2003; Mumford, 2000).

Although organizational learning is a central component of creativity, it is particularly critical in such complex settings as described above. As with creativity, organizational learning is also a multi-level construct (Drazin, Glynn, & Kazanjian, 1999; Glynn, 1996). Clearly, individuals engage in learning when they encounter knowledge gaps and, in response, analyze and solve problems. Organizational learning is neither strictly micro nor macro in nature (Glynn, Lant, & Milliken, 1994) but involves a complex interplay between individuals, work-units and the overall organization. Rather, it is best considered as a group and organizational level process by which new knowledge is created, diffused across the organization, and subsequently integrated into the development of new products, practices, services, or businesses for operational and strategic advantage (Kim, 1998). Therefore, learning has important consequences to organizations, in that it manifests itself in the development and application of new capabilities and the facility for broader strategic adaptation (Kazanjian, Drazin, & Glynn, 2002; Senge, 1994).

As Leonard (1998) notes, organizational learning is the development of new or novel knowledge that is accessible for creative problem solving. By definition then, knowledge management and knowledge building activities are oriented toward creative problem solving. Much of knowledge creation and learning that occurs within organizations is through the development of new products and services pursued in response to emerging customer needs, competitive dynamics and technological capabilities both inside and outside the firm. As organizations develop such new products, the individuals or groups assigned to the task typically break down the overall product design into a series of discrete tasks, each with inherent problems. Analysis of these design problems demonstrates gaps where existing technologies, established design standards, and accepted approaches are inadequate. Through individual and group activities, including problem re-framing, brainstorming, hypotheses generation, and trial and error testing, creative solutions emerge to fill the gaps. This experiential learning, again at the individual and group level, extends existing knowledge while new knowledge also is developed. Learning then occurs at the organizational level as such new technological and operational knowledge is institutionalized (Leonard, 1998; Mumford, 2000).

In this way, new knowledge becomes embodied not only in the product or service being designed, but also in the organization's broader routines and practices (Nelson & Winter, 1982) in such areas as engineering, manufacturing, and customer service, which can be used to create value for customers in the future. Thus, firms that develop leading edge products and services are, of necessity, engaged in the process of knowledge creation (Leonard-Barton, 1992). Embedded within this learning process at the organizational level, the process of creativity is simultaneously unfolding at the individual and inter-personal level. This relationship of creativity to new knowledge development and organizational learning has been examined in only a limited number of cases (Drazin et al., 1999; Mumford, 2000).

Therefore, our purpose in this chapter is to investigate how creativity is related to a range of complex organizational settings and problems and, by extension, to the organizational learning that transpires. In particular, we are concerned with how creativity unfolds over time, and how it is influenced by the organizational context and strategy. The remainder of the chapter is organized into four sections. In the next section, we present a process perspective of creativity that is conducive to the development of a knowledge-based view of the firm. We then, in the second section, develop the centrality of creativity to the knowledge-based view of the firm. In the third section, we describe a continuum of strategies for creativity from incremental strategies that emphasize leveraging and exploiting existing knowledge to strategies that rely more on the importation and development of new knowledge. In the final section, we present specific knowledge management mechanisms that support associated strategies for creativity.

CREATIVITY AS AN ORGANIZATIONAL LEARNING PROCESS

Although a large portion of the literature operationalizes creativity as an outcome, there is ample precedent to view creativity from a process perspective (Drazin et al., 1999; Mohr, 1982). Amabile (1988) has modeled creativity as a cognitive process consisting of multiple stages, while Torrence (1988) defines creativity as a process of sensing problems, making guesses, formulating hypotheses, communicating ideas to others and contradicting conformity. Consistent with an organizational learning and knowledge-based perspective we adopt in this chapter, we define creativity as the engagement of the individual in behaviors and activities directed at the development of novel and useful outcomes (Amabile, 1988, 1996; Drazin, Glynn, & Kazanjian, 1999).

Whether or not the resultant outcomes are considered novel or useful by others, the process of generating new ideas logically is elemental to creativity. Creative engagement is a process in which an individual behaviorally, cognitively and emotionally *attempts* to produce creative outcomes. It is a choice made by an individual to engage in producing novel ideas. Therefore, creativity requires a process component that is a necessary, if not a sufficient condition for creative outcomes. Of course, the level of engagement of individuals, all else being equal, will vary from situation to situation. For example, in one situation, an individual may choose minimal engagement, proposing simple solutions that may not be novel or useful—a behavior Ford (1996) refers to as "habitual action". Alternatively, an individual may chose to engage fully, using all of his or her abilities in an effort to produce creative outcomes. To Kahn (1990), such processes of engagement (and disengagement) will vary over time, ebbing and flowing from moment to moment and from day to day. In developing a new product for example, a creative scientist or engineer may extensively engage in developing a solution to a complex design or manufacturing problem. That individual is seeking to develop a creative outcome that must be evaluated ultimately by peers and supervisors. Although the solution or outcome developed by that individual (or group) might not ever be implemented, the cognitive and interpersonal engagement that leads to these solutions is a process central to creativity (Kazanjian, Drazin, & Glynn, 2000).

This process view of creativity and the problem of employee engagement are highly consistent with the emerging literature on the strategic role of human capital and competitive advantage (Coff, 1997; Kogut & Zander, 1992; Wang, He, & Mahoney, 2009). The resource based view of the firm (Barney, 1996; Wernerfelt, 1984) argues that firm-specific resources serve as the basis of competitive advantage. For example, holding specialized and unique equipment (a tangible resource) might differentiate a firm from its competitors. The knowledge-based view of the firm (emergent from the broader resource-based view of the firm), has argued similarly that knowledge has the potential to serve as the basis of competitive advantage. Knowledge, however, is an intangible resource derived from the human assets or human capital of the firm. As Coff (1997) and others have argued, the central problem is to engage those key individuals who have the potential to create a competitive advantage to contribute their knowledge, energy, and efforts to advance the strategy of the firm, as opposed to extracting all such efforts for themselves. Therefore, the central challenge of exploiting the potential of human capital as a strategic asset is to provide clear strategic direction, access to required resources, and organizational mechanisms that facilitate active engagement of those individuals in the creative process.

ORGANIZATIONAL CREATIVITY AND THE KNOWLEDGE BASED VIEW

A central tenet of the knowledge-based view (KBV) of the firm is that organizations create, maintain, and apply knowledge bases as a means of competing through creativity and innovation (Cohen & Levinthal, 1990; Kazanjian & Drazin, 1987; Kazanjian et al., 2002; Kogut & Zander, 1992). Knowledge bases in organizations are built up through processes of creativity and the exploration of new technical and market developments. In turn, they are utilized through processes of product-line extension and the exploitation of existing domain specific knowledge (Grant, 1996; Grant & Baden-Fuller, 1995; March, 1991).

Organizations consist of multiple bases of knowledge (Ciborra, 1996; Kogut & Kulatilaka, 1994; Kogut & Zander, 1996; McGrath, 1997, 1999), each of which can intersect with a set of products or services to yield innovations and product extensions for a variety of market opportunities (Grant, 1996; Grant & Baden-Fuller, 1995; Prahalad & Hamel, 1990; Sanchez & Mahoney, 1996). It is knowledge that allows an organization to compete in these product areas (Kim & Kogut, 1996). For instance, Honda developed a substantial knowledge of engines and drive-trains that it used to create motorcycles, automobiles, lawn mowers, power generators, and more recently jet engines, each addressing the needs of different market niches. Similarly, Google has used its knowledge of search technologies to extend itself into software development in computing and telecommunications. This knowledge based approach has been central to creativity and innovation in a diverse range of contexts and industries, including automobiles, consumer electronics, consulting, computers, software, power tools, and financial services (McGrath, 1995; Meyer & Lehnerd, 1997; Sanchez & Mahoney, 1996).

A range of distinct but related approaches have emerged over time to describe and conceptually frame the pursuit of knowledge-based growth. These include natural paths of growth (Penrose, 1995), repeated replication (Normann, 1977; Zook & Allen, 2003), growth trajectories (Dosi, 1982), stepping stones (Wernerfelt, 1984), and sequential product introduction (Aaker & Keller, 1990). Additionally, some researchers have examined the viability of these strategies using the related lenses of real options (McGrath, 1997, 1999) and product platforms (Aaker, 1996; McGrath, 1995; Sawhney, 1998). In general, this work tends to focus on the viability of the strategy of knowledge extension, rather than on the related organizational requirements of implementation, with a few exceptions (Kazanjian et al., 2002; Tushman & O'Reilly, 2004).

Consistent with this view, we argue that a detailed understanding of the existing resource and knowledge base of the firm is necessary to frame the learning process around associated creativity centered activities (Zook, 2007). Particular strategies for creativity target specific domains of new products or services that create a shared vision of some new business idea (Galbraith, 1982; Normann, 1977) among key actors. Inherent in this vision are certain attributes, including the market to be pursued, the design and characteristics of the product or service, and the administrative and production mechanisms required. Each of these attributes of the new business idea represents a potential requirement to develop knowledge that goes beyond that currently extant in the firm. Then, the organization must develop competencies beyond those associated with current products and markets to compete in the new businesses.

In such settings, creativity can be understood as an organizational learning process directed at developing the knowledge necessary to compete in a targeted, new, product-market domain (Kazanjian & Drazin, 1987; Normann, 1977; Pennings, Barkema, & Douma, 1994). When an organization targets its efforts at new product development, it necessarily defines the knowledge requirements for implementing that product. The implementation task facing the organization is to learn the knowledge necessary to introduce the targeted product(s). If a targeted product is related to an existing knowledge base, the extent of knowledge development is incremental or small (Henderson & Clark, 1990; Normann, 1977). Alternatively, if the targeted product does not use any of the organization's existing bases of knowledge, then the learning task is more substantial or radical. In effect, the introduction of unrelated products is a process of establishing a new knowledge base that can be exploited in the future (Henderson & Clark, 1990; Kim & Kogut, 1996; McGrath, 1997; March, 1991).

Following this line of argument, we propose that creativity related activities should be assessed relative to a firm's current bases of knowledge (Kazanjian & Drazin, 1987; Kazanjian, Drazin, & Glynn, 2000; Kogut & Zander, 1992). Organizations differ widely in past investments in knowledge and their associated absorptive capacity (Cohen & Levinthal, 1990); thus relatedness, when it is defined relative to an organization's bases of current knowledge, is firm-specific and target-oriented, determined jointly by the knowledge base and the nature of the innovations to be pursued.

STRATEGIES FOR ORGANIZATIONAL CREATIVITY

By viewing organizational creativity through the KBV lens, we establish the foundation for a contingency approach to knowledge management and creativity. Figure 21.1 portrays our view of three archetype strategies for creativity and the types of knowledge development

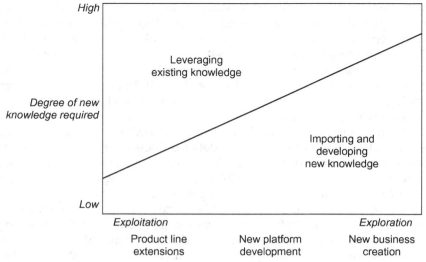

FIGURE 21.1   Matching knowledge to creativity.

necessary for each. For the sake of parsimony, we focus on the broad construct of knowledge relatedness, but this framework could easily be extended to more fine grained or multi-dimensional depictions of knowledge relatedness at the functional (e.g. markets, technology) or sub-functional level. The figure represents the firm's current and potential future knowledge base, demonstrating the possible mix of exploitation of existing knowledge versus the exploration for new knowledge (March, 1991) through importation or internal development. Each such mix represents a distinct strategy for creativity and innovation and hence differing requirements for knowledge management and organizational learning.

Three types of creative activities are displayed on Figure 21.1: product line extensions, new platform development, and new business creation. Each of the three archetypes reflects a different creativity strategy and implies a different level of knowledge to be developed. The computer industry provides a widely observed and easily understood example of the first of these archetypes—product line extensions. With this strategy, established models of existing brands are introduced routinely as variations of a baseline product. In the case of computers, these variations typically incorporate new or upgraded components such as more powerful micro-processors, longer life batteries, monitors with greater image resolution, disk-drives with greater storage capability, or faster software with expanded capabilities. As such, they require little additional new technology development on the part of the PC assembler and are typically directed at existing customers. For example, most PC manufacturers, including IBM, HP, Compaq, Dell and others began by selling desktop systems, initially to sophisticated individuals with strong technology interests or professional needs, and to corporations as a business tool. As the technology of components advanced, specialized portable applications emerged as the first entry into what would later become the laptop market. Within the laptop market, a segment emerged for tablet PCs with specialized capabilities suited to presentation, and capturing notations and addendums. Another segment emerged around highly durable laptops that were able to withstand the rigors of field and shop floor activities. More recently, as wireless networks became more prevalent, "netbooks" emerged in response to the demand for smaller appliances with more limited capability that provided easy access to the internet. Each of these types of product can be seen to be an extension of previous offerings using largely similar components, assembly technologies, and distribution systems.

The second archetype, new product platform, is introduced periodically when companies target a new market and/or technology domain. Here, a firm is either developing some new or more advanced technology to take to existing customers, or is targeting new customers with its own advanced technologies. Meyer and Lehnerd (1997) provide an early but dramatic example of a strategy of new platform development. In the early 1970s, Black and Decker, a consumer power tool company, faced major competitive threats in the form of new global competition and an impending regulatory change which would require substantially increased insulation around power tool motors. Rather than simply redesign each product to meet new insulation requirements, Black and Decker chose to redesign all their tools at the same time, and redesign all manufacturing processes, simultaneously, incorporating the new designs without a price increase to customers. The platform development effort had five objectives:

1. develop a common or "family" look across all products,
2. simplify offerings with standardized parts, interfaces, couplings, and connections,
3. reduce per unit manufacturing costs,
4. improve performance while allowing for the ability to subsequently add new features which could be sold as product line extensions with minimal cost to the firm, and
5. design global products that meet worldwide customer needs and regulatory requirements (opening many new potential markets).

The financial and strategic results were positive and substantial. Labor and development costs dropped markedly, allowing Black and Decker to reduce price to gain market share. At the same time, given that the platform was designed to facilitate product line extension, new product development cycles were dramatically reduced. For several years, Black and Decker introduced on average one new product *per week*. Black and Decker's strategy of new platform development led to a dramatic competitive advantage. Many of the new designs were patented and most competitors were slow to respond. In fact, the Black and Decker strategy of platform development led to a shakeout with several firms exiting the industry.

Finally, with regard to the third archetype, some firms may decide to create entirely new businesses that place them in new markets, with either existing or new technologies. We define a strategy of new business creation as the pursuit of a new business opportunity that is: new to the firm; implemented internally (not via acquisition); and places the firm into an unrelated domain (Block & MacMillan, 1995; Zahra, 1991). Apple's development of a strong position in the music business is an example of a strategy of new business creation. Around 2000, Apple was approached by Tony Fadell, a former employee of General Magic and Phillips. His idea was to develop a new MP3 player built around a small hard disk drive and linked to a content delivery system that would allow users to legally purchase and download music. At the time, Apple was predominantly a producer of computer hardware and software, but it was actively looking for new business opportunities. Apple saw the potential of Fadell's business idea, so he was hired in early 2001, given a development team of around 30 people and a one year deadline. Once introduced, the i-Pod was an immediate success and, over time, the sale of the product expanded rapidly, as did the sale of music through Apple's associated iTunes Music Store. The initial iPod had a 5 GB hard drive, and a distinctive design with a scroll wheel control feature to access menu items and review titles. Through product line extensions, the product has evolved to include a user interface with touch-screen capability and 160 GB of storage with space for up to 40,000 songs, 200 hours of video or 25,000 photographic images. Through the sale of iPods and the associated revenues from the iTunes Music Store, Apple has not only diversified from a reliance on the sale of its computers, but has also altered the structure of the music industry, much to Apple's favor.

CENTRAL TASKS OF KNOWLEDGE MANAGEMENT

The relationship of creativity to learning and knowledge management has typically been discussed in conceptual terms. For example, Dess, Lumpkin, and McGee (1999) offer an interesting analysis of the suitability of modular, virtual, and barrier-free organization designs to the reduction of boundaries which they see as central to innovation related tasks. One contribution of the knowledge management literature is in the movement toward a more problem based, normative perspective (Christensen, 1997; Leonard, 1998). Consistent with this approach, we propose that three distinct creativity based strategies have distinct implementation demands, each with differing needs for new knowledge development.

Leveraging existing knowledge bases is the primary approach to developing new products and services. *Recombining and extending* existing knowledge bases is critical to the development of new platforms for growth. Finally, *importing* or acquiring new knowledge bases is the central approach to the development of new businesses less related to existing competencies and skills. Of course, each of these central tasks entails extending knowledge in some way but they differ in their primacy and focus given the different degrees of creativity required in each setting. These three strategies are consistent with the widely cited knowledge related strategies of exploitation and exploration (March, 1992). As depicted in Figure 21.2, each particular strategy for organizational creativity is associated with a dominant knowledge management task, and further is best supported with specific knowledge management mechanisms related to job design, creation and composition of inter-functional teams, and access to relevant knowledge bases both within and external to the firm. These relationships will be further explicated in this section.

Leveraging Existing Knowledge

Leveraging existing knowledge embedded in products, technologies, and customer relationships presents clear and distinct strategic advantages (Kekre & Srinivasan, 1990). Leveraging utilizes an existing knowledge base and applies it directly to new applications (Hamel & Prahalad, 1993). This might take the form of applying components from existing products to new products (Clark & Fujimoto, 1991), or the use of specialists, such as consultants, who have specific knowledge of a class of problems, to apply their services to customers in different markets. In another setting, companies might make use of existing knowledge by creating ad hoc teams of individual specialists drawn from different parts of the organization

Knowledge Management Mechanisms	Product Line Extension	New Platform Development	New Business Creation
Dominant knowledge management tasks	Leveraging existing knowledge	Recombining and extending existing knowledge	Importing and developing new knowledge
Job design characteristics	Functional generalists	← →	Dedicated specialists
Job and unit boundaries	Within role differentiation and differentiated roles	Team and matrix designs	Dedicated group
Relationships and patterns of communication	Internally focused on existing customers and existing technologies	← →	Externally focused on new customers and new technologies

FIGURE 21.2 Strategies for organizational creativity.

to solve a particular technology or market related problem associated with a creative initiative. Once the problem is solved, team members would then return to their ongoing assignments (Kazanjian & Nayyar, 1994). Across these examples, leveraging is evident when the skills of individual employees, as well as the knowledge embedded in physical resources such as products or equipment, are applied to new applications (Leonard, 1998).

One of the major sources of organizational growth is the extension of existing product lines. Growing companies follow a path of least resistance—that is, they use established products as a base for attempts to grow over larger, but highly related product-market areas. Normann (1977; p52) labels this process as growth through "repeated replication", characterizing it as the sequential introduction of new products that are variations or modifications of current products or brands (Kekre & Srinivasan, 1990; Keller & Aaker, 1992; Kotler, 1996). Such a strategy of product-line extension can be viewed as knowledge exploitation—a process of expansion around an underlying core technology or brand knowledge base (Kim & Kogut, 1996; Kogut & Zander, 1992; McGrath, 1994; Meyer & Lehnerd, 1997; Sawhney, 1998).

The implementation of product-line extensions depends highly on the sharing of knowledge between existing and new products. For example, Chandler (1996) discussed how product-line extension occurred at Allison-Chalmers and International Harvester. Both firms exploited economies of scope in production and technology knowledge to allow them to introduce a set of closely related products.

The diversification literature has clearly established the linkage of organizational performance to the economies of scope that arise from the sharing of resources across related products. Leveraging related assets and knowledge presents two primary tasks to executives of the firm. First, senior managers choose to diversify into product-market areas that are related to the current organization on some basis; such as customers, technologies, manufacturing, or brand. Second this strategy is implemented through an organization design that promotes the sharing of relevant resources. Historians (Chandler, 1962, 1992, 1996) and economists (Panzar & Willig, 1981; Teece, 1980, 1982) have used these concepts to explain the rise of the multi-product firm. Strategy researchers have found that product diversification enhances performance when firms are able to exploit common resources and realize economies of scope (Gimeno & Woo, 1999; Pitts, 1977; Porter, 1985; Rumelt, 1974; Vancil, 1980). Others argue that related diversification improves performance only when it is implemented through organizational designs that promote the sharing of resources (Govindarajan & Porter, 1985; Gupta & Govindarajan, 1986; Hill, Hitt, & Hoskisson, 1992; Markides & Williamson, 1996; Nayyar, 1993; Nayyar & Kazanjian, 1993).

Although a wide spectrum of resources can be shared across business units (Porter, 1985), researchers have focused on the sharing of functional knowledge, such as manufacturing, marketing and brand (Sawhney, 1998), distribution, or research and development (Brush, 1996; Chandler, 1996; Davis & Thomas, 1993; Govindarajan & Fisher, 1990; Montgomery & Hariharan, 1991; Klette, 1996). Despite the utility of understanding the mechanisms of sharing functional knowledge and intangible resources, this literature has not fully addressed the sharing of managerial and professional resources, nor has it addressed resource sharing as knowledge leveraging in the context of organizational creativity. Given the importance of the task of implementing product innovation, such a deficiency is curious. Teece (1982) wrote that the tacit knowledge embodied in managers was critical for achieving economies of scope. Penrose (1995), Nelson and Winter (1982), and Chandler (1996) have all argued that under-utilized management knowledge and professional talent was the incentive for pursuing related product diversification.

Managerial roles subject to resource sharing across old and new products would include all forms of knowledge workers, such as product and project managers, brand managers, and account and relationship managers. Earlier research has suggested that managerial resources are more important than physical resources in implementing growth through product extensions (Ansoff, 1965; Chandler, 1962; Penrose, 1995; Teece, 1982). Penrose (1995) argued that firms develop specialized knowledge that is embodied in managers. The use of that knowledge in the support of existing products may create indivisibilities wherein a specialized expert is under-utilized. This provides an inducement for the firm to share that resource across existing and new products to fully utilize its services.

In the case of our argument, the shared knowledge, diffused across the organization, is held by the knowledge workers of the firm—scientists, engineers and marketing managers—all of whom possess extensive knowledge about existing products, technologies, and markets. The resource being shared is this knowledge, as most of it can be applied to new products as well. Additionally, at least a small amount of knowledge needs to be developed that applies to the new market or technological features of the new product. But, for the most part, the organization is leveraging its existing knowledge by applying a great deal of it towards implementing the new product line. Therefore, there are economies of scope of knowledge sharing.

The key managerial task for product-line extension lies in job design and the creation of teams within and across functions. The associated organizational mechanisms involve sharing knowledgeable managerial resources across old and new products. In such cases, the most direct approach is for a manager or knowledge worker who works on current products to also work on new products. Under such arrangements, a manager or knowledge worker has a dual responsibility for a previously existing product and a new product. In essence, a manager is assigned two jobs simultaneously. Brand managers in a consumer product company are an example (Choi, 1998). A new product may be assigned to a brand manager already responsible for one or more products, or may be assigned to a dedicated manager responsible only for that product. By definition, a new product extension consists of mostly well known facts about technology and marketing.

The primary advantage of this approach is that the manager already has an extended base of knowledge in the existing product and can efficiently transfer that knowledge to the new product extension. In effect, this is the most direct example of leveraging knowledge, because an individual directly is applying his or her knowledge to a new application. However, by differentiating the manager's job into two responsibilities, the manager now also has time to develop the incremental knowledge necessary to launch the new product. The new product or service therefore consists of a high percentage of old knowledge, plus some smaller amount of knowledge necessary to position the new product.

A second organizational mechanism we propose for a product-line extension can incrementally increase the organization's capacity to generate new knowledge. That is, this design is intended to serve extensions that mostly leverage old bases of knowledge, but where the mix of new knowledge required increases. This could be accomplished through a job differentiation design, where a manager or knowledge worker is assigned full time to a product-line extension, but still remains within the department responsible for managing current product lines. In effect the individual is assigned full time to develop the extension, thereby yielding a higher level of knowledge generation capacity. However, the assigned individual comes from, and remains, in the department responsible for the old knowledge base. In this fashion the person is simultaneously freed to engage in creative behavior, but also remains physically and organizationally close to a well-established base of knowledge.

Yet a third option for product line extension is the creation of an intra-functional task team. An ad hoc team may be created within engineering to investigate new technologies which could make existing products cheaper or more responsive to customer needs. The same design of an ad hoc team might be used within marketing to investigate new product features desired by existing customers. Individuals assigned to such teams may be part time or full time, depending on the task. By drawing individuals from the existing functional organization, the company is tapping into several sub-elements of the existing knowledge base. Individuals bring that knowledge with them to the team directly. Part-time individuals are simultaneously supporting existing products and product extension providing a direct opportunity for leverage. When the assignment is completed, the task team is disbanded. Although such assignments could be as short as a few weeks, some may be extended over months or even years when associated with complex product-line extensions for industries such as aerospace.

Each of the three approaches to knowledge leveraging for product-line extension is intended to facilitate the application of existing knowledge to new applications. By having individuals who support existing products and services contribute to the development of new products, they will of course apply what they already know. Further, given that the design builds on a close association with the existing functional organizations (which are the knowledge structures for existing products) those individuals can easily access databases, equipment and colleagues to leverage that knowledge as well. Note however that in all three designs, the degree of differentiation for each individual involved will directly affect the level of knowledge generating capacity. All three options also demonstrate tight linkages to the existing organization, minimizing the barriers to leveraging existing knowledge.

Recombining and Extending Existing Knowledge

Recombining and extending existing knowledge presents opportunities to compete in new domains. Major innovations are often the product of the creative integration of existing technologies or even the integration of existing products in a new way for a different purpose. For example, the first CT scanner was developed by EMI (Teece, 1986), a company with a small presence in medical products, and a larger position in consumer electronics and aerospace. The CT scanner was developed from known technologies associated with data processing, x-ray, and display and yet those technologies were combined in a way to produce a radical application—a three dimensional medical imaging capability. Another such example is offered by Kodama (1992) who describes Fanuc as a company that created a strong presence in computerized numerical controllers for machine tools by combining skills in mechanics, electronics, and materials development. Similarly, 3M developed non-rusting, non-scratching plastic soap pads from capabilities in abrasives, adhesives, coatings, and non-wovens (Leonard, 1998).

We view large, broad-scoped organizations as consisting of multiple bases of knowledge that can be developed as product platforms (Ciborra, 1996, Kogut & Kulatilaka, 1994; Kogut & Zander, 1996; McGrath, 1997, 1999). We earlier defined a product platform as a collection of common elements related to technology and market segments. Product platforms present the opportunity to innovate in a new domain, yet are firmly anchored in existing knowledge related to *either* technology *or* the market. Therefore, the development of a new platform represents the ability to leverage some existing knowledge on at least one dimension, while also combining and extending knowledge in new areas. As demonstrated by the example of Black & Decker described earlier in this chapter, a new product platform is carefully designed to provide the foundation for a number of product-line extensions and the associated benefits of economies of scope and resource sharing. Thus, the development of a new product platform positions the organization to then pursue a strategy of product-line extension within this new class of products, thereby gaining additional economies of scale and resource sharing benefits.

McGrath (1995) has identified product platform strategies in a number of industries. In application software products, platforms are composed of the hardware architecture (mainframe, client/server) and the interfaces (database drivers, user interfaces). In pharmaceuticals, a platform might be the delivery vehicle for a class of drugs; in specialty chemicals, perhaps a core compound itself. In these examples, the:

> "product platform is the foundation for a number of related products...all...unique in some way but related by the common characteristics of the product platform" *(McGrath, 1995, p. 40)*

When developing a new platform, several organizational mechanisms are available to recombine knowledge across disciplines. As we noted in Figure 21.1, new platform development can occupy a range of space relative to the firm's existing market and technology knowledge bases. Some platforms may emanate from bringing a new technology to an existing market, such as the case of emerging biotechnologies in the pharmaceutical industry. In this instance, the platform being developed requires new technological knowledge, but the market for application is the same. This then requires a new and separate group within the technology function dedicated solely to the development of a new class of technologies. Given such a unit's task of developing knowledge, it must be large enough to attain critical mass. However, at the same time, given its focus on new knowledge, it should be buffered from the deadlines and demands of the ongoing technical operations of the organization and perhaps located in a different physical space or off-site. Ultimately, as this new technical knowledge is developed, tested, and codified, it must be integrated with the existing market knowledge of the organization to bring the platform and subsequent product extension offerings to market.

Such initiatives also are typically implemented with multi-functional matrix structures. Teams are designed around the requirement for tapping into the knowledge bases to be combined in some new product, service, or market application. Members are drawn from technical functions as well as representatives of the organizations such as marketing and manufacturing, which serve the existing customers. Some individuals might be assigned part time, others full time depending upon their potential to contribute and the extent to which existing knowledge is being leveraged. The combination of these individuals and groups allows for experimentation on how unorthodox ideas might succeed in a new context.

The deployment of multi-functional matrix teams (Clark & Fujimoto, 1991; Takeuchi & Nonaka, 1986) has been widely discussed in the literature. Clark, Chew, and Fujimoto (1987), Gupta and Wilema (1990), and Womack, Jones, and Roos (1990) have all argued that the use of multi-functional teams creates clear benefits. Clark and Fujimoto (1991), in their global study of product development practices in the auto industry, found that the use of multi-functional teams was a critical factor in influencing success. Similarly, Eisenhardt and Tabrizi (1995) also found that the use of such teams shortened development cycles in their study of new product development in the global computer industry. Although the advantages of using multi-functional matrix teams appears well established, Hitt, Nixon, Hoskisson, and Kochhar (1999) found that contextual factors such as cross-functional politics and the role of institutional leadership may be more important than internal team processes and activities. While recognizing the scope and contribution of this work, we note that the design of multi-functional matrix teams has not been explicitly related to the knowledge management requirements of a creativity context.

In the case of new platform development, multi-functional teams integrate the combination of knowledge by allowing all team members to consider their contribution to the platform relative to the objectives of the project and the possible contributions of other team members (Gerwin & Moffat, 1997). In the case of particularly complex platform assignments (automobiles, aircraft, computers), this process may be facilitated through the extensive use of information technology tools such as computer-aided design and computer-aided manufacturing (Argyres, 1999; Cordero, 1991). Associated benefits include reduced time to market, reduced development costs, and the development of more competitive products (Imai, Nonaka, & Takeuchi, 1985; Liker & Hull, 1993).

Combining and extending knowledge for a new platform development requires considerable individual creativity. In the case of Black and Decker (cited earlier), it is likely that

D. ORGANIZATONAL LEVEL INFLUENCES

product design engineers deconstructed the product into sub-systems and then into individual components. Similarly, manufacturing process engineers may have been presented with specifications which call for faster manufacturing cycles for a product that may be more complex than previous ones. In both cases, existing knowledge had to be extended to satisfy the new specifications. The interaction of these groups, combining their understanding of the state of the art in each of their specialties, searching for insights from seemingly unrelated contexts, and experimenting with emerging but unproven approaches generates the new knowledge necessary for the new platform to become a reality. Note that much of the creativity required to successfully implement this strategy may emerge from the recombination of knowledge from previously unconnected disciplines, or from the recombination of functionally based knowledge. This recombination constitutes new knowledge, but the process of development undoubtedly leverages and extends existing knowledge.

Importing Knowledge

Importing knowledge entails a net new addition to the stock of knowledge in the organization. It is driven by either observed gaps in the knowledge base of the firm or by an emergent strategic intent (Hamel & Prahalad, 1989) of senior management to target a new domain. Imported knowledge can take multiple forms, including new employees, purchased equipment, licensed technologies or acquisitions of other companies. Sources of imported knowledge include customers (Von Hippel, 1988), suppliers (Leonard, 1998), alliance partners (Gomes-Casseres, 1993; Kogut, 1988), universities, government labs, and consultants.

Firms that create new businesses internally diversify their position through market developments or by undertaking technological innovations (Zahra, 1993). A strategy of creating new businesses therefore places a firm in the upper right corner of Figure 21.1. Although this move initially may be from a base of existing knowledge, it nonetheless requires considerable new knowledge about the market and technology. We earlier defined a strategy of new business creation as the pursuit of a new business opportunity that is: new to the firm; implemented internally (not via acquisition); and places the firm into an unrelated domain (Block & MacMillan, 1995; Zahra, 1991).

New business creation strategies have been attempted by a number of companies in different industries. Allied-Signal, Colgate, 3M, and Kodak have all, at various times, engaged in new business creation (Block & MacMillan, 1995). Some of these companies went so far as to create a new venture division (Fast, 1978). More recently, companies such as Intel, Microsoft, McKinsey, and others have engaged in related activities to position themselves into businesses related to the internet and e-commerce.

One detailed example of new business creation completely unrelated to the existing knowledge of the firm is offered by Sykes (1986), through his analysis of the establishment of Exxon Enterprises. Exxon was a large oil and petro-chemical company that was vertically integrated from exploration and production through to retailing. The oil embargoes of the 1970s created windfall profits for much of the industry. Exxon decided to pursue diversification into unrelated markets with products new to the market based on new electronic technologies. The company acquired very early stage ventures, and then internally funded development and commercialization of a range of businesses including a micro-processor, an early text editor, a fax machine directed at the consumer market as well as some voice recognition technologies. Overall, approximately 40 new businesses were created, most by acquiring very early stage firms, then developing them internally to Exxon. Over one billion dollars was invested in these ventures. Many of these businesses later were grouped into a division called Exxon Information Systems. In this example, neither the new technology nor the market was related to any of Exxon's existing knowledge in any way. Ultimately, Exxon exited these unrelated businesses to concentrate on their core operations. More recently, Hamel (1999) has described a new business creation initiative at Royal Dutch Shell that appears to rely much more fundamentally on the existing knowledge of the company at least for the original source for the idea. He cites one new business focused on renewable geothermal energy sources. Although the idea originated within the firm, it involves unrelated technology and new markets.

The creation of a new business within the bounds of an established firm requires developing or adopting new organizational structures that spur innovation and new knowledge development (Zahra, 1993). As we argued earlier, the creation of a new business that is not reliant on the existing knowledge of the firm will be implemented largely through importing new knowledge into it. Such businesses are typically unrelated to existing businesses and therefore require no coordination or sharing of resources. Further, the task of the new business entity early in the process relies extensively on innovation processes that benefit from a degree of differentiation from existing operations. Therefore, many new businesses that are being created by existing firms are structured as independent business units.

A new and separate unit established to create the new business serves as a vehicle to amass resources, both capital and human, and by extension, to build new knowledge. As defined above, importing knowledge entails a net new addition to the stock of knowledge in the organization, taking multiple forms. With a clear focus on establishing a knowledge base related to the new market and technology, an independent business unit becomes the vehicle for knowledge building: new employees can be hired, specialized equipment can be purchased, and license agreements or alliances can be negotiated (Leonard, 1998).

The building blocks of this knowledge importing process are the primary functional groups of the firm such as marketing, engineering, or research and development. A number of authors have argued that knowledge manifests itself as the ability to perform the basic functional activities of the firm more efficiently and effectively than the competition (Amit & Schoemaker, 1993; Collis, 1994). Grant (1991) and Kogut and Zander (1992) have also discussed how routines established within functional groups facilitate the institutionalization of functional-based knowledge. By establishing an independent business unit, each of the functions can be created from scratch, importing (and also extending) knowledge relevant to the new business opportunity. That knowledge only becomes institutionalized when it is firmly established in a set of explicit operating routines or standard operating procedures as well as in the shared cognitive models of a critical mass of functional specialists. Such institutionalized knowledge also becomes manifest in newly offered products and the associated plant, equipment, and other supporting infrastructure.

In addition to each function serving as a base for imported knowledge, they also might search out additional knowledge to import from their natural constituency. For example, the marketing function, or sub-elements within it, might scan the customer base for relevant new knowledge. Research indicates that certain customers may be a source of knowledge about emerging market trends, user preferences, and possible products. Many commercially important products are conceived and sometimes even prototyped by customers (von Hippel, 1988). Von Hippel, Thomke and Sonnack (1999) describe 3M's Medical Surgical Markets Division development of low cost, infection-resistant surgical drapes through close cooperation with leading customers.

In such cases, the marketing function can then import knowledge in the form of new product ideas, designs, prototypes, and sometimes new employees who might be attracted to join the company. Engineering and production functions within the technical core of the company might also work closely and cooperatively with suppliers, again to identify solutions to technical problems or suggestions for product improvements. HP was able to offer more reliable and cheaper keyboards for PCs because of the adoption of new injection modeling equipment from a plastics supplier which was modified to HP's needs (Leonard, 1998). In this way, these newly created functions can search for and import new knowledge relevant to their domain.

Some companies have outlined a strategy to create multiple new businesses, each of which might be established as an independent new business unit. The oversight of these new businesses requires dedicated managerial resources. Earlier these units were called new venture divisions (Fast, 1978) and in the past few years have been called corporate incubators (Hansen, Chesbrough, Nohria, & Sull, 2000). As an example of the number of new businesses within such an incubator, Hansen et al. (2000) cite Lucent, which has created more than 20 new businesses from technologies originated within the firm, but that do not fit with the company's existing businesses. Another example is Ford, which also created an incubator to create internet businesses with some tie to the automotive industry. The head of Ford's incubator reports directly to the CEO of Ford. In describing the Ford incubator, Hansen et al. (2000) noted that Ford staffed these new businesses partly with managers and knowledge workers from inside Ford, but also with new employees from outside of both Ford and the auto industry. History indicates that some of the new businesses may be integrated into the portfolio of existing businesses. In fact, three businesses originally established by Lucent in their incubator were subsequently integrated into their existing operations, based on their increasing relevance to Lucent's overall business strategy as seemingly unrelated technologies converged with existing businesses.

CONCLUSIONS AND IMPLICATIONS

In this chapter, we have proposed a series of organizational mechanisms related to job design, teaming, and the management of organizational boundaries that meet the knowledge management tasks demanded by different strategies for organizational creativity. More specifically, we suggest that the different tasks of knowledge leveraging, recombining, and importing—present to varying degrees in different types of creativity strategies—establish contingencies requiring different organizational responses to attain the desired mix of the exploitation of existing knowledge with the importation and development of new knowledge. Designing appropriate organizational forms to address these critical contingencies enhances the management of knowledge, and, ultimately, the effectiveness of any strategy for creativity.

We argue that each of these distinct creativity settings also require different knowledge management tasks. Building on our re-framing of relatedness as a construct referencing the underlying resources of the firm (Collis & Montgomery, 1998), we propose that a detailed understanding of the existing resource and knowledge base of the firm is necessary to frame the knowledge management process associated with success. Strategies that target related domains to develop product-line extensions must leverage existing knowledge. A new platform development strategy requires the recombination and extension of existing knowledge. Finally, the creation of a new business or technologies calls for the importation and/or the creation of new knowledge.

Although each strategy is predicated on one of the central knowledge management tasks, it also might contain elements of the other two central tasks of knowledge management as well. Therefore, none of the three knowledge management tasks is effectively utilized in isolation, but must be viewed as a building block deployed to maximally manage the exploitation of existing knowledge or the development of new knowledge. The difference is in the emphasis or primacy of the knowledge management tasks to the type of creativity required. Finally, in all three instances, new knowledge is being created, but the amount and type depends on the relatedness of the targeted domain. In other words, exploitation of existing knowledge typically involves developing new knowledge in the process and vice versa. Within this theoretical discussion, we have offered numerous specific organization design options which have been observed in a wide range of organizational settings, and which we expect will have immediate relevance to practicing managers.

Of course, there are several opportunities for additional theoretical development related to knowledge management, creativity, and organizational learning. In concluding our discussion, we highlight one unexplored area relating to the barriers to organizational learning (or the process of institutionalization) once new knowledge has been imported into the organization. The experience of Xerox's development of technology at their Palo Alto Research Center (Parc) is a commonly cited example of a failure of organizational learning. Created in 1969 near Stanford University as a second research and technology development center for Xerox, Parc was located across the US continent from the corporate headquarters in New York, and effectively served as an incubator for new technologies and businesses. In their removed and buffered location, the management of Parc was able to import significant new knowledge via employees hired from the surrounding emerging computer industry and more mature defense industry. This knowledge was used to develop many significant advances in computer hardware and software. Much of what we today understand as the components of the personal computers of the 1980s and later was, in fact, developed by the Parc engineers. Their creative efforts resulted in the development of a graphical user interface, object oriented programming, the ethernet, and laser printers.

Although Xerox had targeted a new domain for development as their stated strategy for creativity, and then adopted the appropriate organization design and knowledge management mechanism, these actions did not result in a process of organizational learning; the new technology and products were not institutionalized into Xerox's functional and operational routines and processes so as to allow them to exploit their own creativity. In fact, much of that technology was ultimately commercialized by Apple Computers, first through a product called the Lisa, and then in the Macintosh. Although Xerox received a block of Apple's pre-IPO stock in return for access to the technology, nonetheless this is an example of a situation where a clear strategy for creativity aligned with an appropriate knowledge management mechanism did not result in organizational learning.

Therefore, a deeper understanding of the organizational and psychological barriers to organizational learning would certainly comprise a worthy extension to existing research related to creativity. Such work might build on recent research by Zollo and Singh (2004) who argued in their study of M&A transactions that firms learn how to manage acquisition processes by forming and refining organizational routines that might influence performance of subsequent integration efforts. By this logic, in studying creativity and the institutionalization of new knowledge into the firm, this might entail, for example, detailed qualitative investigations of the specific capabilities and skills of advocacy for investment in the adoption, advanced development, and commercialization of the products that emerge from new knowledge within the firm. In this way, it might be possible to articulate a "learning by doing" logic that articulates a finer-grained understanding of the specific skills and routines that institutionalize new knowledge, demonstrating organizational learning.

References

Aaker, D. A., & Keller, K. L. (1990). Consumer evaluation of brand extensions. *Journal of Marketing, 54*, 27–41.

Aaker, D. A. (1996). *Building strong brands*. New York, NY: The Free Press.

Amabile, T. M. (1983). *The social psychology of creativity*. New York, NY: Springer-Verlag.

Amabile, T. M. (1988). A model of creativity and innovation in organizations. In B. M. Staw & L. L. Cummings (Eds.), *Research in organizational behavior* (Vol. 10, pp. 123–167). Greenwich, CT: JAI Press.

Amabile, T. M. (1996). *Creativity in context*. New York, NY: Westview Press.

Amit, R., & Schoemaker, P. J. H. (1993). Strategic assets and organizational rent. *Strategic Management Journal, 14*, 33–46.

Andrews, F. M. (1979). *Scientific productivity*. Cambridge, UK: Cambridge University Press.

Ansoff, H. I. (1965). *Corporate strategy: An analytic approach to business policy for growth and expansion*. New York, NY: McGraw Hill.

Argyres, N. S. (1999). The impact of information technology on coordination: Evidence from the B-2 "stealth" bomber. *Organization Science, 10*, 162–180.

Barney, J. B. (1996). The resource-based theory of the firm. *Organization Science, 7*, 469.

Barron, F., & Harrington, D. M. (1981). Creativity, intelligence, and personality. *Annual Review of Psychology, 32*, 439–476.

Basadur, M., Graen, G. B., & Green, S. G. (1982). Training in creative problem solving: Effects on ideation and problem finding and solving in an industrial research organization. *Organization Behavior and Human Performance, 30*, 41–70.

Bennis, W., & Biederman, P. W. (1997). *Organizing genius: The secrets of creative collaboration*. Reading, MA: Addison-Wesley.

Block, Z., & MacMillan, I. C. (1995). *Corporate venturing: Creating new businesses within the firm*. Boston, MA: Harvard Business School Press.

Brush, T. H. (1996). Predicted change in operational synergy and post-acquisition performance of acquire businesses. *Strategic Management Journal, 17*, 1–24.

Carson, P. P., & Carson, K. D. (1993). Managing creativity enhancement through goal setting and feedback. *Journal of Creative Behavior, 27*, 36–45.

Chandler, A. D. (1992). Organizational capabilities and the economic history of the industrial enterprise. *Journal of Economic Perspectives, 6*, 79–100.

Chandler, A. D. (1996). *Scale and scope: The dynamics of industrial capitalism*. Cambridge, MA: Belknap.

Chandler, A. I. (1962). *Strategy and structure*. Cambridge, MA: MIT Press.

Christensen, C. M. (1997). *The innovator's dilemma: When new technologies cause great firms to fail*. Boston, MA: Harvard Business School Press.

Choi, J. P. (1998). Brand extension as informational leverage. *The Review of Economic Studies, 65*, 655–669.

Ciborra, C. U. (1996). The platform organization: Recombining strategies, structures, and surprises. *Organization Science, 7*, 103–118.

Clark, K. B., Chew, W. B., & Fujimoto, T. (1987). Product development in the world auto industry. *Brookings Papers on Economic Activity, 3*, 729–781. New York, NY: Brookings Institution.

Clark, K. B., & Fujimoto, T. (1991). *Product development performance: Strategy, organization and management in the world auto industry*. Boston, MA: Harvard Business School Press.

Coff, R. (1997). Human assets and management dilemmas: Coping with hazards on the road to resources-based theory. *Academy of Management Review, 30*, 374–402.

Cohen, W. M., & Levinthal, D. A. (1990). Absorptive capacity: A new perspective on learning and innovation. *Administrative Science Quarterly, 3*, 128–153.

Collis, D. J. (1994). How valuable are organizational capabilities?. *Strategic Management Journal, 15*, 143–152.

Collis, D. J., & Montgomery, C. A. (1998). Creating corporate advantage. *Harvard Business Review, 76*, 70–83.

Cordero, R. (1991). Managing for speed to avoid product obsolescence: A survey of techniques. *The Journal of Product Innovation Management, 8*, 283–294.

Davis, R., & Thomas, L. G. (1993). Direct estimation of synergy: A new approach to the diversity-synergy debate. *Management Science, 39*, 1334–1346.

DeMaio, A., Verganti, R., & Corso, M. (1994). A multi-project framework for new product development. *European Journal of Operational Research, 78*, 178–191.

Dess, G. G., Lumpkin, G. T., & McGee, J. E. (1999). Linking corporate entrepreneurship to strategy, structure, and process: Suggested research directions. *Entrepreneurship Theory & Practice, 23*, 85–102.

Dosi, G. (1982). Technological paradigms and technological trajectories. *Research Policy, 11*, 147–162.

Drazin, R., Glynn, M. A., & Kazanjian, R. K. (1999). Multi-level theorizing about creativity in organizations: A sense-making perspective. *Academy of Management Review, 24*, 286–308.

Drazin, R., Glynn, M. A., & Kazanjian, R. K. (2004). Dynamics of structural change. In M. Poole & A. Van de Ven (Eds.), *Handbook of change and innovation* (pp. 161–211). Oxford, UK: Oxford University Press.

Dumaine, B. (1993). Payoff from the new management. *Fortune, December 13*, 103–110.

Eisenhardt., K. M., & Tabrizi, B. N. (1995). Accelerating adaptive processes: Product innovation in the global computer industry. *Administrative Science Quarterly, 40*, 84–110.

Fast, N. D. (1978). New venture departments: Organizing for innovation. *Industrial Marketing Management, 7*, 77.

Ford, C. M. (1996). A theory of individual creativity in multiple social domains. *Academy of Management Review, 21*, 1112–1134.

Gardner, H. (1993). *Multiple intelligences: The theory in practice*. New York: Basic Book.

Galbraith, J. R. (1982). Designing the innovating organization. *Organizational Dynamics, 11*, 5–25.

George, J. M., & Zhou, J. (2007). Dual tuning in a supportive context: Joint contributions of positive mood, negative mood, and supervisory behaviors to employee creativity. *Academy of Management Journal, 50*, 605–622.

Gerwin, D., & Moffat, L. (1997). Authorizing processes changing team autonomy during new product development. *Journal of Engineering and Technology Management, 14*, 291–313.

Gimeno, J., & Woo, C. Y. (1999). Multimarket contact, economies of scope, and firm performance. *Academy of Management Journal, 42*, 239–259.

Glynn, M. A. (1996). Innovative genius: A framework for relating individual and organizational intelligences to innovation. *Academy of Management Review, 21*, 1081–1111.

Glynn, M. A., Lant, T. K. & Milliken, F. J. (1994). Mapping learning processes in organizations: A multi-level framework linking learning and organizing. In *Advances in managerial cognition and organizational information processing*, Vol. 5, pp. 43–83. Greenwich, CT: JAI Press.

Gomes-Casseres, B. (1993). Computers: Alliances and Industry Evolution. In D. B. Yoffie (Ed.), *Beyond free trade: Firms, governments, and global competition* (pp. 12–79). Boston, MA: Harvard Business Press.

Govindarajan, V., & Fisher, J. (1990). Strategy, control systems, and resource sharing: Effects on business unit performance. *Academy of Management Journal, 33*, 259–285.

Grant, R. M., & Baden–Fuller, C. (1995). A knowledge based theory of inter-firm collaboration. *Academy of Management Journal*, 17–25. Best Paper Proceedings.

Grant, R. M. (1996). Knowledge, strategy, and the theory of the firm. *Strategic Management Journal, 17*, 109–122.

Gupta, A., & Govindarajan, V. (1986). Resource sharing among SBUs: Strategic antecedent and administrative implications. *Academy of Management Journal, 29*, 695–714.

Gupta, A. K., & Wilemon, D. L. (1990). Accelerating the development of technology-based new products. *California Management Review, 32*, 24–44.

Hamel, G., & Prahalad, C. K. (1993). Strategy as stretch and leverage. *Harvard Business Review, 71*, 75–84.

Hamel, G. (1999). Bringing silicon valley inside. *Harvard Business Review, 77*, 70–84.

Hansen, M. T., Chesbrough, H. W., Nohria, N., & Sull, D. (2000). Networked incubators: Hothouses of the new economy. *Harvard Business Review, September–October*.

Henderson, R., & Clark, K. (1990). Architectural innovation: The reconfiguration of existing product technologies and the failure of established firms. *Administrative Science Quarterly, 35*, 9–30.

Hill, C. W. L., Hitt, M. A., & Hoskisson, R. E. (1992). Cooperative versus competitive structures in related and unrelated diversified firms. *Organization Science, 3*, 501–521.

Hitt, M. A., Nixon, R. D., Hoskisson, R. E., & Kochhar, R. (1999). Corporate entrepreneurship and cross-functional fertilization: Activation, process and disintegration of a new product design team. *Entrepreneurship Theory & Practice, 23*, 145–167.

Hoffman, E. (1997). NASA project management: Modern strategies for maximizing project performance. *Project Management Journal, 28*, 4–6.

Horwitch, M. (1982). *Clipped wings: The American SST conflict*. Cambridge, MA: MIT Press.

Imai, K., Nonaka, I., & Takeuchi, H. (1985). Managing the new product development process: How Japanese companies learn and unlearn. In K. Clark, R. Hayes & C. Lorenz (Eds.), *The uneasy alliance* (pp. 553–561). Boston, MA: Harvard Business School Press.

Kahn, W. A. (1990). Psychological conditions of personal engagement and disengagement at work. *Academy of Management Journal, 33*, 692–724.

Kanter, R. M. (1988). When a thousand flowers bloom: Structural, collective, and social conditions for innovation in organization. In B. M. Staw & L. L. Cummings (Eds.), *Research in organization behavior* (Vol. 10, pp. 169–211). Greenwich, CT: JAI Press.

Kazanjian, R. K., & Drazin, R. (1987). Implementing internal diversification: Contingency factors for organization design choices. *Academy of Management Review, 12*, 342–354.

Kazanjian, R. K., Drazin, R., & Glynn, M. A. (2002). Implementing strategy for corporate entrepreneurship. In M. A Hitt, R. D. Ireland, S. M. Camp & D. L. Sexton (Eds.), *Strategic entrepreneurship: Creating a new mindset (strategic management society)* (pp. 173–192). Oxford, UK: Blackwell Publishers.

Kazanjian, R. K., & Nayyar, P. R. (1994). Attaining technological synergies in diversified firms. In M. W. Lawless & L. R. Gomez-Mejia (Eds.), *Advances in global high-technology management* (Vol. 4, pp. 121–138). Greenwich, CT: JAI Press.

Kekre, S., & Srinivasan, K. (1990). Broader product lines: A necessity to achieve success? *Management Science, 36*, 1216–1231.

Keller, K. L., & Aaker, D. A. (1992). The effects of sequential introduction of brand extensions. *Journal of Marketing Research, 29*, 35–51.

Kim, L. (1998). Crisis construction and organizational learning: Capacity building in catching-up at Hyundai Motor. *Organization Science, 9*, 506–521.

Kim, D. -J., & Kogut, B. (1996). Technological platforms and diversification. *Organization Science, 7*, 283–301.

King, N., & Anderson, N. (1990). Innovation and creativity in working groups. In M. A. West & J. L. Farr (Eds.), *Innovation and creativity at work: Psychological and organizational strategies* (pp. 81–100). Chichester: Wiley.

Klette, T. J. (1996). R&D, scope economics, and plant performance. *The RAND Journal of Economics, 27*, 502–523.

Kodama, F. (1992). Technology fusion and the new R&D. *Harvard Business Review, 70*, 9.

Kogut, B. (1988). Joint ventures: Theoretical and empirical perspectives. *Strategic Management Journal, 9*, 319–332.

Kogut, B., & Kulatilaka, N. (1994). Options thinking and platform investments: Investing in opportunity. *California Management Review, 36*, 52–72.

Kogut, B., & Zander, U. (1996). What do firms do? Coordination, identity, and learning. *Organization Science, 7*, 502–518.

Kotler, P. (1996). *Marketing management: Analysis, planning, implementation, and control* (9th ed.). Englewood Cliffs, NJ: Prentice Hall Press.

Leonard, D. (1998). *Wellsprings of knowledge*. Boston, MA: Harvard Business School Press.

Leonard-Barton, D. (1992). Core capabilities and core rigidities: A paradox in managing new product development. *Strategic Management Journal, 13*, 111–126.

Liker, J. K. & Hull, P. (1993). What works in concurrent engineering?: Sorting through the barrage of practices. Paper presented at the Academy of Management Conference, Atlanta, GA.

Mackinnon, D. W. (1965). Personality and the realization of creative potential. *American Psychologist, 20*, 273–281.

March, J. G. (1991). Exploration and exploitation in organizational learning. *Organization Science, 2,* 71–87.

Markides, C. C., & Williamson, P. J. (1996). Corporate diversification and organizational structure: A resource-based view. *Academy of Management Journal, 39,* 340–367.

McGrath, M. E. (1994). *Product strategies for high-technology companies: How to achieve growth, competitive advantage, and increased profits.* New York, NY: Irwin.

McGrath, R. G. (1995). Advantages from adversity: Learning from disappointment in internal corporate ventures. *Journal of Business Venturing, 10,* 121–142.

McGrath, R. G. (1997). A real options logic for initiating technology positioning investments. *Academy of Management Review, 2,* 974–996.

McGrath, R. G. (1999). Falling forward: Real options reasoning and entrepreneurial failure. *Academy of Management Review, 24,* 13–30.

Meyer, M. H., & Lehnerd, A. P. (1997). *The power of product platforms: Building value and cost leadership.* New York, NY: The Free Press.

Mohr, L. (1982). *Explaining organizational behavior.* San Francisco, CA: Jossey-Bass.

Montgomery, C., & Harihran, S. (1991). Diversified entry by established firms. *Journal of Economic Behavior and Organization, 15,* 71–89.

Mumford, M. D. (2000). Managing creative people: Strategies and tactics for innovation. *Human Resource Management Review, 10,* 313–351.

Mumford, M. D., & Gustafson, S. B. (1988). Creativity syndrome: Integration, application, and innovation. *Psychological Bulletin, 103,* 27–43.

Nayyar, P. R., & Kazanjian, R. K. (1993). Organizing to attain potential benefits from information asymmetries and economies of scope in related diversified firms. *Academy of Management Review, 18,* 735–759.

Nayyar, P. R. (1993). On the measurement of competitive strategy: Evidence from a large US multiproduct firm. *Academy of Management Journal, 36,* 1652–1669.

Nelson, R., & Winter, S. (1982). *An evolutionary theory of economic change.* Cambridge, MA: Belknap.

Normann, R. (1977). *Management for growth.* New York, NY: Wiley.

Panzar, J. C., & Willig, R. D. (1981). Economies of scope. *American Economic Review, 71,* 268–272.

Payne, R. (1990). The effectiveness of research teams: A review. In M. A. West & J. L. Farr (Eds.), *Innovation and creativity at work* (pp. 101–122). Chichester, UK: Wiley.

Pennings, J. M., Barkema, H., & Douma, S. (1994). Organizational learning and diversification. *Academy of Management Journal, 37,* 608–641.

Penrose, E. (1995). *The theory of the growth of the firm.* Oxford, UK: Blackwell.

Pitts, R. A. (1977). Strategies and structures for diversification. *Academy of Management Journal, 20,* 197–208.

Porter, M. E. (1985). *Competitive advantage.* New York, NY: The Free Press.

Prahalad, C. K., & Hamel, G. (1990). The core competence of the corporation. *Harvard Business Review, 68,* 79–92.

Quinn, J. B. & Pacquette, P. (1988). Ford: Team Taurus, Amos Tuck School, Dartmouth College.

Redmond, M. R., Mumford, M. D., & Teach, R. (1993). Putting creativity to work: Effects of leader behavior on subordinate behavior. *Organization Behavior and Human Decision Processes, 55,* 120–151.

Rumelt, R. P. (1974). *Strategy, structure, and economic performance.* Cambridge, MA: Harvard Business School Division of Research.

Sabbagh, K. (1996). *Twenty-first-century jet: The making and marketing of the Boeing 777.* New York, NY: Scribner.

Sanchez, R., & Mahoney, J. T. (1996). Modularity, flexibility, and knowledge management in product and organization design. *Strategic Management Journal, 17,* 17–63.

Sawhney, M. (1998). Leveraged high-variety strategies: From portfolio thinking to platform thinking. *Journal of the Academy of Marketing Science, 26,* 54–61.

Sayles, L. R., & Chandler, M. K. (1971). *Managing large systems: Organizations of the future.* New York, NY: Harper and Row.

Scudder, G. D., Schroeder, R. G., Van De Ven, A. H., Seiler, G. R., & Wiseman, R. M. (1989). Managing Complex innovations: the case of defense contracting. In A. H. Van de Ven, H. L. Agle & M. S. Poole (Eds.), *Research on the management of innovation* (pp. 401–438). New York, NY: Harper & Row.

Senge, P. (1994). *The fifth discipline: The art and practice of the learning organization.* New York, NY: Doubleday.

Singh, B. (1986). Role of personality versus biographical factors in creativity. *Psychological Studies, 31,* 90–92.

D. ORGANIZATONAL LEVEL INFLUENCES

Stahl, M. J., & Koser, M. C. (1978). Weighted productivity in R&D: Some associated individual and organizational variables. *IEEE Transactions on Engineering Management*, 20–24. EM-25

Sykes, H. B. (1986). Lessons from a new ventures program. *Harvard Business Review.*

Takeuchi, H., & Nonaka, I. (1986). The new product development game. *Harvard Business Review, 64*, 137–146.

Teece, D. J. (1980). Economies of scope and the scope of the enterprise. *Journal of Economic Behavior and Organization, 1*, 223–245.

Teece, D. J. (1982). Towards an economic theory of the multiproduct business. *Journal of Economic Behavior and Organization, 3*, 39–63.

Teece, D. J. (1986). Transactions cost economics and the multinational enterprise: An assessment. *Journal of Economic Behavior and Organization, 7*, 21–46.

Torrence, E. P. (1988). The nature of creativity as manifest in its testing. In R. J. Sternberg (Ed.), *The nature of creativity: Contemporary psychological views* (pp. 43–75). Cambridge, UK: Cambridge University Press.

Tushman, M. L., & O'Reilly, C. A (2004). The ambidextrous organization. *Harvard Business Review., 82*, 74–81.

Vancil, R. F. (1980). Managing the decentralized firm. *Financial Executive, 48*, 34–43.

VonHippel, E. (1988). *The sources of innovation.* New York, NY: Oxford University Press.

VonHippel, E., Thomke, S., & Sonnack, M. (1999). Creating breakthroughs at 3M. *Harvard Business Review, 77*, 47–57.

Wang, H. C., He, J., & Mahoney, J. (2009). Firm specific knowledge resources and competitive advantage: The roles of economic and relationship-based employee governance mechanisms. *Strategic Management Journal, 30*, 1265–1286.

Wernerfelt, B. (1984). A resource-based view of the firm. *Strategic Management Journal, 5*, 171–180.

West, M. A. (1989). Innovation amongst healthcare professionals. *Social Behavior, 4*, 173–184.

Womack, J. P., Jones, D. T., & Roos, D. R. (1990). *The machine that changed the world: The story of lean production.* New York, NY: Harper Perennial.

Woodman, R. W., Sawyer, J. E., & Griffin, R. W. (1993). Toward a theory of organizational creativity. *Academy of Management Review, 18*, 293–321.

Zahra, S. A. (1991). Predictors and financial outcomes of corporate entrepreneurship: An Exploratory study. *Journal of Business Venturing, 6*, 259–285.

Zahra, S. A. (1993). Environment, corporate entrepreneurship, and financial performance: A taxonomic approach. *Journal of Business Venturing, 8*, 319–340.

Zollo, M., & Singh, H. (2004). Deliberate learning in corporate acquisitions: Post-acquisition strategies and integration capability in US bank mergers. *Strategic Management Journal, 25*, 1233–1256.

Zook, C. (2007). Finding your next core business. *Harvard Business Review, 85*, 66–75.

Zook, C., & Allen, J. (2003). Growth outside the core. *Harvard Business Review, 81*, 66–73.

Organizing for Change, Innovation, and Creativity

Danielle D. Dunne[1] and Deborah Dougherty[2]

[1]Binghamton University, State University of New York, School of
Management, NY; [2]Rutgers University, Management and Global Business
Department, NJ

INTRODUCTION

Innovation, the development and use of new ideas within an organization, almost always implies change. However, managing organizational innovation is challenging for both managers and organizational theorists (Drazin, Glynn, & Kazanjian, 1999; Leonard-Barton, 1995; Dougherty, 2006). One reason this is so challenging is because organizational innovation depends on fostering creativity within and among employees across the entire organization (Amabile, Conti, Coon, Lazenby, & Heroin, 1996; Drazin et al., 1999). A second reason is that the familiar model of organizational change—a brief episode of transformation versus continuous evolution—does not adequately harness creativity or innovation, and so fails to explain how organizations can be both creative and innovative.

In this chapter we develop a model for managing organizational change that leverages the vast literatures on creativity, innovation, and change. We identify three tensions in creativity and innovation research, and map the conflicting perspectives onto different types of organizing. Understanding these qualitatively different ways of organizing explains why these tensions exist. We then theorize about a new type of organizing that accommodates these conflicting perspectives and articulates a context in which change supports creativity and innovation; and creativity and innovation drive change. In developing our model we follow existing research and consider creativity and innovation in the same context, but it is important to note that creativity and innovation are not the same thing. Amabile (1988) defines creativity as:

> "the production of novel and useful ideas by an individual or small group of individuals working together"

Handbook of Organizational Creativity.
DOI: 10.1016/B978-0-12-374714-3.00022-7

and organizational innovation as:

"the successful implementation of creative ideas within an organization" *(p. 126).*

Creativity and innovation are different but clearly related concepts. We start with existing models of organizational change.

Models for organizational change have been around since the rise of modern management (e.g., Chandler, 1962, on the transformation of General Motors and the development of McKinsey and other consulting for change models in the 1920s). Yet organizational change remains deeply problematic, with many organizations either failing to change in time or implementing change very poorly. While there are many reasons why change is so challenging, we address two in particular. The first challenge is theoretical: the change literature tends to be hung up on a simple dichotomy of episodic versus incremental change, and therefore cannot address organizing to engage in both dynamics. The second challenge is lack of substance, or change to what from what, and why? With limited substance the various change models tend to be theories of anything, and mix together a variety of processes and practices, which may be why they do not explain much. The dichotomy with limited causal dynamics combined with limited focus on actual activities means that generic change models fail to explain how to build creativity and how to foster innovation.

One familiar model of organizational change is based on Weick and Quinn's (1999) discussion of two categories: the episodic or discontinuous change versus the continuous and evolving but mostly incremental change. This generic model seems to fit many of the changes that are observed, but its underlying explanations are suspect. Episodic change or punctuated equilibrium presumes that organizations cannot in fact change continually but rather become inert, and focus on existing operations based on existing business models and processes. Over time, processes and procedures become rigid, managers become inured to shifts in their environment, and employees are assumed to almost automatically resist change. According to this perspective, change is only possible in brief episodes, and the organization returns to long periods of stable and inert operations—provided of course it survives the transformation. These episodes are often discontinuous, radical transformations that are occasioned either by the failure of the organization to adapt more smoothly to evolving markets or technologies, meaning they must shift significantly to survive, or by more sudden shifts in technologies (Gersick, 1991; Romanelli & Tushman, 1994). Other sources of abrupt change include new management, jolts such as strikes or economic recessions, and mergers and acquisitions. The underlying assumption for sudden change is of equilibrium, and more, that people just do not want to or like to change. Related models come from population ecology that assumes that once a population of organizations arises, institutional forces prevent much change, so change occurs at the population level (Baum & Amburgey, 2002).

However, there is another very different model, in which organizations can and do engage in continuous, albeit mostly incremental change, and in so doing adapt over time, at least to relatively slower changes in environmental conditions. Brown and Eisenhardt (1997) argue that some firms continuously adapt and change, or can. Additionally, there is another model of continuous and radical change. Plowman and colleagues (2007) suggest that small changes can accumulate into big ones over time if the dynamics of complexity—disequilibrium and positive feedback—are incorporated. We address the first challenge in the change literature by building on this research to suggest that organizations can accommodate both types of changes simultaneously. To address the second challenge, the one of substance, we focus on organizing for activities that incorporate change, specifically creating a context for creativity and innovation.

A review of academic literature in the areas of creativity and innovation reveals three important tensions for creating a context that supports creativity and innovation: 1. the relative importance of supportive vs. demanding managers; 2. the value of weak vs. strong ties; and 3. the role of job vs. product complexity. Next, we explore these tensions and begin to identify why they might exist, and how a new model of organizational change might accommodate these conflicting perspectives.

Supportive versus Demanding Managers

Research on creativity and innovation converge around the basic idea that relationships, connections between people who work together, are important for developing and implementing new ideas. However, research conflicts over exactly what types of relationships between managers and coworkers are most beneficial for stimulating creativity and innovation.

One perspective explores contextual characteristics of creativity and innovation from the individual or team level of analysis, suggesting that the presence of supportive managers, leaders, and coworkers are important antecedents to increases in the intrinsic motivation and creativity of employees (Shalley, Zhou, & Oldham, 2004). Shalley and colleagues explain that being supportive means showing:

> "concern for employees' feelings, [providing] nonjudgmental, informational feedback about their work, and [encouraging] them to voice their own concerns" (Deci, Connell, & Ryan, 1989). (p.938).

In their meta-analysis of team-level antecedents of creativity and innovation at work Hulsheger, Anderson, and Salgado (2009) seem to agree:

> "A supportive, cooperative work atmosphere, where coworkers socialize and help each other and collaborate in problem solving is…expected to be conducive to innovation (e.g. Amabile et al., 1996; Keller, Julian, & Kedia, 1996; Tiwanta & McLean, 2005)" (p. 1131).

A contrasting perspective suggests that in order to promote innovation, managers and coworkers need to be reasonably demanding. Demanding managers are defined as managers that are more concerned with strategic factors, such as deciding which projects to support with scarce resources. They are responsible for sourcing projects, and ensuring that those projects are progressing efficiently and are tied in with strategic organizational goals. These types of responsibilities often involve making difficult decisions. Some innovation research even suggests that when people are given too much support and encouragement, without a significant amount of structure, it can be detrimental to innovation, particularly for younger workers (Bailyn, 1980). Managers that are overly concerned with supporting people may inhibit what Leonard-Barton (1995) refers to as "creative abrasion" when "different ideas rub against each other, sparks fly" (p.63). This research explains that the energy from the conflict can be creative and synthesizing (Leonard-Barton, 1995).

While the presence or absence of supportive managers does not preclude other organizational mechanisms, most work from the demanding managers' perspective suggests that rules or structures to guide behavior and integrate knowledge are essential to creativity and innovation (Dougherty & Tolboom, 2008). This contrasts with the first perspective that emphasizes positive correlations between supportive managers and coworkers, and creativity and innovation (Hulsheger et al., 2009; Shalley et al., 2004). These divergent perspectives suggest an important tension between the relative importance of supportive versus demanding managers and coworkers.

Weak versus Strong Ties

Research on the value of weak vs. strong ties for creativity and innovation highlights the second tension. Strong ties represent closer relationships, connections in which people invest more significant amounts of social resources, while weak ties represent more distant relationships (Fleming, Mingo, & Chen, 2007). While the content of these relationships is not often considered in network research, we assume that different types of knowledge and potential learning may be attributable to weak vs. strong ties.

Perry-Smith and Shalley (2003) suggest that weak ties are relatively more important than strong ties in facilitating creativity. Additional research suggests that teams that participate in external communication may be more innovative and efficient (Edmondson & Nembhard, 2009). Communication with people outside of a specific team may enable team members to bring together diverse viewpoints and absorb new knowledge (Edmondson & Nembhard, 2009; Hulsheger et al., 2009). Hulsheger and colleagues (2009) find a significant relationship between the team process variables of external communication and innovation. They explain:

> "Our findings confirm that communication, especially with individuals outside one's own team, is a crucial element in fostering innovation in the workplace. If individuals maintain social relationship with people outside their core work team, they are more likely to be exposed to new kinds of information and diversity viewpoints and thus generate fresh ideas" (Hulsheger et al., 2009, p. 1139).

Being exposed to diverse viewpoints and new information may be more likely through weak ties. However, this perspective also seems to assume that the knowledge people have is freely shared.

Creativity research often depicts knowledge and the potential for learning as being readily accessible (Amabile, 1988; Woodman, Sawyer, & Griffin, 1993). In their multi-level interactionist model of organizational creativity Woodman and colleagues (1993) point out that knowledge and expertise play an important role in individual creative abilities; they explain that groups are a context in which people can access each other's knowledge to augment what they already know. Amabile's (1988) model suggests that domain and creativity relevant skills, along with task motivation affect creativity. She explains the importance of domain-relevant knowledge:

"The individual builds up or reactivates a store of information relevant to the problem or task, including a knowledge of response algorithms for working problems in the domain in question. In the case where domain-relevant skills are rather impoverished at the outset, this stage may be quite a long one, during which a great deal of learning takes place. On the other hand, if the domain-relevant skills are already sufficiently rich to afford an ample set of possible pathways to explore during task engagement, the reactivation of this already-stored set of information and algorithms may be almost instantaneous" *(p. 139)*.

This work depicts knowledge as a store of information that can be readily drawn on for a particular task or problem; and if the knowledge does not exist, then time is considered to be the primary constraint for accessibility.

A contrasting perspective emphasizes the challenges of integrating knowledge for product innovation (Bechky, 2003; Carlile, 2002, 2004; Dougherty, 1992). From this perspective, knowledge is caught up in everyday practice, and important knowledge for innovation may not be readily accessible. Knowledge that is embedded in practice is unlikely to be surfaced or created in weak ties (McFadyen, Semadeni, & Cannella, 2009). Additionally, other research suggests that strong ties may be more integral than weak ties to creativity and innovation:

"Although social interaction is generally thought to enhance creativity (Sutton & Hargadon, 1996; Leonard & Swap, 1999; Paulus & Nijstad, 2003; McFadyen & Cannella, 2004), there is still controversy over the optimal structure of that social interaction and, in particular, over the relative creative benefits of brokerage between otherwise disconnected people" *(Fleming et al., 2007, p. 443)*.

Brokers are intermediate people such that the two people only interact through the broker. These findings suggest that weak and strong ties have differential effects on creativity and innovation (Fleming et al., 2007). Specifically, Fleming and colleagues (2007) explain that strong ties are a positive factor when the focal inventor has broader experience, has worked in multiple organizations, and also works with external collaborators (Fleming et al., 2007). Brokers may enable creativity, but be disconnected from innovation (Hargadon & Sutton, 1997).

McFadyen and colleagues (2009) examine the knowledge creation process; specifically the value of strong ties to disconnected others. They explain that high levels of connectivity may aid in the development of collectively held beliefs and norms but may be less likely to provide people with new information (McFadyen et al., 2009). However, while weak ties may work for job hunters, they may not work for innovation; this more complex innovative activity will likely require trust and norms of communication and cooperation (McFadyen et al., 2009). More specifically, people involved in innovation work need to understand how to design products, leverage organizational capabilities, and tap into current strategies and market knowledge (Brown & Eisenhardt, 1997; Dougherty, 2006). This type of situated learning may not be possible through weak ties. These conflicting perspectives suggest an important tension between the value of weak versus strong ties.

Job versus Product Complexity

The third tension is concerned with the boundaries of complexity. One perspective suggests that jobs should provide the boundaries for complexity and another suggests a much broader product boundary for complexity. In the creativity literature, job complexity is

TABLE 22.1   Tensions in Creativity/Innovation Literatures Explained Across Forms of Organizing.

	Bureaucratic Organizing	Adaptive Organizing	Transformative Organizing
Managers and coworkers are beneficial when they are	Supportive	Demanding	Focused on knowledge objects
Relationships are valuable when ties are	Weak	Strong	Found in communities of practice
Complexity is valuable when it is related to	Jobs	Product	Emergence across entire systems

viewed as an important contextual antecedent for creativity (Shalley et al., 2004). In Shalley and colleagues' (2004) own words:

> "The design of jobs has long been considered an important contributor to employee creativity (West & Far, 1990). When individuals work on complex jobs (i.e. those characterized by high levels of autonomy, feedback, significance, identity and variety (Hackman & Oldham, 1980) they are likely to experience high levels of intrinsic motivation and to respond to this motivation by developing creative ideas." *(p. 938)*

When the complexity of work moves from the individual job to the overall work of a team, project complexity is viewed as a challenge for new product development (Edmondson & Nembhard, 2009). However, even as this work explains that complexity may be problematic, it also suggests that it is an inherent part of innovation (Edmondson & Nembhard, 2009). Innovative products involve integrating knowledge from numerous groups, each working on different phases of development (Bechky, 2003; Wheelwright & Clark, 1992;). This type of product development faces continual problems that need to be set and solved (Dougherty, 2006; Schon, 1983), and this makes it nearly impossible to keep complexity within the bounds of job design. While the first perspective suggests that complexity may be limited to job complexity, a contrasting perspective suggests that innovative products may be growing increasingly complex (Dougherty & Dunne, in press). These conflicting perspectives suggest the third important tension between job and product complexity.

In the next section we explain why these tensions exist in the literature. We explain that these conflicting perspectives may be understood in the context of qualitatively different ways of organizing for change. We find that by mapping these conflicting perspectives onto two different types of organizing, the tensions are explained. Then, we theorize about a third type of organizing; a new model that accommodates rather than separates these tensions. The key ideas for the next section are also depicted in Table 22.1.

BUREAUCRATIC ORGANIZING

The first form of organizing is likely the most familiar. The bureaucracy is an organizational structure characterized by functional departments and a clearly outlined hierarchy (Weber, 1946). Creativity and innovation occur in the bureaucracy, but are largely limited to separate functions. In analyzing the three tensions in the context of the bureaucracy we find that the first perspective presented in each section fits well here. More specifically, in bureaucratic organizing, supportive managers, weak ties, and job complexity explain how and why change, creativity, and innovation are fostered in bureaucratic organizing.

Supportive Managers

Understanding bureaucratic organizing helps us to sort out the tension between the conflicting perspectives on supportive versus demanding managers and coworkers. Bureaucratic organizing emphasizes task specialization and efficiency, and in order for creative activities to happen in this type of structure, they need to be legitimized by managers in the hierarchical structure. In this context supportive managers may be integral to motivating employees to move from clearly outlined routine activities to incorporating new ideas into their work (Hulsheger et al., 2009; Shalley et al., 2004). In order for creative activities to occur in Weber's (1946) bureaucracy, creativity, and the change that it implies needs to be a part of articulated work definitions, and that is only likely to happen with supportive managers.

Looking a little closer at some earlier creativity research it is unsurprising to note that the finding that supportive and non-controlling supervision is associated with creativity is from research that examined employees at manufacturing facilities (Oldham & Cummings, 1996). Other research that examines the activities of research and development (R&D) scientists suggests a more nuanced view of the contextual characteristics that promote creativity. For example, Amabile's (1988) model draws on work that emphasizes the importance of freedom in work activities and good project management, defined in part as management that provides "clear direction without managing too tightly" (p. 147).

Weak Ties

An important part of stimulating creativity is being exposed to different points of view, and an important part of innovative work is understanding different functional perspectives (Dougherty, 1992; Edmondson & Nembhard, 2009; Hulsheger et al., 2009). However, bureaucratic organizing groups work by function. In order to access views that are different from those found within a single function, people must form relationships with those outside their line of work. These ties are likely to be relatively weak relationships because there is less interaction with people outside of functional groupings. Additionally, people from different specializations may have different perspectives on their work, making it difficult for them to find the common ground that might form the basis for a relationship (Bechky, 2003; Dougherty, 1992).

In bureaucratic organizations, weak ties may be more important than strong ties for two reasons. First, in these types of functional groupings people are exposed to very little diversity on a regular basis. Weak connections with other functions may be the only way in which different points of view are integrated into the work process and are able to make an important relative contribution. People may not have strong ties to people with different knowledge. Second, most of the innovation within the bureaucracy is likely to take place within a specific function. For example, changes in accounting processes or procedures are likely innovations. These types of process innovations may not require cross-functional collaboration as long as they do not affect how the accounting team interfaces with the rest of the organization in any significant way. In other words, as long as the innovations stay within the function, close ties to those in other areas of the organization may not be necessary.

Functional specialization is one of the underlying drivers of this type of bureaucratic organizing, so it follows that knowledge creation and learning are also occurring within functions. Given this focus it may be more likely that an established body of knowledge may be readily accessible in terms of being easily articulated and readily drawn on. The perspective that knowledge is something that is readily accessible may fit well with bureaucratic organizing.

Job Complexity

Complexity, specifically job complexity plays an important role in bureaucratic organizing (Oldham & Cummings, 1996; Shalley et al., 2004). Jobs are clearly defined in the bureaucracy, but clear work definitions may also create a context in which all jobs become very routine and uninteresting. Research suggests that job complexity is good, and it may be particularly important in this type of organizing because there are clear boundaries placed on jobs. These boundaries modularize complexity, keeping complex issues within jobs, and protect the rest of the organization from the challenges that complexity inevitably entails. In this form, enabling increased complexity in these modularized jobs may enhance creativity and innovation.

Change, creativity, and innovation do occur in bureaucratic organizing and may be stimulated by supportive managers, weak ties, and job complexity. Some types of innovations may be particularly well suited for this type of organizing. For example, given the support from upper management, a manager of research and development (R&D) at a manufacturing organization might be able to re-organize an engineering department to stimulate creativity and innovation. The department may innovate within their function by organizing work such that one group works on daily issues of current projects, one group works on incremental innovations for existing platforms, and another group works on breakthrough innovation or new products. Another example might be a marketing department that is capable of shifting their advertising efforts to new forms of digital media. At another organization people might rotate through jobs, and in doing so change the various jobs, increasing job complexity and stimulating creativity and innovation within functions.

However, in bureaucratic organizing much of this creativity and innovation will be limited to functions. The occasional cross-functional team might be used in response to specific internal or external shocks, but the type of constant change that is required for continuous product innovation may not be possible given the structure of the bureaucracy.

ADAPTIVE ORGANIZING

In analyzing the three tensions in the context of the adaptive organizing, we find that the second perspective presented in each section fits well here. More specifically, in adaptive organizing, demanding managers, strong ties, and project complexity explain how and why change, creativity, and innovation are fostered in adaptive organizing. In adaptive organizing change is fast, continuous, and typically found in terms of product development

(Brown & Eisenhardt, 1997). Work is structured around lateral flows of activities in which multi-functional teams are a staple of the organizing process. Structures here may be best described as "semi-structures", which are defined as:

> "organizations in which some features are prescribed or determined (e.g., responsibilities, project priorities, time intervals between projects), but other aspects are not" *(Brown & Eisenhard, 1997, p. 28)*.

Incremental change and, in turn, incremental innovation are continuous in this type of organizing.

Demanding Managers

In adaptive organizing, project teams work collectively and heedfully, setting and solving the problems that they encounter (Dougherty, 2006; Schon, 1983). The various parts of the organization are linked, such that if there is a change in R&D capabilities there will likely be a ripple effect through the organization, so there is a risk associated with giving people too much support and freedom. Here, managers need to concentrate on making tough decisions and structure the work enough so that there are focused efforts in appropriate areas. Brown and Eisenhardt (1997) quote a manager who calls his group a "giant petri dish", put together to "grow some stuff,"; in this example, the manager notes, "unfortunately we also have to produce results" (pp. 31–32). This type of organizing is defined by flexibility, so that a supportive manager is not as important because the organizing structure supports the continual production of new ideas.

Strong Ties

Whereas the bureaucratic organizing separates work into functional groups, adaptive organizing is concerned with capabilities that are linked to the projects they support. Multi-functional teams drive projects, so that in adaptive organizing a diversity of viewpoints is an inherent part of all projects and processes. Ties to people outside of a team are not necessary to create a diversity of views. Outside connections are integral to staying in tune with product possibilities and constraints. In order to truly understand product possibilities and constraints, people need to build close connections across the organization in order to transform knowledge across boundaries (Carlile, 2002, 2004).

Product Complexity

In adaptive organizing, complexity is considered a common part of innovative work, but it is limited to the product or product platform. Semistructures and simple rules stimulate emergent order in this context, however, it is limited to specific product platforms (Brown & Eisenhardt, 1997; Eisenhardt & Bhatia, 2002). Because the complexity is limited to product platforms, adaptive organizations create continuous streams of innovation that incorporate continuous change, hence the large majority of change and innovation is incremental. However, new learning or radical innovation is managed by separating it out from the everyday work. For example, even a company such as Google—considered a leader in innovation structures—works such that 20 percent of technical employees' time is for projects of their own choosing and managers spend 10 percent on entirely new businesses and projects (Iyer & Davenport, 2008). The time for "radical" innovation is such that:

> "an engineer might spend six months on the core business, and work for a couple months on a discretionary project" *(Iyer & Davenport, 2008, p. 64).*

General Electric, also an important innovator, developed its PC-based ultrasound machine in a local growth team based in Wuxi, China (Immelt, Govindarajan, & Trimble, 2009). The head of the ultrasound business had to personally make sure that the team got the resources it needed and was protected from other responsibilities (Immelt et al., 2009). As these examples show, exploring new areas is done on the margins, in separate parts of the organization, or as separate from core business activities.

Change, creativity, and innovation occur constantly in adaptive organizing and may be stimulated by demanding managers, strong ties, and product complexity. This type of organizing is well suited for some types of creativity and innovation work. For example, Brown and Eisenhardt (1997) study continuous change in the computer industry. This is a good example of an industry in which products have increasingly short life cycles and adaptive organizing is essential (Brown & Eisenhardt, 1997).

TRANSFORMATIVE ORGANIZING

We take this opportunity to theorize about an emerging form of organizing for innovation that goes beyond bureaucratic and adaptive organizing. The idea of a transformative type of organizing has been around for some time, as reflected in Burns and Stalker's (1961) "organic" form, or Mintzberg's adhocracy (see Mintzberg & McHugh, 1985), and a variety of ideas such as the "heterarchy" (Hedlund, 1986), the "shamrock" (Handy, 1989), the "hypertext" (Nonaka & Takeuchi, 1995), or the "edge of chaos" organization especially likely in high technology sectors (Brown & Eisenhardt, 1998). While these forms vary, they present concepts of more flexible, emergent, fluid ways of organizing, which emphasize the process over the state. Plowman et al. (2007) build a new theory for a continuously radically changing organization that highlights the dynamics of complex adaptive systems, and ongoing interactions within and among different entities. The innovation and technology literatures also highlight emergence in technologies such as the digitization of knowledge and media (Boland et al., 2007) that enable networks of innovation across entire sectors of activity such as all the specialties involved in buildings, the "open" or distributed nature of the knowledge needed for R&D and product innovation (Chesbrough, 2003), and open source innovations. Other trends include the reliance on complex and emergent science such as bio-pharmaceuticals, climate and ecology management, health care, and alternative fuels and energy sources (Dougherty & Dunne, 2011). Together, these ideas suggest that, at the very least, the 20th century, large, corporate, divisional organizational form will not dominate all sectors. Another organizing form, which we label transformative organizing, is emerging and will be characterized by open sources of knowledge and innovation, very complex and ambiguous knowledge bases, complicated alliances and networks of partners who together create the knowledge necessary for innovation, and shifting networks of collaborators among particular organizations. We begin to sketch out this new organizing form by leveraging these conflicting ideas.

In transformative organizing there is no longer a tension between the relative importance of supportive versus demanding managers for creativity and innovation. Instead people focus on engagement with the knowledge object (Knorr Cetina, 1997). Building on Knorr Cetina's (1997, 1999) ideas about a new form of social solidarity based on common knowledge objects such as science, we speculate that connections between managers and coworkers in transformative organizing will leverage common knowledge objects. This means that managers will be involved with the people who work with or for them based on a common interest. Motivation will come from intrinsic attachment to the knowledge object (Knorr Cetina, 1997). By focusing on engagement with the knowledge object transformative organizing creates a context where it is not necessary for managers to be supportive or demanding because the work context is supportive and the work itself is inherently demanding.

In transformative organizing there is no longer a tension between weak and strong ties because relationships are part of communities of practice. Communities of practice involve both strong and weak ties, and they connect people on the basis of their participation in common work activities. The importance of communities of practice in transformative organizing builds on the supportive context structured by engagement with a common knowledge object (Knorr Cetina, 1997). Communities of practice bring together people who are engaged in similar pursuits; they are identifiable but not necessarily tightly knit groups of people that are setting and solving similar innovation problems (Brown & Duguid, 1991; Dougherty, 2006; Lave & Wenger, 1991). Communities of practice are self-organizing because these similar pursuits enable them to work separately yet stay in sync. These types of communities of practice already play a central role in scientific inquiry in areas such as the academe.

In transformative organizing there is no longer a tension between job and product complexity because complexity is everywhere. Transformative organizing views the organization as a complex system. In complex systems:

> "organizational members or lower level system participants [interact], [exchange] information, and [act] without coordination from a central decider, resulting in unintended changes at higher levels within and beyond the focal organization—emergence" *(Lichtenstein & Plowman, 2009, p. 617).*

Complex systems are defined by emergence, and enabling emergence is a central concern in transformative organizing. Lichtenstein and Plowman (2009; pp. 619–620) explain four sequential conditions for emergence:

1. dis-equilibrium state, "a notable movement away from stability",
2. amplifying actions or small changes that "escalate in unexpected ways", growing towards a critical point or threshold,
3. recombination/self-organization, "when the system has reached the limit of its capacity, it can either collapse or re-organize", and
4. stabilizing feedback or feedback that slows the system and "keeps the emergent change from spinning the system out of control".

D. ORGANIZATIONAL LEVEL INFLUENCES

Transformative organizing creates a context in which change supports creativity and innovation; and creativity and innovation are constant drivers of change. However, transformative organizing may not be appropriate for organizations in all types of industries. In particular, transformative organization may not be appropriate for more stable industries.

Implications

Transformative organizing creates a context that integrates the conflicting views of creativity and innovation that have been outlined here. Supportive versus demanding managers are not in conflict because a new type of social solidarity is formed based on mutual engagement with the knowledge object. Weak versus strong ties are not in conflict because communities of practice enable self-organization around similar interests. This self-organizing system creates a social context in which people can effectively engage around knowing, and knowledge objects. Job versus product complexity is not in conflict because the entire system is complex. Understanding how creativity and innovation fit with existing ideas of organizing guided the development of a new model for organizing that suggests these tensions can be accommodated and be leveraged to imagine a new context. Additionally, this model integrates existing views of change and begins to theorize about an organization that is capable of managing incremental and radical change together as part of ongoing daily work (Plowman et al., 2007). Transformative organizing creates a context in which creativity and innovation support change and change stimulates creativity and innovation.

Transformative organizing builds on new ideas of complex systems (Lichtenstein & Plowman, 2009; Plowman et al., 2007). However the ideas of complexity are strongly rooted in creativity and innovation literatures and studies that examine job and innovation complexity (Brown & Eisenhardt, 1997; Oldham & Cummings, 1996). In bureaucratic and adaptive organizing, complexity is already a part of the work, it is just localized to jobs and products, and in transformative organizing the entire system is complex. Complex systems are similar to our more familiar forms of organizing, they still have structures and daily activities, but they also enable emergence.

Organizational change is not without risk. False starts and formative challenges are common characteristics of innovative work, and change efforts often fail. Existing research views organizational change as both adaptive and disruptive (Baum & Amburgey, 2002). Findings suggest that older and larger organizations may find change more disruptive (Baum & Amburgey, 2002). However, organizations must weigh the risk of change with the often more significant risk of not changing. Organizations can get trapped in existing ways of doing things and failing to change can be catastrophic (Tushman & O'Reilly, 1996). For example, companies that do not change—such as Sears in the early to mid-1980s—are often faced with significant challenges such as serious drops in their market share (Tushman & O'Reilly, 1997). However, there are ways to mitigate the risks involved with change. One way is to connect changes to the overall strategic context of the organization (Lynn, Morone, & Paulson, 1996). Managers with a good understanding of the content of the work are better equipped to connect projects to the overall strategic context of the organizations.

Transformative organizing opens up numerous questions for future research. In particular, questions include: How to generate common knowledge objects? What kind of common ground or common work will enable these self-organized connections without overwhelming people? How do we continue to deepen people's ability to pull out or draw from their enormous tacit background knowledge in the collective work? There are new interdependencies in this type of organizing, and we need to develop new ways to pull out and work on problems without losing the integrity of the system. We need to enable work projects that are open to new possibilities, enable learning, and still fit with the strategic context of the organization. Innovators need to be able to be able to participate in emergent searching (Dunne & Dougherty, 2010).

Complexity is a central part of transformative organizing and that means emergence needs to be enabled. There are a number of ideas about managing emergence. For example, when existing parameters do not apply and adaptation is required, anyone in an organization can contribute or participate in innovative spurts (Majchrazak, Logan, McCurdy, & Kirchmer, 2006):

> "An engineer who reframes a problem from building a bridge to affecting the flow of traffic is engaged in an innovative spurt. The Red Cross' redirection during the Katrina disaster from a direct-service delivery model to an information broker role was an innovative spurt" *(p. 14)*.

Encouraging interactions and allowing new patterns to emerge so that new paths can be followed is one way to manage emergence. Lichtenstein and Plowman (2009) outline behaviors ascribed to leaders or organizations that may enable emergence in complex systems. These behaviors are: embracing uncertainty, surfacing conflicts and creating controversy, allowing experiments and fluctuations, encouraging rich interactions, supporting collective action, creating a common understanding of the system, recombining resources, having leaders as role models who symbolize something important about the system, and integrating local constraints.

Transformative organizing is a qualitatively new way of organizing around the three tensions outlined in this chapter. This form of organizing pushes research on change, creativity, and innovation into new territory, suggesting that work should be organized around knowledge objects and enabling self-organizing communities as well as emergence. Transformative organizing creates a context in which change supports creativity and innovation, and creativity and innovation drive change, continuously incorporating incremental as well as radical changes.

References

Amabile, T. M. (1988). A model of creativity and innovation in organizations. In B. M. Staw & L. L. Cummings (Eds.), *Research in organizational behavior* (Vol. 10, pp. 123–167). Greenwich, CT: JAI Press.

Amabile, T. M. (1996). *Creativity in context.* Buolder, CO: Westview Press.

Amabile, T.M., Conti, R., Coon, H., Lazenby, J., & Heroin, M. (1996). Assessing the work environment for creativity. *Academy of Management Journal, 39,* 1154–1184.

Bailyn, L. (1980). *Living with technology: Issues at mid-career.* Cambridge, MA: MIT Press.

Baum, J., & Amburgey, T. (2002). Organizational ecology. In J. Baum (Ed.), *The Blackwell companion to organizations* (pp. 304–327). Oxford, UK: Blackwell Publishers.

Bechky, B. (2003). Sharing meaning across organizational communities: The transformation of understanding on a production floor. *Organization Science, 14,* 312–330.

Boland, R. J., Lyytinen, K., & Yoo, Y. (2007). Wakes of innovation in project networks: The case of digital 3-D representations in architecture, engineering, and construction. *Organization Science, 18,* 631–647.

Brown, J. S., & Duguid, P. (1991). Organizational learning and communities of practice. *Organization Science, 2,* 40–57.

Brown, S. L, & Eisenhardt, K. M. (1997). The art of continuous change: Linking complexity theory and time-paced evolution in relentlessly shifting organizations. *Administrative Science Quarterly, 42*, 1–34.

Brown, S., & Eisenhardt, K. (1998). *Competing on the edge.* Boston, MA: Harvard Business School Press.

Burns, T., & Stalker, G. (1961). *The management of innovation.* Cambridge, MA: Oxford University Press.

Carlile, P. (2002). A pragmatic view of knowledge and boundaries: Boundary objects in new product development. *Organization Science, 13*, 442–455.

Carlile, P. (2004). Transferring translating, and transforming: An integrative framework for managing knowledge across boundaries. *Organization Science, 15*, 555–568.

Chesbrough, H. (2003). The era of open innovation. *Sloan Management Review, Spring*, 35–41.

Deci, E. L., Connell, J. P., & Ryan, R. M. (1989). Self-determination in a work organization. *Journal of Applied Psychology, 74*, 580–590.

Dougherty, D. (1992). Interpretive barriers to successful product innovation in large firms. *Organization Science, 3*, 179–202.

Dougherty, D. (2006). Organizing for innovation in the 21st century. In: Clegg and Hardy (Eds.), *The sage handbook of organization studies.* pp. 598–617.

Dougherty, D., & Tolboom, J. N. (2008). Creative organizing to enable organizational creativity: The case of sustained product innovation. *Handbook of creativity.*

Dougherty, D., & Dunne, D. (in press). *Digital science and knowledge boundaries in complex innovation. Organization Science.*

Drazin, R., Glynn, M. A., & Kazanjian, R. K. (1999). Multilevel theorizing about creativity in organizations: A sense-making perspective. *Academy of Management Review, 24*, 286–307.

Dunne, D., & Dougherty, D. (2010). *Searching for clues: The story of leveraging knowledge for exploratory product innovation.* Working paper. Binghamton University.

Edmondson, A. C., & Nembhard, I. M. (2009). Product development and learning in project teams: The challenges are the benefits. *The Journal of Product Innovation Management, 26*, 123–138.

Eisenhardt, K., & Bhatia, M. (2002). Organizational complexity and computation. In J. Baum (Ed.), *The Blackwell companion to organizations* (pp. 442–466). Oxford, UK: Blackwell Publishers.

Fleming, L., Mingo, S., & Chen, D. (2007). Collaborative brokerage, generative creativity, and creative success. *Administrative Science Quarterly, 52*, 443–475.

Hackman, J. R., & Oldham, G. R. (1980). *Work redesign.* Reading, MA: Addison-Wesley.

Handy, C. (1989). *The age of unreason.* Boston, MA: Harvard Business School Press.

Hargadon, A., & Sutton, R. (1997). Technology brokering and innovation in a product development firm. *Administrative Science Quarterly, 42*, 716–749.

Hedlund, G. (1986). The hypermodern mnc—A heterarchy? *Human Resource Management, 25*, 9–35.

Hulsheger, U. R., Anderson, N., & Salgado, J. F. (2009). Team-level predictors of innovation at work: A comprehensive meta-analysis spanning three decades of research. *Journal of Applied Psychology, 94*, 1128–1145.

Immelt, J., Govindarajan, V., & Trimble, C. (2009). How GE is disrupting itself. *Harvard Business Review, October*, 56–65.

Iyer, B., & Davenport, T. (2008). Reverse engineering Google's innovation machine. *Harvard Business Review, April*, 59–67.

Keller, R. T., Julian, S. D., & Kedia, B. L. (1996). A multinational study of work climate, job satisfaction, and the productivity of R&D teams. *IEEE Transactions on Engineering Management, 43*, 48–55.

Knorr Cetina, K. (1997). Sociality with objects: Social relations in postsocial knowledge societies. *Theory, Culture & Society, 14*, 1–30.

Knorr Cetina, K. (1999). *Epistemic cultures: How the sciences make knowledge.* Cambridge, MA: Harvard University Press.

Lave, J., & Wenger, S. (1991). *Situated learning.* Cambridge, UK: Cambridge University Press.

Leonard-Barton, D. (1995). *Well-springs of knowledge: Building and sustaining the sources of innovation.* Boston, MA: Harvard Business School Press.

Leonard, D., & Swap, W. (1999). *When sparks fly: Igniting creativity in groups.* Boston, MA: Harvard Business School Press.

Lichtenstein, B., & Plowman, D. (2009). The leadership of emergence: A complex systems leadership theory of emergence at successive organizational levels. *Leadership Quarterly, 20*, 617–630.

Lynn, G. S., Morone, J. G., & Paulson, A. S. (1996). Marketing and discontinuous innovation: The probe and learn process. *California Management Review, 38,* 8–37.

Majchrzak, A., Logan, D., McCurdy, R., & Kirchmer, M. (2006). Four keys to managing emergence. *MIT Sloan Management Review, 27,* 14–18.

McFadyen, M., & Cannella, A. (2004). Social capital and knowledge creation: Diminishing returns of the number and strength of exchange relationships. *Academy of Management Journal,* 735–746.

McFadyen, M. A., Semadenik, M., & Cannella, A., Jr. (2009). Value of strong ties to disconnected others: Examining knowledge creation in biomedicine. *Organization Science, 20,* 552–564.

Mintzberg, H., & McHugh, A. (1985). Strategy formulation in an adhocracy. *Administrtive Science Quarterly, 30,* 160–197.

Nonaka, I., & Takeuchi, K. (1995). *The knowledge creating company.* Oxford, UK: Oxford University Press.

Oldham, G. R., & Cumming, A. (1996). Employee creativity: Personal and contextual factors at work. *Academy of Management Journal, 39,* 607–634.

Paulus, P., & Nijstad, B. (2003). Group creativity: An introduction. In P. Paulus & B. Nijstad. (Eds.), *Group creativity: Innovation through collaboration* (pp. 3–14). New York, NY: Oxford University Press.

Perry-Smith, J. E., & Shalley, C. E. (2003). The social side of creativity: A static and dynamic social network perspective. *Academy of Management Review, 28,* 89–106.

Plowman, D., Baker, L., Beck, T., Kulkarni, M., Solansky, S., & Travis, D. (2007). Radical change accidentally: The emergence and amplification of small change. *Academy of Management Journal, 50,* 515–543.

Romanelli, E., & Tushman, M. (1994). Organizational transformation as punctuated equilibrium: An empirical test. *Academy of Management Journal, 37,* 1141–1666.

Schon, D. (1983). *The reflexive practitioner.* New York, NY: Basic Books.

Shalley, C. E., Zhou, J., & Oldham, G. R. (2004). The effects of personal contextual characteristics on creativity: Where should we go from here? *Journal of Management, 30,* 933–958.

Sutton, R., & Hargadon, A. (1996). Brainstorming groups in context: Effectiveness in a product design firm. *Administrative Science Quarterly, 41,* 685–718.

Tiwana, A., & McLean, E. R. (2005). Expertise integration and creativity in information systems development. *Journal of Management Information Systems, 22,* 13–43.

Tushman, M., & O'Reilly, C. (1996). Ambidextrous organizations: Managing evolutionary and revolutionary change. *California Management Review, 38,* 8–30.

Tushman, M., & O'Reilly, C. (1997). *Winning through innovation.* Boston, MA: Harvard Business School Press.

Weber, M. (1946). In H. H. Gerth & C. W. Mills. (Eds.), *From max weber: Essays in sociology.* New York, NY: Oxford University Press.

Weick, K. E., & Quinn, R. E. (1999). Organizational change and development. *Annual Review of Psychology, 50,* 361–386.

West, M. A., & Farr, J. L. (1990). Innovation at work. In M. West & J. Farr (Eds.), *Innovation and creativity at work: Psychological and organizational strategies* (pp. 3–13). Chichester, UK: Wiley.

Wheelright, S., & Clark, K. (1992). *Revolutionizing product development.* New York, NY: The Free Press.

Woodman, R. W., Sawyer, J. E., & Griffin, R. W. (1993). Toward a theory of organizational creativity. *Academy of Management Review, 18,* 293–321.

INTERVENTIONS

Careers of the Creatives: Creating and Managing the Canvas

Kimberly S. Jaussi[1] and George Benson[2]

[1]Binghamton University and Center for Leadership Studies, Binghamton, NY;
[2]University of Texas at Arlington, Department of Management, Arlington, TX

INTRODUCTION

As organizations struggle with designing human resource systems to best attract, retain, and motivate employees, career management plays a critical role for human resource professionals (Von Glinow, Driver, Brousseau, & Prince, 1983). However, the career management of an increasingly critical group of employees, creative individuals, is a relatively understudied area of knowledge and practice. To date, little work has considered the implications of a growing focus on creativity and innovation in organizations on career-related individual and organizational factors. For example, research in the areas of individual career anchors and organizational career ladders is noticeably lacking a focus on creative workers. Yet, as creative workers continue to become more valuable to all organizations, human resource systems will need to adopt career-related interventions unique to this employee population. In order to insure these employees are maximally effective and creative at work, HR professionals will need to consider career-related variables and the way which careers are defined, designed, and managed for these high-demand employees.

Today's landscape is different for creative individuals for two primary reasons. The first is that the US economy has continued to evolve towards high-technology, knowledge and service work which has increased the demand for creative and innovative individuals across a wide range of occupations. Creative engineers, designers, artists, and other professionals remain in high demand despite an economic downturn, and now have more opportunity than ever before to change jobs and pursue interesting work within or across

Handbook of Organizational Creativity.
DOI: 10.1016/B978-0-12-374714-3.00023-9

industries. Second, creative individuals are increasingly being placed in traditional jobs in attempts to spur innovation, rather than only in creative jobs such as advertising or new product development. A variety of unanswered questions exist on how to navigate this changed landscape. How do organizations accommodate career development and management amidst this new matrix of creativity and traditional careers associated with more traditional functions and job roles? Further, the impact of organizational context on an individual's creativity at work is well known (Farmer, Tierney, & Kung-McIntyre, 2003; Oldham & Cummings, 1996), but the implications of the ways in which the organization manages the careers of these creative individuals and their creativity has yet to be explicitly considered.

In this chapter, we consider both the individual level of analysis as well as that of the organizational level in efforts to best understand implications for both research and practice. We draw upon research in the areas of careers, creativity, and strategic human resource management in efforts to generate a comprehensive picture of the ways in which creative individuals can be best leveraged in organizational settings. In efforts to build further theory which addresses these issues, we review existing literature concerning both careers of creative individuals as well as career management (human resource management, HRM) for organizational creativity and innovation. In addition to considering extant work, we offer a number of future research questions. Our goal is to present a unique and integrative look at these issues with fresh thought for future actionable research.

In an effort to achieve this goal, we would first like to clarify that we are interested in the *careers* of creative individuals. Careers are evolving sequences of work over time (Anand, Peiperl, & Arthur, 2002). At any point in time, a creative individual will hold a job that makes up part of their career, and that individual may find a tension between the demands of that job and his or her own career goals. Human resource interventions designed to specifically manage this tension will help creative individuals be more effective in those jobs. Thus, one key aim of this chapter is to outline how human resource systems can effectively manage that tension and retain creative individuals by helping them achieve their career goals and be more effective contributors.

We have organized our thoughts by first examining literature on creative people and the kind of work typically done by creative people. We then turn to a discussion of career-related research as it relates to creative workers, focusing on career anchors, occupational types, and career trajectories. We then shift to the HRM implications of the aforementioned, and examine specific HRM practices that may be prudent in leveraging creative employees throughout their careers by effectively helping them navigate their careers. We review the research on HR practices and creativity from the resourced-based perspective that is predominant within the strategic human resource management literature, and which suggests that HRM allows firms to develop a unique set of people and processes. We review how HR practices impact individual creativity through recruiting, selection, performance management, compensation, job design, and training.

As we explore these areas, we first discuss extant work and then conclude the discussion by presenting possible avenues for future research to further explore with respect to each aspect of focus. In doing so, we hope to achieve our goal of connecting literature currently unconnected and raising interesting and relevant questions for future research in the area of careers of the creatives.

CREATIVE PEOPLE AND WORK

Creative People

In order to consider the area of careers of creative people, we must first consider creative people as a unique subset of the general population. Creative people are unique from their colleagues in that they possess a constellation of personality traits and characteristics not found in others. For example, Mumford, Scott, Gaddis, and Strange (2002) found common patterns across research which examined artists and scientists, noting that both groups of these creative individuals possess "openness, flexibility, cognitive complexity, self-confidence, dominance, and introversion." (*p. 710*). In addition, creative people typically have a high need for achievement, a base of expertise, and little concern for power and affiliation (Mumford, et al., 2002). They also tend to have an identity that is strongly linked to their work, and will intensely involve themselves in their work because of this relationship (Rostan, 1998). Over 100 interviews in five contexts done by Goffee and Jones (2007) reinforce Mumford and colleagues' work. Goffee and Jones' research suggests that creative, or "clever" people, can typically be characterized by the following seven characteristics:

1. they know their worth,
2. they are organizationally savvy,
3. they ignore corporate hierarchy,
4. they expect instant access to leaders,
5. they are well connected,
6. they have a low boredom threshold, and
7. they won't thank you.

Similarly Florida (2002) describes creatives as sharing a "common ethos" that emphasizes individuality, diversity, and merit.

These personality attributes and characteristics have definite career implications. In general, they drive creative individuals to seek jobs with high autonomy, and that offer work that is endogenously, not exogenously, motivated (Mumford et al., 2002; Simonton, 2007). While the personality snapshot of a creative individual can help us understand the kinds of jobs and careers they might seek and be best suited for, how they craft their career trajectories, and how their organizations might best develop and manage their careers, the nature of creative work in and of itself suggests career support mechanisms that may help the creative person sustain their energy and motivation for creativity. Therefore, we turn next to a closer look at the task characteristics typically encountered by a person doing creative work.

Creative Work

Creative work requires expertise, and thus the career of a creative individual can be viewed as a collection of opportunities to continue to build expertise. Yet, the expertise underlying creative work does not make it any easier than other work; in fact, it is inherently stressful and uncertain (Mumford et al., 2002). By definition, it involves some aspect that has no known solution (Mumford et al., 2002). As a result, the discovery process in this type of work requires high levels of motivation and attention. In addition, the creative process inherent in this type of work can be lengthy and requires resources. Thus, sustainable motivation and political acumen then become necessary as well; in order to keep the inner fire burning and to garner organizational resources to continue the work (Collins & Amabilie 1999; Dudeck & Hall, 1991; Mumford et al., 2002; Pelz & Andrews, 1966; Simonton, 1984).

As Mumford and colleagues (2002) provide a thorough description and overview of research on creative work, we will not repeat their efforts here. Rather, we would like to consider the implications of this type of work on the careers and career management of creatives. Creatives are needed in all types of organizations and industries today. These jobs go far beyond the artistic endeavor or scientific discovery that was traditionally considered as creative work. Business as diverse as journalism, finance, manufacturing, health care, government and professional services today all require deep expertise and original ideas in order to be successful. All of these organizations need to consider how their HR systems and talent management processes support their ability to attract, motivate, and retain creative individuals.

CAREERS OF CREATIVE PEOPLE

The above discussion of creative individuals and characteristics of the work they do provides a more solid foundation for considering the three aspects of careers that are typically considered in career-based discussions. We turn now to those three aspects, discussing creative people and career anchors, occupational types, and career trajectories.

Career Anchors

Scholarly work regarding careers has been strongly influenced by Edgar Schein's seminal research regarding career anchors (Schein, 1966). Career anchors, according to Schein, reflect one's motivations, interests, and values. Schein's framework considers eight anchors, with one specifically addressing entrepreneurial creativity. According to Schein, employee career anchors can drastically impact satisfaction with organizational career development efforts and trajectories (Schein, 1975, 1978, 1996). Yet, because of rapidly changing market and economic conditions, as well as a shift towards knowledge, virtual, and temporary workers, research suggests that career anchors may well need fine tuning or redefinition (Ramakrishna & Potosky, 2003). This raises a variety of interesting questions for research considering the careers of creatives, starting with one regarding the traditional framework. Are all creative people driven by the entrepreneurial creative anchor? What about the scientist or engineer that does very creative work but in a very traditional organization, vs. the designer in a boutique marketing firm? Creative corporate types are very different from creative entrepreneurs. What do the anchors among these different creative individuals look like? And, even within those creative individuals who are doing the same kind of work, there may be a wide range of career anchors and orientations. For example, Igbaria, Kassicieh, and Silver (1999) found that among R&D professionals, a variety of career orientations were present. Interestingly, the two orientations that would be most expected among this population, technical orientation and entrepreneurship, were the dimensions on which these professionals scored low.

Further, what if the entrepreneur/creative anchor is actually something very different now? If may consist of two distinct parts (at least) now that creativity is so "hot" in today's dynamic environment. Has that increase in the universality of creativity led people to implicitly expect it and/or value it, thereby making it more of a "traditional" anchor?

Occupational Choices

For many years, Holland's (1985) typology of occupational career types dominated the literature on careers. Holland's core proposition is that one's career and choice of occupations are, in essence, an expression of one's personality. Thus, people will pursue careers in occupations that allow them to express their personality. According to Holland, occupations can be grouped into six categories, which are more or less similar to one another based on the constellation of personality traits drawn to those careers. Holland's career types included realistic (e.g., firefighter), social (e.g., nurse), enterprising (e.g., sales), investigative (e.g., engineer), artistic (e.g., author), and conventional (e.g., accountant) (Holland, 1985). If Holland's assertion about the relationship between personality traits and occupational choice is correct, then the personality traits associated with creativity (e.g., openness to experience) should be positively related to occupations and careers that require creativity.

This assertion was examined in a 2003 meta-analysis by Barrick, Mount, and Gupta (2003). Support for a positive relationship between openness to experience and both artistic and investigative occupational choices were found. Yet, much like the above discussion on career anchors, today's work environment follows Mumford & colleagues' (2002) description of creative work as occurring (and being necessary) in all types of jobs. If people who are pre-disposed to creativity in their personalities are gravitating towards occupational choices in the artistic and investigative categories, how will occupations other than those fill their necessary capacity for creativity?

Trajectories

A variety of work has been conducted which examines the careers that creative people craft for themselves. Most of it has looked at scientists, composers, writers, and artists. Typically, creative people craft their careers around opportunities to demonstrate their creativity through their profession. Others are creative through the interaction of several different venues in their lives, taking a more network trajectory (Cohen, 2009). These two perspectives can both be found in the extant literature on careers of creatives.

Simonton's work on career trajectories of creative people (Simonton, 1997) is invaluable for helping the field better understand the careers of creatives. Through his work studying composers and artists, Simonton found that creatives follow a pattern for their "best" work—three key contributions, first, best, and last creative contribution landmarks that exist in a curvilinear fashion: "...the first landmark typically occurs in the late twenties or early 30s, the second in the late 30s or early 40s, and the last in the early 50s, with the output rate maximizing in the late 30s." (Simonton, 2007, p. 162)

While Simonton's work takes a post-hoc approach to identifying the temporal patterns of creative output, other work has considered the careers of creatives as a process for expressing one's identity and manufacturing an image (Svejenova, 2005). This perspective suggests that a creative's career is much like the way in which they approach a task—endogenously, not exogenously motivated. From this perspective, creative careers are indeed more endogenously driven. "The data revealed that creative career is shaped through authenticity work as the duality of identity expression and image manufacturing as well as of continuity and change." (Svejenova, 2005, p. 952)

Shaping one's career is a common theme across most of the careers literature; as the notion of a "boundary-less career" that is completely self-determined by the individual is required in this rapidly changing environment. Gone are the days of the company determining one's career; rather, the individual is the agent of action and control in shaping their own career path (Arthur & Rousseau, 1996). There is a strong argument that the careers of creative individuals have always been boundary-less, as their career choices are more likely to be driven by the opportunity to do interesting work, or to challenge themselves in new ways. Research has begun to consider whether this "boundary-less" path has any identifiable steps or stages for creative individuals.

Conceptualizations of one's career occurring through stages are recurring in extant research, yet the composition of those stages is conceptualized differently. Jones (1996) studied film projects and outlined four stages to a creative career:

1. beginning a career,
2. crafting the career,
3. navigating the career,
4. maintaining the career.

However, Svejenova (2005) found creative individuals to have four stages that help them express their identity and manufacture their image: exploration, focus, independence, professionalism. (Svejenova, 2005).

Adopting a perspective of creatives' careers based on their authentic selves invites us to consider the implication of the inherent tension/duality between creative (private) and public (image) selves. If their careers are a four stage process of reconciling this tension and elevating their expression of their creative selves, the beginning of a creative's career must be, then, accompanied by more of this tension. The question that this raises for organizations is, what kinds of career options can be made available to mitigate this tension, and/or possibly to move individuals onward from the early stages at a more accelerated pace? Imagine the implications of a creative individual trying to "fit in" in a traditionally corporate environment. If they are spending time and energy trying to manage the tension between their private and public selves, how will they have the emotional, motivational, and attentional resources to cope with the inherent aspects of creative work that require those resources?

Career research once focused on organizations as the determinants of a person's career, but more recent research holds the individual more as the agent of action and decision making. "Individuals are increasingly considered the owners and agents of their trajectories, capable of enacting their professional lives in weak situations that are ambiguous and provide few salient guides for action (Alvarez, 2000; Weick, 1996). In such cases, the career contract is not with an organization, it is with the self." (Svejoenova, 2005, p. 955)

Later in this chapter we will cover the organizational HRM practices such as selection, but in considering selection, Svejenova's work (and that of other scholars that consider the locus of a career to be one's self) impresses upon us that there is an individual-level aspect to selection and its relationship to careers as well. People are attracted to certain organizations and jobs for a variety of reasons (Schneider, Goldstein, & Smith, 1995). Individuals may select jobs because of an attraction to the organization, and/or they may be filling in necessary skills to build their career portfolios. Juxtaposing this individual agent perspective vs. the organization HRM perspective of designing careers and designing selection practices to select individuals for those careers allows us to expand our thinking with regards to creating HRM interventions to marry the two.

Career Success of Creatives

One question that is still relatively unanswered is whether creative individuals tend to experience greater success. The answer appears to be "perhaps." Judge, Klinger, and Simon (2010) found that general mental ability (GMA) moderates education, training, and job complexity to career success. Also, since GMA is related to creativity, and creative people have a high need for achievement (thereby suggesting higher education, training, etc.), it leads us to wonder if creative people have more successful careers. Future research may want to investigate this question further. It is likely to become more and more relevant as organizations continue to need increasing amounts of creativity in their organizations; it stands to reason that individuals that can provide this may well have more successful careers, if only because of the growing demand for, and value placed on, creativity.

While career research has considered in some shape or form the implications of the above variables on the careers of creatives, the field of HRM has not moved towards a true integration of these career related variables. We next turn to HRM practices and the interventions that exist and impact the careers of creatives, in an effort to highlight the need for this integration.

HRM IMPLICATIONS OF CREATIVES AND CAREERS

Understanding the trajectories and drivers at work in the case of a creative's career is important because then organizations can help mitigate or foster those inclinations. Now that organizations require creativity and innovation in unprecedented amounts, they have a vested interest in investing in activities to offer creative individuals the tasks and career development opportunities to complement the strengths and mitigate potential threats regarding their creative workforce. Research across a number of different settings has demonstrated that a variety of organizational factors, including HR practices, impact new idea generation and implementation through product and process innovation (Amabile, Conti, Coon, Lazenby, & Herron, 1996). Human resources management plays a role in developing job designs, team processes, goals, incentives, and related management practices that have all been linked to individual creativity and organizational innovation. More broadly, HR practices influence organizational culture (Tushman & O'Reilly, 2002) and climates supportive of innovation and risk taking. HR can create a system or organizational context where employees are able to share suggestions and act on new ideas, or stifle risk taking and knowledge sharing (Amabile, 1997).

Career Trajectories and HR

As discussed above, the career trajectories of creative individuals tend to take either a linear form as they build expertise in one field—or a more networked form, where they creatively create linkages and connect seemingly unrelated realms and experiences throughout their lives in efforts to express their identity. However, accepting either one or the other of these as a career trajectory can have organizational implications for creativity. Linear creatives, in their efforts to deepen expertise, will typically forgo opportunities for cross training. Yet, cross training fosters higher creativity in any field (Cohen, 2009; Root-Bernstein, Bernstein, & Garnier, 1995), and these individuals would be more creative if they engaged in some cross training. Similarly, creative individuals following a network trajectory will be likely to be less "deep" in expertise. Yet, depth of expertise stimulates more creativity. So "...linear creators benefit from cross training and network creators must develop expertise." (Cohen, 2009, p. 239)

Implications like these suggest a quagmire, though, for organizations. They are based on the assumption that an organization knows:

1. which of its employees are the "creatives", and
2. the type of career trajectory each of these "creatives" is pursuing.

While some organizations do indeed know the career patterns of their employees (e.g., GE) they typically only monitor these trajectories for their high performing or high potential employees. Also, how much of that designation is determined by a systematic consideration of creativity is a different question.

In most organizations, "the creatives" are assumed to be found in specific, traditionally "creative" areas like design, marketing, or advertising. However, what about people who do more traditional work, but who are creative with the parameters of those jobs? Imagine the creative engineer, the creative leader, the creative salesperson, the creative accountant. Mumford and colleagues (2002) depict creative work as taking place in any area of organizations, suggesting "...creative work can occur when the tasks presented involve complex, ill-defined problems where performance requires the generation of novel, useful solutions." (p. 707) How are the career trajectories of the individuals doing this creative work similar or different to those doing more traditionally creative work?

HR PRACTICES

HR practices enable organizational performance by getting people with the right sets of knowledge, skills, and abilities (KSA's) into jobs that provide them the motivation and opportunity to perform. At the organizational level, HR also contributes to company culture and signals expectations to employees. The research on HR and creativity comes from two very different perspectives, both motivated by the same premise that individual creativity and organizational innovation are critical for firm survival in today's fast-changing marketplace. Creativity researchers have recognized for some time that individual and team creativity depend on the organizational environment in which they operate. This research has identified a number of organizational characteristics that are conducive or stifling for individual creativity, and many of these are directly related to HR practices.

At the same time, HR researchers have been focused over the last twenty years on examining the link between HR practices and different aspects of organizational performance, including creativity and innovation. Together, all of this work suggests that while HR practices to support creative people and innovative processes are difficult to develop and maintain, they provide a critical competitive advantage (Shipton, Fay, West, Patterson, & Birdi, 2005). Given the importance of change and innovation for survival in today's business environment, using HR to promote creativity continues to be of interest to both managers and researchers. Through integrating career research on creative careers, HR practices stand to better serve the population that increasingly represents a unique resource for their organization.

Our earlier discussions suggested that in general, HRM should offer:

1. opportunities for professional recognition and achievement,
2. promotions into jobs with high autonomy, and
3. avoid requirements for managing others.

In this next section we consider extant research that may help us answer questions such as "How do creative individuals require different approaches in attraction and selection?", "How should organizations incentivize creative individuals?", and "How do these differ from the factors that attract and retain less creative individuals?"

Recruiting and Selection

HR practices impact creativity by recruiting the people with creative abilities and providing an environment for them to perform in. First and foremost, organizations need to recruit, hire, and retain creative individuals with the right skills, intelligence, and temperaments to generate new ideas and act on them. Recruiting, selection, training, and staffing all play critical roles in innovative companies. However, creative individuals also need the situations, opportunities, and incentives to succeed. Researchers have known for some time that creativity and innovation are products of the interaction between individual characteristics and the organizational context. The first step, however, is finding and recruiting creative individuals.

In 2004 a billboard went up above Interstate 10 in the San Jose California on the main commute for Silicon Valley workers showing nothing but an odd mathematical question in black lettering on a white background. The problem yielded a web address which contained additional puzzles. At the end of the puzzle scavenger hunt was the phone number for Google's recruiters, who had placed the billboard as a means for looking for technical talent (Olsen, 2004). Companies have always been creative in their approaches to gaining the attention of potential employees, but today there appears to be much greater focus on how to attract creative people.

Silicon Valley companies in particular have attracted attention for using novel means to recruit top technical talent over the last ten years. These efforts include new recruiting messages and media such as the Google billboard described above. Companies have also begun using techniques, such as reaching out to online communities through gaming, viral video, and social media. Yahoo, Google, and other companies have gone far beyond traditional "help wanted" ads to events such as programming contests, creative internship, treasure hunts, and video games, all intended to attract talented individuals and create a pool of potential job candidates. In addition to using new recruiting methods, these companies and many others have worked hard to develop work environments that specifically attract creative individuals. This includes non-traditional work environments, dress codes, and various perks all intended to make their organizations comfortable for creative types.

Once job candidates have been identified, companies use a variety of traditional and non-traditional ways to select for creative talent. Business and government organizations have tried to systematically identify and select the best people for creative jobs from the very beginning of modern employment testing and selection systems. These efforts have taken various routes over the past several decades with varied success. Today, organizations use an assortment of formal tests that measure a range of personality characteristics, thinking styles, and behaviors associated with creativity. Most of these tests have been validated against criterion measures of job performance. In addition to these tests, however, managers use a variety of informal means to identify creative individuals which may or may not be supported by research.

Psychometric and other formal testing for creativity follows from the tremendous amount of research on the characteristics of creative people going back decades. Studies in the 1960s and 1970s examined the backgrounds and personality traits among architects, engineers, and others (Buell, 1965; McDermid, 1965). This research led to a number of biographical inventories and psychometric tests intended to identify creative ability and cognitive styles. Instruments such as the Creative Behavior Inventory and the Kirton Adaption–Innovation Inventory are intended to identify creativity in particular. In addition to these creativity-specific instruments, companies also use a variety of other tests intended to identify individuals with traits that incline them towards creativity and new ideas. These include willingness to take risks, openness to experience, and proactivity that have been shown to be related to individual creativity (Malakate, Andriopoulos, & Gotsi, 2007).

Formal selection testing for creativity is still widely used in organizations, but today it appears that companies supplement these with a variety of informal tests. Today firms use all sorts of techniques that go beyond formal psychometric testing, including games and puzzles. Puzzle interview questions in particular gained wide popularity in the late 1990s following a series of reports of their successful use at Microsoft. Job knowledge questions have been around for years in interviewing and employment testing, and it has always been common to ask candidates to solve a challenging programming or engineering problem as part of a selection process. Creativity questions go a bit further, in asking candidates to solve a puzzle or reflect on a question that is impossible to answer as an indicator of creativity and analytical thinking styles. While questions such as "Why are manholes round?" or "How many balloons would fit in this room?" have become popular in many companies outside the technical and consulting firms that made them famous, there is little systematic validation research to support their effectiveness in predicting creativity in the workplace.

E. INTERVENTIONS

Despite this investment in testing or interviewing for creativity, the most common way to select for it is to look for evidence of previous creative work. Organizations look first for job candidates with a track record in doing creative work. The problem is that past work does not always translate into future success, which leads to an essential problem for creativity researchers. The challenge for selecting creative employees is whether to focus your methods on past success or future potential.

Job Design

While staffing for creativity is critical, researchers have always been clear that creative individuals are influenced by their organizational surroundings. Such people are influenced by the way in which their jobs are designed as well as the team and organizational context in which they work (c.f., Woodman, Sawyer, & Griffin 1993). It is not enough for HR to recruit and select creative individuals; they also have to be managed in a way that supports creativity and innovation. Job design, team, and organizational influences on individual creativity and organizational innovation have been well established. Research has repeatedly demonstrated the importance of job characteristics, team composition, team process, and organizational culture in providing the freedom and support for creative individuals and teams to generate new ideas, share them within the organization, and ultimately act on them to develop new products and business processes.

In their landmark studies of the effects of business environment on creativity, Amabile and colleagues identified positive managerial practices; which included autonomy or discretion in their jobs as well as challenging assignments that matched their skills and expertise. Moreover they found that creative employees needed to be incentivized through recognition and to have supportive teammates (Amabile et al., 1996; Amabile, 1998).

These practices overlap with the classic theories of employee involvement, which included autonomy in lower level jobs. These systems of work design in traditional manufacturing plants were meant to increase productivity by maximizing the discretion that employees had in their jobs coupled with training, appropriate information, and incentives. These conditions were not only thought to encourage employees to exert more effort due to intrinsic and extrinsic motivation, but also that they would be more productive through process improvement and innovation. Thus employee involvement is largely premised on encouraging creativity in the workplace. Laursen and Foss (2003) and others point out that involvement-oriented job designs encourage problem solving among line employees who have the knowledge and authority to change work processes.

Moreover, HR practices such as self-managed teams, cross-training, and job rotation encourage employees to share information and understand different parts of the business. These types of practices encourage employees to see new connections that generate ideas. Incentive rewards and egalitarianism encourage employees to speak up and act on their ideas. Indeed multiple studies have shown in the US and Europe that firms that embrace involvement-oriented job designs and high performance HR practices in general have a greater ability to innovate new products and compete with and outperform their competitors across a wide range of industries. For example, Beugelsdijk (2008) found that Dutch firms with job designs that emphasized task autonomy and flexible working hours were more likely to produce radical product innovations which accounted for relatively large shares of the firm's total sales.

Goffee and Jones (2007) recommend that in efforts to effectively leverage creative or "clever" individuals and prevent turnover, HR practices that reduce administrative distractions, promote the flow of innovative thinking, and support failure will be most effective. Another interesting recommendation Goffee and Jones put forward involves job design that includes a specific allocation of on-the-job-time to pursue non-work related efforts or pet projects. Companies such as Google, 3M, and Lockheed have adopted such practices, and have reaped the benefits of innovative ideas generated during this time. Other research on creativity at work offers tangential support and perhaps even more "bang for the buck" for this type of job design. Jaussi, Randel, and Dionne (2007) found that when employees apply elements of non-work related problems and solutions to work-related problems, the positive relationship between one's creative identity and creativity at work is significantly strengthened. Thus, job design that facilitates crossovers between non-work and work-related elements is likely to stoke the intrinsic motivation of creative employees.

Performance Appraisal and Incentives

In addition to selection and job design for innovative and creative individuals, research suggests that HRM also influences creativity through goal setting and incentive rewards in particular. Because creatives seek out jobs with opportunities for creativity and craft their careers around those creative experiences, HR practices that either dampen or facilitate those opportunities for creativity will directly impact their careers. Research suggests that reward systems impact creativity; directly by encouraging or discouraging specific behaviors in the workplace, and indirectly through organizational culture and informal norms for information sharing and attitudes towards risk in organizations. It should be noted, however, that incentive rewards for creative behavior has been the subject of vigorous debate over the years with a number of conflicting research findings (e.g. Eisenberger & Cameron, 1998; Hennessey & Amabile, 1998). Taken together this work suggests that creativity goals and incentives for both quality and quantity of creative output are highly context dependent.

When used appropriately and in conjunction with other complimentary HR practices, reward systems can promote new idea generation and implementation in teams and across organizations. For example, pay for performance as part of a larger set of high performance HR practices including validated selection testing, training, and empowerment based-job designs promote suggestions from the shop floor and incremental innovation in new product designs (Beugelsdijk, 2008). This work suggests, however, that goal setting and rewards don't in themselves drive creativity and innovation, but work to promote a larger culture that promotes collaboration, knowledge sharing, and new ideas. Performance appraisals and incentive rewards send strong signals as to the kinds of behavior that organizations actually value. Innovative organizations such as Google or IDEO have reputations as places that celebrate risk taking and view failed ideas as learning opportunities. Sutton (2001) and others have argued that this attitude towards failure, as embodied in performance appraisal and compensation systems, is a defining characteristic of organizations that are able to build and sustain innovative cultures over time. On the other hand, there are many more examples of organizations that stifle creativity with reward systems that end up discouraging risk taking and promoting routinization of work. Sutton (2001) suggests that organizations should reward creative *activity* regardless of the outcome, in order to promote safe environments for experimentation with an open recognition that not all new ideas are good ones. The only activity that should be punished or managed out of the organization is inactivity.

Second, while creative individuals in general are driven by the intrinsic rewards associated with interesting work and problem solving, this does not mean that they are not interested in money or recognition. Research on small firms and start-ups in particular shows that performance incentives and ownership stakes help attract top creative talent and motivate extra effort. For example, Zenger and Lazzarini (2004) found that small firms were significantly more likely to use equity shares, and placed less emphasis on merit pay, based on individual performance or seniority. These firms were also more attractive to top electrical engineers as measured by patents granted, test scores, degrees from top-rated engineering schools, and engineering publications. Preferences for ownership stakes and large potential payoffs that come with the growth of small firms appear to fit well with research on the personality characteristics of creative individuals which emphasize autonomy and merit. Based on these findings, performance management, compensation, and rewards systems to support creative individuals need to emphasize opportunities for interesting work, but also give the individuals some stake in the value of the ideas they produce.

The relationship between incentives and creativity has been examined in the context of individual and group idea generation (e.g., Toubia, 2006), and suggestion systems for organizations (Laursen & Foss, 2003). This research shows that the ways in which creative individuals respond to rewards in general and specific incentives for creativity in particular are complicated at best. This is because, in many organizations, individual creativity appears to be the greatest when individuals are intrinsically motivated by an interesting and challenging task, working without time pressure and using goal oriented self-regulatory strategies (Amabile, 1988; Kanfer & Ackerman, 1989).

While the effectiveness of specific incentives for creative output likely depend on the nature of the work (e.g. complex vs. routine) and the larger organizational context in which individual and teams operate, there are some solid research findings which should be used to guide reward practices for creatives in organizations. For example, meta-analytic findings on team performance demonstrate that goal alignment among the various members of a team is the single most important process variable in driving innovation (Hulsheger, Anderson, & Salgado, 2009). Goal alignment and interdependence, such that all members need others to be successful in their task to meet their own individual goals, is thought to enhance interaction and team cooperation and be crucial to generating and implementing new ideas (Campion, Papper, & Medsker, 1996). Goal alignment in teams can be promoted by measuring and adding team outcomes to individual performance appraisals, providing group feedback, and linking rewards to specific team goals (Wageman, 1995). By considering and utilizing HR rewards and practices such as these, organizations can help creatives fulfill their career goals while being effective for the organization at the same time.

Training and Development

Training and development is a core aspect of career management (Feldman, 1988), and companies that value creative employees and their creativity output put training and development practices on the forefront of their agenda. At Samsung, for example, in efforts to nurture creativity, each employee spends 109 hours each year engaged in training (Samsung website). Corporate creativity training programs can include features such as problem solving (brain storming), divergent and convergent thinking (developing many ideas and then bringing them together to produce a plan), metaphoric thinking (comparing one idea to other things), games, and stories (Hequet, 1992).

Yet, while research on creativity training (Rose & Lin, 1984; Scott, Leritz, & Mumford, 2004) suggests that it increases individual levels of creativity and is linked to millions of dollars in cost savings, the role of creativity training in a creative individual's career path has yet to be examined. More research is needed in this realm, as prior research suggests that individual differences (e.g., in achievement, motivation) will influence the self-selection into creativity training (Kabanoff & Bottger, 1991). Jaussi and colleagues (2004) found that creative individuals found creativity training to be more effective and likely to be useful for their careers than non-creative individuals. This is not surprising considering that other training literatures have found that expertise or prior experience is an important individual difference factor that may affect outcomes (Roberson, Kulik, & Pepper, 2001; Tobias, 1987). In a similar vein, the expertise literature suggests that the effective application of complex problem solving skills depends on the prior acquisition of requisite experience (Mumford, Marks, Connelly, Zaccaro, & Reiter-Palmon, 2000). Similarly, creative people may find the training more salient, in that they can think of ways to immediately apply the creativity techniques in their tasks and jobs. These links for application suggest that creativity training in particular may have unique accelerating effects on the careers of creative individuals.

Career Development

Career development, when designed in a manner that "fits" the employee and type of work the employee is being asked to do, can help keep motivation high. However, what might the appropriate career development be for those doing creative work? The career puzzle becomes more complex when you take into account the stress, political acumen, and need to continuously impact motivation and sustained attention inherently required by the very nature of creative work. Any career development efforts for creatives must balance the need for deepening expertise with the need for purely motivational experiences. As noted earlier, creative individuals value professional achievement and the opportunity to identify with professional groups outside of the organization. This suggests that seizing opportunities to attend and/or present at conferences and other professional networking events may provide the motivational fuel for continued focus and attention on creative work.

AVENUES FOR FUTURE RESEARCH

As the above discussion suggests, we simply do not know how well our existing career models and variables work for today's creative individuals. We also do know not how well traditional HR practices work for people pursuing creative careers, and we have not seen work examining HR practices built upon career variables and career research. A wealth of future research opportunities exists in each of these areas, at both the individual and organizational levels of analysis.

Creative Individuals and Their Careers

While our review highlights several studies that have considered the careers of creatives, a number of unanswered questions remain. For example, future research might investigate questions related to careers of creatives in different types of occupations, such as "Do different types of creative employees view their careers differently from one another? If so, do those views differ by the type of creative work being done or by the type of creativity they exhibit at work (e.g. radical versus incremental creativity)?" The answers to these questions may yield insights that help us understand if there is a level of analysis of "creative people" with respect to creative careers or if it's a more individual level phenomenon that differs between each individual.

Additionally, future research might consider how the changing, competitive economic context (more dependent on creativity yet also filled with more pressure for innovation) impacts the career paths and interests of creative individuals. Given the economic climate in 2010 and loss of jobs, another interesting area for research to consider is, whether the career paths and interests of creative individuals are more complex than those of non-creatives who are now forced into perhaps creating complexity in their own careers.

The recent focus on creativity research on fine-tuning differences in the type of creativity demonstrated (e.g., radical versus incremental creativity), suggests the possibility of a whole new stream of research with respect to Schein's career anchors and values. In addition to considering the new cluster of values (e.g., creativity now more common) and how those may change Schein's career anchor set, future research might also consider people who focus on radical versus incremental creativity. Through considering individuals who gravitate towards each of these types of creativity, new anchors may become apparent and inform future work regarding career anchors.

The area of individual career stages also holds promise for future research regarding creative individuals. For example, it would be interesting to map Svejenova's (2005) four career stages of creative individuals (exploration, focus, independence, professionalism) with a more temporally based, output model based on Simonton's work. Building the two of these camps together would allow us to ask questions such as "What role does opportunities for identity expression play over the three points in time of creative output that Simonton purports? Are those creative outputs generated because of windows of either more, or more complete, identity expression?"

Additionally, future research might also consider the impact of career stages on creative individuals' motivation and satisfaction. This is particularly interesting when one's individual, professionally based career is considered with respect to one's organization's expectations for creativity in stages of the career ladder of the organization. For example, questions such as "How does the influence of expectations for creative work throughout one's career interact with organizational expectations for creativity at different career stages?" might be explored. Finally, future research might continue to untangle the notion of one's career as something purposely constructed to verify one's identity. The lenses of linear versus network trajectories may lend themselves well to this type of enquiry. By considering career stages, scholars may explore questions about whether one's creative identity changes throughout different stages in a creative career.

E. INTERVENTIONS

HR Practices

As noted throughout the chapter, individuals and their careers are enacted in organizations, and HR practices and interventions set the stage for whether creative individuals can achieve their career goals. As the work in this realm has been very limited, scholars have a blank canvas for conducting research and increasing our understanding of how HRM practices and interventions can most effectively leverage creative individuals and their career objectives. Here, we outline several with respect to selection as well as to training and development.

Selection techniques for identifying creative employees is challenging, especially when considering the career stages and career goals of the creative employee. As selecting creative employees brings with it the question of whether to focus your methods on past success or future potential, questions are raised for future research to consider such as "Do recruiting and selection tools used in "creative" companies (e.g., Google) work as effectively in recruiting and selecting employees for more traditional jobs in traditional companies that require creative work?" and "How do new constellations of career anchors and orientations impact recruiting and selection for creative work?" Finally, future research might investigate how creative recruiting and selection can also signal creative career management. Underlying all of these questions is whether recruiting and selection practices for creative employees do in fact require that those practices are indeed creative in and of themselves; we have no research to date that helps us address that assumption.

With respect to training and development practices, future research considering the impact of training on the careers of creatives might consider whether the impact of creative identity and creative expertise on training effectiveness is dependent on whether one is doing a traditionally "creative" job or a traditional job requiring creativity. Additionally, it may prove fruitful to consider whether the rate at which training can influence one's career is different for creatives compared to their non-creative counterparts. Finally, it would be interesting to consider training and its impact on a creative's career from a breadth versus depth perspective—for example, do the careers of creatives benefit more from training that helps them acquire more depth, or more breadth?

The development efforts of organizations are often aimed at either increasing or maintaining employee motivation. Future research may want to investigate the impact of participation in professional conferences and associations on sustaining motivation for creative work, as it offers opportunities for both social support and recognition as well as deepening of expertise. It would also be interesting to compare the impact of these events on the career advancement of creatives, both inside the organization and moving on beyond their current organization and into new ones. Any examination of this question will benefit from a study design that builds in a control group of non-creative individuals given the same kind of professional conference experiences, in order to untangle whether the impact of these experiences on creatives is different than on non-creative individuals.

CREATING THE CANVAS

Our hope is that we have succeeded in bringing together bodies of extant research that have not traditionally been looked at in conjunction with one another. Considering work from areas of careers, creativity, and strategic HRM allows for creative generation of future research questions regarding the careers of creatives. As organizations continue to face escalating pressures for creativity and innovation, demands for (and demands on) these individuals are surely going to increase. Our discussion suggests that not only are careers being redefined, but that they very well may represent something very different for creative individuals than for their non-creative counterparts. Future research has a wide range of new and exciting opportunities to pursue in this area and, with any luck, our discussion has helped point the scholars' compass towards avenues for these pursuits. Potential areas for future research discussed include considering how the spread of creative work to occupations beyond traditionally "creative" occupations impacts the career trajectories of creative individuals. Also discussed as a potentially rich line of questioning was the role of creative identity, how a creative's career is constructed as an expression of that, and how linear vs. network trajectories result from that. Whether or not these specific lines of inquiry are in fact the ones pursued by future research, one thing remains clear: there exists a wide range of exciting research questions for future exploration.

References

Alvarez, J. L. (2000). Theories of managerial action and their impact on the conceptualization of executive careers. In M. Peiperl, M. Arthur, R. Goffee & T. Morris (Eds.), *Career frontiers: New conceptions of working lives* (pp. 127–137). Oxford, UK: Oxford University Press.

Amabile, T. M. (1997). Motivating creativity in organizations: On doing what you love and loving what you do. *California Management Review, 40*, 39–58.

Amabile, T. M. (1998). How to kill creativity. *Harvard Business Review, 76*, 76–87.

Amabile, T. (1988). A model of creativity and innovation in organizations. In B. Staw & L. Cummings (Eds.), *Research in organizational behavior* (Vol. 10). Greenwich, CT: JAI Press.

Amabile, T. M., Conti, R., Coon, H., Lazenby, J., & Herron, M. (1996). Assessing the work environment for creativity. *Academy of Management Journal, 39*, 1154–1184.

Anand, N., Peiperl, M., & Arthur, M. (2002). Introducing career creativity. In M. Peiperl, M. Arthur & N. Anand (Eds.), *Career creativity: Explorations in the remaking of work* (pp. 1–14). New York, NY: Oxford University Press.

Arthur, M. B., & Rousseau, D. (Eds.). (1996). *The boundaryless career: A new employment principle for a new organizational era.* New York, NY: Oxford University Press.

Barrick, M. R., Mount, M. K., & Gupta, R. (2003). Meta–analysis of the five factor model of personality and Holland's occupational types. *Personnel Psychology, 56*, 45–74.

Beugelsdijk, S. (2008). Strategic human resource practices and product innovation. *Organization Studies, 29*, 821–847.

Buel, W. D. (1965). Biographical data and the identification of creative research personnel. *Journal of Applied Psychology, 49*, 318–321.

Campion, M., Papper, E., & Medsker, G. (1996). Relations between work team characteristics and effectiveness: A replication and extension. *Personnel Psychology, 49*, 429–452.

Cohen, L. M. (2009). Linear and network trajectories in creative lives: A case study of Walter and Roberto Burle Max. *Psychology of Aesthetics, Creativity, and the Arts, 3*, 238–248.

Collins, M. A., & Amabile, T. M. (1999). Motivation and creativity. In R. J. Sternberg (Ed.), *Handbook of creativity* (pp. 313–328). Cambridge, UK: Cambridge University Press.

Dudeck, S. Z., & Hall, W. B. (1991). Personality consistency: Eminent architects 25 years later. *Creativity Research Journal, 4*, 213–232.

Eisenberger, R., & Cameron, J. (1998). Reward, intrinsic interest and creativity: New findings. *American Psychologist, 53*, 676–678.

Farmer, S. M., Tierney, P., & Kung-McIntyre, K. (2003). Employee creativity in Taiwan: An application of role identity theory. *Academy of Management Journal, 46*, 618–630.

Feldman, D. (1988). *Managing careers in organizations.* Glenview, Il: Scott Foresman.

Florida, R. (2002). *The rise of the creative class and how it's transforming work, leisure, community and everyday life*. New York, NY: Perseus Book Group.

Goffee, R., & Jones, G. (2007). Leading clever people. *Harvard Business Review, 85*, 1–9.

Hennessey, B., & Amabile, T. (1998). Reward, intrinsic motivation, and creativity. *American Psychologist, 53*, 674–675.

Hequet, M. (1992). Creativity training gets creative. *Training, 29*, 41–46.

Holland, J. L. (1985). *Making vocational choices: A theory of careers*. Englewood Cliffs, NJ: Prentice Hall.

Hulsheger, U., Anderson, N., & Salgado, J. (2009). Team-level predictors of innovation at work: A comprehensive meta-analysis spanning three decades of research. *Journal of Applied Psychology, 94*, 1128–1145.

Igbaria, M., Kassicieh, S. K., & Silver, M. (1999). Career orientations and career success among research and development and engineering professionals. *Journal of Engineering and Technology Management, 16*, 29–54.

Jaussi, K. S., Randel, A. E., & Dionne, S. D. (2007). I am, I think I can, and I do: The role of personal identity, self-efficacy, and cross-application of experiences in creativity at work. *Creativity Research Journal, 19*, 247–258.

Jaussi, K. S., Dionne, S. D., Harder, J., Carroll, E., Korkmaz, N., Silverman, S. (2004). Creativity training: More effective for some? Presented at the national meeting of the *Society for Industrial and Organizational Psychology*, April, Chicago, IL.

Jones, C. (1996). Careers in project networks: the case of a film industry. In M. B. Arthur & D. Rousseau (Eds.), *The boundaryless career: A new employment principle for a new organizational era* (pp. 58–75). New York, NY: Oxford University Press.

Judge, T. A., Klinger, R. L., & Simon, L. S. (2010). Time is on my side: Time, general mental ability, human capital, and extrinsic career success. *Journal of Applied Psychology, 95*, 92–107.

Kabanoff, B., & Bottger, P. (1991). Effectiveness of creativity training and its relation to selected personality factors. *Journal of Organizational Behavior, 12*, 235–248.

Kanfer, R., & Ackerman, P. L. (1989). Motivation and cognitive abilities: An integrative/aptitude-treatment interaction approach to skill acquisition. *Journal of Applied Psychology, 74*, 657–690.

Laursen, K., & Foss, N. (2003). New human resource management practices, complementarities and the impact on innovation performance. *Cambridge Journal of Economics, 27*, 243–263.

Malakate, A., Andriopoulos, C., & Gotsi, M. (2007). Assessing job candidates' creativity: Propositions and future research questions. *Creativity and Innovation Management, 16*, 307–316.

McDermid, C. D. (1965). Some correlates of creativity in engineering personnel. *Journal of Applied Psychology, 49*(1), 14–19.

Mumford, M. D., Marks, M. A., Connelly, M. S., Zaccaro, S. J., & Reiter-Palmon, R. (2000). Development of leadership skills: Experience and timing. *The Leadership Quarterly, 11*, 87–114.

Mumford, M. D., Scott, G. M., Gaddis, B., & Strange, J. M. (2002). Leading creative people: Orchestrating expertise and relationships. *The Leadership Quarterly, 13*, 705–750.

Oldham, G. R., & Cummings, A. (1996). Employee creativity: Personal and contextual factors at work. *Academy of Management Journal, 39*, 607–634.

Olson, S. (July 9, 2004). Google recruits eggheads with mystery billboard. Retrieved from <http://news.cnet.com/Google-recruits-eggheads-with-mystery-billboard/2100-1023_3-5263941.html/>.

Pelz, D. C., & Andrews, F. M. (1966). Autonomy, coordination, and simulation in relation to scientific achievement. *Behavioral Science, 12*, 89–97.

Ramakrishna, H., & Potosky, D. (2003). Conceptualization and exploration of composite career anchors: An analysis of information systems personnel. *Human Resource Development Quarterly, 14*, 199–214.

Roberson, L., Kulik, C. T., & Pepper, M. B. (2001). Designing effective diversity training: Influence of group composition and trainee experience. *Journal of Organizational Behavior, 22*, 871–885.

Root-Bernstein, R. S., Bernstein, M., & Garnier, H. (1995). Correlations between avocations, scientific style, work habits, and professional impact of scientists. *Creativity Research Journal, 8*, 115–137.

Rose, L., & Lin, H. (1984). A meta-analysis of long-term creativity training programs. *Journal of Creative Behavior, 18*, 11–22.

Rostan, S. M. (1998). A study of young artists: The emergence of artistic and creative identity. *Journal of Creative Behavior, 32*, 278–301.

Schein, E. H. (1975). How career anchors hold executives to their career paths. *Personnel, 52*, 11–24.

Schein, E. H. (1978). *Career dynamics: Matching individual and organizational needs*. Reading, MA: Addison-Wesley.

Schein, E. H. (1996). Career anchors revisited: Implications for career development in the 21st century. *Academy of Management Executive, 10*, 80–88.

E. INTERVENTIONS

Schneider, B., Goldstein, H. W., & Smith, D. B. (1995). The ASA framework: An update. *Personnel Psychology, 48,* 747–773.

Scott, G., Leritz, L. E., & Mumford, M. D. (2004). The effectiveness of creativity training: A quantitative review. *Creativity Research Journal, 16,* 361–388.

Shipton, H., Fay, D., West, M., Patterson, M., & Birdi, K. (2005). Managing people to promote innovation. *Creativity and Innovation Management, 14,* 118–128.

Simonton, D. K. (1984). *Genius, creativity, and leadership: Historiometric inquiries.* Cambridge, MA: Harvard University Press.

Simonton, D. K. (1997). Creative productivity: A predictive and explanatory model of career trajectories and landmarks. *Psychological Review, 104,* 66–89.

Simonton, D. K. (2007). Cinema composers: Career trajectories for creative productivity in film music. *Psychology of Aesthetics, Creativity, and the Arts, 1,* 160–169.

Sutton, R. (2001). The weird rules of creativity. *Harvard Business Review, 79,* 94–103.

Svejenova, S. (2005). The path with the heart: Creating the authentic career. *Journal of Management Studies, 42,* 947–974.

Tobias, S. (1987). Learner characteristics. In R. M. Gagne (Ed.), *Instructional Technology: Foundations* (pp. 207–232). Hillsdale, NJ: Erlbaum.

Toubia, O. (2006). Idea generation, creativity, and incentives. *Marketing Science, 25,* 411–425.

Tushman, M. L., & O'Reilly, C. (2002). *Winning through innovation: A practical guide to leading organizational change and renewal.* Cambridge, MA: Harvard Business School Press.

Von Glinow, M., Driver, M. J., Brousseau, K., & Prince, J. B. (1983). The design of a career oriented human resource system. *Academy of Management Review, 8,* 23–32.

Wageman, R. (1995). Interdependence and group effectiveness. *Administrative Science Quarterly, 40,* 145–180.

Weick, K. E. (1996). Enactment and the boundaryless career: Organizing as we work. In M. B. Arthur & D. Rousseau (Eds.), *The boundaryless career: A new employment principle for a new organizational era* (pp. 40–57). New York, NY: Oxford University Press.

Woodman, R. W., Sawyer, J. E., & Griffin, R. W. (1993). Toward a theory of organizational creativity. *Academy of Management Review, 18,* 293–321.

Zenger, T., & Lazzarini, S. (2004). Compensating for innovation: Do small firms offer high-powered incentives that lure talent and motive effort? *Managerial and Decision Economics, 25*(6–7), 329–345.

E. INTERVENTIONS

Can Reward Systems Influence the Creative Individual?

Anthony C. Klotz[1], Anthony R. Wheeler[2],
Jonathon R.B. Halbesleben[3], Meagan E. Brock[4],
and M. Ronald Buckley[1]

[1]University of Oklahoma, Norman, OK; [2]University of Rhode Island, Kingston, RI; [3]University of Alabama, Tuscaloosa, AL; [4]West Texas A&M University, Canyon, TX

INTRODUCTION

Have you ever heard anyone say "If being (blank) was easy, then everyone would be (blank)?" This incomplete statement fits well with the notion of developing creativity in organizations. It is not much of an insight to reveal that it is not very easy and not everyone is creative! We believe that individual possession of creativity is a bit more complex than an either/or proposition. We all probably possess some level of creativity which falls along a continuum from very little to lots. The issue is how we can maximize our varied, individual possibilities with respect to creativity. This promises to be difficult. Should we just throw up our hands and not ev en try to shape creativity? Or, might we look at creative ways to accomplish this? Importantly, can creativity be facilitated by the creative manipulation of reward systems in organizations? We'll first give you what we believe the answer to these questions to be: "it all depends." Our rationale for this answer is the crux of this chapter.

For this chapter, we define creativity as:

"the production of novel and useful ideas in any domain" (*Amabile, Conti, Coon, Lazenby, & Herron, 1996, p. 1195*).

As "production," creativity can be considered a performance behavior of employees. The simple equation *Performance = f (Motivation × Ability)* was introduced over 50 years ago to describe achievement behavior (Anderson & Butzin, 1974; Heider, 1958). Motivation is defined as processes that are utilized in order to energize, direct, and sustain behaviors. Ability is the knowledge and skills that a person possesses. If we consider creativity as a form of performance behavior, the formula suggests that one must have the necessary ability to generate creative ideas (discussed in Chapters 6 and 7 in the present volume), as well as be motivated to engage in creativity. Rewards play a key role in generating motivation and thus are a critical component of organizational efforts to encourage creativity. For example, expectancy theory states that motivation is the product of reward valence, expectancy, and instrumentality (Vroom, 1964). If employees do not value the creativity reward, believe they are capable of achieving the creativity goal, and perceive that managers will reward them for desired creative performance, then motivation and subsequent performance will not be optimal.

The use of reward systems to stimulate creativity is a complex and equivocal topic (see Shalley, Zhou, & Oldham, 2004). Although most managers in today's organizations ostensibly rely upon reward systems to drive creative performance, there is a paucity of empirical evidence of widespread success in using reward systems for this purpose. A number of empirical studies demonstrate that rewards can have both positive and negative influences on both developing and facilitating creative performance. For example, Eisenberger and Aselage (2009) found that college students that expected to be rewarded developed more creative short stories than those that did not anticipate a reward for their performance. In a study of noncommissioned artists, however, subjects not anticipating financial rewards for creativity produced more creative works of art than their commission-based peers (Stewart et al., 1993). Inconsistent findings of the relationships between rewards and creativity have led researchers to call for more extensive research on the role which reward systems might play in driving creative performance in organizations.

Real-world case studies and other qualitative, anecdotal, organizational examples provide us with a clearer view of the value of developing creativity through reward systems. Studies of the most creatively successful organizations exhibit a definite avoidance of traditional reward systems. Rather than focusing on linking rewards to positive outcomes, these organizations use the indirect strategy of creating an environment in which creativity can flourish. Ed Catmull, President of Pixar, the animated motion picture studio responsible for a record of blockbuster movies stretching over a decade, credits the company's creative success to the environment of creativity the company has been able to foster. The result of this environment is:

> "a vibrant community where talented people are loyal to one another and their collective work, everyone feels that they are part of something extraordinary" (Catmull, 2008, pp. 66–67).

Many other creatively and commercially successful companies, from Ferrari (Morse, 2006) to Google (Iyer & Davenport, 2008), also cite cultural and environmental factors, not reward-based incentives, as critical antecedents to the development of creative success. Clearly, creating an environment where employees are free to be creative taps into the intrinsic drivers of individual creative performance.

The purpose of this chapter is to examine the role that rewards play in stimulating creativity. We begin by discussing the role of reward systems in existing models of creativity in organizations. Next, we investigate the function of extrinsic motivation and specifically reward systems in prominent theories of motivation. Drawing from these two bodies of literature, we suggest a simple model of reward systems and creativity. Further, we propose specific intrinsic moderators that influence the relationship between reward systems and creativity at the individual, group, and organization levels. We conclude with a brief discussion of implications for practitioners and future opportunities for research at the intersection of creativity and reward systems.

THE ROLE OF REWARDS IN CREATIVITY MODELS

The Merriam-Webster dictionary defines a reward as "something that is given in return for good or evil done or received or that is offered or given for some service or attainment." Although this definition is seemingly simple and straightforward, even small organizations can use myriad different rewards to stoke employees' extrinsic and intrinsic motivation. Indeed, reward systems have a long history of being used in organizations to impact all types of performance outcomes, including creativity. The primary reason for their prevalence is that:

> "most organisms seek information concerning what activities are rewarded, and then seek to do (or at least pretend to do) those things, often to the virtual exclusion of activities not rewarded" *(Kerr, 1975, p. 769)*.

This is not a new idea as Guthrie (1940) posited many years ago in the Law of Effect: "That which is rewarded tends to be repeated." Typically, rewards are used as a form of extrinsic motivation. Extrinsic motivation has been described by Amabile, Tihge, Hill, and Hennessey (1994) as the motivation to work primarily in response to something apart from the work itself, such as reward or recognition or the dictates of other people.

Although they are most often associated with extrinsic motivation, rewards often have a potent influence on intrinsic motivation as well. For example, when a gift certificate is given to an employee as a reward for good performance in a department-wide meeting, that employee may realize motivation not only by the receipt of a valuable item, but she may also experience an increase in intrinsic motivation from recognition of superior performance by her peers and supervisor. The combination of the reward, the context, the employee, and the behavior of the supervisor combine to deliver an impactful positive outcome for the employee, and everyone else at the meeting.

Rewards can serve a number of additional positive functions in the organization. Rewarding individuals is a signal of good performance (Eisenberger, Armeli, & Pretz, 1998), and provides encouragement to the employee to continue exhibiting the behaviors that have been recognized. At the same time, the mere lack of providing a reward can signal to lower performing individuals that their performance must improve. Superior managers understand their follower's preference for the types and frequencies of rewards they desire, and use rewards strategically to align the behavior of the follower with desired organizational goals.

The diverse and often conflicting findings in research and the real-world examples of the relationship between reward systems and creativity have led scholars to conclude that, although reward systems can positively influence creative behavior, the success of the program will be significantly influenced by four primary factors. First, the type of creativity required to solve the problem will influence the outcome of the reward system (Unsworth, 2001). For example, creating a piece of artwork requires a different type of creativity than suggesting an improvement to an existing manufacturing process. Second, the source of individual or group motivation to be creative can also determine the effectiveness of a reward system. For example, extrinsic motivators, which are most often associated with reward systems, require significantly different methods and produce much different outcomes than intrinsic motivators (Amabile, 1998). Third, an important issue is what type of creativity is desired. Are we trying to facilitate an incremental adaptation or a radical breakthrough in creativity? Finally, the contextual factors that influence creativity all exhibit significant impacts on the outcomes of reward systems. Environmental issues, such as job complexity and supervisory style, have been found to have significant relationships with creative productivity (Oldham & Cummings, 1996).

We use extensive research on extrinsic and intrinsic motivation to demonstrate that reward systems can effectively impact creativity in individuals, groups, and organizations. Reward systems, primarily an extrinsic form of motivation, are only effective if the intrinsic needs of employees have been met. In other words, the relationship between reward systems and creative performance is moderated by intrinsic variables, such that high levels of intrinsic motivation positively influence the relationship between reward systems and creative performance and deficiencies of intrinsic motivation negatively influence the relationship between reward systems and creative performance. These intrinsic variables are complex, difficult to measure, and challenging to manage in employees. Because of the moderating role of intrinsic motivation in our model, it will be necessary to discuss it in some detail in this chapter.

Cummings

In an early theoretical investigation into the influence of organizational variables on creativity, Cummings (1965) contrasted the traditional hierarchical form of the organization with a constructive, alternative structure designed to foster creativity that was based upon organizational variation. The traditional model of organization is not the optimal form of organization for creativity for several reasons. First, conflict over opinions is discouraged in the traditional organization, and creativity can often be derived from differences in opinion. In addition, secrecy is sanctioned in the traditional model, yet the generation of novel ideas is enhanced by a diverse set of inputs from multiple levels and areas within the organization. Third, control systems in the traditional organization foster stability, calculability, and routinization. Creativity however, often arises in environments that are dynamic and in a constant state of flux. Other problems with the traditional model include its omission of an institutionalized appeal system and discouragement of the development of alternative solutions to problems.

Cummings implicates traditional reward systems in the suppression of a creative climate. While reward systems are not a direct muzzle on creativity, the traditional reward system focuses on extrinsic rewards, which encourage predictability of responses in employees. Reward systems that are more carefully sculpted to tap into the intrinsic motivation of employees are necessary for a creative organizational climate but are lacking in the traditional hierarchical model.

In contrast to the traditional organization, Cummings' organization, designed to maximize creativity, would have a number of non-hierarchical characteristics. Organizational positions would not be strongly formalized, and participation and autonomy would be given to individuals in creative positions. The idea generation function in the organization would be severed from idea evaluation function and communication channels connecting all relevant units within the organization would be developed. Importantly, organizational leaders would embrace a management philosophy rooted in the belief that employees are able to be creative while competently completing their assigned job functions.

Cummings' most detailed proposal for the creative organization specifically develops an alternative to the traditional reward system. The extrinsic reward system should be abandoned in favor of one focused on intrinsically motivating the creative employee. This system could include self-selection of task assignments, work scheduling flexibility, increased autonomy regarding how the work gets done, and additional opportunities for professional development and recognition. Extrinsic reward systems are still necessary, but would only be used for an ancillary promotional structure based on more traditional criteria. Clearly, to build a climate that embraces creativity, organizational structures based foremost on maximizing intrinsic motivation and using extrinsic motivation secondarily to add incremental creative performance are necessary.

Amabile

Amabile (1988) develops a five stage model of organizational innovation. In stage 1, the organization sets an agenda for organizational innovation through a mission statement. Stage 2 involves expanding the mission statement into clear goals. In support of these goals, employees gather resources, establish the work context, and carry out market research. The critical stage in this model of organizational innovation is stage 3. In this stage the ideas are produced by individual employees and small groups. In stage 4, the ideas generated in the previous stage are tested and implemented in the marketplace. Stage 5 involves the assessment of the success, failure, or progress of the innovation. If success was not achieved but innovation progress was made, the organization can return to stage 2 and repeat the process again.

Stage 3 in the innovation process is expanded into an additional five stage process of creativity at the employee and team-level. The first stage of this process is task presentation, which involves internal and external sources of motivation. Once the internal and external sources of motivation are derived in stage 1, stage 2 involves the gathering of information and resources. In stage 3 of the micro-level creativity process, employees primarily use intrinsic motivation to produce innovative ideas or products. The ideas are then compared against the task criteria in stage 4. As in the organization-level model, stage 5 is the outcome assessment in which the employees achieve success, failure, or progress, which prompts a return to stage 1.

In this model, reward systems are included as extrinsic motivators in stage 1. Amabile clearly asserts that employee creativity is maximized when it is motivated by the interest, enjoyment, satisfaction, and challenge of the task. External pressures, which include reward systems, produce less creativity than intrinsic motivation. That is not to say that there is not a place for extrinsic rewards in the organization. In fact, recent research has shown that performance pressure increases intrinsic interest in jobs which is positively related to creative performance (Eisenberger & Aselage, 2008). Additionally, for straightforward tasks requiring minimal creativity, reward systems are not only appropriate but necessary.

Extrinsic and intrinsic motivations are not mutually exclusive in this model. Indeed, employees can be creative under extrinsic pressures (Amabile & Gryskiewicz, 1987) and extrinsic motivation can increase creative behavior incrementally beyond the limit of intrinsic motivation (Amabile, Hennessey, & Grossman, 1986). Therefore, the influence of reward systems on creativity is not as strong as intrinsic motivators, but they do have a role in fostering innovation depending on the persons, processes and context.

Woodman, Sawyer, and Griffin

Woodman et al. (1993) use an input–process–output framework to develop their model of organizational creativity. The inputs in this creative process include individual characteristics, group characteristics, and organizational characteristics that either support or hinder the inception of creativity. In this model, rewards are viewed as an organizational antecedent to creativity in the workplace. Individual characteristics that affect creativity include the employees' cognitive ability and style, personality, intrinsic motivation, and knowledge. For example, employees with higher pattern recognition skills may contribute to an organization's creativity more than others (Baron & Ensley, 2006). However, employees that lack intrinsic motivation will likely not have a meaningful input to creativity in the workplace.

Because organizational creativity is the product of many employees, group characteristics can also help or hinder the start of the creative process. The authors identify group norms, cohesiveness, size, diversity, roles, task, and problem-solving approaches as the primary group antecedents to organizational creativity. For example, group norms that contribute to building conformity, and group sizes that are very large, likely hinder the group's creativity. However, norms that support open sharing of information and high levels of diversity will positively relate to creative outcomes.

Organizational characteristics are the final input to Woodman et al.'s (1993) creativity framework. Organizational culture, resources, rewards, strategy, structure, and technology can contribute to the level of creativity in an organization. For instance, an organizational culture that encourages risk-taking and does not punish failure should exhibit more creativity than more conservative environments. Also, an organizational structure that enhances communication within the organization and with outside sources of knowledge will positively relate to the level of creativity in the organization.

Woodman et al. (1993) specifically propose that:

> "individual creative performance will be decreased by reward systems that rigorously evaluate creative accomplishment and link these outcomes tightly to extrinsic rewards". (p. 312).

This assertion is based on previous research which showed that reward systems that have not been carefully constructed tend to suppress creativity (Amabile, 1979). Packaged within this proposition is the notion that creativity in the workplace cannot be developed through "rigorous" evaluation and "tightly" linked reward systems. That is not to say that extrinsic reward systems cannot foster creativity, but the systems must provide employees with the cognitive slack to think, and the emotional space to take risks in the creative process. Another way of saying this is that control systems appear to stifle creativity.

Ford

Ford (1996) develops a theory of creative individual action within the organizational context. In this context, creativity is defined as:

> "a domain-specific, subjective judgment of the novelty and value of an outcome of a particular action" *(Ford, 1996, p. 1115).*

The outcome of the model can be one of two types of competing behavior—creative actions or habitual actions. As demonstrated by Cummings, the typical organizational structure engenders routine, or habitual actions. Creative actions are more difficult to produce in followers, although they are more desirable for many organizational roles. Ford's theory proposes that habitual or creative action is the product of sense making, multiplied by motivation, multiplied by knowledge and ability on behalf of the employee. Sense making refers to cognitive processes that provide meaning and structure to information for individuals in order to facilitate comprehension and action (Gioia, 1986). How employees interpret problems begins the process of using either habitual or creative actions to solve the problems. If the problem is easily solved, the sense-making schemas will facilitate the use of habitual actions, whereas for a difficult problem, creativity may be cognitively engaged.

Motivation encompasses the goals, emotions, receptivity beliefs, and capability beliefs of the individual and their effects on the habitual vs. creative decision. Naturally, an employee's internal goals will impact the amount of creativity that is used to solve a problem. If the problem does not align with individual goals at all, habitual problem solving is the likely outcome. Emotions provide energy for action and reinforce sense-making schemas. For organizations, creating a culture that encourages emotional expression is associated with increased creativity (e.g. Amabile & Gryskiewicz, 1987).

Receptivity beliefs refer to the employee's expectations of the positivity or negativity associated with completion of the task. For example, an employee's past observations of a coworker being scolded for acting in a creative manner will lead to habitual action in similar future activities. Reward systems impact the receptivity beliefs of employees in a direct manner. Although it may not maximize creativity, the presence of a creativity-based reward system demonstrates its organizational importance to employees, which will discourage habitual actions. Of course, the behaviors of managers in support of reward systems must be equally clear in order for them to be effective.

Capability beliefs, similar to self-efficacy, describe the extent to which employees feel they can successfully undertake a specific task. Strong, general capability beliefs lead to a positive self-image which increases the likelihood of creative actions. If a task is associated with past success for the employee, habitual action repeating the prior successful activity is likely. Clearly, it is important for managers to consider not only the abilities and skills of their employees, but also their beliefs in their own abilities before designing a reward system to encourage creativity.

The final multiplier in this model is employee knowledge and ability. Domain-related knowledge of the employee is necessary in order to deliver creative results. Reward systems will not produce creativity if basic job knowledge is not present. Behavioral abilities such as social networking, trustworthiness, and communication skills can support collaboration and increase creative outputs. Although domain-specific knowledge is essential, creative thinking skills can greatly increase the creative output of employees (Amabile & Gitomer, 1984). In Ford's model, intrinsic factors dominate the decision whether to engage in habitual or creative action by employees.

Unsworth

Unsworth (2001) advances a matrix of creativity based on the argument that it is not a unitary construct, but that it emerges from the intersection of the driver of engagement in the creative process and the type of problem that triggers creative behavior. The two types of drivers that initiate a creative act are self-determined choice and external demands. Self-determined creative behaviors are performed because of internally driven causes. For example, a desire to create a work of art is an internal driver of creativity. An external demand is a creativity driver placed on an individual from the outside. Systems that extrinsically reward creativity are external drivers of creativity. Creativity drivers exist along a continuum between these two extremes.

Problems that trigger creative behavior also exist along a continuum from open problems to closed problems. Open problems require the individual to find, invent, or discover a solution to a problem with no precedent to guide them. Creating a painting on a blank piece of canvas is a classic open problem. In closed problems, there is a known process for arriving at a solution to the problem presented to the individual. Problems requiring little creativity to solve, such as simple algebra problems, are examples of closed problems.

Unsworth's matrix describes the four types of creativity that emerge from a matrix with open and closed problems on one axis, and external and internal drivers for engagement on the other. When a closed problem is driven by external factors, responsive creativity is the result. In responsive creativity, a solution is required to a clearly specified problem. When a closed problem is driven by internal drivers, contributory creativity is the result. An example of this type of creativity would be a creative solution or suggestion by a coworker to a specified problem that another employee is solving. An open problem that is driven externally engenders expected creativity. In expected creativity, a unique solution must be developed to a specified problem. An artist commissioned to create a work of art must demonstrate expected creativity. Finally, open problems driven by internal factors result in proactive creativity. An example of proactive creativity would be an unsolicited suggestion by an assembly line worker concerning an improvement in efficiency of the line.

Unsworth (2001) does not elaborate on the positive or negative organizational consequences for viewing creativity through the lens of her matrix. However, the matrix does specify the two types of creativity that can be expected when using reward systems, which are external drivers of engagement. Because they are mandated, expected and responsive creativity do not capture any excitement or passion toward the problem on the part of the creator. Intrinsic drivers tap into those emotions, and produce anticipatory and voluntary creative problem solving. Clearly, for most organizational problems, the latter is preferred. Organizational leaders should consider the type of creativity they expect from their employees before implementing a reward system, which will necessarily result in responsive and expected creative solutions. There seems to be a chasm between motivation, reward systems and creativity and we believe filling this gap may be an important contribution.

MOTIVATION, REWARD SYSTEMS, AND CREATIVITY

Reward systems are designed to motivate specific behaviors. A vast body of work on motivation has developed over the past 50 years, so it is worthwhile to investigate the link between creativity and reward systems through the perspective of the dominant theories of motivation. As we have discussed, although reward systems are viewed as classic examples of extrinsic motivators, they can also affect intrinsic motivation of participants and their effectiveness is likely dependent on the presence of intrinsic motivators. To clarify, given the employee, extrinsic rewards can increase motivation to maximize performance to fill the gap left by intrinsic motivation. Again, one size of incentives does not fit all employees. Some might require extrinsic rewards while others do not need them. Unless you hire a group of intrinsically-motivated creative employees, you're likely going to get a spectrum of creative employees. So extrinsic rewards help make up for the lack of intrinsic motivation of some employees who might not be have the motivation or ability to be creative.

A number of articles have proposed that reward systems actually negatively impact intrinsic motivation, which is a critical antecedent to creative performance. Amabile (1996) argues that rewards systems attempt to control individual behavior, which lowers intrinsic motivation and creativity. In addition, a meta-analytic investigation of the relationship between extrinsic rewards and intrinsic motivation found strong support for the detrimental effect of rewards on intrinsic motivation (Deci, Koestner, & Ryan, 1999). In fact, the authors found that rewards contingent merely on engaging in a task, on completing a task, and on performing well on a task all were found to significantly undermine intrinsic motivation. Further, all rewards, and specifically tangible and expected rewards negatively influenced intrinsic motivation.

Given the numerous empirical associations between creative performance and intrinsic motivation, this unequivocal evidence of the negative influence of extrinsic rewards on intrinsic motivation does not bode well for the efficacy of reward systems. However, a series of more recent research studies from Eisenberger and colleagues have demonstrated strong support for the positive impact of rewards on a number of desirable organizational outcomes. In one such study, a pay-for-performance reward system positively impacted self-determination, competence, task enjoyment, and free time spent performing the task (Eisenberger, Rhoades, & Cameron, 1999). Further, performance-reward expectancy was positively associated with job interest. Rewards explicitly for novel performance also led to higher creativity in subsequent tasks (Eisenberger & Armeli, 1997). In this same study, the requirement of novel performance did not dampen intrinsic motivation. In a later study of 331 employees, the relationship between expected reward for high performance and creativity was mediated by intrinsic job interest (Eisenberger & Rhoades, 2001). These Eisenberger et al. studies demonstrate that intrinsic motivation may be the primary driver of creative performance, but extrinsic rewards can explain significant additional variation in creative performance as well.

So, to further investigate the proper relationship between of reward systems and motivation, we will next analyze the dominant motivation theories in the literature since the mid-1980s (Latham & Pinder, 2005). Through the perspectives of goal-setting theory, social cognitive theory, and organizational justice theory, we will see that reward systems can improve overall motivation as long as intrinsic motivation drivers are well-established.

Goal-Setting Theory

The basis of goal-setting theory is that specific, difficult goals engender higher performance than does merely urging individuals to do their best (Locke & Latham, 1990). Goals drive this higher performance through four mechanisms. First, goals focus attention and effort toward goal-relevant activities and away from other activities. Second, goals energize individuals to exert greater effort on more challenging goals. Third, goals increase the level of persistence that an individual will display in order to achieve the goal. Finally, goals indirectly are the arousal, discovery, and/or use of knowledge relevant to the task.

Goal-setting is an implicit component of most reward systems (Latham & Pinder, 2005). Through the above mechanisms, goals combine with the extrinsic motivation of the reward to increase performance. Creativity however, is often viewed as being maximized when the employee is under minimal constraints. In an investigation of the effect of goal-setting on creative performance, Shalley (1995) demonstrated that the assignment of a creativity goal increases performance, but actually decreases production in a quantity sense. However, another study combining productivity and creativity goals found performance levels of both were maximized when a difficult productivity goal was combined with either a do-your-best creativity goal or a difficult productivity goal (Shalley, 1991). In addition, feedback on creativity goals increases creative performance beyond the effect of mere goal-setting (Carson & Carson, 1993). Creativity is minimized when no creativity goal is provided. In a further investigation into feedback and creativity, the most creative ideas were generated from a combination of feedback style and valence and task autonomy (Zhou, 1998). This empirical support of creativity and goal-setting lends support to the idea that reward systems should incorporate strong creativity goals and feedback mechanisms in order to maximize their effectiveness at increasing creative performance.

Social Cognitive Theory

Social cognition theory posits that cognitive variables, such as self-efficacy and outcome expectancies, mediate the relationship between environmental antecedents and consequences (Bandura, 1977). Individuals cognitively mobilize efforts and resources based on proactive estimates of what is required for goal attainment. Further, goal commitment and self-efficacy predict what action the individual will take upon goal attainment or failure. Cognitive processes have been linked to creative performance and rewards. In one study, extrinsic rewards were positively related to creativity for employees in simple tasks with adaptive cognitive styles, but only weakly related to creativity for employees with an innovative cognitive style in complex jobs. Studies such as this highlight the promise for investigations into the relationship between rewards (extrinsic motivation), cognition, and creativity.

Creative self-efficacy has been established as a distinct construct in creativity research (Tierney & Farmer, 2002). The construct refers to the belief that one possesses the ability to produce creative outcomes. Tierney and Farmer demonstrated that creative self-efficacy predicted creative performance beyond the influence of job self-efficacy. Although no direct connection between creative self-efficacy and reward systems has been made, supportive supervisor behaviors positively relate to creative self-efficacy. Reward systems managed by non-supportive managers will likely be less effective in driving creative behavior than those led by supportive leaders.

In a study of creativity spanning seven companies, Amabile, Barsade, Mueller, and Staw (2005) demonstrated that affect, another cognitive mechanism, has a simple, positive, linear relationship with creativity. The authors subsequently developed a positive cycle of affect and creativity in which the two constructs drive one another in the organizational context. Social cognition theory has also been used to link positive moods to increased attention to rewards (Tamir & Robinson, 2007). In addition, performance-reward expectancy is positively related to positive mood at work and job performance (Eisenberger et al., 1999). The implication of these findings for reward systems is that employees with positive social cognitions such as affect and mood are more likely to respond to reward incentives for creative performance.

The relationship between cognitions, rewards, and creativity was explicitly studied in the context of a manufacturing environment (Baer, Oldham, & Cummings, 2003). The results demonstrated that extrinsic rewards positively relate to creative performance, but only in employees that displayed an adaptive cognitive style and simple jobs. A much weaker positive relationship between rewards and creativity for employees was demonstrated with an innovative cognitive style and complex jobs. Interestingly, employees in complex jobs with adaptive cognitive styles and those in simple jobs with innovative cognitive styles produced a negative relationship between rewards and creative performance. These results indicate that individuals with either innovative or adaptive cognitive styles and in either simple or complex jobs can be motivated to be creative as long as the match between cognitive style and job complexity is correct.

Organizational Justice

Motivations based on organizational justice are derived from the theory that employees develop beliefs about the inputs they provide their employer as well as about the outcomes. These outcomes include tangible benefits, such as compensation or rewards, or intangible benefits such as praise and development. Employees form beliefs regarding whether their input–output ratio is equitable in contrast with comparable coworkers. Two primary subjective considerations that employees make when deciding the fairness of their input–output ratio are, first, whether the outputs or allocations are fair and, second, whether the procedures used by their employer to decide on the allocations were just (Colquitt, Conlon, Wesson, Porter, & Ng, 2001).

Not surprisingly, creative performance has been shown to be higher in individuals who are treated fairly than those who are treated unjustly (Clark & James, 1999). Abbey & Dickson (1983) also demonstrated that a reward system that equitably rewards outstanding performance is the primary characteristic of innovative R&D groups. Although this seems like common sense, this support for the application of organizational justice theory on creative performance has large implications for the administration of reward systems. In order to maximize creative performance, both the outcomes of the reward systems and the procedure by which the rewards are distributed must be clearly communicated and executed. Further, managers that successfully display interactional justice with their employees can foster a supportive environment, which has also been associated with creative performance (George & Zhou, 2007).

One less studied means of influencing motivation, especially as it relates to creativity, is the omission of a reward for desired behavior in one individual while providing a reward for desired behavior in another. In this situation, Equity Theory posits that individuals will compare the two outcomes and take steps to correct the imbalance (Adams, 1965). These correction steps could occur in several different ways. Ideally, the unrewarded individual will increase his or her future creative performance (inputs) in order to match the future reward (outcome). Unfortunately, individuals have demonstrated that they will also engage in negative activities such as stealing to correct equity imbalance (Greenberg, 1990). In another undesirable situation, the rewarded party may see the imbalance and feel that they did not deserve the reward, leading him or her to actually lower their performance to restore the imbalance. The importance for managers is to realize that motivation can be impacted through not only the giving of rewards, but also the absence of rewards vis-à-vis social comparison.

From this analysis of established theories of organizational creativity and motivation, we can derive a simple model of the relationship between reward systems and creative performance. Reward systems can effectively increase the creative performance of individuals, groups, and organizations beyond that of intrinsic motivation alone in many circumstances. However, the influence of reward systems on creative outcomes seems to be mediated by the existence of intrinsic impacts at these three levels of analysis (Shalley et al., 2004).

REWARD SYSTEMS, INTRINSIC FACTORS, AND CREATIVE PERFORMANCE

As we have proposed throughout this chapter, the relationship between reward systems and creative performance is mediated by a number of factors, many affecting intrinsic motivation. We will now take a deeper look at how certain characteristics of individual personality, leadership, teams, and organizational culture interact with reward systems to impact creative performance. In addition, we will explore the entrepreneurship literature on creative and innovative performance to glean additional insight into the rewards that motivate entrepreneurs to constantly develop creative solutions to problems.

Personality

Amabile and Gryskiewicz (1987) found various personality traits were the strongest promoter of creativity in R&D problem solvers. However, finding strong links between personality traits and motivation has been difficult. In a meta-analysis of the Big 5 personality traits and motivation literature, conscientiousness and neuroticism exhibited the most consistent and strong associations with performance motivation; extraversion, openness to experience, and agreeableness demonstrated weaker and sometimes conflicting relationships with motivation (Judge & Ilies, 2002). A self-monitoring personality has also been strongly linked with motivation, job performance, and career advancement (Day, Shleicher, Unckless, & Hiller, 2002). Although not conclusive, this research indicates that individuals high on conscientiousness, self-monitoring, and neuroticism may be more receptive to reward systems than others.

In addition, creativity research has long searched for a set of stable individual characteristics that predict creative performance. This search has led to the discovery of a significant number of characteristics that influence individual creativity including broad interests, intuition, aesthetic sensitivity, tolerance to ambiguity, attraction to complexity, and self-confidence. These characteristics have been developed into the Creative Personality Scale (CPS) (Gough, 1979). Employees that possess high CPS do in fact produce more creative work than those that do not, although this interaction is amplified by contextual variables such as job complexity and supervisor supportiveness (Oldham & Cummings, 1996). In a meta-analysis of the creativity and personality literature, creative people were found to be more open to new experiences, less conventional and conscientious, more self-confident, self-accepting, driven, ambitious, dominant, hostile, and impulsive than less creative individuals (Feist, 1998).

The findings at the intersection of motivation, personality, and creativity highlight the challenge of designing reward systems to increase creativity. As shown in the studies above, while extraversion and openness to experience were unrelated to motivation, they were positively related to creative behavior. Conversely, neuroticism and conscientiousness have not been associated with creativity but have consistently demonstrated a positive relationship with motivation. In a team environment, extraversion and agreeableness enhance performance in a competitive reward system but decrease performance in a cooperative reward structure (Beersma, Hollenbeck, Humphrey, Moon, Conlon, & Ilgen, 2003). So while it would be very difficult to take into account the many aspects of personality that could influence a reward system, these findings can provide guidance for managers dealing with employees on an individual level. For example, if a subordinate is not responding to creativity-based reward systems, it may be prudent to consider that individual's personality to determine whether the problem is one of motivation or creativity.

Leadership

Leaders play a key role in the success of reward programs and the creative performance of employees. In many cases, they play a part in developing, enforcing, providing feedback, and distributing outcomes of reward systems. In addition, leaders can influence the context under which creativity occurs by providing an atmosphere that is conducive to creative performance. Because of the critical role that managers perform at the confluence of rewards and creativity, their understanding of their employees and their ability to craft reward systems based on that understanding is essential.

The leader–member exchange (LMX) model proposes that the leadership position is a conduit for many organizational criteria. This model emphasizes the importance of the dyadic relationship between boss and employee. Employees of leaders high in LMX demonstrate higher levels of creativity than followers of low LMX leaders because high LMX leaders encourage risk taking and non-routine behavior (Tierney, Farmer, & Graen, 1999). Creative performance is also improved when leaders possess similar intrinsic motivation orientation to their followers (Tierney et al., 1999).

Communication between supervisors and subordinates is critical for creative performance. Amabile, Schatzel, Moneta, and Kramer (2004) found that leaders who communicated with their followers on a daily basis can influence the perceptions, feelings, and performance of followers. These daily interactions further drive the overall creative performance in employees. Though moderated by task type, leadership behaviors influence the innovative behavior in employees (Scott & Bruce, 1994). These behaviors can be extended to the overall leadership style of managers. In fact, leaders who supervise in a supportive, non-controlling fashion produce higher levels than those who exert tight control over their employees (Oldham & Cummings, 1996).

Managers can also increase creative performance by providing feedback to employees. Reward systems directly provide feedback by signaling success or failure to the employee, but they also provide opportunities for managers to partake in a discussion with the subordinate concerning the outcome of the reward system. In fact, independent of the impact of rewards on motivation, positive feedback increases intrinsic motivation (Harackiewicz, 1979). Further, feedback related to creativity goals improves creative performance and creative goal commitment (Carson & Carson, 1993).

Clearly, direct supervisors can influence the creative performance of employees not only through their behaviors and leadership style, but through the frequency and quality of interactions with their followers. Also, managers that interact with their employees on a daily basis are more likely to positively influence the organizational justice associated with a reward system. Therefore, we expect managers who interact frequently and form close relationships with their employees will be more successful than less-involved managers at incrementally improving creative performance through the use of reward systems.

Teams

Given that reward systems are not typically designed on an individual level but at a group or organization level, it is important to consider the effect of rewards on creativity in groups. Though traditional creativity research has focused on the individual, there has been a recent surge in creativity literature at the team level that allows us a deeper look into the drivers of creativity in a group setting (George, 2007). The dominant framework in the study of teams is the inputs–process–outputs (IPO) model, and we will use it to explore how reward systems as an input may influence group processes and produce creative outcomes (Mathieu, Maynard, Rapp, & Gilson, 2008).

Goncalo and Staw (2006) investigated the influence of individualistic and collectivist orientation on team creativity. They hypothesized that individualism, which is typically seen as a negative input to team processes, would actually improve the team's creative performance. Indeed, their results demonstrated that groups possessing an individualistic orientation were more creative than collectivist groups when instructed to be creative. These findings imply that reward systems may be more effective at driving creative performance in groups lower in collectivism.

At the center of the IPO model are team processes, which capture the interactions of group members as they work toward task accomplishment. Team process variables have shown stronger effects on creativity than team input variables. Specifically, team vision, external communication, support for innovation, and task orientation all demonstrate strong associations with innovation in meta-analytic results (Hulsheger, Anderson, & Salgado, 2009). Though not as strong, internal communication and cohesion displayed significant positive relationships with innovation as well. Task and relationship conflict did not significantly impact innovation outcomes. Although there is evidence that some amount of conflict is good for the productivity of teams, these results demonstrate that for creative performance, this may not be the case. Reward systems for teams should reward the entire team equitably. Individual-based rewards in a team-based environment are likely to decrease cohesiveness and increase conflict, which will undermine creative performance.

Through a rich qualitative study of professional service firms, Hargadon and Bechky (2006) developed a model of collective creativity that depicts how creative problem solving shifts from the individual to the collective. Help seeking, help giving, reflective framing, and reinforcing behaviors among individuals in a work setting encourage the emergence of collective creativity. Help seeking is the act of reaching out for help from others by an individual faced with a problem. Help giving refers to voluntary act of resource-giving by employees to coworkers seeking help. Reflective reframing represents mindful actions that demonstrate both respect for others' ideas and builds upon them. Reinforcing activities are those that emphasize organizational values that support individuals as they engage in the three prior activities.

Clearly, there is much room for additional research on the inputs and processes impacting creative outcomes in teams. More research, however, has been conducted on the impacts of reward systems on teams. Overall, results from research on the effectiveness of reward systems in positively influencing team behavior has been mixed, with lab studies providing more support for rewards than field studies (DeMatteo, Eby, Sundstrom, Staw, & Cummings, 1998). In their review of team-based rewards, DeMatteo and colleagues highlighted numerous characteristics of the reward system, the organization, the team members, and the overall team that affect team performance. Their review suggested that equal distribution of rewards in teams is likely to foster cohesiveness, while equitable distribution of rewards among team members fosters productivity. Indeed, teams operating under equality rules demonstrate more cooperative behaviors (Sinclair, 2003) and more help giving (Bamberger & Levi, 2009). Additionally, Campion, Medsker, and Higgs (1993) found that interdependent feedback and rewards are positively related to employee satisfaction in teams.

McClurg (2001) highlighted several implications for practitioners based on his review of team-based rewards research. First, employee involvement in all aspects of the reward system design and implementation is critical. Second, communication between human resources and leadership to the team members is essential throughout the process. Third, managers must be prepared for unintended consequences that will likely arise as a result of the execution of a reward system. Team members may put rewards ahead of more critical organizational goals such as safety or quality, or the power of the teams may challenge the power of the leader if disagreement among reward outcomes occurs. Finally, increased managerial time and attention is necessary for reward systems to be successful. The importance of frequent feedback has been stressed throughout this chapter, which may strain managerial resources.

More recent studies provide more insight on the relationship between teams and rewards. Through the development of the team reward attitude construct, Shaw, Duffy, and Stark (2001) demonstrated that individuals with high ability prefer individual rewards whereas lower ability individuals prefer team-based rewards. Reward structure also influences low performance team members more than high performers (Beersma et al., 2003). In the same study, a competitive reward structure enhanced team speed while a cooperative structure improved accuracy. Team role discussion among members can also mitigate some of the differences between competitive and cooperative reward structures (Beersma, Hollenbeck, Conlon, Humphrey, Moon, & Ilgen, 2009).

The scholarly discussions of team-based rewards and team creativity are less ambiguous than the same discussions at the individual level. Reward systems have demonstrated effectiveness in driving team performance in a multitude of contexts. In addition, several specific team inputs and processes have been associated with team creativity. Although much additional research at the confluence of team-based rewards and creativity is needed, the extant research indicates that cohesion and cooperation are likely to engender creative performance in groups whereas conflict and competition may dampen creativity. As with rewards at the individual level, frequent communication and feedback are necessary for motivating creative performance in teams through reward systems.

Organizational Culture

Although the effects of organization culture on creativity have been addressed indirectly through the previous discussion of creativity models, it is important to explicitly consider the interaction of reward systems and creativity at this level of analysis. For employees to be creative, it has been heavily suggested that an environment that encourages risk taking and uncertainty should not be avoided (Shalley & Gilson, 2004). The construct of psychological safety captures the essence of this cultural situation. When employees feel psychologically safe, they share the belief that the environment is safe for risk taking (Edmondson, 1999). Although little empirical evidence exists on the interaction between reward systems and this climate, there is reason to believe that rewards could reduce the level of psychological safety in the workplace. In a study of innovative R&D subsystems, a work climate where risk taking and experimentation with innovative concepts was embraced was associated with greater creativity (Abbey & Dickson, 1983). Performance-contingent rewards add pressure to perform, and the pressure of achieving the reward could reduce the risk-taking propensity that is necessary for creativity (Jehn, 1995). Therefore, creativity-based reward systems may not increase creative output in organizational climates with high levels of psychological safety.

In addition to encouraging risk taking, a healthy creative climate should embrace a certain amount of conflict. Of course, this conflict should be kept at a minimal level and should be task focused (Pelled, 1996). James, Chen, and Goldberg (1992) found that perceptions of conflict promoted creativity within individual's primary area of interest, but decreased creativity outside of it. When reward systems are involved, the level of conflict must be closely managed or it will quickly spiral out of control, resulting in lower levels of creativity and excessive conflict, among other organizational problems. In considering the implementation of reward systems to stimulate creativity, ethical ambivalence must be considered in order to manage the proper level of conflict. Ethical ambivalence refers to situations in which the behaviors, attitudes, and norms that are fostered by the reward system conflict with the ethical values and judgments of employees (Jansen & Von Glinow, 1985). In situations where these reward system characteristics and stakeholder characteristics are not aligned, conflict is likely to result in decreased creative performance.

As Cummings (1965) elaborated, an open organizational structure is critical for maximizing the creative behavior of employees. Amabile (1998; p. 81) suggested that organizations that give employees "the freedom to decide how to climb a particular mountain" will encourage more creativity than organizations with strict hierarchical processes for how to get work done. Indeed, Hage and Aiken (1969) demonstrated that more authoritarian organizations experienced reduced creativity. However, reward systems can be so complex and explicit that employees have little autonomy when it comes to how they achieve the desired outcome. Clearly, to induce creative performance through reward systems, the goal must be clearly specified, but the process regarding how to reach that goal must be left to the employee.

Human resources practices must also be attuned to the creativity goals of the organization. Hiring practices that specifically focus on acquiring creative human capital will amplify the effectiveness of most of the creativity-enhancing practices within the organization, including reward systems. Also, assessing fit and placing employees in roles where their skills and values align with the job and the organization will allow for more slack cognitive resources for the employee to perform creatively (Livingstone, Nelson, & Ban, 1997). Training programs can also be designed by HR to maximize creativity. An integrated HRM system could be designed to reinforce a company's creative culture. For example, you start by finding (recruiting) employees who fit with your culture, who you then hire. You establish reward desired behaviors, and then encourage continuous improvement through performance management. On the job training in creative thought processes and creative problem solving has been shown to increase the creative performance of employees (Basadur, Graen, & Green, 1982; Basadur, Wakabayashi, & Graen, 1990). It is not a stretch to propose that HR departments that are actively engaged in the goals of creativity-based reward systems can have a significant positive impact on creative performance.

In addition, the type of job must be considered in rewarding creativity. Many jobs, such as manufacturing line positions, are firmly rooted within the organization. However, many roles that demand high levels of creativity, such as artists, professors, doctors, and consultants, are more professionally-based. In these roles, individuals may find more extrinsic and intrinsic motivation through professional rewards like tenure, promotions, or public recognition. Therefore, reward systems devised to increase the creative production of professionals should incorporate more external professionally-based rewards if possible.

Reward system design must transpire concurrent with the culture of the organization. Reward systems may be more effective in stimulating creativity in firms that embrace task conflict than those that stymie anything but harmony in the workplace. In addition, organizational structure should specify the desired outcome, not the process that employees must follow to perform creatively. Finally, although some have argued that creativity can only be developed through intrinsic motivation, structured education on creative practices can stimulate creativity at all levels of the organization. To increase the effectiveness of creativity-based reward systems, leaders would be wise to first immerse their employees in this type of training.

E. INTERVENTIONS

ENTREPRENEURSHIP AND CREATIVITY

Entrepreneurship has often been associated with the creation of wealth (Ireland, Hitt, & Sirmon, 2003). This makes it useful to study from the perspective of reward systems and creative performance, because wealth is an extrinsic motivator. Although there are many intrinsic reasons that entrepreneurs start their own companies (see Gimeno, Folta, Cooper, & Woo, 1997), the extrinsic driver of individual wealth is clearly a goal for many business owners. In pursuing this wealth, the entrepreneur has been characterized as an innovative leader that is able to break away from the routine, destroy existing structures, and move the entire economic system away from equilibrium (Schumpeter, 1942). Clearly, if reward systems can engender some of this entrepreneurial behavior in employees, creative performance is likely to ensue.

The construct of entrepreneurial orientation (EO) was developed in an attempt to link entrepreneurial behavior to firm performance (Lumpkin & Dess, 1996). EO is comprised of autonomy, innovativeness, risk taking, proactiveness, and competitive aggressiveness. Although we have discussed the importance of reward systems supporting autonomy, innovativeness, and risk taking, the concepts of proactiveness and competitive aggressiveness merit further attention. Proactive behavior refers to anticipatory action that individuals take to impact themselves or their environment (Grant & Ashford, 2008). Proactivity has been proposed as an antecedent to creative behavior (e.g., Crant, 2000; Frese & Fay, 2001). Therefore reward systems that encourage action through incentives, will likely increase the initiative individuals take to perform creatively. In addition, competitive aggressiveness can be encouraged through reward systems. However, more caution is warranted when using extrinsic rewards to increase competition within an organization. Whereas entrepreneurial competitive aggressiveness is necessary in the dynamic environment in which many small businesses operate, it can quickly destroy the environment within an organization if left unchecked.

REWARD CONTENT

Although this chapter focuses primarily on the process of motivating creativity through rewards, it is important to consider the effect of reward content on creative outcomes. Conventional wisdom suggests the inclusion of a productivity component to reward systems could increase creative performance. Indeed, research supports this position, and demonstrates that creative performance is maximized when creativity goals are coupled with difficult productivity goals (Shalley, 1991). Naturally then, managers would be wise to encourage creative performance through rewards for achieving difficult levels of productivity.

Organizational learning objectives can be easily included in rewards systems. Barrett (1998) argues that organizational learning is critical for creativity, but that it is:

"a risky venture, reaching into the unknown with no guarantee of where one's explorations will lead." *(p. 619)*

Managers can include rewards for organizational learning in their programs to encourage employees to engage in the relatively risky endeavor of organizational learning.

Managers may also be tempted to include incentives for effort in reward systems. The empirical relationship between effort and results, however, is quite murky. For example, Wageman and Baker (1997) found that teams in high-reward conditions exerted more effort than in low-reward conditions. However, in a subsequent and more rigorous test and extension of this study, Allen, Sargent, and Bradley (2003) found no support for this link. As a result of their findings, the authors suggested that task complexity can mitigate the positive influence of rewards on effort. Therefore, managers should consider the complexity involved in the tasks and projects before rewarding employees for effort in creative endeavors.

Clearly, reward system designers must use no small degree of their own creativity to build a program that includes content tailored to their specific organizational situation, focal job, and employee characteristics. Simply rewarding for the end result of creative behavior is likely not enough to drive lasting creative performance. For example, in some organizations, rewarding cooperative behavior may increase creative performance, while in others it may promote groupthink. Managers should consider rewarding a wide range of possible behaviors that are associated with creative behavior in their organization, and then build the reward system with the most promising components of this set.

PRACTICAL IMPLICATIONS

This chapter provides support for both intrinsic and extrinsic motivators of creativity. As we have shown, reward systems are typically considered a form of extrinsic motivation, although, at the margins, they can impact intrinsic motivation both positively and negatively. Managers, for several reasons, should seek to intrinsically motivate their employees' creative behavior before using reward systems. First, intrinsic motivation is unequivocally associated with increased creative performance in a number of organizational settings. In addition, although it is more difficult to foster intrinsic motivation, it requires fewer organizational resources than extrinsic rewards. Finally, because intrinsic motivation, by its nature, comes from within, there is an unlimited supply of it. Extrinsic motivation is dependent on constantly maintaining the valence of the reward in the eyes of the employee.

Only after intrinsic motivation has been established, or attempted, should extrinsic rewards be used to stimulate creativity. In both situations, either once employees are intrinsically motivated or after they have rejected intrinsic appeals, extrinsic motivators can incrementally improve creative performance. As we have discussed, these rewards must align with a number of individual and contextual factors in order to be effective, but they are definitely a valuable arrow in every manager's quiver.

Reward systems have the potential to facilitate, develop, and improve the creative performance of individuals, teams, and entire organizations. However, their design and implementation is far away from a "one size fits all" approach. Indeed, driving performance through the use of rewards and increasing creative performance are two of the most complex and difficult challenges for a manager by themselves. When combined, they make for a daunting task for even the most seasoned leaders. At each stage of the reward system—design, commencement, execution, and conclusion—there are far more opportunities to damage the effectiveness of the system than there are to improve it.

In the design stage, inclusion of individuals at all levels of the organization is paramount. The top leadership in the organization must be present to signal to all of the employees that the reward system and creative performance is important to the mission and vision at the institutional level. These high-level leaders set the tone that risk taking and failure are an accepted part of the creative process. As we have discussed, HR involvement in acquiring the employees that fit the organization's creative vision and training current employees in creative thinking is extremely beneficial.

Middle managers will make or break the success of a reward system. They must tailor their management style to fostering creative behavior. For supervisors accustomed to tightly controlling their subordinates, behavior change, or a transfer to another role in the organization will be necessary. If managers are not capable of creating a climate of psychological safety and allowing employees to find their own unique way to solve problems, creative performance will be thwarted, employees will not receive rewards, and morale will suffer.

Too often, reward systems are designed without the input of the actual employees. Employees are the most important stakeholders in this process, and they must be involved from reward system inception. Honest communication from employees will indicate to attentive managers whether or not the reward systems will actually succeed in driving creative performance. Although reward systems may succeed in increasing general performance in many organizations, this is not always the case with creative performance. If intrinsic factors like personal traits, self-efficacy, and team processes are not properly aligned with creative performance, creativity may actually decrease due to the conflicts that arise from a poorly designed incentive system. Through deep discussions with employees, managers can determine what level of creativity can be realistically expected from their workforce, and design a system that builds on the strengths of their existing employees to incrementally improve creative performance. In this phase of the process, leadership may realize that making organizational changes, like increasing autonomy, can improve creativity through purely intrinsic motivation, and the resources required by a reward system can be conserved.

Communication between managers and employees is critical throughout the execution of the reward system. As we have described, feedback is very important for the stimulation of creativity, so managers must harness this power and positively guide their employees' behavior toward creative outcomes. Not surprisingly, some individuals will require more coaxing than others. Top-level managers must understand that middle-managers need to spend additional time with their subordinates during this time, and support for their other duties may need to be arranged. Finally, although it may be tempting, managers should avoid changing the structure of the reward system too early due to lack of results or push back from workers. Like most aspects of organizational culture, creativity takes time and effort to foster and develop, and reward systems are not a panacea that will deliver rapid creative performance.

Organizational justice comes into play when it is time to begin distributing the rewards for creativity. At this time, it is vital that communication lines remain open, and all levels of the organization assess whether the reward system appropriately compensated the right employees for the desired creative outcomes. In addition, any concerns regarding procedural or distributive justice should be addressed. At this point, small changes in the reward system may be necessary to improve the process for the future.

Clearly, the intersection of two complex phenomena—increasing performance through rewards and motivating creative behavior—presents the opportunity for original and counterintuitive causal relationships in organizations. For example, the rewarding of certain types of failure may increase the psychological safety of a work group and spur creativity. Similarly, offering financial incentives for the creation of a piece of artwork may actually lower the item's creativity. Therefore, to effectively influence creativity through reward systems, traditional causal paradigms must be critically examined. Managers should avoid the trap of applying rewards to creativity just because they may have been effective in positively impacting other organizational outcomes.

FUTURE RESEARCH

In our integration of reward systems and creativity, we have reviewed a large stream of organizational research on both creativity and motivation. Despite the depth of this research, understanding of the impact of extrinsic rewards on creative performance is still unclear. Creative employees allow organizations to develop new products and services, function more efficiently, adapt to change, and survive (Shalley et al., 2004). Therefore, reward systems that can enhance the creative performance of employees can shape the future of the organization for the better. To more conclusively understand the contexts under which reward systems improve or impair creative performance, longitudinal field studies exploring the mechanisms through which reward systems affect creativity over time are necessary. Future research should combine qualitative and quantitative methods to reach the deeper and richer insights into the complex relationship between creative performance and motivation in the workplace. Research on these issues might provide organizations with a yardstick indicating the resource investment necessary for the desired creativity of the workforce and those human resources management systems which may be more conducive to the facilitation of creativity among workers. Furthermore, we need to gain some insight into the multilevel issues which have an influence upon the relationship between reward systems and creativity.

CONCLUSION

Some have argued that reward systems, because of their extrinsic nature, cannot stimulate creative performance. However, we propose that while intrinsic motivation is the primary driver of creativity, reward systems that complement intrinsic motivators can spur incremental creativity in individuals or facilitate the creativity which already exists in individuals. Therefore, organizations should take a portfolio approach to stirring organizational creativity, and use multiple methods to tap into both intrinsic and extrinsic motivators in reward systems. When reward systems are not properly aligned with the individual, team, and organizational characteristics discussed in this chapter, they have the potential to not only be wasted resources, but actually might become a source of malice and perceived injustice in the workplace. Therefore any creativity-based reward system implementation should be meticulously administered with input from many organizational stakeholders. Future research should continue to explore the distinct individual and contextual mechanisms through which rewards enhance the intrinsic drivers of creative performance for scholarly and practical purposes. These findings will be important, as creativity has not only the possibility of propelling the growth of organizations and industries, but has the possibility of propelling entire economies as well.

References

Abbey, A., & Dickson, J. W. (1983). R&D work climate and innovation in semiconductors. *The Academy of Management Journal, 26*, 362–368.

Adams, J. S. (1965). Inequity in social exchange. In L. Berkowitz (Ed.), *Advances in experimental social psychology* (Vol. 2, pp. 267–299). New York, NY: Academic Press.

Allen, B. C., Sargent, L. D., & Bradley, L. M. (2003). Differential effects of task and reward interdependence on perceived helping behavior, effort, and group performance. *Small Group Research, 34*, 716–740.

Amabile, T. M. (1979). Effects of external evaluation on artistic creativity. *Journal of Personality and Social Psychology, 37*, 221–233.

Amabile, T. M. (1988). A model of creativity and innovation in organizations. In B. Staw & L. Cummings (Eds.), *Research in organizational behavior* (Vol. 10, pp. 123–168). Greenwich, CT: JAI Press Inc.

Amabile, T. M. (1996). *Creativity in context*. Boulder, CO: Westview.

Amabile, T. M. (1998). How to kill creativity. *Harvard Business Review, 76*, 76–87.

Amabile, T. M., Barsade, S. G., Mueller, J. S., & Staw, B. M. (2005). Affect and creativity at work. *Administrative Science Quarterly, 50*, 367–403.

Amabile, T. M., Conti, R., Coon, H., Lazenby, J., & Herron, M. (1996). Assessing the work environment for creativity. *Academy of Management Journal, 39*, 1154–1184.

Amabile, T. M., & Gitomer, J. (1984). Children's artistic creativity: Effects of choice in task materials. *Personality and Social Psychology Bulletin, 10*, 209–215.

Amabile, T. M., & Gryskiewicz, S. (1987). *Creativity in the R&D laboratory Technical Report Number 30*. Greensboro, NC: Center for Creative Leadership.

Amabile, T. M., Hennessey, B. A., & Grossman, B. S. (1986). Social influences on creativity: The effects of contracted-for reward. *Journal of Personality and Social Psychology, 50*, 14–23.

Amabile, T. M., Schatzel, E. A., Moneta, G. B., & Kramer, S. J. (2004). Leader behaviors and the work environment for creativity: Perceived leader support. *The Leadership Quarterly, 15*, 5–32.

Amabile, T. M., Tighe, E. M., Hill, K. G., & Hennessey, B. A. (1994). The work preference inventory: Assessing intrinsic and extrinsic motivational orientations. *Journal of Personality and Social Psychology, 66*, 950–967.

Anderson, N. H., & Butzin, C. A. (1974). Performance = Motivation × Ability: An integration-theoretical analysis. *Journal of Personality and Social Psychology, 30*, 598–604.

Baer, M., Oldham, G. R., & Cummings, A. (2003). Rewarding creativity: When does it really matter? *Leadership Quarterly, 14*, 569.

Bamberger, P. A., & Levi, R. (2009). Team-based reward allocation structures and the helping behaviors of outcome-interdependent team members. *Journal of Management Psychology, 24*, 300–327.

Bandura, A. (1977). *Social learning theory*. Englewood Cliffs, NJ: Prentice-Hall.

Baron, R. A., & Ensley, M. D. (2006). Opportunity recognition as the detection of meaningful patterns: Evidence from comparisons of novice and experienced entrepreneurs. *Management Science, 52*, 1331–1344.

Barrett, F. J. (1998). Coda: Creativity and improvisation in jazz and organizations: Implications for organizational learning. *Organization Science, 9*, 605–622.

Basadur, M., Graen, G. B., & Green, S. G. (1982). Training in creative problem solving: Effects on ideation and problem finding and solving in an industrial research organization. *Organizational Behavior and Human Performance, 30*, 41–70.

Basadur, M., Wakabayashi, M., & Graen, G. B. (1990). Individual problem-solving styles and attitudes toward divergent thinking before and after training. *Creativity Research Journal, 3*, 22–32.

Beersma, B., Hollenbeck, J. R., Conlon, D. E., Humphrey, S. E., Moon, H., & Ilgen, D. R. (2009). Cutthroat cooperation: The effects of team role decisions on adaptation to alternative reward structures. *Organizational Behavior and Human Decision Processes, 108*, 131–142.

Beersma, B., Hollenbeck, J. R., Humphrey, S. E., Moon, H., Conlon, D. E., & Ilgen, D. R. (2003). Cooperation, competition, and team performance: Toward a contingency approach. *Academy of Management Journal, 46,* 572–590.

Campion, M. A., Medsker, G. J., & Higgs, A. C. (1993). Relations between work group characteristics and effectiveness: Implications for designing effective work groups. *Personnel Psychology, 46,* 823–850.

Carson, P. P., & Carson, K. D. (1993). Managing creativity enhancement through goal-setting and feedback. *Journal of Creative Behavior, 27,* 36–45.

Catmull, E. (2008). How Pixar fosters collective creativity. *Harvard Business Review, 86,* 64–72.

Clark, K., & James, K. (1999). Justice and positive and negative creativity. *Creativity Research Journal, 12,* 311–320.

Colquitt, J. A., Conlon, D. E., Wesson, M. J., Porter, C. O., & Ng, K. Y. (2001). Justice at the millenium: A meta-analytic review of 25 years of organizational justice research. *Journal of Applied Psychology, 86,* 425–445.

Crant, J. M. (2000). Proactive behavior in organizations. *Journal of Management, 26,* 435–462.

Cummings, L. (1965). Organizational climates for creativity. *Academy of Management Journal, 8,* 220–227.

Day, D. V., Shleicher, D. J., Unckless, A. L., & Hiller, N. J. (2002). Self-monitoring personality at work: A meta-analytic investigation of construct validity. *Journal of Applied Psychology, 87,* 390–401.

Deci, E. L., Koestner, R., & Ryan, R. M. (1999). A meta-analytic review of experiments examining the effects of extrinsic rewards on intrinsic motivation. *Psychological Bulletin, 125,* 627–668.

DeMatteo, J. S., Eby, L. T., Sundstrom, E., Staw, B. M., & Cummings, L. L. (1998). Team-based rewards: Current empirical evidence and directions for future research *Research in organizational behavior, Vol. 20: An annual series of analytical essays and critical reviews* (pp. 141–183). US: Elsevier Science/JAI Press.

Edmondson, A. (1999). Psychological safety and learning behavior in work teams. *Administrative Science Quarterly, 44,* 350–383.

Eisenberger, R., & Armeli, S. (1997). Can salient reward increase creative performance without reducing intrinsic creative interest? *Journal of Personality & Social Psychology, 72,* 652–663.

Eisenberger, R., Armeli, S., & Pretz, J. (1998). Can the promise of reward increase creativity? *Journal of Personality and Social Psychology, 74,* 704–714.

Eisenberger, R., & Aselage, J. (2008). Incremental effects of reward on experienced performance pressure: Positive outcomes for intrinsic interest and creativity. *Journal of Organizational Behavior, 30,* 95–117.

Eisenberger, R., & Aselage, J. (2009). Incremental effects of reward on experienced performance pressure: positive outcomes for intrinsic interest and creativity. [Article]. *Journal of Organizational Behavior, 30,* 95–117.

Eisenberger, R., & Rhoades, L. (2001). Incremental effects of reward on creativity. Journal of Personality & *Social Psychology, 81,* 728–741.

Eisenberger, R., Rhoades, L., & Cameron, J. (1999). Does pay for performance increase or decrease perceived self-determination and intrinsic motivation?. *Journal of Personality & Social Psychology, 77,* 1026–1040.

Feist, G. J. (1998). A meta-analysis of personality in scientific and artistic creativity. *Personality and Social Psychology Review, 2,* 290–309.

Ford, C. M. (1996). A theory of individual creative action in multiple social domains. *Academy of Management Review, 21,* 1112–1142.

Frese, M., & Fay, D. (2001). *Personal initiative: An active performance concept for work in the 21st century* (Vol. 23), pp.133–187. Elsevier Science Ltd.

George, J. M. (2007). Creativity in organizations. *Academy of Management Annals, 1,* 439–477.

George, J. M., & Zhou, J. (2007). Dual tuning in a supportive context: Joint contributions of positive mood, negative mood, and supervisory behaviors to employee creativity. *Academy of Management Journal, 50,* 605–622.

Gimeno, J., Folta, T., Cooper, A., & Woo, C. (1997). Survival of the fittest? Entrepreneurial human capital and the persistence of underperforming firms. *Administrative Science Quarterly, 42,* 750–783.

Gioia, D. A. (1986). Symbols, scripts, and sensemaking: Creating meaning in the organizational experience. In H. P. Simms & D. A. Gioia (Eds.), *The thinking organization: Dynamics of organizational social cognition* (pp. 49–74). San Francisco, CA: Jossey-Bass.

Goncalo, J. A., & Staw, B. M. (2006). Individualism–collectivism and group creativity. *Organizational Behavior and Human Decision Processes, 100,* 96–109.

Gough, H. G. (1979). A creative personality scale for the Adjective Check List. *Journal of Personality and Social Psychology, 37,* 1398–1405.

Grant, A., & Ashford, S. (2008). The dynamics of proactivity at work. *Research in Organizational Behavior, 28,* 3–34.

Greenberg, J. (1990). Employee theft as a reaction to underpayment inequity: The hidden cost of pay cuts. *Journal of Applied Psychology, 75,* 561–568.

E. INTERVENTIONS

Guthrie, E. R. (1940). Association and the law of effect. *Psychological Review, 47,* 127–148.

Hage, J., & Aiken, M. (1969). Routine technology, social structure, and organization goals. *Administrative Science Quarterly, 14,* 366–376.

Harackiewicz, J. M. (1979). The effects of reward contingency and performance feedback on intrinsic motivation. *Journal of Personality and Social Psychology, 37,* 1352–1363.

Hargadon, A. B., & Bechky, B. A. (2006). When collections of creatives become a creative collectives: A field study of problem solving at work. *Organization Science, 17,* 484–500.

Heider, F. (1958). *The psychology of interpersonal relations.* New York, NY: Wiley.

Hulsheger, U. R., Anderson, N., & Salgado, J. F. (2009). Team-level predictors of innovation at work: A comprehensive meta-analysis spanning three decades of research. *Journal of Applied Psychology, 94,* 1128–1145.

Ireland, R. D., Hitt, M. A., & Sirmon, D. G. (2003). A model of strategic entrepreneurship: The construct and its dimensions. *Journal of Management, 29,* 963.

Iyer, B., & Davenport, T. H. (2008). Reverse engineering Google's innovation machine. *Harvard Business Review, 86,* 58–68.

James, K., Chen, J., & Goldberg, C. (1992). Organizational conflict and individual creativity. *Journal of Applied Social Psychology, 22,* 545–566.

Jansen, E., & Von Glinow, M. A. (1985). Ethical ambivalence and organizational reward systems. *Academy of Management Review, 10,* 814–822.

Jehn, K. A. (1995). A multimethod examination of the benefits and detriments of intragroup conflict. *Administrative Science Quarterly, 40,* 256–282.

Judge, T. A., & Ilies, R. (2002). Relationship of personality to performance motivation: A meta-analytic review. *Journal of Applied Psychology, 87,* 797–807.

Kerr, S. (1975). On the folly of rewarding A, while hoping for B. *Academy of Management Journal, 18,* 769–783.

Latham, G. P., & Pinder, C. C. (2005). Work motivation theory and research at the dawn of the twenty-first century. *Annual Review of Psychology, 56,* 485–516.

Livingstone, L. P., Nelson, D. L., & Ban, S. H. (1997). Person–environment fit and creativity: An examination of supply–value and demand–ability versions of fit. *Journal of Management, 23,* 119.

Locke, E. A., & Latham, G. P. (1990). *A theory of goal-setting and task performance.* Englewood Cliffs, NJ: Prentice Hall.

Lumpkin, G. T., & Dess, G. G. (1996). Clarifying the entrepreneurial orientation construct and linking it to performance. *The Academy of Management Review, 21,* 135–172.

Mathieu, J., Maynard, M. T., Rapp, T., & Gilson, L. (2008). Team effectiveness 1997–2007: A review of recent advancements and a glimpse into the future. *Journal of Management, 34,* 410–476.

McClurg, L. N. (2001). Team rewards: How far have we come? *Human Resource Management, 40,* 73–86.

Morse, G. (2006). Sparking creativity at Ferrari. *Harvard Business Review, 84,* 23.

Oldham, G. R., & Cummings, A. (1996). Employee creativity: Personal and contextual factors at work. *Academy of Management Journal, 39,* 607–634.

Pelled, L. H. (1996). Demographic diversity, conflict, and work group outcomes: An intervening process theory. *Organization Science, 7,* 615–631.

Schumpeter, J. A. (1942). *Capitalism, socialism and democracy.* New York, NY: Harper and Row.

Scott, S. G., & Bruce, R. A. (1994). Determinants of innovative behavior: A path model of individual innovation in the workplace. *Academy of Management Journal, 37,* 580–607.

Shalley, C. E. (1991). Effects of productivity goals, creativity goals, and personal discretion on individual creativity. *Journal of Applied Psychology, 76,* 179–185.

Shalley, C. E. (1995). Effects of coaction, expected evaluation, and goal setting on creativity and productivity. *Academy of Management Journal, 38,* 483–503.

Shalley, C. E., & Gilson, L. L. (2004). What leaders need to know: A review of social and contextual factors that can foster or hinder creativity. *The Leadership Quarterly, 15,* 33–53.

Shalley, C. E., Zhou, J., & Oldham, G. R. (2004). The effects of personal and contextual characteristics on creativity: Where should we go from here? *Journal of Management, 30,* 933–958.

Shaw, J. D., Duffy, M. K., & Stark, E. M. (2001). Team reward attitude: Construct development and initial validation. *Journal of Organizational Behavior, 22,* 903–917.

Sinclair, A. L. (2003). The effects of justice and cooperation on team effectiveness. *Small Group Research, 34,* 74.

Stewart, G. B., Applebaum, E., Beer, M., Lebby, A. M., Amabile, T. M., & McAdams, J., et al. (1993). Rethinking rewards. *Harvard Business Review, 71,* 37–49.

Tamir, M., & Robinson, M. D. (2007). The happy spotlight: Positive mood and selective attention to rewarding information. *Personality and Social Psychology Bulletin, 33,* 1124–1136.

Tierney, P., & Farmer, S. M. (2002). Creative self-efficacy: Its potential antecedents and relationship to creative performance. *Academy of Management Journal, 45,* 1137–1148.

Tierney, P., Farmer, S. M., & Graen, G. B. (1999). An examination of leadership and employee creativity: The relevance of traits and relationships. *Personnel Psychology, 52,* 591–620.

Unsworth, K. (2001). Unpacking creativity. *Academy of Management Review, 26,* 289–297.

Vroom, V. H. (1964). *Work and motivation.* New York, NY: Wiley.

Wageman, R., & Baker, G. (1997). Incentives and cooperation: The joint effects of task and reward interdependence on group performance. *Journal of Organizational Behavior, 18,* 139–158.

Woodman, R. W., Sawyer, J. E., & Griffin, R. W. (1993). Toward a theory of organizational creativity. *Academy of Management Review, 18,* 293–321.

Zhou, J. (1998). Feedback valence, feedback style, task autonomy, and achievement orientation: Interactive effects on creative performance. *Journal of Applied Psychology, 83,* 261–276.

E. INTERVENTIONS

Performance Management: Appraising Performance, Providing Feedback, and Developing for Creativity

Ginamarie S. Ligon[1], Katrina A. Graham[2], Aliyah Edwards[3], Holly K. Osburn[4], and Samuel T. Hunter[5]

[1]Villanova University, Villanova, PA; [2]Drexel University, Philadelphia, PA; [3]SAP Americas, PA; [4]University of Central Oklahoma, Edmond, OK; [5]Pennsylvania State University, University Park, PA

INTRODUCTION

Appraising and developing, both integral components of performance management, are complicated endeavors for innovation. DeNisi (2000) defines performance management (PM) as the:

"range of activities engaged in by an organization to enhance the performance of a target person or group." *(p. 121)*

He and other scholars (Mondy, Noe, & Premeaux, 2002; Noe, Hollenbeck, Gerhardt, & Wright, 2007) agree that performance management is a multi-faceted process where employees and managers work together to:

1. set expectations,
2. review results,

Handbook of Organizational Creativity.
DOI: 10.1016/B978-0-12-374714-3.00025-2

3. reward performance, and
4. develop skills.

There is a copious amount of literature on performance management in general (Kline & Sulsky, 2009), as well as accounts of what makes the underlying human resource (HR) interventions legally defensible (Malos, 1995). Although applying these noted best practices to appraise and develop innovative performance will be helpful in several contexts, there is some indication that a blanket application of general HR techniques of performance management may prove less useful—and perhaps even hamper—innovation in organizations.

Before turning to the direct implications for performance management, however, a discussion of innovation as a unique type of performance is warranted. Innovation in organizational settings involves the development of novel, useful products or services. The pursuit of such performance is driven by the need to stay ahead of competition, win new market-share, and grow as an organization. In a recent survey of publicly traded organizations, we found an overwhelming majority of organizations in our sample had innovation, creativity, or a related synonym mentioned in their mission statement and/or core values (Osburn, Ligon, Edwards, Bedford, Bruno, Doran, DiDomenico, & Scherer, 2010).

Innovative performance goals may be accomplished by those working in positions expressly designed for creative problem solving (i.e., innovative positions such as R&D scientists). In addition, "garden variety" innovative performance can be accomplished in more routine positions, and incumbents in such positions are increasingly being asked to do so (Mayfield & Mayfield, 2008; Stafford, 1998). There are various reasons for this increased focus on innovation throughout all levels of an organization, but some of the more prominent causes are the demand for increased worker participation, the transition to a service-based economy, the flattening of organizations, and an increasingly merger and acquisition-rich environment (Cascio, 2006). In short, it seems that employees at all levels in a variety of organizations are being asked to innovate. Whether organizations are able to achieve such innovative performance goals depends on a host of internal and external factors, however. One set of such factors, the factors at hand in this section of the handbook, are organizational interventions for innovation in the workplace.

Indeed, we have three primary goals for this chapter. First, we will review best practices for two well-known interventions for innovation—the performance appraisal process and training/development programs. Second, we will contrast approaches for both practices against similar interventions for other types of organizational performance, specifying when typical interventions are not suited for innovation. Throughout our discussion, we will address how individual differences of those working in creative positions may interact with interventions to enhance creativity. Finally, we propose models for each of these interventions for creative performance, as well as propose a future research and practice agenda for those engaged in work in this area.

Assumptions

Before turning to the present chapter's goals, we must visit three assumptions made in this review and the foregoing intervention models we propose. The most straightforward assumption made is that creativity can indeed be enhanced, and performance appraisal and training/development interventions show a great deal of promise as mechanisms to do so. We see creativity as primarily a cognitive process (Mumford, Mobley, Uhlman, Reiter-Palmon, & Doares, 1991). Thus, providing employees with requisite skills and expertise through training and development, as well as structuring appraisal systems to provide appropriate feedback about those skills and expertise, should motivate employees to engage in the creative process and yield enhanced performance in a host of settings.

Second, to increase innovative performance, work by Baer, Oldham, and Cummings (2003) suggests that those who work in innovative, non-routine jobs may require markedly different interventions from those who work in routine positions. Non-routine positions, when compared to most other positions in an organization, offer more opportunities for task complexity, skill variety, task identity, task significance, autonomy, and feedback (Hackman & Oldham, 1976). This distinction is also useful in differentiating jobs that require innovation (e.g., R&D) vs. those where innovation is a bonus, but is not mandated (e.g., clerical positions).

Garden variety creativity, a concept raised by Stafford (1998) is found in small, everyday innovations that can be undertaken by employees—including those in routine positions. For example, a loading dock attendant may discover a new way to stock trucks, or an administrative assistant may find that sending e-cards to customers in place of traditional holiday cards saves the organization a great deal of capital and time. What Baer and others' findings also suggest is that creativity can be increased in most jobs, given the right conditions and approaches (Baer, Oldham, Jacobson, & Hollinghead, 2008; Mayfield & Mayfield, 2008). However, while such performance in routine positions will benefit the organization, in this chapter we make the case that different approaches must be used to appraise and develop innovation in creative, non-routine positions (e.g., scientists).

In addition to the different performance interventions required for innovative positions, we assume that effective performance management for innovative processes is rooted in the three-component model of creativity (Amabile, 1983, 1996). This view suggests that there are three primary components needed for creativity to occur in an organizational setting: expertise, cognitive creative process skills, and task motivation. Thus, interventions geared at improving creativity should not overlook the importance of these elements. Innovation is more likely to occur when employees' skills and knowledge overlap with motivation, and higher levels of each of the three components should also be related to increased levels of innovation (Amabile, 1996). Given these considerations, there are multiple implications for interventions for innovation, and this is particularly the case for performance management.

PERFORMANCE MANAGEMENT

At all levels of the organization, employees face some type of performance evaluation. There are three related processes to describe activities associated with these formal evaluations. Performance *appraisal* is the process of assessing or evaluating performance to make decisions (e.g., about promotions). Performance *development* refers to the evaluation of performance with the goal of providing feedback and suggesting developmental activities to improve that performance. Performance *management* (PM) is the integration of the two in order to make performance-based decisions and improve organizational performance. Prior to turning our discussion to the specific interventions for innovation, it is necessary to first review the primary goals and history of the performance appraisal in an organizational context, as these two issues drive the development of most HR performance appraisal tools and thus impact those designed for innovation.

Historical Goals of Performance Management and Associated Consequences for Innovation

Performance management consists of two central purposes (Murphy & Cleveland, 1995), and each has potential to enhance (or lessen) innovation. One PM objective is to align employee behaviors with the overarching goals of the organization. Since a key step in performance management involves the setting and evaluation of work goals, one would expect that organizations with more innovative missions would also have PM systems that encourage individual behavior toward this high level objective. Thompson (2007), in a review of the aerospace sector, found that both the industry and the production context influenced PM practices. Using diverse methodologies, it was determined that multi-establishment organizations with different production systems (e.g., high volume vs. custom) also had varied personnel policies, including differences concerning performance appraisals. In organizations where the mission was to produce low volume, high variety products, PM personnel policies reflected looser controls and more autonomy in how the objectives were set and measured. This was different in organizations that specialized in high volume, low variety production goals. In organizations with high volume missions, he found more emphasis on *controlling* appraisal content, such as a focus on absenteeism/tardiness, efficient and error-free work, and adherence to rules and standards.

In a related study assessing organization-level goals of innovation, Searle and Ball (2003) surveyed 88 organizations across a range of industrial sectors in the UK. They found significant differences in the performance appraisal processes of organizations who valued innovation as an organizational objective vs. those who had operating goals such as efficiency or customer service. These and other findings (Forrester, 1994; Noe, Hollenbeck, & Gerhart, 2007) suggest that most PM systems are top–down in nature; objectives are determined at the individual level via the department or group level, which are in turn deduced from organizational level goals and mission (Molleman & Timmerman, 2003).

A second elemental purpose of PM is to enhance the quality and legal defensibility of personnel decisions, such as pay raises, promotions, dismissals, and access to training programs (Murphy & Cleveland, 1995). As a result of this goal, appraisals often attempt to measure standardized aspects of performance that are specific, repetitive, and quantitative (Cardy & Stewart, 1998; Johnsen, 2005). Personnel decisions based on performance appraisals are subject to the same rigorous legal standards as other personnel decision techniques (e.g., selection tests), and, as a result, there must be a defensible explanation of why some employees are promoted, discharged, or provided with pay increases as compared with others. Malos (1998) reviewed court cases where performance appraisals were the source of discrimination claims, and found that litigation resulted in cases of *negligence* (i.e., breach of duty in conducting appraisal with due care), *defamation* (i.e., disclosure of untrue, unfavorable performance information), and *misrepresentation* (i.e., disclosure of untrue, favorable performance information that put others at risk).

After reviewing the court cases associated with performance appraisals, Malos (1995) generated a list of *content* and *process* recommendations that most PM developers strive to follow in their organizations. Some of the recommendations, however, may prove difficult to implement when managing for innovation (and particularly when managing those in creative, non-routine positions with ill-defined goals). For example, one recommendation suggests that appraisals should rely upon objective rather than subjective performance indicators. While this is certainly achievable, the temptation exists for performance appraisals to reward quantity over quality (e.g., number of products vs. strategic advantage of products), consequently promoting more conservative and less innovative performance in an organizational setting.

The goal of legal defensibility also has implications for the format of the rating scale used, whether it is behavior based (e.g., behaviorally anchored rating scales (BARS) and behavioral observation scales (BOS)) or trait based (e.g., innovative). While results concerning the comparative validity of these two approaches are mixed (Kline & Sulsky, 2009; Murphy & Cleveland, 1995), historically, the behavior-based approach is considered much more legally defensible (Latham, Sulsky, & MacDonald, 2008). These behavior-based approaches typically specify behaviors exemplifying performance up front, and then employees are evaluated on demonstration of them during the review period. Another related recommendation presented by Malos (1995) suggests that appraisals should rate work that was within the control of the ratee. Again, by appraising (and perhaps rewarding) such individual-level behavior, team work and peer ratings are less likely to occur. As some empirical work has suggested the benefit of teams for certain aspects of innovation (Axtell et al., 2000), this "best practice" of appraising only individual-level performance (Malos, 1995) may prove to be detrimental when it comes to fostering collaboration and teamwork toward innovation.

Implications for Innovation

The two central purposes of aligning individual goals to organizational objectives and creating legally defensible, systematic methods to make personnel decisions may have additional unintended side effects on innovation beyond the drawbacks already discussed (Mullin & Sherman, 1993; Verbeeten, 2007). Among these side effects are additional internal bureaucracy and paperwork, increased focus on solitary work, gaming of performance measures, and measure-fixation (e.g., over-emphasis on documenting and quantifying performance). Thus, a key issue emerging is that individuals' innovation may decrease rather than increase when it is subjected to the application of standard performance appraisals which are typically used for routine jobs. In short, performance appraisals in their most prototypic (and endorsed, Malos, 1995) form may work well for jobs where the outcomes are predictable, easily quantified, and primarily within the control of the performer, but should be revised to suit the demands of innovative work (Mullin & Sherman, 1993; Mumford, Scott, Strange, & Gaddis, 2002).

Fortunately, there is a cadre of scholars investigating how to best structure aspects of the performance management process to assess and develop innovative performance at work (Carrillo, Robinson, Al-Ghassani, & Anumba, 2004; Molleman & Timmerman, 2003;

Mumford et al., 2002; Mumford & Hunter, 2005; Scott, Leritz, & Mumford, 2004a; Searle & Ball, 2003; Thompson, 2007; West, 2000; Zhou, 2003). While it is important to keep in mind the historically overarching purpose and legal ramifications of performance management as described in the previous section, when managing for innovative performance, particularly goal setting, delivering feedback, and devising developmental programs, one needs to focus on the unique requirements of creative tasks. These tasks, reviewed in more detail in other chapters in this handbook, can be described as ill-defined, complex, and difficult to solve. Most agree that innovative performance in an organizational context is both novel and potentially useful to the organization and can be developed by a recombination of existing practices/materials or generation of new practices/materials (Amabile, 1996; Mumford & Gustafson, 1988). Given the demands required when working on these tasks and solving problems creatively, in the next sections we will highlight some of the suggested practices for appraising, providing feedback about, and developing creative performance.

Appraisals: Contrasting Content and Process for Innovation

The content of the performance appraisal itself may be one of the most important aspects of managing performance (Murphy & Cleveland, 1995), as it focuses attention on objectives within a position and directs behavior. Shalley and Perry-Smith (2001) found there may be a connection between employees' self-rated creativity and perceived methods managers use to set expectations and evaluate results. It seems the approach of some performance appraisal systems is viewed as informational (i.e., providing information to improve performance) while others are perceived as controlling (i.e., measuring performance relative to a set of standards) (Deci & Ryan, 1985; George & Zhou, 2001).

For example, in a study of R&D employees in a pharmaceutical firm, Sundgren and colleagues (2005) found that dialogue-based performance evaluations were related to employee motivation (intrinsic vs. extrinsic) and attitudes toward organizational creativity. It seems that when employees regard expectations as *providing general information about* appropriate behavior (but not as *controlling* behavior), combined with creating an open exchange about ideas, they are more likely to feel intrinsically motivated to work on challenging assignments (Sundgren, Selart, Ingelgård, & Bengtson, 2005). Results of the study showed that organizational creativity was predicted by these types of informational expectations and review processes, providing support for an open dialogue approach. This suggests that when appraising work in positions that require innovation, it is critical that the content of the appraisal be developed in an open and collaborative context between the manager and the employee.

We are not suggesting a diminished role of the manager in determining the goals and objectives of creative positions, as goal setting and project management in general are critical to success in innovation (Mumford & Hunter 2005; West, 1990). More accurately, we suggest that the content of the appraisal should provide direction in a way that allows a view of what the solution may look like, with the realization that how the solution is derived will be an iterative and idiosyncratic process (Hunter, Thoroughgood, Myer, & Ligon, in press). Thus, overly concrete and specific goals in the content of a performance appraisal should be avoided, particularly those that do not acknowledge that multiple paths may be equally effective for meeting challenges (Bolden & Gosling, 2006).

Broadly defined, creative output expectations have been found to contribute to creativity (Madjar & Shalley, 2008; Mumford et al., 2002). One illustration may be found in Cardinal's work (2001), where she examined control strategies and their relationship to drug introductions and drug enhancements in the pharmaceutical industry. Although the presence of specific goals was negatively related to innovation, broader output expectations were positively related to innovation. This occurred for two possible reasons. First, the use of output expectations as opposed to specific goals allows the employee to direct her work without interference concerning the process involved. Second, it may encourage individuals to seek feedback from leaders during the problem definition phase of creative problem solving—a point when they may find their leader's input particularly useful (Mumford & Hunter, 2005).

In order to accommodate Malos' (1995) suggested best practice for specificity, however, more broad goals may be a priori established and specific examples provided later. These examples, provided by managers completing the appraisal, could include exemplary vs. nonexemplary creative performance observations made after the observed process (Catsmull, 2008). For example, at 3M, an organization known for its creative culture, work is evaluated based on overall broad factors—technical, business, and viability. Technical factors include technology strength (e.g., patentability and competitiveness of products), competitive strength (e.g., knowledge of the competition and 3M product performance as it relates to that competition), and manufacturing implementation (e.g., feasibility and cost). Business factors help evaluators appraise the financial potential of the work (e.g., sales and profit potential and actual performance in market, if relevant), competitive advantage (e.g., product value relative to competitors), and probability of marketing success (e.g., potential for increasing market-share). Finally, viability content appraises portfolio mix (e.g., product maintenance relative to new, somewhat related products pursued), number and diversity of skills/expertise (e.g., number of diverse training modules attended), and coordination with other organizational units (e.g., marketing, sales, and manufacturing). Evaluators are able to make ratings on these broader indices of performance, and they are also asked to provide specific examples of performance to justify their ratings. Pixar also engages in a similar post-film review, assessing performance following long projects. While this approach is time consuming and costly to implement (Gupta & Singhal, 1993), it also satisfies Malos' recommendations for legally sound performance appraisals based on specific data without micromanaging the work and the way it is to be accomplished (Krogh, Prager, Sorensen, & Tomlinson, 1988).

Performance appraisal content should also encourage (or at least not discourage) risk taking in innovative positions (Gupta & Singhal, 1993; Hunter et al., in press; Jones, Morris, & Rockmore, 1995; Mumford et al., 2002). Since developing new products and services is a high-risk venture, individuals' time and effort need to be invested, to some degree, in failure (Mullin & Sherman, 1993). Appraisals that focus solely on success may lessen the likelihood of risk taking and initiative. At Raychem Corporation, a supplier of technology-intensive products to aerospace and telecommunications organizations, CEO Paul Cook has said that his performance appraisals:

"don't just reward success, they reward intelligent effort" *(Taylor, 1990, p. 99).*

One aspect of risk taking also involves the tolerance for failed endeavors, and performance appraisal content should reflect this as well. Work by Van Dyck, Frese, Baer, and

Sonnetag (2005) and Sitkin (1996) on error management reveals that embracing failures in pursuit of risky, albeit creative, endeavors can foster innovation and resilience via learning from mistakes. It seems those organizations that embrace failure are especially effective at developing creative solutions. David Kelley's innovative design consultancy IDEO, with clients such as Microsoft, Kodak, and Nike, embraces the motto of:

"fail often to succeed sooner" *(Kelley & Littman, 2001, p. 56)*.

Thus, appraisals that encourage creativity should not solely focus on success of ideas or products, but instead measure progress toward creativity.

In addition to risk taking, performance appraisals should encourage learning orientation—particularly in jobs where individuals may have less intrinsic task motivation for self-development (Yeo & Neal, 2004). Domain expertise is the foundation of creative work (Amabile, 1997; Ericcson, 1999; Ericcson & Charness, 1994), as it provides a set of mental models for solving a given problem or task. Expertise is comprised of factual and procedural knowledge, technical proficiency, and special skills within one's work domain (e.g., knowledge of various statistical packages and techniques). Most scholars agree that while creative problem solving requires creative thinking skills and motivation, domain expertise is fundamental for at least two reasons. First, as the socially-based definition of creativity (Bessemer & O'Quin, 1999) requires that ideas, products, and services have some judged social use, those doing the work of creative problem solving must have the requisite domain expertise to identify what will be a valuable addition to the field. Consequently, a more knowledgeable and experienced employee may find it more facile to determine what has been done and what needs to be accomplished to add value to his organization (Ericcson, 1999). Second, as conceptual combination is a key cognitive process associated with innovation, a number of available cases or mental models must be available to combine and reorganize in new and unique ways (Scott, Lonergan, & Mumford, 2005). Thus, focusing at least some aspects of the performance appraisal on acquiring this expertise, such as measuring society memberships and activities, service to field, and attendance at industry conferences and trainings, should increase innovative capability. However, this may be less critical for individuals who possess high intrinsic motivation for the domain, as they are likely to find ways to acquire such expertise without formal encouragement to do so. Nonetheless, even when evaluating these positions, performance appraisal developers are cautioned to make sure that their content does not discourage such involvement and expertise acquisition (e.g., appraisals should not penalize for time away from the organizational site to attend professional conferences).

In addition to the content of the appraisal, procedural considerations also may impact innovation. For example, the structure of the appraisal may require an absolute or comparative rating. In an absolute rating format, appraisers are asked to evaluate the performance of an employee in an ipsative fashion, making assessments about strengths and developmental priorities within the ratee. In a comparative approach, such as forced distribution or ranking, appraisers are asked to "rack and stack" employees against each other. Wagner and Goffin (1997) argued that it might be easier for raters to accurately evaluate performance in comparative (rather than absolute) terms because social comparisons are a natural byproduct of uncertain decision-making situations such as performance appraisals, particularly in innovative positions. One organization that is well-known for innovations used this approach until recently. Microsoft, after automating its review process with human resource information systems (HRIS) software, was able to provide feedback to managers if their team ratings did not fall on a normal bell curve. If ratings were skewed (i.e., too many managers receiving high performance ratings), appraisers were asked to adjust their group ratings to reflect a normal distribution of performance, thus allowing more clear cut personnel decisions such as promotions, pay increases, and dismissal (Herbold, 2002).

While using a comparative rating system does streamline some personnel decisions, it is not recommended for innovative performance for at least three reasons. First, if not substantiated by specific examples of job-related performance and clearly linked back to job performance criteria, it leaves the organization at legal risk (Malos, 1995). Second, while some administrative decisions are eased by a ranking system, others require more elaborate differentiators that are better directed with an absolute system (e.g., determining proficiency levels prior to training in a given area). Finally, comparative systems often do not provide the rich detail or technical information required to improve creative work (Kline & Sulsky, 2009).

Another process consideration is the frequency with which performance is appraised. Typically, performance appraisals are annual (Murphy & Cleveland, 1995). However, this has implications for the nature of the performance review session; by holding the appraisal once a year only, all outcomes—administrative and developmental—of the performance appraisal are contingent on that one event. Thus, another recommendation is to hold the performance review process at least twice a year for two reasons. First, it allows appraisers to separate sessions where raises and other administrative decisions are determined from sessions where developmental planning is the main focus. Mid-year evaluations provide the opportunity to more frequently assess progress, making corrections and improvement plans. Second, by holding appraisals every six months, managers have shorter time periods to evaluate, and thus may be able to provide more specific time-sensitive feedback to aid in developing progress toward innovation. This is the case at Pixar, where review cycles are determined by film production schedules for most employees, focusing the appraisal on relevant and recent performance (Catsmull, 2008).

The final process consideration revolves around who should conduct the performance appraisal, as well as what sources of information should be used (Kline & Sulsky, 2009). Credibility, power to provide rewards, and opportunity to observe work have all been found to be characteristics of appraisers who are perceived as motivating to employees (Ilgen, Fisher, & Taylor, 1979). Moreover, leaders of innovative teams are typically the best sources of information about the viability, creativity, and quality of ideas, and thus, their feedback will likely have most utility and be most respected by those working in creative domains (Mumford, Connelly, & Gaddis, 2003). Of late, there has also been a push to incorporate data from customers into performance appraisals. Feedback from customers can provide valuable information as to the potential market value of ideas by gaining input about the needs and preferences of customers, such as those gained from focus groups (Kao, 2007). What developers of performance appraisals must be wary of, however, is being overly dictated by customer input. Many radical innovations receive little or no input from customers. In fact, some innovations were met with early criticism and negative evaluations from customers (Christensen, 1997; Hunter et al., in press). Using customer data as a source for performance appraisals for creative positions has not been investigated sufficiently. Research questions that need investigating are:

1. what type of information should be used,
2. how much weight this feedback should hold,
3. at what point during the innovative process should it be delivered, and
4. is the use of customer feedback on performance appraisals legally defensible?

Delivering Performance Feedback for Innovation

Research on how to provide feedback for creative performance is relatively abundant, even considering that the most recent specific review of creativity and performance appraisals was conducted over 15 years ago (Mullin & Sherman, 1993). We know that feedback is essential for creativity in organizations (Mumford et al., 2002) when it is: geared around technical aspects of the work (Mumford & Hunter, 2005), delivered in an informational rather than controlling fashion (George & Zhou, 2001), comprised of compensatory information (Lonergan, Scott, & Mumford, 2004) and recognizing desirable work behaviors (Cardinal, 2001). Though there has been mixed support about the effects of external evaluation and feedback on creativity (Amabile, 1979) and research has demonstrated that the threat of evaluation may lessen effects of artistic creativity (Hennessy, 1989), evaluation and feedback are helpful when managing complex organizational processes, such as decision making and planning. In a study of managerial decision making, Yuan and Zhou (2008) found that evaluation and feedback increased the quality/usefulness factor of ideas developed—a factor that may not be as relevant in the arts, where prior findings of the deleterious effects of feedback were demonstrated (Amabile, Goldfard, & Brackfield, 1990).

Providing feedback may also augment creative performance in routine jobs (i.e., jobs low in autonomy, skill variety, identity, etc; Hackman & Oldham, 1975), in particular for such incumbents who also exhibit an innovative personality (Kirton, 1991, 1994). In these conditions of weak Person–Environment (P–E) fit (Puccio, Talbot, & Joniak, 2000), individuals may view feedback and chance for reward as a means to exert some type of control over their work, and thus may increase their internal motivation for engaging in the challenge of innovative problem solving (Baer, Oldham, & Cummings, 2003).

Feedback should be about technical aspects of the work, with particular emphasis toward the effort and processes used to reach overarching innovation goals (Hunter et al., in press; Mayfield & Mayfield, 2008). Direct but supportive feedback is best for innovation, as problems requiring creative work are often uncertain and ill-defined (Amabile, Schatzel, Moneta, & Kramer, 2004; West, 1990). This support is particularly necessary for creative endeavors in organizations where reactions to originality are typically critical and negative (Blair & Mumford, 2007). As individuals engaging in routine work are likely not used to the ambiguity associated with creative problem solving (Mayfield & Mayfield, 2008), offering supportive and specific process-oriented feedback at various points during projects may reduce anxiety and may encourage these employees to take greater risks. Thus, we encourage having established feedback sessions where managers offer supportive, demonstrative feedback about project progression at critical points during problem definition, generative, and evaluative stages of problem solving. Moreover, by formally taking time to emphasize overarching creativity goals and provide feedback about the processes associated with obtaining them, leaders can remove some of the "sting" associated with critical evaluation. While these formal feedback sessions should mitigate some problems before they arise, managers should also make certain to encourage their teams to bring problems to them on an ad hoc basis given the unpredictable, turbulent nature of most creative problem solving efforts.

When providing this technical feedback, the content should be compensatory in nature. In a study by Lonergan, Scott, and Mumford (2004), participants were asked to revise plans for a marketing campaign—plans that varied on originality and quality/practicality. When participants revised the initial plans using operational criteria (e.g., efficiency standards, cost considerations), the highly original plans were improved. However, when they used innovation criteria (e.g., novelty, variance from standard ad campaigns) to revise plans judged initially higher on quality/practicality, these plans benefitted. In short, providing individuals with feedback that considers alternative aspects of the idea should offset deficiencies. For managing performance, once work has been appraised on quality, originality, and complexity/elegance criteria, the appraiser should be mindful to provide technical feedback to compensate for plan weaknesses along these lines. Again, this suggested best practice necessitates the appraiser's expertise and capacity to evaluate creative ideas.

Of course, the use of appraisals and feedback is likely to prove most successful if accompanied by rewards (Mumford et al., 2002). Although the merits of rewarding creative work have been questioned based on the need for intrinsic motivation (Collins & Amabile, 1999), evidence indicates that rewards can contribute to creativity by providing recognition, encouraging desirable behaviors and work strategies, and establishing creative output expectations (Eisenberger & Cameron, 1996). In keeping with these observations, Cardinal (2001) found that in the pharmaceutical industry, rewards were positively related to both drug enhancements and new drug introductions. What should be noted here, however, is that the leaders' use of a range of rewards, in addition to pay and bonuses, such as granting time to pursue new ventures, providing additional space or equipment, and ensuring professional recognition, may prove particularly useful by capitalizing on both intrinsic and extrinsic motives (Amabile, 1997). The chapter presented by Wheeler and colleagues in this handbook also provides some clarification of the theoretical discourse and practical implications of rewards and creativity.

Performance Appraisal and Feedback: Emerging Issues

The central finding from this review suggests that PM approaches for individuals engaging in creative work should differ from those engaging in routine work for the organization (Hunter et al., in press; Molleman & Timmerman, 2003) (for a summary of principle recommendations, refer to Table 25.1). Specifically, managers of creative employees need more discretion (i.e., freedom from a set of pre-determined HR/organizational criteria) to evaluate creative performance, as they are often the best evaluators of innovation within their area (Mumford et al., 2002). In addition, these leaders charged with PM responsibilities should be trained in practices for innovation, particularly in setting expectations, delivering technical, compensatory feedback, administering rewards, and devising developmental plans.

TABLE 25.1   Content and Process Recommendations for Performance Appraisals of Innovation.

Content

- Directly measure creative and original ideas by using broad output expectations for innovation
- Encourage risk taking by appraising effort toward objectives; do not punish failures
- Measure learning orientation and knowledge development in routine positions to encourage domain expertise acquisition; make certain expertise acquisition is rewarded/acknowledged
- Feedback should be technical, compensatory, and provide information rather than attempt to control future behavior

Process

- Use behavioral observation scales (BOS) to provide specific examples of broad output goals post hoc rather than specifying desired creative behaviors/process steps
- Separate administration of rewards (e.g., raises, promotions) from developmental planning
- Provide training to managers in process of innovation management and appraisal instruments (with particular emphasis on goal setting, feedback delivery, and developmental planning)
- Conduct appraisals at least every other quarter (and allow for informal feedback sessions to occur as problems arise), and help individuals to conduct self-assessments in interim to provide internal feedback

Another issue that emerged is the use of individual vs. team-based appraisals. As those working in creative positions often have personality characteristics that are dominant, introverted, competitive, and autonomous (Feist, 1991, 1999), performance reviews that encourage individual work rather than teamwork are likely to intensify creative performers' individualistic nature. Thus, an opportunity exists to encourage collaboration through the use of the performance appraisal. For example, appraising and rewarding collaboration among other researchers, particularly those in other specialties or departments (e.g., in academia, scientists from different departments or universities serving as co-principal investigators on grants and contracts), may aid in the combination of conceptually distinct practices and products (Scott, Lonergan, & Mumford, 2005; Ward, Patterson, & Sifonis, 2004). This is found at Disney's Pixar, where teams work together throughout the production process, sharing ideas before they are complete to draw from each others' distinct expertise and opinion. President of Pixar, Ed Catsmull, credits the success of movies *Toy Story I* and *II, A Bug's Life,* and *Wall-E* to organizational practices that reward collaborative, trusting relationships among talented and diverse executives (Catsmull, 2008). In addition, appraisals that reward effort toward mentoring and collaboration with junior scientists may also prove useful in developing leadership skills in creative individuals for future positions in management (Mumford, Hunter, Eubanks, Bedell, & Murphy, 2007).

Finally, while leaders of creative efforts are the best source of feedback for the appraisal process, an emerging issue is the increase in the use of multi-source or 360-degree feedback as part of the PM process for other types of positions (3D Group, 2009). Surprisingly little attention has focused on how 360-degree feedback systems—prevalent in most organizations today—might help foster creativity, however. This approach samples feedback, typically via anonymous surveys, from supervisors, direct reports, peers, and more recently customers to compare against the ratee's self-appraisal on the same competencies. Often there are 10–15 behavioral items demarcating competencies, and those providing feedback are asked to make ratings on these about the ratee's performance in various domains. This type of evaluation is often used in managerial positions, and has frequently been implemented to appraise leadership competencies. However, this tool may also be used to provide feedback and develop innovative performance.

One such initiative was recently undertaken in the US Intelligence Community (IC) to encourage a culture that stimulated more innovative problem solving (O'Shea, Allen, Grignon, & Keil, 2010). The IC consists of 16 federal government agencies (e.g., the FBI, the CIA, and the NSA) focused on the collection and analysis of information and the dissemination of intelligence to policymakers. Congress created the Office of the Director of National Intelligence (ODNI) to provide oversight for this community and stimulate cooperation, information sharing, and creative problem solving. A variety of human resource-related interventions have been initiated by ODNI, including the creation of a 360-degree feedback system for all IC Senior Executive Service members. While 360-degree feedback is typically used to help individuals develop and change their behavior, the use of multi-source feedback can also effect organization-wide transformation (Bracken & Rose, 2009), as was the case in the use of the ODNI's 360-degree program.

As such, this feedback program included competencies to encourage collaborative decision making, gathering information from diverse sources, and thinking outside-of-the-box—all related to creative problem solving. This served three main goals. First, by evaluating key leaders on these competencies, the message was sent throughout the organization that these activities were valued. Second, it also encouraged leaders to engage in such creative problem solving efforts as their actions would be assessed by their direct reports, supervisor, and peers (O'Shea et al., 2010). Finally, the multi-source process can also be used to create tailored developmental plans to increase these executives' creative problem solving skills. How this tool and other similar experiential development techniques will be discussed in the following section, training and developing for creativity.

TRAINING AND DEVELOPMENT FOR CREATIVITY

Linking Performance Appraisals to Training and Development for Innovation

The process of performance evaluation as an intervention for creativity should be closely linked to another intervention—training and development (Dransfield, 2000). Personal development plans are often a direct outcome of the performance appraisal and feedback process, with a focus on individual development, to achieve future levels of desired performance. The questions of *if* and *how* creativity can be developed is one that has garnered a great deal of attention (Feldman, 1999; Nickerson, 1999; Ma, 2006; Scott, Leritz, & Mumford, 2004a, 2004b). In organizational settings, efforts to instruct an individual for increased innovation can be categorized in one of two general approaches: training (i.e., efforts to increase an individual's performance in his current role), and experiential development (i.e., efforts to prepare an individual for demands of future roles or organizational change). Training programs are typically geared towards shaping a narrower set of skills (Phye, 1997) or attitudes (Birdi, 2005) associated with creativity, whereas experiential development initiatives may focus on providing individuals with experiences (e.g., mentoring programs, job rotations, 360-degree feedback) upon which they can later reflect to solve organizational problems more creatively. While both of these approaches to increase creativity have merit (Feldman, 1999; Nickerson, 1999), most of the empirical data about planned attempts to improve creativity in organizational settings has been on training.

Meta-Analyses of Creativity and Training

Several scholars have summarized the field of creativity training by conducting meta-analyses to determine a) if creativity training is indeed effective, and b) what program characteristics are linked to success. Torrance (1972) reviewed the results of 142 training programs that used the Torrance Tests of Creative Thinking (TTCT; Torrance, 1966a, 1966b) as criteria. He categorized the programs into nine discrete types, depending on program goals, students, and design characteristics. Using the percentage of attained goals as an indicator of training success, he found that at least 50% of the programs reviewed were successful.

Rose and Lin (1984) updated Torrance's (1972) review, also only using training programs that relied upon the TTCT as criteria. They classified 46 programs into six categories:

1. Covington's Productive Thinking Program (Covington, Crutchfield, Davis, & Olton, 1974), which emphasizes both divergent and convergent processes,
2. the Purdue Creative Thinking Program (Feldhusen, Treffinger, & Bahlke, 1970), which focuses students on divergent thinking skills by providing them 28 audiotapes and workbook exercises,
3. the Osborn–Parnes Creative Problem Solving Program (Osborn, 1963; Parnes, 1966), which uses a variety of techniques to instruct idea generation,
4. other programs that combined multiple theories and techniques,
5. school programs (e.g., gifted and talented classes) designed to increase students overall creative output and academic success,
6. other long-term programs such as imagery training, dramatics, and meditation.

They found that the overall mean effect size was .64, and this finding was driven by scores on the verbal components of the TTCT (rather than figural components). This might have been because the majority of programs analyzed had verbal exercises and lectures, and did not focus on the figural portion of the criteria—a point that emphasizes the importance of how creativity training programs are evaluated. The Osborn–Parnes Creative Problem Solving program had the largest effect size (.63), followed closely by the Purdue Creative Thinking Program (.48).

Scope (1998) reviewed the impact of instruction design variables on creativity, identifying 30 studies (yielding 40 treatment groups) with a mean effect size of .90 ($SD\nabla1.19$). He found that programs that had instructors who were responsive to students and provided one-on-one practice sessions were most effective. He also found a non-significant relationship ($r=-.06$, $p>.05$) between the length of the training program and success.

While the above three reviews were important in gaining consensus about efforts to improve creativity, some have questioned the robustness of creativity training in general (Cropley, 1997; Nickerson, 1999). Specifically, reviews conducted by Torrance (1972), Rose and Lin (1984), and Scope (1998) were comprised mainly of studies with school age samples—and typically in elementary school settings. As a result, it is unclear as to what degree their findings could be generalized to organizational settings on real-world criteria. In addition, perhaps due to the heavy reliance on the TTCT as criteria of interest, the main dependent variables assessed were those of divergent thinking. Problem solving, performance, and on-the-job creativity (Kirkpatrick, 1959) were not examined.

Three subsequent meta-analytic efforts sought to examine these validity concerns. In a review we conducted (Scott et al., 2004a), 156 empirical studies of creativity training were identified. Seventy of these provided sufficient information as to their training methods, study designs, and criteria, allowing us to conduct two separate studies with the goals of understanding:

1. is creativity training effective,
2. what components are most related to success, and
3. what combinations or packages of techniques and training characteristics are optimal (Scott, 2004b).

To answer these questions, the dependent variables used were classified into four categories:

1. divergent thinking (e.g., flexibility, fluency, originality),
2. problem solving (i.e., the production of novel solutions),
3. performance (i.e., the production of novel products), and
4. attitudes and behaviors (e.g., openness toward creative thinking).

Using Glass's Delta (Δ), 97 Δ estimates illustrated that creativity training had noteworthy effects—on all four types of criteria (see Table 25.2 for a summary of these findings). It was also found that these effects held even given concerns of internal validity, and they generalized across different samples and settings (2004a). Programs based on theories of cognitive processes were found to be the most successful, although other approaches also held value (e.g., programs with foundations in personality or motivational theories also showed success, particularly for performance criteria).

A follow-up to this study applied clustering techniques to identify types of training, with respect to core creative process (e.g., problem finding; Mumford et al., 1991) and design techniques (e.g., practice type; Goldstein & Ford, 2001) to assess the effectiveness of varied combinations of training elements (Scott et al., 2004b). Note that in the original (Scott, 2004a) study, 156 programs were identified, but only 70 programs were retained as others did not include substantial information for computing Glass' Δ, leading to a reduced sample size. Thus, in this second study we also applied a judgmental rating of whether the study outcomes were successful, allowing us to examine curriculum elements from all 156 studies. Results of this study showed that there were 11 main types of creativity training, and they represented four major themes of creativity training:

1. idea production training (e.g., Glover, 1980),
2. imagery training (e.g., Flaherty, 1992),
3. cognitive training (e.g., Shively, Feldhusen, & Treffinger, 1972), and
4. thinking skills training (e.g., Baer, 1988).

While imagery training was a widely applied technique ($N = 43$), it was also found to be least effective in terms of both the judgmental and the Δ criteria, whereas the other three types of training were all shown to be relatively effective for enhancing creative outcomes.

TABLE 25.2   Overall Effects of Creativity Training Within and Across Criteria.

	NE	Δ	SE	CI	SD	FS_N
Overall	70	.68	.09	.55–.81	.65	168
Overall with outliers removed	69	.64	.07	.53–.76	.59	152
Divergent thinking	37	.75	.11	.56–.93	.67	101
Divergent thinking with outliers removed	36	.68	.09	.52–.84	.55	89
Problem solving	28	.84	.13	.62–1.05	.67	90
Performance	16	.35	.11	.16–.54	.43	12
Attitude/behavior	16	.24	.13	.01–.47	.54	3

Note: NE = number of effect size estimates; Δ = average effect size estimate using Cohen's delta; SE = standard error of effect size estimates; CI = 90% confidence interval; SD = standard deviation in effect size estimates across studies; FS_N = fail safe N or number of studies needed to decrease effect sizes below .20. Reprinted from "The effectiveness of creativity training: A quantitative review," by G. Scott, L. E. Leritz, and M. D. Mumford, 2004, Creativity Research Journal, 16(4), p. 369. Copyright 2004 by Lawrence Erlbaum Associates, Inc. Reprinted with permission.

Extending the Scott, Leritz, and Mumford (2004a, 2004b) studies, Ma (2006) conducted an updated meta-analysis with the intent of identifying specific techniques of these training packages that were more or less effective. The results of this review indicated an even stronger grand mean effect size (.77), supporting the effectiveness of creativity training on divergent thinking criteria in particular (with strongest effects found for originality and weakest for elaboration). The review also showed that training was more effective for older participants than for younger samples, with the exception of high school students outperforming college-age students (likely due to the large standard deviation in effects found in college samples; Ma, 2006). This review also showed that multiple techniques held promise for creativity training, and among the best were attitude training (Greene & Noice, 1988), Ford and Renzulli's (1976) cognitive program (based on Guilford's Structure of Intellect model, Guilford, 1967), and idea generation training (Glover, 1980). Extending Scott, Leritz, and Mumford's (2004b) findings, programs that did not follow a model or theory per se but instead were a grouping of techniques performed the worst. In addition, Ma (2006) found that programs that focused on imagery alone and rather than providing cognitive strategies/heuristics to solve problems were the least successful (Houtz & Frankel, 1992).

Implications for Organizational Interventions to Increase Creativity

These reviews of the creativity training point to three important findings for the present discussion. First, creativity training is effective—incredibly so given the complex nature of the task at hand. Not only was a large effect size found for an overall success criterion, but large effects were also observed across more specific indices of creativity (i.e., divergent thinking, problem solving, attitudes, and performance). Second, the results indicate the value of cognitive training programs over others when enhancing creativity. Specifically, training which was focused on the core processes underlying creative problem solving (Mumford et al., 1991) was strongly related to program success on a host of criteria

(Scott et al., 2004a). Successful programs are those that are designed to provide participants with strategies to work with information, while those that do not provide participants such heuristics (Mumford & Norris, 1999) to work with their existing knowledge fail to result in even short-term gains (Ma, 2006). Moreover, these reviews show that while there are multiple types of training programs available that offer participants the chance to relax, imagine possibilities, and wait for solutions to come to them, performance improvements in terms of creativity are not be expected from such imagery techniques (Ma, 2006; Scott et al., 2004b). Third, despite the general goal of improving innovation, there is marked variability in the way in which creativity training is designed, delivered, and evaluated. This can be attributed to the heterogeneity of samples and settings in which creativity training is administered; it makes sense that elementary students might require different practice exercises and criteria to evaluate program success than scientists in an R&D lab or production workers on the shop floor. Scholars of creativity training, perhaps by virtue of their focus on models and techniques in school settings, do not seem to apply coherent instructional design methods found in most other types of organizational training initiatives (Goldstein & Ford, 2001).

This limited application of training design best practices poses several problems for creativity training, and particularly for those of us trying to deduce trends and plan interventions. For example, two important steps in Goldstein and Ford's (2001) Instructional Systems Design (ISD) model are the needs assessment and the task analysis. Interestingly, none of the 156 studies in our sample (Scott et al., 2004a) provided expressed detail if (and how) these steps were conducted prior to training. Given the finding that significant aptitude–treatment interactions (Ree, Caretta, & Teachout, 1995) have been found in the training of other complex skills, it seems that understanding the baseline skills, expertise, and motivation of participants is an important step in design for interventions to increase creativity. In addition, as realism of practice was found to be positively related to training performance (Scott et al., 2004a), conducting a task analysis to provide material in constructing exercises also seems important. Another benefit of Goldstein and Ford's (2001) systematic approach to instructional design is the emphasis on linking training outcomes to organizational behavior. While divergent thinking and attitudinal measures are often used as important dependent variables for creativity training, they provide limited insight about real-world organizational innovation, and thus make it difficult for practitioners to demonstrate the return on investment (ROI) of efforts to improve creative performance. In addition, Ford and Goldstsein's (2001) model requires activity to validate efforts. By including this overlooked step when designing interventions to enhance creativity, we may also increase serious empirical efforts to validate initiatives and provide more scientific rigor to our applied interventions (Sternberg & Lubart, 1999). By applying a more systematic model to creativity training, namely the model most used in organizational settings to plan, train and evaluate efforts to improve performance (Goldstein & Ford, 2001), interventions geared to improve creativity may garner more credibility and sustained impact in both academic and applied settings.

Thus, the aim of the following sections is to apply Goldstein and Ford's (2001) prescriptive model for organizational training and development initiatives to efforts to improve creativity by integrating theoretical advancements from meta-analytic reviews (Ma, 2006; Scott et al., 2004a, 2004b), recent empirical evaluations of training (e.g., Benedek, Fink, & Neubauer, 2006; Birdi, 2006; Cunningham & McGreggor, 2008; Memmert, 2007), and development initiatives (Feldman, 1999; Mumford, Connelly, Scott, Espejo, Sohl, Hunter, & Bedell, 2005; Root Bernstein, Bernstein, & Garnier, 1995; Runco, 2003; Simonton, 1999). For an overview of how this model might be applied to interventions to improve creativity, refer to Figure 25.1.

Model for Creativity Training and Development Interventions: Goldstein and Ford (2001)

Needs Assessment

Three activities comprise a typical needs assessment: person analysis, organizational analysis, and task analysis (Goldstein & Ford, 2001). The person analysis is used to assess training participants' pre-training motivation, skill level, and personality characteristics, and data gathered from this step informs training content and structure. In organizations, there is often variability in the motivation an individual displays for the work; those in creative positions—positions where the goal is to generate innovative products and ideas—may have a great deal of intrinsic motivation for the work, while others throughout the organization may find motivation through more extrinsic factors. According to the componential theory of creativity (Amabile, 1997), addressing the motivation issue might be a key step in training design. Specifically, individuals who lack motivation for the work may also be less likely to engage in a training program where the skills being developed are difficult, time consuming, and new. Thus, interventions to increase these individuals' creativity must also address motivation factors. This may be accomplished in two ways.

Recent work on Appreciative Inquiry (AI) techniques (Bushe & Kassam, 2005) show that encouraging employees to focus on the positive outcomes associated with success on a problem may increase the likelihood of innovation, particularly with employees who may not be as naturally inclined to seek out novel solutions. Introduced by Cooperrider & Srivastava (1987) and consistent with work on positive psychology (Nakamura & Csikszentmihályi, 2003; Seligman, 2000; Wallis, Coady, Cray, Park, & Ressner, 2005), AI proposes that the best way to improve an idea is through identification and enhancement of its strongest features (Cooperrider & Srivastava, 1987; Whitney & Trosten-Bloom, 2003). AI has been implemented in a variety of settings, including sales (Skinner & Kelley, 2006), telecommunications (Keers, 2007), health care, education, and hospitality (Bushe & Kassam, 2005). At Longhorn Western riding stables, a UK-based stable that provides horses, equipment, and instructors to a local expedition planning company, employees and management used AI to improve customer service and inter-organizational relations (George & McLean, 2002). While such motivational techniques are likely to increase employees' attitudes toward innovation and change, they may not be effective if not accompanied by skills to solve creative problems (Scott et al., 2004a).

Thus, a second approach for creativity training when working with individuals who lack intrinsic task motivation is to provide them with training on process skills to solve problems creatively, as well as feedback and other extrinsic rewards to use those skills (e.g., tying back into performance appraisal). This may increase individuals overall self-efficacy (Deci & Ryan, 1980) to use the skills on the job, as well as the expectancy (Vroom, 1964) that the use of the skills will result in a desirable outcome.

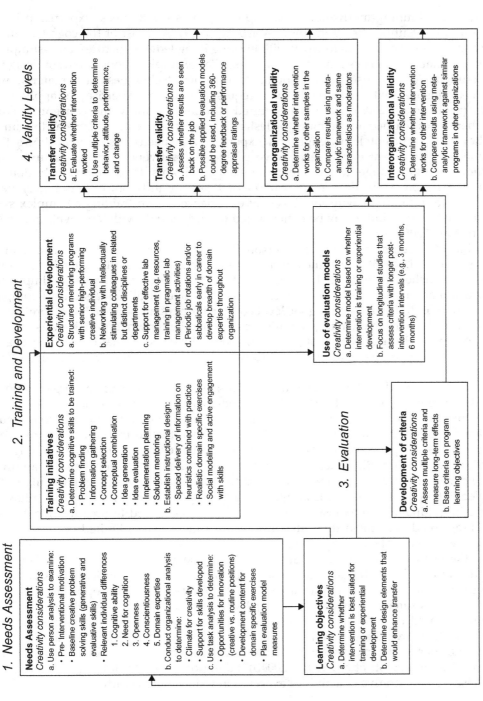

FIGURE 25.1 Model for training and development interventions for creativity, integrating Goldstein and Ford's (2001) Instructional System Design (ISD) model. *Adapted from* Training in Organizations, *4th Ed. (p. 24), by* I. L. Goldstein and J. K. Ford, 2001, *Belmont, CA: Wadsworth. Copyright 2001 by Wadsworth, Cengage Learning.*

Related to pre-training motivation, it is important to assess trainees' expertise prior to designing an intervention (Ericsson, 1999; Weisburg, 1999). As most of the cognitive training programs provide heuristics to work with existing knowledge structures, an assumption is often made that the trainees have such expertise. For example, in one program designed to train students on the use of conceptual combination techniques, task material was generated to insure that participants had requisite domain expertise to apply such heuristics (Scott et al., 2005). Exercises required students to apply the conceptual combination heuristics learned in training to design a new school curriculum—a domain in which they had sufficient knowledge and expertise. If a needs assessment shows that participants lack sufficient expertise to solve problems creatively, then the nature of the intervention should change to one that allows participants to develop such domain knowledge (Ericsson, 1999; Ericsson & Charness, 1994). In addition, exercises may need to be tailored to individuals with low levels of experience. When training a complex skill, the use of case-based training may be better suited for individuals with low levels of experience (Scott et al., 2005).

Individual differences in ability and personality may also require varied instructional techniques (Ree et al., 1995). While the effects of cognitive ability in skill acquisition are relatively well-established (Schmidt & Hunter, 1998; Ree et al., 1995), it may also be important to measure and accommodate personality characteristics. Specifically, in a study of complex skill acquisition, individuals with higher levels of need for cognition (NFC) (i.e., preference to engage in cognitively challenging activities) performed better when practice was massed rather than spaced (Espejo, Day, Scott, & Diaz, 2005). Other individual differences related to creativity training are relevant for future study as well (e.g., Oldham & Cummings, 1996; Zhou, 2003).

The second step in the ISD model's needs assessment is to conduct an organizational analysis (Goldstein & Ford, 2001). This aids in understanding organizational strategy and objectives for innovation (Searle & Ball, 2003), and it also provides a mechanism to measure the climate for creativity—an organizational aspect imperative to the success of interventions (Hunter et al., in press; West, 1990, 2000). In an evaluation of the creativity training in a civil service organization, Birdi (2005) found that poor managerial support and/or an unfavorable departmental climate for innovation limited the impact of training, particularly for idea implementation. This follows from Sternberg and Lubart's (1996) theory that a host of interacting individual and organizational characteristics are related to organizational innovation; failing to address them through a needs assessment leaves limited opportunity to assess the effectiveness of creativity training.

Finally, the task analysis, or a thorough measure of the activities performed in trainees' jobs (Goldstein & Ford, 2001), provides instructional designers with at least two pieces of important information. First, it allows investigators to determine what opportunities exist for employees to exercise creativity in their jobs (Baer et al., 2003; Mayfield & Mayfield, 2004), which should inform criteria to be used in training evaluation models. Second, the task analysis allows for the generation of realistic, domain specific exercises and instructional content. As realistic exercises were found to be a key determinant in the effectiveness of creativity training (Scott et al., 2004a, 2004b), taking time to find out what would make such exercises demonstrative of activities expected in trainees' jobs is advised.

E. INTERVENTIONS

Learning Objectives

The needs assessment should inform the learning objectives, the second critical step in the ISD model (Goldstein & Ford, 2001). Learning objectives focus behavior on what is to be learned, as well as suggesting what approaches are most suitable for skill acquisition. Learning objectives should be based on theoretical models of creativity (Scott et al., 2004a) as well as information learned during the needs assessment. These objectives convey training goals, provide a framework for developing course content, and suggest a basis for determining if the intervention was indeed successful. Goldstein and Ford (2001) recommend three characteristics of effective learning objectives. First, objectives should include the capability or desired terminal behavior (e.g., suggest novel, useful ways to cut costs in one's job role). Second, instructional designers should specify conditions under which behavior will be performed on the job. Finally, learning objectives should make some attempt to state the criterion of acceptable performance. This may include minimum standards (e.g., scores on a test of divergent thinking), time to perform (e.g., within six months on the job), and/or the quality of the work produced (e.g., ideas able to be implemented).

These learning objectives should dictate optimal criteria to be used in evaluation, as well as what instructional vehicle is best suited for development. A key distinction here is to determine whether the creative process should be enhanced via a training program or an experiential development intervention. For example, after a merger of two distinct production organizations, instructional designers had the learning objective of production engineers developing cross-functional expertise to share innovations and foster conceptual collaboration (Beatty & Bremley, 2004). Thus, a job rotation and cross-functional mentoring program was determined to be the best course of action for enhancing creativity, particularly given the amount of cross-organizational domain expertise development required. However, when requisite expertise is already at hand, cognitive training on methods to work with information in a systematic, novel way has been shown to be most beneficial (Ma, 2006; Scott et al., 2004a, 2004b). Thus, in the following sections, we will detail recommended practices for both training and development interventions.

Training Design: Expertise Acquisition and Cognitive Processes

Because one of the most supported findings in the broader creativity literature suggests that domain expertise is the building block for innovative problem solving (Baer, 1998; Weisburg, 1999), it is recommended that any effort intended to increase creativity should first focus on efforts to build domain-specific declarative and procedural knowledge. Recent advances in expertise research indicate that the nature of these efforts should differ at various points in skill acquisition (de Bruin, Rikers, & Schmidt, 2005), focus on mechanisms that support planning, self-evaluation, and feedback about performance (Ericsson, 2005), and be organized in a sequential fashion that promotes improving one specific component of expertise at a time (de Bruin et al., 2005). In short, efforts to develop expertise, or the mental representations and skills needed to direct, evaluate, and revise performance in a given area, should likely precede interventions geared at improving other cognitive process skills associated with innovative performance.

Once the requisite expertise is in place, attention can be turned to improving the process skills needed to work with that knowledge in novel and useful ways. If it is granted that cognitive models provide a particularly effective way to do this, the question remains as to which cognitive processes contribute to training effects (Scott et al., 2004a). The general model of core creative processes developed by Mumford and his colleagues (Mumford et al., 1991) provided our meta-analytic (2004a) framework to assess the cognitive skills used in training including:

1. problem finding,
2. information gathering,
3. concept selection,
4. conceptual combination,
5. idea generation,
6. idea evaluation,
7. implementation planning, and
8. solution monitoring.

The results indicated that programs which emphasized processes closely linked to the generation of new ideas (e.g., problem finding, conceptual combination, and idea generation) were the most powerful positive influences on training effectiveness, although all eight of the core processes showed gains on at least one criterion of interest. Convergent processes (i.e., idea evaluation, implantation planning) may prove more beneficial when the criterion of interest is based on indices other than divergent thinking. In addition, techniques employed in training that provided a set of heuristics for working with already available knowledge, techniques such as critical thinking, convergent thinking, constraint identification, and use of analogies, were positively related to creativity criteria (2004a, 2004b). Thus, it holds that future efforts for creativity training should home in on these types of processes and techniques for optimal gains in a training program.

Training Design: Instructional Strategies

While relying on a cognitive model to develop training content is an important part of creativity training, variation is expected in program effectiveness if appropriate instructional strategies are neglected. Course design variables that appear important can be broken into four main categories:

1. length,
2. delivery method,
3. feedback, and
4. practice exercises (Ma, 2006; Scott et al., 2004a; 2004b).

While the use of training as an intervention is likely shorter than other development techniques (e.g., job rotations), the pattern of results as to what is the optimal length is complex. In the 2004 meta-analysis, longer programs were positively associated with program success, but in Scope's (1998) and Ma's (2006) reviews, no difference was determined between short and long training interventions. One explanation of this finding is the nature of the criteria used to assess success; in programs where divergent thinking (e.g., scores on the TTCT, Torrance, 1966a, 1966b) is the criterion of interest, shorter timeframes may be required. However, when programs rely upon more complex indices of performance (e.g., problem solving or performance), more time is likely required to develop cognitive processing skills.

Delivery methods that performed best were those that presented information in a segmented, step-by-step fashion, particularly in studies that relied upon problem solving and performance criteria (Ma, 2006; Scott et al., 2004a). For example, programs such as the Purdue Program provided short lecturette-training on general principles, with intermittent chances to practice these principles in a particular domain (Baer, 1996). It would make sense then, that other methods which provided information in a distributed fashion would work well to train in the process skills associated with creative problem solving. One avenue for future research is that of computer-assisted training. As few studies utilized this type of training media to deliver training material in the (Scott et al.) 2004 and (Ma) 2006 meta-analyses, it is difficult to draw general conclusions as to how these work for creative training. However, a recent study by Benedek and colleagues (2006) demonstrated the effectiveness of computer-based training for at least some aspects of creative problem solving, indicating that this too is an avenue for future research.

What is proven to enhance the information delivery method, however, is the chance to observe and apply the skills that have been taught in training (Scott et al., 2004a). Social modeling, cooperative learning/discussion, and case based learning were all found to be techniques that facilitated the acquisition of creativity, particularly with regard to problem solving and performance criteria. This suggests that training should be situated in real-world contexts, and that practice and feedback during training is essential to transferring learning into on-the-job behavior. In the case of performance and problem solving criteria, instructor feedback was positively associated with the size of the obtained effect, a finding supported by Yuan's and Zhou (2008) view that organizational innovation requires feedback as to the viability of ideas throughout the problem solving process.

These observations of best practices of delivery, media, and feedback lead us to the discussion of the relationship between practice types and training success. The most clear-cut finding from all three recent meta-analytic reviews suggests that the use of realistic, domain-specific performance exercises was positively associated with training success (Ma, 2006; Scott et al., 2004a, 2004b). It seems that after learning the somewhat abstract and often novel heuristics associated with creative problem solving, participants find that working with familiar information to apply these techniques helps them to better understand how they work. Another explanation is that of expertise; as creative problem solving is heavily reliant on domain expertise, working with familiar information (e.g., situations experienced on the job) should provide an opportunity to execute cognitive heuristics in a productive, useful fashion (Baer, 1998). Using extant knowledge structures in novel ways is also likely to build self-efficacy for applying the skills once on the job. The other noteworthy finding from meta-analytic work is the lack of established effectiveness of imaginative, low-structure practice activities. Thus, training programs should avoid the use of open-ended, ill-structured exercises, as they may lessen, not increase, the effectiveness of creativity training.

Experiential Development

While some learning objectives call for the use of training, other instances require more situated, long-term interventions. Examples of learning objectives that might require the use of experiential development as an intervention are:

1. the acquisition of domain expertise,
2. stimulating exploration and curiosity,

3. encouraging confidence to take risks, and

4. developing meta-cognitive skills (Nickerson, 1999).

Unfortunately, the literature on such planned interventions to increase creativity is scant. Much like those interested in the development of other complex skills (e.g., McCall, 2010), we are able to glean from literature how creativity unfolds naturalistically to determine activities that might prove valuable from an intervention standpoint (Feldman, 1999). Drawing from factors that shape creative potential (Runco, 2003), initial studies examining these questions tended to focus on childhood, or early life experiences (e.g., Roe, 1951, 1953). However interesting, this type of data does not lend itself easily to organizational interventions to increase creativity, and thankfully, development does not cease after adolescence.

Certain kinds of career experiences also contribute to the development of creativity (Gardner, 1993; Gruber, 1996). These experiences may represent more than the development of domain expertise, although domain expertise is likely one important outcome of such interventions. For example, Root Bernstein and colleagues (1995) found that periodic shifts in research programs were necessary for sustained creative output from eminent scientists. Findings such as these play a role in theory development (Feldman, 1999), but also provide some insight as to what types of activities may help foster creativity in an organizational setting. Unfortunately, most studies of this sort are of the qualitative nature, replete with small sample sizes, low base rate behavior (e.g., Gruber's description of Piaget, 1996), and focused on a particular time period.

However, one study was recently conducted on eminent scientists to empirically test theories of creative development (Mumford et al., 2005). Life events from 499 notable scientists in domains of social, physical, life, and health sciences were examined by applying a content coding procedure (Simonton, 1999) to obituaries published in academic journals. Scientists were included whose obituaries were published between 1992 and 2002, and had a mix of academic, applied, or academic and applied careers. Developmental career events were analyzed in eight categories, and markers exemplifying each of these event types were then assessed against a host of performance indicators of creativity. Of the eight types of events examined, three seem most relevant to planned organizational interventions to improve creativity.

First, mentoring was shown to be an important career developmental event, particularly mentoring by an eminent scientist in early career. Perhaps this facilitates creative problem solving transfer, but it also might provide young individuals with a model for how to deal with more pragmatic issues (e.g., running a lab effectively, applying for grants). Thus, it would seem the designation of a mentoring program, particularly one that matches high potential individuals with high performing mentors in the organization, is a fruitful developmental experience.

Second, collaborative colleagues were also important. Particularly, findings showed supportive colleagues—from related but distinct disciplines—who provided intellectual stimulation were related to indices of creativity and sustained success. This finding, similar to mentoring importance, suggests that organizations should encourage and reward such collaborations, perhaps through performance appraisals as well as through establishing formal networking activities to stimulate interaction.

Finally, positive laboratory experiences also proved critical to success. Creative scientists tended to have well-run labs, garnered support from the organization, and supervised high performing junior lab members. While the correlational nature of this research may draw some to question the causality of this finding, it is also important to note that these scientists tended to work in high performing labs well before they obtained eminence, providing at least some evidence of how such experiences may contribute to their performance down the road. One implication of this for organizational interventions is to couple lab-management training with the developmental experience of providing high performing lab members to individuals; by providing skills for effective management practices, as well as resources to execute objectives, organizations may help foster a productive lab environment in which creativity can subsequently occur.

While the obituary study (Mumford et al., 2005) did not explicitly analyze job rotations, it seems this too would be another intervention point for those interested in enhancing creativity at work. Providing exposure to other parts of the organization—and the individuals who work in distinct but related domains—may build expertise and provide additional knowledge structures for conceptual combination activities (Scott et al., 2005). It also may facilitate the subtle shifts in work domains and portfolio diversity that are historically related to creativity (Root-Bernstein et al., 1995). However, it may be difficult to implement such rotations at later points in the careers of creative individuals, as much evidence suggests they tend to select their own careers (rather than be assigned to various paths by others; Mumford, Hunter, Eubanks, Bedell, & Murphy, 2007).

While studies of the naturalistic career event progression of creative individuals provide some indication for experiential development, it is recommended that a more systematic approach be given to the design and evaluation of the effectiveness of such interventions. As an example, domain expertise requires deliberate, effortful, and explicit practice, with some estimates surpassing seven years for mastery in a given area (Bloom, 1985; Ericsson & Charness, 1994). Drawing from what we know about how expertise unfolds during early career activities can shed light on what planned efforts are needed for the domain expertise development that is required for future innovators. Similar to other efforts to develop complex skills, identifying who is ready for such experiential development efforts, as well as what supports are required for individuals to develop from them (Ligon & Hunter, 2010), are two important research activities over the coming years. In addition, although experiential development of other skills has not historically endured the same amount of rigor as the implementation of organizational training programs, we strongly recommend the ISD model be applied to generate well-designed, carefully validated experiential development initiatives.

Evaluation Considerations: Design and Criteria

As scholars have critiqued findings from interventions to improve creativity on the basis of poorly designed studies (Cropley, 1997), again the need for innovation researchers to apply a systematic evaluation paradigm is identified. While we did find that studies that were poorly designed (e.g., no control group, small samples, and fewer treatment groups) evidenced highest (and perhaps inflated; Mansfield, Busse, & Krepelka, 1978) effect sizes, significant effects were also obtained in well-designed studies (Scott et al., 2004a). In particular, the use of multiple dependent variables produced stronger results than studies with a single criterion, and studies that had longer post-test intervals (e.g., Baer, 1988) produced effect size estimates comparable to those with shorter post-test intervals. Such findings of evaluation design have two important implications. First, we should be assessing multiple indices of creativity to evaluate training and development programs. Given the complex nature of organizational creativity, it makes sense that we move beyond the favored dependent variable of divergent thinking to more complex phenomena such as problem solving, performance, and on-the-job behavior. Second, it is important to establish the long-term effects of creativity training and development, and thus it is advised that evaluations of effectiveness be administered at multiple points (e.g., immediately following training, six months, one year, etc) and from multiple sources. Using Kirkpatrick's (1959) model of training evaluation is a good place to start.

In a recent review of the effectiveness of the Creative Problem Solving (CPS) training program, Puccio and colleagues (2006) provided a host of criteria to show the effectiveness of this type of intervention. CPS provides lecture-based training and discussion on the principles of divergent and convergent thinking, and relies upon situated practice to build participant skills and confidence (Puccio, Firestein, Coyle, & Masucci, 2006). For example, Thompson (2001) provided a detailed description of cases in which CPS was applied to reduce costs in a plant setting. Linking to organizational criteria, his team was able to demonstrate effective use of strategies learned from the CPS curriculum at various interval points after training at Quaker Oats and two other publicly traded organizations. In addition, according to Firestien (1996), a CPS session brought a hospital millions of dollars in lost revenue. By carefully planning how programs would be evaluated, these researchers were able to identify what outcomes they expected training to influence and show data demonstrative of training effectiveness in an organizational setting.

Validity

Goldstein and Ford's (2001) concept of validity is closely related to how the program is evaluated. The ISD model proposes that training designers gather four types of validity evidence from developmental interventions:

1. training validity (i.e., did the training work?),
2. transfer validity (i.e., do you see evidence of skills learned back on the job?),
3. intra-organizational validity (i.e., is the training effective with other samples in the organization?), and
4. inter-organizational validity (i.e., is the training effective in other organizations?).

Addressing these four considerations when designing interventions—both training programs and experiential development—should further build the case for the effectiveness of creativity training (Cropley, 1997). Meta-analyses (Scott et al., 2004a, 2004b) and qualitative reviews of training packages and specific programs (Puccio et al., 2006) should continue to be conducted to extend validity evidence for popular programs.

CONCLUSIONS

Before turning to the broader theoretical and practical implications of this review, we should caution readers with at least three of the limitations of the current effort. First, driving our proposed interventions is the assumption that the cognitive process model underlies creative performance (Mumford et al., 1991). While there has been ample empirical support for this model, reliance on it likely precluded us from identifying other types of performance management interventions (Birdi, 2005) as effective options. However, a discussion of each of these models would have made identification of a common set of practices, practices that have a good deal of support in the broader creativity literature, less clear.

Second, while we made some effort to address those working in routine jobs, the bulk of our review was based on interventions for those working in creative positions. This is particularly the case for our section on performance appraisals and feedback, where rote application of typical HR practices for employees in general may cause the most damage. However, we did make some effort to emphasize approaches that would also work for those in routine positions (e.g., appraisals that rewarded expertise acquisition), and the section on training and development is particularly suited for all types of positions.

Finally, the present review focused on only two types of interventions—performance appraisal and training/development. It would be naïve to suggest that these two interventions alone will yield creative performance. As innovation is a complex phenomenon, it makes sense that interventions to encourage it should be integrated with all organizational practices. Thus, related recommendations offered by other authors, and particularly those on reward, leadership, and selection, in this handbook should also be applied to encourage organizational innovation.

Despite these limitations, there are a number of implications based on this review of the literature of performance appraisal, feedback, and training/development. The most unambiguous conclusion is that these are conceptually and practically related activities; developmental planning should flow directly from performance appraisals and skills learned in training should be rewarded through the review process. With the advent of more sophisticated HRIS systems, this linkage should be explicitly made in organizational settings. Related to this, HR practitioners charged with such interventions should familiarize themselves with the unique demands of creative problem solving, as well as the individual characteristics of the people who are most likely to be innovative. This may facilitate the exchange with leaders of innovation—the individuals who will serve as the best evaluators of creative performance as well as the content experts for training design.

Another conclusion flowing from this review is that much more scholarly work needs to be done on the area of performance appraisals and creativity. While some have suggested that highly creative, intrinsically motivated employees are "immune" to poor HR practices (Arnold, 1976; Baer et al., 2003; Hennessey, Amabile, & Martinage, 1989), there is still much room for error given that most performance appraisal instruments were designed for legal compliance in an industrialized, routine work environment (Malos, 1995). Rote application of performance appraisal best practices may result in deleterious effects when trying to improve creative performance. In addition, an opportunity for encouraging desired behaviors (e.g., collaboration, leadership development) in creative individuals also exists that may currently be overlooked. A research agenda devoted to investigating the outcomes of such appraisals on innovative performance should investigate what impact increasing the frequency of reviews providing supervisor training on feedback for creativity may have on innovation criteria at the individual, group, and organizational levels.

This review also highlighted the opportunity for more work on experiential development for creativity. While scholars have provided an in depth offering of creativity training, efforts to design, evaluate, and validate activities such as job rotations, mentoring programs, and other methods for experiential development are limited at best. We pointed to a few well-thought out interventions from our review (e.g., Mumford et al., 2005; O'Shea et al., 2010), but there is much opportunity for advancement. This is particularly timely during economic downturns when investment in large-scale training programs is lessened; the use of opportunities as they present themselves in organizational settings (e.g., mergers) to improve innovation holds promise.

Next, interactions between individual differences and interventions to improve creativity should be examined empirically. While recent theoretical advances have informed thinking on how personal characteristics interact with other contextual factors such as rewards (Baer et al., 2003; Eisenberger & Aselage, 2009) and feedback (Zhou, 2003; Zhou & George, 2001), the same rigor should be applied to understanding how individual characteristics impact the efficacy of performance appraisals, training, and development initiatives. For example, metacognition, or the capacity to plan, monitor, and revise one's approach (Ford & Kraiger, 1995), is one individual difference that likely impacts the effectiveness of interventions for creativity. In addition, applying advances in our understanding about the different knowledge structures of novices and experts, as well as best practices for developing further domain expertise in each, holds promise for investigating what types of creativity training may work best at different levels in one's career.

As a key individual difference contributing to creative performance is domain expertise, our review suggests that future efforts to improve creativity should a) focus first on developing such domain expertise, and b) contain practice exercises that are domain specific in nature. While Baer and his colleagues have conducted empirical investigations illustrative of these points (1993, 1994, 1996; Reiter-Palmon, Illies et al., 2009), future work in this area may shed light on what components of the domain are most critical to be held constant for transfer to outside performance. In addition, investigating the "shelf life", or approximate amount of time on the job we can expect such interventions to yield performance improvements, particularly given the changing nature of domains where creative performance occurs, would be a fruitful area of research.

Finally, as with any intervention in an organizational setting, applying the rigor of a model such as Goldstein and Ford's (2001) ISD model is implored. Particularly when designing training and development efforts, it is critical to specify how results from the needs assessment impacted the design. In addition, both practitioners and academics are urged to move beyond the oft-used criteria of divergent thinking and apply a host of dependent variables to gauge effectiveness. While tying initiatives to real organizational criteria is difficult, messy, and costly, it is important to link our efforts to the ultimate criterion of interest—creativity in organizations—to advance our understanding of these complex relationships.

References

3D Group (2009). *Current practices in 360 degree feedback: A benchmark study of North American companies.* Berkeley, CA: Data Driven Decisions.

Amabile, T. M. (1996). *Creativity in context: Update to "The social psychology of creativity".* Boulder, CO: Westview Press.

Amabile, T. M. (1979). Effects of external evaluation on artistic creativity. *Journal of Social Psychology, 37*, 221–233.

Amabile, T. M. (1997). Motivating creativity in organizations: On doing what you love and loving what you do. *California Management Review, 40*, 39–58.

Amabile, T. M. (1983). The social psychology of creativity: A componential conceptualization. *Journal of Personality and Social Psychology, 45*, 357–376.

Amabile, T. M., Goldfard, P., & Brackfield, S. C. (1990). Social influences on creativity: Evaluation, coactions, and surveillance. *Creativity Research Journal, 3*, 6–21.

Amabile, T. M., Schatzel, E. A., Moneta, G. B., & Kramer, S. J. (2004). Leader behaviors and the work environment for creativity: Perceived leader support. *The Leadership Quarterly, 15*, 5–32.

Arnold, H. J. (1976). Effects of performance feedback and extrinsic reward on high intrinsic motivation. *Organizational Behavior and Human Performance, 17*, 275–288.

Axtell, C. M., Holman, D. J., Unsworth, K. L., Wall, T. D., Waterson, P. E., & Harrington, E. (2000). Shopfloor innovation: Facilitating the suggestion and implementation of ideas. *Journal of Occupational and Organizational Psychology, 73*, 265–286.

Baer, J. M. (1988). Long-term effects of creativity training with middle school students. *The Journal of Early Adolescence, 8*, 183–193.

Baer, J. M. (1996). The effects of task-specific divergent-thinking training. *Journal of Creative Behavior, 30*, 183–187.

Baer, J. M. (1998). The case for domain specificity of creativity. *Creativity Research Journal, 11*, 173–177.

Baer, M., Oldham, G. R., & Cummings, A. (2003). Rewarding creativity: When does it really matter? *The Leadership Quarterly, 14*, 569–586.

Baer, M., Oldham, G. R., Jacobson, G. C., & Hollingshead, A. B. (2008). The personality composition of teams and creativity: The moderating role of team creative confidence. *Journal of Creative Behavior, 42*, 255–282.

Beatty, A., & Bremley, M. S. (2004). Leadership development program after Tyson–IBP Merger. Paper presented at the 2004 Annual Society of Industrial and Organizational Psychology Conference, Los Angeles, CA.

Benedek, M., Fink, A., & Neubauer, A. C. (2006). Enhancement of ideational fluency by means of computer-based training. *Creativity Research Journal, 18*, 317–328.

Birdi, K. S. (2005). No idea? Evaluating the effectiveness of creativity training. *Journal of European Industrial Training, 29*, 102–111.

Blair, C. S., & Mumford, M. D. (2007). Errors in idea evaluation: Preference for the unoriginal? *Journal of Creative Behavior, 41*, 196–222.

Bloom, B. S. (1985). Generalizations about talent development. In B. S. Bloom (Ed.), *Developing talent in young people* (pp. 507–549). New York, NY: Ballantine.

Bolden, R., & Gosling, J. (2006). Leadership competencies: Time to change the tune? *Leadership, 2*, 147–163.

Bracken, D. W., & Rose, D. S. (2009). Using 360 feedback to create large-scale organizational change. Roundtable discussion held at the 24th Annual Conference of the Society for Industrial and Organizational Psychology, April, New Orleans, LA.

Bushe, G. R., & Kassam, A. F. (2005). When is appreciative inquiry transformational? A meta-case analysis. *The Journal of Applied Behavioral Science, 41*, 161–180.

Cardinal, L. B. (2001). Technological innovation in the pharmaceutical industry: The use of organizational control in managing research and development. *Organization Science, 12*, 19–36.

Cardy, R. L, & Stewart, G. L. (1998). Quality and teams: Implications for HRM theory and research. In D. B. Fedor & S. Ghosh (Eds.), *Advances in the management of organizational quality: An annual series of quality-related theory and research papers* (Vol. 3, pp. 89–120). US: Elsevier Science/JAI Press.

Carrillo, P. M., Robinson, H. S., Al-Ghassani, A. M., & Anumba, C. J. (2004). Knowledge management in UK construction: Strategies, resources and barriers. *Project Management Journal, 35*, 46–56.

Cascio, W. F. (2006). Global performance management systems. In G. K. Stahl & I. Björkman (Eds.), *Handbook of research in international human resource management* (pp. 176–196). Northampton, MA: Edward Elgar Publishing.

Catsmull, E. (2008). How Pixar fosters collective creativity. *Harvard Business Review, 86*, 64–72.

Christensen, C. M. (1997). *The innovator's dilemma.* New York, NY: Collins.

Collins, M. A., & Amabile, T. M. (1999). Motivation and creativity. In R. J. Sternberg (Ed.), *Handbook of creativity* (pp. 297–312). New York, NY: Cambridge University Press.

Cooperrider, D. L., & Srivastava, S. (1987). Appreciative inquiry in organizational life. *Research in Organizational Change and Development, 1*, 129–169.

Covington, M. V., Crutchfield, R. S., Davies, L., & Olton, R. M. (1974). *The productive thinking program: A course in learning to think.* Columbus, OH: Merrill.

Cropley, A. J. (1997). Fostering creativity in the classroom: General principles. In M. A. Runco (Ed.), *Creativity Research Handbook* (Vol. 1, pp. 83–114).

Cunningham, J. B., & MacGregor, J. N. (2008). Training insightful problem solving: Effects of realistic and puzzle-like contexts. *Creativity Research Journal, 20,* 291–296.

Deci, E. L., & Ryan, R. M. (1985). The general causality orientations scale: Self-determination in personality. *Journal of Research in Personality, 19,* 109–134.

De Bruin, A. B. H., Rikers, R. P., & Schmidt, H. G. (2005). Monitoring accuracy and self-regulation when learning to play a chess endgame. *Applied Cognitive Psychology, 19,* 167–181.

DeNisi, A. S., & Kluger, A. N. (2000). Feedback effectiveness: Can 360-degree appraisals be improved? *Academy of Management Executive, 14,* 129–139.

Dransfield, R. (2000). *Human resource management.* Oxford, UK: Heinnemann Education Publishers.

Eisenberger, R., & Aselage, J. (2009). Incremental effects of reward on experienced performance pressure: Positive outcomes for intrinsic interest and creativity. *Journal of Organizational Behavior, 30,* 95–117.

Eisenberger, R., & Cameron, J. (1996). Detrimental effects of reward: Reality or myth? *American Psychologist, 51,* 1153–1166.

Ericsson, K. A. (2005). Recent advances in expertise research: A commentary on the contributions in this special issue. *Applied Cognitive Psychology, 19,* 233–241.

Ericsson, K. A., & Charness, W. (1994). Expert performance: Its structure and acquisition. *American Psychologist, 49,* 725–747.

Espejo, J., Day, E. A., Scott, G. M., & Diaz, T. (2005). Performance evaluations, need for cognition, and the acquisition of a complex skill: an attribute–treatment interaction. *Personality and Individual Differences, 38,* 1867–1877.

Feist, G. J. (1991). Synthetic and analytic thought: Similarities and differences between art and science students. *Creativity Research Journal, 4,* 145–155.

Feist, G. J. (1999). Influence of personality on artistic and scientific creativity. In R. J. Sternberg (Ed.), *Handbook of creativity* (pp. 273–296). Cambridge, UK: Cambridge University Press.

Feldhusen, J. E., Treffinger, D. J., & Balke, S. J. (1970). Developing creative thinking: The Purdue creativity program. *Journal of Creative Behavior, 4,* 85–90.

Feldman, D. H. (1999). The development of creativity. In R. J. Sternberg (Ed.), *Handbook of creativity* (pp. 169–188). Cambridge, UK: Cambridge University Press.

Firestien, R. L. (1996). *Leading on the creative edge: Gaining competitive advantage through the power of creative problem solving.* Colorado Springs, CO: Pinon Press.

Flaherty, M. A. (1992). The effects of a holistic creativity program on the self-concept and creativity of third graders. *Journal of Creative Behavior, 26,* 165–171.

Ford, J. K., & Kraiger, K. (1995). The application of cogntive constructs and principles to the instructional systems model of training: Implications for needs assessment, design, and transfer. In C. L. Cooper & I. T. Robertson (Eds.), *International Review of Industrial and Organizational Psychology.* Chichester, UK: John Wiley.

Ford, B. G., & Renzulli, J. S. (1976). Developing the creative potential of educable mentally retarded students. *Journal of Creative Behavior, 10,* 210–218.

Forrester, R. H. (1994). Implications of lean manufacturing for human resource strategy. *Work Study, 33,* 20–24.

Gardner, H. (1993). *Creating minds: An anatomy of creativity seen through the lives of Freud, Einstein, Picasso, Stravinsky, Eliot, Graham, and Gandhi.* New York, NY: Basic Books.

George, M. L., & Mclean, A. J. (2002). Putting the client before the horse: Working with appreciative inquiry in a small business. In R. Fry, F. Barrett, J. Seiling & D. Whitney (Eds.), *Appreciative Inquiry and Organizational Transformation: Reports from the Field* (pp. 27–38). Westport, CT: Quorum Books.

George, J. M., & Zhou, J. (2001). When openness to experience and conscientiousness are related to creative behavior: An interactional approach. *Journal of Applied Psychology, 86,* 513–524.

Glover, J. A. (1980). A creativity training workshop: Short-term, long-term, and transfer effects. *Journal of Genetic Psychology, 136,* 3–16.

Goldstein, I. L., & Ford, J. K. (2001). *Training in organizations: Needs assessment, development, and evaluation* (4th ed.). Belmont, CA: Wadsworth.

Greene, T. R., & Noice, H. (1988). Influence of positive affect upon creative thinking and problem solving in children. *Psychological Reports, 63,* 895–898.

E. INTERVENTIONS

Gruber, H. E. (1996). The life space of a scientist: The visionary function and other aspects of Jean Piaget's thinking. *Creativity Research Journal, 9*, 165–251.

Guilford, J. P. (1967). *The nature of human intelligence*. New York, NY: McGraw-Hill.

Gupta, A. K., & Singhal, A. (1993). Managing human resources for innovation and creativity. *Research Technology Management, May–June*, 41–48.

Hackman, J. R., & Oldham, G. R. (1975). Development of the job diagnostic survey. *Journal of Applied Psychology, 60*, 159–170.

Hennessey, B. A. (1989). The effect of extrinsic constraints on children's creativity while using a computer. *Creativity Research Journal, 2*, 151–168.

Hennessey, B. A., Amabile, T. M., & Martinage, M. (1989). Immunizing children against the effects of extrinsic reward. *Contemporary Educational Psychology, 14*, 212–217.

Herbold, R. J. (2002). Inside Microsoft: Balancing creativity and discipline. *Harvard Business Review, 80*, 72–79.

Houtz, J. C., & Frankel, A. D. (1992). Effects of incubation and imagery training on creativity. *Creativity Research Journal, 5*, 183–189.

Hunter, S. T., Thoroughgood, C., Myers, A., & Ligon, G. S. (in press). Managing the paradoxes of leading for innovation. *Psychology of Aesthetics, Creativity and the Arts—Special issue: Innovation in Organizations.*

Ilgen, D. R., Fisher, C. D., & Taylor, M. S. (1979). Consequences of individual feedback on behavior in organizations. *Journal of Applied Psychology, 64*, 349–371.

Johnsen, A. (2005). What does 25 years of experience tell us about the state of performance measurement in public management and policy? *Public Money and Management, 25*, 9–17.

Jones, F. F., Morris, M. H., & Rockmore, W. (1995). HR practices that promote entrepreneurship. *HR Magazine, 40*, 86.

Kao, J. (2007). *Innovation nation: How America is losing its innovative edge, why it matters and what we can do to get it back*. New York, NY: Free Press.

Kirton, M. (1994). Adaptors and innovators: A description and measure. *Journal of Applied Psychology, 61*, 622–629.

Kirton, M. (1991). Adaptors and innovators: Why new initiatives get blocked. In J. Henry (Ed.), *Creative management* (pp. 209–220).

Keers, C. (2007). Using appreciative inquiry to measure employee engagement. *Strategic HR Review, 6*, 10–11.

Kelley, T., & Littman, J. (2001). *The art of innovation: Lessons in creativity from IDEO, America's leading design firm*. New York, NY: Doubleday.

Kirkpatrick, D. L. (1959). Techniques for evaluating training programs. *Journal of the American Society of Training Directors, 13*, 3–26.

Kline, T. J., & Sulsky, L. M. (2009). Measurement and assessment issues in performance appraisal. *Canadian Psychology: Developments in Psychological Measurement and Assessment, 50*, 161–171.

Krogh, L. C., Prager, J. H., Sorensen, D. P., & Tomlinson, J. D. (1988). How 3M evaluates its R&D programs. *Research Technology Management, November–December*, 10–14.

Latham, G. P., Sulsky, L. M., & MacDonald, H. A. (2008). Performance management. In P. Boxall, J. Purcell & P. Wright (Eds.), *Oxford handbook of human resource management*. Oxford, UK: Oxford University Press.

Ligon, G. S., & Hunter, S. T. (2010). Putting the development into experiential development. *Journal of Industrial and Organizational Psychology: Perspectives on Science and Practice, 3*, 28–32.

Ma, H-H. (2006). A synthetic analysis of the effectiveness of single components and packages in creativity training programs. *Creativity Research Journal, 18*, 435–446.

Madjar, N., & Shalley, C. E. (August, 2008). Multiple tasks' and multiple goals' effect on creativity: Forced incubation or just a distraction? *Journal of Management, 34*, 786–805.

Malos, S. B. (1998). Current legal issues in performance appraisal. In J. W. Smither (Ed.), *Performance appraisal: State-of-the-art methods for performance management* (pp. 49–94). San Francisco, CA: Jossey-Bass.

Mansfield, R. S., Busse, T. V., & Krepelka, E. J. (1978). The effectiveness of creativity training. *Review of Educational Research, 48*, 517–536.

Mayfield, M., & Mayfield, J. (2008). Leadership techniques for nurturing worker garden variety creativity. *Journal of Management Development, 27*, 976–986.

McCall, M. W. (2010). Recasting leadership development. *Journal of Industrial and Organizational Psychology: Perspectives on Science and Practice, 3*, 3–19.

Memmert, D. (2007). Can creativity be improved by an attention-broadening training program? An exploratory study focusing on team sport. *Creativity Research Journal, 19*, 281–291.

E. INTERVENTIONS

Molleman, E., & Timmerman, H. (2003). Performance management when innovation and learning become critical performance indicators. *Personnel Review, 32*, 93–113.

Mondy, R. W., Noe, R. M., & Premeaux, S. R. (2002). *Human resource management* (8th ed.). Upper Saddle River, NJ: Prentice Hall.

Mullin, R. F., & Sherman, R. (1993). Creativity and performance appraisal: Shall never the twain meet? *Creativity Research Journal, 6*, 425–434.

Mumford, M. D., & Hunter, S. T. (2005). Innovation in organizations: A multi-level perspective on creativity. In F. J. Yammarino & F. Dansereau (Eds.), *Research in multi-level issues* (Vol. IV, pp. 11–74). Oxford, UK: Elsevier.

Mumford, M. D., Hunter, S. T., Eubanks, D., Bedell, K., & Murphy, S. (2007). Developing leaders for creative efforts: A domain based approach to leadership development. *Human Resource Review, 17*, 402–417.

Mumford, M. D., Connelly, S., & Gaddis, B. (2003). How creative leaders think: Experimental findings and cases. *The Leadership Quarterly, 14*, 411–432.

Mumford, M. D., Connelly, M. S., Scott, G. M., Espejo, J., Sohl, L. M., & Hunter, S. T., & Bedell K. E. (2005). Career experiences and scientific performance: A study of social, physical, life, and health sciences. *Creativity Research Journal, 17*, 105–129.

Mumford, M. D., & Gustafson, S. B. (1988). Creativity syndrome: Integration, application, and innovation. *Psychological Bulletin, 103*, 27–43.

Mumford, M. D., Mobley, M. I., Uhlman, C. E., Reiter-Palmon, R., & Doares, L. (1991). Process analytic models of creative capacities. *Creativity Research Journal, 4*, 91–122.

Mumford, M. D., & Norris, D. G. (1999). Heuristics. In M. A. Runco & S. Pritzker (Eds.), *Encyclopedia of creativity* (Vol. 2, pp. 139–146). San Diego, CA: Academic Press.

Mumford, M. D., Scott, G. M., Gaddis, B., & Strange, J. M. (2002). Leading creative people: Orchestrating expertise and relationships. *The Leadership Quarterly, 13*, 705–750.

Mumford, M. D., & Hunter, S. T. (2005). The creativity paradox: Sources, resolutions, and directions. In F. J. Yammarino & F. Dansereau (Eds.), *Research in multi-level issues* (Vol. IV). Oxford, UK: Elsevier.

Murphy, K. R., & Cleveland, J. N. (1995). *Understanding performance appraisal: Social, organizational, and goal-based perspectives*. Thousand Oaks, CA: Sage Publications.

Nakamura, J., & Csikszentmihályi, M. (2003). The construction of meaning through vital engagement. In C. L. Keyes & J. Haidt (Eds.), *Flourishing: Positive psychology and the life well-lived* (pp. 83–104). Washington, DC: American Psychological Association.

Nickerson, R. S. (1999). In R. J. Sternberg (Ed.), *Handbook of creativity*. New York, NY: Cambridge University Press.

Noe, R. A, Hollenbeck, J. R., Gerhart, B., & Wright, P. M. (2007). *Fundamentals of human resource management* (6th ed.). Boston, MA: McGraw-Hill Irwin.

Oldham, G. R., & Cummings, A. (1996). Employee creativity: Personal and contextual factors at work. *Academy of Management Journal, 39*, 607–634.

O'Quinn, K., & Bessemer, S. P. (1999). Creative products. In M. A. Runco & S. R. Pritzker (Eds.,), *Encyclopedia of creativity* (pp. 413–422)

Osborn, A. (1963). *Applied imagination*. New York, NY: Scribners.

Osburn, H. K., Ligon, G. S., Bedford, A., Bruno, E., Panik, L., Doran, M., & et al. (2010). Assessing and developing innovative performance. Symposium presented at the 25th Annual Conference for the Society of Industrial and Organizational Psychology, April, Atlanta, GA.

O'Shea, P. G., Allen, M. T., Grignon, J. D., & Kell, C. T. (2010). Organizational innovation through 360 degree feedback. Symposium (G. S. Ligon, Chair) presented at the 25th Annual Conference for the Society of Industrial and Organizational Psychology, April, Atlanta, GA.

Parnes, S. J. (1966). *Instructor manual for institutes and courses in creative problem solving*. Buffalo, NY: Creative Education Foundation.

Phye, G. A. (1997). Inductive reasoning and problem solving: The early grades. In J. G. Ryne (Ed.), *Handbook of academic learning* (pp. 451–471). San Diego, CA: Academic Press.

Puccio, G. J., Firestien, R. L., Coyle, C., & Masucci, C. (2006). A review of the effectiveness of CPS training: A focus on workplace issues. *Creativity and Innovation Management, 15*, 19–33.

Puccio, G. J., Talbot, R. J., & Joniak, A. (2000). Examining creative performance in the workplace through a person–environment fit model. *Journal of Creative Behavior, 34*, 227–247.

Ree, M. J., Carretta, T. R., & Teachout, M. S. (1995). Role of ability and prior knowledge in complex training performance. *Journal of Applied Psychology, 80*, 721–730.

Reiter-Palmon, R., Illies, M. Y., Cross, L. K., Bubolz, C., & Nimps, T. (2009). Creativity and domain specificity: The effect of task type on multiple indexes of creative problem-solving. *Psychology of Aesthetics, Creativity, and the Arts, 3,* 73–80.

Roe, A. (1951). *A psychological study of physical scientists.* Provincetown, MA: Journal Press.

Roe, A. (1953). *The making of a scientist.* New York, NY: Dodd, Mead.

Root Bernstein, R. S., Bernstein, M., & Garnier, H. W. (1995). Correlations between avocations, scientific style, and professional impact of thirty eight scientists of the Eiduson Study. *Creativity Research Journal, 8,* 115–137.

Rose, L. H., & Lin, H. T. (1984). A meta-analysis of long-term creativity training programs. *Journal of Creative Behavior, 18,* 11–22.

Runco, M. A. (2003). Commentary on personal and potentially ambiguous creativity: You can't understand the butterfly unless you (also) watch the caterpillar. *Creativity Research Journal, 15,* 137–142.

Scope, E. E. (1998). Meta-analysis of research on creativity: The effects of instructional variables. Unpublished doctoral dissertation, Fordham University, New York, NY.

Scott, G. M., Leritz, L. E., & Mumford, M. D. (2004a). The effectiveness of creativity training: A quantitative review. *Creativity Research Journal, 16,* 361–388.

Scott, G. M., Leritz, L. E., & Mumford, M. D. (2004b). Types of creativity training: Approaches and their effectiveness. *Journal of Creative Behavior, 38,* 149–179.

Scott, G. M., Lonergan, D. C., & Mumford, M. D. (2005). Conceptual combination: Alternative knowledge structures, alternative heuristics. *Creativity Research Journal, 17,* 79–98.

Searle, R. H., & Ball, K. S. (2003). Supporting innovation through HR policy: Evidence from the UK. *Creativity and Innovation Management, 12,* 50–62.

Seligman, M. E. P. (2000). The positive perspective. *The Gallup Review, 3,* 2–7.

Shalley, C. E., & Perry-Smith, J. E. (2001). Effects of social-psychological factors on creative performance: The role of informational and controlling expected evaluation and modeling experience. *Organizational Behavior and Human Decision Processes, 84,* 1–22.

Shively, J. E., Feldhusen, J. F., & Treffinger, D. J. (1972). Developing creativity and related attitudes. *Journal of Experimental Education, 41,* 63–69.

Simonton, B. K. (1999). Creativity from a historiometric perspective. In R. J. Sternberg (Ed.), *Handbook of creativity* (pp. 116–136). Cambridge, UK: Cambridge University Press.

Sitkin, S. B. (1996). Learning through failure: The strategy of small losses. In M. D. Cohen & L. S. Sproull (Eds.), *Organizational learning* (pp. 541–578). Thousand Oaks, CA: Sage.

Skinner, S. J., & Kelley, S. W. Transforming sales organizations through appreciative inquiry. *Psychology & Marketing, Special Issue: Selling and Sales Management, 23,* 77–93.

Stafford, S. P. (1998). Capitalizing on careabouts to facilitate creativity. *Creativity and Innovation Management, 7,* 159–167.

Sternberg, R. J., & Lubart, T. I. (1996). Investing in creativity. *American Psychologist, 51,* 677–688.

Sternberg, R. J., & Lubart, T. I. (1999). The concept of creativity: Prospects and paradigms. In R. J. Sternberg (Ed.), *Handbook of Creativity* (pp. 16–31). Cambridge, UK: Cambridge University Press.

Sundgren, M., Selart, M., Ingelgård, A., & Bengtson, C. (2005). Dialogue-based evaluation as a creative climate indicator: Evidence from the pharmaceutical Industry. *Creativity and Innovation Management, 14,* 84–98.

Taylor, W. (1990). The business of innovation: An interview with Paul Cook. *Harvard Business Review, 68,* 96–106.

Thompson, G. (2001). The reduction in plant maintenance costs using creative problem-solving principles. *Journal of Process Mechanical Engineering, 215,* 185–195.

Torrance, E. P. (1966a). *The torrance tests of creative thinking: directions, manual, and scoring guide.* (Figural test booklets A & B) Princeton, NJ: Personnel Press.

Torrance, E. P. (1966b). *The Torrance tests of creative thinking: Directions, manual, and scoring guide.* (Verbal test booklets A & B) Princeton, NJ: Personnel Press.

Torrance, E. P. (1972). Can we teach children to think creatively? *Journal of Creative Behavior, 6,* 114–143.

Van Dyck, C., Frese, M., Baer, M., & Sonnentag, S. (2005). Organizational error management culture and its impact on performance: A two-study replication. *Journal of Applied Psychology, 90,* 1228–1240.

Verbeeten, F. (2007). Innovation and control. *Management Control and Accounting, 11,* 45–52.

Vroom, V. (1964). *Work and motivation.* New York, NY: Wiley and Sons.

Wagner, S. H., & Goffin, R. D. (1997). Differences in accuracy of absolute and comparative performance appraisal methods. *Organizational Behavior And Human Decision Processes, 70,* 95–103.

E. INTERVENTIONS

Wallis, C., Coady, E., Cray, D., Park, A., & Ressner, J. (2005). The new science of happiness. *Time, January* 17.

Ward, T. B., Patterson, M. J., & Sifonis, C. M. (2004). The role of specificity and abstraction in creative idea generation. *Creativity Research Journal, 16*, 1–9.

Weisburg, R. W. (1999). Creativity and knowledge: A challenge to theories. In R. J. Sternberg (Ed.), *Handbook of Creativity* (pp. 226–259). Cambridge, UK: Cambridge University Press.

West, M. A. (1990). The social psychology of innovation in groups. In M. A. West & J. L. Farr (Eds.), *Innovation and creativity at work: Psychological and organizational strategies* (pp. 309–333). Oxford, UK: John Wiley & Sons.

West, M. A. (2000). Creativity and innovation at work. *The Psychologist, 13*, 460–464.

Whitney, D., & Trosten-Bloom, A. (2003). *The Power of appreciative inquiry : A practical guide to positive change.* San Francisco, CA: Berrett-Koehler Publishers.

Yeo, G. B., & Neal, A. (2004). A multilevel analysis of effort, practice, and performance: Effects of ability, conscientiousness, and goal orientation. *Journal of Applied Psychology, 89*, 231–247.

Yuan, F., & Zhou, J. (2008). Differential effects of expected external evaluation on different parts of the creative idea production process and on final product creativity. *Creativity Research Journal, 20*, 391–403.

Zhou, J. (2003). When the presence of creative coworkers is related to creativity: Role of supervisor close monitoring, developmental feedback, and creative personality. *Journal of Applied Psychology, 88*, 413–422.

Zhou, J., & George, J. M. (2001). When job dissatisfaction leads to creativity: Encouraging the expression of voice. *Academy of Management Journal, 44*, 682–696.

Organizational Development

Min Basadur[1], Tim Basadur[2], and Gordana Licina[1]

[1]McMaster University, Michael G. DeGroote School of Business, ON, Canada;
[2]University of Illinois at Chicago, Liautaud College of Business, Chicago, IL

INTRODUCTION

In a nutshell, Organizational Development (OD) is a broad, loosely defined field of practice and inquiry that espouses the noble goal of improving organizations and making them more effective. In recent times, this goal has become more complex and challenging, as we experience an era of rapidly accelerating change and frequent major discontinuities and interruptions to the world in which we work. Many organizations that prospered during more stable times—times that rewarded routinized efficiency—now find themselves poorly adapted to today's realities, where adaptability and creativity are necessary. While OD interventions have been used to support creative efforts, overall the field of OD has not made a strong research connection with creativity, probably because creativity, even among creativity researchers, has not been fully understood as a *process* with requisite skills, as opposed to an *outcome*. In this chapter, we show that while OD has gradually evolved to understanding itself as a discipline of change management, virtually no-one in the field of OD has yet envisioned OD as a *continuous process* of change making, as opposed to discrete single or multiple organizational interventions at a single point in time or as an ongoing insertion of interventions over time. As well, such change making has been relegated to outside consulting firms administering various tools and interventions, leaving organizations devoid of these skills and dependent on external experts. Thus, to integrate the fields of OD and creativity, we present Organizational Creativity as a change-making process that includes a set of change-making attitudinal, behavioral and cognitive skills. We show that, just as the field of creativity has many discrete *tools* which can be employed within the creativity process, many OD interventions are also tools that can be employed within the same creativity process. (Similarly, many creativity tools can be applied to enhance typical OD interventions). However, we distinguish between a discrete *tool* and a complete *process*, and between a tool skillfully and unskillfully *applied*.

Handbook of Organizational Creativity.
DOI: 10.1016/B978-0-12-374714-3.00026-4

That once successful companies are finding that their sure-hit formulas no longer work is an outcome predicted by Miller's simplicity theory (Miller, 1993), which suggested that some organizations become so overwhelmingly focused on a single goal, activity, department or worldview that they are incapable of considering other issues. An example, cited by Miller and Chen (1996), is management so obsessed with cost-cutting that they neglect service and design. Long revered icons of organizational excellence have been humbled, and even bailed out of bankruptcy and imminent demise by government intervention. Individuals, families, and entire communities are finding the world shifting beneath their feet as traditional markets, industries, and sources of employment disappear under the impact of new information technologies, global competition, lack of regulation of financial institutions, uncertainty about global warming, transitioning to new energy sources, and a restructuring of the world economy. It is not surprising that organizations whose main virtues during previous times were predictability and reliability should find it difficult to adapt to this increasingly dynamic environment. Their employees, too, are struggling to deal with these changing times, as the vast scale of change has resulted in an unprecedented need for information processing and problem solving skills. There has been a dramatic increase in psychological research aimed at better understanding the cognitive capabilities of employees, in order to improve employee productivity and well-being (Hodgkinson & Healey, 2008).

This chapter addresses the need for organizations to develop more creative ways of thinking and behaving to succeed in a turbulent world. While many organizations possess ample efficiency and analytical capability, successful organizations must also learn to integrate adaptability and creative capability into their repertoire. Business and engineering schools have provided managers with extensive training in analytical thinking and problem solving. While useful for solving efficiency and optimization problems, such training is insufficient for developing tacit-level competencies in adaptability or creative problem-solving. Tacit competency is developed through "learning by doing", to the extent that codification is not required (Fiol, 1991). Polanyi referred to such a degree of competency as subsidiary level tacit knowledge (Polanyi, 1958), meaning skills are so integrated into an individual's repertoire that they become second nature. We argue that creativity attitudes, behaviors, cognitive skills and process must be learned, and developed such that they are second nature if organizations are to survive and thrive. We argue that capability in implementing specific creative behaviors, attitudes, cognitive skills and process are necessary foundations for successful organizational development efforts. Such efforts ultimately all focus on implementing valuable changes that build more effective organizations. First, we summarize a wide array of organizational development approaches, and then we review different approaches to the study of creativity. We then integrate the field of OD into a simplifying system of Organizational Creativity comprised of attitudinal, behavioral, and cognitive skills within a multi-stage process. This system does not exclude analytical thinking and tools; we position developing organizational creativity competency as enhancing or empowering the already present analytical capability as the essential complement. Our goals are to enable a helpful unification of OD research and practice as a subset of Organizational Creativity, and to help apply the field of creativity to real world work.

Prior to the advent of organizational development research in the mid-20th century, the external environment was perceived as the primary determinant of a firm's performance.

This was the standard industrial organizational (IO) neo-classical economics viewpoint (Caves, 1980; Caves & Porter, 1977; Porter, 1980). According to the IO perspective, the source of a firm's profits was ultimately determined by its market position and the structure of the industry to which it belonged, and protected by barriers to entry into the market. This perspective led to the notion that leaders need only to design appropriate organizational structures and continue to make well-reasoned decisions (Edmondson, 1996) in order to achieve continued economic success. The field of organizational development has been built upon the opposite viewpoint, which perceives that the source of superior profitability lies inside the firm. Known as the resource-based view, this perspective regards the firm as a bundle of resources not dependent on external market and industry structures (Ambrosini, 2003; Amit & Shoemaker, 1993; Rumelt, 1984). It suggests these resources—primarily the people of the firm—are responsible for a firm's sustainable competitive advantage, as they are capable of adapting to changing external circumstances. Miller and Shamsie (1996) issued a call for more study of *how* internal resources can be managed in order to keep them, or make them into sources of sustainable competitive advantage, and Beer (2001) supports this need, noting that while there is an overwhelming consensus that companies must become capable of continuous adaptation, there is little agreement on how this can be achieved. We subscribe to the resource-based approach and offer this chapter as a response to that call. Our approach focuses specifically on the capability of the people inside the firm and how they can use their creativity to manage internal or external change, in order to continuously develop and sustain healthy profitability. One well cited example of this is how Southwest Airlines, which is famous for its people-centered management style, continued to be profitable in the post 9/11 period while most US airlines went into near or full bankruptcy.

OPEN SYSTEM ORGANIZATIONS

One of the basic tenets of OD is the view of an organization as a transformational engine comprised of people, equipment, and processes which continuously convert changing inputs from the external environment into changing outputs to the external environment. The extent to which organizations pay heed to their external environments is said to be a measure of how "open" or "closed" they are. The external environment includes things like customers, the ecology, the government, competitors, suppliers, technology, and society as a whole. Closed-system organizations ignore environmental changes while open-system organizations continuously transform environmental changes into improvements in effectiveness. A closed system survives only if the external environment remains stable allowing the organization to endlessly take in the same unchanging inputs and emit the same outputs.

Effective organizations achieve strong relationships with both their external and internal environments. Internal environments can be considered to have three main components—dominant coalition, structures, and culture—which shape the behavior of its employees (Beer, 1980.) The dominant coalition (or thought leaders) is a group of key decision makers whose influence on the system is greatest (Kotter, 1978; Miles & Snow, 1978). The coalition usually includes senior management, but can also include others whose collective job experiences, skills, cognitive orientations, personalities, and values define the internal environment. Structures, such as training, job design, and performance evaluation, are the formal aspects of an organization which signal to people that certain behaviors are desirable and that rewards are likely to result if they practice them. Culture means the composite perception that employees have of their internal environment, expressed by such concepts as "open", "risk-taking", "warm", "soft", "impersonal", "informal", or "rigid". Margulies and Raia (1978) defined the culture of the organization as the shared beliefs and feelings which form an informal set of ground rules about what is expected and what will be rewarded (formally or socially).

An open-systems model that includes the effects of the internal and external environments on the organization as a *transforming engine* is shown in Figure 26.1. It recognizes that the organization is both an economic and social system with multiple purposes and outcomes, and that the people and economic inputs and outputs must filter through both environments. Financial indicators, such as profit and return on investment, are typical economic criteria of organizational performance. People criteria are often summarized as quality of work life and include things like job satisfaction, equitable pay, meaningful work, and a compatible social environment. Beer (1980) suggested organizations must provide a satisfactory quality of work life or will ultimately be unable to attract, motivate, and retain employees and that these two sets of criteria create conflicting demands. Managers often feel forced to trade off one objective against another, such as reducing profits to pay people more, or declaring a dividend while laying-off employees to reduce costs. One purpose of this chapter is to demonstrate how these two outcomes can be accomplished simultaneously without trade-offs.

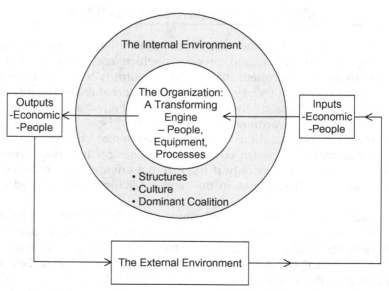

FIGURE 26.1   An organization operating as an open economic and social system.

ORGANIZATIONAL EFFECTIVENESS, ADAPTABILITY AND CREATIVITY

Mott's (1972) field research showed that effective organizations have two major but very different characteristics: efficiency and adaptability. Efficiency means optimizing, stabilizing, and perfecting current methods or routines to attain the highest quantity and quality for the lowest possible cost. High efficiency means mastery of routine, or standard, prescribed methods by which the organization carries out its main tasks. The efficient organization follows well-structured, stable routines to deliver its products or services in high quantities with high quality and at low cost. On the other hand, adaptability means continually and intentionally changing routines and finding new things to do and better ways to do current work. Called opportunistic surveillance by Simon (1977), adaptability means scanning the environment to anticipate new opportunities and problems and deliberately changing methods to attain new levels of quantity, quality, and cost. Adaptability yields both new methods and new products and services. High adaptability means a high rate of positive change of routine. A closed-system organization works diligently to master the routine and focuses only on efficiency. An open-system organization also works diligently to deliberately change the routine to capitalize on its changing environment, and focuses on both internal efficiency and external adaptability.

In a stable world, efficient organizations may be successful. However, in today's changing world, organizations need adaptability to anticipate problems and opportunities, and develop timely solutions and new routines. The people in adaptable organizations accept new solutions promptly and the acceptance is prevalent across the whole organization. While adaptability is a *proactive* process of looking for ways to deliberately change in a planned way, it also includes *reacting* quickly to unexpected events to maintain routines, with minimal disruption, as well as creatively capitalizing on such occurrences. According to Mott's research, the most effective organizations are both efficient and adaptable, while the least effective organizations lack the right amount of either or both attributes. The following equation summarizes the findings:

Organizational Effectiveness = High Skill in Efficiency + High Skill in Adaptability

High skill in adaptability (or efficiency) means the ability to implement higher or lower levels of adaptability (or efficiency) performance as desired (Figure 26.2).

Through the years, many organizations whose success was built on predictable technologies, markets, or other environmental factors learned to become highly efficient but neglected to build capacity for adaptability (Figure 26.3). For example, prior to the 1970s, North American consumers bought almost all of their cars from one of the Big Three domestic automakers. American automakers became accustomed to building large, fuel-inefficient vehicles suitable for a stable environment in which fuel was plentiful and inexpensive. Innovation in the industry was largely limited to cosmetic style changes each model year (low adaptability). As a result, when Japanese automakers began introducing more reliable cars, better options, and smaller vehicles that addressed new problems such as the 1970s oil crisis, they were quickly able to take advantage of the lack of attention the Big Three had paid to both efficiency and adaptability (Figure 26.4).

E. INTERVENTIONS

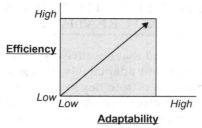

FIGURE 26.2   Balance of efficiency and adaptability appropriate for a rapidly changing, unstable environment.

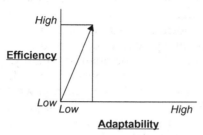

FIGURE 26.3   Balance of efficiency and adaptability appropriate for a predictable, stable environment.

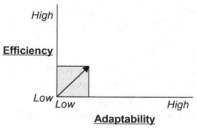

FIGURE 26.4   Balance of efficiency and adaptability inappropriate for any environment.

A similar story can be told about the North American tire industry during the same time period. The radial tire, introduced by France's Michelin in 1945, displaced the bias-ply tire everywhere but in North America. Until about 1975, North America's automotive tire industry enjoyed a predictable environment. Consumers bought their tires from Goodyear, Firestone, or any of their well-known competitors. With the tires basically of the same quality, consumers shopped for the best price and friendly service, and suppliers concentrated on providing these efficiency factors (Figure 26.3). However, management failure to adapt to the radial tire innovation led to the loss of much of the North American market virtually overnight, as consumers discovered the advantages of the new tires. For the North American suppliers, what had appeared to be a predictable environment became anything but. They should have been operating according to Figure 26.2; instead they were operating according to Figure 26.3 (efficient enough but not adaptable enough).

It is also possible for an organization to be too adaptable but not efficient enough (Figure 26.5). Some highly successful organizations—such as 3M, which is famous for continuously

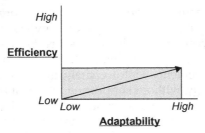

FIGURE 26.5 Balance of efficiency and adaptability overemphasizing adaptability at the expense of efficiency (inappropriate except in the most extremely unstable, unpredictable environments).

creating new products—carefully monitor their own activities so as not to overemphasize adaptability at the expense of efficiency (which would be an appropriate balance only in the most extremely turbulent environment). Microsoft has been criticized for introducing new products too hastily, before ensuring they have been optimized and are error free.

In a rapidly changing, unstable environment, both high efficiency and high adaptability are necessary (Figure 26.2). While all organizations need skills in both efficiency and adaptability in order to be effective, most organizations understand the concept of efficiency and find it easier to mainstream than adaptability. One of the most important factors in determining the appropriate ratio between efficiency and adaptability is the volatility of an organization's environment. Burns and Stalker (1961) suggested that, in rapidly changing environments, organizations with more organic structures (favoring creativity and innovation) would be more effective than organizations with more mechanistic structures (favoring adherence to rules and procedures and routine). In less volatile environments, the reverse was true. The current business environment, characterized by continuous change, requires organizations to become highly competent in adaptability. Adaptable organizations introduce change to both their internal and external environments. An internal focus can include efforts toward innovating new routines or technologies, while an external focus can include developing competitive actions to rattle the stability of competitors. Whether focusing adaptability efforts internally or externally, changes should be planned and deliberate, with an organization regularly setting innovation goals and working toward them. While the former is planned, transformational change, including discovering previously undetected customer problems to solve, the latter results in a planned, steady flow of incremental improvements in the quantity, quality, and cost of current products and services.

HOW HAS ORGANIZATIONAL DEVELOPMENT ATTEMPTED TO SUPPORT CREATIVE EFFORTS AND ADAPTABILITY?

OD Interventions

While it is generally understood that the purpose of the field of Organizational Development (OD) is intended to make organizations more effective, there are many different approaches to defining and understanding OD. Beer and Walton (1987) described one view of OD as comprising a set of actions undertaken to improve organizational effectiveness and employee well-being by applying theory from psychology and organizational behavior (such actions are often called "interventions"). This represents the traditional organizational development approach, which was to provide organizations with tools or interventions designed to solve specific concerns or problems. Unfortunately, these were sometimes prescribed without adequate diagnosis or singly, without supporting interventions. Often they were solutions developed in isolation before problems were adequately defined, and when such interventions failed to make any significant impact, the organization was encouraged to simply reach for another "solution". The specific intervention called total quality management (TQM) has often failed to live up to expectations (Spector & Beer, 1994), partly because it has been introduced as a grab-bag of tools (and management rhetoric) without any change-making skills or process (Basadur & Robinson, 1993). However, TQM has succeeded when installed not only as a tool (intervention), but as part of a continuous process of change making supported by a comprehensive, well-planned system of skill training, additional tools, management leadership, and employee engagement towards well understood, specific, strategic goals (Basadur & Robinson, 1993). We will expand this process and skills view later in this chapter.

Traditional individual OD interventions may be classified into families of tools in Table 26.1 (Beer, 1980; French & Bell, 1984) and summarized as follows:

1. diagnostic interventions, used primarily to gather data about the organization or its parts and to create a setting for sharing and problem diagnosis,
2. process interventions, which affect organizational behavior and process by enabling employees to examine, become dissatisfied with, and change their behaviors, and improve their relationships with others,

TABLE 26.1 A Classification of Traditional OD Interventions.

DIAGNOSTIC INTERVENTIONS	PROCESS INTERVENTIONS
• Survey Feedback	• Processing Meetings
• Confrontation Meeting	• Group Development/Team Building
• Sensing Meetings	— Goal Model
• Manager's Diagnostic Meeting	— Role Model
• Family Group Diagnostic Meeting	— Interpersonal Model
• Organization Mirror	• Inter-group Meetings
• Diagnostic Task Force	• Interpersonal Peacemaking
STRUCTURAL INNOVATIONS AND INTERVENTIONS	**INDIVIDUAL INTERVENTIONS**
• Organization Design	• Counselling and Coaching
• Job Design	• Training and Development
• Reward Systems	• Replacement and Termination
• Performance Management Systems	• Recruitment and Selection
• Control and Accounting Systems	• Career Development

3. structural interventions, which enable the organization to create new designs and systems to address problems and changes in people and environment, and

4. individual interventions, including strategies and methods for selecting, training, and developing individuals, which are intended to change employees.

Each of these interventions is intended to work in a different fashion. Following Lewin's well-known paradigm for the change process called "unfreeze–change–refreeze" (Schein, 1961), by nature, *diagnostic interventions* unfreeze organizational members, i.e., prepare them for change by providing data and identifying problems. *Process interventions* and *individual interventions* provide new attitudes, behaviors, skills, and processes to groups and individuals leading to creativity and innovation, and cause both unfreezing and changing. *Structural interventions* are often designed to refreeze changes, ensuring that new, appropriate behaviors solidify. Structural interventions include changing appraisal and reward systems, jobs (e.g., job enrichment), and organizational designs (e.g., moving from functional design to matrix management or adhocracy) that support the new behaviors learned.

The early work in OD featured diagnostic survey feedback interventions introduced by researchers such as Baumgartel (1967) and Marrow (1969), while Lewin (1947) and Blake and Mouton (1964) became known for their pioneering work in process and individual interventions in developing training groups. As the field of OD has evolved, additional interventions almost too numerous to mention have emerged. Training interventions such as Appreciative Inquiry (Srivastva & Cooperrider, 1990), Emotional Intelligence (Mayer, Barsade, & Roberts, 2008), and Six Thinking Hats (de Bono, 1999), are aimed at increasing individual effectiveness. At the organizational level, terms such as Knowledge Management and Intellectual Capital are now common in the management literature. Practitioners attend seminars on concepts and learn about tools such as "Workout", popularized at General Electric Corporation by Jack Welch (Bunker & Alban, 1996); Organizational Learning (Argyris & Schon, 1978; Edmondson, 2002; Garvin, 1993; Levitt & March, 1988; Senge, 1990); Re-engineering (Hall, Rosenthal, & Wade, 1993); and Six Sigma and Lean Manufacturing (Martin, 2007). Major consulting companies offer sophisticated information systems for knowledge management, and many organizations have established knowledge management or learning systems departments headed up by a "Chief Knowledge Officer".

However, virtually all of these more recent (and perhaps, more sophisticated), interventions are designed to address increased efficiency rather than adaptability, and are usually seen as different and separate from organizational creativity and innovation. One purpose of this chapter is to show how the various disconnected concepts of knowledge management may fit together. We differentiate between the *apprehension* of knowledge and knowledge *utilization* and unite them into a single framework. We argue that this framework allows organizations to do three things:

1. detect errors and implement changes to restore or improve routines,

2. make sense of sudden unexpected events and crises and convert them into opportunities for innovation, and

3. anticipate and seek out new information, and emerging opportunities to develop new products, services, and routines.

Many OD efforts are focused on addressing the first of these three goals—essentially the issue of efficiency. For organizations struggling with issues of adaptability, as expressed in the latter two goals, these OD efforts are inadequate and require creativity.

For example, Levitt and March's (1988) review of the literature shows that Organizational Learning is widely viewed as routine-based. Routines include the procedures and technologies around which organizations are constructed and through which they operate. Argyris and Schon (1978) define two levels of organizational learning, both of which involve detecting and correcting errors in routine. Single-loop learning occurs when the error is corrected without changing the organization's existing norms, policies, or objectives. Double-loop learning occurs when the error is corrected by modifying an organization's norms, policies, or objectives. Thus, both single- and double-loop organizational learning are concerned with organizational efficiency—the maintenance, improvement, and mastery of routine. Single-loop learning restores routine (efficiency), while double loop learning improves or modifies it.

Some companies struggle with innovation, wondering why their continuous improvement programs seem to work smoothly to increase efficiency, while they are unable to sustain meaningful innovation programs. Some researchers and practitioners focus on topics such as "management of technology", viewing information technology as the main source of innovation. However, an organization's success in new technology development and adoption is heavily stymied, not by its technical ability, but its managerial incompetence: its inability to deliberately change its routines as necessary to make the new development or adoption an implemented success, that is, demonstrate adaptability.

Among consulting companies, knowledge management is largely synonymous with knowledge *sharing*. Here, knowledge management consists of converting tacit knowledge (knowledge in individuals' heads) into explicit knowledge (code-able information suitable for electronic storage and transmission) and developing IT systems to spread this knowledge organization-wide so everyone has access to it. Such knowledge-sharing systems require organizations to abandon the "command and control" method of managing, in which knowledge is the cherished and jealously guarded property of managers, and where employees are told exactly what to do, and are provided with the minimum amount of information they need to do it.

However, although knowledge sharing makes more knowledge available to more people, the mere availability of information is insufficient if the goal is to increase efficiency, flexibility, and adaptability. Information must also be put to use, and additional information beyond what is coded in the IT system may be required. We suggest that this requires the adoption of a shared-thinking process for using knowledge innovatively. This approach is consistent with Weick and Roberts' (1993) concept of "collective mind" in which members of an organizational system correlate their actions with those of all the others in the system to achieve optimal results.

Superior organizational performance—whether based on efficiency, adaptability or flexibility—is becoming increasingly dependent on superior thinking. While assets such as labor, capital, processes, and technology continue to be important, the organization's ability to think is now widely recognized as crucial. Innovative organizations make a habit of *using* knowledge creatively. It is true that some organizations derive competitive edge by being superior in efficiency—in continuously restoring and improving routines. Toyota, for example, employs total quality management efficiency tools such as Six Sigma and Lean

Manufacturing to find root causes of errors and reduce waste. Others have their own methods; Procter and Gamble is famous for its willingness to devote years of painstaking analysis to understand what went wrong with company routine procedures when rare failures occur (Swasy, 1993). The methodology we propose offers the opportunity to *operationalize* organizational learning, to make it more than just an academic concept. That is, one might ask, "just how do you *do* double-loop learning?" We suggest that people can learn to do this by becoming skilled in the innovative thinking process and tools we describe.

Adaptability and flexibility are not primarily based on either efficient knowledge sharing (making information widely available) or organizational learning (detecting and correcting errors to restore or modify routine). Adaptability depends on deliberately seeking out new problems, trends, technologies, and information and using them to create new routines, products, and services. Toshiba, for example, deliberately develops adaptability in its employees. Newly hired R&D scientists and engineers start their careers in the sales department to learn that innovation begins by discovering "the problems of the customer" and to develop their problem-finding skills (Basadur, 1992). The 3M Corporation establishes strategic goals for inducing adaptability; for example, one goal is that 30% of the company's products must be new every five years.

Flexibility depends on turning unexpected events, including crises, into opportunities or at least restoring equilibrium quickly. Such opportunities may simply consist of achieving goodwill from the public or even inventing new ways to avoid such a crisis in the future. An excellent example is the Tylenol tragedy in Chicago a few years ago, when several people suddenly died after consuming Tylenol pain relieving capsules. Johnson & Johnson, the manufacturer, quickly removed all Tylenol products from store shelves, reassured the public, confined the danger to the local area, and discovered the root of the problem. Someone had deliberately injected a lethal poison into Tylenol capsules in some stores. The company proceeded to pioneer new innovative tamper-proof packaging that the rest of the industry has since adopted. The public was left with a very favorable image of Johnson & Johnson. The company demonstrated it was both expert about the products it manufactures, and highly skilled in using its knowledge for innovative problem solving.

OD Interventions Supporting Creativity Efforts

Recently Skilton and Dooley (2010) have suggested that structural interventions, such as introducing new members into teams working together over several projects, can support ongoing creativity. Butler (1981) distinguished between two different types of dominant coalitions that top organizations may structure. One is more rigid, permitting little room for the expression of deviant points of view, while the other is looser and allows more risk taking and the emergence of new idea leaders, which are required for innovation. Group development process interventions, which build cohesiveness, also support creativity. Cohen, Whitmyer, and Funk (1960) demonstrated that more cohesive groups produced more unique ideas on work-related problems than non-cohesive groups. However, Angle (1989) suggested that unless an open, confrontive climate for conflict resolution exists within an innovation team, group cohesiveness is negatively related to the level of innovation. Organizational development interventions have also helped to ensure the successful development and implementation of new technology innovations. For example, Wang, Chou, and Jiang found that group cohesiveness significantly improved group performance in organizations that underwent ERP (Enterprise Resource Planning) implementation (Wang, Chou & Jiang, 2005).

OD Supporting Adaptability

Many of these interventions can improve organizations in the short term. However, many seemingly successful and permanent changes regress or disappear within a relatively short time after their implementation. This is sometimes called the fade-out effect (Hinrichs, 1978). This suggests that, beyond changing a single organizational unit or introducing a single, successful intervention, a large organization must understand several strategic considerations in starting, orchestrating, and sustaining an OD effort. For example, training as an individual or team process intervention succeeds only when managers institutionalize the implementation and daily use of the new skills by providing appropriate counseling, coaching, and, above all, modeling of the new skills. Top managers must look at what they practice vs. what they preach (Beer, Eisenstat, & Spector, 1990). They must be proficient in the new skills. New organizational designs, reward systems, performance management systems, and control and accounting systems must also be implemented to ensure employees will use these skills on the job. One of the most obvious examples of the lack of understanding of this systems approach to managing is the inconsistency between organizational rewards and desired behaviors (Kerr, 1995). Table 26.2 details these examples.

Early OD approaches centered on embedding humanistic ideals and values, including personal development, interpersonal competency, participation, commitment, satisfaction, and work democracy (French & Bell, 1999; Mirvis, 1998), into the workplace. Sinangil and Avallone (2001) describe the key defining words most often used during the early years of OD as change of beliefs, attitudes, and values. Some early researchers nevertheless recognized that OD should be viewed from a broader perspective. Bennis (1969) defined OD as a complex educational strategy intended to change the beliefs, attitudes, values, and structure of organizations so they can better adapt to change. Burke (1982) viewed OD as a planned process of change in an organization's *culture* through the utilization of behavioral science technology, research, and theory. More recently, Austin and Bartunek (2003) described OD as an evolving

TABLE 26.2 Examples of Inconsistencies Between Desired Behaviors and Reward Systems.

We hope for.....	But we reward....
• Long term growth; environmental responsibility	• Quarterly earnings
• Setting challenging "stretch" objectives	• Achieving goals: "making the numbers"
• Commitment to total quality	• Shipping on schedule, even with defects
• Teamwork and collaboration	• The best team members
• Innovative thinking and risk-taking	• Proven methods and not making mistakes
• Development of people skills	• Technical achievements and accomplishments
• Employee involvement and empowerment	• Tight control over operations and resources
• High achievement	• Another year's effort

field, and emphasized that OD, at its core, involved the promotion of change and was really one of many approaches to the larger field of study now called planned change. Recent literature contains several definitions which emphasize OD's focus on planned, systematic change, based on the behavioral sciences, with the ultimate goal of improving organizational performance and effectiveness. For Woodman (1993, 1995), OD means creating adaptive organizations capable of repeatedly transforming and reinventing themselves as needed, in order to remain effective. Church (2007) defines OD as a field of professional practice focused on facilitating organizational change and improvement. Beer (1980) defined organizational development as:

> "a system-wide process of data collection, diagnosis, action planning, intervention, and evaluation aimed at developing the organization's self-renewing capacity".

In addition, several authors have suggested the need for OD to address the larger business environment and help businesses accomplish strategic goals (e.g. Seo, Putnam, & Bartunek, 2001).

We believe OD experts have not developed a clear, definite, and complete change-making process to assist in organizational adaptability and to understand change making as a learnable skill. While there is some recognition that individual interventions are not sufficient to create sustained change, and while there is some evidence that progress is being made by organizational and management scholars, the organizational development and change literature remains largely underdeveloped, particularly with regard to its connection to organizational creativity (Pettigrew, Woodman, & Cameron, 2001). As Hodgkinson (2008) noted, challenges in translating strategy into action exist because employees aren't sufficiently equipped to adapt to organizational change initiatives in ways that yield positive individual and collective outcomes. The dominant view of OD and change continues to be one of discrete interventions, tools, or episodes where a change is planned and implemented (Hodgkinson, 2008; Pettigrew, Woodman, & Moore, 2001; Weick & Quinn, 1999; Worren, Ruddle, & Moore, 1999). Interventions are perceived as the activities:

> "through which changes in elements of an organizational work setting are implemented" (*Robertson, Roberts, & Porras, 1993*).

In this interventionist view, OD is designed to focus on specific organizational components that will in turn encourage the adoption of desired new behaviors (Robertson et al., 1993).

Furthermore, when OD researchers such as Schein (Edmonson, 1996) discuss process approaches to OD, they appear to be referring not to a change-making process with change-making skills, but instead to the flow of planned change from the work setting to individual behavior to organizational outcomes when interventions are orchestrated. The goal of such so-called process models is to guide successful organizational change efforts (Armenakis & Bedeian, 1999; Robertson et al., 1993). For example, the consequences of such a planned change activity might include an increase in individual organizational citizenship behaviors and pro-social behaviors (Robertson et al., 1993). However, this is vastly different from our meaning of "process". We advocate a process of organizational creativity with embedded creativity skills at all levels and across all disciplines to effect ongoing change making as an everyday way of life. This is not what is meant by OD researchers when they state that they are taking a "process approach to OD". Also, very importantly, our process equips internal organizational members with creative self-sufficiency, so they may make change without interventionist help from the outside.

In summary, OD has always been interventionist (interventions are discrete, and intended to fix problems), toward the implementation of humanistic ideals. While there is talk of "change process", there is no such process. In our approach, OD is a continuous process of finding and solving problems and implementing solutions, which is synonymous with our Organizational Creativity process. Without a precise change-making process that people can follow, and the necessary attitudinal, behavioral, and cognitive skills needed to make the process work, organizations cannot mainstream adaptability, that is, make it an ongoing routine way of organizational life. Many OD and creativity interventions have failed because they were not embedded in an organizational creativity process and lack requisite skills (e.g., Basadur & Robinson, 1993). Some consultants provide idea generation services to help companies create new product concepts, while others help companies evaluate existing ideas and move them through to commercialization (e.g., Cooper's 1993 stage gate process). The approach we advocate encapsulates both types of interventions within a complete organizational creativity process including all the stages necessary from initial opportunity discovery through definition, optimization, and implementation.

ORGANIZATIONAL CREATIVITY—A DIFFERENT APPROACH TO ADAPTABILITY

Pettigrew, Woodman, and Cameron (2001) concluded with two calls for future OD research. The first is a call to study change as a continuous process, rather than as detached episodes. The second echoes Simon's call to deliver more "how-to" knowledge as opposed to "what is" knowledge. We present a process of organizational creativity that addresses both of these calls.

Organizational Creativity can be defined as a system of knowledge, process, the skills needed to make the process work, tools (such as OD interventions and creativity techniques such as brainstorming), and an appreciation of process style differences (Basadur & Gelade, 2006). Unlike the traditional OD approach, which lacks a strategic perspective and relies on single or multiple interventions to change making, Organizational Creativity involves highly skilled employees at all levels constantly executing a process of finding relevant internal and external problems, solving them, and implementing the solutions. In effect, this defines Organizational Creativity as "implemented change". Such a change-making process is shown in Figure 26.6, beginning with problem finding, then cycling through problem defining and solving and solution implementing.

The most effective organizations know that creative attitudes, behaviors and cognitive skills and a creative process are necessary for successful sustained implemented change (Kriegesmann, Kley, & Schwering, 2005; Stein, 1975). Real, sustained, organizational change comes as a result of a structured process of applied creativity and attitudinal, behavioral, and cognitive skills employed by organizational members and modeled by leadership.

Discussing creativity can be quite difficult because no single, agreed-upon definition exists, and researchers have taken vastly different approaches to its understanding. We focus on demonstrating a circular process of creativity that integrates attitudinal, behavioral,

Environment

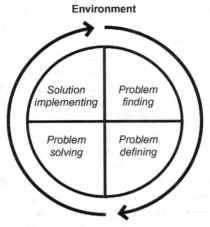

FIGURE 26.6   Creative activity in an organization.

and cognitive skills as part of a continuous system of adaptability (Figure 26.6). We describe creativity in organizations as a continuous process of deliberate problem finding, problem solving, and solution implementation (Kabanoff & Rossiter, 1994) and attitudes, behaviors, and cognitive skills that enable the process to work (Basadur, Graen, & Green, 1982; Basadur, 1994). Problem finding means continuously finding new problems to address. This includes addressing things that are going wrong, but also anticipating and seeking out current or future changes, trends, challenges, and opportunities. Problem finding also includes taking the time to explore problems in depth rather than merely finding quick solutions or "fixes" (Senge, Kleiner, Roberts, Ross, & Smith, 1994). This permits the discovery of not only underlying issues, but also new opportunities and recognition of the interconnectedness of decisions within the organization. This recognition is the essence of systems thinking and the starting point for making long-term, permanent improvements. Problem solving means developing new, useful solutions to identified problems. Solution implementation means making new solutions succeed. Implementation usually leads the organization to find new problems to solve. As Runco (2004) noted, creativity is not only reactive—a response to problems and challenges—but also proactive, as a contributor to change. Thus new problems arise as the system and its environment react to each newly implemented solution. Therefore, organizational creativity can be understood as the fundamental driver of, and virtually synonymous with, adaptability, including a circular process of continuously finding, defining, and solving important problems and implementing new solutions which represent valuable changes that enable the organization to succeed (Figure 26.6).

This approach also removes any distinction between creativity and innovation (despite the views of some researchers, who distinguish between creativity as the generation of an idea and innovation as its implementation). Here, creativity is defined as a multi-stage complete and continuous process driven by attitudinal, behavioral, and cognitive creativity skills at each stage, including problem generation and formulation, idea (solution) generation, and solution implementation. These skills are discussed in detail later in this chapter.

In addition, there are various creativity tools which can be applied in the various stages. However such tools are of little value, and may even be harmful, without the pre-requisite creativity skills to apply them. An example of such a tool is "brainstorming", which is frequently misused due to lack of skill and misunderstanding by researchers who lack experience in real world situations (Basadur & Basadur, 2009). We position most OD interventions as tools which can be employed within our organizational creativity process, but which are not, in and of themselves, useful for creating permanent change.

Some of the above intervention tools (Table 26.1) are very compatible with the problem finding and problem definition stages of our organizational creativity process (Figure 26.6); others within the problem solving and implementation stages. For example, diagnostic interventions like survey feedback or the confrontation meeting are tools for problem generation and formulation; used regularly, they help anticipate and unearth organizational issues that might otherwise remain buried. Other tools, such as group development (or team-building) process interventions, help solve identified problems, such as slow project completion, by improving the way people work together. If employee development is an important problem to solve, structural interventions such as job enrichment may be useful. Structural interventions can also help implement other intervention solutions. For example, installing a new reward system like the Scanlon plan (White 1979), a tool intended to encourage employees to use their creativity by sharing the profits from their productivity improvements, can cement the transfer of creativity skills learned in training to the job. Finally, individual interventions such as counseling and coaching help in the implementation phase of the organizational creativity process. For junior managers who have been given creativity leadership training (individual intervention) to work in a flattened organizational design (structural intervention), it can be helpful for senior managers to provide counseling and coaching (individual intervention) to "cement" the training and ensure implementation.

Effective organizations know how to establish a well-understood process and set of skills for adaptability. They also create a positive climate toward problems and seek them out as opportunities for disruptive change (Mott, 1972). As solutions are implemented, new problems (or opportunities for innovation) are discovered. A positive mindset towards creativity begins with a positive attitude towards *problem finding*, meaning the behavior of continuously and deliberately discovering and formulating new and useful problems to be solved.

THE FOUR DISTINCT STAGES OF AN ORGANIZATIONAL CREATIVITY PROCESS

The evolution of models of multi-stage creative thinking and problem solving processes began with Wallas's (1926) four main stages: preparation, incubation, illumination, and verification. Osborn (1963), and Parnes, Noller, & Biondi (1977) evolved a linear, five step, creative, problem solving model: fact finding, problem defining, idea finding, solution finding, and acceptance finding with divergent (ideation) and convergent (evaluation) thought in each step. Amabile (1988) identified five stages: presentation, preparation, generation, validation, and assessment. Mumford and his colleagues (e.g., Mumford, Mobley, Uhlman, Reiter-Palmon, & Doares, 1991) identified eight core processes commonly used in creative problem solving, beginning with problem identification and ending with implementation planning and solution monitoring. Finke and her colleagues (Finke, 1990; Finke & Bettle, 1996; Finke, Ward, & Smith, 1992; Ward, Smith, & Finke, 1999) proposed that in general, creativity consists of a cycle of generation and exploration to meet specific goals or task demands. Runco and Chand (1995) provided a two tier model in which primary processes (e.g., ideation and evaluation) interact with secondary processes (e.g., motivation and knowledge) to produce novel products.

Reiter-Palmon and Robinson (2009) suggest that the various process models described above all include as a first step a process in which a problem is recognized, identified, and constructed, and that various terms have been used to describe this first step, including problem definition, problem identification, problem recognition, and problem construction. For clarity, they suggest using the term *problem identification and construction* to refer to this first step. This is where the problem is formulated. We suggest something different. We suggest that all of the above models tend to pre-suppose that a problem, task or goal requiring creativity already exists and that a creative process is subsequently applied (which may include problem construction and identification). This reduces these models to mere tools, or problem-solving interventions or episodes, which start with a problem and end with a solution. We offer a more complete process of creativity which begins before a problem is available to be formulated (Basadur, Graen, & Green, 1982; Basadur, Graen, & Wakabayashi, 1990).

Figure 26.6 outlines a continuous circular process that begins with the deliberate seeking out (*generating*) of new problems and opportunities. The second stage of the process is *conceptualizing*, or formulating, defining, and constructing a newly generated problem. In the third stage, *problem solving*, evaluation and selection of solution ideas takes place, while the fourth stage results in *solution implementation*. The process then begins anew, as every implemented solution (action) results in the opportunity to discover (generate) new problems and opportunities. For example, the automobile's invention provided not only a new solution to an old problem (improving transportation) but created many brand-new problems (e.g., pollution, energy, and accidents). Each stage of the process requires specific attitudinal, behavioral, and cognitive skills in order to be successfully completed.

This multistage process and skills approach contrasts sharply with research that confines creative thinking merely to generating ideas to presented problems using techniques such as "brainstorming". Such research has dominated the literature from the 1950s (see review by Basadur, 1994). Such limited process conceptions do not reflect real world situations, and thus their findings are not helpful to practitioners attempting to enact real change (Sternberg, O'Hara, & Lubart, 1997). In terms of the practitioner approach to creativity, Skilton and Dooley (2010) report that OD consultants discovered that attempting a "short burst" brainstorming intervention was ineffective in making any meaningful change in the thinking skills of the team members. Recent literature emphasizes more complete conceptions of creativity (Kabanoff & Rossiter, 1994; Rickards, 1994). Such complete models include not only multiple stages (beyond simply solving presented problems) but other important individual, group, and organizational variables affecting creative performance such as motivation, cohesiveness, environment, linkage to goals, and specific skills, behaviors and attitudes. After reviewing the growth of cognitive models of multi-stage creative thinking and problem solving processes, Kabanoff and Rossiter (1994) defined applied creativity as a *process* occurring in a real-world, industrial, organizational, or social context; pertaining to the finding or solving of complex problems; and having an actual behavioral creative product or plan as the final result. More specifically, our approach focuses on modeling creativity as a cognitive, multi-stage, problem-solving process consistent with Kabanoff and Rossiter's (1994) definition, but we include the process as part of a more complete system requiring attitudinal, behavioral, and cognitive skills to execute the process.

While effective innovation requires strong performance in each of the four stages of the creativity process, our research has found that individuals, teams, and organizations may prefer some stages of the creative process more than others. We call these preferences *styles*, and suggest that effective leaders must learn to synchronize the different creativity styles (Basadur, 2004). In teams, for example, the members must learn to combine their individual preferences and skills in complementary ways. Basadur and Head (2001) showed that heterogeneous teams composed of people with different preferences outperformed homogeneous teams whose members had similar preferences.

CLIMATE, MOTIVATION, AND STRUCTURE

Organizational creativity has also been studied in terms of perception of climate, motivation and strategy. Organizational climate has been defined in several ways. Ivancevich, Konopaske, and Matteson (2005) suggest that it is a set of properties of the work environment, perceived directly or indirectly by employees, that is assumed to be a major force in influencing employee behavior. According to Reichers and Schneider (1990), the concept of climate can be understood as an individual perception and cognitive representation of the work environment and also as a set of shared perceptions of "the way things are around here". Hunter, Bedell, and Mumford (2007) have reviewed numerous approaches to climate assessment for creativity. For example, KEYS is an employee opinion survey that assesses the climate for creativity and innovation that exists in a work group, division, or organization (Amabile, Conti, Coon, Lazenby, & Herron, 1996). It measures specific management practices that impact the work environment. It can be used in a number of ways, including jump starting creativity, communicating the importance of creativity and innovation within an organization, and as an assessment preceding any type of innovation or change intervention. KEYS assesses six managerial practices that support the work environment: organizational encouragement; an organizational culture that encourages creativity through the fair and constructive judgment of ideas; reward and recognition for creative work; supervisory encouragement; work group support; sufficient resources; access to appropriate resources; challenging work—a sense of having to work hard on challenging tasks and important projects; freedom—deciding what work to do; and a sense of control over one's work. In addition, KEYS assesses two management practices that inhibit the work environment: organizational impediments and unrealistic workload pressure.

Ekvall (1996) developed *CCQ, Creative Climate Questionnaire*, to explain creativity within an organization. Studies utilizing CCQ confirmed that innovative organizations in terms of products, services methods and policies exhibit a different climate to those that are conservative. Furthermore, Ekvall (1996) showed that the change-oriented leadership style of managers within an organization influences the climate, thus promoting creativity.

Both the CCQ and KEYS surveys can be considered as discrete organization development interventions under the diagnostic classification of Table 26.1 and as tools for the problem finding and problem definition stages of the organizational creativity process in Figure 26.6.

Kwasniewska and Necka (2004) demonstrated that the level an employee occupies in the organizational hierarchy plays a role in the way he or she perceives the climate for creativity in the organization. It was concluded that managers perceive the organizational climate as significantly more conducive to creativity than non-managers do.

Basadur and Hausdorf (1996) and Basadur, Taggar, and Pringle (1999) identified three specific attitudinal variables that help describe an organization's climate for creativity. Scales to measure these organizational attitudes were labeled; "Valuing New Ideas", "Belief That Creativity Is Not Only For A Select Few", and "Not Feeling Too Busy For New Ideas". These scales measure the extent to which organizations are perceived to truly value new ideas, avoid creating negative stereotypes of "creative people", and prevent employees from feeling too busy for new ideas, respectively. This research suggested that employees are more likely to engage in creative thinking and to try to improve their creative performance if they value new ideas, believe that increased creative behavior and performance is not the sole domain of a select few, and feel they are *not* too busy for new ideas.

Motivation

Research has also been conducted explaining creativity in terms of motivation. Amabile's componential model of creativity (Amabile, 1983, 1988) consists of three components—domain-relevant skills, creativity-relevant skills, and task motivation—that are all essential for creative performance. Each of the three components is necessary for anything creative to result, and as the amount of the components present increases so does the creative output. In Csikszentmihályi's concept of *flow*, when individuals are completely absorbed in the tasks they are working on, creativity resides in the degree to which individuals find their work tasks challenging but within their skill level (Csikszentmihályi, 1996; Csikszentmihályi & Csikszentmihályi, 1988). Early evidence suggested that intrinsic motivation is conducive to creativity and extrinsic motivation is detrimental (Hennessy & Amabile, 1988; McGraw, 1978; Rigby, Deci, Patrick, & Ryan, 1992) and therefore organizations that foster and support intrinsic motivation will encourage creativity by providing the necessary resources and support, and create a work environment that seeks out, develops, and implements creative ideas to nurture creativity, while those that promote extrinsic motivation undermine creativity.

However this simplistic hydraulic view of the relationship between intrinsic and extrinsic rewards and creativity has sparked further research that has indicated that the relationship between creativity and motivation is considerably more complex. Although some studies have found evidence that contingent rewards undermine creativity (Amabile, Hill, & Hennessy, 1994), Eisenberger and colleagues (Eisenberger & Armeli, 1997; Eisenberger & Rhoades, 2001; Eisenberger & Selbst, 1994) demonstrated that the promise of reward can have a positive impact on creativity. In these situations, the extrinsic rewards may act in concert with one's intrinsic motivation, resulting in what Amabile (1993) calls *motivational synergy*. While many researchers continue to believe individuals must be inherently interested in the problem or opportunity in question and intrinsically motivated to generate a solution (Shalley & Zhou, 2008), the question of the role of extrinsic motivation and whether rewards promote or inhibit creativity in the workplace is still not clear (Zhou & Shalley, 2003).

In their review, Hill and Amabile (1993) concluded that the most effective motivation may depend upon multiple factors, including the stage of the creative process that the work

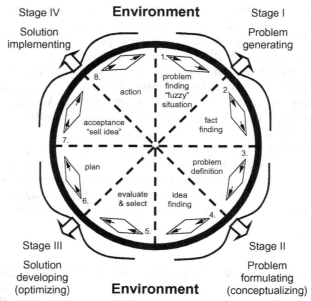

FIGURE 26.7   The organizational change-making process.

is in, and the nature of the person doing the work. According to self-determination theory (Deci & Ryan, 2000; Ryan & Deci, 2000), a person's motivation to perform a particular behavior can range on a continuum from *amotivation* (unwillingness), through external motivation (passive compliance), to intrinsic motivation (active personal commitment). What determines individual motivation is the degree to which the meaningfulness of the activity has been internalized and integrated into the individual's sense of self (Ryan & Deci, 2000). It may be that various types of motivation would be helpful to move people through the four stages of the organizational creativity process that we propose (Figures 26.6 and 26.7). Within this process, it is likely that most individuals are naturally interested in performing some of the necessary process behaviors but not all of them (Basadur, Beuk, & Monllor , 2010). If so, then the creative process activities they prefer are done for their own sake and, therefore, any external rewards given for performance of those activities would seemingly add little additional motivational value. However, it is also likely that individuals are naturally more closely inclined towards being *amotivated* by some of the process activities. In order to motivate individuals to perform these activities conscientiously, it may be necessary to use extrinsic rewards. It may also be that when people are extrinsically motivated to perform tasks for which they already have a pre-existing intrinsic predisposition, creative output can increase through an additive mechanism, as suggested by activity engagement theory (Higgins & Trope, 1990). It is perhaps best to consider the relationship of intrinsic and extrinsic motivation to creative performance is not "either–or", but rather a combinative relationship where both are required if one is to optimally execute the multi-stage creative process.

However, we also propose a radically different explanation of the relationship between creativity and motivation. There is evidence that motivation is a *result* (outcome) of creative activity *not the antecedent*. Support for this is point of view is provided in the next section.

Motivation and Commitment are Outcomes of Creative Activity

Creativity as a means for motivation is an important idea. Establishing adaptability as a daily, continuous process of problem finding and defining, problem solving, and solution implementation to complement efficiency increases employees commitment and motivation. Early animal research and later studies on humans showed that curiosity, activity, and exploration are enjoyed by organisms for their own sake. People develop negative attitudes toward repetitive tasks and experience fatigue and boredom. Permitted to engage in finding and solving problems, workers become motivated and desire even more participation in creative activity. They also work harder at perfecting their routine jobs to increase quality and quantity and reduce costs, thus increasing organizational efficiency and short-term organizational effectiveness. Creative activity also stimulates team-building as people help each other to solve problems. This connection between creative activity and employee motivation is supported by the motivational literature in industrial and organizational psychology. For example, two important motivational need sets—the need for competence, and the need for curiosity and activity—provide the most direct explanations of how creativity motivates people (Berlyne, 1967; White, 1959). When people face new, challenging situations, their need for competence can be satisfied by performing creatively. Many people find that exercising their curiosity and exploring new things is intrinsically motivating. Herzberg, Mausner, and Snyderman's (1959) research also suggested that the way to truly motivate people at work was "job enrichment", or redesigning jobs to require creativity. Neher (1991), although critical of Maslow's motivation theory, supports Maslow's (1954) contention that although lower level motivations can provide important fulfillments and satisfactions, offering people the opportunity to satisfy their higher level needs for self-esteem and for self-actualization through work accomplishment is the best way to motivate them. Encouraging organizational members to use their creativity to seek out work-related challenges of their own (problem finding) and achieve them successfully (problem solving and solution implementation) helps satisfy both higher level needs.

McClelland (1951, 1961) identified the need for achievement as a primary driving force for motivating people in organizations. McClelland showed that a high need for achievement is characterized by a strong desire to assume personal responsibility for finding solutions to problems, and this can be increased by stimulating people to set challenging work goals for themselves. Thus, by giving employees the encouragement and opportunity to find and solve their own challenging problems, and implement their own solutions, organizations can provide intrinsically rewarding work and tap into the need for achievement for motivation.

Problem-finding activity is also the key to other theories of motivation. The goal setting theory of Locke and Latham (1990) showed that when people are given a chance to choose their own goals (problem finding), and the more clear and specific the goals (the problem-definition aspect of problem finding), the more motivated they become to achieve those goals.

Strategy

Ettlie (1984) argued that unique strategy and structural arrangements are necessary for radical innovation, and Kao (1997) emphasized that strategy and creativity must be interconnected permanently. Innovation and innovative capabilities have become important aspects that are necessary in formulating the business strategy of an organization (Mumford, Scott, Gaddis, & Strange, 2002). These things require top–down impetus and strategic alignment. Basadur's (1992) field research found that some Japanese companies use training and a well-developed infrastructure to make creative activity important, and strategically align it with organizational goals. Programs such as a reward-based Employee Suggestion System (ESS) reinforce the importance of creative activity to the company, while clearly articulated company goals result in a close alignment of the system's activity with strategic corporate needs. Managers learn how to influence their subordinates toward including problems which are related to specific goals and objectives for their departments. Managers' performance appraisals are also based in part on their ability to get their subordinates to perform well in the ESS. Other systems, including Quality Circle group activity and Management by Objectives (MBO), are integrated with the ESS. Typically, a manager's objectives will include helping people create and implement suggestions. This emphasis on involving subordinates in creating new ideas is part of the long-range process of management. The belief is that if people are encouraged to use their thinking power on a habitual daily basis, major tangible benefits will accrue to the organization in the long run.

The major discovery of Basadur's (1992) research is that Japanese organizations demonstrate a great deal of knowledge about inducing employee creativity through deliberate strategic means. Top Japanese organizations recognize, emphasize, support, and induce problem finding which is elevated to at least equal priority to problem solving and solution implementation. They recognize all three as separate, important activities—consistent with research that suggests that all three activities need to be nurtured and managed to achieve organizational creativity. Later in this chapter, we will discuss how organizations can induce creativity by setting strategic measurable goals requiring creativity, and including these goals in a program by which the creativity process and skills described in this chapter are learned by employees and applied to achieve the goals within an infrastructure which makes the application possible.

Similar to the OD and creativity interventions described in the earlier part of this chapter, the climate, motivation, and strategy approaches to creativity described above will not result in permanent change unless they are embedded within a process of change making that incorporates the attitudinal, behavioral, and cognitive skills that are required to implement the process. We are making a strong argument that organizational creative performance requires mastery of skills to execute a complete creative process as in Figure 26.6. We argue that none of the other approaches provide the necessary skills. So, what are the skills?

HOW ORGANIZATIONS CAN BECOME SKILLED IN ORGANIZATIONAL CREATIVITY

In order to be considered a resource, an asset has to be *controllable* by an organization (Barney, 1991). Given the creativity "cottage industry" described by Mumford (2000), and the fact that the existing "best practice" for developing creativity in organizations is to screen for and hire creative individuals and "hope for the best", it is fair to say that creative ability is far from a controllable asset for most organizations. Many shortcomings in attitudinal, behavioral and cognitive creativity skills plague individuals, teams, and organizations.

As detailed in Basadur (2004), problem finding is a foreign concept for many people. Conceptual skills in defining problems are lacking and much time is wasted "working on the wrong problem". One of the most difficult creative skills to master for most managers is how to define problems accurately before impatiently leaping to action. This includes new IT projects, where often insufficient effort is devoted to defining the main business problem that the IT solution is intended to solve or the how the project supports the company's strategic objectives. Skills in engaging the potential users of the new IT solution in defining the problem in their own terms are often lacking, leading to a great deal of reworking of the solution when the gap is subsequently discovered between what was really wanted and what was actually delivered. The lion's share of the effort is usually devoted to developing the solution (the new IT system) and then insufficient effort is also devoted to implementation, ensuring that the employees are capable of using the new IT technology.

Even after finding and defining problems, some people find it difficult to solve them creatively and imaginatively. Some individuals are also critical of new ideas, which can prevent productive thinking. While many people may be able to implement routine solutions to routine problems, few can implement creative solutions to new, non-programmed problems. Teamwork is also often uncreative. Group members are unable to communicate clearly in simple terms, for example. Unaware of variations in individual thinking styles, groups fail to synchronize these differences, jump into "solving the problem" without first considering what the real problem is, and then flounder. Meeting leaders steer toward their own points of view rather than facilitating the group to work open-mindedly and cohesively. The design of many organizations remains along bureaucratic, functional lines—a design that itself minimizes creativity. Jobs are programmed for maximum control, highest quality, and lowest cost per unit. Creativity skills and change-making are limited to short-term quick-fixes during emergencies. For organizations without a positive mindset toward creativity, problems and changes stemming from new technology, customer tastes, and foreign competition are viewed as irritants that disrupt well-functioning, established routines, despite the fact that the essence of adaptability and the first phase of the creative process is problem finding. Basadur, Graen, and Green (1982), demonstrated that many of these shortcomings can be overcome by developing specific skills. Training to build these skills is based on two central concepts:

1. **change-making is a process with distinctly different stages:** In practice, it is useful to break the four-stage change process shown in Figure 26.6 into a circular process of eight smaller steps as shown in Figure 26.7. These steps include problem finding and fact finding, which collectively make up "problem generation", or Stage 1; problem definition and idea finding ("problem formulation", or Stage 2); idea evaluation and selection, and planning for implementation ("problem solving", or Stage 3); and gaining acceptance and taking action ("solution implementation", or Stage 4), and
2. **an Ideation–Evaluation process occurs in each stage:** It is vital to use an ideation-evaluation mini-process within each of the eight smaller steps across all four stages as shown in Figure 26.7. The mini-process is shown in Figure 26.8.

Three distinct skills are needed to execute this two-step mini process effectively (Basadur & Finkbeiner, 1985): deferral of judgment, active divergence, and active convergence. By separating divergent thinking from convergent thinking, deferral of judgment resists the tendency to prematurely evaluate and select options, and encourages active

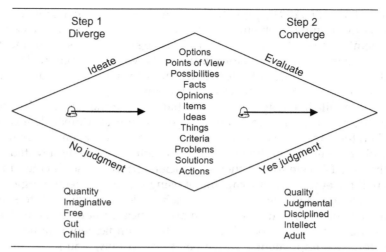

FIGURE 26.8   Ideation–evaluation: A sequential creative thinking mini-process.

divergence. Deferral of judgment also prevents people from leaping to solutions before properly formulating problems, and helps them to separate assumptions from facts. Active divergence enables many options to be generated without judging or analyzing them. Active convergence, which resists the tendency to linger in divergent thinking, then selects and acts on the options that ultimately lead to implementation of change. These three skills all have attitudinal, behavioral, and cognitive components.

BECOMING COMPETENT

It is easier to understand the need for a systematic process to achieve organizational creativity and adaptability (as modeled in Figure 26.7) than it is to become skilled in using such a process. Learning how to use the process involves developing skills in finding, defining, solving, and implementing new opportunities. Most managers have undergone rigorous training in analytical, optimizing, and efficiency thinking processes. However, creativity requires a different set of skills in which competency must now be built belatedly. Building competency has three main components:

1. competency in executing the process as a whole,
2. competency in respecting and helping synchronize different styles in the process, and
3. competency in executing each step and stage of the process.

Organizations which have successfully achieved this set of competencies are described in Basadur (1995) and the competencies are described more fully as follows.

Competency in executing the process as a whole includes being able to distinguish the different steps from each other; for example executing, communicating, and separating (1) problem finding activity from (2) problem defining activity and from (3) solution development activity and from (4) implementing activity. It also includes avoiding unconsciously leapfrogging the process steps, such as jumping backwards from discovering a fresh new problem (step 1) into immediate action (step 8) only to discover later that the problem was not what it seemed to be at all and regretting the time wasted by not permitting the process unfold naturally from 1 *through* 8. This was mentioned earlier in the chapter using the example of IT projects not being defined skillfully at the outset.

Competency in respecting and synchronizing different process styles includes understanding how the creative process depends upon different ways of apprehending knowledge and understanding and utilizing knowledge, however apprehended. Not only are both necessary for creative performance, but frustration and inefficiency in working together can be avoided. For example, if some individuals on a team prefer stage 2, conceptualization, while others prefer stage 4, implementation, it is important that these individuals understand and respect each others' opposite preferred ways of apprehending knowledge (experientially and concretely vs. theoretically and analytically) and of utilizing knowledge (creating options divergently vs. evaluating options convergently).

Competency in executing each step of the process includes competency in executing the ideation–evaluation mini process described previously which combines the three necessary creativity thinking skills within each step:

1. creating options within the step (divergent thinking),
2. evaluating and selecting the most important options within the step (convergent thinking), and
3. skill in separating divergent from convergent thinking within each step (deferral of judgment).

Integrated into early creative problem solving theories and models, including Osborn (1953), Guilford (1967), and Parnes, Noller, and Biondi (1977), these skills in the mini-process have been more deeply explored in more recent empirical research which has described them more completely and identified their attitudinal, behavioral, and cognitive components. For example, in a multi-method, multi-measure field experiment, Basadur et al (1982) identified attitudinal, behavioral, and cognitive effects of training which were readily observable back on the job (along with performance effects). The effects included:

1. attitudinal: more openness to new ideas; more positive reaction when confronted with new unusual ideas,
2. behavioral: more likely to pause to try new, unusual approaches to solving problems; less time spent in negative evaluation while creating options; less likely to jump to conclusions as to the nature of the real problem, and
3. cognitive: increased quantity and quality of options created; more time spent in divergent thought prior to evaluating; more options created prior to selecting one as best.

In a follow-on study, Basadur and Finkbeiner (1985) developed scales to measure two attitudes that they labeled "preference for ideation (preference for active divergence)" and "tendency to (not) make premature evaluations of fledgling ideas (preference for deferral of judgment)". Field research by Runco and Basadur (1993) and Basadur, Runco, and Vega (2000) demonstrated how creativity attitudes and behaviors were associated with cognitive active convergence skills. Puccio, Firestien, Coyle, and Masucci (2006) provided a summary of creativity research relating to attitudes, behaviors, and cognitive skills.

TABLE 26.3   Examples of Deferral of Judgment Skill.

ATTITUDINAL

Tackle problems with an optimistic "can do" attitude.

Enter meetings open to ideas that might disrupt one's own department's routine.

BEHAVIORAL

Visibly value, appreciate, and welcome other points of view.

Avoid making premature, negative judgments of fledgling thoughts.

COGNITIVE

Recognize hidden, unconscious, unwarranted assumptions.

Maintain an awareness that some facts are more difficult to perceive than others.

Understand that some problems require a longer time to solve, and do not expect immediate results.

TABLE 26.4   Examples of Active Divergence Skill.

ATTITUDINAL

Deliberately push oneself to create unusual, thought-provoking ideas.

Turn premature, negative evaluations of ideas into positive challenges to keep the creative process flowing; when others say "We can't because ... " counter with, "How might we ... ?"

BEHAVIORAL

Show leadership in pinpointing changes, trends, problems, and opportunities for improvement throughout the organization.

Share information and ideas freely with other people and departments.

Share "bad news" as quickly as "good news" to aid organizational problem solving.

Facilitate teams to formulate problems in ways that transcend departmental considerations.

COGNITIVE

Search out many different facts and points of view before attempting to define a problem.

Define problems in multiple and novel ways to get a variety of insights.

Additional examples of the attitudinal, behavioral, and cognitive components of each of the three process skills throughout the complete eight step process are provided in Tables 26.3, 26.4, and 26.5 (Basadur, Pringle, Speranzini, & Bacot, 2000; Basadur & Robinson, 1993). It should be noted that there is considerable overlap across attitudinal/behavioral/cognitive distinctions and also across the three process skills distinctions. We do not believe these distinctions are as important as recognizing the various skill components.

The field research by Basadur et al. (1982), provided evidence that unless creativity training was sufficiently impactful to successfully *unfreeze and change* participants, no improvement in creativity skills and performance would be achieved. In other words, the impact of

TABLE 26.5 Examples of Active Convergence Skill.

ATTITUDINAL

Be willing to accept and participate in consensus decisions and move on in the change-making process.

Accept ownership of measures of success of new ideas being implemented.

Take the risk of failing or being criticized for implementing new ideas.

BEHAVIORAL

Take reasonable risks to get action taken within time limits rather than waiting for the "perfect" option to emerge.

Follow up on implementation; do whatever it takes to ensure successful installation of a chosen solution.

COGNITIVE

Select, clarify, and focus on the most significant facts available prior to attempting to define a problem.

Develop unbiased criteria for selecting from among options rather than letting preconceptions or hidden motives sway decisions.

Understand how clear, simple, and specific implementation plans motivate action and overcome inertia.

Understand the importance of including both long- and short-term decision-making criteria.

training must be sufficient to increase the acceptance and practice of the attitudinal, behavioral, and cognitive creativity skills within the multistage creativity process. However, the research also suggested that to *refreeze* the acceptance and use of the new skills, specific strategic structural organizational factors must be established to reinforce and motivate on the job practice (Basadur, 1994). Basadur, Graen, and Scandura (1986) found that the training effects in creativity process and skills as shown in Figure 26.7 on manufacturing engineers were more permanent when they were trained together in intact teams.

Setting up the Internal Environment to Encourage Competency

In the study of the development of expert performance and deliberate practice, the role played by coaches and teachers, and family members in facilitating the eventual success of performers is acknowledged as crucial (Ericsson, 2003; Ericsson, Krampe, & Tesch-Romer, 1993; Salmela & Moraes, 2003). Researchers in this field make it clear that, while the commitment to deliberate practice on the part of the individual is the prerequisite for the development of expertise, the access to knowledgeable and demanding instructors, and parents who re-shape their own personal and social lives to accommodate the demands associated with enabling the continued growth of the performer, is critical. Coaches and teachers structure learning situations so that the performer is always focused on attaining a higher level of performance, and family members make considerable time and financial commitments to ensure the performer remains in an appropriate learning environment (Ericsson, 2003; Salmela & Moraes, 2003).

In terms of the development of creative competency in employees, the internal environment of the organization and its managers must act like the coaches, teachers, and parents that were studied in athletic and artistic expert performance. While the motivation and drive of employees to develop creative thinking skills is critical, management plays the critical roles of instructor and the head of the family. Sacrifices have to be made to structure the environment to enable the continuous growth of employees' expertise, and leaders must monitor the performance and instruct employees using methods that challenge them to reach ever higher levels of competence.

Getting Two for the Price of One

Organizations which provide the right skill training, create the right infrastructure, and participate in and reward continuous problem finding and solution implementing, achieve several outcomes. Some creativity outcomes are directly economically oriented and others are not. As described earlier in this chapter, creativity leads directly to new and improved products and methods; these are economic outcomes associated with adaptability. However, creativity also leads to specific people outcomes which serve as intermediate steps leading to economic outcomes associated with efficiency (Basadur, 1993). Many of these people outcomes are the same as the fundamental aims of the field of OD from its early beginnings. The rest of this chapter will identify these intermediate outcomes, and describe the economic outcomes that result. The first of these people outcomes is motivation.

Despite research showing that most people at work are multi-motivated, the majority of global business is still organized and managed on the overly simplistic "scientific management" concept made popular in the early 20th century by Frederick Taylor (1967). Taylor believed that employees are motivated by one dominant factor—money. Fortunately, using creativity as a formula for motivation can be almost as simple as using money. There are many straightforward ways to encourage people to be creative on the job and achieve a motivated organization. Top Japanese organizations manage their world-class employee suggestions systems to induce creative behavior and to drive creative output including cost savings and new products and procedures. The primary objective of these suggestion systems is not to improve economic outcomes directly but to motivate people and increase their commitment (Basadur, 1992).

Creativity for Job Enrichment

Proactive creative activity, or adaptability, leads to a continuous flow of new methods and new products. However, acceptance of change by employees is assured because they are taking ownership of finding and solving their own problems, and implementing the changes themselves. In effect, they are redesigning their own jobs, which is consistent with a well-documented axiom of social psychology: people do not resist change; they do resist being changed (Coch & French, 1948). Employees enrich their own jobs by being creative.

The Organizational Creative Process as the Transformational Engine

Institutionalizing Organizational Creativity accelerates the identification and solution of problems and opportunities across an organization. These problems and opportunities may originate in either the external or internal environments of the organization, and as they are moved through fact finding, problem definition and then solution

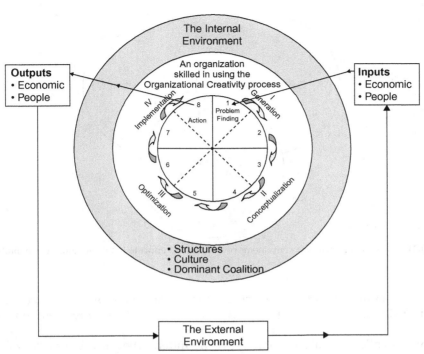

FIGURE 26.9 How the Organizational Creativity process enables an organization to operate as a social and economic open system.

optimization and implementation, the organization is operating as a true open system. How the Organizational Creativity process acts as the transformational engine for an open social and economic system is modeled in Figure 26.9, which inserts the process and skills as the transforming mechanism.

Figure 26.9 illustrates how the Organizational Creativity process provides both economic and people outcomes. As problems and opportunities for change are "inhaled" into Step 1 and then "spun around" the wheel, the resulting implemented change (Step 8) is projected out into the environment as economic and people changes to be mixed in with the environment and cycled back through Step 1. Although some of the economic outcomes result directly from creative activity, the majority are valuable by-products of achieving people outcomes. Creativity leads to such direct economic outcomes as a continuous supply of new and improved products and methods for the organization. It also leads to intrinsically motivated, committed, and job-satisfied people. These people outcomes are valuable in themselves, but more importantly, they lead to the desired economic outcomes.

While adaptability skills are essential, it would be naïve to believe that all that is needed is to train employees in the Organizational Creativity process and the skills needed to make it work. This would only be one third of the battle. To make adaptability performance a normal way of life, an organization must integrate creativity thinking skills and process with

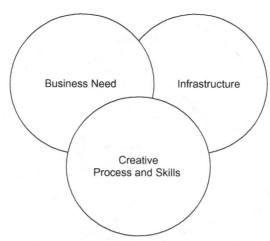

FIGURE 26.10   The three necessary components of a successful effort to institutionalize adaptability.

a clear-cut business need and infrastructure to encourage employees to experience success applying the skills and process. Figure 26.10 illustrates how these three components support each other.

Many worthwhile OD interventions have floundered because the organization lacked at least one of these three components: business need, infrastructure, and change-making process and skills (Basadur & Robinson, 1993). If senior leaders wish to introduce an intervention, they must spell out what specific business need they intend to address (i.e., lower costs, higher sales, fewer defects etc.) to ensure that employees buy in to the intervention and can measure success. An effective infrastructure, such as performance appraisal systems or membership on interdepartmental teams, must be established so that new philosophies and tools are applied regularly. Organizations must also avoid underestimating the effort required to establish people's change-making skills, attitudes, and behaviors, and must provide adequate training.

SUMMARY AND FUTURE RESEARCH

We have offered a new approach to OD in which deep skill in executing creativity as a standard everyday process is the key, equally important to the traditional deep skill of executing traditional efficiency processes. Many executives lack this creative skill and many have turned out to be inadequate leaders, especially in recent times of accelerating change and ambiguity. Some organizations are less effective than others because they value short-term results above all, and reward successful implementers of routines disproportionately. Simply put, organizations favor efficiency at the expense of adaptability.

Many companies still regard innovation as an irritant, something that gets in the way of the "real work". They are content to turn out standard quantities of standard products and achieve the sales, cost, and profit goals for this month, this quarter, this year. Response to greater competition is often to cut staff, reduce costs, lower service levels and, in some cases, lower quality. Too few respond creatively. Sometimes this is because they simply do not know how to go about it. We have tried to demystify various concepts regarding creativity and innovation by integrating them into a single simplified approach focused specifically on improving organizational performance short and long term. Business schools have indoctrinated students with the notion that "maximizing shareholder value" is the holy grail to be pursued. Unfortunately, many managers have taken this to mean "in the short term" rather than "over the long haul". Starbuck (1983) describes such organizations as "action generators" who create behavior programs to repeat their successes and thus are often blind to other events that turn out to be more important. Possibly managers would be willing to attempt to implement Organizational Creativity if they could be shown how it would help achieve even short term results more efficiently. Future research might focus on strategies to help managers grasp and increase comfort with the innovation process, skills, techniques, and style described.

Regardless of the current popularity of creativity and innovation in the media and business publications, most organizations—when given a choice—overwhelmingly favor established routine solutions over unproven novel solutions (Ford & Sullivan, 2005; Staw, 1995). Such efficiency-oriented organizations do not know how to nurture and reward individuals who are capable generators of new opportunities and ideas that will translate into new products, services, and procedures necessary for long-term sustainable success. They have learned to design processes for efficiency, but not adaptability. We define Organizational Creativity as a deliberate and continuous change-making system of attitudes, behaviors and cognitive skills driving a process of problem generation, conceptualization, problem solving, and solution implementation, which is virtually synonymous with adaptability. This definition is consistent with field research, which has established that effective organizations are those which can mainstream both adaptability and efficiency and strike an appropriate balance between the two (Mott, 1972). It requires attitudinal, behavioral, and cognitive skills in deliberate change-making and incorporates interventions into the process as tools. With this approach, organizations can learn to mainstream adaptability by doing two things: encouraging employees to master new skills which increase their creativity, motivation, and engagement; and creating an infrastructure to ensure these skills will be used regularly.

One obvious area for future research is how to most efficiently achieve an abrupt shift in management education to incorporate creativity skills to balance analytical skills. It would also be interesting to investigate the factors that effective organizations consider when balancing adaptability and efficiency, and how to determine an organization's appropriate balance of adaptability and efficiency for a given set of circumstances. Although North American organizations have taken steps to correct the imbalance favoring efficiency over adaptability, they still overwhelmingly favor the former over the latter. More research is needed to reassure innovating organizations that they are on the right track, particularly when the results of emphasizing adaptability may take considerably longer to appear than the results of an emphasis on efficiency. A clue may be found in Japan: whereas much North American decision-making is driven by the next quarter's results, Japanese organizations favor long-term planning and reporting (Dertouzos, Lester & Solow, 1989).

An additional avenue for further research is to identify factors which enable an organization to effectively alter its "appropriate" balance of adaptability and efficiency rather than being caught unaware by upcoming environmental changes. What are the signals that prompt senior management to request more creativity, that motivate middle managers to act upon a top management requirement for more creativity, and that encourage individuals in the organization to act more creatively (assuming in each case that they know how to do so)? A clue may be found in several North American corporations that had the appropriate balance for an earlier era, but had to drastically change that balance during the 1980s in order to react to changes in their environment or circumstances. While suffering through 13 consecutive quarters of huge losses in the early 1980s, Ford made massive top–down training interventions to become a less authoritarian, more innovative and more efficient organization with higher employee involvement. In order to respond to new competition, Xerox reinvented itself, changing from a copier company into a document company and instituted a continuous process to fundamentally change how its employees work and manage. More recently, IBM reorganized itself after seeing its stock price plummet when smaller competitors capitalized on the market shift to personal computers from mainframes. An excellent research question would be how these organizations might have recognized the need to shift their balance much sooner than they did.

Implications for the Field of Organizational Development

In summary, this chapter advocates a new approach to OD. Organizational development must be understood as an ongoing continuous change-making organizational creativity management and leadership process, not just a program of discrete interventions and philosophical values of "what's good" for organizations. Effective OD is really implanting and sustaining a system of organizational creativity that can be learned and mainstreamed to provide continuous and deliberate adaptability. Above all, OD must be understood as a change-making process. In order to implement specific OD interventions, one must first obtain skills in change-making. Specific interventions simply follow as tools and techniques to help implement the steps of the organizational creativity process described in Figure 26.6. These should be attempted as solutions only after careful problem definition and only as part of a complete, system-oriented creativity system. As well, leaders must learn and adopt the corresponding new skills and new ways of thinking and behaving. They must become effective change agents in their everyday work and integrate many of the concepts, values and methods of OD into their own repertoire of capabilities. Team-building, employee engagement, high performance system plant designs, task forces, and other OD concepts are becoming an integral part of enlightened management practice (Beer & Spector, 1985). Managers, who may have been accustomed to a command and control style will need to learn skills in engaging their subordinates in co-creating strategy. By engaging a wider range of people in the process of developing new strategies, ownership and successful implementation of the new strategy is more likely to occur (Coch & French, 1948). Today's managers must learn to think and behave in new ways and to lead others to think and behave in new ways. Mintzberg (1973) documented that most managers operate primarily as short-term implementation doers. Our research (Basadur & Basadur, 2010) found many managers are especially under-skilled in problem finding and problem definition, which represent the essence of strategic thinking and adaptability. Thus the training of managers to improve conceptual thinking skills to combine with optimizing and implementation thinking must become an important intervention to improve fundamental managerial skill.

References

Amabile, T. M. (1983). *The social psychology of creativity*. New York, NY: Springer-Verlag.

Amabile, T. M. (1988). A model of creativity and innovation in organizations. In B. M. Staw & L. L. Cummings (Eds.), *Research in organizational behavior* (Vol. 10, pp. 123–167). Greenwich, CT: JAI Press.

Amabile, T. M. (1993). Motivational synergy: Toward new conceptualizations of intrinsic and extrinsic motivation in the workplace. *Human Resource Management Review*, 3, 185–201.

Amabile, T. M., Conti, R., Coon, H., Lazenby, J., & Herron, M. (1996). Assessing the work environment for creativity. *Academy of Management Journal*, 39, 1154–1184.

Amabile, T. M. (1988). A model of creativity and innovation. In B. M. Staw & L. L. Cummings (Eds.), *Research in organizational behavior* (10, pp. 123–167). Greenwich, CT: JAI Press.

Amabile, T. M. (1993). Motivational synergy: Toward new conceptualizations of intrinsic and extrinsic motivation in the workplace. *Human Resource Management Review*, 3, 185–201.

Ambrosini, V. (2003). The resource-based view of the firm. In V. Ambrosini (Ed.), *Tacit and ambiguous resources as sources of competitive advantage* (pp. 3–6). New York, NY: Palgrave MacMillan.

Amit, R., & Shoemaker, P. (1993). Strategic assets and organizational rent. *Strategic Management Journal*, 14, 33–46.

Angle, H. L. (1989). Psychology and organizational innovation. In A. H. Van de Ven, H. L. Angle & M. S. Poole (Eds.), *Research on the management of innovation: The Minnesota studies* (pp. 135–170). New York, NY: Harper & Row.

Argyris, C., & Schon, D. A. (1978). *Organizational learning: A theory of action perspective*. Reading, MA: Addison-Wesley.

Armenakis, A. A., & Bedeian, A. G. (1999). Organizational change: A review of theory and research in the 1990s. *Journal of Management*, 25, 293–315.

Austin, J. R. and Bartunek, J. M. (2003). Theories and practices of organizational development. In W. C. Borman, D. R. Ilgen and R. J. Klimoski (Eds.), Editor-in-Chief: I.B. *Weiner handbook of psychology, industrial and organizational psychology* (Vol. 12, pp. 309–332). New York, NY: John Wiley & Sons Inc.

Barney, J. B. (1991). Firm resources and sustained competitive advantage. *Journal of Management*, 17, 99–120.

Basadur, M. S. (1992). Managing Creativity: A Japanese model. Academy of Management Executive, Firm resources and sustained competitive advantage. *Academy of Management Executive*, 6(2), 29–42.

Basadur, M. S. (1993). Impacts and outcomes of creativity in organizational settings. In S. G. Isaksen, M. C. Murdock, R. L. Firestein & D. J. Treffinger (Eds.), *Nurturing and developing creativity: The emergence of a discipline* (pp. 278–313). Norwood, NJ: Ablex.

Basadur, M. S. (1995). *The power of innovation*. London, UK: Pitman Professional Publishing.

Basadur, M. S. and Basadur, T. M. (2009). Creativity skills and problem solving style: Impact on creativity social network position. Presented at Academy of Management Annual Conference, Chicago, IL

Basadur, M. S. & Basadur, T. M. (In press). Where are the generators? *Special issue of The Journal of Psychology of Aesthetics, Creativity and the Arts*:

Basadur, M. S., Ellspermann, S. J., & Evans, G. W. (1994). A new methodology for formulating ill-structured problems. OMEGA. *The International Journal of Management Science*, 22, 627–645.

Basadur, M. S., & Finkbeiner, C. T. (1985). Measuring preference for ideation in creative problem solving training. *Journal of Applied Behavioral Science*, 21, 37–49.

Basadur, M. S., Graen, G. B., & Green, S. G. (1982). Training in creative problem solving: Effects on ideation and problem finding in an applied research organization. *Organizational Behavior and Human Performance*, 30, 41–70.

Basadur, M. S., Graen, G. B., & Scandura, T. A. (1986). Training effects on attitudes toward divergent thinking among manufacturing engineers. *Journal of Applied Psychology*, 71, 612–617.

Basadur, M. S., Graen, G. B., & Wakabayashi, M. (1990). Identifying differences in creative problem solving style. *The Journal of Creative Behavior*, 24, 111–131.

Basadur, M. S., & Robinson, S. (1993). The new creative thinking skills needed for total quality management to become fact, not just philosophy. *American Behavioral Scientist*, 37, 121–138.

Basadur, M. S., & Hausdorf, P. A. (1996). Measuring divergent thinking attitudes related to creative problem solving and innovation management. *Creativity Research Journal*, 9, 21–32.

Basadur, M. S., Runco, M. A., & Vega, L. (2000). Understanding how creative thinking skills, attitudes and behaviors work together: A causal process model. *Journal of Creative Behavior*, 34, 77–100.

Basadur, M. S., Taggar, S., & Pringle, P. F. (1999). Improving the measurement of divergent thinking attitudes in organizations. *Journal of Creative Behavior*, 33, 75–111.

Basadur, T. M., Beuk, F., & Monllor, J. (2010). Regulatory fit: How individuals progress through the stages of the creative process. In L. A. Toombs (Ed.), *Proceedings of the seventieth annual meeting of the academy of management (CD)*, ISSN 1543–8643.

Baumgartel, H. (1967). Using employee results for improving organizations. *The Journal of Applied Behavioral Science, 3*, 87–101.

Beer, M. (1980). *Organization change and development: A systems view.* Santa Monica, CA: Goodyear.

Beer, M. (2001). How to develop an organization capable of sustained high performance. *Organizational Dynamics, 29*, 233–247.

Beer, M., Eisenstat, R. A., & Spector, B. (1990). Why change programs don't produce change. *Harvard Business Review, 68*, 158–166.

Beer, M., & Spector, B. (1985). Corporate-wide transformations in HR management. In R. E. Walton & P. R. Lawrence (Eds.), *Human resource management: HRM trends and challenges* (pp. 219–254). Boston, MA: Harvard Business School Press.

Beer, M., & Walton, A. E. (1987). Organization change and development. *Annual Review Psychology, 38*, 339–367.

Bennis, W. G. (1969). *Organization development: Its nature, origins, and prospects.* Reading, MA: Addison–Wesley.

Berlyne, D. E. (1967). Arousal and reinforcement. In D. Levine (Ed.), *Nebraska symposium on motivation.* Lincoln: University of Nebraska Press.

Blake, R. R., & Mouton, J. S. (1964). *The managerial grid.* Houston, TX: Gulf Publishing Co.

Burke, W. W. (1982). *Organization development, principles and practices.* Boston, MA: Little, Brown.

Burns, T., & Stalker, G. M. (1961). *The management of innovation.* London, UK: Tavistock Publications.

Butler, R. J. (1981). Innovations in organizations: Appropriateness of perspectives from small group studies for strategy formulation. *Human Relations, 34*, 763–788.

Caves, R. E. (1980). *Competition in an open economy: A model applied to Canada Cambridge.* Boston, MA: Harvard University Press.

Caves, R. E., & Porter, M. (1977). From entry barriers to mobility barriers: Conjectural decisions and contrived deterrence to new competitors. *Quarterly Journal of Economics, 91*, 241–262.

Church, A. (2007). Organizational development. In S. G. (2007). Rogelberg (Ed.), *Encyclopedia of industrial and organizational psychology* (Vol. 2, pp. 564–568). New York, NY: Sage Publications.

Coch, L., & French, J. (1948). Overcoming resistance to change. *Human Relations, 1*, 512–532.

Cohen, D., Whitmyre, J. W., & Funk, W. H. (1960). Effect of group cohesiveness and training upon creative thinking. *Journal of Applied Psychology., 44*, 319–322.

Csikszentmihályi, M. (1990). *Flow: The psychology of optimal experience.* New York, NY: Harper.

de Bono, E. (1999). *Six thinking hats.* Toronto, Canada: MICA Management Resources, Inc.

Deci, E. L., & Ryan, R. M. (2000). The "what" and "why" of goal pursuits: Human needs and the self-determination of behavior. *Psychological Inquiry, 11*, 227–268.

Dertouzos, M. L., Lester, R. K., & Solow, R. M. (1989). *Made in America.* Cambridge, MA: MIT Press.

Eisenberger, R., & Armeli, S. (1997). Can salient reward increase creative performance without reducing intrinsic creative interest. *Journal of Personality and Social Psychology, 72*, 652–663.

Eisenberger, R., & Rhoades, L. (2001). Incremental effects of reward on creativity. *Journal of Personality and Social Psychology, 81*, 728–741.

Eisenberger, R., & Selbst, M. (1994). Does reward increase or decrease creativity? *Journal of Personality and Social Psychology, 66*, 1116–1127.

Ekvall, G. (1996). Organizational climate for creativity and innovation. *European Journal of Work and Organizational Psychology, 5*, 105–123.

Ericsson, K. A. (2003). Development of elite performance and deliberate practice: An update from the perspective of the expert performance approach. In J. L. Starkes & K. A. Ericsson (Eds.), *Expert performance in sports* (pp. 49–83). Champaign, IL: Human Kinetics.

Ericsson, K. A., Krampe, R. T., & Tesch-Romer, C. (1993). The role of deliberate practice in the acquisition of expert performance. *Psychological Review, 100*, 363–406.

Hennessey, B. A., & Amabile, T. M. (1988). The conditions of creativity. In R. J. Sternberg (Ed.), *The nature of creativity.* New York, NY: Cambridge University Press.

Finke, R. A. (1990). *Creative imagery: Discoveries and inventions in visualization.* New York, NY: Lawrence Erlbaum Assoc Inc.

Finke, R. A., & Bettle, J. (1996). *Chaotic cognition: Principles and applications.* Hillsdale, NJ: Erlbaum.

E. INTERVENTIONS

Finke, R. A., Ward, T. B., & Smith, S. M. (1992). *Creative cognition.* Cambridge, MA: MIT Press.

Fiol, C. M. (1991). Managing culture as a competitive resource: An identity-based view of sustainable competitive advantage. *Journal of Management, 17,* 191–211.

Ford, C. M., & Sullivan, D. M. (2005). Selective retention processes that create tensions between novelty and value in business domains. In J. C. Kaufman & J. Baer (Eds.), *Creativity across domains: Faces of the muse* (pp. 245–259). Mahwah, NJ: Lawrence Erlbaum Associates.

French, W. L., & Bell, C. H. (1984). *Organizational development: Behavioral science interventions for organization improvement* (3rd ed.). Englewood Cliffs, NJ: Prentice-Hall.

French, W. L., & Bell, C. H. (1999). *Organization development: Behavioral science interventions for organization improvement.* Upper Saddle River, NJ: Prentice Hall.

Garvin, D. A. (1993). Building a learning organization. *Harvard Business Review, 71,* 78–91.

Guilford, J. P. (1967). *The nature of human intelligence.* New York, NY: McGraw–Hill.

Hall, M., Rosenthal, J., & Wade, J. (1993). How to make re-engineering really work. *Harvard Business Review, 71,* 104–115.

Herzberg, F., Mausner, B., & Snyderman, B. (1959). *The motivation to work* (2nd ed.). New York, NY: Wiley.

Higgins, E. T., & Trope, Y. (1990). Activity engagement theory: Implications of multiply identifiable input for intrinsic motivation. In E. T. Higgins & R. M. Sorrentino (Eds.), *Handbook of motivation and cognition: Foundations of social behavior* (Vol. 2). New York, NY: The Guilford Press.

Hinrichs, J. R. (1978). Practical management for productivity. Unpublished manuscript.

Hodgkinson, G. P., & Healey, M. P. (2008). Cognition in organizations. *Annual Review of Psychology, 59,* 387–417.

Hunter, S. T., Bedell, K. E., & Mumford, M. D. (2007). Climate for creativity: A quantitative review. *Creativity Research Journal, 19,* 69–90.

Ivancevich, J. M., Konopaske, R., & Matteson, M. T. (2005). *Organizational behavior and management.* New York, NY: McGraw Hill Professional.

Kabanoff, B., & Rossiter, J. R. (1994). Recent developments in applied creativity. *International Review of Industrial and Organizational Psychology, 9,* 283–324.

Kao, J. J. (1997). The art and discipline of business creativity. *Strategy and Leadership, 25,* 6–11.

Kerr, S. (1995). More on the folly-executive fax poll results. *Academy of Management Executive, 9,* 15–16.

Kotter, J. P. (1978). *Organization dynamics: diagnosis and intervention.* Reading, MA: Addison-Wesley.

Kriegesmann, B., Kley, T. M., & Schwering, M. G. (2005). Creative errors and heroic failures: Capturing their innovate potential. *Journal of Business Strategy, 26,* 57–64.

Kwasniewska, J., & Necka, E. (2004). Perception of the climate for creativity in the workplace: The role of the level in the organization and gender. *Creativity and Innovation Management, 13,* 187–196.

Levitt, B., & March, J. G. (1988). Organizational learning. *Annual Review of Sociology, 14,* 319–340.

Lewin, K. (1947). Frontiers in group dynamics: II. Channels of group life; social planning and action research. *Human Relations, 1,* 143–153.

Locke, E. A., & Latham, G. P. (1990). Work motivation and satisfaction: Light at the end of the tunnel. *Psychological Science, 1,* 240–246.

Margulies, N., & Raia, A. P. (1978). *Conceptual foundations of organizational development.* New York, NY: McGraw-Hill.

Marrow, A. J. (1969). *The practical theorist: The life and work of Kurt Lewin.* New York, NY: Basic Books, Inc.

Martin, J. W. (2007). *Lean six sigma for supply chain management.* New York, NY: McGraw-Hill.

Maslow, A. H. (1954). *Motivation and personality.* New York, NY: Harper & Row.

Mayer, J. D., Barsade, S. G., & Roberts, R. D. (2008). Human abilites: Emotional intelligence. *Annual Review of Psychology, 59,* 507–536.

McClelland, D. C. (1951). *Personality.* New York, NY: Dryden Press.

McClelland, D. C. (1961). *The achieving society.* Princeton, NJ: Van Nostrand.

McGraw, K. (1978). The detrimental effects of reward on performance: A literature review. In M. Lepper & D. Greene (Eds.), *The hidden costs of reward.* Hillsdale, NJ: Erlbaum.

Miles, R. E., & Snow, C. C. (1978). *Organizational strategy, structure, and process.* New York, NY: McGraw Hill.

Miller, D. (1993). The architecture of simplicity. *Academy of Management Review, 18,* 116–138.

Miller, D., & Chen., M. J. (1996). The simplicity of competitive repertoires: An empirical analysis. *Strategic Management Journal, 17,* 419–439.

Miller, D., & Shamsie, J. (1996). The resource-based view of the firm in two environments: The hollywood film studios from 1936 to 1965. *Academy of Management Journal, 39,* 519–543.

E. INTERVENTIONS

Mintzberg, H. (1973). *The nature of managerial work*. New York, NY: Harper Collins.

Mirvis, P. H. (1998). Practice improvisation. *Organizational Science, 9*, 586–592.

Mott, P. E. (1972). *The characteristics of effective organizations*. New York, NY: Harper & Row.

Mumford, M. D. (2000). Managing creative people: Strategies and tactics for innovation. *Human Resource Management Review, 10*, 313–351.

Mumford, M. D., Mobley, M. I., Uhlman, C. E., Reiter-Palmon, R., & Doares, L. M. (1991). Process analytic models of creative capacities. *Creativity Research Journal, 4*, 91–122.

Mumford, M. D., Scott, G. M., Gaddis, B., & Strange, J. M. (2002). Leading creative people: Orchestrating expertise and relationships. *The Leadership Quarterly, 13*, 705–750.

Neher, A. (1991). Maslow's theory of motivation: A critique. *Journal of Humanistic Psychology, 31*, 89–112.

Osborn, A. F. (1953). *Applied imagination: Principles and procedures of creative problem solving*. New York, NY: Charles Scribner's Sons.

Parnes, S. J., Noller, R. B., & Biondi, A. M. (1977). *Guide to creative action*. New York, NY: Scribner's Sons.

Pettigrew, A. M., Woodman, R. W., & Cameron, K. S. (2001). Studying organizational change and development: Challenges for future research. *Academy of Management Journal, 44*, 697–713.

Polanyi, M. (1958). *Personal knowledge: Towards a post-critical philosophy*. Chicago, IL: University of Chicago Press.

Porter, M. (1980). *Generic strategies and performance: An empirical examination with American data*. New York, NY: Sage Publications.

Porter, M. (1980). *Competitive strategy*. New York, NY: Free Press.

Puccio, M., Firestien, R. L., Coyle, C., & Masucci, C. (2006). A review of the effectiveness of CPS training: A focus on workplace issues. *Creativity and Innovation Management, 15*, 19–33.

Reiter-Palmon, R., & Robinson, E. J. (2009). Problem identification and construction: What do we know, what is the future? *Psychology of Aesthetics, Creativity, and the Arts, 3*, 43–47.

Rickards, T. R. (1994). Creativity from a business school perspective: Past, present and future. In S. G. Isaksen, M. C. Murdock, R. L. Firestien & D. J. Treffinger (Eds.), *Nurturing and developing creativity: The emergence of a discipline* (pp. 155–176). Norwood, NJ: Ablex.

Rigby, C. S., Deci, E. L., Patrick, B., & Ryan, R. M. (1992). Beyond the intrinsic–extrinsic dichotomy: Self-determination in motivation and learning. *Motivation & Learning, 16*, 165–185.

Robertson, P. J., Roberts, D. R., & Porras, J. I. (1993). Dynamics of planned organizational change: Assessing empirical support for a theoretical model. *Academy of Management Journal, 36*, 619–634.

Rumelt, R. P. (1984). Towards a strategic theory of the firm. In R. B. Lamb (Ed.), *Competitive strategic management* (pp. 566–570). Englewood Cliffs, NJ: Prentice-Hall.

Runco, M. A. (2004). Creativity. *Annual Review of Psychology, 55*, 657–687.

Runco, M. A., & Chand, I. (1995). Cognition and creativity. *Educational Psychology Review, 7*, 243–267.

Ryan, R. M., & Deci, E. L. (2000). Self–determination theory and the facilitation of intrinsic motivation, social development, and well–being. *American Psychologist, 55*, 68–78.

Salmela, J. H., & Moraes, L. C. (2003). Development of expertise: The role of coaching, families, and cultural contexts. In J. L. Starkes & K. A. Ericsson (Eds.), *Expert performance in sports* (pp. 275–293). Champaign, IL: Human Kinetics.

Schein, E. H. (1961). Management development as a process of influence. *Industrial Management Review, 11*, 59–77.

Senge, P. M. (1990). *The fifth discipline: The art and practice of the learning organization*. New York, NY: Doubleday.

Senge, P., Kleiner, A., Roberts, C., Ross, R., & Smith, B. (1994). *The fifth discipline fieldbook*. New York, NY: Doubleday.

Seo, M., Putnam, L., & Bartunek, J. (2001). Dualities and tensions of planned organizational change. In M. S. Poole & A. H. Van de Ven (Eds.), *Handbook of organizational change and innovation* (pp. 73–109).

Shalley, C. E., & Zhou, J. (2008). Organizational creativity research: A historical overview. In J. Zhou & C. E. Shalley (Eds.), *Handbook of organizational creativity* (pp. 3–31). New York, NY: Lawrence Erlbaum & Associates.

Simon, H. A. (1977). *The new science of management decisions*. Englewood Cliffs, NJ: Prentice Hall.

Sinangil, H. K., & Avallone, F. (2001). Organizational development and change. In N. Anderson, D. S. Ones, H. K. Sinangil & C. Viswesvaran (Eds.), *Handbook of industrial, work and organizational psychology* (pp. 332–345). New York, NY: Sage Publications.

Skilton, P. F., & Dooley, K. J. (2010). The effects of repeat collaboration on creative abrasion. *Academy of Management Review, 35*, 118–134.

Spector, B., & Beer, M. (1994). Beyond TQM programmes. *Journal of Organizational Change Management, 7*, 63–70.

E. INTERVENTIONS

Srivastva, S., & Cooperrider, D. L. (1990). *Appreciative management and leadership: The power of positive thought and action in organizations.* San Francisco, CA: Jossey-Bass.

Starbuck, W. (1983). Organizations as action generators. *American Sociological Review, 48,* 91–102.

Staw, B. M. (1995). Why no one really wants creativity. In C. M. Ford & D. A. Gioia (Eds.), *Creative action in organizations* (pp. 161–166). Thousand Oaks, CA: Sage.

Stein, M. I. (1975). *Stimulating creativity, Vol. 2: Group procedures.* Academic Press.

Sternberg, R. J., O'Hara, L. A., & Lubart, T. I. (1997). Creativity as investment. *California Management Review, 40,* 8–21.

Taylor, F. W. (1967). *The principles of scientific management.* New York, NY: W.W. Norton & Company.

Wallas, G. (1926). *The art of thought.* New York, NY: Harcourt Brace.

Wang, E., Chou, H. W., & Jiang, J. (2005). The impacts of charismatic leadership style on team cohesiveness and overall performance during ERP implementation. *International Journal of Project Management, 23,* 173–180.

Ward, T. B., Smith, S. M., & Finke, R. A. (1999). Creative cognition. In R. J. Sternberg (Ed.), *Handbook of creativity* (pp. 189–212). Cambridge, UK: Cambridge University Press.

White, K. J. (1979). The scanlon plan: Causes and correlates of success. *The Academy of Management Journal, 22,* 292–312.

White, R. W. (1959). Motivation reconsidered: The concept of competence. *Psychological Review, 66,* 197–333.

Woodman, R. W. (1993). Observations on the field of organizational change and development from the lunatic fringe. *Organizational Development Journal, 11,* 71–74.

Woodman, R. (1995). Organization development. In N. Nicholson (Ed.) & R.S. Schuler, A H. Van de Ven (Adv. Eds.), *The blackwell encyclopedic dictionary of organizational behavior,* (359–361), Blackwell Business.

Worren, N. A. M., Ruddle, K., & Moore, K. (1999). From organizational development to change management. *Journal of Applied Behavioral Science, 35,* 273–286.

Zhou, J., & Shalley, C. E. (2003). Research on employee creativity: A critical review and directions for future research. In J. J. Martocchio & G. R. Ferris (Eds.), *Research in personnel and human resource management* (pp. 165–221).

E. INTERVENTIONS

CONCLUSIONS

Creativity in Organizations: Conclusions

Issac C. Robledo, Kimberly S. Hester,
David R. Peterson, and Michael D. Mumford
The University of Oklahoma, Norman, OK

THE IMPORTANCE OF CREATIVITY TO ORGANIZATIONS

We have had two overall goals in this *Handbook of Organizational Creativity*. One has been to provide a background for further research in individual, group, and organizational levels that influence creativity and innovation. Another has been to provide managers with practical ideas with regard to encouraging creativity and innovation within organizations. Thus, it is important that we express the importance of creativity and innovation to real-world organizations. For example, today's rapidly changing environment provides a unique context in which creativity occurs (Csikzentmihályi, 1999), a context which needs to be considered for future research.

Specifically, globalization is occurring, changes in technology are now commonplace, market competition is increasing, and economic volatility has also become more of a concern. Some evidence pointing to the importance of this context was provided by James and Drown's (this volume) chapter in the examples they provided of organizations struggling under new, more competitive market conditions. This then leads to the point that organizations must tap into their creative potential or risk dying. Thus creativity may hold more importance to organizations now than in the past, and more in the future than in current times. Given these observations it is important to bear in mind that change and competition are unfolding on a larger scale and it may be important to consider creativity and innovation on this larger scale, with organizations providing a viable starting point.

Handbook of Organizational Creativity.
DOI: 10.1016/B978-0-12-374714-3.00027-6

THE DIFFICULTY OF ENCOURAGING AND MANAGING CREATIVITY

An important point to recognize, given the significance of creativity to organizations, is that encouragement and management of creative efforts are not easy endeavors. Something which should be apparent given the chapters in this *Handbook* is that creativity is complex, leading creative efforts is complex, and planning for creativity is also complex. Thus we are left with an array of interrelated factors affecting creative efforts which are complicated to articulate, and even more complicated to implement successfully within an applied organizational setting. Furthermore, creativity is not necessarily beneficial for all organizations. Thus, as much as some may hope, there does not appear to be one easy and quick approach to implementing creativity in organizations.

As an example, Hunter, Cassidy, and Ligon (this volume) argue that given the complex dynamic nature of planning for creativity, organizations should be strongly committed to an endeavor for plans to be beneficial. This suggests that to attempt to develop certain plans, but not putting enough effort in carrying out those plans appropriately, could create undesirable results for organizational creativity and innovation. Unfortunately, it seems likely that many organizations which have attempted to implement innovation have limited themselves to overly simplistic solutions. Further, there are a variety of contingent relationships noted throughout the *Handbook* that must be taken into account, such as those considered by Reiter-Palmon, Wigert, and Vreede (this volume), and Oldham and Baer (this volume). Thus, focusing extensively on just one aspect of the process will not be very beneficial to the creative production of the organization as a whole.

Having noted some issues that can arise when implementing organizational creativity, it is important to consider how the field as a whole has changed in the past 10 to 15 years. Organizations now place more emphasis on practical late cycle work (e.g., idea evaluation, monitoring progress, and implementation), particularly in teams. However, these are areas that have traditionally been neglected in the extant literature. For example, chapters by Alencar (this volume), Ericsson and Moxley (this volume), and Puccio and Cabra (this volume), among others, have noted a disproportionate emphasis on divergent thinking, an early cycle creativity process, in the literature. Thus they point to the need for researchers to focus more on late cycle forms of creativity, which may be equally important but require a different kind of creative thought.

Our aim herein has been to provide a more accurate perspective to improving creative outcomes in organizations by taking into account multiple factors on multiple levels, thus we believe that the *Handbook* should serve as a basis from which organizations can set up human resources (HR) systems to support innovation. The culmination of key research findings which have been provided in the chapters herein, and summarized in the following pages, should aid as guidelines for setting up such systems to support innovation. In the chapters on interventions, in particular, it becomes clear that these are not necessarily easy and straightforward processes to execute.

Jaussi and Benson (this volume), for example, reveal that human resource practices which support creative people and innovative processes are difficult to develop and maintain. Klotz, Wheeler, Halbesleben, Brock, and Buckley (this volume), in turn, note that reward systems may have the potential to facilitate creative contributions, but they are not necessarily easy to implement, and Ligon, Graham, Edwards, Osburn, and Hunter (this volume) show that project management activities, such as appraising and developing, are complicated endeavors for innovation. Furthermore, Basadur, Basadur, and Licina (this volume) suggest that organizational development is not necessarily straightforward, as it appears to involve a process of enacting continuous change when attempting to increase creative production. An important point, given these caveats, is that these chapters, and others in the *Handbook*, do provide guidelines for managing creativity effectively. However, perhaps more important is that these chapters acknowledge the inherent difficulties of managing for creativity and take them into account. More specific guidelines for managing creativity and innovation will be provided in later sections of this conclusion.

It is important to note that, in line with the lack of readily available simple solutions for implementing creativity and innovation in organizations, there also does not seem to be an option of simply implementing a given system by rote and expecting it to sustain itself without any added input. Contrariwise, in order for sustained innovation to occur, an organization must be prepared to have a system to monitor progress and then come up with viable solutions to any new problems identified from that monitoring (e.g., Hunter et al.). One should note that having HR systems based on principles such as those considered in this *Handbook*, should provide a basis from which sustained organizational innovation can occur.

GENERAL MISCONCEPTIONS

There are a variety of misconceptions about creativity that have been promulgated, and a key contribution of this *Handbook* is that the various chapters have aided in debunking some misconceptions in the field. Thus we will first highlight some of the key misconceptions, as well as what the research findings actually support.

There seems to be a general belief that people who are positive, relaxed, and distracted from their day-to-day hassles are more creative (e.g., Elsbach & Hargadon, 2006; Mainemelis & Ronson, 2006). However, one should note that according to De Dreu, Baas and Nijstad's (this volume) chapter, whether affect is positive does not seem to be the most important factor. Rather, the importance of affect to creative outcomes lies in how affect influences task engagement.

Another misconception has been that divergent thinking is synonymous with creativity. This may have been an outcome from an over emphasis on Guilford's divergent thinking measures in the extant literature. However, creativity actually seems to involve a variety of processes, where divergent thinking represents just one early cycle stage in the creative process (see Mumford, Mobley, Uhlman, Reiter-Palmon, & Doares, 1991). Puccio and Cabra (this volume), aid in undermining this misconception, by stressing that both idea generation and idea evaluation should be effectively executed in order to produce viable creative solutions. Thus it is important to focus on late cycle innovation processes as well.

Further, a frequent thought has been that bureaucracy must be bad for organizational creativity, that it is too structured and thus will stifle creativity. This misconception may stem from the general notion that structure is not conducive to creative contributions. Another consideration is that bureaucracy is generally affiliated with the nuisances one has to deal with in an organization, rather than the more objective view that bureaucracies may help maintain an efficiency of processes. This has led some to assume bureaucratic control would be bad for creative outcomes. In contrast to such lay views, Damanpour and Aravind's (this volume) findings suggest that some structure is beneficial for creativity, in that a structured environment may mean that creative organizational members could free up cognitive resources to come up with novel ideas.

Another belief has been that creativity can occur randomly and that it is not a disciplined process. Frequently there has been a bias among laypersons to thinking that creativity is a spontaneous phenomenon, with insights occurring potentially after waking from a dream or while observing something in nature unrelated to the actual creative problem at hand. Such phenomena may sometimes take place; however, Ward (this volume) points out that an individual's representations of problems as well as their search for solutions are more systematic than random.

Thus, from this section one can hopefully gather that general notions about creativity should be viewed with some caution, as many of them are not entirely accurate. Further, one should note that some of these relationships may be more complex than have been expressed in this brief section. The intent here has not been to oversimplify research findings, but to emphasize that misguided notions exist in the field, and the chapters in this *Handbook* make a contribution by debunking commonly held misconceptions. However, more research may be needed to fully determine why certain relationships exist, do not exist, and under what specific conditions they seem to operate.

WHAT THE *HANDBOOK OF ORGANIZATIONAL CREATIVITY* PROVIDES

The *Handbook of Organizational Creativity* should hopefully enable the reader to make certain sense of a particularly complex phenomenon. First, in the introduction chapters the author presented the background needed to make sense of this complex phenomenon, followed by sections focusing on individual, group, and organizational level influences on creativity and innovation in organizations. This framework should allow for a better conceptualization of the multiple levels in which this phenomenon operates. Furthermore, key variables operating on these levels have been reviewed, such as affect, expertise, leadership, motivation, and organizational structure, to name a few. Practical suggestions were then provided, in the intervention section, for inducing and regulating creativity and innovation within organizations. This layout should hopefully have provided the reader with a framework for understanding organizational creativity and innovation.

Importantly, this *Handbook* also provides a background for further research. Specifically, this *Handbook* operates as a compilation of what is currently known about organizational creativity and innovation by experts in the field, but also provides directions for further research in the context of what is known and what is not known. For example, gaps in the literature often present an opportunity for further research. Thus many of the chapters in this *Handbook* highlight these gaps in the research in key areas. The reader of course, may deduce alternative directions for further research that have not been presented from the content herein, as an exhaustive list of future directions has not been presented.

In addition to providing directions for further research, this *Handbook* provides practical ideas in regard to how leaders and managers can encourage creativity and innovation within an organization, particularly in the section on interventions. Thus far we have mentioned the inherent difficulties involved in encouraging and managing creative efforts and also dispelled key misconceptions in the field. With consideration of these inherent difficulties and misconceptions, the motivated manager who is willing to commit time, energy, and resources to encouraging creativity in the organization will have a firm basis of accumulated research findings from experts in the field to guide the implementation of changes vis-à-vis this *Handbook*.

ORGANIZATIONAL CREATIVITY RESEARCH

Organizations and Creativity

According to James and Drown's (this volume) content analysis assessing the degree to which various topics have been investigated in the organizational creativity literature, we observed a promising status for creativity research whereby the overall amount of research in organizational creativity has grown significantly from 1995 to 2010. However there are clearly certain areas which have plateaued, or even declined in amount, in the literature. For example, most studies have focused on the individual level of analysis, ignoring the team level and how one level may impact another level. Given that creativity in organizations has been identified as a multi-level phenomenon (Mumford & Hunter, 2005), it seems that more multi-level studies would contribute much to the extant literature. Another key issue to address for improving the quality of future research lies in the methods being used. Most researchers seem to have a bias for one given method over others, but James and Drown suggest that there has been a lack of research employing multiple methods.

Methods

As mentioned in Mumford, Hester, and Robledo's (this volume) chapter on methods, there are five key methods which have been used in studies of creativity. These are qualitative, historiometric, survey, psychometric, and experimental. No single method is a complete, adequate description of creative performance. Given the previously noted multi-level nature of creativity, having studies bound by one level can result in ambiguities in interpretation. Each method has strengths and weaknesses that need to be considered, and ultimately using multiple methods is often the most appropriate course of action. Thus, it seems researchers would benefit from learning to effectively use a range of methods in organizational creativity research.

An important implication of these observations is that applied psychologists wishing to implement research findings should consider the methodological limitations present in these different types of studies. For example, there are concerns about the generalizability of results in both qualitative and historiometric studies. While this is not typically a concern in survey studies, these studies do not focus on unobservable attributes of creative performance. Further, with psychometric studies, because these studies focus on individual variability, other sources of variation attributable to the individual cannot be identified. And with experimental studies there is often little exploration of individual difference variables, and typically only two to four variables can be manipulated at a time. These are just some of the general weaknesses of these methods that need to be taken into account by organizational researchers, as well as practitioners wishing to apply experimental findings in the workplace.

Fields, Domains, and Individuals

Historically the literature in creativity has taken the perspective of the individual, while Simonton (this volume) in his chapter, reminds us that creativity does not occur in a vacuum. In fact, Csikszentmihályi (1999) has argued that creativity emerges in a system consisting of three parts: the domain, field, and individual. The interaction of the three systemic components decides whether a contribution is indeed creative. For example, one should consider that different domains allow for varying degrees of creativity. Furthermore, decisions as to which new contributions will be integrated into the domain occur by the field's gatekeepers. It is up to these gatekeepers to decide which innovations will be worth pursuing, and which ones will not. This suggests that an individual's creative contributions may be determined by a greater context. Even given the role of the greater system (e.g., domain and field), research trends indicate that the creative individual should likely be a high achiever with a high degree of motivation. However, Simonton points out that the specific processes by which an individual's abilities and motivation interact with the system have not been well mapped out, and is something that could be of interest to organizational creativity researchers.

Facilitators and Inhibitors

Alencar, in her chapter (this volume), describes some facilitators which have been identified via prior meta-analyses (Runco, 2007): these being positive peer-group, resources, challenges, autonomy, cohesion, intellectual stimulation, and flexibility and risk-taking. Inhibitors were then discussed: intransigency and authoritarian attitudes, protectionism and paternalism, lack of integration between sectors, lack of support for new ideas, and lack of encouragement. Given these findings, Alencar poses a key question: what is the best strategy to nurture creativity? For example, is it optimal to implement an organizational program which would aim to establish facilitators and reduce inhibitors simultaneously, or is it more beneficial to first eliminate inhibitors, then at a later time incorporate facilitators? Research which would address such questions would hold considerable value for applied settings.

INDIVIDUAL LEVEL INFLUENCES

Abilities

For a long time it was held that a focus on divergent thinking alone would increase individual creative performance and thus organizational creativity as well, since organizational creativity is a result, in part, of individual creativity. What we have learned from research in the past few decades, as Acar and Runco (this volume) note, is that divergent thinking is a fairly complex ability, influenced by task type, knowledge, experience, personality, and attitudes.

While divergent thinking is important for creativity, what should be clear from the chapters in this *Handbook* is that creativity involves much more than generating original ideas. In the past, convergent thinking had been considered a hindrance to creativity. However, Acar and Runco (this volume) suggest that both divergent and convergent thinking abilities are needed for creative performance. More specifically, they note that convergent thinking appears to involve both intrapersonal and interpersonal idea evaluation abilities. Intrapersonal evaluation occurs within an individual and interpersonal evaluation involves at least two people. Both types of evaluations are important for organizational creativity (e.g., intrapersonal for leaders and intrapersonal for teams).

The implication of these observations is that creativity is quite complex, with regard to individual abilities, consisting of interactions between ideation and evaluation processes, knowledge, and motivation. In this regard Acar and Runco note that motivation, rather than ability, may be the primary determinant of creative performance. They argue that because motivation varies more than ability and can be more easily manipulated through interventions, motivation may account more for differences in performance. However the relative importance of ability and motivation to creativity is an empirical question that should be addressed in future research.

Expertise

Just a decade or so ago there was little, if any, mention of expertise as an important input to creativity. However, expertise is clearly important to creative performance (Mumford, Scott, Gaddis, & Strange, 2002). Ericsson and Moxley (this volume) note that traditional conceptualizations of expertise have typically relied on the assumption that expertise is developed naturally, or passively, simply from prolonged experience in a given domain. However, these authors also present research which shows that while experience may lead naturally to *acceptable* performance, consistent *superior* performance results from prolonged deliberative practice—specific activities designed to improve specific aspects of an individual's performance.

While it is clear that deliberative practice is important to superior performance, research has not been conducted to determine what the content of that deliberation should be in order to enhance creativity. Ericsson and Moxley (this volume) argue that deliberative practice appears to lead to acquisition of long-term working memory by stimulating the development of knowledge structures which are more accurate, complex, and organized. Thus effective deliberation might be focused on the organization of concepts, problem-solving strategies, or performance parameters (Mumford, 2000). It is less likely that creative people will deliberate much on organizing basic information, as they appear to be very good at building basic models that account for the phenomena at hand (Mumford & Gustafson, 1988). However, such models may be used to generate problem solutions for the task at hand (Finke, Ward, & Smith, 1992). In generating problem solutions such models may also be used to select a particular strategy or set of strategies to apply. Furthermore, creative people seem to be more sensitive to and dwell on anomalous information (Scott, Lonergan, & Mumford, 2005). Thus in generating problem solutions they also appear to deliberate heavily on exceptions.

Creative Problem-Solving

Problem-solving research has traditionally been approached from one of two perspectives—a Gestalt approach, emphasizing problem representation, or an information processing approach, emphasizing search processes from initial problem representation to solution generation. Ward (this volume) points out that recent research has focused on the interplay of these two approaches. What should be recognized here is that creative problem-solving (CPS) is based on the complex interaction of two complex processes.

Adding to this complexity, Ward summarizes evidence suggesting that the nature of this interaction may be contingent upon different task situations (e.g., well-defined vs. ill-defined, arrangement vs. inducing structure vs. transformation). Furthermore, the processes involved appear to be influenced both by people's knowledge structures as well as their recent experiences. These observations point to four critical potential influences on CPS—ongoing representation of problems, cognitive processes, task situations, and knowledge structures. More research is needed to understand the way these four factors converge to influence CPS.

In addition to demonstrating the complexity of CPS, Ward (this volume) also reviews evidence showing that CPS is quite disciplined. This point stands in stark contrast to the misconseption that creativity emerges insightfully when people are relaxed and disengaged. For example, Ward presents research conducted under different problem classification systems (e.g., well-defined vs. ill-defined, insight vs. non-insight, and arrangement vs. inducing structure vs. transformation problems), which suggests that the cognitive processes underlying CPS are executed in a disciplined and purposeful, not a random, manner. However, further research is needed to better understand how these processes might change depending on the type of problem being solved.

Idea Generation/Evaluation

Puccio and Cabra (this volume) summarize research that expands our view of idea generation beyond the contributions of traditional approaches focused on divergent thinking and idea generation. To begin, skills usually associated with divergent thinking (e.g., fluency, flexibility, and elaboration) come from Guilford's divergent thinking work (e.g., Guilford, 1967). However, Puccio and Cabra point out that while much more research has been conducted on idea generation than idea evaluation, Guilford's theory is not the only framework used for identifying skills related to divergent thinking.

On a related note, these authors also review research showing that although the relationship between idea generation and idea evaluation is much more complex than has traditionally been believed to be the case, the skills associated with these processes can be trained and improved. In order for idea generation and idea evaluation to lead to creativity both processes must be implemented effectively. For this purpose Puccio and Cabra summarize criteria used to evaluate creative ideas and products. The resulting list of evaluation methods should prove to be a useful tool for both practitioners and researchers interested in assessment of creativity.

However, given that the research on idea evaluation has not kept pace with research on idea generation, Puccio and Cabra emphasize the need for more research to identify the most effective training methods and how training transfers to the workplace. Of particular interest will be identifying idea evaluation strategies organizations can employ in order to cultivate the most promising ideas. Additionally, given that organizational creativity is a relatively new area within a relatively recent field (i.e., creativity), the authors recommend more field studies be conducted to shed more light on the linkages between individual creative processes, such as idea generation and evaluation, and organizational creative performance.

Affect/Motivation

As noted earlier, there has been an overwhelming belief among practitioners that if people are happy, relaxed, and feel free from various organizational constraints they will be more creative. However, much of the research on the relationship between affect and creativity has demonstrated only mixed effects for the impact of positive moods on creativity, suggesting a more complex relationship than has been previously thought.

De Dreu et al. (this volume) point out that whether a given mood increases (decreases) creativity depends on whether that mood activates (deactivates) the individual. It is the activating effects of moods that lead to higher creative performance. The hedonic tone of moods determines *how* creative performance is increased. Generally, positive activating moods lead individuals to think more flexibly, while negative activating moods lead to increased cognitive persistence. However, more research is needed on the role of negative mood states, especially anger. Further, these studies should employ designs that allow stronger conclusions than those that can be drawn from correlational studies.

To complicate matters further, the activating effects of moods appear to depend, at least in part, on the multiple facets of an individual's motivation. Whether the individual has an approach or avoidance orientation and whether the motivation is intrinsically or extrinsically based are both important considerations. Other motivational influences on creativity include engagement (a prerequisite of achieving flow) induced by fit between the task characteristics and internal states, goal orientation, goal setting, and epistemic motivation.

Clearly, the relationships between affect and motivation and creativity are very complex. De Dreu et al. (this volume), however, propose a framework that is not only useful for researchers seeking to "incorporate, integrate, and understand the effects of different moods, motivations, and motivational orientations" on creativity, but is also valuable for practitioners who want to enhance creativity in organizations. For example, rather than attempting to create relaxed work environments, managers should seek ways of increasing task engagement when trying to enhance employee creativity.

Personality

Similar to affect and motivation, personality is also related to creativity. Hoff, Carlsson, and Smith (this volume) point out that earlier attempts to identify a creative personality resulted in inconsistent findings. However, more recent evidence suggests that what is unique about creative personalities is that they are characterized by opposites (e.g., extraverted and introverted). However, more research is needed to further identify the unique personality characteristics of creative individuals across domains. Perhaps more relevant to organizational creativity, Hoff et al. address the question of whether creativity can be developed vis-à-vis personality development. While such an approach appears to be less effective than other approaches (e.g., problem-solving or divergent thinking training; see Scott, Leritz, & Mumford, 2004), there is evidence to suggest that personality development may still contribute to enhancing organizational creativity. Future research should consider the potential for personality development to enhance creativity above and beyond any effects due to more effective training approaches. Additionally, if such programs provide incremental benefits, additional research will be needed to develop and refine personality development interventions aimed at increasing creativity in organizations.

Context

Throughout the 1980s and 1990s theories began to shift from a focus on individual level factors to also consider organizational influences such as culture, resources, and strategy as well as social influences such as group norms and cohesiveness. Today, while many theories take such factors into account, researchers should give more attention to the impact of contextual variables on organizational creativity. Agars, Kaufman; Deane, and Smith (this volume) suggest using a nested approach to examining organizational creativity, taking into account general thematic areas (e.g., industries), domains (e.g., organizations within an industry), and micro domains (e.g., functional areas within an organization). Theoretically, such an approach should further our understanding of perhaps one of the most complex psychological phenomena being studied today. Pragmatically, this nested approach should help identify what research is most applicable in a given domain, leading to interventions that are more relevant and thus more useful.

Agars et al. point out that both causal relationships and basic criteria for identifying creativity may vary across different contexts. For example, while transformational leadership has been found to increase creativity in some organizations, Robledo, Peterson, and Mumford (2010) have noted that transformational leadership inhibits creativity among scientists and engineers. Regarding definitions of creativity, Agars et al. note that idea generation may be more valued in some contexts while idea evaluation is more valued in others. Furthermore, they note that the way creativity is operationalized and evaluated may differ not just across industries or organizations, but even between different functional areas within a single organization. The inconstancy of creativity across contexts makes it difficult, if not impossible, to provide specific recommendations for enhancing organizational creativity which can be universally applied. Thus, in their chapter, Agars et al. give four broad guiding principles for organizational leaders—emphasize leadership, provide social support, pay attention to culture and climate within domains, and manage resources.

GROUP LEVEL INFLUENCES

Group Composition, Social Processes, and Cognition

As noted in earlier sections, research on organizational creativity has historically focused on the individual. However, it should be recognized that recent work has examined the direct role of groups and teams in the development of creative and innovative products or ideas. Reiter-Palmon et al. (this volume), for example, highlight the importance of group composition, social processes, and cognitive processes for team creativity and innovation. In terms of group composition, there is an important shift from focusing on demographic diversity to more functional diversity when looking to improve creativity and innovation through group composition. This suggests that organizations should focus more on other variables such as diversity in education, function in the organization, and job relevant knowledge, skills, and abilities when seeking to enhance creativity and innovation in teams. It may also be important for teams to have diversity in some individual differences, such as creative ability, cognitive style, and personality, but the extant literature is conflicting and further research in this area would be valuable for applied settings.

Reiter-Palmon et al. also remind us of the known importance of social processes through a review of the extensive literature, but suggest that more emphasis should be placed on cognitive processes where there has been a lack of research. For example, brainstorming in the past has been promoted as a cognitive process which promotes creative processes. However, it is important to consider that this process only focuses on the idea generation phase of creativity and ignores later phases of developing a creative product. In fact, brainstorming is only effective if the correct social processes are in use. Thus the authors suggest considering how cognitive processes interact with social processes, and that caution is called for if emphasizing brainstorming when the desired outcome is a creative product.

Teams and Collaboration

Paulus, Dzindlot, and Kohn (this volume) suggest that cognitive processes such as brainstorming can be used for generating ideas, but they must be used appropriately. Several guidelines are provided in this chapter for brainstorming effectively, in addition to guidelines or strategies for other factors contributing to creativity in teams, such as leadership, conflict, cohesion, and trust. Importantly, caution is called for given that collaborative creativity is very complex. Specifically, a balance of factors such as these must be found, specific combinations of factors must be present at the same time, and stability in team membership may be important for maintaining an appropriate balance of some team factors, especially early in the creative process. The authors conclude that teams will be highly innovative with the right people, the right supporting, motivational, and task contexts, and effective social and cognitive processes. Further, it seems that more research is needed to better identify the optimal patterns and important limiting factors which impact creativity in teams.

Paulus et al. also highlight the importance of considering the phases of creativity in a collaborative team. A review of the literature suggests that different types of people may be better at completing different phases of creativity. For example, divergent thinkers may be better at the exploration phase, which involves idea generation, while others may be better at the exploitation phase, which involves adaptation of creative ideas. However, this does not mean that creativity is unimportant in later phases of product development if an innovative product is desired. This point has important implications for both applied settings and future research. Organizations should consider the types of people assigned to each phase of the creative process, and further research is needed to consider the types of creativity needed in later phases of production of an innovative product.

F. CONCLUSIONS

In addition to reviewing collaborative creativity, the authors discuss an emerging trend in organizations due to technological advances—virtual teams. Although the use of virtual teams is becoming more prevalent, there is still relatively little research examining creativity in virtual teams. It seems that many of the factors impacting traditional creative teams may impact virtual teams in a similar way. Overall, more research is needed in this area, but this chapter does provide some practical guidelines based on the literature on virtual team performance in general. One example is that virtual teams should have some face-to-face meetings, especially during certain phases of the creative process.

Project Management

Paletz (this volume), in her chapter, reminds us of the importance of project management and identifies several important project management variables. Although the extant research on project management is extensive, project management factors have often been ignored as variables in research examining creativity and innovation. Thus, there may be a need for more research examining the relationship between project management and creativity and innovation. A consideration in this chapter is that poor management of teams may be to blame for inconsistent findings in factors impacting creativity and innovation in teams. For example, research which has suggested that brainstorming is less useful as a team cognitive variable has been criticized for ignoring guidelines, such as using a trained facilitator. Therefore, this chapter has highlighted the importance of appropriate use of guidelines, such as those suggested by Paulus et al. (this volume). Her argument that poor project management may be to blame for inconsistent findings may be valid, but at this point more research is needed to find larger effect sizes that would support this argument.

Climate/Environment

West and Sacramento (this volume), in reviewing climate and environmental factors, discuss the longstanding view that strong cultural support for creative efforts is needed to introduce innovative products and procedures, and suggest that organizations could facilitate creativity and innovation by being supportive and creating environments that nurture the individual differences which contribute to creativity. However, it seems to be the case that a shared vision for creativity is even more important. This point leads us to consider that organizations should develop a team climate for innovation. In addition, managers should strive to create a shared vision in which employees at all levels are involved in positive and constructive debates about the best way to achieve that vision and conflict is seen as an opportunity to find creative solutions. Managers may also be interested in the specific instruments identified in this chapter which can help in planning interventions and promoting creative climates. However, further research is needed to examine such instruments to identify how they can best be implemented. In addition, more cross-level research is needed to examine how team and organizational level climate features can enhance or inhibit the effects of individual characteristics on creativity and innovation across varying contexts and time.

Work Context

Oldham and Baer (this volume) discuss the impact of contextual factors on creativity and innovation through a review of an impressive body of research. The authors found that several contextual and environmental conditions appear to strongly impact individual and team creativity. However, many of the contextual factors reviewed appear to differ in direction and consistency across studies. A possible explanation for conflicting findings across studies is that many contextual factors may only impact creativity if certain individual characteristics or other contextual factors are present. Thus, a complex pattern of contextual factors and individual characteristics may exist, which needs to be further researched. In addition, the authors have noted a significant lack of research examining the impact of contextual factors on teams rather than individuals. None the less, this chapter does provide some useful guidelines for applied settings based on the contextual factors that appear to have consistent, positive impacts on creativity, such as job design and social environment, while research examining the most effective ways of changing these contextual factors is still needed.

Leadership

Marion (this volume) contrasts the traditional entity based approach of studying creativity to a complexity leadership approach. Marion argues that a complexity leadership approach allows for research examining how creativity is a function of interdependent interactions under conditions of conflicting constraints, heterogeneity, pressure, and uncertainty. Given this argument, one should note that there is a lack of empirical support for complexity theory, and thus more research in the area is necessary to further support the theory. None the less, Marion's chapter is valuable in that it provides a detailed discussion of the important attributes of leader behavior. Specifically, this chapter has a discussion of the importance of fostering interaction, interdependency, heterogeneity, pressure, task-related conflict, and adaptive rules when creativity is a desired outcome. For example, Danneels and Sethi (2003) found that constructive, or task-related, conflict had a positive effect on creativity in new products. Marion also highlights that creativity is enabled by leaders who champion creative ideas, foster sensemaking, and provide a safe environment. For example, Howell and Boies (2004) found that champions were able to promote creativity due to their enthusiastic support for new ideas and their ability to sell the ideas to the organization. Although more research is needed to support Marion's approach to applying these attributes in a complexity approach, managers should benefit from attending to the leader skills which have been provided in this chapter.

ORGANIZATION LEVEL INFLUENCES

Structure

Kazanjian and Drazin (this volume) remind us that theories of creativity have often neglected that creative tasks might be a function of larger organizational efforts, involving interdependencies between units across organizational systems. Thus, the organizational level has been an important yet often overlooked level of influence on creativity and innovation.

Bearing this point in mind, Damanpour and Aravind (this volume) review the literature on structuring for innovation, where the findings have been divided up by two periods: 1967–1988, and 1990–2009. Overall, the findings for both time periods were generally consistent with each other. Across both time periods some salient determinants of innovation were: technical knowledge resources, specialization, external communication, and complexity. A unique finding across both time periods was that centralization and formalization, measures of bureaucratic control expected to relate negatively to innovation, actually produced mixed results. Essentially, there was no consistent negative effect across both time periods for either one of these bureaucratic measures. This contradicts the general expectation in the field for bureaucracy to inhibit innovation. Given the lack of consistent findings, there may be a complex relationship between bureaucratic control and innovation, and more investigation may be needed into specific mediators and moderators that impact this relationship. An overarching consideration of the authors is that innovation in organizations is planned and structured, thus controlling the process would be important for the appropriate management of innovation.

In light of this observation that bureaucracy in organizations is not necessarily inhibitory for innovation, Damanpour and Aravind identify a trend from organic and mechanistic explanations of organizational structure in the past, to more ambidextrous (e.g., integration of organic and mechanistic) explanations of organizational structure currently. Further, given a lack of focus on research on ambidexterity, this could be a plausible direction for future research.

An example of the possible misguided nature of using organic and mechanistic structure explanations is in arguments that certain organizational conditions facilitate incremental innovations, and other organizational conditions would facilitate radical innovations. As plausible as this may sound, the author's results have not shown a difference in the structures which support incremental vs. radical innovations. Thus ambidextrous frameworks for explaining organizational structure for innovation seem to be more viable.

Planning

Hunter et al. (this volume) point out that given the competitive and challenging context of today's organizations, many organizations can see the advantage in pursuing creativity, but defining the actual path toward creative attainment seems to be less clear. Creativity is a complex endeavor, thus plans appear to provide a mechanism which aids in implementing creativity within organizations. One example showing the importance of planning for innovation is that people left to their own devices will tend to avoid change and prefer what is more familiar to them.

In their chapter, Hunter et al. mention a variety of sub-plan types which are useful for planning for innovation. These sub-plans must then be integrated into a broader organizational plan. Furthermore there are specific planning requirements such as expertise and leadership, which are needed. Given the need for sub-plans, broader organizational plans, and general planning requirements, it seems clear that planning for innovation is a complex and resource intensive process. One should recognize that while the 4-stage framework presented by Hunter et al. shares key characteristics with Mumford et al.'s (1991) 8-stage model, further research is needed to clarify how many stages are truly present in planning for innovation.

An example of properly executing a plan for innovation is when Hunter et al. suggest that pursuing more congruent ideas organizationally can routinize enough processes to allow for more innovation to occur in different areas. Thus organizations can save time and resources on projects that have been built around a common theme, then allowing for more time and resources to delegate to new innovations. However, one should note that a critical issue in organizations is how research themes should be identified in the first place. Thus, given the lack of research in this area, this could be a viable point for further investigation. Furthermore, since acquiring expertise is time consuming, projects being pursued should be integrated, thus allowing expertise to be more concentrated and elaborated to the goals of the organization.

Learning and Knowledge Management

An example of how knowledge can manifest itself is provided by Kazanjian and Drazin (this volume), where experiential learning occurs at individual and group levels, providing a basis from which organizational level knowledge, such as technology, can be institutionalized (Leonard, 1998; Mumford, 2000). Importantly, the relationship between creativity, new knowledge development, and organizational learning has seldom been examined, thus presenting an avenue for future research.

An interesting framework for knowledge management is proposed by Kazanjian and Drazin. In brief, *leveraging* existing knowledge bases is most important for developing new products, *recombining and extending* existing knowledge bases is most important for new platform development, and *importing* or acquiring new knowledge bases is most important for development of a new and less related business. Thus acquiring new knowledge becomes more important the more radically different a new product pursuit is from the current organizational products. A lack of research along these lines has been in resource sharing as knowledge leveraging in the context of organizational creativity.

Change, Innovation, and Creativity

In Dunne and Dougherty's chapter (this volume), we are presented with three tensions in creativity and innovation research. These are supportive vs. demanding managers, weak vs. strong ties, and job vs. product complexity. We are then presented with three types of organizing. There is bureaucratic organizing, used by organizations with functional departments and a clear hierarchy, and adaptive organizing, where change is fast and continuous. A new type of organization theorized is transformative organization, which has been described as being on the edge of chaos and likely occurring in high technology sectors (Brown & Eisenhardt, 1998).

In this chapter creativity in bureaucratic organizations is explained by supportive managers, weak ties, and job complexity, whereas in adaptive organizations it is explained by demanding managers, strong ties, and product complexity. In contrast, transformative organizations are presented as particularly complex, and more integrative, in comparison to bureaucratic and adaptive organizations. For example, transformative organizations exhibit both job and product complexity, and weak vs. strong ties are not in conflict because people focus on the knowledge needs of the organization. It will be interesting to see which industries or situations call for transformative organizing, given that this is a newer area. Specifically, researchers may wish to examine whether transformative organizing is sustainable for long periods, and if so, what would facilitate such sustainability.

INTERVENTIONS

Career Paths and Selection

Jaussi and Benson (this volume) suggest that human resource (HR) practices can play a significant role in the improvement of individual creativity and organizational innovation. They evidence that HR practices which support creative people and innovative processes are difficult to develop and maintain, but highlight the possible value for organizations that do. For example, a current trend is a shift toward placing creative individuals in traditionally non-creative jobs in order to encourage innovation rather than reserving creative individuals for traditionally creative jobs, such as advertising and product development. Examples such as these convey the importance of HR practices in influencing organizational creativity.

These findings highlight the importance of conducting research on creative individuals. Thus Jaussi and Benson review research examining creative individuals' work, career anchors, occupational choices, trajectories, and career success, followed by a discussion of the implications this research has for HR practices. Jaussi and Benson also provide a set of suggestions for organizations seeking to gain a competitive advantage with an HR system that promotes creativity and innovation through recruitment, selection, job design, performance appraisal, incentives, training, and career development. For example, the authors suggest that HR management should offer opportunities for professional recognition and achievement, promotions into jobs with high autonomy, as well as avoiding overly strict management regulations of personnel. Also, for creative employees, administrative distractions should be reduced, innovative thinking should be promoted, and support for failure should be provided (Goffee & Jones, 2007). While the argument presented for the benefit of having one HR system that promotes and supports creativity in all employees is persuasive, more research is needed to determine whether organizations would reap more benefits from having multiple HR systems for different departments. Currently, it is unclear whether traditionally creative departments (e.g., R&D departments) should be handled in the same manner as employees in jobs which have not traditionally required creativity. Thus more research is needed to examine the HR implications that this chapter has drawn from the research on creative individuals.

Rewards

Klotz et al. (this volume), in their chapter, discuss the impact of reward systems on creativity in the workplace. The authors examine the role of creativity in theories of motivation through a review of research on the influence of rewards on creativity and the organizational factors that moderate this relationship. Previous research has suggested that extrinsic reward systems can be detrimental to creative performance. However, a review of current research led Klotz et al. to suggest that extrinsic reward systems can add incremental improvements in creative performance if intrinsic motivation is established first and the right individual and contextual factors are present. Thus, one should consider that reward systems may have the potential to facilitate, develop, and improve creative performance, but they are difficult to design and implement in that they are not "one size fits all" across different organizations. One should recognize that this chapter provides a valuable set of guidelines, including a discussion of key contextual factors, for organizations seeking to use rewards to improve creative performance. Furthermore, it seems that although the present research has provided insight into the impact of reward systems on creativity, more longitudinal, multi-method, and multi-level research is needed to better examine this relationship over time and across levels of an organization.

Training, Development, and Performance Management

Ligon et al. (this volume) discuss the impact of performance appraisal and training/development on creativity in their chapter on performance management. Based on having reviewed the research on these interventions, the authors suggest that a blanket approach to performance management will be less useful, or even detrimental, to innovation in organizations. For example, project management approaches for individuals engaging in creative work should differ from those engaging in routine work for the organization. Another important finding is that creativity training, especially cognitive training, is in fact effective in improving creativity. Based on these key findings, Ligon et al. provide several guidelines for performance management interventions. For example, with regards to evaluation, managers may want to allow creative employees to evaluate their own work because they may be better evaluators of innovation within their area. Beyond these guidelines, it is important to integrate these interventions such that developmental planning should be based on performance appraisals while the skills learned in training should be rewarded. Based on these observations, the authors have proposed a model integrating these performance management interventions. Furthermore, several areas that need further research have been highlighted, such as examining the result of increasing frequency of performance reviews, the role of individual differences, and the amount of time we can expect an intervention to yield performance improvements. Of importance to practitioners is that a review of the available empirical evidence has allowed this chapter to provide some insight for organizations seeking to improve creativity through performance management interventions.

Organizational Development

As a reasonable conclusion to the interventions section, Basadur et al. (this volume) discuss Organizational Development (OD) as an ongoing process of implementing change through organizational creativity management and leadership rather than a set of discrete interventions. The authors provide a viable summary of techniques used in OD, as well as a new perspective on OD that stresses creativity. For example, in the past most OD efforts have focused on improving efficiency, but Basadur et al. point out that a balance must be found between efficiency and adaptability if an organization seeks to be innovative in order to stay competitive in today's environment. This chapter provides an integrated approach to improving organizational adaptability through the encouragement of mastery of new skills and creation of an infrastructure that ensures that the new skills will be used. Specifically, Basadur et al. suggest that many leaders lack the deep skills, such as problem finding and problem definition, which are necessary in executing creativity as a standard everyday process, but that management training can prove to be a successful intervention. However, further research is needed to assess the most efficient way to make this shift in management education. In addition, further research is needed to identify how organizations can best determine the appropriate balance of adaptability and efficiency and what factors, or signals, are best at enabling an organization to effectively modify this balance.

CONCLUDING THOUGHTS

Limitations

At this point we should note some limitations of this *Handbook* as a whole. For one, not all topics relevant to organizational creativity have been presented. Such topics may include economic factors, corporate willingness to invest, and a field's readiness for innovation. Further, while we have encouraged research in a multi-level perspective, we have mostly constrained ourselves to variables operating on the organizational, group, or individual level, and not necessarily variables operating across industries or on a larger societal scale. Another consideration is that the chapters in this handbook have considered influences on organizational creativity in general, and have not limited conclusions to a specific domain, thus the findings in this handbook may not necessarily be generalizable across all domains. These limitations are important to bear in mind, as there may be important variables influencing organizational creativity which have not been considered herein, or have yet to be identified. Even given these limitations, this handbook should provide a noteworthy contribution to the field. Moreover, it is not possible to consider all potential factors within a single handbook.

Summary

In having reviewed the research by the chapter authors in this *Handbook*, we have identified what some significant factors are which contribute to creativity in organizations, how they contribute to organizational creativity, as well as why and when, or under what situations, they contribute to organizational creativity. Importantly, this information has been presented with regard to where the field has been and where it is currently, as well as in terms of where the field is headed. Thus we have provided a context for understanding the current available knowledge base of creativity and innovation in organizations.

Furthermore, we have not only considered the importance of variables that influence organizational creativity, but we have also aimed to provide practical ideas as to how leaders and managers can encourage creativity and innovation within their respective organizations. Ultimately, we have hoped to provide a framework for understanding the key components of organizational creativity from which further research directions can be drawn and mechanisms for sustained innovation can be implemented within the organization.

References

Brown, S., & Eisenhardt, K. (1998). *Competing on the edge*. Boston, MA: Harvard Business School Press.

Csikszentmihályi, M. (1999). Implications of a systems perspective for the study of creativity. In R. J. Sternberg (Ed.), *The handbook of creativity* (pp. 313–335). New York, NY: Cambridge University Press.

Danneels, E., & Sethi, R. (2003). Antecedents of new product program creativity: The moderating role of environmental turbulence. [Proceeding]. A1–A6.

Elsbach, K. D., & Hargadon, A. B. (2006). Enhancing creativity through "mindless" work: A framework of workday design. *Organization Science, 17*, 470–483.

Finke, R. A., Ward, T. B., & Smith, S. M. (1992). *Creative cognition: Theory, research, and applications*. Cambridge, MA: MIT.

Goffee, R., & Jones, G. (2007). Leading clever people. *Harvard Business Review, 85*, 1–9.

Guilford, J. P. (1967). *The nature of human intelligence*. New York, NY: McGraw-Hill.

Howell, J. M., & Boies, K. (2004). Champions of technological innovation: The influence of contextual knowledge, role orientation, idea generation, and idea promotion on champion emergence. *The Leadership Quarterly, 15*, 123–143.

Leonard, D. (1998). *Wellsprings of knowledge*. Boston, MA: Harvard Business School Press.

Mainemelis, C., & Ronson, S. (2006). Ideas are born in fields of play: Towards a theory of play and creativity in organizational settings. *Research on Organizational Behavior, 27*, 81–131.

Mumford, M. D. (2000). Managing creative people: Strategies and tactics for innovation. *Human Resource Management Review, 10*, 313–351.

Mumford, M. D., & Gustafson, S. B. (1988). Creativity syndrome: Integration, application, and innovation. *Psychological Bulletin, 103*, 27–43.

Mumford, M. D., & Hunter, S. T. (2005). Innovation in organizations: A multi-level perspective on creativity. In F. Dansereau & F. J. Yammarino (Eds.), *Research in multi-level issues* (Vol. IV, pp. 11–74). Oxford, UK: Elsevier.

Mumford, M. D., Mobley, M. I., Uhlman, C. E., Reiter-Palmon, R., & Doares, L. (1991). Process analytic models of creative capacities. *Creativity Research Journal, 4*, 91–122.

Robledo, I. C., Peterson, D. R., & Mumford, M. D. (2010). Leadership of scientists and engineers: A three-vector model. *Journal of Organizational Behavior*. Advance online publication. doi: 10.1002/job.739

Runco, M. A. (2007). *Creativity. Theories and themes: Research, development, and practice*. Burlington, MA: Elsevier.

Scott, G., Leritz, L. E., & Mumford, M. (2004). The effectiveness of creativity training: A quantitative review. *Creativity Research Journal, 16*, 361–388.

Scott, G. M., Lonergan, D. C., & Mumford, M. D. (2005). Conceptual combination: Alternative knowledge structures, alternative heuristics. *Creativity Research Journal, 17*, 79–98.

Index

Edwards Brothers Malloy
Ann Arbor MI. USA
August 13, 2014